DATE DUE

Literature Criticism from 1400 to 1800

Guide to Gale Literary Criticism Series

When you need to review criticism of literary works, these are the Gale series to use:

If the author's death date is:	You should turn to:
After Dec. 31, 1959 (or author is still living)	***Contemporary Literary Criticism*** for example: Jorge Luis Borges, Anthony Burgess, William Faulkner, Mary Gordon, Ernest Hemingway, Iris Murdoch
1900 through 1959	***Twentieth-Century Literary Criticism*** for example: Willa Cather, F. Scott Fitzgerald, Henry James, Mark Twain, Virginia Woolf
1800 through 1899	***Nineteenth-Century Literature Criticism*** for example: Fedor Dostoevski, Nathaniel Hawthorne, George Sand, William Wordsworth
1400 through 1799	***Literature Criticism From 1400 to 1800*** (excluding Shakespeare) for example: Anne Bradstreet, Daniel Defoe, Alexander Pope, François Rabelais, Jonathan Swift, Phillis Wheatley
	Shakespearean Criticism Shakespeare's plays and poetry
Antiquity through 1399	***Classical and Medieval Literature Criticism*** for example: Dante, Homer, Plato, Sophocles, Vergil, the Beowulf Poet

Gale also publishes related criticism series:

Black Literature Criticism

This three-volume series presents criticisms of works by major black writers of the past two hundred years.

Children's Literature Review

This series covers authors of all eras who have written for the preschool through high school audience.

Short Story Criticism

This series covers the major short fiction writers of all nationalities and periods of literary history.

Poetry Criticism

This series covers poets of all nationalities and periods of literary history.

Drama Criticism

This series covers playwrights of all nationalities and periods of literary history.

ISSN 0740-2880

Volume 20

Literature Criticism from 1400 to 1800

Excerpts from Criticism of the Works of Fifteenth-, Sixteenth-, Seventeenth-, and Eighteenth-Century Novelists, Poets, Playwrights, Philosophers, and Other Creative Writers, from the First Published Critical Appraisals to Current Evaluations

James E. Person, Jr.
Editor

Gale Research Inc. • DETROIT • WASHINGTON, D.C. • LONDON

STAFF

The paper used in this publication meets the minimum requirements of American National Standard for Information Sciences—Permanence Paper for Printed Library Materials, ANSI Z39.48-1984. ™

Library of Congress Catalog Card Number 84-643570
ISBN 0-8103-7962-7
ISSN 0740-2880

Printed in the United States of America

Published simultaneously in the United Kingdom
by Gale Research International
(An affiliated company of Gale Research Inc.)

Contents

Preface

Literature Criticism from 1400 to 1800 (LC) presents criticism of world authors of the fifteenth through eighteenth centuries. The literature of this period reflects a turbulent time of radical change that saw the rise of drama equal in stature to that of classical Greece, the birth of the novel and personal essay forms, the emergence of newspapers and periodicals, and major achievements in poetry and philosophy. Much of modern literature reflects the influence of these centuries. Thus the literature treated in *LC* provides insight into the universal nature of human experience, as well as into the life and thought of the past.

Scope of the Series

LC is designed to serve as an introduction to authors of the fifteenth through eighteenth centuries and to the most significant interpretations of these authors' works. The great poets, dramatists, novelists, essayists, and philosophers of this period are considered classics in every secondary school and college or university curriculum. Because criticism of this literature spans nearly six hundred years, an overwhelming amount of critical material confronts the student. *LC* therefore organizes and reprints the most noteworthy published criticism of authors of these centuries. Readers should note that there is a separate Gale reference series devoted to Shakespearean studies. For though belonging properly to the period covered in *LC,* William Shakespeare has inspired such a tremendous and ever-growing corpus of secondary material that the editors have deemed it best to give his works extensive coverage in a separate series, *Shakespearean Criticism.*

Each author entry in *LC* attempts to present a historical survey of critical response to the author's works. Early criticism is offered to indicate initial responses, later selections document any rise or decline in literary reputations, and retrospective analyses provide students with modern views. The size of each author entry is intended to reflect the author's critical reception in English or foreign criticism in translation. Articles and books that have not been translated into English are therefore excluded. Every attempt has been made to identify and include the seminal essays on each author's work and to include recent commentary providing modern perspectives.

The need for *LC* among students and teachers of literature was suggested by the proven usefulness of Gale's *Contemporary Literary Criticism (CLC), Twentieth-Century Literary Criticism (TCLC),* and *Nineteenth-Century Literature Criticism (NCLC),* which excerpt criticism of works by nineteenth- and twentieth-century authors. Because of the different time periods covered, there is no duplication of authors or critical material in any of these literary criticism series. An author may appear more than once in the series because of the great quantity of critical material available and because of the aesthetic demands of the series's *thematic organization.*

Thematic Approach

Beginning with Volume 12, roughly half the authors in each volume of *LC* are organized in a thematic scheme. Such themes include literary movements, literary reaction to political and historical events, significant eras in literary history, and the literature of cultures often overlooked by English-speaking readers. The present volume, for example, focuses upon the Scottish Chaucerians. Future volumes of *LC* will devote substantial space to the Restoration dramatists, the English Metaphysical poets and authors of the Spanish Golden Age, among many others. The rest of each volume will be devoted to criticism of the works of authors not aligned with the selected thematic authors and chosen from a variety of nationalities.

Organization of the Book

Each entry consists of the following elements: author or thematic heading, introduction, list of principal works (in author entries only), annotated works of criticism (each followed by a bibliographical citation), and a bibliography of further reading. Also, most author entries contain author portraits and other illustrations.

- The **author heading** consists of the author's full name, followed by birth and death dates. If an author wrote consistently under a pseudonym, the pseudonym is used in the author heading, with the real name given in parentheses on the first line of the biographical and critical introduction. Also located here are any name variations under which an author wrote, including transliterated forms for authors whose native languages use nonroman alphabets. Uncertain birth or death dates are indicated by question marks. The **thematic heading** simply states the subject of the entry.

- The **biographical and critical introduction** contains background information designed to introduce the reader to an author and to critical discussion of his or her work. Parenthetical material following many of the introductions provides references to biographical and critical reference series published by Gale in which additional material about the author may be found. The **thematic introduction** briefly defines the subject of the entry and provides social and historical background important to understanding the criticism.

- Most *LC* author entries include **portraits** of the author. Many entries also contain illustrations of materials pertinent to an author's career, including author holographs, title pages, letters, or representations of important people, places, and events in an author's life.

- The **list of principal works** is chronological by date of first book publication and identifies the genre of each work. In the case of foreign authors whose works have been translated into English, the title and date of the first English-language edition are given in brackets beneath the foreign-language listing. Unless otherwise indicated, dramas are dated by first performance, not first publication.

- **Criticism** is arranged chronologically in each author entry to provide a useful perspective on changes in critical evaluation over the years. For the purpose of easy identification, the critic's name and the composition or publication date of the critical work are given at the beginning of each piece of criticism. Unsigned criticism is preceded by the title of the source in which it appeared. All titles by the author featured in the critical entry are printed in boldface type. Publication information (such as publisher names and book prices) and parenthetical numerical references (such as footnotes or page and line references to specific editions of works) have been deleted at the editors' discretion to provide smoother reading of the text.

- Critical essays are prefaced by **annotations** as an additional aid to students using *LC.* These explanatory notes may provide several types of useful information, including: the reputation of a critic, the importance of a work of criticism, the commentator's individual approach to literary criticism, the intent of the criticism, and the growth of critical controversy or changes in critical trends regarding an author's work. In some cases, these notes cross-reference the work of critics within the entry who agree or disagree with each other.

- A complete **bibliographical citation** of the original essay or book follows each piece of criticism.

- An annotated bibliography of **further reading** appears at the end of each entry and suggests resources for additional study of authors and themes. It also includes essays for which the editors could not obtain reprint rights.

Cumulative Indexes

Each volume of *LC* includes a cumulative **author index** listing all the authors that have appeared in *Contemporary Literary Criticism, Twentieth-Century Literary Criticism, Nineteenth-Century Literature Criticism, Literature Criticism from 1400 to 1800,* and *Classical and Medieval Literature Criticism,* along with cross-references to the Gale series *Short Story Criticism, Poetry Criticism, Children's Literature Review, Authors in the News, Contemporary Authors, Contemporary Authors Autobiography Series, Contemporary Authors Bibliographical Series, Dictionary of Literary Biography, Concise Dictionary of Literary Biography, Something about the Author, Something about the Author Autobiography Series,* and *Yesterday's Authors of Books for Children.* Readers will welcome this cumulative author index as a useful tool for locating an author within the various series. The index, which includes authors' birth and death dates, is particularly valuable for those authors who are identified with a certain period but whose death dates cause them to be placed in another, or for those authors whose careers span two periods. For example, F. Scott Fitzgerald is found in *TCLC,* yet a writer often associated with him, Ernest Hemingway, is found in *CLC.*

Beginning with Volume 12, *LC* includes a cumulative **topic index** that lists all literary themes and topics treated in *LC, NCLC* Topics volumes, *TCLC* Topics volumes, and the *CLC* Yearbook. Each volume of *LC* also includes a cumulative **nationality index** in which authors' names are arranged alphabetically under their respective nationalities and followed by the numbers of the volumes in which they appear.

Each volume of *LC* also includes a cumulative **title index,** an alphabetical listing of the literary works discussed in the series since its inception. Each title listing includes the corresponding volume and page numbers where criticism may be located. Foreign-language titles that have been translated are followed by the titles of the translations—for example, *El ingenioso hidalgo Don Quixote de la Mancha (Don Quixote).* Page numbers following these translated titles refer to all pages on which any form of the titles, either foreign-language or translated, appear. Titles of novels, dramas, nonfiction books, and poetry, short story, or essay collections are printed in italics, while individual poems, short stories, and essays are printed in roman type within quotation marks.

A Note to the Reader

When writing papers, students who quote directly from any volume in the Literary Criticism Series may use the following general forms to footnote reprinted criticism. The first example pertains to material drawn from periodicals, the second to material reprinted from books.

T. S. Eliot, "John Donne," *The Nation and the Athenaeum,* 33 (9 June 1923), 321-32; excerpted and reprinted in *Literature Criticism from 1400 to 1800,* Vol. 10, ed. James E. Person, Jr. (Detroit: Gale Research, 1989), pp. 28-9.

Clara G. Stillman, *Samuel Butler: A Mid-Victorian Modern* (Viking Press, 1932); excerpted and reprinted in *Twentieth-Century Literary Criticism,* Vol. 33, ed. Paula Kepos (Detroit: Gale Research, 1989), pp. 43-5.

Suggestions Are Welcome

In response to various suggestions, several features have been added to *LC* since the series began, including a nationality index, a Literary Criticism Series topic index, thematic entries, a descriptive table of contents, and more extensive illustrations.

Readers who wish to suggest new features, themes, or authors to appear in future volumes, or who have other suggestions, are cordially invited to write to the editor.

Acknowledgments

The editors wish to thank the copyright holders of the excerpted criticism included in this volume, the permissions managers of many book and magazine publishing companies for assisting us in securing reprint rights, and Anthony Bogucki for assistance with copyright research. We are also grateful to the staffs of the Detroit Public Library, Wayne State University Purdy/Kresge Library Complex, and the University of Michigan Libraries for making their resources available to us. Following is a list of the copyright holders who have granted us permission to reprint material in this volume of **LC.** Every effort has been made to trace copyright, but if omissions have been made, please let us know.

COPYRIGHTED EXCERPTS IN *LC,* VOLUME 20, WERE REPRINTED FROM THE FOLLOWING PERIODICALS:

Ambix: The Journal of the Society for the Study of Alchemy and Early Chemistry, v. XII, June-October, 1964. Reprinted by permission of the publisher.—***The Chaucer Review,*** v. 3, December, 1969; v. 14, Winter, 1980; v. 25, 1991. Copyright © 1969, 1980, 1991 by The Pennsylvania State University, University Park, PA. All reprinted by permission of the publisher.—***History Today,*** v. 39, January, 1989. © History Today Limited 1989. Reprinted by permission of the publisher.—***Isis,*** v. 70, September, 1978 for "Hermetic Geocentricity: John Dee's Celestial Egg" by J. Peter Zetterberg. Copyright © 1978 by the History of Science Society, Inc. Reprinted by permission of the University of Chicago Press and the author.—***Journal of the History of Ideas,*** v. XXV, January-March, 1964. Copyright 1964, Journal of the History of Ideas, Inc. Reprinted by permission of the publisher.—***The Journal of Medieval and Renaissance Studies,*** v. 20, Fall, 1990. Copyright © 1990 by Duke University Press. Reprinted by permission of the publisher.—***MLN,*** v. 102, September, 1987. © copyright 1987 by The Johns Hopkins University Press. All rights reserved. Reprinted by permission of the publisher.—***Philological Quarterly,*** v. 53, Summer, 1974 for "Boethius, Chaucer, and 'The Kingis Quair' " by Lois A. Ebin. Copyright 1974 by The University of Iowa. Reprinted by permission of the publisher and the author.—***The Review of English Studies,*** v. XXXV, August, 1984. Reprinted by permission of Oxford University Press.—***Scottish Literary Journal,*** v. 1, July, 1974. Reprinted by permission of *Scottish Literary Journal.*—***Studies in Scottish Literature,*** v. III, July, 1965. Copyright © G. Ross Roy 1965. Reprinted by permission of the editor.—***Texas Studies in Literature and Language,*** v. I, Spring, 1959 for "The Mediaeval Makars" by A. M. Kinghorn; v. II, Autumn, 1960 for " 'The Kingis Quair': An Evaluation" by Mary Rohrberger. Copyright © 1959, renewed 1987; 1960, renewed 1988 by the University of Texas Press. Both reprinted by permission of the publisher and the respective authors.

COPYRIGHTED EXCERPTS IN *LC,* VOLUME 20, WERE REPRINTED FROM THE FOLLOWING BOOKS:

Balz, Albert G. A. From ***Descartes and the Modern Mind.*** Yale University Press, 1952. © copyright, 1952, Yale University Press. Renewed 1980 by Patricia B. Vincent. Reprinted by permission of the publisher.—Bawcutt, Priscilla. From "Aspects of Dunbar's Imagery," in ***Chaucer and Middle English Studies in Honour of Rossell Hope Robbins.*** Edited by Beryl Rowland. Kent State University Press, 1974. © George Allen & Unwin Ltd. 1974. All right reserved. Reprinted by permission of Kent State University Press.—Bawcutt, Priscilla. From ***Gavin Douglas: A Critical Study.*** Edinburgh University Press, 1976. © Priscilla Bawcutt 1976. Reprinted by permission of the publisher.—Bawcutt, Priscilla. From "William Dunbar and Gavin Douglas," in ***The History of Scottish Literature: Origins to 1660 (Mediaeval and Renaissance), Vol. I.*** Edited by R. D. S. Jack. Aberdeen University Press, 1988. © The Contributors 1988. All rights reserved. Reprinted by permission of the publisher.—Benson, C. David. From "O Moral Henryson," in ***Fifteenth-Century Studies: Recent Essays.*** Edited by Robert F. Yeager. Archon Books, 1984. © 1984 Robert F. Yeager. All rights reserved. Reprinted by permission of Archon Books, an imprint of the Shoe String Press, Inc. and Robert F. Yeager.—Clulee, Nicholas H. From ***John Dee's Natural Philosophy: Between Science and Religion.*** Routledge, 1988. © Nicholas H. Clulee 1988. All rights reserved. Reprinted by permission of the publisher.—Coldwell, David F. C. From an introduction to ***Selections from Gavin Douglas.*** Oxford at the Clarendon Press, 1964. © Oxford University Press 1964. Reprinted by permission of Oxford University Press.—Fox, Denton. From "The Scottish Chaucerians," in ***Chaucer and Chaucerians: Critical Studies in Middle English Literature.*** Edited by D. S. Brewer. Nelson, 1966. Copyright © 1966 by University of Alabama Press. Reprinted by permission of D. S. Brewer.—French, Peter J. From ***John Dee: The World of An Elizabethan Magus.*** Routledge & Kegan Paul, 1972. © Peter J. French 1972. Reprinted by permission of the publisher.—Heilbron, J. L. From "Dee's Role in the Scientific Revolution" and "Propaedeumata Aphoristica," in ***John Dee on Astronomy: "Propaedeumata Aphoristica" (1558 and 1568), Latin and English.*** Edited and translated by Wayne Shumaker. University of California Press, 1978. Copyright © 1978 by The Regents of the University of California. Reprinted by permission of the publisher.—Jaspers, Karl. From ***Three Essays: Leonardo, Descartes, Max Weber.*** Translated by Ralph Manheim. Harcourt Brace Jovanovich, 1964. English translation © 1964 by Harcourt Brace Jovanovich, Inc. Reprinted by permission of the publisher.—MacQueen, John. From ***Robert Henryson: A Study of the Major Narrative Poems.*** Oxford at the Clarendon Press, 1967. © Oxford University Press 1967. Reprinted by permission of Oxford University Press.—MacQueen, John. From "Poetry—James I to Henryson," in ***The History of Scottish Literature: Origins to 1660 (Mediaeval and Renaissance), Vol. I.*** Edited by R. D. S. Jack. Aberdeen University Press, 1988. © The Contributors 1988. All rights reserved. Reprinted by permission of the publisher.—Mandelbaum, Maurice. From ***Philosophy, History, and the Sciences: Selected Critical Essays.*** Johns Hopkins University Press, 1984. © 1985 by The Johns Hopkins University Press. All rights reserved. Reprinted by permission of the publisher.—McDiarmid, Matthew P. From an introduction to ***The Kingis Quair of James Stewart.*** Edited by Matthew P. McDiarmid. Rowman and Littlefield, 1973. Introduction © Matthew P. McDiarmid 1973. Reprinted by permission of the author. McDiarmid, Matthew P. From ***Robert Henryson.*** Scottish Academic Press, 1981. © 1981 Matthew P. McDiarmid. All rights reserved. Reprinted by permission of the publisher.—Muir, Edwin. From ***Essays on Literature and Society.*** Revised edition. Hogarth Press, 1965. Copyright Edwin Muir 1949 and The Hogarth Press Ltd. 1965. Reprinted by permission of the Literary Estate of Edwin Muir and The Hogarth Press.—Reiss, Edmund. From "The Ironic Art of William Dunbar," in ***Fifteenth-Century Studies: Recent Essays.*** Edited by Robert F. Yeager. Archon Books, 1984. © 1984 Robert F. Yeager. All rights reserved. Reprinted by permission of Archon Books, and imprint of The Shoe String Press, Inc. and Robert F. Yeager.—Ridley, Florence H. From "A Plea for the Middle Scots," in ***The Learned and the Lewed: Studies in Chaucer and Medieval Literature.*** Edited by Larry D. Benson. Cambridge, Mass.: Harvard University Press, 1974. Copyright © 1974 by the President and Fellows of Harvard College. All rights reserved. Excerpted by permission of the publisher.—Russell, Bertrand, Jacques Barzun, and Mark Van Doren. From "Rene Descartes: A Discourse on Method," in ***The New Invitation to Learning.*** Edited by Mark Van Doren. Random House, 1942. Copyright 1942 by the Columbia Broadcasting System, Inc. Renewed 1970 by Mark Van Doren. Reprinted by permission of the Literary Estate of Mark Van Doren.—Schouls, Peter A. From ***Descartes and the Enlightenment.*** McGill-Queen's University Press, 1989. © McGill-Queen's University Press 1989. Reprinted by permission of the publisher.—Spearing, A. C. From ***Medieval Dream-Poetry.*** Cambridge University Press, 1976. © Cambridge University Press 1976. Reprinted by permission of the publisher and the author.—Yates, Frances A. From ***Theatre of the World.*** University of Chicago Press, 1969. © 1969 by F. A. Yates. All rights reserved. Reprinted by permission of The University of Chicago Press.—Yates, Frances A. From ***The Occult Philosophy in the Elizabethan Age.*** Routledge & Kegan Paul Ltd., 1979. © Frances A. Yates 1979. Reprinted by permission of The Peters, Fraser Dunlop Ltd.

John Dee

1527-1608

INTRODUCTION

English mathematician, astronomer, geographer, and astrologer.

Dee was one of the leading scientists and mathematicians in sixteenth-century England. In addition to advising Queen Elizabeth and her ministers on astrology and geography, Dee provided navigational information to the sponsors and pilots of Elizabethan voyages of exploration, helped further the practical application of mathematics, and wrote on a wide variety of subjects ranging from geometry and astronomy to alchemy and astrology. An intriguing figure in a transitional period, Dee exhibited characteristics of both medieval and Renaissance thought: while his mathematical treatises express the developing Renaissance interest in methodical inquiry and applicable results, Dee's astronomical works manifest the residual influence of the Middle Ages in their abstract and intentionally recondite mysticism. Dee is commonly regarded as both a major contributor to and an exemplar of Elizabethan culture.

According to a horoscope he prepared for himself, Dee was born in London in 1527. His father, Rowland Dee, was a gentleman who attended Henry VIII; his mother was named Johanna Wild. Biographers surmise that he received the classical education typical for a child of his background since he knew Latin well when he entered Cambridge University at fifteen to study Greek. After receiving his bachelor's degree in 1546, Dee was made one of the original fellows and a lecturer in Greek at the newly established Trinity College, Cambridge, where he completed a master of arts degree in the following two years. As the sixteenth-century English university curriculum was devoted exclusively to the liberal arts, Dee had to leave England to study math and science. In 1548, he studied at the University of Louvain in Belgium, then the epicenter of European scientific inquiry, working with such renowned scholars as the mathematician Gemma Frisius and the cartographer Gerard Mercator. Two years later he gave a series of widely attended public lectures on Euclidian geometry in Paris. By this time, Dee had earned a reputation as one of Europe's leading scholars.

Returning to England in 1551, Dee began tutoring and advising several young men who went on to become members of Elizabeth's Privy Council: William Cecil, later Lord Burghley; William Herbert, earl of Pembroke; and Robert Dudley, earl of Leicester. In 1554, Dee was jailed on suspicion of conjuring against Queen Mary, who suspected her younger sister, then-princess Elizabeth, and Elizabeth's sympathizers of plotting against her; however, he was released due to a lack of evidence. Later, Mary rejected his proposal that she establish a national library to consolidate the manuscripts and books scattered when her father, Henry VIII, had dissolved the monasteries. Dee's career as an unofficial royal adviser began in earnest with Elizabeth's ascension to the throne in 1558 (she commissioned a horoscope from him to determine the most auspicious coronation date). Throughout the 1560s and 1570s he traveled frequently on the continent, consulting with physicians about Elizabeth's health, conferring with scholars, advising monarchs, and collecting materials for his library, considered the most extensive in England. Fascinated by astrology, Elizabeth visited Dee often to consult him about such matters, while the preeminent English navigators of the era—Richard Chancellor, Humphrey Gilbert, Martin Frobisher, and Walter Raleigh—sought his advice before embarking to explore North America and search for a northwest passage to the Orient. Dee also continued to tutor prominent young men, among them the poet Philip Sidney and the mathematician Thomas Digges. During this period, Dee produced a wide range of scholarly writings, including the *Propadeumata aphoristica* (1558), a collection of astronomical aphorisms; the *Monas hieroglyphica* (1564), an explication of alchemical and astrological symbols; the *Brytannicae Reipublicae Synopsis* (1570), a set of recommendations for improving England's troubled economy; a "Mathematicall Praeface" to the first English translation of Euclid's geometry (1570); *Parralaticae commentationis* (1573), a commentary on the supernova of 1572; "Certaine verie rare observations of Chester" (1574), an archeological and historical description of that county; "Of Famous and Rich Discoveries" (1576), an apology for what Dee considered English territories; and *General and Rare Memorials Pertayning to the Perfect Art of Navigation* (1577), a treatise on strengthening the English navy.

In the early 1580s, Dee began to redirect his intellectual inquiries, focusing thereafter on efforts to discern the divine design for the universe by conversing with angels. His partner in these endeavors was Edward Kelley, a convicted forger who claimed that the angel Uriel had instructed him to receive the spirits' messages while Dee, unable to hear their voices himself, transcribed the seances. The *Liber Mysteriorum* (1583) comprise Dee's records of the alleged angelic interviews. Dee and Kelley spent the ensuing five years in Europe, vainly soliciting the sponsorship of various monarchs, until a quarrel separated them in 1588. The impoverished Dee returned to his home at Mortlake to find that his library had been ransacked by a mob suspicious of his "black magic." In 1596, Elizabeth granted him the wardenship of Manchester College, but tension with the faculty rendered his stay brief. By the early seventeenth century Dee had outlived most of his benefactors, including Elizabeth, and he spent his final years destitute at Mortlake, selling his remaining books to buy food. He wrote to Elizabeth's successor, James I, pleading for the king's intercession, but received no response. Dee died in 1608.

Two of Dee's most influential works were his expanded version of Robert Recorde's math textbook, *The Grounde of Artes,* and his preface to Henry Billingsley's English translation of Euclid's *Elements of Geometry.* Most previous mathematical treatises had been written in Latin, the esoteric language of scholars. Dee wrote about math in the vernacular English spoken by the crafts-and tradespeople who he hoped would begin utilizing math to simplify their work. Dee also advocated substituting Arabic numerals for the clumsy Roman numerals then in use. Recorde's *The Grounde of Artes,* first published in 1540, was suited to Dee's purposes in that Recorde attempted to familiarize a public ignorant of math with both theory and applications. Dee reworked the text after Recorde's death in 1558, adding a section on fractions; his edition became the standard mathematics textbook of the period and was reprinted twenty-five times during the following century. In 1570 Dee annotated and wrote an introduction to the Billingsley translation of Euclid's *Geometry.* His "Mathematicall Praeface" is a catalogue of sixteenth-century science which describes the integral role of math in various disciplines, including its practical applications in architecture, navigation, surveying, and art. Peter J. French has suggested that "the essential point to be remembered about Dee's preface is that it is a revolutionary manifesto calling for the recognition of mathematics as a key to all knowledge and advocating broad application of mathematical principles."

Dee's expertise in mathematics furthered his scientific interest in astronomy. An affinity for recording sidereal positions (his diaries are largely a collection of such information) provided him with abundant data on which to base his astronomical theories. Dee's premises were articulated in a preface to his friend John Field's *Ephemeris anni 1557,* in the *Propadeumata aphoristica,* in *Paralaticae commentationis,* and in a proposal for calendar reform (1582). In the Field preface, Dee criticized the inaccuracies of older ephemerides and lauded the innovative calculations of Polish astronomer Nicolas Copernicus, who had pioneered the theory of a revolving earth and a heliocentric universe in his *De revolutionibus orbium coelestium* (1543). Yet, although Dee admired Copernicus's methods, he never incorporated Copernicus's conclusions into his own work. The aphorisms of the following year demonstrate Dee's attempts to determine the sizes and distances of the planets; his geometric formula for computing distances is, although difficult to implement, viable. The *Paralaticae commentationis* were occasioned by widespread concern over a supernova that appeared in 1572, prompting the Queen to request an inquiry by Dee. He speculated that the nova occupied the universe's unchanging, outermost belt. He also generated a set of trigonometric theorems to determine why the nova appeared to move in different directions when viewed from different parts of what he treated as a stationary earth. Dee's proposal for calendar reform was contemporaneous with Pope Gregory XIII's 1582 bull reforming, in Catholic countries, the radically inaccurate Julian calendar in effect since 46 B.C. By defining the year as 365.25 days when its actual equatorial length is 365.24 days, the Julian calendar was ten days ahead of the equinoxes and the solstices by Dee's time. Dee's proposal was based on his calculations of the solar position at the time of Christ's birth and, like the papal decree, would have corrected the Julian calendar's cumulative gain, but Anglican bishops rejected it because of its Catholic connotations. England did not adopt the new-style calendar until 1752.

Dee maintained that his diverse scholarly inquiries uniformly sought to apprehend the origins and mechanisms of God's universe. Both the *Monas hieroglyphica* and the seances to which he devoted his last twenty-five years reveal Dee adopting the hermetic approach that he considered the most direct means to this end. Dee subscribed to the medieval hermetic belief that subsequent generations had lost the ancients' understanding of the divine design underlying the cosmos but believed, like the hermetics, that an initiated elite could recover this ultimate knowledge by deciphering ancient texts. In the *Monas,* Dee explicates a hermetic hieroglyphics to empower himself and other enlightened mystics. Because he feared that the uneducated might abuse such abstruse and potent information, Dee wrote the *Monas* in Latin and limited its circulation; at the end of his career he considered it his most important contribution to the advance of knowledge.

The *Liber Mysteriorum* similarly bypass methodical inquiry and empirical corroboration. In attempting to learn the secrets of the universe from the angels he contacted during his seances with Kelly, Dee believed that he was using the most direct approach.

Although scholars and ministers of state alike respected Dee's mathematical ideas, his abandonment of legitimate science for endeavors seemingly akin to necromancy and his relationship with the unscrupulous Kelly confirmed the longstanding popular suspicion that he was either a sorcerer, a charlatan, or a dupe. This view of Dee prevailed until the beginning of the twentieth century, when scholars began to reexamine him as a potentially revealing participant in the early phases of the sixteenth- and seventeenth-century scientific revolution. Led by the influential English scholar Frances Yates, one group of critics has asserted that Dee is best understood as a Renaissance hermetic whose mystical search for the occult principles ordering nature was an early stage in what later became the empirical search for its scientific mechanisms. For example, Dee's astronomical studies presume the hermetic concept of ephemeral, terrestrial qualities emanating from eternal, celestial sources; however, within this framework, Dee often approached astronomy mathematically, applying proven axioms to determine astronomical truths. More recently, critics such as John Heilbrun and Nicolas Clulee have contended that many tenets of Dee's hermeticism—limited access to knowledge, unquestioned exaltation of past precepts, lack of interest in empirical verification—contradict the principles of scientific inquiry. Contemporary historians tend to understand Dee's conceptual framework and purposes as late medieval rather than premodern; however, they generally agree that he provided a relatively backward England with valuable information from the more advanced continental Renaissance. In addition, the recognition that Dee did not consistently adopt an empirical approach to his own endeavors has not decreased admiration for the brilliance of his many mathematical and scientific theories.

PRINCIPAL WORKS

"A Supplication to Q. Mary . . . for the Recovery and Preservation of Ancient Writers and Monuments" (letter) 1556

Propadeumata aphoristica . . . de praestantioribus quibusdam naturae virtutibus (aphorisms) 1558

[*John Dee on Astronomy: Propadeumata Aphoristica (1558 and 1568),* 1978]

Monas hieroglyphica (treatise) 1564

Brytannicae Reipublicae Synopsis: libris explicata tribus (treatise) 1570

"Mathematicall Praeface to The Elements of Geometry of Euclid of Megara" (preface) 1570

Parralaticae commentationis praxeosque nucleus quidam (treatise) 1573

"Certaine verie rare observations of Chester: & some parts of Wales: with divers Epitaphes coatarmours & other monuments verie oderlie and labouriouslie gathered together" (treatise) 1574

"Of Famous and Rich Discoveries" (treatise) 1576

General and Rare Memorials Pertayning to the Perfect Art of Navigation. 4 vols. (treatise) 1577

Liber Mysteriorum (transcribed conversations) 1583

The Compendious Rehearsall of John Dee . . . made unto the two Honourable Commissioners (treatise) 1592

"To the Kings most excellent maiestie" (letter) 1604

John Dee: The Private Diary and Catalogue of His Library Manuscripts (diary and bibliography) 1842

Diary, for the Years 1595-1601, of Dr. John Dee, Warden of Manchester from 1595-1608 (diary) 1880

Walter I. Trattner (essay date 1964)

[*Trattner is an American critic and educator. In the following excerpt, he explains that Dee abandoned his career as a respected geographer because it had not disclosed the "divine wisdom" he subsequently sought in occultism. Trattner maintains that, because Dee's sensibility incorporated both medieval and Renaissance elements, he did not value empiricism over magic.*]

Despite the more than three hundred fifty years that have passed since his death, John Dee still largely remains an enigma. Misunderstood by many of his contemporaries, and called by his later interpreters everything from a "charlatan" and "conjurer of evil spirits," to "the leading pioneer in the English Geographical Renaissance" and a man far "too advanced in speculative thought for his own age to understand," no two authorities paint the same picture of this strange Elizabethan.

Dr. John Dee, a tall, thin man with a long pointed beard and a mysterious manner, presents an interesting problem for the historian. A prolific writer (and almost all of the writings are extant), as well as a man of varied activities, the events of Dee's life are well known. Yet, no satisfactory account of his important life has ever been written. Indeed, even his most sympathetic commentators do not seem to have understood fully this enthusiastic sixteenth-century seeker of wisdom and lover of the secrets of God and nature.

The fascination of his psychic projections has led Dee's biographers to ignore his solid achievements in the science, history, and geography (among other things) of his day. In addition, assuming that there were two John Dees, (1) the utilitarian scientist interested in the practical application of speculative thought, and (2) the evil practitioner of occultism, there has been an inability to see the one true Dee. John Dee was a lover of divine wisdom, a dreamer, and a thinker, living in an age which was becoming increasingly dominated by the middle-class utilitarian ideal. Dee was an intellectually honest, sincere, and pious Christian torn between the passing old and rising new order. He was, in other words, an Elizabethan.

A discussion of two related phases of his many activities not only helps one to better understand John Dee, but it also sheds further light on sixteenth-century England. Dee's rôle in the Elizabethan Geographical Renaissance has not been appreciated fully by his biographers and deserves elucidation.

Secondly, and related, an understanding of why, at the height of Dee's, and England's, overseas operations in 1583 Dee seemingly gave up his interest in those affairs that occupied so much of his time during the previous thirty years helps explain some of the motivations behind the many geographical explorations which played so important a rôle in that turbulent era. In that year John Dee suddenly migrated to the Continent and although he returned six years later, he was never again involved in exploration or colonizing expeditions. Unlike his biographers, I believe that this was a perfectly understandable development. To ask the misleading question about Dee, "How come a man endowed with his gifts and moral attributes could have lapsed into such madness [i.e., his spiritual concerns] as that which he raged?" is to completely misunderstand John Dee and his age. (pp. 17-18)

It was [in 1559] that John Dee turned much of his ceaseless energy to geographical concerns. In this connection two things must be pointed out. First, in the sixteenth century the world location of England had been completely altered. From her slumbers on a remote margin of the Old World, Englishmen now awakened to find themselves on the very threshold of a new one. Secondly, scientific geography has its roots in astronomy—in a knowledge of the shape and size of the earth, of its apparent motion relative to the heavenly bodies—knowledge which allows accurate fixing of position by astronomical means; hence, the debt of geography to astrology, based on just such astronomical knowledge was great. The cosmographer was, in fact, in the first instance a mathematician and an astronomer, so that geographical literature was sought within many astronomical and mathematical works.

Geography owes a large debt to Roger Bacon for his general teaching (as well as specific works) concerning the importance of applied mathematics and the experimental approach to science. Bacon profoundly influenced many of the pioneers of the English Geographical Renaissance, including John Dee. In the words of the leading historian of English geography of the Elizabethan era, after the publication of a new edition of Cabot's world map in 1549, "a new chapter in English geographical thought and practice opened." And that new chapter was, on the practical side, the beginning of the English search for Cathay; on the theoretical side, a story in which John Dee is one of the leading figures.

Keeping in mind the opportunities and stimuli which Dee's personal connections afforded him in his approach to geography, it is no wonder that his interest turned to the seas. His training and Continental travels gave him further opportunities, which he did not neglect, both to confer with the learned and to acquire a fine library of foreign books. No man in all of England was better qualified for the office of technical adviser for various overseas voyages than was the skilled mathematician, astronomer, and astrologer John Dee, with his friendships throughout the Continent and within the Elizabethan Court.

It is known that Dee's advice was sought in 1553 by Sebastian Cabot when he undertook to organize the first Northeast expedition, thus beginning in earnest an era of English expansion. And when the Duke of Northumberland also turned to the promotion of the discovery of Cathay by way of the Northeast (a venture which from the promise it held of new markets for English woolens had gained the support of the great London merchants), it was again Dee who was asked to put his skills at the new company's disposal. In 1559 Dee made his services available to the Muscovy Company. He instructed those heading the voyage (Stephen and William Burroughs) in various mathematical and technical skills. And although the Muscovy Company's discovery of a route to Persia and new trade led in the early 1560's to its practical abandonment of the search for Cathay, others like Jenkinson, Sir Humphrey Gilbert, and John Dee kept Cathay before the public mind.

Dee, however, did not abandon his "other" studies. . . . Sometime in the early 1550's Dee wrote two astronomico-geographical treatises for the Duchess of Northumberland. He also published a number of treatises on subjects apparently remote from geography. The most important of these was his ***Hieroglyphic Monad Explained Mathematically, Cabalistically, and Anagogically,*** written in the Neo-Platonic tradition with additional cabalistic embroideries. In this work, published in 1564 and dedicated to Maximilian, King of Hungary, Dee expressed his belief in the hidden sympathies and antipathies of things, the transmission of the force of the super celestial intellectual world to earth through the stars and planets, and the existence of spiritual beings of a high order not quite synonymous with the angels of Christianity. In addition, it is not surprising that in the text he expressed the belief that the letters of the alphabet embody great mysteries, that medicine is contained in the monad, and that people should raise cabalistic eyes to the sky. Dee indulged in much number mysticism and depiction of characters in the usual Neo-Platonic manner, holding that through the knowledge of superior numbers, one penetrates into the inner mysteries. After proclaiming that such mysteries were not for the vulgar, Dee closed the treatise with a request to the printer to print only a limited amount of copies of the work to be judiciously distributed to the initiated.

In 1570, however, Dee wrote one of his most significant works. In the form of a Preface to Henry Billingsly's *English Translation of Euclid,* he composed a magnificent exposition of the relationship and application of mathematics (especially arithmetic and geometry) to the practice of skilled arts and crafts. It was, in fact, a plea for the scientific method, and it obviously owed much to the great schoolman, Roger Bacon, of whom Dee was so devout a disciple.

Apart from its autobiographical details, the most important sections of the Preface were those dealing with mathematics as the essential foundation for the practice of surveying, navigation, cosmography, and hydrography. The twofold aspect of mathematics, as a pure and an applied science, was constantly on Dee's mind. And the discussion of navigation, and its obvious grounding in mathematics gave Dee an opportunity to remind his countrymen of their duties and privileges in the matters of discovery. In a passage which foreshadowed his later masterpiece, Dee asserted to his fellow Englishmen in a good Christian manner that

> In navigation none ought to have greater care to be skilful than our English pilots. And perchance some would more attempt, and other some willingly would be aiding, if they wist cer-

> tainly what privilege God had endued this island with, by reason of situation most commodious for navigation to places most famous and rich. . . . I say . . . some one or other should listen to the matter: and by good advice and by discreet circumspection, by little and little win to the knowledge of that trade and voyage; which now I should be sorry (through carelessness, want of skill and courage) should remain unknown and unheard of. Thereof verily might we grow commodity to this land chiefly, and to the rest of the Christian Commonwealth, far passing all riches and earthly treasure.

The final phrase on "riches" and "treasure" is a reference to that secret hope which really lay behind all Dee's efforts, the hope of a revelation of occult mysteries in the East.

In 1573, Dee's friend, the expansionist Edward Dyer, was restored to the Queen's favor, while another favorite, Christopher Hatton, was also rising to a position of importance. By now Dee obviously already had begun to dream of England as mistress of a Northern empire based on a command of the seas. And it was through the influence of these two men, both of whom had their hearts set on the discovery of Cathay, that Dee urged his expansionist schemes. In 1577 it was "To The Right Worshipfull, [*sic*] discrete, and singular fauorer, of all good Artes, and sciences, M. Christopher Hatton, Esquier: Captain of her Maiesties Garde, and Ientleman of her privy Chamber," that Dee dedicated the first volume (***A Pety Navy Royall***) of his *magnum opus*, ***General and Rare Memorials Pertayning to the Perfect Arte of Navigation.*** This work, ***A Pety Navy Royall,*** addressed to all those who "carefully desire the prosperous state of the Common Wealth, of this Brytish Kingdom, and the Politicall SECVRITIES therof," does not bear directly on discovery. But it has as its object the setting forth of the advantages of having a navy of vessels in permanent commission and the means whereby such a scheme could be financed. Such a fleet was, of course, a pre-requisite of the policy of expansion which Dee was advocating, namely that of establishing a British maritime Empire. And while many have dismissed Dee as a fanatic and a megalomaniac, his picture (on the front piece of the work in 1577) of Queen Elizabeth at the helm of the Christian ship of Europe, had in it an element of the prophetic.

Mingling what has become the traditional elements of expansion with God and patriotism, Dee urged the importance of establishing a *Pety Navy Royall* of "three score tall ships or more, but in no case fewer," of 80 to 200 tons burden to be thoroughly equipped and manned "as a comfort and safeguard to the Realme." He shows the security this navy would give to English merchants:

> I report me to all English Marchants . . . of how great value to them, and Consequently, to the Publik-Weale, of this Kingdom, such a securitie were? Whereby, both outward, and homeward (continually) their Marchantlike Ships (Many or few, great or small) may, in our Seas, and somewhat farder, pas quietly vnpilled, vnspoyled and vntaken, by Pyrates, or others. . . .

This navy would also "decipher our coasts," sound channels and harbors, and observe tides. Thousands of soldiers, he says, "will thus be hardened and well broke to the rage and disturbance of the sea, so that in time of need we shall not be forced to use all fresh water soldyers" ready at hand.

Dee then touched on the question of unemployment: "hundreds of lustry handsome men will this way be very well occupied and have needful maintenance, which are now idle or want sustenance, or both." Quoting the ancient advocate of sea strength, Pericles, Dee reminded his audience that "These skilful sea-soldyers will be more traynable to martiall exploits, more quick-eyed and nimble than the landsmen." Not only will the *Pety Navy Royall* look after pirates, but it also would protect England's valuable fisheries with the result that "many a hundred thousand pounds yerely Revenue, might grow to the Crown of England, more than (now) doth."

Coming to the financial side, he asserts that every natural born subject of the "Brytish Impire" will willingly contribute towards this "perpetuale benevolence for sea security" the hundredth penny of his rents and revenues, and the five-hundredth penny of his valuation. Dee would end the carrying off of English gunpowder and saltpeter from the realm. "Good God," he cried, "who Knoweth not what provise is made and kept in other Common Weales against armour carrying out of their limits?" He deplores the wholesale destruction of English forests and timber (which is needed for ships) to keep the iron works going.

The question of the limits of sea jurisdiction was also carefully discussed by John Dee. At that time it was commonly held that the diversity of natural products between one country and another was divinely appointed to promote intercourse between nations, and hence that God intended the seas to be free to all. Dee, however, declared for a "closed sea." He held that closed waters extend for 100 miles from a nation's shore, or in the case of narrow seas (less than 200 miles across) to a point mid-way between the home and foreign coasts. By laying claim for England to the shores and islands conquered by the former British Kings, Arthur and Madoc, and hence to a stretch of sea for a hundred miles around each of these, Dee was able to establish fairly well a rightful jurisdiction across the North Atlantic and Arctic Oceans (the recent discoveries of Stephen Burroughs having extended British rights toward the Northeast).

Dee devoted a final chapter to the history of "that Peaceable and Proudest Saxon, King Edgar," whose "yerely chief sommer pastymes [were] . . . sayling round about his whole Isle" guarded with "hys grand nauy of 4,000 sayls, at the least." Then he asks, "Shall we . . . not Iudge it, some parte of wisdome, to Imitate carefully, in some little Proportion . . . the prosperous Pastymes of Peaceable King Edgar, that Saxonicall Alexander" who "so Highly, and Faithfully [served] . . . the glory of God . . . ?"

Dee then concludes by asserting that England must attain this "incredible politicall mystery"—the supremacy of the seas. England must be "Lords of the Seas" in order that its "wits and travayles" may be employed at home for the enriching of the Kingdom, that "our commodities (with due store reserve) may be carried abroad," and that peace and justice may reign, for, as he earlier stated, "It is an olde Proverb, A Sword Keepeth Peace."

Enough has been said of this book to show that, among other things, it was a remarkable contribution towards the history of the naval and fishing industries of Great Britain. Dee's treatise voiced the ideals of many sixteenth-century Englishmen, and twelve years later with the defeat of the Armada they were to be realized. A. L. Rowse, in his *Elizabethans and America* recently wrote: "Strange to say—and everything about Dee is strange—the megalomaniac proved prophetically right: perhaps he was not a clairvoyant for nothing after all."

In spite of John Cabot's early failure, in 1497, to reach Cathay by sailing west and north from England, the belief in a Northwest Passage around America persisted for many years. Englishmen sent voyage after voyage in this profitless and discouraging quest. The most recent examples of the search for the Northwest Passage were the three voyages of Martin Frobisher in 1576, 1577, and 1578. Dee was intimately involved in these attempts, dealing with the expedition both as a promoter and an official geographer. As a promoter he had subscribed some money to Frobisher but although a shareholder in the venture, George Parks is quite correct in maintaining that Dee's "economic interest was in all likelihood a result and not a cause of his intellectual interest; he was probably adviser first and investor second." As early as 1576, even before the writing of his ***General and Rare Memorials*** Dee had been called upon to give lectures in the art of navigation to Frobisher's company.

At about this same time (1577-1580) Francis Drake was making his successful voyage around the world. There is strong evidence that Dee was also in the counsels of those responsible for that venture. The promoters of Drake's voyage included the Earl of Leicester, Walsingham, a Court Secretary and leader of the colonial party, Hatton, and Dyer, all of whom were close acquaintances of Dee. And the earliest entries in Dee's ***Private Diary*** refer to visits from Drake's friends and backers at precisely this time.

By the year 1577 the active, restless brain of Humphrey Gilbert was at work on the problem of the exploration and colonization of America, and it is perhaps more than a coincidence that Gilbert called on Dee the day before he affixed his signature to the document entitled: "How her Majesty May Annoy the King of Spain." On November 6th, 1577, Dee recorded, "Sir Umfrey Gilbert cam to me at Mortlak." Shortly thereafter Gilbert was awarded a patent for his colonizing scheme in the New World. Only about three weeks later Dee was summoned to the Court to explain to both the Queen and Secretary Walsingham (who was behind both Drake's and Gilbert's voyages) her title to the land to be colonized.

While most Englishmen justified England's right to land in the New World on John Cabot's 1497 voyage, Dee declared the Queen's title rested on discoveries first made under King Arthur, then Madoc and later by the British merchant-explorer Thorne (1494) as well as Cabot three years after. And it was on this priority that Gilbert's patent rested. To accompany his views on the matter Dee also drew up a map of Atlantis (the New World) as well as several tracts on the "hydrographic description of the Atlantis." Dee thought that the term generally used at that time for America, "West Indies," was misleading; he preferred the term "Atlantis," even over "America." In all probability Dee took the term "Atlantis" from Plato's *Timaeus* which opens with the tale of the old Athenian State that fought for its own and others' freedom against the people of Atlantis until the earthquake ended the old Athenian race, and the Atlantean continent was swallowed in the sea. John Dee owned copies of many of Plato's works, including the *Timaeus.*

In 1579, as his ***Diary*** mentions, Dee was already in touch with Adrian Gilbert and John Davis, the two men later associated with the Northwest Passage attempts of 1585-1587. In June 1580, he was in touch with the two men again, while in August of the same year Dee obtained from Humphrey Gilbert a grant to what essentially amounted to the royalties of discovery of all the land north of the fiftieth latitude (the abandoned Frobisher region). Queen Elizabeth graciously commanded Dee to attend her Court more often and he was not slow to avail himself of the invitation. On October 3, 1580, he brought her further proof of her ***Titles to Foreign Lands,*** written by his hand on two parchment rolls. A week later the Queen called at his Mortlake estate and "withall told me," he inscribed in his ***Diary,*** "that the Lord Threasorer [Burghley] had greatly commended my doings for her title, which he had to examyn, which title in two rolls he had brought home two howrs before . . . ."

In 1581 Dee's thought centered upon America and apparently he wrote a great volume in Latin on the propagation of the Christian Faith among the Infidels of Atlantis. A year later Dee involved himself with Richard Hakluyt in an entirely new plan for reaching Cathay. At the same time another of Gilbert's chief backers, Sir George Peckham, came to see Dee and inquire into the English title to North American lands. In addition the "young [sea captain] Mr. Hawkins, who had byn with Sir Francis Drake, cam to . . . Mortlak." The following year, 1583, however, saw Dee far more actively involved in overseas exploits than previously.

Early in 1583 the definite formulation of Adrian Gilbert's plans to search for a Northwest Passage, based on Dee's technical advice, came to a head. A clear picture of numerous meetings held both at Dee's home and elsewhere is preserved in his ***Diary.*** On January 23, 1583 "the Ryght Honorable Mr. Secretary Walsingham cam to my howse, where by good lok he found Mr. Awdrian Gilbert, and so talk was begonne of Northwest Straights discovery." And on January 24th, 1583, Dee, "Mr. Awdrian Gilbert, and John Davis went by appointment to Mr. Secretary to Mr. Beale his howse, where only we four were secret, and we made Mr. Secretarie privie of the N. W. passage, and all charts and rutters agreed uppon in generall." Once again, on March 6th, 1583, Dee recorded that "I, and Mr. Adrian Gilbert and John Davis, did mete with Mr. Alderman Barnes [one of the most influential Directors of the Muscovy Company]. Mr. Townson [a London merchant who was often associated with discoveries] and Mr. Yong [?] and Mr. Hudson [Thomas Hudson, father of Henry, and one of the founders of the Muscovy Company], about the N. W. voyage." One of the results of this project was the license granted to Adrian Gilbert and John Davis to explore and plant colonies in the Northern part of Atlantis (observe Dee's influence in the name).

Dee lived for 25 years after 1583, the date of the last extract from his ***Diary,*** and he continued to make notes of important events as they occurred. Yet we find no further allusion in his journal to any of the other expeditions that ensued, nor do we find any further reference made to those who were engaged in them.

Besides immersing himself in geographical pursuits, Dee, over the years, had continued to nourish his interests in astrology and alchemy. In addition, for some time he had engaged in séances with a series of mediums to call up spirits from whom he hoped to learn the secrets of God and nature; those very secrets he sought from his geographical exploits. During the previous year Dee made the acquaintance of a young man, Edward Kelley, who, in Dee's mind, had marked mediumistic powers. Daily crystal-gazing séances again were resumed and Dee believed himself to be conversing with Neo-Platonic angelic spirits. In May 1583, Dee was introduced to the Polish Prince, Laski, then on a visit to England. Laski, too, was a disciple of the occult and when he visited Dee at Mortlake, Laski, Dee, and Kelley spent the entire night prying into hidden mysteries. Shortly thereafter, on September 21, 1583, Dee and Kelley, along with their families, left England in favor of the Continent. It was now that Dee abandoned his geographical activities for others that, perhaps he believed, would bring him more quickly to his ultimate goal.

If the actual attainment of the goal is a measure of success, then John Dee, notable mathematician, philosopher, astronomer, and keen student of geography and discovery was a failure. Nevertheless, it was such failures, both on the practical and theoretical side, that paved the way for the successes and clearer knowledge of the following decades. In claiming for Dee an important place in the history of sixteenth-century English geography it is sufficient to state that he was the teacher, technical instructor, friend, and adviser to most of the English mathematicians, astronomers, and geographers of his day. His pupils include such illustrious men as Richard Chancellor, Stephen and William Burroughs, Anthony Jenkinson, Martin Frobisher, Christopher Hall, Humphrey Gilbert, Adrian Gilbert, John Davis, Walter Raleigh, and Francis Drake, as well as Thomas Digges, Sir Edward Dyer, and Sir Philip Sidney. For his unceasing efforts in instructing mariners and scientists in their attempts to unveil hidden corners of the earth, John Dee is entitled to an honored place in the history of geography.

Prior to 1583 John Dee appeared as a man of learning and a Court favorite—astronomer, mathematician, a brilliant lecturer and a diligent prober in chemical and alchemical secrets. He had written on navigation, history, logic, travel, geometry, astrology, and a host of other subjects. He had essayed to found a national library and he was contemplating a great work upon the reformation of the calendar. Had he remained in England, Dee doubtless would have taken a conspicuous part in later geographical ventures. It was in the critical year of 1583, however, that this man engaged in respectable popular efforts turned aside earthly wisdom in favor of the spiritual, and thereby came into disrepute in the eyes of so many of his contemporaries. Increasingly, reports were spread that Dee was initiated into the magical arts, helped by demons, and the label of "sorcerer" and "conjurer" of evil spirits became permanent. He was to die in poverty in 1608.

Dee did not abandon his geographical interests, as Rowse suggests, because having "no terrestrial preferment, nothing to live by . . . [he] at last . . . accepted better prospects from the Continent and went off to raise the spirits. . . ." John Dee was an Elizabethan, and like many of his contemporaries he was part Medieval and part Renaissance. In true Renaissance style, Dee was a devotee of the new learning, but the sole object of that learning for Dee was the attainment of the older ideal of divine wisdom. Geographical exploration for Dee had not been a matter of material rewards. Beyond a concern for enough money to support himself and his family Dee was not primarily interested in financial matters, for if he had been, he would not have refused the yearly stipend of 200 French crowns offered him in Paris. A revealing paragraph from Dee's ***Autobiographical Tracts*** further bears this point out and is worth quoting.

> To be most briefe . . . as concerning my forraine credit, . . . I might have served five Christian Emporers; namely, Charles the Fifth, Ferdinand, Maximilian, this Rudulph, and this present Moschovite: of every one their stipends directly or indirectly offered, amounting greater each, then other: as from 500 dollars yearely stipend to a 1000, 2000, 3000; and lastly, by a Messenger from this Russian or Moschovite Emporer, purposely sent, unto me at Trebona castle . . . of my coming to his court at Moskow . . . there to enjoy at his Imperial handes £2000 sterling yearely stipende . . . .

Once again, if Dee was interested in financial betterment would he not have accepted any one of these positions rather than die in poverty, as he did?

For Dee, rather, overseas exploration was part of the search for something deeper; it was a probing for the heart of all knowledge, for the Infinite, for the Unknowable. Signs of this already were clearly visible in his ***Pety Navy Royall*** when Dee declared the reasons that he "doth wish and advise part of the publik threasory to be bestowed upon some two or three honest men who should be skilful in Forreyn languages." For "within the next few years," Dee continued, "in farder Cuntries great Affayres are by some of our Country-Men to be handled: If God continue his Gracious Direction and Ayde thereto, as he hath very comfortably begun: and that, *by means not yet published.*" For more than thirty years Dee had sought true wisdom in spirits, books, men, and distant new lands—always, however, unsuccessfully. If concentrated geographical activities failed, perhaps the shew-stone and angels would bring him to his goal.

To Dee the spirits he called upon were angels; he could not believe that he had broken the ideas of Christianity. But by the popular verdict of Elizabethan Christianity they must be devils; angels would have no such commerce with men. The case, therefore, for Dee's contemporaries was one in which the scientist abandoned his profession to resort to the supernatural. For Dee, however, that distinction was meaningless, for as he repeatedly said throughout all his life, *all* knowledge served God. In order to pursue that knowledge as he now saw fit, Dee was forced to turn once again to the Continent.

Beginning with Prince Laski's visit in May 1583, the accounts of his doings with spirits were minutely written down by Dee. They later were printed and published under the title of ***A True and Faithfull Relation of What Passed for many Years Between Dr. John Dee and Some Spirits.*** This illuminating work which throws a great deal of light on the reason behind Dee's psychical activities suggests that Dee's ultimate aims in both his geographical and spiritual exploits were one and the same. Especially revealing is Dee's confession that he

> began and declared by long course of study for forty years, alwayes, by degrees going forward, and desirous of the best, and pure truths in all manner of studies, wherein I had passed, and that I passed as many as were commonly known and more than are commonly heard of. But that at length I perceived onely God (and by his good Angels) could satisfie my desire; which was to understand the natures of all creatures, and the best manner how to use them to his divine honor and glory. . . . And herein I had dealed sundry wayes: And at length had found the mercies of God such as to send me the instruction of Michael, Gabriel, Raphael, and Uriel, and divers other his good and faithful Messagers. . . .

Dee, the astrologer, had always been in close touch with psychic phenomena. The old idea of access to certain stores of wisdom which God had withheld from man, but presumably gave to spiritual creatures of a higher order, had long attracted him. In addition, this profoundly pious man was convinced that God desired to hide nothing from the faithful seeker. This was confirmed for Dee by the sacred words of the angel Gabriel who uttered to him: "If thou remain my servant, and do the works that are righteous, I will put Solomon behind thee, and his riches under thy feet." Therefore, man with God's aid, may establish a real communication with the spiritual world through the calling of good spirits. Once convinced of his mediumistic powers, God's wish to enlighten him through His angels became a reality for Dee. In fact, the voice of another of the divine messengers even had told him to "pluck up . . . thy heart and be merry" and "pine not thy Soul away with inward groanings," for "I will open unto thee the Secrets of Nature and the riches of the world" and "I will disclose unto you such things, as shall be wonderfull, and of exceeding profit." It is, then, no wonder that Dee unhesitatingly left the island empire in favor of the Continent to seek and receive the true wisdom needed to fashion him according to his Maker. In John Dee's own words, all his endeavors, material and spiritual alike, only sought to "highly please, the eternall and almighty God, in executing for him the verity of his mercifull promises, generally made to all his sincere worshippers."

English science in the sixteenth century was, on the whole, practical and experimental. Most leading scholars were not interested in abstract theory, except in so far as it was necessary for determining fundamental principles. They had a clear vision of the practical utility of science for the relief of man's estate. A few, on the other hand, were infused with the older medieval attitude and sought knowledge for its revelation of the truths of God. For Dee, however, the two traditions, did not conflict; rather, they were in harmony and indeed complemented each other. John Dee should be recognized as a particular variant of the proto-typical Elizabethan marriage of science, pseudoscience, and religion in the search for that divine unity which lay like a pattern behind the façade of nature. (pp. 22-34)

Walter I. Trattner, "God and Expansion in Elizabethan England: John Dee, 1527-1583," in Journal of the History of Ideas, *Vol. XXV, No. 1, January-March, 1964, pp. 17-34.*

C. H. Josten (essay date 1964)

[*Josten was curator of the Museum of the History of Science at Oxford University. In the following excerpt, he explicates Dee's* Monas hieroglyphica, *asserting that his alchemy is metaphysical rather than practical and proposing likely sources.*]

In the opinion of Dr. Meric Casaubon (1599-1671), John Dee "was a Cabalistical man, up to the ears, . . . as may appear to any man by his ***Monas Hieroglyphica,*** a book much valued by himself". Casaubon had read the book; " . . . it is soon don", he continues, "it is but a little book, but I must profess that I can extract no sense nor reason (sound and solid) out of it: neither yet doth it seem to me very dark or mystical".

If Casaubon failed to detect anything dark or mystical in the treatise, he cannot have given much attention to its perusal. To any reader conversant with mystical or alchemical writings Dee's ***Monas Hieroglyphica*** bristles with difficult problems of interpretation. The author of the ***Monas*** seems to be taking his reader on a conducted tour through a dark room where, every now and then, he strikes a light to illuminate one out of a multitude of objects apparently assembled there for a distinct purpose. The reader guesses soon that other objects, which he perceives dimly glistening in the background, are probably more pertinent to that purpose than the one set before him for which bland and seemingly lucid explanations are offered. Dee goes so far as to assert that, although he called the work hieroglyphic, it is endowed with a clarity and rigour almost mathematical; yet at the same time he leaves it to the reader even to guess that the subject of the elaborate display, which he is asked to view in such dim light, is the hermetic quest. The semblance of clarity is achieved by discussing that dark subject under the guise of a symbolic sign invented by Dee, which is his monad. This symbol indeed lends itself easily to digressive secondary interpretations of a numerological, cabbalistic, astrological, cosmological, or mathematical nature, all which, however, are without any doubt given so as to establish significant connexions with the all-embracing central theme, alchemy, which is barely mentioned.

The specific message which Dee tried to convey by his symbol of the monad, and by his treatise thereon, is lost. His explanations are sometimes explicitly addressed to *mystae* and *initiati* whose secrets we do not possess. In particular, a full understanding of the alchemical import of the treatise would presuppose a knowledge of the oral tradition of the alchemists which, so far, has resisted the onslaught of historical research. It is also unknown whether it was Dee's purpose merely to illustrate by a new symbol the existing fund of alchemical thought, or whether he meant to add to that fund novel experiences of his own whose veiled interpretation, compressed into a symbol, would enlighten the few as it would baffle the many. He was at any rate anxious lest what he was writing—and indeed what he had written—should fall into the hands of worldlings who would be confused by their imagined understanding, or of imposters. He feared also that an unlawful knowledge of mysteries might be gained by unworthy persons who would correctly interpret, but abuse, his all too candid exposition. (pp. 84-5)

In Dee's [***Monas Hieroglyphica***] the courteous language of modesty is strangely blended with expressions of an excessive pride. [This] gift to King Maximilian [of Hungary], he asserts, is small in bulk, but of the very rarest quality. In his scheme of rarity, the *Arbor Raritatis,* he places the book at the lowest degree of philosophizing and dares but hope that every now and then it may rise a little above that level. Yet in the same context he explains that only one out of a thousand honest and dedicated philosophers may be expected to have had more than a foretaste of the fundamental truths of natural science, whilst only one in a million of them will combine a thorough knowledge of things natural, especially of astronomy and astrology, with an insight into supracelestial virtues and metaphysical influences. "That probably singular hero", who finds himself alone among a thousand millions of men of the common sort, is not only Dee's ideal, but also an image with which, at times at least and perhaps in a somewhat hesitant manner, he inclines to identify himself. Clearly he is himself a philosopher who—rightly—claims to have access to the best of such natural knowledge as his time is able to offer, especially in the kindred sciences of mathematics, astronomy, and astrology, in which he is a recognized authority. At the same time he is undeniably a philosopher of strong metaphysical aspirations, as the argument of the ***Monas Hieroglyphica*** bears out on almost every page. Since he never doubts the quality of his work in either the natural or the metaphysical field, one may infer that only good manners or scholarly diplomacy prevent him from saying expressly how far removed, by elevation, he considers himself to be from the multitude of his contemporaries, even the learned ones: The ***Monas Hieroglyphica*** will rectify the concepts of the grammarians. Admiring arithmeticians will be taught a new notion of number. The geometers will find their science insufficiently established. Those using or making instruments—the musicians, the astronomers, and the opticians—will realize that their labours have become obsolete, when they learn how the doctrine of the *Monas* performs the work of their instruments by itself. The cabbalists will be made to realise that their art is universal, not confined to the language of the Jews, and that there is, besides the common and vulgar cabbalistic interpretation of the spoken and written word, another "real" cabbala, exemplified by the *Monas,* a divine gift, which explores the whole of Creation by new arts and methods.

At this point of his argument Dee calls his ***Monas Hieroglyphica*** a magic parable. The psychological situation in which the treatise was written, therefore, suggests itself as that of an intellectually bold and lonely man, driven back on himself by speculations so daring that he wishes to withhold them from the many, a man to whom ideas are more important than their application, and consequently one who wishes to discover learned men—and, surely, also patrons—of a similarly rare and introspective bent of mind. It may indeed have been the principal purpose of the treatise to arouse the interest and sympathy of such men. The message would reach them even if King Maximilian proved to be not of their number. To them alone, at any rate, the code signals of Dee's magic parable appear to be addressed.

The Platonist Dee, to whom the power of a cosmic symbol invented by himself could seem to make the astronomers' work superfluous, also reveals himself in a passage of his dedicatory letter to King Maximilian, where he declares his restitution of the planetary and zodiacal symbols to their proper shapes to be such as either in times past these symbols had actually been or as our forebears would have wished them to be; he is not sure, therefore, whether he is the restorer of an old discipline or the founder of a new one. In other words he asserts that, by means of anamnesis, he had found the past within himself such as it was, or had reached a level of introspection from which it was possible for him to develop the thoughts of his spiritual ancestors, the ancient sages, precisely as they would have wished. There does not appear to exist for him any material difference between those alternatives. Indeed the object of the true Platonist is to get nearer to the one ideal truth, which is secretly, and more or less perfectly, mirrored in the depths of the human mind just as it may, with more or less clarity, be recognized in the vestiges of a venerable past that had been nearer to the golden age of knowledge than the debased present.

This reconstruction of Dee's impassive attitude towards the world of external appearances and of action, and of his sceptical view of the chances of spiritual attainment remaining in his own age, is confirmed by his opinions on alchemy. The alchemists, i.e. those labouring in the transmutation of metals, are denounced as wretched and inexperienced impostors. In the context a hint is given to the effect that man, not metal, is the subject of alchemical transmutation, if rightly conceived. Yet Dee does by no means regard the alchemical quest as lying entirely in the spiritual field. Man may be the primary subject of transmutation, but he who has been transmuted will be able to produce the philosophers' stone in the external world. This, at least, seems to be the only interpretation of Dee's

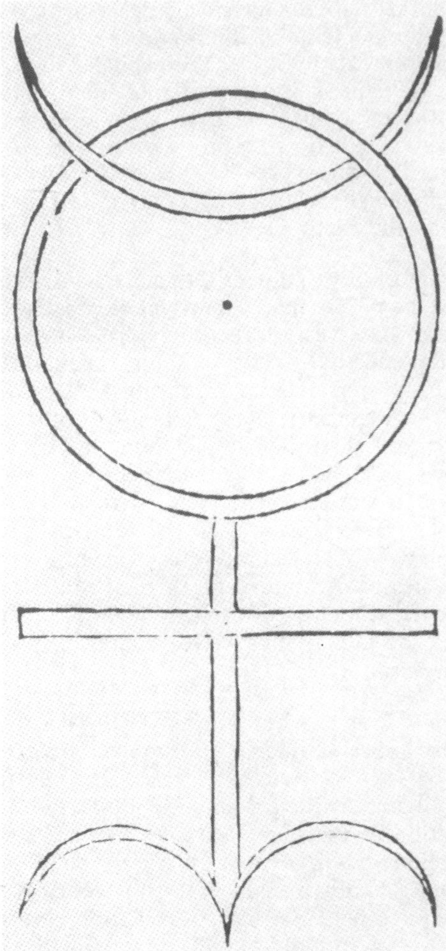

Dee prepared this drawing of the Monas emblem for the Monas hieroglyphica. *The figure is composed of interlocking symbols representing interrelated alchemical elements and celestial bodies.*

views on alchemy compatible with his assertion that, besides certain mystical vessels (darkly described in Theorem XXII), certain common vessels will also be required in the process, vessels whose shapes and materials, he says, it is unnecessary for him to discuss. In another dark passage, which alludes to the philosophers' mercury and its replacement by the Sun, i.e. gold, Dee asserts that this operation (which is the final stage in the transmutation of metals) can no longer be performed in the present age, as it was in the past performed by some great experts, unless indeed one let the work be governed by a certain soul which has been severed from its body by the art of controlling the fire (*ars pyronomica*), a work very difficult and fraught with dangers because of the fiery and sulphurous fumes which it occasions. This passage defies complete and certain interpretation, but indicates beyond doubt that, in Dee's view, the chances of alchemical success in the external world are diminishing as that world, by progressing in time, descends into spiritually darker ages, and that any palpable success in the transmutation of metals may, if at all, be hoped for only after the successful completion of a most unusual and dangerous work. If one assumes that the soul, which in this dangerous adventure is to be separated from its body, is the human soul (or part thereof), then the *ars pyronomica* by which the work is to be performed must be primarily spiritual alchemy, the very *astronomia inferior* of which the monad is Dee's chosen symbol. The fiery and sulphurous fumes attendant on the work would thus seem to denote spiritual, or psychological, dangers rather than poisonous vapours. Yet another passage suggests that the subject which is to be transmuted in the process symbolized by the monad is the artist, or *magus,* himself, and that it is his soul which, in a mystical sense, has to be separated from its body: When the terrestrial centre of the monad (which centre may here well mean the human body) has been united in a perpetual marriage to a certain supernal influence of solar and lunar quality, the monad can no longer "be fed or watered on its native soil", and he who fed it will himself undergo a metamorphosis as a result of which he will henceforth only rarely be beheld by mortal eye; he will then enjoy that invisibility of the *magi* which the doctrine of the monad has the power to confer. It would seem, therefore, that the aim of the secret discipline which Dee wished to express as well as to conceal in his treatise was the elevation of certain chosen and most rare mortals to an existence transfigured by direct participation in astral and supracelestial influences, an existence in which they would be masters of Nature and free from the humbling limitations of ordinary life in the body. Those alchemists of his own time who were merely trying to produce gold, therefore, appeared to him as impostors and as the unworthy heirs of a doctrine whose essential parts were not only unknown to them, but also beyond their reach. In this light it becomes less surprising that Dee should never have given the name of alchemy to the process of spiritual transmutation with which his treatise is chiefly concerned, though in doing so he would not have contravened ancient alchemical tradition or the usage current among the more spiritual alchemists of his time.

The symbol of the monad, as it appears on the title-page and in the illustrations of the text, is essentially the common alchemical and astronomical sign of Mercury to which the common sign of the first division of the zodiac, Aries, has been added at the bottom. The half-circle and the circle forming the upper part of the common Mercury symbol are represented as intersecting so as to convey the idea of a conjunction of Moon and Sun. Besides, the lunar half-circle has been enlarged into a crescent, and a central point has been added to the solar circle, in order to achieve complete identity of those upper elements of the monad symbol with the common signs of Moon and Sun. The central point of the solar circle symbolizes also the Earth around which the Sun, the Moon, and the other planets, revolve; it is what Dee calls the terrestrial centre of the monad.

The sign of Aries appended to the cross at the bottom of the Mercury symbol, thus modified to suit Dee's intentions, is the first of three signs in the zodiac which the astrologers assigned to the element of fire, the so-called fiery triplicity (Aries, Leo, Sagittarius). Its addition to the symbol of the monad is intended, as Dee states expressly, to signify that in the work of his monad (*in huius Praxi Monadis*) the aid of fire is required.

If one leaves aside all refinements and all secondary interpretations with which Dee so confusingly invests his concept of the monad, the most general and obvious idea conveyed by its symbol is, therefore, that of the alchemical process: Mercury, i.e. the philosophers' mercury, is seen as being activated by alchemical fire (*Ignis ille Arietinus*). The inclusion of the monad symbol in an egg-shaped escutcheon points not only to the supposedly oviform orbit of the planet Mercury, but also to the hermetic vessel, or philosophical egg, in which the sublimation of the philosophers' mercury, resulting in the philosophers' stone, takes place.

The symbol of Mercury represents in alchemy the matter, the method, and the result of the alchemical process. Accordingly the modified mercurial symbol which is that of Dee's monad may be assumed to stand for the subject, the method, and the final achievement in Dee's notion of the hermetic discipline. It represented to him in its broadest interpretation, therefore, the principle of transmutation itself, that principle of which Mercury is the universal agent and of which mercurial man, i.e. the true alchemist or *magus,* as a fit recipient of that influence, is the noblest subject. In this light, man appears most clearly not only as the subject, but also as the agent of the process in a passage of our text where Dee goes so far as to identify the philosophers' mercury with the microcosm and with Adam:

> Et, (Nutu Dei,) iste est Philosophorum Mercurius ille Celeberrimus, Microcosmus, & Adam.

Thomas Tymme observed, therefore, correctly in the "Epistle Dedicatorie" of the English translation of the ***Monas Hieroglyphica*** which he intended to publish [in or after 1602] that Dee's "whole purpose & drift is to give unto [Mercury] the Mastery in Alchemy, & the [alpha] and [omega] in the worke", though he was not in the least aware of the stress which Dee intended to give to the preeminently spiritual and non-chemical character of his message.

One would try in vain to go any further in the alchemical interpretation of Dee's symbol and to derive from the text any information on the practical, or psychological, application of Dee's hermetic doctrine. Though he claims to provide not only starting points, but conclusive proofs of its validity to those "in whom inwardly there blazes fiery strength and a heavenly origin", the sum total of his learned circumlocutions, allusions, and digressions, though informative at their own level, does not give any access to that jealously guarded central secret, at least not to the modern reader who finds himself cut off from the oral traditions of the alchemists. It is, all the same, not possible to regard the ***Monas Hieroglyphica,*** even hypothetically, as a fraudulent mystification or as a learned hoax. The solemn sincerity of Dee's language, the known integrity of his character, the circumstances of the dedication of the treatise to King Maximilian, and the importance which Dee attributed to it in his later life, all argue strongly against any assumption of that nature.

One practical application of the symbol of his doctrine is, however, indicated in the text. Theorem XXIII contains elaborate instructions for the mathematical construction of the symbol of the monad, each part of which has to be of a size that is in strict numerical proportion to the size of every other part. Characteristically, no reasons are given for these rules:

> . . . if we put before you the reasons (which we possess) for the proportions here stated, or showed the causes of our design otherwise than we have done throughout this small work, [that is to say] in a manner explicit enough (to the wise), we should be skipping over limits that were judiciously prescribed to us.

These instructions are intended for the benefit of readers who would like to bear the symbol of the monad "on rings or seals, or to use it in other ways". They are addressed to the *Mechanicus,* i.e. the goldsmith or engraver, who manufactures such articles. Dee's own "London seal of Hermes", mentioned in the dedicatory letter, may indeed have been thus engraved. The "other ways" here mentioned of using the symbol may be an allusion to its supposed efficacity as a talisman or magic sigil. Dee states in the fifty-second aphorism of his [***Propaedeumata Aphoristica***], London, 1558 and 1568, that by the art of *κατοπτικη*, i.e. by reflection, an expert may impress any chosen stellar influence into any kind of matter much more strongly than this is done by Nature; this art, he continues, had been by far the most important part of natural magic to the ancient sages. In the next sentence of this aphorism Dee mentions *astronomia inferior* (i.e. alchemy), which evidently he regards as a proximate subject, as a discipline only slightly superior in dignity to the science of fixing stellar influences in this manner and then commends the symbol of his monad to Gerard Mercator (to whom the work is addressed) as the *insignia* of alchemy. It seems, therefore, reasonable to assume that Dee attributed to his symbol a power similar to that of other magic characters which were supposed to perpetuate stellar influences, beneficial or maleficent, when they were engraved, on metal or other materials, at astrologically suitable times.

It has not been possible to identify any ancient author as the principal source of Dee's ideas on the *monas* and on numbers. The writings of Plato, Nicomachus of Gerasa, Theon of Smyrna, Proclus Diadochus, and Michael Psellus, all contain passages which might have influenced Dee's thought; but he leaves the philosophical and mathematical implications of his concepts so vague that one cannot go any further in one's conjectures than indicate that editions of the works of Plato and of the mathematical treatises of Theon, Proclus, and Psellus, were in his library in 1583.

Trying to determine why Dee chose to name the universal principle of transmutation, and his symbol thereof, *monas,* i.e. an essential oneness (or, in the English terminology of his own coinage, a unit), one recalls the *una res* of the *Smaragdine Table* [an ancient alchemical text which in the middle ages was ascribed to Hermes Trismegistus]; but a more immediate source is perhaps to be found in chapter iii, of book II, of Henry Cornelius Agrippa von Nettesheym's work *De Occulta Philosophia,* which chapter is entitled "De unitate, & eius scala". The *scala unitatis,* at the end of the chapter, is a scheme listing the manifestations of essential oneness in the archetypal, the intellectual, the celestial, the elementary, the microcosmic, and the infernal worlds. The *lapis philosophorum* is there given as the representative of oneness *in mundo elementali* and is in the same scheme defined as *unum subiectum & instrumentum omnium virtutum naturalium & transnaturalium.* The text, which this scheme is intended to support and to elucidate, describes the principle of oneness in the elementary world in a passage which does not mention the philosophers' stone, but which, as the description of an agent, might more immediately be applied to the philosophers' mercury. As has already been noted, to the alchemists there was, however, no essential difference between the two, in so far as the philosophers' mercury stood for the matter, the method, and the result, of the alchemical process. Like Dee's *monas,* Agrippa von Nettesheym's notion of oneness in the elementary world, denotes, therefore, the principle of mercurial transmutation itself. Its definition, which follows, might indeed serve, without any modification, as one of Dee's concept:

> Una res est a Deo creata, subiectum omnis mirabilitatis, quae in terris, & in coelis est, ipsa est actu animalis vegetalis & mineralis, ubique reperta, a paucissimis cognita, a nullis suo proprio nomine expressa; sed in numeris figuris & aenigmatibus velata, sine qua neque Alchymia, neque naturalis magia, suum completum possunt attingere finem.

Essential oneness, or *monas,*—the constituent of numbers, though not itself a number—is the notion which links the alchemical contents of Dee's message with those many digressions on number symbolism, especially that of the Pythagorean tetraktys, and on the symbolism of geometry and of letters, with which his magical parable is enriched. Only some examples of such digressions will here be discussed: The doctrine of the *monas* is said to make numbers concrete and, as it were, corporeal by separating from them their formal quality, which the *magus* utilizes in a manner left unspecified. In geometry the principle of the *monas* is represented by the point. Straight line and circle, from which all manifestations take their origin, are inconceivable without that monadic point by whose action they are produced. The cross, which forms the lower part of the common symbol of Mercury and which in Dee's symbol of the monad lies between the circle of the Sun and the sign of Aries, is stated to signify the ternary (in particular the ternary of body, spirit and soul) inasmuch as it consists of two straight lines and the point of their intersection, and the quaternary inasmuch as it may be regarded as composed of four right angles whose eight sides (a secret octonary) coincide in four lines issuing from one point. The cross, by a combination of ternary and quaternary, therefore, also expresses the septenary. In the "mechanical magic" of the process which the symbol of the monad represents, the quaternary of the cross is to be understood as signifying the four elements issuing from a central source by drops becoming a flow. The addition of the numerical elements of the quaternary (one, two, three, and four) yields the denary, which is said to explain the *una res,* and whose virtue, further on in the treatise, is associated with the tetragrammaton.

The alchemical relevance of these seemingly extraneous and logically defective speculations is indicated by Dee's somewhat baffling conclusion that Sun and Moon contained in the monad desire their elements, in which there is a strong denarian proportion, to be separated by means of fire.

Interesting parallels to Dee's alchemical interpretation of the tetraktys, and of the denary derived therefrom, are found in a treatise of a German contemporary of Dee, the Paracelsian physician and alchemist Gerhard Dorn, who also employs the notion of *monas.* According to Dorn—as according to Agrippa von Nettesheym—oneness is the quality (*virtus*) by which all wonderful effects of Nature are induced. Ternary and quaternary lead towards the denary which, as a reproduction of the number one, gives access to the *monas* on a higher level; there is between those levels a continuous flow of exchanges by way of *ascensus* and *descensus.*

Agrippa von Nettesheym, Gerhard Dorn, and Dee may have derived their hermetic interpretation of the monad and the idea of its effect on the *magus* from Johannes Trithemius (1462-1516). There is at any rate a remarkable affinity between their concepts and those alluded to in two letters of Trithemius from which undated extracts are quoted in *Iac. Gohorii De Usu & Mysteriis Notarum Liber,* Paris, 1550, ff. H[iv]-I[iv]^{v}: the master who teaches a student of magic, Trithemius says in the first of these letters (which was addressed to a Prince Elector of the Holy Roman Empire called Joachim, should educate his pupil

> . . . per rectificationem a ternario in unitatem per binarium divisum: Clarius declarare tibi literis non possum nec velim. Deinde necesse est ut universi divisionem sciat, & totius tam inferioris quam superioris ab uno usque ad quaternarium in ternario quiescentem, noveritque ordinem ascensus & descensus, gradum, numerum, fluxum, refluxum, esse & non esse, unum & tria. Quod scire difficillimum est, & omnium mirandorum effectuum radix est fundamentum in magia tam naturali quam supernaturali.
>
> [. . . by rectification from the ternary, through the divided binary, to unity. I cannot explain [this] to you more clearly in writing, nor would I want to do so. Furthermore, it is necessary that he [i.e. the *magus*] should know the division of the universe, and the order of ascent and descent in the inferior as well as the superior worlds from one to the quaternary resting in the ternary, [what be] degree, number, flowing, flowing back, being and non-being, [what] one and [what] three. All which is very difficult to know and is the root [and] foundation of all wonderful effects in natural as well as in supernatural magic.]

The second letter, which was directed "ad amicum quendam", correlates the monad and the tetraktys with the ascent of the element of earth, first to the region of celestial water, then to that of fire which is the region of the angels, and lastly to the "unum simplex, id est anima mundi". This essential oneness, which is the soul of the world and the monad, is stated to be not God, but an *imago* of the human mind, neither alive nor dead, but most powerful.

> "Et dico quicunque huius purae simplicitatis & simplicis puritatis notitia sublimatus est, in omni scientia naturali & occulta consummatus erit."
>
> [And I say that whoever is sublimated by a knowledge of this pure simplicity and simple purity will be accomplished in every natural and occult science.]

The ascent to the monad is effected "per ignem & amorem". Without this experience and knowledge, Trithemius affirms, the *magus* would not be able, without committing a crime, to impart any power to images, nor would a *chimista* without it be able to imitate Nature or to command to spirits (*spiritus compellere*); vaticination also would be impossible, as likewise it would be impossible to understand the laws governing any ingenious experiment. Further on in this letter Trithemius summarizes the processes of *ascensus* and *descensus,* which are simultaneous, as follows:

> Ad ipsum a ternario & quaternario, id est monadem progressus est, ut denarius compleatur, per ipsum est numero regressus ad unum, simul ascensus cum quatuor, & descensus ad monadem. . . . Omnes hoc monadis principium ignorantes, nihil in ternario proficiunt, & sacrum quaternarium non pertingunt.
>
> [To it, i.e. to the monad, one may proceed from the ternary and the quaternary, so that the denary be completed, from which, through number, there is a return to one[ness]; [there is thus] simultaneously an ascent and a descent to the monad through the tetraktys. . . . All those who do not know this principle of the monad will not gain anything in the ternary, and will not attain the sacred quaternary.]

It is the more likely that these ideas inspired the invention of Dee's symbol of universal transmution as he mentions expressly that by the doctrine of his ***Monas*** the element of earth may be raised "in Ignem, per Aquam".

The signs of the Sun, of the Moon, of Aries, and the cross of the elements (i.e. the component parts of the monad symbol which had been derived from straight lines and parts of the circumference of a circle) are shown to be the component parts also of the five remaining planets. Their shapes, inasmuch as they are at the same time the signs of metals (lead, tin, iron, copper, mercury) are subjected to a symbolical analysis bristling with alchemical allusions, whose interpretation defeats the powers of the present writer. A different allegedly old, symbol of Mercury is introduced, denoting a lunar kind of Mercury which is "the uterine brother" of the *mercurius philosophorum* and apparently precedes it in the alchemical process. The symbols of Saturn, of Jupiter, of the Moon, and of this lunar Mercury, are singled out as "geogamic" and are conflated into a fifth symbol which Dee leaves without comment; but for the missing element of the solar symbol, it is identical with that of the monad. In this context, as in other alchemical passages of the treatise, certain "revolutions" are mentioned—there are apparently four (or seven?) revolutions in all—for which no satisfactory explanation has been found, but which appear to refer to stages of the alchemical process.

One is equally at a loss to provide any elucidation of the deliberately veiled description of mystical vessels serving in the process, which Dee derives from an interpretation as an alpha and an omega of, respectively, the top and bottom parts of his monad symbol. The inscriptions of a scheme listing the mystical correspondences resulting from a consideration of the monad symbol as constituted by an alpha, a cross, and an omega, have, therefore, been left untranslated; likewise an even less intelligible scheme which seems to correlate the monad symbol—here, as in two other places, mysteriously appearing in a reversed position—with cosmic and alchemical interpretations of the tetraktys.

The principal enigmas of the ***Monas Hieroglyphica*** have thus been stated. The present writer cannot provide a better conclusion to his tentative comments than the one given by Thomas Tymme, at the end of his short introduction to Dee's treatise:

> Thus breifly I haue deliuered my Coniecture; if any can ayme more neere the Marke, I refuse not to learne.

(pp. 99-111)

C. H. Josten, "A Translation of John Dee's 'Monas Hieroglyphica' (Antwerp, 1564), with An Introduction and Annotations," in Ambix: The Journal of the Society for the Study of Alchemy and Early Chemistry, *Vol. XII, Nos. 2 & 3, June-October, 1964, pp. 84-111.*

Frances A. Yates (essay date 1969)

[*Yates, an English critic and educator, is highly regarded for her numerous studies of the Renaissance. In the following excerpt, she catalogues Dee's library to demonstrate the intellectual breadth and idiosyncrasies that rendered him a "perfect exemplar" of the English Renaissance. She further asserts that Dee's "Mathematicall Praeface," deriving from the Roman Vetruvius, represents the advent of Renaissance neoclassical architectural principles in England.*]

[Modern] historians of science have rehabilitated Dee, have drawn aside the veil of the ridiculous and deluded conjuror of nineteenth-century legend to show behind it the practical scientist fully abreast of the latest scientific thought, translating it into practical use for the service of his countrymen. Dee comes out now as in the van of Elizabethan movements, the maritime expansion, the scientific activity of all kinds, and moreover as particularly Elizabethan in spirit in his appeal to the rising artisan classes. His was a new and modern kind of learning which included technology as well as abstract speculation, which made an appeal to new social classes, as well as to the queen and to courtiers. In these most essential and important respects, no more complete mirror of the Elizabethan age could be found than John Dee.

The historians of science have made a great step forward towards the much needed new assessment of Dee but the picture which they have drawn is only a partial one. By concentrating on aspects which interest them, they have given the impression that Dee and his library have nothing to tell the historian of literature and the arts. But Dee's knowledge cannot be canalized into separate disciplines; it must be seen in the religious, philosophical, and magical contexts in which it was generated. The Cabalistic conjuror of the spiritual diaries was not different man from the practical scientist, adviser of mariners and life and soul of the movement for encouraging mathematical studies who interests the historian of science. He was the same man operating, or rather somewhat pathetically attempting to operate, on a different level.

In an unpublished doctoral thesis of 1953, I. R. F. Calder made an extensive study of Dee's life and work, attempting to cover the mathematics and science, the astrology and alchemy, the spiritualism, the magic and the Neoplatonic philosophy and religion. This thesis is the best effort so far made at dealing with Dee as a whole, though since it was written advances have been made in the understanding of the Renaissance Hermetic tradition to which Dee belonged. And the author omitted a full scale study of Dee's mathematical preface and of the catalogue of his library since he intended the thesis as a preparation for further studies.

The history of thought should not isolate out of the work of a personality those elements which seem of importance in the light of later developments. The history of thought is vitiated and distorted by this process. A man's thought should be seen in the round, including not only those aspects of it which a modern can admire but also those which moderns find difficult. The nineteenth century which excluded Dee from serious consideration because of his 'conjuring' was wrong as the historians of science have discovered. But to include him as a scientist whilst excluding his other sides is also incomplete. We need to see the man as a whole, and it is here, I would suggest, that the catalogue of the library can help.

In what follows I shall omit nearly all mention of the scientific works which have interested the historians of science, the works on geography extracted from the catalogue by Miss Taylor, the works on astronomy which bear on F. R. Johnson's researches on Dee as astronomer, the works on applied mathematics which relate to his importance in the busy development of instrument making in London in the later sixteenth century. I shall select works from the catalogue which seem of significance for Dee's outlook as a whole, to build up from them a picture of the context in which he saw his scientific work as a whole. This attempt to use the catalogue in this way will be but fragmentary and superficial but it may at least serve to draw attention to this absolutely basic document for the understanding, not only of Dee himself, but of the courtiers, noblemen, poets, scholars, scientists of the Elizabethan age for whom this was the best library in the country.

I take first the *De occulta philosophia* of Henry Cornelius Agrippa, copies of which are listed in the catalogue. This book gives the clue as to how the same man could be a mathematical scientist and at the same time a 'conjuror'. Agrippa divides the universe into the three worlds of the Cabalists, the natural or elemental world, where the Magus operates with natural magic, the middle celestial world where he operates with mathematical magic, and the supercelestial world where he operates with numerical conjurations. This was how Dee thought. His concentration on mathematics as the key to all sciences included operating with number in genuine science and operating with number to conjure angels.

The researches of recent scholarship have brought out that Agrippa's book was the logical, though extreme, outcome of the whole movement which is loosely called Renaissance Neoplatonism. This movement included a Hermetic and magical core to which Ficino gave expression in the *Libri de vita* and to which Pico della Mirandola added Cabalist magic. Thus from the Neoplatonic movement there grew as auxiliaries to it a host of writers of occult literature of the most varied kinds. As one would expect, Dee's library was extremely rich in all this literature.

It included all the major works of Ficino, both his own works and his translations from Plato and the Neoplatonists, and of Pico della Mirandola. There was a special section devoted to Cabalist books. Another section was devoted to Lullism, rich not only in Lull's own works but in those of later Lullists; this section is representative of the Renaissance revival of Lullism in association with Cabala, and includes the pseudo-Lullian *De auditu cabalistico.* Trithemius is strongly represented in the library, also Cardanus and Guillaume Postel. Dee did not forget the French Neoplatonists and had a copy of the *Mantice* of Pontus de Tyard. He had some modern Italian philosophers Patrizzi, Pomponazzi. And there are of course large collections of works on astrology and alchemy.

The arrangement of the catalogue is partially systematic though the system varies. Some groups of books seem arranged according to size, others according to language. There are also subject groupings, Paracelsist books (a large section), Lullist books, historical books, books of travel and discovery. One must therefore read through the whole catalogue in order to collect one author or subject which may appear under different groupings. Nevertheless there is nothing haphazard about the catalogue; the entries are clearly written and usually include date and place of publication as well as author and title.

Books of controversial theology are conspicuous by their absence. Dee had bibles in his library, and the psalms; he had some scholastic theology; he had Ficino's *Theologia Platonica,* and of course he had the *Pimander* and *Asclepius* of 'Mercurius Trismegistus', that is to say the *Corpus Hermeticum* and the *Asclepius.* He had Lactantius and Pseudo-Dionysius and Augustine's *Civitas Dei.* On the whole the catalogue gives the impression that Dee, though passionately interested in the supernatural, avoided dogmatic theology.

Science is of course dominant, the genuine sciences intermixed with the pseudo sciences. But Dee was also interested in the fine arts. . . . [He] had copies of Vitruvius and of Renaissance commentators on Vitruvius in his library;

he had Dürer on proportion; Luca Pacioli on proportion; many books on perspective; and Vasari's lives of the painters.

He had Greek and Latin poets, Homer and Hesiod, Pindar, Ovid of course, Catullus, Lucan. An interesting feature is the good representation of ancient dramatists. It is not surprising that he should have had the comedies of Plautus and the tragedies of Seneca, but he also possessed the comedies of Aristophanes and the tragedies of Sophocles and Euripides in Greek. These collections should perhaps be connected with an interest in the production of classical plays, of which we know of one certain example—namely that he made a theatrical machine for a production of the *Pax* of Aristophanes at Trinity College, Cambridge.

The library was well equipped with the usual Renaissance reference books, the *Hieroglyphica* of Pierio Valeriano, the *Mythologia* of Natalis Comes, the *Emblems* of Alciati. It was well stocked with dictionaries and grammars of various languages.

Musical theory was represented by Zarlino and other standard works. And the library possessed the leading Renaissance textbook on cosmic harmony, the *Harmonia mundi* of Francesco Giorgi. (pp. 7-11)

History is richly represented in the catalogue, history both ancient and modern. There is a large section on it and historical works appear here and there throughout the catalogue. The historical books reflect an important side of Dee's activities, his love of semi-mystical antiquarian scholarship and the passion for ancient British history used in compiling his genealogy of Queen Elizabeth. The list of books in English in the library contains many chronicles. The following is a selection from the list of English books: Holinshed's *Chronicles;* Thomas Cooper's *Chronicles;* Leonard and Thomas Digges's *Geometrical Practice;* John Bale's *Pageant of Popes;* William Bourne's *Art of Shooting;* Littlewood's *Tenures;* Robert Recorde's *Urinal of Physics;* Stowe's *Chronicles;* Grafton's *Abridgement of Chronicles.* A reader who knew no Greek and not much Latin could use Dee's library. He could browse to his heart's content in English chronicle history and study technical works in English written by members of Dee's scientific school—Leonard and Thomas Digges, Robert Recorde, William Bourne—and the English Euclid with Dee's famous preface to it.

Poets like Sidney and Dyer would find in the library not only all the books needed for their philosophical and scientific studies under Dee, but might glance in passing at his copy of Petrarch's sonnets, at Dante's *Inferno* with Giambullari's commentary, at Joachim Du Bellay's *Défense et illustration de la langue française.* The historians of science have done well by Dee but they have put other people off by giving the impression that his library was purely scientific in the modern sense of the word.

The whole Renaissance is in this library. Or rather it is the Renaissance as interpreted by Ficino and Pico della Mirandola with its slant towards philosophy, science, and magic, rather than towards purely grammarian humanist studies. It is a Renaissance without doctrinal ferocity, either Reformation or Counter Reformation, but with very strong mystical and magical leanings, a Renaissance which prefers to read of the hierarchies of angels with Pseudo-Dionysius (well represented in the library) rather than the works of Calvin. And it is a Renaissance situated in England, with its characteristic development of popular science with a strong practical bent, with an outlook towards navigation and the sea, and new lands beyond the sea, a Renaissance which includes in its historical studies the British History of Geoffrey of Monmouth (represented in the library) and the chronicles of England, a Renaissance which values poetry, ancient and modern, Greek and Latin, Italian and French. Though there are no English poets in the list of English books, one wonders whether the major Elizabethan poets may not all have used this library.

It is natural to compare the catalogue of Dee's library with the catalogue of another great library, drawn up in 1609, and which, unlike Dee's catalogue, has achieved the honour of learned publication. The catalogue of the Lumley Library, edited by Sears Jayne and F. R. Johnson, was published by the British Museum in 1956. The Lumley library possessed the works of Ficino and of Henry Cornelius Agrippa and a fair sprinkling of works containing Hermetic influences of various kinds. But that library has nothing like the scientific importance of Dee's library with its wealth of works of genuine scientific value. And the Lumley catalogue begins with theology, with an array of Fathers, commentaries on the Scriptures, works of controversial theology of a type which are conspicuously absent from Dee's library. The Lumley catalogue suggests a more conventional mind than the mind behind the Dee catalogue, yet the Lumley catalogue is published and available whilst the Dee catalogue is not. One asks oneself whether, in spite of the useful efforts of the historians of science, the ancient prejudice still operates, and Meric Casaubon's publication of the spiritual diaries still stands in the way of a proper historical and critical approach to one of the most important figures of the Elizabethan age.

It is surely time that Dee should be judged objectively and without prejudice, and that critical historical enquiry should be made, not only into the nature of his science and its place in the history of thought, but also into the nature of his religion and its place in the history of religion. What was Dee's religion? He certainly had one and a very strong one. He defined it in 1592, in a letter to the Archbishop of Canterbury, in which he says that from his youth up it has pleased the Almighty

> . . . to insinuate into my hart, an insatiable zeale, & desire to knowe his truth: and in him and by him, incessantly to seeke, and listen after the same; by the true philosophicall method of harmony: proceeding and ascending (as it were) *gradatim,* from things visible to consider of thinges inuisible: from thinges bodily to conceiue of thinges spirituall: from things transitorie or momentarie, to meditate of things permanent: by thinges mortal (visible and inuisible) to haue some perceiuerance of immortality. And to conclude, most briefely: by the most meruailous frame of the *whole world,* philosophically viewed, and circumspectly wayed, numbred,

> and measured (according to the talent, & gift of God from aboue alotted, for his diuine purposes effecting) most faithfully to loue, honor, and glorifie alwaies, the *framer* and *Creator* thereof. In whose workmanship, his infinite goodnesse insearchable wisdome, and Almightie power, yea his everlasting power, and diuinity, may (by innumerable meanes) be manifested and demonstrated.

It was the religion of a mathematician who believed that the divine creation was held together by magical forces. If we substitute mechanics for magic as the operative force used by the Creator, Dee's religion was perhaps not altogether unlike that of Isaac Newton.

The most fruitful and influential period of Dee's life, from the accession of Elizabeth until his departure from England in 1583, ended with the visit in May of that year of the Polish Prince Alasco, or Laski, who persuaded Dee to go with him to Poland. The Queen commanded that Laski should be received with honour on his visit to Oxford. In spite of the profusion of Latin plays, dinners, fireworks, and disputations which the university strained every nerve to provide, one has the impression—not only from Giordano Bruno's satires but from the subsequent sharp reproof of the Queen and the chancellor's harassed efforts at reform—that this public occasion focused attention upon certain weaknesses in post-Reformation Oxford. Laski's subsequent action is significant. For on the return journey from Oxford to London by river in the royal barge lent for the occasion, and on which he was accompanied by Philip Sidney and other distinguished people, he stopped at Mortlake in order to call upon Doctor Dee. Here is the entry in Dee's diary which records the event:

> June 15th, abowt 5 of the clok cam the Polonian Prince Lord Albert Lasky down from Bissham, where he had lodged the night before, being returned from Oxford whither he had gon of purpose to see the univerityes, wher he was very honorably used and enterteyned. He had in his company Lord Russell, Sir Philip Sydney, and other gentlemen: he was rowed by the Quene's men, he had the barge covered with the Quene's cloth, the Quene's trumpeters, &c. He cam of purpose to do me honor, for which God be praysed.

Surely it is of interest that we might now reconstruct the library in which Dee probably received these splendid guests. The divisions in the catalogue into books of different sizes, its partial subject divisions, books on history, books on geography, the Lullist section, the Paracelsist section, and so on, may actually represent the arrangement of the books on Dee's shelves. Around these shelves we may imagine Philip Sidney strolling, displaying the best library in England and one worthy to rank with some of the best in Europe. Oxford had nothing to show like this; the Reformers had turned out its scientific works—manuscripts of a type which Dee had taken the opportunity of rescuing—so that the Oxford of Roger Bacon and of the medieval Merton school was represented in his collection, which was also kept up to date by the acquisition of modern books.

Laski was so much impressed by Dee that he invited him to join him abroad. Feeling that there was little future for him in England, Dee accepted the invitation, and early in the autumn of 1583 he and Kelly left for Lascoe, the prince's seat near Cracow. The brains drain really began in 1583 when this most eminent mathematician, technologist, and magician was tempted to leave his native country. Before he left, Dee made the catalogue of his library, which is dated September 6th, 1583. Shortly after he left, an angry crowd broke into his house at Mortlake smashed his scientific instruments, and damaged the library.

The lamentable story of these events is told by Dee himself in the ***Compendious Rehearsall,*** under the heading 'A briefe note and some remembrance of my late spoiled Mortlake library.' He estimates the value of the books and manuscripts in it at £2,000, and says that it had taken him about forty years to collect them 'from divers places beyond the seas, and some by my great search and labour here in England.' He complains that he has had no compensation for the loss of his books and manuscripts, but it would seem that he did not lose them all. He speaks of there being above five hundred missing 'I mean of such as may be gotten for money, and so their value known; for some wanting are not to be gotten for money in any mart.' It would thus seem that only a part of his total collection had disappeared. But his other treasures were irrevocably destroyed or had disappeared, his quadrant made by Richard Chancellor, his great cross staff, the two globes of Gerard Mercator's best making. The cases containing documents were rifled, only the chalk marks on their exteriors remaining to give note of their former contents. This was 'a loss of great value in sundry respects as Antiquarians can testify', also the loss of a box containing a collection of seals. 'Clerks of the Records of the Tower', says Dee, 'satt whole dayes at my house in Mortlake gathering raritys to their liking out of them', an interesting glimpse of the use of Dee's house as a kind of combined British Museum and Public Record Office.

The period of the greatest splendour and usefulness of Dee's library was from about 1570 to 1583, a very important decade in English history. Nevertheless he was evidently able to rescue a considerable proportion of his books on his return to England in 1589 and perhaps to acquire more—he could not live without books. All the more lamentable therefore is the report transmitted by Anthony á Wood that Dee in his extremely penurious old age was forced to sell his books one by one to buy dinners. He died in 1608 at the age of eighty-one at his house at Mortlake, apparently a complete failure, but a tradition gathered about his name and his influence survived.

Dee comes straight out of a main Renaissance Hermetic stream which has reached him at rather a late date and bearing with it accretions gathered in the sixteenth century during which it had developed, both in more extremely occult directions and in more precisely scientific directions. The two aspects cannot be separated; they belong together at that date. In no way could this be demonstrated more clearly than by study of the catalogue of Dee's library in which books on his genuine scientific interests are inseparably mixed up with the pseudo-scientific literature.

As an example of this it is interesting to look at a page of the catalogue . . . on which appears a book entered as:

Copernici Revolutiones Nuremberg 1543.

This is Copernicus's epoch-making work in the original edition. It is marked in the margin with a triangle, denoting that Dee considers this an important book. It is immediately followed by Francesco Giorgi's *Harmonia mundi,* the Hermetic-Cabalist work of the Franciscan friar of Venice, also marked with a triangle as important. It is preceded a little way up the page by the *Polygraphia* of Trithemius, also marked with a triangle, the abstruse work on ciphers by one of the most intensely and abstrusely magical of Renaissance writers. And at the bottom of the same page, also marked with a triangle, is a work on chiromancy or palmistry. To Dee all is science, all is important, and this mysterious world of magic and science in which he moves is the world of the Elizabethan Renaissance.

Dee, however, might have looked less eccentric had he not lived in Elizabethan England where the mystico-magico-scientific movement ran counter to the official surface of learning, to the Protestant humanism of normal education. In Venice, as a member of some esoteric academy, he would have seemed more natural. But the esoteric academic movement had not developed in England. Dee's circle may have been something of the kind but it did not have the protection of some Cabalistic cardinal, such as Cardinal Egidius of Viterbo who patronized Francesco Giorgi. In the landscape of Elizabethan London Dee looked peculiar, and might have been suspected of being a Papist as well as a conjuror.

On the other hand this lack of security in his background this sense of belonging nowhere which he must have had, the lack of any public recognition—for the support of Leicester and the Queen was clandestine, not official—in itself made for greater freedom than he might have found elsewhere, freedom both to indulge in more outrageously magical practices, such as the angel-conjuring, and in more intensive 'mathematical magic', that is in applied science and technology. All his activities illustrate Dee's practical bent, his desire to get results. He set about conjuring in a most serious way, filling up innumerable squares with tiny numbers; anyone who has looked at the angel-conjuring manuscripts in the British Museum will be impressed by the detailed labour involved. He would spare no pains to get hold of an angel by correct use of number in the supercelestial sphere because from no one but an angel could he better learn the secrets of nature. Similarly, he meant to perfect the mathematical instruments, using number in lower spheres, which would enable mariners to voyage over unknown seas. In his intense sense of nature as a hierarchy completed at the top by omniscient unseen beings, and in his intense desire to explore also every aspect of the visible world, Dee is the perfect Elizabethan. In him Prospero and Sir Francis Drake meet and are one.

He illustrates also the peculiar social conditions of the Elizabethan age. His contacts with the rising artisan and middle classes, the practice of himself and his school of writing scientific works in English to spread knowledge among those not learned in the ancient tongues, are sides of Dee which differentiate him most strikingly from the learned Renaissance scholar of Italy, France, or Spain, Yet there is also an aristocratic side; there are mysterious noblemen behind him. There is a secret or courtly sphere for his activities as well as the popular side. He is both extremely exoteric and practical, and at the same time esoteric among some vaguely defined inner circle. It is this type of situation which makes the Elizabethan Renaissance so peculiar, as compared with Renaissances in other countries, where there is neither this new social situation with rising new classes who participate in the Renaissance, nor this mystery about patrons and inner groups of cognoscenti. I do not think that it is sufficiently realized how very peculiar the Elizabethan Renaissance was, both socially and intellectually. John Dee is the perfect exemplar of its peculiarities, perhaps even one of their chief sources. To solve Dee would go far towards solving, not only the Elizabethan age itself but also its place in the history of thought. Its 'world picture' was not medieval but Renaissance; it was the world picture of John Dee, the half magical world which is moving, not backwards into the Middle Ages, but onwards towards the seventeenth century. (pp. 11-19)

In the countries of Europe, the progress of the Renaissance was accompanied by intensive building in the new neoclassical style of architecture, stemming ultimately from the revival and study of the work on architecture by the Roman writer Vitruvius, who was contemporary with Augustus. By 1570, the date of the publication of Dee's preface to Euclid, the Vitruvian revival had given birth in Italy to a wealth of works on classical architectural theory, such as Leone Baptista Alberti's *De re aedificatoria* or Daniele Barbaro's commentary on Vitruvius. The year 1570 was actually the year of the publication of Palladio's great work, which was to be the bible of the neoclassical architect throughout Europe for many generations. In all the countries of Europe, palaces and mansions were arising and churches and public buildings were being erected in the new style which, perhaps more than anything else, characterizes the Renaissance and marks its break with the Middle Ages.

In England no such development had taken place. In 1570, Elizabethan London still presented a medieval aspect; Queen Elizabeth was not building a Louvre; no neoclassical churches were being built or planned; Old St. Paul's still dominated a city which would have to wait for Sir Christopher Wren to give it a Renaissance cathedral. It is true that many new manor houses were built but these, although they may be decorated with classical ornament, show no understanding in their basic design of the classical principles of proportion. England was a provincial backwater so far as the new architecture was concerned, and the English literary Renaissance was not matched by an architectural Renaissance.

Not only was there no new building on the European monumental scale, but the whole theory of proportion and symmetry as underlying all the arts and sciences which is so marked a feature of Renaissance thought, is assumed to have been relatively unknown in Elizabethan England.

It has been said in a recent book on Elizabethan architecture that the Renaissance idea of the architect, based on Vitruvius, as the universal man, had not reached Tudor England where the very word 'architect' was unfamiliar and seldom used.

No more striking illustration of the extraordinary neglect by modern scholars of the work of John Dee could be found than this widespread conviction that the Renaissance 'idea of the architect' must be discounted in studies of Elizabethan England as likely to have been unfamiliar to the general public. For in his **'Preface'** to Euclid, Dee expounds the Renaissance idea of the architect, with long quotations from Vitruvius and Alberti. Moreover the whole **'Preface'** is really based on Vitruvius; the mathematical subjects which Dee wishes to encourage are those which Vitruvius states that an architect should know. Nearly fifty years before Inigo Jones, the 'Vitruvius Britannicus', began belatedly to initiate neoclassical building in England, John Dee was teaching the middle-class Elizabethan public, through his popular **'Preface',** the basic principles of proportion and design, and demonstrating that all the mathematical arts subserve Architecture as their queen.

Some analysis of Dee's **'Preface'** must now be made in order to demonstrate the truth of the above statement which must come as a great surprise to historians of architectural theory and to all those interested in the general culture of Elizabethan England.

The **'Preface'** opens with general Pythagoro-Platonic mystical discussion of number. Then he enumerates the sciences dealing with number, which are arithmetic, algebra, geometry and goes through other sciences showing their dependence on number. Military art uses number in the science of tactics; law uses it in its study of just distribution. Geometry is essential to the 'mechanician' in his sciences of measuring. Here Dee lists as among the geometrical arts, geodesy, or surveying, geography, or the study of the earth, hydrography, or the study of the ocean, 'Stratarithmetrie' which is again military art or the disposal of armies in geometrical figures. Next he comes to perspective, a science in which he was particularly interested; then to astronomy, then to music. Astrology is also an 'art mathematical' and one which particularly shows forth the glory of God who made the heavens in his wisdom. Next comes 'statike' an art mathematical which demonstrates the causes of the lightness and the heaviness of things.

With 'anthropographie' he comes to number in relation to man. He has been speaking of 'number, measure, and weight' in the universe at large, and of how the mathematical sciences explore this. The same 'numbering', the same principles of number, measure, and weight are to be found in man, for man is a Microcosmus or 'Lesse World'. He speaks of the noble position of man in the universe, the being for whom all else was made, who 'participates with spirits and angels' and is made 'in the image and similitude of God.' The Macrocosm-Microcosm analogy, the world harmony in its relation to the harmonious constitution of man, brings Dee now to the fine arts, and he mentions 'the excellent Albert Dürer', alluding to Dürer's work on proportion. To this 'Harmonious and Microcosmical' constitution of man all the arts are related, the art of 'Zographie', or painting, of sculpture, and, above all, architecture.

And here he refers his readers to Vitruvius. 'Looke in Vitruvius, whether I deal sincerely for your behoufe, or no.' The reference in the margin is to 'Lib. 3. Cap. 1', that is to the first chapter of the third book of Vitruvius's *De architectura.*

That chapter is on the design of temples, which, says Vitruvius, depends on the symmetry and proportion of the human body which are to be reflected in the symmetry and proportion of the temple. Vitruvius states that a man's body with arms and legs fully extended fits into a square and a circle. This figure of a man in a square and a circle was the subject of a famous drawing by Leonardo da Vinci and was illustrated in some editions of Vitruvius, for example in that by Cesare Cesariano. The geometry of the square and the circle, with the analogies implied by Vitruvius, became the guiding principle in the construction of Renaissance round churches. John Dee, writing in Elizabethan England in 1570, a time and place where no churches of any kind were being built, let alone Renaissance churches, and little interest in neoclassical theory has been assumed, confidently expects his readers to be able to 'look in Vitruvius' and there find Vitruvius's application of the geometry of the square and the circle to man and to the building of temples which shall reflect the cosmic and human proportions in basic geometrical terms.

Dee gives two other references for the geometry of the square and the circle as basic for the theory of proportion. The reader is not only to look in Vitruvius; he is also to 'looke in Albertus Durerus, De symmetria humani corporis' where he would find these principles applied to art. And there is the further significant direction that he is to 'Looke in the 27 and 28 Chapters of the second book, De occulta philosophia'. This is of course a reference to Agrippa's textbook on magic. The 27th chapter of the second book of Agrippa's work is on the proportions of the human body; it quotes Vitruvius (though not by name) on man's body and the square and the circle, and illustrates the extended body of man within a square and a circle, these figures now being marked with the characters of the signs of the zodiac and of the planets. The following (28th) chapter is on the composition and harmony of the soul of man and on the effects of music in harmonizing it with the universe. That is to say, Dee refers his readers not only to Vitruvius on man and the square and the circle, but also to Agrippa where this conception is given an astrological and magical interpretation.

Continuing with the mathematical arts, Dee next speaks of 'Trochlike' which studies the properties of circular motions, and is of value for making wheels, mills, and in mines where wheel work is used. Then comes 'Helicosophie', an art mathematical dealing with spirals, cylinders, cones, of use in architecture and for many instruments and engines such as the screw. 'Pneumatithmie' discusses pneumatics, mechanical devices using air or water, such as the water organ. 'Menadrie' is a mathematical art used in devices for moving weights, such as cranes and pulleys; useful also in engines of war. 'Hypogeiodie' demonstrates how to make underground measurements and surveys; 'Hydragogie' teaches how to lead water from springs and rivers; 'Horometrie' is the art of measuring time by clocks and dials.

With 'Zographie' he is again among the fine arts. This is the skill in geometry, arithmetic, perspective, and anthropography which underlies the work of an artist, the basic understanding of number on which all true works of art are built. The painter is called by Dee a 'Mechanical Zographer'; he is marvellous in his skill and seems to have a certain divine power. Sculpture is a sister art to painting, and of both excellent artificers have written great books; here he cites Pomponius Gauricus and Giorgio Vasari.

And now comes the main section on architecture. . . . (pp. 20-4)

Dismissing the crude idea that because buildings are made of materials whereas 'arts mathematical' do not deal with material and corruptible things he points out that architecture, above all other arts, is based on the abstract sciences of number, making use of all of them, and indeed of all the arts and sciences. And here he quotes 'Vitruvius the Roman' who wrote ten books of architecture addressed to the Emperor Augustus 'in whose daies our Heauenly Archemaster [Christ] was borne'. After invoking this Christian blessing on Vitruvius he embarks on an English translation of selected portions of the first book of the *De architectura.* This is the book in which Vitruvius sings the praises of architecture as the queen of all the arts and sciences and the one which includes them all, for the education of a true architect must include some acquaintance with every branch of the whole encyclopaedia of knowledge.

> An Architect (sayth he) ought to understand languages, to be skilfull of Painting, well instructed in Geometrie, not ignorant of Perspective, furnished with Arithmetike, haue knowledge of many histories, and diligently haue heard the Philosophers, haue skill of Musike, not ignorant of Physike, know the answers of Lawyers, and haue Astronomie, and the courses Celestiall, in good knowledge. He geueth reason, orderly, wherefore all these Artes, Doctrines, and Instructions, are requisite in an excellent Architecte.

Dee then translates the reasons which Vitruvius gives as to why an architect must know so much. Geometry is basic, which teaches first 'the use of the Rule and the Compasse', how to make plans, and 'the hard questions of Symmetrie, are by Geometricall Meanes and Methods discoursed on'.

Music is essential for the architect, and here the English reader heard, in English, about those mysterious amplifiers or 'sounding vessels' in the ancient theatres, for Dee translates the whole of the passage about them in the first chapter of Vitruvius's first book.

> Moreouer, the Brasen Vessels, which in Theatres, are placed in Mathematicll order, in ambries, under the steppes: and the diuersities of the soundes . . . are ordred according to Musicall Symphonies & Harmonies: being distributed in ye Circuites, by Diatessaron, Diapente, and Diapason. That the conuenient voyce, of the players sound, when it came to these preparations, made in order, there being increased; with ye increasing, might come more cleare & pleasant, to ye eares of the lokers on.

Thus the Elizabethan reader of Dee's preface, which was to be the inspiration of artisans and was to foster all that burgeoning movement of new endeavour in so many different spheres of activity, was introduced to the ancient theatre in its aural, acoustic, and musical aspects. These words about the voices of the players coming clear and pleasant to the ears of the lookers on may bring us close to the genesis of the Shakespearean type of theatre.

Struck, as everyone must be, by the vast scope of the architect's education as defined by Vitruvius at the beginning of his work, Dee cries excitedly that all these subjects are actually treated by Vitruvius in the *De architectura.*

> And if you should, but take his boke in your hand, and slightly loke through it, you would say straight way: this is Geometrie, Arithmetike, Astronomie, Musike, Anthropographie, Hydragogie, Horometrie and (to conclude) the Storehouse of all workmanship.

If, following Dee's advice, we take Vitruvius's book in hand and slightly look through it, we find that these words are true. Here, in Vitruvius, are discussions of geometry and arithmetic and their applications in military art, missiles, water supply, geography, dials, fortifications. Here are very long chapters on astrology, on the signs of the zodiac, the planets, the northern and southern constellations, all needful for the architect to know. And Vitruvius's tenth and last book on motion is entirely on mechanical contrivances, which he says are fundamentally the business of the architect, both in building and for public spectacles and plays with a theatrical setting which also come within the purview of the architect. Here he discusses machinery of all kinds, whether for military uses or for peaceful use, pulleys, wheels, pumps, screws, water organs, engines for military defence and attack, as well as pleasing mechanical toys worked by pneumatic devices and devices for theatrical effects. Vitruvius was undoubtedly the storehouse of all workmanship.

And if we reflect on the subjects of Dee's **'Preface'** to Euclid which we have just been slightly looking through, we realize that they are the Vitruvian subjects. The link between the subjects in the **'Preface'** is not only that they are all mathematical arts but also that they are all in Vitruvius. Dee is following Vitruvius throughout.

Thus, though the actual quotation from Vitruvius in the section on architecture consists only of the first chapter on the education of an architect, Vitruvius was clearly one of the main inspirations of the **'Preface'** as a whole. That busy movement among the Elizabethan artisan classes which the **'Preface'** did so much to stimulate was indebted to the revival of Vitruvius, popularized in England by John Dee long before the appearance of Inigo Jones. (pp. 25-7)

Frances A. Yates, "John Dee and the Elizabe-

than Age" and "John Dee and Vitruvius," in her Theatre of the World, *The University of Chicago Press, 1969, pp. 1-19, 20-41.*

Peter J. French (essay date 1972)

[*In the excerpt below, French notes that Dee's mathematical writings demonstrate a concern with both applied and theoretical mathematics and maintains that his "Mathematicall Praeface" remained influential through the seventeenth century.*]

Being a magus in the most complete sense of the term, John Dee was deeply involved in mathesis, the mystical aspects of number, but his interest in mathematics was practical as well as theoretical. It was Dee's concern for the advancement of applied science that inspired him to write a treatise on the great benefits to be gained from everyday use of mathematics. To make this part of his philosophy readily available to his less learned contemporaries—those mechanicians who would use mathematics in their trades—Dee wrote his **'Mathematicall Preface'** to *Euclide* in the vernacular.

Dee conceived of the mechanician as one 'whose skill is, without knowledge of Mathematicall demonstration, perfectly to worke and finishe any sensible worke, by the Mathematicien principall or derivative, demonstrated or demonstrable'. Builders, mechanics, navigators, painters, surveyors, and makers of optical glasses were among the mechanicians whose arts, in Dee's mind, were applied mathematics. Although mechanicians were not held in especially high esteem by most Elizabethan university graduates, Dee respected practical craftsmen and perceived clearly the role they would play in the advancement of knowledge.

The attitude of Dee and others like him represented a basic change in the scientific outlook, and this change was largely responsible for the tremendous advances in technology that occurred during the Renaissance. It is commonly known that, despite their first-rate scientific minds, the Greeks never fully applied their discoveries. As a consequence, they never even achieved the technological sophistication of the ancient Egyptians. S. Sambursky suggests that, though they invented the scientific method, the Greeks never fully understood its ramifications. 'Logic and deduction', he explains, 'were more important than induction and experience, and the teleological view of nature hampered the increase in physical knowledge.' The Greeks lacked the impulse to operate with their cosmos; instead, they wished primarily to understand it. Given this tradition, what was it that inspired Renaissance men like John Dee to *apply* their scientific philosophy? The Hermetic texts that influenced Renaissance philosophy so profoundly and emphasized magical operation may also have fostered practical application of scientific knowledge; at least this possibility must be considered. [The] Hermetic texts encouraged a basic psychological change that released the human spirit and thus prompted magi like Dee to experiment with the powers of the universe, in spite of the dangers involved. Also, as Festugiére has stressed, Hermetic science was diametrically opposed to Aristotelian science, which was essentially disinterested, did not attempt to seek practical applications, and neglected the particular for the general. Hermetic science, on the other hand, attempted to study the specific characteristics of everything in nature. The mysticism and secrecy involved with Hermetic science originally made it a science of the *cognoscenti,* but the urge to experiment, to examine particulars, was none the less inherent in it.

Paolo Rossi has demonstrated [in *Francis Bacon: From Magic to Science*] that Francis Bacon's ideas on utilitarian science were rooted in the magical tradition. Dee's were even more so. The desire of the Hermetically inspired Renaissance magus was to control nature, to use it for the benefit of mankind; and, as in Dee's case, this hope frequently prompted an interest in technology. Dee expostulates:

> My entent in additions is not to amend *Euclides* Method, (which nedeth little adding or none at all). But my desire is somwhat to furnish you, toward a more general art Mathematical then *Euclides* Elementes, (remayning in the termes in which they are written) can sufficiently helpe you unto. And though *Euclides* Elementes with my Additions, run not in one Methodicall race toward my marke: yet in the meane space my Additions either geve light, where they are annexed to *Euclides* matter, or geve some ready ayde, and shew the way to dilate your discourses Mathematicall, or to invent and practise things Mechanically.

When coupled with an increased familiarity with the mechanical arts, the attempts of the theoretical scientists—the magi—to understand and use nature drew attention to the gap between traditional scientific learning and the practical potential of science.

Francis Bacon, who is often portrayed as the first English exponent of the experimental method, was by no means original in his call for experimentation, as Rossi has shown. Indeed, almost every magician of the sixteenth century advocated some sort of methodological experimentation, and the forms suggested were often more meaningful than Bacon's. Perhaps in reaction to Aristotelianism, Bacon never fully accepted the role that hypotheses play in a truly productive experimental process. After all, the successes of modern science are based on an interplay between induction and deduction. As F. R. Johnson pointed out some time ago, John Dee proposed a viable theory of experimental science considerably before Francis Bacon formulated his own. It is quite possible that Bacon knew of Dee's treatise in which he terms experimental science 'Archemastrie', an art that 'teacheth to bryng to actuall experience sensible, all worthy conclusions by all Artes Mathematicall purposed, & by true Naturall Philosophie concluded'. Dee continues to explain, 'Bycause it procedeth by *Experiences,* and searcheth forth the causes of Conclusions, by *Experiences:* and also putteth the Conclusions them selves, in *Experience,* it is named of some, *Scientia Experimentalis.*' Dee's entire **'Mathematicall Preface'** is a paean to the fusion of theoretical knowledge with mechanical application. Though he was secretive about religious matters and speculative science because of being in the Hermetic tradition, Dee tried desperately to help his countrymen make progress in their knowledge of applied science. He wanted people to understand how they could use the powers of the cosmos for their benefit.

Dee's first published effort along this line appeared in 1561 when he produced an augmentation of Robert Recorde's *Grounde of Artes,* an arithmetic textbook in English that was originally published in 1540. Recorde's series of mathematical textbooks was the first in English to present coherently and simply the newly developing subject of algoristic mathematics, or that based on Arabic numbers. The changeover to Arabic mathematics was very slow in taking effect, and government accounts, for instance, continued to be kept in Roman numerals throughout the Tudor period. Recorde's works, like Dee's preface, were aimed specifically at mechanicians, or non-university men, as is indicated in the introduction to the *Grounde of Artes:* 'Therefore gentle reader, though this boke can be but small aide to the learned sort, yet unto ye simple ignorant (which nedeth most helpe) it may bee a good furtheraunce and meane to knowledge.' Mathematical education was so elementary that Recorde had to assume little or no knowledge on the part of his reader and consequently had to start with the most basic concepts and gradually work up to the more complex and difficult aspects of mathematics.

Recorde's various scientific works had extremely practical aims: he wished to arouse the interest of his pupils and encourage them to use mathematics in everyday affairs. The secret of Recorde's method of teaching is to combine, in clear and concise prose, the theoretical and applied aspects of mathematics. He does not condone a system that simply presents the empirical side of the mathematical sciences without giving the student a comprehensive understanding of the principles underlying the application. Using a dialogue form in which the master answers questions and corrects observations made by the student, Recorde leads the pupil through the subject in a carefully ordered fashion. Recorde's series of textbooks was thus meant to give the reader a solid understanding of the subject, and it appears that the books were also meant to be studied in the sequence in which they were published, beginning with the *Grounde of Artes* and ending with his fourth work, the *Castle of Knowledge,* which was first printed in 1556. The *Grounde of Artes,* which Dee augmented after Recorde's death, went through no less than twenty-six editions before 1662; it was the standard arithmetic text of the period.

Dee revised some of Recorde's text, improving and correcting it in various details, but he also enlarged the volume by adding a section entitled, **'The Second Part of Arithmetike Touching Fractions, briefly sette forthe'.** Dee may have based his additions to the *Grounde of Artes* on an existing treatise on fractions which is in his hand. The treatise, however, is not in dialogue form, which is one of the notable features of Recorde's work and is continued by Dee in his augmentation. We can be fairly sure that Dee viewed his work on the *Grounde of Artes* as preparation for the first English *Euclide.* In conjunction with John Mellis, a Southwark schoolmaster, Dee produced another edition of the *Grounde of Artes* in 1582, and this edition included some verses by Dee addressed to 'the earnest Arithmetician'. Though not published in the earlier volume, the verses were apparently written while Dee was working on the 1561 edition because he mentions that there is not yet an English *Euclide.* They express his conception of the relationship between arithmetic and geometry:

> My loving friend to Science bent,
> Something thou hast by this booke woone
> But if thou wilt be excellent,
> Another race thou must yet runne. . . .
>
> The famous Greeke of Platoes lore,
> EUCLIDE I meane Geometer:
> So true, so plaine, so fraught with store,
> (as in our speach) is yet no where.
>
> A treasure straunge, that booke wil prove,
> With numbers skil, matcht in due sort,
> This I thee warn of sincere love,
> And to proceede do thee exhort.

The first English *Euclide* was translated by Sir Henry Billingsley, an alderman and later Lord Mayor of London, and was printed as a beautiful folio volume by John Day in 1570. The earliest translation of Euclid into Latin was made by Adelard of Bath around 1130, and this version, to which Campanus of Novara added commentaries, became the popular one. It has usually been assumed that the English *Euclide* of Dee and Billingsley was based on the Adelard-Campanus version, which was first published at Venice in 1482. It seems almost certain, however, that the first English *Euclide* was translated from the Greek edition of the *Elements* produced by Simon Grynaeus and published at Basel in 1533 by John Hervagius. Though Billingsley probably had the Latin version before him, it appears that he used it only for reference. To Billingsley's admirable translation, Dee added his important and influential **'Mathematicall Preface',** as well as annotations throughout the body of the text, and the introductions which appear before the various books.

In the **'Preface',** which he claims was hurriedly written under constant pressure from the publisher, Dee manages to outline the entire state of science as it was known in the sixteenth century. The **'Preface'** opens with a discussion of philosophical mathematics and its mystical implications, which was of interest to magi; but when Dee begins to explain the practical applications of the mathematical sciences, he pointedly states:

> From henceforth, in this my **'Preface',** will I frame my talk, to *Plato* his fugitive Scholers: or, rather, to such, who well can, (and also wil,) use their utward senses, to the glory of God, the benefite of their Countrey, and their owne secret contentation, or honest preferment, on this earthly Scaffold. To them, I will orderly recite, describe & declare a great Number of Artes, from our two Mathematicall fountaines [arithmetic and geometry], derived into the fieldes of *Nature.*

This he clearly does.

In the text accompanying the 'Groundplat', Dee explains

the natures of the various sciences, the relationships among them, and the levels of advancement achieved in each. The explanations are usually trenchant rather than detailed. Dee also makes suggestions, which are sometimes prophetic, for future scientific developments. As an example, under 'Pneumatithmie', he discusses the power of a vacuum and says that, by understanding its force, 'two or three men together, by keping Ayre under a great Cauldron, and forcying the same downe, orderly, may without harme descend to the Sea bottome: and continue there a tyme &c'. The most striking of the scientific suggestions offered in the preface is that architecture henceforth be based on classical rules of harmony and proportion, in other words that the architects in England follow the lead of their Continental counterparts and institute a neoclassical revival. The essential point to be remembered about Dee's preface is that it is a revolutionary manifesto calling for the recognition of mathematics as a key to all knowledge and advocating broad application of mathematical principles.

One major aspect of the **'Mathematicall Preface'** must be discussed in more detail. Dee advocates an essentially utilitarian form of education based on the quadrivial subjects and thus is very much in the mainstream of educational reformers of the sixteenth century. His thoughts on the subject are similar to those of Robert Recorde, whom he succeeded as the leading scientist and scientific teacher in England, and they parallel those that Peter Ramus, Dee's friend, was advocating in France. In their idea about educational reform and their interest in practical mathematics, Dee and Ramus had an intellectual meeting ground. The two corresponded about mathematical texts; but . . . it is likely that Dee perceived of Ramus's approach merely as an introduction to method. On this account, the theories of the Frenchman would have been acceptable to Dee, but they would not have provided a means of exploring the higher—and to Dee all-important—philosophical and mystical aspects of thought. It is improbable that Dee would have found much in Ramus's works that would have improved on the pedagogical method of Recorde. As Johnson and Larkey have shown, Robert Recorde's ideas on education, though in some ways similar to those of Ramus, were arrived at quite independently. Dee carried on the tradition of educational reform that Recorde introduced in England during the 1540s, before Ramus published anything. It seems logical to assume, therefore, that Dee was most indebted to Recorde and only secondarily indebted, if at all, to Ramus.

Like Dee, Recorde was by choice primarily a mathematician and scientist, whereas Ramus, until quite late in his career, remained chiefly a logician wishing to reform and simplify dialectic in relation to the Aristotelian system. Ramus turned to mathematics principally to apply his logical method to the restructuring of its subject matter, but before he was able to apply the dialectical method that marks his system, Ramus had to learn the mathematical sciences. He never approached Dee's profundity as a mathematician, and it is a minor irony that Ramus should have recommended Dee to Elizabeth as worthy of holding a mathematical chair at either of the English universities. Ramus's textbooks present a revision and simplification of old mathematical knowledge rather than a critical remodelling of material in light of the latest discoveries. The textbooks of Recorde and Dee also simplify the subject matter, but they reflect a much more comprehensive understanding of the mathematical sciences than do the comparable works by Ramus. This is probably why Ramus's works on geometry and arithmetic, though translated into English, had little success in England, though use of his dialectical system was fairly widespread in the last part of the sixteenth century. The mathematical works of the Englishmen were simply better.

To Peter Ramus, for example, 'Geometrie is the Arte of measuring well'. To John Dee, this is only one aspect of the science's complex function:

> But, well you may perceive by *Euclides Elementes,* that more ample is our Science, then to measure Plaines: and nothyng lesse therin is tought (of purpose) then how to measure Land. An other name, therefore, must nedes be had, for our Mathematicall Science of Magnitudes: which regardeth neither clod, nor turff: neither hill, nor dale: neither earth nor heaven: but is absolute *Megethologia:* not creping on ground, and dasseling the eye, with pole perche, rod or lyne: but liftyng the hart above the heavens, by invisible lines, and immortall beames: meteth with the reflexions, of the light incomprehensible: and so procureth Joye, and perfection unspeakable.

Their diverse conceptions of the role of geometry exemplify the difference between the minds of Dee and Ramus. The latter would have nothing to do with the theoretical aspects of mathematics; for example, he thought Euclid's tenth book on irrational magnitudes was useless. Dee and Recorde, on the other hand, both considered theory necessary for any real understanding of the subject. In his study of Ramist attempts at educational reform, Hookyaas outlines its purpose: 'They wanted to make education easier, more interesting, and more concrete by inserting into it examples borrowed from everyday practices because, in Ramus's opinion, the natural method is also, inevitably, the easiest method.'

Recorde, Ramus and Dee all published their mathematical texts in the vernacular, which was necessary to the furtherance of their attempts at educational reform. Dee was fully aware of the revolutionary aspects of presenting an edition of Euclid's *Elements* in English, and at the end of the **'Preface'** he defends himself against possible attack by disapproving university men. Dee assures the universities that they really have nothing to fear and comments: 'great Comfort, with good hope, may the *Universities* have, by reason of this *Englishe* Geometrie, and **"Mathematicall Praeface,"** that they (hereafter) shall be the more regarded, esteemed, and resorted unto.' He was probably not quite so solicitous about the universities as might be imagined since he did leave them because they were so backward in the teaching of science, and he did make it plain in other writings that they had nothing to offer in the profounder sciences. Dee makes his attitude somewhat clearer when he adds:

> Besides this, how many a Common Artificer, is

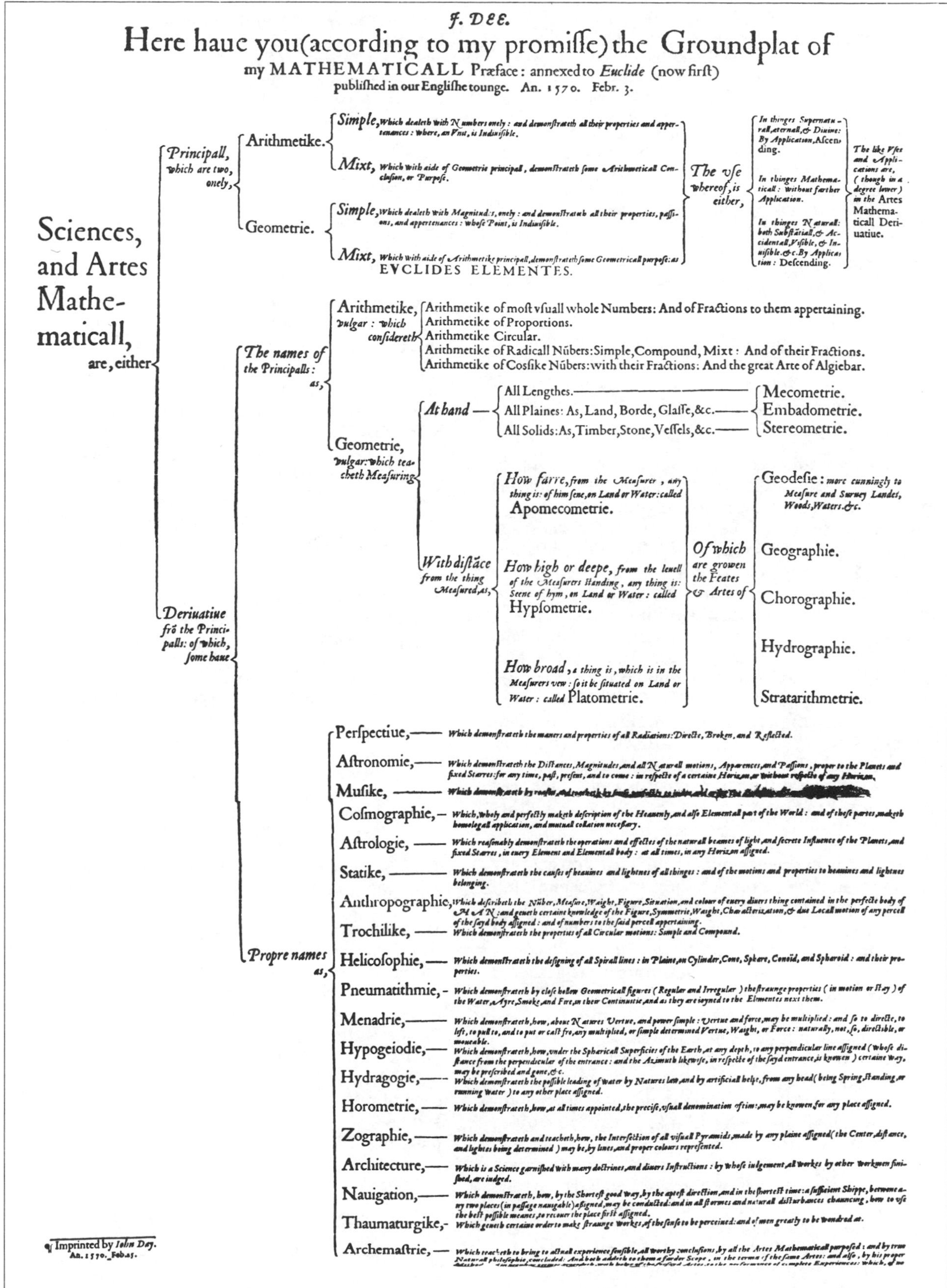

J. DEE.

Here haue you(according to my promiſſe) the Groundplat of my MATHEMATICALL Præface: annexed to *Euclide* (now firſt) publiſhed in our Engliſhe tounge. An. 1570. Febr. 3.

Sciences, and Artes Mathematicall, are, either

- *Principall, which are two, onely,*
  - Arithmetike.
    - *Simple, Which dealeth with Numbers onely: and demonſtrateth all their properties and appertenances: where, an Vnit, is Indiuiſible.*
    - *Mixt, Which with aide of Geometrie principall, demonſtrateth ſome Arithmeticall Concluſion, or Purpoſe.*
  - Geometrie.
    - *Simple, Which dealeth with Magnitudes, onely: and demonſtrateth all their properties, paſſions, and appertenances: whoſe Point, is Indiuiſible.*
    - *Mixt, Which with aide of Arithmetike principall, demonſtrateth ſome Geometricall purpoſe: as* EVCLIDES ELEMENTES.
  - *The vſe whereof, is either,*
    - *In thinges Supernaturall, æternall, & Diuine: By Application, Aſcending.*
    - *In thinges Mathematicall: without farther Application.*
    - *In thinges Naturall: both Subſtãtiall, & Accidentall, Viſible, & Inuiſible. &c. By Application:* Deſcending.
  - *The like Vſes and Applications are, (though in a degree lower) in the* Artes Mathematicall Deriuatiue.
- *Deriuatiue frõ the Principalls: of which, ſome haue*
  - *The names of the Principalls: as,*
    - Arithmetike, *vulgar: which conſidereth*
      - Arithmetike of moſt vſuall whole Numbers: And of Fractions to them appertaining.
      - Arithmetike of Proportions.
      - Arithmetike Circular.
      - Arithmetike of Radicall Nũbers: Simple, Compound, Mixt: And of their Fractions.
      - Arithmetike of Coſſike Nũbers: with their Fractions: And the great Arte of Algiebar.
    - Geometrie, *vulgar: which teacheth Meaſuring*
      - *At hand*
        - All Lengthes. — Mecometrie.
        - All Plaines: As, Land, Borde, Glaſſe, &c. — Embadometrie.
        - All Solids: As, Timber, Stone, Veſſels, &c. — Stereometrie.
      - *With diſtãce from the thing Meaſured, as,*
        - *How farre, from the Meaſurer, any thing is: of him ſene, on Land or Water: called* Apomecometrie.
        - *How high or deepe, from the leuell of the Meaſurers ſtanding, any thing is: Seene of hym, on Land or Water: called* Hypſometrie.
        - *How broad, a thing is, which is in the Meaſurers vew: ſo it be ſituated on Land or Water: called* Platometrie.
        - *Of which are growen the Feates & Artes of*
          - Geodeſie: *more cunningly to Meaſure and Suruey Landes, Woods, Waters. &c.*
          - Geographie.
          - Chorographie.
          - Hydrographie.
          - Stratarithmetrie.
  - *Propre names as,*
    - Perſpectiue, — *Which demonſtrateth the maners and properties of all Radiations: Directe, Broken, and Reflected.*
    - Aſtronomie, — *Which demonſtrateth the Diſtances, Magnitudes, and all Naturall motions, Apparences, and Paſſions, proper to the Planets and fixed Starres: for any time, paſt, preſent, and to come: in reſpecte of a certaine Horizon, or without reſpecte of any Horizon.*
    - Muſike, — *Which demonſtrateth by reaſon, and teacheth by ſenſe perfectly to iudge and order the* [illegible]
    - Coſmographie, — *Which, wholy and perfectly maketh deſcription of the Heauenly, and alſo Elementall part of the World: and of theſe partes, maketh homologall application, and mutuall collation neceſſary.*
    - Aſtrologie, — *Which reaſonably demonſtrateth the operations and effectes of the naturall beames of light, and ſecrete Influence of the Planets, and fixed Starres, in euery Element and Elementall body: at all times, in any Horizon aſſigned.*
    - Statike, — *Which demonſtrateth the cauſes of heauines and lightnes of all thinges: and of the motions and properties to heauines and lightnes belonging.*
    - Anthropographie, *Which deſcribeth the Nũber, Meaſure, Waight, Figure, Situation, and colour of euery diuers thing contained in the perfecte body of MAN: and geueth certaine knowledge of the Figure, Symmetrie, Waight, Characteriȥation, & due Locall motion of any percell of the ſayd body aſſigned: and of numbers to the ſaid percell appertaining.*
    - Trochilike, — *Which demonſtrateth the properties of all Circular motions: Simple and Compound.*
    - Helicoſophie, — *Which demonſtrateth the deſigning of all Spirall lines: in Plaine, on Cylinder, Cone, Sphære, Conoïd, and Sphæroid: and their properties.*
    - Pneumatithmie, — *Which demonſtrateth by cloſe hollow Geometricall figures (Regular and Irregular) the ſtraunge properties (in motion or ſtay) of the Water, Ayre, Smoke, and Fire, in their Continuitie, and as they are ioyned to the Elementes next them.*
    - Menadrie, — *Which demonſtrateth, how, aboue Natures Vertue, and power ſimple: Vertue and force, may be multiplied: and ſo to directe, to lift, to pull to, and to put or caſt fro, any multiplied, or ſimple determined Vertue, Waight, or Force: naturally, not, ſo, directible, or moueable.*
    - Hypogeiodie, — *Which demonſtrateth, how, vnder the Sphæricall Superficies of the Earth, at any depth, to any perpendicular line aſſigned (whoſe diſtance from the perpendicular of the entrance: and the Azimuth likewiſe, in reſpecte of the ſayd entrance, is knowen) certaine way, may be preſcribed and gone, &c.*
    - Hydragogie, — *Which demonſtrateth the poſſible leading of water by Natures law, and by artificiall helpe, from any head (being Spring, ſtanding, or running water) to any other place aſſigned.*
    - Horometrie, — *Which demonſtrateth, how, at all times appointed, the preciſe, vſuall denomination of time, may be knowen, for any place aſſigned.*
    - Zographie, — *Which demonſtrateth and teacheth, how, the Interſection of all viſuall Pyramids, made by any plaine aſſigned (the Center, diſtance, and lightes being determined) may be, by lines, and proper colours repreſented.*
    - Architecture, — *Which is a Science garniſhed with many doctrines, and diuers Instructions: by whoſe iudgement, all workes by other workmen finiſhed, are iudged.*
    - Nauigation, — *Which demonſtrateth, how, by the Shorteſt good way, by the apteſt direction, and in the ſhorteſt time: a ſufficient Shippe, betwene any two places (in paſſage nauigable) aſſigned, may be conducted: and in all ſtormes and naturall diſturbances chauncing, how to vſe the beſt poſſible meanes, to recouer the place firſt aſſigned.*
    - Thaumaturgike, — *Which geueth certaine order to make ſtraunge workes, of the ſenſe to be perceiued: and of men greatly to be wondred at.*
    - Archemaſtrie, — *Which teacheth to bring to actuall experience ſenſible, all worthy concluſions, by all the Artes Mathematicall purpoſed: and by true Naturall philoſophie, concluded: And both addeth to them a farder Scope, in the termes of the ſame Artes: and alſo, by his proper* [illegible]

¶ Imprinted by *John Day*. An. 1570. Feb. 25.

A copy of Dee's Mathematicall Praeface *to the 1570 Billingsley translation of Euclid's* Elements of Geometry.

> there, in these Realmes of England and Ireland, that dealeth with Numbers, Rule, & Cumpasse: Who, with their owne Skill and experience, already had, will be hable (by these good helpes and informations), to finde out, and devise, new workes, straunge Engines, and Instrumentes: for Sundry purposes in the Common Wealth? or for the private pleasure? and for the better maintayning of their owne estate? I will not (therefore) fight against myne owne shadowe. For, no man (I am sure) will open his mouth against this Enterprise. No man (I say) who either hath Charitie toward his brother (and would be glad of his furtherance in vertuous knowledge): or that hath any care & zeale for the bettering of the Common state of this Realme.

There is, of course, one particularly strong reason why the universities would have been annoyed with Dee's **'Preface':** not only does it implicitly attack the standard Oxford or Cambridge education, but it is definitely *not* Aristotelian in spirit.

Like Recorde, but unlike Ramus, Dee was not particularly anti-Aristotelian. It is well known that Ramus, for his M.A. at Paris, defended the notorious thesis that everything Aristotle said was wrong. In contrast, Dee accepted and used the doctrines of Aristotle that he felt had validity; he did not denounce Aristotle indiscriminately. Dee's attitude was one that tended to destroy rigid Aristotelianism from within rather than from without by a vicious onslaught. In his attempt to give the English mechanicians the means to think for themselves about the sciences, Dee advocated testing old beliefs by experiment in the Platonic tradition supported at medieval Oxford, which was more hospitable to science than the predominating Aristotelianism of Renaissance Oxford and Cambridge. This was hardly an approach that the universities would condone, but it did lead to the establishment of scientific method and did encourage the practical application of the mathematical arts.

The centre of English science during the sixteenth century was in London, not at the universities. In the capital, numerous non-university people, as well as university men like Dee and Recorde, formed a kind of amorphous third university. Functioning at Syon House, along with Dee's circle at nearby Mortlake, was the group that gathered around Henry Percy, the 'Wizard Earl', during the latter part of the sixteenth and the early seventeenth centuries. Some of the greatest intellects in England were in this circle; Anthony Wood includes Thomas Hariot, John Dee, Walter Warner and Nathaniel Torporly—'the Atlantes of the mathematical world'. To these should be added Thomas Allen, a mathematician who in many ways resembled Dee, Christopher Marlowe, John Donne and Walter Ralegh. There was apparently considerable communication between Dee's circle and that of Percy. Ralegh did favours for Dee at court and had considerable respect for the man who directed the exploratory voyages of his half-brothers, Adrian and Humphrey Gilbert. Thomas Hariot, who was educated at Oxford and was subsequently employed by Ralegh as a mathematical tutor, has been neglected, but his substantial contributions to science are beginning to be recognized. His biographer claims with good reason that Hariot was as great a mathematician and scientist as Galileo; Hariot was certainly studying the moon with a telescope by July of 1609. One of Hariot's primary interests was optics, which was also a preoccupation of Dee's; in fact, the interests of these two scientists usually coincided. And there is no doubt that they were good friends.

Besides the Dee and Northumberland circles, the first formal scientific academy in England, Gresham College, was situated in London. The methods of teaching and the orientation towards the quadrivial subjects at the college were in direct contrast to the educational system at Oxford and Cambridge.

It was particularly among extra-university mechanicians and scholars living in the capital, that Dee's **'Mathematicall Preface'** enjoyed popularity. Since it was so commonly known and so highly respected, it is probably almost impossible to estimate its true influence on the development of scientific and philosophical thought in England during the Renaissance. Dee's personal role as a teacher and adviser to mechanicians and scientists may have been even more important. Yet, Dee and his treatise have often been neglected by historians of science. A brief history of the dispersion of the preface subsequent to its publication in 1570 will demonstrate its popularity.

When George Gascoigne decided to publish Sir Humphrey Gilbert's *A Discourse of Discoverie for a new passage to Cataia* in 1576, he claimed that one reason for publication was Dee's approval:

> Now let mee say that a great learned man (even *M. Dee*) doth seeme very well to like of this *Discoverie* and doth much commende the Authour, the which he declareth in his **'Mathematical Preface'** to th'english *Euclide,* I refer thee (Reader) to peruse the same, and thinke it not strange though I be encouraged by so learned a foreleader, to set forth a thing whiche hee so well like of.

This is one of the earliest printed indications of the respect that contemporaries afforded Dee's **'Preface'.**

William Bourne, a popularizer, a Londoner, a self-educated individual, and the first of a series of non-university teachers and writers, published *A Booke called the Treasure for Traveilers.* Though Bourne terms his borrowing from Dee, 'A briefe note, taken out of *M. Dees* **'Mathematical Preface'** that goeth before *Euclides Elementes* nowe extant in our Inglishe tongue, as touching what the *Mathematical* sciences are', he reproduces the entire breakdown of the sciences offered by Dee. Edward Worsop, another Londoner and popularizer of practical mathematics, styles Dee the foremost mathematician in Europe. He adds that Dee

> hath put unto these englished elements, many scholies, annotations, corollaries, and expositions which give great light, and facilitie to the understanding of them. Also his mathematical preface unto these elements, is a worke of such singularitie and necessitie to all students of the Mathematicals, that I wish them to make it a manuel.

One of the most glowing contemporary tributes accorded Dee's **'Mathematicall Preface'** was made by Thomas Hylles in *The Arte of Vulgar Arithmetic.* Hylles was also a Londoner and a popularizer and translator of practical scientific works; he published on everything from gardening to the interpretation of dreams. Hylles exhorts the reader,

> I refer you to the prefaces of *M. Rob Record* in his Ground of artes and Whetstone of wit, & to the notable **'Preface'** of *M. John Dee* prefixed to *Euclid,* where you shal finde matter aboundant touching that argument, delivered with such grace & sweetnes of stile that the very memory thereof forceth my rustick pen, as quite abashed, all amased & astoined, here sodenly to stop, & abruptly to stay.

Hylles suggests, interestingly, that the frenzied and emotionally charged prose that Dee uses in the preface is of considerable merit. Dee certainly rises to heights of lyrical enthusiasm in his praise of the mathematical sciences, and his contemporaries apparently found this extremely effective, though the style now seems at first obscure and alien. In his own century Dee's **'Preface'** fully achieved the objectives which he had in mind: it did impress on his compatriots the significance of the mathematical sciences and the benefits to be gained from their study.

The fame of Dee's **'Mathematicall Preface'** continued well into the seventeenth century. In his edition of the first six books of Euclid's *Elements* printed in 1651, Thomas Rudd does not bother adding any significant comments of his own in evaluation of the mathematical sciences. Instead, he reprints the preface of 'that pious and learned Mathematician M^r^. JOHN DEE . . . (which deserves perpetual commendations) having beene so large in the explanation and use of all the parts' of the mathematicals.

Perhaps the most telling evidence of the widespread admiration that the preface continued to command is found in the correspondence between John Worthington, who was Master of Jesus College, Cambridge, during the Protectorate, and Samuel Hartlib, an educational reformer and friend of John Milton. Writing to Worthington on 20 November 1655, Hartlib begs him to have some outstanding Latinist translate Dee's preface because, as he says:

> Mr. Dee's large **'Preface'** before his Commentary upon Euclid (wch hath been epitomized and printed last year as I take it with the s^d^ Preface) is deservedly extolled as a Substantial, solid, and learned discourse to shew the Necessity and Excellency of Mathematicks, I should think, if this were added also to Jungius's Discourse, it would put many more young Scholars throughout the world, into a Mathematical Conversation. That great Scholar of *Christ's Coll.* in Camb. (I mean Sr W. Boswell,) was pleased to attribute all his proficiency in learning whatever it was, to the goodness of the forementioned **'Preface'** of Dee's. Methinks, this should be a sufficient Incentive to stir up some able pen at Camb. to turn it in Latin.

Apparently nothing came of this suggestion because Hartlib comments to Worthington on 12 December 1655: 'You say nothing whether any body may be found, that will undertake the translating of Dee's mathematical preface. I pray be pleased to answer categorically to this particular.' Hartlib obviously considered this a project of some moment. It is, none the less, slightly ironic that he was so anxious to see the preface in Latin when Dee had so pointedly avoided that language.

About the same time that Hartlib wrote to Worthington, John Webster, the Puritan divine, was examining the state of education at the universities and, in the course of his study, had special praise for Dee's preface. When recommending the introduction of a form of education very like that which Dee envisages in the **'Mathematicall Preface',** Webster says,

> What shall I say of *Staticks, Architecture, Pneumatithmie, Stratarithmetrie* and the rest enumerated by that expert and learned man, Dr. *John Dee* in his **'Preface'** before *Euclide?* What excellent, admirable and profitable experiments do every one of these afford? truly innumerable, the least of which is more use, benefit and profit to the life of man, than almost all that learning that the Universities boast of and glory in.

It is revealing that, in his attack on the Aristotelians, Webster defends natural magic, apparently understanding that there is a close relationship between magic and the development of science; this relationship is, of course, especially exemplified by Dee. One cannot help but wonder if that other Puritan, John Milton, who was so deeply interested in mathematics, also had Dee's **'Preface'** in mind when he wrote *Of Education.* Certainly Milton knew the edition of the *Grounde of Artes* with Dee's augmentation, and it is highly probable that he knew the English *Euclide,* or at least the **'Mathematicall Preface',** in one of its reprintings since it was also a standard mathematical work.

Almost a hundred years after it was written, the **'Preface'** was reprinted in an edition of Euclid published in 1661. The editors assert, 'We have thought good to insert . . . that full and learned **"Preface"** of the famous Mathematician *John Dee,* then which nothing of that nature can be more ample or satisfactory.' As much as Bacon's *Advancement,* Dee's **'Mathematicall Preface'** is a milestone in the history of English scientific thought. (pp. 160-76)

Peter J. French, in his John Dee: The World of An Elizabethan Magus, *Routledge & Kegan Paul, 1972, 347 p.*

J. Peter Zetterberg (essay date 1978)

[*In the excerpt below, Zetterberg examines Dee's hermetic writings, which he claims reveal Dee's cosmology better than his astronomical treatises, concluding that despite his respect for Copernicus, Dee never renounced the doctrine of geocentrism in favor of Copernican heliocentrism.*]

In this paper I will reconsider John Dee's opinion of the Copernican hypothesis, especially the claim that Dee's Hermeticism predisposed him toward heliocentricity. I grant at the outset that Dee may have been a Copernican, since it is always possible that he may have held in private what he would not advocate in print. However, I believe that Dee never accepted Copernican cosmology. And I will argue that he never accepted it because he was instead deeply committed—and the commitment was Hermetically inspired—to what he believed to be the geocentric cosmology of the ancient magi.

Not until 1573, when Thomas Digges, in his *Alae seu scalae mathematicae,* accepted the Copernican system as a physical theory, did any Englishman openly defend the new system as something more than a useful mathematical device or, as Osiander had cautioned, a hypothesis, which "need not be true nor even probable." Robert Recorde had included a brief discussion of the Copernican system in his *Castle of Knowledge* (1556), letting any examination of the cosmology of the theory "passe tyll some other time," and several of Recorde's English contemporaries were undoubtedly familiar with the work of Copernicus. But as a physical theory, the novel hypothesis of *De revolutionibus* generated no debate in England prior to Digges' work. Even Dee, who tutored Digges in mathematics and astronomy, never expressed an opinion regarding the cosmology of the new system.

Despite Dee's silence, a number of historians have speculated that Dee may have been a true Copernican. As evidence they commonly cite the laudatory references to the mathematical achievement of *De revolutionibus* that Dee makes in his earliest extant work, a preface to John Feild's *Ephemeris anni 1557* (London), and also Dee's association with Digges. Lynn Thorndike, for example [in *A History of Magic and Experimental Science,* Vol. VI], grudgingly concedes that Dee may have quietly accepted the Copernican cosmology, although he adds that Dee "believed in so many things that were wrong, that we could not give him personally any high credit, even if in this one instance he believed in something that happened to be right."

More recently Peter French has drawn attention to another factor that he regards as relevant to the question of Dee and the Copernican hypothesis—Dee's Hermeticism. French believes that Renaissance magi like Dee, far from retarding the rise of science in the sixteenth and seventeenth centuries, may actually have stimulated the movement. He cites [in *John Dee: The World of an Elizabethan Magus*] Dee's supposed Copernicanism in support of this view, arguing that

> . . . magic did not impede the acceptance of heliocentricity. Indeed, the Renaissance magus was ready and willing to embrace the Copernican hypothesis. Dee apparently did so, but without fanfare. Thus, we come to the conclusion that, although the Renaissance magus worked his magic within a geocentric system, he had a spiritual affinity with heliocentricity. . . . In this case, then, scientific advance was spurred by the renewed interest in the magical Hermetic religion of the world.

As I will demonstrate, the geocentric system in which Dee worked his magic was far from conventional. According to Dee, ancient magi had known the true structure of the heavens and preserved their knowledge for subsequent generations in the common planetary signs that they carefully designed not only to represent the heavenly bodies but also to reveal cryptically what was true of them. In the ***Monas hieroglyphica*** (1564), his principal Hermetic work, Dee claims to have discovered the truth of geocentric cosmology by deciphering these ancient signs and other hieroglyphs and symbols. In this ancient cosmology, the sun occupies a very special place. Indeed, the sun may well be the body about which one planet turns, for Dee suggests in a veiled way that Mercury's deferent is sun-centered. The sun itself, however, orbits the earth, which retains its position as the true center of the universe.

When Dee first learned of the work of Copernicus is not known; however, it must certainly have been no later than May of 1547, when he traveled to the Continent to study with Gemma Frisius among others. Frisius, in his "Epistola" to the *Ephemerides novae* (1556) of Joannes Stadius, was among the first to comment favorably on the work of Copernicus, although he never accepted Copernican cosmology.

Dee's first published reference to the work of Copernicus was in 1557, several years after his return to England. In 1555 he had been arrested with John Feild and charged with "endeavoring by enchantmentes to destroy Queen Mary." Feild was planning an ephemeris, and Dee, evidently during their confinement together, suggested that he base it on the work of Copernicus and Reinhold. Feild accepted the suggestion and asked Dee to write a preface to the work.

The preface itself is brief. Dee begins by explaining that there were many errors in the old astronomical tables—a theme of the "Epistola" of Frisius, who like Dee cites errors in the position of Mercury as an example. These had been corrected by the "Herculean" labors of Copernicus, Reinhold, and Rheticus, whom he lauds as "restorers of the heavenly discipline," especially the "god-like" Copernicus, whose splendor "blinds the eye." Dee concludes by urging his countrymen to use the work of these reformers, noting that it was he who had convinced Feild to base his tables on their work. Dee does speak highly of the work of Copernicus. However, he defers from any discussion of the heliocentric hypothesis, claiming that the preface is not the proper place to consider such things. Dee's support of Copernican planetary theory is thus qualified and limited, as it is also in his proposal for calendar reform, which was written twenty-five years later and contains his only other significant reference to Copernicus.

It was at Queen Elizabeth's request in 1582 that Dee submitted a proposal for calendar reform. In the proposal he relies on what he regards as the most accurate astronomical data available: the "Calculation and Phaenomenies" of Copernicus and the Prutenic Tables of Reinhold. As in the preface to Feild's *Ephemeris,* Dee accepts the work of Copernicus in this proposal, but again only in a qualified way. For after acknowledging his dependence on the "Calculation and Phaenomenies" of Copernicus, Dee hastens to add that this is "excepting his Hypotheses Theoricall: not here to be brought in question."

The works considered above contain Dee's only discussions of Copernican planetary theory. In neither is there any indication that he accepted the heliocentric hypothesis as anything more than a useful mathematical fiction. Both works deal with practical concerns, and in both the Prutenic Tables of Reinhold, who never accepted heliocentricity, are as much the object of Dee's support as the planetary theory used in their computation.

Dee and Digges were closely associated as master and pupil for a period of time after Dee had written his preface to Feild's *Ephemeris* and well before he composed his calendar reform proposal. That Dee's qualified acceptance of Copernican theory is markedly similar in both works suggests that Dee did not share his student's enthusiasm for heliocentric cosmology. So too do the known facts of their association, the decisive event of which was the appearance of a supernova in the constellation of Cassiopeia in November of 1572.

Both studied the nova carefully and established that it was a phenomenon located in the supposedly unchangeable celestial region of the universe. Dee's contribution to the literature on the nova was a book of trigonometric theorems for use in determining stellar parallax [**Parallaticae commentationis praxeosque nucleus quidam**]. Among Dee's unpublished treatises is another work on the nova, now lost, in which he evidently discussed the star's diminishing appearance. The title of this work indicates that he believed the nova to be moving perpendicularly away from the earth ("in coeli penetralia perpendiculariter retracta"). Digges parted company with Dee on this issue and considered another possibility. In the *Alae* he wondered whether "the motion of the Earth set forth in the Copernican theory is the sole reason why this star is diminishing in magnitude." His attempts to verify this supposition were inconclusive and confused. Nonetheless, Digges was clearly willing to treat the heliocentric hypothesis as a physical theory, while Dee, who from all indications left the earth at rest and assumed instead that the star was moving, was evidently not.

Several years after his work on the nova, Digges published an English translation of the principal sections of the first book of *De revolutionibus.* Included with the translation were arguments offered by Digges in support of heliocentric cosmology. Digges gives no indication in either of the works in which he defends the Copernican system that Dee shared his views. References to Dee are limited to an apology to him in the *Alae,* in which Digges explains why he is issuing his work on the nova prior to Dee's ***Parallaticae commentationis,*** and a note of indebtedness to Dee, whom Digges refers to as his "second parent in Mathematics and Astronomy."

As in both of the works in which Dee briefly refers to Copernicus, nothing in his association with Digges justifies the conclusion that he was a true Copernican. Nor does a remark by the Elizabethan Richard Forster in his *Ephemerides meteorographicae* (1575) lend itself to such a conclusion: "Astronomy, which in England, first began to revive and emerge from darkness into light through the efforts of John Dee, Keen champion of new hypotheses and Ptolemaic Theory, will, as a result of the interference of unskilled persons, go to ruin with the heavens of Copernicus and Reinhold unless Dee again interposes his Atlantean shoulders." The remark is admittedly ambiguous, but it seems to be based on nothing more than what Dee says in his preface to Feild's *Ephemeris.* To resolve the general ambiguity that surrounds the question of Dee's cosmological views it is necessary to leave his works on practical science and turn instead to his occult interests. For only in his occult works, in particular the ***Monas hieroglyphica,*** the subject of which is alchemy, does Dee reveal a cosmology.

In the **"Mathematicall Preface,"** the work in which Dee's interest in both practical and occult science is evident, "Cosmographie" is defined to be "the whole and perfect description of the heavenly, and also elementall parte of the world, and their homologall application, and mutuall collation necessarie." With other Renaissance alchemists, Dee believed that there was a direct correspondence between celestial bodies and terrestrial bodies, and he claimed to have a "Globe Cosmographical" that demonstrated this by matching "Heaven, and the Earth, in one frame, and aptly applieth parts Correspondent." Through study of the relations among celestial bodies, one could learn of the relations among terrestrial bodies. In particular, one could learn of alchemical processes through study of the heavens, provided that the correspondences between the celestial and terrestrial realms were known. As defined by Dee, cosmography was, in part, the study of such correspondences, and hence cosmological considerations play an important part in the ***Monas hieroglyphica*** and its alchemical mysteries.

In the ***Monas*** Dee claims to disclose the secrets of alchemy by means of a special hieroglyph: the "hieroglyphic monad." Throughout the work he analyzes this hieroglyph "mathematically, magically, cabbalistically, and anagogically," as he outlines his scheme in a subtitle. Dee cautions the reader in a prefatory letter that as there is a difference between a body and its shadow, so too is there a difference between what words and symbols appear to mean and what they really mean. He adds: "The ignorant, rash, and presumptuous apes grasp mere shadows, naked and inane, while the wiser philosophers enjoy the solid doctrine and very pleasing effects of the [real] bodies." Students of the ***Monas*** are thus advised by Dee to search deeply for the mysterious truths that he claims to reveal.

The caution to readers of this difficult and abstruse work applies not only to the work itself but also to all symbols and signs in it. They too may have multiple, hidden meanings. Indeed, at least one thing is clear in the ***Monas,*** and that is Dee's belief that the common planetary signs have hidden meanings. They are cryptic representations of cosmic truths, carefully crafted by ancient magi to preserve God-given truths through time. According to Dee, to understand the universe one need only decipher the signs of the heavenly bodies, for "the common astronomical symbols of the planets (instead of being dead, dumb, or up to the present hour at least, quasi-barbaric signs) . . . [are really] characters imbued with immortal life and should now be able to express their especial meanings most eloquently in any tongue and to any nation."

Dee demonstrates in the ***Monas*** that the planetary signs are each "composed of [elements derived from] the symbols of Moon and Sun and [from] the hieroglyphic sign[s] of the elements and of Aries." These are the four special signs or symbols that combine to form the hieroglyphic monad. The powers, virtues, and place of each planet in the universe are supposedly evident in the symbols of which it is made. Jupiter, for example, is somehow under the influence of the moon and Venus the sun, since the former contains the symbol of the moon, the latter that of the sun.

What then of the sun; what does its symbol reveal to Dee about the most important of celestial bodies? Among other things, it reveals that the sun orbits the earth. Not only is the cosmology Dee reveals through his interpretation of planetary symbols geocentric, it is geocentric as a matter of mathematical necessity. Dee begins in the ***Monas*** with these three theorems:

> Theorem I: The first and most simple manifestation and representation of things, nonexistent as well as latent in the folds of Nature, happened by means of straight line and circle.
>
> Theorem II: Yet the circle cannot be artificially produced without the straight line, or the straight line without the point. Hence, things first begin to be by way of a point, and a monad. And things related to the periphery (however big they may be) can in no way exist without the aid of the central point.
>
> Theorem III: Thus the central point to be seen in the centre of the hieroglyphic monad represents the earth, around which the Sun as well as the Moon and the other planets complete their courses. And since in that function the Sun occupies the highest dignity, we represent it (on account of the superiority) by a full circle, with a visible centre.

These theorems clearly depict a universe that is geocentric, and they are intended, moreover, as an explanation of why the universe is so structured.

According to Dee, the universe was created by God in a mathematical way. This is a recurrent theme in his works, especially the **"Mathematical Preface,"** in which he expounds upon it at length and refers to God's creating as His "Numbryng." The sun, like all other things, had been created by God in a mathematical way (Theorems I and II); in particular, it had been created to travel in a circular orbit. However, as the circle cannot be produced without the aid of a central point (Theorem II), so God could not have created the sun and its orbit without first creating a central point: the earth or "terrestrial monad." For this reason God placed the earth in the center of the universe (Theorem III). The ancient magi, according to Dee, have sent this truth to us hidden in a symbol, the sun circling the earth, which was the primal point in the chaos to which God affixed His celestial ruler and compass when constructing the rest of the world. This is the cryptic truth that the symbol reveals.

Peter French acknowledges in his study of Dee that a geocentric cosmology is assumed in both of Dee's major works on occult science, the ***Propaedeumata aphoristica*** (astrology) and the ***Monas hieroglyphica*** (alchemy). He regards this geocentric framework as strictly conventional, however, and after noting that in both works the sun "is accorded a place of primary importance," he goes on to argue that despite Dee's silence on the matter "for a Hermeticist like Dee, the sun-centered universe of Copernicus would have been a mysterious, mystical and pregnant religious revelation." French here echoes the view of Yates that "for Bruno [and by implication other Hermetic philosophers of the period] the Copernican diagram is a hieroglyph, a Hermetic seal hiding potent divine mysteries of which he has penetrated the secret."

Dee, like Ficino and Fludd, as well as Bruno, did regard cosmological diagrams as hieroglyphs of a kind. Indeed, he regarded the pattern of the heavens itself in this way, as is evident throughout the ***Monas*** and also in the **"Mathematicall Preface,"** in which he scolded those who merely "looke upon the *Heaven, Sterres,* and *Planets,* as an Oxe and an Asse doth." The heavens are instead a cryptic message to man from God, who "made the *Sonne, Mone,* and *Sterres,* to be to us, for *Signes.* . . . I wish every man should way this word, *Signes.*" But neither Dee's view that the heavens are a cosmic hieroglyph nor the reverence for the sun that, to some degree at least, is evident in the ***Monas;*** is in any way proof of heliocentric convictions on his part. Dee may have had a spiritual affinity with the sun, but that does not mean, as French argues, that he had "a spiritual affinity with heliocentricity." Both Ficino and Fludd, for example, while singing eulogies to the sun, were perfectly content with its traditional place in the middle of the heavens, which they regarded as special. This seems to have been Dee's position, although he gave a unique rationale for the traditional ordering of the planets and made the sun's place in the center of the heavens an even more special one.

Dee's cosmological diagram in the ***Monas*** is a curious celestial egg. The egg, which represented the primordial chaos out of which the ordered world had emerged, was a favorite symbol of alchemists. In the ***Monas*** the egg in which Dee places the planets serves as a reminder to the reader that knowledge of the heavens must precede knowledge of alchemical mysteries—that, as Dee teaches, "celestial astronomy is like a parent and teacher to *Astronomia inferior* [sc. alchemy]." It is more than a reminder, however. It is this diagram of the heavens that supposedly will reveal alchemical truths to those who can decipher it, and therefore the cosmology expressed in it cannot be regarded as merely conventional. Indeed, the diagram, although geocentric, has unique features.

In Dee's figure the sun, moon, and planets circle the earth, as clearly indicated by the dotted lines depicting their orbits. The cosmology revealed is geocentric and consistent with the first three theorems of the work. The sun is in the middle of the egg, in the center of the yolk. This, and not the center of the universe, is its special place. Planets most subject to a lunar influence—as indicated by the [lunar crescent] in their symbols—are placed in the white of the egg with the moon; those most subject to a solar influence—as indicated by the [solar sphere] in their symbols—are placed in the yolk of the egg with the sun. After presenting his diagram, Dee addresses other alchemists.

"May those very inexperienced imposters, in their desperation, hereby understand what is the water of the white of eggs, what the oil from the yolks, [and] what the chalk of eggs [sc. egg-shell], and many more things like these." He explains that the white of the egg is the "aqueous moisture of the Moon" and that the yolk is the "fiery liquid of the Sun," both of which "infuse their corporeal virtues into all inferior bodies." The rationale for the order of the planets within the white and the yolk, as explained above, is clear, and their order from moon outward to Saturn is the usual one, needing no explanation. Only the eggshell or "chalk" is left unexplained, although Dee does hint at an interpretation.

"They [the alchemists] have called this secret 'the Egg' but all of them [really] mean 'Mercury' "—so wrote the Greek alchemist Zasimo, and in alchemical texts the egg symbol is indeed often associated with the element mercury. In the ***Monas,*** also, I would suggest that Mercury is associated in a special way with an egg symbol. For I believe that the "chalk" of Dee's celestial egg is meant to depict Mercury's suncentered deferent. Dee writes:

> Raising toward heaven our cabbalistic eyes (that have been illuminated by speculation on these mysteries) we shall behold an anatomy precisely corresponding to that of our monad, which, in the light of Nature and of life, will at all times reveal itself to us as is here shown, and will, by its pleasures, quite openly discover the most secret mysteries of this analysis of the physical world.

The anatomy to which Dee refers is his celestial egg. Where in the heavens could one observe it? Dee suggests an answer.

> While we were once contemplating the motions, in theory and in the heavens, of the celestial messenger [sc. Mercury], we were taught that the figure of an egg adds [pertinent information] to this scheme. For it is well known to astronomers that he [sc. Mercury] on his course in the ether performs an oval orbit. And this, [once] said, should be enough to the wise.

A number of astronomers had attributed an oval deferent to Mercury, including Reinhold, whose work Dee knew. From the passage above it seems clear that he adopted this novel view, which is further indication that the geocentric framework of the ***Monas*** is far from conventional.

In the preface to the ***Monas*** Dee singles out Mercury as a special planet, which "may rightly be styled by us the rebuilder and restorer of all astronomy [and] an astronomical messenger." The special importance of Mercury in Dee's scheme of things is evident in the hieroglyphic monad itself, which is nothing more than the common symbol for Mercury with the sign of Aries affixed to its base. The title page of the ***Monas*** contains the inscription "Mercury becomes *the parent and the King of all planets* when made perfect by a stable pointed hook"—that is, when the sign of Aries is placed on the base of the sign of Mercury. The unique feature of Mercury's symbol is that it alone of all the planetary signs contains both the sign of lunar influence and the sign of solar influence. It would be fitting, then, that Mercury (in refined form the philosopher's stone) has as the center of its deferent the sun (the gold of the heaven), for this would then make Mercury subject in a special way to solar influence and not only lunar influence, which is all that its place in the white of the egg would otherwise suggest. Certainly such a cosmic design, reflecting as it does the mercury-gold relationship of the alchemy of the terrestrial world, would have appealed to Dee, who believed so strongly in the correspondence between celestial and terrestrial realms. Such a geocentric cosmology, unique in its features, and not heliocentricity, is, I contend, the revelation of the ***Monas hieroglyphica,*** a revelation from the ancient magi who, according to Dee, devised the planetary signs to be cryptic messengers of such truths.

In a prefatory letter to the ***Monas,*** Dee ridiculed the strenuous labors of the common astronomer, writing of the geocentric cosmology he was to reveal:

> And will not the astronomer be very sorry for the cold he suffered under the open sky, for [all his] vigils and labours, when here, with no discomfort to be suffered from the air, he may most exactly observe with his eyes the orbits of the heavenly bodies under [his own] roof, with windows and doors shut on all sides, at any given time, and without any mechanical instruments made of wood or brass?

It was in ancient signs and symbols, not in the naked heavens, that Dee, the Hermetic magus, searched for cosmological truths. And I would argue, in conclusion, that the geocentric cosmology he claimed to have discovered by deciphering the planetary signs—a Hermetic activity—was the one which he believed in throughout his life. For the ***Monas hieroglyphica*** was the work Dee was most proud of. He seems never to have lost faith in the truths he claimed to have revealed in this work. In the ***Compendious Rehearsall*** (1592), a rambling autobiographical account of his achievements, Dee singled out the ***Monas*** as the most significant product of his active and diverse career, even though it was never appreciated by his countrymen, including, he lamented, "University graduates of high degree, and other Gentlemen who . . . disprаysed it because they understood it not."

As Robert Westman has argued, there is no indication that Hermetic philosophers, with the exception of Bruno, accepted a heliocentric cosmology, although some like Dee did appreciate the work of Copernicus and did welcome the derivative Prutenic Tables of Reinhold. In Dee's case, at least, Hermetic interests seem on the contrary to have reinforced a belief in geocentric cosmology. And, importantly, Dee's expressed reverence for the sun, even granting it to have been deep and Hermetically inspired, was in no way incompatible with this geocentric cosmology. For the sun, the center of the yolk of Dee's celestial egg, was not denied its very special place. (pp. 385-93)

J. Peter Zetterberg, "Hermetic Geocentricity: John Dee's Celestial Egg," in Isis, *Vol. 70, No. 253, September, 1978, pp. 385-93.*

J. L. Heilbron (essay date 1978)

[*In the following excerpt from his extensive introduction to the* Propadeumata aphoristica, *Heilbron contends that Dee and other Renaissance hermeticists contributed only indirectly to the development of modern scientific methodology. Heilbron then examines Dee's sources for the* Propadeumata aphoristica *and its departures from contemporary cosmology.*]

There is no doubt that Dee was a competent and knowledgeable mathematician and that he played an important part in making the mathematics and the occultism of the Continental Renaissance known in England. His technical advice and lessons and his constant advertisements for mathematics, culminating in the stirring long-winded **"Preface,"** encouraged people to study geometry who might otherwise have neglected it. Several of the mathematical masters active in London at the end of the sixteenth century learned their art either directly from him or from others inspired by him. All this gives Dee a modest place in the intellectual history of Tudor England. To this may be added a part in justifying, encouraging, and attempting to realize the imperial ambitions of Elizabeth.

Recently historians have found a larger role for Dee: he was not only an important link between English and Continental savants, but also a prime mover and necessary forerunner of the Scientific Revolution. Here is the opinion of Peter French, the latest Dee monographer [as explained in his *John Dee: The World of an Elizabethan Magus,* 1972]: "The more overtly scientific attitudes of men like Francis Bacon and William Harvey evolved from the approach of Dee and his [magician] colleagues. . . . Dee's theories about mathematics, architecture, navigation and technology—all part of a broader magically oriented philosophy—achieved results: they helped to pave the way for the momentous scientific advances of the seventeenth century." Dr. French takes his theme from Frances Yates of the Warburg Institute. Dr. Yates, an imaginative and resourceful historian, has come to see the Renaissance magus as "the immediate ancestor of the seventeenth-century scientist," and the magicians' frame of mind as "the necessary preliminary to the rise of science." Her argument [in *Art, Science, and History,* ed. by Singleton, 1968] runs roughly as follows.

The science of Galileo, whom no one refuses a place in the revolutionary van, is characterized above all by the application of mathematics to physics and by appeal to experiment; it also disdains the school philosophy, finds some of its concerns in the technical problems of engineers, mariners, and military men, and uses special materials, instruments, and apparatus. According to Yates, the same characteristics may be found in Renaissance hermeticism, which she makes a mixture of Neoplatonism, magic, numerology, cabala, alchemy, and the teachings of Hermes Trismegistus. Her mixture may be dissolved into two distinct ingredients.

First is the Neoplatonic/magical, which rests upon the old scheme of Emanations from the original, indifferent One. The Emanations, ordered in strength and dignity, each in turn created and creating, decline from the first immaterial hypostases down to and beyond the first visible incarnation, the sun, the material image of God. The hermetist believed himself capable of tapping the energies, or exploiting the "sympathies," in the chain of creation that holds the cosmos together. Alchemy and astrology hinted how he might proceed, how the sun's creative power or the derivative planetary influences might be concentrated in appropriate talismans, amulets, and symbols. In performing these operations, in bringing together the magical material, in resorting to his furnace, burning mirror, harp, or dung heap, the hermetist became a magus and, according to Yates, the ancestor of the experimental physicist.

The second ingredient in Yate's hermeticism in Pythagorean/cabalistic. It links to the hermetic complex by locating Number among the early Emanations, among the Ideas sprung from the One, and by invoking practical cabala, or number magic, to help tap the Neoplatonic power line. And it links or leads to Galileo in two ways: it endorses the promiscuous study and use of mathematics, including the applications of arithmetic and geometry spelled out by Dee; and it authorizes the natural philosopher to search for the simple mathematical relations among physical quantities that constitute the Pattern of the Universe.

Yates's thesis gains much of its plausibility from its inclusiveness. There is scarcely an interesting writer on mathematics or physics from Ficino to Galileo who does not touch one or another of her hermetic themes. But that does not make them magicians. We know, for example, that from the first Parisian printing of Euclid in 1516 the *Elements* customarily carried a preface praising Plato; yet few editors or students were Pythagoreans, much less hermetists. One can even be a magician and not a hermetist. Whoever taps the world's energies or sympathies merely by manipulating ordinary, given powers, practices natural magic, Dee's thaumaturgy; he designs mechanical tricks, makes up philtres and cosmetics, invents cryptograms, plays with mirrors and magic lanterns, in short does the thousand amusing, silly, practical, or useless things set forth in the books of Giambattista della Porta, Athanasius Kircher, Gaspar Schott, and Francesco Lana. If, on the other hand, one attempts to influence the sources of power, to alter the course of nature, one must cajole alien intelligences; one sings them songs or shows them pictures, summons spirits, invokes demons, conjures up angels good and bad. These were the tendencies of true hermetic magic. The natural variety could be respectable and successful; its practitioners acquired knowledge and experience of materials, particularly metals and glass, that went into building the apparatus of the scientific revolution. Needless to say, invoking spirits was useless and dangerous; conjurers might learn at great risk to their souls the hierarchies of demons and the unutterable names of God, but their exuberant animism blocked investigation of the ordinary and the regular, and they ended no wiser than they began.

In the 1920s Lynn Thorndike began to uncover what he took to be examples of the intercourse and offspring of magic and empiricism, of alchemy, astrology, mysticism, medicine, and natural history. From Thorndike's huge and heterogeneous inventory, Paolo Rossi [in his *Francis*

Bacon, 1968] has chosen Francis Bacon as a capital test case. Certainly Bacon, whom many seventeenth-century scientific revolutionaries took as their warlord, profited from the writings of the magicians. He took the magus to be a manipulator, a midwife, able to accelerate, retard, or prepare the operations of nature; an impresario who thoroughly understood natural powers and sympathies and, what is more, the terminology in which sixteenth-century adepts expressed them. Bacon saw in the industrious study and subsequent manipulation of natural powers the needed antidote to his favorite evil, the ills of traditional learning: "the aim of magic is to recall natural philosophy from the vanity of speculations to the importance of experiments."

But is Bacon's magic that of the adepts of Hermes? Rossi observes that although Bacon accepted some of the metaphysical principles of hermeticism, such as natural sympathies and antipathies, he opposed the adepts at a crucial point. The knowledge of the magi was the property of the initiated; it had to be acquired by direct teaching or by inspiration and passed on to the enlightened in riddles opaque to fools. Agrippa says that he writes so as to "confound the ignorant," and Dee, despite his essays in general education, insisted on restricting and obscuring his higher knowledge. The printing press put these good men in a quandary. Should they use it to reach the enlightened everywhere, or should they continue the practice of the ancient Pythagoreans, passing on their wisdom only to initiates chosen by them? Dee characteristically shifts the problem to someone else: he gives his manuscript to the printer and beseeches him to keep the resultant book—in this case the incomparable ***Monas***—from falling into the hands of the vulgar. His reasons are curious. Some people, unable to extricate themselves from the "labyrinth" of his thought, will "torture their minds in incredible ways [and] neglect their everyday affairs"; while others, "imposters and mere spectres of men," may deny the truths Dee revealed and question his integrity.

Bacon reproved the hermetists for their secrecy, for their obscurity, and, above all, for their belief that knowledge advances by individual inspiration and limited circulation. Cardano had said that in making discoveries there is no need for partnership; Bacon insisted upon slow, plain, orderly, cooperative investigations. He would organize, set up committees, systematically extract the lore of philosophers, artisans, mechanics, and magicians. Unconfirmed effects, false claims, illusions, and fallacies would be exposed, rooted out, and thrown away with the refuse of the school philosophy. Bacon's concept of an open, natural-magical research organization was an important ingredient of the Scientific Revolution. We find it already adumbrated in the little society della Porta set up in Naples; and we see it expressed in Kircher's museum, in the Accademia del Cimento, in Lana's Filoesotici, and in the royal societies of London and Paris. There is no doubt that a denatured, democratic hermeticism and alchemy inspired some of the members of these groups.

Bacon and the natural magicians of the seventeenth century also differed from Yates's hermetists over the business of conjuring. Although the hermetist might draw back from invoking demons explicitly, he always flirted with spirits, for even the most benign hermetic rites implicitly addressed superior intelligences. Ficino, for example, strums Jovial music, burns Jovial incense, and contemplates Jovial pictures to prepare (he says) his own soul or an appropriately marked seal for the absorption of the beneficent rays of Jupiter; his idea is to bring his soul or the talisman into harmony with the planetary spirit so that they all might vibrate together. But as appears from the writings of Ficino's disciple, Francesco da Diacetto, the music, the incense, and the talismanic symbols were also part of a rite aimed to conciliate the planetary soul; indeed, it could not be otherwise, for as St. Thomas had proved two hundred years earlier, symbols, songs, and prayers can secure the ends intended by the magician only if directed at superhuman intelligences. The use of intelligible signs to attract celestial powers presupposes an appeal to demons. The demonic side of Ficinian astral magic is emphasized by the chief of the sixteenth-century magicians, Heinrich Cornelius Agrippa von Nettesheim, who openly describes, though he does not endorse, the standard methods for coaxing planetary spirits.

One could give sound reasons for believing that astral intelligences could be summoned and commanded. First, analogy to the practices of the Church, to prayer, to the efficacy of the sacraments, and, above all, to the mystery of the eucharist: on every side one saw, or believed one saw, the intervention of superpowers mobilized by human operations. Agrippa made much of parallels in the workings of priests and magicians. Second, there was excellent authority for the efficacy of hermetic astral magic, no less an authority than God; for the disciples of Hermes believed that their master had his wisdom from Moses, who had had his by divine revelation. As Agrippa tells it, God presented Moses with two revelations, one to be made public in Scripture, the other, too heady for the vulgar, to be passed down through a line of sages. Why Moses chose to confide in an Egyptian on the eve of the flight of Israel is a hermetic mystery. That the revelation of Hermes does not derive from remote antiquity but from inspired Alexandrian Greeks given to pseudepigraphy was a discovery of the seventeenth century.

Among the hermetic books is one, the *Asclepius,* that teaches how to prepare objects for the acceptance of celestial influences and how to animate a statue with, or with the help of, astral intelligences. The hermetist consequently accepted the existence of astral influences as part of his magical revelation. But he was not necessarily an enthusiastic astrologer. Agrippa, for example, always had doubts about traditional astrology, which he finally attacked as baseless and superstitious. Likewise Ficino's disciple Pico della Mirandola, who had no difficulty with astral magic, devoted an entire book to the confutation of astrology. The resolution of the apparent paradox in their position turns on a distinction important for understanding the significance of Dee's astrological aphorisms.

The traditional astrology, the star lore the Latin Middle Ages took from the Arabs, was deterministic: the stars govern everything here below, and cannot alter the future they announce. The Catholic Church had utterly condemned this fatalistic doctrine in late antiquity; but when it returned in the twelfth century, enriched with the learning and mathematical obscurities of the Arabs, theologians thought rather to Christianize than to fight it. The compromise worked out by Thomas Aquinas allows the stars full rights over matter, including the human body and its appetites, but exempts the soul. The doctrine turned out to be more useful to theologians than to common men, because, alas!, we only too often allow ourselves to be carried away by passions driven by our appetites. "And so it is," says St. Thomas, "that astrologers are able to foretell the truth in the majority of cases. . . . " Only those able to rule their passions can escape them; only the wise man can win the endless struggle with the stars.

This compromise did not satisfy the hermetists. Their revelation promised that they could not only evade, but also exploit, stellar influences. They opposed theoretical constraints on their freedom of action; man is a maker, a magus, a miracle; he operates as a god. "And so, O Asclepius," Hermes tells his disciple, "man is a *magnum miraculum,* a being worthy of reverence and honor," half divine, a cousin or brother of demons. What might he not accomplish through revealed wisdom and family connections? Pico sounds the same note in his *Oration on the Dignity of Man,* and goes on to emphasize freedom of the will and action. Now these rhapsodies, however sunny and optimistic they may appear, in fact menace the very dignity

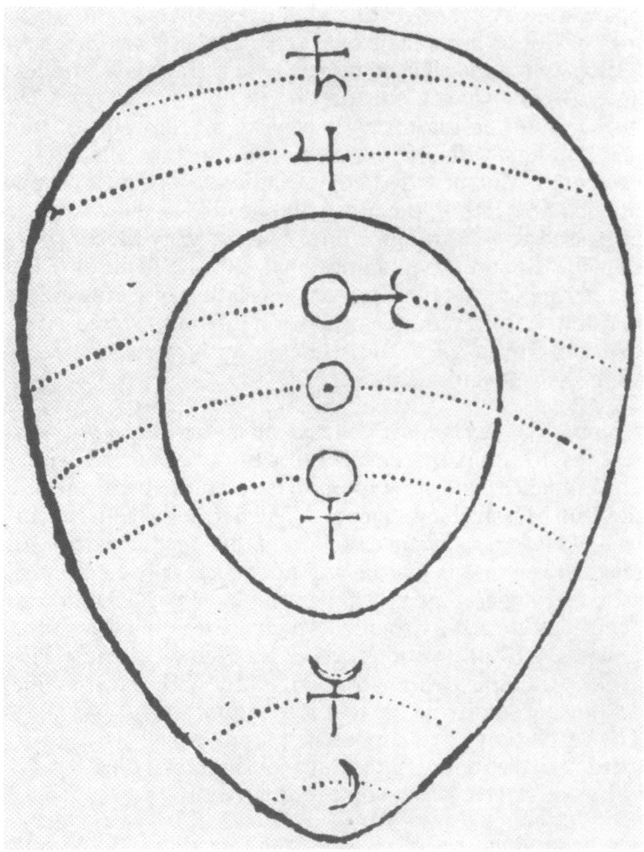

A diagram which Dee prepared for the Monas hieroglyphica, *the celestial egg represents Dee's conception of an ovoid, geocentic universe.*

they declare; for man's reason, which might be urged to be the first mark of his excellence, can neither discover nor explain the magic that hermetists applauded as evidence of his, or rather their, high state. Belief in the efficacy of unintelligible operations on the basis of revelation does not stem from confidence in the power of the human mind. And with the erosion of confidence in reason comes a willingness to accept reports of strange isolated occurrences, of singular events, of prodigies; one loses the basis of judgment, or, to use a favorite sixteenth-century image, one goes adrift without the only compass that can provide safe passage through seas of uncertainty and confusion. The connection between faith in Hermes' revelation, depreciation of reason, and gullibility appears clearly in Agrippa, who swings between occult philosophy and extreme scepticism, and finishes in fideism.

We are left with the supposition that hermetic astral magic may be antithetic to the traditional rationalistic, computational, deterministic astrology. Astrologers may be closer to physicists than to magicians. The course of Dee's work confirms the conjecture. He began optimistic in his power to understand and develop a full mathematical astrology, free, as will appear, from appeal to demons. He presently lost his compass (which perhaps was never tightly secured) and wandered through Europe without reason or direction, asking recalcitrant angels for revelations that never came.

Yates is by no means the first modern historian to emphasize the importance of mystical Platonizing mathematics in the transition from peripatetic to early modern science. The thesis, as started by E. A. Burtt [in *Metaphysical Foundations*] in 1924, emphasizes the importance of considerations of mathematical harmony and simplicity to Copernicus, Kepler, Galileo, Descartes, and Newton, considerations that might override objections to their novelties drawn from traditional physics, direct experience, or common sense. The appeal to "reason" over "sense," to ideas over experience, is supposed to mark the difference between Plato and Aristotle. Galileo made it the ground of his spokesman Salviati's admiration for the Copernicans: "they have through sheer force of intellect done such violence to their own senses as to prefer what reason told them over that which sensible experience told them to the contrary." The new criterion of truth is mathematical appropriateness: God is a geometrician, and so, in our weaker way, are we. If we can but shed the prejudices of our senses we may recapture at least part of the Divine Plan, the figures, forms, and numbers—in short the mathematics—of creation. This is, as we know, a constant element in Dee's thought, and the inspiration, if not for his best mathematics, for his most ecstatic prose. "O comfortable allurement, O ravishing perswasion, to deale with a Science, whose subject, is so Ancient, so pure, so excellent, so surmounting all creatures, so used of the Almighty and incomprehensible wisdome of the Creator, in the distinct creation of all creatures: in all their distincte partes, properties, natures and vertues, by order, and most absolute number, brought, from *Nothing,* to the *Formalities* of their being and state."

Burtt counts the early Copernican revolutionaries, Copernicus himself and Kepler, as Platonists chiefly because they took mathematical elegance as the touchstone of true physical theory. They may be admitted Platonists—or rather Neoplatonists—on another ground as well. Ficino had emphasized the prerogatives of the sun in words that virtually declared a heliocentric universe. Copernicus recalled in *De revolutionibus* that the thrice-great Hermes had named the sun "a visible God"; for himself, he preferred to imagine it "resting on a kingly throne, govern[-ing] the family of stars that wheel around." These remarks, together with the emphasis on mathematics and the fact that Copernicus cultivated humanism during ten years' study in Italy, show that at some level—whether of enabling inspiration, congenial confirmation, or incidental decoration—Platonism figured in the composition of *De revolutionibus.*

In the case of Kepler, the matter is plainer. He began his astronomical work with the conviction that God had the Platonic solids in mind when arranging the planets, and he came to his greatest discovery, the elliptical orbits, following an odd celestial dynamics derived from his belief that the sun, an image of God the Father, literally drove the planets around. In middle age he returned to the riddle of the number and spacing of the planets. To answer it, he took the notion of mathematical harmony to its literal extreme: he worked out that the Pythagorean music of the spheres, a music for the intellect, not the ears, is written with chords fixed by the ratios of the distances of the planets from the sun. The precise part assigned to each member of the choir depends upon its velocity. Kepler's search for harmonies caused him to examine many possible relations between the solar distances of a planet and its speed; and among the discoveries of his Pythagorean quest was the true and important "law" connecting the average solar distance (a) and the heliocentric period (T) of the planets.

Galileo had little patience with Kepler's procedures. He can therefore plausibly be held to be a Platonist only on the ground of his insistence that to understand the universe one must be able to read mathematics. For mathematics is the language in which the book of the universe is written; without a knowledge of its alphabet, of "triangles, circles and other geometrical figures," one cannot understand a word of it. Many similar Platonic commonplaces may be gathered from Galileo's works. Historians of science have taken them very seriously. Under the influence of the late Alexandre Koyré it became fashionable to reckon Galileo's Platonism so strong as to have kept him from the experiments that had been considered his greatest glory. But recently Stillman Drake and others have restored him to his weights and inclined planes. They may thereby save Galileo from Koyré's brand of Platonism, but—and this is a capital point—not necessarily from Yates's. Galileo's experimentalism, which embarrassed Koyré, is to Yates a natural development from the combination of elements first united in men like Dee. The novelty in her position, perhaps the chief cause of current interest in Dee, is the claim that hermetists helped to arrange the wedding of scholar and manipulator, of geometry and experiment.

We may consider Yates's claim as part of an explanation of the remarkable growth of interest in, and knowledge of, mathematics in the sixteenth century. There were of course other causes of this phenomenon than the program of the hermetists. One frequently invoked is the activity of the humanist translators, the new masters of Greek, who, having exhausted the ancient writings closest to their hearts, turned to making good Latin editions of the classic mathematicians. These translations, disseminated by the new printing presses, made accessible almost the entire range of extant Greek mathematics. Euclid, already available in incunabular printings of a medieval translation from an Arabic original, was reedited directly from the Greek into Latin and vernacular languages. Ptolemy's *Almagest* first came into Latin directly from Greek in 1528; Archimedes's *Opera* did the same in 1544, and the first four books of Apollonius's *Conics* in 1566.

Another cause for sixteenth-century interest in mathematics was utility. The new warfare based on gunpowder required the skill of practical geometers for both fortification and sieges, for constructing cannon-proof ramparts, running trenches, designing siege equipment. Dee's student, Thomas Digges, to name but one among many mathematicians, made part of his career as a military engineer. Then there was civil engineering, the new architecture of Brunelleschi and Alberti, or rather the old architecture of Vitruvius. And, most important of all, the voyages of discovery and exploration, the lengthening trade routes to Africa and Russia, the governance and defense of vast empires made necessary the services of crowds of navigators, surveyors, and cartographers. It was this need that inspired Gemma's teaching and brought Dee to Louvain.

We have observed that the connection of mathematics with practice helped to earn it the disfavor of dons unwilling or unable to study it. The academic mathematician often met this prejudice by calling up the Greeks. Editors of Euclid, for example, liked to dwell upon the prerequisite for admission to Plato's Academy, a knowledge of geometry, without which one cannot fully grasp higher philosophical studies. Others met the prejudice head on, by extolling the incomparable Archimedes, the exemplar of the mathematician pure and applied. The sixteenth century took much from the ancient engineer of Syracuse. His elegant mathematics helped inspire its algebra; his studies of mechanics and hydrostatics gave it a model for quantitative descriptions of physical phenomena; and, above all, his traditional exploits, his destruction of the Roman fleet by burning mirrors, his single-handed moving of a great ship by a system of pulleys, taught it what a little mathematics, appropriately applied, could do.

Plato and Archimedes could, of course, be more than convenient symbols in academic disputes about the value of mathematics. They might also inspire fruitful lines of study. If Plato was Kepler's cicerone, Archimedes was Galileo's; while Kepler pondered the cosmological significance of the five regular solids, Galileo, who had learned his mathematics at the Florentine Accademia del Disegno along with painters, architects, and engineers, was composing essays on Archimedean themes such as centers of gravity and floating bodies. Now Yates promotes Hermes as a third major inspirer and director of mathematical studies in the sixteenth century, particularly of studies that realized, or at least anticipated, an amalgamation of mathematics and experiment. Among those she likes to point to is Dee.

Students of the scientific revolution are therefore challenged to discover how far (if at all) applied mathematics and Yates's hermeticism interacted fruitfully in the sixteenth century. Did a significant number of applied mathematicians then derive their interest, direction, and legitimization from the Pythagorean elements in hermeticism? What in their writings is conventional or purely rhetorical? What part did astrology and other quantitative pseudo-sciences play? Forty years ago, E. W. Strong [in his *Procedures and Metaphysics,* 1936] attacked some of these questions in an attempt to answer Burtt's claim about the Platonic underpinnings of early-modern science. Strong pointed out that the chief contributors to pure mathematics in the sixteenth century did not concern themselves much, if at all, with numerology, while those most Pythagorean in spirit produced relatively little. Hermes did not figure at all. Strong's polemical purpose, however, took him beyond the mark; and he ends by denying that Neoplatonic impulses assisted in any way in the birth of modern science.

The example of Kepler, or of the algebraist and cabalist Stifel, show that Strong went too far. Yates, too, has overplayed her hand. The secretive "experimentation" of her magi, their tendency to accept reports of prodigies, and their anti-rationalism ran against the currents of the scientific revolution. Yet, the hermetists' emphasis on wisdom, on studying subjects depreciated or ignored in the schools, and their promise of ultimate knowledge, may have provided psychological support for many to master and to promote neglected studies that had no necessary connection with magic. In this connection, the ***Propaedeumata aphoristica*** take on great interest. On the one hand, they represent an inclusive, quantitative, physical science, assisted by experiment and aimed at both understanding and control of natural processes. On the other, they echo the harmonies of the world and the sympathies among all things, and dimly announce the hermeticism that was to inform the ***Monas.*** The sources of Dee's aphorisms and the manner in which he reworked them consequently claim our attention. (pp. 34-49)

The cosmology underlying Dee's astrological aphorisms may appear to be traditional. The framework of the whole is the Aristotelian earth-centered universe, finite in size and divided into two qualitatively distinct regions, the unalterable celestial and the corruptible sublunary. The devices of Ptolemaic astronomy regulate the motions of the heavenly bodies; the old doctrine of the four elements, with an admixture of alchemy, applies to the world beneath the moon. Neoplatonic sympathy ties everything together; according to Dee, it originates in the heavenly bodies and propagates through space as prescribed by the respectable medieval theory of the multiplication of species. When received on earth, the species or radiated sympathy gives rise to effects that depend upon its own nature and on that of its terrestrial absorber. Knowledge of elective sympathies, of the capacities of sublunary substances for soaking up or concentrating celestial species, enables the astrologer to set up as a magus or physician, and, perhaps, to alter the course of events.

Dee reworked these received qualitative propositions in the manner of the applied mathematician. He took as his guide the exemplar of all radiations, the pattern of multiplication of species, "the first of God's Creatures," namely visible light. That immediately put at his disposal all geometrical optics then known. He came to assimilate invisible species so closely with light that, in the **"Preface,"** he defined the art of perspective as the description of "all Actions, and passions, by Emanation of beames perfourmed." Not only did optical theory give Dee a way to estimate the relative strengths of astrological radiations in different planetary configurations; it also enabled him to prescribe how to confirm and extend the reach of the calculations by experiment. The main apparatus required was a parabolic speculum, a burning mirror, supposed to concentrate all stellar emanations precisely as it intensified light.

Dee's approach to astrology, although not entirely original with him, deviated in several ways from that of the ordinary literature. There is no trace of the hermetic planetary souls, for example: stars are not intelligences to be cajoled but unalterable sources of exploitable power; they are not like people but like radiators; their influences may be concentrated by optical instruments, not by songs, prayers and incense. Again, Dee takes literally the demands of optical theory; and since the intensity of radiation diminishes with distance and increases with the size of the luminous source, he insists that an exact astronomy, one that yields precise values of the sizes and distances of all planetary configurations, is a prerequisite to a competent astrology. The general practitioner did not care for such refinements, which he could neither use nor understand. We may take the grasp of arithmetic of Andrew Borde, M.D., as representative: "Euery one of the sygnes [of the zodiac] is deuydyd in lx degres," he says, and "euery degre doth contayn .vi. mynutes [!];" from which he works out that "y^{e}.zodiack [has] .CCC.vi.degres."

A more instructive contrast with Dee is furnished by Cardano, who published some 1173 astrological aphorisms in 1547. Cardano dismisses Trithemius and Agrippa as crackpots; like Dee, he has no place in his astrology for demons, an ineffectual race in his experience (his father had kept one) who have no effect on stars. But Cardano, although a good mathematician and a professor of mathematics, had no program for a quantitative astrology. "Vita brevis, ars longa," he says, "experience is not subject to our will and judgment is difficult." We must collect rules and guides from reading books and comparing nativities with biographies. To be sure, some knowledge of arithmetic and geometry is needed, but not much: the motions of the stars cannot be known perfectly, ephemerides need continual adjustment, and in any case no planet ever returns precisely to the same place in the heavens. The surest guide is the study of genitures. Cardano analyzes a great many of them, some of famous men; and he emerges with a welter of aphorisms impossible to reduce to general principles. "When the moon is under the sun she makes melancholics and great thinkers." "If the moon is in the second degree of Taurus, and either in quadrature or opposition to Jupiter and moving into trine with the sun, he [the subject of the geniture] will acquire not inconsiderable riches." "When the moon and Mercury are in conjunction in Taurus, he will be studious and even erudite." Cardano alternately encourages and bullies the fledgling astrologer who may have difficulty swallowing several hundred of these morsels. "Constant repetition is necessary in this science," he says, for it is exceedingly hard. "[My] book is more difficult than Ptolemy's great composition [the *Almagest*] or the ars magna [algebra], than Archimedes' spheroids, Aristotle's physics, or Plato's aenigmata."

Dee's aphorisms differed from Cardano's in offering explanations rather than recipes and mathematics in place of mush. Among precedents for such an approach is Ptolemy himself, who tried to reduce astrological practice to intelligible rules based upon physical properties assigned to the planets. Envious or malevolent contemporaries accused Dee of plagiarizing from closer to home, from his friend Mercator or from medieval authorities, from old Urso of Salerno or from Alchabitius (al-Qabīsī, fl. 950), the author of an introduction to astrology often reprinted in the sixteenth century. Had these peevish prattlers known that their man had borrowed a manuscript containing several works of al-Kindi (fl. 850), including *De radiis stellarum,* from Oxford in 1556, they could have made a better case. Al-Kindi taught a straightforward determinist astrology, urged its merits as a mathematical science, and grounded it physically in the interplay of radiations continually and invariably pouring out of celestial bodies. He also recommended magic to accumulate useful rays, as had the Greek Neoplatonists from whom he took his theoretical underpinnings. Al-Kindi's views had enjoyed the advertisement of formal condemnation at Paris and Oxford during the thirteenth and fourteenth centuries, and of special attention in the widely read *Errores philosophorum* of Giles of Rome.

Another astrological writer who doubtless poured his influence on Dee was one Joannes Franciscus Offusius. Like Dee, Offusius understood that astrology could not become a science until it could compute celestial influences precisely; and having made this charge his own, he spent many years searching the world (in vain as it happened) for a suitable scientific collaborator. He stayed with Dee in 1553, and perhaps propounded a few of the three hundred astrological aphorisms that his host then confided to a manuscript now unfortunately lost. He no doubt learned much from Dee, and perhaps even more after leaving him; and in an ephemeris for 1557 he was able to publish the results of his new system of astrology. As one might expect, he concluded that astral influences propagate in rays that obey mathematical laws; in particular, the influences diminish in power with distance from their sources according to curious laws of the inverse square and cube, and the average distances between earth and the planets, among other parameters of interest, spring from the geometry of the Platonic solids. Offusius's system was more Pythagorean than Dee's, but otherwise much like it; Dee could not miss the affinity and cried plagiarism when, in 1570, a full account of his old collaborator's ideas was printed. These priority disputes have at least one merit: by showing that Dee's program to base astrology on mathematical physics was not unique, they give his ***Propaedeumata*** the interest of a representative work.

Whoever tried to father Dee's aphorisms on Mercator came closest to the mark. Indeed, Dee acknowledged his obligations to his friends at Louvain in the dedicatory letter to the ***Propaedeumata,*** where he singled out not only Mercator and Gemma, but also Gaspar a Mirica (Caspar vander Heyden) and Antonius Gogava. Vander Heyden was a goldsmith and engraver who had worked for many years for Gemma and who had probably taught Mercator his art; he made instruments too and may have instructed Dee in the manufacture and use of astronomical and optical apparatus. Gogava was a twenty-year-old prodigy who had just finished a translation of Ptolemy's *Tetrabiblos* when Dee arrived in Louvain. It is the first complete Latin version made directly from Greek. In the same volume, Gogava gave two medieval tracts, one on conic sections, the other on burning mirrors; he thereby provided the modern astrologer with all he needed to make use of vander Heyden's practical instruction, and to philosophize in the foreign, or at least the Louvain, manner. Dee says that the "earnest disputations" of Gogava did much to "provoke" him to a serious study of astrology.

As for Gemma and Mercator, both firmly believed in the power and reach of astral influence. Gemma, who with his fellow physicians held astrology to be essential to correct medical practice, endorsed Gogava's translation of Ptolemy for its up-to-date practical utility. Mercator, although a cartographer by profession, preferred philosophy, and understood the structure and operation of the universe. The sun and stars occupy the chief place in his world. They are perfect and unchanging, as Aristotle taught, the most noble instruments of God, sympathetically and genetically tied to the sublunary world. If they were to alter it would go hard with us, for it is their business to constitute, preserve, and perpetuate things here below, "ad maturandos inferioris mundi foetus, eisque obstetricandum." Mercator's sunny conviction that stellar influences are inherently good (evil arises from irradiating corrupt or inappropriate matter) recurs in Dee.

The sizes and distances of the planets, the main parameters of Dee's mathematical astrology, were also of vital interest to Gemma and Mercator. The hope of learning something new and precise about these parameters, about a world "hitherto described [only] within uncertain limits," had aroused in Gemma a great desire to read the work of Copernicus. He had gone so far as to urge Copernicus's bishop to shake the long-awaited book out of him. "I do not care [Gemma wrote] whether he says that the earth revolves or stands still . . . ; the only bad thing is delay." As will appear, planetary distances are determined more directly from Copernicus's theory than from Ptolemy's. It was precisely on this head that Gemma later argued the superiority of Copernicus's hypotheses: "they do not bring anything absurd into natural motions, since they allow us a fuller knowledge of the planetary distances than do [Ptolemy's]."

Gemma's endorsement of the new astronomy served as preface to a set of ephemerides calculated by Joannes Stadius after the *Prutenic Tables* of Erasmus Reinhold, who had worked from the parameters and hypotheses of Copernicus. Stadius's work appeared in 1556; a year later, Dee's friend John Feild brought out similar tables, with a similar preface by Dee. In the same vein as Gemma, Dee emphasized the inaccuracies and stupidities of the older ephemerides and the promise of the new, computed according to the "divine studies of Copernicus." As for Copernicus's hypotheses, Dee declined to discuss them; he may have considered them to be no more than the best available calculating device, as did Reinhold and perhaps also Feild. But we may be sure that Dee shared Gemma's interest in the computation of planetary distances according to the new astronomy. In the **"Preface"** he gives Copernicus's values for the solar and lunar distances. Moreover, he there makes the first service of astronomy the "certification" of "the distance of the Starry Skye, and of eche *Planete* from the Centre of the Earth; and of the greatness of any Fixed Starre sene, or *Planete*, in respect of the Earthes greatness." A traditional definition would rather emphasize the planetary motions.

And why the consuming interest in dimensions? Because they give us the thickness of the "heauenly Palace" in which the planets do their exercises, and "meruailously perfourme the Commandement and Charge given to them by the omnipotent Maiestie of the king of kings." As we know, Dee contributed to the technique of determining planetary distances, which he advertised as "a most beautiful part of philosophy, and most necessary to man." His method is ingenious if seldom practicable. (pp. 50-8)

Dee could have taken a second principal ingredient for his astrology from his friends at Louvain. The tract on burning mirrors published by Gogava was often wrongly attributed to Roger Bacon; and it may have been the concern of Gemma's group with Bacon that brought Dee to recognize the bearing of the work of his medieval countryman on the computation of astral influence. By 1556, medieval optics was the subject best represented in Dee's collection of manuscripts, which included several tracts by Bacon, Alhazen, and John Peckham, the author of the standard *Perspectiva communis.* Dee's interest in Bacon was to extend well beyond optical theory. He later developed and . . . algebraized, Bacon's idiosyncratic calculus of the graduation of qualities, and he undertook to clear him of charges of practicing unwholesome magic and devilish arts. His aphorisms in particular owe much to Bacon's notions of the propagation of force.

The occasion for the aphorisms, in which Dee "mathematically furnished up the whole Method of astrology," was an inquiry from Mercator about the progress of his studies. What better answer than a little book to commemorate the lively discussions of astrological matters from which he had profited at Louvain? That, at least, is the motivation Dee gives for his first essay into print. But we may suppose that he also fired off the aphorisms to anticipate Offusius. And he might have wished to do his part in silencing those loud local critics then recently blasted by Leonard Digges, those "busy byghtinge [backbiting] bodyes" who rejected "the secret truthes" of astrology. Digges had discovered that these bodies byghted out of "ignorantie, the grete enemie of all pure learning." John Feild took the same tack: the ignorance and bumbling of the vulgar chart-makers and nativity-casters have brought disrepute and even ruin to the discipline. Dee's aphorisms offer a stronger defense. Although full of the usual sneers at the ignorant and uninitiated, they set out a rational astrological method open to anyone prepared to study them. (pp. 58-9)

J. L. Heilbron, "Dee's Role in the Scientific Revolution" and "Propaedeumata Aphoristica," in John Dee on Astronomy: "Propaedeumata Aphoristica" (1558 and 1568), Latin and English, *edited and translated by Wayne Shumaker, University of California Press, 1978, pp. 1-99.*

Frances A. Yates (essay date 1979)

[*In the following excerpt, Yates explains the shifting focus and eventual waning of Dee's career in terms of his interest in occult philosophy.*]

The subject of John Dee's thought, science, position in the Elizabethan age, is, at the time at which I am writing this, in the melting pot. New factual material is constantly turning up; many scholars are trying to assess his scientific thought; the old prejudices against him as a ludicrous figure still subsist, though very much diminished in force as it becomes more and more apparent that Dee had contacts with nearly everyone of importance in the age, that his missionary journey to Bohemia had enormous repercussions, that, in short, the life and work of John Dee constitute a problem the solution of which is not yet in sight.

Under these circumstances my plan in the present [essay] is to avoid, as far as possible, the unsolved problems, and to concentrate on bringing together indications that the label 'Christian Cabalist' might cover his outlook, or the greater part of it. If this can be done at all convincingly a step will have been taken towards the solution of the general problem of Dee, and his place in the history of thought, even though many factual matters are left untouched, and great gaps, awaiting the new synthesis, will have to be evaded.

I believe it to be most important to distinguish carefully between the three periods of Dee's life. I therefore divide this chapter into three parts, corresponding to the three periods.

Dee's First Period (1558-83): The Leader of the Elizabethan Renaissance

John Dee was the son of an official at the court of Henry VIII. He was thus born into the Tudor world at a time immediately before the break with Rome, when the divorce issue was looming. His connections and patrons during the early part of his life were the noblemen whose families had been influential in the Tudor Reformation. He was particularly close to the Dudley family, strong adherents of radical reform. Robert Dudley, afterwards Earl of Leicester and favourite of Queen Elizabeth I, had been Dee's pupil when a child; throughout his life he encouraged Dee and his enterprises. Dee's memories went back to the time of Edward VI and the radical reform of that reign; and he served with zeal the last of the Tudors, Queen Elizabeth I, promoting with enthusiasm the Elizabethan expansion.

He was of Welsh descent, and believed himself to be descended from an ancient British prince, even claiming some relationship to the Tudors and to the queen herself. He associated himself intensely with the Arthurian, mythical, and mystical side of the Elizabethan idea of 'British Empire'. (pp. 79-80)

[Dee] had a considerable collection of Lullist works. He possessed the works of Pico della Mirandola and of Reuchlin. He owned several copies of Agrippa's *De occulta philosophia.* He had the 1545 edition of the Latin version of Giorgi's *De harmonia mundi.* There is no doubt that he was fully conversant with these works and with many others of similar tendency. Though such works may have formed the core of Dee's library, and filled the centre of his mind, that library and that mind also included a vast wealth of scientific knowledge of all kinds, and of literary and historical material. It was the library of a man of the Renaissance, bent on assimilating the whole realm of knowledge available in his time.

This library was at the disposal of friends and students. Here came courtiers and poets, like Sir Philip Sidney (nephew of the Earl of Leicester), navigators and mathematicians, historians and antiquaries, all learning from Dee's stores.

The manifesto of Dee's movement was his preface to Henry Billingsley's translation of Euclid, which was published in 1570. (p. 80)

With the opening invocation to 'Divine Plato' we are at once in the world of 'Renaissance Neoplatonism'. The subject of the **'Preface'** is the importance of number and of the mathematical sciences, and this is confirmed by quotation from one of Pico della Mirandola's Mathematical Conclusions: 'By number, a way is had, to the searching out and understanding of every thyng, hable to be knowen.' Dee's outlook is that of Renaissance Neoplatonism as interpreted in Pico della Mirandola's synthesis. And Dee's Neoplatonism is associated with Renaissance Cabala, for the outline of the Preface is based on Agrippa's *De occulta philosophia* on the three worlds. Like Agrippa, Dee thinks of the universe as divided into the natural, the celestial, and the supercelestial spheres. The tendency of the movement towards concentration on number as the key to the universe, which is apparent in Agrippa and in Giorgi, and which Reuchlin had accentuated through his emphatic association of Pythagoreanism with Cabala, is carried forward by Dee in a yet more intensely 'mathematical' direction.

Dee's mathematics were applied in the practical sphere through his teaching and advice to navigators, artisans, technicians. He also had a grasp of abstract mathematical theory, particularly the theory of proportion as taught in the work on architecture by the Roman architect, Vitruvius. The **'Preface'** contains many quotations from Vitruvius; Dee follows Vitruvius on architecture as the queen of the sciences and the one to which all other mathematical disciplines are related.

Dee's numerical, or numerological, theory is closely related not only to Agrippa's basic statement about number, but also to the more extended treatment of this theme in a Cabalist setting by Francesco Giorgi. Dee does not mention Giorgi in the **'Preface'**—the only Cabalist whom he mentions is Agrippa—but he had Giorgi's work in his library and there is no doubt that he had studied the *De harmonia mundi* carefully. Yet Dee seems to be coming to his subject of proportion in relation to number more through Agrippa and the Germans than through Giorgi and the Italians. Giorgi's architectural symbolism was related to his knowledge of Italian architectural theory. . . . [He] applied the theory of architectural harmony to the plan for a Franciscan church in Venice. Dee, however, refers for the theory of proportion to the German artist and theorist Albrecht Dürer.

It is significant that, at the point in the **'Preface'** at which Dee advises the reader to consult Vitruvius on theory of proportion, he also advises him to consult, on the same subject, Agrippa and Dürer. Thus the reader of the **'Preface'** would look at the diagrams in the *De occulta philosophia* on proportion in relation to the human figure, and also at the same diagrams in Dürer's basic *Four Books of Human Proportion* (*Vier Bücher von Menschlicher Proportion,* 1528) which transferred to the north the Italian art theory on proportion.

Dee and his readers are coming to theory of proportion through Agrippa, the occult philosopher and Cabalist; he cites the German artist, Dürer, as the exponent of the theory. This is an interesting indication that Dürer's work was known to Dee, and presumably to the English readers whom he is addressing, and it suggests that Dee's artistic theory, which was one form of his concentration on number, came to him through the German Renaissance rather than the Italian, though he would find the same theory in the Italian tradition on which Giorgi depended.

Like Reuchlin, Agrippa, and the Christian Cabalists generally, Dee was intensely aware of the supercelestial world of the angels and divine powers. His studies in number, so successful and factual in what he would think of as the lower spheres, were, for him, primarily important because he believed that they could be extended with even more powerful results into the supercelestial world. In short, as is well known, Dee believed that he had achieved, with his associate Edward Kelley, the power of conjuring angels. In one of the descriptions of his séances with Kelley, Dee speaks of the book of Agrippa as lying open on the table, and there is no doubt that Agrippa was Dee's main guide in such operations. The sensational angel-summoning side of Dee's activities was intimately related to his real success as a mathematician. Like the Christian Cabalists generally, he believed that such daring attempts were safeguarded by Cabala from demonic powers. A pious Christian Cabalist is safe in the knowledge that he is conjuring angels, not demons. This conviction was at the centre of Dee's belief in his angelic guidance, and it explains his pained surprise when alarmed and angry contemporaries persisted in branding him as a wicked conjuror of devils.

The angel-conjuring is not apparent in the **'Preface,'** which can be read as a straightforward presentation of the mathematical arts. The underlying assumptions are, however, indicated in the fact that Dee is certainly following Agrippa's outline in the *De occulta philosophia* and that was a work founded on Renaissance Magia and Cabala. Also he hints in the **'Preface'** at higher secrets which he is not here revealing, probably the secrets of the angel-magic.

The extremely complex nature of Dee's mind and outlook baffles enquirers, many of whom have begun to become aware of his importance and are impressed by the **'Preface,'** but would like to forget the angel-magic. Real progress in the understanding of the past cannot, however, be made on obscurantist lines. The facts about Dee must be faced, and one fact certainly is that this remarkable man was undoubtedly a follower of Cornelius Agrippa and attempted to apply the 'occult philosophy' throughout his life and work.

Another very important aspect of Dee's mind was his belief in alchemy. The studies prosecuted with Kelley included not only the angel-magic, but also, and above all, alchemy. Kelley was an alchemist and was believed, according to some rumours, to have succeeded in effecting transformations and in making gold. Practical Cabala and practical alchemy thus seemed to go together in the Dee-Kelley partnership.

I am faced here with a historical question. What place had there been in the Hermetic-Cabalist tradition, stemming from Ficino and Pico, for the Hermetic science of alchemy? The Ficinian outlook, with its emphasis on astral correspondences, would, one would think, have been a philosophy favourable to application as alchemy. Little has, however, as yet been heard of alchemy as an interest of Ficino or of Pico, and their followers. Yet there is a point at which alchemy does enter this tradition, and that very decidedly, and that is with Cornelius Agrippa.

In Agrippa's mysterious travels he was in contact with alchemists in many different places. Sometimes he is heard of performing alchemical operations in a laboratory; he certainly sought out alchemical books and was deeply interested in the subject. He cannot, surely, have been the only Cabalist to be interested in alchemy. Was there a Cabalist alchemy, or an alchemical Cabala, which represented some new kind of combination of such interests already formed in the time of Agrippa? This is at present an unanswered question. Here I am only concerned to state that some close connection between alchemy, Cabala, and his other interests, existed in Dee's mind.

A curious diagram, to which Dee attached the greatest importance as a statement of his whole philosophy, was the ***Monas hieroglyphica,*** published in 1564 with a dedication to the Emperor Maximilian II, and an explanatory text which leaves the reader thoroughly bewildered. Dee's *monas* is a combination of the signs of the seven planets, plus the symbol for the zodiacal sign, Aries, representing fire. It must have some astral significance; alchemical operations seem implied through the fire sign; it is also some kind of mathematics or geometry; but above all it is Cabala. It is related to 'the stupendous fabric of the Hebrew letters'. It is a 'Cabalistic grammar'. It can be mathematically, cabalistically, and anagogically explained'. It is a profound secret which Dee wonders whether he has sinned in publishing.

There are no Hebrew letters in the *monas* sign itself, yet one gathers that the parts of the planetary signs of which it is composed were to be manipulated in a manner analogous to the manipulation of Hebrew letters in Cabala. There is also a mathematical process going on, though the mathematical side is not so prominent in the ***Monas hieroglyphica*** as it is in the ***Aphorisms,*** a work published by Dee a few years earlier (1558) with which he states that the ***Monas hieroglyphica*** is closely connected. The ***Aphorisms,*** in which the *monas* sign appears, would seem to be stating in a more obviously mathematical form the Cabalist meaning of the ***Monas hieroglyphica.***

I would suggest that an important source in which to study the mode of thought out of which Dee evolved his *monas* sign is Giorgi's *De harmonia mundi.* Here he would have found numerological theory combined with Cabalist theory as the double key to the universe in a manner which is closely analogous to the double meaning of the *monas,* numerological and Cabalist. Giorgi begins with the One, or the *monas,* out of which, as expounded in the *Timaeus,* the numbers one to twenty-seven proceed to form the universal harmony in both macrocosm and microcosm. Combining Pythagoro-Platonic theory with Cabalist letter-mysticism, Giorgi arrives at his synthesis. Dee's mind would work in a similar way in the *monas.* His composite planetary symbol would imply a composite Cabalist symbol. Behind its planetary cosmology would be the 'tremendous structure' of the Hebrew alphabet.

The *monas* symbol includes a cross. It is a Christian Cabalist symbol, no doubt believed by its creator to have great magical power.

Dee was not only an enthusiast for scientific and mathematical studies, in the strange contexts in which he saw them. He wished to use such studies for the advantage of his countrymen and for the expansion of Elizabethan England. Dee had a politico-religious programme and it was concerned with the imperial destiny of Queen Elizabeth I.

I have discussed in my book, *Astraea. The Imperial Theme in the Sixteenth Century* (1975) the nature of Elizabethan imperialism. It was not only concerned with national expansion in the literal sense, but carried with it the religious associations of the imperial tradition, applying these to Elizabeth as the representative of 'imperial reform', of a purified and reformed religion to be expressed and propagated through a reformed empire, the empire of the Tudors with their mythical 'British' associations. The glorification of the Tudor monarchy as a religious imperial institution rested on the fact that the Tudor reform had dispensed with the Pope and made the monarch supreme in both church and state. This basic political fact was draped in the mystique of 'ancient British monarchy', with its Arthurian associations, represented by the Tudors in their capacity as an ancient British line, of supposed Arthurian descent, returned to power and supporting a pure British Church, defended by a religious chivalry from the evil powers (evil according to this point of view) of Hispano-Papal attempts at universal domination.

Though these ideas were inherent in the Tudor myth, Dee had a great deal to do with enhancing and expanding them. Believing himself to be of ancient British royal descent, he identified completely with the British imperial myth around Elizabeth I and did all in his power to support it.

Dee's views on the British-imperial destiny of Queen Elizabeth I are set out in his ***General and rare memorials pertayning to the Perfect art of Navigation*** (1577). Expansion of the navy and Elizabethan expansion at sea were connected in his mind with vast ideas concerning the lands to which (in his view) Elizabeth might lay claim through her mythical descent from King Arthur. Dee's 'British imperialism' is bound up with the 'British History' recounted by Geoffrey of Monmouth, based on the myth of the hypothetical descent of British monarchs from Brut, supposedly of Trojan origin, and therefore connecting with Virgil and the Roman imperial myth. Arthur was the supposed descendant of Brut, and was the chief religious and mystical exemplar of sacred British imperial Christianity.

In the ***General and rare memorials*** there is a complicated print, based on a drawing in Dee's own hand, of Elizabeth sailing in a ship labelled 'Europa', with the moral that Britain is to grow strong at sea, so that through her 'Imperial Monarchy' she may perhaps become the pilot of all Christendom. This 'British Hieroglyphick', as Dee calls the design, should be held in mind at the same time as the ***Monas hieroglyphica,*** as representing a politico-religious expression of the *monas* in the direction of a 'British imperial' idea.

Much of the material on Dee which I have here resumed is familiar but Dee and his activities may appear in a somewhat new light when viewed in relation to [Renaissance occult philosophy]. In what light would this deep student of the sciences of number, this prophetic interpreter of British history, have been seen, both by himself and by his contemporaries?

I suggest that the contemporary role which would exactly fit Dee would be that of the 'inspired melancholic'. According to Agrippa, and as portrayed by Dürer in the famous engraving, the inspired melancholic was a Saturnian, immersed in those sciences of number which could lead their devotees into great depths of insight. Surely Dee's studies were such as to qualify him as a Saturnian, a representative of the Renaissance revaluation of melancholy as the temperament of inspiration. And after the first stage of inspiration, the inspiration coming from immersion in the sciences of number, Agrippa envisages a second stage, a prophetic stage, in which the adept is intent on politico-religious events and prophecies. And finally in the third stage, stage of inspired melancholy, the highest insight into religion and religious changes is revealed.

It may seem suggestive that not only was Dee's programme for the advance of science based on Agrippa on the three worlds in the *De occulta philosophia,* but also that the stages of his prophetic outlook might be clarified from the same source. First Dee as Saturnian melancholic studies the sciences of number; then he gains prophetic insight into British imperial destiny; and finally vast universal religious visions are revealed to him. Yet all the time he was, like Agrippa, a Christian, a Christian Cabalist with leanings towards evangelicalism and Erasmian reform.

It must be remembered that Dee's ideas, which we have to try to piece together from scanty and scattered evidence, would have been known to contemporaries through personal contact with this man, who was ubiquitous in Elizabethan society and whose library was the rendezvous of intellectuals. And there were many works by Dee passing from hand to hand in manuscript which were never published. In his ***Discourse Apologetical*** (1604), Dee gives a list of his writings, many, indeed most, of which are unknown to us but which may have been available to his contemporaries in manuscript. From that list I select the following titles of lost writings by Dee:

> ***Cabala Hebraicae compendiosa tabella, anno 1562.***
> ***Reipublicae Britannicae Synopsis, in English,*** 1565.
> ***De modo Evangelii Iesu Christi publicandi . . . inter infideles,*** 1581.
> ***The Origins and chiefe points of our auncient British histories.***

Through these lost titles, we catch glimpses of Dee studying Cabala, immersed in his 'British History' researches, and interested in missionary schemes for publishing the Gospel of Jesus Christ to the heathen.

Dee is not a person who can be lightly dismissed as a 'sorcerer', in accordance with the labels affixed to him in the witch scares. He must have been one of the most fascinating figures of the Elizabethan age, appealing to that brilliant world for his learning, his patriotism, and for the insight associated with Christian Cabala.

Dee's Second Period (1583-9): The Continental Mission

In 1583, John Dee left England and was abroad for six years, returning in 1589. During these years on the continent Dee appears to have been engaged in some kind of missionary venture which took him to Cracow, in Poland, and eventually to Prague where the occultist emperor Rudolf II, held his court. It is possible, though there is no evidence for this, that when in Prague, Dee was in contact with the Rabbi Loewe, famous Cabalist and magician, who once had an interview with Rudolf. Dee stayed for several years in Bohemia with a noble family the members of which were interested in alchemy and other occult sciences. His associate, Edward Kelley, was with him, and together they were fervently pursuing their alchemical experiments and their attempts at angel-summoning with practical Cabala.

To this period belong the séances described in Dee's spiritual diary, with their supposed contacts with the angels

Uriel and Gabriel and other spirits. Dee was moving now on the more 'powerful' levels of Christian Cabala through which he hoped to encourage powerful religious movements.

The evidence about Dee's continental mission is somewhat obscure and incomplete. It is referred to thus by a contemporary observer:

> A learned and renowned Englishman whose name was Doctor Dee came to Prague to see the Emperor Rudolf II and was at first well received by him; he predicted that a miraculous reformation would presently come about in the Christian world and would prove the ruin not only of the city of Constantinople but of Rome also. These predictions he did not cease to spread among the populace.

Dee's message appeared to be neither Catholic nor Protestant but an appeal to a vast, undogmatic, reforming movement which drew its spiritual strength from the resources of occult philosophy.

In the context of the late sixteenth century in which movements of this kind abounded, Dee's mission would not have seemed incredible or strange. Enthusiastic missionaries of his type were moving all over Europe in these last years of the century. One such was Giordano Bruno, who preached a mission of universal Hermetic reform, in which there were some Cabalist elements. Bruno was in Prague shortly after Dee; he had been in England preaching his version of Hermetic-Cabalist reform, and was to go on into Italy, where he met the full force of the Counter-Reformation suppression of Renaissance Neoplatonism, and its allied occultisms, and was burned at the stake in Rome in 1600. Dee was more cautious, and was careful not to venture into Italy.

For Dee's mission, the ***Monas hieroglyphica*** is probably the most important clue, for it contained in the compressed form of a magic sign the whole of the occult philosophy. And it had reference to contemporary rulers who were to be the politico-religious channels of the movement. The first version of it had been dedicated to the Emperor Maximilian II, Rudolf's father. Dee may have hoped that Rudolf would step into his father's role, and accept the *monas* as his occult imperial sign. In England, Dee had transferred to Queen Elizabeth I the destiny of occult imperial reform, signified by the *monas.*

There is some kind of congruity between the ideas associated with Rudolf and those associated with Elizabeth. As R. J. W. Evans has said [in *Rudolf*]: 'Both the unmarried Emperor and the Virgin Queen were widely regarded as figures prophetic of significant change in their own day, as symbols of lost equilibrium when they were dead.' It is perhaps in some such sense of occult imperial destiny linking Elizabeth and Rudolf that the true secret meaning of Dee's continental mission may lie. On the more obvious level it would seem to have been a movement antagonistic to the repressive policies of Counter-Reform, and as such it would have made dangerous enemies.

The emperor did not enthusiastically support Dee, and when he returned to England in 1589 it must have been far from clear to the queen and her advisers whether he had accomplished anything at all, beyond making extremely dangerous enemies.

However he had sown powerful seeds which were to grow to a strange harvest. It has been shown that the so-called 'Rosicrucian manifestos', published in Germany in the early seventeenth century, are heavily influenced by Dee's philosophy, and that one of them contains a version of the ***Monas hieroglyphica.*** The Rosicrucian manifestos call for a universal reformation of the whole wide world through Magia and Cabala. The mythical 'Christian Red Cross' (Christian Rosencreuz), the opening of whose magical tomb is a signal for the general reformation, may perhaps, in one of his aspects, be a teutonised memory of John Dee and his Christian Cabala, confirming earlier suspicions that 'Christian Cabala' and 'Rosicrucianism' may be synonymous.

Dee's Third Period (1589-1608): Disgrace and Failure

When Dee returned to England in 1589, he was at first received by the queen, but his old position at the centre of the Elizabethan world was not restored. During his absence, the Armada victory of 1588 had occurred, and this, one would think, might have been seen as the triumph on the seas of the patriotic movement in which Dee had had so large a share. On the other hand, the Earl of Leicester's movement for landward extension of the Elizabethan ethos in his military expedition to the Netherlands in 1586 had failed; his nephew Philip Sidney lost his life in that expedition; and the whole enterprise was checked by the queen who withdrew Leicester from his command in disgrace. Leicester never got over this; he quietly died in 1588. Thus Leicester and the Sidney circle, Dee's supporters in the old days, were no longer there except for some survivors, such as Edward Dyer, Sidney's closest friend, who had been in touch with Dee and Kelley in their recent adventures.

Shunned and isolated, Dee was also confronted with a growing witch-hunt against him. The cry of 'conjuror' had always been sporadically raised but in the old days the queen and Leicester had protected his studies. Now the enemies were increasingly vocal. Dee felt obliged to defend himself in a letter to the Archbishop of Canterbury, printed in 1604 but written earlier. It is illustrated with a woodcut which shows Dee kneeling on the cushion of hope, humility, and patience with his head raised in prayer to the cloudy heavens wherein can be seen the ear, eye, and avenging sword of God. Opposite to him is the many-headed monster of lying tongues and unkind rumour, its heads malevolently turned in his direction. He earnestly assures the archbishop that all his studies have been directed towards searching out the truth of God, that they are holy studies, not diabolical as his enemies falsely assert. From his youth up it has pleased the Almighty

> to insinuate into my hart, an insatiable zeale, and desire to knowe his truth: And in him, and by him, incessantly to seeke, and listen after the same; by the true philosophical method and harmony: proceeding and ascending . . . *gradatim,* from things visible, to consider of things inuisible; from thinges bodily, to conceiue of thinges

> spirituall: from thinges transitorie, and momentarie, to meditate of things permanent: by thinges mortall . . . to have some perceiuerance of immortality. And to conclude, most briefeley, by the most meruailous frame of the *whole world,* philosophically viewed, and circumspectly wayed, numbred, and measured . . . most faithfully to loue, honor, and glorifie alwaies, the Framer and Creator thereof.

One hears in these words the voice of the pious author of the **'Mathematical Preface,'** rising with number through the three worlds. But the admired Dee of other days, mentor of Elizabethan poets, must now defend himself from being a black conjuror of devils.

The implications of the angel-conjuring side of Dee's doctrine had come out more prominently during his continental mission; probably rumours of this, and of Jesuit opposition to it, had reached England. Elizabeth and her advisers, always nervous of committing themselves to the rash projects of enthusiasts, would now be understandably nervous of Dee. Elizabeth had withdrawn her support from Leicester's continental enterprise; Leicester and Sidney were both dead. No wonder that Dee's position in England was very different from what it had been before his continental journey and that many people might now refuse to believe that the famous mathematician was a Christian Cabalist, and not a conjuror of devils.

Of Dee's three periods, the first one, the successful one, has been the most explored. We are all now familiar with the idea that John Dee, dismissed in the Victorian age as a ridiculous charlatan, was immensely influential in the Elizabethan age, an influence which is far from being, as yet, fully assessed or understood. Of the second period, the period of the continental mission, we are beginning to know a good deal more than formerly, enough to realise that it had some very large religious or reforming scope, and that its influence long persisted in ways difficult to decipher. The third period, the period of failure verging on persecution of this once so admired and important figure, has been the least studied of all. What I now say about it must be provisional, awaiting further much-needed research. For the third period is most essential for the understanding of Dee as a whole.

Dee was very poor after his return and in great anxiety as to how to provide a living for his wife and family. A former friend with whom he was, apparently, still in contact was Sir Walter Raleigh, with whom Dee dined at Durham House on 9 October 1595. Raleigh, however, was himself out of favour, and would be unlikely to be able to help him to a position. At last, in 1596, he was made warden of a college in Manchester, whither he moved with his wife and family. It was an uncomfortable place and he had difficulty with the fellows of the college. In fact the Manchester appointment seems to have been something like a semi-banishment where he was, for reasons not quite clear, unhappy.

One of his activities when at Manchester was to act as adviser about cases of witchcraft and demonic possession. He had books on these subjects in his Manchester library which he lent to enquirers investigating such cases. One of the books which he thus lent was the *De praestigiis daemonum* by Weyer, the friend of Agrippa, in which it is argued that witchcraft is a delusion, witches being only poor, melancholy old women. Another book which Dee lent was the *Malleus maleficarum,* a work which is very positive as to the reality of witches.

It would seem strange that the conjuring suspicions against Dee should have taken the form of turning him into an expert on demonology to be consulted in trials, but such seems to have been the case.

The reality of witches and witchcraft was being forcibly maintained in these years by no less a person than the King of Scotland, soon to succeed Queen Elizabeth as James I. In his *Daemonologie* (1587), James is profoundly shocked by the 'damnable error' of those who, like Weyer, deny the reality of witchcraft. He refers the reader to Bodin's *Démonomanie* where he will find many examples of witchcraft collected with great diligence. And for particulars about the black arts the reader should consult 'the fourth book of Cornelius Agrippa'. This was the spurious fourth book of the *De occulta philosophia* which James accepted as genuine (Weyer had said that it was not by Agrippa). James has much more to say about 'the Divel's school' which thinks to climb to knowledge of things to come 'mounting from degree to degree on the slippery scale of curiosity', believing that circles and conjurations tied to the words of God will raise spirits. This is clearly 'practical Cabala' interpreted as a black art, a fruit of that tree of forbidden knowledge of which Adam was commanded not to eat.

James's work, if read in Manchester, would not have helped Dee's reputation.

Dee appears to have been away from Manchester from 1598 to 1600; eventually he returned to his old house at Mortlake, living there in great poverty, though still partially in touch with 'great persons'.

The accession of James I in 1603 boded little good for the reputed conjuror. Nevertheless Dee made desperate appeals to the new monarch. In a printed pamphlet, dated 5 June 1604, John Dee appeals to the king asking that those who call him a conjuror should be brought to trial: 'Some impudent and malicious forraine enemie or English traytor . . . hath affirmed your Maiesties Suppliant to be a Coniuror belonging to the most Honorable Priuie Counsell of your Maiesties most famous last predecessor. . . .' Note that Dee suspects foreigners or traitors of fomenting the rumours against him, and that he hints that such rumours might implicate the late queen and her council.

All was in vain. Dee was not cleared. He died in great poverty at Mortlake in 1608.

The last act of Dee's extraordinary story is the most impressive of them all. The descendant of British kings, creator (or one of the creators) of the British imperial legend, the leader of the Elizabethan Renaissance, the mentor of Philip Sidney, the prophet of some far-reaching religious movement, dies, an old man, in bitter neglect and extreme poverty.

I am not interested here in the sensationalism which has gathered round Dee's story and which has tended to obscure his real significance. That significance, as I see it, is the presentation in the life and work of one man of the phenomenon of the disappearance of the Renaissance in the late sixteenth century in clouds of demonic rumour. What happened in Dee's lifetime to his 'Renaissance Neoplatonism' was happening all over Europe as the Renaissance went down in the darkness of the witch-hunts. Giordano Bruno in England in the 1580s had helped to inspire the 'Sidney circle' and the Elizabethan poetic Renaissance. Giordano Bruno in 1600 was burned at the stake in Rome as a sorcerer. Dee's fate in England in his third period presents a similar extraordinary contrast with his brilliant first, or 'Renaissance', period.

The Hermetic-Cabalist movement failed as a movement of religious reform, and that failure involved the suppression of the Renaissance Neoplatonism which had nourished it. The Renaissance magus turned into Faust. (pp. 80-93)

Frances A. Yates, "John Dee: Christian Cabalist," in her The Occult Philosophy in the Elizabethan Age, *Routledge & Kegan Paul Ltd., 1979, pp. 79-93.*

Nicholas H. Clulee (essay date 1988)

[*In the following excerpt, Clulee examines the* Liber Mysteriorum, *concluding that this transcription of Dee's angelic seances expresses both his anxiety about salvation and his fear that science will not enable him to discover God's design for the universe.*]

The body of material resulting from Dee's actions with spirits dwarfs, in its bulk, all of his other works combined, and it may well be the vehicle for the most intimate view of Dee's personality and spiritual and intellectual life. The topics of the actions range across religion, politics, the reformation of the church, cosmology, theology, eschatology, and natural philosophy, and both what the angels say and Dee's and Kelley's reactions provide a reflection of their deepest religious beliefs and concerns and their perceptions of and attitudes toward the world outside the closed room in which they carried on their practice. Thus far, however, this material has received little concentrated scholarly attention, providing rich resources for romantic biography and writers of occult sympathies but something of an embarrassment to any attempt to consider Dee as a significant figure in the history of philosophy and of science. Whether or not his activities with Kelley are considered one of his productive endeavours, they represent such a large period of his life that they need to be considered for their bearing on Dee's natural philosophy and his intellectual career.

This material cannot be considered as science or natural philosophy in its own right, but there are elements that reflect Dee's concerns in natural philosophy and that draw upon and develop themes from his earlier writings. . . . [Dee's] previous thinking may look forward to these angelic conversations considered as a kind of spirit magic. Since Dee's thinking changed in the course of his career and his mathematical and scientific interests often drew upon different influences, it is of interest to consider the relation of these activities to his previous thinking and to the varieties of magic current in the sixteenth century. Furthermore, while the circumstances of his disappointments with his fortunes in England and the apparent opportunity offered by [Albrecht Laski, the need of a powerful Polish family and a patron of alchemists] help to understand the particular shift in his career in 1582 and 1583, they do not fully explain why he was so amenable to the revelations offered through Kelley. It is also necessary to assess the motives that were influential in this kind of activity assuming such prominence in his consideration and becoming so addicting that even after separating from Kelley and returning to England in 1589 he never resumed any significant work in natural philosophy or science. (pp. 203-04)

The records of Dee's spiritual actions or angelic conversations comprise two distinct classes of material. The actual conversations are recorded in what amount to minutes of the séances. These are divided into a large number of 'books', each with a title that is usually some variation on ***Liber mysteriorum.*** The second class of material comprises several books based on the angelic revelations, either directly dictated by the angels or abstracted from the minutes by Dee to represent the angels' teaching.

Unlike [other of] Dee's published works . . . , these records do not present the problem of discerning in the text a possibly esoteric level intentionally disguised from the uninitiated reader. Dee never intended this material for publication and never mentions it in public accounts of his writings. The revelations of the angels were private communications to Dee and Kelley, so there was little motive for secrecy. Other individuals were at times admitted to the actions, but only after Dee and Kelley had become confident, sometimes mistakenly, of their trustworthiness. The conversations do, however, present another problem, since the majority of the records consist of minutes of séances in which Dee neither saw nor heard the angels. It was through Kelley's account that Dee recorded what Kelley saw and what the angels said to Kelley, bracketed by Dee's record of his own opening and closing prayers and his and Kelley's comments, questions, and requests for clarification.

To what extent the revelations of the angels represent Dee's thinking presents a considerable problem that hinges on a judgement about what actually transpired in these séances and the role of Kelley as scryer. About Dee there is little difficulty. He never doubted that the spirits were real and was only rarely doubtful that they were good angels bearing genuine messages from God. Dee's records of noises, voices, apparitions, and prophetic dreams in his diaries quite independently of Kelley's influence, as well as his episodes with other scryers, indicate a personal belief in the reality of a spirit world, and while it may present interesting psychological issues, this belief was supported both by his readings and the broader cultural conditioning that spirits existed. The closest Dee came to questioning the 'angelic' character of the spirits and the trustworthiness of Kelley's vision was near the end of their association when Kelley announced that the spirits commanded that they share everything in common, including their wives, but his scruples were soon put to rest when the spirits assured him that this was a special dispensation from God for them as his elect.

Kelley presents greater difficulties but a full assessment of his personality and motives will lead too far afield. He may well have consciously fabricated everything to deceive Dee, but his bouts of emotional anxiety and arguments with the spirits in the course of his visions, his reluctance to continue except for Dee's desperate pleadings, and his admission of the visions to religious authorities in Prague when that might have had serious consequences all suggest that more than conscious deception was involved. Although Kelley often questioned the divine character of the angels, he seems to have believed in their reality as firmly as did Dee, and while it is clear that the revelations of the angels through Kelley were often prejudiced in favor of Kelley's interests in particular circumstances, they also reflect what Kelley knew of Dee's interests. In a number of places in the minutes Dee has noted the similarity of the angelic revelations to material in Agrippa, Reuchlin, Trithemius, and Peter of Abano, and since Kelley lived with Dee and had access to his library, the revelations are very likely the joint product of Kelley's imagination and stock of knowledge and what he knew of Dee's thinking from their discussions and his reading among books of current interest to Dee.

Dee, therefore, was more than just the passive recipient of the revelations. Keith Thomas's observation [in *Religion and the Decline of Magic*] regarding séances and divination in popular magic that the client's imagination was the chief asset of the cunning men, whose services usually amounted to confirming the convictions of the client that were familiar to the seer, applies equally to Dee and Kelley. Dee's interests determined the major themes of the revelations and his ideas as Kelley may have gleaned these from discussions and Dee's books contributed a considerable amount of their actual content. This, combined with Dee's abiding faith in their divinely inspired character, suggests that the records are evidence of Dee's and not just Kelley's thinking.

Dee did not consider these actions a type of magic but as a variety of religious experience sanctioned by the scriptural records of others to whom God or his angels imparted special illumination. In contrast to the 'wicked Conjurers' who 'have their Devils to write Books at their commandments', Dee thinks that as 'an honest Christian Philosopher' he should 'have the help of God his good Angels to write his holy Mysteries'. The practice of the actions therefore takes place in the simple religious atmosphere of Dee's oratory following a period of silent prayer and ending with a short prayer of praise and thanksgiving. There is no element of invoking angels and compelling their services; rather it is a question of humbly petitioning God to send his angels, who are in no way thought to be doing Dee's or Kelley's bidding. The opening prayer Dee most often used was addressed to God and Jesus as the source and the embodiment of wisdom, and asks that he be worthy of their aid in philosophy and understanding and that they send their spiritual ministers to inform and instruct him in the arcana of the properties and use of all God's creatures. There are no elaborate ritual preparations, quasi-sacramental ceremonies, or incantations that are part of the ceremonial magic of Agrippa's third book, nor are there the music and Orphic hymns, fumigations, candles, talismans, or foods and substances that figured in the magic of Ficino and Campanella for attracting the beneficent influences of the planets or planetary demons.

The only piece of seemingly magical apparatus at the outset was the 'shew-stone' through which Dee's scryers had their visions. Dee eventually had several of these, one of which was supposedly brought by the angels themselves. Such polished translucent or reflective objects were the traditional instruments for catoptromancy. Dee's earliest stone, which he says was given to him by a friend, was probably the circular flat black mirror of polished obsidian. This was most likely brought by the Spanish from Mexico where the Aztecs deified obsidian and used it for divinatory mirrors. It may have come to Dee with tales of mysterious or magical powers, for he says that he was informed that good angels were 'answerable' to it and associated it with the 'shew-stone' he believed had been used by 'high priests' of Israel at the order of God to seek his light in resolving their doubts and questions about his secrets. Another significant distinction of Dee's practice from Ficino's and Agrippa's magic is that, except for rare requests for direct benefits, such as the alleviation of [his son] Arthur's or [his wife] Jane's illness, Dee's objective is not the attraction of beneficial influences or the invocation and manipulation of spirits for specific purposes; rather it is to learn and follow God's will and to receive 'true knowledge and understanding of the laws and ordinances established in the natures and properties of his creatures'.

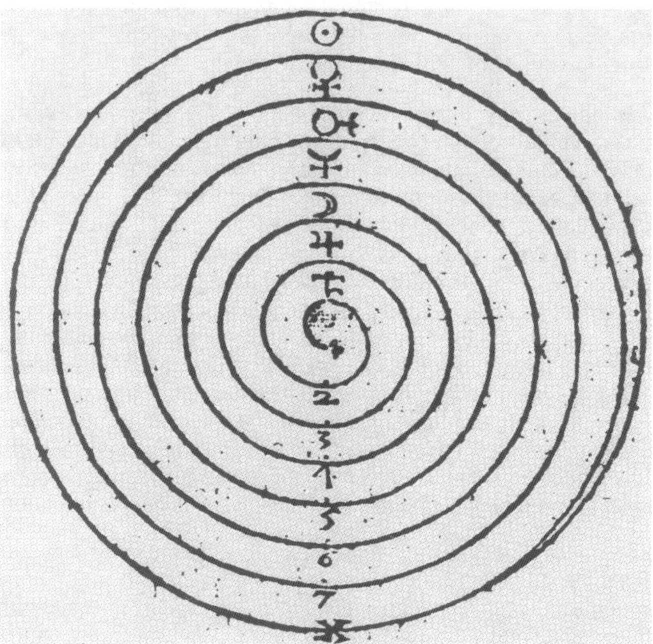

One of Dee's drawings for the Monas hieroglyphica, *this diagram depicts the revolutions of the four lunar-influenced, "egg white" planets (Moon, Saturn, Jupiter, and Mercury) and the three Solar-influenced, "egg yolk" planets (Sun, Mars, and Venus) around the earth.*

The revelations often shift in their day-to-day focus and in their specific content, but there is an underlying coherence to the actions. What ties everything together is the notion that Dee and Kelley are the elect of God, specially chosen to receive a divine revelation. Despite the fact that they are apparently in God's special favour, they are not spared frequent homilies and exhortations on their sins, the nature of salvation, and the necessity of unflinching obedience to the angels as part of their obedience to God as a prerequisite to receiving the full revelation. These pronouncements often bear on issues of contemporary religious significance, and their tenor is most often Protestant and even Calvinist in the emphasis on the intrinsic sinfulness of mankind and the impossibility of salvation without God's gift of faith as a token of God's election. In keeping with earlier indications of Dee's flexibility in adapting to prevailing religious practice, the religious teachings of the angels do not have any specific denominational preference and in Prague they recommend that Dee and Kelley reconcile themselves to the Roman church and support a Catholic interpretation of transubstantiation and the Mass. . . . The investigation of Dee's religious views, for which there is much material in these records, is not germane to this study except to the extent that the atmosphere of his spiritual concerns conditioned his intellectual choices. He seems to have had a rather Protestant view of salvation by faith through God's grace and election that centred on the individual's direct relation to God independent of any organized church; yet he was quite latitudinarian in the acceptance of varying forms of religious observance and went beyond all the organized churches, both Protestant and Catholic, in accepting the validity of continuing divine revelation independent of scripture and church teachings. The frequent concern with his spiritual worthiness and with the angelic revelations as a token of his special spiritual merit speaks to a profound sense of spiritual anxiety and insecurity.

The special revelations of the angels to Dee and Kelley fall into two large categories. In one category are prophetic revelations of often apocalyptic import regarding great religious and political changes in eastern Europe. These are closely tied to their personal fortunes with Laski and others with whom they became associated during their travels. . . . In the other category is the reception of a revealed esoteric wisdom promising a universal knowledge of creation. From the point of view of Dee's intellectual career, this is by far his preeminent concern in the actions. It is the element that is most closely tied to his earlier concerns in natural philosophy, it is the issue that he unfailingly pursues to the very end of his association with Kelley, and it is the motive that originally prompted him to seek the aid of the angels.

Dee is quite clear about his motive for initiating his actions with the spirits. The earliest record of angelic conferences is prefaced by a long prayer to God in which Dee confesses how he has prayed to God ever since his youth for 'pure and sound wisdome and understanding of your [God's] truthes naturall and artificiall' to be used for God's honour and glory and the benefit of Dee's fellow men. Although he has studied in many books and in many places and conferred with many men, Dee has concluded that 'I could find no other way to such true wisdome attayning but by thy extra-ordinary gift, and by no vulgar schole doctrine or humane invention', and cites the examples of Enoch, Moses, and others from scripture to whom God sent his angels and imparted special wisdom. Likewise, when Edward Kelley first came to [Dee's home at] Mortlake and asked Dee to show him something in 'spiritual practice', Dee said that he was 'neyther studied, or exercised' in the 'vulgarly accounted magik', but that he had for a long time been 'desyrous to have help in my philosophical studies through the company and information of the blessed Angels of God'. For Dee the angelic conversations were thus a continuation of his philosophical studies 'to fynde or get some ynkling, glimpse, or beame, of such aforesaid radicall truthes'.

The 'pure and sound wisdome and understanding' of God's natural and artificial truths is delivered by the angels in a long and haphazard dictation of what are called the 'Books of Enoch'. The historical Ethiopic Book of Enoch was unknown in Europe in the sixteenth century, but there was a long tradition in which the Patriarch Enoch was a pseudepigraph for a number of works in the Middle Ages. Some of these included occult hermetica, Arabic sources in particular equating Enoch with Hermes, and Christian mystical and visionary apocalyptic thought often drew upon the biblical account of Enoch as the recipient of God's special revelations and one of the two Old Testament figures to have been directly carried to heaven. Enoch also figured in Jewish mysticism and kabbalah, identified following his metamorphoses as the angel closest to God, the celestial scribe, and the teacher of divine mysteries. When appealing for the special instruction of God's angels Dee mentions the example of Enoch as enjoying direct conversation with God. Dee was certainly familiar with the biblical account of Enoch but his familiarity with Roger Bacon's notes on the *Secretum secretorum* and Guillaume Postel's *De originibus* are the likely source of a more elaborate idea of Enoch.

Roger Bacon mentions Enoch as a recipient of an ancient, divine wisdom, and equates Enoch with Hermes. Postel had met an Ethiopian priest from whom he had learned about the Ethiopic Book of Enoch, and in *De originibus* he presents Enoch as the first to record in writing an esoteric wisdom received by oral tradition from Adam and eventually dispersed. Significantly, Postel considers the various arts of magic and divination as fragments of this wisdom and considered that this wisdom could be attained through angels and spirits. Likewise Dee's angels refer to Enoch as receiving and recording the wisdom of God that had been lost with Adam's sin. This wisdom was again corrupted and lost through men's unworthiness, but Dee and Kelley are now chosen to receive 'this Doctrine again out of darknesse'. Dee's books of Enoch are therefore a restoration of the understanding of the creation that Adam had before his loss of innocence. In this prelapsarian state, Adam was a

> partaker of the Power and Spirit of God: whereby he not onely did know all things under his Creation and spoke them properly, naming them as they were: but also was partaker of our [the

> angels'] presence and society, yea a speaker of the mysteries of God; yea with God himself.

Dee and Kelley are not quite to recover the full 'innocency' of Adam; they are told that heavenly understanding and spiritual knowledge are closed to them in this life but that they shall have the keys to a knowledge of creation.

What this adamic understanding amounts to is difficult to grasp because of the haphazard way in which it was received over the course of many months of séances interrupted by sessions dominated by apocalyptic visions and homiletic exhortations. This is complicated by the fact that at several points the angels seem to repudiate everything and begin delivering their teaching in a new form. Some idea of what this teaching involved is nonetheless offered by the books Dee abstracted from the minutes of the séances. What all of these have in common is that they are catalogues of the angelic and spiritual hierarchies that govern the various regions of the earth and levels or domains of creation with descriptions of their characteristics, powers, their sigils, and the 'calls' or incantations by which they may be summoned. The ***De heptarchia mystica,*** drawing on the earliest revelations in 1582 and 1583, presents creation as divided into various sevens. There are seven kings, each with a subordinate prince and forty-two ministers, who rule various regions of the world and the affairs of men as well as being associated with each of the seven days of the week. There are also forty-nine good angels and, below them, other orders of angels whose purview seems to be physical nature, since there are groups for the cure of disease, for metals, for transformation, for the elements, for local change, for the mechanical arts, and for human knowledge of all secrets.

Beginning in 1583 the angels introduced an entirely new language purporting to be the angelic language of Adam and of Enoch. This was dictated in the form of numerous grid-like tables of forty-nine rows by forty-nine columns in which letters, sometimes interspersed with numbers, occur in apparently random order. These tables comprise the ***Liber mysteriorum sextus et sanctus,*** which is also referred to as the Book of Enoch. By some method of selection the angels chose from these tables letters to form words and sentences, which amount to another set of calls pertaining to angels. These became the basis for the ***48 Claves angelicae,*** written in Cracow in 1584, which consists of a catalogue of the forty-eight angels, their characteristics and subordinate spirits, and their invocations in the 'Enochian' language with English translations. A further catalogue from 1585, again different from the previous, is the ***Liber scientiae auxilij et victoriae terrestris*** listing the governing angels and their ministers for ninety-one different regions of the world. The spirits that most often figure in the séances—Annael, Michael, Gabriel, Raphael, and Urial—are the traditional arch-angels, although other less familiar names such as Salamian, Nalvage, and Madimi also appear. Nalvage and Madimi, who began as a young child and grew to maturity in the course of four years, played a particularly important role as time went on. It is through these spirits that Dee and Kelley learn of the hosts of lower angels and spiritual governors of the terrestrial realm such as King Naspol, his Prince Lisdon, and their forty-two ministers. Some of these are also invoked during the actions and reveal their characteristics and powers.

What this amounts to is a vast, overlapping, and confusing angelology or demonology compounded from a hodgepodge of sources. Various references to Peter of Abano, Trithemius, Reuchlin, and Agrippa indicate that Dee was aware of the similarity of these schemes both in general and in many details to their schemes. At one point Kelley emerges from his study with Agrippa's *De occulta philosophia,* indicting the angels as frauds because they have plagiarized Agrippa, perhaps to forestall Dee's conclusion about who was the actual fraud. There are also some figures with letters and numbers on concentric circles, perhaps reflecting some imitation of Ramon Lull's *ars combinandi* which Pico had associated with kabbalah. Dee, however, seems to have taken these similarities as confirmation of the validity of what other authors recorded. Another very likely source upon which Kelley drew for his visions of these angelic/demonic hierarchies were medieval manuals of ritual magic with their catalogues of demons, spirits, and angels and their sigils and incantations. Not all of these manuals consisted of 'black' magic directed at evil demons or diabolical agents; some present parallel spirit worlds in which a legitimate, or 'white', magic directed at divine angels is derived from God and may be used for pious purposes. Kelley's personal expertise was more in the area of this 'vulgar magik' as Dee termed it. Not only was there the story of necromancy in Kelley's background, but at several points during his association with Dee he voiced his interest in practising magic from his own books and raising reprobate spirits, which he admitted doing on his own despite the prohibitions of Dee and the angels, who eventually command him to bury his own books of magic.

The similarity of the books dictated by the angels to some of the medieval treatises of ritual magic is not surprising since . . . Renaissance magical works were [dependent] on these sources for their specific content. While Agrippa seemingly elevates this material by integrating it within the framework of a Neoplatonic and kabbalistic cosmology, Trithemius's *Steganographia,* with which Dee was particularly impressed, takes it over with little modification other than Christianizing it. Dee also notes a parallel to Arbatel, the pseudonym for the author of a work of doubtful provenance published in 1574 with the title *De magia veterum.* This likewise presents a ritual magic in a Christian context as the revelation from God through his ministering angels as a means of restoring a lost wisdom and gaining knowledge of the secrets of nature. It is perhaps noteworthy that shortly after Kelley's tenure began the angels not only dictate these tables of spirits, they also give directions for a 'table of practice' decorated with various mystical symbols and for a 'sigillum Dei' to be inscribed on wax disks to be placed under the legs of the table and beneath the shew-stone on the table. The practice of the actions thus seems to take on a much greater aura of magic under Kelley's influence. One of the ironies of the angelic conferences is that, while Dee considered their conduct as in no way magical, what the angels deliver as the embodiment of the greatest and most arcane secrets of God's creation is essentially a system of demonic magic.

Sorting out in detail the sources of what the angels deliver is of little purpose since it pertains mostly to how Kelley constructed the visions. What is significant is that Dee accepted these revelations as legitimate. The angelic revelations never fulfilled Dee's desire for an understanding of the divine arcana, as we might expect given their source, but it is worth considering why he considered them his most promising medium for that knowledge. As the angels present it, the divine wisdom of Adam's innocence consisted of two interrelated aspects: his command of a divine language and his participation in the society of the angels. The language the angels impart to Dee is the *'Lingua Angelica, vel Adamica'*, now for the first time since Adam's fall disclosed to mankind, and is the same as the discourse by which God created everything. In this language every word signifies the essence of a substance so that this language contains the secrets and keys to the world because through it the true natures of all things are known. In reference to one of the tables of seemingly random letters, an angel explains that it embodies all human knowledge; physic (medicine); knowledge of all elemental creatures and why they were created; the nature of fire which is the secret life of all things; the discovery, virtues, and uses of metals and stones; the conjoining of natures and their destruction; movement from place to place; knowledge of all mechanical crafts; and, not least, *transmutatio formalis, sed non essentialis.* The tables of letters the angels give are, however, not the *lingua adamica* itself because the letters are disorganized. The great secrets they contain are only revealed when the letters are selected and arranged according to some mystifying process involving the numerical values attached to the letters and their place in the tables. In one instance a group of letters yield the sum 4723 which the angel calls both the 'Mystical roote in the highest ascendent of transmutation' and the 'square of the Philosophers work', and although Dee comments on the inconsistency between root and square he does not unduly trouble the angel. The angels refer to this language as the 'cabala of nature' echoing the 'cabala of the real' of the ***Monas,*** and clearly the promises of the angels to reveal the original divine language of creation responds to the same interests that had been at work in the ***Monas.*** This 'cabala' does not operate according to any apparent rules or key, so that even with the tables Dee was perpetually at the mercy of the angels for instruction which the angels never seem to complete although they continue to make promises to the very end.

The catalogues of angels and spirits with the calls by which they may be summoned serve to recover the second aspect of Adam's innocence: his society with the angels and command over all creatures. The knowledge of and ability to communicate with this vast spirit world is essential for an understanding of nature because the creation is presented in a vaguely kabbalistic fashion as the self-revelation of God through his attributes in the form of angels and spirits. The term kabbalistic may be ill-advised in this context because we have previously noted that Dee's knowledge of kabbalah was very slight and Kelley's was likely no better, but what little there is of cosmology and cosmogony in the conversations inclines in a vague and Christianized way more toward a kabbalistic than toward a Neoplatonic view. These angels, spirits, and divine governors hold the secrets to the various realms of creation and by recovering their society, by means of magical conjurations, their knowledge will become available to Dee. The recovery of the *lingua adamica* is the key to this because it is the language all God's creatures understand and through which they can be summoned. The calls derived from the tables thus have the power to call forth and make obedient the spirits so that they will open the 'mysteries of their creation' and their secret knowledge.

Thus magic, and a spirit/demonic magic of the most unabashed variety, becomes the key to the knowledge and understanding of the secrets of creation Dee sought. The situation is somewhat comical if we consider that, while Dee patiently recorded what he thought were divine revelations through the angels and not a kind of magic, Kelley was practising the only thing he knew, which was magic, and presented this demonic magic as the means to fulfilment of Dee's thirst for knowledge, Dee accepting in the end what he had set out to avoid. What the angels provided was a kind of knowledge but it was not the direct knowledge of the secrets of creation that Dee sought. Rather, it was a magic in the form of the angelic language and the description of the spiritual hierarchies and their calls that was the means to this knowledge. It is a magic that is far removed from both the philosophical magic and occult philosophy of the Renaissance and the natural magic he seems to have derived from Roger Bacon. Despite the similarity of the angelology and demonology to material in someone like Agrippa, there is no hint here of the Neoplatonic/Stoic theory of the spirit as the vehicle of magical influence, or of the role of the imagination, or of the sympathetic use of the divine qualities in lower things to draw down the influence of higher things. Nor is there any remnant of the quasi-physical concept of occult virtues as a mechanism of magical effects that is found in al-Kindi, Bacon, and the ***Propaedeumata.*** There is simply the idea of the world populated by hosts of spirits and magic as the straightforward theurgic conjuration of them.

The conversations do pick up on themes from Dee's earlier career and from his previous writings on natural philosophy, and it is worth looking at these both for what they reveal about the conversations and what the conversations reveal about his basic motivations in natural philosophy. Dee's idea of archemastrie clearly encompassed a variety of magic involving divination with optical devices, and his 'other optical science' may well have referred to a technique by which man might 'participateth with Spirits, and Angels' as he puts it elsewhere in the ***Praeface.*** The conversations are, in fact, very much a practical expression of the conception that had emerged in the 1560s of the philosopher as theologian who seeks out an esoteric wisdom of secret divine science that reveal a knowledge of God through his creation independent of scripture. He expresses this goal in his 1562 letter to [William] Cecil and particularly in the ***Monas*** where the highest vocation of the philosopher as the *adeptiuus* is the exploration of 'supercelestial virtues and metaphysical influences' through a combination of kabbalah, magic, and alchemy. As with the *lingua adamica* of the conversations, in the ***Monas*** the key to this wisdom is Dee's recovery through divine inspiration of a sacred art of writing, his kabbalah of the real, hitherto lost or unknown. It is this holy language of divine creation that provides the medium for an intimate knowledge of God through his creation and for communication with God. The pursuit of knowledge in the ***Monas*** is a gnostic quest to overcome the fallen state of mankind in which a religious magic, which he absorbed in the 1560s both in a Neoplatonic form and in Trithemius's openly angelic/demonic form, provided the path for a mystical ascent to divine illumination. As a mysticism, the angelic conversations are odd in that Dee only participated in the visions vicariously through his scryers as a blind and deaf spectator.

The conversations as a quest for an understanding of the secrets of divine creation are therefore interwoven with themes that had already been of central importance to him when he wrote the ***Monas*** and that very directly build upon Dee's intellectual and spiritual aspirations of the 1560s. Like the ***Monas,*** what transpires in the conversations is not science. Even more so than in the ***Monas,*** the conversations are antithetical to science as both empirical investigation and rational inquiry with their emphasis on passivity and subservience in the reception of revelation. As knowledge the revelations are utterly banal, lacking even the redeeming value of ingenuity and inventiveness that give the ***Monas*** some interest. The greatest irony of Dee's career is that his attempts to get progressively closer to the truths of nature in fact lead to a progressive distancing from nature.

This, of course, was not Dee's perspective. For Dee they were the epitome and not the nadir of his 'philosophical exercises'. This centres on his fundamental intent in philosophy. We have previously touched on this in particular instances, but it is time to assemble the scattered indications. What these point to is that Dee considered all of his philosophical studies as having the ultimately religious purpose of knowing God and attaining 'heauenly wisedome' and an understanding of divine truths. Dee reiterates this theme, frequently embellished with a heart-rending recitation of the numerous years, the considerable expenses, the difficult travels, and the great personal sacrifices he has made in pursuit of his studies, in all of his pleas for patronage and all of his apologies defending the legitimacy of his studies against charges of conjuring. The polemical and self-serving purpose to which Dee put these protestations should not, however, detract from his sincerity in making them. He presents natural philosophy as having this religious purpose in contexts where self-justification is not an issue, and in the private context of the minutes of the angelic conversations he uses identical terms to present that activity as the culmination of his life-long philosophical endeavour.

Natural philosophy was, for Dee, preeminently a theology in which he sought

> by the true philosophicall method and harmony: proceeding and ascending (as it were), *gradatim,* from things visible, to consider thinges invisible: from thinges bodily, to conceive of things spirituall: from things transitorie, and momentarie, to meditate of things permanent: by thinges mortall (*visible and invisible*) to have some perceiverance of immortality, and to conclude, most briefely; by the most marvailous frame of the *whole World,* philosophically viewed, and circumspectly wayed, numbered, and measured (according to the talent, and gift of God, from above allotted, for his divine purposes effecting) most faithfully to love, honor, and glorifie alwaies, the *Framer,* and *Creator* thereof.

The notion of the book of nature as a divine revelation equivalent to scripture was a frequent common-place used to justify natural philosophy but Dee invested the idea with significant ramifications. He seems to have considered it not merely a parallel revelation to supplement scripture but a self-sufficient and adequate alternative to biblical theology with the advantage of greater certainty than scripture which was prone to varieties of human interpretation. He also invested this natural theology with considerable spiritual and emotional significance. The knowledge he sought through nature served a soteriologic as much as a noetic function; recovering the secrets of the creation would overcome original sin, heal and deliver the soul from distress, and lead 'from this vale of misery and the misery of this vale, and from this realm of shadoes and the shadows of this realm, to the sacred mount of Sion and to the heavenly temple.' This last statement occurs in an apologetic piece to the Archbishop of Canterbury in which Dee defends his philosophical studies as fundamentally religious and Christian, but it is revealing that he uses almost identical terms in one of the prayers initiating the spiritual actions in which God is asked to guide him to 'Holy Mount Sion and to Thy celestial tabernacles'. Thus, the stakes were high and Dee was willing to make a significant commitment, explaining to Cecil in 1562 that if necessary 'my flesh, blud, and bones shuld make the mechandyse' to acquire this divine wisdom.

Despite his appeals to the study of natural phenomena in the ***Propaedeumata*** and the ***Praeface*** however, the letter to Cecil of 1562 indicates that Dee looked for this wisdom less in nature itself than in books and from other men and ultimately these never took him far enough. While he was quite confident in 1562 that he had found the precious books that would show him the way, and in the ***Praeface*** he is rhapsodic about the vision offered by the mirror of creation, by the 1580s he admitted that 'I found (at length) that neither any man living, nor any Book I could yet meet withal, was able to teach me those truths I desired, and longed for'. The only alternative to human inquiry was the 'extra-ordinary gift' of angelic revelation, which was of such value that more than his 'flesh, blud, and bones' he now had, Faust-like, 'unto E.K. [Edward Kelley] offered my soul as a pawn, to discharge E.K. his crediting of them, as the good and faithful Ministers of Almighty God'. In this context the frequent concern in the conversations with salvation and election, and the religious anxiety this speaks to, are of significance. While the angels voice the Protestant idea of salvation as God's individual election of individuals through the unmerited gift of faith and grace, the constant angelic reassurance that Dee and Kelley are elect and that the revelations represent a particular covenant between them and God indicates that Dee was less than comfortable with the reduction of the church as a source of supernatural sanctions and the sacramental dispensation of grace that resulted from the Protestant attempts to eliminate the magical elements in religion, thereby leaving the individual believer alone and often insecure in his relation to God.

Keith Thomas has shown that religion was commonly considered in magical terms as a medium for obtaining supernatural powers and that religion and magic performed parallel functions in the sixteenth century, and he suggests that the many popular varieties of magic flourished at just this time because they filled the vacuum left as Protestantism diminished the magical functions of religion in favour of self-help. Dee's allegiance to the Catholic Mass and to the conversations with their sacred and sacramental aura may well derive from the same emotional source. In his third book on 'theological magic' Agrippa includes Christian practices among prayers, sacraments, and rites that are elements of ceremonial magic, and Peter of Abano explicitly compares the Mass with magic, arguing that the magical effect of transubstantiation certifies the general effectiveness of incantations. Like the popular magic studied by Thomas, the intellectual magic of the Renaissance also served an essentially religious function.

It is in its liturgies that religion is most similar to magic, and the fundamental element in the intellectual vogue of magic in the Renaissance was the ceremonial and ritualistic aspect of spiritual magic that made it an alternative form of religious life and path to salvation. This is most prominent in Reuchlin, Trithemius, Agrippa, and Arbatel, the authors explicitly cited in the ***Liber mysteriorum*** and to whose thinking Dee's angelic conversations bear the closest affinity. Not only do they present the idea of a vast spiritual world permeating and governing all creation and the theurgic techniques for invoking these spirits and angels from whom miraculous knowledge and power may be derived. They present magic as a vehicle for salvation through which the soul may escape the material realm and the limitations of human understanding and ascend to the supercelestial realm and union with the divine through divine illumination. Significantly, magic in Reuchlin and Agrippa appears in the context of an explicit disillusionment with sense experience, natural knowledge, and human reason as sources of infallible religious knowledge and a concomitant dissatisfaction with both scholastic theology and humanist philology and rhetoric for the attainment of true wisdom. Both considered the mystical divine illumination and inspiration of the mind prepared by faith to be the only adequate source for an understanding of the deepest religious truths. Such a revelation was typically considered to be embodied in the occult wisdom of the ancient theology and in the kabbalah where magic functioned as a sacramental rite for attaining direct and personal mystical illumination and gnosis. In Reuchlin and Agrippa magic was part of a broad occult philosophy considered both as a science of non-rational agents and as the science of their operation for the attainment of wondrous powers and religious knowledge. For them magic was the key element in a fusion of philosophy, religion, and magic that would renew philosophy by making it operative and reform religion by infusing it, by means of a divine and angelic magic, with a reinvigorated ceremonial, ritual, and sacerdotal character. With Trithemius divine illumination is also considered the necessary preliminary to any valid human knowledge, and magic is considered the vehicle by which the soul achieves mystical experience. Likewise in Arbatel the magical evocation of God's ministering spirits is the only way to the recovery of wisdom which is the necessary foundation for all other human knowledge. While much of the intellectual magic of the Renaissance was derived as much from medieval demonic magical texts as it was from late antique Neoplatonic treatments of ancient theurgy, the cultural function of this philosophical revival of magic was as an instrument of religious regeneration that alleviated the often intense despair over the limits of human intellectual abilities, answered the quest for esoteric wisdom, and offered the spiritual assurance of direct illumination.

Although the angelic conversations reveal little of the Neoplatonic philosophical framework through which Reuchlin and Agrippa attempted to legitimate their presentations of magic, they have very strong affinities with the religious impulse that motivated the Renaissance interest in magic. The first indications of Dee's conception of the religious function of natural philosophy emerge in the early 1560s with Trithemius's idea of a mystical theology as a kind of magic. His discovery of Trithemius's *Steganographia* at the same time may well have established in his mind an association between mystical theology and spirit magic that continued through his later readings and the hints in the ***Praeface.*** Other than the serendipitous discovery of successful scryers, it is difficult to isolate the exact motivation for the angelic conversations, but Dee's definitive and all-absorbing turn to angelic revelation and spirit magic in the 1580s seems very likely to have resulted from the combination of an intensified religious anxiety and a growing pessimism about his ability either through books or his unaided abilities to achieve his goal of a natural theology. (pp. 204-20)

Nicholas H. Clulee, in his John Dee's Natural Philosophy: Between Science and Religion, *Routledge, 1988, 347 p.*

Ian Seymour (essay date 1989)

[*In the excerpt below, Seymour maintains that Dee used his diverse, esoteric knowledge in Elizabeth I's political service because he believed that English expansion would engender international harmony.*]

Despite the vast bulk of his surviving works and no less than four full-length biographies, John Dee remains one of the most enigmatic of Elizabethans. A brilliant Renaissance polymath, skilled in the most practical of sciences, he is best known by such inadequate titles as 'Queen Elizabeth's Astrologer', or worse, 'a roving James Bond of Tudor times'. In reality Dee was that archetypal figure, the magus or magician, the focal point of an occult subworld of extraordinary scope and power that remains little explored. The relationship of magic and the Renaissance state was not simply one of persecution. At some levels magic arts could become a tool of policy.

Dee's contemporaries acknowledged a powerful distinction between *malificarum* (witchcraft) and *magia* (the study of the hidden powers of nature). Magic, still largely undistinguished from experimental science, claimed, like Marlowe's Faustus, 'a dominion that . . . stretcheth as far as doth the mind of man'.

These infinite powers were of obvious use as instruments of statecraft. Greene's play *Friar Bacon and Friar Bungay* (1589) has the magician, Bacon, announce:

> I will strengthen England by my skill, that if ten Caesars liv'd and reigned in Rome, with all the legions Europe doth contain, they should not touch a grass of English ground.

Such feelings were not restricted to the cheering groundlings at the Rose theatre. Dee's magic was patriotic, well-intentioned and thoroughly Christian. It held out the prospect of world peace and order at minimal expense (always a Tudor concern) and so occupied the greatest minds in England, amongst whom we must rank Dee himself.

To discover how this was so we must return to the basis of so much Renaissance thought; the hermetic books. The *Corpus Hermeticum* originated in a Greek manuscript presented to Cosimo de' Medici around the year 1460. It professed to be the work of one Hermes Trimegistus, a contemporary of Moses. In reality the volume dated from the late pagan Egypt of the second and third centuries AD. The often deeply contradictory texts set out a path to unity with God that was seized on as the earliest and hence most accurate account of the deity. Hermes joined the ranks of the *prisci theologi,* the enlightened pagans to whom Christianity was revealed long before Christ. Hermes had seen man as divine; a reflection of God, with whom he sought reunion. The beautiful Neoplatonic phrase 'as above so below' showed the universe to be a continuous chain of descent from sacred perfection, bound together by love.

The image of microcosm perfectly fitted the needs of the Tudor and Stuart states. Both monarchs wished to be seen as restorations; Elizabeth as Astraea, establishing light and justice, James as the restorer of the ancient unity of Britain. Their work was the political equivalent of that of Hermes; the recreation of the primordial harmony of the golden age. Such ideas were taken very seriously. They motivated the Emperor Rudolf of Bohemia and Henry III of France, while both Lorenzo de' Medici and Charles VIII of France extended protection to a pseudo-messiah, one Giovanni Mercurio da Correggio, who claimed to be the son of Christ and Hermes, come to reassert divine order.

The microcosmic ideal suggested that an act performed on one level affected conditions in another. It provided the intellectual vindication of magic and held out the prospect of unlimited power. In Sir Francis Bacon's *New Atlantis* (1610) this potential is expressed in the most dramatic of terms:

> The end of our foundation is the knowledge of causes and secret motions of things; and the enlarging of the bounds of the human empire to the effecting of all things possible.

Occult traditions of magical commonwealths encouraged such aspirations. Many hermeticists firmly believed their art could repair the shattered remains of Christendom and restore order to Europe. The Golden Age seemed once more within grasp.

The life of John Dee provides ample evidence of the use of magic and magical thinking in the practical politics of his time. (pp. 29-31)

It was inevitable that Dee's spiritual interests would spawn active political involvement, simply due to the breadth of the hermetic world view. If the universe was innately harmonious and the principal of 'as above so below' generally applicable, social disharmony was a reflection of disorder in the cosmos. It was the magician's duty to bring light and balance into all things. This is what Dee attempted, only to earn the reputation of a necromancer. The late Peter French's superb biography of Dee has succeeded too well in restoring his name, however. Dee's esteem as a scientist has not been higher since the sixteenth century, but his magical aspect remains to be critically explored. French complained 'there are always those angels in the background', but to Dee those angels were his great work.

The earliest indication of Dee's involvement in politics occurs in 1551, when William Cecil presented him to Edward VI, who in turn granted him a pension of 100 crowns. Dee's friends at court seem to have been of the most radical reformist party, including the Earl of Pembroke and the Lord Protector Northumberland. Both were, of course, caught in the web of intrigue regarding the accession of Queen Mary; so was Dee. Shortly after Mary had taken the throne Dee was asked to cast her horoscope, and that of her husband, Philip II of Spain. Soon afterwards he entered into correspondence with Princess Elizabeth, for whom he constructed a similar chart.

On May 28th, 1555, the Privy Council instructed Sir Francis Englefelde to:

> Make search for one John Dye, dwelling in London, and tapprehend him and send hym hither, and make searche for suche papers and bookes as he maye thinke maye towche the same Dye.

Dee was arrested and imprisoned at Hampton Court only a week before Elizabeth suffered a like fate. The charges were unquestionably false and he was swiftly and fully aquitted, but found himself sent to Star Chamber to be tried on religious grounds. (He shared a cell with Barthlet Grene, a Protestant martyr, but was soon released, becoming the friend and adviser of his captor, Bishop Bonner.) Although it is inconceivable that Dee would ever have worked evil magic, least of all against his queen, he was undoubtably active in Elizabeth's cause. As he later reminded her:

> Before her Majestie's coming to the Crown, I did shew my dutifull good will in some travailles for her Majestie's behalf to the comfort of her Majestie's favourers then.

On Elizabeth's accession his support became blatant. Sponsored at court by Pembroke and Dudley, afterwards Earl of Leicester and sometime Dee's pupil, his first duty had been to set by astrological means the date for the new queen's coronation. Elizabeth was well pleased with the result and promised him preferment. It has always been assumed that frustration when this failed to appear drove Dee abroad. This is unlikely. He had other strange but serious preoccupations and purposes. Dee was a personal friend of William Cecil, Elizabeth's Lord Treasurer, with whom he maintained a correspondence throughout the trip. His letters reveal he was deeply excited (as was Cecil) by the discovery of a book of magic.

The work in question was the *Steganographia* of Abbot Trithemius. The work is divided into three books, all seeming to be concerned with the evocation of angels. The first two parts are elaborate hoaxes; their real subject is codes, but the third is simply concerned with contacting spirits. It is generally agreed that the first sections were devised as camouflage for the latter part. This supposition is supported by the fact that Trithemius, who died only in 1516, was quite open about performing 'lawful magic', dedicating one magical text to the Emperor Maximilian. A personal friend, Charles Bouelles, wrote that Trithemius had been in possession of magical techniques for gaining and communicating knowledge in an instant, regardless of distance. It is easy to imagine how exciting such a prospect must have appeared to the Lord Treasurer. Dee wrote that he had learnt things 'by diligent serche and travaile (for so short a time) almost increadible'. The *Steganographia* was, he said, a treasure for which:

> . . . a thowsand crownes have ben offred, and yet could not be obtayned . . . a boke for which many a lerned man has long sought and dayly doth seeke; whose use is greater than the fame therof is spread.

Cecil was delighted, and on Dee's return granted him a certificate stating that his time abroad had been well spent on issues of national importance. In a world where magic and science were by no means distinct it would have been a betrayal of Cecil's duty not to investigate the potential power of such knowledge.

Curiously enough, when Dee and his co-worker Edward Kelley believed they had mastered such intelligence-gathering techniques Cecil was among those they observed. On February 18th, 1584, while in Prague, 'a litle wench' appeared in their magic crystal, who said:

> 'How do you Sir? . . . Sir I have been in England at your house, where they are all well'.
>
> [Dee] 'Thankes be to God'.
>
> [Spirit] 'Amen . . . The Queen said she was sorry she had lost her Philosopher but the Lord Treasurer [Cecil] answered "He will come home soon".'

The rather sad and obvious wishfulness of the news is immediately apparent. In actual fact Dee's house had just been looted by a pious mob.

The use of magical shortcuts to English security was by no means a rare aspect of Cecil's policy however. He enthusiastically endorsed a project of 1565 which intended to produce 50,000 marks of pure gold a year for the royal treasury by the transmutation of metal.

While Dee was abroad he published his ***Monas Hieroglyphica,*** a bizarre hermetic work whose meaning is exceptionally obscure. Dee's contemporaries 'dispraised it, because they understood it not', and he writes that Elizabeth herself participated in the 'Gracious defending of my Credit'. Cecil stated it was 'of the utmost value for the securities of the Realme'. On the surface the book is conventional alchemical mystification, but it may also contain a parallel political significance.

The monad of the title is a diagram linking Venus, Mercury, Aries, Taurus, the Moon, Sun, and Christian cross in a sigil, or magic sign. It is showered by celestial dew and situated on a broad highway. Such symbolism deserves investigation. Firstly we must note that Aries was the astrological sign of England while Mercury was the ruling planet of technology, arcane knowledge and the principality of Wales. Dee was quite probably himself of Welsh descent and devoted much effort to proving the Tudor state was a restoration of Arthur's kingdom; a British rather than English nation. The symbol thus indicates the union of the two realms. The presence of Venus indicates harmony and evokes Elizabeth herself; Astraea reborn, who will bring peace and justice to all. Likewise the image of the Moon is familiar through the Elizabethan iconographic tradition of depicting the Queen as Diana; purity and holiness. It also symbolises the sea. Taurus stands for stubbornness and determination while the Sun signifies God and glory. The presence of the cross gives a Christian tone to the whole, which forms a shape resembling the Egyptian Ankh, then understood as the *prisci theologi's* vision of Christian redemption.

The divine dew (*'ros'*) puns on the Tudor rose, while the wide path surely refers to the Anglican religious settlement. The whole forms an image of a united British state, in harmony with itself and under godly rule, armed with technological and magical knowledge. This is exactly the idea expressed in all Dee's writings. Magical thinking identified the symbol with the signified; 'as above so below'. In making the monad, Dee was bringing its symbolised reality nearer. It was presumably this that excited Cecil.

Dee believed in the establishment of a British empire (a phrase he coined) that would unite Europe from Muscovy to Greenland. Dee cites Abbot Trithemius as proving that all these lands are:

> . . . due to the Royall Government and allso the Enheritance of his [King Arthur's] posterity, the awfull Kings and Quenes of this British Monarchie.

Dee's imperialism was not purely based on ancient precedent. The dream of a united Europe was a common one in an age of chaos. One aspect of his vision was unique however; Dee believed himself to be in contact with a group of spirits through his 'Shewstone' or magic crystal. The policy he urged was theirs. Whether such supernatural intelligence was taken seriously by men like Cecil is not certain, but we may be sure that Dee's views were.

One of the most prominent of these was his belief that technological knowledge must be spread to all levels of society, especially artisans. As early as 1570 he was working on a project entitled *'Make this Kingdome Flourishing, Triumphant, Famous and Blessed'* which systematically reviewed national industry and suggested paths for progress. Such concerns were part of Dee's overall interest in practical mathmatics, of which astrology and cabala were aspects.

Dee did not intend merely to assert English power through trade and conquest; magic was another instrument to spread Elizabeth's dominions. Proof of this is contained in an extraordinary manuscript entitled ***Liber Scientia Auxilli et Victoria Terrestris,*** now in the Sloane collection; The book of the Science of Help and Victory in the World'. This consists of a list of all the spirits ruling the various kingdoms of the earth, with the information required to evoke them. The spirits assured Dee:

> Hereby you may subvert whole countries without armies, which you must and shall do, for the glory of God.

The information contained in this slender work serves to highlight one of the most remarkable aspects of Dee's political life; his period at the court of Rudolf II, Holy Roman Emperor. The Rudolfine court was a haven for unconventional thinkers. The monarch's melancholic interest in magic and alchemy made Prague a centre for such studies. In 1606 Rudolf 's foes would claim:

> His majesty is interested only in wizards, . . . and the like, sparing no expense to find all kinds of treasures, learn secrets and use scandalous ways of harming enemies.

It was even claimed that he had used evil magic against his brother Mathias.

The general atmosphere of Rudolf 's Prague would have attracted Dee, but he also had a more serious purpose. The Bohemian Lutheran, Budovec, gives perhaps the most succinct account of his mission:

> A learned and renowned Englishman whose name was Doctor De: came to Prague to see the Emperor . . . [He] predicted that a miraculous reformation would presently come about . . . and would prove the ruin . . . of [the Turks and] Rome also. These predictions he did not cease to spread among the populous.

As we shall learn, Dee's predictions had a less than purely spiritual significance.

Dee was granted an audience by the emperor in late 1584. He defiantly claimed that no human knowledge now sufficed for him and that he had come to rebuke the monarch and set him on a godly course. Rudolf had presumably expected a display of magical pyrotechnics and was not amused. After a stay of many months the religious authorities rose against Dee and commanded that he be arrested and sent to Rome. Dee evaded this but was interrogated by the papal nuncio. Kelley, Dee's coworker did most of the talking, urging universal reformation with a conviction that must dismiss doubts as to his sincereness. The magicians were able to stay in Bohemia until 1589, when personality clashes parted them, but by this time Dee at least had performed important intelligence work.

Dee's home at Mortlake was only a short distance from that of Sir Francis Walsingham, Principal Secretary, Privy Councillor and director of the secret service. As early as 1571 he had, with Elizabeth's blessing, sent Dee to France with regard to her projected marriage to the Duc d'Anjou and the two men were old friends. It seems likely therefore that Dee was involved in what may have been one of the greatest acts of deception in history.

In 1587 Europe was abuzz with wild stories concerning the imminent defeat of a great empire. In Spain the morale of the seamen gathered for the Armada began to crack and the authorities arrested rumour-mongers while the church furiously denounced the arts of prophecy. It was said that a stone containing a similar message had been discovered at Glastonbury, and was the work of Merlin. This instantly reminds one of Dee, who had a deep regard for the ancient abbey and claimed that he had found magical secrets amid its ruins. As we have seen, during the critical months prior to the fleet setting sail Dee was in Prague, presenting the Emperor Rudolf with awful prophecies of the fall of a mighty kingdom amid fearsome storms. Rudolf informed the Vatican, as he was presumably intended to.

One of the remarkable features of the outburst of prophetic frenzy was its point of origin. The story seems to have begun with the printers of Amsterdam, whose almanacks were read across the Continent. It is not without interest that Dee was an intimate personal friend of William Silvius, one of the largest Dutch publishers of the time. Silvius had not only seen some of Dee's books through the press but actually lived with him. The magician's connection with those now foretelling doom was therefore excellent.

The situation is further complicated by the fact that in England such prophecies were played down. The almanacks for 1588 were unusually mundane, although the national atmosphere seems to have been little short of hysterical. It seems almost certain that official restraint on the Stationer's Company was responsible; indeed works denying the truth of the rumours appear to have received official support.

The whole situation bears the marks of an elaborate plot, in which Dee at, the very least, played an important part. The tales significantly undermined the morale of the Spanish at a critical moment and made support for this cause less easily forthcoming. Dee would have been aided by the fact that he believed the essential truth of his prophecies. On April 30th, 1586, the spirits had told him that God declared:

> In the yeare 88 I will send out my visitation that the ends of world may be known and that justice may appeare in the garments of her unmeasurable honor.

Justice was perhaps Astraea, a name applied to Elizabeth.

Although Dee was undoubtably a passionate patriot, as is reflected in his work on behalf of the English government, he also had wider loyalties. His service to Elizabeth was merely a part of a general scheme literally to save Europe. The spirits bluntly told him that his work alone was preserving England from God's righteous anger. His devotion was not so much to the country as to an ideal mythical order. Elizabeth, he claimed, was the direct descendant of King Arthur and he had cast himself as Merlin. Great things were on the edge of coming to pass, and, to quote the Dee-inspired Rosicrucian Manifestos:

> The World shall awake out of her heavy and drowsy sleep, and with open heart, barehead and barefoot, shall merrily and joyfully meet the new arising sun.

Dee was in the service of this dream; he was a Prospero attempting to reconcile the kingdoms of the earth into divine harmony.

Dee's political vision of a restored Arthurian monarchy uniting Europe in an 'incomparable BRYTISH IMPIRE' remained a fantasy, but it was not without influence. His visionary combination of imperialism and a sense of supernatural mission undoubtably struck deep chords in the minds of many contemporaries. He knew and inspired Raleigh, Hawkins, Frobisher and Gilbert, particularly directing their attention towards the Americas, which he believed to be Atlantis. Dee was a highly able cartographer and scientific adviser to many other Elizabethan mariners, although always apt to over-estimate their capacity and exceed the bounds of possibility. His final project (1583) was nothing less than the exploration, colonisation and conversion to Christianity of North America. The voyage was to be led by Adrian Gilbert and John Davis. Dee questioned the angels as to the mission's success, but, as normally was the case when direct requests were made, they proved curiously vague. A few months after the seance Dee began his continental travels and it was quietly forgotten.

Dee's dream of an Atlantic empire based on the principal of justice and directly under God became, through various paths, one of the aspirations of the founders of the United States of America. Likewise his belief in a British duty to bring order to a savage world initiated a new theme in English perceptions of imperialism.

The last years of Elizabeth's reign saw the steady decline of Dee's influence. His patrons were dead or shadows of their former power, and the new forces in the land were more concerned to ingratiate themselves with the aging queen than with wild designs to reform the world. Dee had outlived his time. Unprotected, he became subject to growing abuse as a necromancer, which the coming of James did nothing to diminish. Dee complained that 'Brainsicke, Rashe, Spiteful and Distainfull Countrey men' persecuted him. He died in 1608, transformed from Elizabeth's 'philosopher' into a bogey to scare children to bed.

It may be asked how Dee survived so successfully for so long; there is little reason for wonder. His mind moved in a borderland between science and the supernatural that he shared with the major intellects of his day; although undoubtably a magician, his was a magic of debatable illegality whose potential power was enough to find influential friends and protectors. Certain personalities at court, chief amongst them the queen, recognised his genius and made him secure. Those who knew Dee's work would have felt he was simply speaking to angels, as many godly men had done. There was no intrinsic evil in this.

Dee's irrational and intuitive researches were becoming less significant however. The scientific method he had done much to encourage was beginning to reject the subjective world of spirits and angels. Only fifty years after his death, Dee's magical records would become a by-word for self delusion and credulity. Yet for all his personal failings Dee's influence was enormous and played an active part in the development of England's imperial conciousness.

Strange as it would seem to him, Dee's bequest to future ages would not be his angelic conversations, but his conviction that England's future lay in her commerce and beyond the seas. (pp. 31-5)

Ian Seymour, "The Political Magic of John Dee," in History Today, *Vol. 39, January, 1989, pp. 29-35.*

William H. Sherman (essay 1990)

[*In the following excerpt, Sherman examines Dee's* Brytannicae Reipublicae Synopsis, *maintaining that both its pragmatic recommendations for the Reipublicae and its dichotomous format reveal Dee as a product of the Elizabethan Renaissance.*]

There are significant, primary Renaissance texts which remain virtually unread. This fact comes as no surprise to anyone who has done historical or textual-historical research; yet the rediscovery or drastic reinterpretation of texts reveals an "unreading" which is simultaneously intoxicating and sobering in its challenge to our historical accounts. This unreading—not something which simply happens to texts—ranges from forms of innocent overlooking (i.e., not noticing or not identifying) to intentional misreading, abridging, or excluding (i.e., rewriting or writing out). The works of John Dee (1527-1608) provide abundant examples of unreading of every variety, despite the existence of a considerable tradition of Dee scholarship. In a group of studies collectively putting forth what can be labelled the Yates thesis Dee has been described as "the characteristic philosopher of the Elizabethan Age," an age, for Yates, dominated by hermetic, Neoplatonic ideas and ideals. Roy Strong and Graham Yewbrey have found in Dee a mystical imperialism (or "Cosmopoliticall Philosophy") which posited Queen Elizabeth as the virgin empress of a united, Protestant Europe, Charles Nicholl has found a source for the "alchemical theatre" produced by Shakespeare and his contemporaries. Nicholas Clulee has found a "Natural Philosophy" situated somewhere "between Science and Religion." Peter French suggests that Dee was "Renaissance England's first Hermetic magus, a philosopher-magician in the Continental tradition" and Yates herself believed that "the contemporary role which would exactly fit Dee would be that of the 'inspired melancholic'."

In this essay I want to suggest some of the forms of unreading that have accompanied, and in some ways allowed, this picture of Dee by reading one of his many unread texts, a manuscript currently housed in the British Library as Cotton Charter XIII, art. 39. Its full title reads ***Brytannicae Reipub [licae] Synopsis: libris explicata tribus. Synopseos Adumbratio, a Joanne Dee. L**[ondinensis?]. Designata: A°. 1570.* The text is written in a clear italic hand which is unquestionably Dee's own. It consists of a table, now taking the form of a roll, measuring approximately 107.8 cm (42.5 in) × 75.5 cm (29.75 in) and composed of five sheets or partial sheets of paper pasted together with a slight overlap. From the horizontal and vertical creases that are still visible the document appears to have been kept in a folded state in an earlier period, but the whole was mounted on a single sheet of linen backing in the British Museum bindery during the nineteenth century. Damage to the upper edges of the topmost sheets has resulted in some loss of text. In addition to the text's even, premeditated distribution on the constructed page, the lack of revisions and the uses of italic script and rubrics suggest that it was a presentation (as opposed to a working) copy. It is the only copy presently known. The catalogue of the Cotton Charter collection suggests that the document is "a table of matters belonging partly to ethics and partly to political economy": Dee describes the work as a "synopsis of the British commonwealth" and more specifically one relating to "politics." In a confusing revision, providing neither a reason nor a substitute, he crossed out the latter description, ironically prefiguring what twentieth-century readers would make of his works.

Perhaps the most pressing question regarding this text is Why has an Elizabethan synopsis of the British commonwealth been left out of socioeconomic, intellectual, and textual histories? As a tentative answer, I suggest three tendencies or habits in the reading practices of modern (intellectual) historians which have contributed to the unreading of Dee's text.

The first is of a broad, theoretical nature: studies of Renaissance texts have usually been carried out under the assumption (or paradigm) that a text is an autonomous, ideational vehicle rather than a contingent, interpersonal transaction. This has led to a distorting focus on the historical facts that can be gleaned from a text, or on that text's contribution to timeless traditions of ideas. As historians of the book (e.g., Roger Chartier, Robert Darnton, and Natalie Zemon-Davis), sociological bibliographers (e.g., D. F. McKenzie and Jerome McGann), students of literacy (e.g., Walter Ong, Brian Street, and Ruth Finnegan), and even social theorists (from M. M. Bakhtin to Anthony Giddens) have asserted, our focus must rather be on texts as forms of interaction, communication, and negotiation.

The occasion of Dee's construction of his ***Synopsis*** (and the act of patronage it engenders) must not be ignored or explained away by a mere attention to historical facts: to do so would be to miss the specific ways in which Dee read and was read and, more importantly, the specific ways in which reading and politics were related in Elizabethan England. The ***Synopsis*** . . . is a reader's guide to the British

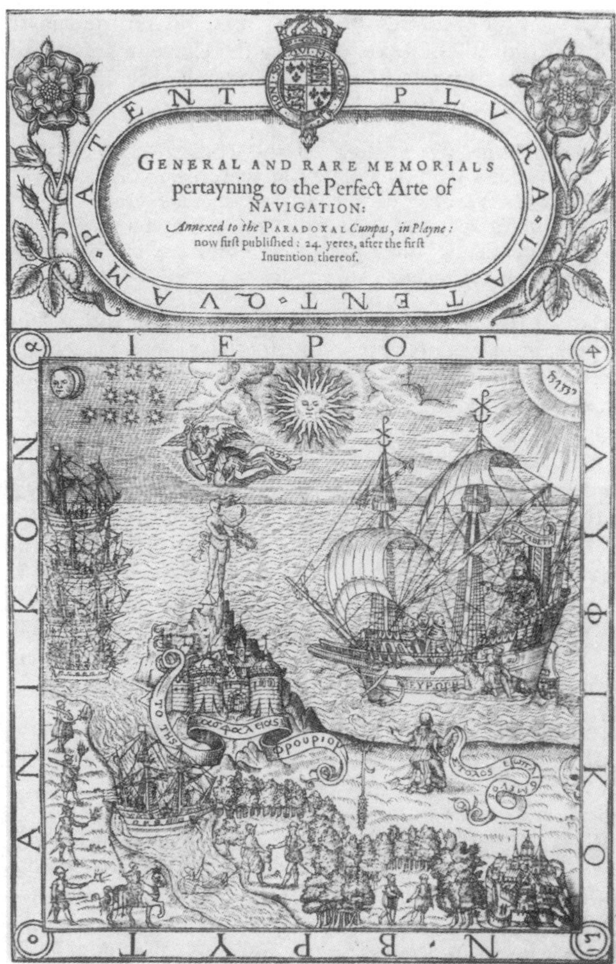

Dee's illustration for the title page of General and Rare Memorial pertayning to the Perfect Arte of Navigation. *The kneeling figure on the right represents the Republic of Britain beseeching Elizabeth, at the helm of the imperial ship, to use the naval power to secure and expand British territories.*

commonwealth. It represents Dee's scholarly mediation between a body of knowledge and a body of political readers (specifically Privy Councilors): it was designed to clearly present information about the state of the commonwealth to a politician who needed a working knowledge of the situation and was in a position to affect governmental policy. If, on the other hand, we look at the ***Synopsis*** in terms of the original contribution of ideas to recognizable intellectual traditions, it is at best boring and at worst unintelligible. It only becomes readable when seen in the context of specific practices, both in Dee's written facilitation and in the privy councilors' political application.

To see this activity or process is to restore both a fuller sense of the ***Synopsis***'s signification and a more tangible sense of Dee's textual agency. This restoration is [according to Michel de Certeau in his *Practice of Everyday Life*] part of a larger critical project to "challenge 'consumption' as it is conceived and (of course) confirmed by these 'authorial' [intellectual] enterprises." To concentrate on active reading practices—to study, in Chartier's terms, the "appropriation" of texts and, in de Certeau's evocative phrases, "Reading as Poaching" and "the ideology of 'informing' through books"—means

> holding any process of the construction of meaning . . . as situated at the crossroads between readers endowed with specific competencies . . . and texts whose meaning is always dependent on their particular discursive and formal mechanisms.

This shift in our reading position is academically and politically empowering: not only does it reveal aspects and avenues of Renaissance culture that we have since lost, but, as de Certeau asserts, "we may be able to discover creative activity where it has been denied that any exists." In most of the cases that de Certeau discusses, this means recovering the creativity of everyday activities and strategies for the "masses" or the working classes; in the case of Dee and those like him it means recovering the creativity of advisors and servants behind the elite historical surface. Inasmuch as this study can restore that which has been written out, in terms of both Renaissance history and Renaissance historiography, a key to the rewriting of the Renaissance may well be found in the readings of its texts.

Within Dee studies, two further tendencies toward unreading have been especially pronounced: one concerns manuscripts and the other politics. Both are strikingly revealed by statistics regarding Dee's written output. Clulee's comprehensive bibliography lists 76 surviving items, ranging from fragments, letters, and diaries to elaborate and completed texts. Of these 76 texts, 64 (approximately 84 percent) are manuscripts, all of which, as far as can be determined, were never intended for publication. Given this statistic, I think two incorrect assumptions have been made in the reading and unreading of Dee's manuscripts. The first is that, in Yates's words, "there were many works by Dee passing from hand to hand in manuscript . . . many, indeed most, of which are unknown to us." On the contrary, not only do many of the manuscripts that Dee mentions in an autobiographical inventory of 1592 survive, but many that he does not mention as well. The other assumption is that those manuscripts which have survived are trivial and insignificant. This can be clearly detected in Yewbrey's lament that "despite the great number of his manuscripts presently extant, research in the life and thought of John Dee . . . is frequently hampered by the non-survival of important works." While I despair, with Yewbrey, over the apparent loss of such intriguing works as ***Cabalae Hebraicae compendiosa tabella; De modo Euangelij Iesu Christi publicandi, propagandi, stabiliendique, inter Infideles Atlanticos;*** and ***The Originals, and Chiefe points, of our auncient Brytish Histories,*** I cannot agree that research opportunities are exhausted while texts such as the ***Synopsis*** remain unexamined. This antimanuscript bias, apparent in the very structure of Clulee's authoritative study (three of four sections of which focus on what Clulee considers Dee's three major printed works), reaches its most blatant and illogical form in the entry on Dee in the *Dictionary of Welsh Biography,* which declares that "it is not possible to assess the value of Dee's works, as most of the seventy-nine he composed still remain in manuscript form." It is apparent, then, that for one reason or another a large body of Dee's manuscripts (a "great number of his manuscripts" indeed) have been neglected.

The other general area of exclusion in Dee studies has been that of his political theories and practices. Considering again Dee's written works—this time excluding letters and diaries but including known texts which have not survived—it is possible to categorize each item under the headings, Magic (or Natural Philosophy), Science, and Politics. Assigning each item to only one category—not an easy task, nor a desirable one except to make such a general point—results in the following distribution: 13 items on magic, 21 on science, and 30 on politics. And yet, with the notable exception of one short chapter in Clulee's book (the title of which, *John Dee's Natural Philosophy,* proclaims its nonpolitical scope), the major studies of Dee have either ignored his politics or subordinated them to his occult philosophy. It seems at least logically inconsistent to claim for Dee, as do Yates and French, a central role in the intellectual life of the Elizabethan court and then to treat that sociopolitical milieu so slightly. And the virtual absence of any political writings from Gerald Suster's collection, *John Dee: Essential Readings,* seems even more unjustifiable. At the very least, remembering the extent of Dee's political writings ought to confirm his authorship of the ***Synopsis,*** a thoroughly political document whose recovery here might well be a first step in assessing and revising Dee's intellectual career.

In turning to a reading of the ***Synopsis,*** it is reasonable to begin with whatever illumination—and confusion—Dee himself provides as to its composition. His first reference to the ***Synopsis*** comes in ***General and Rare Memorials pertayning to the Perfect Arte of Navigation*** (published in 1577; written in 1576). Having mounted an argument that a "Pety Nauy Royall" would deter "malitious and subtile Attempts, intended against the weale Publike of this Noble kingdom," Dee breaks off with a personal address to his reader:

> But, such matter as this, I judge you haue, or mought haue hard of, ere now, (by the worshipfull *M. Dyer,*) and that, abundantly: Seeing, ***Synopsis Reipub. Brytanicae,*** was, at his Request (six yeres past) contriued. . . .

This passing reference is telling. First, it provides an occasion for the ***Synopsis:*** not only a date (1570), but a commission. Second, it suggests the milieu within which it circulated: Christopher Hatton, Edward Dyer, and, through them, select Privy Councilors. Third, it explains that Dee considered "such matter" as naval policy and national security to have been adumbrated in the ***Synopsis.*** Most importantly, it allows us to avoid the confusion that has arisen from Dee's second reference to the ***Synopsis.*** In the above mentioned inventory of 1592 Dee lists ***Reipublicae Britannicae Synopsis*** among his unpublished manuscripts; the problem is that he dates it "Anno 1565." This has driven Clulee, in turn informed by Yewbrey, to postulate the existence of a 1565 ***Synopsis,*** of which the 1570 manuscript is merely a summary. The claim is perhaps supported by the full title of the 1570 text, ***Brytannicae***

Reipub. Synopsis: libris explicata tribus: while "libris" need not mean books it probably does not denote divisions as short as Dee's. On the other hand, it is difficult to see why Dee would have bothered to make a presentation copy of such a summary; the 1570 manuscript was clearly one intended to be displayed and read by others. Ultimately, my feeling is that this hypothesis, whether right or wrong, is unnecessary. The fact remains that the ***Synopsis*** we have is dated 1570, and that Dee thought enough of it to refer to it six years after the fact instead of twenty-two as the ***Synopsis.***

The content and the purpose of the ***Synopsis*** are suggested most clearly by the lead caption in the center of the diagram:

> To make this Kingdome flourishing,
> Triumphant, famous, and Blessed:
> Of necessitie, in it, are required
> these thre principall things.

The "thre principall things," indicated by the three principal branches, are Vertue, Welth, and Strength. Dee's middle section, by far the most detailed and context-specific, requires the most elucidation. It is accompanied by the Latin epigram, "Nihil est vtile, quod no*n* sit Honestum" [Nothing is expedient which is not honest]. In his attention to home industries and foreign trade, Dee touches on such landmark economic issues as lapsed standards in the cloth industry, debasement of the coinage, and "lamentably decayed towns." Dee's terms are overtly critical, suggesting ways to improve England's position internationally and the commons' position at home. These ends, not surprisingly, are to be achieved by the increase of wealth: the section begins, "Welth: which Chiefly growet[h] or may gr[o]we." The sources of income are equally straightforward: either by "Naturall Commodities of this monarchy," themselves either used "Within this Land" or "The ouerplus Transporting (to our most gayne) into foreyn places convenient," or "by things . . . browght in." Dee goes so far as to provide a tabular overview of British foreign trade, outlining seven regions and, presumably to be filled in later, the volumes or goods involved in import and export trade. His presentation culminates in a classic statement of what C. H. Wilson [in "Trade, Society, and the State," *The Cambridge Economic History of Europe,* 1966-, vol. 4] has called "the central principle" of late Tudor economics, "the balance of trade." Wilson cites the well-known definition from the *Discourse of the Common Weal* (1549): "We must alwaies take care that we bie no more of strangers than we sell them." Dee's version is more ambitious:

> It wold be pollitikly cumpassed (and not co*m*mandeme*nt* publik) that of our Commodities (in totall summe) more be carried out, than in waies do come in, yerely; by 1/3: or 1/4 at the least.

Wilson concludes his survey of early mercantilist theory with the suggestion that "perhaps the most important thing about the mercantilists was that they believed that material change was possible and desirable and supported their belief with an unprecedented concentration on organized human energy." Whether or not Dee is to be considered a mercantilist, this comment is certainly true of his analysis of the cloth trade. That he considered material change to be possible and desirable is clear from his proposition, "if this new encrease of Cloth making were ordayned to be in sundry townes of England, which now are lamentably decayed" then ("besides many other commodities publik, hereby arrising") British money would be better spent and British cloth would be of higher esteem abroad. More explicitly,

> Our Wooll: Of it, (at the least) a quarter more, than now is, wold be dr[a]ped here: As well for relieving of innumerable pore folk by th[e] working of it: and restoring of decayed Townes: As also, for that our cloth and wooll, with the forayner, Wold be of more estimation.

As is by now apparent, Dee does indeed support his beliefs in change with a "concentration on organized human energy." His twofold suggestion for reforming the corruptions in the industry also involves the employment and deployment of human resources:

> And withall the Testimony of appointed honest skylfull overseers, for eue[ry] principall point belonging to good and perfect cloth, by Severall Seales of lead to euery cloth [ms faded] And also sufficient warning, by apt mark in the said Seales of lead, of any notable fault fownd in the said cloth, by negligence or fraude in workmanship, in any of the principall points.

What is most striking in Dee's analysis is its currency: that is, the extent to which it corresponds with contemporary problems, practices, and discourses. *Leake's Treatise on the Cloth Industry, with Proposals for the Reform of Abuses* (1577) makes the need for reformed legislation emphatically clear:

> I am fullye of opinion that, for all Colored Clothes dressed and dyed within this realme, and generallye for all other Clothe, the lawes were never yet observed in any one place with in the Realme. . . . And therefore I conclude that these deceiptes vsed by the makers is the Cause whye our commodityes are the lesse sett by in forraine nations.

Leake's complaints, both in substance and in style, uncannily echo Dee's, implying not that Dee was a source for Leake but that they both felt the same needs, had similar knowledge, and utilized recognized discourses. The same goes for his suggestions about "the best waye to reforme these abuses." First, "I suppose no way so meete as the findinge out and appointinge of one meete man to be a Supervisor . . . and giuinge him sufficient power and authority." Second,

> the weaver [ought] to present his Clothe wouen before the Masters of his Companye, and ther to be proved, the Fullier or Clotheworker likewise, and the Dyer for his parte also; which beinge founde perfect euery of them might sett to their seales particulerly, with a Confirmation of the town seale wher it was made. And if it be faultie in any pointe materiall, then the seales wherin the offence is shall wante, and therby give knowledge to the buyer.

These correspondences are not fortuitous; nor was Dee's

choice to discuss the cloth trade at such length an arbitrary one. As Ramsay explains, "from the point of view of the government, especially with the raising of the cloth export duty in 1558, the yield of taxes from the woollen industry was vital." It was, in fact, the prime source of income: "Customs receipts, mostly connected with the cloth trade in one way or another, continued to provide the major source of royal revenue." The cloth industry was not just any industry, therefore: it was "the largest and most important of the country's manufacturing industries." But this had been true for some time. The importance of the convergence in the 1570s of suggestions for reform (of which Dee and Leake were only a part) is that it testifies to a crisis within that crucial industry. Both Bowden and Ramsay have drawn a picture of extreme crisis within the Staplers' Company—responsible not only for wool exports but for lead as well, a trade which Dee also mentions in this context—which reached its worst proportions around 1570. The most immediate cause was the loss of the thriving Antwerp market in 1569: that year saw a "brusque rupture of the traffic to Antwerp, which was never fully resumed." This is not to suggest, then, that Dee was a radical and innovative economic theorist; it is to suggest that he provided, in a schematic nutshell, a topical and informed critique of England's important and promising, though recently threatened, cloth trade.

Dee concludes this section on trade with general advice for merchants regarding the shrewd and beneficial handling of money:

> Of Necessitie, all o' Marchants (trading with forayners) owght to be very perfect in the true valew of all currant coynes, Syluer and Gold . . . And So To Bargayne wisely: and Skyllfully to vnderstand theyr gayne: in marking with reckoning of the difference in vale[w] bethwene the standerds of any diuerse coynes in theyr handling.

This may seem like common sense, but it responds to the substantial confusion and loss that had resulted from shifting metal standards and general debasement of the coinage. The doctor in the *Discourse of the Common Weal* explained in no uncertain terms what he felt had been the result of these changes:

> What oddes soeuer theare happen to be in [exchaunge] of thinges, youe that be merchauntes can espie it anone; ye lurched some of the coyne as sone as euer ye perceived the price of that to be enhaunced; ye, by and by perceivinge what was to be wonne theare in beyond the sea, raked all the old coyne for the moste parte in this realme, and founde the means to haue it caried ouer; so as litle was lefte behind within this Realme of such old coyne at this daye; which, in my opinion, is a greate cause of this dearthe that we haue now in all thinges.

An "enhancement" of the exchange rate had led directly to the drainage of precious metal from the realm, which in turn had led to the renowned mid-Tudor economic crisis.

As with the case of the cloth trade, Dee presented his material on the exchange of currency in terms of beneficial reform. Not only would the education of merchants in the dynamics of currency "wynn vnto at the length: for the marvaylous benefyt of this Realme," but indeed serve to make "England both abroad and at home to be Lord and ruler of the Exchange." It is likely that he also had more modest, pedagogic motives, that this was part of his broader program for the scientific education of England's unlearned (and specifically merchant and mechanical) subjects. This project is clearly glimpsed in Robert Recorde's mathematical textbook, *The Ground of Artes,* first published in 1542 and reprinted in 1582 with additions by John Dee and John Mellis. Most of the examples, significantly, use current English coins as units. Moreover, the second edition added the practical section entitled *The Rules of Practice for Merchants.* Chapter 14 of this section, for example, "entreateth of exchanging of money from one place to another, with diuers necessarie questions incident thereunto." Even more practical and to the point is chapter 16: "a brief note of the ordinarie Coines of moste places of Christendome for traffique." Finally, Dee refers in a section on mixed numbers to "an example of mixture of Gold and Siluer." A manuscript marginal note in the Cambridge University Library copy suggests that this addresses the "pollution of the currency."

The top section, "Vertue," is accompanied by the Latin phrase, "Sola Virtus vitam efficit Beatam" [Only virtue brings about the prosperous life], and is broken down into Wisedome, Iustice, Fortitude, and Temperance. This section of the manuscript has been severely damaged (it is, in fact, impossible to discern further divisions within the topic of Wisedome). Fortunately, this is the section which requires least development, as it is the most conventional. The section is included, in the first place, because of the Aristotelian convention that makes a discussion of politics impossible without reference to ethics. Furthermore, Dee's four virtues correspond exactly to the classical four cardinal virtues. These virtues are well described by Quentin Skinner, who suggests [in *The Foundations of Modern Political Thought,* vol. I, 1978] that they were a commonplace in Renaissance commonwealth literature. While this section is on the whole thoroughly traditional, Dee has elaborated the concept of "Iustice" in a clear, unique, and critical way. He suggests, first, that all laws "ought to be ordred to gither in a Body Methodicall: and not to be a Confused Chaos (and Worse) as they are." This can be taken as a critique of the state of English Law in terms of one of the qualities which Dee, and his humanist contemporaries, valued most: method. In fact, in ***General and Rare Memorials*** he can be found referring to himself as "the Methodicall Author". His second and third suggestions are less contentious: that the laws ought to be made more readily available and that they should be authorized and amended, when necessary, by Parliament. One might assume that these were derivative or amateurish recommendations, since most studies of Dee do not indicate any training or experience in legal matters. However, not only does Dee claim that he studied civil law, at least informally, but it is clear that Dyer and others respected him for it. While visiting the University of Louvain, he claimed,

> I did, for recreation, look into the method of the civile law, and profited the rein so much, that in

> the antimonys, imagined to be in the law, I had good hap to finde out (well allowed of) their agreementes; and also to enter into a plaine and due understanding of divers civill lawes, accounted very intricate and darke.
>
> (***Compendious Rehearsall,*** 7)

This reference to "antimonys" and "their agreementes" can be read in two ways. Dee might have meant that he was studying comparative—i.e., international—law. He was later called upon to utilize this knowledge in several commissioned works on the complicated issues of British sea limits and royal titles to foreign lands. But it is more likely that Dee was referring to the Roman Law which he would have studied on the continent. This law was based on generalities and inferences, whereas the English common law was based on specifics and precedents. In this light, Dee's comment may mean that he was actually engaged in the attempt to reduce the English law's compendium of examples to a collection of general rules; in other words, to order all laws "in a Body Methodicall."

Two aspects of the ***Synopsis***'s final section, on Strength, merit special attention. First, Dee provides a figure on the size of the Royal Navy—whether actual or ideal it is hard to gauge—and more general descriptions of the deployment of defense resources that have not, as far as I know, been compared with other contemporary accounts. Second, this section provides the clearest example of the efficiency and clarity afforded by the diagrammatic form Dee has used. It is a classic use of an expository form Dee inherited from his humanist predecessors, a form described by Walter Ong [in *Ramus, Method, and the Decay of Dialogue,* 1958] as "tidy bracketed tables of dichotomies."

Having read, albeit briefly, the ***Synopsis*** for its content, I now want to examine its form. This form is not just the product of what appears to be an obsessive harping on method: it is the product of Dee's education in and mastery of the humanist method of pedagogical presentation. In presenting his material in a system that scholars have found in frequent use by humanist writers and have labelled the "divisive technique," characterized by "dichotomous tables" or "a series of dichotomous synoptic tables," Dee once again proves the product of his times. As William Temple, Dee's humanist colleague at Cambridge, asserted in a debate with Everard Digby over the nature and uses of dialectical method, "the divisive technique . . . is indeed the one and only *methodus.*" What we must remember is that the *Synopsis* was written within what Ong has characterized as a "cult of dichotomies."

It is an amusing irony—one of the many lurking in Dee studies—that the presentation of Dee as in any way a traditional humanist should today be a radical proposition. He did, of course, have his quarrels with the educational institutions of his day, and after leaving his appointment as a founding fellow of Trinity College, Cambridge he consistently resisted contact with the English universities. Yet, it seems that his use of the dichotomous method is in absolute concord with that of the mainstream, Ramist tradition. Lisa Jardine's description of this method [in *Francis Bacon: Discovery and the Art of Discourse,* 1974] is particularly resonant:

> Ramus' dichotomous method is a procedure for displaying material . . . in the most clear and most easily grasped fashion for comprehension by the student. The teacher commences with the most general definition of the subject . . . followed by the division of that subject into two parts . . . with explanations and examples. . . . He then proceeds to key down each arm of the array in turn, conveniently displaying the material under each head in a tabular form. . . . Dichotomous keying became an extremely voguish way of proceeding.

Walter Ong, in a discussion of "The Method of Method," quotes Ramus's own description: "The method of teaching . . . is the arrangement of various things brought down from universal and general principles to the underlying singular parts, by which arrangement the whole matter can be more easily taught and apprehended." This movement (of "bringing down") is clear in Dee's diagram: he progresses—to follow one "arm of the array"—from "Strength" to the category of things "Moveable" to things "Lyving" to "MAN: trayned vp in all Martiall skyll and feates: necessary against all kinde of Enemyes." Another feature of the dichotomous method is that, "theoretically, no material is omitted." This comprehensiveness can be sensed by following another other part of the same branch in the subject of Strength: from things "Lyving" (as opposed to "Vnlyving") to "Beast" (as opposed to "MAN") to "Horse" (as opposed to "Ox") to "Great Horse/Dimilance/Light horse/Hackenye/Cart horse."

The dichotomous method was not without its problems. It is not hard to imagine—and Dee's diagram provides abundant examples—how the presentation will fall short of the total coverage of its subject: this is dependent both on the comprehensiveness of the subject headings and on their pairings into absolute dichotomies. In a case such as Dee's necessarily in complete analysis of British industry, or in his division of all English subjects into either "Students" or the "Vulgar," we can see that the treatment is neither full nor natural. Furthermore, as Francis Bacon pointed out, the method was limited both in range and effect: he saw that dialectic and rhetoric are "very properly applied to civil business and to those arts which rest in discourse and opinion" but that they are unsuitable for exploring the truth in any area of natural knowledge. This is to suggest that "dialectic . . . is concerned with the presentation of ideas which are already fully formed." These points add to the appropriateness of Dee's dichotomizing: in the ***Synopsis*** he organizes (for Dyer) his already acquired knowledge of "civil business." Despite its practical faults and limitations the dichotomous method was both an effective and an apt choice for Dee's ***Synopsis.*** In the final analysis, the dichotomous method is simply one of those techniques which are "particularly effective as vehicles for transmitting new or difficult knowledge to an audience." This, I am suggesting, was Dee's skill; it was the service he provided to a range of clients from Frobisher, Gilbert, and Bourne to Dyer, Hatton, and the queen herself. (pp. 293-308)

William H. Sherman, "John Dee's 'Brytannicae Reipublicae Synopsis: A Reader's Guide to the Elizabethan Commonwealth," in The

Journal of Medieval and Renaissance Studies, Vol. 20, No. 2, Fall, 1990, pp. 293-315.

FURTHER READING

Aubrey, John. "John Dee." In his *Letters Written By Eminent Persons in the Seventeenth and Eighteenth Centuries,* vol. 2, pp. 310-15. London: Longman, Hurst, Rees, Orme, and Brown, 1813.

Personal anecdotes about Dee and speculation concerning the whereabouts of his letters and manuscripts.

Clulee, Nicholas H. "Astrology, Magic, and Optics: Facets of John Dee's Early Natural Philosophy." *Renaissance Quarterly* XXX, No. 4 (Winter 1977): 632-80.

Examines his earliest extant work, the *Propadeumata aphoristica,* to demonstrate how Dee's sources, interests, and approaches evolved.

———. "At the Crossroads of Magic and Science: John Dee's Archemastrie." In *Occult and Scientific Mentalities in the Renaissance,* edited by Brian Vickers, pp. 57-71. Cambridge: Cambridge University Press, 1984.

Asserts that the portion of Dee's "Preface" in which he discusses "archemastrie," or experimental methods, indicates most accurately the hegemony of magic and religion over science and math in his work. Clulee modifies this opinion somewhat in his 1988 book on Dee.

Deacon, Richard. *John Dee: Scientist, Geographer, Astrologer and Secret Agent to Elizabeth I.* London: Frederick Muller, 1968, 309 p.

Often-conjectural biography in which Deacon claims that Dee served Queen Elizabeth as a spy. Deacon's scholarship and conclusions are often questioned.

Gwyn, David. "John Dee's *Arte of Navigation.*" *The Book Collector* 34, vol. 3 (Autumn 1985): 309-22.

Explains composition, publication, and reception of the *Arte of Navigation.*

Johnson, Francis R. "The Advancement of Astronomy in England, 1550-1573." In his *Astronomical Thought in Renaissance England: A Study of the English Scientific Writings from 1500 to 1645,* pp. 120-60. 1937. Reprint. New York: Octagon Books, 1968.

Survey of mid-sixteenth-century English astronomical theory which holds that Dee's importance lies in his teaching and advising "most of the English mathematicians, astronomers, and geographers of the day." Johnson also discusses Dee as a typically neoplatonic Renaissance scientist, as a pioneer of "the experimental method," and as a leader in research on the supernova that appeared in 1572.

Knoespel, Kenneth J. "The Narrative Matter of Mathematics: John Dee's *'Preface'* to the Elements of Euclid of Megara (1570)." *Philological Quarterly* 66, No. 1 (Winter 1987): 27-46.

Discusses the relationship between language and numbers in Dee's "Mathematicall Praeface," asserting that his subject categories and style conduce to practical applications of mathmatical theory, and that he was fundamentally language-oriented despite his conviction that numbers disclose "the divine structure of the universe."

Mackay, Charles. "The Alchymists: Dr. Dee and Edward Kelley." In his *Extraordinary Popular Delusions and the Madness of Crowds,* pp. 170-84. 1841. Reprint. Wells, Vt.: Fraser Publishing, 1932.

Biographical sketch which focuses on the last twenty-five years of Dee's life, maintaining that "his heart was in alchymy" and that he was both a "quack" and a deluded "fanatic."

Meadows, Denis. "John Dee, the Queen's Astrologer." In his *Elizabethan Quintet,* pp. 176-237. London: Longmans, Green and Co., 1956.

Appreciative biographical essay which describes Dee's education, his highly-placed acquaintances and patrons, and his wide-ranging intellectual activities.

Smith, Charlotte Fell. *John Dee, 1527-1608.* London: Constable and Co., 1909, 342 p.

The first extensive biographical study of the "persistently misjudged" Dee, maligned for three centuries, Smith proposes, because "he was too far advanced in speculative thought for his own age to understand."

Taylor, E. G. R. "John Dee and the Search for Cathay: 1547-1570," "John Dee, Frobisher and Drake: 1570-1579," and "John Dee and the Search for Cathay: 1580-1583." In his *Tudor Geography, 1485-1583,* pp. 75-139. London: Methuen and Co., 1930.

An attempt to reconstruct the "intellectual background" of sixteenth-century English "voyages of discovery" which includes discussion of Dee's contributions: mathematical expertise, knowledge of early cartography and navigational instruments, astronomical and navigational theory, and ardent patriotism.

René Descartes

1596-1650

French philosopher and mathematician.

INTRODUCTION

Descartes is considered one of the seminal figures of modern thought. In his philosophical program, as presented by such important works as *Discourse on Method* and *Meditations on First Philosophy,* he "brought together," as Wilhelm Windelband wrote, "the scientific movement of his time to establish rationalism anew, by filling the scholastic system of conceptions with the rich content of Galilean research." Descartes posited that philosophy must be based on a clear, rational method of inquiry. In order to establish a firm basis for this method, he rigorously subjected popularly held assumptions concerning the nature of the self and the universe to a process of universal doubt. Descartes effectively reduced verifiable reality to the thinking self, though he eventually accepted the objective reality of the external world and the existence of God. Critics affirm that the most significant result of Descartes's methodical skepticism was his radical separation of the thinking subject from the physical world, which he viewed in purely scientific, mechanistic terms, suggesting the modern metaphor of the world conceived as an intricate machine.

Descartes was born on 31 March 1596, at La Haye in Touraine. His family belonged to the *noblesse de robe,* or juridical nobility, as attested by his father's position as *councilor* of the *parlement* of Rennes in Brittany. From his mother, who died of a lung infection a few days after his birth, Descartes inherited a delicate constitution, and his health was a subject of great concern for his doctors. Nonetheless, in 1604 he was sent to the Jesuit college of La Flèche in Anjou, where he received a largely classical education but also familiarized himself with new discoveries in optics and astronomy. After graduating from La Flèche in 1612, he studied law at the University of Poitiers until 1616, though he appears never to have practiced. Weary of studying, Descartes finally decided on a military career and served under the banners of Maurice of Nassau and the German emperor Ferdinand during the early phases of the Thirty Years War. During 1618-19 at Breda, Holland, Descartes became acquainted with the famous mathematician Isaac Beeckman, who encouraged him to return to the study of science and mathematics.

In April 1619 Descartes began travelling, settling in Neuberg, Germany, where he secluded himself "dans un poêle" ["in a heated room"] for the winter. On 10 November 1619 Descartes experienced a series of extraordinary dreams which led him to believe that he was destined to found a universal natural science based on mathematics. During the next few years Descartes continued travelling in Europe. He returned to France in 1622, eventually establishing himself in Paris, where he continued to refine his philosophical theories in the company of mathematicians and scientists. In 1628, Descartes publicly presented his philosophical ideas in a confrontation with the chemist Chandoux, who upheld a probabilistic view of science. Demonstrating to the audience through brilliant argumentation that any philosophical system not grounded in certainty would inevitably fail, Descartes was taken aside after the lecture by Cardinal de Bérulle, who urged him to complete his method, explaining that it was God's will for him to do so. Shortly afterwards, Descartes completed his first substantial work, *Regulae ad directionem ingenii* (1701; *Rules for the Direction of the Mind*), explicating the methodological foundations of the new system.

At the beginning of 1629 Descartes moved to Holland, where he was able to work in an atmosphere of tranquility and intellectual freedom. In 1633 Descartes completed *Le monde de M. Descartes, ou le traité de la lumière* (1644; *The World*), wherein he supported the Copernican theory of the earth's movement around the sun. However, he suppressed publication of this work after hearing from his friend Marin Marsenne of Galileo's condemnation by the Roman Catholic church for upholding the same thesis. Four years later, Descartes published *Discours de la méthode de bien conduire sa raison et chercher la vérité dans les sciences; plus la dioptrique; les météores; et la géométrie, qui sont des essais de cette méthode* (1637; *Discourse on the Method of Properly Guiding the Reason in the Search for Truth in the Sciences; also the Dioptric, the Meteors and the Geometry, which are Essays in This Method*). The four-part treatise defined the principles of modern scientific method and applied them to matters of current academic interest. Written in French in order to reach a wider audience, the work caused a critical uproar and was immediately challenged by a number of prominent mathematicians. The years 1641 and 1642 marked the appearance of two editions of the *Meditationes de prima philosophia in qua Dei existentia et animae immortalitas demonstratur* (1641; *"Meditations on First Philosophy, in which the Existence of God and the Immortality of the Soul are Demonstrated"*) and *Meditationes de prima philosophia, in quibus Dei existentia et animae humanae a corpore distinctio demonstrantur* (1642; *Meditations on First Philosophy, in which the Existence of God and the Distinction between Mind and Body are Demonstrated*), a comprehensive exposition of his epistemological and metaphysical theories. The work did much to augment Descartes's influence in Europe's intellectual circles. However, many of Descartes's positions were attacked by such notable scholars as Pierre Gassendi and Gysbertus Voetius, president of the University of Utrecht, who accused the author of atheism. Throughout the controversy, Descartes was supported by his many friends and admirers, including the refugee Princess Elizabeth of the Palatinate, to whom Descartes dedicated the *Principia philosophia* (1644; *Principles of Philosophy*), a four-part treatise that provided further explanation of the principal ideas of the *Meditations.* Descartes visited Paris in 1647, where he met Blaise Pascal and attended court, securing the promise of a pension from the crown. However, the rebellion of the Fronde in 1648 promptly rendered the promised stipend unavailable, and Descartes again returned to Holland. The following year, Queen Christina of Sweden, who decided to found an academy of scholars, requested Descartes to come to Sweden and instruct her in philosophy. After overseeing the publication of *Traité des passions de l'âme* (1649; *The Passions of the Soul*), which sought to explain psychological events in mechanistic terms, Descartes left Amsterdam on 1 September 1649, and reached Stockholm a month later. Descartes was required to tutor the queen in philosophy at five o'clock in the morning, a schedule he found extremely taxing. Returning to his lodging one bitter January morning, he caught pneumonia and died within a fortnight on 11 February 1650.

During the seventeenth century, Descartes was as famous for his scientific treatises as he was for his philosophical works. However, he is known today primarily for the *Discourse on Method* and the *Meditations,* which are numbered among the principal works of modern philosophy. The *Discourse on Method* amplified Descartes's project for a universal methodology adumbrated in his *Rules for the Direction of the Mind.* The *Discourse on Method* is actually an extended preface to a much larger treatise comprising three separate works—*Dioptrics, Meteors,* and *Geometry,* all of which are technical discussions of scientific subjects. The *Discourse* itself is divided into six chapters. The first three are primarily autobiographical, touching on Descartes's early education as well as the three dreams of 10 November 1619. Chapter four is concerned with traditional metaphysical questions concerning the nature of reality and contains the formula "I think, therefore I am." The fifth chapter investigates the subjects of physics and biology, while the final chapter serves as a general conclusion. The six-part *Discourse* is generally upheld as an indispensable introduction to the Cartesian system. Commentators agree that the cornerstone of the work is Descartes's presentation, in Chapter Two, of the four methodological principles that established the frame for his scientific method. Here Descartes demonstrated that useful knowledge must be founded on clear and distinct judgments, which should be as irrefutable as mathematical formulae based on pure intuition and deductive reasoning.

The second edition of the *Meditations on First Philosophy* appeared in 1642 with a compendium of "objections" by such notable thinkers as Thomas Hobbes, Antoine Arnauld, and Pierre Gassendi. Whereas Descartes's previous works were essentially theoretical discussions on methodology, the *Meditations* address specific philosophical issues: skepticism, the nature of God, the metaphysical foundation of truth, and knowledge of the physical world. The work is divided into six separate Meditations, each of which focuses on a particular problem.

The First Meditation invokes Descartes's principle of methodological doubt, which he saw as indispensable to creating a positive foundation for knowledge. Beginning with the assumption that all knowledge derives from sensory perception or rational intuition, Descartes purports that sensory perception is questionable. He demonstrates, for example, that in our dreams we perceive objects as clearly as in an awakened state. On the other hand, purely intuitive ideas such as those pertaining to mathematics would appear to be irrefutably true, yet Descartes maintains that their relation to objective reality cannot be verified through reason alone. The Second Meditation elaborates on the relation of the thinking subject to objective reality. Descartes maintains that while sensory perceptions and pure intuitions are possibly illusory, the thinking subject cannot be doubted because the "I" accompanies every thought. Therefore, existence must be seen as a predicate of thought, as expressed in the formula "I think, therefore I am." Descartes defines man as a thinking being whose mental operations are separate and distinct from the existence of the external world.

In the Third Meditation Descartes attempts to establish formal proof of the existence of God. He reasons that as God is an infinitely perfect being and is not a deceiver, there is no reason to doubt that clear and distinct perceptions correspond to objective reality. In the Fourth and Fifth Meditations, Descartes provides further proofs for the existence of God and contends that the external world can be known with absolute certainty so long as we operate in the realm of clear and distinct ideas. The Sixth Meditation is considered by many critics Descartes's most original contribution to modern philosophy. Here he methodically analyzes the relation between the human soul and the body. Descartes defines the mind (or soul) as a purely volitional and indivisible thinking "substance." However, he views the body as a passive object for sensations and says that it is no different from any other physical object, whose essence is "extension." Although he later suggests that the mind and body are closely related, he maintains a clear distinction between the two, explaining that he can imagine the mind existing independently of the body. This distinction is seen by many commentators as the starting point of modern philosophy, and is the basis for Cartesian dualism.

The *Meditations* suggested new ways of conceiving of the rational universe, both physical and spiritual. It is generally agreed that Descartes's ideas were extremely influential in directing the course of the scientific revolution of the seventeenth century as well as the rationalist program of the eighteenth-century French Enlightenment. Descartes's rationalist dualism was eventually eclipsed by the powerful monistic systems of Benedictus de Spinoza, Gottfried Wilhelm von Leibniz, and Georg Wilhelm Friedrich Hegel. However, as late nineteenth-century philosophy turned away from grand systems and focused its attention on the thinking subject, Descartes's ideas elicited renewed interest among philosophers and scientists. For example, the influence of Cartesian rationalism can be discerned in such important modern schools of thought as phenomenology and structuralism. Furthermore Cartesian thinking has affected researchers in a variety of fields, including psychology and linguistics, as evidenced by Noam Chomsky's strong emphasis on innate, mental, non-empirical factors operant in the process of language acquisition. Therefore, the *Discourse on Method* and the *Meditations* continue to be seen as central to the Western intellectual tradition.

PRINCIPAL WORKS

Discours de la méthode de bien conduire sa raison et chercher la vérité dans les sciences; plus la dioptrique; les météores; et la géométrie, qui sont des essais de cette méthode (philosophical prose) 1637
[*Discourse on the Method of Properly Guiding the Reason in the Search for Truth in the Sciences; also the Dioptric, the Meteors and the Geometry, which are Essays in This Method,* 1649]

Meditationes de prima philosophia, in quibus Dei existentia et animae humanae a corpore distinctio demonstrantur (philosophical prose) 1641-2
[*Meditations on First Philosophy, in which the Existence of God and the Distinction between Mind and Body are Demonstrated,* 1680]

Le monde de M. Descartes, ou le traité de la lumière (philosophical prose) 1644
[*The World,* 1979]

Principia philosophia (philosophical prose) 1644
[*Principles of Philosophy,* 1983]

Traité des passions de l'âme (philosophical prose) 1649
[*The Passions of the Soul,* 1650]

Regulae ad directionem ingenii (philosophical prose) 1701
[*Rules for the Direction of the Mind,* 1952]

Oeuvres de Descartes 13 vols. (philosophical prose) 1897-1913

Philosophical Works of Descartes 2 vols. (philosophical prose) 1955

The Essential Writings of René Descartes (philosophical prose) 1977

Samuel Taylor Coleridge (lecture date 1819)

[*An English poet and critic, Coleridge was central to the English Romantic movement and is considered one of the greatest literary critics in the English language. In the following excerpt from a public lecture on continental philosophy originally given on 22 March 1819 in London, Coleridge evaluates Descartes's theory of the cogito, or thinking self.*]

Descartes was the first man who made nature utterly lifeless and godless, considered it as the subject of merely mechanical laws. And having emptied it of all its life and all that made it nature in reality, he referred all the rest to what he called "spirit", consequently "the faculty of spirit" in relation to this "matter". What must be then the perception? What was it then to perceive? What was it not? For mechanical laws prevented his admission of that. (Not, as the old Platonists would have said, perceiving the things outward; physiology had advanced too far to render that attainable.) He therefore conceived what he called "material ideas". That is, he supposed that as there were in the soul causative powers which produced images for it, so there were in the brain certain modes that pre-existed in itself and which determined it to receive such and such impressions rather than others, and these he had called "material ideas". And in consequence of their origin being in the organization itself, he had named them "innate ideas", in both senses; first of all, the true ideas, or spiritual ones, he conceived as having their birth place in the mind; and secondly, those material ideas he considered innate, as having their birth place in the organization. But the Jesuit, Voetius, . . . had attacked this on the ground that Locke proceeds on, but the answer Descartes (who was a truly great man) makes is this: "I said innate not connate, I spoke of the birthplace not the time. Do you suppose that either I or any man in his senses, nay, I will add, that any man out of his senses, could imagine such an absurdity as that men heard *before* they heard, that they had images *before* they saw? These things are too absurd to be attributed to any man in his senses, much more to a philosopher." But still admitting that, and taking Descartes without his material hypothesis at all, nothing can be more simple than what he says or more agreeable to common sense. And what indeed was not first stated by Descartes it would <*not*> be difficult to find anywhere among the Schoolmen in which you will find the same things said, or among the ancient metaphysicians, which is simply this: that there must be a difference in the perceptions of a mouse and a man, but this difference cannot be in the object perceived but in the percipient; that therefore, says Descartes, we have reason to suppose that there are two sorts of ideas or thoughts. If, says he, two really be two, (these are Descartes' own words and I am now speaking logically and as a grammarian, not as a mathematician) if there are two, *they show these* differences. One is of those thoughts or images in which we are conscious of being passive; those which are impressed upon us whether we will or no, and those (as appearing to have their causes externally) we call external ideas. But, says he, there are others in which the mind is conscious of its own activity, and tracing its own operations, forms notions which from the place of their origin are all innate ideas. He then goes on with a definition which is noticeable (you may see it in his answer to Voetius) by being word for word the same as Locke's definition of the ideas of reflection, so that in truth the man-of-straw that was to be thrown down never existed, but the real assertion to be opposed was not merely in substance but *totidem verbis* [*identical with*] the idea in Locke's "ideas of reflection." (pp. 376-78)

Samuel Taylor Coleridge, "Descartes, Spinosa, Leibnitz, Locke, Kant, Schelling," in his The Philosophical Lectures of Samuel Taylor Coleridge, *edited by Kathleen Coburn, Philosophical Library, Inc., 1949, pp. 368-91.*

L. Lévy-Bruhl (essay date 1901)

[*Lévy-Bruhl was a French philosopher and sociologist noted for his studies of the psyche and religion of primitive peoples. In the following excerpt, Lévy-Bruhl gives a general overview of Descartes's philosophical system.*]

With Descartes a new period of modern philosophy begins. It is not, indeed, a beginning in a literal sense: there is no such thing in the history of ideas, nor elsewhere. Descartes, who came after the great scientific and philosophical illumination of the sixteenth century, had profited largely by it. He owed much to the Italian Renaissance, and not less to the Renaissance in France and in England. He was acquainted with the discoveries of contemporary men of science, such as Galileo, Torricelli, and Harvey. Even scholastic philosophy, which he was to combat, left a lasting impression upon his mind.

However, after we have considered all the influences, both of the past and of the present, which were exercised upon him, the originality of Descartes shines out all the more conspicuously, and we see the more clearly that he initiated a new philosophic method. Hegel called him a hero, and this hyperbole may in a certain sense be justified. Descartes had, indeed, no vocation for martyrdom. But nature had endowed him with that higher sort of courage which is love of truth and devotion to science; and if the name of hero is due the men whose exertions have laid open new paths for human thought, Descartes is undoubtedly entitled to the name.

The attitude of Descartes toward the philosophers who preceded him is remarkable,—he deliberately ignores them. Although well acquainted with their works, he builds his own system as if he knew nothing of them. He wishes to depend solely on his own method and reason. Not that he personally holds in contempt either the ancient or the modern philosophers. He is not so presumptuous as to believe that his mind is superior to theirs. He even acknowledges that many truths had been discovered before he created his method, but these truths he does not wish to accept on tradition. He is determined to discover them for himself. By means of his method he proposes to obtain these truths, no longer mixed pell-mell with the mass of doubtful or erroneous opinions, but set in their right places, and accompanied with their proofs. Thus only do they become valuable and useful. For a truth, when isolated, sporadic, and floating and unconnected with the truths that have gone before it, and consequently powerless to develop those that are to come after it, is of slight interest in itself. To acquire such a truth is not worth the trouble we must take in order to understand ancient books, and the time we lose in learning the ancient languages. All this time were better employed in training our reason to grasp the necessary concatenation of truths as deducible one from another.

This is already a first motive, and a quite sufficient one, for Descartes to dispense with erudition and to take no account of traditional doctrine. But he has another and more weighty one. He seeks not what is probable, but what is true. Now the first requisite in finding what is true he takes to be the casting aside of the philosophy taught in his time, which contented itself with probability and gave no satisfactory demonstrations. Therefore, though he occasionally retains the vocabulary of scholasticism (for instance in the greater part of his ***Meditations***), though he even borrows some of his matter from it (for instance, in the ontological argument, in the theory of continuous creation), nevertheless Descartes broke distinctly and completely with the method and spirit of the philosophy which had been handed down from antiquity through the vicissitudes of the Middle Ages and the struggles of the Renaissance. Even what he seems to borrow from it, he really transforms. Cartesianism not only has a positive meaning, which we shall presently study, but it has to begin with a critical function, and proposes first of all to do away with a philosophical system which, appealing to substantial forms and occult causes, claimed to explain everything and could demonstrate nothing.

There is accordingly something more in his attitude to his predecessors than a mere protest against the authoritative method,—a protest which had already been raised by eloquent voices in the sixteenth century and even earlier. We have in it, in fact, a set determination to consider the generally accepted philosophy as null and void, and to replace it with another which shall owe nothing to the former. A bold undertaking, not merely of a reformative but of a revolutionary nature. In England, Bacon, while combating the Scholastic Philosophy in the matter of experimental method, nevertheless derived from it his conception of physical reality. Hobbes, however much he may have freed himself from traditional metaphysics, is nevertheless the heir of the later great English scholastics. In Germany likewise, the genius of Leibniz is one of conservatism as well as of innovation. He openly disapproves of Descartes's excessive severity toward scholasticism, of which, for his part, he preserves a great deal, in his doctrine as well as in his terminology. Therefore we see his successor Wolf restoring, so to speak, a new scholastic system based on the philosophy of Leibniz. It was this philosophy that Kant imbibed; and later on, after Kant's *Kritik,* a kind of new scholasticism appeared (in the school of Hegel for instance), indisputably related to that of the Middle Ages. Thus, in Germany, the thread of philosophical tradition was never entirely broken.

In France, owing to Descartes, the case was altogether different. The Cartesian philosophy aimed at nothing less than the utter destruction of its rival. It prevailed; and, as early as the latter part of the seventeenth century, the victory was complete. This was both favorable and unfavorable to the progress of French philosophy. Of course, it was no small advantage for the latter to free itself from the prestige of antiquity, from the tyranny of scholasticism, to regain its full independence, and to draw its inspiration freely from the spirit of the mathematical and physical sciences, the increasing power of which was a genuinely new element in the life of mankind. To this the success of Cartesianism, and the fact that its method persisted, even after the doctrine was discarded, bear sufficient testimony. But on the other hand, certain displeasing characteristics of French philosophy in the eighteenth century may, at least in some measure, have originated in this breaking with tradition. A taste for abstract and too simple solutions, a conviction that it is sufficient to argue soundly upon evident principles in order to discover the truth, even in the most complex problems of social life—in short, a lack of historical spirit, with which the French philosophy of that period has been reproached—all these faults are owing in some measure to the spirit of Cartesianism. Certain it is that Descartes and his followers, in their contest with tradition, failed to appreciate its value and necessary function.

Nothing is so significant in this respect as the way in which these writers speak of history. As it is not a science, it cannot possibly be the basis of a school. It may entertain us, but it cannot really teach us. It is even liable to beget false ideas, and to be an encouragement to extravagant undertakings. And, logically speaking, whatever rests on historical claims only is insufficiently justified. This last maxim may, in practice, have most serious consequences. Descartes foresaw the attempt that would be made to extend its application to political and social problems. He therefore openly disclaims beforehand this application, which he personally refuses to make. Yet if he wishes us to abstain from criticising existing institutions, it is in his case, as in Montaigne's, for reasons of utility alone. One can easily imagine circumstances in which considerations of utility would favor the other side. It is, then, a mere question of expediency.

This tendency to claim that reason alone ought to be the basis of opinion, because reason alone can demonstrate it to be true, and the consequent tendency to make free use of rational criticism, appear in the history which Descartes gives us of his mind. Of all that he learned at school, nothing satisfied him except mathematics. Hardly had he freed himself from the sway of his masters (the best, he says, there were then in Europe), when he deliberately set about forgetting their teaching. He speaks only with irony of the various sciences, or so-called sciences: medicine, law, philosophy, as they were taught in his day. He coolly turns his back on belles lettres, and holds history in contempt. Geometry alone found favor in his eyes; still he wondered greatly at its being used only as an object of amusement for the curious, and that "on so firm a basis nothing more lofty had been established." The ground was now cleared; Descartes could begin to build.

According to some, Descartes is first of all a man of science, and secondly a philosopher. According to others, the philosopher in him predominates over the man of science. In point of fact, philosophy and science were not separated in Descartes's view. He seeks to establish the system of truths accessible to man—a system which he conceived as unique, and which may be figured as an endless chain. And he seeks it in order to find the means of living as uprightly and happily as possible. Thus the end which Descartes has in view is a righteous and happy life: wherein he agrees with the philosophers of his time, and, we may also say, of all times.

In order to attain to this righteous and happy life, leaving out of account the teachings of religion, Descartes sees no sure way but the possession of truth or science. Now science, in its turn, rests on metaphysics, or primary philosophy, whence it derives its principles. Therefore Descartes proposes to be a metaphysician; but this he will be for the sake of science itself. Metaphysics is to him a road, but indeed a road of paramount importance, since all the rest depends upon the principles discovered therein. Besides, mathematics, physics, and other theoretical sciences are also roads, the terminal point lying in the applied sciences, to which they lead. "The whole of philosophy," says Descartes, in the Preface to the ***Principes de la Philosophie,*** "is like a tree, the roots of which are metaphysics; the trunk is the science of physics; and the branches shooting from that trunk are all the other sciences, which may be reduced to three main ones, viz., medicine, mechanics, and ethics, by which last I mean the highest and most perfect ethics, which, since it presupposes a complete knowledge of the other sciences, is the supreme degree of wisdom."

Thus if Descartes is careful to make a distinction between the sphere of action and that of knowledge, and if, before undertaking the long and difficult task of seeking after truth, he provides himself with a "provisional" ethics, which he unquestioningly accepts from authority and custom, he nevertheless proclaims the principles of action to be dependent upon knowledge. It is the business of reason not only to enlighten, but also to guide us. Descartes, believing in the future progress of mankind, considers it to be dependent on the development of the sciences. We even observe, in several passages, that the progress of ethics appears to him subordinate to that of mechanics and of medicine. But these in their turn depend for their advancement upon the establishment of a sound and rigorously demonstrated physical science. Thus, although science is not its own end, the fundamental problem of philosophy according to Descartes is finally reduced to the problem of the establishment of science.

Now there is no breach of continuity between metaphysics and physics; on the contrary, there is a natural and necessary transition from the one to the other. Descartes attempted to build up a system by means of which one could proceed uninterruptedly from the first principles of cognition and of being, in a world, from God, down to the most specific scientific proposition of physiology or of ethics, without one link missing in the chain. A bold conception, which dominates the whole system and is inseparable from the famous method of Descartes.

Up to this point mathematics alone appeared to Descartes worthy of being called a science. It differs from everything else he had learned in the perfect lucidity of its principles, in the rigorous demonstration of its propositions, and in the inevitable sequence of its truths. But to what does it owe these characteristics, if not to the method from which mathematicians make it a rule never to depart? Therefore, in order to establish the science or philosophy sought by Descartes, it was sufficient to find a method that should be to philosophy what the method of mathematical deduction is to arithmetic, algebra and geometry.

To apply to that universal science conceived by Descartes the method so effectively employed in the above-mentioned sciences would evidently be the simplest solution of the problem proposed. But this solution is impracticable. The mathematical method, as we see it practiced in "the analysis of the ancients and the algebra of the moderns" is a special method, limited to the study of figures in geometry, and confined in algebra to symbols and rules which hamper the mind. How could one pass from these processes, which are especially adapted to particular sciences, to the general method required by general science or philosophy? Descartes would undoubtedly never have conceived such an audacious hope, had not a great discovery of his set him on this track. He had invented analytical geometry, or the method of expressing by means of equations the properties of geometrical figures, or, inversely, of representing determinate equations by means of geometrical figures. In this way, Descartes substituted for the old methods, which were especially adapted to algebra and geometry as distinct branches, a general method, applicable to what he called the "universal mathematical science," viz., to the study of "the various ratios or proportions to be found between the objects of the mathematical sciences, hitherto regarded as distinct." Not only did this discovery mark a decisive epoch in the history of mathematics, which it provided with an instrument of incomparable simplicity and power, but it furthermore gave Descartes a right to hope for the philosophical method he was seeking. Ought not a last generalization to be possible, by means of which the method he had so happily discovered should become applicable, not only to the "universal mathematical science," but also to the systematic combination of all the truths which our finite minds may permit us to attain?

Thus was formed in Descartes's mind the method which he summed up in the ***Discours de la Methode,*** and which was destined in his plan to replace the useless and sterile ancient logic. It is inexpedient here to explain these rules minutely. We must, however, observe that the first one, "Never to accept a thing as true which I do not clearly know to be such," is not, properly speaking, a precept of method. Such precepts are set forth in a subsequent set of rules, where Descartes successively prescribes analysis for dividing difficulties into parts, and synthesis for constructing and expounding science. But the first rule is quite different. It does not lay down a process to be used in order to discover truth. It concerns method only in so far as method is not separated from science itself (and such indeed was Descartes's meaning). If such is the case, the first step of method—or of science—must be to determine accurately by what mark we can recognize what is to be regarded as true, and what is to be set aside as being only probable or dubious. This mark is what we call evidence. This first rule may have been suggested to Descartes, as the others were, by mathematics. Even as in his method he generalized the processes used for mathematical researches and demonstrations, so in this formula he laid down the regulating principle to which this science owes its perfection, and which was also to become the regulating principle of the new philosophy.

Thus the famous rule of "evidence" reaches far beyond the scope of a mere principle of method. Both from what it excludes and what it implies, it may be looked upon as the motto of the Cartesian philosophy. It rejects, to begin with, any knowledge grounded upon authority alone (excepting the truths of religion). Even though Aristotle and all his commentators were agreed on one opinion, this would be no proof of its being true; and should it really chance to be so, the authority of Aristotle would count for nothing towards establishing its standing in science. Nothing can be admitted in science but what is evident; i. e., nothing but what is so clear and plain as to leave no possible doubt, or is soundly deduced from principles which rest on such evidence. The whole system of scholasticism: metaphysics, logic, physics, thus stand irretrievably condemned *in toto.* The so-called moral sciences, which cannot attain to a degree of evidence comparable to that of mathematics, and which have to content themselves with more or less strong probability, are likewise rejected by the Cartesian formula; in fact, Descartes, as has already been observed, had but little esteem for history and erudition.

But what makes this rule of paramount importance is, that it establishes reason as supreme judge of what is false or true. Reason thus proclaims its own sovereign right to decide without appeal. What we are to think, to believe, and to do should be determined solely by evidence; and of that evidence reason alone is judge (except in the case of urgency compelling us to immediate action). It is true, reason being identical in all men, that such truth as becomes evident to one of them becomes so to all other men likewise. Therefore the assent given to evidence by one mind is by implication equivalent to the universal consent of mankind; so that the individual reason which distinguishes between true and false is precisely the universal feature in every man.

Nevertheless, Descartes felt the danger that lay in his formula. He foresaw the very serious misunderstandings to which it might give rise, and he endeavored to prevent these by taking multifarious precautions. First of all, the truths of religion are carefully set apart and withdrawn from the criticism of reason. They do not fall under its jurisdiction. It is not ours to examine them, but to believe them. According to Descartes, we must seek neither to adapt them to our reason, nor to adapt our reason to them. They belong to another domain. Then Descartes makes a distinction between the sphere of knowledge and that of conduct; he submits to provisional ethics, which is to be replaced by definitive ethics only when science is completed, that is to say, in a still remote future. Moreover, even in the province of speculative thought Descartes refrains from touching upon political and social questions. He censures "those blundering and restless humours" ever ready to propose unasked-for reforms. Thus, after moral and religious problems, political problems in their turn are cautiously set aside. Where, then, shall the absolute sovereignty of reason be exercised? In philosophy, in abstract sciences, in physics; in short, wherever men generally have no other interest but that of pure truth.

Well-meant precautions these were, no doubt, but vain precautions, too. Let reason rule supreme over this apparently limited province, and by degrees it will invade the others. If we allow it, as a principle, the right to decide without appeal between falsehood and truth, it soon will admit of no restrictions but those it sets of its own accord through the works of a Kant or of an Auguste Comte. In fact, French philosophy in the eighteenth century was in the main an endeavor to apply the spirit of the Cartesian method to the very objects: politics, ethics, religion, which Descartes had carefully set apart. By holding nothing as true until I have evidence of its being so, do I not in advance deprive all historical rights of the means of securing recognition; do I not thereby summon all privileges, institutions, beliefs, and fortunes to produce their title deeds before the bar of reason? By solemnly paying homage to Descartes, the "Assemblée Constituante" proved that the spirit of the Revolution was conscious of one of its chief sources.

Being now in possession of his method, did not Descartes have all that was necessary to construct his philosophic system with absolute mathematical certainty? No, for in mathematics the foundation principles: axioms and definitions, are so plain and evident that no reasonable mind will question them. But philosophy had until his time been wanting in such principles, and the object which Descartes has in view is precisely to establish them.

To attain this end, he first casts aside as false (at least provisionally) all the opinions which he has hitherto held as true, and which are only probable. In order to avoid tedious enumerations, he proposes to consider opinions from the point of view of their sources. "For instance," says he, "having sometimes found my senses deceitful, I will distrust all that they teach me. As I have sometimes erred with regard to very simple reasoning, I will distrust the results of even the most positive sciences. Lastly, I may suppose that an evil genius, who is all-powerful, takes delight in making me err, even when I believe I see the truth most plainly. Therefore, by a voluntary effort, which is always possible since I am free, I will suspend my judgment even in cases where the evidence seems to me irresistible. "Is there any proposition which is not affected by this 'hyperbolical' doubt? There is one, and one only. Let my senses deceive me, let my reasonings be false, let an evil genius delude me concerning things which appear to me most certain; if I am mistaken, it is because I am—and this truth 'I think, therefore I am,' *cognito, ergo sum,* is so self-evident and so certain that the most extravagant doubt of skeptics is unable to shake it." Here, then, is the first principle of philosophy sought for by Descartes. And even as Archimedes asked only a standing-place to lift the world, so Descartes, having found a *quid inconcussum,* an indisputable proposition, set to work to erect his whole system upon this foundation.

However, if according to the custom of philosophers we distinguish the sphere of knowledge from that of existence, this proposition, or, as it is called, Descartes's *cogito,* is certainly first in the sphere of knowledge; for I may have doubts about whatever I may think, but about my thinking I can have no doubt, even in the very moment when I doubt. But in the sphere of existence the Absolute—that is, God—comes first. Therefore Descartes, as soon as he had established the *cogito,* turned to demonstrating the existence of God. He knows that he thinks, but he also knows that he doubts, and therefore that he is imperfect; for not knowing instead of knowing is an imperfection. He therefore has an idea of perfection. Whence comes this idea? Descartes examines all the conjectures which may be made as to its origin; he eliminates them one after another as inadequate until one only remains, viz., that the idea of perfection cannot have sprung from experience, that we could not have it if the all-perfect Being—that is, God—did not actually exist, and that therefore this idea is as "the stamp left by the workman upon his work."

Descartes was bound to demonstrate the existence of God at the very outset. Otherwise, the supposition of an evil genius, who was able to deceive him even when he conceived things with perfect clearness, would have cast suspicion upon all propositions but the *cogito;* the doubt which he himself had raised would have paralyzed him. In order to do away with such a supposition, Descartes at once proceeds to demonstrate the existence of an all-perfect God, who cannot possibly wish to deceive us. But is not this a syllogistic circle? If the plainest argument, in order to be accepted as valid, needs the guaranty of God, what will guarantee the argument intended to prove the existence of God?

A syllogistic circle, indeed, had not Descartes escaped from it with the help of the following reasons: God's guaranty is necessary, not for the sake of the evidence, which is quite sufficient in itself so long as it lasts (whereof the *cogito* is a proof); but in order to assure me of the truth of propositions which I remember having admitted as evident without remembering for what reasons. It is necessary, in short, wherever memory intervenes, but only in that case. Now if we have no need of memory to know that we think, neither do we need it to know that God exists. In spite of the syllogistic form which Descartes gave to the proof of the existence of God, this proof is rather intuitive than grounded on formal reasoning. In the act of conceiving the idea of the all-perfect Being, I *see* at the same time the impossibility of His not existing. The existence of all other things is looked upon as only possible; but the existence of God appears as evidently necessary, being comprised in the very notion of God. This is no argument, but rather an immediate apprehension. It is, as Malebranche said shortly afterward, a proof "from mere vision." The syllogistic circle therefore was only apparent. Descartes was right in establishing the existence of God immediately after the *cogito.* Henceforward he could in all confidence make use of the faculties given him by God, who never deceives. He only needed now to follow out his method carefully, and to link propositions together in the requisite order, in order to arrive infallibly at the truth.

Now, the requisite order is, to begin with things which are most general, simple and easy to grasp; that is, with the primary principles from which the other truths are to be deduced. Physics therefore is not to be studied until metaphysics is well grounded. Acting upon this precept, Descartes first established the existence of an absolute and perfect Being—that is, God; for the same reason he now proceeds to ascertain the essence of the soul and of the body. To reach this end his starting-point is again the *cogito.*

I think, I am; but what am I? A creature that thinks; that is to say, judges, remembers, feels, imagines and wills; a being whose existence is not linked to any place, nor dependent upon any material thing. Descartes has just got out of his universal doubt by means of the *cogito.* The only thing the existence of which he can maintain at this point is his own thought. Now, the existence of his thought does not appear to him to be necessarily linked to that of his body and dependent upon the latter. On the contrary, he may suppose that his body does not exist and that the perception of the external world and of his own members is an illusion. He is even unable for the present to reject this supposition; he cannot do so till later on, and even then with some difficulty. Nevertheless, since he thinks, he is certain he exists. But, conversely, let him for a moment suppose that he ceases to think; upon this supposition he ceases to exist, although all external bodies and his own body should remain real. Therefore, the cognition of his own being, which is his thought, by no means depends on material things, the existence of which is still problematic. Therefore his whole nature is to think.

"You suppose," some opponent said to Descartes, "that your own body does not exist, and you say that nevertheless you continue to think. But should your supposition prove true—that is to say, should your body and your brain be dissolved—can you affirm that *even then* you would continue to think?" To which Descartes answered: "I do not assert this—at least not now. My present object is not to demonstrate the immortality of the soul. This is a metaphysical question I am not now able to solve—for I know only one fact as yet, viz., that I think (and also that God exists). The whole question I am examining is merely: 'What am I?' Now it appears from what has been said that my existence is known to me as that of a being endowed with thought and endowed only with thought; for, whilst I am as certain as possible of the existence of my thought, the existence of anything else is still wholly doubtful to me. The existence of this thought may possibly be actually connected with that of the brain. I know nothing about that. I am not discussing that for the present. One thing is certain: I know myself as a thought, and I positively do not know myself as a brain."

This is one of the leading features of the philosophy of Descartes, and one which may enable us to measure his influence, by comparing what had been thought before him with what was thought after him. The *cogito* of Descartes displaced, so to speak, the axis of philosophy. To the ancients and to the scholastics (theology excepted) the thinking mind appeared inseparable from the universe, regarded as the object of its thought, just as the soul itself was conceived to be the "substantial form" of the living body. According to Descartes, on the contrary, the existence of the thinking mind, far from being dependent on any other existing thing, is the essential condition of every other existence conceivable to us; for if I am certain of the existence of anything but myself, with far better reason am I certain that I, who have that thought, am in existence. The only reality I cannot possibly question is that of my own thought.

Both the adversaries and the successors of Descartes started from this point. All the modern forms of idealism, so utterly different from the idealism of the ancients, have a common origin in the *cogito.* The tempered and prudent idealism of Locke, the Christian idealism of Malebranche, the skeptical idealism of Hume, the transcendental idealism of Kant, the absolute idealism of Fichte and many other doctrines derived from these, which have appeared in our century, are all more or less closely related to the foundation principle of the Cartesian philosophy. Moreover, the conception of nature in modern science must also be connected with it. For, as we shall see farther on, when Descartes set thought—that is, the soul—so distinctly apart from everything extraneous to itself, in so doing he made necessary a new conception of force and life in the material world.

Now, let us add to the Cartesian formula, "I am a thing which thinks," the following principle, "All that I conceive clearly and distinctly is true." Then, since I conceive clearly and distinctly that the nature of the body and that of the soul have no attributes in common, therefore it is true that these two natures or substances are separated one from the other. Not only is there no need of my having any notion of the body in order to comprehend the soul, but also the soul has no need of the body in order to exist.

Descartes, therefore, had a right to infer that "the soul is more easily known than the body." This does not mean that, according to his doctrine, psychology is an easier science than physics or physiology. Psychology as we conceive it has no place in the system of Descartes; there is at most a mere sketch of it in the ***Passions de l' Ame.*** But this maxim is metaphysical, not psychological. It means that there is no more evident knowledge than that which the soul has of itself, since there is none which it is more impossible to doubt; that the body, on the contrary, is known only representatively, and that, far from our being unable to doubt its existence, we cannot overcome such a doubt, when once raised, save by means of laborious and complicated reasonings.

In order to make all this clearer still, let us remember Descartes's oft-repeated caution to "cast off all the impressions of the senses and imagination and trust to reason alone." There are not two kinds of evidence: one which tells us that the sun shines, that honey is sweet, that lead is heavy; and another which informs us that if equals be added to equals the sums are equal. Only the latter proposition is self-evident; the former statements, in spite of any prepossession to the contrary, are not so. The impressions of the senses are vivid, but confused; we cannot account for them, and nothing can warrant them to be true. The water which is warm to me seems cold to you. Cold and heat, as well as all other qualities pertaining to bodies, with the exception of extension, are not inherent in them; they are relative to the sentient subject. Therefore, if we think we know bodies by what our senses teach us of them, we fall into error, as will happen every time when, through overhastiness or prejudice, we form a judgment before the evidence is complete. For can I not have in a dream all the perceptions I now have and be as firmly persuaded of their reality? But whether I am dreaming or waking it is true that two and two are four, and it is true that I, who think so, am in existence.

Thus, previous to philosophical reflection, nothing seems to us so well known as the body and its qualities, because we form images of them continually and without any difficulty; whereas it is not easy for us to realize what the soul is, seeing that it is not an object for the imagination to grasp. The first task of the philosopher consists precisely in disengaging himself from the false light of the senses and seeking the true light of reason. It is an effort akin to the one demanded by Plato, when he termed philosophy the science of the invisible, and recommended the study of mathematics as a preparatory training. The body and the organs of the senses, far from making us acquainted with what really is, are a hindrance to the proper activity of the mind. Even matter, which we fancy our hands, eyes, ears, etc., can apprehend immediately, we really know only by means of our understanding. For the latter alone can give us a distinct notion of it, viz., the notion of a thing measurable in length, breadth and depth.

The other qualities of bodies are not really inherent in them. "Look at this piece of wax; it has just been taken from the hive; it has not yet lost the sweetness of the honey it contained; it still retains something of the fragrance of the flowers from which it was gathered; its color, figure and size are apparent; it is hard, cold, easily handled, and if you strike it will give forth some sound. But now, while I am speaking, somebody brings it near the fire; whatever taste remained in it is exhaled, the odor evaporates, its color changes, its shape is lost, its size increases, it becomes liquid, it is warmer, one can hardly handle it, and when we strike it, it will no longer give forth a sound." And yet the same wax is there. Therefore this wax was neither the honey-sweet flavor, nor the pleasant flowery smell, nor the whiteness, nor the form, nor the sound, but merely a body which, a short time before, was apparent to my senses under these forms, but now presents itself under other forms. Therefore all I can *conceive* clearly and distinctly about this body is its extension.

Descartes's definition of the soul is "a thing that thinks"; of the body, "a thing that has extension." This doctrine is strangely at variance with the metaphysics taught in his time. The scholastic philosophers, who on this point followed the teaching of Aristotle, regarded the soul as both the principle of life and the principle of thought. The same soul which in plants is purely nutritive, becomes locomotive, then sensitive in animals, and lastly, in man, rational. And though such a doctrine made the immortality of the soul a difficult thing to conceive, it was no cause of embarrassment to the schoolmen, for immortality to them was an object of faith, not of demonstration. There is neither a nutritive nor a locomotive soul, says Descartes. There is but one kind of soul, which is the thinking soul, for feeling is thinking. Nutrition and locomotion are explainable simply by the laws of mechanics. Animals, which do not think, do not feel either. They may be looked upon as automatons, and the perfection of some of their actions may be compared to the perfection of the workings of a clock. After this we can no longer suppose that the destiny of man after death is the same as that of flies and ants.

Scholastic physics likewise assumed the existence of forces and occult causes inherent in matter, and thought the specific nature of certain natural phenomena could not otherwise be accounted for. Here again Descartes adopts the reverse of their doctrine, rejecting *in toto* these assumed principles, forces and causes, which to him are but confused notions, hypotheses convenient to sluggish minds, explanations which explain nothing, but merely repeat the enunciation of the problem under another form. Given matter, that is, extension as considered by geometricians, he wants no other data than number, motion and duration. These are sufficient, he considers, to account for all the phenomena which take place in bodies either inorganic or living.

Thus Descartes's physical science is purely rational in character and in scrupulous accordance with the rule of his method which forbids him to "accept anything as true unless it appears by evidence to be so." It tends to assume a geometrical form, and all questions of physics are reduced, at least in principle, to problems of mechanics. "Give me matter and the laws of motion," says Descartes, "and I will build a universe exactly like the one that we behold, with skies, stars, sun and earth, and on the earth minerals, plants and animals; in short, everything that experience introduces to us, except the rational soul of man."

No doubt Descartes imagined all natural phenomena, and in particular those of animated beings, to be less complicated than they really are. His conceptions are those of a great mathematician, living at a time when physics and chemistry hardly existed and when biology did not exist at all. He thinks he can determine *a priori* the number of the fixed stars. He imagines he can describe accurately the formation of the fœtus. He hopes, by taking due care of the human machine and by repairing it when necessary, to protract the life of man indefinitely, to conquer disease and even death. Scientific men in our days are better acquainted with the difficulties of such problems and are consequently less pretentious. But the scientific ideal they aim at, though indefinitely removed from that which we are considering, has remained pretty much the same as Descartes conceived it: to discover the laws of every phenomenon by reducing them, as far as possible, to number and measure, and to discard every metaphysical hypothesis meant to explain any class of physical phenomena.

This geometrical conception of the material universe was repeatedly attacked by the successors of Descartes. Leibniz endeavored to prove that the Cartesian definition of matter was incompatible with the laws of motion. Leibniz is fond of connecting Democritus and Descartes, and is wont to quote them together. The parallel is an ingenious one, but should not be followed up too closely. No doubt Descartes, like Democritus, requires only matter and motion in order to explain the genesis of the physical universe. But, to say nothing of the very considerable differences between the explanation of Democritus and that of Descartes, can anyone forget that the physical science of Democritus and his metaphysics are all one and the same thing? Atoms and vacuum are to him the primal elements of all things, and, as was objected to him by Aristotle, he does not take the trouble even to explain the origin of motion. With Descartes, before physics is begun a complete metaphysical system has first been established, and it is from this that physics is to derive its principles: the primordial laws of phenomena (for instance, that light propagates itself in straight lines) are deduced from God's attributes. Moreover, Descartes is not compelled by his system, as Democritus is, to deny the existence of final causes. On the contrary, he maintains their existence. It is true that he forbids us to seek them out, but the reason is that, according to him, it would be highly presumptuous in us mortals to try to comprehend God's designs; the more so as God's liberty is absolute and infinite, and since, in consequence, His acts may be wholly unintelligible to our reason. And lastly, far from looking upon matter as self-existent, Descartes believes that bodies, as well as all other finite things, exist only by God's express will and constant help. Should this help cease for an instant all bodies would at once sink back into nothingness.

The mechanical character of Descartes's system, if mechanical it be, is therefore far removed from the materialism of Democritus. Descartes firmly maintained the reality of freewill, to which he ascribes an essential part in his theory of judgment and of error. It is only as physicist, not as philosopher, that Descartes may be termed mechanical. But in this sense nearly all men of science are so, too; for, to use F. A. Lange's striking expression: "Mechanism is an excellent formula for the science of nature."

But is not, however, the strictly deductive science conceived by Descartes very remote from the modern science of nature, which employs the experimental method with so much zeal and success? True, Descartes often thought deduction easy when it was difficult, and possible when it was impracticable. But this was a question of fact, not of principle. As this or that branch of science (at least, of physical science) is gradually brought nearer to perfection, we see it grow from the experimental into the rational. Such has long been the case with astronomy and celestial mechanics, and later, successively with optics, with acoustics, with hydrodynamics, with the theory of heat and electricity and other fields of physics, all so many confirmations of the Cartesian ideal.

Moreover, Descartes himself assigned an important rôle to the experimental method. Anecdotes depict him to us as rising very early, in Amsterdam, in order to choose in a butcher's shop the joints he wished "to anatomize at leisure"; or answering an inquirer who wished to see his library, "Here it is," at the same time pointing to a quarter of veal which he was busily dissecting. In the last years of his life he devoted only a few hours a year to mathematics, and not much more to metaphysics. He busied himself almost exclusively with experiments in physics and physiology. How could he have failed to appreciate the importance of a method which he was himself so assiduously putting into practice?

"Anticipating causes with effects," is Descartes's felicitous definition of experimenting. It clearly shows the functions he ascribed to it. Were there only one way in which a certain effect might be deduced from given causes, experimenting would be unnecessary. But natural phenomena are so complex, and the possible combinations of causes are so numerous, that we may nearly always explain in several ways the production of a given effect. Which is the right way? Experiment alone can decide. Let us make a distinction between science already developed and science which is developing. To expound a developed science the suitable method is deduction,—descent from causes to effects. But science which is developing cannot yet adopt this method; and to discover unknown laws, it must employ the experimental method, must anticipate causes with effects.

Descartes had written a ***Traite du Monde*** and was about to publish it, when the condemnation of Galileo for heresies concerning the motion of the earth altered his resolution. Being, above all, desirous to work in peace, and to postpone as long as he could a perhaps inevitable conflict with the theologians, he published only a few fragments of his physical theories, and put a summary sketch of it into the admirable fifth part of the ***Discours de la Methode.*** We must certainly deplore the loss of this great work, which would throw light upon many an obscure point in the Cartesian philosophy. But, after all, the essential part of the doctrine did not lie here, any more than in the well-known hypothesis of "vortices," which the Cartesian philosophers of the eighteenth century vainly tried to set up in opposition to the principle of universal gravitation discovered by Newton, and with which some physicists now partly agree in their theories of matter.

The main interest lies elsewhere, viz., in the perfect character of the science of nature, of which Descartes had such a clear and precise notion, even though he was far from being able to put it into practice save in a few points (for instance, by his discoveries in optics). It is said that the man who invented the plough still walks, invisible, beside the peasant who drives his own plough in our days. I might almost say that, in our laboratories, Descartes stands invisible and present, investigating with our scientific men the laws of phenomena.

If he had lived, would he have passed on from the sciences of life to the ethical and social sciences, as he had done already from mathematics to physics, and from physics to anatomy and physiology? This may be doubted. To say nothing of considerations of prudence, to which Descartes was most susceptible, he held in slight esteem the visionaries and political reformers of the sixteenth century, and would have been sorely vexed if any comparison had been drawn between their fancies and his own doctrines. On the other hand, he could not but find it extremely difficult to make social facts fall in with his method, since, as Auguste Comte very aptly observed, so long as biology is not sufficiently advanced, social science must needs be out of the question. Now, in the time of Descartes, biology was still unborn. Even ethics he does not seem to have taken into deep consideration. He borrows the rules of his provisional ethics from Montaigne and from the Stoics. Stoicism, modified in some respects, also forms the fundamental part of Descartes's moral letters to Princess Elizabeth. It is a peculiarity of French philosophy, that it has produced many moralists and few moral theorists. The reason for this we shall seek elsewhere. Certain it is that Descartes was not one of these theorists. Perhaps he believed that scientific ethics (ethics not grounded on religious authority) could not be established till the science of man was established, and the connection of the physical and the moral better known. To this knowledge he opened the way in his ***Traite des Passions de l'Ame.***

All the precautions taken by Descartes, all his prudence, did not shield him from the attacks his philosophy was to bring upon him, as being "subtle, enticing, and bold." After hesitating a long while, the Jesuits, by whom he had been brought up at La Flèche, and among whom he had still some friends, declared themselves against his philosophy. The seventh series of *Objections,* by Father Bourdin, express the opinion of this society. Descartes wrote a vigorous reply. His quarrel with the Jesuits was one of his motives for not living in France. He established himself in Holland, where he lived a long while in undisturbed peace. But as his philosophy spread, attention was drawn to him, and as the universities of the country were beginning to quarrel about his theories, he felt that his life there would soon become unbearable. He therefore resolved to yield to the entreaties of Queen Christina, who earnestly urged him to come to Sweden. But he could not endure the severe climate of that country, and hardly six months had elapsed when he died of inflammation of the lungs. Later, his body was brought back to France.

The philosophy of Descartes was in accord with the leading tendencies of his time. The success which attended it from the moment it appeared is a proof of its opportuneness, and it is difficult to determine whether it formed, rather than expressed, the spirit of the age. Doubtless it did both. As has been said, the seventeenth century in France was preeminently the "age of reason."

> Aimez donc la raison; que toujours vos écrits,
> Empruntent d'elle seule et leur lustre et leur
> prix,

said Boileau; yet perhaps, had it not been for the Cartesian philosophy, this taste for reason might not have asserted itself so earnestly and have been so perfectly conscious of its existence.

This philosophy of "clear ideas" prevailed in France in the second half of the seventeenth century, and from France its influence spread over all Europe. Though vigorously attacked in the eighteenth century, both as to its metaphysics and its physics, it nevertheless remained discernible even in the methods of its adversaries. Locke, Hume, and Condillac had not the same conception of evidence as Descartes; but their empiricism was as fond of clearness as his rationalism had been. Newton combated the hypothesis of "vortices," but he preserved the Cartesian notion of a mechanical explanation of physical phenomena. For a thorough-going and express negation of the Cartesian spirit we must go to the end of the eighteenth century. Then the German romantic writers spring up, and maintain that the philosophy of clear ideas is false from its very principle. According to them, reality is not clear, and the more satisfactory a doctrine is to the human understanding, the surer it is to reproduce only the surface of things, while the essence of them is mysterious, intangible and inexpressible. Whence it follows that religions, arts and literatures are spontaneous philosophies, incomparably deeper than the systems produced by the conscious labor of the understanding, even as the works of nature are artistically superior to the articles manufactured by man.

The philosophy of Descartes, to tell the truth, affords but little scope to sentiment, and still less to the imagination and to the hidden and unconscious activities of the mind. It places value on evidence alone, whose vivid, but glaring light, dispels the *chiaroscuro* so dear to romantic writers. This fixed and rigid purpose has its drawbacks, which were not long in making their appearance among the followers of Descartes.

But apart from the fact that in Descartes himself the rational effort was uncommonly sincere and vigorous, at the time when this philosophy appeared it was really necessary. It was a deliverer. It put an end to superannuated doctrines, the domination of which was still heavily felt. It cleared the ground, and set physics free, once for all, from the clogs of metaphysical hypotheses. Lastly, it formulated problems which needed formulation. Descartes wished to furnish science not only with a powerful and flexible instrument such as Bacon had already sought, but also with an unchanging and immovable basis. Thence sprang the "provisional doubt," with which his method bids him begin, which obliges him to test all previously acquired information, and which may be looked upon as the starting-point of all modern theories of knowledge. For this doubt, which affects successively perception, imagination, reasoning power, and stops only before the immediate self-intuition of thought, is itself a criticism of the faculty of knowledge. It studies it in its connection both with the outward object and with the very mind which is thinking; in short, it heralds Kant's *Critique of Pure Reason.*

An innovating and fruitful doctrine nearly always develops in various directions. The various minds that receive it gradually draw from it diverse and sometimes contradictory conclusions, most of which were overlooked and would often have been disapproved of by the founder of the system. This is perhaps even truer of Descartes than of any other philosopher. Being chiefly preoccupied with the method and structure of science, he did not hesitate to leave open, at least temporarily, many important questions which his method did not require him to solve immediately. Thus it happened that metaphysical systems very different from one another were soon founded on the Cartesian principles. Spinoza adopted the definition which Descartes had given of soul and matter, but in thought and extension he saw only two attributes of one and the same substance. Beside this pantheism, appeared the idealism of Malebranche, which proceeds no less directly from Descartes; for did not the latter say that "truth is the same thing as being?" And does not the theory of continued creation lead directly to that of occasional causes? Locke, who combated Descartes on the subject of innate ideas, without understanding him exactly, has on the other hand many points in common with him; the very idea of inventorying and examining the ideas in our minds is singularly akin to the critical examination of our knowledge which, in Descartes, precedes the *cogito.* And lastly, into the idealism of Leibniz the Cartesian element enters in large measure; for instance, the notion of sensation being but a dim intellection, which is the central point of Leibniz's theory of knowledge, had already been clearly stated by Descartes.

The philosophy of Descartes is therefore a sort of crossroad whence diverge the chief ways followed by modern thought. Still, outside of France, his method has not been followed without restrictions, and his philosophy has been accepted only to be immediately combined with other elements either traditional or modern. In France, the influence has been far deeper and more enduring. There, while the Cartesian philosophy may have lost its prestige rather quickly, the Cartesian spirit, owing, doubtless, to its close affinity with the very genius of the nation, has never disappeared, and we shall recognize its influence, not only throughout the whole eighteenth century and in the French Revolution, but in all the greatest thinkers of the nineteenth century. (pp. vii-xxx)

L. Lévy-Bruhl, "Essay on Descartes," in The Meditations and Selections from the Principles of René Descartes (1596-1650), *translated by John Veitch, The Open Court Publishing Company, 1901, pp. vii-xxx.*

Sir Leslie Stephen (essay date 1902)

[*Stephen is considered one of the most important English literary critics of the late Victorian and early Edwardian era. In the following excerpt, Stephen reviews the essential philosophical principles outlined by Descartes in his* Meditations.]

Descartes' initial principle of provisional scepticism was intended to exclude [the] danger of possible prepossession. He resolved to doubt whatever could be doubted. Propositions which proved to be insoluble under this process, carefully and systematically applied, were to be regarded as definitively established. Here was the solid rock upon which to erect a flawless and imperishable creed, free from the futile logomachies of the old scholasticism. Descartes, in fact, denies the dogma of authority which asserts more or less clearly that a doctrine is to believed simply because other people have believed it. Every traditional faith was to have its credentials strictly scrutinised before its soundness could be admitted. Reason, in fact, is openly asserting its claims to be a judge of supreme and independent authority, instead of a mere accessor in the court of authority. The doctrine was gradually working its way to recognition throughout the century, though Descartes himself shrank from certain obvious applications.

This, however, is the negative side of the doctrine. Descartes did something more than protest against a blind submission to arbitrary authority. When resolving to test by his new method all existing beliefs, he did not in fact doubt that some such residuum as he sought would be discovered. He did not really expect that the provisional would have to be converted into an absolute scepticism. The method, indeed, already indicates the character of the truths which will be discovered. It is likely to disperse any doctrines articulately stated in the dogmatic form, and of which it is evident, upon inspection, that they rest upon prescription rather than reason. But it is less likely to be efficacious as against doctrines which have insinuated themselves more thoroughly, because by subtler methods. A belief which is implied in the very mode of conceiving the universe, which the philosopher, like other men, had unconsciously imbibed from his infancy, might easily pass itself off as implied in the very structure of the mind. The only test for discovering the true nature of such beliefs is afforded by the comparative method, which enables us to trace their origin and development in minds different from our own. But this mode of examination was implicitly repudiated by Descartes' first principle. The individual mind is regarded as competent to test the validity of its own beliefs by a process of direct inspection. Descartes, therefore, assumes that it is possible—and he of course converts the possibility into an actuality—that we may discover in the mind some 'innate ideas' and first principles which are a sufficient evidence for themselves. This doctrine might take various forms to evade the criticism of opponents; but in some shape or other it is implied in all the philosophical speculations to which Descartes gave the impulse, that, by passing under review the contents of our minds, we can discover some primary truths, which either reveal themselves, or are recognised as soon as revealed, and which have a validity altogether transcending that of any knowledge acquired by experience. They need no further test than their inherent clearness; and to deny them is to fall into a contradiction in terms.

The method thus announced seemed to be sanctioned by a great precedent. Mathematical knowledge was at that time not merely the typical example of deductive reasoning, but the only department of science which had been pushed far beyond its rudiments. It was natural to infer, as was inferred by Descartes and his whole school, that mathematics exhibited the normal process of all philosophy. If other sciences had not advanced equally, it was because in them men had not been faithful to the same methods of speculation. Now mathematics start from certain primary axioms which may be plausibly regarded as independent of all experience. If we know things as they are, or recognise truths independently of experience, the knowledge must necessarily be the same in every man. It is easy to invert the argument, and say what is the same to every man must be independent of experience. Every man agrees in the first principles of mathematics; therefore a mathematical truth is independent of the personal peculiarities which determine this or that man's intellectual conceptions; and therefore, it is again inferred, it is independent of all men's modes of conception, or it is a universal and absolute truth. From the primary axioms of mathematics are evolved a vast body of mutually coherent truths, each of which has equal validity with the primary truths. The mathematician defines a curve, and by the help of his axioms deduces the most remote properties. Let the metaphysician once discover the axioms suitable to his problems, and define with equal clearness the conceptions with which he is to deal, and he will be able to construct a science as complete and unalterable as that of the mathematician.

That is the vision which Descartes endeavoured to realise, and one difficulty immediately occurs. The mathematician might argue with confidence about his triangles (or so it seemed) without troubling himself to inquire whether there ever was or ever could be a triangle in the world. The propositions are certainly true on the hypothesis that there are triangles, for they flow by a logical necessity from the very definition of triangles. But to make the logic useful, we must know that the idea has a counterpart in reality. In the same way metaphysicians might construct a complete logical framework without being certain that it had any more substance than a dream. Hence the first step is to find a point of contact with reality. Once get hold of a reality, and then we have a firm centre from which our knowledge may spread along every line of thought. The logical nexus by which the properties of the idea are inferred from its definition must correspond to a causal nexus by which the properties of the object are evolved from its essence. Given the reality of space, and our geometry must correspond to fact. The celebrated *je pense, donc je suis,* supplies us with one such reality—namely, ourselves; and by a more laborious and more easily assailable reasoning, Descartes endeavours to exhibit the other great idea—God—as proving its own reality. We have only to contemplate it to be forced to acknowledge that it corresponds to the fact which lies at the centre of the universe.

Another discovery follows—What is our self ? It is the single, indivisible, and therefore indestructible unit, which we call the soul, and from the very mode of proof it is evident that the essence of the soul is thought. Knowing the nature of the soul by direct intuition, we also know the nature of its necessary opposite—matter. For matter must be that which does not think, and, further, must be that abstraction which exists under all the varying forms of the visible world. Matter, that is, becomes almost identical with space. Its essence is extension, though we may perhaps throw in the quality of impenetrability, just, as we may say, to stiffen it into the necessary consistency. Matter, in short, is simply the world as conceived by the pure mathematician in his dealings with geometry and mechanics. All other qualities vary from man to man; and it is plain, therefore, that we cannot know them as they are.

Here then we have our realities. The antithesis between subject and object is represented by the two absolute substances—the soul and matter; whilst God, the eternal and self-existent substance, sustains and regulates their relations. And now, having the necessary starting-point, we might proceed to deduce the world from our ideas, in full security that the ideas must correspond to facts. But here, unluckily, occurs the great difficulty which perplexed Descartes and his followers. What is the soul? It is the opposite of matter, and utterly devoid of all material qualities. And what is matter? It is the opposite of the soul, and by no alteration or manipulation can thought be got out of it. If so, how are we to bridge over the gulf between two contradictories? How are we to conceive of any reciprocal action between the two or of one upon the other? All our reasoning is to be guaranteed by the absolute clearness of our ideas; and yet, here at the very root of the system is a fatal contradiction. The action of any being upon another must follow from their definitions; yet the definitions show that matter cannot be brought into relation to spirit, whilst all scientific knowledge rests on their mutual connection. The difficulty suggested various so-called solutions, which really admit it to be insuperable by calling in the aid of the Deity. Matter, it was suggested, does not affect the soul, but when a change happens in one, God

"Descartes as a Young Man," from an anonymous seventeenth-century portrait.

causes a change in the other; or, the soul cannot be directly conscious of matter, but 'sees all things in God;' or, the soul and matter are like two separate clocks wound up by God to go in perfect correspondence. Thinking, and the object of thought, being torn asunder by the metaphysical analysis, God is introduced as the correlating and unifying principle. But a philosophy which begins by making a difficulty only to be overcome by Omnipotence might well alarm sober minds. (pp. 22-6)

Sir Leslie Stephen, "The Philosophical Basis," in his History of English Thought in the Eighteenth Century, Vol. I, *third edition, 1902. Reprint by John Murray, 1927, pp. 1-73.*

Jacques Maritain (essay date 1928)

[*A French philosopher and educator, Maritain was the foremost spokesman for the Catholic Literary Revival in France. In the following excerpt, Maritain elaborates on the "spiritual bearing" of Descartes's philosophical system, purporting that ultimately "the spirit of Descartes has led us astray."*]

1. I or my mind, he said. He produced his effect not, like Luther and Rousseau, by reproducing in souls the waves of his sensibility, the vast tumult of his heart, but by leading the mind astray, by captivating the reason with sines and clear ideas.

It would be little to our purpose to study the career and moral physiognomy of Descartes: the head superbly heavy and vehement, the low forehead, the discreet, stubborn, fanciful eye, the mouth proud and earthly; a strange life, secret and cunning, yet for all that strong and great from a single plan followed to the very end and a singularly clear and precocious understanding of the first condition of an intellectual amongst men, which is to flee them; the moment, short as a wing-beat, of that obscure dream by the German stove and of the call to philosophize until death for the renewal of humanity. What matters is his system; in it is his destiny formed.

I shall not undertake here an analytical examination of that system. I shall try to make its spiritual bearing clear. I address myself to readers familiar with Descartes in the confidence that they will recognize the points of doctrine to which I refer. Therefore I leave aside the human element which, in every philosopher and perhaps especially in this one, confuses the absolute of ideas and diminishes their pure force, and I want to give a bare, unadorned presentation, more direct than the original expression, not so much of the philosophic work as of the *spirit* of Descartes.

2. Leon Bloy saw every commonplace of common speech as a sphinx crouching over the mystery of creation. It is an admirable way of experiencing ecstasy at every utterance of, say, our hall-porter, or member of Parliament. There is as much hidden wisdom in the commonplaces of philosophy, even of the history of philosophy. What do they tell us about Descartes?

As Luther discovered *the Human Person* and Jean-Jacques *Nature and Liberty,* Descartes discovered *Thought.* "He really revealed thought to itself," wrote M. Hamelin. Let us not protest. That proposition is very true in the sense in which Hamelin took it. Let us say that Descartes unveiled the face of the monster which modern idealism adores under the name of Thought.

3. Let us try to find the right names for things: the sin of Descartes is a sin of *angelism.* He turned Knowledge and Thought into a hopeless perplexity, an abyss of unrest, because he conceived human Thought after the type of angelic Thought. To sum it up in three words: What he saw in man's thought was *Independence of Things;* that is what he put into it, what he revealed to it about itself. Surely, you say, the crime is wholly mental, perpetuated in the third degree of abstraction; does it concern anyone but lunatics in long pedants' robes, those who have themselves bound in calf, as Councillor Joachim des Cartes said of his son? It has influenced some centuries of human history and havoc, of which the end is not in sight. Before indicating its consequences let us consider it in itself, and try to show its chief characteristics.

According to St. Thomas's teaching, the human intellect is the last of the spirits, and the most remote from the perfection of the divine Intelligence. As the zoöphyte bridges the gap between two kingdoms, so the rational animal is a transitional form between the corporeal world and the spiritual world. Above it, crowded like sea sand, rise in countless multitude the pure spirits in their hierarchies. These are *thinking substances* in the true sense of the word, pure subsistent forms, who certainly receive existence and *are* not existence, as God is, but they do not inform matter and are free from the vicissitudes of time, movement, generation and corruption, of all the divisions of space, all the weaknesses of individuation by *materia signata;* and each concentrates in himself more metaphysical stuff than the whole human race together. Each by itself is a specific type, and exhausts the perfection of its essence, and therefore they are borne, from the moment of their creation, to the complete fullness of their natural possibilities, incorrupt by definition. They raise above our heads a canopy of immensity, an abundance of stability and strength which, in comparison with us, is infinite. Transparent each to his own glance; each with full perception of his own substance *by* that substance, and at a single leap naturally knowing God also—by analogy, no doubt, but in what a mirror of splendour: their intellect, always in act with regard to its intelligible objects, does not derive its ideas from things, as does ours, but has them direct from God, Who infuses them into it when He creates it. And by these innate ideas, which are in it as a derivation from the divine Ideas, their intellect knows created things in the creative light itself, rule and measure of all that is. Infallible, then, and even impeccable in the natural order, considered apart from the supernatural end: autonomous and self-sufficing, so far as a creature can be self-sufficing: the life of the angels is an endless outflow of thought, knowledge, and will, without weariness or sleep. Piercing, in the perfect clearness of their intuitions, not, of course, the secrets of hearts nor the unfolding of future contingencies, but all essences and all laws, the whole substance of this universe; *knowing the power and actions of fire, water, air, the stars, the heavens, all other bodies, as distinctly as we know the different occupations of our workmen,* they are finally, without hands or machines, *as masters and possessors of nature,* and can play upon nature as on a guitar by modifying the movement of the atoms at their will. In all this we are speaking of the attributes of the angelic nature considered in itself, and, apart from its elevation to the supernatural order, as it subsists in fallen and faithful spirits alike. That is the model on which a son of Tourraine set out one day to reform the human mind.

4. Consider the three great notes of angelic Knowledge—Intuitive, as to its mode, Innate, as to its origin, Independent of Things, as to its nature. You find these three same notes again, transposed certainly, but not less fundamental and not less manifest, in human Knowledge according to Descartes.

5. Descartes's first effort, as we know, aims at freeing philosophy from the burden of discursive reasoning, at opposing to the laborious farrago of the School and its swarm of syllogisms raised one on another a ready, distinct, level science, a sheet of clearness. But see where that search for the simple actually leads. When our understanding apprehends, judges, and reasons, it is no longer tied down to three operations irreducibly distinct in nature. It has but one function: vision. A fixing of the pure and attentive intelligence on such or such object of thought, with well defined lines, with nothing of the implicit or virtual, grasped fully and wholly by absolutely original and primary vision and with a certitude grounded on itself alone—that is what Descartes calls intuition, "intuitus," and it is to that henceforth that everything in the cognizant understanding is reduced.

For Descartes makes the judgement, the operation of assenting, of interior conviction, no longer belong to the understanding, but to the will, which alone is active: it is a decision of the will, which comes to *agree* to an idea as a faithful representation of what is, or may be.

And after "intuition," he does indeed admit another operation, which is "deduction," the operation of reasoning; but that consists of nothing more than constructing new objects of apprehension by combining intuitions; a concession perforce to discursive reasoning but clumsy and contradictory, which destroys the unity belonging to reasoning and the continuity of logical movement and replaces it by a discontinuous succession of motionless glances. To reason is no longer *to be led* by the principle to see the consequence, it is to *see* the principle and its connexion with the consequence *together.* Behind the banal attacks on the syllogism in the ***Regulae,*** we must see a tenacious zeal to reject that work of patient production of certitude which constitutes the life of the reason as such, and by which, considering one truth in the light of another, a new light is born and rises in us, in which what was virtual and hidden in the truth already known shines out clearly.

6. This logical denial is of peculiar importance. To lay hands on the syllogism is to lay hands on human nature. What Descartes really attacks, in his impatience of the servitude of discursive work is the potentiality of our intellect, that is to say, its specifically human weakness, what makes it a *reason.* So by curious chance the first move of rationalism is to disown reason, to do violence to its nature, to challenge the normal conditions of its activity. Behold it reconstructed after an intuitive type, stiff in the tinsel of pure intelligence and in a parcelling-out of comprehending immobilities.

The secret desire of the intelligence in search of a superhuman condition is to reduce all to simple perception—but this is a desire which only grace makes truly realizable, in the transluminous night of contemplation. Descartes, for his part, set himself to that from the first, and in the very work of the reason. He wanted to effect such a concentration of evidence that the whole train of conclusions might be grasped by simple intuition of the principle: that alone is worthy of Science! And as he could not manage that, he would despair and confess himself beaten by the evil Genius, did he not think that, in the initial certitudes of the *cogito* and the ontological proof, he had found an argument as ready and direct as simple intuitive perception. He would despair, did he not also think that by making the thought of God and the divine truthfulness coexistent and coextensive with the whole advance of knowledge, and by setting the philosopher in the ever-present light of the idea of God, he could remedy the impossibility in which we are (and to which he will never submit), of having, at the actual moment when we make the inference, gathered up in one single and indivisible present (in which memory has nothing to do) the present—and compelling—evidence of all the previously established conclusions which serve us as premisses.

What does this mean, but that the sole authentic and legitimate archetype of Knowledge is, for him, angelic Knowledge? The angel neither reasons, nor proceeds by reasoning: he has but one intellectual act, which is at once perceiving and judging: he sees consequences not successively from the principle, but immediately in the principle; he is not subject to the progressive actualization of knowledge which constitutes logical movement properly so called; if his thought travels, it is by intuitive leaps, from perfect act to perfect act, from intelligible fullness to intelligible fullness, according to the discontinuity of wholly spiritual time, which is not a succession of instants without duration, (like the time, also discontinuous, which Descartes attributes to our world) but the permanence of a stable instant which lasts motionless so long as it does not give place to another motionless instant of contemplation. That is the ideal limit, the pure type of reason conceived in the manner of Descartes.

7. The angelic intellect is not made of faked-up intuitions, like the Cartesian understanding; it is genuinely intuitive. It is true that it is infallible, at least in the natural order, and that is so necessary a consequence that the fact of error is very troublesome to Cartesian optimism, the most difficult of humiliations to admit and the most difficult to explain.

How is it possible that I should be mistaken, I who am spirit? How can a substance whose whole nature is to think, think wrongly? It is so serious an anomaly that the author of things seems compromised by the scandal. I am mistaken only because I will have it so, my free will alone is to blame. And therefore human error is explained for Descartes in the same way as theologians explain angelic error; I mean, more precisely, than the Cartesian theory of error, so little consistent with his position, would only become coherent and logical if one brought to it, with suitable emendation, the case of the errors of fallen spirits. Precipitancy of judgement! When they err (which only happens to them when they are dealing with the supernatural order), they see in full light an object whose natural reality they completely apprehend, and they also see not less clearly the contingent and conjectural bond between that object and any other—for example, some future event—which remains dark to them. And when they impetuously extend their affirmation beyond what they see, and give their assent precipitately, I mean by deliberate inadvertence, to a thing which is not evident to them, it is because they are carried away by the malice of their will: "*sciens et volens non se detinet, sed judicat ultra quam potest.*" Such, according to Descartes, is man when he affirms and judges beyond what he perceives clearly and distinctly, from a weakness of his free will, from an impetuosity for which his will is solely responsible, and that just in so far as it is free. Due allowance being made, we cannot help remarking here a strange likeness between this psychology of error in the fallen Angel and the psychology of error in us according to Descartes.

In consequence of this angelist psychology the philosopher will demand such a criterion of certitude that to avoid error it shall be enough for us at every moment to survey the field of our representations with a true will not to be deceived. To look into ourselves, to separate the obscure from the clear, and the confused from the distinct, and agree only to the clear and distinct, so that it shall rest as much and as rightly with our will that we should not err in speculation as that we should not sin in action: that is the art of infallibility which the criterion of clear ideas should teach us. Obviously such a science ought to be constructible—under ideal conditions, instantaneously—at the worst easily and quickly: the greater the speed, and the fewer the minds concerned with its construction, the better. Was not one enough for it? If he were in a position to make all the experiments he needs, would not Descartes himself refound and complete the whole body of wisdom? He has no time to lose, he is a man in a hurry (like all moderns). If he can only snatch some tens of years from death, the great work on which the happiness and perfection of humanity depend will be done. In any case it will not need more than two or three centuries—this we now have the pleasure of verifying.

If Cartesianism showed itself so savage a ravager of the past in the intelligible order, it is because it began by disowning in the individual himself the essential intrinsic dependence of our present knowledge on our past, which makes our establishment in truth, humanly speaking, necessarily and of itself a strangely long and laborious thing. In a general manner, whether the poor effort of the individual or the common work of generations is in question, the Cartesian angel only submits to time as to an external compulsion, a force repugnant to his nature; he does not understand the essential function of time in bringing human cognition to maturity.

8. The ideas of the angel, as we have said, are innate: they do not come from objects, like our abstract ideas; they are infused into him, received at the beginning like a dowry of light. They are certainly accidents, really distinct from the angelic substance and its intellective power, and superadded gifts, but they are required as of right by the nature of the pure spirit.

From the fact that Descartes refuses to acknowledge the reality of accidents distinct from substance, his innatism remains bound in inextricable difficulties. Sometimes innate ideas are proximate dispositions to think this or that, yet still confused with the thinking nature itself, which puts in the latter, as it were, hidden preformations which already foreshadow the Leibnitzian virtualities. Sometimes the soul differs from its thoughts as extension from its shapes, and for Descartes, (who, by one of his frequent clumsinesses, here wrongly applies the scholastic notion of mode,) that means that the act of thinking this or that is not an accidental but a substantial determination, a completion of the thinking substance in its very substantiality. As if an operation could be substantial elsewhere than in the Pure Act! He thus pictures mode as a substantial completion in the operative order. Spinoza took this bastard notion and made a pretty monster of it.

It remains—and this is what concerns us—that the Cartesian ideas come from God, like angelic ideas, not from objects. Thus the human soul is not only subsistent as the ancients taught, causing the body to exist with its own existence; it has, without the body, received direct from God all the operative perfection which can befit it. There is the destruction of the very reason of its union with the body, or rather, there is its inversion. For if the body and the senses are not the necessary means of the acquisition of its ideas for that soul, and consequently the instrument by which it rises to its own perfection, which is the life of the intelligence and the contemplation of truth, then, as the body must be for the soul and not the soul for the body, the body and senses can be there for nothing but to provide the soul—which needs only itself and God in order to think,—with means for the practical subjugation of the earth and all material nature, and this reduces the soul's good to the domination of the physical universe. This universe, the whole of which has not the value of one spirit, will make it pay dear for this deordination. This angel is iron-gloved, and extends its sovereign action over the corporeal world by the innumerable arms of Machinery! Poor angel turning the grindstone, enslaved to the law of matter, and soon fainting under the terrible wheels of the elemental machine which has got out of order.

9. But to come back to the Cartesian theory of Knowledge. If our cognition is like an outflow of the creative truth into our spirit, if wisdom, of which we bear all the innate germs in the nature of our soul, is a pure unfolding of our understanding, human science must be *one,* with the oneness of the understanding; there can be no specific diversity of sciences. And thus there will be no specific diversity of knowledge ruling the judgement, no varying degrees of certitude. Certainly it is so with the angel, for all his certitudes in the natural order are unique in degree,—even the degree of perfection of his own immateriality and his innate knowledge. In Descartes the result is the most radical

levelling of the things of the spirit: one same single type of certitude, rigid as Law, is imposed on thought; everything which cannot be brought under it must be rejected; absolute exclusion of everything that is not mathematically evident, or deemed so. It is inhuman cognition, because it would be superhuman! There is the source not only of Descartes' proclamation of brutal contempt for the humanities, for Greek and Latin: "It is no more the duty of a sound man to know Greek or Latin than to know Swiss or Low-Breton,"—for history, for erudition, for all the huge realm of positive and moral studies which his successors later reduced to absurdity in the desire to make of them a "mathematics of the contingent"; but it is the principle and the origin of the deep *inhumanity* of our modern science.

Moreover, innatism, making of the intellect a power predetermined by nature to all the objects of its knowledge, does not allow that our understanding should be intrinsically determined and raised as by a grafting in it of the object to be known or the end to be attained, in order to produce a perfect work wherever it be, whether in the speculative or practical order. No more than with the angel in the natural order, are there elevating qualities or *habitus* in the Cartesian intellect.

Hamelin noticed rightly that one of the causes of the passion for method in the time of Descartes—at that time when modern man, the better to start his attack on the world, left the old supports of intellectual tradition—was the need to justify so much confidence by replacing these supports by a good insurance against error. To tell the truth, what the *guaranteed success* of the process and the recipe had to do duty for was not only the aids of the *via disciplinae,* but also and especially the interior vigour of the *habitus.* And thus common sense will do for everything. The shop of clear ideas is the *Bon Marche* of wisdom. After Descartes, prices will go up again, and that fine universal facility will give way to the most fearful complications. But it is always by method, or by methods, and no longer by the spiritual quality ennobling the intellect, that the austerity of knowledge will be measured. We see in our days the cheering effects of this materialization of science, and the astonishing intellectual beggary that an advance, admirable in itself, in technical specialization and operative processes can bring about: for the flame remains feeble on which piles of green wood are flung.

10. The deepest quality of angelic cognition is not that it is intuitive or innate, but that it is independent of external objects. The ideas of pure spirits have no proportion with ours. As they are resolved in the very truth of God and not in the truth of external objects, these infused ideas are a created likeness, and as it were a refraction, in the angelic intellect of the divine ideas and the uncreated light where all is life. So that they represent things just in so far as things derive from the divine ideas, for the angels have thus received, at the first instant, the seal of likeness which made them full of wisdom and perfect in beauty—*tu signaculum similitudinis, plenus sapientia et perfectus decore*—and God, as St. Augustine says, produced things intelligibly in the knowledge of spirits before producing them really in their own being.

Moreover, these ideas, unlike our abstract ideas, are universal not by the *object* which they present to the intelligence immediately, but only by the means which they constitute of reaching from the same point of view a multitude of natures and individuals distinctly apprehended even to their ultimate differences. Their universality is not the universality of representation due to the process of abstraction, but the universality of causation or activity belonging to the creative ideas, whence things descend into being, and of which the angel's ideas are a likeness cut to his measure. They are, John of St. Thomas tells us, like copies of models—but sparkling with spiritual vitality—like models imprinted on the angelic intellect, in which is figured the countless swarm of creatures flowing from the supreme art, as God sees it even before bringing it into existence: though doubtless not in the absolute unity of the divine vision, but distributed according to the capacity of created spirits, under certain great categories, by the unity of objects in their relation to such or such an end, and in the mode in which they proceed from their divine exemplars. And so, like the divine causality and the divine ideas, the ideas of the angel go down to existence itself: they directly touch the individual existence, comprehensively known by pure intelligences so far as it receives being and responds, in the concrete of matter then given, to its eternal archetype refracted in the pure spirit.

It is thus that the angelic cognition, depending solely on the knowledge of God, is independent of objects, from which it does not draw its ideas, and which are not its formal rule—independent, we may say, if at least we are talking of the lower world, in regard to its very objects of intellection, which it precedes, which it awaits, of which it is the measure, which it fully apprehends by the very efficacy of the creative knowledge, and to the intelligibility of which it has not to proportion the degree of immateriality of its ideas. We see in what eminent sense the angel knows all the things of this lower world *a priori* and by their supreme causes, since he knows them by a participation in the very ideas which make them, since he knows the work of art—I mean all this universe—in what the artist tells him about his operative science, the very cause of being and all beauty.

11. Now look at the Cartesian understanding. Does not that also hang immediately on God, rising above and measuring all material nature without receiving anything from it? By one of those slips due to his resolve to go quickly in the work, Descartes applies to the certitudes of reason and science the classical solutions of the traditional teaching about the formal motive of faith: *veritas prima revelans,* the authority of God revealing. It is because God cannot lie that clear and distinct ideas deserve our assent, and he who does not know the divine truthfulness is strictly certain of nothing. If we could not lean on the guarantee of the truthfulness of the Creator, author of things and author of our mind, we could not *know* on trustworthy authority that there is a material world, or that there exist outside our thought things in conformity with our ideas, or even that these ideas deliver to us anything of the authentic, intelligible object or of the eternal truths, and do not deceive us even in what we conceive as most evident. That well shows that rational cognition is for Descartes

a sort of *natural revelation,* and that our ideas, like the infused species of the angel, have their immediate pattern in God, not in objects.

Yet, surely, unlike the angelic intellect, the Cartesian understanding reaches directly neither individuality nor existence. Be undeceived. However ill or hastily Descartes may have expressed himself on general ideas, it seems clear that in his eyes they are essentially incomplete notions—Spinoza later called them inadequate. Human science, if it is to be perfect, must reach singular essences by direct apprehension. A universal *means* of thinking, in the angelic fashion, all well and good! A universal *object* of thought, an abstract quiddity whose singular mode of realization we know only by a return to images, that is not worthy of the spirit to which all matter is subjected. Hardly indicated in Descartes, that disregard of nature and of the importance of the universal *in praedicando*—of the properly human universal—that sort of intellectualist nominalism developed fully with Leibnitz and Spinoza; with them it became one of the signs of the claim to be as the angels which characterizes absolute intellectualism, until, falling into English heads and rejoining the old sensationalist nominalism, it helped to ruin every sound notion of abstraction.

As to the perception of the existent as such, we may say that the transition to existence, the grasp of existence by the help of the intelligence alone and starting from pure ideas, forms just the crucial problem of the Cartesian philosophy. For as our ideas are no longer resolved (materially) in things by means of the senses, whose data have no longer anything but pragmatic and subjective value, existence and the placing of things outside nothingness is no longer conveyed to us at once by our fleshly contact with the world. We must arrive at being, we must rejoin it, or deduce it, or beget it, from an ideal principle set or discovered in the depths of thought. There is the impossible task to which, from Descartes to Hegel, the metaphysics of the moderns is condemned. Descartes kept the scholastic teaching that the perception of our human intelligences reaches directly only essences, and therefore cannot by itself cross the vast sky which separates the possible from existent reality. For him, meanwhile, pure thought must be self-sufficient, and the philosophizing intelligence cannot, even in the order of the *resolutio moralis,* essentially need to have recourse to the senses, which of themselves yield to us only modifications of our consciousness, appearances, uncertainty. Must one, then, renounce for ever any meeting with Being? No. There are privileged cases in which the pure intelligence suffices to reach it; it is so with the *cogito,* in which thought transparent to itself knows its own existence not by an empirical verification, but by an immediate grasp of its substantial ground in an act of intellection; it is so with the proof of God by the idea, in which thought has only to fix itself on the imprint of Perfection in it to read there openly Its real existence. It is a twofold intellectual revelation of existence in which alone human reason reaches its full spiritual measure, and behaves like the angel knowing himself and his author.

My thought exists, God exists. All flows from that. It is from God that the Cartesian science descends to things and deduces Physics. It is perfect science, science by causes, the only one proportioned to the philosopher's ambition. It also knows this universe *a priori* and according to the very order of creative reasons. (If it fails in the task, it will be to hand it over to the metaphysics of Spinoza.) Does it expect anything from the senses, for after all one does not quite forget that one is human? The senses have only an accidental part, in particular that of selecting between the equally possible different ideal combinations and of showing us which has actually been realized.

Such, in its first manifestation, appears to us the independence of the Cartesian reason in regard to external objects; separation between the intelligence and the senses by which the intelligence was in continuity with external objects, with the existent singular. Contempt of the body in the work of science, refusal of animal cognition which first binds us to creation, refusal of that properly human condition of being able to know only by the senses and the intellect together what the angel knows by intellect alone. See that fine science set out. Is it fairly sure of itself? It will go far. But Kant is waiting for it at the turn of the road. If the senses, he will say to it, only yield pure appearances to us and are not to our minds the vehicle of what is, to reach being you would need, O presumptuous one, a supersensible intuition, even that enjoyed by the pure spirits in whose image you have been re-formed. But you have no such intuition in your luggage. Ergo, you will never know that which is, and all your *a priori* is only a phenomenal structure.

12. There is a second aspect, perhaps more specific, of the independence of the Cartesian reason with respect to things. This time it is less a question of sensible things as such than of their intelligibility, and therefore of the proper object of the intelligence.

For St. Thomas, and it is a logical consequence of the abstractive nature of our intelligence, the sole absolutely first object reached by it is Being in general, and in that it resolves all its conceptions, learning at the dictation of experience to make explicit the differences contained in it. Now it is most evident that Being, which permeates all things, is hostile to no reality; it welcomes them all, it is the Abraham's bosom, if I may venture to call it so, in which rest all the fauna of creation, all the forms which flow from the Poetry of God, however noble and rare, poor or luxuriant they may be. Hence it follows that an analysis carried out in terms of Being, elaborating the concepts of our science according to the requirements of reality, docile to the analogy of transcendentals, following with fidelity and obedience, with tenderness and devotion, the outlines of that which is, will be able to penetrate into things and put essences into intelligible communication without any injury to their originality, their unity, their own secret. That is why although the brain of a Thomist may be as limited and hard as every human brain and very disproportioned to the wisdom he defends, yet none the less he has the consolation of telling himself that, considering the doctrine in itself, if not the doctor, there is nothing in heaven and earth which is not at home in his theology.

For Descartes, on the contrary, and it is a logical consequences of his innatism, thought finds in itself a plurality of ideas, ready made, irreducible, irresolvable, each clear by itself, each the object of primary intuition, intelligible elements to which everything that knowledge has to do with must be reduced. These are the "simple natures" which are like atoms of obviousness and intelligibility. As he suppressed the material resolution of our concepts in external objects, Descartes suppresses their formal resolution in Being.

Nor do the angels cut out their ideas from the common cloth of Being, but that is because they fully apprehend the whole reality of a section of creation by a single one of their comprehensive ideas. Whereas to replace resolution in being by reduction to simple natures—to thought, for things of the soul; to extension and motion for things of the body—can only produce incalculable mischief in an understanding which, however much it may dislike it, remains discursive, and whose whole work consists in advancing by composition of concepts.

What the Cartesian revolution introduces here is nothing less than a radical change in the very notion of intelligibility, and correlatively in the very type of scientific intellection and "explanation."

Unqualified in principle to comprehend the analogy of being and to use it, and so from the first closing to itself approach to divine things, the Cartesian analysis, cutting up and levelling down, can only break the internal unity of beings, destroy alike the originality and diversity of natures, and violently bring everything back to the univocal elements which it has been pleased to select as simple principles. Henceforth, to understand is to separate; to be intelligible is to be capable of mathematical reconstruction. To take a machine to pieces and put it together again, that is the high work of the intelligence. The mechanical explanation becomes the only conceivable type of scientific explanation.

Criterion of obviousness! There is nothing more equivocal and less loyal than the Cartesian clearness and distinctness. Let us clearly understand that Cartesian obviousness is wholly different from the obviousness designated by the ancients, and by the common usage of men, as the criterion of certitude. That obviousness is a property of Being, *fulgor objecti,* and it manifests itself to our mind in self-evident propositions known of themselves, first principles of our knowledge. It forces us to difficult elaborations in order to keep these principles faithfully, yet without in any way disregarding experience, in order to sin neither against reason nor against reality. The more it makes our science grow, the more it makes us perceive that Being is our measure and that there is nothing of which we know the whole. Finally, whether it is question of power, matter, contingency, of what is in itself least intelligible, or of the things of the spirit and of God—to a sovereign degree intelligible in themselves but to our intellect as the sun to an owl's eyes—it leads us to objects dark either in themselves or for us, and makes us issue out on mystery, mystery of imperfection or perfection. What does it matter? It is a luminous night, in which the necessities of thought trace for us a surer way than the orbits of the planets.

Cartesian obviousness, on the contrary, is a subjective obviousness, a quality of certain ideas, and it is not in the *propositions* regulating the progression of our certitudes, it is in *notional objects,* the term of the analysis of things, that it is manifested to our mind. There are *ideas* which are self-evident and perfectly penetrable by our thoughts. These ideas are the matter of science. All the others must be reduced to them or be eliminated. These are the things which lie open to the Cartesian angel. Far from the corporeal world concealing a residue of relative unintelligibility, it is perfectly clear to our human perception, being nothing but geometrical extension, perfectly subject to our spirit in cognition before being perfectly subject to it in practice. With this fatal meeting of pantheism and absolute intellectualism, we soon have, confronting an intelligence which imagines itself as in pure act of intellection, a universe which is imagined as in pure act of intelligibility. We really have all things forcibly adjusted to the level of human ideas, the treasures of experience squandered, creative art profaned, and the work which God made replaced by the inane world of rationalism.

To tell the truth, as our reason drifts and has no rule in it when separated from Being, clear ideas understood in Descartes' sense furnish no consistent criterion. Actually they are reduced to ideas which are easy or "easy to conceive"; and the Cartesian clearness is synonymous with facility. Ought not science, then, to be easy to man as it is to the angel? That is why Mathematics becomes the Queen of Sciences and the norm of all knowledge. Everywhere else, under cover of this pretended strictness, the arbitrary creeps in, following a law of irony which we see daily verified (of which German exegesis gives a good illustration in the nineteenth century). Bossuet says in a celebrated passage, "Under the pretext that we must not accept anything but what we understand clearly—which, within certain limits, is very true—everyone gives himself liberty to say, 'I understand this, and I do not understand that,' and on this sole basis they admit and reject whatever they like." In practice, for truth measured by Being Cartesian obviousness could not but substitute facility in reasoning and tractability of ideas. The Philosophy of Illumination, lighting heaven with the candles of the Encyclopædia, will thus very naturally continue the philosophy of clear ideas.

Let us say that, in all that, the Cartesian understanding claims independence with respect to its object, with respect not only to things as the object of the senses, but to things as the object of science. Descartes is an out-and-out dogmatist, and from this point of view the very opposite of a subjectivist. But with him human science, drunk with mathematics, begins no longer to be measured by the object. For its constitution, its existence as a science, it no longer asks the object to impose its law upon it, it imposes on the object a measure and a rule which it thinks it finds in itself. Thus while the science of the Angel, although independent of external objects, does not deform the object which it reaches, because it reaches it by a likeness of the creative ideas, cause and measure of that object and of its being, the Cartesian science does violence to reality in order to reduce it to the predestined scale of "scientific" explanations. Thence-forward the human intelligence becomes the law-giver in speculative matters; it fashions its object. We may say that Cartesian reason practised Kantian *apriorism* before it was named (*in actu exercito*). Kant afterwards only had to observe that in good logic an understanding which fashions its objects without producing them in being can only have phenomena for its objects and not things in themselves. Cartesian dogmatism, after a long flight, will have become agnosticism when it falls to earth.

13. The Angel knows himself immediately by his substance, in a perfect intuition which yields him the ground of his being. His natural cognizance of God is consummated not only in his beholding external objects, but primarily and above all in beholding himself, in the most pure mirror of his own essence. His own essence is the first object of his intellection, and he is always in act of intellection of himself. Everything he knows, he knows by first being cognizant of himself and by a sort of prolongation of his cognizance of himself.

All that appears again, transposed and lessened, in Cartesian thought. But why is the soul easier to know than the body? Why does everything it knows reveal first its own nature to it? Not because its essence is the transparent object through which it sees all things, but because its glance stops at itself, ends in an idea which is something of itself, congeals in self-consciousness. My act of apprehension, as such, only grasps my thought, or a representation, an effigy depicted in it, with which, by reason of the divine truthfulness, some outward model corresponds. The idea thus becomes the sole term immediately attained by thought, the thing, portrait or representation, itself first known before making anything else known. This reification of ideas, this confusion of the idea with an "instrumental sign" and an "object *quod*" is, as we have shown elsewhere, the original sin of modern philosophy. It governs all the Cartesian doctrine of knowledge, the Cartesian first proof of the existence of God, the Cartesian theory of eternal truths; without it, Descartes as a philosopher is unintelligible.

Now it is curious to note here, yet again, a collusion with the angelic world. The divine ideas, in the light of which the Angel knows external objects, are creative or operative ideas, an artist's ideas: models in imitation of which a thing is made (*forma intelligibilis ad quam respiciens artifex operatur*). The object seen in such an idea is not a nature drawn from external objects and transported into the knowing spirit, it is a model issuing from the creating spirit, according to which the thing is placed in being. Confuse these ideas of the divine art with the concepts of human knowledge, and for both it will mean going from the idea to the object from thought to being, and you will have made of the object immediately grasped in the concept something different from what is:—a model, a picture of what is. You will thus have come back to the Cartesian ideas and the principle of all modern idealism.

With this theory of representational ideas the claims of Cartesian reason to independence of external objects reach their highest point: thought breaks with Being. It forms a sealed world which is no longer in contact with anything but itself; its ideas, now opaque effigies interposed between it and external objects, are still for Descartes a sort of lining of the real world. But as Hamelin says, the lining was to consume the cloth. Here again Kant finishes Descartes' work. If the intelligence when it thinks, reaches immediately only its own thought, or its representations, the thing hidden behind these representations remains for ever unknowable.

14. The retreat of the human mind on itself, independence of the reason with respect to the sensible origin of our ideas, to the object as the rule of our science, to real natures as the immediate term of our intellection—absolute intellectualism, mathematicism, idealism—and, finally, irremediable breach between intelligence and Being—that, then, is how Descartes revealed Thought to itself.

The result of a usurpation of the angelic privileges, that *denaturing* of human reason driven beyond the limits of its species, that lust for pure spirituality, could only go to the infinite: passing beyond the world of created spirits it had to lead us to claim for our intelligence the perfect autonomy and the perfect immanence, the absolute independence, the *aseity* of the uncreated intelligence. Of that claim, Kant was the scholastic formulator, but the origins lie much deeper: and though the world's experience has already been wretched enough and humiliating enough to give it the lie, it remains the secret principle of the breakup of our culture and of the disease of which the apostate West seems determined to die.

The old philosophy knew the nobility of the intelligence and the sublime nature of thought. It knew that in its purity, and freed from every condition alien to its formal notion, it is only fully realized in the infinitely holy God. It knew that if the human intelligence is the last of the intelligences, it yet partakes of the life and liberty which belong to the spirit; that if it depends on the senses, it is to draw from them wherewith to transcend the whole sensible universe; that if it depends on the object to which it is proportioned, it is to gush out in spontaneous action and become all things; that if it depends on the being which makes it fruitful, it is to conquer Being itself and rest only in it. You pay dear for rejecting these truths.

That which is the measure has, as such, that which is measured under its complete rule, imposes its specification upon it, holds it bound and subject. Because it no longer understands the life which belongs to it as a created spirit, which interiorizes within itself what is its measure and finds its true liberty in that subjection, and because it wants an absolute and undetermined liberty for itself, it is natural that human thought, since Descartes, refuses to be measured objectively or to submit to intelligible necessities. Freedom with respect to the objective is the mother and nurse of all modern freedoms; it is the finest achievement of Progress, which makes us, as we are no longer measured by *anything,* subject to anything whatever! Intellectual liberty which Chesterton compared to that of the turnip (and that is a libel on the turnip), and which strictly only belongs to primal matter.

Thus the Cartesian reformation is not only at the source of the torrent of illusions and fables which self-styled "immediate clarities" have poured on us for two centuries and a half; it has a heavy weight of responsibility for the immense futility of the modern world and that strange condition in which we see humanity to-day, as powerful over matter, as informed and cunning to rule the physical universe, as it is weakened and lost in face of the intelligible realities of which the humility of a wisdom subject to Being once made it partaker. To fight against bodies it is equipped like a god; to fight against spirits it has lost all its weapons, and the pitiless laws of the metaphysical universe crush it in mockery.

15. I apologize for having dwelt so much on the Treatise on the Angels in this attempt to discern the spirit of Descartes. It was very necessary to show that the word "angelism" is not a more or less picturesque approximation, but that it designates the special character of the Cartesian reformation in the metaphysical order, and that a number of the clearest and most precise analogies between Descartes and the angelic knowledge can be found.

The Angelic Doctor, when he elucidated, in one of the most splendid parts of the Summa—in that very part which the philosopher of the *cogito* heavily derided in front of young Burman, thinking himself witty, but only betraying, as he would have said, his own incompetence in the subject—when he elucidated, as a metaphysician who knows what thought is, the properties of pure spirits, he not only introduced us to the best philosophy of the intellectual life, but prepared for us the means of penetrating the deepest meaning of the reformation of the human mind effected by Descartes, and of showing the true face of the masked reason which then moved on to the world's stage.

Luther bore witness that it was the devil in person who convinced him of the inanity of the Mass. The "Genius" who taught Descartes was more wary. But what man in his sober senses could imagine that pure spirits are indifferent to philosophers, and only set themselves to control sorcerers? At the source of the error conceived by Descartes by his German stove it is very curious to note the simple application to human reason of the collection of properties and characteristics which are true of the physiology of separated forms.

We must not forget the importance of the stake. We must not forget that Descartes finally reversed the order of human cognition and made Metaphysics an introduction to Mechanics, Medicine, and Ethics, from which we shall henceforth gather the invigorating fruits of learning. In the higher order of Cognition, the Cartesian reformation gave the irretrievable stability of the things of the spirit to the moral attitude of turning towards perishable goods. See what the great name of Science has since become. It is to-day hardly applied to anything but the knowledge of matter, and science, *par excellence,* is regarded by most modern thinkers as belonging to a museum. In the modern world, reason turns its back on eternal things and is ordered to the creature. It rates the mathematics of phenomena above theology, science above wisdom. From the mountain of its excellence it has descried all the kingdoms of the material universe and the glory of them, and it goes down to possess them.

16. I do not claim that one can reduce to this *angelism,* or deduce from it, the whole of Descartes's doctrine. So complex a system involves a number of primary aspects and principles. We will not speak of the contributions of scholasticism (of a scholasticism, moreover, more or less pure). The taste for simple and easy strictness, for a venture strongly and reasonably conducted, a healthy aversion for pedantry and empty contention, a brave resolution to save the deposit of naturally Christian truths by force of good sense, by some quite simple and well worked out piece of boldness, closely relate Descartes to the best minds of his time. The naturalist and utilitarian tendency of his wisdom, the harsh and zealous love he vowed for his Physics, his radically mechanistic conceptions, his showy and reckless cosmology, which the Newtonians were to call the "romance of nature," all that belongs at once to the powerful physico-mathematical movement, which had been a passion with learned Europe for half a century, and to the gifts of his astonishing analytical genius which made him the initiator and prince, not of physical experiment, in which Pascal towers above him, but of all modern theoretical Physics. Descartes's angelism is, to my mind, only the deepest spiritual and metaphysical *intention* of his thought. It remains the fact that there would be no difficulty in showing how well the articles of his system derive from this secret principle. His dualism, in particular—which makes man, despite vain efforts to maintain the old notion of the substantial unity of the human compound, a complete spiritual substance (this as much from the point of view of specific nature as from that of subsistence) joined in an absolutely unintelligible manner to an extended substance which is also complete and exists and lives without the soul—is only the translation into the order of Being of a doctrine which, in the order of knowledge, attributes to the human soul the functions of the pure spirit. We can also note in what concerns Descartes's mechanicism that, for a human reason made angelic, before which all the secrets of the material world lie open, a Physics which is nothing but Geometry was the only possible physics.

17. But the quality of Cartesian angelism is again best shown in its remote consequences, in the fruits of an ideal logic decanted by time.

The very notion of the rational animal takes a turn to the divine after Descartes. The inhuman breach by which the modern age feels itself, as it were, mystically obliged to free itself from the past, is only explicable if we understand that at the dawn of this age an angel began to emerge from the chrysalis of humanity.

And so, while the novelties of the Renaissance and the Reformation were introduced in the name of an antiquarian zeal for the pure springs of former days—classical antiquity and the primitive Church—the sense of the worth and rights of what is modern, as modern, springs into life with the Cartesian revolution. We know well the part played by the Cartesians in the quarrel of ancient and modern, the Georges Sorel has well shown the Cartesian origins of the dogma of Progress.

Man is a political animal because he is a rational animal. If we go some distance in his chief operation, which is the operation of the intelligence, he does not naturally need to be taught, but should, as a perfect intellectual nature, proceed by the way of discovery alone, the deepest root, and the most spiritual, of sociability disappears. In spite of a strong personal attachment to discipline and authority in politics, Descartes is thus in a very high sense at the origin of the individualist conception of human nature. From afar, but most certainly, he paves the way for the man of Jean-Jacques. Nor is his *rationalistic naturalism* without proclaiming in its fashion the naturalism of negative education. Is not Nature—leaning, it is true, on the philosopher's complete works—is not Nature enough for the building up of knowledge, and common sense enough for the approach to the most rare sciences? Now we have human nature quite naked, naked as a pure spirit, and reason *in the state of nature,* without the outward helps of human experience and the traditional *magisterium,* without the inward helps of the *habitus* and the virtues developed in the depth of the intellect, charged to scale the metaphysical heaven, until it sets itself to govern its own history and make happiness and goodness reign in the world.

How, finally, should we not find in the transference of the angelic independence of external objects to our understanding the spiritual principle not only of idealism but also of rationalism properly so-called? The essence of rationalism consists in making the human reason and its ideological content the measure of what is: truly it is the extreme of madness, for the human reason has no content but what it has received from external objects. That inflation of reason is the sign and cause of a great weakness. Reason defenceless loses its hold on reality, and after a period of presumption it is reduced to abdication, falling then into the opposite evil, anti-intellectualism, voluntarism, pragmatism, etc. It must be a very superficial inquiry which would classify under a single heading, as M. Louis Rougier lately tried to do, such a malady of the mind and the great realism of the *philosophia perennis*—which smashes rationalism as roughly as anti-intellectualism and, because it respects the natural humility of the reason, allows it to go forward victoriously in the knowledge of Being.

18. As the Lutheran Reformation is the great German sin, I have said that the Cartesian Reformation is the great French sin in the history of modern thought. Truly Descartes gave a philosophic and rational *form,* and, by the same stroke, a spiritual consistence and indefinite vigour of expansion, to tendencies which were prevalent in Europe before him under very difficult aspects. This remains true, that France has made the success of the Cartesian philosophy, and thus allowed those tendencies to penetrate inside Catholic thought. It remains true that if the most subtle and most profound principle of the Cartesian philosophy, as I have tried to expose it in this study, came down from the land of pure spirits—a land, need we say? essentially cosmopolitan,—it has fallen on earth and germinated in our home climate. I am well aware that the triumph of Cartesianism in France marked the first crack in our house, recently rebuilt and beaten by all the winds of Europe. Yet much more than the ideology of the eighteenth century, all contaminated by influences first English, then German, Cartesianism is in the image, not of the French spirit—I would not advance so foolish an idea—but of certain typical deformities against which we have to be on our guard; in the image not so much of what is life and moderation in us, but especially of what is excess and weakness.

Let no one characterize it as the model of French thought: it still keeps much of its native strength, but its features are thinned and stretched even to grimace. Nor should we have the frivolity to see in it with M. Lanson the vivifying principle of our classical art. On this point Brunetière was right: "The influence of Cartesianism in the seventeenth century is one of the inventions, one of the errors with which Victor Cousin formerly infested the history of French literature." Moreover the direct influence of a philosophical system on the arts is always very sporadic and superficial; it only truly makes impression on them indirectly in consequence of the effect it has on the general intellect,—and then with notable delay. We must seek the Cartesian brand in literature in the last years of the seventeenth century and at the beginning of the eighteenth, at the time when La Motte was sorry that Homer and Virgil had written in verse, and when that poet—one of the finest geniuses France possessed, according to Fontenelle, Mme. de Tencin, and the Abbé Trublet—sang:

> La nature est mon seul guide;
> Représente-moi le vide
> A l'infini répandu;
> Dans ce qui s'offre à ma vue
> J'imagine l'étendue,
> Et no vois que l'étendu . . .
> La substance de ce vide
> Entre ce corps supposé
> Se répand comme un fluide;
> Ce n'est qu'un plein déguisé.

A little later Abbé Terrasson was to announce, "No man who does not think in questions of literature as Descartes told us to think in questions of Physics is worthy of the present age."

All we can grant is that there are correspondences, because they have common causes, between the Cartesian philosophy and the parts of less resistance, or of less fullness, of an art whose substance and virtues depend on very different principles and have their origin in the twofold treasure, ancient and Christian. If Cartesianism attached itself to the fine working reason of the age of Louis XIV, it was to be its parasite. It was not Racine, nor La Fontaine, nor Boileau, it was their opponents, who sucked the milk of Descartes. It was Perrault, who wrote seriously, "Plato is condemned: he does not please the ladies," and stirred up the sex against Boileau. ("Don't be disturbed," said Racine to his friend, "you have attacked a very numerous body which is nothing but tongue; the storm will pass.") It was the *gentlemen* whom Racine recalled to respect for antiquity: "I advise these gentlemen no more to make up their minds so lightly about the works of the ancients. Such a man as Euripides deserved at least their examination, since they were anxious to condemn him. They should remember those wise words of Quintilian: '*Modeste tamen et circumspecto judicio de tantis viris pronuntiandum est*'." It was the "Hurons" and the "Topinambours" of the Academy, who were imperilling the classical deposit—"the whole thing is that they all club together against Homer and Virgil, and especially against good sense, as against an ancient, much more of an ancient than Homer and Virgil." Whether it is authentic or not the saying attributed to Boileau is still very significant: "I have often heard him say to M. Despréaux," wrote J.-B. Rousseau to Brossette on the 14th July, 1715 "that Descartes' philosophy had cut poetry's throat." How many other pallid victims were already lying in the street!

19. The Cartesian angel has aged a good deal, he has moulted many times, he is weary. But his undertaking has prospered prodigiously, it has become world-wide and it holds us under a law which is not gentle. He is an obstinate divider and he has not only separated modern and ancient, but he has set all things against each other—faith and reason, metaphysics and sciences, knowledge and love. The intelligence turned by him to the practical utilization of matter overflows in action which is external, transitive, and also material. And by that poor thing, the intelligence replaces the normal complement of its true life, which is the immanent and spiritual activity of love; for knowledge is only truly perfect when it flows out in love. The world sighs for deliverance; it sighs for wisdom, for the wisdom, I say, from which the spirit of Descartes has led us astray, for the wisdom which reconciles man with himself and, crowned with a divine life, perfects knowledge in charity. (pp. 53-89)

Jacques Maritain, "Descartes," in his Three Reformers: Luther—Descartes—Rousseau, *1928. Reprint by Sheed & Ward, 1950, pp. 53-89.*

Descartes's friend "Princess Elizabeth of the Palatinate" by Guillaume van Houthorst.

Bertrand Russell, Jacques Barzun, and Mark Van Doren (essay date 1942)

[*A respected and prolific author, Russell was an English philosopher and mathematician known for his support of humanistic concerns. Barzun is a French-born American educator and writer whose wide range of learning has produced distinguished works in several fields, including history, culture, musicology, literary criticism, and biography. Van Doren, the younger brother of the poet Carl Van Doren, was one of America's most prolific and diverse twentieth-century writers. In the following dialogue taken from the transcript of a conversation recorded in 1942, Russell, Barzun, and Van Doren consider the merit and influence of Descartes's philosophical ideas, focusing primarily on* The Discourse on Method.]

Van Doren: The full title of Descartes' essay, you remember, is ***Discourse on the Method of Rightly Conducting the Reason and Seeking Truth in the Sciences,*** but one notices immediately upon starting to read the essay that it has narrative form; it is cast, as Descartes himself says, in the guise of a tale. Mr. Russell, does it seem to you that this fact is purely accidental in its interest, or has Descartes been assisted in saying what he wants to say by assuming the posture of a narrator?

Russell: I think it assists him very greatly to say what he has to say. It helps the reader to be interested, and it helps the reader to be able to follow the chain of thought. Most philosophers are extraordinarily dry and very dull; Descartes is neither dry nor dull, and that is very largely because he doesn't confine himself to strict logic, but puts in picturesque material of a biographical sort.

Barzun: I should go farther, Mr. Russell, and say that for me the autobiographical element is the only value I find in the essay. It is interesting to note that the present title is a second choice. The essay was first called ***History of My Mind,*** and it was the preface to three purely scientific essays. I've often thought that if authors kept to their first titles less dangerous consequences would follow. In the present case we are misled into thinking that here is a discourse on method. I, for one, find no method whatsoever propounded in the essay.

Van Doren: Doesn't he at least propound a method which, according to him, came to him while he was lying in bed?

Russell: I disagree radically with what you say. A great deal of what he has to say about method is extremely good; I have found it valuable myself.

Barzun: But perhaps it's only the putting into somewhat rigid form of rather ordinary and self-evident rules: how to avoid mistakes. Certainly the account he gives of how he arrived at his method is unconvincing to me. I don't believe that he went through this process at all.

Russell: Oh, I dare say not! A great deal of that is just picturesque talk. But it's talk of a sort that helps you to understand what he means; therefore it's justifiable.

Barzun: It helps us to understand, but it formed a school of Cartesians who really believed that all this had happened.

Van Doren: I take the narrative form to be more than accidental. It seems to harmonize with the method itself. The impression finally given by the essay is that there is a truth about things which can be discovered in time. At first there is nothing and then there is something—the discovery of a principle of philosophy becomes in Descartes by implication almost a creation of the world.

Russell: You're both very unfair to Descartes.

Barzun: Well, you go ahead.

Russell: He says he's going to have nothing except what is clear and distinct. That is not having nothing.

Barzun: Well, he does say that after his education, for which he was properly grateful, he found that he had to undo it all. That is a common enough experience, but then he goes on to say that the first step was the achievement of a *tabula rasa.* Unlike Locke, who started the infant with a *tabula rasa,* Descartes achieved his with great effort, and then came the clear and distinct ideas. Why are those ideas valid, according to Descartes, Mr. Russell?

Russell: Because he was a mathematician. Of course it won't do as a method in empirical matters at all. But it does do in mathematics, and he was primarily a mathematician; all his remarks are those of a mathematician, and in mathematics it is, after all, the clear and distinct that the mathematician trusts to.

Barzun: That's where my objection comes in, because after setting aside the truths of poetry and literature and art and morals he leaves us only with mathematical truth, which, as I hope you'll admit, is truth about something conceived and not something existent. Yet at the end of the essay he invites us to consider physiology and medicine and the practical arts.

Russell: All that historical explanation is also historical justification. In his day mathematics was the chief machine for discovering facts about nature, and it did discover the most important facts, as in the case of Galileo who was a mathematician. He discovered things about the world, and mathematics was his instrument for doing it.

Barzun: But isn't there a kind of misleading uniformity in the attempt to make a very successful science in one realm apply to other realms?

Russell: It certainly is, and we see that now. Now, I think, his method isn't the right one, because on the whole the mathematical part of the job has been to a great extent done. But in his day it hadn't.

Barzun: But it has taken us three hundred years to get over this little essay of sixty pages. That's where my animus originates.

Russell: It goes back further than that. It goes back to Plato. The undue emphasis on mathematics goes back, in fact, further than Plato. It goes back to Pythagoras; Pythagoras is the villain of the piece.

Barzun: You are admitting then that there is a villain in the piece!

Russell: Well, he's become a villain. For two thousand years he was a saint.

Barzun: In other words, Descartes must have the credit of repeating a great error—is that your position?

Russell: Well, the thing has become an error. It was not an error in his day.

Barzun: I'm afraid I must agree with you there, but there is a further objection in my mind, and that is the tone and temper of the man and the ***Discourse.*** He was a singularly unamiable, vain, malicious, timid person whose ideas could appeal only, it seems to me, to the narrowest and most sectarian of philosophic minds.

Van Doren: You say he was both vain and timid. Would there be any difficulty in reconciling those two terms, or do you mean both?

Barzun: I hadn't thought of it, but I mean both.

Russell: They are quite easy to reconcile. Newton was both, obviously. But I don't agree with you. When one reads most philosophers they're mostly much worse than he is in all these respects. Philosophers are perhaps a narrow-minded sect.

Barzun: Oh, I don't know! I think if you take a man like Berkeley or Locke you find a fuller, richer atmosphere. I suppose we can overdo this point of the atmosphere of a philosopher, but I think it has a great influence historically.

Van Doren: I find Aristotle to be less vain, if vain at all, than Descartes, and for this reason. He seems to begin with the assumption that a world already exists, a world which is very thick and full about him, a world that he did not create and did not conceive himself. Descartes has the air of being the first, or at any rate the only man. Nothing shall be before him; he wants to clear away all former conceptions and all former ways of talking, so that there will be complete barrenness and emptiness and dryness in the world.

Russell: Well, I wish he'd done it more subtly. The trouble was merely that he didn't do it enough. The world was encumbered with rubbish in his day, intellectual rubbish, and the first thing was to be a scavenger, to get it all out of the way.

Van Doren: When the world is full of rubbish, which it always is, of course, thank God—I much prefer a world full of rubbish to an empty one—isn't the wisest thing to do to order that rubbish?

Barzun: Or a corner of it!

Van Doren: If you can.

Russell: Well, it isn't the custom, if you want to build a fine public building, to leave all the ruins of some previous buildings there; you clear them away.

Barzun: Now we fall back into one of Descartes' metaphors—

Russell: We do!

Barzun:—in the introduction, and we come upon one of

his major inconsistencies. First he divides the world into thought on the one hand and matter on the other, and that is a cleaning-up process in itself, since his matter is simply extension and his thought is whatever he finds by the test of clarity and distinctness. But then on top of that he brings in the established social order and a curious set of mixed morals—ethics—partly stoical, partly epicurean. At bottom he is profoundly indifferent, it seems to me, to everything except his few leading principles, which can lead in any direction without producing much result.

Van Doren: His morals, incidentally, he explicitly calls provisory. That is to say, they are temporary morals which he will adhere to until the moment when he knows everything. In Part Three of the ***Discourse,*** you will remember, he says: pro tem, I shall observe the following rules, not because I think they conduce necessarily to right living but because they are the safe ones to follow; they are the rules that will get me into the least trouble. First, I shall obey the laws and customs of my country if only to escape notice and be left free to think. Then I shall be as firm and resolute in my action as possible; that is to say, not knowing yet what is true, nevertheless, when I do see a course of action or a course of thought, I shall take it straight away—here is the metaphor once again—as a man lost in a forest should do. A man lost in the middle of a forest should keep going in one direction, because anything is better than remaining in the middle of the forest. Then, third, I shall be something of a stoic. I shall try to conquer myself rather than fortune, I shall not ask for things which I cannot have. He is nowhere more contemptuous of morals than here where he assumes that they are but ways of being safe.

Russell: But, look, I must stand up to this. When you come to what he really does feel you learn that he has the most passionate desire to be of use to the human race—to be of use through the discovery of knowledge, which was the way in which he could be most useful. I very much doubt whether any other manner of life that he could have adopted would have made him as useful as he was.

Barzun: But wouldn't you admit that he was perhaps a little bit too adroit and diplomatic, not only in his relations to life but in his writings? For example, many of his contemporary critics said that it is very well to divide thought from matter for purposes of science, but that surely they must unite in the human organism: the mind and the body are connected. There is then a third original idea, which is the union of soul and matter and we feel it or sense it through the senses; but we have to go to his letters to a princess who was interested in philosophy in order to learn that, just as we have to go to other letters and other writings to discover that he believed in the value of the emotions and the passions, that he thought they were all perfectly good, provided that they were used in moderation—which contradicts his stoicism. We have to go again to his letters to discover that he was—oh, almost a Christian Scientist. He said that he had been cured of early tuberculosis by looking on the bright side of things, which simply does not go with the image of Descartes as we see him historically.

Russell: I quite agree, of course, but that is so with any man. Any man, if you take him in his letters, where he's discoursing more or less accidentally, doesn't have the same statuesque appearance that he does when he writes his great works; that's just common humanity.

Van Doren: We don't mean to be as savage as we sound. We're expecting you to annihilate us within the next few minutes. Descartes' claim that he is doing good in the world interests me a great deal. He says, to me if you please, that he is doing me good. Well, that reminds me of my failure ever to believe a scientist when he tells me that he is in the world to do me good. I do not find that he is very much interested in me. I am not, you understand, being personal now; I am putting myself in the place of any human being. I find a curious lack of warmth in his voice as he says he wants to do me good. What he really wants me to believe is that if I shall agree with him—

Barzun: He will tolerate you!

Van Doren: He will tolerate me.

Russell: Let's take this up. It's perfectly true that the pure man of science, as such, is not actuated by philanthropy directly, but he knows perfectly well that the outcome of what he does is likely to be beneficial. Let's take, say, a man who is doing medical research. He is not interested in patients because he's not dealing with them; he is engaged in discovering a method by which others can deal with patients.

Van Doren: I wonder how much good a man like Descartes could do medicine in view of the fact that he distinguished body and mind as sharply as he did? It strikes me as possible that all the good one could do in medical experiment might not balance the harm done by that distinction.

Barzun: And I, for one, am certainly not requiring philanthropy in scientists. They should do things for the ordinary, good enough human reason that they're interesting and ultimately valuable, without any particular love for this or that group of human beings. But the reason I feel so strongly against Descartes—I might as well reveal it—is that his insistence on method has had a bad influence on science and more particularly on French education. It has led, it seems to me, to an over-emphasis on the formal side of all thinking, to organization on a mechanical basis, rather than on the organic unity of thought and the capacity for insight. Now, Descartes was not without insight but he trampled it underfoot. His four rules are simply scaffolding, of very little importance in actual use and of very great harm in the sequel.

Van Doren: What are those four rules, by the way? Have you found them useful, Mr. Russell?

Russell: His four rules may as well be set forth. Never accept anything not known to be true or clear and distinct. Divide difficulties into as many parts as possible. Proceed from the simple to the complex. Make complete enumerations to be sure that nothing is omitted. Now, the second and third especially—divide difficulties into as many parts as possible and proceed from simple to complex—I personally have found it always necessary to insist upon with advanced students who were beginning research. Unless they were very able they tended to take vast problems far beyond their powers, and I find Descartes' rules exactly what one has to tell them.

Barzun: Of course, simple and complex are terms relative to almost any single subject matter, and it is possible to lose the view of the whole through looking at detail. I can take an example from Descartes' own life. He wrote his ***Meditations,*** of which the full title was ***Meditations in Which Are Proved the Existence of God and the Immortality of the Soul,*** and, as usual, he sent the manuscript to his friend and critic, Father Mersenne, who read it and said: "It's splendid, but there isn't a word in it about the immortality of the soul!" So that Descartes's enumeration there was imperfect. I don't blame him for that. Geniuses have often made those silly errors. But it shows that he didn't use his method.

Russell: He proved the soul was immaterial and forgot to stick in that what was immaterial is immortal.

Van Doren: Possibly, Mr. Russell, the greatest defect of the higher learning today is that students are too much discouraged from considering hard subjects. If I were going to reform graduate schools, for instance, in the United States, I should begin by insisting that students be encouraged to begin in a very large field and then refine it. There is too much suspicion of the capacities of students. This seems to be a direct result of Descartes's own thought, whose scorn of anything except the clear and the distinct, which often became in his mind the small, means that the capacities of students have actually diminished with the failure to occupy them with larger things.

Russell: There is a compromise at that point, which I think is important. When one is engaged upon a smaller matter it should always be in its relation to a large one and because of its relations, not in itself.

Van Doren: That is precisely, it seems to me, where we can see one unfortunate result of Descartes. Take his discussion of God, which might be considered unessential to an explanation of his method, but which I think is very interesting. He pays all sorts of lip service to God, insists that God exists, and indeed spends time proving that He exists; yet what he is really proving is that after one has said all that one can forget God. God started the world, to be sure, and it is now working as He started it going, or as any mathematician might have started it going; Descartes almost says: "I could have done the same thing. I have proved the world to be exactly what it ought to be because it is intelligible to me." That is his test of existence, namely, intelligibility.

Barzun: It is a reduction of experience to something much more abstract and limited.

Van Doren: I don't want to be fantastic, but why wouldn't it be a good thing to expect students to begin with the contemplation of God? We act as if we thought they should begin with a worm.

Russell: Supposing you do begin with the contemplation of God—I should still uphold Descartes, and say that here he sees a large subject that can be divided into heads which can be taken one at a time.

Barzun: I should be perfectly willing to arrive with Descartes at any conclusions that seem to be useful in physics and mathematics, if he would be wholly candid. But, for example, he never tells us except in letters that the main ideas of his philosophy occurred to him when he was twenty-three in a dream, in a series of dreams on one single night in the year 1619. Instead of that, he gives us the wholly false and "public" view that you can arrive at truth by sitting down in a porcelain stove, as he did, and excogitate truth.

Van Doren: That's curious behavior for a scientist, isn't it?

Russell: I don't think it is. He confesses once that you may happen to hit upon the truth in dreams, especially, he says, in matters that are purely intellectual, and I think that's as much as you can expect of him. If he had come before the public and said that something was revealed to him in a dream it wouldn't have had the right effect.

Barzun: No, but he wouldn't have had to say that. He would have had to say that upon the basis of glimmerings acquired in a dream, his ideas were thought out and verified. I'm comforted, however, by the fact that history took its revenge upon him. When he died in Stockholm, since he was an infidel in a Protestant country, he was buried first in the cemetery devoted to children who die before attaining the age of reason.

Van Doren: How did he happen to die, by the way?

Russell: He died of getting up early! He never used to get up till twelve o'clock, in the middle of the day. Then he went to teach Queen Christina of Sweden, and she insisted on his getting up at five in the morning in the Arctic winter. The poor man died of it.

Van Doren: How soon? How many mornings?

Russell: Oh, in a little time. He died the first winter.

Van Doren: Mr. Russell, I wonder if Mr. Barzun and I have not exaggerated the influence of Descartes and rendered too malicious an account of his thought.

Russell: I do not think Mr. Barzun has exaggerated his influence in France. I, too, if I were French, might agree with all he says. But in other countries his influence has been less, and I think one may say of any man, however great and good, that his influence is bad—everybody's influence is bad if it's great.

Barzun: A very philosophical principle!

Van Doren: Will you go on to elaborate that?

Russell: Yes. It produces a set of disciples who repeat what the man has said instead of thinking. And so Descartes, by the mere fact that he had a great influence, undoubtedly became harmful in France. So would anybody else who had a great influence, but, if you contrast him with the scholastics who went before, I think he was better.

Barzun: And he did start Locke on his path. It was a very different path, but Descartes was the necessary stimulus. And the *Discourse*—I don't want to be misunderstood—

remains a wonderful piece of autobiographical writing. Wonderful if only in this: that every sentence has at least two or three intentions and must be deciphered before one quite gathers where Descartes stands and what he wants his readers to believe.

Van Doren: What kind of sentence does he write, Mr. Barzun?

Barzun: In France he is considered one of the first modern prose writers. He writes a rather long and tortuous and complex sentence, but one perfect in its fulfillment of hidden meanings. He's a malicious writer.

Van Doren: But also delicate.

Barzun: A very delicate writer.

Van Doren: Do the translations manage to convey all that is there?

Barzun: They tend to break it up into smaller units of prose that spoil his rhythm.

Van Doren: I have not read him in French, although it is clear to me, as I read him in English, that he must have these qualities. However, I suspect them rather than find them.

Barzun: It is interesting that at the end of the autobiography he says that he wants a subsidy. He was thinking ahead to the large foundation, I think, that supports scientists without asking them to produce anything definite.

Russell: I'm not sure that he didn't want them to produce anything. He certainly wanted a subsidy. He wanted it solely for the purpose of experiments.

Van Doren: I think it would be fair, Mr. Russell, to ask you to read something from Descartes.

Russell: I'll read the last paragraph of his ***Discourse on Method,*** which will give one, perhaps, a better all-around picture of him than what we've been saying. He says:

> In conclusion, I am unwilling here to say anything very specific of the progress which I expect to make for the future in the sciences, or to bind myself to the public by any promise which I am not certain of being able to fulfill; but this of me I will say, that I have resolved to devote what time I may still have to live to no other occupation than that of endeavoring to acquire some knowledge of Nature, which should be of such a type as to enable us therefrom to deduce rules in medicine of greater certainty than those at present in use; and that my inclination is so much opposed to all other pursuits, especially to such as cannot be useful to some without being hurtful to others, that, if, by any circumstances, I had been constrained to engage in such, I do not believe that I should have been able to succeed. Of this I here make a public declaration, though well aware that it cannot serve to procure for me any consideration in the world, which, however, I do not in the least affect; and I shall always hold myself more obliged to those through whose favor I am permitted to enjoy my retirement without interruption than to any who might offer me the highest earthly preferments.

(pp. 93-104)

Bertrand Russell, Jacques Barzun, and Mark Van Doren, "Rene Descartes: A Discourse on Method," in The New Invitation to Learning, *edited by Mark Van Doren, Random House, 1942, pp. 91-104.*

Albert G. A. Balz (essay date 1952)

[In the following excerpt, Balz addresses Descartes's understanding of the physical world, arguing that his position is not as revolutionary as is commonly held.]

The most fateful achievement of Descartes was his apportionment of Nature's substantiality, of what was previously called the existential indefinitude. The critical factor in this was the redefinition of matter. The consequences are beyond simple estimate. In every field of modern thought and action—in art, in poetry, in science, in religious aspiration—the apportionment and the Cartesian definition of matter are governing elements even when unnoticed. In so far the modern world is Cartesian, however deficient his conception of matter.

In many ways the Cartesian apportionment and definition are distillates from the historical fund of opinions. Throughout the history of the Western mind the problem of reckoning with man's exceptional status was conditioned by ideas concerning the relation of things to the spatiotemporal structure of existence. Despite appearances, Descartes' work was conservational rather than revolutionary, simplificatory rather than additive, an effect rather than a cause. Descartes' redefinition of matter as a substance whose essential nature must be found in the dimensionalities inseparable from corporeality was not as revolutionary a change as it may seem to be. It was an economical fixation of ideas effected by a genius in response to a revolutionary situation. The revolutionary situation was not initiated by Descartes but rather by St. Thomas, while Descartes defined rather than initiated it. The filiations of ideas are often obscured by similarities and differences of terminology. Perhaps it would have been more expedient had Descartes elected to discard such terms as "substance," "matter," "essence," "attribute," "idea," and "soul." In retaining older terminology, while revising the meanings of terms, continuities and discontinuities become obscured. Existence being what it is, and exerting pressure upon thought by way of its apparency, mind is constrained to devise ideas corresponding to its general structure. There is no more notable instance of this than the ideas for which the word "matter" has been the vehicle. Descartes' retention of traditional terms represents, it may be, his sense of continuity rather than a mask to disguise revolutionary intent.

The Idea of Nature, it has been previously contended, defines the horizon of the sciences. After the discoveries of the Sixth Meditation, Descartes could realize the complexities of the situation. How can the Idea of Nature be made functional in the sciences? The over-all substantiality of the existential indefinitude, if there is such a thing, remains to be discovered—at any rate, if specific content is to be supplied for the expression. For the pursuit of the sciences, the Idea of Nature must receive specification. The first stage in this, as was seen, is the apportionment of Nature's substantiality. This substantiality once given a provisional apportionment, the subordinate ideas reflecting the apportionment must be defined for the uses of the sciences. Figuratively, it may be said that there are three such ideas: the Idea of Material Nature, the Idea of Apparent Nature or of Natural Signs, and the Idea of Psychophysical Nature. These must be examined under the tension produced by the functional necessity of employing two referents for the sciences concerned with Nature. There must be some disclosure of Nature's economy, and the disclosure must provide an inquiry program, not for the thinking thing, but for men when they function as conductors of inquiry. Under the auspices, the Ideas of Nature and of Creation must be maintained as functionally distinct, even though Descartes seems to imply that in the end they may be constructively interactive, especially if the provisional moral code is to be expanded to a doctrine that will assure man's mastery and possession of himself.

Descartes perceived that the architectonic supports the search for truth in the sciences *by limiting the scope of the search.* The sciences need not be encumbered by questions concerning the relation of Nature's indefinitude of substantiality to infinite substance. Their functionally final referent is Nature and its order. In so far as the sciences are speculative, they are speculative within these limits. In so far as something of Nature's substantiality or "substances" comes to be known in the sciences, the referent receives more adequate definition and may the more effectively control the processes of inquiry. In return, Nature's substantialities and order are represented by ideas in the scientific fund which are subject to revision and reorganization in the history of inquiry. Scientia's metaphysical tasks are, of course, reciprocally influenced by this accumulation. Thus, under the auspices, Scientia provides and implements a relative independence and freedom for the sciences.

The allotted task of man, Descartes emphatically asserts, is not merely to know but also to act, for the mastery and possession of Nature by men is the practical objective. Now there seems to be an infinitude of things comprised within Nature's substantiality. Its order is made manifest in each and every thing, but in different ways and degrees in each and every thing. If men did not need, or propose, to act, the sciences need not be replete with detail. Mind could be contemplatively content with an austere perception of Nature's general economy. Indeed, it could be said that metaphysics would suffice. Or, on the assumed condition, the search for truth in the sciences would be enjoined only for the purpose of enriching metaphysical speculation. But this is not in the spirit of Descartes. Action is enjoined. Somewhere Descartes declares that he had given but a few hours a year to metaphysical speculation. Human beings, since they are equipped with cognitive powers which conduce toward efficient action, it is clear that the search for truth in the sciences can and should serve the interests of action no less than the interests of speculation and contemplation. The mastery and possession of Nature defines the art corresponding to truth-in-the-sciences.

What, then, must be the character of the sciences if they are to assure the mastery and possession of Nature? Everything here pivots upon a fact which may be described as the *singularity* of the existent. Aristotle had said that science is of the universal. The Christian theologians came to declare that that knowledge, impossible for man—knowledge of the singular in its inexhaustible singularity—indicates what Divine Knowledge may be. But the mastery and possession of Nature and, correspondingly, the arts of welfare require precise reckoning with the similarities and the differences attendant upon the fact that the indefinitude of existence comprises an indefinitude of singulars. In one set of conditions, differences between singulars may be less important, for inquiry and art, than the similarities which permit them to be understood as instances of kinds. But in another, the differences may be all-important. Every thing, as Aristotle rightly contended, is a unity of matter-and-form, a first substance, a singular. How then are singulars to be known in the sciences when knowledge of the singular as such is impossible?

Were the revelatory resources of Theologia infinitely vaster and replete with infinite detail, the problem would not arise. Every existent—every man (each man), every butterfly (each butterfly), every atom (each atom)—is designed to enact its peculiar contribution to the fulfillment of the Divine Plan of Creation. Final causes, Descartes avers, are useless in physics. But if Theologia had the resources, physics would be useless! If Theologia, by reason of an indescribably detailed and comprehensive Revelation concerning the indefinitude of creatures, could make clear the singular's intended contribution to the consummation of the Divine Plan, the singular would be known in its imprescriptible singularity, and therefore its internal nature and organization would be known. How different patients will react to the same treatment would be predictable by a theological medical art. Theologia, however, as has been made clear, has no such resources. The problem of reckoning with the singular is accordingly that of the sciences. The sciences must find, in their own ways and in terms of their own funds of ideas, that which will serve as a substitute for the immitigable teleological uniqueness which Theologia must attribute to the singular. In sum, the sciences must transmute the singular into the particular, into the case, the instance, the example. Their universals must be such that a precise representation of similarities and differences is possible. Inquirers must ask, not *why* a thing is what it is and *why* it differs from another, but rather *what* is this thing and precisely *how* does this instance differ from that?

The Idea of Nature must be defined in accord with the conditions under which inquiry promotes mastery and insures the arts of mundane welfare. Under the control of the architectonical auspices, Descartes faced a grand problem of reorientation and reorganization. A basis for knowledge must be found that will provide a humanly feasible equivalent, an infinitely remote substitute proportioned to human resources, for a knowledge that deity alone possesses. The unspannable distance between Nature's indefinitude and Perfect Being remains acknowledged in Cartesian metaphysics, but the foundations of the search for truth in the sciences must be defined in such a way as to free such inquiries of concern for that distinction. Singulars, known to Theologia as creatures, are to be transmuted into a manyness of exactly specifiable particulars. Nature must be reduced to comparative simplicity and to an order corresponding to this poverty. Inquiry-claims must represent its ordered multiplicity in two ways: by abstraction from its existential richness, the particular being regarded as a mere instance of something more general, while generality is pushed to a limit where it accords with Nature's indefinitude and unity of order; again, the samples must be distinguishable one from the other, even though they be cases under the same generality and their differences represented with accuracy. Aristotle, whose metaphysics is endorsed by children, indicated a world of nonduplicatable things caught within a web of interrelations. Creation could not be a teleologically ordered whole were there not some all-pervasive shared traits and principles of the proportionment of one creature to another. Scientia, under the Idea of Nature, must disclose for the sciences something quite different but equally all-pervasive and proportioned. Scientific knowledge must be at once a knowledge of particulars and knowledge applicable to particulars.

Creatures, as known to Theologia, are alike in an especial sense. To each the distinction between essence and existence pertains. Their essences provide no grounds for inferring necessities of existence. They are alike in their immeasurable distance from the Being in which essence and existence are unfathomably one. The existence enjoyed by any creature is a *received* existence. They are participants, at far remove, of that Being which is God. Even Aristotle could not appreciate the status of singulars as creatures. Right in that he proclaimed their due measure of reality, and well-advised in ascribing to them what might be called substantiality, he nevertheless could not have brought together in one view the meagerness of received existence's substantiality (because of its distance from the Creator) and the overwhelming magnificence of existence as Creation. It is not the task of Scientia's sciences to hymn this magnificence or to proclaim the distance between existence and its source. Scientia must provide for its sciences ideas defining the meaning (for the uses of sciences) of received existence and participated being. Scientia must equally facilitate the reduction of singulars to particulars and the substitution of precise definition of instances for the enjoyment of singularity. To represent the order and substantiality of Nature's indefinitude, on the one hand, and to achieve an exquisite precision in representing the indefinitely varying particularities of that substantiality—these are the tasks of Scientia's sciences.

Under the control of the auspices, Descartes confronted an excessively difficult situation. Nature is one, in that it corresponds to Creation. It is one, in that it is infinitely remote from infinite and absolute substance. It is one, in that all existence is what Theologia defines as received or participated being. Moreover, on the assurances of Theologia, it is real in its own way. It can be treated as if it were a final object of inquiry and it is for Scientia's sciences the final referent of claims. The divine governance of Creation must have its correlate in the sciences—in the laws of Nature, in its ordered uniformity. The sciences must assume that principles of order extend throughout the indefinitude of Nature. The pebbles with which children play and the stars are within a single indefinitude. Nature is resplendent, not impoverished, but it or some portions of it must be treated *as if* it were impoverished. Were it possible for mind to achieve a complete teleological metaphysics, no similarities and no dissimilarities could be neglected. The sciences, however, must neglect some similarities and some dissimilarities. The vexatious problem, however, is to determine what likenesses and differences can be neglected, so that great portions of Nature can be known by means of human cognitive equipment. What *does suffice* to express the diversity of things in the indefinitude of Nature? The question is peculiarly acute with respect to man, for this thing too is a part of Nature to be mastered and controlled and possessed. In the perspective of Scientia, the most notable fact concerning man is that he is endowed with the powers of inquiry and with a capacity to seek the good life and to use the results of inquiry in the seeking. What, then, of man in reference to Nature's substantiality and order?

How can Nature's substantiality and order be defined? For Descartes, assuredly, the Idea of Nature refers to all that can be described as finite or indefinite. But the traditional notion of the hierarchical ordering of creatures cannot be elided by reducing all things to a monotonous uniformity. This would offend children and Aristotle and St. Thomas. The latter had made sturdy efforts to define the singular existent by an adaptation of the Aristotelian metaphysical analysis. A finite thing, a singular, is a unity of matter-and-form. But this applies to corporeal existents alone. It could be said that a thing is corporeal if the form-matter analysis applies to it, and that if a thing is corporeal the form-matter analysis does apply to it. An existent's intelligibility depends upon a tension between the two poles of analysis, the one signified by "form." the other by "prime matter." If this be the case, Descartes' problem was to define an equivalent polarity for the sciences—a problem all the more crucial if existential science is to become mathematical. The matter of terminology, whether to conserve the language of "form" and "matter" and associated terms while redefining them for the uses of inquiry depended upon many considerations. If the term "form" should be retained, it must be adjusted to the changed meaning of matter. Now if all things comprised within Nature, assuming that the scope of the term is to be comparable with that of Creation, are unities of matter and form, "matter" would signify something pertinent to the understanding of the whole of Nature. It could be defined in such a way as to be equivalent in universality to the notion of received existence, of participated being, to a mark whereby every thing that exists and yet is not to be identified with God can be defined in its status as being other-than-God. Matter would then indicate some universally shared trait of everything in Nature's indefinite substantiality. This trait would then serve as the final referent for the sciences, for all the sciences, and the variable characters of particulars could be related to it. But this would be permissible only upon the proviso that every thing is corporeal and can be construed as a unity of matter-and-form. According to St. Thomas, however, this is not the case. Not all singular existents are corporeal, or, what amounts to the same thing, such that their intelligibility is conditioned by the polar tension expressed in the matter-form distinction. The angels are incorporeal. They are not unities of matter-of-form. In this sense they are immaterial. They are, of course, singulars, individuals. Each is a substance. But each is a substance in a sense to be distinguished from that in which a unity of matter and form is a substance. Now doubtless it is the case that Descartes accepted the existence of angelic beings and must urge that, if they exist, they have their hierarchical place in the existential indefinitude. In view of the difficulties of knowing anything about angels, he must have thought, it would be well for the sciences to treat the existential indefinitude as if it does not comprise angels. The hierarchy of existence, for the sciences, must be viewed as having man at its apex. So understood, the problem can be restated. In this existential indefinitude, is there anything of such a nature that the form-matter distinction does not basically condition knowledge of it? If this be the case, then the term "matter" cannot be reinterpreted as the (or a) final referent for all possible sciences. Nature's indefinitude of substantiality cannot then be defined as "matter" and the order of Nature cannot be interpreted as the laws of matter. The term will not designate a factor underlying all possible existence.

The conclusions of the Sixth Meditation, which Descartes felt he was compelled to accept, shows that he faced a dilemma. Either the term "matter" signifies something less than the dependent indefinite substantiality of Nature, or else the scope of the Idea of Nature must be less than that of the Idea of Creation. In view of the unity of Creation, we are constrained to anticipate that Nature is somehow one. In view of the distinction between Creator and Creation, between Being and derivative existences, between Being and received existence, a distinction between infinite substance, which alone is rightly substance, and dependent and conditioned substantiality is imposed. Putting together these considerations we are impelled to grant to the term Nature a scope equivalent to that of Creation and to assign to Nature a single dependent substantiality. But if this be done the notions of matter-and-form, corporeality, materiality are unavailable for describing this substantiality without violent collision with St. Thomas' notion of the contents of Creation. Now it might be urged: abandon the angels to Theologia and exclude them from Scientia's sciences. What if the scope of the Idea of Nature be less than that (alleged) to pertain to Creation? Cut across the hierarchical order of creatures and confine inquiry to men and all other things which are like men at least in that they are not above men and are not angels. But this counsel entails a great deal more than appears. Is the notion of a hierarchy of beings in Nature to be retained? Are we to retain and adapt the notion, making it functional for scientific inquiry? Conceiving Nature on this reduced scale, the upper levels of the hierarchy of creatures being lopped off, shall we regard this reduced Nature as a single indefinitude of substantiality? An adjustment with the auspices might be effected. Beings higher than men would be perceived in the perspective of Theologia alone. If there were a "science" of such beings as angels, then it would be exclusively a theological science and presumably a teleological science. The adjustment would conform to the Angelic Doctor's own dualism, a dualism represented, on the one hand, by beings with respect to which the matterform distinction is irrelevant and, on the other hand, by beings whose intelligibility is dependent upon the distinction. In this case, "matter" could appropriately be taken as designating the substratum, the indefinite dependent substantiality of Nature. All sciences established by Scientia would be sciences about Nature and all would have matter-substance as their final referent. Since all natural beings, in these conditions, are unities of matter and form, their respective singularities could be particularized by reference to the intrinsic constitution of this matter-substance. The referent, matter, could be called "substance," the substance of Nature, reserving to Scientia's metaphysics the distinction between "finite" and infinite substance. It could be urged that by this adjustment the freedom of scientific inquiry, affirmed in principle by the architectonic of Wisdom, could be realized in fact. As mind in the future surveys the fruits of scientific inquiry, the content of the Idea of Nature could be vastly enlarged. Moreover, the Idea would contain what, and *only* what, the exercise of cognitive powers can attain when they function in complete independence.

Despite these advantages the scheme presents difficulties. Of these, the crucial one concerns man. There must be a science, or sciences, of man. Now man is a corporeal being, at least in part. He is a thing among things. Presumably, his intelligibility is in so far conditioned by the polarity of matter and form. The sciences must reckon with the exceptional status and extraordinary singularity of this being. There seem to be but two alternatives. Nature's substantiality must be construed in such a way that everything in Nature, even its most exceptional manifestations, all animate and inanimate existence, can be interpreted in terms of constitutive attributes of a single substance. The Sixth Meditation, however, conveys Descartes' conviction that this cannot be done. A dualistic apportionment of Nature was necessary. If the matter-form distinction is then not universally applicable throughout the range of Nature's indefinitude, what serves a like purpose with respect to those existents, "souls" let us say, where the matter-form distinction does not apply? If the matter-form distinction does apply, with these exceptions, to everything else in Nature, how can the distinction be transmuted into ideas serviceable in the corresponding sciences? The mastery and possession of physical or corporeal nature means power over *things*—stones, plants, animals—and the making of things—watches, plows, steam engines. For St. Thomas, one of the two fundamental questions for metaphysics had been: what is a thing? The analysis of thingness was indispensable. In the transition to modernity and in Descartes' efforts to devise a basis for the sciences' economy, the problem of the transformation of "thingness" was of major importance. In the philosophical tradition, of course, the analogy of human construction had exercised a powerful influence. A product of human making, such as a watch, a house, or a hoe, once it is made, has an independent career like things whose existence does not depend upon human making. If Nature be thought of as consisting of "things," all things could be roughly divided into two groups: those whose coming-into-being depend in part upon human activity, whose existence could not be wholly accounted for without reference to man and the nature of man expressed in his activities; and all other things, things that are what they are and seemingly would be and be just what they are, even if the world did not contain human beings. The analysis of human making and its conditions would be indispensable for understanding the first group of things. The four causes of Aristotle would emerge from the analysis. Then, if things made by men are similar to many things not made by men, the four causes could be extended by analogy to the latter, at least to the extent that the similarity would undergird the analogous uses. By a reductive process, the four causes can be resolved into matter and form. Under the architectonical apportionment, however, the four causes, the analogy, and the matter-form distinction must be revised and transformed.

The Cartesian problem, accordingly, was not one of replacing the matter-form distinction by some new one, rejecting the former as meaningless. It was rather a problem of reinterpreting the distinction under the Idea of Nature and for the purpose of efficiency in the search for truth in the sciences. The Thomistic query remains: what is a thing? The reinterpretation of "form" and "matter" must be such that the distinction will be relevant to everything which, in the tradition, could be designated as a unity of matter and form. But if there are existents to which the matter-form analysis, as traditionally understood, is not relevant, then we should expect a revised conception of matter and form to have a correspondingly restricted applicability. The analogy between the coming-into-being of things through human agency and the coming-into-being of other things must be either discarded or reinterpreted. The very words, the mastery and possession of nature, convey the suggestion that the analogy could be made fruitful. The phrase implies the general *availability* of portions of Nature as resources exploitable in human making. The exploitation of these resources, however, depends upon a science permitting accurate and precise representations of the specificities of things. If mastery and possession, however, is to include man's mastery and possession of man, and man is thus to be viewed as a part of Nature's availability as means for making, exploitation reaches its maximal difficulty. If Nature's tendency to produce singulars from its substantialities attains its maximal expression in human beings, the problem of reckoning with the specificities and diversities of "things" becomes extraordinarily difficult. The making activities of men, their incorporations of new forms into portions of Nature, become most precarious and desperately dangerous when mankind itself and men themselves are viewed as parts of the availability of Nature. How can the sciences proceed economically unless the singular, the individual thing, is construed as a case, a particular, an instance, an example? But how can Nature in its maximal singularity be reduced to instances without maximal loss of reality? It is not a matter of wonder that the modern age, so largely foreseen by Descartes, should be marked by a new demand for freedom, for the full recognition of the significance of individuality. If the sciences are to serve the cause of human welfare, it is the welfare of teach and every individual human being, in his extraordinary singularity, that must define objectives. The Cartesian revision of the concepts of matter and form must not imperil human welfare while disclosing the basis for its attainment.

The revision of the notion of "form" may be reserved for later consideration. How then is the remaining term, matter, to be defined so that it may represent as much as possible of Nature's substantiality for the uses of science and also be adjusted to the singularity of things, on the one hand, and to the generality of Nature's order, on the other hand? Matter may be taken to signify that (relative) independence of being historically conveyed by the term "substance." Matter, then, is the name of a substance. Nature's substantiality, or this substantiality so far as Nature is corporeal, may then be indicated by the term "matter." It may be helpful to note that, in the perspective of Theologia, it would be inappropriate to define *Creation,* or some great region of it, as a substance. In that perspective, every creature has its unique role to play in the design of Creation. Teleologically viewed, accordingly, it is singularly appropriate to regard each creature, each thing, each unity of matter and form as a substance. In the perspectives defined for physical science by Scientia, however, economy requires that "things" become particularizations of a widely embracing substantiality. "Substance" is a term, then, that may appropriately be used of Nature. Or, if Nature is not adequately represented unless its general quasi substantiality be divided into several substances, in any case the word "substance" fitly indicates the finality of Nature as the referent of the sciences.

With respect to the Cartesian use of the term "matter" to signify Nature's substantiality—in whole or in part—the question is one both of idea and of terminology. Abstractly considered, the issue concerns the transition from the negative to the positive aspects of the Idea of Nature. Nature corresponds to what Theologia describes as received existence or participated being. This is a negative correspondence. But how shall Nature be understood in a positive sense as is suggested by its substantiality for inquiry? On the one hand, if Theologia defines every creature as a unity of matter-and-form, and if matter be signate for form, then "matter" might well be adapted as a term for Nature's total substantiality. The phrase, matter-and-form, could be regarded as representing a polarity of analysis pertinent to every case of received existence and expressing what it means to have the status of received existence or participated being. The equivalence of Scientia's dependent being and Theologia's participated or created being would be neatly expressed by the unrestricted applicability of the matter-form distinction. Now prime matter does not exist. A form is not a thing. An existent is a unity-of-matter-and-form. It is informed matter. If the relationship between matter and form be reciprocal, then, in the conditions proposed, Nature's substantiality could be signified by the term "matter" and every existent within that substantiality could be regarded as a specification of matter-substance, as a restricted concretion of and within matter. In sum and in simple terms, every thing would be a case of organized matter. But the conditions presupposed do not obtain in either Thomistic or Cartesian doctrine. St.

Thomas does not define matter in such a manner that it and it alone is everywhere a factor in the analysis of created or received existence. The angels and, to a certain extent, men are excluded. And with Descartes, whatever the soul of man is, it is at least immaterial. With respect to Thomistic no less than Cartesian doctrine, the case of man is quite complicated—as will appear later. In these circumstances, if Descartes is to adjust his use of terms with some regard for tradition, matter cannot be defined as the substance of all Nature. It can be defined as the substance of all corporeal things, of all things whose intelligibility depends upon the polarity expressed by means of the distinction between matter and form and of the reciprocal relation between matter and form.

Briefly, the point can be expressed in this way: a portion of Nature's existential indefinitude is corporeal and nucleations within this portion may be called bodies. Matter designates the ("finite") substance of all corporeality. Since Nature's corporeal substantiality appears to be richly diversified, its diversifications must be conceivable in relation to this substantiality, that is, to matter. The formal factor in the unity of matter-and-form must undergo a revision corresponding to the definition of matter as substance. If "form" traditionally signified factors in Nature not susceptible of this readjustment, then such factors must be related to something else in Nature's apportioned substantiality.

Substance, however, is a mere empty shell unless it possesses an intrinsic inherent and constitutive nature. Substance deprived of inner constitution would reduce to the equivalent of a gesture whereby it is acknowledged that existence is existence. It becomes the equivalent of prime matter, which does not exist, but serves to point out how analysis of any existent must move if the bare fact that the existent does exist is to be admitted. But if matter-substance be identified with prime matter, and prime matter be conceived as deprived of all intrinsic constitution, then matter-substance tends to become the equivalent of privation, of nothingness. It could not then serve as a referent for sciences dealing with bodies or with Nature's corporeal substantiality. It is impossible to understand how unrelieved nothingness, naked privation, can contribute to the existential status of anything, a stone, a rose, a dog. The Angelic Doctor, it appears, was fully aware of this. At the limit, then, even "prime" matter must signify something real, something internally organized, something having an intrinsic structure. It must be neither *a* thing nor yet nothing. Since there are many corporeal things comprised within Nature, and since they are extremely diversified and yet similar, matter must be such as at least to render possible many bodies and their diverse properties. Assuredly, if matter were unqualified nothingness, it could not prevent the existence of anything; but neither could it contribute to the existence of any thing, to any thing whose positive existence and limited dependent status requires the polarity of "matter" and "form" for inquiry's reckoning with that thing. Prime matter must then signify a range of possibility comparable to the range of Nature's corporeal substantiality. Yet it must signify a certain limitation of possibility, in accord with the fact that Nature's corporeal substantiality is a *corporeal* substantiality. Prime matter is not signate for every possible form, unless we are to conclude that every actual or possible existent within Nature's indefinitude is and must be a unity of matter-and-form. But this alternative has been rejected, as was seen previously. However generously comprehensive prime matter's undifferentiated signateness may be, it is not unrestricted because prime matter's undifferentiated signateness may be, it is not unrestricted because prime matter is not the nothingness of mere privation. It is then clear that an intrinsic constitution must be assigned to prime matter. If, then, this be accomplished, prime matter has become transformed into what may rightly be called a substance. It can function in the sciences as a final referent.

What, then, shall be attributed to prime matter as intrinsically constitutive of its nature and definitively contributive to the existence of things? To make the notion serviceable in the sciences—one conjectures this to have been the thought of Descartes—the intrinsic constitution of matter-substance must economically combine universality and inexhaustible specifiability. In a sense, the conditions are simple. The multitude of inquiry-claims convincingly indicate the reliability of common sense, or, if you will, the point of view of children and Aristotle. The world comprises many things. The many, each of which is a thing, a this and of such and such a kind, somehow fall together within a comprehending whole. Things move and nothing so fully suggests the entitative integrity of each thing as the fact that each may move as a unit without jeopardizing too gravely its persistent unity of existence. The many are there to be reckoned with, whether they are reported upon by children or by scientists. Modifications accruing to each thing because of its interactions with other things vary greatly from triviality to destruction. The thing and its motion; this thing as distinct from and other than that thing; the thing and the space in which it is; the thing and its career in time; the thing with its effects upon other things and the effects of other things upon it; the coming-into-being and the passing-out-of-being of the thing; the persistent core of existence that defines thinghood as distinct from qualitative and quantitative changes without necessarily destroying the persistent thing: these statements and many similar ones guide the report of common sense concerning Nature. They represent the way in which the profane mythos is commonly read and understood. The higher criticism of the sciences cannot blandly dismiss this reading, for it must render this very report intelligible. The reading of common sense suggests that common denominators for the existence of corporeal things are indicated by relatively few traits. There is the stuff of things; there are space and time; there is motion. To which trait shall priority be given?

Priority here means basically conditioning the intelligibility of things for the reckonings of the sciences, for reckonings that can never achieve exhaustive knowledge of singulars but must anticipate practical art in dealing with these very singulars. Things must be approached by noting the universal traits of received existence and by noting also the specifications nesting within the fund of common existence. The hierarchy of genera and species may be admirably fitted to express the survey of things in the perspective defined by the Idea of Creation. The problem, however, is to find a suitable equivalent under the Idea of Nature. It is therefore a problem of the attributes which, because they are universal in Nature's corporeal substantiality, transform the emptiness of prime matter into authentic character. From the standpoint of common sense, it would appear that the definition of matter's internal constitution would require a selection from the several common denominators seemingly possessed by things or else their coalescence into a single universally shared property. Yet the continuity of space and time seemingly stands opposed to the nucleated existence of things about which common sense reports. Existence comes in chunks, in more or less separable bits, and despite continuities it suggests that there are elementary portions. The book of Nature appears to consist of words, and words of syllables and letters. It cannot be a book of nonsense syllables. For the uses of scientific inquiry, surrogates for the distinctions of common sense are indispensable. It could be urged that the Cartesian problem is one of reconciling Plato and Aristotle. If it be true, as is sometimes alleged, that "matter" in the Platonic tradition tends to become identical with privation, with nothingness, the Cartesian definition of matter must escape this identification. On the other hand, the "things" of Aristotle and their hierarchical ordering, highly appropriate to the description of the world in the perspective of Creation, must be correlated with equivalents specifiable in terms of matter's constitution. Now whatever may be the tendency of "matter" in the Platonic tradition to reach the emptiness of bare privation—the statement is questionable—the tendency is arrested here and there by a virtual identification of "matter" and space. In the tradition fathered by Democritus there are constantly present myths based upon the notion of particles moving about in containers, that is, in time and space, things being somehow resoluble into such particles. In Aristotle's world singulars have their several careers to the character of which space, time, and motion contribute. Descartes could not possibly have escaped the forces which gave rise to these diffused traditions. The definition of matter-substance must be, as it were, a distillation from many ingredients. As we know, matter is defined as a substance whose primary or essential attribute is extension. Participation in extension defines the minimal likeness of all existents in Nature's corporeal substantiality. Whatever "things" in their severalty may turn out to be, as inquiry comes to know more and more about them, they are one and all at least participants in extension. Once this basis of economy is attained, the sciences can proceed to define with exactitude and approximative exhaustion the resemblances and differences of corporeal existents.

St. Thomas frequently employed the phrase, *materia quantitate signata.* The reciprocal causality of matter and form, to use Forest's expression, is then a causality between form and a matter, ultimately a prime matter, readied for giving rise to things that, whatever else they may be, are at least possessed of quantity. In this measure they could be brought together for an inquiry based upon quantitative ideas. Corporeality seems to imply space-occupancy. Prime matter is then indeed not a term signifying bare privation, propertylessness. All corporeal things share in something contributed by the restricted but generously receptive nature of prime matter. Is it too much to contend that Descartes brings together in his conception of matter-substance, as in essential constitutive attribute extended, many factors in the traditions? The definition may represent Nature's corporeal substantiality in an exceedingly impoverished manner. Something must be done about the apparent riches of that substantiality. Either they do belong to Nature's corporeal substantiality or else they must only appear to belong to it while in truth belonging to another substantiality of Nature. But at least corporeal existents present themselves as prepared for an economical accounting in terms of quantity and extension. The indefinitude of figures will suffice for the representation of the details discoverable in Nature's corporeality. To the sciences organized to explore Nature's corporeality—this appears to be the conviction of René Descartes—with instruments suitable for reckoning with modes of extension, matter is extension. In the subordinate perspective of the Idea of Matter—subordinate to the more comprehensive perspective of the Idea of Nature—only Nature's corporeal substantiality will be perceptible. Accordingly, to sciences adapted to this perspective, the Idea of Matter and the Idea of Nature will seem to be equivalent. They may rightly be taken, functionally, as if they are equivalent. But in fact they are not. Nature, according to Descartes—and assuredly he here follows St. Thomas in spirit if not in letter—comprises a great deal that cannot be seen in the perspective of matter. (pp. 249-64)

Albert G. A. Balz, in his Descartes and the Modern Mind, *1952. Reprint by Archon Books, 1967, 492 p.*

Karl Jaspers (essay date 1953)

[*Jaspers was a German psychologist and philosopher whose writings explore modes of man's being and freedom. In the following excerpt from an essay originally published in 1953, Jaspers considers the philosophical ramifications of Descartes's "fundamental operation" in the* Discourse on Method—*his positing of universal doubt in order to assert the supremacy of the Cogito and God's existence.*]

The fame of Descartes is uncontested; his influence has been enormous, and the study of his principal works is still indispensable to anyone who wishes to philosophize. Thus there is no need to demonstrate his *historical* greatness, especially as German philosophers, since Hegel and Schelling, have looked upon him as the beginning and source of modern philosophy.

We know Descartes's irreplaceable discoveries in mathematics. We know his extraordinary achievement in renewing the form of thought; anyone who comes to Descartes after reading the philosophers of the Renaissance feels that he has suddenly emerged into clearer air; the thought is pregnant, each sentence is undeviatingly in its right place; the superfluous and incidental are disregarded; the development is resolute and conscious of its aim; the reader feels that he has been taken in hand.

We see the great style of his disciplined life, his courage and nobility and practical wisdom; we note how he withdrew into solitude, and went to a foreign country for the peace and quiet he required for meditation; how he devoted his life entirely to the task in which he believed, the renewal of all knowledge.

Nevertheless, it is not an easy matter to go beyond such a general characterization of the man, his work, and his influence, to show more clearly and definitely wherein the *philosophical* greatness of Descartes resides. This greatness has been called into doubt. The literature on Descartes includes so-called exposures, purporting to unmask him as a hypocrite who did not say what he thought, as a coward whose fear and mistrust led him to hide his true colors; as a man who, for all his intolerable pride, was jealous of other men's achievements, who schemed and plotted to ensure his fame; as a revolutionary who wished to destroy the whole existing order. We hold with none of these judgments. But with all our admiration for his historical greatness, we are among those who doubt whether his philosophy, either in content or in method, constitutes an eternal embodiment of philosophical truth. For when it is asked: In what sense can we make this philosophy our own?—we come to see, behind the rational clarity of the surface, an extraordinarily complex philosophical operation, which seems to by-pass the truth whenever it tackles a crucial problem. If we go on to observe how Descartes's thinking developed in other minds, we are also led to wonder whether, by virtue of his greatness, he may not, in addition to kindling the philosophizing of all those who followed in his footsteps, have led it astray through his method as well as the content of his thinking. Because he dealt with matters essential to the modern era, he was able to influence the greatest minds; but since, by his way of approaching it, he missed or even perverted the meaning of what was true in his discovery, he became a danger to all those who fell under his spell. It seems quite possible that philosophy was corrupted by the tendencies whose fountainhead and foremost representative was Descartes, and that the depth of truth reached since Descartes has been achieved more in spite of Descartes than because of him.

Opposition to Descartes—which has been continuous from his lifetime until today—has sprung from very diverse and even mutually exclusive motives. Thus the mere fact of being against Descartes means nothing—it is the nature of the opposition that matters. The more opposition to Descartes is based on critical understanding, the more it gains in truth. Anyone who ventures to disclose the seeds of untruth in the source of truth, must at the same time keep in mind that original truth without which historical greatness would be incomprehensible.

Our analysis derives its sequence from the following consideration: Descartes is famous for having tried, through *method,* to raise philosophy to the rank of a science coinciding with science as a whole. His method is related to his equally famous *fundamental operation,* by which he sought to make certainty spring from universal doubt.

These two elements—the problem of method and the problem of the origin—merge into a whole in his philosophy, but this whole was formed from two originally different sources. In his search for method, Descartes seems to take the same path as what was then modern science. The fundamental operation which, while providing the foundation for certainty, develops the principles of all being, is, on the contrary, rooted in the age-old philosophical tradition. In this new form philosophy strove to create a foundation not only for modern science, but for man's life as a whole.

In . . . this essay we shall analyze the "fundamental operation". . . .

1. HOW IT WAS EFFECTED

Let us briefly recapitulate the steps taken by Descartes:

1. Dissatisfied—he said in substance—by the instability of human opinions, by the doubt that has been cast upon every philosophical assertion made until now, and by disputations which thus far have not yielded a single secure result, I shall aim for real and enduring certainty.

In order to attain it, I shall first carry doubt to the extreme. If with plausible reason I have doubted everything that I ever regarded as certain, and if I then find a certainty that is secure against all modes of doubt, this certainty must be the foundation of all further knowledge that is accessible to us.

I can doubt the existence of the things outside me and the existence of my body; I can go so far as to doubt mathematical truths, even if these are compelling as such; for an evil genius might have created me and so organized me that for all my subjective certainty I might still be deluded; if that were so, I should be defenseless and might even fail to recognize the most evident truth. Then I should be un-

A portrait of Descartes's patron Queen Christina of Sweden by Sébastien Bourdon.

able to know any truth; I might, to be sure, defend myself against the demon by resolutely refusing to accept any statement involving a doubt. Does this mean that I can no longer accept any statement?

2. In taking the decision to doubt and radically to withhold my judgment, I observe that even if all grounds for doubt are justified, one thing remains certain: as long as I think, even if I am mistaken in supposing my thought to be compelling, I am certain that I myself exist (*cogito ergo sum*): of this certainty I can no longer doubt. If an evil spirit, who was my creator, deceived me in everything else, he could not deceive me in regard to the fact that I, even while allowing myself to be deceived, nevertheless know that I am.

3. Once I have gained a basis in indubitable certainty, how shall I go on?

In the process of attaining this certainty, I also learn what is requisite for certainty in any matter, namely: to conceive clearly and distinctly. But I formerly believed that I conceived many things clearly and distinctly and yet fell into doubt, suspecting that even in clarity and distinctness a demon might be giving me an illusion of truth. Thus a universal rule, such as: everything must be true that I conceive as clearly and distinctly as the *cogito ergo sum*—will be valid only if I can convince myself beyond any doubt that I was not created by a demon of deception. The next step must lead to this certainty.

Now I see not only that I did not create myself, but also that consciousness of my existence is inseparably bound up in me with the idea of infinity, which is the standard by which I measure my finiteness. In other words: I find within myself the idea of an infinite and perfect being, that is, the idea of God. In order to understand this idea, which was given me with my existence, I must clarify a fundamental insight in terms of a rational idea, which I call a proof of God's existence. I proceed as follows: I cannot have produced the idea of God any more than I can have brought forth my own existence. This I know on the strength of an axiom which is given to me by natural insight, namely, that there must be as much reality in a cause as in its effect. But since there is finiteness and imperfection in me, which I am enabled to appraise by the standard of my idea of the infinite and perfect, this idea of the infinite cannot have its source in me, who am finite, but can only come from God Himself. Therefore God *is,* and He is an infinite and perfect being. In knowing that I am, I know at the same time—even if everything else is illusion—that I am not alone in the world. "We must of necessity conclude from the fact alone that I exist, or that the idea of a Being supremely perfect—that is, of God—is in me, that the proof of God's existence is grounded on the highest evidence."

But this being cannot be evil, for evil is imperfection. He must be good in every way and therefore cannot deceive. Thus through what follows inevitably from the *cogito ergo sum,* I can rely, also in every other realm of my knowledge, on the clarity and distinctness which in the *cogito ergo sum* were able to withstand even a possible demon.

4. After clear and distinct knowledge has thus, on the two foundations of the *cogito ergo sum* and the certainty of God's existence, been proved to be reliable and beyond doubt, most of the truths I had previously doubted are restored at one stroke, in particular, the mathematical truths and the existence of corporeal things outside me, in so far as these are clearly and distinctly recognized, that is, in so far as they have quantity, extension, form, position, and motion.

Descartes sums up this whole development in the statement of Eudoxus in the dialogue ***Recherche de la vérité:*** "For it is really from this universal doubt, which is like a fixed and unchangeable point, that I have resolved to derive the knowledge of God, of yourself, and of all that the world contains."

2. CRITIQUE OF THIS CERTAINTY

The most evident purpose of this operation is to provide an indubitable certainty, valid for every thinking being. In inquiring to what degree this certainty is achieved, we shall have to ask: *to what* does this certainty refer? what does *doubt* mean in this operation? and, is there *a way to further development* from the ground of certainty thus acquired?

1. *To what does the first certainty refer?* As Descartes himself expressly states, the *cogito ergo sum* is not an inference; for an inference would presuppose other truths from which the *sum* followed, whereas this thought itself is represented as the origin. We interpret Descartes: The *ergo* is employed only as an analogy to the syllogism, in order to bring out the fact that this is not an immediate, perceived certainty, but a fundamental reflexive certainty, a self-certainty. I become aware, in reference to myself, that I think, that I am. Here we have the unity of a unique act of thought, which in thought refers back to itself and becomes aware of this relation as something existing in itself. Any attempt to state this adequately raises insuperable difficulties. Since *cogito ergo sum* suggests an inference, but Descartes rejects the notion of an inference, we might attempt to change the wording. We might say: *cogito, sum,* but then we should merely have two unconnected words. We might say: *cogitans sum* (if I think, I am); then, however, we should have a relation of consequence, the possession of being resulting from the fact of thinking, but this relation would be almost empty and, moreover, it would be stated in a definite form implying temporal existence; besides, the emphasis would be solely on the *sum,* whereas the *cogito* is of equal importance; the origin of the idea would not be appropriately rendered. Accordingly we shall use Descartes's formula *cogito ergo sum* in the following, even though its syllogistic form lends itself to misunderstanding.

To recognize thought in myself as being is to attain overwhelming certainty concerning the indispensable medium of all being that is being for me. But such certainty does not know what it possesses, for it can have no definite content.

Thus the *cogito ergo sum* as such cannot be doubted. But both its power and its weakness reside in the fact that its meaning remains utterly indeterminate and for that reason cannot be clearly apprehended. I am supposed to be certain of my existence as a thinking being. But in order to attain clarity concerning this certainty, we must find out what *thought* is, what the *I* is, and what the *being* of this *I* is.

What is thought in Descartes? Let us consider, without reference to explicit statements of Descartes's, what he may have meant by thought: it is the unique action which in acting knows itself, which consequently has immediate certainty of itself through its relation to itself. Because the object of certainty is here at the same time its subject, subject and object coincide; they are one and the same thing, which is neither subject nor object and at the same time both subject and object. This is what Descartes seems to mean when he expresses his full confidence in the fundamental certainty of the *cogito ergo sum* as the foundation of objective reality. But thought, which Descartes may originally have conceived in this way, becomes something more definite as soon as he begins to examine it more closely. If he takes pure thought to be *self-sufficient,* it becomes an emptiness that can never be filled; if he *describes* thought in greater detail, he is led to a psychological phenomenology. Both of the following extreme interpretations of thought are possible on the basis of his work:

Either: It has the character of divine thought (a conception that goes back to the ancients) which is and has all Being in itself, because *in the process of thinking it creates what is thought.* But human thought finds in itself only the punctual emptiness of the "I think" without the being that gives it content; for human thought requires something other, the object that is given to it and confronts it, without which it would vanish into the void of self-thinking.

Or: The thinking that has immediate certainty of itself is not the identity of a self-certain one, but is split into two things, namely, that within me which thinks, and that which this thinking as thinking knows. But then the certainty is no longer immediate; it relates to something other, which must, in order to be thought, have existed previously. This seems to be what Descartes means when he calls that which has absolute self-certainty in the *cogito ergo sum* a "thinking thing, which doubts, understands, affirms, negates, wills and does not will, and which also has imagination and sensation." This means that the thought which is certain of itself has the same scope as consciousness. But then everything that my consciousness is is real in the same sense as the "I am." Then thought becomes consciousness and the being of thought is the *being of consciousness as a whole,* or the being of everything that is dealt with in a phenomenology of consciousness or in a psychology that analyzes and describes consciousness. If thought is conceived of as the totality of the acts and states of consciousness, my original certainty is replaced by an aggregate of highly uncertain insights.

Consequently—as we pursue our inquiry into the definite meaning of thought in Descartes—the certainty refers either to the punctual emptiness of self-thinking or to the reality of consciousness with all its innumerable vacillations. Whether we define thought in one or the other sense, the original certainty on which everything was supposed to rest vanishes.

What is the I in Descartes? Descartes, it is true, says that the statement *ego sum ego existo* is indivisible; but when he calls this *ego* a *res cogitans* as distinguished from a *res extensa,* he fails precisely to ask what distinguishes the *I* from the being of any other *res non extensa,* that is, from all mere consciousness, whatever form it may assume. The being of the *I* never became a philosophical question for him. In fact, because he reduced the self-certainty of the existence that thinks itself to an infinitesimal point that thinks itself, or denatured it by introducing psychological elements, the existence of the *I,* conceived of as an objectively existing thing like any other object of thought, remained outside the field of his investigations.

Because the *cogito ergo sum* expresses the I's discovery of its own reality, the philosophy of Descartes became in a later day the starting point for the philosophizing which, since Kant, Fichte, and Schelling, has investigated the riddle of the I. But before that, it led to subjectivist philosophies which soon took on a psychological character.

What is being in Descartes? Descartes's certainty relates to the being of the *cogito.* His propositions are not meant as formal truths; they are meant to express a thinking rational being's certainty of its own existence. But he does not question the meaning of being in his *cogito ergo sum.* He takes being for granted, and soon it becomes for him the mere presence of the *cogito.* In order to show what is lacking, let us compare Descartes's statement with ideas pointing in the same direction in Augustine, Kant, and Schelling:

In Augustine the *cogito ergo sum* is a function of my all-embracing need to gain certainty concerning the inner significance of Being, which is a mirror of the Trinity and speaks to me and through me in existence, life, knowledge, and love. By reducing this thought to a general idea, useful as the starting point of a chain of reasoning, Descartes makes it into a certainty analogous, and in his opinion even superior, to mathematical certainties. But through the next step, the idea loses the depth of its content: a distinction is drawn between the substantiality of the *res extensa* and the substantiality of the *res cogitans,* and the being of the *res cogitans* becomes vitiated with an empty and by no means demonstrated durability. Descartes took a long leap from Augustine's self-certainty of the immortal soul to the purely rational idea of a substantial point, whose being consists solely in thought.

Kant elucidated the enigma of being by pointing out that the "I am" is an empirical statement (in so far as it affirms my existence as an object of psychology) and it is not an empirical statement (in so far as it designates the indispensable condition of all thought). Then he realized that the "I am" does not tell me how I appear to myself or what I am as myself, but only *that* I am and this in an utterly indeterminate sense. Instead of considering these enigmas raised by the *cogito,* Descartes proceeded to identify the being of the *I* with the being of a *res cogitans* as a substance.

In an exposition of Descartes, Schelling criticized the meaning given to being in the *cogito ergo sum.* He recognized the justification of doubt as a means of arriving at being. But the doubt that is a doubt of being presupposes on the one hand that what is doubted exists in a certain sense, though not in the full sense of the word. As far as things are concerned, "one can only doubt that they *are* in an absolute sense; but that they are *in some sense* can be inferred in the same way as Cartesius infers his *sum.* It is just as correct to infer: I doubt the reality of things, therefore they are, or at least: they are not entirely without being. For I cannot even doubt what exists in no sense and not at all." On the other hand, I must also doubt *my own being.* For what is immediately certain, my own being, is incomprehensible to me. I must doubt my own being in the sense that my being, like everything that is doubted, is not a being grounded in itself, but a species of being, a being whose "reality is derived and therefore doubtful." Like all empirical existence, my own existence is a mode of being, situated between being and nonbeing; for thought, too, is only a state, a mode, of existence. Accordingly Schelling says: "The *sum* comprised in the *cogito* has not the significance of an absolute 'I am,' but only the significance of an: 'I am in a certain way, namely, as a thinking being.' "

Precisely because Descartes does not make the meaning of being into a question, because he neither looks into the abyss of the being of the I, nor conceives of absolute being as a standard, he slips from the certainty of his *cogito ergo sum* directly into a knowledge of the being of thought as *res cogitans* distinguished from a *res extensa.* Consequently the "I am" cannot for Descartes signify the absolute being of possible Existenz, which I know myself to be if I am relative only in reference to transcendence. Or at least it cannot preserve this significance in Descartes, who, on the contrary, takes it as a relative being, a certain mode of being as opposed to other being. And the *cogito ergo sum* becomes empty, in so far as it becomes a mere mode of being among other modes of being.

Schelling had no great esteem for the mode of being concerning which Descartes achieves certainty in the *cogito ergo sum.* He did not desire to follow Descartes, "who was not concerned with understanding things, but only with knowing that they are (the least one can know of things). . . . "

But if with the *cogito ergo sum* it is merely demonstrated that I exist in some way, the step I have taken away from universal doubt is by no means as weighty as it first seemed. I have not achieved a grounding in authentic being. Then, according to Schelling, "I doubt the being of the things outside me, therefore they are, is an inference no less valid" than that of Descartes: "I doubt, I think, therefore I am."

The consequence of Descartes's failure to inquire into the meaning of being in the *cogito ergo sum* is that every definition of this being annuls the philosophical force which was present, though unclearly, in the original idea.

2. *What is the meaning of doubt?* Descartes was accused of having sinned by his doubt: had he not gone so far as to doubt the existence of God and to suggest the hypothesis of a demon of deception? This gave Descartes an opportunity to characterize his type of doubt (in a letter replying to Buitendijck's question as to whether it was permissible to doubt the existence of God). Descartes declared that a distinction must be made between the doubt which concerns the reason and the doubt which concerns the will. Intellectual doubt is not a matter of choice or justification, for insight is a matter not of will but of capacity. Consequently, many must doubt the existence of God in their reasoning, in so far as their reason is unable to prove His existence, and still believe in His existence. For faith is the affair of the will, and if I believe, I can nevertheless examine the question of God's existence with my innate reason and so doubt it, without doubting in my faith. Anyone who sets himself the goal of doubting in God in order to persist in this doubt, is committing a grave sin. But the conduct of one who undertakes to doubt as a means of more clearly knowing the truth, is pious and beyond reproach. In the ***Responsiones*** Descartes repeats what he has already said in the ***Discours*** and the ***Meditations,*** namely, that he had always excluded from doubt "everything relating to piety and in general to customs."

Thus as he speaks of it here, Descartes's doubt is a methodological doubt in reason, not an existential doubt in faith. It is a systematic, intellectual attempt to arrive at rational certainty; it is not an existential experience. It is an activity, of which Descartes remains master, not a fall into the abyss of unbelief. His only standard is theoretical evidence, not an awareness of the truth in the practical course of life and action. Hence this doubt has not the earnestness of an existential risk, but only the earnestness of a conscientious effort at logical thinking. This doubt is merely a means of ascertaining the source of the theoretical certainty of reason by finding a clear and distinct concept that no one can doubt. It is not despair, it is not a crisis through which I can achieve certainty of a truth to live by. Thus Descartes's doubt presupposes that, even when I doubt, I continue to live by a source other than the truth with which this doubt is concerned.

Descartes's doubt also presupposes the acceptance of an absolute truth which is accessible to our human judgment. For a moment this absolute stands even higher than God; for if God were to deceive us as to this truth, He would be judged evil. The thinking man who doubts thinks on the basis of this truth, which, however, in the last analysis, is guaranteed only by God.

Now this truth is either a definite, particular truth—and then it is *indeed compelling* and universally valid; in this case it is scientific truth, but never the truth by which I live. Or else, it purports to state, in the *form* of compelling certainty, the certainty that is the ground of my Existenz; in that case, it must necessarily err, because we are unable to express such a certainty clearly and adequately in the form of a proposition. For this reason authentic philosophy, which follows this second path, cannot have as its aim the certainty that characterizes the *rationally compelling* sciences. An indirect indication of this is that every explicit philosophical position has had opponents, and that philosophy never achieves the scientific kind of knowledge which is valid for all men and capable of gaining universal acceptance. Descartes, who follows the philosophical tradition of Aristotle and St. Thomas in holding philosophical and scientific truth to be of the same kind, doubts, *because* all philosophical propositions put forward up until his time have been contested. But the fact that Descartes's own theses incurred the same fate was a source of insight to later generations: the radical method by which Descartes sought certainty confronted later philosophers with the task of distinguishing scientific and philosophical certainty.

Because of this unquestioned assumption that the one universally valid truth is the form of all truth and because of this certainty, both of which are fundamental to Descartes's thinking, Kierkegaard—despite his esteem for Descartes—spoke ironically of his doubt and Nietzsche said that he hoped to be a better doubter than Descartes. Both understood that Descartes had taken the nature of truth in general as something self-evident, which it is not.

3. *Descartes's certainty leads nowhere.* Despite the indefinite and ambiguous content of the *cogito ergo sum,* it nevertheless represents an incontestable advance from radical doubt. For all its indeterminateness, it is correct for a mind that is looking only for a compelling argument. Before Descartes, the step had already been taken by Augustine. The difference between Augustine and Descartes is that Descartes regarded the step as an essentially rational argument and made it the principle of his whole philosophical system, whereas for Augustine it is on the one hand an all-encompassing confirmation of the self, enriched with the full content of one's self-awareness, while, on the other hand, he employs it only incidentally as an argument against skepticism.

Thus Descartes takes an unquestionable certainty as his starting point. But his next step is intended to show that clarity and distinctness are *universally* valid criteria of true knowledge. For this he requires the proof of the existence and essence of God (who must not be a demon of deception, capable of provoking false evidence). This proof required first of all a new assumption, namely, that the cause of an idea must be as perfect as its content; on the strength of this premise, the idea of God, which is present in our minds, cannot have been created by ourselves, but must have its ground in God Himself. This idea—having its sources in Descartes's religious belief—seems, indeed, to have the depth of a metaphysical elucidation of human existence; it possesses a force of conviction capable of appealing to a man without specific religious ties but fundamentally predisposed to faith; its meaning is inseparable from its undemonstrability. But once this idea is transformed from an inspiring appeal into a proof of the kind that gives us mathematical certainty, it collapses; it loses the truth that is peculiar to it and fails to achieve compelling validity.

Thus this first certainty is such that with it Descartes *runs aground.* From this certainty he can take no further step to a new certainty, having the same character of compelling evidence. He has struck ground, but his ground is a sandbank: he cannot go on, and he cannot even stay where he is.

This sterile certainty of the *cogito ergo sum* finds its expression in the peculiarly negative form of the reasoning that leads to it. The self-certainty of consciousness is achieved by the negation of all possible skeptical negations. Its outcome is doubt and not a source of its own. The primary "no" never gives rise to a creative "yes." Like all philosophical ideas that spring from a refutation and not from a positive source, Descartes's idea is striking in its simplicity, but at the price of leading nowhere. The same is true of another well-known idea, used to refute skepticism: The skeptic says there is no truth; in so saying, he maintains something that he regards as true; thus he contradicts himself, for in his statement he is doing something which his statement says to be impossible. Like Descartes's idea, this one is correct and useful as an answer to the negations of skepticism, but it too leads nowhere.

Self-certainty may be of two kinds. One is that of the absolute skeptic who can effect no judgment, because in thinking he is certain only that he thinks. The other opens the prospect of attaining to a deeper truth by seeking to confront all certainty with the certainty of the self—the actual presence of the truth—in other words, to raise all certainty to the level of self-certainty.

Descartes often gives the impression of choosing the second path, for a move in that direction is unquestionably present in the initial impulse of his thinking. Even in so abstract an expression of self-certainty as the *cogito ergo sum* there is something at work which speaks to the reader, which sets up a sympathetic vibration, and a more explicit indication of this impulse in Descartes is that he believes in God and needs Him as the indispensable source of all knowledge of the truth. But he does not incorporate God—taken as the fullness of Being, as the real source of real existence—into his philosophical movement. He makes use of Him as the mere idea of God, a God who, once His existence is proved, is no longer needed, because His sole function was to establish clarity and distinctness as criteria of knowledge, so rendering this knowledge absolutely independent. But a God who serves only to establish a criterion of truth is just as vague and empty as the *cogito ergo sum.* Where, on the contrary, the "I am" is bound up existentially with the idea of God, a reciprocal bond is present in the source: the "I am" becomes as rich as the idea of God. Then the "I am" is actual Existenz oriented toward transcendence; it can no longer be adequately apprehended in any abstract logical idea and cannot be the first link in a chain of reasoning tending to establish compelling certainty.

Because of this striving for compelling certainty, Descartes's first fundamental thought is without richness and content. In every further step he attempts to recapture richness and content, but he *never again attains certainty.* He starts out with an empty certainty; but at the very next step even this certainty is lost.

3. THE ENCOMPASSING

However, there is, in Descartes's fundamental operation, something more than a striving for indubitable certainty. In basing his confidence in clear and distinct knowledge of the fact that God is the creator and cannot be a deceiver, he gains awareness of the Encompassing which we are and in which we are. Though in Descartes's system God is reduced to a mere function, and serves solely as the guarantor of compelling certainty, nevertheless his thinking reveals an echo of profound philosophical reflections relating to his own being as indissolubly bound up with transcendence. Despite the precision with which Descartes's propositions are formulated, the content is so indeterminate as to make them meaningless. But for all this indeterminateness, they point to the Encompassing. We shall try to show how in Descartes a philosophical meaning speaks through these pointers but also how, because of his method of philosophizing, it immediately falls silent.

We call *transcendence* the Encompassing in which we authentically are. We call *Existenz* the Encompassing that we ourselves are. The mode of our *Existenz* depends on the *meaning of truth for it,* and achieves reality through *inner action.* Consequently we shall examine successively, in Descartes's fundamental operation, the presence of transcendence, the starting point in my consciousness of my Existenz, the meaning of truth, and inner action. In conclusion we shall show how Descartes's thinking marks the beginning of a break in man, who saw the ground receding beneath his feet and then began consciously to look for new and reliable ground.

The presence of transcendence. Descartes's philosophy begins with the indissoluble bond between the thinking being's certainty of his existence and the idea of God. Even though this inseparability is taken at once as the basis for a rational proof of the existence of God, its source is no mere rational position but the Encompassing. This lends his subsequent steps a meaning which, however, gradually seems to lose itself in mere rationality.

We read, for example, at the end of the Fifth Meditation: "And so I very clearly recognize that the certainty and truth of all knowledge *depend* alone on the knowledge of the true God, in so much that, before I knew Him, I could have a perfect knowledge of no other thing." Although the explicitly stated meaning of this passage is merely that knowledge of God's existence gives us confidence in clarity and distinctness as the criteria of knowledge, the original idea contains far more than this application which seems poor by contrast. In Descartes, however, *this* original idea is not developed.

We find in Descartes passages which not only bear witness to his piety, but show that he was aware of transcendence. At the end of the Third Meditation, he writes: "But before . . . I pass on to the consideration of other truths . . . it seems to me right to pause for a while in order to contemplate God Himself, to ponder at leisure His marvelous attributes, to consider and admire, and adore the beauty of this light so resplendent, at least as far as the strength of my mind, which is in some measure dazzled by the sight, will allow me to do so. For just as faith teaches us that the supreme felicity of the other life consists only in this contemplation of the Divine Majesty, so we continue to learn by experience that a similar meditation, though incomparably less perfect, causes us to enjoy the greatest satisfaction of which we are capable in this life." In such passages it is as though Descartes had abandoned his role of sober rationality. The style here is not that of his demonstrations. In his innermost attitude Descartes preserved something of what he had taken over from scholasticism. His thinking—for brief moments at least—carries a transcendent mood, which does not express itself directly, but which is present and can be discerned by the perceptive reader despite the rationality which carries Descartes so far away from it.

The starting point: my consciousness of my existence. The self-certainty of the thinking being is more than one insight among others. It is for Descartes the starting point, and not only in the sense of a first statement in a series; it is being itself, one and incomparable, and only in relation to this being can anything else acquire being and truth for us. Consequently Descartes holds that whatever is inseparably bound up with this self-certainty of the thinking being—e.g., doubt, negation, affirmation, will, sensation, imagination—is just as real and true as the "I am." It is inseparable from my consciousness (*a mea cognitione*) and my self (*a meo ipso*). Consequently an interpreter of Descartes can say quite rightly: " . . . and everything which is as closely bound up with the idea of your existence as existence itself exists for you and with you with equal necessity, equal certainty!" One is tempted to think of Kant's words about the "starry heavens above me" and the "moral law within me": "I do not merely conjecture them and seek them as though obscured in darkness or in the transcendent region beyond my horizon; I see them before me and I associate them directly with the consciousness of my own existence. The former begins at the place I occupy in the external world of sense. . . . The latter begins at my invisible self . . . and exhibits me in a world . . . which is comprehensible only to the understanding—a world with which I recognize myself as existing in a universal and necessary . . . connection." We seem to find the same impulse at the source of Descartes's fundamental idea.

But in Descartes this original impulse is not preserved. What he designates as inseparable from consciousness (*cogitatio*) is not only thought in the sense of judgment and not only freedom to affirm or deny, but over and above these, or rather far below them, the multiple contents of consciousness: "What then am I? . . . a thing which doubts, understands, affirms, denies, wills, refuses, which also imagines and feels. Certainly it is no small matter if all these things pertain to my nature. . . . " In restricting the Encompassing to consciousness, Descartes reduces it to a field of psychological phenomena to be considered by the methods of psychology. This is no longer the Encompassing but a kind of stage on which psychological phenomena are displayed. Both empirical existence as the dark background of our reality, and possible Existenz, as the absoluteness of a selfhood, that knows itself to be in the presence of transcendence, are lost. Hence, in elucidating what is no longer the Encompassing Descartes loses himself in psychological (phenomenological and epistemological) reflections. Thus he can no longer attain the language of Existenz, often present in speculative thinking (and that is why there is next to nothing of Anselm's "ontological proof" in Descartes's second proof, which reduces it to a mere logical operation); moreover, he attains neither the reality of empirical existence nor the imperative that speaks to us out of the possible Existenz of the self. And indeed the connection between truth and my consciousness of my Existenz, or, in other words, this Encompassing which is authentic Being, is not brought out in Descartes. Only by interpreting Descartes on the basis of what is known to us from other sources, can we discover the seed of the idea that moved Kant and Kierkegaard.

The Encompassing and truth. Our conception of the Encompassing is always correlative to a specific conception of the nature of truth. Thus the idea of the equality of all men is correlative to the mode of knowledge that is identical for all; and the idea that men differ from one another in rank and essence is correlative to a conception of truth, according to which the content of thought is by no means the same for all men.

After starting from the self-certainty of his existence, Descartes's thinking breaks away from its roots in the totality of the Encompassing; and this is reflected by the way in which he regards all men as capable, and then again incapable, of apprehending the truth.

On the one hand, the accent is on the idea that the essential is always identical to itself and therefore accessible to all. All men become identical for him in an Encompassing which is nothing more than consciousness and reason. For example: "I have observed, in examining the natural aptitude of several men, that virtually none are so crude or slow-witted as to be incapable, if properly directed, of achieving the state of mind necessary for the acquisition of the highest sciences." Another example: "Good sense is of all things in the world the most equitably distributed, for everybody thinks himself so abundantly provided with it. . . . It is unlikely that this is an error on their part; it seems rather to be evidence in support of the view that the power of forming a good judgment and of distinguishing the true from the false, which is properly speaking called good sense or reason, is by nature equal in all men. Hence too it will show that the diversity of our opinions does not proceed from some men being more rational than others, but solely from the fact that our thoughts pass through diverse channels and that the same objects are not considered by all."

Nevertheless Descartes speaks of "weak minds," he finds men's aptitudes very unevenly distributed, and expresses the belief that fewer men are fit for metaphysical than for geometrical studies, and even goes so far as to say: "The minds of all men are subject to certain limits which they cannot surpass." But here we need not necessarily see a contradiction; for thanks to what is common to all men, they might all be guided into the right way. For Descartes, every individual as a human being has the possibility of participating in this reason which is common to all men: "There is no soul so lacking in nobility, so attached to the things of the senses, that it does not sometimes turn away from them to desire some greater good. . . . "

On the other hand, Descartes not only sees men varying in rank according to their aptitudes; he also seems to presuppose so radical a difference among men that he warns them against his own ideas, which were supposed to carry compelling, universally valid certainty and intended to provide sound methodological guidance for all. Considering the possibility that revolutionaries might make use of his ideas for their own purposes, he wrote: "My design has never extended beyond trying to reform my own opinion. . . . I do not do so because I wish to advise anybody to imitate it . . . the simple resolve to strip oneself of all opinions and beliefs formerly received is not to be regarded as an example that each man should follow. . . . "

The contradiction is astounding. Certain dangers incite him to warn others not to take the same path as himself, although his is the only methodical path to the truth. The only possible explanation for this is that Descartes senses the presence of certain powers of empirical existence and Existenz, which he had *not* gathered into his purely rational Encompassing—which is common to all men alike. Since Descartes unquestioningly posits only one interpretation of truth—that of compelling validity for all men—the meaning of truth in all its multiplicity is no problem for him. Consequently, his Encompassing narrows down to consciousness and reason. It becomes an island cut off from the actual world. When he speaks in this way, he has no inclination to concern himself with those who do not follow him in his cautious conception of a truth far removed from action in the world; he expressly shuts himself off from them.

Inner action. The thinking of the Encompassing is identical with a continuous inner action, in which I elucidate, produce, and transform myself. Descartes's doctrine of liberty makes it clear that he philosophizes in the Encompassing, even though he immediately loses sight of it in developing the content of his ideas.

In his fundamental operation, Descartes performs an inner action which he examines more closely when he takes freedom as a philosophical theme: in submitting to universal doubt, freedom of thought gains self-awareness. A man need submit to no judgment, to no received truth; he can suspend his own judgment until, having considered, penetrated, and surveyed all possible critical objections, he arrives at a certainty which he accepts as so indubitable that he recognizes his own eternal essence in it forever.

In dealing with "freedom," Descartes reasons as follows: the world that we have learned to take for granted in the course of our physical and historical development does not disclose things to us as they intrinsically are. It discloses them to us in a form corresponding to our physical needs, ranging, according to the conditions of our existence, from sensory needs to the practical requirements of human society. The judgments which such experience has imprinted upon us are prejudices, and they are well-nigh insurmountable. The traditional philosophy which Descartes rejects is in his opinion nothing more than a kind of unconscious justification of these prejudices; in practice, he holds, its system of the world merely reflects our needs and interests.

But once we have awakened to maturity, he believes, we can think independently of these needs and interests, that is, we can think not only in order to live, but also for the sake of thought itself. Then the aim of thought ceases to be our empirical existence alone, and becomes first and foremost truth as such. The power to engage in this thinking, which is a striving for pure knowledge of the truth, detached from the conditions of existence which formerly pressed in upon us, deceived us, and nourished our prejudices—that is the freedom possible for man. Descartes expresses the beauty of this freedom, of this philosophical upsurge which frees us from the old blind prejudices:

Freedom of judgment, that is, freedom to affirm or negate or to suspend judgment, is unlimited. I can restrict my affirmation or negation to what is absolutely clear and distinct to the eyes of my mind. In my freedom of decision I am secure against all error if I abstain from decision until the object of my judgment has attained the highest clarity and distinctness. Judgment is an act of the will; freedom of will enables me to confine myself to true judgments, and makes me responsible for every error, because in case of error I have judged without having previously attained full clarity and distinctness.

This freedom is complete only in thought, that is, in the realm of *theory.* In *action* we do not have time to achieve full certainty of judgment; but in action the indecision of theoretical judgment is not permissible; time presses and every situation demands a decision. In the realm of theory what counts is *compelling certainty,* which convinces by its evidence and is as such indestructible. In action, on the other hand, what counts is the *determination* which leads me unflinchingly to carry out my decision once made, even though its theoretical foundation may be inadequate.

In the realm of theory, freedom is unlimited. Here alone can I venture—in action it would be disastrous—to doubt everything with a view to attaining compelling certainty. To conceive this certainty with perfect clarity and distinctness—that is freedom. As long as clarity and distinctness have not been attained in the course of my methodic progression, I can decline to affirm or deny, so preserving at least the freedom of indecision.

It is therefore my task, as a potentially free being, to find myself in inner action, by thought and only by thought. In order to arrive, through reason, at full certainty of the truth and at the same time of my own Being, I must detach myself from everything else. In order to achieve such detachment, I must, by means of universal doubt, free myself from prejudice—that is, from all opinions taken unquestioningly for granted—and I must free myself from sense perception and imagination by practice in pure thought, free from the sensory representations that cloud our thinking and prevent it from becoming clear.

Descartes speaks with proud self-assurance of this possible freedom. Otherwise everything in human nature is weak, finite, and limited over against God, in whose image we are made: "It is free-will alone or liberty of choice which I find to be so great in me that I can conceive no other idea to be more great; it is indeed the case that it is for the most part this will that causes me to know that in some manner I bear the image and similitude of God." This freedom consists "in our having the power of choosing to do a thing or choosing not to do it (that is, to affirm or deny, to pursue or to shun it), or rather it consists alone in the fact that in order to affirm or deny . . . we act so that we are unconscious that any outside force constrains us in doing so."

With this grandiose conception of freedom of judgment, Descartes idealizes man's ability to disregard whatever he pleases, so that his thinking remains in a state of suspension. Such thinking can open up a vast area of freedom, but this freedom is empty. If it is to acquire content, the thinker must enter into his own historical substance and realize his relationship to transcendence. The weakness of Descartes's first operation is that, though he attains compelling certainty, its content remains questionable. This may be clarified as follows:

a) *Freedom of judgment* depends entirely on the clarity and distinctness of the content. Without a given substantial content, the clarity and distinctness are empty, and with them the judgment. The truth resides not only in clarity and distinctness as such, but also in the nature and origin and evidence of the content of my thinking. How I become aware of this content, how I perceive it and assimilate it—that is the decisive question. Indispensable as they are, clarity and distinctness are merely secondary conditions of truth. Moreover, suspension of judgment is in itself merely a renunciation, devoid of content.

b) *Pure thought*—detached from everything—is no longer the Encompassing as such; it is divorced from the total Existenz of man. In greater or lesser degree, it loses its ties with the reality of life and makes for an attitude of isolation, which has less and less content. The man himself in his Existenz, his all-encompassing possibility, is lost sight of.

c) Scientific inquiry and life itself can be fruitful only if we recognize the existence of contradictions, not in order to resign ourselves to them, but in order to surmount them. One who decides from the start to *sidestep all contradiction,* can only revolve in a barren circle, and his supposedly sound judgments can carry him no closer to eternal truth. It is worth remembering what great mistakes were made by Descartes, who hoped to exclude all error by confining himself to self-evident truths. Descartes is perhaps the greatest example of a thinker who erred precisely because of his striving for compelling certainty and who lost the truth by succumbing to the temptations of rationality.

As in the doctrine of freedom, inner action is discernible in Descartes's philosophizing wherever method ceased to be a mere technique and became a means of communicating with himself. Several of the Meditations end with an appeal for inner action; the First: ". . . a certain lassitude leads me into the course of my ordinary life. And just as a captive who in sleep enjoys an imaginary liberty, when he begins to suspect that his liberty is but a dream, fears to awaken and conspires with these agreeable illusions that the deception may be prolonged, so insensibly of my own accord I fall back into my former opinions, and I dread awakening"; the Second: "But because it is difficult to rid oneself so promptly of an opinion to which one was accustomed for so long, it will be that I should halt a little at this point, so that by the length of my meditation I may more deeply imprint on my memory this new knowledge"; the Fourth: "Nor have I only learned today what I should avoid in order that I may not err, but also how I should act in order to arrive at knowledge of the truth; for without doubt I shall arrive at this if I devote my attention sufficiently to those things which I perfectly understand; and if I separate them from these which I only understand confusedly and with obscurity."

To be sure, this inner action is not much more than a self-administered treatment of the intellect; it has to do with the purification of thinking, with intellectual exercise, and the discipline of clarity. Nevertheless it carries a vestige of the philosophical Encompassing that is at work in every method. For philosophy does not merely strive, like the sciences, to achieve methodical knowledge of something; it strives through knowledge to fulfill the encompassing essence of the philosopher.

Abyss and foundation. Although Descartes's doubt is presented merely as an attempt to prove that rational certainty is beyond doubt, it actually has deeper implications. The radical doubt which culminates in the hypothesis that my creator was an evil spirit of deception, opens up to me for a moment the possibility that my existence is without foundation. If the clarity and distinctness of compelling insight as such are no longer absolutely reliable, rational certainty ceases to be a foundation; reason is called into question. The only thing that prevents this shattering of all certainty is that Descartes does not think this thought in earnest, but only experiments with it. Anyone who is really convinced of this idea that Descartes puts forward experimentally—and here the idea of the creator-demon can be dropped as long as his illusory world with its innumerable ambiguities remains (as often in Nietzsche) the sole reality—has not only lost confidence in reason but is faced with a bottomless abyss if there is no other ground than reason to sustain him.

Philosophically speaking, Descartes took an extraordinary step when, holding rational evidence in itself to be inadequate, he tried to confirm it from a deeper source. For a moment he was aware that rational evidence has its source in a prerational act. But taking the form of a purely rational and compelling statement, this insight was instantly lost. Wishing to disclose the irrational source of rational evidence by rational arguments, he lost sight of it. In questioning reason, he did not depart from the solid ground of reason; no sooner was his question formulated than he was back at his starting point.

In order to make fully clear the relationship in Descartes between his fundamental operation and the evidence of rational insight in mathematics and the sciences, we should first have to realize the existence of two distinct types of certainty, and then derive one from the other in a new way which transcends all particular scientific intelligibility.

And it may be noted that Descartes actually tends to distinguish two kinds of certainty, when, on the basis of the proof of the existence of God, he writes that "the existence of God would pass with me as at least as certain as I have ever held the truth of mathematics," and when, comparing the evidence of the existence of God with the evidence of geometrical insight, he writes: "*Whereas,* on reverting to the examination of the idea which I had of a Perfect Being, I found that in this case existence was implied in it in the same manner in which the equality of its three angles to two right angles is implied in the idea of a triangle . . . or even more evidently still." But how can anything be more evident than the absolute evidence of mathematical insight? This passage might be explained by the existence of two different kinds of certainty. With his fundamental operation Descartes tries to gain a certainty on the basis of which mathematical certainty, already supreme among certainties, can be made absolute. From this we must infer that for Descartes mathematical certainty was lacking in the absolute necessity with which I must think God's being and my own existence. He seems to have in mind a certainty which is not rational, but is the ground of rational certainty, to believe that anterior to compelling certainty there is a still more compelling certainty. Stepping out of the purely rational cognition of mathematics and science, we must find a new approach to knowledge, the ground of another certainty.

It would be going too far to say that Descartes subordinated the compelling certainty of reason to the existential certainty without which rational certainty would sink into nothingness. Originally Descartes's ideas may have moved in this direction, but clothed in a rational, argumentative, demonstrative form, they soon lost whatever existential content they might have had. After having experimentally doubted rational certainty, Descartes found no other foundation for it than rational certainty itself, from which he had never seriously departed. (pp. 61-93)

Karl Jaspers, "Descartes and Philosophy," in his Three Essays: Leonardo, Descartes, Max Weber, *translated by Ralph Manheim, Harcourt Brace Jovanovich, 1964, pp. 59-186.*

Jean-Paul Sartre (essay date 1955)

[*A French writer and philosopher, Sartre was one of the chief contributors to the philosophical movement of Existentialism. In the following excerpt, Sartre analyzes Descartes's conception of intellectual freedom.*]

Freedom is one and indivisible, but it manifests itself in a variety of ways, according to circumstances. The following question may be asked of all philosophers who set up as its defenders: in connection with what exceptional *situation* have you experienced your freedom? It is one thing to test your freedom in the realm of action, of social or political activity, or of artistic creation, and another thing to test it in the act of understanding and discovering. A Richelieu, a Vincent de Paul or a Corneille would, had they been metaphysicians, have had certain things to tell us about freedom because they grasped it by one end, at a moment when it manifested itself by an absolute event, by the appearance of something new, whether poem or institution, in a world that neither asked for it nor rejected it. Descartes, who was primarily a metaphysician, grasped things by the other end: his primary experience was not that of creative freedom "ex nihilo" but of autonomous thinking which discovers by its own power intelligible relationships among existing essences. That is why we Frenchmen, who have been living by Cartesian freedom for three centuries, understand implicitly by "free will" the practice of independent *thinking* rather than the production of a creative act, and our philosophers have finally come, like Alain, to identify freedom with the act of judging.

The fact is that the exhilaration of understanding always includes the joy of feeling ourselves responsible for the truths we discover. Regardless of who the teacher is, there always comes a moment when the pupil confronts the mathematical problem unaided. If he does not bring his mind to grasp the relationships, if he himself does not produce the conjectures and diagrams which are to be applied like cipher-stencils to the figure under consideration and which reveal the major features of its construction, if he does not finally acquire a decisive insight, the words remain dead signs; everything has been learned by rote. Thus, if I examine myself, I can feel that intellection is not the mechanical result of a pedagogic procedure, but rather that its origin lies solely in my deliberate willing, my application, my refusal to be distracted or hurried, in the undivided attention of my mind—to the radical exclusion of all external forces. And such indeed was Descartes' primary intuition. He was more fully aware than anyone else that the slightest act of thinking involves all thinking, an autonomous thinking that posits itself—in each of its acts—in its full and absolute independence.

But, as we have seen, this experience of *autonomy* does not coincide with that of *productivity.* The reason is that thought must obviously have *something* to understand, whether it be the objective relationships among essences and among structures, or the sequence of ideas, in short, a pre-established order of relationships. Thus, as a counterpart to freedom of intellection, nothing is more rigorous than the path that lies ahead: "As there is but one truth concerning each thing, whoever finds it knows all that can be known about it. For example, a child who has been taught arithmetic and who has done a sum in accordance with its rules can be certain that, as far as the sum which he examined is concerned, he has found all that the human mind can find. For the method which teaches how to follow the true order and to indicate exactly all the circumstances of what is sought, contains everything that gives certainty to the rules of arithmetic."

Everything is stated: the object to be discovered and the method. The child who sets himself to doing a sum in accordance with the rules does not enrich the universe with a new truth. He merely repeats an operation that has been performed by a thousand others before him and that he will never be able to push beyond the same point they have reached. The attitude of the mathematician is therefore a rather striking paradox. His mind is like that of a man who walks on a very narrow path where each of his steps and the very posture of his body are rigorously conditioned by the nature of the ground and the necessities of the walking, but who is nevertheless imbued with the unshakable conviction that he is performing all these acts freely. In short, if we start with mathematical intellection, how shall we reconcile the fixity and necessity of essences with freedom of judgment? The problem is particularly difficult owing to the fact that, in Descartes' time, the order of mathematical truths seemed to all right-thinking people the product of the divine will. And since this order could not be eluded, Spinoza preferred to sacrifice human subjectivity to it: he showed the true as developing and asserting itself by its own power *through* these incomplete individualities, these finite modes. Confronted with the order of essences, subjectivity can be only the simple freedom of adhering to the true (in the sense that, for certain moralists, we have no other *right* than to do our *duty*) or else it is only a jumbled thought, a mutilated truth, the development and elucidation of which dissipate its subjective character. In the second case, man disappears. There remains no difference between thought and truth. The true is the totality of the system of thoughts. If anyone wants to save man, the only thing to do, since he cannot *produce* any idea but only contemplate it, is to provide him with a simple negative power, that of saying *no* to whatever is not true. Thus, we find in Descartes, under the appearance of a unitary system, two rather different theories of freedom, according to whether he is considering this power of understanding and judging which is his or whether he simply wants to save the autonomy of man when confronted with the rigorous system of ideas.

His spontaneous reaction is to affirm the responsibility of man in the presence of the true. Truth is a human thing, since I must affirm it in order for it to exist. Before my *judgment,* which is an adherence of my will and a free commitment of my being, there exist only neutral and floating ideas which are neither true nor false. Man is thus the being through whom truth appears in the world. His task is to commit himself totally in order that the natural order of existants may become an order of truths. He must ponder the world, must will his thinking and must transform the order of being into a system of ideas. Ever since the ***Meditations,*** he has appeared as the "ontico-ontological" being of whom Heidegger speaks. Descartes therefore begins by providing us with entire intellectual responsibility. At every moment, he experiences the freedom of his thought, and his solitude as well, in the face of the sequence of essences. As Heidegger has said, nobody can die for me. But Descartes had said earlier that nobody can understand for me. In the end, we must say yes or no and decide alone, for the entire universe, on what is true. This adherence is a metaphysical and absolute act. Commitment is not relative. It is not a matter of an approximation that can be called into question again. But just as Kant's moral man acts as a legislator for the community of ends, Descartes, as a scientist, decides as to the laws of the world. For this "yes," which must finally be uttered in order for the reign of the true to come into being, requires the commitment of an infinite power that is given in its entirety all at once. We cannot say a "partial" yes or a "partial" no. And man's "yes" is no different from God's. "Only the will do I perceive within me to be so great that I cannot conceive the idea of anything wider or more far-reaching, so that it is chiefly the will which enables me to know that I bear the image and likeness of God. For, though it is incomparably greater in God than in myself, either because of knowledge and power, which, being joined to it, make it more stable and more efficacious, or because of its object . . . nevertheless it does not seem to me greater, if I consider it strictly and precisely in itself."

It is evident that, precisely because this entire freedom is not a matter of degree, it belongs equally to every man. Or rather—for freedom is not a quality among other qualities—it is evident that every man *is* a freedom. And the famous assertion that common sense is the most common thing in the world does not mean only that every man has the same seeds in his mind and the same innate ideas, but also that "it bears witness to the fact that the power to judge soundly and to distinguish the true from the false is equal in all men."

A man cannot be more of a man than other men because freedom is similarly infinite in each individual. In this sense, no one has shown better than Descartes the connection between the spirit of science and the spirit of democracy, for universal suffrage cannot be founded on anything other than this universal faculty of saying yes or saying no. We can, no doubt, observe a wide difference among men. One man has a better memory, another a richer imagination, another understands things more quickly, another embraces a wider field of truth. But these qualities are not constitutive of the notion of man. They are to be regarded as corporeal accidents. The only thing that characterizes us as human creatures is the use that we freely make of these gifts. It makes no difference whether we have understood more or less quickly, since understanding, however it come, must be total for all or it does not exist. If Alcibiades and the slave understand the same truth, they are entirely alike in that they understand it. In like manner, the situation of a man and his powers cannot increase or limit his freedom. Descartes has here made, after the Stoics, an essential distinction between freedom and power. To be free is not to be able to do what one wants but to want what one can: "There is nothing that is entirely in our power, save our thoughts, at least if you use the word thinking, as I do, for all the operations of the soul, so that not only acts of meditation and of will, but even the functions of seeing, hearing, determining to perform one movement rather than another, etc. . . . , in so far as they depend upon it, are thoughts. . . . I did not mean thereby that external things are not at all in our power, but simply that they are so only in so far as they can follow from our thoughts, and not *absolutely* or *entirely,* because there are other powers outside us which can interfere with the results of our intentions."

Thus, with a variable and limited power, man has total freedom. Here we perceive the negative aspect of freedom. For if I do not have power to perform such and such an action, I must abstain from desiring to perform it: "I must always try to conquer myself rather than fortune and to change my desires rather than the order of the world." In short, I must practise Eποχη in the moral realm. Nevertheless, the fact remains that freedom, in this primary conception, has a certain "efficacity." It is a positive and constructive freedom. It probably cannot change the quality of the movement that is in the world, but it can modify the direction of this movement. "The main seat of the soul is in the small gland which is in the middle of the brain, from which it radiates throughout the rest of the body by the agency of the [animal] spirits, the nerves and even the blood. . . . And the entire action of the soul consists in this, that merely by willing something, it makes the small gland to which it is closely joined move in the way requisite for producing the effect relating to this desire."

It is this "efficacity," this constructiveness of human freedom that we find at the origin of the ***Discourse on Method.*** For the method is *invented:* "Certain paths," says Descartes, "have led me to considerations and maxims from which I have formed a method." Better still, each rule of the Method (except the first) is a maxim of action or invention. Does not the analysis prescribed by the second rule call for a free and creative judgment which produces schemes and which conceives hypothetical divisions which it verifies shortly afterwards? And must not the order recommended in the third rule be sought and prefigured in the midst of disorder before we submit to it? The proof is that it will be invented if it does not actually exist: "Supposing even that there is order between [those objects] which do not naturally precede each other." And do not the listings of the fourth precept suppose a power of generalization and classification characteristic of the human spirit? In short, the rules of the Method are on the level of Kantian schematism. They represent, in sum, very general directives for free and creative judgment. Was not Descartes, at a time when Bacon was teaching the English to look to experience, the first to call upon the physicist to give precedence to hypothesis? We thus discover in his works a splendid humanistic affirmation of creative freedom, which constructs the true, piece by piece, which at every moment anticipates and prefigures the real relationships among essences by producing hypotheses and *schemata* which equal for God and for man, equal for all men, absolute and infinite, forces us to assume a fearful task, *our* task par excellence, namely, to cause a truth to exist in the world, to act so that the world is true—and which causes us to live with *generosity,* a "sentiment that each one has of his own free will and that is joined to the resolution never to be lacking in it."

But the established order intervenes at once. For a philosopher like Kant, the human mind constitutes the truth. For Descartes, it merely discovers it, since God has fixed for all time all the relationships which essences maintain among themselves. In addition, however the mathematician has chosen to handle his problem, he cannot doubt the result once it has been reached. The man of action who contemplates his enterprise can say, "This is mine." But not the scientist. As soon as the truth is discovered, it becomes foreign to him. It belongs to everyone and no one. He can merely recognize it, and, if he has a clear view of the relationships that constitute it, he cannot even doubt it. Transpierced by an inner illumination that animates his entire being, he can only give his adherence to the theorem that has been discovered and thereby to the order of the world. Hence, the judgments "two and two are four" and "I think, therefore I am" have value only inasmuch as I affirm them, but I cannot help but affirm them. If I say that I do not exist, I am not even shaping a fiction. I am assembling words whose meanings destroy each other, just as if I spoke of squared circles or three-sided cubes. Thus, the Cartesian will is forced to affirm. "For example, examining recently whether anything really existed in the world, and knowing that by virtue of the fact that I was examining the question, it very manifestly followed that

I myself existed, I could not help but judge that a thing which I conceived clearly was true, not that I found myself forced to do so by any external cause, but only because the great light that was in my understanding was followed by a great inclination in my will."

Descartes persists in using the word "free" to qualify this irresistible adherence to evidence, but he does so because he is here giving a quite different meaning to the word freedom. The adherence is free because it is not caused by the pressure of any constraint external to us, that is, it is not caused by a movement of the body or by a psychological impulsion. We are not in the realm of the passions of the soul. But if the *soul* remains independent of the body during the unfolding of the evidence *of the soul,* and if, in the terms of the definitions in the ***Treatise on the Passions,*** we may call the affirmation of relationships that are clearly and distinctly conceived an action of the thinking substance taken in its totality, these terms cease to have meaning if we consider the will in relation to the understanding. For we have called freedom the will's self-determined possibility of saying yes or no to ideas conceived by the understanding, which meant, in other terms, that the die had never been cast, that the future had never been foreseeable. Whereas at present, the relation of understanding to will, as concerns evidence, is conceived in the form of a rigorous law in which the clarity and distinctness of the idea play the role of determining factor in relation to the affirmation. In short, Descartes is here much closer to philosophers such as Spinoza and Leibniz who define the freedom of a human being by the development of his essence, apart from any external action, though the moments of this development follow on each other's heels with rigorous necessity. It is at this point that he goes so far as to deny the freedom of indifference or rather so far as to make it the lowest degree of freedom: "In order for me to be free, it is not necessary that I be indifferent to choosing one of two alternatives, but rather, the more I incline toward one, whether because I know from evidence that the true and good meet there or because God thus disposes the inner working of my thinking, the more freely do I choose and embrace it."

The second term of the alternative, "whether God thus disposes the inner working of my thinking," concerns faith in the strict sense of the term. In this domain, as the understanding cannot be the sufficient reason of the act of faith, the entire will is shot through and illuminated by an inner and supernatural light that is called grace. We may be shocked to see this autonomous and infinite freedom suddenly *affected* by divine grace and *disposed* to affirm what it does not see clearly. But, at bottom, is there a great difference between natural light and this supernatural light which is grace? In the second case, there can be no doubt that it is God Who affirms, through the intermediary of our will. But does not the same obtain in the first case? If ideas have being, they do so insofar as they come from God. Clarity and distinctness are only signs of the inner cohesion and the absolute density of being of the idea. And if I am irresistibly inclined to affirm the idea, it is exactly insofar as it weighs on me with all its being and all its absolute positiveness. It is this pure and dense being, flawless and entire, which affirms itself within me by its own weight. Thus, since God is the source of all being and all positivity, this positivity, this fullness of existence which is itself a true judgment, cannot have its source in me, who am nothing, but in Him. And let us not regard this theory merely as an effort to reconcile a rationalistic metaphysics with Christian theology. It expresses, in the vocabulary of the time, the consciousness that the scientist has always had of being a pure nothingness, a simple beholder in the face of the obstinate and eternal consistency, the infinite weight of the truth he contemplates.

Three years later, in 1644, Descartes did return to conceded to us the freedom of indifference. "We are," he says, "so certain of the freedom and indifference that are within us that there is nothing we know more clearly. Consequently, the omnipotence of God should not prevent us from believing in them." But this is a simple precaution. The tremendous success of the ***Augustinus*** had worried him, and he did not want to run the risk of being condemned by the Sorbonne. We must rather point out that this new conception of freedom without free will began to extend to all subjects on which he reflected. He wrote to Mersenne: "You reject what I have said, *that it is sufficient to judge correctly in order to act correctly;* and yet it seems to me that the common scholastic doctrine is *Voluntas non fertur in malum, nisi quatenus ei sub aliqua ratione boni repraesentatur ab intellectu,* whence the saying: *omnis peccans est ignorans;* with the result that if ever the understanding proposed to the will anything which was not a good thing, the will could not fail to make the proper choice." The thesis is now complete. The clear vision of the Good entails the act as the distinct vision of the True entails assent. For the Good and the True are one and the same thing, namely, Being. And if Descartes is able to say that we are never so free as when we do Good, it is in doing so that he substitutes a definition of freedom by the *value* of the act—the freest act being that which is the best, the one most in conformity with the universal order—for a definition by autonomy. And this is in accordance with the logic of his doctrine: if we do not invent *our* Good, if Good has an *a priori,* independent existence, how could we perceive it without doing it?

Nevertheless, we find in the quest for the True, just as we do in the pursuit of the Good, a veritable autonomy of man, but only insofar as he is a nothingness. It is as a nothingness and insofar as he is involved in Nothingness, Evil and Error that man escapes God. For God, Who is infinite fullness of being, can neither conceive nor govern nothingness. He has placed that which is positive within me. He is the author who is responsible for everything in me which is. But because of my finiteness and my limits, because of that side of me which is in shadow, I turn away from Him. If I retain freedom of indifference, I do so in relation to what I do not know or what I know imperfectly, in relation to fragmentary, mutilated and obscure ideas. I, who am a nothingness, can say *no* to all these nothingness. I am able *not* to decide to act or affirm. Since the order of truths exists outside of me, that which will define me as an autonomy is not creative invention but refusal. It is by refusing to the point of being unable to refuse any more that we are free. Thus, methodical doubt becomes the very model of the free act: "*Nihilominus . . . hanc in nobis libertatem esse experimur, ut semper ab iis credendis, quae non plane certa sunt et explorata possimus abstinere.*" And elsewhere he writes: "*Mens quae propria libertate utens supponit ea omnia non existere, de quarerum existentia vel minimum potest dubitare.*"

This power of escaping, disengaging oneself and withdrawing is recognizable as a prefiguration of Hegelian negativity. Doubt strikes at all propositions which affirm something that is outside our thought, that is, I can place all existants between parentheses; I am exercising my freedom fully when I, who am myself a nothingness and a void, make of everything that exists a nothingness. Doubt is a breaking of contact with being. Through doubt, man has a permanent possibility of disentangling himself from the existing universe and of suddenly contemplating it from above as a pure succession of phantasms. In this sense, it is the most magnificent affirmation of the reign of the human. The hypothesis of the Evil Genius shows clearly that man can escape from all traps and illusions. There is an order of the true because man is free, and even if this order does not exist, it would be enough for man to be free for there never to be a reign of error, because man, who is a pure negation, a pure suspension of judgment, can, provided he remains motionless, like someone holding his breath, withdraw at any moment from a false and faked nature. He can even withdraw from everything within himself which is nature, from his memory, his imagination, his body. He can withdraw even from time and take refuge in the eternity of the moment. Nothing reveals more clearly the fact that man is not a being of "nature." But at the very moment that he attains this unequalled independence, against the omnipotence of the Evil Spirit, and even against God, he discovers that he is a pure nothingness. Confronted with the *being* that is placed, in its entirety, between parentheses, all that remains is a simple *no,* bodiless and without memories, without knowledge and without *anyone.*

It is this translucent refusal of everything that is achieved in the *cogito,* as the following passage testifies: "*Dubito ergo sum, vel, quod idem est; Cogito ergo sum.*" Although this doctrine is patterned on the Stoic Ε*πoχη* no one before Descartes had stressed the connection between free will and negativity. No one had shown that freedom does not come from man as he is, as a fullness of existence among other fullnesses in a world without lacunae, but rather from man as he *is not,* from man as a finite, limited being. However, this freedom can in no way be creative, since it is *nothing.* It has no power to produce ideas, for an idea is a reality, that is, it possesses a certain *being* that I cannot confer upon it. In addition, Descartes himself limited its scope, since, according to him, when being finally appears—absolute and perfect being, infinitely infinite—we cannot refuse it our adherence. We can thus see that he did not push his theory of negativity to the limit: "Since truth consists in *being* and falsehood in *non-being* only." Man's power of refusal lies only in his refusing the false, in short, in saying no to nonbeing. If we are able to withhold our assent to the works of the Evil Spirit, it is not because they are true or false—they have at least, insofar as they *are* our conceptions, a minimum of being—but insofar as they are not, that is, insofar as they relate falsely to objects that do not exist. If we can withdraw from the world, it is not insofar as it exists in its full and high majesty, like an absolute affirmation, but insofar as it appears to us confusedly through the mediation of the senses and insofar as we ponder it imperfectly by means of a few ideas, the foundations of which escape us. Thus, Descartes constantly wavers between the identification of freedom with the negativity or negation of being—which would be the freedom of indifference—and the conception of free will as a simple negation of negation. In short, he failed to conceive negativity as productive.

A strange freedom. It ends by decomposing into two phases. In the first, it is negative and an autonomy, but confines itself to refusing our assent to error or confused thoughts. In the second, it changes meaning; it is a positive adherence, but the will then loses its autonomy, and the great clarity which exists in the understanding penetrates and determines the will. Is this what Descartes wanted, and does the theory he constructed really correspond to this proud and independent man's primary feeling about his free will? This does not seem to be the case. This individualist, whose very person plays such an important role in his philosophy, whether he is tracing the history of his thinking in the ***Discourse on Method*** or whether he is encountering himself, as an unshakable fact, on the path of his doubting, conceived a freedom that disembodied and deindividualized, for, if we are to believe him, the thinking subject is at first *nothing* but a pure negation, a nothingness, a slight trembling of air which alone escapes the act of doubting and which is *nothing other* than the doubt itself, and, when it emerges from this nothing, it does so in order to become a pure assumption of being.

There is not much difference between the Cartesian scientist, who is, in the last analysis, only the simple *vision* of eternal truths, and the Platonic philosopher, dead to his body and dead to his life, who has become only the contemplation of Forms and who ends by being identified with science itself. But *man,* in Descartes, had other ambitions. He conceived his life as an undertaking. He wanted science to be *made* and to be made by him; but his freedom did not allow him to "make" it. He wanted the passions to be cultivated, provided they were put to good use. He perceived, to a certain extent, the paradoxical truth that there are *free* passions. He prized true generosity above all things, defining it as follows: "I think that true generosity, which leads a man to esteem himself as highly as he can legitimately do so, consists only partly in his knowing that there is nothing that really belongs to him but the free disposing of his will nor any reason why he should be praised or blamed except for his using it well or badly, and partly in his feeling within him a firm and constant resolution to use it well, that is, never to lack the will to undertake and execute all things which he judges to be best: which is to follow virtue perfectly." This freedom, which he invented and which can only restrain desires until the clear vision of Good determines the resolutions of the will, cannot justify his proud feeling of being the veritable author of his acts and the continuous creator of free enterprises, any more than it gives him the means of inventing operative schemata in accordance with the general rules of the Method.

The reason is that Descartes, who was a dogmatic scientist and a good Christian, allowed himself to be crushed by the pre-established order of eternal truths and by the eternal system of values created by God. If man does not invent his God, if he does not construct Knowledge, he is only nominally free. Cartesian freedom here joins hands with Christian freedom, which is a false freedom. Cartesian man and Christian man are free for Evil, but not for Good, for Error, but not Truth. God takes them by the hand and, through the conjunction of natural and supernatural lights which He dispenses to them, leads them to the Knowledge and Virtue He has chosen for them. They need only let themselves be guided. The entire merit in this ascension reverts to Him. But insofar as they are nothingness, they escape Him. They are free to let go of His hand on the way and to plunge into the world of sin and non-being. *Per contra,* they can, of course, always beware of intellectual and moral Evil. They can beware and preserve themselves, can suspend judgment, can check their desires and stop their acts in time. In short, they are only asked not to hinder God's intentions. But Error and Evil are, in the last analysis, non-beings. Man has not even the freedom to produce anything in this domain. If he persists in his vice or his prejudices, what he creates will be a *nothing.* The universal order will not even be ruffled by his stubborness. "The worst," says Claudel, "is not always sure." In a doctrine that confuses being and perception, the only field of human initiative is the "bastard" terrain of which Plato speaks, the terrain that "is never seen except in dream," the borderline between being and non-being.

But since Descartes warns us that God's freedom is no more entire than that of man and that one is in the image of the other, we have a new means of investigation for determining more exactly his personal exigences, exigences which philosophic postulates have not allowed him to satisfy. If he conceived divine freedom as being quite like his own freedom, then it is of his own freedom, such as he would have conceived it without the fetters of Catholicism and dogmatism, that he speaks when he describes the freedom of God. We have here an obvious phenomenon of sublimation and transposition. The God of Descartes is the freest of the gods that have been forged by human thought. He is the only creative God. He is subject neither to principles—not even to that of identity—nor to a sovereign Good of which He is only the executor. He had not only created existants in conformity with rules which have imposed themselves upon His will, but He has created both beings and their essences, the world and the laws of the world, individuals and first principles:

"The mathematical truths which you call eternal have been established by God and are entirely dependent upon Him, as are all other creatures. To say that these truths are independent of God is to speak of Him as one speaks of Jupiter or Saturn and to subject Him to the Styx and the fates . . . It is God Who has established these laws in nature, as a king establishes the laws of his kingdom . . . As for eternal truths, I repeat that they are indeed true or possible because God knows them as true or possible and that they are not, on the other hand, known as true by God as if they were true independently of Him. And if men quite understood the meaning of their words, they would never say without blasphemy that the truth of something precedes God's knowledge of it, for to God willing and knowing are one. With the result that by virtue of His willing a thing He knows it and by that very fact the thing is true. It should therefore not be said that if God did not exist, these truths would nevertheless be true."

"You ask who obliged God to create these truths; and I say that He was as free not to make all the lines drawn from the centre to the circumference not equal as not to create the world. And it is certain that these truths are not more necessarily co-existent with His essence than other created things. . . . " "And though God wished that some truths be necessary, this does not mean that He wished them necessarily, for it is one thing to wish them to be necessary and quite another thing to wish necessarily or to be the necessity of wishing."

The meaning of the Cartesian doctrine is revealed here. Descartes realized perfectly that the concept of freedom involved necessarily an absolute autonomy, that a free act was an absolutely new production, the germ of which could not be contained in an earlier state of the world and that consequently freedom and creation were one and the same. The freedom of God, though similar to that of man, loses the negative aspect that it had in its human envelope;

Portrait of Descartes by Frans Hals.

it is pure productivity; it is the extra-temporal and eternal act by which God brings into being a world, a Good and eternal truths. Thenceforth, the root of all Reason is to be sought in the depths of the free act. It is freedom which is the foundation of the true, and the rigorous necessity that appears in the order of truths is itself supported by the absolute contingency of a creative free will. This dogmatic rationalist might say with Goethe, not "in the beginning was the word," but "in the beginning was the act." As for the difficulty of maintaining freedom in the face of truth, he glimpsed a solution to it in conceiving a creation which is at the same time an act of intellection, as if the thing created by a free decree somehow encounters the freedom that sustains it in being and thereby yields to understanding. In God, willing and intuition are one and the same; the divine consciousness is both constitutive and contemplative. And, in like manner, God invented Good. He is not disposed by His perfection to decide what is the best; rather, that which He has decided is, as a result of His decision itself, absolutely Good. For Descartes, the divine prerogative is, in the last analysis, an absolute freedom which invents Reason and Good and which has no limits other than itself and its fidelity to itself. But, on the other hand, there is nothing more in this freedom than in human freedom, and he is aware, in describing his God's free will, that he has merely developed the implicit content of the idea of freedom. If we examine the matter closely, we shall see that this is why human freedom is not limited by an order of freedoms and values which might offer themselves to our assent as eternal *things,* as necessary structures of being. It is the divine will that has laid down these values and truths and that supports them. Our freedom is limited only by the divine freedom. The world is only the creation of a freedom that preserves it for an indefinite time. Truth is nothing if it is not willed by this infinite and divine power and if it is not taken up, assumed and confirmed by human freedom. The free man is alone in the face of an absolutely free God. Freedom is the foundation of being, its secret dimension. Freedom, in this rigorous system, is the inner meaning and the true face of necessity.

Thus, in his description of divine freedom, Descartes ends by rejoining and explicating his primary intuition of his own freedom, of which he says that it is "known without proof and merely by our experience of it." It matters little to us that he was forced by the age in which he lived, as well as by his point of departure, to reduce the human free will to a merely negative power to deny itself until it finally yields and abandons itself to the divine solicitude. It matters little that he hypostasized in God the original and *constituent* freedom whose infinite existence he recognized by means of the *cogito* itself. The fact remains that a formidable power of divine and human affirmation runs through and supports his universe. It took two centuries of crisis—a crisis of Faith and a crisis of Science—for man to regain the creative freedom that Descartes placed in God, and for anyone finally to suspect the following truth, which is an essential basis of humanism: man is the being as a result of whose appearance a world exists. But we shall not reproach Descartes with having given to God that which reverts to us in our own right. Rather, we shall admire him for having, in a dictatorial age, laid the groundwork of democracy, for having followed to the very end the demands of the idea of *autonomy* and for having understood, long before the Heidegger of *Vom Wesem des Grundes,* that the sole foundation of being is freedom. (pp. 180-97)

Jean-Paul Sartre, "Cartesian Freedom," in his Literary and Philosophical Essays, *translated by Annette Michelson, 1955. Reprint by Collier Books, 1962, pp. 180-97.*

Leonard G. Miller (essay date 1957)

[*In the following excerpt, Miller assesses the philosophical implications of Descartes's doctrine of necessity associated with mathematical and metaphysical inquiries in the* Meditations.]

In Descartes' first *Meditation* the propositions of mathematics survive the criticism of the perception and dream arguments, but they do so only to be unsettled by the demon argument. Could not an all-powerful demon make me believe these propositions are true when, as a matter of fact, they are not? As Descartes suggests, "How do I know that I am not myself deceived every time I add two and three, or count the sides of a square, or judge of things yet simpler, if anything simpler can be suggested?" Now this is a puzzling statement. If someone tells me that I may always be mistaken about such simple matters, I immediately think he is not talking about the sort of mistake I occasionally make, and so I expect some explanation. In this case I expect Descartes to tell me what a square would be like if it did not have four sides, and what the sum of three and two would be if it was not five. Unfortunately, however, although he insists that the propositions of mathematics are not reliable unless their truth is guaranteed by God, he is not at all clear about how it is possible for them to be false, or what may be the case if they are. This is a crucial matter, for upon it hinges the meaning and significance of his basic contention, the contention that clear and distinct ideas require metaphysical support. In this paper I am going to delve into this matter by examining what Descartes does say or imply about the nature of the necessity associated with mathematical truths in particular and the eternal verities in general.

I must start by making it clear that Descartes really does adopt a skeptical attitude toward even the simplest propositions of mathematics, and I must do this because he sometimes argues that his readers have done him an injustice on this point. When he is accused of arguing in a circle in the third *Meditation,* he replies to the effect that axioms are never dubitable and that theorems are dubitable only if we are not attending to their proofs. As we shall see, he never abandons this position even though he frequently asserts even more emphatically that all knowledge depends upon the will of God. The latter view is asserted or implied in the ***Discourse,*** the third and fifth *Meditations,* the replies to ***Objections V*** and ***Objections VI,*** and in the ***Principles.*** It is also asserted very emphatically in a number of letters spaced from 1630 to 1648. In these he says, for example, that God could have arranged it so that triangles would not have three angles, the radii of a circle would be unequal, mountains would occur without valleys, and two times four would not equal eight, or, in brief, " . . . we see that nothing can have obliged God to make it true that contradictories cannot be together, and that consequently He could have done the contrary . . . " This brings us right back to the first *Meditation,* the demon, and the questions I asked about Descartes' treatment of two plus three and squares. The diversion indicates that Descartes is puzzled by the nature of these propositions whose truth appears to be self-evident, for he is inclined to say both that we cannot possibly be mistaken about them provided that we apprehend them clearly and distinctly and that we can be deceived by the demon no matter how clearly and distinctly we perceive them. When he introduces the demon Descartes really is raising a question about the nature of logical or mathematical necessity.

To reveal the nature of his perplexity I must first locate the context in which this necessity occurs. In all of his works Descartes maintains or implies that knowledge is ultimately based upon what he calls in various places simple natures, principles of knowledge, primary data, or common ideas. His view is not altogether clear, since he refers to the simples in different ways in different places and gives neither a complete analysis of his final position nor a clear indication of the evolution of the details. He always maintains, however, that the simples are revealed to us by "intuition" or the "natural light," that they are the ultimate objects of clear and distinct apprehension, and that they are all to be found within our consciousness if only we attend carefully enough. Descartes is not as specific as he might be about the nature, number, and kinds of simples, but in his fullest lists he divides them into four main categories: those which apply to all things, such as existence, substance, duration, number, unit; those which apply to physical things, such as extension, shape, straight, motion; those which apply to mental things, such as thought, ignorance, doubt; and, depending on the particular list, either relations such as equals, like, and cause and effect or axioms such as "If equals be added to equals the results will be equal," "Things the same as a third are the same as one another," and "Everything has a cause." The items in this fourth category provide the links whereby knowledge is generated out of those listed in the first three. According to Descartes, some of the resulting connections hold necessarily. He says, for instance, that we cannot conceive of extension not being related to substance, or of three and one not equaling four. It seems, then, that the necessity we are investigating characterizes the manner in which certain simples or complexes of them are related to each other by certain simple relations.

His inclusion of axioms requires no essential modification of this conclusion, since axioms are really statements about simple relations. This is indicated not only by the way in which axioms replace relations in his lists, an axiom about cause and effect replacing the relation cause and effect, axioms about equals replacing the relation equals, and so on, but also by the way in which he speaks about intuition and deduction. Consider, for instance, a very simple deduction where we might expect an application of the axiom "If things are equal to a third they are equal to one another." After intuiting that three plus one equals four and that two plus two equals four we then see, he says, that three plus one equals two plus two. There is no mention of the axiom here; the deduction is explained completely in terms of three intuitions, each involving the relation equals. The third insight, that three plus one equals two plus two because each is equal to four, is especially important not only because it makes the deduction possible but also because it is closely related to the axiom. Indeed, the axiom is just the generalization of this sort of insight; it is a statement about a particular feature of the relation equals, that is, that if it holds between X and Y and between Z and Y, then it also holds between X and Z.

Two things need to be said about this axiom. In the first place, Descartes would admit that we can use it as a premise in place of the third insight and so construct a "syllogistic" argument having the same conclusion as the original argument, but, as his discussion shows, he would not admit that this is either necessary or desirable. It is not necessary because we would not comprehend the axiom in the first place unless we were capable of insights of the very sort the axiom is to replace or obviate, and it is not desirable since in any given case understanding is more likely and error less probable if we develop our argument not by applying general principles but by tracing out the specific relations discovered by a close scrutiny of the terms themselves. He concludes that syllogistic reasoning may be of considerable use in presenting knowledge but that it has little use and is best avoided in research. In principle, axioms can be eliminated from deductive reasoning. In the second place, if it be said that as a matter of fact axioms do occur and therefore that the nature of their truth must be accounted for, it must be pointed out that to see that the axiom is necessarily true is really to see that in a certain sort of situation a certain relation necessarily holds. Both these points indicate that axioms, far from constituting a fifth kind of simple which is indispensable for deductive reasoning, are really to be explained in terms of relations. Consequently, their occurrence does not jeopardize the conclusion that we are concerned primarily with the manner in which certain simple relations hold between certain other simples or complexes of simples.

Having located the context in which mathematical necessity arises, I can go on to consider its nature. Perhaps the most important point to be established is that Descartes' eternal verities are, in later terminology, synthetic rather than analytic. This point would hardly need defense were it not for the fact that he frequently says a proposition is necessarily true because one concept is implicated or contained in another. The synthetic nature of necessary propositions is indicated by his treatment of the propositions "Body has extension" and "Extension exists only in body," both of which are necessarily true even though we "understand by the term 'extension' something other than body." He supports this belief not by analyzing meanings but by pointing out that it is impossible to imagine either body or extension without imagining the other.

> For though the understanding is *in strictness attending only to what is signified by the word,* the imagination ought nevertheless to form a true idea of the thing, in order that the understanding

> may be able, at need, to direct its attention to such other conditions belonging to it *as are not expressed by the word* . . .

Notice that to say the concepts "extension" and "body" are contained in each other is not to say something about the relationship between meanings, for the necessity of the connection between them is not revealed by anything "signified" or "expressed by the word." The propositions under consideration are necessarily true but not analytic.

There is an implication in the passage just quoted that an understanding of a simple per se will not reveal any necessary relationship between it and others. This conclusion is born out in other places where Descartes says or implies that simples have been distinguished from one another in such a way that apprehending the essential meaning of one does not involve apprehending that of any other. Furthermore, this conclusion follows in a number of ways from the things he says about simples. In the first place, simples are not things which can occur or exist independently of each other; they are distinguished from each other or from the things they characterize by a process of abstraction. Since this process must be continued until further distinctions are impossible if composites are to be eliminated, and since it is always possible to distinguish between a thing and its properties or relations, it follows that the idea of a simple per se does not contain the idea of any relationship whatsoever, to say nothing of one that is necessary. Second, as he frequently points out, the simples are indefinable. Emphasizing this point, he says an attempt to define them will result in the substitution of a composite for a simple or in the explanation of something else or nothing at all, thus indicating that simples do not have the sort of meaning which would make analytic statements possible. Once more it follows that it is impossible to analyze a simple and see that it necessarily subtends certain relationships. In the third place, we not only can but must be able to apprehend the simples apart from their relations, for, as he says, we cannot judge that simples are related unless we have first apprehended them by themselves. In the fourth place, the nonanalytic nature of necessary truths is required by the doctrine that God could have made the eternal verities other than they are. For instance, the radii of a circle are necessarily equal, but this necessity does not follow from the meaning of "circle," for God could have made circles so that their radii were unequal. These various considerations show quite conclusively that for Descartes a necessarily true proposition is not an analytic proposition.

As his very examples indicate, this conclusion applies also to propositions involving composites. The proposition I have cited, "Body has extension," is a case in point, for body is a composite of extension and substance. It might seem that the proposition is really analytic, since it can be replaced by "Extended substance is extended" or, in Descartes' words, "That which is extended is that which is extended," but despite the appearance of these propositions he does not think the point they are meant to express can be discovered by inspecting the meanings of terms or the forms of statements. In giving his equivalent he implies that the important thing is the relation between substance and extension, and he emphasizes that this relation is revealed by the understanding aided by imagination, not by the understanding dissecting meanings. The important point is not that imagination is involved, for he gives up this view in his later works, but rather that the relation is not revealed by an analysis of meanings. Descartes never gave up this view, nor could he give it up, for the things related are simples. Even if he had explicitly introduced definitions which would lead to analytic statements, he would have insisted that such statements are quite trivial. The whole point of the doctrine of simples is that starting with the simple terms and the simple relations and observing that various relations necessarily hold between various terms, we could, in principle, generate the whole body of knowledge. Terms like "body" need not be introduced. In such a system the truth of every proposition would be logically necessary, but no proposition would be analytic. If terms such as "body" were introduced as convenient abbreviations, (1) they could always be eliminated if we so desired, and (2) the analytic propositions which come in their wake would not give us additional knowledge; that is, they would not add to the stock of knowledge implicitly contained in the simples. Conceiving of the system of knowledge as he does, Descartes would not think analytic propositions are of much significance; rather, he is concerned with the nature of the necessary connections which make possible the definitions leading to the analytic propositions, the necessary but nonanalytic connections upon which all knowledge rests.

From our discussion so far we can conclude that, according to Descartes, the necessary connections between simple concepts must be revealed by some mental operation which involves more than grasping their meanings. But how does this capacity operate, and exactly what does it mean to say that certain simples are necessarily related to each other in certain manners? Unfortunately, Descartes does not give an analysis. Instead, adopting an analogy with vision, he simply reiterates again and again that the necessity is revealed by the "eyes of the mind," "mental vision," "spiritual illumination," or the "natural light." It is quite clear that the natural light is the light of reason and that this light is cast upon the simples, thus revealing the necessary relations between them, but the exact manner in which reason inspects its objects and the exact nature of the relations it observes remain obscure.

We can see, without pushing him farther than he wants to go, that Descartes is courting trouble. Since he does want to say that the seeing, apprehending, or understanding of simples reveals the necessity of the relationships, we can consider what it is that is seen that does reveal this. Is it something about the simple or simples, some property that necessitates the relation? No, for in the first place, if the property were necessarily conjoined with the simple, a fresh instance of the very thing we are investigating would arise; and if it were not necessarily conjoined, the simple would not be related necessarily to anything in virtue of it. And in the second place, as we have seen, we cannot attribute a property to a simple, for a thing with a property is a composite. If it is not something about the simple then is it the simple per se that necessitates the relation? Will an apprehension of the simple as such reveal the relation? Hardly, for a simple, regarded as that which may subtend relations, must be understandable apart from its relations. Apprehending a simple does not involve apprehending any relationships at all, to say nothing of necessary ones. This is true of all simples, including simple relations. Therefore, according to the doctrine of simples, there is nothing about simple *A,* simple *B,* and simple relation *C* which can lead us to conclude that *C* necessarily holds between *A* and *B.* Speaking logically and not temporally, after we have apprehended the nature of *A, B,* and *C,* we still have to recognize that they are related and related necessarily. However, whenever Descartes speaks of intuition and later of the *lumen naturale,* he does say that a contemplation of the simples will reveal the necessity of the connection. He now has a puzzle on his hands, for according to the doctrine of simples he cannot discover the necessity in the nature of the simples, but according to the doctrine of the *lumen naturale* he can discover it by beaming the natural light upon them. For Descartes the *lumen naturale* reveals necessary connections but does not illuminate the source of nature of this necessity. It simply is an unanalyzable fact that there are necessary connections and that we can apprehend them.

We are now in a position to understand the skeptical attitude expressed in the first *Meditation.* Descartes' uneasiness stems in part at least from the nature of the two major doctrines I have mentioned, that of simples on the one hand and that of the *lumen naturale* and the apprehended necessity of certain relations on the other. We have seen that he finds it very difficult to describe or analyze the necessity he apprehends and that he therefore refers to it in terms of an analogy with vision or indicates that it is an unanalyzable fact of our intellectual life. That he is not as clear about this matter as he would like to be is itself a sufficient reason why he should adopt a questioning attitude and why he should look for support from some other quarter. This uneasiness is intensified by an examination of the doctrine of simples, which suggests that we have good reason for thinking that the allegedly "necessary" relations are not necessary at all. Since a simple is such that its nature can be apprehended independently of any relation, it would be unaffected if its relations were other than they happen to be, and consequently it could subtend a relation other than the one we apprehend to be necessary. For instance, since we cannot say why two and three should total five despite the full illumination of the natural light, and since the meanings of the concepts are quite distinct from one another, there is no reason why they should total five rather than, say, nine. Descartes will not consider such an alternative, however, for despite the analysis of simples, the understanding cannot make sense of it. We come back then to the basic inconsistency hovering in the background: according to the theory of simples an awareness of the simples will not reveal the necessary relations between them, but according to the doctrine of the *lumen naturale* it will.

The confusion and perplexity is only increased by a view I have not yet mentioned, the view that for all we know, the necessity we apprehend may stem from the nature of the apprehending apparatus. It is quite conceivable, Descartes suggests in a number of places, that my mind is such that certain relations seem necessary to me when, as a matter of fact, they are not. This view is compatible with the theory of simples, insofar as it requires that the simples themselves do not determine what relations hold, and with the doctrine of the *lumen naturale,* insofar as the analogy with vision suggests the possibility of distortion and deception. Furthermore, this view follows directly from Descartes' belief in the supreme power of God. He had firm convictions on this matter, convictions which were only strengthened by his attempts to confute those whom he thought were elevating the Divine Reason at the expense of the Divine Will. According to Descartes, if God really is all-powerful He is indifferent to "every reason of truth and goodness" in the sense that all truths, contingent, necessary, and moral, are alike His creatures and might very well have been other than they are if He had so chosen. It is perplexing enough that God could have made the eternal verities other than they are. But it is worse still that, having determined them, He not only could have made us so that we apprehend them in a mistaken way but also that He is not constrained from doing so by any moral considerations. It is a matter about which He is quite indifferent.

If Descartes had asserted throughout his work that the necessity of the truth of the so-called "eternal" verities may arise not from the nature of the simples themselves but from the nature of the created mind that apprehends them, his position would be more consistent, for this view, unlike the one which maintains that the necessity is something objective revealed to us, is consistent with both his theory of simples and his theology. Despite these by no means trivial considerations, however, he really cannot bring himself to accept this view, for it strikes at the very heart of his rationalism. He cannot discount the conviction that the necessity of certain relations is revealed clearly and distinctly by the light of reason. As a result, when he asks why he cannot conceive certain relations to be other than they are, he finds himself caught between two opposing explanations. In his later writings he wavers constantly between them, stressing one whenever he makes use of self-evident truths and whenever he emphasizes that knowledge is possible and the other whenever he is concerned with his skepticism or with the power of God. Added to the difficulties I have already mentioned, his inability to decide between these conflicting views only compounds his perplexity.

There are, then, a number of reasons why Descartes is puzzled by the reasoning found in mathematics and why he looks for a justification elsewhere. Those very same reasons, plus the fact that mathematics is bound up intimately with substance, attributes, and modes, lead him to look for this justification in the realm of metaphysics. Consequently, in the later writings the demon hypothesis is raised and, after the familiar arguments, rejected.

I do not intend to discuss this well-known line of reasoning, but I would like to examine the conclusion it is supposed to support, the conclusion that since God exists and is not a deceiver we see the eternal verities as they really are. Two points follow immediately. First, we seem to have confirmed our strong conviction that in recognizing that the eternal verities are necessarily true we are recognizing an objective fact about the verities themselves, or rather about the constituent simples. Second, it follows not only that we see the eternal verities as God sees them but also, of course, that He sees them as we do. This is not to say that we know as much about them as He does, for He knows them in a context which we cannot possibly apprehend, but so far as our knowledge goes it is exactly like His. With respect to the eternal verities, we know just as He does that they are necessarily true.

This familiar position must be considered, however, in the light of the doctrine that God created the eternal verities and is therefore responsible for their truth. Descartes usually introduces this doctrine on the ground that it must be true since its denial is incompatible with the belief in the supreme power of God. This is an important consideration for him, but the doctrine is also suggested and influenced by the theory of simples, for if the relations between simples are not determined by the simples themselves, they must be determined by some external source. When Descartes supposes that God might have created the eternal truths other than He did, he supposes that He would have used the same notions but related them differently, thus implying that He is responsible for the relations which do hold. Descartes is understandably vague about the manner in which God did establish these relations. He does say that God produced them by willing them or by willing-thinking them and that they are necessarily true for Him either because He has chosen not to change His mind about them or because He has created them "from all eternity," but when he is pressed further he says the whole matter must remain incomprehensible to us.

This doctrine leads to the final difficulty in Descartes' thought, for it involves as a consequence the very possibility it is supposed to eliminate, namely, that God is a deceiver. The eternal verities cannot be necessarily true for God in the same sense they are for me, for if they were He could not have envisaged alternatives to them and thus could not have created them other than they are. Descartes must and does maintain that God can conceive of alternatives in cases where I apprehend that they are impossible. Consequently, despite my "insight" to the contrary, the denial of an allegedly necessary truth really is not inconceivable and really is not self-contradictory. For me, a proposition is necessarily true if its denial is inconceivable, but for God it is necessarily true only in the sense that He chose to make it true and decided it would always be so. Concepts are contradictory only for a creature like me and only because God has made me so that I must apprehend them as such. It would seem, then, that the necessity is one thing for me and quite another for God. The necessity I perceive is not the necessity that really characterizes the eternal verities; it is at best a distorted view of a connection which must remain incomprehensible. My mind does not work like God's, even in a finite way.

It is not possible to accept Descartes' view that my insight is accurate so far as it goes because it parallels God's. If this were so the major difference between my insight and God's would be that He sees more clearly and in full detail why it is impossible to think of alternatives to the eternal verities, but this, of course, is not the difference. Looking at it the other way, if my insight differs from His in extent only and not in nature, then I should be able to conceive of the possibility of alternatives. According to Descartes, however, I cannot. The crucial difference between our understandings is not that I cannot think of an alternative while He can, but rather that I see it is senseless to think of there being one, while He does not. When I recognize that a proposition is necessarily true, I also recognize that it would be a mistake to suppose it could be false. Consequently, if I were able to admit the possibility of an alternative, the very nature of my belief would change. Since this is not so for God, we are not aware of the same thing when we each apprehend what is supposed to be the same truth. Descartes cannot escape the conclusion that God has put exceedingly misleading ideas in my mind.

One possible way of avoiding this conclusion would require that Descartes abandon the view that the simples are necessarily related in certain ways. But he cannot do this even after he has supposed that God could have connected the simples differently from the way He did; for whenever he attends to the eternal verities themselves he is confronted by a fact that refuses to be upset by any belief about God and His powers, the fact that he cannot sensibly think of them as being false. God would be absolved if Descartes could suspend judgment about the nature of the necessity, but since he cannot conceive the propositions to be false, he cannot do this. The only other way he could avoid the conclusion would involve abandoning the belief that the truth of the eternal verities depends on God, but he will not do this. As a result, the metaphysical guarantee he has developed really destroys the significance of the criterion it is supposed to support. Descartes believes that reason is able to reveal the basic nature and structure of the universe and that it can do this by apprehending the manner in which simples are and are not necessarily related to each other. After the guarantee of the criterion of clear and distinct ideas has been elaborated, however, it turns out that the relations apprehended by reason are but misleading representatives of the true relations whose basic nature must remain a mystery to us. There is a powerful and basic undercurrent of irrationalism in Descartes, the first of the modern rationalists.

The contrast between this tendency to irrationalism and the opposing tenacious adherence to rationalism together with his refusal, even at the expense of inconsistency, to allow either to overcome the other brings us back once more to what has become the principal theme of this paper: Descartes' work is characterized by two conflicting patterns of thought. One pattern contains the closely related views that the simples are the ultimate building blocks from which knowledge is constructed, that simples must have a strict meaning which is neutral with respect to their relations, that all propositions are synthetic, that God is all-powerful, that God could have connected the simples other than He did, that we are finite, that we do not understand why the eternal verities are necessarily true, that the necessity we apprehend may be imposed by our own understanding, and that the criterion of clear and distinct ideas requires metaphysical support. The other and opposing pattern contains the related views that knowledge is possible, that reason can reveal the basic nature of the universe, that there is no circle in the third *Meditation,* that the truth of a proposition does not depend on us, that in the case of the eternal verities truth is determined by the notions involved, that the *lumen naturale* can and does reveal these necessary connections clearly and distinctly, that we cannot conceive of such insights being false, and therefore that such insights do not require metaphysical support. If Descartes had accepted this second pattern and had been able to reject such portions of the other as are inconsistent with it, the evil-demon hypothesis, the questions about two plus three and squares, and the search for a metaphysical support would not have arisen. But, for reasons I have discussed, he cannot bring himself to do this. Insofar as he views simples in the way he does and insofar as he emphasizes the power of God, he is led almost inevitably to the evil-demon argument and the search for a metaphysical support. But unfortunately he is also accepting a position which makes it impossible for him to find that support; he cannot avoid the demon. (pp. 451-65)

Leonard G. Miller, "Descartes, Mathematics, and God," in The Philosophical Review, *Vol. LXVI, 1957, pp. 451-65.*

Robert Champigny (essay date 1959)

[In the following excerpt, Champigny challenges Descartes's theory of the Cogito, or thinking self, asserting that "the seductiveness of the Cogito in the Meditations *seems to me due to dramatic technique."]*

Descartes doubts that there is this or that; he does not doubt that something is. If he claimed to apply doubt not only to what is, but also to being (in Heideggerian terms), then the word "doubt" which he uses would become meaningless.

There is something else that Descartes does not question: the meaningfulness of language as a whole and of a particular tongue in so far as he uses it as he does. The doubt bears on the way the mind, or language, divides and composes what is: this and that thing, this and that relation. The quest of Descartes may, I think, be interpreted in this way: Is there a word, or group of words, which can safely be assumed to isolate a definite object of thinking which, *as determined,* would be more than an object of thinking, or creature of language? (This "more" may be specified in various ways, including a Cartesian way. I shall remain non-committal about it for the moment.)

The phenomenological reduction of this and that does not leave a bare "there is," but a "there is thinking (this or that)." Descartes does not doubt the meaningfulness of the word "thinking" any more than the meaningfulness of the verb "to be"; and he does not doubt the meaningfulness of such words as "doubting," "feeling," "willing," *in so far* as doubting, feeling, willing, etc., involve unreflective thinking.

A conclusion is thus reached which may be phrased as follows: "Thinking" is a minimum definition of "being." Whatever else may be said to be, there is thinking. This is an echo of Parmenides. And a translation into Heideggerian terms might run like this: Thinking is not on the ontic, but on the ontological level. Thinking as doubting reveals the nihilating power of being.

But this is not the goal of the Cartesian quest; or at least its goal is not just that. The preoccupation is centered on definite objects of thinking. The kind of object which is wanted has not been found through unreflective thinking, since this thinking has taken the form of doubting. But this kind of object is believed to be found through the intervention of reflective thinking. In one of the versions of the Cogito, the reflective leap is indicated by "therefore" (*donc, ergo*). The value of this conjunction is less logical than psychological. It means something like "thus, I realize it." It is equivalent to the pseudosyllogistic Greek conjunction *ara.*

The effect of the reflective leap is not simply to permit the affirmation: "There is thinking." In order to obtain a properly isolated object of thinking, distinct from thinking (about thinking), the formula objectifies unreflective thinking (doubting). The realization indicated by the word "therefore" is an objectification. And thus, as it is made an object of thinking, thinking becomes an-ego-who-thinks, a particular thinking thing.

This extrapolation effects a radical alteration which, along with other critics such as Sartre, I cannot accept. I reject it not because of any formal rule of logic (the Cogito lies outside the scope of formal logic), but because the way in which I interpret the text and the way in which I interpret my experience do not tally.

As far as I am concerned, words like "to think," "to feel," may be used to refer to experiences, or activities, lived as such (lived infinitively), and not as an ego who thinks and feels: they are not lived substantively, or personally. The ego appears only when I translate these experiences, or activities, within the frame of some I-thou pattern, as, for instance, when I write a philosophical essay.

What can be said about these experiences or activities is that a certain quality inhabits them, or haunts them, a quality which may be called "selfness" rather than "self." I say "selfness" as I might say "blueness," or "dryness." "Selfness" is a substantive, like "self," but it stands as a pro-adjective. This quality of selfness is a matter of experience and comprehension. It can not be detached from the experiencing so as to be made an isolated object of thinking, of knowledge and belief.

On the other hand, what can be an object of thinking, knowledge and belief is the personal, or social, self. This self is posited as an object among other objects, as a person among other persons. It is this self which can properly be designated with the help of personal pronouns. Selfness is a quality inherent in feeling, the self is an object of thinking, in particular of imaginative thinking (thinking according to thing-concepts). It is a tool of sociopragmatic thinking, a creature of imagination.

Now, as I interpret it, the methodical doubt is precisely designed to reject this kind of object. A methodical doubt, or phenomenological reduction, shows the inauthenticity of the category of the person. It encloses the I-thou pattern within the conventions of the human comedy, or tragedy. It reduces the social, or personal self to a theatrical persona.

But it appears to me that what the Cartesian formula affirms is not the quality of selfness which is felt in one way or another (for instance as an ideal), but the personal self, this theatrical persona which should have been dissolved by the methodical doubt. To be more precise, the Cartesian "ego" stands for a particular person and also for the category of the person, for a quasi-Platonic idea of the self.

The first ground for this interpretation has already been presented. No doubt the ego which Descartes extrapolates is pretty empty. It is not a personality. But it can be considered as the almost empty conceptual frame for a personality. It is an *être de raison* which can serve as a frame for a being of imagination. If Descartes had only wanted to translate into language what I call selfness, then this elaborate show was not needed. It could only, as it does, confuse the issue by assuming the appearance of a reasoning sequence.

A search for a definite object of knowledge and belief can only encounter the self, not selfness. What appears once the reflective leap has been taken is the self. As a matter of fact, reflection can be said to create the self.

My interpretation also relies on what follows the Cogito: the verbal establishment of the existence of God. What Descartes calls "God" is not equivalent to "divine": this god is a personal god. He is a "being," a "creator." He is supposed not to be deceitful, unlike the *malin génie.* No doubt this god is said to be "infinite," but this does not prevent him from being an object of thinking and belief.

If, in the formula "I think, I am," "I" were meant only to refer to what I call selfness, it would be possible to proceed to an examination of the experience of the divine, of the ideal, but not to the examination of the idea of a god. The "I" has to be conceived as personal in order to call forth the idea of a personal god. There has to be a *dramatis persona* on the philosophical stage in order that a *deus* may appear *ex machina.* (I am not concerned here with the quality of the mechanism.)

In the demonstration, much use is made of the idea of finitude. The idea of the finite calls forth the idea of the infinite: these two ideas are correlative. What I call selfness can be described as neither finite nor infinite. The word "infinitive" might be used instead. If the phrase "I think" were equivalent to "there is thinking," Descartes could not abstract from it the idea of finitude. The *res* has to be posited apart from *cogitans* in order that the idea of finitude may appear. The demonstration of the existence of God relies on a rift between the substantive and the participle. If we restore the participle to its full infinitive value (altered by the association with a substantive), the rift is between a substantive and an infinitive.

This rift and the privilege granted to the substantive are also made evident in a passage of the answer to Hobbes's objections: "It is certain that thought can not be without a thing which thinks, and in general no accident or act can be without a substance of which it is the act."

Let us now return to the part of the ***Méditations*** which precedes the Cogito, i.e., to the doubting sequence. There is no denying its seductiveness. But this seductiveness is dramatic rather than philosophical. It is fitting that the establishment of a belief in a persona should be effected with the help of theatrical technique.

The first person is used constantly: a verb-ending in the Latin text, a pronoun in the French text. A narrator is put on the stage. Advantage is taken of the structure of a language in which the category of the person, of the personified thing, plays a fundamental role. Actually, it is in the very nature of language (prosaic, socio-pragmatic language) to betray uniqueness. On being translated into language, uniqueness necessarily becomes singularity or universality, or both (as in the case of the Cartesian ego). Yet uniqueness is no more singular or universal than blue is round or square. There are ways of tricking language, of betraying with words the betraying words. Thus in certain anti-theatrical plays, the characters seem to say: "We are characters in a play, we are your dream; we are creatures of language and so are you." There is also the poetic conversion of language. But in the ***Méditations,*** an *honnête homme* addresses *honnêtes gens.*

So there is an expository monologue. "I" designates a singular person who is busy removing all props from the stage. But as we enter into the spirit of the game, this persona becomes invisible: we assume that it is not on the stage. For this persona has a universal as well as a singular value. The reader identifies himself with the persona in order to live the experiment. In this way, the personal selves of both the narrator and the reader are discounted. This is good in a way: this persona must not obtrude too much, for we might say: "Since the *tabula* must be *rasa,* why is not this narrating ghost, this theatrical convention, taken out of the way too?" On the other hand, this character must reappear on stage, in "clear and distinct" light. It is this very mask "I," universal and singular, which must be affirmed.

In the ***Méditations,*** this is done with the help of a conjuring trick. Once the stage has been emptied of props and characters, the character "I" is called back on stage by another character. The difficulty consists in having this other character appear on stage and play his part without stirring suspicion. The trick is similar to one which has been used by mystery novelists in a closed-room situation: the character does not enter the stage as a "real" character, but, say, as a prop-man.

We are told: "Now in case we had been remiss and left something on stage which escaped our notice, I call a prop-man to check." We admire the thoroughness of the conjurer. Lost in admiration, we do not notice that what seems to make the trick impossible makes it in fact more easy.

For the hypothetical *malin génie* who is thus brought into play is deceitful. We might have balked at seeing an ego pulled out of the hat of thinking. But undoubtedly, if there is something deceived, this something has to be a person. The verb "to be deceived" requires a personal subject such as may be legitimately detached from the verb. The verb has meaning only within the scope of an I-thou pattern.

The monologue has become a dialogue. This is theatrically effective: It is more compelling to "believe" in a character engaged in a dialogue than in a character engaged in a monologue. The narrator was somewhat ghostly; but the deceived persona is a "real" character.

"At the moment of entering the stage of this world, where I have stood so far as a spectator, I walk masked." *Larvatus prodeo:* this phrase of Descartes appears identical to the Cogito in the perspective of my critical interpretation. There is walking, advancing, for instance thinking, under the mask of the ego.

But Descartes means the mask to be affirmed as something more than a socio-pragmatic convention. Or rather there are two masks. The first mask (the materially involved ego) is exposed and the second mask appears all the more authentic.

Thus characters in a play appear more "real" if they are made to watch a play within the play. The reflective leap is meant to have this effect in Descartes. Likewise, I may realize that I am dreaming, but stop there and fail to notice that the realization itself takes place within a second dream. Thus, perhaps Descartes, in one of the ***Songes,*** according to his biographer: "Doubting whether what he had just seen was dream or vision, not only did he decide, while sleeping, that it was a dream, but he also interpreted it before sleep left him."

However, the spectacle of the play within the play or the experience of the dream within the dream may provide an incentive for further doubt instead of confining the doubt to a chosen domain. If theatrical characters can watch a play, what are we who watch these characters watch a play? If a dream can be recognized as such while sleeping, what is waking? The doubting sequence in Descartes is induced in part by such a preoccupation. But on what should the attention fasten to break the spell of the waking dream, or play? On "errors" of the senses? I should rather think on language, language as it is molded by sociopragmatic categories such as that of the person.

To sum up. My critical interpretation has not consisted in saying that the self was not a reliable object of knowledge and belief. Any object of knowledge, any tool used in a cognitive language, can be considered as certain or uncertain according to the perspective, the mood or the situation. Thus, belief in the self and selves is normal in a dramatic situation, and the seductiveness of the Cogito in the ***Méditations*** seems to me due to dramatic technique. But if the situation appears as theatrical rather than dramatic, the self is reduced to a persona, to a theatrical mask. Beliefs are as fitful as barometers. There is something approaching: this is a person, there is belief in a person. Words are heard and interpreted: there is belief in my self. Now there is thinking about this event: there may be no more belief in the two selves. "Good reasons to believe" do not alter the picture radically. Beliefs come before reasoning. Reasoning, as long as it lasts, may dispel a belief; it cannot produce a belief. And to try to bolster a belief with reasons is quite superfluous, or inefficacious.

My critical interpretation has rather consisted in saying that the Cartesian experience, as I live it, can not furnish any object of knowledge and belief, certain or uncertain, because it dissolves objects of knowledge: the experience of radical doubt annihilates the perspective of knowledge, a perspective which it is necessary to enter in order that objects of knowledge and belief may appear. Descartes needs a reflective leap, or a *malin génie,* in order to reenter a perspective of knowledge.

This is why I have been concerned with showing that the self posited by Descartes *was* a person, or persona, that is to say an object of knowledge and belief, rather than just a name for a quality of the experience.

An experience does not ask for belief. Names for qualities of experience do not ask for belief: they are to be comprehended. They may appear ill-chosen: "selfness" is probably a poor choice. "Coherence" would be a better word, if it were not too narrowly intellectual. What about "logos"?

The result of my critical interpretation is not the assertion that persons, or selves, "just do not exist." "To exist" has meaning only if the mode of existence is specified. Persons exist as objects, or tools, of knowledge in socio-pragmatic language and thinking. They exist as objects of belief in socio-pragmatic acting. My person, or self, exists as persona in social role-taking. The assumption of the persona may range beyond its domain of usefulness and tend toward hypnotic identification. (pp. 370-77)

Robert Champigny, "The Theatrical Aspect of the Cogito," in Review of Metaphysics, *Vol. XII, No. 3, March, 1959, pp. 370-77.*

Maurice Mandelbaum (essay date 1984)

[In the following excerpt, Mandelbaum asserts that Descartes's principle of methodological doubt is contradicted by his causal theory of perception.]

"Seeing is believing" is a phrase with which we are all familiar. On the other hand, near the beginning of a well-known book [by H. H. Price] entitled *Perception* one finds the statement, "When I see a tomato there is much that I can doubt." This essay is concerned with believing and doubting, and I shall begin where these two remarks would lead you to expect me to begin: with a discussion of doubt and belief as they occur with respect to the testimony of our senses. What I hope to establish in considering such cases will then lead me to formulate some tentative suggestions regarding the bases of belief in other, wider contexts as well. Although my approach to these problems is in large measure both phenomenologically and psychologically oriented, diverging therein from most recent philosophic discussions of belief, the claim that I shall initially advance concerning the relations of doubt and belief is by no means unprecedented, having also been pressed in different ways by Peirce and by Wittgenstein. I shall be claiming that doubt is always parasitic on belief, that belief precedes doubt, not only temporally, but also in the logical sense that every act of doubting presupposes a full acceptance of one or more other beliefs, such that if these beliefs were themselves to be doubted no reason would remain for the doubt that was initially entertained. Peirce put his view of the matter succinctly in one of his many criticisms of Descartes' method of doubt when he said, "We cannot begin with complete doubt. . . . A person may, it is true, in the course of his studies, find reason to doubt what he began by believing; but in that case he doubts because he has a positive reason for it." This, as I shall now show, is a justified claim with respect to each of the stages through which Descartes' doubt proceeded in his ***Meditations.***

In the ***Meditations,*** . . . Descartes began his methodological doubt with doubts concerning sense-perception, because he found that in some instances his senses had deceived him. It was his contention that even though his senses might not always deceive him, the fact that they were sometimes deceptive was a sufficient reason for distrusting them. As he said, "It is wiser not to trust entirely to any thing by which we have once been deceived." Let us, however, look at one case to which Descartes himself alludes in his sixth *Meditation.* There he refers to a tower that appears to be round when seen from a distance, but is later seen to be square when viewed from closer at hand. In such a case, in order to characterize our earlier experience as having been deceptive, three assumptions must be made. First, we must hold that this particular tower, which we are now seeing, is not in fact round; second, we must assume that what we saw from a distance is the same tower which we are now seeing; and, third, we must assume that towers, unlike some objects, such as hedgehogs, do not change shape as we approach them. In the absence of any one of these assumptions, it could not be claimed that our senses had deceived us. Yet, the sole basis on which each of these assumptions rests is to be found in sense-experience. Thus, it is only because we accept some of the testimony of our senses as trustworthy that we are in a position to reject other experiences as illusory. On what basis we grant precedence to some forms of sense-experience rather than to others will later occupy me. First, however, I must proceed to a second argument which Descartes offered for doubting what was presented to him in sense-experience: the fact that in dreams he often supposed himself to have been in familiar surroundings when in fact he had been asleep.

This argument, too, is directed against the trustworthiness of sense-experience, and it, too, rests on assumptions that contradict the general thesis it is designed to prove. In this case, however, the contradiction is less immediately obvious, and we must examine the presuppositions of the argument more closely. In this connection, we must first note that Descartes could not seek to undermine our reliance on sense-experience through appealing to dreams if he did not from the outset assume that a distinction of some kind is to be drawn between actually seeing, hearing, and touching objects and whatever is occurring in dreams. At this point Descartes noted that our waking experiences are clearer and more distinct than our dreams, but he rejected that difference as capable of authenticating waking experience. As he said, "There are no certain indications by which we may distinguish wakefulness from sleep." Nevertheless, one finds that he did in fact assign precedence to waking experience, for why else should he have said in ***Recherche de la verité,*** "How can you be certain that your life is not a perpetual dream and all that you imagine you learn by means of your senses is not as false now as it is when you sleep?" Yet, had Descartes really assumed that both types of experience are equally convincing, why view as *false* that which occurs in dreams? Bernard Williams [in *Descartes: The Project of Pure Inquiry* (1978)] has suggested one basis for doing so: the fact that following a dream we awaken in our own room, in our own bed. On awakening, we reject what we have dreamt, no matter how convincing it was at the time, because we cannot have been where we dreamt we were, nor could we have done the things we had dreamt we had done, unless we believe—contrary to all our other experience—that where we are at one moment, and how we then act, is discontinuous with the situations in which we find ourselves at the next moment. Thus, in order to characterize dreams as false, Descartes must have accepted the truth of a particular set of sense-experiences: those which occurred on his awakening. But on what must that acceptance have been based? If Descartes was indeed serious in denying that we can distinguish between dreams and waking experience in terms of how clearly we apprehend what is present in each, he must have relied on some other criterion. Near the end of the sixth *Meditation* he suggests what that criterion was: the coherence of waking experience as contrasted with dreams. Thus, his willingness to characterize dreams as illusory rested on a belief that the regularities among natural events with which he was acquainted in waking experience provided evidence that those events were not illusory. Thus, the dream argument fails to avoid the charge that I have levelled against Descartes: in this case, too, his doubt could only arise insofar as he had antecedently accepted another set of beliefs as true.

It was not, however, by appealing to specific illusions in sense-experience, nor by introducing his argument from dreams, that Descartes ultimately sought to undermine all faith in the senses. For that purpose he feigned the hypothesis that a malignant demon might be deceiving him, implanting in him thoughts that led him to believe that his sense-experience informed him of objects existing in an external, independent world, even though no such objects did in fact exist. I shall now try to show that in this hypothesis Descartes again relied on assumptions that were incompatible with the doubts he wished to instill.

Why, we may ask, did Descartes hold that his thoughts were deceptive if they had in fact been implanted in him by the demon? It could only be because his direct experience carried no hint that there was a demon causing him to see, hear, touch, taste, or smell what he was perceiving; on the contrary, his experience seemed to depend directly on the existence of a world of objects which appeared to be independent of him. To be sure, not all of our ideas have this characteristic: we distinguish, for example, between *seeing* something and remembering or imagining it. As Descartes suggested near the end of the ***Meditations,*** our ideas of sense are livelier, clearer, and in a way more distinct than are those of memory or imagination. Furthermore, they differ with respect to the fact that we have a lesser degree of control over them. As he says, "I found

"Queen Christina of Sweden Surrounded by Scholars" by Dumesnil.

by experience that these ideas presented themselves to me without my consent being requisite, so that I could not perceive any object, however desirous I might be, unless it were present to the organs of sense; and it was not in my power not to perceive it, when it was present." Here Descartes obviously presupposed a causal theory of perception, in which what we perceive depends upon the functioning of our sense-organs, and this is in fact the test that he cannot, in the end, avoid using. He could not simply appeal to liveliness, clarity, and distinctness in order to distinguish between perceiving and, say, remembering, because some memory-images possess these characteristics in a very high degree. For example, the memory of a faux pas one has just committed may displace any clear awareness of what one is presently seeing, hearing, or tasting. Nor is it merely the involuntariness of our sense-perception which distinguishes perceiving from remembering or imagining, because there are many occasions on which our thoughts and our memories come to us unsought and seem to be as little under our control as are our sense-perceptions. Thus, it is the role of the senses in perception which Descartes must stress, and even though he does not develop his causal theory of perception until the sixth *Meditation,* that theory was presupposed by him all along. Had he not assumed it, he could not have claimed that if his ideas had been implanted in him by the demon they would not, like a dream, be false. In short, he could only use the demon hypothesis to cast doubt on our sense-perceptions because it contradicted another theory that he did not doubt: the causal theory of perception which he had developed in his earlier work, particularly in the first chapter of ***Le Monde*** and the sixth *Discourse* of his ***Optics.*** That Descartes claimed that only an appeal to God's existence provided an escape from doubt should not be allowed to obscure the point that at every stage in his methodological doubt, including his use of the demon hypothesis, his argument presupposed the truth of a causal theory of perception. In fact, even in terms of his own argument, Descartes was saved from skepticism regarding the senses only because God's veracity guarantees that our perceptions are in fact caused by the existence of an independent, external world. (pp. 3-6)

Maurice Mandelbaum, "On Doubting and Believing," in his Philosophy, History, and the Sciences: Selected Critical Essays, *Johns Hopkins University Press, 1984, pp. 3-22.*

Emmet T. Flood (essay date 1987)

[*In the following excerpt, Flood proposes that "the intelligibility of the* [Meditations] *as a whole, its success as a piece of philosophy, and . . . its significance for Western philosophy all depend upon the unity of the* Meditations *as a narrated whole."*]

It is a truth universally acknowledged that modern philosophy commences with Descartes. Subsequent thinkers may differ as to the meaning and relevance of Descartes's thought, but critics and sympathizers alike agree that he is a father to us all.

Still the nature of his parentage (a good father or bad?) and the extent of his current philosophical influence (are we still spectator-philosophers? should we be?) remain at issue. His influence on the common sense understanding of self among Western men needs no glossing. In one way or another we are all Cartesians.

When we encounter Descartes in his writings, and try to make philosophical sense of them as the fresh and lively speculations they once were, we always place them against some broader background; such backgrounds offer us a tacit understanding of his historical place, and thereby give us an intelligible starting point for our own inquiries. In effect we locate him in a historical sequence which, far from being a mere chronology of persons or works, has a deeper narrative quality, a valorized, significant structure in which Descartes, through his ***Meditations,*** plays a key role. One of the first things every student of Descartes learns is that he is a pivotal figure in the drama of Western philosophical thought.

Of course the precise, even the general, significance of his thought is subject to debate and any notion of Descartes's importance will depend in large measure on the role we assign him, implicitly or explicitly, in the stories we tell about our philosophical past. Histories of philosophy that begin with the modern period usually paint Descartes as a kind of patriarch, the founder/discoverer of a new problematic and of a truly philosophical (if not true philosophical) methodology. Histories that begin with Thales or Socrates make Descartes seem less an originator and more a peripetal figure; he becomes a philosophical prophet of return, calling philosophy out of the misty darkness of medieval theology and back toward the humble path of unencumbered reason. Or he may be represented as a disastrous evil genius who obscures the self-disclosing movement of Truth by forcing philosophy into an epistemological gridlock of subject-object, mind-body oppositions. He then becomes an enemy to be overcome in violent battle. Or he may seem a figure of tragic irony, naively repeating, in slightly altered form, the mathematical, foundation-directed mistakes of Plato, and for his punishment is condemned to a life-term in a solipsistic prison of his own construction.

The point I want to make here is not that one of these stories is the correct account, but rather that in approaching Descartes an essential element of the horizon of our expectations is provided by the place and shape of some narrative historical continuum. To begin to understand him at all is to have already located him in a story we tell ourselves about philosophy. Descartes's ***Meditations*** play an important if disputed role in the drama of philosophy; this essay is devoted to a reading of the ***Meditations*** and to uncovering the dramatic element within it. As part of this reading, I hope to show why, in spite of all philosophical differences as to its meaning, the work retains its powerful hold on our imaginations.

Let us begin by noting what is so obvious that it has seldom been given attention: the fact that *the* ***Meditations*** *is a series of meditations.* If this were only a trivial truth, we could understand why it is so infrequently mentioned but not then why it has not found its way into the standard readings of the work. Since it is not a trivial truth, one wonders not only why it is not more noticed than it is, but also just what its importance might be.

What makes this a particularly pressing concern is the fact that, while Descartes put forth the fundamental elements of his thought in a variety of discursive modes, it is the ***Meditations,*** with its narrative structure, that survives as the pre-eminent Cartesian text. Why is this? How can it be that ***The Rules for the Direction of the Mind*** or ***The Principles of Philosophy*** with their propositional forms of writing (the traditionally recognized ones) have not yet superceded the ***Meditations?*** Why do we not look to these others for a truly philosophical presentation of his thought independent of the literary clutter that is part and parcel of the *meditatio* form? Can it be that a thinker so brilliant and a writer so versatile would willingly settle on so unsuitable a form for the writing of *philosophy?* Let us see.

What of the meditation form? It is personal, introspective: it reenacts the state of withdrawal from ordinary concerns he had described in the ***Discourse.*** Though it is the form of the solitary thinker, it is also an exemplary one, mapping a fresh route through intellectual terrain that is "so untrodden." And unlike the other works mentioned, it is a *prima facie* narrative structure, a series of recollections in the form of interior dialogue, told from memory with some awareness of the problematic status of the power of memory, that fundamental precondition for the story's telling.

The focus of this essay will be precisely this narrative quality informing the ***Meditations.*** The intelligibility of the work as a whole, its success as a piece of philosophy, and I believe, its significance for Western philosophy all depend upon the unity of the ***Meditations*** as a narrated whole. The attention paid here to the narrative quality of his thought is not motivated by perversity, nor by an excess of "literary sensibility." On the contrary, understanding the ***Meditations*** for what it is means beginning with the fact that it is a meditative narrative and not a treatise or a list of propositions. We are closer to the work itself and less prisoners of our own interpretive conventions when we recognize this.

The usual accounts of the ***Meditations*** tend to isolate certain key arguments for analysis and evaluation (in express contrast with Descartes's stated wishes), or attempt to detail the architectonic structure of the work as if it were a treatise. I don't deny that there are arguments in the ***Meditations,*** nor do I disagree with Descartes's own claim that there is a complex philosophic structure offered to the reader. But I do insist that an essential, and not merely accidental, formal dynamism is given the work by its narrative form. Attending to that form may cause us to alter our understanding of Descartes, since that understanding is typically mediated by the forms of philosophic imagination that inhabit the received picture of philosophy. A closer view of the work's narrative thread helps us to reorient our perspective on Descartes and his achievement. And, if it is successful, this reading will expose certain tensions latent in Descartes's own thought between the nature of knowledge and the temporal modes of its organization and reception.

The argument of the ***Meditations,*** though its precise form is a matter of perennial dispute, is well-known. Descartes, recognizing that much of what he once believed is untrue or uncertain, resolves to do away with his old opinions and "start again right from the foundation" since he "wanted to establish anything at all in the sciences that was stable and likely to last." Through strenuous application of hyperbolic doubt, he proceeds to strip away in great chunks all those previous beliefs that do not stand the test. Because of the deception of the senses, the vivacity of dream-experiences, and most powerfully and sweepingly because of the (logical) possibility of a deceitful evil genius, Descartes realizes that all, or nearly all, his beliefs are dubitable and therefore uncertain. But his descent into the ever-darkening twilight of doubt is halted when he realizes that, as he puts it, "I am, I exist, is necessarily true whenever it is put forward by me or conceived in my mind." The acquisition of indubitable knowledge of his own existence through the act of thinking has a two-fold import. Like Augustine before him, Descartes seems to have discovered a powerful counterexample to the skepticism of latter-day academics like Montaigne. And, as Archimedes had hoped for himself, Descartes seems to have positioned himself at "just one firm and immovable point" upon which he can base his new system and thereby catapult the world of philosophy into the modern scientific age. Having persuaded himself of his existence, he then concludes that it is actually his existence as a thinking (one who doubts, understands, affirms, denies, etc.) being that is not in doubt. He then proceeds to establish that God exists (as the cause of Descartes's idea of perfection and as the cause of his being) and that God's nature is such as to prevent his being universally deceived (though it is true that he is sometimes deceived). And further, material things are by nature extended, and they are in principle knowable (as possible objects of mathematical study) if they exist. Ultimately, material objects do exist pretty much as we do perceive them; they are really and completely distinct *res extensa* from the *res cogitans,* the thinking subject. Though perceptual error and misunderstanding are still possible, in the last analysis the universal doubt is vanquished, and the universe of common-sense knowledge is more or less restored.

So goes the standard account of the ***Meditations*** and this summary would be difficult to contest at this level of generality. More detailed accounts will highlight this or that argument (the nature of the *cogito* argument, the arguments for God's existence, etc), investigating the internal coherence of these and their place and function in the argument of the whole. What commentaries on the ***Meditations*** typically neglect to report is the fact that these arguments are knit together by a narrative synthesis without which the ***Meditations*** would be a fragmentary, unsuccessful pastiche of discrete arguments. A collection of scattered clear and distinct ideas does not make for a scientific philosophy.

Meditation I begins "today" in a state of delivery from those cares and passions that impede clear philosophical speculation. But the "today" of the first ***Meditations*** has a historical setting, for it is to be understood as occurring in a time of personal maturity that contrasts favorably with the unreflective time of his earliest youth and the doubt-full days that followed his first detecting the falsehood of his earlier opinions. "Today" has a future-directed aspect as well; his thought-project is undertaken with certain expectations, certain hopes in mind; the critical phase, if all goes well, should give way to a rebuilding of the now precarious edifice of metaphysical knowledge.

"Today" is also the first of six such days of meditation, skeptical reflection and philosophical rebuilding. The project of the ***Meditations,*** particularly from *Meditations* II-VI, is cumulative; the doubt corrodes, but in time all is restored. The continuity and coherence of the arguments in the "restorative" phase of the work depend entirely (though nearly always implicitly) upon the veracity of the recognitive power of *memory.* Yet Descartes has very little to say about memory *per se.* We might wonder why this is so. This heavy reliance upon memory may be unwitting, perhaps even unwilling. Nonetheless, as we shall see, memory plays an important, all-embracing part in the unfolding of the ***Meditations.***

These two facts: that the senses occasionally deceive and that in dreaming we often seem to be awake, are together sufficient to demonstrate the general dubitability of sense knowledge, because, as a methodological principle, "it is prudent not to trust completely those who have deceived us even once." Further, the metaphysical possibility of a "malicious demon of the utmost power and cunning" who "has employed all his energies in order to deceive me" makes all knowledge of external things questionable in principle. The situation in which Descartes finds himself at this point is twice difficult. To remain aware of the overwhelming possibility of universal deception is a "hard labour," an "arduous undertaking," and to slip from such an awareness into the cognitive posture of ordinary life would be to slumber when wakefulness, however difficult, is needed. Meditation I ends with a recognition of both the procedural and epistemic problems caused by the evil genius.

The second Meditation commences with the memory of "yesterday" and all its unforgettable doubtings; it proceeds with the assurance that, should something indubitable present itself to him, he will "hope for great things" for his task. Then, reconsidering the hypothesis of the malicious demon, he realizes that whether such a demon actually deceives him or no, "I am, I exist, is necessarily true whenever it is put forward by me or conceived in my mind." This discovery is his salvation from the bottomless pit of absolute skepticism; it is also his undoing.

Note that the *cogito,* that fixed fulcrum on which all is subsequently leveraged, is a discovery that is certain "whenever it is put forward by me." This discovery, this fixing of the cornerstone of modern thought is a discovery made at a particular time, the certainty of which depends upon its being thought or pronounced *simultaneously.* This fact is consistent with the individual, personal quality of Descartes's meditations; the 'cogito' is discovered in the existential time of a living, inquiring mind.

As Hintikka has shown [see Jaako Hintikka, "Cogito, Ergo Sum: Inference or Performance," *Descartes: A Collection of Critical Essays* ed. Willis Doney (South Bend: University of Notre Dame Press, 1968), pp. 108-139.], the certainty Descartes has of his existence is not the result of his having logically deduced it from previously established premises. None exist. Rather, the *cogito* is indubitable because, when uttered, it is existentially self-verifying. Thought or uttered, it must *ipso facto* be true of the thinker. But a dear price is paid. The sought-after certainty is attained, but only at the moment of the performing of the utterance.

If Descartes is entitled to be certain of his existence at the moment he pronounces it or mentally conceives it, then his discovery is valid and the foundation safely laid. But the negative question presents itself: what happens to the certainty of his existence when the "I think" is not being uttered or thought? And the answer can only be "It is lost."

The certainty of the *cogito,* being momentary, cannot, on Cartesian principles, persist. Though the discovery of the *cogito* is sufficient formally as a counter-example to the demon-induced universal doubt, it so far provides only a single exception to the malicious demon's skein of deception. Having discovered the *cogito,* Descartes is entitled only to affirm his existence at the moment of its discovery and at the times of its reaffirmation. As [H. A.] Prichard says: "Admitting as he does the existence of the general doubt, he would have done better to admit that it was irremovable . . . our certainty of anything could only be momentary."

Descartes continues with his argument, taking account of his various attributes and ruling them all out as non-essential with the exception of 'thinking.' And what of "thinking? At last I have discovered it—thought; this alone is inseparable from me. I am, I exist, that is certain. But for how long? For as long as I am thinking . . . ". When Descartes is not thinking, it is possible that he may cease to exist.

The question I will raise here is necessary to evaluate the restorative phase of his overall argument; it is a question raised before by other commentators. Granted that Descartes establishes one thing firmly—that he exists when he affirms the fact—how and why is he entitled to pass beyond this insight? Must he not take more as given if he is to proceed with his argument?

Descartes knows that he must and admits that he does. Not absolutely everything has been called into doubt. In the ***Principles of Philosophy,*** Descartes wrote that "the proposition 'I think, therefore I am' is the first and most certain of all to occur to anyone who philosophizes in an orderly way. . . . " Still, he adds that he "did not in saying that deny that one must first know what thought, existence and certainty are. . . . " Does Descartes exempt memory from the scope of the doubt or is it too subject to the devastating deceptions of the evil genius? Can we or should we regard its functioning as constantly reliable in the way in which we somehow continually and indubitably know what thought and existence are? Descartes is truly justified in proceeding with his argument (arguments are cumulative) only if his memory is fundamentally reliable.

Yet he does not include the power of memory among those things not susceptible to the malicious demon and so it would seem that, while the demon cannot prevent him from affirming his own existence at the moment he thinks it, the demon might well prevent him from reliably recalling the fact at any later moment. An additional reason to think that memory is not immune to doubt is provided by his discussion of the problem of memory in Meditation V which I will quote at length.

> . . . my nature is such that so long as I perceive something very clearly and distinctly I cannot but believe it to be true. But my nature is also such that I cannot fix my mental vision continually on the same thing, so as to keep perceiving it clearly; and often the memory of a previously made judgement may come back, when I am no longer attending to the arguments which led me to make it. And so other arguments can now occur to me which might easily undermine my opinion, if I did not possess knowledge of God; and I should thus never have true and certain knowledge about anything, but only shifting and changeable opinions. . . . I can convince myself that I have a natural disposition to go wrong from time to time in matters which I think I perceive as evidently as can be. This will seem even more likely when I remember that there have been frequent cases where I have regarded things as true and certain, but have later been led by other arguments to judge them to be false.

The reliability of memory in general is secured by the existence of a benevolent, non-deceiving God. It is possible to be certain of things clearly and distinctly perceived, but propositions become doubtful when past because "other reasons" may intervene to make dubious what was once certain. The passage of time could vitiate even certain judgments from the past unless God were there to uphold them.

The insuperable difficulty for the advancement of his argument in the segment of the ***Meditations*** after the middle of Meditation II is the fact that Descartes has not yet proven the existence of God, and so God is not available to guarantee the general veracity of memory. The progress of his argument ought to be absolutely suspended by this impediment. There are no valid memories without a proven God and no God is provable without a veracious memory securing the steps of the argument.

Unfortunately for Descartes's reader, he has no explicit theory of memory. But from the scattered observations on memory it is possible to conclude that memory is a capacity of the mind by which past ideas are brought to present consciousness. Remembering is not the same as intuiting, for in intuition we have clear and distinct perception, while in memory we may be mistaken. Intuitions are momentary, they are what Derrida would call acts of (putative) pure presence-ing. To remember is to know or think that one knows something intuited or imaged in the past. Memory is naturally fallible, for it is one thing to intuit a proposition clearly and distinctly in the present and quite another to recall having done so with a present guaranteed certitude. Between the original intuition and the later recollection a lot can go wrong.

Perhaps because of this fact, most of Descartes's comments on memory in the ***Meditations*** have to do with doubtful reliability and with the process by which that doubtfulness can be overcome. As we have seen, God is the being who, if only his existence be established, can supply the cure.

Before attempting the proofs of God's existence, Descartes pauses at the end of Meditation II and states that his last clear and distinct intuition—that nothing is more easily known than his own mind—now needs to be more deeply fixed in his memory. One would think that such propositions, when clearly and distinctly intuited, could not be more firmly grounded. And this is true. But a clear and distinct intuition becomes dubitable again once it is past, and so memory must, if it can, secure the continued reliability of such intuitions. And how is this to be accomplished? Descartes indicates that this imprinting upon the memory is effected by meditating for some time. To meditate is to remember past knowledge and so to have it at hand for present consideration. As Descartes says in his Preface to the Reader, "those who desire to meditate seriously with me" must leave aside consideration of isolated portions selected arbitrarily and try to "grasp the proper order of my arguments and the connections between them." Meditation is a process wherein discursively elaborated intuitions and arguments are conjoined and fixed in a unitary thought.

In a similar vein, at the end of Meditation III, he adverts to meditation again, picturing it as a displaced version of the contemplation of God, a less perfect device for achieving unity of vision. And near the end of IV, he states that meditation is that form of thought by which memory is secured, its natural fallibility overcome. Although "I am aware of a certain weakness in me in that I am unable to keep my attention fixed on the same item of knowledge at all times" (because of forgetfulness, but primarily because of the temporal progression of thought), he says that *"by attentive and repeated meditation I am nevertheless able to make myself remember it as often as the need arises. . . .* " (italics mine). Again, meditation is an act by which something temporally known is imprinted upon the mind in such a way as not to be forgotten. And so, a fortiori, the ***Meditations*** itself as a thought-project is an elaborate *mnemonic,* a formal device for uniting in memory his discursively and temporally extended intuitions into a single vision.

What is most striking about this recurrent sense of the word "meditation" is its affinity, even identity, with a thought process fundamental to the construction of a valid *science.* In the ***Rules for the Direction of the Mind,*** Descartes says that there are three basic ways to arrive at the knowledge of things, First, *intuition* is "the conception of a clear and attentive mind which is so easy and so distinct that there can be no room for doubt about what we are understanding." To be an object of intuition, a proposition must first be clear and distinct and second, "the whole proposition must be understood all at once and not bit by bit." But true science must be more than a collection of separate clear and distinct intuitions.

Therefore, a second access to indubitable truth is provided by simple *deduction,* a mental process whereby we can infer with necessity some new facts from previously known certainties (learned in intuition). Deduction differs from simple intuition by, among other reasons, the fact that in deduction "we are aware of a movement or a sort of sequence." Intuition occurs in a pure present, deduction in a temporally extended span "through the continuous and uninterrupted movement of thought." And, curiously, the deductively inferred conclusion "gets its certainty from memory."

The third way of arriving at certain truths is by a lengthier and more complex process of deduction which Descartes calls *enumeration.* This species of deduction involves long chains of inferences in which the conclusions are remote from the original intuition(s). The middle links in these deductive chains are difficult to keep before the mind in a single survey. The mind's attention is such that it normally can fix only on a single fact, relation, or deductive connection at a time. In attending to the early steps in a long deduction, we may forget the initial premise. In thinking the later steps, we may forget the earlier. And so forgetfulness is an ever present threat to certainty, ready to seep in through the chinks in our deductive armor. However, Descartes writes that:

> I run through them (the steps of the argument) several times in a continuous movement of the imagination, simultaneously intuiting one relation and passing on to the next, until I have learnt to pass from the first to the last so swiftly that memory is left with practically no role to play, and I seem to intuit the whole thing at once. . . . In addition, this movement must be nowhere interrupted. . . .

This enumeration process is essentially an act of condensation, a compression of a discursively articulated and temporally extended pattern of thought into a non-discursive and instantaneous unit. Paradoxically, the forgetfulness of memory that makes this process necessary, is overcome by a repeated movement (repetition itself depends on memory) of, of all things, the *imagination.*

This is an astonishing observation. For it places the active synthesizing power of the imagination at the very center of that most rigorously philosophical of thought processes—deduction. Any science worthy of the name depends upon the power of the mind to deduce conclusions from established premises, and at the heart of the deductive process, the temporal function of imaginative synthesis performs its crystallizing role. *Imagination is a cornerstone of Cartesian science.*

What can be made of the paradoxical process Descartes calls *enumeration?* Undeniably, something like the process Descartes describes really does take place. But how can the imagination intuit "one relation" while it is simultaneously "passing on to the next"? There is an oxymoronic quality to the very idea of "simultaneously passing on." And how precisely is fallacious memory conquered by repeated, and therefore remembered, mental surveys?

There do not seem to be ready answers for these questions. Certainly Descartes, with his theory of time as a linear sequence of discrete instants, cannot explain the process. If "time, the duration of things," as he says in the ***Principles,*** "is such that its parts are not mutually dependent and never co-exist," then it is a veritable wonder how memory and imagination can bring together the discursively articulated and temporally transient elements of a deductive argument into the form of a single instantaneous intuition. Yet, the possibility of science depends upon this wondrous activity; we are forced to conclude that Descartes's scientific theory is at odds with the synthetic practice of scientific activity.

But that is not all. The act of enumerative condensation that compresses an extended complex of intuitions and deductions is an essentially poetic act, a troping process, metaphoric in character. A plurality of meanings collapses into a single intuition in which they are unified and concealed. Though such an intuition could be analyzed into its constituent elements, in order to function in the present of thinking consciousness it must be single, unitary. When it is, as for example when we think "The Pythagorean Theorem," the complex argument summarized and named in that expression then functions in reverse as a kind of synecdochic trope. Such conceptual tropes are what enable Cartesian science to be more than a mere aggregation of separate insights. For a lengthy deduction, a single intuition is substituted; it stands in as a concentrated representative, a single thought representing a deductive thought-complex, a temporally frozen intuition somehow capturing the temporal extendedness of the argument. This enumeration has a double practicality; it effectively seals the temporal chinks, preventing memory failure, and it reduces the unwieldy ganglia of intuitions and deductive inferences into an abbreviated, manageable whole, permitting knowledge to accumulate hierarchically, rather than simply piecemeal.

It is impossible not to notice that the imaginative act of enumeration performs the same task for lengthy deduction that the imaginative act of emplotment does for temporal narrative. Each unifies an extended whole, combatting the natural entropic drift of long arguments (into discrete, disconnected, forgettable propositions) and temporal forms (into mere sequence, linear transience). Each culminates in a single "thought." Once "enumerated" the elaborate argument can be intuited as a single unit in a way paralleling precisely the summary act through which we unite temporal processes as completed, integral wholes, an act that Louis Mink calls configurational judgment. In fact the pure temporal present occupied by the Cartesian intuition of the enumerated argument mimics perfectly the false eternity in which temporally extended stories are grasped in the single moment of configurational judgment. Both actions "telescope" something complex and extended into a form that is basic and instantaneous, promising totality and simplicity in a *totum simul.*

Returning to the ***Meditations,*** it is now clear that Descartes may fairly continue with the later meditations if, at the end of II, he has truly meditated, that is fixed the whole of what has gone before in an enumerated-argument-become-singular-intuition. Meditation and enumeration are essentially identical functions, alike processes of overcoming *fallax memoria* by repeated actions of imaginative synthesis, performed in order to progress cumulatively in the attainment of knowledge. If Descartes can successfully repeat this process of meditation/enumeration (he repeatedly refers to meditation as an aid to memory, at the ends of Meds. II, III, and IV), the restoration of the realm of everyday knowledge can proceed unhindered—but proceed through the temporally progressive, cumulative logic of *story,* not "philosophic argument." Imagination and memory, not analysis and deduction (or rather *under and through* analysis and deduction) bind the stages of the ***Meditations*** into an integrated totality.

At this point let us sidestep the traditional philosophic bones of contention (the proofs for God's existence, the justification of mind-body dualism) and simply recall that in Meditations III-VI Descartes does restore the world of ordinary experience alluded to in the first sentence of the first Meditation. Though a profound shift in the philosophic basis of experience occurs, the practical facts of common knowledge return by the end essentially unaltered. As the ***Meditations*** closes, it becomes, as an extended argument for a new foundation in metaphysics, fitting matter for the same type of enumerative condensation as any other lengthy deduction. The discursive and temporal consecution of the ***Meditations*** can, through repeated running through of the overall argument, be conflated into a single thought. And since the ***Meditations*** are arranged in a temporal sequence as well as in a metaphysical order of discovery, the temporal pattern of the work comes to the fore as we scrutinize the work "in a continuous and wholly uninterrupted sweep of thought. . . . "

This movement of thought is simultaneously logical and temporal. And just as there is a temporal, successive dimension to any discursive chain of argumentation, so also there is a configuration, a shape, to the temporal ambit of the work. *The temporal form, the imaginative configuration discovered in the meditation that is the* ***Meditations,*** *is comic narrative.* The plot of the work, the internal history assumed by the six episodes (and their subparts), is comic because it is a temporal sequence in which an orderly (if naive) world is disrupted, debased, and restored. This temporal process of disturbance, discovery, and recuperation is the essential thread, the defining quality of the comic. "Comedy has a U-shaped plot, with the action sinking into deep and often tragic complications, and then suddenly turning upward into a happy ending." Whatever the logical validity of the arguments for God's existence or for the existence of external objects, the contour these assume is indisputably that of the comic in its later recuperative phase.

If the ***Meditations*** is comedy in the formal quality of its temporal arrangement, it is no less so in the thematic element of the text. According to Northrop Frye, "The theme of the comic is the integration of society," and in Christian comedy, "it is the theme of salvation. . . . " Descartes's technique of integration emerges through his concern for "the order and connections" of his reasonings. The procedural order of reasons, an advancement through "evidenced stages of inquiry" secured by individual certainty, replaces the Aristotelian order of topics with its ordering borrowed from a pre-established metaphysic. In recasting the order of knowledge along the axis of personally secured evidence, he creates a new sense of philosophical justification and reintegrates the field of philosophical perceptions with the self at the center, initiating a Copernican revolution of his own. His success in this project amounts to a secular species of salvation, both from the skeptical abyss of the first Meditation and from the doubts of his later youth. This quest for integration and the hope of salvation are the ordering motives of the work. They give it its urgency and convince us that it is more than a dispassionate analysis of traditional issues. The common-sense but divinely sanctioned knowledge that Descartes reacquires at the end of the ***Meditations*** is literally an individual, personal discovery. But it is still fair to say that the conclusion has a public social importance insofar as Descartes is a representative figure. His purpose in writing the ***Meditations,*** as is clear from the Preface, is strongly didactic. "So, first of all, in the Meditations, I will set out the very thoughts which have enabled me in my view to arrive at certain evident knowledge of the truth, so I can find out whether the same arguments that convinced me will convince others." The narrative of the ***Meditations*** is thus both invitation and allegory. The Descartes who meditates represents a new way of thinking, a fresh ethic of metaphysical reasoning open to all willing to try it, and he invites his readers to see for themselves.

Frye might say that the drama enacted in the ***Meditations*** is in the "low mimetic" comic mode. Through the process of Descartes's reasonings, we follow a protagonist who is down to earth, who shuns the terminological subtleties of scholastic thought. The problem-setting, complicating phase of the ***Meditations*** constitutes an *ordeal* for the thinker, a true test of his powers of thought. The prose of the latter part of Meditation I exudes a sense of laborious effort and impending frustration. This effort is expended in the attempt to sail the treacherous sea of sensory illusion created by the deceitful evil genius, himself a type of the impostor, a blocking character used to heighten the danger and produce the web of illusion to be resolved and cleared away in the restorative phase.

The whole work may be said to exemplify the classic comic theme of illusions dispelled, and in two ways. The ***Meditations*** displaces the illusory metaphysics Descartes had been spoonfed as a youth through a rigorous, self-critical method; as autobiography it is a classical example of maturation, a growth in knowledge and a putting away of the things of youth. And internally, establishing a new foundation in the *cogito* rends the genius's veil of illusion, and puts Descartes for the first time on secure epistemological footing. Then the protagonist can move vertically up Plato's ladder of knowledge, away from mere opinion and toward knowledge of true reality. The Descartes who emerges at the end of Meditation VI seems a liberated man, slave neither to Scholastic metaphysics nor to the demon and his spell.

Not surprisingly, the ***Meditations*** is comic even to the point of utilizing the classic salvific device of the *deus ex machina.* One of the ironies of Cartesian thought is that in breaking with the effete scholastic method and metaphysic, with all its emphasis on God's power and providence, Descartes actually assigned God a more active and interventionist role than any late Scholastic would have dared or even been tempted to do. The subject-centered epistemology and metaphysic of Descartes demanded that God guarantee his memories, safeguard most (though not all) of his judgments, and underwrite his clear and distinct ideas of the material world. And though the need for God in his system is clear, the proofs for his existence have remained suspect even to the point of being thought artificial. Indeed they have evoked the same kind of criticism as has the *deus ex machina;* both are artificial, non-realistic escape mechanisms. In a pattern that parallels the evolution of drama, in the history of philosophy the importation of God into the metaphysical picture came to seem more and more otiose. Modern philosophy soon no longer had any need for the God-hypothesis. Still it is impossible to imagine Meditations IV-VI without the proofs in III. Together they constitute a second *anagnorisis,* absolutely essential to repair the early skeptical breach.

Just as the discovery of the *cogito* is the peripetal moment in Descartes's story, the proofs for the existence of God in III are an essential discovery, catalyzing the recovery of knowledge of material bodies. Nothing beats an omnipotent, morally reliable ally in the struggle against error. In fact, having inserted God directly into the process of knowing, Descartes must then take pains (in Meditation IV) to show how error is ever possible. The infinite power of a non-deceiving God now must be reconciled with the empirical fact that he nevertheless does make errors of judgment. The problem is analogous to the traditional theological difficulty of squaring the omnipotence and omniscience of God with human moral freedom. Descartes's solution to the question of human error in judgment turns on the freedom of the will to affirm propositions that it does not yet fully understand due to the finitude of the intellect. God guarantees the basic soundness of the mind and its operations; he does not intervene to stop every abuse of its powers. In the end, the *deus ex machina* supports him not only in the knowledge he has of his memories, but also in the cognizing of such ideas as extension, figure, and quantity which, in their material instantiations, constitute that *machina ex deo,* the external world.

As in comedy, philosophy itself undergoes a difficult but rewarding transformation in Descartes's ***Meditations.*** His original conception of metaphysics (alluded to, but not elaborated in Meditation I) was a species of realism overgrown with a tangled jungle of scholastic verbiage. The movement of the ***Meditations*** is a breaking down of that medieval picture, specifically by attacking the most fundamental of scholastic philosophical principles inherited from Aristotle: *"Principium nostrae cognitionis est a sensu."* After dynamiting the foundation of the scholastic edifice, Descartes replaced it with one of his own, constructing it not on the shifting sand of the senses, but on the firm bedrock of his own mind. Ultimately, he projects philosophy along a new orbit, shifting the foci from sense and world to mind and self.

As a consequence of the comic structure of the work, the reader of the ***Meditations*** feels a certain satisfaction in reaching its end. The malicious demon has been expelled, order restored, and the "hope for great things" of Meditation II at least partially realized. An artful incongruity is produced by the juxtaposition of the sophisticated, critically defensible metaphysic exhibited toward the end and the naive, indefensible knowledge of his youth. Still the "happy ending" is not a complete apotheosis; while radical error is driven out, we must in the end "acknowledge the weakness of our nature."

This cautionary conclusion is an essential element in the completing action of the ***Meditations,*** and it serves both a "literary" and "philosophical" function. The warning against recurrent error checks the ascending movement of the later meditations, keeping them from rising to a mystical state (the object of a different, more ecstatic, kind of meditation), that would be error free and on a par with God. After all, the work is essentially comic and not a romance.

The final admonition also reminds the reader of a crucial feature of the new metaphysic: its heightened degree of critical methodological self-awareness. The sense of superiority over the metaphysics of the schools that is attained in the end is based in large part on a strengthened awareness of the fact that error lurks ever near and must be kept at bay by severity of thought and restraint of judgment. Thus the triumph over error is real but provisional. The decay of memory into time proves a challenge continually to be met.

These effects are as much a product of Descartes's poetry as they are of philosophy. It should be clear by now that there is no slur in saying this. While it is superficially surprising to discover these "literary" forms in the greatest apostle of science and philosophic method, the poetic element in the ***Meditations*** is as unmistakeable as it is necessary. The work is a splendid fusion of philosophy and narrative. Enumeration, the mental conspectus that enables us to picture temporally and discursively elaborated structures in an integrated unity, is both conceptual and metaphorical knowledge. And the profile of his logical arguments, skeptical and constructive, shapes and is shaped by the temporal contour of the comic narrative.

I believe that the narrative, temporal form of the ***Meditations*** represents a radical departure from the Cartesian theory of time as a sequence of separate moments. The memories that make knowledge and science possible, and the progressions and hopes that dynamize the ***Meditations,*** occur in a continuous, narratively organized time, a time closer to myth than to the indifferent parade of discrete instants that is scientific time. The time of the ***Meditations*** is charged with the threat of radical doubt and the supervening hope of discovery and return.

Science, says Santayana, lives in a world of expurgated mythology. In the world of Descartes's ***Meditations,*** at the dawn of the age of science, the outlines of the mythical are visible in narrative form, presiding at the birth of a new metaphysics. For those with eyes to see, those outlines are visible yet. (pp. 847-66)

Emmet T. Flood, "Descartes's Comedy of Error," in MLN, *Vol. 102, No. 4, September, 1987, pp. 847-66.*

Peter A. Schouls (essay date 1989)

[In the following excerpt, Schouls argues that Descartes was a revolutionary thinker who rejected accepted philosophical ideas yet succeeded in creating a new rationalist philosophical canon.]

Among the concepts of freedom, mastery, and progress, that of freedom is the most fundamental to Descartes' works. For mastery presupposes freedom from prejudice and oppression and consists in having the liberty to shape one's own destiny. Progress, in turn, is measured in terms of the extent to which mastery has been achieved. (p. 13)

To establish the fundamental nature of Descartes' concept of freedom, I shall consider some general features of his position in [this] chapter. . . . In presenting Descartes as a revolutionary, I shall focus on those acts of freedom which he believes can deliver us from the confinement imposed by our physical and cultural contexts.

In this chapter I shall argue first that Descartes' position may be called that of a revolutionary because his method dictates that if we are to obtain knowledge we must begin by rejecting all beliefs and opinions which we have absorbed from the contexts in which we live. Secondly, I want to make it clear why Descartes holds that his revolutionary procedure, although it involves a radical form of epistemic individualism, does not lead him into relativism. It is important to see how strongly Descartes means his position to oppose relativism, for this allows us to understand . . . how the freedom of revolutionary activity can become firmly linked with an absolutism dictated by reason.

I shall go on to deal with both the bondage and the liberation of reason. Because reason is misdirected by what Descartes considers pernicious habits, it is like someone caught in what he regards as a vast web of prejudice. He believes that the impediments can be destroyed in a revolt which calls for the exercise both of freedom and of methodic doubt. (pp. 13-14)

Descartes saw the need for what he called a "reformation"

of the sciences. Not that he expected himself fully to bring about such a "reformation," but he did expect to make a beginning. For he believed that he had available to him the necessary instrument: his "method of rightly conducting reason." In this section I will, therefore, begin with an exploration of Descartes' use of his method in the rejection of all beliefs which we have absorbed from the contexts in which we live. In other words, I want to begin with a preliminary exploration of what I shall call Descartes' "revolutionary procedure."

First, *Descartes as revolutionary.* Although he speaks of the necessity of bringing about a reformation in the sciences, it seems to me that Descartes should instead be seen as bringing about a revolution. He should not be considered as a revolutionary in some narrow sense of that word; for, as we shall see, he intended to bring about a totally new outlook in all areas of life. The term "reformation" does not cover so radical an activity. Although reformation does away with the old and replaces it with what is new, it is an activity which takes place within an accepted framework within which certain key aspects are considered inviolate by the reformer. Reformation may therefore exist in improving the old by removing imperfections or faults or errors. By contrast, revolution may be taken as radical substitution of everything within a certain framework and of that framework itself. If the term "reformation" is restricted to the activity of amending and the term "revolution" to that of radical substitution, then Descartes' "reformation" ought to be seen as a revolution and Descartes himself should bc characterized as a revolutionary rather than as a reformer. He had no sympathy with a reformation which set out merely to amend. Indeed, the only instrument which he considered adequate for the task of bringing about a "reformation" in the sciences precluded mere amendment. This instrument, the method of the ***Rules for the Direction of the Mind*** and of the ***Discourse on the Method of Rightly Conducting the Reason,*** called for radical substitution. If revolution consists in two parts, the first being to do away with the old and the second to present the new, then Descartes was sometimes modest with respect to his achievements in the second area but never with respect to his accomplishments in the first.

In the ***Discourse,*** where he often speaks of the need for *réformer le cors des sciences,* Descartes makes it quite clear that he considers himself to have been entirely successful in carrying out one of his major self-imposed tasks. That task was not limited to removing much of what was old in the realm of science; instead, it was the total rejection of all his own beliefs and opinions, and this of course included total rejection of whatever he had up to then taken to be science. He writes that "as regards all the opinions which up to this time I had embraced, I thought I could not do better than endeavour once for all to sweep them completely away . . . ." Well before the end of the ***Discourse*** he is confident that he has been successful in this endeavour. Old opinions are to be swept "completely away, so that they might later on be replaced, either by others which were better, or by the same, when I had made them conform to the uniformity of a rational scheme." Thus what is new may appear similar to, even identical with the old.

This ostensible re-incorporation of the old may give Descartes' revolution the appearance of being less radical than it in fact is meant to be. However, that is appearance only. For it is crucial that nothing old be retained unless it "conforms to the uniformity of a rational scheme." As he puts it later in the ***Discourse,*** with respect to doctrines and discoveries to be presented in the ***Dioptrics*** and the ***Meteors,*** "And I do not even boast of being the first discoverer of any of them, but only state that I have adopted them, not because they have been held by others . . . but only because Reason has persuaded me of their truth." But before one can be persuaded by reason, the old, regardless of whether it is to reappear as the new, is to be swept completely away. The old, as such, can never truly and legitimately find a place in the new.

Descartes did not believe that any of the old would in fact find a place in the new. This is clear from what he says about the ***Principles of Philosophy.*** In the final paragraph of the "Author's Letter" which serves as preface to the French edition of the ***Principles,*** he states that what he is about to present is genuinely new rather than the old, partly or even largely, transformed. Its newness is a consequence of the fact that the principles upon which it is founded are themselves new, a "difference which is observable between these principles and those of all other men." This stress on newness comes to the fore in all of Descartes' works.

Take, for example, ***The Passions of the Soul,*** the last work which he prepared for publication. In its first article he speaks of "the defective nature of the sciences," and therefore seems to sound the typically-thorough reformer's note when he says "There is nothing in which the defective nature of the sciences which we have received from the ancients appears more clearly than in what they have written on the passions . . . " However, that the internal correction of defects holds no appeal becomes clear from the continuation of this sentence: "that which the ancients have taught regarding them is both so slight, and for the most part so far from credible, that I am unable to entertain any hope of approximating to the truth excepting by shunning the paths which they have followed." Thus a strategy naturally presents itself. It is the strategy of the person who denies the existence of links with the past rather than that of the one who holds that there is continuity. It is the procedure of the revolutionary rather than that of the reformer: "I shall be here obliged to write just as though I were treating of a matter which no one had ever touched on before me."

Of course, speaking of ***The Passions'*** contents as new was not an idle boast, for there existed no precedent of a consistent attempt at an explanation of mental and physiological phenomena entirely by means of simple mechanical processes. What was presented as new looked new and was in fact different from what had gone before. But its newness in appearance should not obscure the important point that whether or not it looked new, it would, in Descartes' view, be new simply because it could have been presented only after the old had been completely swept away. And this stress on newness is not dictated by the particular subject-matter of ***The Passions.*** It pertains to the entire realm of knowledge, whatever its subject-matter. As Descartes writes in ***The Search after Truth,*** with respect to "upsetting all the knowledge . . . hitherto acquired": "I do not wish to be placed amongst the number of these insignificant artesans, who apply themselves only to the restoration of old works, because they feel themselves incapable of achieving new."

If we take seriously the metaphor from the ***Discourse*** that no systematic knowledge can be attained unless one first takes all one's opinions and "sweeps them completely away," then whatever takes their place can arise only in this newly created void and that which arises in a void cannot fail to be new. Although as we shall see it cannot be *creatio ex nihilo* it is certainly meant to be *creatio de novo.*

Sometimes Descartes speaks as if the *hubris* or, perhaps, the cultural solipsism which seems implicit in these statements is meant to be taken as quite innocent because it is entirely idiosyncratic. In the ***Discourse,*** for example, we read that "My design has never extended beyond trying to reform my own opinion and to build on a foundation which is entirely my own." In the sentence immediately following he even seems to warn against taking his action as an example. But these warnings are meant for only two groups of people. They hold, in the first place, for those who are "precipitate in judgement." Such persons simply cannot follow Descartes' example even if they would, for they do not have "sufficient patience to arrange their thoughts in proper order" and therefore can not reach valid new results. Not paying attention to "order" is attempting to gain truth unmethodically, and the outcome of that exercise can only be opinion and uncertainty rather than knowledge and certainty. This result is shared by the second group: those who believe "that they are less capable of distinguishing truth from falsehood than some others from whom instruction might be obtained." Such people "are right in contenting themselves with following the opinions of these others rather, than in searching better ones for themselves." These warnings amount to saying that attempts at "reformation" are for neither the foolish nor the timid. That leaves the wise and the courageous. And as Descartes well knew, men are more apt to classify themselves as wise and courageous than as foolish or timid. Thus for anyone not satisfied with mere opinion and uncertainty, the complete sweeping away of all beliefs is a necessary condition for obtaining knowledge and certainty.

Even apart from these warnings to the precipitous and timid, Descartes has to say that his design does not extend beyond trying to reform his own opinion and to build on a foundation which is entirely his own. He must say this because his method forces it upon him: everyone has to do it for himself and can only do it for himself. No one, therefore, can build upon anything which we might call a "primary given," on something given through the senses or tradition, by education or by contemporary thought. None of these can provide a solid foundation on which to build a system of knowledge. As he writes in the first of the ***Principles,*** "in order to examine into the truth it is necessary once in one's life to doubt of all things." Modest though Descartes' "reformation" may seem in some of his comments, very little probing is needed to show it up for what it is, namely a complete and universal revolution. Its intended completeness and universality are dictated by Descartes' method, the instrument whose use he considered necessary for the attainment of truth. For it is this method which requires of whoever searches for truth "to strip oneself of all opinions and beliefs formerly received."

It may seem an exaggeration to speak of the intended universality of Descartes' revolution if the basic principle of the revolution's manifesto merely forbids the acceptance of a primary given as a foundation on which to build science. It will seem less of an exaggeration once we remember that, for Descartes, no action can be called truly human unless it can be called rational; that it cannot be called rational unless it is dictated by knowledge; and that there is no knowledge apart from science. Hence when it is said that no primary given may be accepted as a foundation on which to build science, what does this imply? It implies that no primary given may be accepted as a basis on which to order any part of life, if that part of life is to qualify as truly human. Hence my earlier statement that Descartes intended to bring about a totally new outlook in all areas of life.

The completeness and universality of Descartes' revolution are dictated by his method. This relationship between revolution and methodology will be a topic for further discussion. But I should first turn to consider the fact that this revolution's intended universality is also closely related to Descartes' epistemology. This introduces the second topic of this section, namely, that contrary to what some might expect from one who advocates universal and thoroughgoing revolution, Descartes is nevertheless *a thorough opponent of relativism.*

For a set of connected statements to qualify as a (part of a) system of knowledge it must have a "solid foundation"; and this foundation must consist of items which are known not in terms of something else but in terms of themselves. The point of connection of this aspect of Descartes' epistemology with his insistence on sweeping former opinions "completely away" is perhaps clear enough from the outset: the items known in terms of themselves are by definition known in a void, that is, they are known out of context of other items. To make this connection quite clear let us look at intuition, the power through which we are said to "grasp" these foundational items of knowledge, and at clarity and distinctness, the criteria which these items of knowledge are said to meet.

It is in the ***Rules for the Direction of the Mind*** that Descartes introduces "intuition." As a definition he gives:

> By intuition I understand, not the fluctuating testimony of the senses, nor the misleading judgment that proceeds from the blundering constructions of imagination, but the conception which an unclouded and attentive mind gives us so readily and distinctly that we are wholly freed from doubt about that which we understand.

The mind is said to consist of the understanding (comprising both "intuition" and "deduction"), imagination, sense, and memory. Memory is never taken to be a source of knowledge for it can only present that which it has first received from the understanding, imagination, or sense. But it is clear that Descartes also rules out both the senses and the imagination as sources of knowledge, or at least knowledge which may be called "foundational." His purposeful juxtaposition of "fluctuating," "misleading," and "blundering" with "unclouded," "attentive," and "wholly freed from doubt" points to his belief that if we are to gain foundational knowledge we must depend upon the understanding alone. What Descartes wants to dispute is that any "givens" ought to be accepted. For Descartes himself it is beyond dispute that, for example, whatever we sense, or whatever we learn from others, cannot be accepted as a "given." What is thus "given" may be accepted as a point of departure for analysis but, because it lacks clarity and distinctness, must be rejected as a suitable starting point for synthesis.

It must be rejected as a suitable starting point for synthesis, for the construction of systematic knowledge, because what we sense or what we learn from others is always complex. What is complex is not originally clear and distinct, and therefore cannot be grasped in an intuition, which means that it cannot be known. Whatever is sensed or learned can therefore only function legitimately as a point of departure for analysis, for in analysis we attempt to break up the given complex item into ultimate items which are simple, clear, and distinct. It is only from these items that we can commence our synthesis. They are the first that can be intuited. If we cannot break up a given complex item, it is to be rejected, for by definition it will remain opaque to the understanding. And if it can be broken up, that also constitutes its rejection, because even if the same complexity as is given in the original results from the synthesis which is to follow analysis, the item which results is different from the original given. It is now no longer *given* to the mind but is *put together* by the mind itself. In either case, because of the role of intuition, Descartes' epistemology demands the rejection of any complex givens as knowledge. And because whatever is given by means of the senses, or by means of the senses and the imagination combined, is always complex, it is initially to be rejected as knowledge. We come to the same conclusion if, rather than focus on intuition, we say more about the criteria of clarity and distinctness.

The criteria of clarity and distinctness jointly apply to an item if it is legitimately called an item of knowledge. It is not difficult to show that these criteria dictate the contextlessness of items of knowledge grasped as the foundational items of science. Descartes calls "clear" that which "is present and apparent to an attentive mind"; and "the distinct" "is that which is so precise and different from all other objects that it contains within itself nothing but what is clear." Therefore to be capable of judging anything properly it is not sufficient just to be fully aware of all of that "thing." That much is compliance with the first criterion, clarity, only. And such compliance may leave the "thing" intricately enmeshed with many other "things," themselves not necessarily clearly in mind. "Clarity" only demands of that on which we pronounce judgement that it be before the mind fully. But that is not sufficient "to be capable of judging of it properly. For the knowledge upon which a certain and incontrovertible judgment can be formed, should not alone be clear but also distinct." And "distinctness" demands that we have before the mind nothing but what pertains to having that item fully before the mind.

Thus these criteria dictate that we cannot initally accept anything as knowledge which is not utterly simple in the sense of not synthetically derived. Even if we are confronted with a complex item which is clear and distinct to others, it cannot be so to us. For, as complex, it is a compound of other items all of which we must ourselves intuit as clear and distinct. Only then can the relations which hold between and among such items be intuited; only then can a complex item be clear and distinct. These criteria therefore demand that at the foundation of science there be utterly simple items, that is, items known apart from any other items. These criteria dictate that at the foundation of science there be items known *per se* rather than *per aliud.*

If they can be known at all, items to be known *per se* can only be known clearly and distinctly. Anything known *per aliud* can be known only if that from which it is derived is also before the mind clearly and distinctly (or at the least is remembered as having been so before the mind). Thus anything known *per aliud* ultimately can be known only if it can be seen as following from the relevant foundation or first principles, i.e. from what is known *per se.* Therefore that which the senses give us cannot, as given, be known immediately by the understanding. For what is thus given is concrete, enmeshed in its context.

The implications for us at this point are clear. For Descartes, "nature" can be understood only once it has been fitted into the "rational scheme" of mechanics, medicine, or morals. These rational schemes themselves cannot be developed prior to the advancement of the "rational schemes" called metaphysics and physics. Metaphysics and physics, in turn, rest on the prior intuited knowledge of certain concepts and principles known *per se.* And therefore "nature" cannot be known immediately. Neither can we know immediately that which our education or cultural environment places before us. Neither Euclid's *Elements* nor Aristotle's *Ethics,* neither Aquinas's *Summa Theologica* nor Galileo's *Two New Sciences* show that they derive their conclusions from indubitable principles known *per se.* None of them even went so far as to attempt to state these principles. But even had they stated them, and even had they derived their conclusions from them by uninterrupted chains of arguments, I cannot begin at the end, with conclusions. If I am to understand I must start where they began to understand, at the level of items known *per se.* But such items are not "given."

Descartes' epistemology, therefore, dictates that, whether it is my physical or my cultural context which I attempt to understand, if I am to understand I must understand for myself, radically so. Using words from the opening paragraph of the first Meditation, someone else's "firm and permanent structure in the sciences" is of little use to me for I will not be able to understand it unless I myself "commence to build anew from the foundation." And no foundation is ever given. The foundation is always to be established. Whoever wants to understand will first have to establish his own foundation. Moreover, no foundation can be established apart from obeying the precepts of the method which Descartes proposes. Thus, when he writes that "my design has never extended beyond trying to reform my own opinion and to build on a foundation which is entirely my own," Descartes speaks for himself and, he believes, for whoever seeks to understand. The need for universal revolution is dictated by a methodology which goes hand-in-hand with the criteria of clarity and distinctness, with a doctrine of radical epistemic individualism.

Such a radical form of epistemic individualism at once raises questions about relativism. If each can only "reform" his own opinion, if each must build on a foundation which is entirely his own, how can there be talk of science if (as Descartes does) by science we refer to a system of objective universal truth? How, for that matter, can Descartes without contradiction hold that he speaks for himself and for whoever seeks to understand when he says that one can only "reform" one's own opinion and must build from a foundation entirely one's own? The answer to these questions introduces one of Descartes' fundamental assumptions, and assumption which he shares with all major figures of the Enlightenment. It is that each person's reason is like every other person's reason, and that therefore a correct description of the workings of one person's reason holds for all. . . . It might be an innocuous assumption if Descartes did not take the workings of reason to be those articulated in his methodology.

Descartes assumes that truth is objective, absolute, and attainable only in one particular way. Because of this assumption he concludes that a description of the way in which a *particular* (set of) truth(s) has been attained is a description of the way reason functions *whenever* it is successful in its pursuit of truth. But once written down, that description may be read by others. And, says Descartes, if these others have also been successful in their pursuit of truth and have become conscious of their reason's operation in this pursuit, then they will find their reason's mode of operation reflected in the statement they read. That statement, being a picture of reason's procedure, is to that extent reason's self-portrait. The fact that others find themselves in this picture indicates that the portrait is not of a single person's idiosyncratic way of procedure but that it is a self-portrait of rational thought wherever it occurs. Of course, this move to the universal is not warranted by any finite number of corroborating experiences; and it is not taken to be invalidated by contrary claims about reason's manner of operation. For example, Descartes would be quite unperturbed by contrary claims which Aristotelians might make—as is clear from what he says in the second of the ***Rules for the Direction of the Mind.*** The universality of reason, with reason's mode of procedure as that described by Descartes, therefore remains an assumption. It is an assumption which comes to the force in all of Descartes' works, but most especially in the ***Rules,*** the ***Discourse,*** and the ***Meditations.***

Descartes did not deny the existence of relativism, nor did he deny the existence of what might seem to provide grounds for such a position, namely, widespread divergence of opinion on almost anything worth having an opinion about. But he did not take the existence of relativism and of its apparent grounds to be a consequence of epistemological and methodological tenets like his own. Instead, he explained all controversy as the result of prejudice, and prejudice he explained as flowing from wrong habits.

In the Preface to the ***Principles*** Descartes writes that "the principles are clear and nothing must be deducted from them but by very evident reasoning" and anyone has "sufficient intelligence to comprehend the conclusions that depend on" these principles. If that is so why did not all who read the ***Principles*** and reflected on the issues which Descartes raised come to the foundations and the conclusions he himself reached? He points to the permeating influence of habit and prejudice on the one hand, and the pervasive absence of method on the other. One way of introducing his answer is to consider what Descartes took to be the conditions for doing scientific work. Going this way will lead us back to the notions of objectivity and absolute truth, and will allow some further discussion of one of Descartes' fundamental assumptions, that of the universality of a rational faculty which is held to function only in the ways described through Descartes' methodological principles.

As stated at the end of the second part of the ***Discourse,*** the prerequisites for doing scientific work are: (i) overcoming partiality, (ii) observing life, and (iii) obtaining facility in the method. Overcoming partiality focuses especially on the task of freeing oneself from philosophical preconceptions. But, in general, overcoming partiality results in the kind of disinterestedness which enables one to distinguish between opinions or beliefs held because of the cultural epoch or geographical area in which one happens to live, and beliefs or items of knowledge accepted on rational grounds. Observing life has a double reward. It is, first, an aid to overcoming partiality. The experience that manners, customs, and opinions which in one country may be signs of sophistication are elsewhere deemed inconsequential or even silly is an important step on the way towards disinterestedness. Second, and at least as important, the observation of life provides one with a stock of experiences which can become starting points for analysis at various stages in one's scientific work. Finally, facility in method is needed for the simple reason that method is necessary for finding out the truth.

Observing life is a prerequisite for doing scientific work. On the other hand, the very fact that we must observe life in order to overcome partiality is an indication that life itself has spoiled our ability to do scientific work. We need to observe life in order to recognize that the very process of growing up in a certain place at a certain time has saddled us with attitudes and beliefs peculiar to that place and time:

> Since we have all been children before being men, and since it has for long fallen to us to be governed by our appetites and by our teachers (who often enough contradicted one another, and none of whom perhaps counselled us always

> for the best), it is almost impossible that our judgments should be so excellent or solid as they should have been had we had complete use of our reason since our birth, and had we been guided by its means alone.

Our teachers "often enough contradicted one another." In this they themselves reflect the world around them, in which there are "many conflicting opinions . . . regarding the self-same matter, all supported by learned people"; a world in which philosophy, though "it has been cultivated for many centuries by the best minds that have ever lived" is nevertheless a discipline in which "no single thing is to be found . . . which is not subject of dispute, and in consequence which is not dubious." Descartes' observation of life, his confrontation with a bewildering variety of opinion and conflict in doctrine, rather than leading him into thorough-going scepticism or relativism, instead prompts him to assert the absoluteness and universality of truth: never mind "how many conflicting opinions there may be regarding the self-same matter . . . there can never be more than one which is true." If only we had possessed "complete use of our reason since our birth" so that we would not have been ensnared by the bias of our teachers and the controversies of our tradition, we would not now have our natural light obscured and would live in the realm of truth. For, as he writes somewhat later in the ***Discourse,*** since there is "but one truth to discover in respect to each matter, whoever succeeds in finding it knows in its regard as much as can be known." To illustrate his point he introduces the example of a child "who has been instructed in Arithmetic and has made an addition according to the rule prescribed; he may be sure of having found as regards the sum of figures given to him all that the human mind can know." Crucial, however, is that the addition be made "according to the rule prescribed." This rule is a specific application of the general method, of "the Method which teaches us to follow the true order and enumerate exactly every term in the matter under investigation" and which, if followed, gives "certainty" in the sciences.

At the very end of the first part of the ***Discourse,*** that is, immediately prior to turning his attention to the articulation of the methodological precepts in the second part, Descartes writes:

> . . . I learned to believe nothing too certainly of which I had only been convinced by example and custom. Thus little by little I was delivered from many errors which might have obscured our natural vision and rendered us less capable of listening to Reason. But after I had employed several years in thus studying the book of the world and trying to acquire more experience, I one day formed the resolution of also making myself an object of study and of employing all the strength of my mind in choosing the road I should follow. This succeeded much better, it appeared to me, than if I had never departed either from my country or my books.

Study of the book of the world helped to overcome partially, a victory which made his natural vision clear. This, in turn, allowed him to succeed much better in studying himself. The outcome of this self-study is presented in the ***Discourse's*** second part: the method which is to be used to gain truth in whatever area man believes he can obtain the truth. Clearing the natural vision, or releasing reason from the bondage of habit rooted in sense and in education, is to lead reason to become conscious of its own operations unhindered by sense or prejudice. The cause of relativism is uncritical acceptance of the data provided through one's cultural context. The consistent use of reason gives objectivity and truth in spite of the fact that through the operation of analysis it involves rejection of whatever is given through one's context. Because the use of reason leads to objectivity and truth it bears important additional "fruits."

One result of the consistent application of the method is the ***Principles of Philosophy.*** A "fruit" born of these principles is "that the truths which they contain, being perfectly clear and certain, will remove all subjects of dispute, and thus dispose men's minds to gentleness and concord." This is in sharp contrast to "the controversies of the Schools" which "by insensibly making those who practice themselves in them more captious and self-sufficient [*plus pointilleux et plus opiniastres*]" are therefore "possibly the chief causes of the heresies and dissensions which now exercise the world." Gentleness and concord will be the lot of those who practise the use of Descartes' principles; the employment of reason carries the promise of healing for broken communities. The context of this passage emphasizes the point that such practice consists in working methodically at the foundation of the sciences.

The emphasis on method is not surprising for, according to Descartes, only the unhampered exercise of reason can lead to truth and hence to concord, and only methodic procedure allows (or better: *is*) the unhampered exercise of reason. Practice in working methodically, that is, learning to think reductionistically, leads to peace and tranquillity rather than dissension and opinionated conceit. Although unanimity is not a criterion for truth, it may function as a mark indicating its presence; unanimity can come about once the method for gaining truth becomes available to man.

Overcoming partiality and obtaining facility in the method is to allow one to break through cultural relativism into the realm of absolute truth. But one cannot break into the realm of truth without "stripping oneself of all opinions and beliefs formerly received." That revolutionary act is not at all easy to carry out, for the "received opinions" are so firmly rooted in the mind that they hold reason captive. (pp. 14-27)

Peter A. Schouls, in his Descartes and the Enlightenment, *McGill-Queen's University Press, 1989, 194 p.*

FURTHER READING

Beck, L. J. *The Metaphysics of Descartes.* Oxford: Clarendon Press, 1965, 307 p.

Comprehensive analysis of the *Meditations.*

Belloc, Hilaire. "René Descartes." In his *Characters of the Reformation,* pp. 292-302. 1936. Reprint. Freeport, N. Y.: Books for Libraries Press, 1970.

Comparative analysis of two pivotal seventeenth-century French philosophers, René Descartes and Blaise Pascal.

Blom, John J., ed. *Descartes: His Moral Philosophy and Psychology.* Translated by John J. Blom. New York: New York University Press, 1978, 288 p.

Features correspondence between Descartes and important seventeenth-century personages, addressing issues of moral philosophy and psychology.

Bouwsma, O. K. *Philosophical Essays.* Lincoln: University of Nebraska Press, 1965, 209 p.

Contains three previously published essays on Descartes exploring prominent themes in the *Meditations.*

Chomsky, Noam. *Cartesian Linguistics: A Chapter in the History of Rationalist Thought.* New York: Harper and Rowe, 1966, 119 p.

Analytical study limited to "a preliminary and fragmentary sketch of some of the leading ideas of Cartesian linguistics with no explicit analysis of its relation to current work that seeks to clarify and develop these ideas."

Curley, E. M. *Descartes against the Skeptics.* Cambridge, Mass.: Harvard University Press, 1978, 242 p.

Assessment of Descartes's thought that seeks to determine what his "views and arguments really were."

Davidson, Hugh M. "Descartes and the Utility of the Passions." *Romanic Review* LI, No. 1 (February 1960): 15-26.

Detailed exposition of Descartes's treatise *The Passions of the Soul.*

Derrida, Jacques. "Cogito and the History of Madness." In his *Writing and Difference,* translated by Alan Bass, pp. 31-62. Chicago: University of Chicago Press, 1978.

Advances that Michel Foulcault's "reading of Descartes and the Cartesian Cogito proposed to us engages in its problematic the totality of [his] *History of Madness* as regards both its intention and its feasibility."

Deutscher, Max. "Stories, Pictures, Arguments." *Philosophy* 62, No. 240 (April 1987): 159-70.

Considers the significance of central images in the *Meditations.*

Fitzgerald, Desmond J. "Descartes: Defender of the Faith." *Thought* XXXIV, No. 134 (Autumn 1959): 383-404.

Assesses Descartes's attempt to reconcile his philosophical initiatives with his personal commitment to Roman Catholicism.

Flores, Ralph. "Cartesian Striptease." In his *The Rhetoric of Doubtful Authority: Deconstructive Readings of Self-Questioning Narratives, St. Augustine to Faulkner,* pp 66-87. Ithaca: Cornell University Press, 1984.

Argues that in the context of the *Meditations* "the Cartesian narrator offers to 'conjoin past and present knowledges [*connaissances*]' and to dismiss his erstwhile doubts as 'hyperbolic and ridiculous'."

Frankfurt, Harry G. *Demons, Dreamers and Madmen: The Defence of Reason in Descartes's "Meditations."* 1970. Reprint. The Philosophy of Descartes, edited by William Doney. New York: Garland, 1987, 193 p.

Critique of Descartes's philosophy limited to "those parts of the *Meditations* that . . . are indispensable to understanding Descartes's attempt to provide a justification of reason."

Gueroult, Martial. *Descartes' Philosophy Interpreted According to the Order of Reasons.* 2 vols. Translated by Roger Ariew, Robert Ariew, and Alan Donagan. Minneapolis: University of Minnesota Press, 1984-85.

Systematic analysis of the *Meditations.*

Haldane, Elizabeth S. *Descartes: His Life and Times.* 1905. Reprint. New York: American Scholar Publications, 1966, 398 p.

Well-regarded survey of Descartes's life and work.

Heffernan, George. Introduction to *Meditations on First Philosophy,* by René Descartes, pp. 1-54. Notre Dame: University of Notre Dame Press, 1990.

Critical resume of Descartes's philosophical works, emphasizing the preeminent position of the *Meditations.*

Hooker, Michael, ed. *Descartes: Critical and Interpretive Essays.* Baltimore: John Hopkins University Press, 1978, 322 p.

Collection of previously unpublished critical essays written between 1965 and 1978. Essayists include Harry G. Frankfurt, Willis Doney, Ruth Mattern, and Margaret D. Wilson, among others.

———. "René Descartes." In *European Writers: The Age of Reason and the Enlightenment,* Vol. 3, edited by George Stade, pp. 1-22. New York: Charles Scribner's Sons, 1984.

Biographical and critical summary intended for the student beginning the study of Descartes.

Huxley, Thomas Henry. "On Descartes' 'Discourse Touching the Method of Using One's Reason Rightly, and of Seeking Scientific Truth'." *Macmillan's Magazine* XXII, No. 127 (May 1870): 69-80.

Evaluates Descartes's essential philosophical propositions, concentrating on those enunciated in the *Discourse on Method.*

Keeling, S. V. *Descartes.* London: Oxford University Press, 1968, 325 p.

Study of Descartes's metaphysics which aims "not merely to assemble into one connected story doctrines that Descartes elaborated piecemeal in various contexts, but rather to interpret those doctrines through conceptions and in language more readily understood to-day."

Kennington, Richard. "Descartes' *Olympica.*" *Social Research* 28, No. 2 (Summer 1961): 171-204.

Detailed interpretation of Descartes's autobiographical *Olympica,* upheld as a "primary source for the question of the rationalism of Descartes."

Krutch, Joseph Wood. "One of the Greatest of Men Who Made One of the Greatest of Mistakes." In his *And Even If You Do: Essays On Man, Manners & Machines,* pp. 289-95. New York: William Morrow & Company, 1967.

Considers the foundations of Descartes's philosophic

method, arguing that "Descartes is . . . the real father of the mechanistic theories of man current today."

Laudan, Laurens. "The Clock Metaphor and Probabilism: The Impact of Descartes on English Methodological Thought, 1650-65." *Annals of Science* 22, No. 2 (June 1966): 73-104.

Traces Descartes's influence on the formation of scientific method in seventeenth-century England.

Mackenzie, Ann Wilbur. "Descartes on Life and Sense." *Canadian Journal of Philosophy* 19, No. 2 (June 1989): 163-90.

Identifies "the fundamental conceptual innovations at work in Descartes' attempt to extend the new [mechanistic philosophy] to include biology.

Magnus, Bernd, and Wilbur, James B., eds. *Cartesian Essays: A Collection of Critical Studies.* The Hague: Martinus Nijhoff, 1969, 147 p.

Articles, arranged by topic, investigate key themes in Descartes's philosophy. Includes an extensive bibliography for further reading.

Maritain, Jacques. *The Dream of Descartes.* 1944. Reprint. Port Washington, N. Y.: Kennikat Press, 1969, 220 p.

Compilation of previously unpublished essays and reprints which purport "to try to determine the value and significance of the Cartesian reform with regard to metaphysical and theological wisdom."

Merrylees, W. A. *Descartes: An Examination of Some Features of His Metaphysics and Method.* Melbourne: Melbourne University Press, 1934, 330 p.

Comprehensive study of Descartes aiming "not so much to give an exposition of Descartes' philosophy, as to arrive at the true answers to the questions he raises."

Popkin, Richard H. "Descartes: Conqueror of Scepticism" and "Descartes: Sceptique Malgré Lui." In his *The History of Scepticism from Erasmus to Spinoza,* pp. 172-92, 193-213. Berkeley and Los Angeles: University of California Press, 1979.

Considers Descartes's apparent triumph over scepticism in the *Meditations.*

Read, Herbert. "Descartes." In his *The Nature of Literature,* pp. 183-95. New York: Horizon Press, 1956.

Assesses modern critical responses to Descartes's philosophy.

Rorty, Amélie Oksenberg, ed. *Essays on Descartes' "Meditations."* Berkeley and Los Angeles: University of California Press, 1986, 534 p.

Selection of articles written by leading commentators on Descartes "organized to follow the sequence of Descartes' *Meditations* as closely as possible." Included are essays by E. M. Curley, Geneviève Rodis-Lewis, and Jean-Luc Marion, among many others.

Roth, Leon. *Descartes' Discourse on Method.* Oxford: Clarendon Press, 1937, 142 p.

Critical and historical assessment of the *Discourse on Method.*

Sebba, Gregor. *Bibliographia Cartesiana: A Critical Guide to the Descartes Literature 1800-1960.* The Hague: Martinus Nijhoff, 1964, 510 p.

Annotated guide to Descartes criticism from 1800 to 1960.

Smith, Norman Kemp. *New Studies in the Philosophy of Descartes: Descartes as Pioneer.* London: MacMillan & Co., 1963, 369 p.

General evaluation of Descartes's major philosophical and scientific writings.

Spinoza, Benedictus de. *The Principles of Descartes' Philosophy.* Translated by Halbert Hains Britan. La Salle, Ill.: Open Court, 1905, 177 p.

Modern translation of Spinoza's commentary on the Cartesian system originally published in 1663.

Valéry, Paul. Introduction to *The Living Thoughts of Descartes,* translated by Harry Lorin Binsse, pp. 1-33. London: Cassell and Co., Ltd., 1948.

Introduction to Descartes's life and work rendered "in terms of altogether elementary impressions."

Vendler, Zeno. "Descartes' Res Cogitans." In his *Res Cogitans: An Essay in Rational Psychology,* pp. 144-205. Ithaca: Cornell University Press, 1972.

Investigates Descartes's psychological theories, concluding that "the *Cogito* is, briefly, a dramatic account of the rise of self-consciousness."

Versfeld, Marthinus. *An Essay on the Metaphysics of Descartes.* London: Methuen, 1940, 192 p.

Affirms that "the metaphysic of Descartes arises . . . from the need to restore a self-confidence shattered by a profound sense of discontinuity between the human mind and the rest of reality."

Vrooman, Jack Rochford. *René Descartes: A Biography.* New York: G. P. Putnam's Sons, 1970, 308 p.

Focuses on "six periods in [Descartes's] life that were crucially important for his personal development and for the works he produced."

Weinberg, Florence M. "The Idea of Soul in Descartes and Pascal." *French Forum* 8, No. 1 (January 1983): 5-19.

Argues that for Descartes and Pascal the "central idea of the soul remains remarkably traditional in conception."

Williams, Bernard. *Descartes: The Project of Pure Enquiry.* Atlantic Highlands, N. J.: Humanities Press, 1978, 320 p.

Exegesis of Descartes's metaphysical doctrines conceived more as "a study in the history of philosophy rather than in the history of ideas."

Wilson, Margaret Dauler. Introduction to *The Essential Descartes,* edited by Robert Paul Wolff, pp. vii-xxxii. New York: New American Library, 1969.

Concise critical introduction to Descartes's central philosophical works.

———. *Descartes.* London: Routledge & Kegan Paul, 1978, 255 p.

General appraisal of Descartes's achievement "presented in the form of a sort of semi-commentary on Descartes's *Meditations Concerning First Philosophy.*"

Windelband, W. *A History of Philosophy: With Especial Reference to the Formation and Development of its Problems and Conceptions.* Translated by James H. Tufts. New York: The MacMillan Company, 1921, 726 p.

A history of Western philosophy focusing on key problems and concepts.

Gavin Douglas

1475?-1522

Scottish poet and translator.

INTRODUCTION

Douglas is widely recognized as an important literary figure in the transitional period between the Middle Ages and the Northern Renaissance. An inheritor of the traditions of the Latin classics and Chaucerian verse, he is best remembered for his translation of Virgil's *Aeneid*—published under the title *The XIII Bukes of the Eneados*—which was the first endeavor to transpose a Roman epic into an English dialect. While his other major work, *The Palice of Honour,* is a poem written in the medieval genre of dream allegory, the moral, political, and religious sensibilities expressed throughout his translation of Virgil significantly anticipate the views of the humanistic revival of the sixteenth century.

Although details of his early years are few, it is believed that Douglas was born in the Scottish Lowlands around the year 1475 into a powerful and politically contentious noble family. Reared with a strong sense of honor and zeal for his house, he learned early to promote his family's interests during a turbulent period in Scottish history. In 1490 the poet began his formal education at Saint Andrews, the oldest of the Scottish universities, and upon completion of the course of studies, it is supposed that he attended the University of Paris, where he likely encountered the humanist ideologies of the "new scholars," most importantly, Desiderius Erasmus. Returning to Scotland around the year 1497, he entered the service of the Catholic church, briefly holding minor ecclesiastical offices in the Scottish towns of Hauch and Linton. His first noteworthy benefice came in 1503, when, by royal appointment of King James IV, he became provost of the collegiate church of Saint Giles in Edinburgh. While little is known of his ministerial activity, his involvement with secular affairs is well-documented. Douglas served both as a legal procurator on behalf of his family and as burgess of Edinburgh in 1513. Although it seems that Douglas was preoccupied with political advancement, he was also engaged in literary activities during this period, in which both *The Palice of Honour* and the *Eneados* were produced.

The poet's literary career came to an abrupt end in 1513 with the death of James IV and the subsequent marriage of Douglas's nephew Angus to the widowed queen, Margaret Tudor. Suspicious of the queen's relationship with her brother, Henry VIII of England, for fear of English involvement in their country's affairs, a faction of Scottish nobles vehemently opposed the regency of Margaret—who ruled for her young son—and sought to install the Duke of Albany in her place. Douglas, naturally, favored the regency of his niece and became involved in the internecine feuds of the Scottish nobility, affairs which occupied him for the remainder of his life. In 1516 he was given the bishopric of Dunkeld amidst great controversy, during which he was imprisoned for a year. His episcopacy was fraught with intrigue, and, in 1521, caught between shifting political alliances, Douglas fled to London to escape prosecution for treason. It was there in exile that he spent his last months, eventually succumbing to the plague in September 1522.

The formation of Douglas's poetic canon has occupied critics and historians for centuries. Early records attribute to Douglas a number of works which are no longer extant. One poem which does survive, the allegorical *King Hart,* was long believed to have been written by Douglas, but recent scholars have disproved this ascription. The earliest authenticated work still extant is *The Palice of Honour.* This work is a highly conventional dream allegory—the dominant poetic form of the day—closely following the genre's tripartite structure of dream, journey, and arrival. Douglas employed this popular literary vehicle to explore the nature of honor. The poet-narrator of *The Palice of Honour* contemplates, through allusions to works of classical antiquity, the Bible, and medieval romance, the many ostensible paths by which honor may be attained. Learning that the ways of wisdom, asceticism, and love are futile, the poet concludes that moral excellence offers the true road to honor.

For centuries, scholars and critics deemed *The Palice of Honour* of historical interest only, a derivative work by one of the "Scottish Chaucerians." The Scottish poet forthrightly acknowledges that he is a disciple and devotee of Geoffrey Chaucer, and critics observe that Douglas did indeed imitate Chaucer's humor, phraseology, archaisms, and imagery. Moreover, scholars note, *The Palice of Honour* is strongly influenced by two of Chaucer's dream poems, *The House of Fame* and the Prologue to *The Legend of Good Women.* Douglas's debt to "the master" has been judged so great that some critics have charged that he plagiarized Chaucer. Others, however, have taken the more moderate view that his borrowings constitute an act of homage to his predecessor. Many commentators have focused on the great amount of detail in Douglas's creation, with some lauding *The Palice of Honour* for its linguistic intricacy and others viewing it as tedious and laboured. Abstract vocabulary, complex syntax, and a complicated rhyme scheme all contribute to the poem's density. Like Chaucer, Douglas loved lists and used them as a basic structural device. In addition, he filled the allegory with many latinate words, following a poetic fashion of the day.

Some twentieth-century critics have found that *The Palice of Honour* offers a philosophic vision of the poet as a "conductor to virtue." According to this view, the allegory is a meditation on the nature of the poet and his special insight into the meaning of life. Even though he himself may not comprehend the depth of what he has learned, the poem suggests, the poet is compelled to share the revelation through his craft. As Gerald B. Kinneavy has noted, "That [the poet] has chosen poetry as his path to honor, that he sees virtue and thereby honor as 'finall end' of his art is . . . emphasized in that his last action within the poem is creative, a ballad in praise of virtue and honor."

Scholars agree that Douglas's most important work is the *Eneados.* As Douglas himself states, this Scottish rendering of the twelve books of Virgil's *Aeneid,* together with the thirteenth book of Mapheus Vegius, was begun in 1512 at the request of his cousin, Lord Sinclair, and completed sixteen months later on 22 July 1513, a remarkably short period of time for such an immense undertaking. To the various books Douglas appended Prologues, original compositions on a range of subjects, from discussions of the difficulties of translation to depictions of nature. These Prologues make clear that fidelity to the original text was not an important consideration, for Douglas did not attempt to produce a word-by-word translation; rather, the poet sought to make Virgil comprehensible to his Scottish contemporaries.

The propriety of the poet's attempt to transpose Virgil to Scottish vernacular was long the subject of critical debate. Scholars throughout the eighteenth and nineteenth centuries admired Douglas's spirited verse but considered the Scottish language—and the poet's particular use of it—crude and poorly developed. In the twentieth century critics have increasingly applauded his efforts to discover cultural analogues for the conditions described by Virgil while simultaneously attempting to enrich and improve Scottish. As Lauclan Maclean Watt has observed, in the *Eneados* "we find a fresh and individual attempt to create a new vehicle of utterance." Some critics now consider Douglas's work superior to John Dryden's 1697 English translation of the *Aeneid.* Modern scholars have also stressed that in his commentary throughout the *Eneados,* Douglas places the poet in the role of teacher. To help his native audience grasp Virgil's timeless wisdom, Douglas introduced into the text explanations of historical and geographical allusions so that no part of the poem would be left incomprehensible and Scottish society as a whole might, in turn, benefit from Virgil's insights into human nature. Valuing Douglas as a teacher and storyteller has likewise led to a renewed interest in the *Eneados* as a political and moral treatise. As a pedagogical device, the work is meant to induce rulers to govern benevolently and to motivate citizens to valiant deeds. As Bruce Dearing has stated, "It is not the history of Aeneas, but the *myth* of Aeneas which engages Douglas. . . . [The] idea of Aeneas as the embodiment of manly virtue and political sagacity [is] the informing principle of the entire translation."

The Prologues to the thirteen books are often treated as independent poetic works and are considered the most accessible of all Douglas's writings. Some critics have viewed these poems as "pedantic breaks," or respites, in the lengthy, unfolding epic, while others have regarded them as revelations of the poet's distinctive personality as a keen observer of, and participant in, the harmony of the natural world order. Most noteworthy are Prologues VII, XII, and XIII, which are often admired as "nature poems," meticulous descriptions of the changing seasons of the year. To capture the vitality of natural phenomena, Douglas employed a number of poetic devices, including onomatopoeic words that imitate the sound of birds chirping, exaggeratedly long catalogues of flowers and animals, and alliterative expressions that ornament the descriptions and enhance the overall rhythmic quality of the verse. Though Douglas was not the first poet to write of the beauty of nature for the sake of beauty itself, Priscilla Bawcutt has remarked, "No other poet writing in English before Douglas devotes so much space to the continuous description of the natural world. . . . [For] accuracy and close observation of detail Douglas seems unrivalled at this time."

Although *The Palice of Honour* is esteemed by scholars as a work of literary value and interest, Douglas's critical reputation is based on the *Eneados.* For the Scottish poet, Virgil possessed an eternal insight into the human condition, which he sought to preserve through his translation for the benefit of his native people. As Alastair Fowler has remarked, "The *Eneados* is one of those few works that looks directly across the centuries. By sharing something of Douglas's perspective, we may arrive at a better sense of his situation, of Virgil's, and our own."

PRINCIPAL WORKS

The Palice of Honour (poetry) 1501 (published c. 1540)

**The XIII Bukes of the Eneados* (poetry) 1513 (published 1533)

The Poetical Works of Gavin Douglas, Bishop of Dunkeld. 4 vols. [edited by John Small] (poetry) 1874

Selections from Gavin Douglas [edited by David F. C. Coldwell] (poetry) 1964

*This work was translated and adapted from Virgil's *Aeneid* and the thirteenth book of the *Aeneid* by Mapheus Vegius.

Sir David Lyndsay (essay date 1530)

[*Lyndsay was a sixteenth-century Scottish poet and satirist of the Reformation. His most famous work is the morality play* Ane Satyre of the Thrie Estaitis *(c. 1540). In the following excerpt taken from the prologue to* The Testament and Complaynt of Our Soverane Lordis Papyngo, Kyng James the Fyft (1530), *the poet extols Douglas's literary achievements.*]

[As] Phebus dois Cynthia precell,
So Gawane Dowglas, Byschope of Dunkell,

Had, quhen he wes in to this land on lyve,
A bufe vulgare Poeitis prerogatyve,
  Boith in pratick and speculatioun.
I saye no more, gude Redaris may descryve

His worthy workis, in nowmer mo than fyve;
And speciallye, the trew Translatioun
Of Virgill, quhilk bene consolatioun
To cunnyng men, to knaw his gret ingyne,
Als weill in naturall science as devyne.

Sir David Lyndsay, in his The Poetical Works of Sir David Lyndsay of the Mount, Lyon King of Arms, Vol. I, *revised edition, William Paterson, 1871, 400 p.*

George Mackenzie (essay date 1711)

[*Mackenzie was a Scottish biographer and physician. In the excerpt below, he offers a biographical sketch of Douglas, particularly noting the poet's literary contributions to the Scottish nation.*]

[Douglas] apply'd himself closely to Theology, entred into Holy Orders: And, by the Recommendation of the King, who was a Good Judge of the Merits of his Subjects, he was Advanced to be Provost of the Collegiate Church of S. *Giles* in *Edinburgh,* a Place then of great Dignity and Revenue; and Rector of *Heriot*-Church, some few Miles from it. He continued for several Years, in this Station, as became his Holy Character, Noble Birth and Liberal Education. Then it was, he Composed and Published the most of his Poetical Works, as we may Learn from himself. The First of which was his ***Palace of Honour,*** which he Composed about the 27th Year of his Age, in the Year of GOD 1501, and 12 Years before he Finished his Translation of *Virgil,* as it appears from these Verses of his to my Lord *Sinclair.*

To zou, my Lord, what is thare mare to say?
Ressaue zour Werk desyrit mony ane Day,
Quharin also now am I fully quytt,
As twichand *Venus,* of my auld Promytt,
Quhilk I hir maid weill Twelf Zeris tofore,
As witnessith my *Palace of Honoure:*
In the quhilk Werk, ze red, on hand I tuke
For to Translate at hir Instance ane Buke;
Sa haue I done aboue, as ze may se,
Virgillis Volume of hir Son *Enee.*

The Author's Design in this Poem is, under the Similitude of a Vision, to represent the Vanity and Inconstancy of all Worldly Pomp and Glory; and, as it is expressed in his Life prefixed to the late Edition of his Translation of *Virgil,*

To shew, That a Constant and Inflexible Course of Vertue and Goodness, is the only Way to True Honour and Felicity, which he Allegorically Describes, as a Magnificent Palace, situate on a very high Mountain of a most Difficult Access. He illustrates the whole, with Variety of Examples; not only of those Noble and Heroic Souls, whose eminent Vertues procured them Entrance into that Blessed Place; but also of those Wretched Creatures, whose Vitious Lives have Fatally Excluded them for ever, notwithstanding of all their Worldly State and Grandeur. This Work is Addressed to King *James* IV. on purpose to Inspire that Brave Prince, with Just Sentiments of True Honour and Greatness; and incite him to Tread in the Paths of Vertue, which alone could Conduct him to it. And, to make it the more Agreeable and Entertaining, he hath Adorned it with several incident Adventures, and, throughout the Whole, Discovers a Vast and Comprehensive Genius, an Exuberant Fancy and Extraordinary Learning, for the Time he lived in. He seems to have taken the Plan of it, from the Palace of Happiness, Described in the *Picture of Cebes.*

After this, he Wrote his ***Aureæ Narrationes,*** mentioned by *Dempster,* and *Vossius;* and which seems to be the same, he speaks of himself, in his Epistle to the Lord *Sinclair,* at the End of his *Virgil,* in these Words:

I haue also ane schorte Commend compyld,
To expone strange Historiis and Termes wylde.

And if so, 'tis Probable, as the Authors of the fore-cited Life say, since now it is intirely lost, that it might have been a short Treatise of the Poetical Fictions of the Ancients, with an Explication of their Mythology, with which our Author was very well acquainted, as his Works, that are still extant, sufficiently Testify.

His next Work was his ***Comœdiæ Sacræ,*** which are now intirely lost: But, if they were Wrote with the same Design, as that of the ***Palace-Honour,*** and Dedicated to the same Prince, as *Vossius* seems to insinuate, 'tis probable, that they were composed out of the Sacred History, to excite People to Vertue.

His Last and Noblest Performance in Verse, was his Translation of *Virgil*'s *Æneis.* This Work he compleated in Eighteen Months or rather Sixteen, (he being, for Two Months, diverted from it by some troublesome Affairs, in which he was involved,) and Finished the 22d of *July* 1513; a Month and 17 Days before the Fatal Battle of *Flowden.* All which we have, from his own Words, in these Verses.

Completit was this Werk *Virgiliane,*
Apoun the Feist of *Marye Magdalane,*
Fra *Christ*'s Birth, the Date, quha list to here,
Ane thousand fyue hundreth and threttene Zere:
Quhilk for vthir grete Occupacioun lay
Vnsterit clois beside me mony ane Day:
And neuirtheless, quhidder I serf Thank or Wyte,
Fra tyme I thareto set my Pen to Wryte,
(Thocht GOD wate gif thir boundis wer full myde
To me, that had sic Besines beside,)
Apoun this wyse, as GOD list len me Grace,
It was compilyt in Auchtene Monethis space:
Set I feil syith sic Twa Monethis in fere
Wrate neuir ane Wourd, nor micht the Volume stere,
For grave Materis, and grete Sollicitude,
That all sic Lauboure fere beside me stude.

So that it was begun in *January* 1512, and probably, betwixt that and *December* following, he met with these Two Months of Interruption. For he began the Seventh Book in *December* 1512; the Twelfth, in *May;* and *Mapheus*'s Supplement, or the Thirteenth, in *June* 1513, as he tells us in the **Prologues** to these Three Books. So the Seven last Books took him up only Eight Months; whereas Ten

Months were employ'd in the First Six. And tho' he did not closely set about this Translation, till the Year 1512; yet he had Projected it long before, as it appears from his ***Palace of Honour,*** wherein *Venus* is brought in, enjoining him to make this Translation, to atone for a Ballad, (as he calls it) written by him, against her and her Court. This Translation he undertook, at the Desire of *Henry* Lord *Sinclair,* a great Patron of Learning and Vertue. (pp. 296-98)

[Douglas's] Translation of *Virgil* is highly Commended by a great many Learn'd Men, whose Testimonies, concerning him and his Works, have been very Diligently Collected and Annexed to his Life, in the late Edition Published at *Edinburgh.* (pp. 300-01)

But of all these I shall only trouble the Reader with Two. The one is that of the Learned Bishop of *Carlisle,* who, speaking of his Treatise *de Rebus Scoticis,* says,

> How well Qualify'd he was for an Undertaking of this Nature, we may well guess by his Admirable Translation of *Virgil*'s *Æneids,* which (in Eighteen Months time) he turned into most Elegant *Scotish* Verse, thereby wonderfully improving the Language of his Country and Age. *F. Lesly,* that was a good Judge of the Work, assures us, That 'tis done in such a Masculine Strain of True Poetry, that it may justly vye with the Original; every Line whereof is singly render'd, and every Word most appositely and fully.

The other is that of *Hume* of *Godscroft,* who was an excellent Judge in Poetry: And tho' he was an extraordinary Friend to the *Douglasses;* yet he was a Sworn Enemy to those of our Author's Character.

> He wrote (says he) in his Native Tongue, diverse things: But his Chiefest Work is, his Translation of *Virgil,* yet extant, in Verse, in which he ties himself to strictly as is possible; and yet it is so well expressed, that whosoever shall essay to do the like, will find it a hard Piece of Work, to go through with it. In his **Prologues** before every Book, where he hath his Liberty, he sheweth a Natural and Ample Vein of Poesy, so Pure, Pleasant and Judicious, that, I believe, there is none, that hath Written before or since, but cometh short of him. And, in my Opinion, there is not such a Piece to be found, as is his **Prologue to the Eighth Book,** beginning thus, *Of Drevelling and Dremys,* at least in our Language.

After our Author had Finished this Translation; he Wrote no more in Verse, but apply'd himself to the more Weighty Affairs of Church and State, as he tells us in the Conclusion of this Work.

> Thus up my Pen and Instrumentis full zore
> On *Virgilis* Past I fix for euermore,
> Neuir from thens sic Matteris to diserive:
> My Muse sal now be clene contemplative,
> And solitare, as doith the Bird in Cage;
> Sen fer by worne all is my Chyldis Age
> And of my Dayis nere passit the half Date,
> That Nature suld me granting, wele I wate.
> Thus sen I feile doun siveyand the Ballance,
> Here I resigne up Zounkeris Obseruance;
> And wyl derek my Laubouris euermoir
> Unto the Commoun-Welth and GODDIS Gloir.
>
> (p. 301)

George Mackenzie, "The Life of Gawin Douglas, Bishop of Dunkeld," in his Lives and Characters of the Most Eminent Writers of the Scots Nation, Vol. II, *1711. Reprint by Garland Publishing, Inc., 1971, pp. 295-308.*

John Campbell (essay date 1741)

[*The following excerpt is taken from* The Polite Correspondance; or, Rational Amusement, *a collection of essays written in the form of letters. Here, in "Celadon to Phaon," Campbell praises the* Eneados *as a great translation.*]

I have taken some Pains in gathering all the Translations from the *Latin* Poets that I could meet with, both old and new, and so great is the Pleasure I take in comparing these, that I am sometimes alone in my Study two or three Hours, when I think I have not been there a Quarter, and it is certainly a Sign that a Man is employed to his liking, when Time runs away unperceived. Amongst these Translations I have met with one made from *Virgil,* by *Gawin Douglass,* Bishop of *Dunkell.* What you say . . . , of the *Ever-green,* put me upon reading, though I confess to you with some Difficulty, this Translation; but it is scarce possible for me to express my Surprize, when after a short Acquaintance with this Author, I discovered that he was by far the ablest Translator ever attempted the Works of this Prince of the *Latin* Poets. His Translation in my Judgment, has all the Advantages a Translation can have; it is close, concise, and comparable in its Beauties, to the Original itself: In short I know nothing equal to it, unless it be *Chapman*'s *Homer,* which, take it altogether, is a wonderful Book, but then its Excellency lies in the Author's Genius, and not in the Justness of the Translation; whereas the Bishop of *Dunkell,* shows himself to have been a Great Man, by showing him a Great, that is an exact Translator. (pp. 301-02)

John Campbell, "Celadon to Phaon," in his The Polite Correspondence; or, Rational Amusement: Being a Series of Letters, Philosophical, Poetical, Historical, Etc., *1741. Reprint by Garland Publishing, Inc., 1971, pp. 296-302.*

Alexander Campbell (essay date 1798)

[*Campbell was a Scottish musician who wrote several works on the poetry and music of his country. In the following excerpt, he briefly sketches Douglas's life and poetic output.*]

In one of these corners, where nature seems to retire amidst her deepest solitudes, in former days chosen as a fit place for rearing an alter to the most high, did Gawin Douglas dedicate his time to the God of nature and the muses. Dunkeld, is delightfully situated on the river Tay—tradition mentions it as once, a strong fortress, and one of the passes to the Highlands. This district was at an early period errected into a Bishoprick. Douglas, on the death of George Brown, was raised to the dignity of Bishop and appointed to this Diocess After some opposition, he was left in quiet posession of his appointment. He died at London in the 48th year of his age, and was intered by the side of Thomas Halsay Bishop of Laghlin in Ireland in the Hospital church in the Savoy—their epitaphs appear on one stone. Our business is not with the Eclesiastic, but with the poet. Gawin Douglas stands confessedly at the head, in the age he lived, of those his cotemporaries, as a first rate poet. His chief work the ***Bukes of Eneados*** of the famose poet Virgill translated out of latyne verses into Scotish metir, by the reverend Father in God, Mayster Gavin Douglas Bishop of Dunkel, and unkil to the Erle of Angus. Every buke having its particular prologe. Imprinted at London 1553. 4to is a performance of uncommon merit—it is the labour, as he himself tells us, of eighteen months only! a proof what genius can achieve when in full vigour. The prologues to each book, are in a stile truely original, and shews what a rich vein, he possessed for discriptive poetry. The learned, ingenius Ruddiman has given, with the addition of a very complete gloslary, an elegant edition of this work, (printed at Edinburgh 1718 for Symson and freebairn) to speak of the merits of Douglas as a poet would far exceed the bounds prescribed to this short sketch—his works must be read—and to read them, is the highest pleasure. Besides the ***Eniad,*** he has written other pieces, among which are *King Hart* and ***The Palice of Honour*** both allegorical poems—the former is in the Maitland collection and printed among the ancient Scotish poems 1786—the latter is very scarce and hardly to be met with. (pp. 56-7)

Alexander Campbell, in an excerpt in his An Introduction to the History of Poetry in Scotland, from the Beginning of the Thirteenth Century down to the Present Time, *1798. Reprint by Garland Publishing, Inc., 1972, pp. 56-7.*

David Irving (essay date 1810)

[*Irving was an English biographer and recognized authority on Scottish poetry. In the excerpt below, he extols Douglas for his poetic genius, especially as evinced in his use of allegory, descriptive images, and language.*]

The works of Douglas exhibit specimens of varied excellence. Of literary perfection however, if such a term may be adopted, our notions are not absolute but relative. This eulogy must therefore be understood to bear reference to a particular scale of merit: and a comparative estimate must be formed of the characters of different ages, nations, and languages. Yet after every requisite indulgence is granted, the intrinsic beauty of his compositions will not fail of exciting the admiration of those whom a previous knowledge of the Scotish dialect has constituted judges. His writings present us with constant vestiges of a prolific and even exuberant imagination; and his very faults are those of superabundance rather than of deficiency. In his descriptive poems, so admirable in many respects, he sometimes distracts the attention by a multiplicity of objects, and is not sufficiently careful to represent each new circumstance in a definite and appropriate manner. His allegorical sketches are efforts of no common ingenuity: but what chiefly renders his works interesting, is the perpetual occurrence of those picturesque and characteristic touches which can only be produced by a man capable of accurate observation and original thought. He is minute without tediousness, and familiar without impertinence. We are delighted with the writer, and become interested in the man. The beauties of external nature he seems to have surveyed with the eyes of a poet; the various aspects of human life with those of a philosopher. Our attention is alternately attracted by picturesque descriptions of material objects, and by pointed observations on the manners and pursuits of mankind.

To his inherent qualifications was superadded the necessary aid of scholastic discipline. He was perhaps the most learned of the early Scotish poets. The intimacy of his acquaintance with ancient literature was in that age rarely paralleled. His favourites among the heathen poets were apparently Virgil and Ovid: and among the Christian fathers his favourite was St Augustin, whom he denominates the chief of clerks. Of the Latin language his knowledge was undoubtedly extensive: and as he has informed us that Lord Sinclair requested him to translate Homer, we may conclude that he was also acquainted with Greek. At present his secular learning is alone remembered; but Myln has informed us that he was likewise eminently skilled in theology and in the canon law.

His style is copious and impetuous: but his diction may be considered as deficient in purity. In his translation of Virgil he professes to be scrupulous in rejecting Anglicisms: and indeed his language is generally remote from that of the English poets. But he has imported many exotic terms from another quarter; his familiarity with the Latin authors betrays itself in almost every page of his writings. His verses, though less smooth and elegant than those of Dunbar, are not unskilfully constructed. With regard to the quantity of syllables he has not displayed the same unbounded licentiousness as sometimes appears in the writings of our ancient poets. In many of his lines deficiencies or redundancies may be discovered; but they are commonly to be imputed to the inaccuracy of transcribers, or to our ignorance of the true mode of pronunciation. What Mr Tyrwhitt has suggested in defence of the versification of Chaucer [in his *Essay on the Language and Versification of Chaucer*], may with equal propriety be applied to that of Douglas: "The great number of verses, sounding complete even to our ears, which is to be found in all the least corrected copies of his works, authorizes us to conclude, that he was not ignorant of the laws of metre. Upon this conclusion it is impossible not to ground a strong presumption, that he intended to observe the same laws in many other verses which seem to us irregular; and if this was really his intention, what reason can be assigned sufficient to account for his having failed so grossly and repeatedly as is generally supposed, in an operation which every ballad-monger in our days, man, woman, or child, is known to perform with the most unerring exactness, and without any extraordinary fatigue?" (pp. 25-8)

The following is Mr Sage's criticism on ***The Palice of***

Honour [in his *Life of Bishop Douglas*]: "The author's excellent design is, under the similitude of a vision, to represent the vanity and inconstancy of all worldly pomp and glory; and to shew that a constant and inflexible course of vertue and goodness is the only way to true honour and felicity, which he allegorically describes as a magnificent palace, situate on a very high mountain, of a most difficult access. He illustrates the whole with variety of examples, not only of these noble and heroic souls, whose eminent vertues procured them entrance into that blessed place, but also of those wretched creatures, whose vicious lives have fatally excluded them from it for ever, notwithstanding of all their worldly state and grandeur. This work is addressed to James IV. on purpose to inspire that brave prince with just sentiments of true honour and greatness, and incite him to tread in the paths of vertue, which alone could conduct him to it. And to make it more agreeable and entertaining, he hath adorned it with several incident adventures; and throughout the whole discovers a vast and comprehensive genius, an exuberant fancy, and extraordinary learning, for the time he lived in. He seems to have taken the plan of it from the palace of happiness described in the *Picture of Cebes;* and it is not improbable that his country-man Florentius Volusenus had it in view, and improv'd his design, in his admirable (but too little known) book *De Tranquillitate Animi.*"

Between the description however of Cebes and that of Douglas, it will perhaps be difficult to discover any very remarkable affinity. If it can be evinced that a striking resemblance prevails between those two compositions and the work of Florence Wilson, it seems more safe to conclude that he imitated Cebes rather than Douglas. Wilson's dialogue *De Animi Tranquillitate* appeared in 1543; whereas ***The Palice of Honour*** was not printed till ten years afterwards. If therefore he ever perused this poem, it must have been previously to its publication.

It has also been surmized that the work of Douglas is *probably* founded on the *Sejour d'Honneur* of St Gelais; for no other apparent reason than the obvious affinity of their respective titles. If imitation must thus be so zealously inferred, it would perhaps be more proper to fix upon Chaucer's *House of Fame* as the exemplar. But till other arguments shall be produced, ***The Palice of Honour*** may safely be regarded as an original composition.

Douglas's spirited translation of the ***Æneid*** has often been highly commended, though seldom beyond its merits. Without pronouncing it the best version of this poem that ever was or ever will be executed, we may at least venture to affirm that it is the production of a bold and energetic writer, whose knowledge of the language of his original, and prompt command of a copious and variegated phraseology, qualified him for the performance of so arduous a task. And whether we consider the state of British literature at that æra, or the rapidity with which he completed the work, he will be found entitled to a high degree of admiration. In either of the sister languages few translations of classical authors had hitherto been attempted; and the rules of the art were consequently little understood. It has been remarked that even in English no metrical version of a classic had yet appeared; except of Boëthius, who scarcely merits that appellation. On the destruction of Troy Caxton had published a kind of prose romance, which he professes to have translated from the French: and the English reader was taught to consider this motley composition as a version of the *Æneid.* Douglas bestows severe castigation on Caxton for his presumptuous deviation from the classical story; and affirms that his work no more resembles Virgil than the Devil resembles St Austin. He has however fallen into one error which he exposes in his predecessor: proper names are often so disfigured in his translation, that they are not without much difficulty recognized. In many instances he has been guilty of modernizing the notions of his original. The Sibyl, for example, is converted into a nun, and admonishes Æneas, the Trojan baron, to persist in counting his beads. This plan of reducing every ancient notion to a modern standard has been adopted by much later writers: many preposterous instances occur in the learned Dr Blackwell's *Memoirs of the Court of Augustus.*

Of the general principles of translation however Douglas appears to have formed no inaccurate notion. For the most part his version is neither rashly licentious nor tamely literal. In affirming that he has always rendered one verse by another, Lesley and Dempster have committed a mistake. This regularity of correspondence he either did not attempt or has failed to maintain. Such a project would indeed have been wild and nugatory. The verses of Virgil and Douglas must commonly differ in length by at least three syllables; and they may even differ by no fewer than seven. (pp. 58-62)

In the poems appended to his translation, Douglas has fortunately specified the origin and progress of the undertaking. The work, he there informs us, was begun and finished at the request of his cousin Henry Lord Sinclair; whom he represents as an accomplished and liberal patron of literature. It was the labour of only sixteen months, and completed on the twenty-second day of July, 1513, about twelve years after he had composed his ***Palice of Honour.*** This task must be understood to comprehend, not merely a version of the twelve books of Virgil, but also of the supplement of Mapheus Vegius, together with the original prologues and epilogues.

Hume of Godscroft, who was himself a poet, has remarked that "in his prologues before every book, he sheweth a natural and ample vein of poesy, so pure, pleasant and judicious, that he believes there is none that hath written before or since but cometh short of him. There is not such a piece to be found as is the prologue to the eighth book, at least in our language."

His prologues to the seventh and twelfth books display an admirable vein of descriptive poetry. They have been exhibited in an English dress by Mr Fawkes. The prologue to the twelfth book has also been modernized by Jerom Stone. The prologue to the supplement of Vegius presents us with a poetical description of an evening in June.

These are the only works of Douglas which have descended to our times. In the ***Conclusion*** of his Virgilian task, he avows a resolution to devote his future days to the glory of God and the service of the commonwealth. (pp. 64-5)

David Irving, "The Life of Gavin Douglas," in his The Lives of the Scottish Poets, Vol. II, *second edition, Longman, Hurst, Rees, & Orme, 1810, pp. 1-67.*

Joseph Robertson (essay date 1821)

[*In the following excerpt, Robertson acknowledges Douglas's accomplishments, both as a translator and as an allegorist.*]

As a man of letters, Douglas stands distinguished as the first poetical translator of the classics in Britain. Besides the translation . . . of Ovid's *De Remedio Amoris,* he translated the *Æneid* of Virgil, with the additional sixteenth book of Mapheus Vigius. It was printed at London, in quarto, in the year *1553,* under the following title: "The XIII Bukes of ***Eneados*** of the Famose Poet Virgill. Translatet out of Latyne Verses into Scottish Meter by the Reverend Father in God, Mayster Gawin Douglas, Bishop of Dunkel and Unkil to the Erle of Angus. Euery Buke hauing hys perticular Prologe."

It appears that he had projected this work as early as the year 1501, but did not actually engage in it till eleven years after, when he completed it in the short space of eighteen months.

No metrical version of a classic had yet appeared in English, except one of Boëthius, who wrote at so late a period of Roman declension, as scarcely to deserve the appellation. All that was commonly known of Virgil was through Caxton's distorted romance on the subject of the *Æneid.* Douglas's translation, therefore, could not fail of attracting considerable notice; and its merit acquired it a popularity which it preserved until the close of the last century, when it was superseded by other versions, probably more elegant, but not more faithful nor more spirited.

Douglas's Virgil possessed one excellence, to which no succeeding translation has any pretension. The **Prologues** of his own composition, which he has prefixed to the different books, are such as almost place him on a level with the divine poet he has translated. Many of them, says Mr. Pinkerton, are "quite wonderful, particularly that to B. VII. describing a summer morning; and that to Maffei's B. XIII. a summer evening. Mr. Warton has put Milton's "L'Allegro" and "Il Penseroso" as the earliest descriptive poems in English; if so, we have examples in Scottish near a century and a half before. And what examples! Suffice it to say, that they yield to no descriptive poems in any language."

It may be a matter of some interest to the lovers of Scottish poetry to observe, that, in these **Prologues,** the author has preserved the names and characterizing lines of several ancient Scottish songs, which have been long ago lost. He mentions,

> I come hidder to wow.

And,

> The jolly day now dawis;

both of which lines have been made the burden of modern adaptations: as also the following;

> The schip sailis over the salt fome
> Will bring thir merchands, and my leman home.
>
> I vill be blyth and licht;
> My hart is bent upon sa gudly wicht.

Douglas wrote two other works, both of an allegorical character, the one entitled ***The Palace of Honour,*** and the other *King Hart.*

The Palace of Honour is addressed, as an apologue for the conduct of a king, to James the Fourth. It was written prior to 1501, and printed at London in *1553,* and at Edinburgh in *1579.* Both editions are extremely rare; and the work, though it appears to have been once well known in Scotland, is now only read by one in the million. The printer of the Edinburgh edition of 1579 says, in his preface, that "besides the copy printed at London, there were copyis of this work set furth of auld amangis our selfis." The purpose of the allegory is to shew the insufficiency and instability of worldly pomp, and to prove that a constant and undeviating habit of virtue is the only way to true Honour and Happiness, who are poetically said to reside in a magnificent palace, situated on the summit of a high and almost inaccessible mountain. The allegory is illustrated by a variety of examples of illustrious personages, who, by a steady perseverance in noble deeds, have scaled the envied eminence; and of others, who, from debasing dignity of birth and station by vicious and unmanly practices, have been tumbled to the bottom. "It is a poem," says Mr. Warton, "adorned with many pleasing incidents and adventures, and abounds with genius and learning." (pp. 59-62)

Joseph Robertson, "Gavin Douglas," in his Lives of Scottish Poets, Vol. I, *Thomas Boys, 1821, pp. 54-69.*

A. Lang (essay date 1880)

[*A translator, poet, and revisionist historian, Andrew Lang is perhaps best known for his extensive research into early languages and literature. In the following excerpt, he examines Douglas's reliance upon Virgil and Chaucer. In addition, the critic observes that Douglas's writings reveal him to be a humanist as well as a cleric.*]

The chief original poem of Douglas, ***The Palice of Honour,*** is an allegory of the sort which had long been in fashion. Moral ideas in allegorical disguises, descriptions of spring, and scraps of mediaeval learning were the staple of such compositions. Like the other poets, French and English, of the last two centuries, Douglas woke on a morning of May, wandered in a garden, and beheld various masques or revels of the goddesses, heroes, poets, virtues, vices (such as 'Busteousness'), and classical and Biblical worthies. In his vision he characteristically confused all that he happened to know of the past, made Sinon and Achitophel comrades in guilt and misfortune, while Penthesilea and Jeptha's daughter ranged together in Diana's company, and 'irrepreuabill Susane' rode about in the troop of 'Cleopatra and worthie Mark Anthone.' The diverting and pathetic combinations of this sort still render Douglas's poems rich in surprises, and he occasionally does poetical justice on the wicked men of antiquity, as when he makes Cicero knock down Catiline with a folio. To modern readers his allegory seems to possess but few original qualities. His poem, indeed, is rich with descriptions of flowers and stately palaces, his style, like Venus's throne, is 'with stones rich over fret and cloth of gold,' his pictures have the quaint gorgeousness and untarnished hues that we admire in the paintings of Crivelli. But these qualities he shares with so many other poets of the century which preceded his own, that we find him most original when he is describing some scene he knew too well, some hour of storm and surly weather, the bleakness of a Scotch winter, or a 'desert terribill,' like that through which 'Childe Roland to the dark tower came.' . . .

The little piece of verse called ***Conscience*** is not bad in its quibbling way. When the Church was young and flourishing, *Conscience* ruled her. Men wearied of *Conscience,* and cut off the *Con,* leaving *Science.* Then came an age of ecclesiastical learning, which lasted till the world 'thought that Science was too long a jape,' and got rid of *Sci.* Nothing was left now but *ens,* worldly substance, 'riches and gear that gart all grace go hence.' The Church in Scotland did not retain even *ens* long after the age of Douglas. Grace, on the other hand, waxed abundant.

The work by which Douglas lives, and deserves to live, is his translation of the *Aeneid.* It is a singular fruit of a barren and unlearned time, and, as a romantic rendering of the *Aeneid,* may still be read with pleasure. The two poets whom Douglas most admired of all the motley crowd who pass through ***The Palice of Honour*** were Virgil and Chaucer. Each of these masters he calls an *a per se.* He imitated the latter in the manner of his allegorical verse, and he translated the former with complete success. We must not ask the impossible from Douglas,—we must not expect exquisite philological accuracy; but he had the 'root of the matter,' an intense delight in Virgil's music and in Virgil's narrative, a perfect sympathy with 'sweet Dido,' and that keen sense of the human life of Greek, Trojan, and Latin, which enabled him in turn to make them live in Scottish rhyme. If he talks of 'the nuns of Bacchus,' and if his Sibyl admonishes Aeneas to 'tell his beads,' Douglas is merely using what he thinks the legitimate freedom of the translator. He justifies his method, too, by quotations from Horace and St. Gregory. He is giving a modern face to the ancient manners, a face which his readers would recognise. In his prologues, his sympathy carries him beyond orthodox limits, and he defends the behaviour of Aeneas to Dido against the attacks of Chaucer. He is so earnest a 'humanist' that he places himself in the mental attitude of Virgil, and avers that Aeneas only deserted Dido at the bidding of the gods:—

> Certes, Virgill schawis Enee did na thing,
> Frome Dido of Cartaige at his departing,
> Bot quhilk the goddes commandit him to forne;
> And gif that thair command maid him mans-
>   worne,
> That war repreif to thair divinitee
> And na reproche unto the said Enee.

But though Douglas is a humanist in verse, all the Bishop asserts himself in prose. In his prose note he observes that 'Enee falit then gretly to the sueit Dido, quhilk falt reprefit nocht the goddessis divinite, for they had na divinite as said is before.' Though he adores the Olympians in verse, Douglas adopts the Euhemeristic theory in prose: 'Juno was bot ane woman, dochter to Saturn, sistir and spows to Jupiter king of Crete.' In spite of these edifying notes, Douglas's conscience pricked him, 'for he to Gentiles' bukis gaif sik keip.' Even if he knew Greek, he probably would not have translated Homer, as a friend asked him to do. The prologue to the Thirteenth Book of the ***Aeneid*** (i.e. of the book 'ekit' to Virgil by Mapheus Vergius,) proves that there were moments when he thought even Virgil a perilous and unprofitable heathen.

The language of Douglas, as he observes (**Prologue to the First Book**), is 'braid and plane,' that is to say, it is good broad Scotch, and still 'plain' enough to a Scotch reader. He does not, however, 'clere all sudroun refuse,' when no Scotch word served his turn, and he frankly admits that

> the ryme
> Causis me to mak digressioun sum tyme.

Douglas's rank is that of an accomplished versifier, who deserted poetry with no great regret for the dangerous game of politics. (pp. 160-62)

A. Lang, "Gawain Douglas," in The English Poets: Chaucer to Donne, Vol. I, *edited by Thomas Humphry Ward, Macmillan and Co., 1880, pp. 159-74.*

W. J. Courthope (essay date 1895)

[*Courthope was an English scholar, author, and professor of poetry at Oxford. In the following excerpt from his study of allegory in medieval literature, the critic singles out Douglas as a transitional figure between the chivalrous school represented by Geoffrey Chaucer and the classical or moral school represented by Edmund Spenser. In this essay, he briefly discusses* King Hart, *a work he ascribed to Douglas but which is now believed to be the work of another poet.*]

Scarcely less celebrated as a poet in his own age than Dunbar, and certainly on the whole a more important figure for the historian of poetry, Gavin Douglas heralds the introduction into the chivalrous school of allegory of the classical style, which received its fullest development from the hands of Spenser. (p. 374)

The Palace of Honour, poor as a composition, is historically interesting as marking the transition from the old allegory on the subject of love, to the moral style which came into favour through the influence of the Classical Renaissance. Here, as in Dunbar's *Golden Targe,* we find the poet preserving the conventional machinery of allegory: the ideal landscape, the Vision, the complaint about the cruelty of Fortune (of whom at this period Gavin had certainly no personal right to complain), and the Court of Venus, in which he is put upon his trial for writing a ballad against the goddess and her votaries. In this part of the poem it is noticeable that Venus is the prominent personage; that Amor, or Cupid, or Love, who in the earlier allegories is sovereign of the court, occupies a subordinate place; while the poet actually disputes the competence of the tribunal on two grounds: first, that *ladies may not be judges;* and, secondly, that Gavin himself, being "a spiritual man," is not accountable to a lay court. Judgment is about to be given against the poet, who fears that he will be put to death or transformed into a beast, when suddenly the Court of the Muses appears upon the scene, and, at the intercession of Calliope, Gavin is pardoned, on condition that he shall compose a ballad in praise of Love. Promptly complying with this requirement, he is then taken by the Muse on a tour round the habitable world, in the course of which he comes to a rock of "hard marble stone," shining like glass in the sun, on which is built the Palace of Honour. This he ascends with the help of his guide, but near the top he beholds the place of punishment for idle people, the sight of which fills him with so much alarm, that he is only prevented from making his way down by Calliope, who, seizing him by the hair of his head, "as Abacuk was brought to Babylon," drags him to the top. There he beholds the tempestuous sea of the world with a "lusty ship" tossing upon it, which Calliope, who, though a pagan Muse, is well versed in the dogmas of the Christian religion, informs him is the "carwell," or ship, of the state of Grace, necessary for man's salvation. A minute description of the Palace of Honour follows, in the course of which the poet finds an opportunity to enumerate all the leading characters of sacred and secular history, together with the cardinal and theological virtues, and to show his knowledge of the Ptolemaic system. Having penetrated through the gates of the castle, he is on the point of following "his nymph" over a narrow bridge into an inner enclosure, when (happily for the reader) he falls into the moat, which wakes him from his dream, and enables him to end his poem with a ballad in praise of honour and virtue.

King Hart is an allegory descriptive of the progress of human life, in which the various faculties of the body and mind are impersonated. The idea was suggested by that description of the Castle of Inwyt in the *Vision of Piers the Plowman* which furnished Spenser with his allegory of the Lady Alma and the House of Temperance in the *Faerie Queen. King Hart* shows a great advance on ***The Palace of Honour*** in narrative power and in versification. The influence of the study of Virgil is particularly visible in the metrical syntax, and though the vocabulary is exceedingly archaic, yet compared with the hobbling verse of contemporary English poets, like Hawes, Skelton, and Barclay, the rhythmical movement in Douglas's stanzas is the very soul of melody, as may be seen from the opening of the poem:—

> King Hart, into his cumlie castell strang,
> Closit about with craft and mickle ure,
> So semlie was he set his folk amang
> That he no doubt had of misáventure:
> So proudlie was he polist, plane and pure,
> With youthhead and his lusty levis grene;
> So fair, so fresh, so likely to endure,
> And als so blyth as bird in simmer schene.

Here it will be observed that nothing is wanting to develop the measure into the nine-line stanza used in the *Faerie Queene* but an added Alexandrine. The eight-line stanza had been introduced into English poetry by Chaucer, who took it from the French; but a great advance is noticeable in Douglas's versification both as regards swiftness of movement and disposition of accent. The first of these improvements is due to the protraction of the sentence. Instead of a number of short sentences, many of them confined within one line, and few of them extended beyond two, a single sentence, linked together by subordinate clauses in the Latin fashion, may now, as in the example just given, be carried through a whole stanza. The more regular distribution of the accent is due to the disappearance, from the Northern dialect used by Douglas, of the final *e,* the surviving symbol of inflection; and also to the fact that, in many of the words imported from the French, the accent, forced to follow the Teutonic law, has been removed from the final syllable to one of the syllables of the stem. Thus the following words which in Chaucer's verse would have been usually, if not invariably, pronounced Pleasánce, Jealousýe, Honoúr, Mirroúr, Natúre, Discretioún, Tresoúr, Beauté, Pité, become in *King Hart,* Pleásance, Jélousy, Hónour, Mírrour, Náture, Discrétion, Treásour, Beaútye, Pítie. The alteration in the general rhythmical effect may be gathered from a comparison of the following stanza from Chaucer's *Fortune* with that from *King Hart* already cited:—

> O Socrates, thou stedfast champioun,
> She never mighte be thy tormentour;
> Thou never dreddest hir oppressioun,
> Ne in her chere founde thou no savour.
> Thou knewe wel the deceit of hir colour,
> And that hir mostë worshipe is to lye.
> I knowe hir eek a fals dissimulour,
> For fynally, Fortune, I thee defye!

Gavin Douglas anticipates Spenser, not only in his metrical style, but also in his use of allegory as a method of interpreting nature. As the expectation of the approaching end of the visible world, which had for so many centuries haunted the imagination of men, waned, the desire to realise the nature of the unseen universe also began to disappear, leaving, however, behind it, in minds of a religious temper, a profound sense of the vanity of mortal things. This feeling, blended with the growing habit of moral reflection and the quickened perception of beauty, was fostered by the love which the pioneers of the Renaissance entertained for Virgil, an author whose depth of religious sentiment was only equalled by his profound knowledge of the resources of his art. No poet, not even Dante himself, ever drank more deeply of the spirit of Virgil than Gavin Douglas. Deeply versed in Catholic doctrine, he read into his theological studies the gravity, the melancholy, the sweetness, of his master in poetry. He showed his love for him by turning the *Æneid* for the first time into English ten-syllable rhyming couplets, and even more by the sentiment and style of the original **Prologues** which he prefixed to each book of his translation. Particularly notable are the **Prologues** to the sixth and seventh books. In the former, while he proclaims his fervent belief in the Christian religion, he indignantly rebukes those who regard the tale of Æneas' descent to the nether world as a narrative of "ghosts and brownies," and maintains that the sixth book of the ***Æneid*** is an inspired allegory of the future life. The Prologue to the seventh book contains a description of winter of extraordinary beauty and power, showing how thoroughly Douglas had learned from Virgil the art of associating human feelings with the varying aspects of external nature. He describes how in winter—

> Rivers run on spait with water brown
> And burnis hurlis all their bankis down;

and how—

> O'er craggis and the front of rochës sere
> Hang gret ice schoklis lang as ony spere;

and again,—

> So bustuysly Boreas his bugle blew,
> The deer full dern doun in the dalis drew.
> Small byrdis flocking through thick ronnis th-rang,
> In chyrming and with cheping changed their sang,
> Seeking hidlis and hernys thaime to hyde
> From fearfull thudis of the tempestuous tyde.

While he lay awake,—

> The wyld geese, clacking eke by nichtis tyde,
> Above the citie flying heard I glyde.

As the night wore on,—

> Approaching near the greiking of the day,
> Within my bed I wakened where I lay.
> So fast declinis Cynthia the moon,
> And kais keklis on the roof aboon.
> Palamedes' byrdis, crouping in the sky,
> Flying at random, shapen like a Y,
> And as a trumpet rang their voices soun,
> Whose crying bene pronosticatioun
> Of windy blastis and ventosities.

All this is quite in the spirit of the first *Georgic;* and Douglas goes on to assimilate these appearances of nature to his own mood:—

> And as I bound me to the fyre me by,
> Both up and down the house I did espy,
> And seeing Virgill on a lectern stand,
> To write anon I hynt a pen in hand,
> For to perform the poet grave and sad,
> Whom so far forth, ere then, begun I had,
> And wox annoyit some dele in my hart
> There rested incomplete so gret a part.
> And to myself I said: "In guid effect
> Thou man draw forth, the yoke lies on thy neck."
> Within my mind compassing thought I so,
> No thing is done while ought remains to do.

(pp. 375-80)

W. J. Courthope, "The Progress of Allegory in English Poetry," in his A History of English Poetry, Vol. I, *Macmillan and Co., Limited, 1895, pp. 341-92.*

Louis Golding (essay date 1922)

[*Golding was an English poet and author of several novels on Jewish themes. In the following excerpt, he considers the "Scottish Chaucerians" as poets in their own right, in some ways superior to Chaucer. Regarding Douglas, the critic praises his versification and imagery, but finds that his poems are more concerned with form than content.*]

In the weak eyeballs of academicians the virtues of the Scottish Chaucerians are blurred in the glory thrown about them by the sun of Chaucer. But it is possible to overestimate even Shakespeare as we can impute thirty thousand feet to Everest. So Chaucer is rather lost wholly than loved wholly by the declaration that he was greater in each respect than each member of this community of poets who derive their immortality, alas! more from his name than from their own high merits. Chaucer's greatness lies not in his detail but in his mass, in so much being less than Shakespeare, whose greatness is surpassed in neither mass nor detail. It is the multiplicity of the man, Chaucer, the abundance of his large lungs breathing, this laughing colossus standing wind-towsled over his age, that so cheats the airs from our puny pinnaces. Obviously enough none of the Scottish company is a colossus. They are great in their detail rather than their mass. And it is in the beauty of their texture, their delight in the threads they weave into comely silken patterns like Henryson's 'Robene and Makyne,' stout tapestries like the **Prologues** of Douglas, that they anticipate the marvellous housewifery of Spenser, and, at their highest, in the sweetness and strength of 'The Golden Targe,' that they anticipate John Keats, the last of their line.

Their mediaevalism is imputed to them now as a virtue, now a fault. It is no more a virtue than a man's skin. Or the term is applied to them as a statement of their limitations. This seems a graver consideration. They are not, we learn, original "makers." Without Chaucer they fall to the ground; once more these poets seize the antiquated orange of allegory, attempting once more to squeeze thence new drops of invention. James has his allegory, 'The Kingis Quair,' Henryson his Chaucerian Testament; Dunbar and Douglas, poets who should have known better, still embrace their fruits of allegory. These critics state an obvious enough truth. These poets certainly made use of long-familiar forms. Yet apart from the fact that at least three of them were highly original elsewhere in their writings (and who knows but that Time has ruthlessly swallowed other work of James than his 'Quair' and 'Good Counsel,' and work no less original than a prologue of Douglas?), yet the criticism is parallel to a condemnation of the Elizabethans for not forging entirely new plots. Whether the form of the Scottish Chaucerians was native or derivative, or their language a blend of northern and southern modes, their achievement was poetry, of which there is so little in the world, of which there cannot be too much. One feels that if Gower had lived to-day, he would not have attempted Parnassus's slope. He would have found the cinema a more effective instrument of moral suasion and have written scenarios for films of religious propoganda. Lydgate would have been a Civil Servant writing letters to the reviews mildly repudiating Mr. Bayfield on Shakespearian versification. The Scottish Chaucerians, who were poets of the fifteenth century, would have been poets to-day.

It is the fashion to sneer at the Chaucerians, when any attention is paid them at all, for their "aurification" of the

English tongue—their deliberate introduction of Latinisms. No critic who finds this a fault can have a keen insight into the making of poetry. These poets were conscious of an abounding sensuous delight in the world. It was perhaps a courtly, almost a sophisticated delight; yet it was sincere and urgent; they sought for a vocabulary to express their emotion in the language as left by Chaucer; but the language of Chaucer was not meticulous enough, not adequately jewelled. Hence we find in them that deliciously inquisitive search for musical Latin trisyllables, for fine melodies—a process which, though essentially smaller in nature, anticipates the majestic Latinizings of Milton and the later trilingual symphonies of Francis Thompson. (pp. 782-83)

Douglas in some senses marks the decadence of this burst of poetry briefly examined here. He is more of a litterateur, an Alexandrian, than the rest. We feel that the tremendous versatility of Dunbar, his feverish experimentation with many techniques is implicit in the man, native to him. In Douglas we feel a sense of deliberation, form a greater stimulus than matter. Take, for instance, the amazing virtuosity of the **'Ballade in Commendation of Honour'**; how the rhymes dance and sparkle like ascending and descending watery arrows in a sunlit fountain!

> Haill, rois maist chois til clois thy fois greit micht!
> Haill, stone quhilk schone upon the throne of licht!
> Vertew, quhais trew sweit dew ouirthrew al vice . . .

Not that even here poetry is lacking. But the tone here is of cunning silver rather than of plain fine gold.

So too we find a new formalism invading, not unpleasantly, the prologues to his translation of the *Æneid.* The prologues describing the winter landscapes and the May morning are adjectival poetry *in excelsis.* Never was there such a plethora of adjectives. Whilst, in sooth, adjectives are not lacking from 'The Golden Targe,' they are subordinate to the scheme. In Douglas the scheme is subordinate to the adjectives. *Passing away,* saith simplicity, *passing away.* And yet never was the adaptation of sound to meaning carried to a more masterly degree. The poem on winter, in its each syllable, is a translation of winter's essential music, hard, dry, jagged, craggy. The sea spumes bitterly, howls along livid coasts. Marrow freezes. A man reading in summer crouches for warmth over his empty fire-grate.

. . . Until the reader recalls the May morning of this same poet, this May morning of English poetry:

> The twinkling stremowris of the orient
> Sched purpour sprangis with gold and asure ment. . . .
> And al smal foulis singis on the spray
> Welcome the lord of licht and lampe of day!

The freshness of Chaucer, the lyric of Henryson, the skill of Dunbar, are fused in this *aubade.* Spring poets since that day seem curiously belated. When Shakespeare came, he sang the summer of his race. There are moments when it seems that to Shelley, wild, dying bird, was left only the threnody of autumn. (p. 783)

Louis Golding, "The Scottish Chaucerians," in The Saturday Review, *Vol. 134, No. 3500, November 25, 1922, pp. 782-83.*

Bruce Dearing (essay date 1952)

[Dearing is an American educator and authority on English medieval and Renaissance literature. In the following excerpt, he regards the Eneados *as a politically motivated, didactic tool created by Douglas to educate and enlighten rulers as to what constitutes the "ideal prince." Thus, the critic contends, "Douglas cannot be dismissed as a 'mere Chaucerian,' provincial and essentially medieval in scope and outlook. He deserves instead a place in the honored company of Erasmus, among the serious and humanistic scholars of the English Renaissance."]*

In the general scorn and neglect by modern literary scholars of the entire area in English literature between Chaucer and Spenser, few poets have fared so ill as the sixteenth-century Scottish Chaucerian Gavin Douglas. To be sure, his name appears frequently enough in histories of literature, and occasionally in studies of Chaucer, or Surrey, or Henryson, Lindsay, Dunbar. But one suspects that Douglas has less often been carefully and sympathetically read than he has been hustled into a dusty place of honor by conventional encomium, or relegated to the ranks of the inconsiderable on the ground that he is a mere "Chaucerian," a petty tracer of his master's matchless strokes.

This meager attention may be due primarily to the admitted difficulty of Douglas' language. While the intrinsic difficulty of Middle-Scots dialect is easily exaggerated, Douglas' own blend of Scots, Latin, French, and "Sudroun" may be sufficiently thorny to disquiet a reader of Chaucer, Henryson, and Dunbar. George Eyre-Todd [in his *Medieval Scottish Poetry,* 1892] has no hesitation in ascribing to Douglas the greatest degree of obscurity in language to be found among the Scots poets, and even such an enthusiast for Middle-Scots poetry as Gregory Smith is so preoccupied with his unusual diction as to conclude [in the *Cambridge History of English Literature,* 1932] that the primary interest in Douglas' work must be philological.

Moreover, the "Chaucerians" are by the very designation taxed with lack of originality. Though some have thought to defend them by the lame suggestion that the allegorical machinery of the May morning, the dream in the garden of the rose and the rest, outworn in England by the fifteenth century, was yet fresh enough in Scotland, such a defense condemns as much as it commends. Such an assumption licenses the critic to dismiss Douglas with a few polite comments on the genuine feeling for nature which lifts fragments of his poetry to creditability by modern standards. In consequence that poet is ordinarily read, if at all, only through the anthologists' unvarying choice of the prologues to the seventh and twelfth books of the ***Eneados:*** one a description of a Scottish winter, and the other of the conventional May morning.

Even among the admirers of the Chaucerians Douglas has had scarcely his due. While Dunbar has enjoyed at least in Scotland a major revival and Henryson has recently been subjected to a good deal of critical attention, most scholars seem to have been content to accept Gregory Smith's disparagement of Gavin Douglas as the "last and least" of the poets of one of Scotland's golden ages. The pronouncements of so distinguished a scholar cannot have failed of effect in fixing critical opinion. Unhappily, this judgment of Douglas appears to arise less from a sober evaluation of his poetry than from violent reaction against an earlier portrayal of the poet as a child of the Renaissance, writing in "the pure Virgilian strain" [W. J. Courthope, *A History of English Poetry,* 1897], who is "thoroughly interpenetrated with the Virgilian atmosphere and succeeds in communicating this to the reader" [T. F. Henderson, *Scottish Vernacular Literature,* 1898]. The elaborate depreciation of the poet in Gregory Smith's *The Transition Period* is essentially polemical rather than critical. It may be argued that in his zeal for correcting one common misconception, the author has substituted another which is even wider of the mark. Certainly his conclusion that Douglas' "Vergil is, for the most part, the Vergil of the dark ages, part prophet, part wizard, master of 'illusions by devillich werkis and coniurationis' " is demonstrably mistaken.

Examination of this line in context reveals that Gregory Smith, perhaps too mindful of the familiar legends traced by Comparetti in his *Vergil in the Middle Ages,* has leaped to a hasty conclusion unsupported by the full text. Actually, the poet is only arguing reasonably that not only the sixth book of the *Aeneid,* which Caxton "callis it fenyeit" and omits ostensibly on that ground, is fable, but that "Sa is all Vergill perchance, for, by his leif, / Juno nor Venus goddes neuer wer," and that Eneas could as well tour hell as Theseus or Hercules. Moreover,

> Quha wait gif he in visioun hiddir went,
> By art magik, sorcery, or enchantment,
> And with his faderis saul did speik and meit,
> Or in the liknes with sum wthir spreit,
> Lyke as the spreit of Samuell, I ges,
> Rasit to King Saul was by the Phitones?
> I will nocht say all Virgill bene als trew,
> Bot at sic thingis ar possible this I schew;
> Als in thai days war ma illusionis
> By deuillich werkis and coniurationis,
> Than now thair bene, so doith clerkis determe,
> For, blist be God, the faith is now mair ferme.

Douglas is saying simply that although the age of miracles and magic is past, there is no more reason to question the authority of Vergil on Aeneas' descent through Avernus than to cavil at the scriptural account of the Witch of Endor. In no way, either here or elsewhere, does Douglas imply any notion of Vergil himself as a wizard, a *master* of "illusionis by deuillich werkis and coniurationis." For him the days when there were "ma illusionis" are clearly the misty times of heroic legend, and not the enlightened age of Augustan Rome.

Thus it appears that Gregory Smith's scoffing at Douglas' claim to any Renaissance quality rests upon a frail foundation: a mistaken imputation to the poet of ignorant acceptance of the necromancy tradition, an "unillumined thirteenth-century erudition," and "his indifferentism, his inability to care for full artistic enjoyment." This is nineteenth-century Romantic criticism, and far enough from the literary theory of the Renaissance, to which we must return for a sounder estimate of the place of Douglas' ***Eneados*** in literary history.

But Gregory Smith is by no means alone in establishing or perpetuating misconceptions which could not survive a careful reading of Douglas' text. His translation of the *Aeneid* has since his own time been recognized as his most important accomplishment in letters, but such a catalogue of notices of the poem as appears in Lauchlan MacLean Watt's discussion entitled "The Man and his Fame" [in his edition of Douglas's *Aeneid,* 1920] serves only to illustrate the astonishing ignorance of his work which has characterized the perpetuators of his fame. It is all too evident that with few exceptions the historians and scholars who for something over four centuries have allowed Douglas some measure of literary reputation knew the translation only through earlier accounts of it, or at best through first hand acquaintance with one or two of the prologues. These authors exhibit a confusion as to the number of books the poet translated, an extreme looseness and generality of language, and the persistent error of praising the ***Eneados*** as a strict line-for-line rendering of the *Aeneid.* This error is the less excusable in light of the poet's having in his prologue to Book I disclaimed any such attempt:

> Sum tyme the text mon haue ane expositioun,
> Sum tyme the colour will caus a little additioun.

As he doubtless intended from the first, Douglas has added several hundred lines over the total of the Latin original.

The revival of interest in Middle Scots poetry stimulated by the intense Scottish nationalism of the eighteenth century allowed Douglas some attention, but understandably led to no very critical estimate of his work. The scholar-patriot Thomas Ruddiman edited in 1710 *The Threttene Bukes of Eneados* in a handsome volume including "Testimonies of Learned Men" full of traditional inaccuracies, a *Life* by Bishop Sage, and notes and glossary. It is surprising that Ruddiman and his Jacobite circle should have chosen to republish a poet who suffered persecution and exile because of his English sympathies and alliances, and noteworthy that they managed to overlook Gavin Douglas' somewhat unsavory intrigues for ecclesiastical preferment as a protege of Henry VIII. These intrigues, for which the poet was banished as a traitor in 1519, evidently alienated many of his nineteenth-century critics. In any event, it is evident from Ruddiman's remarkable notes and glossary that his attention was focussed rather upon Douglas' dialect than upon his ideas: the poet as Scot, rather than the Scot as poet.

Those nineteenth-century critics and historians of poetry who did not allow themselves to be offended by his political morality seem to have been interested in Douglas principally as a nature poet or, in an excess of enthusiasm, as "a lonely scholar in the midst of Vandal surroundings," "a bright herald of the New Learning" [Andrew Lang, in

Ward's English Poets, 1880]. It is the latter view, presented largely as an unsupported assertion, that Gregory Smith has been at such pains to discredit.

Since Gregory Smith's studies, only one extended discussion of Gavin Douglas has appeared, Lauchlan MacLean Watt's *Douglas's Aeneid.* The author announces in his preface an admirable design: "This is an attempt to elucidate Gawain Douglas's work, and to place it in its proper setting as a literary document, in the hope that, until something better is achieved, this may fill a blank in Scottish Literature. My excuse is that it has not before been done." In his approach to the poem, however, Watt has relied too much on the tools of the rhetorician. In one aureate generalization he asserts: "Douglas's ***Aeneid*** is, in fact, an open door through which the spirit of Northern poetry walked into the wide fields of the South. *The Kingis Quair* was a window ajar, letting in the melody of the World's music, Northward blown. This poem of Douglas is, however, not a passive thing but an actively originating force. For the first time, Scottish poetry crosses the Borders and stirs the sleepers." This otherwise unaccountable statement is based upon the similarity [George Frederick Nott, in his *The Works of Surrey and Wyatt* (1815),] finds between Surrey's translation of the *Aeneid* and Douglas' version, first published in 1553 and therefore readily available to Surrey. But this striding spirit of Northern poetry is nowhere explicitly defined, and one is reluctant to credit such extravagant claims for Douglas' influence on English poetry.

The entirely curious history of Gavin Douglas' literary reputation suggests that assignment of the poet to his appropriate position in literary history must depend upon a fresh examination of the whole of the ***Eneados*** with a scrupulous effort to avoid some of the biasses, patriotic, sentimental, philological, and biographical, which have vitiated most criticism of the poem as a work of literature. This paper undertakes such a reexamination.

The very considerable undertaking of ***The XIII Bukes of Eneados of the famose Poete Virgil*** "Translatet out of Latyne verses into Scottish metir, bi the Reuerend Father in God, Mayster Gawin Douglas" was completed after eighteen months' labor, in June 1513. Its composition falls thus within the period of English translations from the classics justly described by Henry B. Lathrop [in his *Translations from the Classics into English from Craxton to Chapman,* 1933] as stylistically helpless, "without regularity of syntax, or definiteness of emphasis, or clearness of connection" and for the most part simply crude. Very few translators worked directly from the Latin, preferring like Caxton a French recension; when they did translate directly from the original, they flabbily multiplied synonyms and rendered metaphors in distressingly literal and pedestrian fashion. If Gavin Douglas is to be measured against his contemporaries—translators among whom Lathrop finds Caxton only the least inept—his achievement in the ***Eneados*** stands out boldly. It is incontestably the first translation of Vergil's *Aeneid* into any English dialect; it is unmistakably translated from the original Latin, with a sure hand, and with a humanistic scholar's scorn for the French recension substituted by Caxton for the masterpiece. Douglas translated the entire twelve books (and appended the Mapheus Vegius thirteenth) in contrast to the completion of two books by Surrey, four by the graceless Stanyhurst, and nine by Phaer. In this respect Douglas is so far in advance of his age as to outdistance almost all of the English translators before Golding. Even in the Erasmian period described by Lathrop it was rare for a translator to render more than a fraction of his original, and it was not until the early seventeenth century that complete translations were ordinarily even projected. But it is on grounds quite other than mere bulk or successful Latinity that Douglas' ***Eneados*** is to be established as a work of literary and historical significance, and not dismissed as the "happy accident" which Gregory Smith would have it.

The first step by the literary historian, and one too often "orhippit quyte" in evaluating Gavin Douglas, might well be to examine the poet's own statements of his intent and his literary theory. Douglas is astonishingly explicit for an age considered so unselfconscious; in his prologue to the first book he has much to say and to intimate on his score. To be sure, he begins with a thoroughly conventional "commendacyon" of Vergil, piling up the familiar series of aureate terms:

> Mast reuerend Virgill, of Latyne poetis prince,
> Gemme of ingine and fluide of eloquence,
> Thow peirles perle, patroun of poetrie,
> Rois, register, palme, laurer and glory,
> Chosin cherbukle, cheif flour and cedir tree,
> Lanterne, leidsterne, mirrour, and *a per se,*
> Master of masteris, sweit sours and springand
> well . . .

It is a commonplace that Vergil and Ovid were the unfailing favorites throughout the Middle Ages, and the enthusiasm and veneration Douglas is expressing is quite as characteristic of the Renaissance. Nevertheless, the manner of expression here is as much a formula as is the praise of Chaucer which appears later in the same prologue. Probably Douglas' references to his own "bad harsk speche and lewit thong," his "ignorant blabring imperfyte," and "corruptit cadens imperfyte" are to be interpreted similarly. In the light of Douglas' spirited defense of his method and of his accomplishment isseems clear that these phrases represent conventional humility, and not scorn for "Scottis metir" or contempt for his own poetic powers. One is reminded of the literary modesty of Douglas' acknowledged master Chaucer and of most of his contemporaries.

If the reader continues though the latter portion of the prologue—which appears to have been too rarely, or too casually read—he is refreshed by the tone of individuality and conviction which is there so unmistakable. Douglas is surely not posturing when he exclaims against "that Caxtoun" who

> In pross hes prent ane buik of Inglis gros,
> Clepand it Virgill in Eneados,
> Quhilk that he sais of Frensch he did translait,
> It hes na thing ado therwith, God wait,
> Nor na mair like than the devill and Sanct Aus-
> tyne.

The charges laid against Caxton illuminate both translations. George Saintsbury [in his *History of English Prosody,* 1906] has called Douglas "furiously angry with Caxton for not doing what he never pretended to do with Virgil." But actually Caxton seems to have invited such an attack by his representation of the "lytyl book in frenshe, which late was translated out of latyne by some noble clerke of fraunce" as "made in laytne by that noble poete and grete clerke vyrgyll," and by his suggestion that if "only man . . . fyndeth such termes that he cannot vnderstand, late hym goo rede and lerne vyrgyll (or the pystles of ouyde) and there he shall se and vnderstande lyghtly all." Caxton's *Aeneis,* actually a translation of *Le Livre des Eneydes,* follows the French romance in so altering the emphasis that the great original is barely recognizable. As a churchman and a classicist, Douglas may have had little taste for romances in any circumstances; certainly he has reason to bridle at the spectacle of an adapted chivalric romance masquerading as Vergil. Douglas is convinced that poor Caxton "Knew neuer thre wowrdis of all that Virgile ment." The translator has done violence to the fable, Douglas asserts, by omitting wholly the first three books (save "ane little twiching Polidorus" and the tempest sent by Æolus), and the fifth and sixth books. He has consistently confused his gods and garbled his geography:

> For Caxtoun puttis in his bulk out of tone,
> The storme furth sent be Eolus and Neptone;
> Bot quha that redis Virgill suthfastlie
> Sall fynd Neptune salf Eneas navie.
>
> Thus ay for Tibir, Touyr puttis he,
> Quhilk mony hundreit mylis sundry be.

At the clumsy huddling together of the final six books, "I hald my toung for schame bytand my lip." This rehearsal of Caxton's perversion of Vergil's epic concludes on a note of resignation as well as of horror:

> Quhat suld I langar on his errouris dwell?
> Thai bene sa plaine, and eik so mony fald,
> The hundreith part tharof I laif ontald.

But it is something much more important to him than Caxton's irritating minor inaccuracies, or the perverse delight in flyting which is common enough among Scots and scholars, that has led Douglas to this outraged attack. It is unnecessary to doubt his sincerity when he exclaims:

> I nald ye trast I saide this for dispyte,
> For me list with na Inglis buikis flyte,
> Na with na bogil na browny to debait,
> Noder auld gaistis nor spretis deid of lait,
> Nor na man wil I lakkin or despyse,
> My werkis till authoreis be sik wyse.
> Bot tuiching Virgillis honor and reuerence,
> Quha euer contrarie, I mon stand at defence.

It is the righteous indignation of the moralistic man of letters that Caxton has aroused when he

> So schamfully that storye did pervert;
> I red his werk with harmes at my hert.

Douglas' bitterest objection, significantly, scores the wildly disproportionate emphasis accorded the story of Dido, which though scarcely the twelfth part in Vergil's text makes up more than half of Caxton's, and is there clearly the center of interest. As Douglas well knew, neither Caxton nor his French original was initially responsible for this romanticizing of the *Aeneid.* As early as the twelfth century, French poets were restyling the epic poem in precisely the manner of *Le Livre des Eneydes;* the *Roman d'Encas* is characteristic of the tradition Caxton is merely perpetuating. Indeed, as Miss Nitchie demonstrates in her *Vergil and the English Poets,* it is Douglas and not Caxton who is taking a new tack in his conception of the story:

> Gower and Lydgate, as we have seen, made many references to Dido and Aeneas, but they were in the main conventional, and the result of a knowledge of the romantic conception of the story rather than a scholarly acquaintance with the original. There is a certain amount of survival of this conventional attitude in the poems of the Renaissance, especially in the lyrics of the Elizabethan collections of songs and sonnets. Dido is still in many cases the forsaken woman, and Aeneas the false traitor, the type of unfaithfulness in man as Cressid is of unfaithfulness in woman, and Penelope of faithfulness faithfulness and Helen of beauty.

Douglas cannot countenance the romantic conception of the *Aeneid* which others found palatable, for one compelling reason. With his interpretation of the epic the notion of Aeneas as a traitor, either political or venereal, is utterly incompatible. In the context of the Middle-Scots translation Dido symbolizes, not the forsaken woman, but "unlesum luve." For Douglas, she is necessarily and properly renounced, albeit not without pain and regret, by the "trew prynce Enee." Although in the ***Palice of Honour*** (1509) Douglas has been content to place in the train of Venus "Dido with her fals lufe Enee," four years later he is at considerable pains to acquit the hero of all stains whatever. So strongly does he feel that he even takes issue with his master Chaucer. In the *Legende of Good Women,* Douglas remembers, Chaucer has said Aeneas was "forsworne' to Dido, and has gone so far as to style him "fals tratour." If this be accepted, Douglas argues, then Vergil's diligence has come to nought, and "His twelf yeris labouris war nocht worth a myte." Defending Aeneas, his apologist asserts that the hero forsook Dido only at the command of the gods and in fulfillment of his high destiny:

> That war repreif to thair diuinite,
> And na reproche vnto the said Enee. . . .
> Sen the command of God obey suld all,
> And undir his chargis na wrangus deid may fall.

Douglas is quite willing to indulge Chaucer in his particular misinterpretation and misemphasis:

> Bot sickirlie, of resoun me behuvis
> Excuse Chaucer fra all maner repruvis,
> In loifing of thir laydis lilly quhyte
> He set on Virgile and Eneas this wyte;
> For he was euer, God wait, wemenis frend.

No such charity is extended to Caxton, and it may not have occurred to the poet that Caxton's *Aeneid* was directed to the very taste that found Chaucer's *Legende* and Henryson's *Testament of Cresseid* both charming and affecting. Though most of the abuse Douglas heaps upon

Caxton belongs more justly upon the head of the anonymous author of *Le Livre des Eneydes,* the real object of his attack is an idea and not a man. Caxton's unforgivable sin is that in substituting a French romance under the title and color of the Latin epic, he has degraded into something mean the work which was to the scholar-moralist a "myrrour of verteu" of all but canonical authority. Late in the first prologue Douglas makes his own reading of the Trojan hero explicit:

Our werk desiris na lewit rebaldaill,
Full of nobilite is this story alhaill.
For euery vertu belangand a noble man,
This ornait poet bettir than ony can
Payntand descrivis in persoun of Eneas;
Nocht for to say sic ane Eneas was,
Yit than by him perfitlie blasonis he
All wirschep, manheid and nobilite,
He hated vice, abhorring craftineis,
He was a myrrour of verteu, and of grais,
Just in his promys euer, and stout in mynd,
To God faythful, and to his frendys kynd,
Verteous, vyse, gentil, and liberall,
In feates of war, excelling vderis all,
Witht euery bountie belangand a gentle knycht,
Ane prince, ane conquerour, or a vailseand wycht.

It is not the history of Aeneas, but the *myth* of Aeneas which engages Douglas, as he clearly recognizes and admits. And the idea of Aeneas as the embodiment of manly virtue and political sagacity becomes the informing principle of the entire translation.

In Douglas' ***Eneados,*** then, appears a prototype of the ideal prince who is to occupy so much of the attention of the poets of the English Renaissance. While in Boccaccio's *De Casibus Virorum Illustrium* and in Lydgate's *Fall of Princes* the melancholy tales of princes and noblemen come to grief are taken as examples of the mutability of fortune, Douglas' rendering of Vergil insists upon the superiority to fortune of a prince who possesses humanity, integrity, and resolution. In his typically Renaissance view Douglas looks to and beyond the *Mirror for Magistrates,* which concerns itself not only with "how frayle and unstable worldly prosperity is founde, where Fortune seemeth most highly to favour," but with the manner in which "vices are punished in great princes and magistrates." Douglas' Turnus would fit as well into the *Mirror* as did Douglas' king, who found his way into that work in consequence of his stubbornness and impetuosity at Flodden. His Dido, as presented in the prologue to Book IV, fits into the same pattern:

Allace, thi dolorus cace and hard myschance!
From blis to wo, fra sorow to fury rage,
Fra nobillnes, welth, prudence and temperance,
In brutall appetite fall, and wild dotage;
Danter of Affrik, Quene fundar of Cartage,
Vmquhile in riches and schynyng gloir ryngyng,
Throw fuliche lust wrocht thi awin vndoing.

The real focus of Douglas' attention, however, is upon the ideal ruler and the virtues to be imitated, using by way of contrast the vices to be eschewed. And it is more plausible, as well as more generous, to find in Douglas' approach to the *Aeneid* evidence of a scholarly understanding and appreciation of his original rather than proof of naivete and a quaint medievalism which [according to Watt] "lead[s] Douglas, as with a bias, away from the New Birth." That original, it must be remembered, was designed to glorify Rome and Augustus through identification with the epic hero. Aeneas is held up as a moral and religious ideal, and it is not too much to say that in his championship of peace, reconciliation, law and piety, rather than military glory, Vergil is writing as a political apologist for Augustus. Evidence that Douglas the humanist knew well enough what Vergil meant Aeneas to represent to the Romans appears in one of his own notes inscribed on the Cambridge manuscript: "Bot ye sall knaw that the principall entent of Virgill was to extoll the Romanys, and in specyal the famyllye or clan Julyan, that commin from this Ascanyus, son to Eneas and Crevsa, otherwais callyt Iulus: because the empryour August Octauyan, quhamto he direkkit this wark, was of that hows and blud, and sistyr son to Cesar Julyus."

If Douglas was thus clear in his statements of intent, in his vigorous disavowal of chivalrous or romantic interest in the *Aeneid,* and his scholarly appreciation of the historical context of the original, it remains only to demonstrate that the political and moral focus of the allegory is borne out in the translation as a whole.

Aside from the prologues and notes, it is in his expansions that the poet most obviously reveals his preoccupation with the political implications for the sixteenth century of Vergil's great symbol. A few examples should suffice to point up the nature of the lessons wise and virtuous princes were expected to glean from these pages. Beside the passage in the Sixth Book concerning the unhappy Tantalus, the 1553 editor of Douglas' ***Eneados*** has placed the rubric: "He signifies Tirannis lyfis to be vncertane, ful of fear, and nocht durabyl." The peculiarities of William Copland's editorship is a matter for later discussion, but in this instance Douglas has clearly invited such interpretation by expanding three and a half lines into seven and identifying as Tantalus the tyrant an eternally frustrated shade who is not directly named in the original. A more striking example of Douglas' method appears a few lines later in the account of Phlegyas and Sisyphus. Vergil has written:

Saxum ingens volvunt alii, radisque rotarum
Destricti pendent; sedet aeternumque sedebit
Infelix Theseus, Plegyasque miserrimus omnis
Admonet et magna testatur voce per umbras:
'Discite iustitiam moniti et non temnere divos.'

The Scottish translator renders the passage

For sum weltris a gret stane wp the bra,
Of quhom in number is Sisyphus ane of tha:
On quhelis spakis speldit vtheris hingis;
The maist wrechit of all princis and kingis,
Phlegias, wmquile king of Thessaly,
All mortale wychtis admonises, with his cry
And lowd voce throw the dirk awitnessing:
Be myne example all wychtis, prince and king,
Lernis, quod he, to hant justice and rycht,
And nocht to contemne the goddis strenth and mycht.
Thair sittis eik, and sall sit euermair,
The fey wnhappy Theseus full of cair.

Whereas in Vergil the unspecifically miserable Phlegyas voices a general warning against injustice and impiety, in the Scottish version he is a "wrechit *prince*" exhorting "all wychtis," to be sure, but principally "*prince and king*" to heed his example.

Interestingly and perhaps significantly, Douglas foregoes an attack upon the notorious Tarquins in favor of an extended eulogy of Brutus:

> Vis et Tarquinios reges animamque superbam
> Ultoris Bruti, fascesque videre receptos?
> Consulis imperium hic primus, saevasque secures
> Accipiet; natosque pater, nova bella moventes,
> Ad poenam pulchra pro libertate vocabit.
> Infelix! Utcunque ferent ea facta minores:
> Vincit amor patria laudamque immensa cupido.

> Pleas the behald the Tarquynes, kingis tuo,
> And the stout curage of Brutus also,
> Quhilk can revenge the wrang in his cuntre;
> His gret honour gif thow list heir or se,
> And ensen yeis send fra Ethurianis,
> This ilk Brutus sall first amang Romanis
> Ressaue the dignite and stait consulare:
> With heding swerd, baith felloun, scherp, and gair,
> Befoir hym borne throw all Romis toun,
> In takin of justice executioun,
> His awin sonnis, moving vnkyndlie weir,
> To pvnitioun and deid sall dampne in feir,
> To keip fransches and souerane libertie;
> And thus onsilly fader sall he be.
> How sa evir the peple his fatale deides
> In tyme to cum sall blasoun, quha thaim redis,
> The fervent luif of his kynd native land,
> And excedand desyre he bair on hand
> Of honour and hie glory to ressaue,
> Mot al evil rumour fra his lawd bywaif.

If one is prepared to accept Gregory Smith's judgment of "the garrulous Provost of St. Giles" this may be set down as mere diffuseness. Read more sympathetically, it echoes the characteristic abhorrence of rebellion and civil strife found throughout sixteenth-century English literature, and most eloquently expressed in Shakespeare's history plays. Again, Vergil's famous lines:

> Tu regere imperio populos, Romane, memento,
> Hae tibi erunt artes, pacisque imponere morem,
> Parcere subjectis et debellare superbos.

in Douglas become:

> Bot thow, Romane, remember, as lord and syre,
> To rewle the pepill vndir thyne impyre;
> Thir sall thi craftis be at weil may seme,
> The paix to modyfy and eik manteme,
> To pardoun all cumis yoldin and recreant,
> And prowd rabellis in batale for to dant.

Douglas is careful to spell out Aeneas' defense of his motives in waging the "onhappy weyr" and his reiterated desire for peace and amity.

> Quaequam vos tanto fortuna indigna, Latini,
> Implicuit bello, qui nos fugiatis amicos?
> Pacem me exanimis et Martis sorte peremptis
> Oratis? equidem et vivis concedere vellem.
> Nec veni, nisi fata locum sedemque dedissent,
> Nec bellum cum gente gero: rex nostra reliquit
> Hospitia et Turni potius se credidit armis.
> Aequius huic Turnum fuerat se opponere morti.

> O Latyn folkis, quhat misfortoun onglaid
> Hes you involuit in sa onhappy weyr,
> That ye chais ws away, your frendis deir?
> Desyre ye pece bot for thame that bene lost
> By marcyall fayt, and slane into this ost?
> And I, forsuyth, tyll all that levand be
> Wald glaidly grant the sammyn, I say for me.
> Neuir hydder had I cummyn, war nocht, perfay,
> Into this steid the fatis hecht for ay
> Our resting place providit and herbry,
> Ne na weirfeir with your pepill leid I.
> Bot your kyng hes our confiderans vpgeve,
> And rather hes settin all his beleve
> On Turnus vassalage and his hie prowes:
> Thocht moyr equale and ganand war, I ges,
> To this Turnus, the brekar of our pece
> Till aventur hymself to de in prece.

Jupiter's ten-line remonstrance against the strife between the Trojans and the Rutilians is expanded in Douglas to a twenty-four-line invective against war. Even in the translation of Vegius' Thirteenth Book of the *Aeneid,* devoted as it is to Christian allegory, Douglas is still preoccupied by the noble and magnanimous prince, who should seek always for peace. Where Vegius has written:

> Turnus ut extremo devictus Marte profudit
> Effugientem animam, medioque sub agmine victor
> Magnanimus stetit Aeneas, Mavortius heros.

and Thomas Twynne translates simply:

> When Turnus in this finall fight downthrowne, his flittring ghost
> Has yeelded up into the aire, in middest of all the host
> Aeneas valient victour stands, god Mavors champion bold.

Douglas reminds us again of Aeneas' position in the state:

> As Turnus, in the lattyr bargan lost,
> Venquest in feild, yald furth the fleand gost,
> This marciall prynce, this ryall lord Enee,
> As victor full of magnanimite,
> Amyddis baith the rowtis baldly standis.

In the eleventh prologue the poet has outlined the doctrine of the mean as "Aristotill in his Ethikis doith expres," with particular concern for the

> verteu souerane
> According princis, hecht magnanymite,
> . . .a bonte set betwix vicis tuane.

Never in Douglas' Vergil does Aeneas fall short of the magnanimity proper to a "crysten knycht and kyng." Turnus, however, brave and noble as he is, exhibits the extremes of foolhardiness, stubbornness, and impetuosity that lead inevitably to his ruin. It is ironical that James IV, who was unquestionably intended to profit by the example, was too nearly of the temperament of Turnus. Barely three months after the completion of the ***Eneados,*** Douglas' luckless king, whom the poet's father had tried in vain to dissuade from an assault upon the forces of that English Aeneas, Henry Tudor, fell at Flodden Field and became himself a melancholy example for the instruction of princes and magistrates.

Though Gavin Douglas is throughout his translation deliberately emphasizing the political lessons to be gleaned by a sixteenth-century prince from the pages of Vergil, and though topical political allegory lay ready to hand, it is noteworthy that he gains his emphasis not by perverting the original, but by making unmistakable the *sentens* that could be obscured by a merely literal rendering of the Latin. The result is not merely a textbook for schoolboys, nor a tale interesting only for its fable, nor a mere exercise in scholarship, as various scholars have styled it. It is instead a prototype of the Renaissance cultural and political epic.

In his illuminating discussion of the epic before Milton, E. M. W. Tillyard [in *The Miltonic Setting, Past and Present,* 1938] has provided an admirable summary of a tradition with which we now have every reason to identify Gavin Douglas. He says in part:

> This notion of the great 'example' was to dominate much Renaissance literature . . . in its beginnings, it was connected with contemporary politics. . . . Serious men were cruelly aware how vital it was to train the prince to be a good ruler; and the energies of serious literature were directed to that object. Its highest work was to educate the growing prince or to instruct the mature one. And its peculiar and most effective method was through the great example.

Although he is perhaps the earliest, Douglas is not alone among Renaissance translators with this political bias. Barclay's dedication of his version of Sallust's *Jugurtha* (ca. 1520) to the Duke of Norfolk recommends it as "fruytful, profitable, and ryght necessary" to noblemen who would attain fame and honor. Sir Anthony Cope in his dedication of a recension of Livy (1554) took occasion to advise Henry VIII to go to war with France and Scotland on the worthy examples of "Anniball of Carthage, and Scipio of Rome." In the year of Douglas' first printing, 1553, appeared the translation by John Brende of Quintus Curtius' *History of the Acts of Alexander.* This version was dedicated to the Duke of Northumberland, in the office of Earl Marshall, and in the preface appears the familiar moral:

> There is required in all magistrates both a fayth and feare in God, and also an outward policye in worldly thynges, whereof as the one is to be learned by the scryptures, so the other must chiefly be gathered by the reading of histories. . . . In histories it is apparent how dangerous it is to begyn alteracions in a commen wealthe. How enuy and hatredes oft rising vpon smal causes, haue ben the destruction of great kyngdomes. And that disobeyers of hygher powers, & suche as rebellyd agaynst magystrates, neuer escapyd punishment, nor came to good end.

The bitter experiences of civil strife which so exercised the Renaissance humanists in England, and the habits of mind they gave rise to, are evident outside Douglas' poetry. His memorandum to Henry VIII against the Duke of Albany is eloquent of his concern for political parallels. The poet-politician makes much of the fact that the proud Duke's father "deyt banneist, forfaltit and rebell to the Crovne of Scotlaund," and hints darkly that Albany as regent of Scotland has opportunities and ambitions dangerously akin to those of Richard III:

> Item, all sik thingis beand saddlie rememberyt, sik mysordour and crudelite bypast considerit aucht wele to reduce the cruell example of King Rycharde to remembrance; and how a man of sik mynde, and beand suspect be euident tokynys preceding, havand the hole reule of ony realme, and beand also thairin, may find mony wayis to vsurpe the crovne, and all to layt war to provyde remede tharfor quhen the harme may not be redressit, as God forbyd so suld fall, for als moche as than the said Duke wald or mycht allege and pretend sum coloratt tytill or clame to the crovne, quhare now he has non sik, for in the Kyng of Scottis, God saufe his Grace! restis and regnis the trew ondowtyt bloode of Inglaund Scotlaunde and Denmerk.

Never in Gavin Douglas' lifetime was Scotland free from the factional strife in which his powerful family was deeply involved, and which ultimately forced the poet himself into exile for his English sympathies. As poet and as politician Douglas was steadfastly on the side which advocated peace with England and the suppression of the turbulent noblemen at home. It may be reasonably argued that his political and poetical careers are thus essentially consistent and intimately related; the long standing notion that Douglas the poet must somehow be excused and forgiven for his unaccountable degeneration into a disreputable politician need no longer concern us.

The status as a political document which the ***Eneados*** had assumed by the date of its first printing is established simply by the nature of the 1553 Black Letter edition. This volume has been called the Protestant edition because Douglas' allusions to the Virgin are systematically omitted, along with the discussion of Purgatory and other elements which smacked of Roman Catholicism. For the purposes of this inquiry, however, the significant alteration of Douglas' text is the addition by William Copland, the printer, of marginal rubrics. Whenever by any stretch of the imagination a given passage can be interpreted as a precept for princes, there appears a marginal rubric to direct the reader's attention; when that element is not in evidence, tens of pages are left innocent of marginal comment. Copland's enthusiasm for the instruction of princes led him into occasional excesses and far fetched applications. In the passage concerning Æolus, for example, opposite the line "Gaif theme ane kyng, quhilk as thar lord and juge" appears the note: "The office of a Prince." Where Aeneas is scanning the sea for traces of his scattered fleet, Copland offers: "He descriueth ane prince to haue more cure of his people then of himself." Of the words to comfort the "drery cheir" of his companions: "A constant orison of Eneas full of consolation wyth the which as a nobyl valyeant Prynce he exhortes his men to pacience in aduersity." To call attention to Ilioneus' eulogy of Aeneas: "The iustice, wisdome, fortitude, and temperance of Eneas." Where Douglas has translated the account of Priam's mercy toward Sinon without embellishment save for the section heading

> Yit of the traitouris fals contfrivit slycht,
> That was beleifit, allace! with euery wycht

the editor moralizes in the margin to this effect: "Nobill princys of simplicite are oft tymes deceuyed be crafty men, whyche is a gret falt and negligens in princis." Of Anchises' reluctance to flee fallen Troy, which Douglas has rendered simply

> Bot he refusis or euir to leif in joye
> Eftir the rewyne and destructioun of Troye;
> To suffir exile he said at he na couth.

the zealous Copland insists: "A good prince desyreth not to liue seinge the destructyon of his natiue countre."

It is unnecessary to multiply examples of the 1553 editor's passion for the instruction of magistrates. Though it is probable that neither Vergil nor Gavin Douglas would have pressed some of the interpretations of individual passages, the morals drawn are rarely inconsistent with the tone of either the *Aeneid* or the ***Eneados.*** The interpretation of the epic which Douglas implies or boldly states through prologues, notes, expansions, and shifts of emphasis is seen to be wholly acceptable to the sixteenth-century reader. Within "dirk poetry," Douglas has said, lies hidden much practical instruction for all Christian men, but most particularly for princes and magistrates. Much has been written about the moralistic bias which characterizes the English Renaissance; too little has been written of the roots of that tradition, with which Gavin Douglas must properly be identified. He can but unjustly be dismissed as a "mere Chaucerian," provincial and essentially medieval in scope and outlook. He deserves instead a place in the honored company of Erasmus, among the serious and enlightened humanistic scholars of the English Renaissance. As Bush has so brilliantly shown in *The Renaissance and English Humanism,* the new learning represented no sudden and complete emancipation from medievalism. If Douglas emerges as a transitional figure, it is because there existed side-by-side in the ***Eneados*** the allegory of the ideal Christian Prince and that of the individual Christian soul. Heretofore, when Douglas' allegory has been examined at all, it is the second element which has been noted to the exclusion of the first. But even when both are considered, the result is not an incongruous wedding of incompatible "medieval" and "Renaissance" elements.

Douglas is actually a consistent Christian humanist whose attitudes parallel closely those of the brilliant array of scholars at the court of Henry VII and Henry VIII. Douglas' Vergil, far from the "Virgil of the Dark Ages, part prophet, part wizard, master of 'devillich werkis and coniurations'," is essentially the Vergil of the Renaissance, recognized as the court poet of Augustan Rome, and as instructor alike of first- and sixteenth-century princes and noble men. (pp. 845-62)

Bruce Dearing, "Gavin Douglas' 'Eneados': A Reinterpretation," in PMLA, *Vol. LXVII, No. 5, September, 1952, pp. 845-62.*

Arms of Bishop Gavin Douglas.

C. S. Lewis (essay date 1954)

[*A logician, Christian polemicist, and mythopoeic writer, Lewis is an acknowledged authority on medieval and Renaissance culture. He is also highly regarded as a perceptive literary critic and as a writer of fantasy literature. In the excerpt which follows, he presents Douglas as a transitional figure between the medieval and Renaissance periods and notes that the poet possessed a unique sense of history, in which he viewed Virgil more as a contemporary than a figure from the distant past.*]

[Our consideration of the sixteenth century] opens with the appearance (1501) of the ***Palice of Honour*** by Gavin Douglas, a young churchman of a great house, almost exactly the same age as the king. The problem of the poem 'Where does true Honour lie?' was one that probably had more than literary interest for the poet; and if his own political career after Flodden does not suggest that he solved it very well in practice, we need not thence assume that he did not ask it in good faith. It was perhaps not very easy during the regency of the Queen Dowager to see where Honour lay. Not, certainly, a modern will reply, in those intrigues with England (he almost begs Henry VIII to invade) of which Douglas stands convicted by his own letters. But even that was not quite obvious. The intrigues were family intrigues, the ambitions family ambitions. 'Your blood is maid for ever' was the bait the tempter, Adam Williamson, held out to him. External greatness for one's house—that certainly was one of the things that Honour meant in 1514. The word was ambiguous; it wavered before men's eyes with the same dazzle as (in later ages) 'Nature' or 'Wit' or 'Democracy'. But there is no denying that Douglas was wiser about it in 1501 than he was twelve years later; for when it comes to virtue, experience, as Kant tells us, is the mother of illusion.

The poem is substantially an original work and owes little to the *Séjour d'Honneur* of Octovien de St. Gelais. In the dream which it relates the various paths to Honour are represented by various processions or courts on progress. Sapience and her court pass by and 'To the Palice of Honour all thay go'. That may be the true path—nay, that certainly is *one* of the paths—to Honour; the way of intelligence, whether practical like Ulysses', or contemplative like Pythagoras'. One might become a great philosopher or a great statesman; only in the latter event—this is where Douglas's youthful vision was clearer than his mature vision—one must distinguish very carefully between true wisdom and 'craftynes, deceyt, and wit abused'. Sinon and Achitophel follow Sapience in vain on her journey to the Palice; 'our horsis oft, or we be thair, will founder'. Then there is, of course, the way of virginity (the court of Diane goes by). Women and men too have won immortal Honour by the triumph over the flesh. 'Bot few I saw with Diane haunt', says the poet. The truth is, he is in haste to describe the court of Venus which next rode by; the dazzling glory of courtly love and (no doubt) of a poetical career spent in its celebration. He spends stanza after stanza on it; and yet perhaps he likes even better the court that follows next. This is the 'court rethoricall':—

Yone is the court of plesand steidfastnes,
Yone is the court of constant merrines,
Yone is the court of joyous discipline.

Joyous discipline, the gay science, is poetry—and rhetoric too, for our modern distinction would have been unintelligible to the writer. When he represents this court as rescuing him from the anger of Venus, and when he follows it through the whole world to the Palice, he is in his own fashion saying like Keats and many another young poet:

Oh, for ten years that I may overwhelm
Myself in poesy!

But, like Keats again, he recognizes that there is a stage beyond that, and when we reach the Palice we find that it is founded on the craggy rocks of moral virtue, that the officers of true Honour have such names as Charity, Conscience, and Justice, and that Honour himself, seen only for a moment through 'a boir', a keyhole, and, in that moment blinding the seer's eyes, is God.

All this is, in my opinion, very well contrived and is, on the emotional level at least, a real resolution of the conflict with which the poet started; not a mere 'moral' stuck on as an afterthought. But to say only this is to leave out most of the quality of the work. That quality is prodigality; its vice is excess. The poet is still too delighted with the whole world of poetry, as he understood it, to control his delight. He is happily overwhelmed, like a surf-bather. All his reading, too often in the form of mere catalogue, pours into his poem. Everything that can be either gorgeously or terrifyingly described is introduced—May morning, desolate wilderness, journey, the pleasant plain by Hippocrene, stormy sea, late Gothic palace with 'Pinnakillis, fyelles, turnpekkis mony one', a magic mirror full of 'excelland schaddouis gracious', and the final presence chamber blazing with birds, flowers, and curious knots of burnished ivory and enamelled gold. He has chosen for his work—inevitably—the most difficult metre he can think of; the nine-lined stanza which has only two rhymes, and even this varied at certain points in Parts I and II by the almost impossible addition of a tenth line and in Part II by a different nine-lined form which gives a concluding couplet. Aureation with its indefinite licence of coinage makes such verse possible. It may also be supposed that the dullness of mere lists of names was concealed from the writer by the pleasure he took in fitting them in. One may call such ingenuity perverse, but one must not call it affected—unless the very young cyclist is affected when he first revels in the discovery that he can ride with his hands off the handle bars; and amidst all this virtuosity the imagination of the poet is alert and sensitive. In his opening lines Dawn has a 'russat mantill' (Horatio yet unborn), 'Eous' lifting his head from the sea restores 'the new collour that all the nicht lay deid', sweating horses shine as if they had been oiled, streams chattering over stones make a 'sober' noise in contrast to the 'birdis sang and sounding of the beis', and the sea-nymphs sit on the rocks 'dryand thair yallow hair'. Nor is the inner world neglected. Where the dream passes into nightmare and Douglas is alone in the frightful wilderness, his feelings are brought before us by the statement that, at this moment, the mere squeak of an unseen mouse would have been to him 'mair ugsum than the hell'. But then, later, and just as it ought to be in a dream, all his fear vanished, 'bot yit I wist not quhy'. Best of all is the passage in which, fearing that Venus may transform him into a beast (for angry goddesses have been known to do such things), he keeps on passing his hand over his face to make sure that it is still human.

It is worth noticing that these deliberate contrasts between scenes of beauty and scenes of terror are much helped by a variation in the language—a variation which would hardly have been possible to Chaucer and which depends on the fact . . . that Scotch poetry had become a bow with more than one string. You rendered beauty by aureation; for terror (as for bawdy or invective) you became 'boisteous' and native. Thus in a stanza from the Prologue describing the May morning the rhyming words run *lamentabill, sabill, circumstance, honorabill, amiabill, observance, plesance, amiabill, varyance;* but in a stanza from Part I describing the 'laithlie flude' the list is *routit, schoutid, fordeifit, doutit, sproutit, unleifit, leifit, moutit, reifit.* Douglas could have learned this from Henryson, in whose *Swallow and Other Birds* the stanzas on the seasons undergo a similar change as we reach winter. The young student will soon discover that in the 'Makers' the hard words which send him to the glossary tend to bunch at particular places. This is not an accident; just as the increase of Doric forms in the lyric parts of a Greek play is not an accident.

We can date the ***Palice of Honour*** from Douglas's own reference to it at the end of his Virgil. The lost works cannot be dated. Bale's *Index Brittanniae Scriptorum* credits him with 'golden stories' (*aureas narrationes*); Tanner's *Bibliotheca* adds *De Rebus Scoticis, Comoedias aliquot,* and a version of Ovid's *Remedium Amoris.* The punning poem *'Conscience',* which survives, is of no importance. *King Hart* is, but we have no conclusive evidence that Douglas wrote it. (pp. 76-80)

The plan of translating the *Aeneid* had been in Douglas's mind ever since 1501, for in the ***Palice*** Venus commissions him to perform that work. He finished it in 1513, having spent only eighteen months on the actual translation; but it bears in almost every line the impress of a mind so long steeped in Virgil that when he set pen to paper he knew exactly what had to be done and many of his problems (we may suppose) had been subconsciously solved. If I speak of this great work at some length I trust the reader will bear with me. Its greatness easily escapes modern eyes. The public for which it was intended no longer exists; the language in which it was written now awakes false associations or none; its very original has been obscured first by classicism and then by the decay of classicism. An effort is required of us.

The ***XIII Bukes of the Eneados,*** as Douglas called his version, were undertaken partly as a correction of Caxton's *Eneydos* (1490) which Douglas claims to have read 'with harmes at his hert', and he piques himself on the fidelity of his own version and even hopes that it will be fit for use in the schoolroom:

> a neidfull wark
> To thame wald Virgill to childryng expone;
> For quha list note my versis one by one
> Sall fynd tharin hys sentens every deill
> And almaiste word by word.
> (***Dyrectiown of his Buik.***)

The modern reader, whose Latin is likely to be better than his Scots, will test this claim most easily in the reverse manner—that is by keeping an open Virgil on his knees for glossary and comment while he is reading Douglas. He will find that *almaiste word by word* is an exaggeration: Douglas expands freely both for literary effect and also for the inclusion of explanations, and himself, in another place, has reminded us that Saint Gregory 'forbiddis ws to translait word eftir word'. But if he often inserts, he never omits; and the two texts are generally so close that a glance at one serves to elucidate anything that is difficult in the other. At worst, Douglas is a very honest translator and always lets you see how he is taking the Latin; his mistakes—for some he makes—are never sheltered by the vagueness of Dryden or Pope. His Virgil differed from the received text of our own days. In it the division between Books I and II came thirteen lines later than in ours. It had the reading *de collo fistula pendet,* which modern editors reject, at iii. 661, and *campus* for *campos* at vi. 640, and *lectisque* for *tectisque* at vii. 12. I suspect that it also gave *patriae* for *patrios* at vii. 636; and at ii. 737 and vi. 203 it had readings I am unable to identify.

Poetically, the first impression which Douglas's version makes on a modern English reader is one of quaintness. I am glad that the question of quaintness should cross our path so early . . ., let us get it out of the way once and for all. To the boor all that is alien to his own suburb and his 'specious present' (of about five years) is quaint. Until that reaction has been corrected all study of old books is unprofitable. To allow for that general quaintness which mere distance bestows and thus to be able to distinguish between authors who were really quaint in their own day and authors who seem quaint to us solely by the accident of our position—this is the very *pons asinorum* of literary history. An easy and obvious instance would be Milton's 'city or suburban' in *Paradise Regained.* Everyone sees that Milton could not have foretold the associations that those words now have. In the same way, when Douglas speaks of the Salii 'hoppand and singand wonder merely' in their 'toppit hattis' it is easy to remember that 'top hats', in our sense, were unknown to him. But it is not so easy to see aright the real qualities of his Scots language in general. Since his time it has become a *patois,* redolent (for those reared in Scotland) of the nursery and the Kailyard, and (for the rest of us) recalling Burns and the dialectal parts of the Waverley novels. Hence the laughter to which some readers will be moved when Douglas calls Leucaspis a 'skippair', or Priam 'the auld gray', or Vulcan the 'gudeman' of Venus; when *comes* becomes 'trew marrow' and Styx, like Yarrow, has 'braes', when the Trojans 'kecklit all' (*risere*) at the man thrown overboard in the boat race, or, newly landed in Latium, regaled themselves with 'scones'. For we see the language that Douglas wrote 'through the wrong end of the long telescope of time'. We forget that in his day it was a courtly and literary language,

> not made for village churls
> But for high dames and mighty earls.

Until we have trained ourselves to feel that 'gudeman' is no more rustic or homely than 'husband' we are no judges of Douglas as a translator of Virgil. If we fail in the training, then it is we and not the poet who are provincials.

About this first mental adjustment there can be no dispute; but there is another adjustment which I think necessary and which may not be so easily agreed to. Virgil describes Aeneas, on hearing Turnus's challenge, as *laetitia exsultans;* Douglas says 'he hoppit up for joy, he was so glad'. To get over the low associations of the verb 'hop' in modern English is the first adjustment. But even when this has been done, there remains something—a certain cheerful briskness—in Douglas which may seem to us very un-Virgilian. Here is another example; Virgil writes:

> Quamvis increpitent socii et vi cursus in altum
> Vela vocet, possisque sinus implere secundos.

Douglas translates:

> Ya, thocht thi fallowis cry out, Hillir haill!
> On burd! ane fair wind blawis betwix twa schetis!

It is admirably vivid; but it sounds very unlike the Virgil we knew at school. Let us suspend judgement and try another passage.

> lumenque juventae
> Purpureum et laetos oculis adflarat honores.

Douglas says that Aeneas' mother made him 'Lyk till ane yonkeir with twa lauchand ene'. The picture is fresh and attractive; yet somehow unlike the Aeneas of our imagination. But is that because Virgil has never said anything about the beauty of Aeneas, both here and in other places? On the contrary, Virgil quite clearly has told us that his hero was of godlike beauty. There has been something in our minds, but not in the mind of Douglas, which dimmed the picture; our idea of the great king and warrior and founder apparently shrinks (as Virgil's and Douglas's did not) from the delighted vision of male beauty. Douglas shocks us by being closer to Virgil than we. Once a man's eyes have been opened to this, he will find instances everywhere. *Rosea cervice refulsit:* 'her nek schane like unto the rois in May'. Do you prefer Dryden's 'she turned and made appear Her neck refulgent'? But *refulsit* cannot possibly have had for a Roman ear the 'classical' quality which 'refulgent' has for an English. It must have felt much more like 'schane'. And *rosea* has disappeared altogether in Dryden's version—and with it half the sensuous vitality of the image. Thus, again, Douglas translates *omnibus in templis matrum chorus* by 'in caroling the lusty ladeis went'. If this seems altogether too merry and too medieval, turn to Dryden again, and you will find that Dryden has flatly refused to translate those five words at all. And that brings us to the real point.

It is hard to blame Dryden for suppressing *matrum chorus.* In the style which he is using it simply cannot be translated. As long as we are under the spell of schoolroom 'classicality' we can do nothing; 'women', 'wives', 'matrons' are all equally fatal. But it will go at once and delightfully into the medieval line about ladies 'caroling.' And the reason is that at this point there is a real affinity between the ancient and the medieval world, and a real separation between both of them and the modern. And as soon as we become aware of this we realize what it is that has made so many things in Douglas seem to us strangely un-Virgilian. It is not the real Virgil; it is that fatal 'classical' misconception of all ancient poets which the humanists have fastened upon our education—the spectral solemnity, the gradus epithets, the dictionary language, the decorum which avoids every contact with the senses and the soil. (Dryden tells us that though he knew *mollis amaracus* was sweet marjoram, he did not so translate it, for fear 'those village words' should give the reader 'a mean idea of the thing'.) Time after time Douglas is nearer to the original than any version could be which kept within the limits of later classicism. And that is almost another way of saying that the real Virgil is very much less 'classical' than we had supposed. To read the Latin again with Douglas's version fresh in our minds is like seeing a favourite picture after it has been cleaned. Half the 'richness' and 'sobriety' which we have been taught to admire turns out to have been only dirt; the 'brown trees' disappear and where the sponge has passed the glowing reds, the purples, and the transparent blues leap into life.

I must not be taken to mean that Douglas attends only to the more vivid and sensuous elements in his original, that he fails to respond to its grandeur. He has indeed his own theory of the style which a great poem demands from its translator, and develops it in his **Ninth Prologue.** He calls it the 'knychtlike stile' in which we 'carp of vassalage'. This goes back to the doctrine of the three styles as we find it in Johannes de Garlandia; it has left its mark on Dante's *De Vulgari Eloquentia.* It must be admitted that when Douglas says that the 'knychtlike' style should, among trees, prefer the laurel, the cedar, and the palm, to broom and heather, we seem to be heading for something as false as Dryden's feeling about 'village words'; yet the theory, at worst, is based not on the superstition of 'the Classical', but on some dim perception of social and psychological facts. In practice it means that 'thar suld na knyght reid bot a knychtly tale' and that horses, hounds, and hawks will naturally interest such a reader more than goats. More important than his theory is his practice. He is not always great in the great passages; but he has often rendered the sublimity of Virgil in lines that no translator, and not many original poets, have surpassed:

> The langsum luife drinkand inwart full cauld.
>
> Wet in the mindless flude of Hell, Lethe.
>
> Mychtfull in hevin and dym dungeon of helle.
>
> And the paill furowr of Tysiphonee
> Walkis wod wroth amydwart the melee.

He has even done more than this. One of the things that test a translator's quality is that mass of small additions which metre inevitably demands. In Douglas what is added is often so Virgilian that when we turn back to the Latin we are surprised not to find it there. Thus *caeco marte resistunt* becomes 'Quhen blindlingis in the battell fey thai fycht'; or Creusa cries 'Quham to sall we be left *in this waist hous*'; or the single word *fessum* gives the line 'Wery and irkit in ane fremmyt land'. The words themselves are not in Virgil, but they are so true to the dominant emotion of the Third Book that it is, in a sense, from Virgil that Douglas is getting them. Even when, in the Tenth, there is really nothing at all to correspond to

> Than thus fra deid to deid, from pane to pane,
> Be catchit on and euery day be slane.

I find it impossible not to forgive lines which so pierce to the very heart of the *Aeneid.*

He is not, of course, a perfect translator. He does not succeed with *lacrimae rerum* nor *possunt quia posse videntur.* He knew much more than Virgil about ships; hence while his landfalls are as good as Virgil's (they could not be better) his storms and embarkations are almost too good—in the sense that his poem as a whole smells much more strongly of salt water than the original; Palinurus becomes almost a character. He puts into his text explanations that a modern translator would relegate to the notes—stopping to tell us that nymphs and fauns are 'fair-folkis' and 'elvis' or that the 'gammis Circenses' were what we call 'justing or than turnament'. At times these interpolated explanations are wildly wrong. Where Pallas, falling, bites the earth in Book X, Douglas says this was done on purpose 'as was the gys' in order that a warrior might not cry out in his death pains. Surely this is a happy error?

These faults—for so, I suppose, we must call them—are part and parcel of the general medievalization to which he subjects the *Aeneid.* The whole Virgilian underworld is mapped out in circles and limbos on the Christian pattern, the gods become planets, the Aegis is blazed like a 'coat',

Mercury has a 'fedrame' like Volund, and Camilla a Turkish bow. *Suos patimur manes* is rendered 'Ilkane of us his ganand Pugatory Maun suffir', the Sibyl is a 'holy religious woman clene', and Chloreus 'ane spiritual man'. In other words, Douglas pays for his freedom from the specific blindness of the *renascentia* by a specifically medieval blindness of his own. But the price is not really a very heavy one. The fact . . . that the medieval world and the ancient world (still more, the imagined prehistoric Italy of Virgil) have so much in common goes far to palliate the anachronism. *Phrygios leones* loses very little by becoming 'The lionis that the Phrygiane armis bene'. *Fulvo nutricis tegmine laetus* and 'Cleid in his nureis talbart glaid and gay' belong to the same world of legendary emblem and symbolic costume. Only once, if I remember rightly, does Douglas foist upon Virgil the confidential manner of a medieval poet and pull him up from a digression with a 'bot to our purpos'. At the very worst, I am convinced that even where Douglas is out, he is no further out in one direction than many Virgilians are out in the other. To the present day a reading of his version is the best possible preparation for a re-reading of the Latin. Douglas gives us new eyes—unless, of course, we approach him with the assumption that wherever medieval Virgilianism differed from humanistic, the medieval must have been simply wrong.

An account of Douglas's ***Aeneid*** which confined itself to his version of the text would be very incomplete. His work contains, in addition, **Prologues** to every book, a Thirteenth Book, an epilogue, a note between the Sixth and Seventh Books, and a **Commentary,** most unluckily incomplete and covering only part of the First. The Thirteenth Book is translated from the work of Maffeo Vegio, an Italian humanist of the fifteenth century who appears to have been dissatisfied with the abrupt ending of Virgil's poem—and very un-Homerically abrupt it is—and had the audacity to continue it, working out the happy ending in full. He concludes foolishly enough, but his earlier scenes, at least if you read them in Douglas, are far from contemptible; it is a little odd that he refuses, as resolutely as Virgil himself, to make a character of Lavinia. The book which Douglas has given us is, therefore, a composite work, and it ought to be read as a whole. The mere presence of the Thirteenth Book and the **Prologues** shows no lack of respect for Virgil; but it shows a lack of that particular species of respect which came in with the *renascentia.* The sacrosanctity of the epic form and of the number twelve mean nothing to Douglas. He is ready to interrupt his master with comic, familiar, or devotional poetry of his own at the beginning of every book. The resulting volume is thus the fine flower of medieval Virgilianism.

The **Prologues** have a threefold interest, as poems, as criticism, and as familiar self-portraits of the artist. His habits both in winter and summer, his reading, his difficulties as a translator, his haunting consciousness that a man is not made a bishop in order to translate Virgil, and the excuses which he makes to himself, are here all faithfully set out. His delight in his own work, wrestling and successfully wrestling with his modesty, is expressed with humorous frankness:

> Yit by myself I fynd this proverb perfyte,
> 'The blak craw thinkis hir awin byrdis quhite'
> Sa faris with me, bew Schirris, will ye hark,
> Can nocht persaue a falt in all my wark.
>
> **(Prol. ix.)**

His criticism is to be found chiefly in the **First, Fifth, Sixth,** and **Ninth Prologues.** Much of it is simply a good statement of the ordinary medieval opinion of Virgil. He is a heathen poet and all his work, in a sense, is *fenyeit;* but under the *derk poetrye* lies *great wisdome.* He has described the *stait of man baith life and deid* and it is wonderful how often he is substantially right even about *mysteris fell* which we have learned by revelation. Augustine quoted him freely, we must remember, and Ascencius in modern times has gone so far as to call him a *hie theolog sentencious.* Presumably this wisdom was learned by Virgil from *Sibillis sawis.* On the moral plane, his story is plainly full of *nobilitie,* and Aeneas a mirror of *wirschap* and *manheid.* Douglas defends his desertion of Dido (in the **First Prologue**), rejecting the opinion of Chaucer who *was ever, God wait, wemenis frend* and showing a much better understanding of Book IV than many modern critics. Douglas, in fact, regards the *Aeneid* much as Malory and Caxton regarded the *Morte:*

> Weill auchtin eldris exemplis ws to steyr
> Tyll hie curage, all honour till ensew.
>
> **(Prol. xi.)**

and while *churlish wychtis* are simply to be told that his translation is correct, *nobillis* are invited to *amend* it. This choice of nobles rather than scholars is significant.

For sheer poetry his best **Prologues** are the **Seventh, Twelfth,** and **Thirteenth**—three nature poems of such discriminating sensibility and effortless technical power that they set us wondering why (in that field) we ever needed a romantic revival, just as Douglas's translation makes us wonder why we needed a *renascentia.* The history of literature is very far from being one of simple progress. The least good of these (the **Seventh,** on winter) leaves nothing to be improved, and much to be corrupted, by Thomson. Douglas himself in the midst of the scenes he describes—Douglas baking himself by the fire, and creeping into bed under *claythis thrinfauld,* Douglas watching the bitter moonlight shining in his room all night, Douglas next morning opening the window *a lytill on char* and hastily shutting it after a glance that prints the landscape indelibly on our imaginations—all this saves the poem from the flatness of mere description. Sometimes a single line evokes not only the momentary scene, but the sensation of many winter days on end:

> The wind made wayfe the reid weyd on the dyk.

But the **Twelfth** and **Thirteenth** are better. The former is as hackneyed in subject as any medieval poem could be—a description of spring—but after we have read it, Chaucer and the Elizabethans in this kind seem tepid. It begins with a regular salvo of mythology and personification; but the shining figures which Douglas makes move across his sky are no more conventional or merely ornamental than the similar figures in Botticelli. Saturn draws off into dim distances *behind the circulat warld of Jupiter*—Aurora opens the windows of her hall—crystalline gates are unfolded—the great assault is ready and marches forward with banners spread,

> Persand the sabill barmkyn nocturnall.

This is not simply a better or worse way of describing what we *see.* It is a way of making us see for always what we have sometimes felt, a vision of natural law in its angelic grandeur, a reminder of something that Chaucer ignores—of the pomp and majesty mingled even in the sweetest and most gracious of Nature's workings. It is a true spiritualization (true, at least, to our experience) of the visible object; Douglas here reaches out in one direction to Wordsworth or even Blake, and in another to the Homeric hymns. The greatness of the opening, contrasted with the humbler sweetness that follows, enables Douglas to hit off to a nicety the experience of any man who wakes early and walks out on such a morning; for the intimate pleasures of the lanes and woods, once reached, as the dew begins to ascend, do thus decline from the more august splendours of the dawn—decline so amiably that we welcome the declining. Throughout this part of the poem his observation is admirable; his attention to shadows and his use of shadows to tell us about the light could hardly be bettered. The **Thirteenth Prologue** is gentler. It records a visionary meeting with *Mapheus Vegius* which the poet feigns as his excuse of the Thirteenth Book. The angry humanist appears *Lyke to sum poet of the auld fassoune*—for Douglas has been reading Henryson—and the interview is described with considerable humour. But the real value of the **Prologue** lies in the setting—a northern summer night, described in full, from its late twilight to its early dawn. The best lines (where nearly all are good) have been quoted, I doubt not, by many others; but they are so characteristic of the whole that I cannot help giving them again:

> Yondyr dovn dwynis the evin sky away,
> And vpspryngis the brycht dawing of day
> Intill ane other place nocht far in sundir,
> That to behald was pleasans and half wondir.

About Douglas as a translator there may be two opinions; about his ***Aeneid*** (**Prologues** and all) as an English book there can be only one. Here a great story is greatly told and set off with original embellishments which are all good—all either delightful or interesting—in their diverse ways. The couplet in which most of the book is written seems very rough if we read ten lines. It seems less so after ten pages. When we have finished a volume we find it an admirable medium for narrative—a happy mean between the severity of Pope and the rambling of Keats. Often it has the ring and energy of Dryden; I would particularly recommend to the reader's attention the twenty-four lines entitled ***Conclusioune of this Buik*** as an example of Douglas's skill in bringing out the proper powers of this metre.

After the publication of his ***Aeneid*** (unless *King Hart* is later) Douglas concerns us no more. He is the queen's man and flies from Scotland at Albany's return, to live on an English pension and die of an English plague at London in 1522. (pp. 81-90)

C. S. Lewis, "Late Medieval: The Close of the Middle Ages in Scotland," in his English Literature in the Sixteenth Century: Excluding Drama, *Oxford at the Clarendon Press, 1954, pp. 66-119.*

Kurt Wittig (essay date 1958)

[*In the essay below, Wittig highlights the alliterative and descriptive beauty of Douglas's* Prologues. *The critic also discusses Douglas as a religious thinker and precursor of the Scottish Reformation.*]

It would no doubt be very rewarding to study Gavin Douglas (*c.* 1474-1522), later Bishop of Dunkeld, against the wider European background of his time. Such a study would reveal how in his work the Middle Ages overlap with the New Learning, presenting a continuity, not a break. Douglas's ***Eneados*** is one of the great Renaissance translations. In it he makes it his purpose to bring one of the very greatest classical authors within reach of the common reader. He shows a respect for the letter of his original that is wholly new; and such is his reverence for Virgil, both as a man and as a poet, that he reviles Caxton's so-called *Aeneis,* and even censures the liberties that Chaucer had taken with his author (**Prol. I,**). In many ways the **Prologues** of the ***Eneados*** represent the beginnings of literary criticism (**Prols. I, V, VI, IX**), and Douglas ponders the problem of choosing between a literal translation and one that attempts to reproduce the style as well as the meaning of the original (**Prol. I; "Dyrectioun of his Buik**"). He quotes his authorities, and adopts the educated Renaissance man's slightly patronising attitude towards the unlearned; yet he includes a translation of the "Thirteenth Book" of the *Aeneid,* by Mapheus Vegius (Maffeo Veggio). His style and his theory of the epic show a similar mixture of old and new. Douglas retains the Christian interpretation of Virgil and the Catholic system of thought, and he writes allegories—but he fills them with a new meaning, and he comes within striking distance of Sir Philip Sydney's theory of an epic as a sugar-coating for a moral pill (**Prol. I**). But Douglas has been unduly neglected; none of these studies has been undertaken; and (though it is in progress) not even the Scottish Text Society edition of his works has yet been published.

Not less interesting is Douglas's place in the Scottish tradition. His ***Eneados*** (1513) is the most sustained work in Scots poetry, and, considering the scale, the most consistent. In order to achieve this result, he had had to labour away at the problem of widening the Scots tongue's range of expression, forging it and reforging it until it was capable of expressing anything. He does not go in for Scottish concision or understatement; dogmatically he will sometimes say a thing three times over in different words. Like Dunbar (and, to a lesser extent, Henryson), Douglas moves freely from one level of poetry to another, with appropriate modulation of language, style, and metre. In this connexion, it is illuminating to compare the May idyll of the Prologue to the ***Palice of Honour*** (1501) with the grotesque eldritch episode in the same poem (1.7-8, especially "the fisch yelland as eluis schoutit"), with its harsh final consonants and heavy alliteration. In the ***Eneados,*** there is a similar contrast between the aureate magnificence of **Prol. I** and the rhymed alliterative bob-and-wheel of **Prol.**

VIII, a passionate flyting against the corruption of this false world. Here we have plain Braid Scots, containing words of Norse and Gaelic origin, with stressed metre and knotty alliteration up to six times in a line and often of two initial consonants. The rugged dynamic force of **Prol. VIII** contrasts no less sharply with the serenity of **Prol. XII,** (the "May Prologue"), or with the hymnlike severity of Douglas's invocation of the Creator in **Prol. X,** where there is a rich admixture of Latin words, in forms terminated by the stress: *etérn, glór, creát, generát, incommíxt,* etc. There is also a wealth of long vowels, with consonants checking the movement here and there, and an occasional pause for an unstressed syllable. This creates a slow solemnity, like the heavy pealing of a cathedral bell.

There is nothing artless or inadvertent about Douglas's use of these different levels. At the beginning of **Prol. IX,** in three stanzas of rich internal rhyme suggestive of Latin hymns, he first appeals for sincerity and constancy, but then breaks off—

> Eneuch of this, us nedis prech na moyr,
> Bot, accordyng the purpos said tofoyr,
> The ryall style, clepyt heroycall,
> Full of wirschip and nobillness owr all,
> Suld be compilit but tenchis or voyd word,
> Kepand honest wys sportis quhayr thai bourd,
> All lous language and lychtnes lattand be,
> Observand bewte, sentens, and gravite.

Further, he suggests

> we aucht tak tent
> That baith accord, and bene convenient,
> The man, the sentens, and the knychtlike
> stile. . . .

And, still more specifically, in writing of dignified deeds:

> Full litill it wald delite
> To write of scroggis, broym, haddir, or rammale:
> The laurer, cedir, or the palm triumphale,
> Ar mayr ganand for nobillis of estait:
> The muse suld wyth the person aggre algait.

Douglas strictly observes this rule, not only in his choice of language, but also in his use of alliteration. In allegorical, courtly, or discursive passages like those quoted above there is, very occasionally, an almost unintentional alliteration. The more "hamely" the subject and language, the more dominant does alliteration become. It bursts forth whenever the flyting mood takes charge, as above, in the exceptional line "All lous langage and lychtnes lattand be," in **Prol. VIII** and in **Prol. I:**

> I spittit for despyt to see swa spilt . . .

It is noticeable, too, that Douglas's nature scenes are heavily alliterated, as, for example, in his descriptions of May **(Prol. XII)**, a June evening **(Prol. XIII)**, and winter **(Prol. VII)**; in the latter we are forcibly reminded of Henryson's verse-portrait of Saturn. This points rather to native seasonal songs, than to Chaucer and the May convention, as being here the ultimate source of Douglas's inspiration.

The usual verdict is that with all its fidelity Douglas's translation of the ***Aeneid*** has more rugged vitality, more rustic vigour, more fire, more self-assertion than Virgil's *Aeneid.* Douglas, it is said, is more rugged, Virgil more supple. C. S. Lewis maintains, however, that we have too classically solemn a picture of the *Aeneid,* and that Douglas's ***Eneados*** has more of the essential Virgil; while Ezra Pound is convinced (in *How to read*) that the translation is better than the original. Be that as it may, Douglas's characteristics are closely akin to those of the Scottish tradition, and there is no doubt that in some passages—notably the sea scenes—Douglas's imagery is more vivid and more concrete than Virgil's and shows more delight in detail. Douglas's language, too, has more life in it: it teems with images of nature, and seems racier and closer to the soil.

Gavin Douglas's poems reveal a man of distinctly virile, almost angular, character, who has no sympathy with the softness for women that had led Chaucer **(Prol. I)** to

> set on Virgile and Eneas this wyte,
> For he was ever, God wait, wemenis friend.

Douglas is disgusted at weak undignified indulgence in love and lust, and in **Prol. IV** he points to the medieval legend of Aristotle's debasement:

> Men sayis thow bridillit Aristotle as one hors
> And crelit up the flour of poetry.

Virgil can teach us, he adds, to be moderate in love and wine:

> Childir to engener ois Venus, and nocht in vane;
> Have na surphat, drink nocht bot quhen thow
> art dry.

This leaves no place for courtly love or amorous play, any more than in the *Kingis Quair* or *The Testament of Cresseid.* That is "unlefull luffe" **(Prol. IV)**. Yet Douglas is remarkably concrete when thundering against the "schamefull play" in May, with its stealthy whisperings and meetings.

This brings us to the question of Douglas's religious and moral attitude. ***The Palice of Honour*** is more than a pageant of figures in allegorical trappings; it tries to *solve* a genuine moral question: how, and on what basis, to achieve honour. In the **Prologues** of the ***Eneados,*** his most important original contribution to portray, Douglas stresses the fact that he does not, like Virgil, intend to glorify false gods or to preach the transmigration of souls—a doctrine for which he seeks a Christian interpretation, concluding that his "philosopher naturall" must have had intuitions of Hell, Purgatory, and the Deadly Sins, of Mary in the shape of the Sibyl, of Satan in that of Pluto, and so forth **(Prols. VI, X).** This is truly medieval, and, as Douglas points out, Augustine himself had quoted the Sixth Book of the *Aeneid* **(Prol. VI).** There is, of course, in this bishop-to-be, much theological orthodoxy, as in his account of the Trinity: according to him, its three Persons correspond to the soul's three faculties, namely intelligence or understanding, which "considers the thing before" "raison," which "decernis"; and "memor," which "kepis the consait" **(Prol. X).** Douglas also vividly compares the Trinity with fire, which combines flame, light, and heat. Most of this is highly conventional; here and there, however, he strikes an original note.

In this same **Prologue,** Douglas invokes God as the Creator of all things, who also in His wisdom ordained the course of the world and the seasons. He is "incomprehensabill," and not even from His creation can man comprehend Him. God is in everything, with no diminution of Himself. These arguments are not exceptional in the medieval Church, and are to be found in Augustine; but nowhere are they expressed so absolutely. Still more surprising is a passage **(Prol. XI)** on grace and redemption:

I say, be grace; for quhen thou art in grace,
Thou may eik grace to grace, ay moyr and moyr,
Bot quhen thou fallys be syn tharfra, allace!
Off thy meryte thou gettis hyr nevirmor:
Yit quhen thou dewly disponis the tharfor,
Doing all that in the thar may be done,
Of hys gudnes the etern Lord alssone
Restoryis the meryt, wyth grace in erlis of glore.

Here there is no mention of confession and absolution, of the intercession of the Church, or of the mediation of the saints; even more than in Barbour and Henryson, the individual has to settle his account with God Himself, and salvation is not the reward of good works, but the free gift of God to a soul that has striven hard to respond to God's offer. This passage is almost exactly attuned to the innermost principle of the Kirk of Scotland, as defined by a former Moderator, G. D. Henderson [in his *The Claims of the Church of Scotland,* 1951]: "The Christian privilege and responsibility of each child of God, the freedom of the individual Christian to study and reflect, and to make his personal response to every divine offer and challenge." The emphasis that Douglas lays on the prevenience of God's grace can be traced back to Augustine; but Calvinism itself was baesd on this aspect of Augustinian teaching. Those passages in which Barbour, Henryson, and Douglas lay so much stress on the *personal* response of the individual to the challenge of the Divine Will clearly foreshadow the predominant ideas of the Scottish Reformation. Indeed, it may be said that Protestantism and Presbyterianism would never have taken such firm root in Scotland if the soil had not long been ready for them. Like Barbour and the Declaration of Arbroath, Douglas is very close to Calvin (and Augustine) in his insistence on law and justice as the divinely ordained foundations of freedom. In **Prol. XI** he discountenances war (and chivalry) except in so far as "the ground of batale" is "fundyt apoun rycht":

Nocht for thou lyst to mak discentioun,
To seik occasionis of contentioun,
Bot rype thy querrell, and discus it plane:
Wrangys to redres suld weyr be undertane,
For na conquest, reif, skat, nor pensioun.

Without God's help, the power of man is indeed feeble. Citing Aristotle's *Ethics,* Douglas then goes on to distinguish "hardyment" from "fuyl hardyment" and from cowardice. (The parallel with Barbour is, however, even more striking than that with Aristotle, in view of Douglas's insistence on the importance of being "auyse".)

It is, however, in the tone of his religious and moral teaching that Douglas is closest to the spirit of Presbyterianism, for he seems to have been gripped by a haunting suspicion that we shall have to pay for all our happiness:

All erdly glaidnes fynysith with wo.

Temporall joy endis with wo and pane.

. . . erdlie plesour endis oft with sorrow, we see.

and there is even an occasional outburst of fire-and-brimstone sermonising **(Prol. IV).** Like so many other Scottish writers, Douglas displays a deep delight in rational argument. Barbour and Henryson had been able to indulge their love of argument in the bygoing: Douglas is no less impatiently assertive, but has to save up his comment until he has finished a book of the *Aeneid*—but then it bursts forth all the more impetuously. On contemplating Caxton's mutilations of Virgil's *Aeneid,* Douglas is filled with righteous indignation **(Prol. I),** and the mere thought that his own translation will have its critics causes him to flare up as in a flyting. At one moment he will observe the poetic convention of modesty and will apologise for his rough verse—but it is not so bad as to give anybody the right to criticise it, and damnation take all who despise it or mutilate it! "After all," he exclaims **(Prol IX),** "I myself

Can nocht persaue a falt in all my wark,
Affectioun sa far my raysson blyndis."

Quite as impatiently as Carlyle, he rails **(Prol. III)** at those who see nothing more than a fable in the story of the Minotaur:

Tharfore wald God I had thair eris to pull,

and **(Prol. VI)** at those who think the Sixth Book of *Aeneid* was all "japis" or "auld idolatreis":

O hald your pece, ye verray goddis apis!

"Na, na," he stamps his foot **(Prols. I, IV, V,** etc.); he will not report any mere "gabbing" (II.9.25). His impatience breaks forth **(Prol. VI)** in rhetorical questions:

Schawis he nocht heir the synnis capitall?

Ar all sic sawis fantasy and in vane?

It is only natural, of course, to speak like this in the midst of an argumentative outburst. In Scotland, however, as Sir Walter Scott often points out, questions are commonly used instead of statements or answers; and in Gaelic it is a perfectly normal way of telling a story. This imparts a subjective colouring, and greatly intensifies the dramatic quality latent in all Scots speech; in Douglas's poetry it has the same effect, though it occasionally tends to produce an inflated style.

But as a rule Douglas's language is pithy, richly and vividly descriptive and pungently realistic: on occasion, it is also scurrilous—even in passages of "knychtlike stile." The sharp clarity of Douglas's pictures is due chiefly to the precision with which he marks the details, as when in ***En.*** V.iv. he describes the laughter which arises when one of the Trojans falls into the sea during the Naval Games:

The Troianis *lauchis fast* seand him fall,
And, hym behaldand swym, thei *keklit* all;
Bot *maist,* thai maiking *gem* and *gret riot,*
To see hym *spout salt wattir* of his *throt.*

Often, too, he heightens the effect by means of comparisons and contrasts, through which, more even than the other Makars, he projects into the context an image of his own that is a great deal more vivid than the thought he is actually expressing; often, indeed, this gives the subjective impression more emphasis than the objective fact. Where, he asks in **Prol. I,** is there a vernacular that provides such clearly-defined terms as *"genus, sexus, species, obiectum, subiectum"*:

> He war expert culd fynd me termes twa,
> Quhilkis ar als rife amange clerkis in scule
> As euir *fowlis plungit in laik or puile.*

Intensification of this subjective element leads on occasion to that extravagant, grimly humorous exaggeration which we have so frequently remarked elsewhere, as in **Prol. I:**

> Beis nocht our studious to spy a mote in my ee,
> That in your awin a *ferry bote* can nocht see.

Douglas strove consciously to widen the scope of "Scots"—as he was the first to call it instead of "Inglis"—by making it more flexible, more academically precise, more copiously rhetorical, more aureate. What higher standard could he have chosen than Virgil's *"di parlar sì largo fiume"*? What better task than that of translating the *Aeneid?* Yet his own characteristic idiom, so pithy and so picturesque, is closely akin to folk-speech; and the proverb, sometimes Biblical, sometimes vernacular, is one of its essential ingredients **(Prols. I and IX)**:

> And do to me as ye wald be done to.

> Do tyll ilk wyght as thou done to wald be.

> The blak craw thinkis hir awin byrdis quhite.

Douglas's imagery is largely derived from nature, as seen in Scotland, and also from Scottish folklore. Thus in introducing the Sixth Book of the ***Eneados,*** he says **(Prol. VI)**:

> All is bot gaistis and elriche fantasies,
> Of browneis and of bogillis full this buke.

This was what enabled him to write his great nature poems, the first in Scots or English in which landscape is depicted solely for its own sake.

Apart from a passing reference to Boreas and Eolus the whole of the winter poem **(Prol. VII)** is founded solely on Scottish experience, and it contains a wealth of sharply-defined sense images drawn from a multiple awareness of nature that was to remain unrivalled until the eighteenth century. The sun hangs low down on the horizon, the days are short, and rivers run "reid on spait with watteir broune." For winter in Scotland is not so much a time of sharp ringing frost, with a thick blanket of snow, but rather of biting winds, sleet, hail, and blinding snowstorms, of low drumly clouds racing across white skies; a time of miry roads, when the land lies bleak and barren, and long icicles bedeck the crags. All this is wonderfully depicted, with frequent alliteration, and a wealth of epithets coldly expressive of privation: "barrand, strypyt [stripped], nakyt, fadyt, widderit." Even the stars look hostile. We hear the wind whining, we see the husbandman drenched and exhausted; the birds shiver on bare branches, the deer come down into the glens, the sheep bield themselves as best they can against the braeface, and in the byre the cattle huddle together for warmth. It is not a winter in which warmth is to be got by exercise, but one that cuts to the bone and dazes the blood. The cold gets inside you: there is no defence against it.

Douglas's picture of all this—and here he excels even the nature poets of the eighteenth century—is not static. Often—as in the expressive line:

> The wynd maid wayfe the reid weyd on the dyk

—his sharp eye registers a movement, slight in itself, which yet serves to emphasise the stark fixity of the wintry landscape. Douglas's picture of winter, like Henryson's, is highly subjective: we are made aware of the cold by the poet's account of his own reactions to it, and see him at his fireside, trying to defeat it by means of a "mychty drink" and double wraps, or in bed, beneath three blankets, with his head wrapped up against the frost. Through the window-panes he sees the wintry constellations, hears the "wyld elriche screik" of the hideous owl, the whistle of the "gled [kite]," or the cry of the wild geese in their Y-formation high in the "lift." At daybreak, he opens the window "on char [ajar]": the day is "bla," "wan," "har"—a powerfully evocative use of bleak vowel sounds and wintry Norse words. The dew has frozen, the "branchis brattlys," hail hops on roof and road. Quickly he shuts the window, "chiverand for cauld," and tries:

> . . . wyth hait flambe to fleme the fresyng fell.

The Virgil on his desk, with so much still to be translated, makes his spirit sink lower still. With a sigh, however, he takes up his yoke—Book Seventh, and how well it matches this dreary environment!—and goes on with his translation. This is not really a description of winter: it is rather the evocation of a winter mood, and by his choice of metres, words, and sounds, he enables us to relive his own wintry impressions of intense cold, of eldritch uncanny noises, and of scenes the mere sight of which is enough to induce shivering.

Douglas's elaborate descriptions of a May day and a June evening **(Prols. XII, XIII)** contain more classical mythology, and the diction is more aureate. But the things to which he applies these aureate terms are native to Scotland—like **(Prol. XII)** the "Nymphis and Naedes,"

> Syk as we clepe wenchis and damysellis,
> In gresy gravis wandrand by spring wellis.

And elsewhere, in speaking of Philomene, Esacus and Peristera, Douglas explains:

> I meyn our awin native bird, gentill dow . . .

and then paints in the sheen of its coloured plumage. The scene is decidedly Scottish: the midsummer sun setting far in the north, the cobwebs, the insects—"midgeis, fleyis [flies], emmitis [ants], byssy beis" **(Prols. XII, XIII)**: what other poet had ever evoked vibrant summer heat so vividly by painting the incessant flitting to-and-fro of so many different insects, or used the sudden stillness, when all this movement ceases, half so skilfully to suggest the close of day? These two prologues mark the climax of the heightened sensibility that we found in the older Scottish literature. Colours, forms, smells, sounds are seized with a precise and instantaneous awareness of shades and values such as no Scots or English poet had previously attained. Observing the pale flowers, Douglas remarks **(Prol. XII)**:

> Sum wattry hewit as the haw wally see,
> And sum depart in freklys red and quhyte,
> Sum brycht as gold with aureat levys lyte.

Elsewhere **(Prol. XIII),** he comes very close to impressionism:

> The dewy grene, pulderit with daseis gay
> Schew on the sward a cullour dapill gray.

And in this description **(Prol. XII)** of a lily, the concentration of sensuous images—smell, touch, taste, and sight—is so intense and so varied as almost to constitute a synœsthesia:

> The balmy vapour from thar sylkyn croppis
> Distylland hailsum sugurat hunny droppis,
> And sylver schakaris gan fra levis hyng,
> Wyth crystal sprayngis on the verdour yyng.

"Crystal," "bedit," "perlis," "pulderyt"—by means of such words, Douglas tries always to transmit an *exact* image; we see the fire in a dewdrop or the pattern of the shadow of trees and towers contrasting with the light, and the "illuminate air" **(Prol. XII).** The local accuracy of such images, and the frequency with which they occur in the May Prologue and elsewhere, are both reminiscent of Gaelic poetry. But Douglas also instils a sense of the *rhythms* of nature, and his May Prologue is no mere catalogue. It has little in common with the emblematic background tapestry of the conventional May prologue in medieval poetry. Far more than James I, Henryson or Dunbar, he conveys an impression of the changes, the *stirrings,* great and small, that are incessantly in progress. Sometimes the hint is so delicate that it may easily be missed:

> Soft gresy verdour *eftir balmy schowris*
> On curland stalkis *smyling* to thar flowris . . .

> The dasy *dyd on breid* hir crownell smaill.

> The flour delice *furth spred* his hevinly hew. . . .

But here is his description **(Prol XIII)** of the "gloaming"—Scotland's long, long summer evening:

> All byrnand reid *gan walxin* the evin sky,
> The son enfyrit haill. . . .

In this slow-fading light, with its soft shades, the tip of every blade of grass catches the dew, which falls

> as lemand beriall droppis . . .
> Lyke cristall knoppis or small silver bedis.
> The lycht *begouth* to *quynkill owt* and *faill,*
> The day to *dyrkyn, decline,* and *devaill.*

Presently the shadows grow deeper, up goes the bat with "hir pelit ledderyn [naked (*lit.* peeled) leathern] flycht," the lark settles down to rest,

> Out owr the swyre swymmis the soppis of mist,

and night at length casts her mantle. Darkness enfolds man, beast, "fyrth," and forest; peace descends on cattle and deer; even the restless activities of the insects cease. Metrically, too, this remarkable passage shows fine modulation and masterly control of pace. Line by line, a reader who cares to make the experiment of reading it aloud will find himself lowering his voice in expectation of the final cadence: but cadence succeeds cadence, and the long syllables go on soothing the reader's ear, till his voice sinks finally to its lowest pitch, and the last cadence of all leaves behind it a sense of absolute tranquillity.

Equally enchanting is Douglas's description of the short June night, during which, in Scotland, it never becomes completely dark. Waking after his dream of Mapheus Vegius, Douglas looks about him, and this is what he sees:

> Yonder doun dwynis the evin sky away,
> And upspryngis the brycht dawing of day
> Intill ane other place nocht far in sundir,
> That to behald was plesans, and half wondir.

The stars fade one after another, and morning is here. Douglas paints it in with a wealth of adjectives richly expressive of joyous activity—"blyth," "bissy," "blyssful"—and full of lively vowels:

> Sone our the f*ei*ldis sch*i*nis the l*y*cht cl*ey*r.

What a contrast here with winter's "bla," "wan," "har"! The scene is alive with Nature's creatures—birds, cattle, poultry—and as part of the slow awakening of the world we see

> The mysty vapouris springand up full sweit.

And in **Prol. XII,** Nature's underlying rhythms are interpreted as those of one vast living organism:

> The sulye spred hyr braid bosum on breid,
> Zephyrus' confortabill inspiratioun
> For till ressaue law in hyr barm adoun.

As here portrayed, nature breathes, loves, cherishes. Many of the countless details which go to produce this impression are, in themselves, so trivial, that we ourselves may scarcely be conscious of them. But the final effect is that in these **Prologues** we see for always what we have sometimes felt. . . . (pp. 77-90)

Kurt Wittig, "Full Tide: The Makars," in his The Scottish Tradition in Literature, *Oliver and Boyd Ltd., 1958, pp. 33-90.*

David F. C. Coldwell (essay date 1964)

[*A distinguished member of the Scottish Text Society, Coldwell is a scholar of Scottish history and literature. In addition to contributing to numerous periodicals, he has edited two volumes of Douglas's works. In the excerpt below, he evaluates Douglas's merits as a translator of verse and as a poet in his own right. The critic judges Douglas's translation of the* Aeneid *superior in many respects to William Caxton's and John Dryden's renderings of the same work; however, he considers Douglas's own poetry—as evidenced by the* Prologues *and the* Palice of Honour*—merely competent.*]

[Gavin Douglas] makes little attempt to have his characters act in foreign, ancient ways, or to make them stately.

He is proud of his fidelity to the text: *he* did not mangle the text as the unconscionable Caxton did; but his characters speak and fight like knights of the late fifteenth century, and the action takes place in terms the fifteenth century would readily recognize. Hence 'Sir' Diomeid, or 'Dan' Virgil, or 'child' Cillenyus, or Neptune's 'mattock', or the somewhat implausible 'nuns of Bacchus'. For all the reverence accorded to Virgil, the ***Aeneid*** seemed far closer and more natural in 1500 than it did in 1700 or 1900; improved Latinity seems to have cut off the Latin classics from popular imagination. Douglas's anachronisms should not be objectionable. He had an authoritative model in Virgil himself, for Dryden remarks on the 'famous anachronism, in making Aeneas and Dido contemporaries. For it is certain that the Hero lived almost two hundred years before the building of Carthage. . . . Chronology at best is but a Cobweb-Law, and he broke through it with his weight.' Furthermore, one of the aims of the translator is to produce a poem that might have been written in his own time. It may be that anachronism shows a kind of cultural vitality, where a careful antiquarianism would suggest the undertaker laying out the corpse. Douglas saw far less difference between the lives of Scots and Romans than Dryden did: his descriptions of ships, battlefields, and ghosts are therefore so much the more lively than Dryden's, where the dignified and decorous Romans always seem to be on parade.

Dryden's purpose, determined by his view of the graces of epic poetry, was to make all things 'grave, majestical, and sublime'. He is, therefore, at his best, perhaps, in the formal, dignified speeches that make up much of the poem. It is fitting that Juno should speak with god-like decorum:

O Eolus! for to thee the King of Heav'n
The Pow'r of Tempests, and of Winds has giv'n:
Thy Force alone their Fury can restrain,
And smooth the Waves, or swell the troubl'd Main.
A race of wand'ring Slaves, abhorr'd by me,
With prosp'rous Passage cut the Thuscan Sea:
To fruitful Italy their Course they steer,
And for their vanquish'd God design new Temples there.
Raise all thy Winds, with Night involve the Skies;
Sink, or disperse my fatal Enemies.
Twice sev'n, the charming Daughters of the Main,
Around my Person wait, and bear my Train:
Succeed my Wish, and second my Design,
The fairest, Deiopeia, shall be thine;
And make thee Father of a happy Line.
(I. 97-III.)

For Douglas she is rather a sharp-tongued Scottish housewife:

'Eolus, a pepill onto me ennemy
Salis the sey Tuscane, cariand to Italy
Thar venquyst hamehald goddis and Ilion;
Bot sen the fader of goddis every one
And kyng of men gave the power,' quod sche,
'To meys the flude or rays with stormys hie,
Infors thi wyndis, synk all that schippis infeir,
Or skattir widquhar into cuntreis seir,
Warp all thar bodies in the deyp bedeyn.
I have,' quod sche, 'lusty ladeis fourteyn,
Of quham the farest, clepit Diope,
In ferm wedlok I sal conjune to the
For thi reward, that lilly quhite of swar,
With the forto remane for evermar,
Quhilk propir spous and eik thi lady myld
Sal mak the fader to mony fair child.'
(I. ii. 25-40.)

Dryden's pace, though majestic, is slow, and has disadvantages when the speed of the original quickens:

Thus while the Pious Prince his Fate bewails,
Fierce Boreas drove against his flying Sails,
And rent the Sheets: The raging Billows rise,
And mount the tossing Vessel to the Skies:
Nor can the shiv'ring Oars sustain the Blow;
The Galley gives her side, and turns her Prow:
While those astern descending down the Steep,
Thro' gaping Waves behold the boiling deep.
Three Ships were hurry'd by the Southern Blast,
And on the secret Shelves with Fury cast.
Those hidden Rocks, th' Ausonian Sailors knew,
They call'd them Altars, when they rose in view,
And show'd their spacious Backs above the Flood.
Three more, fierce Eurus in his angry Mood,
Dash'd on the Shallows of the moving Sand,
And in mid Ocean left them moor'd a-land.
(I. 146-61.)

'Moor'd a-land'! Douglas is able to summon to his translation more nautical energy, and to capture something of the thunder and confusion of the shipwreck:

And al invane thus quhil Eneas carpit,
A blastrand bub out from the north brayng
Gan our the forschip in the baksaill dyng,
And to the sternys up the flude gan cast.
The aris, hechis and the takillis brast,
The schippis stevin frawart hyr went gan wryth,
And turnyt hir braid syde to the wallis swyth.
Heich as a hill the jaw of watir brak
And in ane hepe cam on thame with a swak.
Some hesit hoverand on the wallis hycht,
And sum the swowchand sey so law gart lycht
Thame semyt the erd oppynnyt amyd the flude—
The stour up bullyrrit sand as it war wode.
The sowth wynd, Nothus, thre schippis draif away
Amang blynd cragis, quhilk huge rolkis thai say
Amyd the sey Italianys Altaris callis;
And othir thre Eurus from the deip wallis
Cachit amang the schald bankis of sand—
Dolorus to se thame chop on grond, and stand
Lyke as a wall with sand warpit about.
(I. iii. 14-33.)

Dryden can be bad when his dignity becomes stilted and artificial:

No Vessels were in view: But, on the Plain,
Three beamy Stags command a Lordly Train
Of branching Heads; the more ignoble Throng
Attend their stately Steps, and slowly graze along.
(I. 259-62.)

Douglas makes it simpler:

Na schip he saw, bot sone he gat a syght
Of thre hartis waverand by the cost syde,
Quham at the bak, throu out the gravis wide,
The mekil herdis followit in a rowt
And pasturit all the large valle about.
(I. iv. 48-52.)

The simpler version seems closer to Virgil's Latin:

navem in conspectu nullam, tris litore cervos
prospicit errantis; hos tota armenta sequuntur
a tergo et longum per vallis pascitur agmen.
(I. 184-86.)

Ignoring the enchantment of the rhythm, one can see in this a plain meaning: 'He observed no ship in sight, but three stags wandering on the shore; whole herds follow behind them and in a long line graze through the valley.' A reader unaccustomed to the statuesque treatment of Latin might find Dryden's version of the passage empty and insincere. And yet it must be admitted that on occasion Douglas's rough-hewn vigour may become incongruous:

For to the madynnys of Tyre this is the gyis
To beir a cays of arowis on this wys,
With rede botynys on thar schankis hie.
(I. vi. 55-8.)

This is not Douglas at his best; he succeeds in vigorous passages describing action, and in passages where there is more human warmth and emotion than Dryden's stately composure and dignity allow him to transmit.

Douglas is closer to the common reader than Dryden is. He was less of a Latinist. He translated from an inferior text, by modern standards; he had few technical aids; he had no models; he worked fast: it is not surprising that he sometimes made mistakes. Yet his methods were sound, for he depended heavily on a monument of contemporary scholarship, the commentary made about 1500 by the Dutch humanist Ascensius. Ascensius made a running prose commentary on the poem, identifying the mythological allusions, providing alternative, simpler wording, and explaining the metaphors. When Douglas borrowed from this somewhat pedantic paraphrase, he was making his poem translation and commentary at the same time. Thus where Virgil has simply 'sola', Douglas may expand to 'allane in wedowheid', because Ascensius had the explanatory note 'idest in viduitate'. Or Virgil's 'auditque videtque' can be combined with Ascensius's 'audit & videt. scilicet per fantasiam & imaginationem illum scilicet amatum absentem' to produce Douglas's version:

And of him absent thinkis scho heris the soun,
His voce scho heris, and him behaldis sche,
Thocht he, God wait, fer from her presence be.

Or a line with no equivalent in Virgil, 'And all that to the schippis langis of rychtis' (XI. vii. 80) can come wholly from Ascensius, 'Atque cetera ad constructionem navium necessaria'. When Virgil was obscure or allusive, Douglas examined Ascensius. Part of the diffuseness of the poem is due to his determination to embody explanatory material in the text—and this was appropriate, because he wished to make Virgil available to schoolboys, and because almost every English writer of the early Renaissance seems to have been haunted by a sense of the impermanence of language, and determined to lay synonyms as props against decay. One may suspect that Virgil without the commentary was not wholly available to Douglas, and that some of the explanatory expansions borrowed from Ascensius mark the places where his own classical scholarship was uncertain.

Why did Douglas undertake the translation of the ***Aeneid,*** beyond assenting to the proposal of his cousin Lord Sinclair? He was not influenced by the medieval transformation of Virgil into a necromancer addicted to clandestine meetings with women, to whose window he was hoisted in a basket; to this body of legend Douglas alludes but once, when he says that the power of love 'crelit up the flour of poetry' (**Prol. I.** 32). Nor was he affected by the medieval legend that Virgil was the unconscious prophet of Christianity; though he alludes to it in **Prologue VI:**

Thus faithfully in his Buikolikis he saith,
The maid comith bryngis new lynage fra hevin.

Rather he adopts the Renaissance attitude towards Virgil, reverence for the master-poet, humility before the master-achievement:

Maist reverend Virgill, of Latyn poetis prynce,
Gem of engyne and flude of eloquens,
Thow peirless perle, patroun of poetry,
Roys, regester, palm, lawrer and glory. . . .
(Prologue I.)

The hie wysdome and maist profund engyne
Of myne author Virgile, poete dyvyne,
To comprehend, makis me almaist forvay,
So crafty wrocht his wark is, lyne by lyne.
(Prologue V.)

In face of such excellence, Douglas sinks into self-depreciation:

. . . set that empty be my brayn and dull,
I have translait a volum wondirfull:
So profund was this wark at I have said,
Me semyt oft throw the deip sey to waid;
And so mysty umquhile this poecy,
My spreit was reft half deill in extasy . . .
Not as I suld, I wrait, but as I couth.

And yet on occasion, particularly on the occasion of completing the work, he abandons his pose of ignorance and unlettered stupidity, and praises himself for doing, rather well even, what no one had attempted in Scots before.

Douglas has, then, a double attitude towards himself, on the one hand a sense of insufficience before the masters of the past, on the other a sense of supremacy over his contemporaries. As the first translator of a major classical poem into English, he had no immediate rivals. Surrey's less lively blank-verse version of the *Aeneid* was in the future, as were the tongue-twisting hexameters of Stanyhurst and the graceless septenaries of Phaer. It is illuminating to compare Douglas's work with Caxton's translation, if that loose rendering can so be called. In **Prologue I** Douglas attacks Caxton's shameful perversion of the story, and in **Prologue V** he remarks complacently on his own superiority:

Now harkis sportis, myrthis and myrry plays,

Ful gudly pastans on mony syndry ways,
Endyte by Virgil, and heir by me translate,
Quhilk William Caxton knew nevir al hys days,
For, as I sayd tofor, that man forvays;
Hys febil proys beyn mank and mutulate,
Bot my propyne com from the pres fute hait,
Onforlatit, not jawyn fra tun to tun,
In fresch sapour new from the berry run.

He offers the heady wine of scholarship, inebriating after the poor dregs set out by Caxton. Caxton went wrong in three fashions: he offended the exact scholar by his mistakes in names; the poet, by his mutilated, feeble prose; and the humanist, by his omissions and expansions that changed the harmonious structure of the original. Nor is this last charge unjustified, for Caxton made his *Eneydos* a romance on Dido, so much is the Fourth Book expanded; and in fact he did not translate Virgil, but a French version of an Italian version of some parts of the ***Aeneid.*** So passionately did Douglas revere the Virgilian text that he reproved even Chaucer, a master and lantern for poets, for impugning the moral integrity of Aeneas, and thus of Virgil too.

It may be objected that Douglas himself departed from the sacred text by including the Thirteenth Book, the sequel composed in 1428 by Mapheus Vegius. The inclusion of the supplement is not surprising. For a century and a half after Vegius wrote the Thirteenth Book it was considered an inseparable part of the poem, even enjoying the same sort of scholastic comment that Badius Ascensius lavished on the other twelve books. Nor was Vegius's the only attempted sequel: it was commonly felt that hero-worship of Aeneas was incomplete without his death and deification and some account of the realized glory of Rome. Vegius paid Virgil the compliment of close imitation, and his contemporaries called him 'doctissimus' and an 'alter Maro'. Douglas was not, therefore, taking the same startling liberties with the text that Caxton did, yet nevertheless, in the **Thirteenth Prologue,** he seems to have had doubts (as did the printer Aldus Manutius) of the decorum of including even this very respectable supplement.

It may also be objected that he almost doubled the number of lines in the original. The considerable expansion of Virgil's bulk is partly due to the form: while Douglas did not translate strictly line by line, the couplet is his unit of composition corresponding to the hexameter, so that he has twenty syllables for Virgil's fifteen or so. This in part accounts for the *extra* words, the makeweight phrases such as 'I wene', 'full weill I wait', 'quod he', 'as was the gys', and 'I wis', and the doublets so characteristic of the translation, such as 'clepe and call', 'braid and large', 'begynnyng and original', 'wyse and sage', and 'reuthfull and devote'. These are minor verbal additions, and it is clear that within the limits of his powers Douglas aimed at equivalence, that is, capturing all the sense of the original and transferring it without distortion into Scottish verse. He sacrificed many of the levels of suggestion that make the Latin so haunting and evocative; he may not have known they were there. But he captured the clear sense of the poem, especially in passages that rush with energy and effort. At best many translations make the poem a *tableau vivant,* at worst a *tableau mort.* Douglas felt life in the original and infused it into his translation.

Douglas's greatest achievement was the translation of the ***Aeneid;*** he recognized the *magnitude* of the task when he challenged harsh critics to

assay als lang labour agane,
And translait Ovid, as I have Virgill.

But what of his original poetry? It is not strikingly original; Douglas was simply competent in the manipulation of the standard forms of the late fifteenth century. Students of literary theory find much of interest in the **First, Third, Fifth, Sixth, Ninth,** and **Thirteenth prologues,** and in the **Conclusion, Direction,** and **Exclamation** that follow Book XIII. In these poems Douglas developed his somewhat inchoate theories of translation and aesthetics, indicating that the translator must aim at a just rendering of the 'sentence', or significance, of the poem; that he so aimed; that nevertheless he translated 'al maste word by word'; that he would have done better if he had not been limited by the existing text; that the style should fit the subject; that Virgil's transcendent meaning escaped him; that he was too rudely ignorant to capture Virgil's music; that the poem is 'translatit rycht'; that Scots was a poverty-stricken language; that critics should not be censorious; and that composing a vernacular version of the ***Aeneid*** was an honourable and useful task. Another group of prologues develops various philosophic, theological, and ethical ideas. The **Second,** as an introduction to the fall of Troy, is a meditation on a common, melancholy, medieval theme, 'All erdly glaidnes fynysith with wo'. The **Fourth** attacks Venus and Cupid as fosterers of burning, carnal delight, and solemnly warns young and old, male and female, against the power of love. In the **Fifth** (as incidentally in the **First**) Douglas disposes of the pagan gods and their claims to divinity; in the **Sixth** he demonstrates that Virgil, although a pagan, had philosophic insights nearly Christian. The **Eighth,** interesting for its intimidating vocabulary and as the author's sole exercise in the alliterative form (which by 1513 had lost the freshness of its prime), is a fairly conventional attack on the society of the day, its irrationality, its dispirited materialism, its permissive surrender of old moral values; though Douglas perhaps evaded responsibility for the charges by placing them in the mouth of a disgruntled misanthrope in a dream. The **Tenth** runs through the principal points of theology, Creation, the Trinity, the Incarnation, the Atonement, Transubstantiation, the sovereignty of God, the insufficiency of human understanding, and universal order. The **Eleventh** describes Douglas's idea of moral chivalry, tying the theological **Tenth** to the ***Aeneid*** by citing the virtues and prowess of the Christian knight, the perfect theologian and yet, like Aeneas, the perfect soldier. Most modern readers will find these moralizings tedious and prolix. Finally, among the prologues there are the nature poems. The **Seventh,** the description of winter, is probably the best because it captures authentic experience, the chill of an Edinburgh December. In contrast the **Twelfth,** more conventional in response and subject than the **Seventh,** is ecstatically lyrical in praise of May, piling up the 'flowers white and red' that dot medieval tapestries and perfume medieval lyric verse, coming to life with the singing country girls and the leering young men, and achieving point when the generative processes of nature in springtime inspire Douglas to complete the task of translation. The **Thirteenth Prologue** begins with a June evening, and ends—delightfully—with the world's awakening the following morning; the middle narrates Douglas's dream in which Mapheus Vegius appears and compels the reluctant translator to add one more book to the tale, the Vegian supplement that carries Aeneas to heaven. Some of these poems were evidently inspired by and are intimately connected with the books they precede, others seem to be affixed for form's sake when critical inspiration failed.

The ***Palice of Honour*** is a good example of a common medieval form, the dream allegory. It explores the various roads humanity can follow to honour, the roads of wisdom, chivalric love, chastity, poetry, valiant knighthood, and, the surest way, moral virtue. It begins with a splendid aureate prologue, an invocation of nature, not, one fancies, the real natural world around Edinburgh, but the stylized, half-imaginary world of medieval tapestries. Indeed, Douglas himself is at pains to remind the reader that this is an artificial dream-world, a world '*depaint* as paradice amiabill', 'powderit with mony a set Of ruby, topas, perle, and emerant', a world in which the blooming flowers 'Ovirspred the levis of *natures tapestreis*', and in which the umbrate trees 'War *portrait,* and on the eirth yschappit Be goldin bemis vivificative'. The poem must be admired for its exuberance and energy, and for the sensuous pleasure of language-play, not for its evocation of the real world. (pp. viii-xvii)

The poem has more to offer than ornamental flourishes, though here, more than elsewhere, Douglas displays his facility with aureate diction, the dulce, mellifluate, flowered, redolent rhetoric that impedes so many readers of sixteenth-century Scottish poetry. Douglas speaks of his 'rurall termis rude', but he manipulates to his purpose a difficult stanza (nine lines with but two rimes, as in *skatterit, batterit, odious, swatterit, tatterit, vennemous, contagious, clatterit, sulphurious*), and can even marshal his vocabulary in complicated internal rime:

> Haill rois maist chois till clois thy fois greit micht,
> Haill stone quhilk schone upon the throne of licht,
> Vertew, quhais trew sweit dew ovirthrew al vice,
> Was ay ilk day gar say the way of licht;
> Amend, offend, and send our end ay richt.

The lists become oppressive: poets, virtuous Greeks, the terms of music, the terms of architecture are displayed with pointless erudition—or is it the author's pleasure to fit as many items as possible into his rimes to display his virtuosity? He is enchanted with his own skill, and his enthusiasm is enough to carry the reader through most of the poem. But beyond the decorative skill, the poet shows flashes of wit, and finally rises to modest heights of philosophic vision.

Douglas must be regarded, then, as a competent poet in his own right—beyond this as a great translator. He had doubts about Scots, for it had not been dignified by age and use as Latin had. But he faced the difficulty of language with individuality and vigour, asserting the rightness of Scots as it was right for Virgil to use Latin, and aiming at a vitality unrestrained by the stately decorum of Neo-classicism. History on the whole has been kind to his reputation, and it would be an error in taste to find now nothing in his work except an archaic level of sensibility. His ***Aeneid*** differs from Virgil's, being less sensuous and melodic, more spirited and lively, and, above all, more nautical. But if the reader can accustom himself to the curiosities of Scottish orthography, then he may find here the most satisfying translation of the Latin original. (pp. xviii-xix)

David F. C. Coldwell, in an introduction to Selections from Gavin Douglas, *Oxford at the Clarendon Press, 1964, pp. vii-xix.*

Denton Fox (essay date 1966)

[*Fox is an American educator specializing in Middle Scots and English literature. In the following excerpt, he examines the relationship between Douglas's version of the* Aeneid *and Virgil's original as well as the poet's debt to Chaucer in the* Palice of Honour. *Furthermore, he assesses Douglas's poetic strengths and limitations, focusing particularly on the rhetoric, rhythm, vocabulary, and structure of his poetry.*]

Both of Douglas's major poems, ***The Palace of Honour*** and his translation of the ***Aeneid,*** seem to have some affinities with later English poetry. In ***The Palace of Honour*** we see a world that is immensely rich but confusing and baffling, a world in which the traditional ways of acting and perceiving no longer appear effective. Dunbar's poems, on the other hand, tend to be either amoral or to follow a simple and traditional morality, while Henryson is an extremely subtle but also very traditional moralist. Douglas's ***Aeneid*** is in many ways a Renaissance translation: he is interested in Virgil's *Aeneid* as a literary whole, and in Aeneas as 'the mast soueran man', a pattern of conduct. He follows the Latin text conscientiously, although he does not aim at a literal translation: 'Sum tyme the text mon haue ane expositioun, / Sum tyme the collour will caus a litill additioun, / And sum tyme of a word I mon mak thre . . . ' (**Prologue to Book I,** 347-49). Here again, Douglas is very different from Henryson, who allegorises the myth of Orpheus and Eurydice, from Dunbar, with his lighthearted and traditional references to the 'ornate stilis so perfyte' of 'Omer', and, as Douglas self-righteously points out at length, from Chaucer's rather lop-sided treatment of the *Aeneid* in *The House of Fame.*

Douglas's aristocratic, self-seeking and mercurial life is appropriate to his poetry, for with him we seem to have a new image, the poet as gifted amateur, rather than the old image of the poet as a professional and semi-anonymous bard. It is not that his poetry is technically casual or incompetent, but that he gives the impression of writing only at his own pleasure, and only on subjects which interest him. It is curiously fitting, in view of his transitional position in Scottish literature, that his poetry should be exactly contemporary with Dunbar's (***The Palace of Honour*** was written about 1501, and his ***Aeneid*** was finished in 1513), but that most of his public life should take place in the radically changed new world of James V.

The most important thing to say about Douglas's ***Aeneid*** is what Ezra Pound and C. S. Lewis have already said loudly, just that it is an exceedingly good poem. It seems likely, especially now that a competent edition has appeared, that the poem will in the future be valued for what it is: one of the first and best of the English translations of the Renaissance; a translation of the *Aeneid* which is at least as good as Dryden's; and therefore necessarily an important English work in its own right. C. S. Lewis has helped to clear away two misapprehensions about the poem which a modern reader is likely to fall into. One is that Douglas's language may seem to us quaint and rustic, because 'We forget that in his day it was a courtly and literary language'. The other is that the characters in the translation may seem to us too brisk, colloquial and modern because we have been falsely trained to see them as venerable, antique and stiff. Lewis's point here is surely sound, though perhaps Douglas went a little too much to the opposite extreme from us. One suspects that Aeneas seemed more of a contemporary to Douglas than he did to Virgil.

But there is still a third misapprehension which may block our understanding of the poem. It is easy to think of Douglas as an untaught genius who forcibly, brilliantly and instinctively threw the *Aeneid* into English. But nothing could be farther from the truth, since Douglas's ***Aeneid*** is an exceptionally self-conscious and rhetorical translation. He warns us of this clearly enough in his prologue to the first book, a critical and polemical general introduction running to more than five hundred lines. The first few lines show both Douglas's opinion of Virgil, as a master of rhetoric, and Douglas's ambition to raise his own language to an equal pitch of eloquence.

> Lawd, honour, praysyngis, thankis infynyte
> To the and thy dulce ornat fresch endyte,
> Maist reuerend Virgill, of Latyn poetis prynce,
> Gem of engyne and flude of eloquens,
> Thow peirles perle, patroun of poetry,
> Roys, regester, palm, lawrer and glory,
> Chosyn charbukkill, cheif flour and cedyr tre . . .

Modern readers have been misled, perhaps, by the contrast which Douglas goes on to draw between his 'blunt endyte' and the 'scharp sugurate sang Virgiliane', between his 'ignorant blabryng imperfyte' and Virgil's 'polyst termys redymyte' ('wreathed' or 'adorned'). But this conventional mock-modesty is of course itself a rhetorical flourish. In the rest of the prologue Douglas demonstrates rather ostentatiously the range and skilfulness of his styles, and at the same time takes up some technical matters. He states that he will use some Latin, French and southern English words, which means that he will use an artificial poetic diction; he discusses, with examples, the difficulty of translating some Latin words; and he derides the blunders of earlier translators. Douglas provides a most revealing image when he remarks,

> Quha is attachit ontill a staik, we se,
> May go na ferthir bot wreil about that tre:
> Rycht so am I to Virgillis text ybund . . .

His translation, then, is a green plant winding around a stake, ornamenting and covering it, but attached to it at all points—or almost all, for Douglas says he may 'mak digressioun sum tyme'. The simile also works in a way which Douglas may not have intended, for a plant's stake is designed, of course, to support and guide the plant. Douglas laments that he could have made a poem 'twys als curyus' if he had not been constrained to follow Virgil's text, but if he had attempted to write a poem of this magnitude without a support and guide, the results would surely have been more curious than organised.

Douglas's famous prologues, original poems which are prefixed to each book of the ***Aeneid,*** offer another guidepost to the nature of the translation. These prologues are in a great variety of metrical forms, and on a great variety of subjects: some provide literary criticism; some are satirical, moral, philosophical, or religious; and some are descriptions of nature at different seasons. Critics have usually concentrated on these last ones, and complimented Douglas on his feeling for nature and his close observation of the Scottish landscape. But this is to put the emphasis on the wrong place, for the prologues are above all a series of set pieces intended to demonstrate Douglas's competence at writing in various styles on various subjects. To be sure, the seasonal prologues are very good, but Douglas wrote them more because the seasons were a standard topic for Scottish poets than because he had any eighteenth-century feeling for nature. The prologues might be compared with the *Shepherd's Calendar:* in both cases there is the same purposive and partly experimental variety of forms, the same self-conscious use, and abuse, of traditional genres, and the same obtrusive concern with poetical techniques.

Douglas's ***Aeneid*** is so huge and so variegated that it is impossible to treat it in any detail here, but perhaps a single quotation will indicate some of the qualities, as well as some of the problems, of the translation.

> The rage of Silla, that huge swelth in the see,
> Ye haue eschapit, and passit eik haue yhe
> The euer rowtand Charibdis rolkis fell;
> The craggis quhar monstruus Ciclopes dwell
> Yhe ar expert. Pluk vp your hartis, I you pray,
> This dolorus dreid expell and do away.
> [I iv 73-8]

> vos et Scyllaeam rabiem penitusque sonantis
> accestis scopulos, vos et Cyclopia saxa
> experti; revocate animos maestumque timorem
> mittite . . .
> [I 200-03]

One notices first Douglas's characteristic habit of expanding and elucidating his original. *Mittite* is doubled into the downright 'expell and do away'; *accestis* into the explicit 'eschapit, and passit eik'. These expansions seem reasonable enough, but a purist would object that Douglas has unwarrantably introduced Charybdis into the passage, and moreover has mistakenly made Scylla, instead of Charybdis, into a whirlpool *(swelth)*. This confusion is unimportant, but the passage shows how he generally takes a freer approach to the Latin than a modern translator would. If one reads Douglas's translation while holding an annotated edition of Virgil, one will find that Douglas incorporates directly into his text many of the modern annotations. Usually, though not always, these additions are correct and helpful. But a modern translator would no more dare to do this than he would dare to insert his own original compositions between each book. Douglas often throws new and valuable light on the meaning of a particular passage, just as his translation as a whole brings out powerfully and unexpectedly some overlooked aspects of Virgil, but he is not a reliable guide to Virgil's actual words. To an unusually large degree, the excellence of Douglas's translation is derived more from the translator than from the original.

This passage also shows some of the reasons for Douglas's excellence. One of them, rather ironically, is precisely the quality which makes him difficult for a modern reader: his vocabulary. In some cases he was simply fortunate in his inheritance: *rowtand,* for instance, is an admirable word for *sonantis,* being more exact than *roaring* and less bookish than *resounding,* while *dolorus dreid* is a very happy equivalent for *maestum timorem.* Douglas is particularly skilful in taking advantage of the flexibility of literary Scots: he moves freely from the most colloquial to the most ornate diction and makes a forceful but never pedantic use of Latinisms and neologisms. The first four lines of this passage, for instance, lead up to the emphatic Latinism, *expert* (which ordinarily meant 'experienced' in Middle Scots, but is here used in a Latinate construction), and then this climax is followed by the semi-colloquial *Pluk vp.* Similarly, in the last line the Latinate *expell* is complemented by *do away.*

Douglas's felicitous handling of rhetoric and rhythm is also demonstrated in this passage. There are, for instance, two separate patterns in the first three lines. On the one hand, the first and third lines, describing the dangers, are balanced against the second line, describing the safety. On the other hand, these three lines are divided syntactically into two clauses, each a line and a half long, and arranged in a careful chiasmus: object, subject, auxiliary verb, past participle—past participle, auxiliary verb, subject, object. The next phrase, *The craggis . . . ar expert,* is parallel with the first line and a half, so that the reader expects Douglas to repeat the whole three-line pattern again. But instead there is an abrupt and rhythmically jarring full stop, emphasising the *expert,* and a shift into a broken and colloquial rhythm, imitating the tone of Aeneas's earnest plea. Throughout the passage there runs an alliteration so constant as to be almost structural, but used purposefully to link words together: *Silla—swelth—see, craggis—Ciclopes, dolorus dreid—do away.*

Douglas's ***Palace of Honour,*** though a less important poem than his ***Aeneid,*** is especially interesting here because it so clearly stands in the Chaucerian tradition. In genre, it is like *The House of Fame:* a dream-vision about a journey to a lofty and allegorical building. Douglas seems to have borrowed many of the details of his plot from Chaucer, though of course one cannot always be certain that he did not go directly to Chaucer's sources, or on the other hand borrow from *The Temple of Glass* or other fifteenth-century imitations of Chaucer, some of which are perhaps no longer extant. But there are enough verbal reminiscences of Chaucer in ***The Palace of Honour,*** and enough direct references to Chaucerian characters, to make us safe in assuming that Douglas, most of the time, was borrowing immediately from Chaucer.

By looking at the plot of ***The Palace of Honour*** one can see not only how much Douglas was indebted to Chaucer, but also how well he understood him—Douglas's poem is a very useful commentary on *The House of Fame.* ***The Palace of Honour*** has the same traditional beginning as *The Legend of Good Women:* the narrator goes out on a May morning, sees the spring flowers, hears spring songs, and then has a visionary dream. But Douglas's narrator, like the narrator in *The House of Fame,* dreams that he is in a 'desert terribill'. In both poems, this desert stands for the desolate and barren spiritual condition of the narrator, caught in the wastes of the temporal world, and is equivalent to Dante's *selva oscura* or Eliot's wasteland, though the actual detailed description of Douglas's desert makes it seem oddly like the landscape in Browning's *Childe Roland.* Douglas's narrator sees Minerva, the 'Quene of Sapience', go by with her train, on the way to the 'Palace of Honour', and then Diana, but he himself remains and does not follow either the way of wisdom or the way of asceticism. Then, after a learned digression on sound waves, in imitation of the lecture which Chaucer's eagle gives, Venus appears, with Mars, Cupid and the rest of the court of love. This court is composed mostly of the heroines of *The Legend of Good Women* and of the figures from the temple of Venus in *The House of Fame,* together with a few characters who are even more Chaucerian: Arcite, Palamon and Emily, Troilus and Criseyde, and Griselda. The narrator finally feels constrained to sing a song, set off from the narrative by being in a different stanzaic form, in which he laments his own woes and denounces Venus. As a result, he is seized by the court, tried and condemned. There is an obvious parallel here with *The Legend of Good Women,* where Chaucer's narrator is condemned by the god of love for having made songs against love, and the parallel is carried on by the sequel. In Douglas's poem the 'court rethoricall' of muses and famous poets appears, and Calliope intercedes for mercy, using the same arguments that Chaucer's Alceste uses: the sin is small, the victim is unworthy of a god, and he won't do it again. So Douglas's narrator, like Chaucer's, goes free after having promised to make poetic amends.

Douglas makes it clear that he is using this material because it is meaningful, not simply because it is traditional. He emphasises, for instance, the difference between sexual love, with its power to brutalise or destroy (the dreamer is afraid that Venus will transform him into an animal or kill him) and the intercessory charity of Calliope. The complicated relationships between love and poetry are neatly implied, too: they are at odds, not only because poetry is often anti-feminist, but also because perfection of the work conflicts with perfection of the life; yet they are reconcilable, partly because poetry celebrates and immortalises love, and partly because poetry is a parallel but independent road to the Palace of Honour. So after the narrator is saved by Calliope and her band of muses and poets, who sweep on stage almost like a rescuing army,

Calliope entrusts him to the charge of a nymph and they go off together on their way to the palace.

This guiding nymph fulfils the same functions as Chaucer's eagle and, though less loquacious, shows her similarity to him by encouraging the fearful narrator and telling him where to look. Their journey is a terrestrial one, yet no less extraordinary and extensive than Chaucer's aerial one: 'Now into Egypt, now into Italie, / Now in the realme of Trace, and now in Spane.' But at one place there seems to be a humorous glance at Chaucer's air transport, for the nymph seizes the narrator by the hair and carries him over a hell-like ditch and up to the palace at the top of a hill.

The third and last part of ***The Palace of Honour,*** as of *The House of Fame,* is concerned with the narrator's adventures at his destination. Douglas's building is obviously modelled on Chaucer's: both are very beautiful, are made out of beryl, have intricately carved golden gates, and have immensely rich interiors which are full of precious stones. But they are also very different, as the titles of the poems suggest: 'Palace' is grander than 'House', and 'Honour' less equivocal than 'Fame'. The difference is neatly symbolised by the hills the buildings are on: both hills appear to be made of glass, but where Chaucer's turns out to be of ice, Douglas's is of hard marble, and so equally hard to climb but infinitely more durable. Chaucer emphasises the arbitrariness of earthly fame and, with his revolving wicker house, gives an image of mutability. Douglas's honour is supernatural, just and eternal (it is always the same season at the palace), and so is contrasted with earthly mutability: from the top of the hill one can look down and see the earth, which appears in the guise of a stormy sea filled with drowning mariners.

But there is a curious similarity between the climactic revelations of the two poems. In *The House of Fame,* of course, Chaucer breaks off just as the 'man of great auctorite' is apparently about to make an important statement. Although ***The Palace of Honour*** is a finished poem, the climax is almost as equivocal and tantalising: the narrator peers through a hole, sees 'ane God omnipotent', swoons, and is laughed at by his nymph for being such a coward. It would seem as though each poet was forced by the very nature of his poem to produce such an ambiguous climax, or perhaps more exactly such a lack of climax. Dante could end his serious and Christian poem with a Paradiso, but Chaucer and Douglas can only make an ironic gesture towards an ultimate revelation in their half-humorous and ostensibly unchristian poems. Dante, the pilgrim, is educated by his travels so that he can understand the truths of the Paradiso, but neither Chaucer's nor Douglas's narrators are very educable, and perhaps neither the eagle nor the nymph are the best possible pedagogues.

It would be possible to show other Chaucerian borrowings in ***The Palace of Honour***—it seems likely, for instance, that there is a bond of relationship between the Chaucerian *persona* and Douglas's narrator, who is shown as being dazed, curious, timid, and, as he himself admits, knowing no more than a sheep. But for all of Chaucer's influence, it must be admitted that the poem seems to a modern reader profoundly un-Chaucerian. In *The House of Fame,* for all its preposterous plot, there is a smooth and plausible narrative line, and the narrator always seems to be present in his flesh and blood. But ***The Palace of Honour*** is a glittering and artificial poem: Douglas seems to make no effort to preserve any reasonable narrative coherence, or to impart any feeling of verisimilitude.

Douglas's metrical forms are partly responsible for the special quality of his poem, and they also give us an indication of his purposes. The first two books are in the nine-line stanza, rhymed *aabaabbab,* which Chaucer used in *Anelida and Arcite,* and which Dunbar was to use in *The Golden Targe,* a poem very similar to some parts, particularly the prologue, of *The Palace of Honour.* The third book is in the different nine-line stanza, rhymed *aabaabbcc,* which Chaucer used in *The Complaint of Mars.* In several places Douglas uses a ten-line stanza to mark off rhetorically ornate songs, and at the end of the poem, perhaps taking a hint from the internal rhyme in *Anelida and Arcite,* he has three stanzas, the first with double internal rhyme, the second with triple and the third with quadruple, while he preserves in all of them the normal end-rhyme of the *Anelida* stanza. Douglas's use of the forms of these two poems reminds us of an aspect of Chaucer which was very important in the fifteenth century but which has often been overlooked: Chaucer as a metrical innovator and as a technical virtuoso. And these intricate stanzaic forms show us that Douglas is not trying to conduct a realistic narrative, but to achieve a highly wrought poetic brilliance. The elaborate burst of rhyme with which Douglas concludes ***The Palace of Honour*** is only an extreme example of the artificial splendour which he has been striving for throughout the whole work.

It is surely no accident that Douglas's narrator is rescued and given a guide by Calliope, the muse of epic poetry and so, as Douglas says, of the 'kinglie stile'. Douglas's narrator rises above the world by the aid of a muse, not by the aid of a philosophical and humanly loquacious eagle: Douglas himself raises his poem off the ground by sheer rhetoric, not by structural design or by sympathetically human characters. Douglas's preoccupation with rhetoric and style is of course very evident throughout the poem. The prologue is a dazzling set piece in the aureate mode, and Douglas begins the first book with a dramatically rhetorical stanza—in which he pretends to disclaim any rhetorical ability. The poem is filled with rhetorical figures and with explicit comments on the styles of Douglas himself, of his characters and of other poets, while at the end there is a three-stanza epilogue that is largely Douglas's mock-apology for his 'barrant termis' and 'vile indite'.

But there is also a connection between the poem's emphasis on rhetoric and its very structure. Visionary poems about allegorical journeys tend to be richly variegated and comprehensive, as if their authors wished to set up allegorical worlds that were as complex and multitudinous as our ordinary world. Dante and the author of *Piers Plowman* achieve this comprehensiveness by the sheer magnitude and seriousness of their poems; Chaucer, in *The House of Fame,* uses a variety of devices—the re-telling of the *Aeneid,* which brings a metamorphosed classical world into the poem, the exhaustive logical rigour with which the various applicants to Fame are classified, and the stupidity of the narrator, which allows Chaucer to hint at worlds seen but not understood. *The Parliament of Fowls* offers a tidier example, with its three figures of Scipio, Venus and Nature balanced against each other so as to form the corners of an all-embracing triangle. But Douglas has a simpler way to make his poem inclusive. He merely brings every possible sort of subject matter into his poem, fits it all neatly into the tissue of his rhetoric, and passes on. One of the most characteristic parts of the poem is the section where the narrator looks into Venus's magic mirror and sees 'The deidis and fatis of euerie eirdlie wicht': Satan's fall, Noah's flood, over thirty Old Testament figures, about fifty figures from classical history and mythology, medieval falconers and necromancers, and the heroes of contemporary popular poetry.

The basic structural device of ***The Palace of Honour,*** then, is the list: the different parts of the poem are joined together by simple juxtaposition and these parts are themselves largely made up of catalogues. Chaucer himself is a great master of lists—one thinks of the description of the House of Fame, or of the more brilliant description of the temples in *The Knight's Tale*—but the difference between the two poets is shown by their methods of describing a journey. Chaucer conveys the length and the marvellousness of the flight in *The House of Fame* by letting us see it through the surprised eyes of the narrator; Douglas achieves something of the same effect by simply giving a long, preposterous, but skilful list of the geographical places through which his narrator passes.

One may, if one wishes, repeat the old truism to the effect that medieval critical theories perniciously emphasised rhetoric and ornamentation at the expense of structure and unity. But it is perhaps more helpful to note that Douglas's techniques are justified by their results. The suddenness of his scene shifting, for instance, the quick juxtaposition of apparently disparate passages, works to produce the strange mixture of clarity and lack of causality that is so typical of dreams, and also is used to reinforce Douglas's themes. In particular, the pervasive theme of the contrast between earthly mutability and transcendental perfection is repeatedly brought out by the juxtaposition of contrasting scenes. And even Douglas's catalogues are something more than a medieval vice: it is interesting to observe that Auden, another poet who is fond of allegory and ostentatious rhetoric, uses catalogues frequently. Like Dunbar, who is also addicted to lists, Douglas uses them to group similar or contrasting elements, to balance entities against each other and to freeze them into a comprehensive and rigid rhetorical form. Dunbar's catalogues perhaps reveal a finer ear and a greater meticulousness, but Douglas's are far from slovenly. The following passage, for instance, shows not only Douglas's skilful variation of pace and rhythm, but also his ability to lead a catalogue up to a climax:

> The miserie, the crueltie, the dreid,
> Pane, sorrow, wo, baith wretchitnes and neid,
> The greit inuy, couetous dowbilnes,
> Tuitchand warldlie vnfaithfull brukilnes.

The Palace of Honour is doubtless not one of the world's great poems, but it is, I think, a very deft and interesting piece which has been undervalued because misunderstood: readers have hunted in it for a philosophical richness or a Chaucerian humanity which is not there, and have dismissed as faults and digressions the obtrusive rhetoric and the perpetually shifting subject matter which are actually the poem's essential qualities. (pp. 188-99)

Like the other Scots poets, [Douglas] can be seen in several contexts. One is the familiar 'History of English Literature'. Here Douglas, Henryson and Dunbar appear as poets inheriting the Chaucerian wealth, partly through fifteenth-century intermediaries, but using it for profoundly un-Chaucerian purposes: there is a vast gulf between *The House of Fame* and ***The Palace of Honour.*** These poets seem themselves to leave no direct heirs, except for some relatively minor sixteenth-century Scots, but Douglas, at least, foreshadows the Elizabethan poets. Just as his ***Aeneid*** is the precursor of the Elizabethan translations (and was plagiarised by Surrey), so the prologues to it seem to point towards the experiments in different metres and dictions of the sixteenth-century English poets, and so his ***Palace of Honour*** makes a bit more evident the connection between Chaucer and the *Faerie Queene.*

Another context is the general European background, the tradition that Dante suggested in his famous phrase for Arnaut Daniel: 'fu miglior fabbro del parlar materno' (*Purgatorio* XXVI, 117). Douglas, Henryson and Dunbar have an honourable place among the countless medieval and Renaissance poets who tried to refine their various maternal tongues by concentrating arduously on perfection of form and rhetoric, and who successfully attempted to produce a literature that could rival their classical inheritance.

But Dante's phrase, with its use of the word *fabbro,* 'smith, craftsman, maker', for *poet,* leads us back again to Douglas, Henryson, Dunbar and the short-lived apogee of Scottish literature which they represent. The word *poet* itself, of course, like many of its synonyms in different languages, has an etymological meaning of something like *maker,* but it is surely not coincidental that in modern English the term *maker,* in the sense of *poet,* is reserved almost exclusively for the Middle Scots poets. Their poetry is a poetry of craftsmanship, and they are united by their devotion to their craft, even though each poet manifests it differently: Henryson with his pervading decorum and his art that conceals art; Dunbar with his succinct brilliance; Douglas with his gaudy rhetorical flowers. These poets, in their different ways, all seem to have channelled their passion towards the idea that a poem ought to be as finely wrought as possible. This implies their limitations: these poets are not profoundly interested in philosophy, in nature, or in self-revelation. But their poems are well made, which is perhaps all the praise that any poet can demand. (pp. 199-200)

Denton Fox, "The Scottish Chaucerians," in Chaucer and Chaucerians: Critical Studies in Middle English Literature, *edited by D. S. Brewer, Nelson, 1966, pp. 164-200.*

Gerald B. Kinneavy (essay date 1969)

[*Kinneavy is an American educator who has written several articles on the literature of the late Middle Ages. In the excerpt below, he purports that the* Palice of Honour *is a multi-leveled work of great imaginative and poetic power. Skillfully structured, this allegory, the critic maintains, is a meditation on the poet's journey to discover the tools of his craft and his own creativity.*]

Though Gavin Douglas's poem, ***The Palice of Honour,*** has been described most frequently as an unoriginal composition in which the conventions current in his day abound and in which details are "piled on aimlessly," it has—by its most recent critics—been given a place as "substantially an original work" [C. S. Lewis, in his *English Literature in the Sixteenth Century: Excluding Drama,* 1954]. And though the poet's employment of the conventions current in medieval literature is extensive, those conventions are "skilfully shaped to the present purpose" [David F. C. Coldwell, in his edition of *Virgil's Aeneid,* 1957-64] of the poem. The artistry of Douglas is such, says C. S. Lewis [in his *Allegory of Love,* 1936], that the conventions of the dream and so on are shaped to appeal directly to the imagination and not simply to evoke the "memory" of the conventional usage:

> Douglas is no dreamer like Hawes, for he is not the servant of his dream, and he writes with a clear head and a learned and practised pen; but what he describes is sheer wonderland, a phantasmagoria of dazzling lights and eldritch glooms, whose real *raison d'être* is not their allegorical meaning, but their immediate appeal to the imagination.

Lewis calls attention to the freedom and sense of space created in the poem by figures "hithering and thithering" apparently without narrative consequence as particularly appropriate to a poem in which the persona is, in fact, dreaming. I am not so sure that there is no narrative consequence to the events and figures in the poem, but Lewis' general point supports the view that Douglas is here employing many of the traditional conventions of his time but in a way which gives those conventions a new shape, an originality and a purposeful pattern. That pattern has been described most often in moral terms, and certainly there can be no doubt that the poem deals with honor and that attention is given by the poet to matters of morality. The sermon of Calliope's nymph would seem evidence enough for this. But the more immediate concern of the poet in this poem deals with the possibility, it seems to me, of his art as a conductor of honor—"honor" not in the sense of worldly fame but of his art as a justifiable occupation or endeavor, one of value. Many paths are available—wisdom, chastity, poetry and virtue. And though his guide instructs the speaker in moral virtue as *the* way, we are shown poets who have achieved entry into the Palice of Honour and we find the speaker ultimately desiring to seek his entrance through that particular kind of endeavor. This does not negate the morality of the theme; it merely focuses or channels those moral concerns to the realms of poetry, to the speaker's view of his art as it grows in the poem itself. What we finally discover in the poem is the speaker-poet's own recognition and desire for honor through or by means of his imaginative power as poet. He chooses the imaginative path to honor, the path of poetry.

The Prologue to ***The Palice of Honour*** opens with the usual conventions of the medieval dream-vision. The time of year is May. The speaker rises to do his "obseruance, / And enterit in a Gardyne of plesance . . . " (ll. 6-7). The ritualistic aura suggested by "obseruance" is sustained by the description of the garden, in which

> The siluer droppis on Daseis distillant;
> Quhilk verdour branches ouir the alars yet
> With smoky sence the mystis reflectant.
> (ll. 16-18)

This is the traditional May ritual of the medieval poet. The garden is seen in terms of "altars" and "incense," and choirs of birds who make "heuinly Harmoneis" (21)—all recognizable trappings of religious ritual. But the conventional association of May with love observance is not the point of emphasis here.

Rather, the broader archetypal significance of May, of spring as a form of rebirth, is the focus in Douglas's poem. The garden suggests to the speaker the essentially restorative power of the season. The paradise is "Replenischit and full of all delice" (29); birds, flowers and brush all "Recomfort was" (36). The sun provides beams which are "viuificatiue" (42), heat which is "maist restoratiue" (43) and "nutritiue" (48). In short, "Richt hailsome was the sessoun of the yeir . . . " (46). The natural setting, then, is appropriate to regenerative acts, to "obseruances" which honor that particular power in nature.

But the effect "Paill Aurora" and the spring have is not restricted only to things vegetative. The speaker himself is affected by "The purgit Air with new engendrit heit" (56): "Sa reioycit and comfort was my Spreit / I not was it a vision or fantone" (59-60). And he hears a voice singing praise to May, that "Maternall Moneth" (65), as a "Mirrour of soles" (64), as the power which "Causis the eirth his frutes till expres, / Diffundant grace on euerie creature" (71-2). The productive power is seen not only in terms of external nature, but is linked to man himself, to his internal faculties. May as "Mirrour of soles" providing "grace" associates the regenerative motif with the moral realm as well. The apostrophe to May is conventional to be sure; but it is important also to notice that it is functional. It focuses attention on that particular restorative quality which the speaker sees literally in spring and links that external material to what he will center on thematically in the poem, the restorative process of the poet, the creative soul's own revitalization.

After hearing the song to May, the speaker is sore afraid and "half in ane frenesie" (90) and begins his own apostrophe to May. Significantly, he pleads with nature's queen to "recounsell" him out of his present fear. The "re-" prefix of the verb is not out of place in light of the continued emphasis given to the regenerative, the renewing qualities of the season and situation. The speaker wants to be relieved of fear so that he "may sing yow laudis day be day" (95). In effect, he is pleading for her to restore his powers to sing, and this power—for the poet—is that of creating poetry. To state the idea so soberly, of course, loses the sense of comedy involved in our first direct meeting with the speaker of the poem. He describes himself as half in a frenzy and a feeble wit—not an uncommon self-description by a narrator of a medieval dream-vision. But the further detail—"My desie heid quhome laik of brane gart vary" (101)—begins the portrait of the speaker as pleasantly comic. He is not knocked down by the ensuing vision immediately into a swoon as is usual in such poems. Rather, he first falls into the shrubbery all in confusion: "Amyd the virgultis all in till a fary / As feminine so feblit fell I doun" (107-08). *Then* he falls into the swoon in which "thair remanit nouther voice nor sicht, / Breith, motion, nor heiring naturall" (110-11). The point of emphasis is again the reduction of powers. The fear, the "dreidfull terrour" (117), has not, however, merely put him in a faint. Attention is directed specifically to his wit—corrupted, made inactive by the "ouir excelland licht" (113), as when the heart malfunctions, "memberis wirkis not richt" (116).

The prologue seems little different, then, from the many instances of the dream-vision format in medieval literature. Even the light self-mockery on the part of the speaker is not unusual. But these conventions are brought together to create a specific and individual situation for Douglas's immediate purposes. The May convention is clearly depicted for its regenerative quality. That quality is sustained in the speaker's treatment of his own art of "singing." And finally, the swoon itself and the ensuing awakening are given in terms of intellectual powers lost and regained. The initial fact about the speaker—his rising to do observance to May, the "creating month"—ends in the prologue with his performing an equally creative act, the description of a vision caused by that "richt hailsome" season. Nor is the depiction all external. The speaker concentrates on himself and on his understood duties as poet or singer. And the faculties which he draws attention to are specifically those which in the course of the prologue and vision proper were deadened and which he seeks to revitalize (as the flowers of the garden were deadened in winter and reborn in spring). The conventional treatment of spring in *her* creative aspect is made to conform functionally with the concern of the poet himself in *his* creative act. The language whereby the poet describes the situation which gave rise to the vision—soon to be described—is not inappropriate to the concern of the speaker with his psychological state. His consistent concern is with his interior faculties, "spreit," "wit." These details, it seems to me, suggest not only that we have here an essentially self-conscious attitude toward the experience of the vision, but that the vision is in fact not simply the conventional description of one kind of dream but a truly visionary description by the poet of his own creative powers.

Part I of the poem, too, sustains the essentially poetic concerns of the poet-speaker. He opens the poem with a conventional apostrophe to his own feeble wit and laments his lack of power to write effectively.

> Thow barrant wit, ouirset with fantasyis,
> Schaw now the craft þat in thy memor lyis.
> Schaw now thy schame, schaw now thy bad nystie. . . .
> Schaw furth thy cure and write thir frenesyis,
> Quhilks of thy sempill cunning nakit the.
> (127-29, 134-35)

There is nothing extraordinary here. Familiar with the convention, a reader recognizes that such apostrophes are not to be taken at face value. But when the speaker returns in the next stanza to the situation at hand, his "rauist spreit in that desert terribill" (136), we are brought directly back to the concern expressed in the prologue. We recall that he had been in the beautiful garden, "ful of all delice," when the "impressioun" in the form of light came to him and caused him to lose all consciousness, to lose his faculties. Here, within the vision, his spirit remains ravished and the setting is not a garden but a desert filled with ugliness and horror:

> My rauist spreit in that desert terribill
> Approchit neir that vglie flude horribill,
> Like till Cochyte the riuer Infernall,
> With vile water quhilk maid a hiddious trubil. . . .
> (136-39)

In contrast to the fruitful and lovely trees and flowers in the garden, here rotten trees sprout without bloom, without leaves:

> Not throw the soyl bot muskane treis sproutit,
> Combust, barrant, vnblomit and vnleifit,
> Auld rottin runtis quhairen na sap was leifit,
> Moch, all waist, widderit, with granis moutit—
> A ganand den quhair murtherars men reifit.
> (149-53)

The sudden shift from the May garden to this wilderness and wasteland, where instead of soft breezes "The quhissilling wind blew mony bitter blast" (158), has its natural effect on the speaker: "Quhairfoir my seluin was richt sair agast" (154). The understatement by the speaker, of course, further sustains his comic image, but it does not destroy the essentially plausible motivation for the following three-stanza lament on the inconstancy of fortune. Such laments abound in medieval poems, but Douglas's use of the conventional lament seems functional. A ravished spirit transported abruptly from the most pleasant of gardens and from the most productive of seasons to a wintry heath might well reflect on the inconstancy of fortune as the speaker does. It is another instance of the poet's integrating the convention, assimilating it, making the convention function within the poem's larger structure.

The speaker, in his frightened state, has lodged himself in a tree from which vantage point he witnesses the court of Dame Sapience as it passes. The lords and ladies of that court, who all have grave minds and abound in wit, pass without noticing the tree-bound poet. The speaker whose wit is "barren" and "corrupt" and whose character is comic could hardly communicate directly with these "grave minds." The second, much smaller group which passes before the speaker, who retains his perch in the tree, is the train of Virgins, led by Diana. But like the court of Sapience, this court of Chastity "All on thay raid and left me in the tre" (345).

In both these instances, the speaker has no possible way

of joining the entourages—for purely literal reasons. Allegorically, the paths of wisdom and chastity, though surely means of achieving honor, are not available to him. After each episode, he reminds us of the horror of his situation in the desert where

> The water stank, the feild was odious,
> Quhair dragouns, lessertis, askis, edders swatterit,
> With mouthis gapand, forkit taillis tatterit,
> With mony a stang and spoutis vennemous
> Corrupting Air be rewme contagious.
> Maist gros and vile enpoysonit cludis clatterit,
> Reikand like hellis smoke sulfurious.
>
> (348-54)

Though he can describe himself comically—"My daisit heid fordullit disselie" (355)—he is nonetheless in need of salvation. And it is a matter of both literal and allegorical fact that neither Sapience nor Chastity has provided that salvation.

After these two episodes, the speaker—"half in ane litargie, / As dois ane Catiue ydrunkin in sleip" (356-57), raises himself up

> And sa appeirit to my fantasie
> A schynand licht out of the North eist sky,
> The quhilk with cure to heir I did tak keip.
> Proportion sounding dulcest hard I peip,
> In Musick number full of Harmonie
> Distant on far was caryit be the deip.
>
> (358-63)

Though the image of a shining light appearing to his "fantasy" joined to the sound of harmonious music is suggestive of the kind of harmony the dreamer experienced in the garden of the prologue, he is so overcome by the previous "grislie fantasyis" that "This Melodie Intonit heuinlie thus / For profound wo constranit me mak cair" (398-99). His condition—his present need of aid—remains centrally before us.

The "heavenly sound" announces the arrival of the third court, that of Venus, and the speaker minutely describes the goddess as "sa peirles excellent womanheid" (474). He recognizes Venus' court as one of earthly love, but further views its unsurpassable power in creating music and minstrelsy—presumably the "heavenly melody" he had heard before:

> Bot yit thair mirth and solace neuertheles,
> In Musick tone and menstralie expres,
> Sa craftelie with curage aggreabill—
> Hard neuer wicht sic Melodie, I ges.
>
> (486-89)

There follows a *digressio* on music and a catalogue of lovers, classical, biblical and romance. The sight of all these lovers in mirthful situations is not without its effect on the narrator. The great variety in the catalogue ranging from joyous love to despair points up to him once again the inconstancy of fortune and moves him to sing his ballad of inconstant love, in the course of which he accuses Venus of falsehood:

> Loude as I mocht, in dolour all distrenyeit,
> This lay I sang and not ane letter fenyeit.
> Tho saw I Venus on hir lip did bite. . . .
>
> (637-39)

The moment of courage lapses, however, when the court of Venus demands he come down, and

> All in ane Feuir out of my muskane bowre
> On kneis I crap and law for feir did lowre.
> Than all the Court on me thair heidis schuik,
> Sum glowmand grim, sum girnand with visage sowre.
>
> (646-49)

The remaining part of this first section of the poem sustains the growing comic image of the speaker as we see him worrying over what punishment he will be made to suffer. His most serious concern is that Venus will transform him into some kind of beast:

> That Venus suld throw hir subtillitie
> In till sum bysning beist transfigurat me. . . .
>
> (739-40)

That worry is carried over into gesture: he keeps feeling his face and gazing at his hands to see if any transformation has occurred without his knowing—"Oft I wald my hand behald to se / Gif it alterit, and oft my visage graip" (743-44). Part I ends with the speaker "rolland thus in diuers fantaseis" (763), with no hope of mercy from Venus nor aid from any friend: "My febill minde seand this greit suppryis / Was than of wit and euerie blis full bair" (770-71).

As the courts of Sapience and Chastity provided him with no salvation from his plight in this wilderness, the court of Venus does not either. The need for being saved, in fact, has been intensified. Not only is he in need of being taken from this wilderness, but he also needs salvation from the court of Venus itself. In terms of a path to the Palice of Honour, love cannot be his way since he recognizes and cries out against the inconstancy of love. Further, the association usually expected with May-time and love is seen as no longer (if at all) at work in this poem. The poet here is not a devotee of Venus in her office as the goddess of love. The "obseruance" of the prologue, then, by this point in the poem is clearly not to be seen as relative to the usual love matters of the May setting. The emphasis observed in the prologue and sustained in Part I of the poem is on the regenerative functions of spring, on the creative or productive faculties or powers of the poet.

It is the idea of salvation of one sort or another which opens Part II of the poem. The speaker attempts to console himself with faith in

> The glorious Lord ringand in persounis thre,
> Prouydit hes for my Saluatioun
> Be sum gude spreitis Reuelatioun,
> Quhilk Intercessioun maid, I traist, for me.
> I foryet all Imaginatioun.
>
> (776-80)

And having resolved his fear on grounds of faith, almost as if by Providence the "heuinlie rout" which will, in fact, effect his salvation appears—"Singand softlie full sweit on thair maneir, / On Poet wise all diuers versis seir . . . " (795-96). Douglas is again directing attention to a number of things brought together in a single context. First of all is the literal situation of the narrator, his need to be extracted from the physical circumstances of the wilderness and from the clutches of the court of Venus, whom he has offended. That need is underscored as a kind of "salvation" by the initial reference to theological salvation, faith in the Lord's saving him though the means remain unknown. The speaker simply believes the Lord "Prouydit hes for my Saluatioun." He does not intellectually know the reason why, he says, "Saue that I had sum hope till be releuit . . . " (783). Immediately ensues the sight of the "heuenlie rout" which is composed of "singers," of poets—a group whose association with the speaker is direct and appropriate. The ladies of that court astound him by their peerless skill in the poetic art:

> I had greit wonder of thay Ladyis seir,
> Quhilks in that airt micht haue na compeir;
> Of castis quent, Rethorik colouris fine,
> Sa Poeit like in subtell fair maneir
> And eloquent firme cadence Regulair.
> (817-21)

It is of some significance to note that when the speaker was incited to sing his ballad of inconstant love before the court of Venus he was moved to "courage" by his sense of the instability of love evident among the examples he had seen. Here he is moved to courage for a quite different reason—he is simply pleased by their "estate," their office, their position as poets:

> My curage grew; for quhat caus I nocht wait,
> Saif that I held me payit of thair estait. . . .
> (829-30)

And he remains passive. They come to Venus' court "To Iustifie this bysning quhilk blasphemit" (834). "Iustifie," of course, means to bring to justice, perhaps even to punish. But this is the first instance of any of the several courts in the wilderness coming voluntarily into association with the speaker. And the fact that it is the court of poetry, the court of the Muses, is not without special meaning in terms of their ultimately leading him to the Palice of Honour. His and their "estate" is the same: poet.

This court of poetry is "the facound well Celestiall," "the Fontane and Originall," and "the well of Helicon" (838-40). The images of the fountain and the well, perhaps, recall to us the initial stress in the garden on the quality of productivity, of fecundity and fertility, which we saw soon related to the speaker's own art, his song. At any rate, the description serves to delineate the essentially creative nature of poetry, a power not unlike that attributed to May and Aurora in the prologue of the poem. In addition, the members of that court—the Muses—are the sources of comfort, delight and angelical sayings:

> Yone ar the folk that comfortis euerie spreit
> Be fine delite and dite Angelicall. . . .
> (841-42)

The terminology itself is identical to the regenerative power of spring which in the prologue "replenischit," "restorit," and "recomfort [it]." The means whereby comfort is attained is the prescribed medieval aesthetic requirement of combining *mirthe* and *doctryn*—"delite" and "dite angelicall." The principle is further underlined in the immediately following lines in which Douglas repeats the basic notion in each line and joins the lines themselves in a curiously interlocking scheme:

> Yone is the Court of *plesand* steidfastnes,
> Yone is the Court of constant *merines,*
> Yone is the Court of *Ioyous* discipline. . . .
> (844-46)

The notion of "mirth" is repeated as "plesand," "merines," and "Ioyous." The *doctryn* or complementary principle in the aesthetic is given in terms of stability, "steidfastnes," "constant" (which though ambiguously in adjectival form nonetheless by virtue of its context takes on the sense of its noun counterpart, constancy), and "discipline." The principle is stated with greater explicitness in the lines which follow. This court is that

> Quhilk causis folk thair purpois to expres
> In ornate wise, prouokand with glaidnes
> All gentill hartis to thair lair Incline.
> (847-49)

It is the view of poetry as an impetus through "gladness" or "ornate wise" ("delite") toward "lair," learning or knowledge ("dite angelicall"). But the expression of that aesthetic criterion is not in itself what is most interesting here. That is commonplace. What the description continually emphasizes is the role of the muse as "cause," as a force or power (fountain, well) leading to renewed spirit, to doctrine and mirth. Such emphasis is indeed appropriate to the speaker's current situation: he is in fact in dire need of *doctryn* and *mirthe* in his literal predicament as well as in his psychological state, his "corrupted wit." And he as a poet in need of renewed spirit, and the muses and poetry as powers which do renew spirit, seem not an inadvertent juxtaposition. Further, the catalogue of muses which follows is composed of three stanzas, two devoted to eight of the muses and one full stanza solely on "The nynt, quhome to nane vther is compeir" (871), Calliope. The intention of Douglas here to focus attention and value on poetry cannot be questioned. The speaker himself underlines the value in his reaction to the arrival of the muses and their court:

> Reioysand weill my Spreit, befoir was cauld.
> The suddane sicht of that firme Court foirsaid
> Recomfort weill my hew, befoir was faid.
> Amid my spreit the Ioyous heit redoundit. . . .
> (888-91)

When he was accused by Venus, he had a quaking voice and a "hart cald as a key" (674). Here, the mere presence of the court of poetry "recomforts" him, warms his spirit, restores heat to his heart. This "spreit" which before was "cauld" and in a wilderness has begun a process of restoration, "salvation" on a literal level, through the power of poetry, "the facound well Celestiall." The literal situation of the persona, of course, has not yet been resolved. But even at this point the salvation or acquittal or renewal of the narrator literally or "spiritually" is clearly to be effected through the powers Douglas has been describing, through the court which the persona has just been witnessing, through the art of poetry.

The defense of the poet which Calliope makes before the

court of Venus underscores the basic relationship between the speaker and the muse of poetry. She speaks of his "lak," his deficiency—literally his crime against Venus—as a minor offense since "Your excellence maist peirles is sa knaw" (962), and petitions the goddess to give the poet over to her:

> Giue me his life and modifie the Law,
> For on my heid he standis now sic aw
> That he sall efter deserue neuer mair blame.
> (964-66)

She seeks custody of him, possession of his life. And she recognizes the "aw" which the speaker has for her personally as muse of poetry. Further, the word "aw" perhaps is used ambiguously here. Without doubt the context demands our reading it as "awe" or "fear." But the word also has a possessive meaning, "owe, owned." And the fact that Calliope seeks to get his life, that he already is a poet and thereby in her control, as it were, perhaps will allow the operation of both meanings together. And if she is, in fact, given "ownership" of him, the ensuing promise—"he sall efter deserue neuer mair blame"—establishes an even closer alliance of the speaker with the muse of poetry.

Venus accedes to the requests of Calliope and gives two conditions: 1) he must compose a ballad "Tuitching my Laude and his plesand releif" (996), and 2) fulfill the next reasonable command Venus will give him, which of course prepares the ground for the later order of Venus for the poet to render Virgil into his dialect. The ballad which the speaker then writes does make token fulfillment of Venus' demands for praise, but the emphasis is clearly put on the speaker himself, and on a particular faculty of his wit "deliucrit of dangair" (1015). The language indicates his sense of a spirit revived. His spirit is "deliuerit," "releuit," "fre of seruice and bondage." He addresses his wit to "Behald thy glaid, fresche, lustie, grene curage" (1021). The piling up of the adjectives—glad, fresh, lusty and green—indicates the regeneration felt in his spirit, his "curage." The literal reason, of course, is quite obvious. He has been saved from death or transformation into a beast—for him, a fate worse than death. But in terms of the regenerative powers implicit in poetry and attributed to the muse of poetry, the ballad further indicates the renewal of the speaker's own imaginative or poetic powers. After all, he is involved at this moment in the creative act itself. The association of the revived spirit of the speaker with his poetic powers is made even more explicit as he directs his wit to "Incres in mirthfull consolatioun, / In Ioyous sweit Imaginatioun" (1035-36). The lines are again suggestive of the basic aesthetic principle, the union of *mirthe* or *solas* and *doctryn* so that the "Incres" can only be a direction to create. And if there were any question in the matter, "mirthfull consolatioun" is given a gloss within the text: "In Ioyous sweit Imaginatioun." His final direction—after making token praise and thanksgiving to Venus—is again to his wit: "Be glaid and lycht now in thy lusty flouris" (1043). The state of the speaker's faculties is presented as being "in bloom," as having the vigor of creativity which was so evident in the initial garden scene in May. What is more, the poet is ending a ballad here, finishing a creative act, evidence of his "sweit Imaginatioun" functioning once again.

The focus on the poetic faculty is sustained as the narrator thanks Calliope for her aid. He addresses her as his "protector," "help," "supplie" and "redemption," and voluntarily submits his life to Calliope:

> And in that part your mercie I Imploir,
> Submitting me my lifetime Induring
> Your plesure and mandate till obeysing.
> (1065-67)

The poet's commitment to Calliope, to poetry, is complete. Not only has the goddess Venus—through Calliope's own suggestion—commanded it, but the speaker himself has submitted to her control without qualification. Her immediate will is that he go and visit "wonderis moir" (1069). And what possible function is there in a poet's experiencing wonders at the direction of the muse of poetry if not as a kind of imaginative preparation for the creative act? He is put in the keeping of one of Calliope's nymphs, given a horse, and together the nymph and the persona ride "Als swift as thocht" (1077). Though the simile makes perfectly good idiomatic sense, given the context of the poet's concern with his poetic faculty, "swift as thocht" may well suggest the flight of a poet's imagination where he can accumulate the material of his art. For instance, the nymph conveys him "Amid the Musis to se quhat thay wald mene, / Quhilks sang and playit bot neuer a wreist yeid wrang" (1079-80). The apparent function of his trip is to show him, to make him "see." But "see" is not used simply in its visual sense; it is linked to the intellectual kind of "seeing"—"quhat thay wald mene." And those whom he is witnessing are singers expert in their art, never striking a wrong note. The materials he views or hears in the voyage itself are, then, enclosed in the contexts of song or poetic rendition since after six stanzas in which he was "caryit in twinkling of ane Eye" (1084), he is brought "Straicht to the Musis Caballine Fontane" (1134). The echoes of Chaucer and his *House of Fame* here are telling. The eagle informs Chaucer that the purpose of the flight, the experience "Is for thy lore and for thy prow." The speaker in ***The Palice of Honour,*** too, is intended to profit from the flight. And it is perhaps not irrelevant to notice that the geographical areas he views in the flight are not only the real world—such places as high mountains of Germany, Rome, the rivers Rhine, Po, and Tiber—but mythic or legendary "places" as well—Acheron's well, the hill of Helicon, Parnassus. That the flight is one of the imagination seems implied from its universal nature, from its encompassing both the real and the legendary worlds of all times, and by the repeated "now" formations which suggest something of the flitting quality of a voyage of the imagination:

> Now out of France tursit in Tuskane,
> Now out of Flanders heich vp in Almanie,
> Now into Egypt, now into Italie,
> Now in the Realme of Trace and now in Spane.
> (1086-89)

The remaining stanzas of Part II are devoted to the occurrences at the "Musis Caballine Fontane." It is here, significantly, that they pause to rest. Of all the places they have been, only here—at the fountain of poetry—do they stop. The scene is that of a banquet, rich in variety of drink and "Delicait meitis, dainteis seir alswa" (1179). Poets and poems of different poetic genres provide the courses in this rich and delightful banquet. Ovid shows "full mony transmutatiounis / And wonderfull new figuratiounis" (1216-17), followed by Virgil, who "playit the sportis of Daphnis and Corydone" (1226), Terence, who "playit the Comedy / Of Parmeno, Thrason and wise Gnatone" (1227-28); Juvenal "Stude scornand euerie man as thay yeid by" (1230), and Martial "was Cuik till roist, seith, farce and fry" (1231). The speaker's summary statement after this catalogue of poets and poetic types identifies the banquet as one of poetry:

> With mirthis thus and meitis delicait
> Thir Ladyis feistit according thair estait. . . .
> (1234-35)

Once again the aesthetic of *mirthe/doctryn* comes into view, this time varied in terms to suit the particular banquet context, "mirthis / meitis." What other kind of banquet could occur at the "Musis Caballine Fontane"?

As swiftly as the speaker and his guide had flown to the fountain, the court of poets—now including the nymph and her charge—move "Ouir mony gudelie plane" (1243), until they lift up their eyes and "se the finall end of our trauaill" (1248), the mountain of rock which holds the Palice of Honour. It is significant that the speaker has identified with this court of poets not only in terms of his physically being with them, "*we* se," but also in terms of their office as poets, "*our* trauaill." Further, the tautology, "finall end," suggests not only that the voyage itself is nearing completion, but that a teleology is involved: that this place, which we finally see identified as the Palice of Honour, is the goal, the end toward which their work ("trauaill") as poets leads.

The intricacy and expertise of a single line such as this in which so much is done reduces the possibility of taking at face value the final two stanzas of Part II in which the poet laments once again his inability to recreate what he saw in his vision, what is in his imagination. This "inability" topos is a self-conscious device not uncommon in the Middle Ages as a technique of heightening anticipation of what is about to be described. And the concern here is clearly with his own artistry. He has before him a plan, a form which he intends to give poetic expression. The problem is the artistic one of reproducing as accurately as possible the effect of what he sees:

> Howbeit I may not euerie circumstance
> Reduce perfitelie in remembrance,
> Myne Ignorance yit sum part sall deuise,
> Tuitching this sicht of heuinlie sweit plesance.
> (1279-82)

The point of interest is that regardless of the mode the persona assumes at a given point, the concerns remain those of the poet's art. In the last two stanzas the poet, who has already experienced the flight of his imagination to the Palice of Honour, evokes his frustration in not being able to represent it accurately. Though the lament of his inability, the comments on the marvels to be described are devices intended to win acceptance by the audience of what he is about to tell, the terms of those devices are interior ones. The poet is directing attention to his powers as poet, to what his imagination offers. The second voice, too—the persona under the care of Calliope's nymph who joins the court of poets and identifies with them to "the finall end of our trauaill"—is concerned directly with his office as poet, with his imagination. His spirit has now passed through the wilderness to begin the last stage of his regeneration, the seeking of the Palice of Honour itself. The speaker changes, or more accurately, has a variety of poses. But the one constant is the introspective concern with the faculties which make him a poet, with his imagination.

It is in the voice of the active poet rehearsing his former flight that Part III of the poem begins. The close connection between the speaker and the muse of poetry once again is underscored by the language and emphasis of the opening invocation. He speaks of the muses as those who "maid me se" (1289). The loaded verb again suggests not only a physical but an intellectual kind of vision and indicates the quality of the muse as cause or source for his art. Further, he petitions her directly to "caus me dewlie till Indite this storie . . . " (1292). The notion of the muses as "caus" of both seeing and composing constitutes really a description of the poetic act itself. First the poet must have the vision of subject matter; his imagination must first of all operate to acquire the materials of the poem. And secondly, it must operate to order and express that vision. Though the stanza is on the surface wholly conventional, those very conventions are seen to play an organic role. The narrator in all his poses as we have seen is consistently concerned with the inspiration for and the operation and execution of his art. He has identified completely with the court of the muses, with poetry, and he invokes that court in exactly those terms which he has found most needful to him—the operation of his imagination (represented allegorically by the muses as sources of inspiration). He seeks their aid in the immediate creative act of constructing this poem at this moment. He further seeks their aid in his prior pilgrim voice for the journey to the Palice of Honour. In effect, Douglas is describing the two phases of the art, inspiration and execution, both as products of the imagination. To claim such subtlety in the use of conventional devices, it might be argued, is to disregard the frequency, the very conventionality of them. However, it would seem that the frequent attention provided in medieval commentary on the ambiguity of language, on the necessity of reading closely, justifies such an interpretation. Douglas himself demands such close reading, word by word, line by line, taking time and paying close attention: "Bot redis leill, and tak gud tent in tyme"; "Consider it warly, reid oftar than anys / Weill at a blenk sle poetry nocht tayn is . . . ". Besides that fact, the technique, though formally a conventional device, seems clearly to be shaped to the thematic concern which has been developing from the very beginning of the poem.

They have arrived at "the Roche of slid, hard Marbell stone" (1300), on whose summit lies the Palice of Honour. The muses and the court of poets at this point have left the nymph and the narrator alone and "clam the Roche in hie" (1304). *Their* passage to the Palice of Honour was not difficult apparently, but the passage for the speaker was perilous and full of pain: "With mekill pane thus clam

I neir the hicht" (1313). The court of poets has already executed their art, has already gained entry to the Palice; the speaker, however, is as yet unproved: "Still at the hillis fute we twa abaid" (1306). What follows—his ascent up the mountain and tour through the palace—carries the overtones of initiation. He sees a "grislie sicht," a kind of inferno:

> Ane terribill sewch birnand in flammis reid,
> Abhominabill and how as hell to se,
> All full of Brintstane, Pick and bulling Leid,
> Quhair mony wretchit creature lay deid
> And miserabill catiues yelland loude on hie. . . .
> (1316-20)

Our attention is again directed not so much to the "grislie sicht" itself as to its effect on the persona, here once again in his comic role: "Trimbland I stude, with teith chatterand gude speid" (1330). The juxtaposition of an inferno soberly described and serious in tone with the speaker's teeth "chatterand gude speid" reduces the seriousness of the inferno scene, but does not negate the direction of our attention to the speaker in his reaction to the experiences he undergoes. Further, the nymph recognizes the lapse of confidence in the poet and consoles him by the reminder that he shall not perish: " 'and lo the caus' quod sche. / "To me thow art commit; I sall the keip' " (1332-33). He seems to grow comic at those times when he forgets his total commitment to poetry, when he forgets that he is in the care of Calliope's nymph. The comic voice, then, not only amuses the reader and lightens the tone, but functions to underscore the as yet incomplete development of the speaker as a poet. He is still being initiated in the art of the imagination.

His role as apprentice is further illustrated by the ensuing allegorical vision of the world. Like Chaucer's eagle in the *House of Fame,* the nymph commands the persona to "Luik doun" and see "in quhat estait / Thy wretchit warld thow may considder now" (1343-44). The nymph's role is seen not simply as protector of the poet; it is she who interprets the allegory. "Tho at my Nimphe breiflie I did Inquire / Quhat signifyit that feirfull wonders seir" (1378-79). The speaker is within a learning process, as it were, and it is not without significance that the context of that process is allegorical, a basic framework of medieval art, the basic device of the poem in progress. After explicating the allegory, the nymph directs our attention again to the quality of the speaker as "learner" or "apprentice" in the art. The purpose of his voyage with the nymph of Calliope is clearly to prepare him for his specific occupation as poet:

> "Considder wonders, and be vigilant
> That thow may better endyten efterwart
> Things quhilkis I sall the schaw or we depart.
> Thow sall haue fouth of sentence and not scant.
> Thair is na welth nor weilfair thou sall want.
> The greit Palice of honour thow sall se.
> Lift vp thy heid, behald that sicht," quod sche.
> (1398-1404)

The sights he is shown by the nymph are intended to provide him with the materials of his art, materials "fouth of sentence" which will improve his art. The time reference is telling. The present sights provide the substance of what will be "better endyten efterwart." The voyage, then, is indeed the description of the imaginative process preceding the actual writing of the poem. The point is again emphasized after brief descriptions of the "plane of peirles pulchritude" before the Palice of Honour—but this time with comic overtones. Our speaker is overwhelmed by the beauty of the architecture and the surroundings, the wonders of the place. The situation is analogous to that in the *House of Fame,* where the eagle startles the equally dazed Chaucer with "Awak!" Here the nymph describes her protégé:

> Thus in a stair quhy standis thow stupifak
> Gouand all day, and nathing hes vesite.
> (1460-61)

The description of the poet wandering about and seeing the wonders but missing the whole point of them not only relaxes into comedy but further underlines the fact that there *is* a point, a reason that he has been committed to her care. "Follow me and pay attention," she says, "Quhat now thow seis, luik efterwart thow write . . . " (1464). In the space of eight stanzas, the notion of "preparation" for his later "endyting" is repeated in similar language. Such repetition and emphasis ought not go unnoticed as distinctions between two parts of the poet's creative process, the initial "imagining" experience and the final execution of that experience into poetry. The distinction in context defines that former experience as what is presently taking place in the speaker. That is, by calling attention to the creative process as a two-part operation and by portraying a poet—not writing, but "preparing" to write—the current happenings within the poem are clearly to be seen as an illustration of the first part of the creative act.

The scene of Venus' mirror which follows immediately is not unrelated to the attention continually directed to the creative act, particularly to the "imagining" phase. The nymph has taken the speaker to a garden in which they find the mirror of Venus, richly and elaborately decorated in gold and stones. But the outstanding quality of the mirror is its healing power:

> Bot all the bordour, circulair euerie deill,
> Was plait of gold, cais, stok and vtter hem,
> With verteous stanis picht that blude wald stem;
> For quha that woundit was in the Tornament
> Wox haill fra he vpon the Mirrour blent
> (1481-85)

The description is grounded in the literal context of knights in a tourney, particularly apropos since it is, after all, the mirror of Venus. But the restorative virtue of the mirror carries further overtones since "restoration" has, as we have seen, been a recurrent motif throughout the poem. It is described, further, as a "royall Relick," a term for the Middle Ages necessarily associated with restoration, both physical and spiritual. Such overtones, of course, have particular significance in terms of the poet-speaker who is in fact being rescued from the wilderness, whose powers are being renewed under the auspices of the muse of poetry. What he views in the mirror, moreover, is in effect the history of the world and the history of literature—"The deidis and fatis of euerie eirdlie wicht" (1496).

The catalogue includes both scriptural and profane "histories" from Adam to Piers Plowman and Ralph Coilyear:

> And breiflie euerie famous douchtie deid
> That men in storie may se or Chronikill reid
> I micht behald in that Mirrour expres,
> The miserie, the crueltie, the dreid,
> Pane, sorrow, wo, baith wretchitnes and neid,
> The greit Inuy, couetous dowbilnes,
> Tuitchand warldlie vnfaithfull brukilnes.
> I saw the Feind fast folkis to vices tyst,
> And all the cumming of the Antechrist.
> (1693-1701)

The catalogue is the longest in the poem, running for twenty-two stanzas, and this summary statement suggests that his vision has been not only of names and of historical, literary and mythic facts and figures, but that he has to an extent experienced human events from creation to the coming of the Antichrist, which is but another way of saying he has seen all things imaginable. The mirror of Venus possessed a restorative faculty. The wounded who looked on it were made "haill." In the context of the poet's own condition, he too was wounded. He was traumatically swept from the pleasant and fertile May garden to the barren wilderness where his faculties as poet became equally barren and inoperative. Is it possible that the vision presented to him in Venus' mirror is but a visual mode of describing the poet's own imaginative faculty as also restored or made "haill"? The idea is not contrary to the concerns which have been uppermost in the poem thus far.

The ascent to the Palice of Honour continues in an essentially conventional frame—descriptions of elaborate and richly wrought architecture and a catalogue of the court of "hie Honour" in personification terms. Once again, the speaker is overwhelmed by the exquisite "warkmanschip" (1862), the artistry of the engravings and designs of the mythic stories on the walls, and is prodded on gently by the nymph and led to the closed door of Honour's court. They do not enter, however. He views the actual court through the keyhole—a comic touch—but perhaps significant thematically in that the speaker is not yet qualified to enter the court at all. In terms of the initiation motif, such a detail operates rather precisely as an indication of the speaker's unfulfilled status. Further, his brief vision of Honour throws him into another ecstatic swoon:

> Enthronit sat ane God Omnipotent,
> On quhais glorious visage as I blent,
> In extasie be his brichtnes atanis
> He smote me doun and brissit all my banis.
> (1921-24)

C. S. Lewis [in his *Allegory of Love*] draws attention to this passage as "the nerve of the whole allegory." The pun on "ane" as "a" and as "one," he says, suggests ironically the pilgrim's discovery that Honour is with God. The persona when he saw Honour was not equipped to understand that fact, but the poet who is recreating himself in the past has made that discovery and is showing the process wherein it was made. This seems indisputable. The ensuing dialogue and action between the guide and the poet are comical for a reason: to show the inadequacy of the poet at this point. He is indeed not yet equipped for the discovery: he remains in the *process* of discovery. The nymph recognizes the speaker's inadequacy as she responds to his complaints "richt merilie" and laughs and says she understands his "mad hart weill aneuch" (1953). But there is no question that her "sermon" which follows is intended to point up to him a basic moral fact, that the path to honor is single, the path of virtue:

> And in this countrie Prince, Prelate or King
> Allanerlie sall for vertew honourit be,
> For eirdlie gloir is nocht bot vanitie. . . .
>
> Vertew is eik the perfite sicker way,
> And nocht ellis, till lestand honour ay.
> (1976-78, 2008-09)

The poet is reprimanded strongly and explicitly by the nymph for his inadequate perception of the experience:

> "Waryit," quod scho, "ay be thy megir hart!
> Thow suld haue sene, had thow biddin in yone art,
> Quhat wise yone heuinlie companie conuersit.
> Wa worth thy febill brane, sa sone was persit.
> Thow micht haue sene remanand quhair thow was
> Ane hudge pepill puneist for thair trespas. . . ."
> (2029-34)

At his expression of desire to see "thair torment fane" (2059), the nymph suggests that he will "be reioisit, / Quhen thow hes tane the Air and better appoisit" (2060-61). The literal context, of course, is clear. His "dazed" state will be remedied by air. But "appoisit" perhaps suggests something further—that his vision, his understanding of what he has seen will be corrected too when he is better disposed, when he has become more perceptive of the "moral" nature of his vision, when the "final end" of this travail is consciously recognized by him.

It is important to notice, however, the essentially literary context in which this discovery is made. His "dazed spirit" is once again to be refreshed by entrance into a garden, but a garden of rhetoric:

> Bot first thow sall considder commoditeis
> Of our garding, lo, full of lustie treis!
> All hie Cypres, of flewer maist fragrant.
> Our Ladyis yonder, bissie as the beis,
> The sweit flureist flouris of Rethoreis
> Gadderis full fast, mony grene tender plant. . . .
> (2062-67)

The passage into the garden is so perilous, though, that the poet falls from the bridge-entrance into a stream and is awakened from his dream. The detail has at least a dual function. It first of all operates as a device to end the vision; secondly, and perhaps more importantly, it allegorically underscores both the recognition that poetry as an art has its pitfalls, is difficult to achieve, and that the poet-speaker is himself as yet not fulfilled as poet. The initiation motif is seen both in its moral and in its artistic senses.

The garden which was sweet to his spirit at the beginning of the poem, now, by comparison to the vision he has experienced, holds little for the poet:

> The birdis sang nor yit the merie flouris

Micht not ameis my greuous greit dolouris.
All eirdlie thing me thocht barrane and vile.
Thus I remanit into the Garth twa houris,
Cursand the feildis with all the fair coluris,
That I awolk oft wariand the quhile.
Alwayis my minde was on the lustie Ile.
(2098-2104)

The value which he attaches to his vision is its relationship to his art. He laments that he has not gained entrance into the garden of rhetoric: "I purpoisit euer till haue dwelt in that art, / Of Rethorik cullouris till haue found sum part". The intention to pursue *that* path to honor is explicit. And its connection to virtue as "the finall end of our trauaill" is recognized finally by the poet as he explains further that

maist of all my curage was aggreuit,
Becaus sa sone I of my dreme escheuit,
Not seand how thay wretchis war torment,
That Honour mankit and honestie mischeuit.
(2107-10)

The poet has discovered the full texture of his art, its imaginative nature and its role or function as a conductor to virtue. That he has chosen poetry as his path to honor, that he sees virtue and thereby honor as "finall end" of his art is further emphasized in that his last action within the poem is creative, a ballad in praise of virtue and honor. He seeks Honour's aid in preparing him for appointment to his court: "Delite the tite, me quite of site to dicht, / For I apply, schortlie, to thy deuise" (2141-42). The internal rhyme which has been accruing in the ballad approaches the absurd here as poetry. But the language is fraught with overtones linking the basic strands of initiation, preparedness and virtue with the art of "endyting," of devising, with poetry.

The progression in this poem, then, is multi-leveled. On the one hand, the speaker himself rises from comic ignorance of the end of his art to knowledge of it and intention to apply that knowledge to his art. The end of the poem is didactic and moral: it is to lead to honor, to establish virtue. A life of virtue is the important value learned. At a different level, however, we see the poet-speaker seriously concerned with the nature of the path which he is to follow toward virtue, that is, the operation of his poetic faculties. That operation is seen to be a dual one—first, the need for a fertile wit, for a refreshed imaginative faculty. The poet's spirit must be sharp and aware and observant and fresh as the gardens in the poem. When it is barren, in the wilderness, it is in need of regeneration, of that fecundity so apparent in nature's springtime. And what has happened to this particular poet-speaker in the poem is precisely portrayed as regenerative. As a poet, his "wit" is cleared, given new life—an action that enables him to create this particular vision. As a man—his "vision" also is cleared. His comic obtuseness, his tendency to be awed so much by the artistry and fantasy of the vision that he is unable to recognize the significance of that vision is rectified through his final recognition that honor is achieved by virtue "And nocht ellis" (2009). This latter recognition perhaps makes it possible to agree with one critic's description of ***The Palice of Honour:*** "We reach a later period of allegory when the didactic purpose is superseding the more spontaneous love cult" [Janet Smith, *The French Background of Middle Scots Literature,* 1934]. But to leave it at this is to ignore a most emphatic element in the poem, the concern of the poet for his imaginative faculty and for the end product of that faculty. The didactic element, the ultimate stress on virtue, does not preclude the poet's introspective examination of the powers which produce his poetry nor the related examination of poetry itself as subject matter within the poem. (pp. 280-303)

Gerald B. Kinneavy, "The Poet in 'The Palice of Honour'," in The Chaucer Review, *Vol. 3, No. 4, December, 1969, pp. 280-303.*

Priscilla Bawcutt (essay date 1976)

[In the excerpt below, Bawcutt offers an overview of the Prologues, *regarding them as inventive introductory prefaces to the poet's person, purpose, and work.]*

[Prologues VII, XII, and XIII] have been much praised, and commonly linked together as 'nature poems' [David F. C. Coldwell, in his edition of *Virgil's Aeneid Translated into Scottish Verse by Gavin Douglas,* 1957-64] or 'portraits of the seasons' [A. M. Mackenzie, "The Renaissance Poets," in *Scottish Poetry: A Critical Survey,* edited by J. Kinsley,

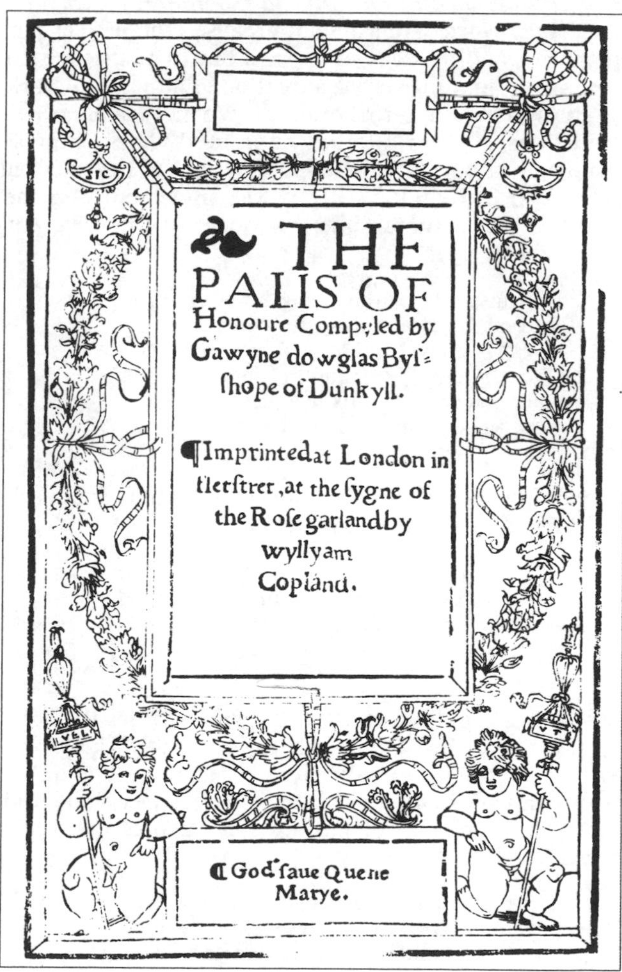
THE PALIS OF Honoure Compyled by Gawyne dowglas Byſhope of Dunkyll.

¶Imprinted at London in fleteſtret, at the ſygne of the Roſe garland by wyllyam Copland.

God ſaue Quene Marye.

Facsimile of the title page of the first edition of The Palace of Honor, *printed at London in 1553.*

1955]. These **Prologues** indeed resemble one another in subject and descriptive technique, and within the framework of the whole ***Eneados*** each functions similarly, as a much expanded *chronographia.* Such ornate and ceremonial descriptions of the time of day or season were popular with both medieval and classical poets, and Virgil himself may have supplied a model to Douglas in his many descriptions of the dawn. Yet each **Prologue** has its distinctive structure and significance which may be obscured by over-insistence on such group labels.

Prologue XII has provoked strikingly different reactions from modern readers. L. M. Watt found its description of May 'vibrant with the freshness of the living air [*Douglas's Aeneid,* 1920], whereas Coldwell said dismissively that 'convention to a large extent dictated what Douglas was to see . . . the poem might as well have been written in his stall at St Giles' as in the fields of Midlothian'. Douglas's contemporaries had a different approach to the **Prologue,** stressing its learning and its 'craft'. The 1553 side note terms it 'ane singular lernit Prologue', perhaps following a manuscript comment such as the Cambridge manuscript's *explicit scitus prologus.* Douglas himself calls it a 'lusty crafty preambill' (307). No one can fail to observe the learned, Latinate character of much of the diction: *purpurat, nocturnall, diurnall, obumbrat, rubicund, venust.* Such words are used not because Douglas has particularly recondite ideas to express but in the interest of rhyme, rhythm, and verbal aureation. The natural world is often presented in terms of myth. We meet familiar personifications: Nature, Flora, Priapus and Ceres. We read not of the owl but 'Nycthemyne' (II), not of the cock but 'Phebus red fowle' (155), not of the spider but 'Aragne' (170). We are in the ambiguous world of the *Metamorphoses,* where

Progne had or than sung hir complaynt,
And eik hir dreidfull systir Philomeyn
Hyr lays endyt, and in woddis greyn
Hyd hir selvyn, eschamyt of hir chance;
And Esacus completis hys pennance
In ryveris, fludis, and on euery laik.
(282-87)

The opening lines of this **Prologue** abound in Ovidian echoes. The stars are put to flight; Aurora opens

the wyndois of hir large hall,
Spred all with rosys, and full of balm ryall,
And eik the hevynly portis cristallyne
Vpwarpis braid, the warld till illumyn.
(17-20)

The sun has a golden chariot, drawn by 'Eous the steid' (25) and flames burst from his nostrils (29). The face of Phoebus and his bright throne are dazzling: 'For quhais hew mycht nane behald hys face' (38). All these find parallels in Ovid's account of the sun and his palace in *Metamorphoses,* II:

ecce vigil rutilo patefecit ab ortu
purpureas Aurora fores et plena rosarum
atria: diffugiunt stellae, quarum agmina cogit
Lucifer
(112-15)

aureus axis erat, temo aureus, aurea summae
curvatura rotae
(107-08)

quadripedes animosos ignibus illis,
quos in pectore habent, quos ore et naribus efflant.
(84-5)

neque enim propiora ferebat
lumina.
(22-3)

The artifice of this **Prologue** is as striking as its learning. As in the ***Palice of Honour*** and Dunbar's *Goldin Targe* the natural world is described in imagery that derives from man's artefacts. Nature provides a tapestry (102), and the soil is embroidered (65); Douglas speaks of 'the fertill *skyrt lappys* of the ground' (85), 'the variand *vestur* of the venust vaill' (87), and terms corn a 'glaidsum *garmont revestyng* the erd' (78). Images of jewels and other precious substances abound: silver and gold and ivory (22, 31, 36, 55, 14, etc.); Phoebus's hair is 'brycht as chrisolyte or topace' (37); and we read of 'beriall' streams (60) and emerald meadows (151). Such imagery both reinforces the sense of radiant light—the world sparkles and gleams—and suggests the idealized nature of this description. Coldwell comments incredulously on Douglas's phrase 'fervent heit' (174): 'In May? In Scotland?' But the **Prologue** has several other distinctly un-Scottish features, such as the trellised grapes (99-100) and the olive trees (165). These clearly derive from the Mediterranean tradition of the *locus amoenus.* **Prologue** XII was never conceived as a naturalistic description of one particular Scottish landscape—the picture is an idealized and composite one. Yet there is evidence that Douglas saw through his own eyes as well as through those of earlier poets. He describes

The syluer scalyt fyschis on the greit
Ourthwort cleir stremys sprynkland for the heyt,
With fynnys schynand brovn as synopar,
And chyssell talys, stowrand heir and thar.
(55-8)

Fishes' silver scales had been noted by many earlier poets, but Douglas draws our attention to other features: the distinctive colour (cinnabar is a reddish-brown mineral), the chisel-shaped tail, and above all their quick, wriggly movement. Here and elsewhere in the **Prologue** Douglas revivifies traditional themes through vivid and minute observation.

Convention by no means 'dictated' everything that Douglas saw, but it prescribed to him many features of his style, above all the poetic technique that dominates the **Prologue:**

The dasy dyd onbreid hir crownell smaill,
And euery flour onlappyt in the daill;
In battill gyrs burgionys the banwart wild,
The clavyr, catcluke, and the cammamyld;
The flour delys furthspred hys hevynly hew,
Flour dammes, and columby blank and blew;
Seir downys smaill on dent de lyon sprang,
The yyng greyn blomyt straberry levys amang;
Gymp gerraflouris thar royn levys onschet,
Fresch prymros, and the purpour violet;
The roys knoppys, tutand furth thar hed,
Gan chyp, and kyth thar vermel lippys red.
(113-24)

James Russell Lowell [in his *Literary Essays,* Vol. IV, 1893] denounced this '*item* kind of description':

> It is a mere bill of parcels, a *post-mortem* inventory of nature, where imagination is not merely not called for but would be out of place. Why, a recipe in the cookery book is as much like a good dinner as this kind of stuff is like true word-painting.

One answer to Lowell is that catalogues have had a perennial appeal to poets; we find them as early as Homer and as recently as Auden. Douglas is using a descriptive technique that was popular not only with medieval poets but with many classical ones, such as Ovid, Statius and Lucan. It is perhaps more important to note that Douglas does not give us a *post-mortem* of the natural world. He describes movement, change, and growth—'onlappyt', 'furthspred', 'sprang', 'tutand furth thar hed'; his nature is living, not static or inanimate. Where Douglas is most open to criticism is in his lack of selectivity. His catalogues are often long—this list of flowers runs to over thirty lines, three times the length of a similar list in the *Culex* (398-407)—and there are so many of them that they form not a decorative set-piece, not even a 'purple patch', but the whole fabric of the poem.

It is perhaps this aspect of his style, together with Douglas's allusiveness and the occasional unfamiliarity of his vocabulary, that has obscured for many readers the structure of this **Prologue,** and consequently its meaning. Even appreciative critics, such as John Veitch [in his *The Feeling for Nature in Scottish Poetry,* Vol I, 1887], speak of its 'lack of unity'. A brief analysis of its structure may therefore be helpful. I do not think that Douglas intended primarily to describe 'a day lived through in every detail' or 'the fields of Midlothian' or even the *locus amoenus.* **Prologue** XII is, above all, a hymn of praise to the sun, and implicitly to the sun's Creator. God is not named in the **Prologue,** but there are frequent references to God's vicegerent, Nature (e.g. 84, 102, 154, 230, 248). The **Prologue** celebrates first the glory of the sun-rise—Douglas later revealingly speaks of it as a 'tryumphe' (275)—and then of the month in which the revitalizing power of the sun is most apparent (Douglas dates the **Prologue** as written on the 9 May).

The splendid ceremonial opening shows the sun rising, emerging like a monarch from his palace. The planets flee from his presence, and Aurora casts open before him the 'hevynly portis cristalline'. The first rays of light

> Persand the sabill barmkyn nocturnall,
> Bet doun the skyis clowdy mantill wall.
>
> (23-4)

The regal imagery is sustained by allusions to the sun's 'palyce ryall', crown, and throne (35, 36, 47). Later in the **Prologue** it is recalled in allusions to 'the cummyng of this king . . . Newly aryssyn in hys estait ryall' (273 ff.; see also 141).

Douglas then turns to the sun's influence upon the earth. We move from light itself—'twynklyng', 'lemand', 'glytrand', 'illuminat', reflected in streams and casting shadows (60 ff.)—to its effects upon flowers and plant life (73-148); upon birds and animals (151-86); and upon man (187-230). Plants respond to the 'yong sonnys' warmth (96) by fresh growth and unbudding:

> The dasy dyd onbreid hir crownell smaill,
> And euery flour onlappyt in the daill . . .
>
> (122 ff.)

Birds and animals respond by procreating: swans are pictured 'seirsand by kynd a place quhar thai suld lay' (154). In Douglas's beguiling account of the animals each is accompanied by its young:

> The sprutlyt calvys sowkand the red hyndis,
> The yong fownys followand the dun days,
> Kyddis skippand throu ronnys efter rays;
> In lyssouris and on leys litill lammys
> Full tayt and tryg socht bletand to thar dammys,
> Tydy ky lowys, veilys by thame rynnys;
> All snog and slekit worth thir bestis skynnys.
>
> (180-86)

Here there are no barren or diseased animals; instead the calves are 'sowkand', the cows 'tydy', that is, 'giving milk', and their coats are 'snog and slekit'. Up to this point the picture is highly idealized. Nature is plentiful, joyful, and harmonious. Only from man is the response to the season discordant. Side by side with the Maytime courtship and 'caralyng' of young people is practised 'bawdry and onlesum meyn' (210). To Douglas this appears

> schamefull play,
> Na thyng accordyng to our hailsum May,
> Bot rather contagius and infective,
> And repugnant that sesson nutrytyve
>
> (225-28)

The climax of the **Prologue** comes when the birds sing a hymn of praise to the sun, a skilful rhetorical summing-up of earlier themes:

> Welcum the lord of lycht and lamp of day,
> Welcum fostyr of tendir herbys grene,
> Welcum quyknar of floryst flowris scheyn . . .
> Welcum the byrdis beild apon the brer,
> Welcum master and rewlar of the yer,
> Welcum weilfar of husbandis at the plewys,
> Welcum reparar of woddis, treis and bewys,
> Welcum depayntar of the blomyt medis,
> Welcum the lyfe of euery thyng that spredis . . .
>
> (252 ff.)

The last section (267-310) is in a different key; personal, conversational, and humorous, it forms the transition to book XII. The bird-song rouses Douglas—as it rouses other sleeping poets—and fills him with the desire to see the dawn (273). Their last word, 'sluggardy', pricks his conscience and calls him back to his 'langsum wark / Twichand the lattyr buke of Dan Virgill' (270-71).

In this **Prologue** Douglas clearly owes much to other poets. There are echoes not only of Ovid but also of Chaucer and Henryson, and the central section of the **Prologue** seems highly Virgilian. Several details—above all the conception of an almost sentient universe in 'The sulye spred hir braid bosum on breid' (74)—were inspired by the *laus veris* in *Georgic* II. Much else in the shape and subject matter of the **Prologue** is highly traditional. Many poets before Douglas had celebrated the revivifying power of the sun, the rebirth of the world in spring, and the fecundity of Nature, 'Seand throu kynd ilk thyng spryngis and revertis' (230). The most famous example is perhaps Chaucer's opening to the *Canterbury Tales.* Yet Douglas uses his inheritance to good effect. He conveys in a way of his own both the cosmic grandeur of the season and its many tiny consequences: 'seir downys smaill on dent de lyon sprang'. **Prologue XII** is impressive as a whole, not simply for scattered details; it is in the best sense what Douglas himself calls it: 'a lusty crafty preambill'.

Many critics have praised **Prologue VII.** They find it 'the most original of the three', the most realistic, and the most genuinely Scottish. **Prologue VII** seems to me indeed original both in conception and execution, yet I feel that the nature of Douglas's achievement here needs to be more precisely defined. It does not consist solely in his descriptive realism, nor in his first-hand observation of a Scottish winter. Douglas could be a remarkably accurate and vivid observer, alert not only to visual images but to very small movements and sounds:

> Ryveris ran reid on spait with watir brovne
> (19)
> The wynd maid waif the red wed on the dyke
> (19)
> scharp hailstanys mortfundeit of kynd
> Hoppand on the thak and on the causay by.
> (136-37)

Yet I think there has been a critical over-emphasis on this aspect of the **Prologue.** Here, as in the other **Prologues,** Douglas's inspiration was partly literary in kind. His imagination was fired by the writings of others, not just by looking directly at the natural world. There are several passages in this **Prologue** which are clearly indebted to other writers. It is quite false to say of it that 'apart from a passing reference to Boreas and Eolus the whole . . . is founded solely on Scottish experience' [K. Wittig, *The Scottish Tradition in Literature,* 1958].

The very first lines of the **Prologue** illustrate this:

> As bryght Phebus, scheyn souerane hevynnys e,
> The opposit held of hys chymmys hie,
> Cleir schynand bemys, and goldyn symmyris hew,
> In laton cullour alteryng haill of new,
> Kythyng no syng of heyt be hys vissage,
> So neir approchit he his wyntir stage;
> Reddy he was to entyr the thrid morn
> In clowdy skyis vndre Capricorn:
> (I-8)

Douglas is adhering to tradition both in his syntax—the suspended temporal clause, with 'as' or 'when'—and in his dating of the poem by a reference to the sun's position in the Zodiac. Lydgate had opened his Prologue to the *Siege of Thebes* similarly:

> Whan briyt Phebus passed was þe ram
> Myd of Aprille & in to bole cam
> And Satourn old wt his frosty face
> In virgyne taken had his place . . .
> (I-4)

Lydgate is recalling still more famous opening lines: 'Whan that Aprill with his shoures soote . . . '. Spring openings were clearly the most popular, yet other medieval poems, such as the *Kingis Quair* and Lydgate's *Temple of Glas,* purport to start in winter, and Chaucer dated his *House of Fame* on 10 December. Douglas seems here, however, to be echoing another poem of Chaucer's. The striking image of the sun's change from gold to 'laton' (i.e. copper) derives from Chaucer's

> Phebus wax old, and hewed lyk laton,
> That in his hoote declynacion
> Shoon as the burned gold with stremes brighte.
> (*Franklin's Tale,* v. 1245-47)

Another poet also contributed to Douglas's opening. His lines on the constellation Orion

> Rany Oryon with his stormy face
> Bewavit oft the schipman by hys race.
> (27-8)

allude to Orion's shattering of Aeneas's fleet (*Aeneid* I.535). Douglas certainly recalls Virgil's epithets for Orion—*nimbosus* (I.535), *aquosus* (IV.52) and *saeuus* (VII.719). In such a Virgilian context Douglas's mention of 'Frawart Saturn, chill of complexioun' (29), though highly traditional, may also echo Virgil's *frigida Saturni . . . stella* (*Georgic* I.336).

Such allusiveness is not confined to the opening of the **Prologue.** When Douglas describes the birds that he hears as he lies awake in bed (105-25), he is giving new life to an ancient literary genre, the bird-catalogue. He recalls and seems to challenge comparison with well-known lists of birds in Chaucer's *Parliament of Fowls* and Virgil's *Georgic* I. There are clear echoes of Chaucer in Douglas's reference to the cock as the 'nyghtis orlager' (113—cf. *Parliament of Fowls,* 350), and to the 'trumpat' voice of the crane (121—cf. *Parliament of Fowls,* 344). In *Georgic* I.360 ff. the birds figure in the guise of weather prophets. So too for Douglas the cry of the cranes

> bene pronosticatioun
> Of wyndy blastis and ventositeis.
> (122-23)

Nonetheless, here—and also in **Prologue XII**—Douglas makes his contribution to the genre memorable and distinctive. He puts it into a realistic-seeming context: the birds are heard 'on the ruyf aboyn' (118) or 'by my chalmyr in heich wysnyt treis' (124). Although he notes some visual details—the owl has a 'crukyt camscho beke' (107), and cranes fly 'on randon, schapyn like ane Y' (120)—Douglas concentrates on one particular aspect of the birds: their cries. For the most part he characterizes them effectively and accurately through their distinctive calls: the 'claking' of the wild geese, the 'crowpyng' of the cranes, the 'pew' of the kite, and the 'wild elrich screke' of the owl. A modern naturalist [R. S. R. Fitter, in his *The Pocket Guide to British Birds*] speaks similarly of the barn owl's 'prolonged, strangled, eldritch screech', and Douglas is clearly attempting to suggest the sound made by these birds in his choice of onomatopoeic words.

Henryson had devoted two stanzas to winter in an account of the Seasons (*Fables,* 1692-1705), and supplied a bleak, wintry Prologue to his *Testament of Cresseid.* A generation after Douglas, Lindsay described winter in the Prologue to his *Dreme.* From this it has been inferred that 'a welcome and refreshing realism' was a mark of the Scottish descriptive tradition. I think, however, that the native tradition to which Douglas owed most in this **Prologue** was less Scottish than alliterative. When we read his

> Scharp soppys of sleit and of the snypand snaw
> (50)

we may be reminded of a line from *Sir Gawain* (2003):

> þe snawe snitered ful snart, þat snayped þe wylde.

The comparison highlights the greater economy and verbal energy of the *Gawain*-poet; yet it also illustrates that Douglas was familiar not necessarily with a specific poem such as *Sir Gawain* but with the traditional collocations of alliterative poetry. In the *Awntyrs of Arthure* (stanza vii) we read similarly of 'þe slete and þe snawe, þat snayppede þame so snelle'. Alliteration contributes many stock epithets and collocations to **Prologue VII:** 'raggit rolkis', 'schouris snell', 'firth and fald'; but it is far more than an ornament. The rhythmical structure of many lines is emphatically alliterative:

> So bustuusly Boreas his bugill blew,
> The deyr full dern doun in the dalis drew;
> Smale byrdis, flokkand throu thik ronys thrang,
> In chyrmyng and with chepyng changit thar sang,
> Sekand hidlis and hyrnys thame to hyde . . .
> (67-71)

From poems such as *Sir Gawain* or the *Morte Arthur* or *The Destruction of Troy* Douglas may have acquired a greater sensitivity to stormy weather and wild and remote scenery, and a greater readiness to describe them. He certainly shared with the authors of these alliterative poems a much wider vocabulary than Chaucer or Lydgate possessed for describing natural phenomena.

Yet Douglas was unusual in devoting such a long, sustained piece of writing to the subject of winter. There are hundreds of medieval descriptions of May or spring, but no poet writing in English before Douglas seems to have made the experience of winter the centre of his poem. Earlier English poets refer to winter, it is true, but usually briefly and in long poems chiefly as a means of dating the action. Often, as in Dunbar's 'In to thir dirk and drublie dayis' or the Harley lyric 'Wynter wakeneth al my care', the season serves as a symbolic starting point for a meditation on death or mutability. There are traces of both these functions in Douglas: the **Prologue** marks a stage in the composition of the whole ***Eneados,*** and to the poet who had just translated *Aeneid* VI winter appears

> a symylitude of hell,
> Reducyng to our mynd, in euery sted,
> Gousty schaddois of eild and grisly ded.
> (44-6)

Nonetheless, the chief object of the **Prologue** seems to be to characterize the complexity and multifariousness of winter. Douglas's originality consists partly in this, and partly in his revitalization of ancient poetic themes and images. He draws on many diverse traditions, and successfully blends material from earlier poets with material from his own experience. In this as in other **Prologues** first-hand observation co-exists with tradition; the one does not necessarily exclude the other.

Prologue VII has been subject to the same criticisms as **Prologue XII**—a lack of unity and too much of the '*item* kind of description'. Yet if it is read attentively this **Prologue** consists of far more than a mere collection of vivid but haphazard details. It has a structure, and conveys a distinct sense of progression. Its movement might be compared to that of a film, which ranges over a wide panoramic landscape and gradually moves in to a close-up. The subject is the winter solstice—'tha schort days that clerkis clepe brumaill' (14). Douglas purports to be writing on the third morning after the sun had entered Capricorn, that is, not on Christmas Eve but on 15 December. The time of year and even the mood resemble the opening of Donne's *Nocturnall upon St Lucies Day:* ''Tis the yeares midnight and it is the dayes'. The first thirty-four lines of the **Prologue** are learned and abstract. The season is characterized chiefly in astronomical and mythological terms: Phebus, Neptunus, 'Mars occident', 'Rany Oryon'—

> Frawart Saturn, chill of complexioun,
> Throu quhais aspect darth and infectioun
> Beyn causyt oft, and mortal pestilens,
> Went progressyve the greis of his ascens;
> And lusty Hebe, Iunoys douchtir gay,
> Stude spulyeit of hir office and array.
> (29-34)

The last two lines clearly refer to the cupbearer of the gods, who slipped and was disgraced, and succeeded by Ganymede. But what is Hebe doing in this **Prologue?** It is worth explaining her presence, not only because it illustrates Douglas's highly allusive technique but because it clears him from the charge of irrelevance. Douglas seems to have in mind the symbolic interpretation of the myth, such as he would find it in Boccaccio [in his *Genedogy of the Gods*]. Hebe primarily signifies youth . . . and the renewal of life associated with spring, but her nakedness and loss of 'array' is linked with the fall of leaves in autumn. Ganymede, who took over her 'office', is identified with the sign Aquarius into which the sun moves on leaving Capricorn:

> Tandem adveniente tempore partus, id est vere novo, Hebem parit [Iuno], id est iuventutem et rerum omnium renovationem, frondes, flores, et germina omnia ea emittuntur tempestate. . . . Tandem adveniente autumno, in quo Sol incipit versus solstitium hyemale tendere . . . virentia omnia cessare, et frondes arborum cadere incipiunt, et sic Hebes, dum deteguntur que occultaverunt frondes nudari dicitur, et obscena monstrare, et a pincernatu etiam removetur, et Ganimedes substituitur, qui Aquarii signum dicitur,eo quod eo tempore pluviosa sit hyemps.

Douglas then moves from this grand, cosmic picture of the season quite literally 'down to earth'. The symbolic image of Hebe, 'spulyeit of hir office and array', foreshadows the wintry landscape that follows, studded with 'epithets coldly expressive of privation':

The grond stud barrant, widderit, dosk or gray,
Herbis, flowris and gersis wallowyt away.
Woddis, forrestis, with nakyt bewis blowt,
Stude stripyt of thar weid in euery howt.
(63-6)

Yet this is still a composite picture of many aspects of winter. We move from mountain to plain, from snow and ice to muddy roads, 'full of floschis, dubbis, myre and clay' (54). With line 68 occurs an important shift of focus. Living creatures had hardly been mentioned in the first section of the **Prologue,** but now they come into the foreground and their response to winter is sympathetically described. Animals and men are linked together in a shared endurance of the elements:

The deyr full dern doun in the dalis drew . . .
Puyr lauboraris and bissy husband men
Went wait and wery draglit in the fen.
The silly scheip and thair litil hyrd gromys
Lurkis vndre le of bankis, woddis and bromys.
(68 ff.)

Finally we move to the poet himself—from man in general to one individual. Both the place and the time are more precisely indicated, and the scene has the vividness of a Flemish genre painting:

The callour ayr, penetratyve and puyr,
Dasyng the blude in euery creatur,
Maid seik warm stovis and beyn fyris hoyt,
In dowbill garmont cled and wily coyt,
With mychty drink and metis confortyve,
Agane the stern wyntir forto stryve.
Repatyrrit weil, and by the chymnay bekyt,
At evin be tyme dovne a bed I me strekyt,
Warpit my hed, kest on clathis thrynfald,
Fortil expell the peralus persand cald.
(87-96)

In his search for warmth and shelter Douglas is at one with the other living creatures he had described earlier. He describes how he opens the window to look out, and is repelled by what he sees:

The schot I closit, and drew inwart in hy,
Chyvirrand for cald, the sesson was so snell,
Schupe with hayt flambe to fleym the fresyng
fell.
(138-40)

In this **Prologue** there is no sense of delight in a snowy landscape. . . . The mood is rather one of 'shivering repugnance'; this is indeed a *tristis prologus.*

The bridge passage (141-62) is managed skilfully. Douglas awakes, and the day's labours recommence—the theme, in part, of **Prologues XII** and **XIII.** He employs the traditional plough-imagery to express his weariness, but the images arise appropriately from what has preceded. Like the 'dantit grettar bestiall' (79) and the 'puyr lauboraris and bissy husband men' already described, the poet must pick up the work he has started despite his own reluctance and the inclement weather.

It is something of a misnomer to call **Prologue XIII** a 'nature' **Prologue.** The description of a June evening is not the centre of the poem, but a beautiful and symbolic setting for the poet's dreamdialogue with Maphaeus Vegius. The **Prologue** is one of Douglas's most accomplished pieces of writing, and makes one regret that he abandoned poetry—as he seems to have done—shortly after composing it. It has an ease and fluidity of style. There is no straining after extreme aureation. By contrast with **Prologue XII,** far less space is devoted to astronomy, and there are fewer mythological allusions and jewel images. Yet Douglas still cannot refrain from a three-fold description of dew as 'beryall droppis' and 'cristall knoppis or smal siluer bedis' (26-8). The tone is largely conversational, and often humorous. Douglas makes fun both of himself and Maphaeus, and is jocular in his use of number symbolism. He undertakes to translate Maphaeus's book as well as the twelve books of the *Aeneid*

in honour of God
And hys Apostolis twelf, in the number od.
(151-52)

There is a skilful modulation of tone, from the near-slapstick of the dream to the sense of awe that dawn provokes:

Yondyr dovn dwynys the evyn sky away,
And vpspryngis the brycht dawyng of day
Intill ane other place nocht far in sundir
That tobehald was plesans, and half wondir.
(159-62)

Yet the **Prologue** is unified by a prevailing serenity, even cheerfulness of mood: June is 'the ioyus moneth' (3), the birds and beasts are tranquil, 'at thar soft quyet' (48), and the planets—Venus and Jupiter—are auspicious (70-2).

Douglas's sense of form is apparent in this **Prologue:** its structure is simpler and more dramatic. The **Prologue** begins at twilight and ends at dawn, and there is much patterning of contrasted images: the setting and the rising sun; the evening star and the morning star; bat and lark (symbolic creatures of dusk and dawn). Verbal antitheses sometimes reinforce these oppositions: Phoebus declines, but Esperus 'vpspryngis' (20); and

Vpgois the bak with hir pelit ledderyn flycht,
The lark discendis from the skyis hycht . . .
(33-4)

Yet Douglas is not blind to the similarity between these periods of half light. In the evening, as later in the dawn, he notes how

Owt our the swyre swymmys the soppis of myst.
(37)

I take this patterning to be intentional, and to serve as more than ornament. The contrasts enforce a sense of natural rhythm, the repeated cycle of night and day. This in turn has a symbolic correspondence to the poet's own changing mood. The opening lays stress on the night's function—'eftir laubour to tak the nychtis rest' (10)—and

Still war the fowlis fleis in the air,
All stoir and catall seysit in thar lair,
And euery thing, quharso thame lykis best,
Bownys to tak the hailsum nychtis rest.

(43-6)

Douglas, too, thinks that he has completed his labours on the *Aeneid.* But the **Prologue** ends with a new beginning. Dawn—*referens opera atque labores* (*Aeneid* XI.183)—brings the resumption of activity by bird, beast, man and the poet himself:

> Belyve on weyng the bissy lark vpsprang,
> To salus the blyth morrow with hir sang;
> Sone our the feildis schynys the lycht cleir,
> Welcum to pilgrym baith and lauborer;
> Tyte on hys hynys gaif the greif a cry,
> 'Awaik, on fut, go till our husbandry' . . .
> Tharto thir byrdis syngis in the schawys,
> As menstralis playng 'The ioly day now dawys.'
> Than thocht I thus: 'I will my cunnand kepe,
> I will not be a daw, I will not slepe,
> I wil compleit my promys schortly, thus
> Maid to the poet master Mapheus.'

(167 ff.)

The **Prologue** is thus far from static; there is a sense of change and progression both in the outside world and in the poet's mind.

At the centre of **Prologue XIII** are two stock medieval forms: the dream and the interview. The ***Palice of Honour*** indicates very clearly Douglas's familiarity with the many and varied uses to which the dream form had been put by medieval poets. In this **Prologue,** however, Douglas says quite explicitly that one particular dream was in his mind:

> I wait the story of Iherom is to you kend,
> Quhou he was dung and beft intill hys sleip,
> For he to gentilis bukis gaif sik keip.

(122-24)

Maphaeus replies contemptuously:

> 'Ya, smy,' quod he, 'wald thou eschape me swa?
> In faith we sall nocht thus part or we ga!
> Quhou think we he essonyeis hym to astart,
> As all for consciens and devoit hart,
> Fenyeand hym Iherom forto contyrfeit,
> Quhar as he lyggis bedovyn, lo, in sweit!
> I lat the wyt I am nane hethyn wight,
> And gif thou has afortyme gayn onrycht,
> Followand sa lang Virgill, a gentile clerk,
> Quhy schrynkis thou with my schort Cristyn wark?'

(131-40)

Jerome's dream was famous and influential. It was sometimes represented in art—as we may see from Botticini's painting in the National Gallery—and memories of it shaped the dreams of other Christians besides Douglas. The twelfth-century bishop, Herbert of Norwich, had a vision in which he was told that 'the same mouth should not preach Christ and recite Ovid' [*Epistolae Heberti de Losinga*]. Douglas is thus giving a new and humorous slant to what was clearly a well-known story. In so doing Douglas lets his readers know that he is aware of a classic discussion of the Christian's attitude to pagan literature. At the same time he is associating himself with a great saint and scholar, and what is more significant, the translator of the Vulgate. The pretension is at once ridiculed by Maphaeus—'Fenyeand hym Iherom forto contyrfeit'—yet the link has been made.

The poet's interview with someone who commands him to write was a popular theme, and often linked with the dream. It perhaps originated partly as a humorous development of the humility topos: the poet writes not out of 'vane presumptioun' but at the request of another. Chaucer experienced a vision in which Cupid commanded him to write poems in praise of love and women; the *Legend of Good Women* followed. Douglas recalls this situation in his own ***Palice of Honour,*** and humorously tells us that the ***Eneados*** was prompted by the request of Venus (**Directioun,** 120-27; ***Palice of Honour,*** 1749-57). Other writers well known to Douglas had put the form to many and different uses. In Lydgate's *Fall of Princes* (II.3844-4212) Thyestes and Atreus demand that the poet put their stories into verse; later in the *Fall of Princes* (Prologue VIII) Lydgate has an imaginary conversation with Boccaccio and Petrarch. In *Prohemium* III of the *Genealogy of the Gods* Boccaccio describes an interview of a different kind, in which an attempt is made to dissuade him from writing; an old man, Numenius, chides him for harming the *numen* of the gods.

The closest parallel to **Prologue XIII,** however, is provided by Henryson. In his Prologue to the Fable of the Lion and the Mouse Henryson takes a walk on a June day, falls asleep beneath a hawthorn, and has a vision of the poet Aesop. Douglas clearly recalled Henryson when writing this **Prologue.** He describes Maphaeus as 'lyke to sum poet of the ald fasson' (88)—a line which in slightly different form Henryson used twice, of Aesop (*Fables,* 1353), and of Mercury (*Testament of Cresseid,* 245). Yet the differences are as striking as the resemblances. The hawthorn is replaced by the laurel (64, and cf. 87), traditionally associated with epic poetry. And instead of the grave dialogue between Henryson and Aesop Douglas gives us something more like a 'flyting'. At first he addresses Maphaeus 'with reuerens' (89), but Maphaeus's tone towards Douglas is consistently contemptuous—his use of the slighting 'thou' and 'thee' should be noted. Douglas uses the form for his own ends, to dramatize a conflict within his own mind. Maphaeus is Douglas's *alter ego,* and voices some of Douglas's own views. The dialogue embodies a kind of literary criticism. It puts forward Douglas's defence for translating book XIII, yet shows that he is aware of its inferiority and the impropriety of adding it to Virgil. Yet this is all a humorous ploy; Douglas is making a show of being forced into something that he really wants to undertake. **Prologue XIII** is thus a successful piece of writing in itself, yet closely linked with the book that it precedes.

It will be clear that I depart from some earlier critics in my interpretation of these three **Prologues.** I do not think that in any of them 'landscape is depicted solely for its own sake' [Wittig], or that Douglas was 'the first poet in our language to take landscape in itself and for itself as a subject' [Mackenzie]. This seems no more true of Douglas than of Virgil in the *Georgics* or Milton in *L'Allegro* or *Il Penseroso.* Nonetheless, I think Douglas is a figure of some importance in the writing of descriptive poetry. Nature is still celebrated in moral or philosophical terms, or designed in part as a setting or correlative to the poet's mood, but it is given enormously increased prominence in these **Prologues.** No other poet writing in English before Douglas devotes so much space to the continuous description of the natural world. Again, for accuracy and close observation of detail Douglas seems unrivalled at this time. The presence of conventional features cannot detract from this. Douglas not only imitated Virgil but learnt from him, and seems to have been the first to introduce the *Georgics* into the English poetic tradition. In this he anticipates Thomson, but does not seem to have influenced him. (pp. 175-90)

Priscilla Bawcutt, in her Gavin Douglas: A Critical Study, *Edinburgh University Press, 1976, 245 p.*

Priscilla Bawcutt (essay date 1988)

[*In the excerpt which follows, Bawcutt offers an overview of Douglas's literary achievements, examining his poetic technique in the* Palice of Honour *and the* Prologues, *as well as assessing the merits of his translation of Virgil's* Aeneid. *Placing Douglas in his historical context, the critic outlines the poet's adherence to, and departure from, the traditions and literary conventions of his time.*]

Douglas is exceptional among early Scottish poets for his learning. He abounds in references to other writers, telling us whom he likes and dislikes, praising Virgil's 'maist excellent buke' (**Prol I,** 80), or castigating Caxton's 'febil proys' (**Prol V,** 51). He bids us read some authors (such as Boccaccio), but to cast others (such as Caxton) contemptuously to the floor. Characteristically, when he wishes to praise his patron, he calls him a bibliophile. Henry, Lord Sinclair, is a 'fader of bukis', who

> Bukis to recollect, to reid and se,
> Has gret delyte as ever had Ptholome.
> (**Prol I,** 99-100)

Respect for the written word informs all Douglas's poetry. In ***The Palice of Honour*** he celebrates the power of literature to teach, to delight, and to preserve a knowledge of the past; but he also recognises its destructive power—there is a quirky but revealing episode when Catiline tries to sneak into the Palace of Honour through a window, and 'Tullius' strikes him down 'with ane buik' (1772). The invention of printing did not cause Douglas's love of books, but may have fostered it. He reveals an impressive awareness of new publications, consulting recently printed editions of Ovid and Virgil, and reading John Major's *History of Britain* almost as soon as it appeared. Despite occasional pedantry there is great liveliness in his response to what he reads. He flytes with 'Inglis' books, translating his scorn into physical manifestations-spitting 'for dispyte', 'bytand my lip' (**Prol I,** 150, 252). Yet he also communicates wide and generous enthusiasms, for poetry, epic and, above all, Virgil.

Douglas had a learned circle of friends, and was aware of the passionate scholarly debates taking place on the continent. Although not strictly a Humanist (he did not read Greek, nor teach *studia humanitatis*), he shared many of the Humanists' values: an antipathy to some aspects of scholasticism, a respect for the text of ancient authors, and a belief in the high importance of the classics. He was fired by a missionary zeal, not simply to translate one particular great poem but to teach and educate his countrymen, and also to transfer to his native 'Scottis' tongue something of the richness and felicity of 'fair Latyn, / That knawyn is maste perfite langage fyne' (**Prol I,** 381-82). He was a translator in the widest sense—a transmitter of ideas and values. Douglas saw vernacular poetry not as something wholly divorced from that written in Latin, but as inheriting the same rich tradition. The central section of ***The Palice of Honour*** is dominated by the Muses and their procession. Symbolically placed at the very end appear three English and three Scottish poets (one of whom is Dunbar); beside the multitude of Latin authors their number is small, yet they are all equally followers of the Muses. Douglas also puts himself there, half-comically and half-seriously, as an aspirant poet, who has much to learn. Douglas often represents himself as a follower of Virgil, which is true in a double sense: as a translator he follows Virgil's words closely; as a poet he sees Virgil as a model, and aspires to write in that great tradition which Chaucer introduced to Britain and which flowered in Spenser and Milton. Douglas had high ambitions. At the beginning of his career he represented poetry as his personal road to honour; at its end he proudly claimed that his work would bring him immortality, and that he would be read 'Throw owt the ile yclepit Albyon' (***Conclusio,*** 11). He saw his poetry as having public importance, of value to Scotland as well as to himself.

The Palice of Honour (*c.* 1501) employs an ancient form, the allegorical dream, to explore the nature of honour, its connection with love and poetry, and its distinction from fame, or glory. This was a topic that had long interested moralists, but peculiarly fascinated poets from the fourteenth to the sixteenth century, who frequently deified Honour, and placed him in temples, castles and palaces. . . . In November 1501 elaborate pageants welcomed Katherine of Aragon to London; in one, placed upon a throne, the figure of Honour declaimed that many pursued him but failed through lack of virtue. Honour was Virtue's reward. Douglas makes a similar point, at greater length, but far more imaginatively. The dreamer encounters three processions, led by Minerva, Diana, and Venus, who are making their way towards the palace of Honour. He joins a fourth procession, that of the Muses, and learns eventually that virtuous Honour, which is immortal, must be distinguished from 'eirdlie gloir', which is vain and transient. Yet such a brief summary fails to do justice to the poem's complexity. Douglas's notion of honour has caused some puzzlement. At times he seems to equate Honour with the Christian God, and his abode with heaven. But Honour's palace accommodates Venus, the Muses, Hercules, Robert Bruce, and—more surprisingly—Medusa and Semiramis. Douglas here follows a tradition that regarded Medusa and Semiramis, along with the Amazons, as heroic representatives of women. . . . In thus peopling the inmost court with heroes of both sexes Douglas gives pre-eminence to heroic honour, won by martial virtue, or valour. This is fore-shadowed in earlier parts of the poem, which is studded with 'knichtlie deidis', tournaments, and 'battellis intestine'. Among the Muses

Douglas gives priority to Calliope, who inspires epic poets to write of heroes, 'in kinglie style, quhilk dois thair fame incres' (878). Douglas's great contemporary, Erasmus, wrote on a theme more congenial to many modern readers—*dulce bellum inexpertis.* But the ideas here expressed by Douglas were probably more acceptable to his own age. The king to whom he dedicated the poem delighted in tournaments, and by a sad irony his own fame largely rests upon his courageous but foolhardy death at Flodden.

At a climactic point, when the dreamer first sees the palace, his guide promises him 'fouth of sentence' (1401). 'Fouth', or a rich copiousness, of words and things, is the most striking feature of ***The Palice of Honour.*** Douglas characteristically uses words like 'repleit' or 'pleneist' to signify approval. He likes to be all-inclusive—the Muses' court contains 'Everie famous poeit men may devine' (850). The poem abounds in lists, of sages and lovers, rivers and mountains. The palace itself well illustrates his descriptive technique—idealised, glistening with precious metals, outdoing Troy or Solomon's Temple, and crowded with small architectural details:

> Pinnakillis, fyellis, turnpekkis mony one,
> Gilt birneist torris, quhilk like to Phebus schone,
> Skarsment, reprise, corbell and battellingis . . .
> (1432-34)

But this modish late-Gothic edifice is set in a timeless landscape, recalling the earthly paradise:

> I saw ane plane of peirles pulchritude
> Quhairin aboundit alkin thingis gude,
> Spice, wine, corne, oyle, tre, frute, flour, herbis grene,
> All foullis, beistis, birdis and alkin fude,
> All maner fisches, baith of sey and flude,
> War keipit in pondis of poleist silver schene,
> With purifyit water, as of the cristall clene.
> (1414-20)

Douglas's favourite verbal ornament is *repetitio,* yet he is also mindful of another rhetorical category, *dispositio.* ***The Palice of Honour*** is a carefully composed and remarkably patterned poem. Douglas delights in symmetry, both in small features (the English trio of poets matching the Scottish one), and in large, such as the series of processions, all led by divinities. Yet again and again such parallelism highlights differences: the scantiness of Diana's court humorously contrasts with the multitude that follows Venus; and the dreamer's response varies significantly—mingled fear and delight at the sight of Venus, unqualified joy at the arrival of the Muses. Despite its symmetry ***The Palice of Honour*** is full of surprises. The basic pattern is that of the quest, Honour being the 'finall end' (1248), to which all, including the dreamer, are travelling. But it is a journey with many detours and interruptions—the digression on the properties of sound, for instance, where we learn that fish cannot hear, 'For as we se richt few of thame hes eiris' (377), or the comical incident, when the poet angers Venus and fears metamorphosis into 'a beir, a bair, ane oule, ane aip' (741). The poem abounds in odd, freakish, and sometimes terrifying images. The presiding deities (with the significant exception of the Muses) are often wrathful. As a dream ***The Palice of Honour*** hovers between celestial vision and nightmare.

The story of Aeneas was extremely popular in the Middle Ages, but to those who could not read Latin *The Aeneid* was known only through partial or abridged versions, in which the characters of Dido and Aeneas were distorted and striking changes of emphasis occurred. In the early 1500s no major classic had yet been translated into English. Douglas's ***Eneados*** (1512–13) was thus a pioneering work: it was a translation, not a loose paraphrase, of the whole *Aeneid;* and it was based directly on Virgil not on some intermediary version. Douglas was aware of both novelty and the magnitude of his undertaking, and voiced pithy criticisms of the perversion of the *Aeneid* published by Caxton:

> It has na thing ado tharwith, God wait,
> Ne na mair lyke than the devill and Sanct Austyne.
> (**Prol I,** 142-43)

He proudly asserts his own fidelity to Virgil: 'Rycht so am I to Virgillis text ybund' (**Prol I,** 299). But in the sixteenth century 'Virgillis text' was rather different from that we read today. The edition that Douglas used, almost certainly that published by Jodocus Badius Ascensius in 1501, differed from a modern one in wording as well as in spelling and punctuation; it omitted or inserted whole lines, and completed some of the famous half-lines. Any assessment of Douglas's accuracy as a translator must take account of this. Many apparent blunders or barbarisms originated not in his ignorance but in the peculiarities of his Latin text. Much else in ***The Eneados*** that might seem extraneous is modelled on the lay-out and contents of contemporary editions of Virgil, such as the marginal commentaries or the *monosticha argumenta* (twelve one-line summaries of the different books). Douglas's decision to translate the so-called Thirteenth Book, written by the Italian humanist, Maffeo Vegio, might well seem inconsistent, but we should remember that it formed a regular supplement to *The Aeneid* in almost all editions from 1470 to the seventeenth century.

Douglas's scholarly zeal also affects his style. His undoubted diffuseness springs partly from his innate love of 'fouth', partly from an intense desire to convey Virgil's 'sentence', i.e. to draw out the full implications of even the smallest word. When Virgil calls the treacherous Sinon *turbatus* and *pavitans* (*Aeneid,* II, 67 and 107) his dissimulation is largely contextual; but Douglas leaves us in no doubt, translating as '*semyng* ful rad [terrified]', and 'quakand . . . *as it had bene* for dreid'. Again and again he thus explains Virgil's hints and ambiguities, making explicit what is implicit in the Latin. He gains clarity and introduces vivid details of his own, but often loses Virgil's brevity and rich suggestiveness. The relationship between ***The Eneados*** and *The Aeneid* has been much discussed, and Douglas's achievement compared to that of later translators, such as Surrey and Dryden. But critics sometimes ask us to consider ***The Eneados*** as a work of art in its own right. This poses a difficult question. How do we divorce ***The Eneados*** from *The Aeneid,* when story, larger structural features, and major themes, all derive from Virgil? Douglas took great pride in retaining the proportions of his original, and invited his detractors to compare his work to Virgil's. His own contribution is essentially a matter of expression—he gives us Virgil 'in the langage of Scottis natioun' (**Prol I,** 103). In fact his language is inventive and remarkably wide-ranging: sometimes he uses harsh onomatopoeic words, of storms or bird-cries, sometimes he anticipates Milton in his use of sonorous Latinisms. Not surprisingly he is most successful when given an opportunity to do what is most congenial to him—descriptions of the natural world, for instance, or portraits, such as that of Venus, disguised as 'a wild hunteres / With wynd waving hir haris lowsit of tres', and Charon:

> Terribil of schap and sluggart of array,
> Apon his chyn feil cannos harys gray,
> Lyart feltrit tatis; with burnand eyn red,
> Lyk twa fyre blesys fixit in his hed.

Douglas provided each book of ***The Eneados*** with a **Prologue,** and paid a leisurely farewell to it in a series of epistles and epilogues. Anyone new to Douglas should start with these **Prologues;** designed chiefly to introduce readers to Virgil, they form an excellent introduction to Douglas himself. Their variety is startling: one **Prologue** contains only three stanzas, but many run into hundreds of lines; metrically, they range from the elaborate thirteen-line alliterative stanza of **Prologue VIII** to the five-beat couplet adopted for the translation itself. Their tone and contents are so varied that critics debate how closely they are integrated with the translation, whether some were written for a different purpose, and whether it would be better to regard them as independent poems. Some indeed, such as **Prologues X** and **XI,** form virtually self-contained essays on moral or theological themes. Yet many other Prologues, particularly the first six, are highly relevant to the books they introduce. Subtle attempts to fit the **Prologues** into a pre-meditated, over-all scheme, calendric or thematic, are not convincing. What unity they possess seems more casual and organic, proceeding from Douglas and his pre-occupations—in particular his enthusiasm for Virgil and his view of translation as a great and creative enterprise. One persistent theme arises from the tension in Douglas between poet and churchman; almost every **Prologue** touches on this in some way. **Prologue I** opens with a magnificent eulogy of Virgil, 'of Latyn poetis prynce', but corrects this significantly with a later prayer:

> Thou prynce of poetis, I the mercy cry,
> I meyn thou Kyng of Kyngis, Lord Etern,
> Thou be my muse, my gydar and laid stern . . .
>
> In Criste is all my traste, and hevynnys queyn.
> (**Prol I,** 452-54; 462)

For the Christian, Virgil and his pagan inspiration are ultimately transcended by Christ.

Since the eighteenth century the so-called **Nature Prologues (VII, XII** and **XIII)** have been particularly admired. In the past it was claimed that they sprang from Douglas's direct experience of nature. But books were an important element in Douglas's experience. It does not detract from his originality to note how these **Prologues** were partly shaped by his reading of Chaucer and Henryson, as well as Virgil's *Georgics,* Ovid's dawn descriptions, or the storm scenes of alliterative poetry. No vernacular poet before Douglas (or for long afterwards) described the natural world so well, or devoted so much space to it. Grand panoramic vistas are combined with accurate observation of tiny details. Long before Hopkins Douglas delights in dappled things—flowers, 'depart in freklys red and quhite' (**Prol XII,** 111), or the 'dapill grey' of a lawn, powdered with daisies (**Prol XIII,** 177-8). **Prologue VII** opens with a vivid but composite image of winter: the eye is led from the heavens down to earth, from mountain tops, 'slekit with snaw', to muddy roads and the activity of 'Puyr lauboraris and bissy husband men'. Yet the final focus is upon the poet, preparing for bed and later awakening:

> Fast by my chalmyr, in heich wysnyt treis,
> The soir gled quhislis lowd with mony a pew:
> Quhar by the day was dawyn weil I knew,
> Bad beit the fyre and the candill alyght,
> Syne blissyt me, and in my wedis dyght,
> A schot wyndo onschet a litill on char,
> Persavyt the mornyng bla, wan and har . . .
>
> The schot I closit, and drew inwart in hy,
> Chyvirrand for cald, the sesson was so snell,
> Schupe with hayt flambe to fleym the fresyng fell.
> (124 ff.)

The subject might better be termed 'Poet in a wintry landscape' than 'winter'. So too with **Prologue XIII**—the description of a June night, beautiful though it is, is primarily a frame for the dreaming poet. (It has striking parallels of structure with **Prologue VIII,** including the topos of the weary poet, anxious to finish his 'buke'.) Douglas's chief purpose is to justify his inclusion of the Thirteenth Book, which he accomplishes, skilfully and humorously, in the dream-dialogue with its author, Maffeo Vegio. **Prologue XII** is dominated by the splendid image of the sun as monarch, making a triumphal progress, and receiving the homage of his subjects, who hail him as 'master and rewlar of the yer'. It celebrates 'dame Nature' at her most fecund and benign, the month is 'hailsum May', and the season not spring (as repeatedly stated) but the first day of summer (Douglas speaks of the 'lang symmyris day' in line 93; cf. also 204). Of the three, **Prologue XII** is the most wholeheartedly a 'nature poem'. (pp. 81-6)

Douglas's works were printed in the sixteenth century, in England as well as Scotland, and clearly influenced later poets, notably Surrey and Sackville. From then to the present day there has been continuous critical awareness of 'the learned bishop of Dunkeld'. . . . about him in the later sixteenth century, and throughout the seventeenth century. Dunbar's re-discovery was initiated by the publication of some of his poems in Ramsay's *Ever Green* (1724); thenceforth there was ever-growing critical interest and admiration. Scott called him 'the darling of the Scottish Muses'; to Crabbe he Douglas's name has always been linked with that of Virgil; although this once aided his reputation, sadly this is no longer true. Today there is increasing appreciation of him not just as a translator but as an original poet, with wayward slightly eccentric gifts. (pp. 86-7)

Priscilla Bawcutt, "William Dunbar and Gavin Douglas," in The History of Scottish Literature: Origins to 1660 (Mediaeval and Renaissance), Vol. I, *edited by R.D.S. Jack, Aberdeen University Press, 1988, pp. 73-89.*

FURTHER READING

Bawcutt, Priscilla. "Gavin Douglas and Chaucer." *The Review of English Studies* XXI, No. 84 (November 1970): 401-21.

Studies the relationship between Douglas and Chaucer, highlighting the themes, dialogue, and spirit which links them. In addition, Bawcutt analyzes the strengths and diversity of the poetic traditions inherited by the Scots poet.

Bennett, J. A. W. "The Early Fame of Gavin Douglas's *Eneados.*" *Modern Language Notes* LXI, No. 2 (February 1946): 83-8.

History of the publication of the *Eneados* and its use by subsequent writers.

Coldwell, David F. C. "Introduction." In *Virgil's Aeneid Translated into Scottish Verse by Gavin Douglas, Bishop of Dunkeld,* Vol. I, edited by David F. C. Coldwell, pp. 1-127. Edinburgh: William Blackwood and Sons, 1964.

Provides a general overview of Douglas's life and his translation.

Conington, John. "The English Translators of Virgil." *The Quarterly Review* 110, No. 219 (July 1861): 73-114.

History of the attempts to render the Roman poet's works into English. The critic praises Douglas's translation as a noble effort while simultaneously noting its "primitive workmanship."

"On Gawin Douglas's Translation of Virgil's Aeneid." *The Edinburgh Magazine and Literary Miscellany* (January 1820): 41-4.

Commendation of Douglas's *Eneados* with portions of the translation reprinted.

Elton, Oliver. "The Fifteenth Century." In his *The English Muse,* pp. 77-100. London: G. Bell and Sons, 1937.

Examines the Scottish Chaucerians in their historical context. Elton offers qualified praise of Douglas, considering his translation of the *Aeneid* "a poem in its own right," but judging his versification faulty.

Fowler, Alastair. "Virgil for 'every gentil Scot'." *The Times Literary Supplement,* No. 3932 (22 July 1977): 882-83.

Elaborates upon Priscilla Bawcutt's studies of Douglas, emphasizing, in particular, the originality and creativity of Douglas's works.

Lewis, C. S. "Allegory as the Dominant Form." In his *The Allegory of Love,* pp. 232-96. Oxford: Oxford University Press, 1936.

Presents *King Hart* and the *Palice of Honour* as part of a long medieval tradition of poetic allegory, and commends the poems as highly imaginative works of art.

Minto, William. "Chaucer's Contemporaries and Successors." In his *Characteristics of English Poets from Chaucer to Shirley,* pp. 45-113. Boston: Ginn and Co., 1904.

Includes an analysis of Douglas's versification and philological efforts in the Prologues of the *Eneados.*

Parkinson, David J. "Gavin Douglas's Interlude." *Scottish Literary Journal* 14, No. 2 (November 1987): 5-17.

Discusses Prologue VIII as a dramatic entertainment featuring two distinct voices—"the translator" and a "dream figure"—engaged in a dialogue.

Pound, Ezra. "Exhibit: Gavin Douglas 1474/1522." In his *ABC of Reading,* pp. 101-13. London: George Routledge and Sons, 1934.

Extracts of the *Eneados* with commentary and notes. Pound maintains that in certain passages, he gets "considerably more pleasure" from Douglas than Virgil.

Preston, Priscilla. "Did Gavin Douglas Write *King Hart*?" *Medium Aevum* XXXVIII, No. 1 (1959): 31-47.

Questions Douglas's authorship of *King Hart,* citing differences in tone, style, and syntax between the allegorical works and the poet's acknowledged writings.

Ridley, Florence H. "Did Gawin Douglas Write *King Hart*?" *Speculum* XXXIV, No. 3 (July 1959): 402-12.

Investigates the historical attribution of the allegorical poem to Douglas. Ridley concludes that there is "no shred of evidence" to suggest that Douglas was the writer of *King Hart.*

Ross, John M. "Gavin Douglas." In his *Scottish History and Literature to the Reformation,* pp. 293-374. Glasgow: James Maclehose and Sons, 1884.

Presents Douglas as a transitional figure between the Middle Ages and the English Renaissance whose works reflect the influence of the chivalric traditions as well as heralding the advent of humanism.

Saintsbury, George. "The Prosody of the Scottish Poets." In his *A History of English Prosody, Vol. I,* pp. 265-87. 1908. Reprint. New York: Russell and Russell, 1961.

Examines Douglas's poetic technique in a general historical overview of fifteenth-century Scottish poets.

Small, John. "Biographical Introduction." *The Poetical Works of Gavin Douglas, Bishop of Dunkeld, Vol. I,* edited by John Small, pp. i-clxvii. Edinburgh: William Paterson, 1874.

Traces the development of Douglas's works and his philological impact on the standardization of the Scottish language.

Smith, Sydney Goodsir. "The *Aeneid* of Gawin Douglas." *Life and Letters and the London Mercury* 55, No. 123 (November 1947): 112-25.

Challenges the contention that Douglas was merely an imitator of Chaucer.

Speirs, John. "The Scots 'Aeneid' of Gavin Douglas." In his *The Scots Literary Tradition,* pp. 165-97. Revised Edition. London: Faber and Faber, 1962.

General appreciation of the *Eneados* as a great poetic work unrivalled by any other translation.

Tillyard, E. M. W. "The Great Translations." In his *The English Epic and Its Background,* pp. 338-44. New York: Oxford University Press, 1954.

Compares Douglas's *Eneados* to Virgil's original, concluding that the translation falls short of a true epic and is, at best, a meritorious long poem.

Watt, Lauchlan Maclean. *Douglas's Aeneid.* Cambridge: University Press, 1920, 252 p.

Study of the historical and literary movements which affected Douglas in his writing of the *Eneados.*

William Dunbar

1460?-1530?

Scottish poet.

INTRODUCTION

Dunbar is recognized as one of the most accomplished poets in Scottish literary history—second, in many critics' estimation, only to Robert Burns in capturing the unique spirit of his country. His poetry encompasses many diverse styles and forms, including devotional compositions, flytings (exchanges of personal abuse in poetic form), satire, and petitionary verse, but he is best remembered for his ceremonial poems, "The Thrissil and the Rois" and "The Goldyn Targe," composed during his tenure as a court poet to King James IV. As James Kinsley has remarked, Dunbar "is a keen and humorous observer of . . . the human pageant, a moody but finely reflective moralist, a word-hurler and castigator on a grand scale, and a persistent experimenter. . . . [In] linguistic and metrical variety, assurance and exuberant imagination he is the richest of our poets."

Born in East Lothian around the year 1460, Dunbar began his formal education in 1477 at Saint Andrews in Edinburgh. He completed his studies two years later and became a mendicant friar of the Order of Saint Francis. Travelling extensively throughout Europe, he went to France in 1491 where he encountered the French rhetoriqueurs, among them François Villon, whose writings were to have a lasting influence on Dunbar's poetry. He returned to England in 1500 and abandoned the Franciscan habit, opting instead to be ordained to the secular priesthood. While the circumstances and date of his appointment are uncertain, the poet eventually became a laureate to the Scottish court of James IV and was paid an annual pension. Hoping to gain a benefice from the king, he wrote many petitionary poems in which he voiced his dismay to the sovereign and mocked his court rivals who were, in his opinion, receiving preferential treatment. Dunbar was also involved in diplomatic missions on behalf of the king, making voyages to both Scandinavia and the Netherlands. As part of a Scottish delegation to the English court of King Henry VII, the poet was involved in arranging the betrothal of James IV to Henry's daughter, Margaret Tudor. It was for their nuptials in 1503 that he composed "The Thrissil and the Rois," his first major work. During his lifetime he wrote between eighty and one hundred poems which scholars contend are difficult, if not impossible, to date. Nothing certain is known about his death, although some researchers have suggested that the poet perished in the Battle of Flodden in 1513 or that he received his long desired benefice and retired. All concur that Dunbar died sometime before the year 1530, since in that year Sir David Lyndsay referred to him as being deceased.

Critics generally agree that Dunbar's fame rests on his remarkable employment of a variety of literary forms. In particular, the poet was adept in his use and embellishment of the dream allegory. His most acclaimed such work, "The Thrissil and the Rois," an epithalamion to James and Margaret, combines the medieval genre with heraldic pageantry reminiscent of Geoffrey Chaucer's *Parlement of Foules.* Like Chaucer's dream vision, the work is a praise of love in which a convocation of animals and birds, derived from traditional literary bestiaries, pays tribute to the Thistle and the Rose, armorial insignie for James and Margaret. While acknowledging that the poem is conventional, scholars have lauded the highly original way in which Dunbar weaves the conventions together. With his vivid descriptions of singing birds, colorful flowers, and the extended procession of admirers, the poet transforms a depiction of an otherwise ordinary human event into a pantheistic celebration. As John Baxter has written, "Had [Dunbar] written nothing else, 'The Thistle and the Rose' would alone have established his fame." While some commentators argue that "The Goldyn Targe" is just another courtly poem exploring man's vulnerability to feminine beauty or a confection written to compliment James IV's interest in the navy and gunnery, others value the piece as an enlargement upon the dream allegory form. The poem is ornamented with a wide range of imagery, from the reflection of leaves on a lake and the sound of birds chanting matins, to archers, catalogs of gods and goddesses, and the discharge of artillery from a white-sailed ship. The imagery is enhanced by highly formal diction, rich with descriptive terms such as "twinkling," "silver," and "crystalline." Although an energetic creation applauded for its graceful and witty language, the poem has also been judged to have considerable philosophical merit. More than simply an idealization of love, "The Goldyn Targe" is a meditation upon humanity's rational desire to be in harmony with nature: a wish which, the poem suggests, is often thwarted by the sensual appetites. Many scholars have also admired the satirical "Tretis of the Tua Mariit Wemen and the Wedo" as a work which further manifests Dunbar's poetic versatility, scope, and ingenuity. Although structured as an allegory, this work draws upon a number of conventions, especially in its use of unrhymed alliterative verse, which had been popular in English literature in the fourteenth century, and its theme of matrimony, a common subject in the French poetry of Dunbar's time. Dunbar brilliantly satirizes traditional concepts of marriage, however, by radically shifting from what appears at first to be an allegory of idealized love to a lascivious commentary on the reality of married life. Three women discuss the details of their marital experiences, not in the language of courtly love typical of allegory, but in explicit, bawdy terms that deride men as objects of scorn and revulsion. This reversal of expectations is accompanied by a sharp alteration of tone from solemn and dignified to scornful and mocking.

Standing in marked contrast to such raucous satires are Dunbar's numerous devotional or moral poems. Some critics contend that poems of this type, which form a large portion of his canon, were written toward the end of his life, although no historical evidence supports this claim. Perhaps most noteworthy among them is "The Dance of the Sevin Deidly Sinnis," a macabre piece in which the vices and their followers leap through the flames of hell while piercing each other with knives. Critics have observed that Dunbar infused even a grisly scene like this with humor, by combining the joy of dance with the ghastly pain of hell. C. S. Lewis has noted, "Dunbar and his contemporaries seriously believed that such entertainment awaited in the next world those who practised (without repentance) the seven deadly sins. . . . They believed and (doubtless) trembled; yet they also laughed." In the stern and somber "Lament for the Makaris," with its poignant refrain, "Timor mortis conturbat me" ("fear of death disturbs me"), Dunbar mourns his Scottish poetic predecessors while contemplating the finality of death. Many critics claim that liturgical works such as "Ane Ballat of Our Lady," "On the Resurrection of Christ," and "On the Nativitie of Christ," are among the most lyrical of all English-language poems. Resonating with vibrant energy, these spirited compositions are like songs which summon all creation to participate in the divine mysteries.

The flyting, a contrived half-playful exchange of personal insults between poetic competitors, was another literary form Dunbar employed with skill. Derived from medieval Latin verse, the genre provided a framework for the poet to display his mastery of arcane vocabulary, internal rhyme, rhetoric, and alliteration. In the most famous, "The Flyting of Dunbar and Kennedy," Dunbar trades verbal scurrilities with contemporary and rival, Walter Kennedy. Although some scholars have censured the piece for its vulgarity, the "Flyting" is generally lauded for its spirit and acknowledged as a masterful example of the genre. While less roundly abusive than the flytings, some of Dunbar's petitionary verse is also noted for its invective. In such poems as "Complaint to the King," "Remonstrance to the King," and "Birth of Antichrist," the poet voices his frustration to James IV over his lack of a benefice and satirically attacks the disreputable followers of the king. As some critics have asserted, these aesthetic denunciations, rich in alliteration and rhyme, are perhaps the best examples of the poet's versification.

Critics unanimously commend Dunbar's ability to vary the poetic style in accordance with the form and subject of each work. In "The Thrissil and the Rois" and "The Goldyn Targe" Dunbar skillfully used the technique of aureation, ornamenting these poems with dignified and solemn adjectives to evoke strong visual images and employing a formal, stately diction. The poet further enriched the verse with neologisms derived from Latin, giving his native Scottish a rich rhetorical quality. In the devotional piece, "On the Nativitie of Christ," he juxtaposed liturgical Latin with aureate Scottish dialect to produce a sober and reverent air, but in "The Testament of Mr. Andro Kennedy," Dunbar, like Villon, set Latin and vernacular verse side by side to create a comic effect. In other works Dunbar employed the "eldritch" style. In contrast to the aureate style which tended towards the abstract and descriptive, the eldritch was characterized as concrete, noun-dense, and alliterative. Widely used in the Middle Ages in satires and comedies, the swift-moving eldritch manner was boisterous and powerful and thus well-suited to Dunbar's flytings and petitionary verse in which he disparaged rivals and mocked seemingly serious situations.

Many critics have suggested that the merit of Dunbar's poetry lies not only in its technical aspects, but also in its overall content and vision. Although his works are often divided into the ceremonial and satirical, all share an ironic perspective of the medieval world. As a realistic chronicler of the human drama in such pieces as "The Dance of the Sevin Deidly Sinnis," "Of Lyfe," and "Of the Changes of Lyfe," Dunbar wrestled with the dilemma of how to negotiate change in a supposedly immutable universe. To believe that the cosmos is perfectly ordered is naive, these poems suggest, since life reveals discord. For the poet, the perpetuation of such a myth was a source of amusement. A similar commentary on the inability of human beings to discriminate between fantasy and reality is found in "The Tretis of the Tua Mariit Wemen and the Wedo," with its mocking of notions of idealized love. Critics have found elements of irony and humor even in "The Goldyn Targe," detecting satire on the insincere behavior which governed the Scottish court, especially in regard to women. Pamela King has remarked that "The Goldyn Targe" "has the dual function of parodying the matter of courtly artifice surrounding the battle of the sexes, while mimicking its manner."

Dunbar's literary contribution to the Scottish nation was acknowledged by contemporaries like Gavin Douglas and David Lyndsay, but it was not until the eighteenth century that literary historians began to collect and edit his works. As David Laing observed, "During [Dunbar's] own age he received the homage due to his genius, and his writings for a time continued to be admired and imitated by succeeding poets; yet he was doomed to total and absolute neglect during the long period which elapsed between the year 1530, when Sir David Lyndsay mentions him among the poets then deceased, and the year 1724, when Allan Ramsay published a selection of his poems." In the nineteenth century Dunbar's poetry increasingly found admirers, Sir Walter Scott prominent among them. Two scholarly editions of the poems were published in the period, giving rise to the first modern assessments of Dunbar's work. Some commentators, such as James Russell Lowell, found the poetry coarse, tedious, and pedantic, while others, including William J. Courthope, praised it as highly original and diverse. Much critical contention in the late nineteenth and early twentieth century surrounded the question of the extent of Dunbar's reliance on the medieval poetic conventions and, especially, on the works of Chaucer. Though Dunbar's poetry was faulted by some as highly derivative, most scholars took a moderate view and argued that Dunbar himself recognized his dependence on the traditional styles of English verse and forthrightly admitted his debt to Chaucer, whom he hailed as the "rose of rethoris all." In the latter half of the twentieth century, critical attention has shifted from the consideration of Dunbar as a Scottish Chaucerian to an evaluation of him as a poet in his own right, as an enlarger of the poetic conventions of his day. Commentators have focused on his technical brilliance, his impressive range of styles and subject matter, and his unique poetic vision comprehending many facets of the human condition. As Lewis has noted, "Dunbar is the first completely professional poet in our history. Versatile to the point of virtuosity, he practices every form from satiric pornogram to devotional lyric and is equally at home in the boisterous language of the alliterative pieces, the aureation of his allegories, and the middle style of his ordinary poems."

PRINCIPAL WORKS

**The Chepman and Myllar Prints* (poetry) 1508
†"The Thrissil and the Rois" (poetry) 1724
The Poems of William Dunbar. 2 vols. [edited by David Laing] (poetry) 1834
The Poems of William Dunbar. 3 vols. [edited by John Small] (poetry) 1884-89
The Poems of William Dunbar [edited by W. McKay Mackenzie] (poetry) 1932
The Poems of William Dunbar [edited by James Kinsley] (poetry) 1979

*These separately printed sheets include "The Ballade of Bernard Stewart," "The Ballad of Kynd Kittok," "The Flyting of Dunbar and Kennedy," "The Goldyn Targe," "Lament for the Makaris," "The Testament of Mr. Andro Kennedy," and "The Tretis of the Tua Mariit Wemen and the Wedo."

†This poem was originally composed in 1503.

Thomas Warton (essay date 1778)

[*Warton was an English poet and literary critic of the eighteenth century. The following excerpt, taken from a work first published in 1778, is a general recognition of Dunbar's merit and marks the beginning of modern criticism of the Scottish poet.*]

I am of opinion, that the imagination of Dunbar is not less suited to satirical than to sublime allegory: and that he is the first poet who has appeared with any degree of spirit in this way of writing since Pierce Plowman. His **"Thistle and Rose,"** and **"Golden Terge,"** are generally and justly mentioned as his capital works: but the natural complexion of his genius is of the moral and didactic cast. The measure of [**"The Dance of the Seven Deadly Sins"**] is partly that of Sir THOPAS in Chaucer: and hence we may gather by the way, that Sir THOPAS was anciently dewed in the light of a ludicrous composition. It is certain that the pageants and interludes of Dunbar's age must have quickened his invention to form those grotesque groupes. The exhibition of MORALITIES was now in high vogue among the Scotish. A morality was played at the marriage of James IV. and the princess Margaret. Mummeries, which they call GYSARTS, composed of moral personifications, are still known in Scotland: and even till the beginning of this century, especially among the festivities of Christmas, itinerant maskers were admitted into the houses of the Scottish nobility (p. 505)

Thomas Warton, "Digression to the Scotch Poets," in his The History of English Poetry from the Eleventh to the Seventeenth Century, *1778. Reprinted by Alex. Murray and Son, 1870, pp. 491-505.*

Sir Walter Scott (essay date 1829)

[*A Scottish author of historical romances, Scott was one of the leading proponents in the early nineteenth century of verisimilitude and historical accuracy in literature. He clearly represented the increased tolerance of the Romantic age towards all literature, and his criticism was usually based on a high regard for realism and the desire to assess an author's place in literary history. The following is a portion of a memoir written in honor of George Bannatyne, an early compiler of sixteenth-century poetry, including some of Dunbar's works. Scott notes Dunbar's place in the history of English literature and lauds the poet's versification and the entertainment value of his works.*]

This darling of the Scottish Muses [Dunbar] has been justly raised to a level with Chaucer by every judge of poetry, to whom his obsolete language has not rendered him unintelligible. In brilliancy of fancy, in force of description, in the power of conveying moral precepts with terseness, and marking lessons of life with conciseness and energy, in quickness of satire, and in poignancy of humour, the Northern Maker may boldly aspire to rival the Bard of Woodstock. In the pathetic, Dunbar is Chaucer's inferior, and accordingly in most of his pieces he rather wishes to instruct the understanding, or to amuse the fancy, than to affect the heart. It is with pleasure we understand that an edition of the excellent poet, unrivalled by any which Scotland ever produced, is soon to appear under the auspices of [David Laing]. We shall then be in possession of what a correct text can give. But where is the Dryden to be found, who is to translate, for the benefit of more modern times, the wisdom, the wit, the humour, which can now only be comprehended by the scholar and antiquary? (pp. 14-15)

Sir Walter Scott, "Memoir of George Bannatyne," in Memorials of George Bannatyne, *n.p., 1829, pp. 1-24.*

James Russell Lowell (essay date 1875)

[*Lowell was a celebrated American poet and essayist, and an editor of two leading journals, the* Atlantic Monthly *and the* North American Review. *He is noted for his satirical and critical writing, including* A Fable for Critics, *a book-length poem featuring witty critical portraits of his contemporaries. In the excerpt which follows, from an essay originally published in 1875, he of-*

fers an unfavorable review of Dunbar's poetry as pedantic, coarse, and tedious.]

On the whole, the Scottish poetry of the fifteenth century has more meat in it than the English, but this is to say very little. Where it is meant to be serious and lofty it falls into the same vices of unreality and allegory which were the fashion of the day, and which there are some patriots so fearfully and wonderfully made as to relish. Stripped of the archaisms (that turn every *y* to a meaningless *z,* spell which *quhilk,* shake *schaik,* bugle *bowgill,* powder *puldir,* and will not let us simply whistle till we have puckered our mouths to *quhissill*) in which the Scottish antiquaries love to keep it disguised,—as if it were nearer to poetry the further it got from all human recognition and sympathy,—stripped of these, there is little to distinguish it from the contemporary verse-mongering south of the Tweed. Their compositions are generally as stiff and artificial as a trellis, in striking contrast with the popular ballad-poetry of Scotland (some of which possibly falls within this period, though most of it is later), which clambers, lawlessly if you will, but at least freely and simply, twining the bare stem of old tradition with graceful sentiment and lively natural sympathies. I find a few sweet and flowing verses in Dunbar's **"Merle and Nightingale,"**—indeed one whole stanza that has always seemed exquisite to me. It is this:

Ne'er sweeter noise was heard by living man
Than made this merry, gentle nightingale.
Her sound went with the river as it ran
Out through the fresh and flourished lusty vale;
O merle, quoth she, O fool, leave off thy tale,
For in thy song good teaching there is none,
For both are lost,—the time and the travail
Of every love but upon God alone.

But except this lucky poem, I find little else in the serious verses of Dunbar that does not seem to me tedious and pedantic. I dare say a few more lines might be found scattered here and there, but I hold it a sheer waste of time to hunt after these thin needles of wit buried in unwieldy haystacks of verse. If that be genius, the less we have of it the better. His **"Dance of the Seven Deadly Sins,"** over which the excellent Lord Hailes went into raptures, is wanting in everything but coarseness; and if his invention dance at all, it is like a galley-slave in chains under the lash. It would be well for us if the sins themselves were indeed such wretched bugaboos as he has painted for us. What he means for humor is but the dullest vulgarity; his satire would be Billingsgate if it could, and, failing, becomes a mere offence in the nostrils, for it takes a great deal of salt to keep scurrility sweet. Mr. Sibbald, in his "Chronicle of Scottish Poetry," has admiringly preserved more than enough of it, and seems to find a sort of national savor therein, such as delights his countrymen in a *haggis,* or the German in his *sauer-kraut.* The uninitiated foreigner puts his handkerchief to his nose, wonders, and gets out of the way as soon as he civilly can. Barbour's "Brus," if not precisely a poem, has passages whose simple tenderness raises them to that level. . . . The "Brus" is in many ways the best rhymed chronicle ever written. It is national in a high and generous way, but I confess I have little faith in that quality in literature which is commonly called nationality,—a kind of praise seldom given where there is anything better to be said. Literature that loses its meaning, or the best part of it, when it gets beyond sight of the parish steeple, is not what I understand by literature. To tell you when you cannot fully taste a book that it is because it is so thoroughly national, is to condemn the book. To say it of a poem is even worse, for it is to say that what should be true of the whole compass of human nature is true only to some north-and-by-east-half-east point of it. I can understand the nationality of Firdusi when, looking sadly back to the former glories of his country, he tells us that "the nightingale still sings old Persian"; I can understand the nationality of Burns when he turns his plough aside to spare the rough burr thistle, and hopes he may write a song or two for dear auld Scotia's sake. That sort of nationality belongs to a country of which we are all citizens,—that country of the heart which has no boundaries laid down on the map. All great poetry must smack of the soil, for it must be rooted in it, must suck life and substance from it, but it must do so with the aspiring instinct of the pine that climbs forever toward diviner air, and not in the grovelling fashion of the potato. Any verse that makes you and me foreigners is not only not great poetry, but no poetry at all. Dunbar's works were disinterred and edited some thirty years ago by Mr. Laing, and whoso is national enough to like thistles may browse there to his heart's content. I am inclined for other pasture, having long ago satisfied myself by a good deal of dogged reading that every generation is sure of its own share of bores without borrowing from the past. (pp. 267-71)

James Russell Lowell, "Spenser," in his Literary Essays: Among My Books, My Study Windows, Fireside Travels, Vol. IV, *Houghton, Mifflin and Company, 1890, pp. 265-353.*

W. J. Courthope (essay date 1895)

[*Courthope was an English scholar, author, and professor of poetry at Oxford. In the following excerpt he offers a brief overview of Dunbar's major poems, noting their vitality and versification.*]

The chief place among the Scottish poets who flourished before the Reformation has been assigned to William Dunbar. Specimens of his poems, including **"The Golden Targe," "The Thistle and the Rose,"** and **"The Dance of the Seven Deadly Sins,"** were published by Lord Hailes in 1770, and, appearing at a time when the current of taste, both in England and Scotland, was setting in the direction of antiquity, were welcomed with a somewhat exaggerated enthusiasm. Warton [in his *History of English Poetry*] was generous in his appreciation of Dunbar's merits. Scott, in the next generation, proclaimed him to be the greatest of Scottish poets [in *Memorials of George Bannatyne,* 1829]. Campbell [in his *Specimens of the British Poets,* vol. 11] compared him with Chaucer. His poems, collected in 1834 by David Laing, allow us to form a cooler estimate of his genius, and show us that Dunbar, while possessing a rich, vigorous, and versatile imagination, wanted the qualities which entitle a man to the front rank in the history of national poetry. Essentially a poet of the court, his talents were always employed in satisfying the momentary tastes of his patrons, so that though his works are of great importance to the antiquary, he rarely touches those notes of human interest which are the passport to the sympathy of the general reader. (p. 370)

As a poet he may be described as a jongleur transformed to meet the requirements of a literary age. His poems show a shrewd knowledge of men and manners, and remarkable skill in presenting, under a variety of novel aspects, the somewhat narrow range of themes acceptable to a court. His favourite poetical device was to carry a single burden or refrain through a number of stanzas, each containing a different turn of thought; but he frequently amused the king and queen with personal satires on the courtiers, or with rapid sketches of scenes in actual life, which have all the character of improvisations.

His allegories, like those of Henryson, indicate the influence both of classical studies and court pageants on the older forms of chivalric symbolism. **"The Golden Targe"** has a plot of some ingenuity. Falling asleep, in the orthodox fashion, one May morning, by the side of a river, the poet beholds in his dream a ship approaching from which a hundred ladies land. This is the Court of Venus, which includes all the heathen goddesses, the chief of whom are duly enumerated; and it is presently joined by the Court of Cupid, equally well attended by the gods of Latin poetry. The two companies combine, and please themselves with music, singing, and dancing. Coming out of his concealment to view the sight, the poet is espied by Venus, who orders her archers to arrest him; whereupon Dame Beauty assails him with a whole troop of feminine Attractions, such as Fair Having, Fine Portraiture, Pleasaunce, and Lusty Cheer. Reason, however, appears in his defence, and protects him from these assailants behind a Golden Targe or Shield, with which Youth, Innocence, Dread, and Obedience are also successfully repulsed; but at last Venus orders Dissimulation to bring up her reserves in aid of Beauty, and the eyes of Reason being blinded with a powder, the poet is taken prisoner. Beguiled by Dissimulation, he continues in the company of Cherishing and New Acquaintance, till Danger at last hands him over to the keeping of Heaviness; at which point Æolus blows a great blast upon his trumpet; the abstractions vanish; and the poet, waking out of his dream, concludes his composition with some stanzas in praise of "reverend Chaucer," "moral Gower," and "Lydgate laureate."

"The Thistle and the Rose" is a complimentary poem, written to celebrate the marriage between Margaret, daughter of Henry VII. of England, and James IV. of Scotland. Great ingenuity is shown in the conduct of this allegory, which in some parts seems to have been suggested by Chaucer's *Parlement of Foules.* Nature first summons the animals to receive her orders, and gives instructions to the Lion, king of beasts—the emblem of the Scottish nation—for the good government of his realm. She then addresses herself to the flowers, and, committing sovereignty to the "awful Thistle," bids him cherish above all others the "fresh Rose," which at the same time she crowns, and hails as Queen of Flowers. The poem is concluded with the conventional concert of birds, who praise the Rose, and of course awake the poet.

"Beauty and the Prisoner" describes, in a succession of stanzas all ending with the word "prisoner," the manner in which the poet was taken captive by Beauty, his lady, and of his various fortunes up to the point where Slander appeared to be master of the field:—

Than Matrimony, that noble king,
  Was grievit, and gatherit ane great host,
And all enermit without leising
  Chased Sklander to the West Sea coast;
Than was he and his liniage lost,
  And Matrimony, withouten weir,
The band of friendship has indost
  Betwix Beauty and her Prisoneir.

This stanza will enable the reader to perceive how far abstraction and impersonation, originally modes of philosophical thought, had been carried as mere ornaments of poetical style.

"The Dance of the Seven Deadly Sins" is an allegory of a different kind, in which the spirit of parody and burlesque predominates. Lord Hailes, Warton, Campbell, and other critics, have regarded this poem as a proof of Dunbar's original genius,—credit to which he is hardly entitled. Little invention was in fact required for the composition, which is merely a literary adaptation of the "Dance of Death," a long-established pageant in the carnivals of the Continent. Lord Hailes observes: "The drawing of the picture is bold, the figures well grouped. I do not recollect ever to have seen the Seven Deadly Sins painted by a more masterly pencil than that of Dunbar." In the grouping of the sins the Scottish allegorist merely followed the usual theological order; and, as regards the drawing, no reader of the *Vision of Piers the Plowman* will be prepared to admit that there can be any comparison between Langland's portrait of "Envy" and the following description:

Next in the dance followit Envy,
Filled full of feud and felony,
  Hid malice and despite;
For privy hatred that traitor tremlit,
Him followit mony freik dissemlit
  With fenyeit wordis quite:
And flatterers in to men's faces,
And backbiters in secret places,
  To lie that had delight;
And rownards of false leasings,
Alace! the courts of noble kings
  Of them can never be quit.

(pp. 371-74)

W. J. Courthope, "The Progress of Allegory in English Poetry," in his A History of English Poetry, Vol. I, *Macmillan and Co., 1895, pp. 341-92.*

George Saintsbury (essay date 1898)

[Saintsbury was an English literary critic and historian. In the following excerpt, he discusses Dunbar's reputation based on the range of his poetic output. The critic maintains that Dunbar is ranked as a great poet second only to Robert Burns.]

It is usual to rank William Dunbar as the chief of all this group [the Scottish Chaucerians], and in fact the greatest Scottish poet except Burns. Nor is there much reason for quarrelling with the estimate, since Dunbar, though he has perhaps nothing equal in their own kinds to [Robert Henryson's] *Testament of Creseide* and to *Robene and Makyne,* has a larger collection to show, both of good and of excellent work, a somewhat wider range, and above all, a certain body and fulness of poetical wine which is not so evident in the pensive though not uncheerful schoolmaster of Dunfermline. (pp. 185-86)

The poems known to be by, or reasonably attributed to, him are tolerably numerous, but not very bulky, none exceeding some 600 lines, while most are quite short. The entire number in Dr. Small's edition is 101, of which eleven are given as "attributed," while seven, having been . . . printed in the poet's own lifetime as his, have a higher degree of certainty than any of the others in text. The two most considerable are **"The Twa Maryit Wemen and the Wedo"** and the **"Friars of Berwick,"** the latter only "attributed," but displaying a *verve* and an accomplishment of form not known to be possessed by any other Scottish poet of the time. Both are very strongly Chaucerian, and the **"Friars"** is in Chaucerian "riding-rhyme"; the other piece is perhaps the most accomplished specimen of . . . revived alliteration. . . . Dunbar does not limit himself to three alliterations, often giving four or even five, and he is somewhat less distinct in his middle pause than Langland. On the other hand, his whole verse, which averages thirteen or fourteen syllables, has a distinctness and evenness of rhythm which are only found in parts of *Piers Plowman.* The matter of the poem is an ultra-Chaucerian satire on women. The three personages are represented as all young and all pretty; they are drinking freely in a goodly garden on Midsummer Eve, and the poet achieves a triumphantly contrasted picture of physical beauty in scene and figure and of moral deformity in sentiment. The Wife of Bath, the undoubted model of these three young persons, is neither mealy-mouthed nor straight-laced, but she is always good-natured. Dunbar's wives and widow combine sensuality with ill-nature in a way not elsewhere to be paralleled in English literature till we come to the rakes of the Restoration. Yet the ugliness of the picture is half redeemed by the mastery with which Dunbar makes them expose their own shame, and sets their figures for us with a touch of grave irony worthy of Butler, and less purely caricatural in style than *Hudibras.* The **"Friars of Berwick"** is a version of a well-known *fabliau,* in which two friars, treated with scant hospitality by a woman who in her husband's absence has made an assignation with her lover, revenge themselves upon her (though not to extremity), taking advantage of the husband's unexpected return. It is therefore much less of an original and more of a commonplace than **"The Twa Maryit Wemen,"** but the story is told with the true *brio* of the *Canterbury Tales* themselves.

Next to these two may be ranked the **"Golden Targe,"** the **"Flyting of Dunbar and Kennedy,"** the famous **"Dance of the Seven Deadly Sins,"** and **"The Thistle and the Rose."** The first of these is a typical fifteenth-century poem, allegorical in tone and very "rhetorical" in language, with the usual praise of Chaucer, "Rose of rhetors all," and "light of our Inglis," as well as of the "sugared lips and aureate tongues" of Gower and Lydgate. The **"Targe"** is in nine-lined stanzas; **"The Thistle and the Rose,"** in rhyme-royal, is of the same stamp and style, but adjusted to convey a welcome full of grace, good sense, and good taste to the youthful Margaret, the "rose" married to the "thistle." Many who know nothing else of Dunbar's, know the **"Seven Deadly Sins"** from its early inclusion in anthologies. The vigour of its lurid pictures has not been exaggerated, nor the real command of metre (Romance eights and sixes) which the poet here as everywhere displays, and which contrasts so strikingly with the staggering gait and palsied grip of his English contemporaries. The **"Flyting,"** one of a group of such things, is a curiosity no doubt, but a curiosity of a kind which could perhaps be spared. Literary Scots at all times, up to the eighteenth century, admitted . . . a coarseness of actual language which is rarely paralleled in literary English; and these "flytings" consisted of alternate torrents of sheer Billingsgate poured upon each other by the combatants. There is not much doubt that many of the strange terms of abuse used are mere gibberish, coined for the occasion; but there was considerable legitimate accommodation in Scots for the purpose, and the poem, like others of its kind, is at worst a quarry for lexicographers.

Of the very numerous minor poems must be mentioned the touching and interesting **"Lament for the Makers,"** "when he was sick," with its passing-bell refrain of *Timor Mortis conturbat me,* and its list of poets, most of whom are shadows of shades; the lively if irreverent **"Ballad of Kind Kyttok,"** and her reception at Heaven's gates; the **"Testament of Mr. Andro Kennedy,"** a macaronic pendant to the **"Flyting"**; two rhetorical pieces on the Lord Bernard Stewart, living and dead; a sharp satirical description of Edinburgh Session; a quaint contrast of merry Edinburgh and distressful Stirling; the very vivid if not very decorous **"Dance in the Queen's Chamber,"** which, with other poems to the Queen, shows that Margaret had the full Tudor tolerance of broad speech; the not unamusing **"Poem to ane Blackamoor"**—"My lady with the meikle lips"—a negress who, as a rarity, had been imported to be maid to the Queen. The rest are pious or profane, personal or general, rhetorical or direct. But they are nearly always out of the common way of literature of their time; and the contemptuous fashion in which they have been sometimes spoken of is not a little surprising. (pp. 186-88)

George Saintsbury, "The Four Great Scottish Poets," in his A Short History of English Literature, *The Macmillan Company, 1898, pp. 180-92.*

W. Mackay Mackenzie (essay date 1932)

[*In the following excerpt, Mackenzie praises Dunbar's diversity of style, noting the scope of his poetic output. He also esteems the poet as a "technically accomplished, self-conscious artist."*]

An obvious but, for the time, a novel characteristic of Dunbar's verse is that his poems are never long. In distinction from so much of the poetic manner both before and after he is neither voluble nor shapeless. His longest effort,

"The Tua Mariit Wemen and the Wedo," runs to but 530 lines, and most of his poems are short and lyrical in fashion.

Further, he is novel in many of his themes, these including not only personal grievances but also the occasion of a headache, the condition of the streets of Edinburgh, the way in which a certain Mure had treated one of his poems, the character of the tailors' and shoemakers' crafts—any topic that lent itself to emotional or satiric treatment in verse. And verse was still the only medium proper to one aiming at literature.

These features, however, must not be taken to imply a complete break with the literary past. His appeals on the matter of his benefice may fall within the established category of "Complaints." Of another current type, however, the "Testament" (or Will), there is but one example, and that in a burlesque vein. But several of the most pretentious efforts are cast in the form of "allegory," the poetic form which had supplanted the old long-drawn romance. Even in metre there may be a reversion. In **"Kynd Kyttok,"** if it really be by Dunbar, we have a comic use of the stanza of the later romance poems in rhyming alliterative verse, while in **"The Tua Mariit Wemen and the Wedo"** the unrhymed alliterative lines repeat a very old convention, of which this is the last example, save one, in the language. More generally an apt alliteration is a feature of his rhythms throughout. But on all his compositions Dunbar imposes his own freedom of treatment, and he is indeed less fettered by mediaeval convention than his younger contemporary, Gavin Douglas.

Dunbar was, indeed, a technically accomplished, self-conscious artist. He quite often draws attention to his "writing," and the misfortune of his headache was that, when he set himself to write, "the sentence lay full evil to find." He was as anxious as Chaucer that no one should spoil his "meter," and his anger at an outrage of this kind, in the **"Complaint Aganis Mure,"** which was communicated to the royal court, indicates both one mode of circulation and the reputation of Dunbar, to whose supposed utterance so much importance could be attached.

This, too, is a point which should be considered in relation to his appeals for ecclesiastical preferment. One critic [G. Gregory Smith, in *The Transition Period*], has denied seriousness to such of his compositions, claiming that they have "all the unreality of these fifteenth-century exercises" on the part of other writers and that Dunbar "wrote with his tongue in his cheek." This is hard to believe in face of the bitterness and passion which in so many places beat behind his words:

> For owther man my hart to breik,
> Or with my pen I man me wreik.

Harder still, perhaps, in respect of his apologetic manner in addressing the king:

> I say not, sir, yow to repreiff,
> But doutles I ga rycht neir hand it.

It does not appear how "merriment at His Majesty's Court" could be extracted from such strains. (pp. xxiv-xxvi)

It is more reasonable to hold that Dunbar's angry sarcasms could not have failed to sting, because they were so obviously true. It cannot have been amusing for engrossers of parish livings, bishops or abbots or others to hear:

> Swa thay the kirk have in thair cuir,
> Thay fors (care) bot litill how it fuir,
> Nor of the buikis, nor bellis quha rang thame;
> Thai pans (think) nocht of the prochin (parish) pure,
> Had thai the pelfe to pairt amang thame.

For the inferior clergy his contempt is unmistakable and, by all accounts, fully warranted. The clerical order must have been inhumanly callous to remain unruffled by Dunbar's lashings, and, in that case, their influence against him must have weighed heavily with a king, like James IV, so sensitive to their appeal. The friars cannot have loved Dunbar, yet with the king they were most powerful. And even the king personally cannot but have been pricked by the vicious satire on his Italian protégé, John Damian, or the scorn the poet poured upon the hangers-on at his court. Bitter contempt exudes even from the obscure terms and compounds which he finds necessary to characterise the upstarts, charlatans, and avaricious persons who benefited by patronage:

> Soukaris, groukaris, gledaris, gunnaris; . . .
> Gryt glaschew-hedit gorge-millaris.

Conscious, probably, of his outspoken manner and its effect he, in **"The Dream,"** puts these words in the mouth of "Ressoun," protesting that he has long been a servant to the king but

> all his tyme nevir flatter couthe nor faine,
> Bot humblie into ballat wyse complaine.

At the same time it must be kept in mind that satire on the shortcomings of the clergy was always and everywhere a mediaeval practice, contributed to by many saintly censors as well as by mere laymen.

Yet it was the life of court and town that was most congenial to Dunbar. Action, colour, music, the dance, "sangis, ballatis, and playis," were the elements of environment proper to a temperament such as his, subject to fits of despondency as Burns was to melancholia. Particularly was he depressed by the winter season. For him, as for the mediaeval folk of his class, there were substantially but two seasons—winter with what he calls its "dark and drublie" days, its enforced restraint on outdoor activity, its confinement in crowded, draughty, and smoky apartments, its few indoor amusements:

> My hairt for languor dois forloir
> For laik of symmer with his flouris.

Yet delight in the season does not lead to any pronounced pleasure in the aspect of the open country or, least of all, to finding in its features any mystical suggestiveness. A rare reference to the Highlands is but a shudder at the "dully glennis."

Dunbar, indeed, like all the other poets of the time, was fascinated by the garden described in the great French poem translated by Chaucer (or another) as *The Romaunt of the Rose.* This model garden is the scene of **"The Goldyn**

Targe" and of the allegories generally, as inevitably as the month of May is their time. Only occasionally, and not then with any appreciation, does a more local element appear, as when the May of **"The Thrissil and the Rois"** is first thought by the poet to be disfigured by "busteous blasts," so that the birds have more reason to weep than to sing. But this was an intrusion of reality; in his dream the poet enters "a lusty gairding gent."

The landscape, in fact, must consort with the mood; of itself it does not call for notice; and there is nothing in Dunbar to set beside such nature pictures of Gavin Douglas, as are wholly Scottish in detail. The devotion of poets to the garden was probably due to the feeling that it was the proper artistic setting, a Nature not spontaneous, wild, and formless but (in Pope's phrase) "Nature methodised" and made rational, Nature as it aimed to be or at its best. Such an outlook was in agreement with Aristotle's aesthetic theory and so with mediaeval idealism in general.

Another inheritance from the same French poem was the allegory, a form which has never died and once again blossomed on a great scale in Spenser's *Faery Queen.* It had a special appeal to the mediaeval mind with its interest in abstraction and symbol. For serious work it became as inevitable as the symphony in music. The poet dreams, and in his dream enters the property garden, to which repair the allegorical personages who are to carry out in action the poet's conception. To our minds the reality of the performance may be less concrete than to the mediaeval listener, who was already familiar with the personification of ideas in his stage plays or in pictorial art. Particularly is it so in such a case as **"The Dance of the Sevin Deidly Synnis,"** which also is set in the classical framework of the allegory, since the vision came to the poet "in a trance," in which, instead of the usual garden, he "saw baith hevin and hell." But the figures of "Pride," "Envy," "Gluttony," etc., were already defined for the mediaeval observer by artistic representation, and the transition was easy to those of "Reason," "Fair Having," "Dame Homeliness" and abstractions generally. The vital difference between the two fields of allegory was in the language. For the pleasant or didactic and dignified type there had to be chosen "dulce and redolent" terms of description—the "grand style." For the other class the poet could safely dredge all the resources of the native tongue. To the latter belongs **"The Birth of Antichrist,"** where the traditional setting of the dream ("a swevying") is used to express a violent satire on Dunbar's *bête noire,* the abbot of Tungland.

This Scots vocabulary, too, is the material of his more exuberant satires. In these no class quite escapes his censure, though there is perhaps some tenderness towards rank, but kirkmen, the law courts, "mediciners" or doctors, and certain crafts he does not spare. This sensitiveness to what he considered abuses and injustices need not be wholly attributed to a sourness of mind engendered by his fruitless longing for a benefice. For one thing, it was quite in the manner of his time. Further, he, latterly at least, in his handsome pension had most of what such preferment would give him, and with money in his purse he could not feel his disappointment continuously bitter—not, as he himself said,

> quhill thair is gude wyne to sell.

It cannot have been because he was "poisoned with a grievance" that he wrote the satire on Edinburgh, which is rather the expression of one whose aesthetic sense is offended. That the capital city, the seat of "the Court and the Session," should be noisy, smelly, and cluttered with beggars seemed to him shameful, but not less so that its houses should be darkened by forestairs and its minstrels should limit themselves to a couple of tunes. Moreover, if he chastened Edinburgh, it was because he loved "the mirry toun," as many allusions show. He emphasised its shortcomings not because of a realistic cynicism that is claimed to have distorted his perceptions, but because he genuinely disliked them, just as he did the charlatanism of the *Fenyeit Freir,* the nature of the *Sevin Deidly Synnis,* and his Gaelic-speaking countrymen. Indeed, he mixes up the two latter groups, a confusion which some regard as an anti-climax but which is just Dunbar's fun, and shows how real to him were his allegorical personifications. The mediaeval poet, too, like the mediaeval artist generally, was better at sinners than at saints. With the same hilarious spirit he introduces himself into the **"Dance in the Queenis Chalmer,"** while a bold humour informs the **"Dregy,"** as it does also **"The Testament of Mr. Andro Kennedy"** and **"Kynd Kyttok."**

No great stress, however, need be laid on the fact that, in these latter poems, Dunbar seems to indulge a mocking, irreverent spirit; in others a vein of physical grossness. To a social life like that of the Middle Ages, at once coarse and naïve, such pleasantries were not out of place. Since the mid-thirteenth century there had been a practice of parodying portions of the church services, and a parody of Scripture in ridicule of the Scots and their leaders is one of the English memorials of the War of Independence.

A similar mingling of apparently discordant strains is to be observed in his treatment of love. Just as the mediaeval mind found room on the religious side for both abject devotion and in decorous gesture, so in the matter of love writers oscillated from an extreme idealisation of the female sex to an equally extreme defamation. Dunbar has examples of both fashions—not, indeed, to a greater extent than poets before and after him. Most of these poems are in a mode very similar to that of the allegory. In a certain season, on a certain day, and at a particular time the poet goes forth and overhears a lover or lovers, whose utterance or dialogue he records. That is the general type, and the numerous examples have been classed under the name of *Chansons d'Aventure,* France having been the origin of this mode as of so many others. Thus we get Dunbar starting off with:

> In secreit place this hyndir nycht,
> I hard ane beyrne (man) say till ane bricht
> (maid),

just as the writer of *The Murning Maidin,* an anonymous poem in the *Maitland MS.,* begins:

> Still undir the levis grene,
> This hindir day I went alone;

I hard ane May sair murne and meyne,
To the King of Luif scho maid hir mone.

Like the May morning, the beautiful garden, the river and the singing birds it is an established opening, of which **"The Tua Mariit Wemen and the Wedo"** gives a complete example. This poem, however, is of a particular species, that telling of unhappy marriage, usually on the part of a wife (*chanson à mal mariée*) but in some cases of a husband. Despite the many French and English exercises in this class also, Dunbar's contribution is in several respects unique. The personages in number are unusual, and in their parts unlike those of any other example. The work is too long for a *chanson;* it is a poem, while its elaborately alliterative unrhymed metre removes it still further from the general category. In its character as a satire it comes nearer to Chaucer's *Prologue* to *The Wife of Bath's Tale.*

The matter of the poem, too, goes beyond anything hitherto attempted on this line. "From the mysteries of religion," wrote Landor, "the veil is seldom to be drawn, from the mysteries of love never." Landor, however, was much too late with his admonition for Dunbar, and even since his time it has scarcely been honoured with strict observance. The author of the *Introduction* to the S. T. S. edition of the poems holds this one to be a picture, perhaps a caricature, of the "moral disease" of the time, which was to undergo the cure of the Reformation. Mrs. Taylor [in her *William Dunbar*], on the contrary, describes it as "this very modern debate" and says that "the first lady's doctrine would suit a Bloomsbury novel to-day." Professor Saintsbury contrasts the beautiful opening and close of the poem with its "ugly" content [*A Short History of English Literature,* 1898]. As to expressions used here and in some other poems it is well to remember Macaulay's comment on Restoration Dramatists: "Whether a thing shall be designated by a plain noun substantive or by a circumlocution, is a mere matter of fashion." The brief moralising at the close is artistically an anti-climax, but something of the sort would be expected. On the poem as a whole Dunbar has obviously expended much pains.

Of all his compositions, however, the most bizarre to modern taste is **"The Flyting"** or "The Scolding," in which, of course, he is but one of the two protagonists. Yet this sort of verbal tournament *à outrance* as a form of literature has wide relationships. The *agōn* or "altercation" was one essential element of the Old Comedy of Greece, while in a more personal vein it has parallels in other literatures, Arabic, Italian, Provençal, Celtic. The Provençal *tenson,* or debate in alternate verses between troubadours, was of this class, but rarely exceeded half a dozen stanzas and, though often lively enough, was not of a scurrilous character. The contention of **"The Merle and the Nychtingaill"** is more of this type. It therefore cannot have served as a model, while the stimulus need not be searched out. Such a bout reflects a common human resort under passion to improvised personal abuse, a stray example of which may still crop up even in more polite times, as in the case of Tennyson's retort to "the padded man who wears the stays." But in the present or similar literary examples no impulse of real animosity need be assumed King James V and Sir David Lindesay engaged in a *Flyting,* while King James VI included this exercise in his not unworthy treatise on poetical forms. Such a contest, indeed, seems to have caused amusement in the best circles. Its psychology may be illustrated from a passage in a contemporary (1931) novel: "They were good friends, these two, so they called each other insulting names and explained how little they thought of each other." As regards the present "jocund and merrie" interchange of vigorous but often coarse abuse we are invited in one MS. to "juge quha gat the war (worse)."

Dunbar's moralising and religious poems are individually characteristic only in the metrical quality of certain examples. In the fifteenth century the Middle Ages were in their twilight; there was a poverty of ideas, and a sententious preaching manner was popular. Reflections on the instability of life, on the certainty of death, and on man's subsequent destiny chimed in a particular harmony with the spirit of the time. For much of this frame of mind the emotional teaching of the friars was answerable. Other results of the same influence were the new attitude towards such themes as the crucifixion of Christ and praise of the Virgin. In the former, Christ has become primarily the Suffering One, and there is an almost morbid tendency to dwell in detail on every incident of the Passion. Dunbar's poem on the subject opens in the conventional dream-form, and it is significant that the place is within a cloister of the friars, after which no harrowing feature of the tragedy is overlooked. In the practical precision of the details we further trace the ocular effects of the mystery plays. A similar particularity marks the triumphant outburst, *Done is a battell on the dragon blak,* with its march of vivid, sonorous lines. The conception of the Virgin, again, has reverted to the Byzantine figure of the Empress of Heaven—Villon's *haute déesse,* Dunbar's "Empryce of prys, imperatrice"—but now with an added significance as the protectress and "oratrice" of mankind.

All this, of course, was common at the time to Western Christendom, of which Scotland was just a part, and was expressed in the contemporary graphic arts as well as in literature. And Dunbar, though showing no profound spiritual quality, was devout in his observances. That he satirised the clergy is no discordance, for the reason already given. Kennedy's gibe at him as "Lamp Lollardorum" is but topical abuse with no religious significance. Editors, however, have tended to agree in assigning the religious poems to the closing years of the poet's life. But, apart from a somewhat naïve psychology, there is no reason for such a conclusion. A temperament like that of Dunbar was open to religious impressionism and devotional outpouring at any period of life, though the more laboured efforts may well be taken to suggest a stage of failing power.

Over all, then, Dunbar is one of the poets who illuminate the life of their time but do not idealistically transform it. Robert Browning in an essay distinguishes the class of poet as "fashioner," or as the Scots, after the Greeks, would say, "makar," from that of the poet as "seer"—the objective from the subjective type. Dunbar is of the former class; he does not proffer "intuitions" as reflections of an "absolute mind," as Browning held himself to do. Poetry was for him a social art, not the functioning of a seer or diviner, the latter being an assumption which by now as surely dates itself as does Dunbar's "mellifluate" diction. This restriction may or may not be a disparagement, but other poets, from Aristophanes and Juvenal downwards, flourish in spite of it. Further, he is without the sentimentalism incident to Burns, though, like him, he tended to become, at times, "literary" in the prevailing fashion. Most poets carry dead weight of this character. But he and the rest of his school saved their share of the island literature from the blight which fell upon the successors of Chaucer in the southern kingdom. And so they worthily repaid the debt they owed to that great master. (pp. xxvi-xxxiv)

W. Mackay Mackenzie, in an introduction to The Poems of William Dunbar, *edited by W. Mackay Mackenzie, Faber & Faber Limited, 1932, pp. xi-xxxix.*

C. S. Lewis (essay date 1936)

[*A logician, Christian polemicist and mythopoeic writer, Lewis is an acknowledged authority on medieval and Renaissance culture. He is highly regarded as a perceptive literary critic and as a writer of fantasy literature. In the excerpt below, he argues that Dunbar's poetry reveals a shift in the use of allegory. Such works as "The Thistle and the Rose" and "The Golden Targe," Lewis claims, retain the allegorical form as decoration, designed simply to entertain.*]

The reader will have observed that all the Chauceriana, with the possible exception of the *Flower and the Leaf*, display a weakening of the genuinely allegorical impulse. The trappings of allegory are retained but the true interest of the poets lies elsewhere, sometimes in satire, sometimes in amorous dialectic, and often in mere rhetoric and style. Before we can proceed to the true allegories of this period in which the impulse is by no means decadent and is indeed preparing itself to pass on to the new triumphs of *The Faerie Queene*, there are a number of other poems to be considered which fall into the same class with the Chauceriana.

Dunbar is, perhaps, the first completely professional poet in our history. Versatile to the point of virtuosity, he practices every form from satiric pornogram to devotional lyric and is equally at home in the *boisteous* language of his alliterative pieces, the aureation of his allegories, and the middle style of his ordinary lyrical poems. His content is everywhere as central and obvious, as platitudinous if you will, as that of Horace; but like Horace he is such a master of his craft that we ask nothing more. His allegories are not of historical importance. They have no purpose in the world but to give pleasure, and they have given it abundantly to many generations. The **"Thistle and the Rose"** is an allegorical epithalamion after the manner of Chaucer's *Parlement*, though any comparison between the two is rather unfair to Dunbar. Into the *Parlement* Chaucer has put the whole of his early strength and made a paradise of tenderness and fun and sublimated sensuality. Dunbar's poem does not aspire to be more than a festal exhibition of fine language adding a new touch of magnificence to a royal wedding and strictly comparable to the court dresses of its first hearers. As such it is a brilliant success, but it yields to the **"Golden Targe."** In the **"Targe"** the language is more splendid, the stanza more adapted to support such splendour, and the images more dazzling. To notice the abundance of such words as 'crystalline', 'silver', 'sperkis', 'twinkling', and the like is to indicate sufficiently the quality of the poem. And this peculiar brightness, as of enamel or illumination, which we find long before in *Gawain* and *Perle* and again in Douglas, is worth noticing because it is the final cause of the whole aureate style—the success which enables us to understand the aims of all the poets who did not succeed. And when the thing is successful it silences all *a priori* objections (such as the Wordsworthian heresy) against artificial diction: when the thing is well done, it gives a kind of pleasure that could be given in no other way. From our own point of view the poem might almost be classified as a radical allegory. It has an intelligible allegoric action: the poet's mind, though long defended by reason, becomes at last the prisoner of beauty. But this action is so slight and degenerates so often into a mere catalogue of personifications (which is the only serious fault of the **"Targe"**) that we are right to neglect it. The real significance of the poem lies elsewhere: in it we see the allegorical form adapted to purposes of pure decoration, as the Pastoral form was adapted by Pope or the elegiac by Matthew Arnold—we might add, by Milton. For this also is one of the things that happens to a dominant form. (pp. 250-52)

C. S. Lewis, "Allegory as the Dominant Form," in his The Allegory of Love: A Study in Medieval Tradition, *Oxford at the Clarendon Press, 1936, pp. 232-96.*

John Speirs (essay date 1940)

[*Speirs is a critic, scholar, editor, and author of several books on medieval Scottish and English poetry. In the excerpt below, from an essay originally published in 1940, he argues that Dunbar's achievement is greater in the comic and satiric poems than in the more frequently studied ceremonial pieces.*]

To Dunbar Chaucer has become the 'rose of rethoris all'; the phrase is sufficient to awaken doubt as to the substantiality of Dunbar's appreciation of Chaucer. An examination of his poetry reveals that as a poet he is in fact as different from Chaucer as it was possible for another medieval poet to be. Of course he inherits some of the Chaucerian modes and themes, as he inherits others which, though medieval, are not specifically Chaucerian. But even when Dunbar borrows from Chaucer it is always the differences from Chaucer that are more striking than the resemblances. Plainly, to begin an account of Dunbar from a comparison between his work and that of Chaucer would not be much to the point, unless to bring home the inaccuracy of styling Dunbar a Scottish Chaucerian. He is at a still further remove from Chaucer than Henryson, and, perhaps because he was 'a court man', being nearer the European centre in his time than the latter, he belongs to the very latest medieval phase.

But to find the explanation of Dunbar's power in the influence, already, of the Renaissance would, again, be a misrepresentation. What gives him (in spite of, and because of, his 'lateness') his extraordinary power, whereby he is perhaps the greatest Scottish poet, is his skilled command of the rich and varied resources of language open to him, and, related to this, his command of varied metres adapted from what were by his time the rich accumulations of medieval French and medieval Latin verse, as well as, and often united together with, indigenous alliteration and assonance used as Hopkins rather than as Swinburne uses it. This variety of language and of metres has its counterpart in a variety of modes so bewildering that our first difficulty must be to determine where the centre of Dunbar's work as a whole is. Dunbar's technical skill and versatility are what may first strike the reader. It may be that his poetry appears to be more various than it really is. There is a variety of modes and moods, a vigour and directness, but not a Chaucerian large view of experience. It is my object in this [essay] to suggest that the core of his living achievement, that part of his achievement which we read as if it were contemporary, consists, not of the ceremonial poems, **"The Goldyn Targe," "The Thrissil and the Rois,"** but of the comic and satiric poems, **"The Twa Mariit Wemen and the Wedo," "The Dance of the Sevin Deidly Sinnis,"** the goliardic blasphemies, **"The Flyting," "The Satire on Edinburgh,"** and the more acrid and radical satires that merge into the saturnine poems that give his work as a whole, for all its intense vitality, its dark cast.

These comic and satiric poems are not less traditional than the ceremonial poems. The difference is in the nature of their several traditions, or, to put it otherwise, in the ways in which they are traditional; and this again works down to a difference in their language, and social and moral implications of which should appear. The language of the comic and satiric poems is essentially the language of what was living speech in Dunbar's 'locality', which was not without its place in the still homogeneous medieval European community; whereas the 'aureate diction' of the ceremonial poems of Dunbar, the court poet, is at a distinct remove from living speech, and therefore from life, including Dunbar's own, in any locality; is in fact purely 'literary' or 'poetical', rootless, without actuality. The difference between the former and the latter is in consequence that between a greater and a much lesser degree of inherent life. Without life informing it, language, however brilliant its surface, and however aristocratic its lineage, is verbiage.

Yet **"The Goldyn Targe"** and **"The Thrissil and the Rois,"** though they may be pressed to one side, for the lively reader, by the vitality of the comic and satiric poems, are what in Dunbar's case had become of the direct line of European allegorical poetry descending from the *Roman de la Rose,* and on this ground they demand some attention in any attempt to give an account of Dunbar's work as a whole. To Dunbar himself and to his contemporaries they doubtless seemed the centre of his work, as indeed they might be if the value of a poem is in proportion to the amount of conscious effort that seems to have been expended on it. But even to Dunbar's first readers I doubt if they were the poems which really yielded the most enjoyment. These heavily ornate poems, with their bejewelled formal landscapes, dazzle the eye; but, except here and there, life has largely escaped from them. There is little that is spontaneous about these show-pieces.

The terms of Dunbar's celebration of Chaucer and Gower at the end of **"The Goldyn Targe"** are inappropriate in everything else except that they fit their context. It is Dunbar himself in **"The Goldyn Targe,"** not Chaucer, whose 'term–is' are 'enamelit' and 'celicall' and whose 'lippis', 'tonguis' 'mouthis' are 'sugarit', 'aureate', 'mellifluate'. He goes wrong here as a critic, at the same time unconsciously revealing why here he goes wrong also as a poet. The first five stanzas of the poem are a dazzling exercise in the rhetoric, the heavy ornamentation, the overloaded decorativeness, then, in that 'late' century, fashionable. But the poem is inadequate as a poem not because it is rhetoric, but because of the nature of that rhetoric itself. Rhetoric must be something more fundamental, more deeply rooted, than this, to be at the same time fully satisfactory as poetry. Dunbar's highly conscious interest in language carried with it certain obvious dangers. There is a kind of mechanical delight generated in the sheer verbal exercise; but it is not the same thing as the life, the abundant energy of the living language which Dunbar elsewhere successfully shares. **"The Goldyn Targe"** remains a monument to the fact that a poem cannot be made out of an interest purely in language, and the manipulation and arrangement of it; and when the interest is in 'poetic' language artificially enriched by over-lavish borrowing from alien sources, the resulting kind of richness may easily be fatal to life. Where this kind of rhetoric wears off, as in the beautiful passage about a hundred ladies who land in a meadow from a ship, it is significant that the poetry is revealed as something much more like Spenser than even the Chaucer of the translation of the *Roman de la Rose.* Medieval allegory is here seen changing into something else; it is the death of allegory, its swan-song.

The ceremonial poems were of course written for ceremonial occasions; they correspond to the pageants and processions of these royal and other occasions. To this extent they correspond to something in the public life of Dunbar and the Scotland of Dunbar's time in which ritualistic pomp and show, pageants and processions, played a part such as to suggest, the times being late, that this heightening of the outward forms, this colouring up of the outward shows, is the symptom of some inner spiritual corruption rather than simply what it may at first seem, the spontaneous expression of the natural joy of life in a rather primitive people; there is nothing spontaneous about **"The Goldyn Targe."** We cannot afford to ignore this in trying to understand the meaning of Dunbar's work as a whole. Together with the conscious interest in language the ceremonial poems exhibit, it may have a bearing on the other poems of Dunbar that are so unlike the ceremonial poems.

At this point we may well have begun to ask whether Dunbar gained anything by being, in his particular place and time, a court poet. What he did gain may be exemplified most purely by the small poem **"To a Ladie."** If the ceremonial poems show that he was among other things a professional court poet, the lyric **"To a Ladie"** shows him capable also of a genuine courtliness. It would seem absurd to claim uniqueness for this trifle, except in the obvious sense that every poem is unique; but in Dunbar's work it is something of a rarity, something of a surprise in itself; it is at one end of his range; in it the main European tradition is alive, not as in the ceremonial poems dead. Nor is it simply a concentration of what Dunbar does diffusely in the ceremonial poems; it contains something that is not there present; there is in it a certain unexpectedness, almost wit.

> Sweit rois of vertew and of gentilnes
> Delytsum lyllie of everie lustynes.

You would expect 'lily' where you get 'rose', and 'rose' where you get 'lily'; they are interchanged: the lady is virtuous and desirable at the same time. The poem shows Dunbar's skill as a metrist; but that skill is, here, not merely metrical; it is part of the unexpectedness; it contributes, for example, to the surprise of the final line of the first and, again, the second stanza. Allegory and wit are thus brought together, the *Roman de la Rose* and, except that the poem remains in itself completely medieval, the conceitedness of the sixteenth century Petrarchan sonnets. This intellectual element in it, balancing the emotional, is exactly what the purely 'local' love songs of Burns are without.

But, as has been indicated, **"To a Ladie"** is not representative of Dunbar's characteristic achievement. It is in the comic and satiric poems in colloquial Scots that the sap flows vigorously, that Dunbar's central creative energy finds in various shapes and forms its free and full expression; and it is (I think) in **"The Twa Mariit Wemen and the Wedo"** that the comic zest, the sheer enjoyment and appetite, reaches its maximum of bursting exuberance; for this poem, though in the tradition of the *chanson à mal mariée* (This is how these women, when they get together in secret, tear their husbands limb from limb), is primarily comic, not satiric; in it we devour the ripe grapes. The force of vulgar gossip is raised to the degree of art; ribaldry assumes this proportion.

> I wald me prunya plesandly in precius wedis,
> That luffaris myght apone me luke and ying lusty gallandis,
> That I held more in daynte and derer be ful mekill
> Ne him that dressit me so dink; full dotit wes his heyd.
> Quhen he wes heryit out of hand to hie up my honoris,
> And payntit me as pako, proudest of fedderis,
> I him miskennyt, be Crist, and cukkald him maid:

What the poem seems essentially to represent is the force of the impudent ('lowd thai lewch') natural self rising up from among the people and asserting its right according to the 'law of luf, of nature and of kynd' without respect for moral authority, the dogmas and restraints of the Church.

> Ladyis, this is the legand of my lif, though Latyne it be nane.

But the profane figure of the widow in church is an object of purely comic contemplation; there is no hint of arbitrary condemnation.

> Than lay I furght my bright buke one breid one my kne,
> With mony lusty letter ellummynit with gold;
> And drawis my clok forthwart our my face quhit,
> That I may spy, unaspyit, a space me beside: . . .
>
> Quhen frendis of my husbandis behaldis me one fer,
> I haif a watter spunge for wa, within my wyde clokis,
> Than wring I it full wylely and wetis my chekis,

(The consequence is she is provided with no dearth of lovers in secret.)

> And all my luffaris lele, my lugeing persewis,
> And fyllis me wyne wantonly with weilfair and joy:
> Sum rownis; and sum ralyeis; and sum redis ballatis;
> Sum raiffis furght rudly with riatus speche;
> Sum plenis; and sum prayis; some prasis mi bewte,
> Sum kissis me; sum clappis me; sum kyndnes me proferis;

In spite of the dramatization we to an appreciable extent share, we are made partakers of the comforts of 'these creatures of the kyn of Adam', the stolen delight in unrestrained sin; the eavesdropper behind the hawthorn is scarcely an intruder.

> Apon the Midsummer evin, mirriest of nichtis,
> I muvit furth allane, neir as midnicht wes past
> Besyd ane gudlie grein garth, full of gay flouris,
> Hegeit, of ane huge hicht, with hawthorn treis
> Quhairon ane bird, on ane bransche so birst out hir notis . . .
> I saw thre gay ladeis sit in ane grene arbeir . . .
> Thir gay Wiffis maid game amang the grene leiffis;
> Thai drank and did away dule under derne bewis;
> Thai swapit of the sweit wyne, thai swanquhit of hewis.

There is no essential contrast between the natural scene (described, because background, in more conventional language, but still bursting with the opulence of midsummer) and the gossips; the beauty of nature and the ugliness of vice, as some moralist has suggested. The hawthorn, the birds and the gossips are filled with the same heady wine, the same exuberance of life; they are equally on the plane simply of nature and instinct.

"The Dance of the Sevin Deidly Sinnis" comes from the same common source in the popular speech, though in another of these traditions, and exhibiting another variety of this humour The humour here is savage, primitive, uncivilized. Its expression is conditioned by the dance frenzy in the rhythm; for the poem is a *dance* of the Sins. It goes to the pipes or fiddle. The caricature figures of the satanic pageant are caught up in the dance which ends in a wild reel of Highlandmen, smothered by the Devil with smoke.

And first of all in dance wes Pryd,
With hair wyld bak and bonet on syd,
Lyk to mak waistie wanis;
And round abowt him, as a quheill,
Hang all in rumpillis to the heill
His kethat for the nanis:
Mony prowd trumpour with him trippit,
Throw skaldand fyre ay as thay skippit
Thay gyrnd with hiddous granis.

The poem has been commended for a conscious blending of the comic with the horrible, the ghastly, the macabre; but that is to misunderstand the essential nature of this savage folk-humour. There is no such dichotomy and no such sophistication in this poem. There is no fantasy or supernatural element in it either. It shares the vigorous, earthy actuality of the popular sermons of the Middle Ages.

Syne Sweirnes, at the secound bidding,
Come lyk a sow out of a midding,
Full slepy wes his grunyie:
Mony sweir bumbard belly huddroun,
Mony slute daw and slepy duddroun.

Him followit mony fowll drunckart,
With can and collep, cop and quart,
In surffet and exces;
Full mony a waistles wallydrag,
With wamis unweildable, did furth wag.

There is no incongruity, intentional or otherwise, in introducing the figure of the Highlandman at the end; Pride ('bonnet on side') and Ire are just as 'local'. But they are at the same time 'local' against the whole medieval religious (and ecclesiastical) background.

Quhill preistis come in with bair schevin nekkis,
Than all the feyndis lewche and maid gekkis,
Blak Belly and Bawsy Brown.

"The Dance of the Sevin Deidly Sinnis" belongs to the grotesquerie of the late medieval popular imagination.

We shall by this time have observed that there is a good deal of the goliard even in those poems of Dunbar which are not, as **"The Dregy of Dunbar"** and **"The Testament of Kennedy"** are, primarily goliardic. The goliardic parodies should be read with Dunbar's own serious hymns in mind. These latter are scrupulously on the model of the Latin hymns, ritualistic, formal, stiff. The symbolism (I think of the beautiful 'Rorate celi desuper') is the extremely conventional symbolism of the Latin hymns. Latinized diction is used; and lines of Latin are inserted. But the ecclesiastical world, the language of which was Latin, was something actual in Dunbar's own world; the lines of Latin fit, without incongruity, into even his profane poems, as they would not into the purely 'local' poems of Burns. The incongruity in the goliardic poems is not essentially between the Latin lines and the Scots (most goliardic poems were wholly in Latin), but in the clash between sacred associations and the profane sentiments of lustfulness, eating and drinking.

Ego pacior in pectore,
  This night I myght nocht sleip a wink;
Licet eger in corpore,
  Yit wald my mouth be wet with drink.

Nunc condo testamentum meum,
  I leiff my saull for evermare,
Per omnipotentem Deum,
  In to my lordis wyne cellar;
Semper ibi ad remanendum,
  Quhill domisday without dissever,
Bonum vinum ad bibendum,
  With sueit Cuthbert that luffit me nevir.
A barell bung ay at my bosum,
  Of warldis gud I had na mair;
Corpus meum ebriosum
  I leif on to the toune of Air.

The blasphemy of the goliardic poems is the complement of the dogmatic belief accepted (there is no reason not to suppose sincerely) in the serious hymns. Dunbar is one of the last of the goliards, a descendant of the *clerici vagantes* of the earlier Middle Ages; in many of his lyrics he is more like his near-contemporary Villon, in this respect, than Chaucer.

Dunbar's satire when it is serious is, as we should expect, predominantly ecclesiastical and, at its deepest, religious. **"The Satire on Edinburgh"** is not satire of this serious kind; it is again (unless I am much mistaken, for it has been found scathingly bitter) less satiric than comic.

May nane pas throw your principall gaittis
For stink of haddockis and of scattis,
For cryis of carlingis and debaittis,
For fensum flyttingis of defame:
  Think ye not schame,
Befoir strangeris of all estaittis
That sic dishonour hurt your name!

Your stinkand Scull, that standis dirk,
Haldis the lycht fra your parroche kirk;
Your foirstairis makis your housis mirk,
Lyk na cuntray bot heir at hame:
  Think ye not schame,
Sa litill polesie to wirk
In hurt and sklander of your name!

At your hie Croce, quhar gold and silk
Sould be, thair is bot crudis and milk;
And at your Trone bot cokill and wilk,
Pansches, pudingis of Jok and Jame:
  Think ye not schame,
Sen as the world sayis that ilk
In hurt and sclander of your name!

Plainly Dunbar is here thoroughly enjoying himself, even if the enjoyment is subordinated to a fairly serious and respectable intention. The poem conveys the character of the town, its noises and smells, what it was like to live in. The impression is of a lively place, the habitat of a boisterous and vigorous community crowded together among high houses that shut out the sun from one another and from the streets. **"The Flyting of Dunbar and Kennedy"** is a poem of essentially the same nature. The two poets abuse each other like two fishwives, though it is of course a kind of game. It is a comic *tour de force* of sheer language, but because the language is in this case living language, the coarse-textured vigorous language of the actual popular speech, it does not separate the poet from life but carries him towards it, its own life, wild, savage, uncivilized as its humour again is here.

Thow bringis the Carrik clay to Edinburgh Cors
Upoun thy botingis, hobland, hard as horne;
Stra wispis hingis owt, quhair that the wattis ar worne;
Cum thow agane to skar us with thy strais,
We sall gar scale our sculis all the to scorne,
And stane the up the calsay quhair thow gais.

Off Edinburch the boyis as beis owt thrawis,
And cryis owt ay, 'Heir cumis our awin queir Clerk!'
Than fleis thow lyk ane howlat chest with crawis,
Quhill all the bichis at thy botingis dois bark,
Than carlingis cryis, 'Keip curches in the merk,
Our gallowis gaipis: lo! quhair ane greceles gais.'

Than rynis thow doun the gait with gild of boyis,
And all the toun tykis hingand in thy heilis;
Of laidis and lownis thair rysis sic ane noyis,
Quhill runsyis rynis away with cairt and quheilis,
And cager aviris castis bayth coillis and creillis,
For rerd of the and rattling of thy butis;
Fische wyvis cryis, Fy! and castis doun skillis and skeillis,
Sum claschis the, sum cloddis the on the cutis.

Flyting passages, monstrous pilings-up of language, are a feature of both Dunbar's comic and satiric poems, and serve their various ends.

But there are many poems, many of them satiric, and together forming a considerable part of Dunbar's poetry, in which plainly the poet is not enjoying himself, in which he is something of a malcontent. To these sardonic or morose poems we must finally turn to complete the meaning of Dunbar. At the root of these poems is the overpowering feeling that the times are late and evil everywhere dominant in the world.

The clerkis takis beneficis with brawlis,
Some of Sanct Petir, and some of Sanct Pawlis.
Take he the rentis, no cair hes he
Suppois the devill tak all thair sawlis.
["Of Discretion in Taking"]

Sic pryd with prellatis, so few till preiche and pray;
Sic hant of harlettis with thame bayth nicht and day.
["A General Satyre"]

Wyld haschbaldis, haggarbaldis, and hummellis;
Druncartis, dysouris, dyvowris, drevellis,
Misgydit memberis of the devellis;
Mismad mandragis off mastis strynd,
Crawdonis, couhirttis, and theiffis of kynd;
Blait-mowit bladyeanes with bledder cheikis,
Club-facet clucanes with clutit breikis,
Chuff-midding churllis, cumin off cart-fillaris,
Gryt glaschew-hedit gorge-millaris . . .
Panting ane prelottis contenance
Sa far above him set at tabill
That wont was for to muk the stabell;
Ane pykthank in a prelottis clais,
With his wavill feit and wirrok tais,
With hoppir hippis and henches narrow,
And bausy handis to beir a barrow; . . .
With gredy mynd and glaschane gane,
Mell-hedit lyk ane mortar-stane.

The monstrous exaggeration develops into caricature, as again, for example, in **"A General Satyre."**

Sic fartingaillis on flaggis als fatt as quhaillis,
Facit lyk fulis with hattis that littill availlis,
And sic fowill tailis, to sweip the calsay clene,
Thet dust upskaillis; sic fillokis with fucksaillis. . . .

'This is the end' is the final feeling conveyed. Distrust infects the air.

Is na man thair that trestis ane uthir . . .
["Tydingis fra the Sessioun"]

Fra everie mouthe fair wordis procedis
In everie harte deceptioun bredis
Flattrie weiris ane furrit goun.
["Into this World may none Assure"]

The sugurit mouthis with myndis thairfra
The figurit speiche with faceis twa . . .
["Of the World's Instabilitie"]

The disillusion is mature and deep-seated; it proceeds from an ultimate dissatisfaction with everything that was connoted by the phrase 'the world'.

. . . the warld, feignid and false,
With gall in hairt, and honied hals.

I have ventured to call the satire in these poems, directed as it is chiefly (though by no means wholly) against ecclesiastics, not merely ecclesiastical but religious (though negatively so) because of the consciousness in them of the loss or absence of goodness and of any assurance of spiritual reality. The nearest Dunbar comes to such an assurance seems to me perhaps to be here:

Lord sen in tyme sa sone to cum
De terra surrecturus sum,
Rewarde me with na erthlie cure
Bot me ressave in regnum tuum
Sen in this warld may non assure.

The question, to what extent the morbidity in these poems was temperamental, in Dunbar's case, and to what extent it was imposed on his poetry by his world, need not trouble us. It is plainly something both profoundly personal and, since it is common to late medieval poetry, much more than personal. In the **"Meditatioun in Wyntir"** it is given unusually *personal* expression. Winter was no doubt, especially for Dunbar, wretched enough in itself, but it is explicitly from something more even than winter that he turns with such anxiety to the new season.

For feir of this all day I drowp;
No gold in kist, nor wyne in cowp,
No ladeis bewtie, nor luiffis blys,
May lat me to remember this,
How glaid that ever I dyne or sowp.

Yit, quhone the nycht begynnis to schort,
It dois my spreit sum pairt confort,
Off thocht oppressit with the schowris.
Cum, lustie symmer! with thi flowris,
That I may leif in sum disport.

It is not only winter that oppresses his spirits, but his morbid moods and thick-coming fancies. He turns with anxiety to summer, as he has turned to song, dance, plays, wine, some lady's beauty, to escape from oppressive fears of age and death. This morbidity in fact explains the Epicurean strain in Dunbar's poetry, the desperate grasping at vivid enjoyments and vivid delights; Dunbar's mirth is often of a violent character.

> Now all this tyme lat us be mirry
> And sett nocht by this warld a chirry,
> Now, quhill thair is gude wyne to sell,
> He that dois on dry breid wirry,
> I gif him to the Devill of hell.

The frequent images of dancing, music, drinking of red wine,

> Sangis, ballatis, playis,

symbolize these delights, and the sprightly dance measures of many of his poems express them. But just as frequent is the sinister image of the gallows gaping, the violent images of cut-throats and cut-purses, and 'cartes' and 'dyce' associated with evil. It is here that a comparison with Villon suggests itself. The obsession with death was inevitable to some part of Dunbar's poetry coming where it did; Dunbar inherited a world, sensed as fallen, mouldering in decay. That the sense of mortality is not more pervasive in his poetry than it is is due to the force of that tremendous principle of life (represented in **"The Twa Mariit Wemen and the Wedo"** and the other primarily comic poems) he could at times share with the Scottish people. But where there is no assurance of a spiritual reality behind a clairvoyant recognition of the vanity of earthly things, the worm of death and corruption finally devours everything that is,

> Death followis life with gapand mouth
> Devouring fruit and flowering grane.

and the human procession becomes Death's.

> On to the ded gois all Estatis,
> Princis, Prelotis, and Potestatis,
> Baith riche and pur of al degre;
> *Timor mortis conturbat me.*
>
> He takis the knychtis in to feild,
> Anarmit under helme and scheild;
> Victour he is at all mellie;
> *Timor mortis conturbat me.*
>
> That strang unmercifull tyrand
> Takis, on the moderis breist sowkand,
> The bab full of benignite;
> *Timor mortis conturbat me.*
>
> He takis the campion in the stour,
> The capitane closit in the tour,
> The lady in bour full of bewte;
> *Timor mortis conturbat me.*

The Latin phrase lends a liturgical solemnity to the contrasting familiar Scots, like a funeral bell tolling. But what makes Dunbar's poem speak directly to us is its homely personal note—the makar's concern about his friends and, finally, himself as subject to the inevitable common fate.

> The flesche is brukle, the Fend is sle;
> Timor Mortis conturbat me.

(pp. 54-68)

John Speirs, "William Dunbar," in his The Scots Literary Tradition: An Essay in Criticism, *revised edition, Faber & Faber, 1962, pp. 54-68.*

James Kinsley (essay date 1955)

[*Kinsley was a well-known scholar, editor, and critic. In the excerpt which follows, he compares Dunbar to Chaucer finding little commonality between the poets. While criticizing Dunbar as "deficient in matter," he simultaneously lauds the poet as "a keen and humorous observer of. . . the human pageant."*]

Henryson and Dunbar, though writing about the same time in neighbouring parts of Scotland and in the same general tradition, make one of the strangest contrasts in our literary history. Henryson read English poetry with critical respect, and his very individuality grows from firm roots in the school of Chaucer; Dunbar, despite his formal recognition of Chaucer's eminence, is startlingly unique. Henryson's interests are those of almost any educated man of his time in Europe; Dunbar's best poetry is the reflection of the manners and culture of a Stuart court. His historical and personal virtues lie in the range of his metrical skill, his inventive manipulation of innumerable poetic kinds, and his command of the now rich resources of the Scottish tongue. French and Latin lyrical measures, English modifications of Continental forms, and the old indigenous alliterative verse are all drawn in to serve his need; and he uses them with an assured versatility. He turns his restless hand to allegory and dream-poem, panegyric, complaint, religious and didactic lyric, debate, comic narrative and satire. His diction ranges from the strong speech of the Edinburgh streets and the obscenities of the boudoirs of Holyrood to the aureate language of official praise.

He is a volatile, chimerical character: now paying compliments to the King, now importunately begging the royal bounty; celebrating public occasions and recording court scandal with equal facility; eloquent in cursing and in prayer; cutting a caper with trim Mistress Musgrave in the Queen's chamber, and at other times bemoaning his headaches or his penury and lamenting the impermanence of earthly delights. He throws into relief the contrasting scenes of court life and the crowds who clustered round a fascinating, versatile and (if we believe Dunbar) injudicious king. A few poems are written in praise of other airts, and one describes the noise and odorous vitality of a Royal Mile that has changed little with the centuries:

> May nane pas throw your principall gaittis
> For stink of haddockis and of scattis,
> For cryis of carlingis and debaittis,
> For fensum flyttingis of defame . . .

But Dunbar's milieu was the court of Holyrood in its splendour and sordidness; and of the culture and the 'rash fierce blaze of riot' of that court his verse is the most lively memorial.

His moral and religious verse, although the least novel and in some ways the least personal part of his work, has not received the attention it deserves. In serious mood he shows a strong piety and a sombre wisdom grounded in experience. His religious poetry is not illuminative, and to the modern reader some of it is marred by extravagant virtuosity. 'In all poetry which attempts to represent the intercourse between an individual soul and its Maker there is a conflict between the ostensible emotion—adoring love, absorbed in the contemplation of its object, or penitence, overwhelmed by the sense of personal unworthiness—and the artist's actual absorption in the creation of his poem'; in the religious poetry of Dunbar the conflict disappears in verbal ornament and formal artifices. It is a poetry almost devoid of tenderness and imagination. His account of the Passion, for instance, has all his characteristic vividness and force—

Onto the crose of breid and lenth
  To gar his lymmis langar wax,
Thay straitit him with all thair strenth,
  Quhill to the rude thay gart him rax . . .

The erde did trimmill, the stanis claif,
  The sone obscurit of his licht;
  The day wox dirk as ony nicht,
Deid bodiis rais in the cite;
  Goddis deir Sone all thus was dicht,
O mankynd, for the luif of the . . .

—but this is passionless rhetoric beside the imaginative pity of Langland's lines:

Consummatum est quod Cryst and comsed for
  to swowe,
Pitousliche and pale as a prisoun þat deyeth;
Þe lorde of lyf and of liyte þo leyed his eyen to-
  gideres.
Þe daye for drede withdrowe and derke bicam
  þe sonne,
Þe wal wagged and clef and al þe worlde quaued.
Ded men for that dyne come out of depe graues,
And tolde whi þat tempest so longe tyme dured.

It is, however, just Dunbar's power in rhythm and phrase that enables him to celebrate a festival of the Church in splendid exultation:

Done is a battell on the dragon blak,
Our campioun Christ confountet hes his force;
The yettis of hell ar brokin with a crak,
The signe triumphall rasit is of the croce . . .

Dungin is the deidly dragon Lucifer,
The crewall serpent with the mortall stang;
The auld kene tegir with his teith on char
Quhilk in a wait hes lyne for us so lang,
Thinking to grip us in his clows strang . . .

Few of his reflective poems are mere rhetorical exercises in conventional modes. Behind traditional turns and commonplace sentiments is the intimate, admonitory tone of a man saddened and made wise by the world. He voices, in a style which 'maintains majesty in the midst of plainness', the sage melancholy of the later Middle Ages, their sense of the futility of earthly joy and their quiet acceptance of ultimate loss:

For feir of this all day I drowp:
No gold in kist, nor wine in cowp,
  No ladeis bewtie, nor luiffis blis
  May lat me to remember this,
How glaid that evir I dine or sowp.

The finest example in these poems of a common convention adapted to a personal mood is the **'Lament: Quhen he was Sek'**, a poetical *danse macabre*. The solemn and reluctant procession of humanity towards the grave was a frequent theme in fifteenth-century mural painting, sculpture and poetry. Whatever examples of the *danse macabre* Dunbar may have come across on his travels, he probably knew Lydgate's 'Daunce of Death' and the stone carvings in Rosslyn Chapel near Edinburgh, which were completed about 1480. The **'Lament'** opens on a subjective note:

I that in heill wes and gladnes,
Am trublit now with gret seiknes,
And feblit with infermite;
  Timor mortis conturbat me.

These reflections on disease and death serve as a prologue to the grey procession of the *morts:*

On to the ded gois all Estatis,
Princis, Prelotis, and Potestatis,
Baith riche and pur of al degre;
  Timor mortis conturbat me.

Representatives of human society pass in review—the knight, the infant, 'the campion in the stour [conflict]' and 'the lady in bour ful of bewte', the scholars and the poets. All 'playis heir ther pageant, syne gois to graif'; and so must Dunbar:

Sen he hes all my brether tane,
He will nocht lat me lif alane,
On forse I man his nixt prey be;
  Timor mortis conturbat me.

Dunbar drastically reduces the number of type-figures—most versions of the *danse macabre* have upwards of thirty *morts;* but he keeps to the traditional scale by cataloguing twenty-four of his own profession. The column which unrolls from his dejected mind is led by the shadowy great of the earth; but the ghosts become more familiar and significant as the poets pass, and the reiterated response from the Office for the Dead rises into a cry from the poet's heart.

The procession in the **'Lament'** illustrates a favourite technique of Dunbar's. Catalogues are commonplace ornament in mediaeval and renaissance poetry; but Dunbar's are rarely mere artifice. His imagination is cumulative: and the catalogue is one of his most natural modes of expression, whether he is reflectively analysing human nature, compiling black-lists of court hangers-on, or liberating floods of abuse on his rival Kennedy. In his graver verse, the catalogue adds point and concrete illustration to abstract thought:

The slidand joy, the glaidnes schort,
The feinyeid luif, the fals confort,
The sweit abayd, the slichtful trane,
  For to considder is ane pane.

The sugurit mouthis with mindis thairfra,

The figurit speiche with faceis twa,
The plesand toungis with hartis unplane,
For to considder is ane pane.

His catalogues have not always this measured dignity, in which the bitterness of his mind is softened in rhetorical grace. In the **'Remonstrance to the King'**, for instance, the roll of James's court servants becomes a crescendo of vituperation as the poet gathers in the charlatans and opportunists who stand in his light:

on your hienes follows eik
Ane uthir sort, more miserabill,
Thocht thay be nocht sa profitable:
Fenyeouris, fleichouris, and flatteraris;
Cryaris, craikaris, and clatteraris;
Soukaris, groukaris, gledaris, gunnaris;
Monsouris of France, gud clarat-cunnaris.

The catalogue is used to greatest effect in this torrential style; the poet's wrath and verbal resourcefulness expand together to confound the reader and destroy the victim. Dunbar's most astonishing performance is **'The Flyting of Dunbar and Kennedy'**. The *flyting,* for which James VI justly recommended 'Rouncefallis or Tumbling verse', was a popular Renaissance exercise. Skelton tried it; Sir David Lindsay 'flyted' James V; and Montgomerie fought in verse with Polwarth. In so far as it is an abusive dialogue between rival poets, the *flyting* may be distantly related to the French *tenson;* and is clearly an offshoot of the ubiquitous mediaeval *débat.* Whatever its ancestry, it appealed to the contumelious Scot. Centuries later Burns made jottings for a 'literary scolding'; and the habit is not yet dead. But for calculated volubility Dunbar holds the palm among 'flytaris'. He takes the part of the true poet against the pretender Kennedy, whose eloquence he says is only that of Gaeldom, with 'littill feill of fair indite'. He offers the virtuous disclaimer of the classical satirist—'Flyting to use richt gritly I eschame': scurrility is the wretched Kennedy's familiar art, but Dunbar stoops to it only under provocation. Yet he gives a terrible description of the power of his satiric muse:

The erd sould trimbill, the firmament sould schaik,
And all the air in vennaum suddane stink,
And all the divillis of hell for redour quaik,
To heir quhat I sould wryt with pen and ink.

Dunbar and Kennedy use different methods of attack. Kennedy takes a characteristically 'Hielant' line: he defends his noble lineage and assails Dunbar's, which does not seem to have been without spot. He defends Gaelic against 'Inglis' (Dunbar's Scots) as the true national tongue. He is pretentiously allusive, and depends for effect chiefly on history and on coarse anecdote. Dunbar, on the other hand, uses the more direct method of vivid caricature. His picture of Kennedy's outward gracelessness is one of the best pieces of grotesquerie in Scots poetry:

. . . hiddowis, haw, and holkit is thine ee;
Thy cheik bane bair, and blaiknit is thy ble;
Thy choip, thy choll, garris men for to leif chest;
Thy gane it garris us think that we mon de:
I conjure the, thow hungert heland gaist.

. . . Thy rigbane rattillis, and thy ribbis on raw,
Thy hanchis hirklis with hukebanis harth and haw,
Thy laithly limis are lene as ony treis;
Obey, theif bard, or I sall brek thy gaw,
Fowll carribald, cry mercy on thy kneis.

The quality of Dunbar's invective is variable; but in such a bizarre kind of writing, the only requisite is a rolling flood of alliterative abuse. Nowhere else does he so fully illustrate the richness and power of colloquial Scots. Saintsbury too hastily dismissed the **'Flyting'** as 'alternate torrents of sheer Billingsgate', overlooking the poets' resourcefulness in language and figure and their sustained rhetorical power. Dunbar's second appearance is a *coup de théâtre.* He holds the stage in dramatic monologue: he postures, mimicks and gesticulates; he rants and whispers; he sniggers and guffaws uproariously; and swaggers off in a cascade of verbal fireworks.

His versatility in metre and diction is equalled by his skill in adapting established poetic kinds to serve an occasion or reflect a passing humour. It is easy to sort his work into conventional categories; but everywhere a restless, irrepressibly comic temperament is turning old conventions to original uses. Such a perspicacious humorist as Dunbar is easily provoked to laughter by a personage or an event; but he contrives to give his merriment a literary colour in parody and adaptation. In **'The Petition of the Gray Horse, Auld Dunbar'**, the begging-poem is given a new, ironical twist. He uses the beast-fable form to record the reprehensible **'Wowing of the King . . . in Dumfermeling'**. The old device of the poetic testament goes to make the self-revealing and self-destructive monologue which Burns later perfected in 'Holy Willie's Prayer':

I, Maister Andro Kennedy,
Curro quando sum vocatus,
Gottin with sum incuby,
Or with sum freir infatuatus;
In faith I can nought tell redly,
Unde aut ubi fui natus,
Bot in treuth I trow trewly,
Quod sum diabolus incarnatus.

The Office for the Dead is parodied with blasphemous ingenuity for a witty epistle in the **'Dirige to the King, Bydand our Lang in Stirling'**. In **'The Fenyeit Freir of Tungland'** Dunbar, in his daftest mood, uses the dream convention to deride the ill-fated flying experiment of an eccentric charlatan about the court. The metre and the exaggeration of the romance are parodied in **'Of Sir Thomas Norny'** to ridicule a Holyrood Braggadocio. Called to celebrate a court tournament of 1508, the **'Emprise du Chevalier Sauvage à la Dame Noire'**, Dunbar gently mocks the conventional praise of a lady's pink and white beauty:

Lang heff I made of ladyes quhytt,
Now of ane blak I will indytt,
That landet furth of the last schippis;
Quhou fain wald I descryve perfitt,
My ladye with the mekle lippis.

The French trick of recording a courtly lovers' dialogue which the poet claims to have overheard *en cachette* is used in **'In Secreit Place'** to open a licentious wooing; and the conventional protestations of unrequited love—'How lang will ye with danger deill? Ye brek my hart, my bony ane'—give way to the giggles, the playful abuse and the baby-talk endearments of a man and a willing maid:

> 'Tehe!' quod scho, and gaif ane gawfe,
> 'Be still my tuchan and my calfe . . .
> My belly huddrun, my swete hurle bawsy,
> My huny gukkis, my slawsy gawsy,
> Your musing waild perse ane harte of stane,
> Tak gud confort, my grit heidit slawsy.'

The *chanson pastourelle* is made fit for Holyrood. In **'The Dance of the Sevin Deidly Synnis'** the traditional procession of the Sins is not, as in less volatile poets, an elaborate pictorial allegory, but a wild revel probably inspired by a spectacle at court. The **'Dance'** is a lurid carnival of vice. The Sins and their cronies wheel grotesquely through swirling verse; but their obscene and ghastly merriment heightens rather than obscures the diabolical agonies of Hell.

'The Tretis of the tua Mariit Wemen and the Wedo', Dunbar's longest poem, is the fullest illustration of his original treatment of literary conventions. Formally, the **'Tretis'** is a debate on love among three ladies celebrating Midsummer Eve in a garden bower. The poet, *en cachette* behind a hedge, overhears their conversation. The Widow assumes the rôle of president of the court, and sets her companions a *demande d'amour.* They take it up in turn, answering pragmatically from their experience in and out of wedlock. On the setting of the debate, and on the participants, Dunbar lavishes all the rich ornament and 'enamellit termis' of sophisticated descriptive poetry: the garden is an earthly paradise, and the ladies are heroines of romance. They are familiar with the diction and ideas of *amour courtois,* practise adultery with art, and profess the virtues of secrecy and 'pitee'. No one, says the Widow generously, will go from me unloved;

> And gif his lust so be lent into my lyre quhit,
> That he be lost or with me lig, his lif sall nocht danger.

But this is only a jocular echo of courtly sentiment. The Widow's 'honour' is an accessible commodity; she claims noble birth, but she is less a courtly lover than an amateur strumpet. Her use of the rules and language of *amour courtois* is deliberately comic; and when she ends her defence of promiscuity as the exercise of 'pitee', her companions laugh loudly and promise to 'wirk efter hir wordis'. She is a vivacious cousin to the Wife of Bath. Despite their courtly veneer, all three ladies are drawn from Edinburgh town. One confesses she is tied to a 'hur maister', a dashing man-about-town 'brankand and blenkand [swaggering and casting an eye] to the brichtest that in the burgh duellis'. They have a highly coloured vocabulary and a reserve of strong simile which still enliven vernacular conversation in street and closemouth in Scottish towns:

> I have ane wallidrag, ane worme, ane auld wobat carle,
> A waistit wolroun, na worth bot wordis to clatter;
> Ane bumbart, ane dron bee, ane bag full of flewme . . .
> With goreis his tua grym ene are gladderrit all about,
> And gorgeit lyk twa gutaris that war with glar stoppit.

The debate has been described as 'cold obscenity'. But the ladies have a hot vitality both in imagination and in speech. Dunbar draws a satiric contrast between their outward beauty and delicacy, and their inward corruption. Ideal loveliness is revealed as the whited sepulchre of lust, and what seems to be of the bower is seen to belong to the street. Even as they expose themselves, these three bawdy, jesting 'cummaris' cynically pretend, as part of their festive joke, some allegiance to courtly love.

In the **'Tretis'** the old alliterative measure is used on two levels. It is possible that Dunbar had Scottish models for the alliterative abuse of the **'Flyting'**; it is much more certain that by his day this measure was associated with serious poetry. In the ornate prologue to the **'Tretis'** he shows his skill in the sophisticated style. The smooth, rapid run of the verse and the rich phraseology give the listener what he expects in this measure, and seem to set the tone of the poem. Metre, diction and portraiture harmonize. Then the alliterative line, retaining its flexibility but gradually increasing in force, is turned to a new and startling use in the speech of the first lady. The centre of the poem is a contrast between appearance and reality, between the ideal world of courtly poetry and the 'spotted actuality' of the women's minds and habits; and the alliterative line, with its romance associations, is the formal base on which Dunbar develops a tonal contrast between the conventional description and 'enamellit termis' of the prologue, and the coarse sentiment and coarser conversation in the debate which follows.

In his poetic vision **'The Goldyn Targe'**, Dunbar praises Chaucer as the 'rose of rethoris all'. This formal recognition of one of the less significant characteristics of Chaucer, repeated by fifteenth-century poets *ad nauseam,* has been too much emphasized. The aureate style is not obviously a major interest of Dunbar's, though he may have earned his bread by it; and he is not, save in a few points, a disciple of Chaucer. He is an assured and independent inheritor of a European tradition, far removed from Chaucer in temperament. There is nothing in him of Chaucer's love of philosophy, theology and classical letters; and he has not Chaucer's sophisticated courtliness, his tolerance, his oblique humour or his 'high seriousness'. Chaucer, on the other hand, has not the turbulent, masculine fancy of Dunbar, or his intoxication with language. Dunbar is much more, however, than a wild court poet with fire in his belly. He is a keen and humorous observer of a part of the human pageant, a moody but finely reflective moralist, a word-hurler and castigator on the grand scale, and a persistent experimenter in an age when the English poetic tradition had hardened into derivative formalism. The vocabulary of his poems awaits critical analysis; but it is clear at least that he had a sense of the weight and colour of words, and a resourcefulness in marshalling and deploying words, unequalled in his generation or the next. Whether through some inner inadequacy or because of the circumstances of his life at court, he is too often deficient in matter. His intellectual interest is more restricted than

Henryson's; he has neither the humour nor the humanity of a Henryson or a Burns. 'The people of Scotland,' Sir Herbert Grierson remarks, 'clannish as they are, have never taken Dunbar to their hearts: "he wants the natural touch".' Yet in linguistic and metrical variety, assurance and exuberant imagination he is the richest of our poets. (pp. 24-32)

James Kinsley, "The Mediaeval Makars," in Scottish Poetry: A Critical Survey, *edited by James Kinsley, Cassell and Company Ltd., 1955, pp. 1-32.*

Denton Fox (essay date 1959)

[*Fox is an American educator specializing in Middle Scots and English literature. In the following excerpt, he reassesses "The Golden Targe," taking exception to the characterization of the work as conventional and "artificial." While admitting that the poem does borrow from earlier allegorical pieces, he contends that its deviations from fixed medieval traditions reveal the poet's deliberate intention to create an aureate style of composition.*]

Although the love allegory, **"The Golden Targe,"** is one of the most widely known poems of William Dunbar or, for that matter, of any of the so-called "Scottish Chaucerians," it is not a work in very good repute today. Modern critics have generally given the preference to Dunbar's humorous poems, notably **"The Tua Mariit Wemen and the Wedo,"** or to the moral lyrics, such as the **"Lament for the Makaris,"** and have tended either to pass over the **"Targe"** in discreet silence or to say frankly that "the poem is inadequate" [John Speirs, *The Scots Literary Tradition,* 1940]. Their principal grounds for objection to the poem are its ornate and lavishly decorated style, and in particular its profusion of the polysyllabic Latinate words which are usually called "aureate terms." Patrick Cruttwell [in his "Two Scots Poets: Dunbar and Henryson," in *The Age of Chaucer,* edited by Boris Ford, 1954] sums up the prevailing opinion when he says that the poem is written "in that medieval 'poetic diction' which is just as lifeless and conventional as the worst that the eighteenth century can show . . . In such a diction, fixed and prefabricated, living poetry can hardly be made." Some of the modern antagonism to the poem, however, may really stem from the poem's matter, which is fully as conventional and "artificial" as its style. Dunbar handles the traditional *Roman de la Rose* themes in an extremely conservative manner: with a few minor exceptions, every part of the **"Targe"** can be paralleled many times over in earlier poems.

Facsimile of the Opening Lines of The Goldyn Targe.

But while recognizing that the poem is in many ways very traditional, it is still possible, I think, to show that it deserves a much higher evaluation than it has generally been given. Such a rehabilitation would, if successful, be important for a number of reasons. In the first place, of course, there is the value of the poem itself: it is a pity that an excellent and successful poem should remain inaccessible to the modern reader. More generally, our estimation of the **"Targe"** must affect our understanding and evaluation of Dunbar as a poet, since it has in some ways a central position in his work. Dunbar is principally an occasional poet: a surprisingly large proportion of his poems are prompted by some specific event, and the great majority of the remainder are "occasional" in a looser sense, being short, casual, and unpretentious. But in the **"Targe,"** Dunbar adopts a large, important, and constantly treated theme in which he has room to extend himself to the limit of his powers and, in particular, to write in the most polished and skillful manner that he can. With this poem, much more than with his others, we are able to make comparisons between Dunbar and earlier poets, and so to see how he fits into the literary tradition and what the essential qualities of his poetry are. It might seem, of course, that the **"Targe"** should be set apart from the rest of Dunbar's work precisely because of its being non-occasional, a set piece in a high style. This is, indeed, the general modern opinion, but it is truer, I think, to say that in this poem one can see clearly displayed the technical methods that are equally important but perhaps more unobtrusive in his occasional poems.

Any revaluation of the **"Targe"** necessarily involves a reappraisal of the richly decorated "aureate" style in which it is written. It is significant that this poem, which has been held up by modern critics as an example of Dunbar's worst style, was apparently selected by his contemporaries as an example of his best. In one of the very few early allusions to Dunbar, Sir David Lyndsay, in the *Testament of the Papyngo,* speaks of "Dunbar, quhilk language had at large, / As maye be sene in tyll his golden targe." This difference of opinion is plainly caused by different theories of style: where Dunbar's contemporaries placed a high value on an ornate "aureation," modern critics have dismissed this style as an unhappy literary fashion, a disease which blighted a great deal of fifteenth-century and early sixteenth-century poetry. Aureation has lately found some defenders, notably C. S. Lewis [in his *Allegory of Love,* 1936], who claim, quite properly, that an artificial and highly wrought style is not necessarily pernicious, but even Lewis is forced to admit that the aureate style "along with some beauties, has many vices." It is no part of my intention to maintain that all verse written in an aureate style is good, but only that this style can be used to produce entirely successful poems. It is obviously a very narrow and specialized style, for which it has been condemned, but the fact that its limitations are more than compensated for by corresponding advantages has not, I think, been sufficiently recognized. In order to see these advantages, however, it is necessary to understand the special functions of this style, the particular uses for which it was intended, and this can only be done by making a fairly thorough study of a particular poem. I hope to provide such a case study by an examination of the **"Targe,"** and so both to show some of the essential qualities of the style and to justify the high opinion which Dunbar's contemporaries had of it.

C. S. Lewis has tried to defend the **"Targe"** as being "pure poetry," brilliant language lavished on banalities. He says of the poem:

> Its simple allegory (that the poet is temporarily defended from love by reason) is little more than a peg, but an adequate peg, on which to hang its poetry . . .
>
> (*English Literature in the Sixteenth Century*)

> It has an intelligible allegoric action: the poet's mind, though long defended by reason, becomes at last the prisoner of beauty. But this action is so slight and degenerates so often into a mere catalogue of personifications (which is the only serious fault of the **"Targe"**) that we are right to neglect it. The real significance of the poem lies elsewhere: in it we see the allegorical form adapted to purposes of pure decoration, as the Pastoral form was adapted by Pope or the elegiac by Matthew Arnold—we might add, by Milton.
>
> (*Allegory of Love*)

But though one can see Lewis's point when he says that the elegiac form became purely decorative in Milton, one wonders whether this statement does not obscure a more important truth. And, in the same way, a dismissal of the framework of the **"Targe"** seems to me dangerous: even though its style is admittedly of primary importance, perhaps the best way to approach it is through the structure.

For the convenience of the reader, I will give here a brief synopsis of the poem. The first five stanzas (lines 1-45) are a traditional description of a May morning as seen by an early-rising poet. In the next two stanzas (46-63) the poet goes to sleep and dreams that he sees a ship which comes to land and disembarks a hundred ladies. The eighth stanza (64-72) is a traditional disclaimer of the poet's ability to describe the cargo, and the next six stanzas are a description of it. There is the court of Nature and Venus (73-108), which contains such figures as Flora, Juno, Apollo, Fortune, and May, all of whom are joyously saluted by the birds. There is also the other court of Cupid (109-26), which contains Mars, Saturn, Mercury, and other gods. The poet, ravished by their singing and dancing, draws near, with the inevitable results:

> Than crap I throu the levis, and drew nere,
> Quhare that I was rycht sudaynly affrayit,
> All throu a luke, quhilk I have boucht full dere.
>
> And schortly for to speke, be lufis quene
> I was aspyit, scho bad hir archearis kene
> Go me arrest; and thay no time delayit . . .

The next six stanzas (145-98) are a description of the assault carried on by various groups of Venus's archers under the command of Beauty, Youth, High Degree, and "Dissymilance" against the poet, who is defended successfully by "Resoun, with schelde of gold so clere." But in the following two stanzas (199-216), Presence casts a powder in Reason's eyes and blinds him, with the result that the poet is "woundit to the deth wele nere, / And yoldyn as a wofull prisonnere / To lady Beautee." In the next stanza and a half (217-28), the poet enjoys briefly the company of Fair Calling and New Acquaintance, and afterwards the more doleful attentions of Danger and Heaviness. But then Eolus blows his bugle and everything turns back into wilderness (229-34). All the company go back to their ship and sail away, firing off guns which wake the poet, and he discovers that he is again back in a beautiful May morning (235-52). The last three stanzas (253-79), which form a sort of epilogue, are about poetry.

Even this sketch shows how traditional the main lines of the poem are, and a more minute examination would strengthen this impression immeasurably. The vocabulary, the phrases, and the smaller motifs, such as the "mery foulys armony" upon the "tender croppis," and the "hundreth ladyes . . . als fresch as flouris . . . in kirtillis grene . . . with . . . mydlis small as wandis," all can be paralleled many times over in earlier poetry. The great temptation for the critic is, in fact, to annotate the poem, listing its sources and analogues. But any sort of a complete list would be extremely long and would not, moreover, be particularly useful, since it is rarely possible to point to a passage in an earlier poem that Dunbar used as his sole source for a passage in the **"Targe."** Nevertheless, it is important to keep in mind that the **"Targe"** is, in many ways, an extremely derivative poem.

The more the **"Targe"** is compared with earlier allegorical poetry the greater its borrowings seem, indeed, but also the greater its originality. This originality is plainly not derived from the novelty of the poem's matter, yet there are a few apparently new elements even here, unimportant in themselves but, I think, indicative, though for the present I will simply list them.

The maritime aspects of the **"Targe,"** the ship on which the two courts of love arrive and depart, may be original with Dunbar. In Machaut's *Dit dou Lion* and in *The Isle* *of Ladies* there are islands, and hence naval operations, but ones very different from those in the **"Targe."** In Hawes' *Example of Virtue* the hero falls asleep, meets a lady, and takes ship; while in his *Pastime of Pleasure* there is a ship with a "pele of gonnes" (line 5028); but neither of these poems can definitely be shown to antedate the **"Targe,"** and in any case they do not furnish good parallels. Ships are common enough in other medieval poetry, to be sure, but it seems probable that Dunbar is responsible for using them in a new way. Then too, as far as I know, W. A. Neilson [in his *The Origin and Sources of the "Court of Love"*, 1899] is correct in saying that the **"Targe"** is the first poem to collect a number of Roman gods and goddesses in the court of love meadow. Again, this is an effective but not a surprising innovation: Venus, Cupid, Nature, and Flora were stock figures, and Froissart and the author of *The Flower and the Leaf* had at least gotten as far as introducing heroes of romance among the courtiers of love.

These additions are much less startling than the omissions which Dunbar makes in the traditional court of love plot. This is a more tenuous matter, since there exists no single fixed plot common to all the poems that derive from the *Roman de la Rose:* each of the poets who worked in this tradition felt free to disregard or to amplify the different parts of the pre-existing material. But Dunbar's omissions are radical to an unprecedented degree. Most of the customary amplifications are neglected: though there are two courts, one ruled by Cupid and one by Nature and Venus, there is neither any of the usual differentiation between courtly and natural love nor any establishment of a king and queen of love. There are no rules for the lover to follow, though Dunbar of course knew this tradition, and used it in his short poem, **"Gude Counsale."** More basically, there is a complete absence of dialogue, which necessarily results in the absence of many other usual features: there can be no mediating or explaining figure such as the usual "Amis" or "Frend," and it is impossible for the dreamer to be questioned angrily by any member of the court. The whole battle between the dreamer and Venus's servants is, in fact, reduced to the simplicity of a dumb show. Nor is there any real interior monologue: the dreamer does not give us any account of his past life or even of his feelings, with the exception of a few brief statements, "Thair observance rycht hevynly was to here" (132), "That sory sicht me sudaynly affrayit" (207), and the single traditional apostrophe:

> Quhy was thou blyndit, Resoun? quhi, allace!
> And gert ane hell my paradise appere,
> And mercy seme, quhare that I fand no grace.
> (214-16)

Though it does not seem to have been previously noticed, the whole structure of the **"Targe"** is, strictly speaking, elliptical. Courts of love, though they might spend their spare time being debating societies, existed to punish or reform recreants against love. Poems dealing with courts of love typically show the dreamer to be such a recreant, who is reprimanded by the court and given a lady to woo, though many other variations are possible. In the **"Targe,"** Venus spies the dreamer, as he is watching the courts of love, and then sends her warriors to capture him. But the allegorical meaning of this is not immediately apparent, since *love* is a transitive verb, and there is no woman available for the dreamer to love. It was customary, of course, for the heroine to be represented by a number of allegorical figures and not to appear as a single person, but Venus's warriors can hardly be combined into a single woman. Guillaume de Lorris, with considerable perception, created both Daunger and Bialacoil out of one woman, but even with due respect for feminine complexity it is hard to find in a single woman "Grene Innocence," "Wantonnes," "Contenence," "Libertee," "Humble Obedience," "Hie Degree," and "Schamefull Abaising."

It is already possible to see some of the negative implications, át least, of the additions and deletions that Dunbar makes in his inherited material. The allegorical form has certain technical advantages: it offers a general method for seizing on the universal elements that underlie the accidental, and in the case of love allegory it gives a particular technique for penetrating and vivid psychological description. Dunbar uses the traditional allegorical framework, but he strips it of almost all the elements that make these advantages possible. The lack of dialogue or monologue prohibits on the one hand the subtle psychological analyses of Guillaume de Lorris and on the other hand the concrete immediacy of Chaucer's allegorical figures. There is no treatment of the nature or anatomy of love, though some steps towards this could have been taken simply by complicating the allegory slightly, for instance by opposing Cupid's court (courtly love) to the court of Venus and Nature (natural love). But Dunbar does not, in fact, seem to be much interested in the allegory of his poem. The innovations which he may have made, the ship and the companies of gods, do not have any apparent allegorical significance; while the elliptical structure of the poem again suggests that Dunbar was not primarily concerned with maintaining a clear allegorical narrative.

Broadly speaking, then, the changes which Dunbar makes in the form all work towards an elimination, or at least a decrease, of the human and psychological elements. But in order to justify his special approach and to see what compensating advantages he gained through it, we must, of course, look at the poem itself. Perhaps it will be useful to quote here a fairly long passage, the first five stanzas, which set the scene, and the sixth stanza, with which the allegory begins, in the hope of showing both the structural and the stylistic techniques of the poem.

> Ryght as the stern of day begouth to schyne,
> Quhen gone to bed war Vesper and Lucyne,
> I raise and by a rosere did me rest;
> Up sprang the goldyn candill matutyne,
> With clere depurit bemes cristallyne,
> Glading the mery foulis in thair nest;
> Or Phebus was in purpur cape revest
> Up raise the lark, the hevyns menstrale fyne
> In May, in till a morow myrthfullest.
>
> Full angellike thir birdis sang thair houris
> Within thair courtyns grene, in to thair bouris
> Apparalit quhite and red wyth blomes suete;
> Anamalit was the felde wyth all colouris,
> The perly droppis schake in silvir schouris,
> Quhill all in balme did branch and levis flete:

To part fra Phebus did Aurora grete,
Hir cristall teris I saw hyng on the flouris,
Quhilk he for lufe all drank up wyth his hete.

For mirth of May, wyth skippis and wyth hop-
pis,
The birdis sang upon the tender croppis,
With curiouse note, as Venus chapell clerkis:
The rosis yong, new spreding of thair knopis,
War powderit brycht with hevinly beriall drop-
pis,
Throu bemes rede birnyng as ruby sperkis;
The skyes rang for schoutyng of the larkis,
The purpur hevyn, our scailit in silvir sloppis,
Ourgilt the treis, branchis, leivis, and barkis.

Doune throu the ryce a ryvir ran wyth stremys,
So lustily agayn thai lykand lemys,
That all the lake as lamp did leme of licht,
Quhilk schadowit all about wyth twynkling
glemis;
That bewis bathit war in secund bemys
Throu the reflex of Phebus visage brycht;
On every syde the hegies raise on hicht,
The bank was grene, the bruke was full of bre-
mys,
The stanneris clere as stern in frosty nycht.

The cristall air, the sapher firmament,
The ruby skyes of the orient,
Kest beriall bemes on emerant bewis grene;
The rosy garth depaynt and redolent,
With purpur, azure, gold, and goulis gent
Arayed was, by dame Flora the quene,
So nobily, that joy was for to sene;
The roch agayn the rivir resplendent
As low enlumynit all the leves schene.

Quhat throu the mery foulys armony,
And throu the ryveris soune rycht ran me by,
On Florais mantill I slepit as I lay,
Quhare sone in to my dremes fantasy
I saw approch, agayn the orient sky,
A saill, als quhite as blossum upon spray,
Wyth merse of gold, brycht as the stern of day,
Quhilk tendit to the land full lustily,
As falcoune swift desyrouse of hir pray.

This passage is rather a special case, being in a style even higher than the rest of the **"Targe,"** and immeasurably above the equally traditional but more restrained descriptions of a spring morning with which Dunbar opens **"The Merle and the Nychtingaill"** and **"The Thrissil and the Rois."** But these stanzas are still a beautiful, if exaggerated, demonstration of Dunbar's usual techniques, and they seem to me to be very successful. The passage is a particularly interesting one to examine, not only because Dunbar's techniques can be more easily seen in such an exaggerated case, but also because the first five of these stanzas have previously been singled out as an example of an extremely lifeless style.

For the most part, the vocabulary of these stanzas is as thoroughly traditional as the subject matter: in the first stanza, for instance, there is hardly a phrase that was not a poetic commonplace in the fifteenth century. But Dunbar renovates these commonplaces by a number of techniques, of which one of the most obvious is simply the mechanical structure of the verse. The stanzaic form of the **"Targe,"** apparently first used by Chaucer in the *Complaint of Anelida,* is an uncommon one, and Dunbar probably took it from Douglas's *Palace of Honour,* its only other important occurrence. It is an extremely demanding form, having only two rhymes for its nine lines (*aabaabbab*), but this paucity of rhyme makes it an exceptionally close-knit strophe. Dunbar, unlike Douglas, takes full advantage of this feature, scrupulously preserving the unity of the strophe by a careful adjustment of subject matter and by a variety of rhetorical devices: in two cases, for instance, where a single subject extends over two stanzas (the lists of gods and goddesses, 73-90 and 109-26), the stanzas are linked together in one case by a repeated rhyme and in both cases by the ingenious use of anaphora.

The poem's meticulous construction is shown plainly in its opening stanza, quoted above. This stanza is divided into three main parts, each three lines long. In the first section, the poet rises; in the second, the sun springs up; and in the third, the lark rises up. This structural parallelism is made explicit verbally: the first words of the third line, "I raise," are matched by the first words of the next line, "Up sprang [the sun]," and both these phrases are recapitulated by the "Up raise the lark" of the eighth line. The basic image of the stanza is the sunrise, which is responsible for the arousal of the poet and of the birds, and accordingly each of the three sections opens with a line about the sun. The stanza's theme of arising is imitated in its structure: the first three-line section deals with the small human arising of the poet; the second section shows the sun, rising in a loftier and more important way, and "Glading the mery foulis in thair nest"; while in the third section the lark, one of the "mery foulis," flying up out of its nest to become the "hevyns menstrale," presents us with the most vivid and soaring image of ascending. The stanza ends with the line "In May, in till a morow myrthfullest," and the three alliterating words, each longer than the one before, complete the crescendo.

But this sort of mechanical analysis emphasizes the stanzaic unity at the expense of the unity of the whole poem. Even in so short a passage as the six stanzas quoted above, one can see how Dunbar uses recurrent and interlocking images to bring out the poem's twin theme of spring and love. The images are, in fact, so intertwined that it is difficult to divide them into groups for the purposes of analysis, but one might distinguish these categories: the act of arising and getting dressed; rich bright colors and sunlight; and birds. To take these up in order, the arising image that we have seen in the first stanza is of course connected with spring: the poet, the birds, and all of nature arise from their winter sleep. But this arousal is also connected with the erotic theme, both by the natural sequence "love-bed-arising" and by the poetic tradition of the *aubade.* This connection is made explicit by the description of Phoebus arising from Aurora's bed (16-18), and by the amorous connotations of the birds' curtained bowers (11). The next step after arising is to get dressed, and accordingly we find the whole world putting on gaudy spring clothes. Phoebus wears a "purpur cape" (7), the birds' bowers are "apparalit quhite and red" (12), the field is enameled (13), the trees are gilded (27) and bathed in light (32, 39, 45), and the purple heaven wears clouds like silver garments (26). Finally, the whole garden is painted and arrayed by Flora (40-42), and the poet goes to sleep on "Florais mantill" (48). All these colors are the result of sunlight and are themselves bright and sparkling, while there is a repeated emphasis on reflection (23-24, 30-33, 44-45). This predominance of brilliant colors and light is one of the chief characteristics of the poem, and it is also a powerful unifying factor. In the first five stanzas, the sky, the bright earth, and even the water, reflecting light (30, 44) and with its pebbles "clere as stern in frosty nycht" (36), are all bound into a single luminescent whole. This world is both springlike, being fresh and bright, and erotic, being rich and luxurious, while the luminescence is made explicitly erotic by the strong image of Phoebus drinking up dew with his hot love (18), and, more subtly, by the last of the stanzas quoted above. This stanza, which is the beginning of the second part of the poem, connects the ship that carries the court of love to the description of spring by the line "A saill, als quhite as blossum upon spray" (51). Even more important, however, is the equation made between the approaching ship and the rising sun. The ship, like the sun, appears "agayn the orient sky," and its most striking feature is that it has a "merse of gold, brycht as the stern of day," which reminds us immediately of the first stanza, where "the stern of day," "the goldyn candill matutyne," rises. When the poet is awake, he sees the spring sun rising with powerful and beneficial effects; when he dreams, he sees its equivalent in the dream world, the ship bringing its cargo of love and beauty to land.

The birds are the last and in some ways the most revealing of the images which need to be considered here. It is not surprising that there are birds in the poem, of course, since they were traditionally connected with both spring and love, but Dunbar uses them in an unusual and important way. They sum up, in a sense, all of the images discussed above: birds rise into the sky, wear bright colors, and live in light and air. At the same time, they are given a central position in the structure of the poem, becoming even substitutes for mankind. Unlike human beings, the birds fit naturally and easily into the world of the poem; they are the appropriate subjects of the queen of love, not disrupting intruders like the dreamer. The poet rises, only to rest by a rosebush and to go back to sleep, but the birds rise and pay homage to their rulers, Nature, Flora, and Venus (94-108). Yet though the birds replace men, they still remain birds: they are not, as in many other love allegories, given human speech or psychological complexity. They are described in human terms, "hevyns menstrale" (8), as are their actions, "thir birdis sang thair houris / Within thair courtyns grene, in to thair bouris" (10-11), but they never have any human depth. Instead, Dunbar uses them as symbols which embody love and spring, and which at the same time characterize the brilliant but inhuman atmosphere of the poem. A neat example of this is the likening of the birds to "Venus chapell clerkis" (21). This phrase, which echoes the earlier "thir birdis sang thair houris," sums up succinctly and graphically both the traditional connection of birds with Venus and the religious aspect of courtly love, but also indicates that the birds stand in the same relation to the deities of the poem as men do to Christianity. Even the goddesses themselves get drawn into the world of the birds when Dunbar compares the approaching ship to a "falcoune swift desyrouse of hir pray" (54). The ship, or rather its cargo, is like a falcon in that the goddesses are the rulers of the birds, but it is also like a falcon because its passengers attack the dreamer.

The structure and imagery of the **"Targe"** have much to do with Dunbar's success in renovating the old poetic commonplaces, but the sheer compression of the poem is no less important. This compression is immediately evident when one considers the brevity of the **"Targe":** its 279 lines make it one of the shortest poems of its type. And the style of the poem, no less than its structure, reflects this compression. From a negative standpoint, one of the most striking features of this style is its lack of irrelevance and garrulousness. It is perhaps not too sweeping a generalization to say that most of the late medieval English poetry is marred by an inability to come to the point. Some of the poets, like Lydgate at his worst, feel no obligation to be pertinent, and even the poets who know where they are going and intend to get there seem continually compelled to interrupt themselves with "which is to say," "but to resume," and "I mean . . . " These mannerisms can sometimes be justified as intentional humor, as imitations of colloquial speech, or simply as devices for producing an easy conversational style, but very often this loquaciousness is simply a vice. Douglas's *Palace of Honour* is frequently quite close in style to the **"Targe,"** and Douglas is certainly no contemptible poet, but a single stanza of the *Palace* makes clear the immense difference between the poems:

> Aneuch of this, I not quhat it may mene;
> I will returne till declair all bedene
> My dreidfull dreame with grislie fantasyis.
> I schew befoir quhat I had hard or sene,
> Particularlie sum of my panefull tene,
> But now, God wait, quhat feirdnes on me lyis:
> Langer (I said) and now this time is twyis,
> Ane sound I hard of angellis, as it had bene,
> With harmonie fordinnand all the skyis.

This stanza, which follows a two-stanza digression on the comparative acoustical properties of water and earth, gives an example of the typical structural digressions as well as of the verbal parentheses and asides: "Aneuch of this," "I schew befoir," "as it had bene." Douglas, as a person, is so amiable that we are apt to like him the better for his asides and for finishing a long rhetorical Latinate description of music with the lines:

> Na mair I vnderstude thir numbers fine,
> Be God, than dois a gekgo or a swine,
> Saif that me think sweit soundis gude to heir.

But this should not blind us to the fact that these digressions effectually prevent any sustained high style.

Some of the methods by which Dunbar achieves a compressed high style can be seen by comparing three lines from the **"Targe"** with their probable source, three lines from the prologue of the *Palace of Honour:*

> Up sprang the goldyn candill matutyne,
> With clere depurit bemes cristallyne,
> Glading the mery foulis in thair nest . . .
> **("Targe,"** 4-6)

Richt hailsome was the sessoun of the yeir,
Phebus furth yet depured bemis cleir,
Maist nutritiue till all thingis vegetant.
(*Palace of Honour*)

Douglas's "depured bemis cleir" is virtually echoed in Dunbar's "clere depurit bemes," but there the resemblance between the two passages ends. Douglas's abstract and platitudinous line "Richt hailsome . . . " has no equivalent in the **"Targe,"** and his equally vague and flat line "Maist nutritiue . . . " is replaced by the concrete and specific "Glading the mery foulis in thair nest." Douglas's "Phebus furth yet," which is adequate but not inspired, suggesting a beneficent gardener with a watering can, is replaced by the full line "Up sprang the goldyn candill matutyne." Dunbar's changes are all in favor of the vivid and pictorial. Douglas's Phoebus, for instance, has no particular function here, so Dunbar replaces him with the precise image of a candle, though he is ready enough to use mythology when it can be made vivid, as in the line "Or Phebus was in purpur cape revest" (7). Douglas characteristically relies heavily on copulatives, while Dunbar uses sharp and vigorous verbs, such as *up sprang* and *glading.*

In these passages, Dunbar is more "aureate," in the common sense of the term, than Douglas. *Matutyne, depurit,* and *cristallyne* are all obtrusively Latinate, while Douglas's *nutritiue* and *vegetant,* though equally Latinate, are specific technical terms and do not have the rich ornamental qualities that are usually associated with "aureate terms." It might be expected, then, that Dunbar's passage is more "ornamental," in a pejorative sense, than Douglas's. But *matutyne* cannot be considered superfluous: it is a precise adjective qualifying *candill,* and the unusualness of the word is functional in that it prevents our passing heedlessly over it. By the phrase "goldyn candill matutyne," Dunbar emphasizes precisely those qualities of the sun which are important to the poem: the sun brings light to the world in the morning, after the night, and in the morning of the year, after the night of winter, and is therefore "goldyn" in value, as well as in color. *Cristallyne,* however, might seem merely decorative, for its meaning has already been given by the adjectives *clere* and *depurit.* But actually, I think, the precise and vivid *cristallyne,* placed in emphatic position at the end of a line, sums up and reinforces the two previous adjectives. This sort of repetition is also used in the larger structure of the poem: the fifth of the stanzas quoted above, for instance, is mainly a recapitulation of the preceding ones. But both the verbal and the structural repetitions work towards concentration rather than diffusion, for they knit together the preceding elements.

The style of the **"Targe"** is undeniably rich: the complicated stanzaic form, the frequent alliteration, and the diction, which, if less Latinate than might be supposed, is still ornate, all contribute to the general feeling of highly wrought opulence. But it is necessary to make a distinct separation between the style of the **"Targe"** and the rich suggestive style that is popularly associated with such different poets as Spenser and Keats. The **"Targe"** is not in the least suggestive or evocative: in this respect, at least, one could characterize it by the term which has been applied to Dryden's work, "a poetry of statement." For all of Dunbar's exuberance of language and his occasional erotic and allegorical themes, he is a very classical poet. Rachel Annand Taylor's curious underestimation of Dunbar [in her *Dunbar: The Poet and His Period,* 1931] is an interesting indication of how little he appeals to someone whose taste is limited to romantic poetry. I have tried to indicate some of the technical means that Dunbar uses to discipline his matter: the intricate and orderly structure into which compressed and interwoven images and themes are fitted; the lack of any sort of garrulous irrelevance; and the precision and tightness of the language. Before considering from a broader viewpoint the essential qualities and the effects of the style, which in this case is the same thing as considering the poem as a whole, it may be useful to look briefly at the allegorical figures who are, after all, the principal actors in the piece.

In the passage from C. S. Lewis quoted above there is a plausible condemnation of the **"Targe's"** allegory: "this [allegoric] action is so slight and degenerates so often into a mere catalogue of personifications (which is the only serious fault of the **"Targe"**) that we are right to neglect it." When Lewis says that the action turns into a catalog of personifications he is simply stating a fact, but when he uses the words "degenerates" and "serious fault" he is giving his own theory about the merits of such catalogs. While there is no *a priori* reason why a poetic catalog is a pernicious thing, Lewis's strictures seem plausible, since personifications presumably are valuable only if they can be given more reality than they receive by being simply listed. But in fact, I think, Dunbar's use of a catalog technique can be fully justified.

Here again, the structure of the catalog passages is worth noting. Leaving aside for the time being the two lists of gods and goddesses, the principal catalogs of the poem are contained in the description of the attack on the dreamer. In the first stanza (145-53), "dame Beautee" advances in a preliminary assault, together with "Fair Having," "Fyne Portrature," "Plesance," and "Lusty Chere," but "Resoun" appears on the scene and repulses them. These assailants are personifications of the most general and most obvious feminine attractions: beauty and friendliness. After the failure of this general assault, the dreamer is attacked by three different and more specialized groups of warriors. Dunbar's description of the first group makes any elucidation superfluous:

Syne tender Youth come wyth hir virgyns ying,
Grene Innocence, and schamefull Abaising,
And quaking Drede, wyth humble Obedience . . .
(154-56)

The second group is led by "Suete Womanhede," who has such followers as "Nurture," "Honest Besynes," and "Benigne Luke." These figures are the attractions of maturity, of the perfect bourgeois matron. In the next group comes "Hie Degree," with such companions as "Estate," "Noble Array," "Libertee," and "Richesse." This group completes the progression: first the young maiden, then the mature woman into whom the maiden ideally develops, and finally the mature woman with all the additional attractions of nobility and wealth. But none of these groups succeed in overcoming the dreamer, and so Venus, perceiving their defeat, sends her last and most dangerous group. "Dissymilance" leads them, and under her are "Presence," "Fair Callyng," "Cherising," "Hamelynes," and finally "Beautee," pressed back into service. Except for Beauty, all of these characters are connected either with carnal love or with feminine wiles, and even Beauty seems less virtuous in this company than she did before. These more redoubtable warriors conquer the dreamer after Presence blinds Reason by throwing powder in his eyes.

These stanzas make the poem's allegory a little less elliptical. The dreamer, assaulted by sexual desire (Venus), is protected by his reason, which prevents him from succumbing to maidens, matrons, or noblewomen. But, as with many another man, his reason is finally overcome by a combination of purely sensual attractions and of feminine deceitfulness. This orderliness of structure explains the particular personifications that Dunbar chose, but it does not, of course, explain why he used the technique of personification. He could, on the one hand, have dropped the allegory in favor of a simple description. He would have had a precedent for this in a passage from Douglas's *Palace of Honour* which is probably a source for some of his personifications:

> The fresche bewtie, the gudelie representis,
> The merie speiche, fair hauingis, hie renoun
> Of thame, wald set a wise man half in swoun.

Alternatively, he could have turned the personifications into full-fledged allegorical figures by giving them each specific actions to perform, the method of the *Roman de la Rose* and many of its descendants.

For Dunbar's purposes, however, personification has certain advantages over both the literal and the fully developed allegorical methods. It has, at best, a vividness that is lacking in the literal method, as is immediately apparent when one compares the three lines from Douglas quoted above with Dunbar's rehandling of them. And it has a conciseness that would necessarily be destroyed by attempting to clothe the personifications with flesh. The danger, of course, is that personifications, unless handled very delicately, may become a mere empty list, neither vivid nor concise. Dunbar avoids this danger by a variety of devices. One, certainly, is simply the careful order in which the figures are arranged. The groups are kept carefully distinct, and each group contains closely related but still separate figures, so that there is no vague disorder. Another important technique is the skillful use of descriptive adjectives. Many of the personifications have an adjective as part of their proper name: "Gude Fame," "Fair Having," and so on, while others have only a single name: "Youth," "Innocence," to which a descriptive adjective is added: "tender," "grene." When one stops to consider, one can generally tell whether the adjective is an integral part of the name or not, though it is not always easy, particularly with "Fyne Portrature," "Suete Womanhede," and "Honest Besynes." But the two types of adjectives tend to blend into each other, much more so, of course, in the manuscripts and early print of the poem, which did not capitalize them in either case. The final result is that all the figures appear to have the type of name that is illustrated by "Honest John," "Blind Harry," "Patient Griselda," and to be simultaneously highly particularized individuals and embodiments of an abstract quality. Occasionally Dunbar replaces or assists these adjectives by short descriptive phrases:

> Perilouse Presence, that mony syre has slayne . . .
>
> (196)
>
> Than saw I Dangere toward me repair,
> I coud eschew hir presence be no wyle.
> On syde scho lukit wyth ane fremyt fare . . .
>
> (223-25)
>
> There saw I May, of myrthfull monethis quene,
> Betuix Aprile and June, her sistir schene . . .
>
> (82-83)

These phrases, like the adjectives, produce a quick and vivid characterization. The most brilliant examples of this technique are in the lists of the gods and goddesses:

> Fair feynit Fortune . . .
>
> (79)
>
> Thare saw I crabbit Saturn ald and haire,
> His luke was lyke for to perturb the aire . . .
>
> (114-15)
>
> Thare was the god of wyndis, Eolus,
> With variand luke, rycht lyke a lord unstable . . .
>
> (122-23)

The catalogs and personifications are, in a way, simply the obverse side of Dunbar's scrupulous avoidance of any human elements. The **"Targe"** is an exceptionally flat and two-dimensional poem: it makes no pretence of being rounded and lifelike, or, on the other hand, of containing any complexities of thought. Both ideas and the corporeal world have a reality that is independent of any poem, but which a poet can, by innumerable methods, evoke. The **"Targe,"** as I have suggested, is not in the least evocative, but as a compensation it attains a singularly high degree of self-completeness. The personifications of the poem are an excellent example of how Dunbar shuns both the physical (lifelike characters) and the intellectual (abstract qualities). Though the two-dimensional quality of the **"Targe"** is undeniably a limitation, it is also an advantage. For one thing, there is a clarity and precision of line and of structure that would be impossible in any three-dimensional writing. Nothing is left vague or hidden: with the exception of the "hundreth ladyes . . . in kirtillis grene," who are themselves sharply delineated, all the characters are named and put into an exact context, which is unusual in a poem of this genre. The poem's lack of depth does not preclude a clear hard vigor: in the lines "For mirth of May, wyth skippis and wyth hoppis, / The birdis sang upon the tender croppis" (19-20), the forceful brevity of the sketch is as effective as any longer and more rounded description could be. Dunbar's method is to condense, to simplify, and then to render this simplification by a vivid and comprehensive phrase.

The **"Targe"** deals constantly and explicitly with surfaces:

as we have seen, the imagery of the first few stanzas, and indeed of the whole poem, is largely concerned with light, color, and garments. These surfaces are not in any way symbolic, but are completely sufficient in themselves, and are able to carry the whole weight of the poem. This is possible because the surfaces are not, in a pejorative sense, superficial, but are rich, formal, and yet have a precise brilliance. It is beautifully characteristic that the most striking of the images in the opening stanzas describe reflected light. The poem is filled with references to gems, but it uses them for their sharp brilliance and not for any vague encrusted richness. The novelties that Dunbar may have introduced into the *Roman de la Rose* tradition, the ship and the companies of deities, have again the same function of contributing to the poem's bright full vividness.

There are two different, though complementary, ways of justifying the **"Targe's"** emphasis on surfaces. In the first place, there is the peculiar appropriateness of the style to the matter. The **"Targe"** is, formally, a dream poem, which is to say that, like its predecessors, it uses a dream both as a convenient and plausible frame and as a way of entering into a world more mysterious and in some way more significant than the waking world. But unlike most of its predecessors, the **"Targe"** does not emphasize the fantastic, vague, and yet symbolic qualities of dreams. If dreams are at times shadowy and only dimly perceived, it is equally true that they are occasionally preternaturally vivid, and have, at least for their dreamer, a clarity and logic far surpassing anything in the waking world. Dunbar concentrates on this clear but unsubstantial surface, and in doing so he brings new vigor to the old themes. The dream becomes not concrete but startlingly vivid, so that it attains its own sort of reality.

Another way to look at the **"Targe,"** and perhaps ultimately a more important way, is to consider it a poem about poetry. This could be said, with some degree of validity, about all of Dunbar's poems, for in all of them the formal manner of transmuting matter into poetry is obtrusive, and more important than the matter itself. But the **"Targe"** is concerned with poetry in a much less vague way. Four of the poem's thirty-one stanzas are explicitly about poetry: one of them is a traditional declaration to the effect that neither Homer nor Cicero, much less Dunbar himself, could do justice to the beauty of the scene, and the other three, which I will quote here, are the conclusion of the poem.

> O reverend Chaucere, rose of rethoris all,
> As in oure tong ane flour imperiall,
> That raise in Britane evir, quho redis rycht,
> Thou beris of makaris the tryumph riall;
> Thy fresch anamalit termes celicall
> This mater coud illumynit have full brycht:
> Was thou noucht of oure Inglisch all the lycht,
> Surmounting eviry tong terrestriall,
> Alls fer as Mayis morow dois mydnycht?
>
> O morall Gower, and Ludgate laureate,
> Your sugurit lippis and tongis aureate,
> Bene to oure eris cause of grete delyte;
> Your angel mouthis most mellifluate
> Oure rude langage has clere illumynate,
> And faire ourgilt oure speche, that imperfyte
> Stude, or your goldyn pennis schupe to wryte;
> This Ile before was bare and desolate
>
> Off rethorike or lusty fresch endyte.
> Thou lytill Quair, be evir obedient,
> Humble, subject, and symple of entent,
> Before the face of eviry connyng wicht:
> I knaw quhat thou of rethorike hes spent;
> Off all hir lusty rosis redolent
> Is none in to thy gerland sett on hicht;
> Eschame thar of, and draw the out of sicht.
> Rude is thy wede, disteynit, bare, and rent,
> Wele aucht thou be aferit of the licht.

It is the imagery of this passage which is important for our purposes, rather than the traditional self-deprecation or the equally traditional but more significant praise of Chaucer, Gower, and Lydgate. Dunbar suggests several metaphors for good writing, a principal one being that of light. Gower and Lydgate are said to have illuminated and made clear the language, while Chaucer is given almost solar powers: he is all the light of English, his celestial terms "This mater coud illumynit have full brycht," and he is compared to a May morning, opposed to the midnight of other terrestrial poets. Bareness is a symbol for bad writing ("Rude is thy wede, disteynit, bare, and rent"), or for the absence of good writing ("This Ile before was bare and desolate"), while poetic beauty is characterized by flowers. Dunbar says that the trouble with the **"Targe"** is that it has none of the roses of rhetoric, but Chaucer's style makes him "rose of rethoris all . . . ane flour imperiall." A good style has the power of gilding ("tongis aureate," "ourgilt oure speche," "goldyn pennis") and of making sweet ("sugurit lippis," "mouthis most mellifluate"). But the most revealing image and the one which connects all the others is "anamalit." Enamel is clear and brilliant, colorful, with a rich sweet beauty, and, most particularly, is a surface adornment, like illumination, flowers, and gold or sugar coating.

The critical theory implicit in these images is not likely to recommend itself to us: we are quite properly suspicious of any tendency towards defining poetry as a decorative frosting. But all the same, Dunbar's aesthetics should not be condemned too hastily. In his practice, at least, he was much less superficial, in a pejorative sense, than the English fifteenth-century poets. The rhetorical figures and ornate diction in Lydgate and his followers are for the most part strictly decorative, being added to make palatable and ostensibly poetic the underlying prose sense, which has the place of honor. But in all of Dunbar's poems the prose sense is negligible and the decoration, the poetic artifices, are everything. Where the typical poem of the Lydgatian school rambles interminably, finding what structure it has in a preconceived logical plan or in a vague narrative thread, Dunbar's poems are static, ending where they begin, but are made tightly unified by technical poetic devices. And, it should be noted, Dunbar's theory is directly connected to his practice. One indication of this is that the images which he uses to describe poetry are taken from the rest of the poem. Brightness, colored garments, flowers, gilt, and enamel are qualities which belong equally to the garden and to Dunbar's description of poetry. What we have here, in fact, is theory and example; the theory being the stanzas stating that poetry should be like enamel and the example being the rest of the poem. Subject, style, and aesthetic theory all coalesce, and the coalescence is made explicit by the imagery: "anamalit" is simultaneously a characteristic of the garden ("Anamalit was the felde wyth all colouris" [13]), of the hard and brilliant style ("fresch anamalit termes" [257]), and of the sort of poetry that Dunbar strives to make.

Perhaps the best way to sum up the essential qualities of the **"Targe"** is through this metaphor of enamel. Dunbar devotes his very considerable poetic energies to fitting words into a meticulously interlocked pattern and creating a hard and beautiful surface as substantial and as self-sufficient as a piece of enamel-work. The poem is intentionally artificial, being based on the previous literary tradition and not on nature. And Dunbar uses this earlier tradition in a parasitic manner: his immediate concern is with the technical and rhetorical manipulation of the form, not with the "meaning" of the genre, the allegorical and courtly love content for which it had been devised. It would be fully as senseless to condemn the **"Targe"** for being artificial and inhuman, or for existing primarily in its surface, as it would be to condemn enamelwork for these qualities: in both cases the limitations are an integral part of the work's virtues and of its ultimate meaning. The **"Targe"** is undeniably an example of a very limited and specialized type of poetry, for in it, even more than in his other poems, Dunbar concentrates on verbal artifice and on an intricate and orderly craftsmanship. Yet we can still say, I think, not only that the poem is, of its kind, unsurpassable, but also that with its clarity, compression, richness, and controlled vigor it achieves a permanent and valuable type of success. (pp. 311-34)

Denton Fox, "Dunbar's 'The Golden Targe'," in ELH, *Vol. 26, No. 1, March, 1959, pp. 311-34.*

Priscilla Bawcutt (essay date 1974)

[Bawcutt is a critic, editor, and author of several books and articles on Scottish and medieval literature. In the excerpt which follows, she examines Dunbar's varied use of imagery, focusing particularly on those that derive from "direct observation of everyday life or from popular tradition."]

Dunbar handles imagery with a brilliance that is still insufficiently recognized. Some critics have limited themselves to the artificial, aureate images in his courtly poems such as **"The Goldyn Targe"** or **"The Thrissil and the Rois;"** some have neglected the subject entirely. Only recently have other critics looked more searchingly and more appreciatively at Dunbar's imagery. Images of every type—symbol, personification, metaphor, and simile—abound in Dunbar; in this respect he contrasts strikingly with his Scottish contemporaries, Henryson and Gavin Douglas. Although his imagery is not outstanding for its intellectual subtlety, it has enormous zest and energy. Much of the visual impact, the wit, and the emotional vitality of Dunbar's poetry is effected by images, which Dunbar handles with versatility. Indeed, the interplay between image and theme may often structure the whole poem.

I propose chiefly to discuss here some of the more colloquial, humorous or satirical poems, whose imagery has been less studied than that of the religious poems or courtly allegories. One reason for this neglect may lie in the occasional difficulties or ambiguities of their language. For example, in **"Of ane Blak-Moir,"** the "blak lady" is described as "tute mowitt lyk ane aep / And lyk a gangarall onto graep." Small [in his *The Poems of William Dunbar,* 3 vols., 1884-93] glossed *gangarall* as "child beginning to walk," and noted that "the line represents her waddling mode of walking." Craigie [in his *The Maitland Folio Manuscript,* 2 vols., 1912-27] glossed *gangarall* as "spider." Mackenzie [in his *The Poems of William Dunbar,* 2nd ed., 1966] and Kinsley [in his *William Dunbar Poems,* 1958], however, preferred "toad," an interpretation supported by other sixteenth-century Scottish writers (see *DOST* and *OED*). The image thus suggests a skin dark and rough to the touch ("onto graep"), possibly even scarred by smallpox. But there are still far too many lines in Dunbar where editors have provided not glosses but comically divergent guesses, as may be seen in the varying explanations of *fepillis* and *hogeart* in **"The Tretis"** (ll. 114, 272). Such differences arise in part from Dunbar's extreme colloquialism, his liking for the sort of word common enough in speech but rarely written down, because it is too technical, too low, too slangy, or too obscene. Unfortunately for modern readers, images which in his own day were crisp and definite become blurred.

My primary concern is not with the sources of Dunbar's images, but with their poetic use; *how* they work, rather than *whence* they derive. Nonetheless I am aware that the source of an image is relevant to its effect in a poem—its associations, sacred or secular, courtly or vulgar, naturalistic or non-naturalistic. Dunbar draws on an enormous variety of literary sources—the Bible and the liturgy, the lapidary, the bestiary, and heraldic lore—but in the colloquial and satirical poems it is perhaps to be expected that the naturalistic images derive mainly either from direct observation of everyday life or from popular tradition. Some of Dunbar's most arresting and apparently original images employ the homeliest objects found in house or street or farm: soap; a tar-barrel; a saffron bag; a chamber-pot ("jowrdane-hedit"); a harrow ("hippit as ane harrow"); a mortar stone ("mell-hedit lyk ane mortar stane"); a smith's pincers ("lyk turkas birnand reid"). He confronts us with the more unpleasant realities of late medieval street life: bull baiting; cock fighting; choked gutters:

> With goreis his tua grym ene ar gladderrit all about,
> And gorgeit lyk twa gutaris that war with glar stoppit.

or a man on the gallows:

> With hingit luik ay wallowand upone wry,
> Lyke to ane stark theif glowrand in ane tedder.

Such images are reinforced by others which, though not of the same imaginative order, stem ultimately from a similar realm of experience. These are the commonplace, semi-proverbial similes, which were the stock in trade of all medieval poets, and often linger in our speech today; swift as an arrow, brim as boars, green as grass, sad as lead, lean as trees, small as wands, white as whalebone. Dunbar disdained their use no more than did Chaucer. Sometimes they are merely metrical and alliterative conveniences; sometimes an ironical twist is given to a trite simile, as in the First Wife's remark about her husband in **"The Tretis,"** "Bot soft and soupill as the silk is his sary lume," or in **"Of the Ladyis Solistaris at Court,"** where Dunbar clearly has tongue in cheek when he terms the ladies "trest as the steill."

Single images in Dunbar strike us first for their vividness and imaginative accuracy. Isabel Hyde has noted [in her "Poetic Imagery: A Point of Comparison between Henryson and Dunbar," in *Studies in Scottish Literature* 2, 1965] Dunbar's "wild delight in light and colour;" Dunbar takes a similar pleasure in recording movement. The animals to which his victims are compared are frequently shown in motion or transfixed in a characteristic grotesque posture:

He stackeret lyk ane strummall aver,
That hopschackelit war aboin the kne. . . .

Than cam in the Maister Almaser,
Ane hommiltye jommeltye juffler,
Lyk a stirk stackarand in the ry.
("A Dance in the Quenis Chalmer")

Than Yre come in with sturt and stryfe;
His hand wes ay upoun his knyfe,
He brandeist lyk a beir.
("The Dance of the Sevin Deidly Synnis")

Dunbar's imagination was not simply visual; many of his images are tactile. "Gangarall," quoted above, is a case in point. But the most striking instance occurs in **"The Tretis,"** where the First Wife complains of her husband:

And with his hard hurcheone skyn sa heklis he my chekis,
That as a glemand gleyd glowis my chaftis. (ll. 107-8)

The reader is made acutely aware both of the sensation of prickly roughness and of the Wife's sense of repulsion. The "heckle" was an instrument for combing flax or hemp.

Single images strike us also for their compression. Just as his poems tend to be short (his longest, **"The Tretis,"** is barely over 500 lines), so Dunbar seems to prefer metaphors and short simple similes to the long, spacious similes of Chaucer's *Troilus and Criseyde.* He favours the succinct combination of two nouns, in which the first noun carries the metaphor: "catt nois;" "bledder cheikis," suggesting fat, white, pendulous cheeks; "hoppir hippis," an image used later by Wycherly (*Love in a Wood,* II.i: "she is bow-legged, hopper-hipped"). The line previously quoted—"And with his hard hurcheone skyn sa heklis he my chekis"—is remarkably compressed, far more than the comparable lines in Chaucer's *Merchant's Tale:*

With thikke brustles of his berd unsofte,
Lyk to the skyn of houndfyssh, sharp as brere—
For he was shave al newe in his manere—
He rubbeth hire aboute hir tendre face.

Elsewhere Dunbar uses verbs in this vigorous, metaphorical way: "My panefull purs so priclis me," or "That fulle dismemberit hes my meter."

Dunbar also achieves economy by exploiting ambiguities in everyday speech: *gillot, gillet* - 1. a wanton woman, 2. a mare; *gammaldis* - 1. a horse's bounds or curvets, 2. leaps or springs in dancing; *brankand* - 1. prancing, tossing the head (of horses), 2. strutting, walking confidently (of humans); *fry* - 1. offspring, in general, 2. the offspring of fishes. The intertwined animal and human associations in these words are highly relevant:

Quhy sould not palfrayis thane be prowd,
Quhen *gillettis* wil be schomd and schroud,
That ridden are baith with lord and lawd? . . .
Quhen I was young and into ply,
And wald cast *gammaldis* to the sky.
("The Petition of the Gray Horse, Auld Dunbar)

And yit he is als *brankand* with bonet one syde,
And blenkand to the brichtest that in the burgh duellis. . . .
I buskit up my barnis like baronis sonnis,
And maid bot fulis of the *fry* of his first wif.
(**"Tretis,"** ll. 180-1, 402-3)

In some of Dunbar's shorter poems a single image serves as the organizing principle of the whole poem. **"Quhone Mony Benefices Vakit,"** a short poem of fifteen lines, pleads with the King for a more just distribution of benefices. Apart from the presence of this word (*benefice*) in the first line, the argument is entirely metaphorical, proceeding in terms of the fair distribution of food at a banquet:

Schir, quhiddir is it mereit mair
To gif him drink that thristis sair,
Or fill a fow man quhill he brist,
And lat his fallow de a thirst,
Quhilk wyne to drynk als worthie war?

The poem is virtually a parable. The tone is light, even jocular; the effect of the metaphor is to veil and tone down Dunbar's criticism of the King. Another poem employs the same image in its opening line, "Off benefice, Schir, at everie feist," but it is not sustained, and its tone is far more outspoken and bitter. Yet another poem, slight but amusing, is organized round one central image, springing from a pun on the name of the unfortunate Keeper of the Wardrobe, James Doig or Dog [**"Of James Dog, Kepar of the Quenis Wardrop"**]. Each stanza presents a different and comic picture of the "Wardraipper:" barking as if "he war wirriand ane hog;" a surly house dog that needs a heavy clog; "ane midding tyk . . . chassand cattell throu a bog;" a huge mastiff far too large to be the Queen's *messan* or lap dog. Dunbar clearly enjoyed this word play because he used it in two other poems. In the refrain to [**"Of the Same James, Quhen He Had Plesett Him"**], a sequal to [**"Of James Dog"**], Dunbar has to eat his words: "He is na Dog; he is a Lam." **"Of a Dance in the Quenis Chalmer"** plays with a similar idea:

The Quenis Dog begowthe to rax,
And of his band he maid a bred . . .
Quhou mastevlyk about yeid he!

Another punning image—Mackenzie observes that "Dunbar does not pun"—is the focus of **"To a Ladye,"** a brief, witty but rather frigid love poem. The first two stanzas draw a parallel between the Lady who possesses every virtue except mercy and a garden that lacks only rue:

In to your garthe this day I did persew,
Thair saw I flowris that fresche wer of hew;
Baith quhyte and reid moist lusty wer to seyne,
And halsum herbis upone stalkis grene;
Yit leif nor flour fynd could I nane of rew.

The last stanza, which opens "I dout that Merche, with his caild blastis keyne, / Hes slane this gentill herbe that I of mene," is allusive and enigmatic in tone. Far from exhausting the comparison, it teases the reader into speculating on its exact significance.

It is more profitable, however, to consider Dunbar's frequent use of groups or clusters of images. The simplest kind of grouping is seen in the torrents of abusive images that occur in **"The Flyting,"** or in certain petitionary poems, such as the **"Complaint to the King":**

Wyld haschbaldis, haggarbaldis, and hummellis;
Druncartis, dysouris, dyvowris, drevillis,
Mysgydit memberis of the devillis;
Mismad mandragis of mastis strynd.

Such catalogues occur at climaxes, moments of high indignation, when—as Dunbar himself puts it—

. . . owther man my hart to breik,
Or with my pen I man me wreik;
And sen the tane most nedis be,
In to malancolie to de,
Or lat the vennim ische all out,
Be war, anone, for it will spout,
Gif that the tryackill cum nocht tyt
To swage the swalme of my dispyt!
("Remonstrance to the King")

What may at first seem a haphazard selection, in reality displays considerable art. **"Complaint to the King"** has a preponderance of images drawn chiefly from the world of the labourer, clearly appropriate in a poem attacking upstarts: "jowrdane-hedit," "club-facet," "bledder cheikis," "hoppir hippis," "mell-hedit lyk ane mortar-stane." They are designed ostensibly to ridicule physical appearance, but they also suggest the tasks for which such men are fitted.

A characteristically witty cluster of images occurs in **"None May Assure in this Warld":**

Towngis now are maid of quhite quhale bone,
And hartis ar maid of hard flynt stone,
And eyn ar maid of blew asure,
And handis of adament laithe to dispone;
So in this warld may none assure.

The stanza has a cumulative effect; the repeated "maid" suggests a Midas-like transformation of warm human beings into insensate stony blocks. The images are complex; eyes are not only as blue but as hard as lapis lazuli; hands are like adamant because their owners are both hard and reluctant to part with money. In its context the stanza is an *amplificatio* of the preceding, echoing it line by line: "Fra everie mouthe fair wordis procedis; / In everie harte deceptioun bredis." The images are similarly related to the following stanza: "Yit hart and handis and body all / Mon anser dethe, quhone he dois call." The rest of the poem is far less tightly integrated.

Elsewhere in Dunbar, however, juxtaposition of images may inform the whole poem. **"In Secreit Place this Hynder Nycht"** has Dunbar making fun of the conventional language of endearment. Pet names, diminutives, baby talk, and above all images are used in such profusion that they jostle incongruously:

Quod he, "My claver, and my curldodie,
My huny soppis, my sweit possodie."

Later the girl replies:

"Welcum! my golk of Marie land,
My chirrie and my maikles munyoun,
My sowklar sweit as ony unyoun,
My strumill stirk, yit new to spane."

Comparison of the loved one to flowers, young animals, and even food has of course a long history, but Dunbar's boorish lovers reduce such imagery to absurdity. The trite "sweit as the hunye" is mockingly echoed by "sweit as ony unyoun." The flowers to which the lover compares his girl are not the courtly rose and lily, but clover (chiefly used for fodder) and the "curldodie," a name which seems to have been applied to various weeds with large round heads. Dunbar's technique partly recalls that of Chaucer in the *Miller's Tale,* but the images have been coarsened and degraded. In the *Miller's Tale* Alison is compared to a weasel, a kid, a calf, and a colt; in context these images are not unpleasing. Dunbar's lovers compare each other not only to a kid and a calf but to a clumsy young stirk [ox] and—what is surely an indignity—a "tuchan," a calf's skin stuffed with straw to persuade the cow to give milk. The *Miller's Tale* emphasizes images of food: Alison's mouth is "sweete as bragot or the meeth, / Or hoord of apples" (I, 3261-2); Nicholas is "sweete as is the roote / Of lycorys, or any cetewale" (I, 3206-7). But Dunbar's lovers compare each other to "possodie" and "crowdie mowdie," which have been respectively interpreted as sheeps' head broth and a gruel of milk and meal!

Particularly subtle is Dunbar's use of imagery in his most ambitious poem, **"The Tretis of the Tua Mariit Wemen and the Wedo."** On the surface its structure is deceptively simple, three monologues on marriage overheard by the hidden poet. Yet it is a carefully and intricately composed poem, in which the elaborately described garden setting and the recurrent bird and animal images are skilfully interwoven to reinforce and at times to anticipate some of the more explicit themes of the poem.

Most readers of **"The Tretis"** are struck by the abundance of animal imagery, particularly in the volley of abuse that explodes from the First Wife:

I have ane wallidrag, ane worme, ane auld wobat carle,
A waistit wolroun, na worth bot wourdis to clatter;
And bumbart, ane dron bee, ane bag full of flewme.

(ll. 89-91)

The vehemence suggests the outburst of pent up feelings expressed by the Second Wife in another image: "Now sall the byle all out brist, that beild has so lang; / For it to beir one my brist wes berdin our hevy" (ll. 164-5). All three women repeatedly compare their husbands to animals: a cat ("that lene gib," l. 120); a dog ("I hatit him like a hund," l. 273); a coward cock that will not fight (the "craudone" of ll. 215 and 326). Their skin is bristly as a hedgehog's (l. 107) or a boar's ("As birs of ane brym bair, his berd is als stif," l. 95). Most common of all is the image of an old cart horse; there are oblique hints either of this or of an ox in the First Wife's desire for a husband who is "Yaip, and ying, in the yok ane yeir for to draw . . . A forky fure, ay furthwart, and forsy in draucht" (ll. 79, 85). This is followed by the use of the particularly contemptuous term "aver:"

> And quhen the smy one me smyrkis with his smake smolet,
> He fepillis like a farcy aver that flyrit one a gillot.
>
> (ll. 113-14)

The "aver" is one afflicted with "farcy," a disease which causes swellings and discharge of mucous matter from the nostrils. Such images cast an ugly light on both partners in the marriage. The Widow triumphs over her last husband:

> I wald haif ridden him to Rome with raip in his heid . . .
> "Se how I cabeld yone cout with a kene brydill!
> The cappill, that the crelis kest in the caf mydding,
> Sa curtasly the cart drawis, and kennis na plungeing,
> He is nought skeich, na yit sker, na scippis nought one syd."
>
> (ll. 331, 354-7)

The husbands are tamed, domesticated beasts of burden. Furthermore, they are often viewed as sick or humiliated animals: a "broddit" beast (l. 33), a plucked heron (l. 382), or a "dotit dog:"

> He dois as dotit dog that damys on all bussis,
> And liftis his leg apone loft, thoght he nought list pische.
>
> (ll. 186-7)

By contrast, the Wives compare themselves to powerful, cruel, predatory animals; the Widow advises them to model themselves on tigers, dragons, and adders (l. 261). Even more revealingly, they picture themselves as birds. The Widow boasts that her last husband "payntit me as pako, proudest of fedderis" (l. 379), and "I thought my self a papingay and him a plukit herle" (l. 382). A few lines earlier she had applied to herself a verb used also of birds trimming their feathers (modern "preen" and "prune" are variants of it)—"I wald me prunya plesandly in precius wedis" (l. 374). The ostensible resemblance is to the beauty and bright plumage of such birds, and the poet in part endorses this. The Wives are indeed beautiful, "swanquhit of hewis" (l. 243). But there is more to the bird imagery than this. It connects with one of the leading themes, stated explicitly in the First Wife's denunciation of marriage:

> Birdis has ane better law na bernis be meikill,
> That ilk yeir, with new joy, joyis ane maik,
> And fangis thame ane fresche feyr, unfulyeit and constant,
> And lattis their fulyeit feiris flie quhair thai pleis.
> Cryst gif sic ane consuetude war in this kith haldin!
>
> (ll. 60-4)

The Second Wife returns to the theme:

> Ye speik of berids one bewch: of blise may thai sing,
> That, one Sanct Valentynis day, ar vacandis ilk yer;
> Hed I that plesand prevelege to part quhen me likit,
> To change, and ay to cheise agane, than, chastite, adew!
>
> (ll. 205-8)

The Wives aspire not only to the beauty of birds but to their whole way of life, with its apparent freedom and joy and total irresponsibility. Yet although they make some show of seeking love and praising the law of nature ("It is agane the law of luf, of kynd and of nature, / Togiddir hairtis to strene, that stryveis with uther," ll. 58-9), their picture of the world of nature is partial and distorted. It is instructive to compare Langland's interpretation of the "law of Kynd," where Kynd shows the dreamer how "reason" informs all the activities of birds and beasts:

> I hadde wonder at whom and where the pye lerned
> To legge the stykkes in whiche she leyeth and bredeth . . .
> Ac that moste moeued me and my mode chaunged,
> That Reason rewarded and reuled alle bestes,
> Saue man and his make.

The Widow's speech makes it clear that what she desires is not love but promiscuity, not freedom but a tyrannical power over others. Some of her images are highly revealing, since they suggest not a natural but a highly unnatural, perverted state of affairs. One remark about her late husband is rich in implications: "I crew abone that craudone, as cok that wer victour" (l. 326). It is not simply that marriage is seen as a cock fight or that the whole of the Widow's speech is characterized by the crowing boastfulness of a cock. The sex reversal implicit in the image—the assumption of the male role by the Widow, who later compares herself not to the peahen but to the peacock—foreshadows the more explicit degradation of the husband into a "wif carll:"

> I maid that wif carll to werk all womenis werkis,
> And laid all manly materies and mensk in this eird.
>
> (ll. 351-52)

It suggests, furthermore, the kind of sexual humiliation which is latent in her boast that she "that grome geldit had of gudis and of natur" (l. 392). The use of "geld" here is extremely forceful. Dunbar seems to have been the first user of the verb in the figurative sense, and we are clearly meant to think also of its literal sense. It both suggests the Widow's sexual preoccupations, and links with the other imagery of mutilated animals.

There are many other aspects of Dunbar's imagery that might be discussed: its cruelty and painfulness, clearly linked to its satirical function; the shock, when Dunbar speaks of Kennedie's "gule" snout and "giltin" hips (**"The Flyting,"** ll. 52 and 99), of dignified aureate epithets incongruously applied. The versatility with which Dunbar uses animal imagery would also repay study; the symbolic and deliberately unnaturalistic picture of the nightingale, "quhois angell fedderis as the pacock schone" (**"The Merle and the Nychtingaill"),** contrasted with the sensuous and exact observation displayed in such phrases as "catt nois" and "hurcheone skyn;" the ordered correspondence between the human and animal hierarchies in a poem such as **"The Thrissil and the Rois",** contrasted with the disordered, topsy-turvy world of **"The Flyting"** and other comic poems, in which the animal analogies degrade and dehumanize. A poet's handling of images is of a piece with his handling of language in general, and Dunbar has a craftsman's care for the choice and placing of his words. A study of his imagery can consequently but strengthen one's admiration for Dunbar, the "makar." (pp. 190-99)

Priscilla Bawcutt, "Aspects of Dunbar's Imagery," in Chaucer and Middle English Studies in Honour of Rossell Hope Robbins, *edited by Beryl Rowland, George Allen & Unwin Ltd., 1974, pp. 190-200.*

A. C. Spearing (essay date 1976)

[*In the following excerpt, Spearing investigates Dunbar's varied use of the dream and concludes that it was a literary device which linked the "world of reality" to the "world of art."*]

The dream-framework was a favourite device of Dunbar's, and he used it for a variety of different purposes; indeed, from his work alone it could be demonstrated that the dream-poem has no single right use. One poem, for example, is a vision of Christ's passion, which is granted to the poet when he suddenly falls into a trance while praying in an oratory—a 'dream' closely parallel to Langland's vision of Piers Plowman in B XIX, and related like it to the visionary experiences of devotional writers such as Rolle and Julian of Norwich. The first part of the vision gives a detailed sensory picture of the Passion itself; the second uses personifications such as Compassion, Remembrance and Grace to describe the poet's own response to his vision, which is brought to an end when he is awakened by the trembling of the earth of Matthew 27:51. Another poem [**How Dunbar was desyrd to be ane Freir**] consists of a comic analogue of those dreams that, according to the *Liber de Modo Bene Vivendi,* 'occur through the illusions of unclean spirits'. In it St Francis appears, to urge the poet to become a friar; Dunbar resists his urging, and the supposed saint turns into a devil and 'vaneist away with stynk and fyrie smowk' (48). One commentator [Tom Scott, *Dunbar: A Critical Exposition of the Poems,* 1966] has asserted that in this poem Dunbar 'is writing about a real dream which he actually had', that he 'is in fact receiving his religious vocation in a dream-vision from one of the great saints in person: to a devout Catholic there could be no other interpretation,' and that his rejection of the call expresses a deep inner conflict. This view of the poem is merely fanciful, and disregards the broad range of types of dream with which a medieval poet is likely to have been acquainted. This *visio* is obviously spurious, and the poem's chief purpose is to satirise the pretensions of the friars, in support of the common medieval view that 'Freres and feendes been but lyte asonder' (*Canterbury Tales* III [D] 1674).

A number of Dunbar's other dream-poems are satirical in intention. Two of them are directed against John Damian, Abbot of Tongland, an alchemist who attempted to fly with wings made of birds' feathers and was patronized by James IV of Scotland. The first hilariously describes how all the species of birds attacked him in his attempted flight, and the satire is the sharper if one recognizes that Dunbar sees it as a travesty of Philosophy's promise to Boethius to 'fycchen fetheris in thi thought' (for 'philosophy' had also come to mean alchemy). In the second, the poet has a vision of Fortune, who informs him that Damian will meet a she-dragon in the heavens and will beget Antichrist. Here the implication of the dream-framework seems to be double: that the abbot's associations are devilish, and that his attempt at flight belongs rather to apocalyptic fantasies than to waking life. Other dream-satires are less personal in their scope. One, in which a single vision incorporates two poems, **"The Dance of the Sevin Deidly Synnis"** and **"The Sowtar and Tailyouris War"** (The Battle of the Shoemaker and the Tailor) offers a comic vision of hell, showing first the personified sins and then the shoemaker and the tailor urged on by the devil to a grotesque tournament. It is a parody, of course, of genuine religious visions of the other world, and its last line declares its status as mere fantasy: 'Now trow this gif ye list!' The comic vision of the other world is completed in a third poem which purports to make amends to the shoemakers and tailors for the joke at their expense. Here an angel appears to the poet in a dream, to promise that, though these tradesmen may be knaves on earth, they will be saints in heaven. Another grotesque dream-satire, but more sombre in tone, is **"The Devillis Inquest",** in which the poet sees people of various callings dedicating themselves by their blasphemies to the devil, who stands close by and encourages them. Here the function of the dream is to provide a genuine insight into an unseen reality: in waking life we hear the blasphemies but do not see the devil who profits by them. Lastly, in a poem called simply **"The Dream",** a vision comes to the poet 'halff sleiping' (1), in which he is visited by various personifications. Distres, Hivines and Langour depress his spirits, while others discuss the fact that the king has not rewarded him with ecclesiastical preferment for his work as a poet. It ends with Patience encouraging the Dreamer to rely on the king's generosity, but at this point a gun is shot off, and the noise wakes him. In this case the function of the dream-setting is, I believe, somewhat complex. Dream . . . is an appropriate setting for debate among personifications (particularly those which stand, as these do, for the various psychological impulses which are really reflected in dreams); in this sense the poem represents a plausible *somnium animale.* This dream, however, discloses a truth—that Dunbar has received no reward—but the plea, and the incidental satire against the pluralism of other courtiers, are softened by the fact that it is 'only a dream'. And finally the assurance of the king's generosity, followed as it is by a rude noise which brings the vision to an end, is exposed as the most insubstantially dreamlike thing of all.

Even in Dunbar's shorter poems, then, the dream can be used for complex purposes. But the poem on which I wish especially to focus is a longer work, **"The Thrissil and the Rois"** which, in my view, has been greatly underestimated by modern commentators. Mr Speirs [in his, *The Scots Literary Tradition,* 2nd ed., 1962] sees it and **"The Goldyn Targe"** as poems from which 'life has largely escaped', while Dr Scott describes it as 'regressive and morbid . . . , forced, contrived, unreal, unconvincing, spurious'. It is a formal occasional poem, written in 1503 to celebrate the marriage of King James IV to the English princess Margaret Tudor, and what takes place inside the dream relates symbolically to this historical event. In the dream (to summarize briefly) Dame Nature summons all the creatures to do homage to her. Among them comes the lion, from the royal arms of Scotland, whom Nature crowns as king of the beasts. Then she crowns the eagle as king of the birds. Lastly she crowns the thistle as king of the plants, gives him good advice about ruling the other plants, and advises him to love no other flower but the rose. The thistle, emblem of Scotland, stands for James IV, and the advice to love none but the rose implies that he should abandon his mistresses when he gets married. Then Nature crowns the rose—a Tudor rose, red and white in colour, set above the lily (the emblem of France), and standing, of course, for the English princess. All the birds sing a song of welcome and praise of her, and with their noise the Dreamer wakes. The concept of the gathering of the creatures under the rule of Nature, and the ending with birdsong which awakens the Dreamer, both derive from Chaucer's *Parliament of Fowls,* but Dunbar's poem is considerably shorter than Chaucer's, and much simpler in structure.

Although the events of the dream, such as they are, stand for historical events, the dream-world in which they are set is not a version of this world, as in the tradition of *Winner and Waster,* but a paradisal other world. It is imagined along traditional lines: it is a May morning, the Dreamer is taken into a 'lusty gairding gent' (44) (pleasant and noble garden), full of green leaves and sweet-smelling flowers, the air rings with the song of birds, and the language used implies the usual analogy with the heavenly world—this time it is the sun which 'In orient bricht as angell did appeir' (51). . . . [This] traditional dream-landscape originated in the Mediterranean area, and then spread over the whole of Europe as a literary convention without any very close relationship to the realities of the climate in any locality. In the south of England, though springtime weather is notoriously treacherous, the convention remained just plausible enough to survive intact. The breaking-point seems to have come when it was carried still further north to Scotland. Not even a Scot could believe that a Scottish spring would be paradisal, even as late as May, and . . . in Henryson's and Douglas's dream-prologues the month was silently changed to June. Dunbar went further, by taking up the contrast between literary convention and climatic reality and making it part of his poem's meaning. The opening section of **"The Thrissil and the Rois,"** before the dream begins, takes place in May. The poet lies sleeping in bed one morning, when it seems to him (and here his dream begins) that Aurora, the goddess of the dawn, looks in through his bedroom window, with a lark on her hand which sings aloud,

> Awalk, luvaris, out of your slomering,
> Se how the lusty morrow dois up spring.
> (13-14)

Then May appears to him, a personification of the season, standing by his bed, dressed in flowers and glittering with sunbeams, and she too tells him to rise up and write something in her honour: the lark has aroused lovers 'with confort and delyt' (25), so why has not Dunbar risen to compose songs for them? (As in Chaucer, it is assumed that the Dreamer, a court-poet, must be a love-poet.) But at this the Dreamer rebels, and in effect tells this literary personification, May, that she is a mere fiction, and that the real Scottish May is a season of bitter winds, cold air, and silent birds:

> 'Quhairto,' quod I, 'sall I uprys at morrow,
> For in this May few birdis herd I sing?
> Thai haif moir caus to weip and plane thair sorrow.
> Thy air it is nocht holsum nor benyng;
> Lord Eolus dois in thy sessone ring;
> So busteous ar the blastis of his horne,
> Amang thy bewis to walk I haif forborne.
> (29-35)

In reply to this rebellious speech, May simply smiles soberly, reminds the Dreamer that he has promised to write something in honour of the rose, and invites him to enter the world of his dream, that garden

> Illumynit our with orient skyis brycht,
> Annamyllit richely with new asur lycht.
> (41-2)

He does so, and the main content of the dream follows.

What Dunbar has done is to admit that the idealized world of his dream is only a fiction, an artifice, as is suggested, by the very words *illumynit* (like a manuscript illumination) and *annamyllit* (like a design painted on precious metal). And the sense of a contrast between the real world and the dream-world is continued when Dame Nature appears in the dream and orders Neptune, the sea-god, to prevent storms at sea, Aeolus, the god of the winds, to make no cold blasts, and Juno to keep the heavens dry:

> Dame Nature gaif an inhibitioun thair
> To fers Neptunus, and Eolus the bawld,
> Nocht to perturb the wattir nor the air,
> And that no schouris, nor [no] blastis cawld,
> Effray suld flouris nor fowlis on the fold;
> Scho bad eik Juno, goddes of the sky,
> That scho the hevin suld keip amene and dry.
> (64-70)

The obvious implication of these precautions is that paradisal weather is not the norm in real life; it belongs to an art based on the exercise of the will in opposition to the natural course of events.

Dunbar, then, pointedly uses the dream-framework as a way of separating the world of art, or poetic fiction, from the world of reality. But this does not mean, as is sometimes assumed, that he is content to write an escapist and merely decorative kind of poetry, to be a 'dreamer of dreams' in the post-Romantic sense. There is of course a paradox involved in Dunbar's contrast between the dream-world of art and the waking world of nature: it is that Nature herself, the personified concept, can be seen only in the dream-world of art. Just so, in *Winner and Waster,* winning and wasting can be identified as the principles underlying everyday life only in a dream. Dream enables one to see more deeply into reality than one can in waking life; it is a form of intuition which, far from escaping from reality, lays bare its deeper structure. In the more specific terms of this particular poem, the art of poetry merges into that of heraldry—both modes of artifice which convey meaning not by imitating the surface appearance of everyday reality, but by stepping back from it, selecting certain objects, and transforming them into the symbols of ideas. The vision of the gathering of the creatures before Nature is a vision of that ordered hierarchy which in medieval times could be seen as underlying the world men directly experienced. And it does not involve pretending that the harsher aspects of experience can be dismissed or disregarded. For example, animals sometimes prey on each other, and Nature cannot be made to order them not to do so; but she can tell the eagle, as king of the birds (and hence James in his role as the enforcer of laws), to ensure that birds of prey should seize only the prey proper to them:

> And lat no fowll of ravyne do efferay,
> Nor devoir birdis bot his awin pray.
>
> (125-26)

And this philosophical vision of hierarchical order merges through heraldry into a political vision of concord between the warring neighbours, England and Scotland. The lion, as well as king of the beasts, is an emblem of Scotland, and is described partly in heraldic terms, standing on a 'field' of gold:

> Reid of his cullour, as is the ruby glance;
> On feild of gold he stude full mychtely,
> With flour delycis sirculit lustely.
>
> (96-8)

It is Nature who lifts him up into the heraldically appropriate rampant posture. By means such as this, political concord is shown as rooted in natural order; but the connection between the two can be seen only through an art which distinguishes itself from nature in order to conceive of nature more clearly. For Dunbar, the image of that art of intellectual vision is the dream; and he is able to re-use the traditional elements of dream-poetry—the paradisal landscape and the comically obstinate dreamer—for a purpose which is at once traditional and new.

A glance at Dunbar's other major courtly dream-allegory, **"The Goldyn Targe,"** will show that its treatment of landscape and weather helps to support what has just been said about **"The Thrissil and the Rois."** In **"The Goldyn Targe"** the dream-world at first is once more a world of conscious artifice, which is also a paradise—it is actually called 'that paradise complete' (72)—beyond the power of the 'ornate stilis' (68) of Homer or Cicero to describe. But this time the subject of the dream is an allegorical love-affair, and, as it proceeds, the paradisal vision collapses, as if in a speeded-up version of the *Roman de la Rose.* The Dreamer is delivered by Danger into the power of Hevynesse, and the paradisal landscape is dissolved by that same god of winds who was the chief representative of the real Scottish climate in **"The Thrissil and the Rois:"**

> Be this the lord of wyndis, wyth wodenes,
> God Eolus, his bugill blew, I gesse,
> That with the blast the levis all to-schuke;
> And sudaynly, in the space of a luke,
> All was hyne went, thare was bot wildernes,
> There was no more bot birdis, bank and bruke.
>
> (229-34)

In the next stanza, the ship which originally brought the personifications through whom the love-affair is recounted sails rapidly away again, firing its guns, and the noise awakens the Dreamer. In this poem, though, dream weather and real weather have changed places, and when he wakes from this dream which has become a nightmare he finds himself in a real paradisal landscape. The love-affair was nothing but a hideous fantasy; the reality is a landscape of rhetorical artifice, in which Dunbar is the humble disciple of the three great English poets, Chaucer, Gower and Lydgate. Like the 'Chaucer' of the dream-poems, he retreats gladly from the pain of love to the comforting artifice of literature; and yet, comparing his work with that of his great predecessors, he feels that 'Rude is thy weid, disteynit, bare and rent' (278)—an obvious parallel to the final state of the landscape in the dream, after Aeolus has been at work. In Dunbar's hands the dream-poem has become a hall of mirrors, in which reality and artifice reflect each other in perpetually recurring paradox. (pp. 191-97)

A. C. Spearing, "The Chaucerian Tradition," in Medieval Dream-Poetry, *Cambridge University Press, 1976, pp. 171-218.*

Lois Ebin (essay date 1980)

[*In the excerpt below, Ebin explores the lasciviousness of Dunbar as exhibited in three of his most popular satires. The poet's introduction of bawdy language into traditional poetic forms, the critic asserts, not only parodies conventional styles but establishes thematic oppositions between illusion and reality.*]

While in recent years critics have devoted a great deal of attention to Chaucer's bawdy, and, as a result of their labors, have left us with more than 25 articles, notes and glosses, and even a book-length commentary on Chaucer's bawdy terms, they have virtually ignored this aspect of Dunbar's writing. Yet bawdy perhaps plays a more significant role in Dunbar's poetry than it does in Chaucer's. Like Chaucer, Dunbar exploits bawdy as an important source of comedy and irony in his work, ranging from the coarse scatalogical humor of the **"Sowtar and Tailyouris War"** and the **"Fenyeit Freir of Tungland,"** not unlike the "ars-metric" of Chaucer's *Summoner's Tale,* to the more sophisticated wit of the **"Dance in the Quenis Chalmer"** and Dunbar's punning address to his purse. But in addition to its humorous function, bawdy in Dunbar's work often serves as a major artistic device by which he revaluates the forms, styles, and traditions to which he turns, and as such it is linked directly to his central techniques as a poet. To illustrate this role of bawdy, I will consider briefly three different kinds of examples—**"Of the Ladyis Solistaris at Court"; "In Secreit Place this Hyndir Nycht"**; and **"The Tretis of the Tua Mariit Wemen and the Wedo."**

In the first of these poems, **"Of the Ladyis Solistaris at Court,"** Dunbar exploits a pivotal bawdy pun to push to its limits a familiar genre of praise—the praise of women—and at the same time to create a potent satire of the contemporary legal system. While his poem, like the many hundreds before it, celebrates "ladyis fair," as we learn at the outset, the lines refer not to courtly ladies but to ladies of the court, solicitors in two senses, suitors who present pleas and prostitutes who trade their favors. From this pun emanates the extensive play with language and meaning in the poem. The "ladyis fair" make "repair," that is, they frequent and they remedy (presumably by their favors) "and in the court ar kend," that is, they are recognized and they are known sexually. In three days, the narrator assures us, they can do more to settle a matter than men can do in ten. "So weill thay ken Quhat tyme and quhen / Thair menes thay sowld mak than." "Menes," according to the *DOST* [*Dictionary of the Older Scottish Tongue from the Twelfth Century to the End of the Seventeenth,* 4 vols., edited by William A. Craigie, 1937-73], suggests both complaints and intercession or remedies in context in the double sense of legal and sexual mediation. With little annoyance, they can end a matter and keep it quiet and "coy," words which gather irony from the surrounding puns. As the narrator assures us, "Thay do no mis, Bot gif thay kis, / And keipis collatioun, / Quhat rek of this? / Thair mater is / Brocht to conclusioun." According to the meanings listed in the *DOST,* these lines suggest at least a triple pun with "collatioun" having the significance of 1) conference or talk, 2) refreshment or reflection before going to bed, and 3) the action of bringing together, while "conclusioun" suggests both an ending, resolution, or agreement and conclusion in the sexual sense.

As we read on, it becomes increasingly difficult to look at even apparently neutral words without suspecting double entendre. The ladies, the narrator reveals, have "grit feill / Ane mater to solist," suggesting a triple pun on "feill," which meant in Dunbar's time not only "touch" but also "understanding" and finally "a large quantity, many." Therefore, the narrator advises men if they have a plea to send in their place their ladies "grathit up gay," for, if they spend (again a bawdy pun), their goods are "nocht the les." Within two hours in a quiet place

They can, percaice, Purches sum grace
At the compositouris.
Thair compositioun, With full remissioun,
Thair fynaly is endit,
With expeditioun And full conditioun,
And thairto seilis appendit.

(35-40)

The lines are loaded with legalistic puns. "Compositioun," according to the *DOST,* refers both to an agreement between parties for the settlement of a dispute, loss, or damage, and to a sum paid in settlement of a claim, a fixed amount agreed upon by both parties. "Remissioun" suggests the act of remitting or paying in both senses, while "expeditioun" refers both to the ladies' assistance or execution of their task and to their promptness, speed, or dispatch. Finally, "Conditioun" legally signifies a point in a compact or agreement, a stipulation or requirement in a bargain, but in context it refers to the fulfillment of the lady solicitors' other sort of bargain as well. Significantly, Dunbar's intricate scheme of internal rhymes in lines 1, 3, 5, 7 of each stanza puts a heavy emphasis on these puns, which regularly occur in the prominent rhyming position.

The narrator concludes by reasserting his admiration for the "ladyis fair." "Sic ladyis wyis Thay ar to pryis, / To say the veretie, / Swa can devyis, And none suppryis / Thame nor thair honestie" (45-48)—playing with the various meanings of "devyis" and "suppryis." Dunbar's persistent punning thus makes shambles of the traditional praise of women and spills over to color even familiar courtly words like "fair," "myld and moy," "coy," "honestie." The nexus of bawdy puns in the poem becomes the vehicle by which the conventional praise is undermined and an anti-genre is erected in its place. Bawdy, however, is a double-edged weapon in this poem. Dunbar's puns also turn his ironic praise of "ladyis fair" into an effective indictment of the contemporary legal system inasmuch as they juxtapose the presumed working of the court and the terms which define it with the subverted version of this activity—the actions of the lady solicitors. The result is a more compelling satire than we find in Dunbar's more direct and impassioned poems like **"Aganis the Solistaris in Court"** which deal with the same subject.

In the second example, **"In Secreit Place this Hyndir Nycht,"** Dunbar exploits, not puns, but levels of diction to revaluate the conventional form he turns to—the pastourelle. Typically, this form involves a seduction of a maiden or a persuasion to love. The man eloquently addresses his plea, the lady responds coyly, and the dialogue usually ends with considerable wit but with little satisfaction for the man. The fun is in the knight's "line" and in the clever evasions of the lady. The humorous possibilities of reversal and variation of this scheme were not lost on Dunbar's predecessors. For example, Henryson in his version of "Robene and Makyne" switches the role of the man and the woman at the outset, making Makyne the eager suitor and Robin the coy and reluctant lover. In **"In Secreit Place this Hyndir Nycht,"** Dunbar begins conventionally enough with the man's impassioned plea for comfort:

My huny, my hart, my hoip, my heill,
I have bene lang your luifar leill,
And can of yow get confort nane;
How lang will ye with danger deill?
Ye brek my hart, my bony ane!

(3-7)

But, as we reach the second stanza, we are jolted by the

diction which Dunbar introduces. Using not the typical langauge of the lover but the colloquial jargon of the cale-besplattered suitor, the "backstairs fornicator," to borrow Kinsley's words [in his *William Dunbar: Poems,* 1958], Dunbar creates a much more extreme version of the effect Chaucer achieves in the *Knight's* and the *Miller's Tales* by his switch from the remote world of ancient Athens and the artificial language of Palamon and Arcite to the contemporary world of Oxford and the banter of "hende" Nicholas. The disparity between the expected diction, the diction characteristic of this genre, and the actual language of Dunbar's characters encourages us to reconsider our assumptions about the form, while the persistent vocabulary of bawdy makes unavoidably explicit the unspoken object of the dialogue. The lover

> . . . wes townysche, peirt, and gukit;
> He clappit fast, he kist, and chukkit,
> As with the glaikis he wer ouirgane;
> Yit be his feirris he wald have fukkit;
> Ye brek my hart, my bony ane!
>
> (10-14)

To create this effect, Dunbar introduces a number of words he uses nowhere else in his poetry, even in his other bawdy works. In the passage above, for example, "glaikis" (sexual desire) is a dialectal word which appears nowhere else in Dunbar, and, according to the *DOST,* not at all among contemporary poets. Again, Dunbar reinforces the impact of his language with rhymes on the most conspicuous words, for example, "gukit / chukkit / fukkit" and later "billie / willie / quhillelillie" (penis).

The density of Dunbar's mixture of colloquial and bawdy diction increases as the lover renews his plea. Combining colloquial terms of endearment with explicit references to his desire, the lover bids the lady, his "claver," his "curldodie" (or ribwort plantain), his "huny soppis," his "sweit possodie" (or sheep's head broth), to be not "oure bosteous" (or hostile) to her "billie." In a ridiculous parody of the language of the love lyric, he concludes, "Your heylis, quhyt as quhalis bane, / Garris ryis on loft my quhillelillie." Clearly moved, but not yet won, the lady describes the lover in an unbroken series of epithets almost as dense as the language of the flyting, though endearing rather than scornful in its effect:

> My clype [big softie], my unspaynit gyane [unweaned giant] . . .
> My belly huddrun, my swete hurle bawsy,
> My huny gukkis [fool], my slawsy gawsy,
> Your musing waild perse ane harte of stane,
> Tak gud confort, my grit heidit slawsy. . . .
>
> (36-41)

The lover musters his linguistic forces for one last valiant attack. His diction becomes even more remote from the courtly as he combines childlike terms of endearment with colloquial Scots and bawdy, addressing the lady as his "kyd," his "capirculyoun" (woodgrouse), his "bony baib," his "tendir gyrle," his "wallie gowdye" (goldfinch), his "tyrlie myrlie," his "crowdie mowdie" (gruel of milk and meal). He ends his plea more explicitly and urgently than before: "Quhone that oure mouthis dois meit at ane, / My stang dois storkyn with your towdie." The lady is overwhelmed, and the poem ends not with their amiable parting, but with consummation as "thai twa to ane play began, / Quhilk men dois call the dery dan"—another version of the Wife of Bath's "olde daunce." The effect of Dunbar's diction in **"In Secreit Place this Hyndir Nycht,"** his mixture of colloquial Scots and explicit bawdy, thus provides a parody of the courtly pastourelle by bringing to the foreground the implicit object of the debate. The unexpected use of bawdy shifts the emphasis of the poem and makes us reconsider our assumptions about the purpose of this traditional form.

In **"The Tretis of the Tua Mariit Wemen and the Wedo,"** Dunbar's use of bawdy is part of a larger system of devices by which he revaluates the courtly tradition, its thematic assumptions, and the poetic medium which embodies them. Like each of the stylistic and structural devices he exploits in the **"Tretis,"** bawdy draws attention to the disparity between appearance and reality, between the glittering surface of the courtly poem and the opposing points of view which lie beneath it. The explicit language of the two women and the widow, though condemned by many critics as "coldly obscene" and "nakedly sexual and lascivious," [H. Grierson and J. C. Smith, *A Critical History of English Poetry,* 1944], provides an important part of the poem's meaning. Dunbar sets the stage for reversal by beginning his poem "Apon the Midsummer evin, mirriest of nichtis," traditionally a time for revelry and for turning topsy-turvy the proprieties and ceremonies of everyday life. But except for his alliterative meter, his style at the outset is familiar and courtly, and we are led to expect a romance or an elegant dream vision like the **"Goldyn Targe"** or the **"Thrissil and the Rois."** The narrator finds himself in the familiar garden of "gay flouris," birds, sweet smells, and "sugarat" sounds of the love vision; similarly, the description of the ladies dressed in fresh flowers, green and gleaming gold, echoes lines from the **"Targe"** and poems of like kind. This courtly diction and detail appear, however, only in the frame. The body of the poem is characterized by a markedly different style and point of view. As the "gay ladies" begin to speak, we are forced to modify our initial expectations. Their explicit, bawdy language is the polar opposite of the idiom of the courtly dame; and the contrast between frame and vision, between the style of the narrator and the style of the dialogue, gradually defines a larger thematic opposition in the poem between what people appear to be and what they are, between the illusions of love and the realities which lie beneath it, and finally between two opposing views of life.

To a great extent, Dunbar establishes these oppositions by his skillful exploitation of bawdy. As the tone shifts in the speech of the first wife, so do our impressions of women, love and marriage. While the Wedo demands, "Think ye it nocht ane blist band that bindis so fast?" the first Wife undoes the meaning of the Wedo's words with her opposing alliterative phrase. "It, that ye call the blist band that bindis so fast, / Is bair of blis, and bailfull, and greit barrat wirkis." To the Wedo's suggestions about free choice, she opposes the view of marriage as "Chenyeis ay . . . to eschew" (53), playing with the Wedo's words "chenyeis" and "changeis." The reversal of meaning becomes even more extreme as the Wife introduces not only reversed phrases but an opposing linguistic mode in the bawdy which dominates the remainder of her speech. Her words, as she continues, work to the opposite end of the aureate speech of the opening frame, not to make their object more splendid and admirable, but, like the language of the flyting tradition which underlies it, to dehumanize, to transform man into an object of scorn and repulsion. The husband becomes a grotesque animal, "ane wallidrag, ane worme, ane auld wobat carle, / A waistit wolroun, na worth bot wourdis to clatter; / Ane bumbart, ane dron bee, ane bag full of flewme, / Ane skabbit skarth, ane scorpioun, ane scutarde behind . . . " (89-92), while his lovemaking is seen as repellent and ugly:

Quhen kissis me that carybald, than kyndillis all my sorow;
As birs of ane brym bair, his berd is als stif,
Bot soft and soupill as the silk is his sary lume;
He may weill to the syn assent, bot sakles is his deidis.

(94-97)

The speech of the second Wife exploits the bawdy mode further to heighten the opposition between what men appear to be and what they are. Though she believed she had "josit a gem," she had in fact "geit gottin." He had the "glemyng of gold, and wes bot glase fundin" (201, 202).

He semys to be sumthing worth, that syphyr in bour,
He lukis as he wald luffit be, thocht he be litill of valour,
He dois as dotit dog that damys on all bussis,
And liftis his leg apone loft, thoght he nought list pische;
He has a luke without lust and lif without curage;
He has a forme without force and fessoun but vertu,
And fair wordis but effect, all fruster of dedis;
He is for ladyis in luf a right lusty schadow,
Bot in to derne, at the deid, he salbe drup fundin. . . .

(184-192)

The Wedo transforms the oppositions the Wives' bawdy defines into a system. Instructing her charges like the "good Wif of biside Bathe" and Jean de Meun's la Veille before her, she teaches the women to exploit the disparity between appearance and reality to their advantage:

Be constant in your governance, and counterfeit gud maneris,
Thought ye be kene, inconstant, and cruell of mynd;
Thought ye as tygris be terne, be tretable in luf,
And be as turtoris in your talk, thought ye haif talis brukill;
Be dragonis baith and dowis ay in double forme,
And quhen it nedis yow, onone, note baith ther strenthis;
Be amyable with humble face, as angellis apperand,
And with a terrebill tail be stangand as edderis;
Be of your luke like innocentis, thoght ye haif evill myndis. . . .

(259-67)

Her speech ends with a marvellously bawdy inversion of the Christian value of *Caritas* as the Wedo offers her love to all, satisfying some from the front and some from behind and those too far away with a suggestive glance.

The narrator abruptly returns to his own courtly idiom in the outer frame as he describes the sun rising and the departure of the ladies, "thir ryall roisis, in ther riche wedis," juxtaposing his elaborate and eloquent words with the women's racy speech:

. . . the day did up daw, and dew donkit flouris;
The morow myld wes and meik, the mavis did sing,
And all remuffit the myst, and the meid smellit;
Silver schouris doune schuke as the schene cristall,
And berdis schoutit in schaw with thair schill notis;
The goldin glitterand gleme so gladit ther hertis,
Thai maid a glorius gle amang the grene bewis.
The soft sowch of the swyr and soune of the stremys,
The sueit savour of the sward and singing of foulis,
Myght confort ony creatur of the kyn of Adam,
And kindill agane his curage, thocht it wer cald sloknyt.
Than rais thir ryall roisis, in ther riche wedis,
And rakit hame to ther rest through the rise blumys. . . .

(512-24)

The linguistic and structural oppositions in the **"Tretis of the Tua Mariit Wemen and the Wedo"** thus establish conflicting realities and perspectives on the action of the poem. The work's two modes of discourse—the aureate and the bawdy—function as polar opposites or inversions of each other, the aureate inflating or enhancing its object, the bawdy dehumanizing or reducing it to an animal level. While the bawdy of the poem's center serves to undercut the splendid vision of the frame and to parody the narrator's courtly point of view and the traditional *chanson de mal-mariée* and *demande d'amour* forms, it is, finally, not accurate to consider the poem simply a parody of conventional styles and forms. In the **"Tretis,"** Dunbar's use of bawdy goes beyond parody to suggest something about the nature of literary language itself and its relation to our perception of reality. The disparity between the poem's styles and the perspectives they embody draws attention to the partial nature of each style as a purveyor of reality. As in Chaucer's *Troilus,* where to a certain extent our conception of the heroine, Criseyde, depends upon the perspective we are allowed by the poet's techniques, with strikingly different impressions being created by the contrasting methods of Books II and IV, so in the **"Tretis"** our vision is dependent upon the specific mode of discourse the narrator chooses to introduce. Like the *Troilus,* the **"Tretis"** ultimately exploits its style to suggest the incomplete nature of human reality and to raise questions about the limits of the poet's medium.

Although this study is confined to three examples of Dunbar's exploitation of bawdy, many equally significant uses of bawdy are found in the other poems, notably in the **"Dance in the Quenis Chalmer," "To the Quene,"** the

"Flyting," the **"Sowtar and Tailyouris War,"** and in the various petitions to the king. As these examples reveal, bawdy is a more important artistic device in Dunbar's work than we have recognized. Bawdy, in Dunbar's hands, is not only a source of humor and irony but often is part of a larger system of techniques by which he reworks the forms, styles, and poetic modes to which he turns. In many poems, bawdy is the means by which Dunbar extends to its limits the medium in which he works and prompts the reader to reconsider the assumptions which underlie his genres and forms. Dunbar's bawdy finally must be considered in the context of his other striking experiments as a poet, that is, as a device which is important to his artistry in ways which often are more central than is bawdy in Chaucer's work. (pp. 278-85)

Lois Ebin, "Dunbar's Bawdy," in The Chaucer Review, *Vol. 14, No. 3, Winter, 1980, pp. 278-86.*

Edmund Reiss (essay date 1984)

[In the following excerpt, Reiss explores Dunbar's use of irony, which, he asserts, the poet employed to express his conviction that the world is basically harmonious yet filled with incongruous elements which confound humanity.]

While acknowledging that William Dunbar may well be the first writer in the English language whose body of work consists almost entirely of short poems, we can hardly help but notice that these more-than-eighty pieces offer such diversity that it is exceedingly difficult to describe the body of poetry itself or the achievement demonstrated by it. Traditional classifications of these poems into such categories as allegories, love poems, invectives, petitions, moralizings, and hymns may give a sense of order, but they actually confirm our impression that Dunbar's poetic offering lacks both unity and a sustained purpose.

We can hardly help but feel that whatever Dunbar may be at one moment, he is apt to be something quite different—unpredictably different—at the next. Though he can put on the garb of the priest—which he was—he can don as easily the motley of the court fool—which, though he was not, he certainly gives the distinct impression of being. And for all the sense we have of his being a sober and serious investigator of the human condition, we have just as great a sense of his being frivolous and zany, indeed a buffoon. We can hardly be blamed for thinking of so protean a poet as the elephant and his readers as the blind men trying to make sense of the strange object before them. With Dunbar's poetry, understanding the parts does not necessarily result in understanding the whole.

Even when we recognize the pervasiveness of the ludic in late medieval literature and the fact the *homo ludens* was at his zenith in the early sixteenth century, we may still have problems knowing just how to view Dunbar. Though we may be able to appreciate much medieval mirth and game and to accept, for instance, Chaucer's bawdy Miller's Tale as a companion-piece to his elegant *Knight's Tale,* we may have difficulty finding in the body of Dunbar's poetry an equally happy marriage of the grave and humorous, the religious and the bawdy, the eloquent and the scatological. We may be more than a little offended that Dunbar, who was capable of writing the perfectly respectable epithalamion **"The Thrissill and the Rois"** and the technically brilliant hymn to the Virgin **"Hale, sterne superne,"** would also pen the embarrassingly vulgar **"Flyting of Dunbar and Kennedie"** and the childishly bawdy **"In secreit place."**

The sense of a schizophrenic division within Dunbar's poetry has been perpetuated by the superficially attractive view of his two voices, one, as John Leyerle would have it [in his "The Two Voices of William Dunbar," *Toronto Quarterly* 31, 1962], eldritch given to pasquinade, and the other aureate given to panegyric. Neat as this distinction may seem, it is unfortunately simplistic and finally misleading. Not only are dozens of Dunbar's poems not accounted for in any kind of meaningful way by Leyerle's two voices, but even Leyerle himself, though maintaining a distinction between them, acknowledges that rarely does Dunbar employ one voice to the complete exclusion of the other. Rather than think that we should speak of two, or for that matter ten, voices—say, one for each mode or genre represented in his work—we should realize that, notwithstanding the various expressions it takes, there is but one main voice in Dunbar's poetry and that is the voice of irony.

No matter whether he is reiterating moral conventions or creating *tours de force* of language, the common denominator in most of Dunbar's eighty-odd poems is his sense of irony. It is this sense that allows for all of the incongruities, for his being both secular and religious, vulgar and aureate; and although he may seem to go from one to the other, we have this impression only because our view is necessarily influenced by our reading one poem at a time. Dunbar is most properly to be understood as blending as well as juxtaposing, offering simultaneously, as it were, the sacred and the profane. His procedure is such that he provides an excellent illustration of what that influential medieval literary theorist Geoffrey of Vinsauf had termed "the conjurer," the poet who transforms the normal order and nature of things. As Geoffrey states it [in his *Poetria nova,* translated by Margaret F. Nims, 1967], the poet's art "causes the last to be first, the future to be present, the oblique to be straight, the remote to be near; what is rustic becomes urbane, what is old becomes new, public things are made private, black things white, and worthless things are made precious." Such is also what the perceptive recent theorist of irony Vladimir Jankélévitch has termed *le confusionisme ironique* [in his *L'ironie,* 1964] where the play with words consciously distorts their sense: it joins together what is different and separates what is similar. Both Jankélévitch and Geoffrey could easily be describing Dunbar's poetry.

But while Dunbar's irony might be most apparent to us through his manipulations of language, we should realize that this irony itself is far more than a matter of surface effects or of tone injected sporadically by the poet into his writing. We may best think of this irony as not so much a particular point, theme, or solution as a general attitude. Hardly what was characterized later in sixteenth-century

England by George Puttenham [in his *The Art of English Poesie*] as "dry mock" or "perverse negativity," this irony is more what Cicero [in his *De orotore*] had termed *perpetuae facetiae,* a pervasive and continuous play that may be seen reflecting the essentially ironic world view of the Middle Ages, and one that was actually quite positive.

Although our modern sense of irony may be the result of doubt about man and the future of this world, irony in the Middle Ages—including Scotland in the late fifteenth and early sixteenth centuries—may be thought of as the result of a sense of certainty. Incongruous as such a notion may appear, we should recognize that Dunbar and his audience knew that regardless of how chaotic and incomprehensible things might seem to be, God was in his heaven and all was right with the world. All things really existed in harmony, and discord was more apparent than real, an aberration created by those unable to see with God's ubiquitous eye. Instead of relying on his faculty of reason, man should realize its limitations. As Nicholas of Cusa had reaffirmed in the mid-fifteenth century [in his *De docta ignorantia*], reason was actually a matter of differentiating; and since its primary rule was noncontradiction, it could never take man to an understanding of the whole, where the ambiguities, confusions, and distortions that fill man's consciousness are resolved.

Not only must man learn to view things *in specie aeternitatis,* he must also appreciate the ultimate harmony of everything, as expressed in the concept of the *connexio rerum*—the joining together of all creation—which, as derived by Thomas Aquinas from Pseudo-Dionysius, led to the formulation by Nicholas that all things, however different they may appear to be, are really linked together in a *concordantia oppositorum,* which stemmed from and relied on a real delight in the diversity of creation. In Aquinas's terms, it is man's awareness of the "heterogeneous whole" as well as the "homogeneous whole" that leads him to praise the *numerositas* and *varietas* of creation [*Summa Theologiae*]. Precisely because of their recognition of the desirability of plentitude and of the real compatibility of apparently disparate entities, as well as their sense of certainty that truth could not be affected by man's confusions or purposeful distortions of it, Dunbar and his audience could delight in the celebration of the ambiguous and the incongruous. The linking together of the improbable as well as the ostensibly contradictory not only provides a basis for the element of counterpoint spoken of by Paul Zumthor [in his *Essai de poétique médiévale,* 1972] in his reference to "the constant possibility of irony" in medieval literature, but also indicates the hallmark of Dunbar's ironic art.

Whereas Dunbar's ironic distortions and plays of antitheses may be seen most readily in such dream fantasies as the **"Dance of the Sevin Deidly Synnis"** and the **"Tournament,"** they should also be recognized in the fictions created by his blendings of the animal and human worlds—in the two James Dog poems, the so-called **"Dance in the Quenis Chalmer,"** and the account of the king's amorous escapades in **"This hyndir nycht in Dumfermeling."** And whereas the irony is obvious in such mythologizings of his contemporary world as the **"Devillis Inquest,"** with its depiction of the marketplace of this world, and in such allegorizations of contemporary events as the two John Damian pieces, it is just as pervasive in his begging poems with their special pleading and all-consuming concern with material gain. The fact that elsewhere Dunbar offers conventional moralizing about man's proper attitude toward earthly wealth may be taken as indicating not his inability to apply this wisdom to himself but rather his ironic use of the personal and the ostensibly autobiographical.

Dunbar's play with conventional attitudes takes a variety of shapes: in **"Sanct salvatour"** he curses money at the same time as he begs for it; in **"He that hes gold,"** he notes man's predicament in this world and concludes by unpredictably counselling merriment instead of concern; and in **"This waverand warldis wretchidnes,"** while addressing the fact of mutability in twenty-five stanzas, he responds in each with the refrain, "to consider is ane pane." Elsewhere he is purposely outrageous in other ways, as when he refers to the lord treasurer of Scotland as "my awin lord thesaurair" and thinks of him as existing for the poet's benefit alone; when he tells the king that he hopes he will be Joan Thompson's man, that is, one who is dominated by his wife; when he urges the king while he is on a religious retreat to quit his purgatory and return to the paradise that is the court; and when he alternates drunken Scottish irreverance and serious Latin liturgical sequences. Still elsewhere Dunbar is purposely contradictory in his treatment of the same subject or issue in several poems: besides begging insistently for advancement and reward while also advocating "discretioun" and the need to be content with little, he presents women as both nonpareils and harridans and both condones all sorts of earthly love and declares that "All lufe is lost bot upone God allone."

Although Dunbar may combine humor and didacticism in a way never imagined by Horace [in his *Ars poetica*], whose dictum that the poet should both delight and instruct was a commonplace in the early sixteenth century, his didacticism is real. Like the second-century Greek writer Lucian—who, perhaps not coincidentally, became known to Northern Europe in Dunbar's lifetime—Dunbar might seem to be an unlikely source of moral and ethical instruction, but we should not assume that ironic fictions are necessarily inimical to eternal values and ultimate truths. If Dunbar had been called upon to define his ironic play, he might have replied as his contemporary Erasmus did when he explained that in his *Praise of Folly* he was taking the *via diversa* and presenting obliquely what he elsewhere presented directly. In being oblique, Dunbar, like Lucian and Erasmus, presents the ridiculous with gravity and the grave ridiculously. Moreover, he may be seen exhibiting vividly the several kinds of humor found in Lucian, which, as described by Erasmus [in his Preface to *Alexander*], include "All the dark humor men attribute to Momus and all the light they ascribe to Mercury."

We may also see in the emphasis on "non-sense" in Dunbar's writing an expression of the compelling notion of learned ignorance (*docta ignorantia*), which while originating with Socrates and developed by Saint Paul and a host of subsequent Christian writers, became in its restatement by Nicholas of Cusa the mark of the age. What this concept emphasized was, paradoxically, the need for man to become the *idiota* so that he might be open to the discovery of truth. Given the sense of the inadequacy of reason and traditional knowledge, the way to wisdom was increasingly seen to lie in accepting the apparently discordant and incomprehensible. By demonstrating the failures of the rational and by emphasizing "unknowing," the poet as well as the philosopher could go beyond the inadequacies of language and the trivialities of its manipulation.

Part of our difficulty in assessing what Dunbar is doing in his poetry comes from our ignorance not only of why a late medieval cleric would even turn to poetry but of what a sixteenth-century Scottish audience expected of its poets. What seems clear, however, is that as a purveyor of sanctity and morality, the court poet was necessarily less effective than the homilist, whose eye was wholly on the sermon and whose writing could be free of such distractions as rhetoric and prosody. The truths expressed by the court poet, though perhaps justifying his work, are hardly original with him, and they certainly do not depend on his poetry for either their existence or their validity. Because these truths are givens, Dunbar is able to employ traditional doctrine without being concerned about validity. Instead of wrestling with doctrinal problems, he can, as ironist, project both the problem and its solution and use the interplay as the structure of his poem.

We can see instances of this procedure in the several moralizings of Dunbar that concern the need for man to understand mutability as the way of the world and turn to that which is unchanging. In **"I seik about this warld unstabille,"** the recognition of mutability leads to the wisdom of the last line, "Sa is this warld, and ay hes bein"; and elsewhere this insight takes the form of a refrain that drives home the lesson of the stanzas: "All erdly joy returnis in pane" and "Into this warld may none assure." These expressions should be regarded not as instances of fatalism but as Dunbar's equivalents to the biblical and liturgical phrases that provide the refrains of other poems: "Vanitas vanitatum et omnia vanitas," "Quod tu in cinerem reverteris," and "Timor mortis conturbat me."

While all these poems have as their premise man's inability or unwillingness to face the fact of mutability, all conclude with full recognition of it and, moreover, with a sense of resolution. In the "makaris" poem that has *timor mortis* as its refrain [**"Lament for the Makaris"**], the initial sickness of the narrator is seen to be due to his recognition of the transitoriness of human life (lines 5-8). The awareness that death takes everyone, not only the noble, powerful, and learned but also the "makaris," extends over twenty-four stanzas as Dunbar shows in instance after instance both the inexorable fact of death and the helplessness of man. But then in the last stanza we are offered the recognition that since there is no remedy for death, it is best for man to prepare for it so that he may live afterwards: "Sen for the ded remeid is none / Best is that we for dede dispone / Eftir our deid that lif may we" (lines 97-99). The *timor mortis* of the refrain, which had begun as a threat to man, becomes by the end of the poem a means of preparing him for his afterlife. Rather than suppose that the last stanza represents an afterthought which Dunbar tacked on to a catalogue of the victims of death, we should realize that it is what the poem has been pointing toward from its outset.

In like manner, other mutability poems of Dunbar offer refrains that, stemming from the recognition of mutability, affirm how man should respond to his new awareness: "For to be blyth me think it best," "Without glaidnes avalis no tresure," and "He hes anewch that is content." What is significant in these pieces is that in all instances comprehension leads to peace of mind and even to happiness: it is hardly accidental that these refrains focus on such terms as "blyth," "glaidnes," and "content." What is ironic is not the transitoriness of life or the inadequacy of this world, or even the awareness of such seen in the course of the poem, but Dunbar's stance in relation to his subject. His simultaneous recognition of the problem and its solution allows him to manipulate the conflict between man's fears and traditional doctrine and to give the sense of a process of discovery even while we recognize that truth has been obvious all along.

To see further how Dunbar's ironic art transforms conventional moralizing into poetry, we may look at one other work, the poem on life [**"Of Lyfe"**], which, taking the form of a single Chaucerian stanza, may be quoted in its entirety:

> Quhat is this lyfe bot ane straucht way to deid,
>   Quhilk hes a tyme to pas and nane to duell;
> A slyding quheill us lent to seik remeid,
>   A fre chois gevin to paradice or hell,
>   A pray to deid, quhome vane is to repell;
> A schoirt torment for infineit glaidnes—
> Als schort ane joy for lestand hevynes.

Though ostensibly beginning as a question, the poem is actually a series of affirmations that take the shape of a definition which is a declaration and not at all an interrogative. That is, while creating a dilemma, Dunbar also offers a reaffirmation of traditional doctrine. His ironic approach to his subject allows him to suggest simultaneously the negative view, that life is the way to "lestand hevynes," and the positive view, that it is the way to "infineit glaidnes." While Dunbar insists that man can make of life what he will, his greatest concern here seems to be with the creation of his paradox, which he brings about through presenting a combination of, on the one hand, contrasting elements and, on the other hand, parallelism of syntax and vocabulary.

The point is that inasmuch as truth is immutable and even obvious, Dunbar is able to play with its shapes and use it as the basis of fictions whose particular significance may be seen to reside less in the traditional doctrine being revealed than in the poetic effort itself. In his various moralizings, as in his other more overtly ironic pieces, Dunbar may be regarded as not so much the preacher or teacher as the poetic craftsman who is concerned with exploring the possibilities of the word and with manipulating its various forms. But, ironically, while appreciating the beauties of language and the potentials of his Scottish vernacular, Dunbar also recognized the essential inadequacy of his writing and the triviality of the poet's activity. Even though the "makar" may seek to imitate the art of his own Maker, he must necessarily be inferior since he has only words to use, and these are both his tools and the products of his creation.

Moreover, as poets are at the mercy of death—they "Playis heir ther pageant, syne gois to graif; / Sparit is nought ther faculte"—so poetry itself is fragile and ephemeral, at the mercy of a host of extraneous factors. As Dunbar's poem on his headache makes clear, even though the poet may intend "to dyt," he can very well be too "dullit" to proceed. Or again, as he shows in **"Sanct salvatour,"** even though he would be delighted to write poems, a lack of spirit prevents him from doing so: "Quhen I wald blythlie ballattis breif / Langour thairto givis me no leif." As he makes clear elsewhere, even harsh weather can take away his desire to write—"Nature all curage me denyis / Off sangis, ballattis and of playis"—and as he indicates in his so-called **"Complaint against Mure,"** the poet's meter may easily be "dismemberit" and his rhetoric turned to "discordis."

Beyond this, as we may see in the **"Flyting of Dunbar and Kennedie"** what comes out of the poet's mouth is not necessarily gold. In fact, although Dunbar may elsewhere affirm that he "will no lesingis put in vers / Lyk as thir jangleris dois rehers," the poet may well be, as Dunbar himself appears in the **"Flyting,"** a raw-mouthed ribald (line 27), whose "wit is thin" (line 354), and who is "imperfyte" in his poetry (line 498). In fact, the actual activity of the poet may be suspect. In the address to the king beginning "Schir, yit remember" [**"To the King"**] although the narrator protests that since he can only write poems—"Allace, I can bot ballattis breif"—he is different from court sycophants who flatter and feign, it is clear that like the flatterers he is asking for preferment. Dunbar may here be ironically linking the activity of the poet with the deceptions of hypocrites and the frauds of the unworthy. As the narrator goes on to complain, even the stable boy who is preferred over him has a false card up his sleeve that is worth all of his poems (lines 68-69).

Whereas, on the other hand, the **"Goldyn Targe"** would seem to offer unambiguous praise of poets and their craft, we should realize that in praising Chaucer's "fresch anamalit termes celicall"—that is, his freshly enameled heavenly phrases—and in noting that Gower and Lydgate "Oure rude langage has clere illumynate, / And fair ourgilt oure spech that imperfyte / Stude," Dunbar treats the famous English triumvirate as though they were painters whose excellence lay in their covering with a gilt veneer that which was crude and ugly. But while the poet may transform what is before him, his powers are clearly limited. The idealized setting of the **"Goldyn Targe,"** for instance, cannot be described even by Homer, no matter how "fair" he could write and notwithstanding all his "ornate stilis so perfyte." Nor, Dunbar adds, could the art of Cicero, for all of its rhetoric, suffice to depict fully this paradise (lines 67-72). Such references indicate that far from being a seer, philosopher, or theologian the poet in Dunbar's view is at best a painter of words and a craftsman of language. Though in offering traditional doctrine he can go beyond being the "lear," the "tratlar," and the "janglar," and though in his singing he may even occasionally participate in the universal hymn of praise to the Creator—"All *Gloria in excelsis* cry, / Hevin, erd, se, man, bird and best"—he most customarily offers his wit, rhetoric, and play for what they are worth in and of themselves.

Dunbar's ironic art, far from being an impediment or alternative to truth, is actually a means of taking his audience to truth. But along with noting the nature and practice of Dunbar's irony, we must do far more if we are to understand fully his poetic achievement. For all of his individuality, Dunbar is also very much a man of his age, and we must examine his individual effort in relationship to those of his contemporaries. How, for instance, is his ironic art distinct not only from that of such early sixteenth-century writers as Skelton, Erasmus, More, and Ulrich von Hutten, with their focus on the foolish and the ridiculous, but also from that of such contemporary artists as Holbein, Dürer, Bosch, and Breughel, with their emphasis on the grotesque and the distorted? Though we can hardly hope to investigate this matter here, we should recognize that, notwithstanding the particular achievements of these poets, thinkers, and artists, they all reveal a "non-sense" that is not a misguided effort but the expression of the natural and the fecund, and as such the way to wisdom. Once we understand Dunbar's place in what may be termed this "age of non-sense," we may most fully appreciate his ironic art. (pp. 321-29)

Edmund Reiss, "The Ironic Art of William Dunbar," in Fifteenth-Century Studies: Recent Essays, *edited by Robert F. Yeager, Archon Books, 1984, pp. 321-31.*

FURTHER READING

Bawcutt, Priscilla. "William Dunbar and Gavin Douglas." In *The History of Scottish Literature,* Vol. 1, edited by Cairns Craig, pp. 73-89. Aberdeen: Aberdeen University Press, 1988.

Provides a general overview of Dunbar's person and poetry with particular emphasis on his craftsmanship.

Baxter, J. W. *William Dunbar: A Biographical Study.* Edinburgh: Oliver and Boyd, 1952, 254 p.

Historical and biographical account of the life, times, and poetry of Dunbar. In particular, Baxter deals with problems of authorship, publication history, and the dating of various works.

Collins, John Churton. "William Dunbar." In his *Ephemera Critica: Or Plain Truths about Current Literature,* pp. 183-92. Westminster: Archibald Constable and Company, 1901.

Negative reaction to Oliphant Smeaton's characterization of Dunbar as a "poet of mighty genius." Collins contends that Dunbar's importance in the history of poetry has been greatly exaggerated since the writer is merely an imitator of Chaucer, Lydgate, and others.

Eddy, Elizabeth Roth. "Sir Thopas and Sir Thomas Norny:

Romance Parody in Chaucer and Dunbar." *The Review of English Studies* XXII, No. 88 (November 1971): 401-09.
Technical comparison of Dunbar's poem "Sir Thomas Norny" and Chaucer's "Sir Thopas," concluding that Dunbar did indeed imitate Chaucer in this piece, particularly in rhyme, language, and humor.

Elton, Oliver. "The Fifteenth Century." In his *The English Muse: A Sketch,* pp. 77-100. London: G. Bell and Sons, 1937.
Examines the Scottish Chaucerians in their historical context. Elton offers qualified praise of Dunbar, calling him a "virtuoso" for his originality and diversity of poetic forms, but also judging his poems occasionally coarse.

Finkelstein, Richard. "Amplification in William Dunbar's Aureate Poetry." *The Scottish Literary Journal* 13, No. 2 (November 1986): 5-15.
Considers the sophistication of Dunbar's poetry. Finkelstein lauds the writer not only for his use of uncommon words, but especially for his rich and varied imagery.

Fox, Denton. "The Scottish Chaucerians." In *Chaucer and Chaucerians: Critical Studies in Middle English Literature,* edited by D. S. Brewer, pp. 164-200. London: Thomas Nelson and Sons, 1966.
Investigates Dunbar's debt to Chaucer, noting "borrowings" of meter, rhetorical devices, diction, and literary genres.

———. "Middle Scots Poetry and Patrons." In *English Court Culture in the Later Middle Ages,* edited by V. J. Scattergood and J. W. Sherborne, pp. 109-27. New York: St. Martin's Press, 1983.
Traces the poetic traditions available to Dunbar, Douglas, and Henryson. Fox assesses how the poets' ties to the Scottish court influenced their choice of one tradition over another.

Fradenburg, Louise O. "Spectacular Fictions: The Body Politic in Chaucer and Dunbar." *Poetics Today* 5, No. 3 (1984): 493-517.
A Freudian interpretation of Chaucer's and Dunbar's use of the "body" as a symbol of the political assembly. Fradenburg hypothesizes that Dunbar's poetry uses the metaphor to reflect upon humanity's immortality: while the physical body perishes, the body politic endures.

Golding, Louis. "The Scottish Chaucerians." *The Saturday Review* 134, No. 3500 (November 25, 1922): 782-83.
Assesses the Scottish Chaucerians as poets in their own right, in some ways superior to Chaucer. Regarding Dunbar, the critic praises his originality and power of speech, but finds that he lacks simplicity and grace.

Gosse, Edmund. "The Close of the Middle Ages." In his *A Short History of Modern English Literature,* pp. 33-72. New York: D. Appleton and Company, 1897.
Outlines the major poems of Dunbar. Gosse refers to the poet as an "oasis" after the desert of fifteenth century English literature.

Grierson, Herbert J. C. and Smith, J. C. "Early Scottish Poetry." In their *A Critical History of English Poetry,* pp. 50-66. 1944. Reprint. London: Chatto and Windus, 1965.
Study of the artistry of Dunbar. Grierson and Smith maintain that Dunbar is the "highest peak" among the range of fifteenth-century Scottish poets.

Hyde, Isabel. "Primary Sources and Associations of Dunbar's Aureate Imagery." *The Modern Language Review* LI, No. 4 (October 1956): 481-92.
A study of the aureate imagery of Dunbar's ceremonial poems. Hyde explores the medieval sources of such images as the dragon, hell, and the pilgrimage, as well as the poet's clever employment of them.

King, Pamela M. "Dunbar's 'The Golden Targe': A Chaucerian Masque." *Studies in Scottish Literature* XIX (1984): 115-31.
General overview of "The Goldyn Targe." King uses the metaphor of theatrical "masque" to analyze the poem as Dunbar's commentary on the false and insincere behavior surrounding the court pageantry of the fifteenth century.

Lewis, C. S. "The Close of the Middle Ages in Scotland." In his *English Literature in the Sixteenth Century Excluding Drama,* pp. 66-156. Oxford: Clarendon Press, 1954.
A categorization of Dunbar's poetic works. Lewis takes exception to the labeling of the writer as a "Scottish Chaucerian" or a "Scottish Skelton," preferring instead to appreciate the poet in his own right.

Leyerle, John. "The Two Voices of William Dunbar." *University of Toronto Quarterly* XXXI, No. 3 (April 1962): 316-38.
Discusses the "aureate" and "eldritch" styles present in Dunbar's works. Leyerle suggests that the varied use of both "voices" qualify the poet as an artist of "brilliance, scope, and variety."

Macdiarmid, Hugh. "Introduction." In his *Selected Poems of William Dunbar,* pp. 7-12. Glasgow: William Maclellan, 1955.
Investigates the dependence of Dunbar on Chaucer. Macdiarmid maintains that there is little commonality between the poets.

Mackay, Æ. J. G. "Introduction." In *The Poems of William Dunbar,* Vol. I, edited by John Small, pp. xi-clii. 1893. Reprint. Hildesheim and New York: Georg Olms Verlag, 1973.
Comprehensive introduction to the study of Dunbar in his historical and social contexts.

Mackenzie, W. Mackay. "William Dunbar." In *Edinburgh Essays on Scots Literature,* pp. 27-55. 1933. Reprint. Freeport, N.Y.: Books for Libraries Press, 1968.
Commendation of Dunbar as a poet of great intensity of expression and originality.

Millar, J. H. "The Golden Age of Scottish Poetry." In his *A Literary History of Scotland,* pp. 46-111. London: T. Fisher Unwin, 1903.
General study of Dunbar's poems with particular stress on their revelations of the poet's personality.

Minto, William. "Scottish Successors." In his *Characteristics of English Poets from Chaucer to Shirley,* pp. 93-115. Boston: Ginn and Company, 1904.
Presents Dunbar as a Chaucerian, but simultaneously emphasizes Dunbar's Scottish temperament, which, he claims, accounts for his originality, rhyme, and use of language.

Moore, Arthur K. "William Dunbar." In his *The Secular Lyric in Middle English,* pp. 195-216. 1951. Reprint. Westport, Conn.: Greenwood Press, 1970.
Presents Dunbar as caught in the tension of a changing

world order between the Middle Ages and the Renaissance. Moore judges that the poet's works exhibit dependence upon medieval conventions, yet are unique in lyricism, rhythm, and overall technical style.

Morgan, Edwin. "Dunbar and the Language of Poetry." In his *Essays,* pp. 81-97. Cheadle, England: Carcanet New Press, 1974.

Discusses the energy of Dunbar's poetry. Morgan extols the writer's syntax and versatility, lauding him as an "outstanding poet."

Nichols, Pierrepont H. "William Dunbar as a Scottish Lydgatian." *PMLA* XLVI, No. 1 (March 1931): 214-24.

Compares Dunbar with Chaucer and Lydgate. Based on an examination of literary themes and vocabulary, Nichols concludes that Dunbar is better termed a "Scottish Lydgatian" than a "Scottish Chaucerian."

Quiller-Couch, Arthur. "After Chaucer." In his *Studies in Literature, Second Series,* pp. 246-78. New York: G. P. Putnam's Sons, 1922.

Unfavorable critique of Dunbar's poetry. Quiller-Couch charges that Dunbar is a "colourist," covering up allegorical deficiencies in his poems with vulgar speech and cluttered images.

Ranken, T. Elliot. "The Scottish Reformation and Vernacular Literature." *The Month* CIII, No. 477 (March 1904): 266-75.

Analyzes the Reformation and its relationship to the development and eventual decline of native Scottish literature. Ranken asserts that Dunbar "is not only the most brilliant poetic genius of his age; he is also incomparably the greatest of all the Scottish poets, and no unworthy rival of Chaucer."

Ridley, Florence H. "The Treatment of Animals in the Poetry of Henryson and Dunbar." *The Chaucer Review* 24, No. 4 (1990): 356-66.

Examines Dunbar's and Henryson's use of animals in their poems and fables. Ridley finds that Dunbar's use of animals is basically "inner-directed," that is, employed to ridicule and satirize the human condition.

Ross, John M. "King James, Henryson, and Dunbar." In his *Scottish History and Literature to the Period of the Reformation,* edited by James Brown, pp. 132-218. Glasgow: James Maclehose and Sons, 1884.

Description of the major poems of Dunbar. Ross contends that the works are responses to the educational, economic, and religious upheavals of the fifteenth century.

Saintsbury, George. "The Prosody of the Scottish Poets." In his *A History of English Prosody,* Vol. I, pp. 265-87. 1908. Reprint. Macmillan and Company, 1923.

Assesses Dunbar's poetic contributions in a general historical overview of fifteenth-century Scottish literature.

Scott, Tom. *Dunbar: A Critical Exposition of the Poems.* Edinburgh: Oliver and Boyd, 1966, 389 p.

Detailed study of the life and poetry of Dunbar.

Shuffleton, Frank. "An Imperial Flower: Dunbar's 'The Golden Targe' and the Court Life of James IV of Scotland." *Studies in Philology* LXXII, No. 2 (April 1975): 193-207.

Provides an historical framework for "The Goldyn Targe" as well as summarizing the major critical contentions regarding the poem's merit.

Sitwell, Edith. "Notes on Certain Poems by Dunbar, Skelton, Gower, and a Poem by an Anonymous Poet." In her *A Poet's Notebook,* pp. 70-84. London: Macmillan and Company, 1943.

Faults Dunbar's works for their harshness of language. Sitwell dismisses the poet himself as an "ungodlike giant of our poetry."

Smeaton, Oliphant. *William Dunbar.* Edinburgh: Oliphant Anderson and Ferrier, 1898, 159 p.

Hails Dunbar as a "poet of mighty genius." Smeaton offers a biographical portrait of the writer with extracts of various poems.

Taylor, Rachel Annand. *Dunbar: The Poet and His Period.* 1931. Reprint. Freeport, N.Y.: Books for Libraries Press, 1970, 87 p.

Negative evaluation of Dunbar. Taylor views the poet as lacking in learning, devoid of technique, and deviant from the cultural folk tradition characteristic of fifteenth-century Scottish literature.

Tilley, E. Allen. "The Meaning of Dunbar's 'The Golden Targe'." *Studies in Scottish Literature* X, No. 4 (April 1973): 210-31.

Elucidates the meaning of "The Goldyn Targe" as a meditation upon humanity's struggle between instinct and reason, and the quest to achieve harmony with nature.

Turville-Petre, Thorlac. "Epilogue: After the Revival." In his *The Alliterative Revival,* pp. 115-43. Cambridge: D. S. Brewer, 1977.

Dissects "The Tretis of the Tua Mariit Wemen and the Wedo" as a literary creation derived from English, French, and Scottish sources.

Wittig, Kurt. "Full Tide: The Makars." In his *The Scottish Tradition in Literature,* pp 33-90. Edinburgh: Oliver and Boyd, 1958.

Compares Dunbar to Henryson, noting the particular milieu and temperament which fashioned Dunbar's singular poetic style.

Robert Henryson

1430?-1506?

(Also Henrysoune and Henrysone) Scottish poet and fabulist.

INTRODUCTION

Henryson is considered the most prominent of the Scottish Chaucerian poets, or *makars,* after William Dunbar. The major characteristics of his works—his ironic humor, his colloquial dialogue, and his talent as a master storyteller—indicate that Henryson was highly influenced by Chaucer. Critics generally agree, however, that Henryson was no mere imitator of Chaucer, for his imaginative powers of observation, his economic style of expression, and his authentic portraits of animals, humans, and their surroundings all demonstrate that he is an important literary figure in his own right. Although he wrote a number of poems, Henryson is primarily known for *The Testament of Cresseid* (1492?), a continuation of Chaucer's *Troilus and Criseyde,* and *The Morall Fabillis of Esope the Phrygian* (1462-88?). Henryson's original treatment of Chaucer's heroine in his own poem and his masterful adaptation of Aesop's fables into the Scottish vernacular attest to his poetic genius and place him among the finest poets in Scottish literature.

The facts of Henryson's life and career are virtually unknown and his biography almost entirely rests on speculation. Based on several historical references, including the title page of the 1569 edition of his *Morall Fabillis,* critics generally surmise that he held the position of schoolmaster at Dunfermline in Fife. Some sources also identify him as "Master Robert Henryson," which implies that he was a master of arts. Presumably, he earned this degree abroad for he is not mentioned in any Scottish university's register until 1462, when a Robert Henryson, who held a master of arts and an additional bachelor in canon law, was incorporated into the University of Glasgow. While it is true that Robert Henryson was a common name at that time, most scholars believe that the poet's knowledge of legal matters and vocabulary, exhibited in some of his fables, confirm that it was he who entered Glasgow, possibly to lecture in law. This conclusion also supports the theory advanced by critics that according to some documents, Henryson witnessed the charters of the nearby Benedictine abbey as a notary public; however, such a function would have required him to be a clergyman. Henryson's works do exhibit a Christian moralism that lends credence to this notion, but no records survive to substantiate such speculation. One of the only details that scholars affirm with any certainty is that Henryson died early in the sixteenth century. This supposition is drawn from Dunbar's reference to the poet's death in *The Lament for the Makars,* written around 1506: "In Dunfermline, he [Death] hes done roune,/ With Maister Robert Henrysoune."

Like his life, Henryson's works cannot be precisely dated, but critics believe that he flourished from 1450 to 1490. Of all Henryson's works, *The Testament of Cresseid* has attracted the most wide-ranging attention from commentators. Written as a sequel to Chaucer's *Troilus and Criseyde,* the *Testament* has generated a significant amount of literary criticism and has prompted several comparative studies. In fact, the structure and style of the two works are so similar that many sixteenth-century scholars and editors mistook the *Testament* as the last book of Chaucer's poem and appended it to their editions of that work. This error was not corrected until 1593 when Henrie Charteris published *The Testament of Cresseid, Complyit be M. Robert Henrysone, Sculemaister in Dunfermline,* although many editions continued to attribute the work to Chaucer well into the next century. Henryson also borrowed subject matter from a Latin translation of Aesop's fables that was immensely popular among medieval audiences, and many critics consider his adaptation, *The Morall Fabillis of Esope the Phrygian,* his most original work. In truth, only seven of the *Morall Fabillis* are Aesopic, while the remaining six are members of the Reynardian cycle, folktales which depict the exploits of Reynard the fox. Chief among the stories found in the *Morall Fabillis* are "The Taill of the Uponlandis Mous and the Burges Mous," "The Taill of Schir Chantecleir and the Foxe," and "The Preiching of the Swallow," all of which demonstrate, according to scholars, Henryson's skillful rendering of such techniques as characterization, visual effect, irony, and humor. Henryson's canon also includes several minor poems, of which the most notable are *Orpheus and Eurydice* (1450-62?), the allegorical *Bludy Serk* (1450-62?), and *Robene and Makyne* (1450-62?), a work many commentators believe to be the first pastoral in the English language.

A. M. Kinghorn has well described the nature of Henryson's critical reception over the past five centuries. According to Kinghorn, "not being an innovator in poetic forms and styles, [Henryson] has not served as a model for later poets, . . . and his firm intellectual rooting in the traditional learning of the Middle Ages, together with a saintly conservatism of temperament, has made of him an occasionally admired, but largely neglected *makar.*" Before the twentieth century, literary studies of the *Testament* only existed in editions focusing on Chaucer's works and in historical literature surveys. During this period, critics uniformly maintained that, if as an imitation of *Troilus and Criseyde* Henryson's work lacks Chaucer's wit and sublime conception, the poem nevertheless compensates by refashioning its source into a compact and highly stylized reflection on the influences and morals of his own time. Consequently, the *Testament* has been variously interpreted as inferior or superior to Chaucer's *Troilus* depending on how commentators have compared the two works. Turn-of-the-century scholars generally upheld their predecessors' opinions, but appreciation for the *Testament* as a literary masterpiece in its own right became more widespread by the mid-twentieth century, when Herbert Grierson declared it "perhaps the most original poem that Scotland has produced. It was no light thing to come after Boccaccio and Chaucer, and to succeed in making a real addition to a great dramatic story, something that without needless challenging of comparison does, in its impressive way, complete that tragic tale."

As critics began to examine the *Testament* more closely, they became increasingly aware of Henryson's skillful manipulation of the conventions found in his source, his economy of expression, and his complex poetic structure. Earlier critics had condemned Henryson for what they considered his overly harsh treatment of Cresseid in the *Testament,* especially in comparison with Chaucer's detached lack of judgement towards his Criseyde. Yet when critics began to probe the medieval influences inherent in Henryson's poem, they found that his use of the themes of leprosy and the planet gods revealed how tightly the poet had constructed his narrative to develop the perfect retribution for Cresseid's apostasy at the beginning of the *Testament.* In the course of the work, Henryson engineered a reunion with Troilus that compelled Cresseid to examine her actions, admit her betrayal of him, and finally, achieve moral elevation through her insight and contrition. As a result of such analyses, recent critics have come to regard the *Testament* as a challenging narrative and to admire the poem for its great complexity and energy.

Henryson's other major work, the *Morall Fabillis,* has a similar critical history to that of the *Testament.* Because of the didactic nature of the collection—each fable concludes with an expository *moralitas*—early critics interpreted the work in connection with the tradition that Henryson was a provincial, moralistic schoolmaster, and many commentators attributed his motivation to adapt Aesop's fables to his commitment to moral instruction. This representation of the poet influenced much of the literary criticism of Henryson prior to the twentieth century, and while he was praised for his ironic humor and his attention to detail, the work was often censured for prolixity and tedious morality. As the twentieth century approached, scholars began to offer increasingly favorable assessments of the *Morall Fabillis,* as is evidenced in John M. Ross's judgement that Aesop's fables "[had] never been illustrated with such wealth of descriptive imagery and fulness of incident, humorous and sentimental, as in the forgotten version of this gifted Scot." Through closer analyses of the *Morall Fabillis,* commentators began to discuss the colloquial structure of the tales in relation to Henryson's naturalistic observations of his medieval Scottish surroundings, noting that this use of local elements exemplified his humanism. In addition, critics perceived in these characteristics some literary commentary on such issues as religious corruption and social problems in Scotland. During the twentieth century, scholars have provided comparative studies on the individual tales in the *Morall Fabillis* with other traditional folktales; Henryson's Reynardian fables have been explored in relation to similar beast tales, and some fables, like "The Taill of Schir Chantecleir and the Foxe," have been portrayed against parallel themes in Chaucer's *The Canterbury Tales.* One frequently recurring observation among critics who have examined the various elements of the *Morall Fabillis* is that Henryson's extraordinary ability to invest his animal figures with human traits and attitudes gives each fable a dimension of full character and symmetry. In addition, commentators have reassessed the importance of Henryson's moral seriousness and the role of the *moralitas* to the understanding of each fable, as well as the entire work. Such evaluations have continued to stimulate analyses of Henryson's fables among modern critics.

Recent critical appreciation of Henryson's works attests to the poet's enduring appeal with scholars. While he was certainly influenced by Chaucer, his success with both conventional and original literary forms helped establish Henryson as one of the foremost Scottish Chaucerians. Commentator Kurt Wittig spared no praise when he summarized the poet's achievements: "In his assimilation of European subject matter, of Chaucer's conception of poetic art, and of Scottish characteristics, Robert Henryson is one of the greatest poets of the whole of Scottish literature, perhaps the greatest of all, and certainly the one with the most marked personality."

PRINCIPAL WORKS*

The Bludy Serk (poem) 1450-62
The Garmont of Gud Ladeis (poem) 1450-62
Orpheus and Eurydice (poem) 1450-62
Ane Prayer for the Pest (poem) 1450-62
Robene and Makyne (poem) 1450-62
Sum Practysis of Medecyne (poem) 1450-62
The Morall Fabillis of Esope the Phrygian (fables) 1462-88
The Thre Deid Pollis (poem) 1462-88
The Abbay Walk (poem) ca. 1488
The Annunciation (poem) ca. 1488
The Prais of Aige (poem) ca. 1488
The Ressoning betuix Aige and Yowth (poem) ca. 1488
The Ressoning betuix Deth and Man (poem) ca. 1488
†*The Testament of Cresseid* (poem) 1492?
The Poems and Fables of Robert Henryson (poetry and fables) 1865
The Poems and Fables of Robert Henryson, Schoolmaster of Dunfermline (poetry and fables) 1933
The Poems of Robert Henryson (poetry and fables) 1981

*The dates below reflect probable composition dates for Henryson's principal works, not publication dates.

†This work was first published in Francis Thynne's 1532 edition of Chaucer's works and was originally attributed to Chaucer.

William Godwin (essay date 1804)

[*An English philosopher, novelist, and essayist, Godwin is remembered as an author whose writings strongly influenced the English Romantic writers. In the following excerpt, Godwin favorably assesses Henryson's* Testament of Cresseid *as an individual work, but judges it an unworthy addition to Chaucer's* Troilus and Criseyde.]

Many marks of approbation have been conferred upon the poem of *Troilus and Creseide*. . . . A poet of a succeeding age, who now appears to have been Mr. Robert Henryson, wrote a sequel to the poem, or sixth book, which ordinarily bears the name of the ***Testament of Creseide.*** This is to be found in most of the editions of Chaucer; is printed by the earlier editors without any notice of distinction, as if it had been the work of Chaucer himself. . . . The sequel however contains in itself the most explicit declaration that it is not the production of Chaucer. . . . (pp. 486-87)

Henryson perceived what there was defective in the close of the story of *Troilus and Creseide,* as Chaucer has left it. It is true that the law of poetical justice, as it has been technically termed by some modern critics, has been urged to a ridiculous strictness, and that the uniform observation of this law is by no means necessary to the producing the noblest and most admirable effects. The scheme of real events, and the course of nature, so far as we are able to follow it, is conducted by no rule analogous to this of poetical justice; and the works of human imagination ought to be copies of what is to be found in the great volume of the universe. Poetry has a right to deal in select nature; but its selections should not be so fastidious as to exclude the most impressive scenes which nature has to boast. No true critic would wish Lear, Othello and the Orphan not to have existed, or scarcely to be in any respect other than as they are. Two of the three could not have been changed in their catastrophe, without the destruction of the main principles of their texture. But, though virtue may be shown unfortunate, vice should not be dismissed triumphant. It is not perhaps necessary that it should always be seen overtaken by some striking and terrible retribution; but it should not appear ultimately tranquil and self-satisfied; for such is not its fortune on the great stage of the world. It is followed in most instances by remorse; or, when it is not, remorse is only excluded by a certain hardness and brutality of temper, which is solitary in its character, and incompatible with genuine delight. Henryson therefore judged truly, when he regarded the poem of Chaucer as in this respect faulty and incomplete. The inconstant and unfeeling Creseide, as she appears in the last book of Chaucer, is the just object of aversion, and no reader can be satisfied that Troilus, the loyal and heroic lover, should suffer all the consequences of her crime, while she escapes with impunity.

The poem of Henryson has a degree of merit calculated to make us regret that it is not a performance standing by itself, instead of thus serving merely as an appendage to the work of another. The author has conceived in a very poetical manner his description of the season in which he supposes himself to have written this dolorous tragedy. The sun was in Aries; his setting was ushered in with furious storms of hail; the cold was biting and intense; and the poet sat in a solitary little building which he calls his "orature." The evening star had just risen.

> Throughout the glasse her bemés brast so faire,
> That I might se on every side me by;
> The northren winde hath purified the aire,
> And shedde his misty cloudés fro the skie;
> The frost fresed, the blastés bitterly
> Fro pole Artike come whisking loud and shill.

Creseide is then represented as deserted of Diomed, filled with discontent, and venting her rage in bitter revilings against Venus and Cupid. Her ingratitude is resented by these deities, who call a council of the seven planets. The persons of the Gods bearing the names of these planets are described with great spirit. Saturn, for example,

> Whiche gave to Cupide litel reverence,
> But as a boistous chorle in his manere
> Came crabbedly with austern loke and chere.
>
> His face frounsed, his lere was like the lede,
> His tethe chattred, and shiver'd with the chin,
> His eien droup'd hole sonken in his hede,
> With lippés blew, and chekés lene and thin.
>
> Attour his belte his liart lockés laie,
> Feltred unfaire, o'er fret with frostés hore,
> His widdred wede fro him the winde out wore.

In the council it is decreed that Creseide shall be punished with leprosy. Cynthia is deputed in a vision to inform her of her fate. She wakes and finds that her dream is true. She then intreats her father to conduct her, unknown, to a hospital for lepers. By the governors of this hospital she is compelled to go as a beggar on the highway, with a bell and clapper, as we read was anciently practised by lepers. Among the passers by, comes Troilus, who in spite of the dreadful disfigurement of her person, finds something in her that he thinks he had seen before, and even draws from a glance of her horrible countenance a confused recollection of the sweet visage and amorous glances of his beloved Creseide. His instinct leads him no further: he does not suspect that his mistress is actually before him. Yet

> For knightly pitie and memoriell
> Of faire Creseide,

he takes "a girdle, a purse of golde, and many a gaie jewell, and shakes them doun in the skirte" of the miserable beggar:

> Than rode awaie, and nat a worde he spake.

No sooner is he gone, than Creseide becomes aware that her benefactor is no other than Troilus himself. Affected by this unexpected occurrence, she falls into a frenzy, betrays her real name and condition, bequeaths to Troilus a ring which he had given her in dowry, and dies. Troilus laments her fate, and builds her monument.

It seemed to be the more proper that we should take thus much notice of the poem of the schoolmaster of Dumferling, that by contrasting Henryson and Chaucer, we might be the better able to judge of the vicissitudes of poetry and the progress of taste between the reigns of Edward III. and Henry VIII. The combat indeed is not exactly equal, since Chaucer possessed at least all the advantages of education which England could afford, if he were not yet a courtier, when he wrote his *Troilus and Creseide,* and Henryson was no more than a provincial schoolmaster. Accordingly the judicious reader will perceive that the Scottish, was incapable of rising to the refinements, or conceiving the delicacies of the English, poet: though it must be admitted that in the single instance of the state of mind, the half-recognition, half ignorance, attributed to Troilus in his last encounter with Creseide, there is a felicity of conception impossible to be surpassed. In some respects the younger poet has clearly the advantage over the more ancient. There is in his piece abundance of incident, of imagery and of painting, without tediousness, with scarcely one of those lagging, impertinent and unmeaning lines with which the production of Chaucer is so frequently degraded.

The principal circumstance however to be remarked respecting the poem of Henryson, is that, whatever eminence of merit may justly be ascribed to it, it does not belong to the *Troilus and Creseide.* Chaucer disowns the alliance of the Scottish poet. The great excellences of Chaucer's poem are its simplicity, its mild and human character, and that it does not sully the imagination of the reader with pictures of disgust and deformity. Highway-beggary, the bell and clapper, the leprosy, and the hideous loathsomeness of Henryson's Creseide, start away from, and refuse to be joined to, the magic sweetness and softness of Chaucer. No reader, who has truly entered into the sentiment of kindness, sympathy and love subsisting between Chaucer's personages, will consent that Creseide, however apostate, shall be overtaken by so savage and heart-appalling a retribution. This is not a species of chastisement that can be recognised in the court of the God whose battery is smiles, and whose hostility averted glances and lips of amorous resentment. (pp. 487-95)

William Godwin, "Sequel to 'Troilus and Creseide' by Robert Henryson—Tragedy of Shakespear on the Subject," in his Life of Geoffrey Chaucer, Vol. I, *second edition, 1804. Reprint by AMS Press Inc., 1974, pp. 486-515.*

David Irving (essay date 1804)

[In the excerpt below, Irving briefly surveys Henryson's principal works.]

The genius of Henryson seems to have been well adapted to didactic poetry, or that species which professes to convey to the mind of the reader important truths decked in an alluring garb. He has however attempted various modes of composition, and few without success. To his skill in versification he unites a power of poetical conception, of which that age did not furnish many examples. His verses, if devested of their uncouth orthography, might often be mistaken for those of some poet of the present day.

The longest of his poems is the ***Testament of Faire Creseide;*** of which the subject was suggested by the perusal of Chaucer's *Troilus and Creseide.* This production contains many strokes of poetical description which a writer of more than ordinary genius could only have produced. Propriety, it must be admitted, is frequently violated: but the beauties of the work are more than sufficient to counterbalance its deformities. (pp. 377-78)

Creseide having returned to the habitation of her father, is represented as despondent and querulous: she shuts herself up in an oratory, and begins to upbraid Venus and Cupid for having permitted her to sink into such hopeless misery:

> Whan this was said, doun in an extasy,
> Ravished in spirite, in a dreme she fel,
> And by apparaunce herde where she did lie
> Cupide the King tinging a silvir bel,
> Which men might here fro hevin into hel;
> At whose sounde before Cupido aperes
> The seven planets discending fro the spheres.

This silver bell is certainly possest of no common virtues: but the reader is not prepared to expect such consequences from its ringing.—Henryson's knowledge of astronomy seems to have been extremely imperfect. According to his notion, the planets are seven in number; namely Saturn, Jupiter, Mars, Phœbus, Venus, Mercury, and Cynthia. And when they are thus introduced, he is by no means sufficiently careful to preserve their personified characters: they are sometimes planets, and sometimes gods and goddesses.

Perhaps the most striking passage which his works contain, is his delineation of the person of Saturn. Though some of the touches may be calculated to excite disgust, the picture is evidently drawn with a bold and masterly hand:

> His face frounsid, his lere was like the lede,
> His tethe chattrid, and shivered with the chin,
> His eyin droupid, whole sonkin in his hede,
> Out at his nose the mildrop fast gan rin;
> With lippis blew, and chekis lene and thin;
> The iseickils that fro his heer doune honge
> Was wondir grete, and as a spere was longe.
>
> Attour his belte his liart lockis laie
> Feltrid unfaire, or fret with frostis hore;
> His garment and his gite ful gay of graie,
> His widrid wede fro him the winde out wore;
> A bousteous bowe within his honde he bore,
> Undir his girdle a fashe of felone flains
> Fedrid with ise and hedid with holstains.

Other figures of the group are also depicted with strength of colouring. The picture of "Lady Cynthia" however is totally devoid of congruity: if the poet regard her as a person, his description is wild and unappropriate; if as the moon, he ought to have recollected that a planet cannot conveniently enter the door of an oratory. It may indeed be urged in his defence, that as these personages are only supposed to have been beheld through the medium of a dream, the utmost congruity was not indispensibly requisite.

The attributes of Mercury, as exhibited by Henryson, are altogether inconsistent with classical notions. He is properly represented as "right eloquent and ful of rethorie;" but why he should be invested with a doctor's gown, it will perhaps be difficult to discover:

Boxis he bare with fine electuares
And sugrid siropes for digestion,
Spices belonging to the potiquares,
With many wholsome swete confection;
Doctor in Phisike cledde in scarlet goun,
And furrid wel, as suche one ought to be,
Honest and gode, and not a worde couth lie.

The honesty of Mercury has always been regarded as somewhat equivocal: and if the precedent character be drawn with impartiality, Horace must have been little acquainted with his history:

Te canam, magni Jovis et Deorum
Nuntium, curvæque lyræ parentem;
Callidum, quidquid placuit, jocoso
Condere furto.

The remainder of this poem, though less remarkable than the visionary scene, may also be perused with pleasure. (pp. 380-83)

Of the ***Fabils*** of Henryson several have been published. That of **"The Lyon and the Mous"** he feigns himself to have received from Æsop in one of his day-dreams. Æsop informs him that the place of his birth was Rome, and that he was there initiated in the mysteries of science. When Henryson is apprized of the character of his aërial visitor; he with profound reverence addresses him by the titles of poet and laureat. From these circumstances it is evident that he was totally unacquainted even with the history of the writings which are commonly ascribed to Æsop the Phrygian, but which Dr Bentley, a critic of admirable sagacity, has demonstrated to belong to the catalogue of spurious productions. The work which he had perused must have been some metrical version in Latin.

The introductory part of this fable possesses uncommon beauty. The following passage in particular is too remarkable to be overlooked:

In myddis of June, that joly sucit sessoun,
Quhen that fair Phebus, with his beamis brycht,
Had dryit up the dew fra daill and down,
And all the land maid with his lemys lycht;
In a morning betwene mid-day and nycht,
I raiss and put all sluith and sleep on syde;
Ontill a wod I went allone, but gyd.

Sueit was the smell of flouris quhyt and reid,
The noyis of birdis rycht delitious;
The bewis brod blwmyt abone my heid;
The grund growand with grassis gratious:
Of all pleasans that place was plenteous,
With sueit odours and birdis armonie;
The mornyng myld my mirth was mair forthy.

The roseis reid arrayit rone and ryss,
The primrose and the purpure viola:
To heir it was a poynt of paradyss,
Sic myrth the mavyss and the merle cowth ma:
The blossoms blyth brak up on bank and bra;
The smell of herbis, and of foulis the cry,
Contending quha suld have the victory.

The apologue of **"The Borrowstoun Mous and the Landwart Mous"** may be regarded as his most happy effort in this department. The same tale has been told by many poets, ancient as well as modern; and among the rest by Horace, Cowley, and La Fontaine; though the latter has substituted rats instead of mice.

The general fault of his fables is, that they are too much protracted. The apologues of the spurious Æsop, of Phædrus, Poggius, and Abstemius, seldom exceed the bounds of a few lines; whereas those of Henryson are extended over a surface of many pages.

The ***Garment of Gude Ladyis*** is a poem of a fanciful construction; but, as Lord Hailes has justly remarked [in his *Ancient Scottish Poems*], "the comparison between female ornaments and female virtues is extended throughout so many lines, and with so much of a tire-woman's detail, that it becomes somewhat ridiculous."

The ***Abbay Walk*** is of a solemn character, and not altogether incapable of impressing the imagination. Its object is to inculcate submission to the various dispensations of providence: and in the management of this theme he evinces some degree of skill in the poetical art. His thoughts are such as the pious mind willingly recognizes; nor are they debased by an unsuitable poverty of diction. (pp. 383-85)

The ***Prais of Ege,*** the ***Ressoning betwixt Deth and Man,*** and the ***Ressoning betwixt Aige and Yowth,*** are of the same religious complexion, though of inferior beauty.

The Bludy Serk, which has been classed among his fables, is an allegorical composition of considerable merit. The poet represents the accomplished daughter of a mighty monarch as having been carried away by a hideous giant, and cast into a dungeon, where she was doomed to remain until some courteous knight should atchieve her deliverance. A worthy prince at length appeared as her champion, vanquished the giant, and thrust him into the loathsome dungeon which he had prepared for others. When he had restored the damsel to her father, he felt that death must speedily be the consequence of the wounds which he had received in the combat. To her he bequeathed his *bludy serk,* and solemnly enjoined her to contemplate it whenever another lover should happen to present himself. (pp. 386-87)

But the most beautiful of his productions is the pastoral entitled ***Robene and Makyne;*** which I regard as superior in many respects to the similar attempts of Spenser and Browne. Free from the glaring improprieties which appear in the eclogues of those writers, it exhibits many genuine strokes of poetical delineation, and evinces the author to have been intimately acquainted with human character. Robene's indifference seems indeed to be rather suddenly converted into love: but this is perhaps the only misrepresentation of the operations of nature into which the poet has been betrayed. The fable is skilfully conducted: the sentiments and manners are truly pastoral; and the diction possesses wonderful terseness and suavity. (p. 388)

David Irving, "The Life of Robert Henryson," in his The Lives of the Scottish Poets, Vol. I, *Alex. Lawrie and Co., 1804, pp. 375-88.*

John M. Ross (essay date 1884)

[*In the excerpt below, Ross favorably comments on Henryson's major works, particularly* Robene and Makyne *and the* Testament of Cresseid.]

Such poems as ***The Abbay Walk, The Prais of Aige, The Ressoning betwixt Deth and Man,*** are fine examples of the grave, serious, and thoughtful spirit of [Robert Henryson]. Their didactic tone is not that of a cold philosophy, but of a warm and living Christianity. As he paces alone the cloisters of an abbey "fair to se," and muses on the changeful fortunes of men, the divine truth is brought home to him that nothing in this world comes by chance, that all happens by the great provision of God, and that the supreme duty of man is loyal obedience to the mysterious Will.

Obey, and thank thy God of all.

The Prais of Aige is distinctly coloured by the public calamities of his time. In the following lines we can read the protest of a meek and gentle and pious nature against the brutal license and greed of the feudal magnates:—

Now trewth is tynt, gyle hes the governance,
And wrachitness hes turnyt al fra weill to wo;
Fredoume is tynt, and flemyt the Lordis fro,
And cuvattyce is all the cause of this.

The burden of the poem is

The moyr of aige the nerar hevynnis blis.

It is supposed to be sung in a garden of roses by a man, old and decrepid, but with a clear and sweet voice. He is full of joy at the thought of parting with this false world, where nought is certain but uncertainty.

This day a King, the morne na thing to spend!
Quhat haif we heyr bot grace us to defend?
The quhilk God grant us till amend our myss,
That till His joy He may our saullis send;
The moyr of aige the nerar hevynnis bliss.

Still more solemn and impressive is the dialogue or ***Ressoning*** between Death and Man. The former proclaims his resistless power. None can withstand him, "paip, empriour, king, barroun, and knycht." Man, for a moment boastful of his youth, refuses to yield to the stranger; but when the dread name of the latter is announced ("They call me Deth"), his arrogance vanishes in confession of sin and humble acceptance of his fate:

Jesus, on thee, with peteous voce, I cry,
Mercy on me to haif on domisday.

Beautiful in its way is ***The Bludy Serk,*** a version in ballad-metre of one of those curious allegorical tales in the *Gesta Romanorum,* in which religious doctrines are expounded through exploits of chivalry. The deliverance of the soul from the power of Hell was, perhaps, never more quaintly or poetically told than in this piece, where each thing seems a part of some mortal adventure in real life, till all is moralized at the last into theology. ***The Salutation of the Virgin*** is a devotional lyric, full of sweetness and grace.

O lady, lele and lusumest,
Thy face moist fair and schene is!
O blosum blith, and bowsumest,
Fra carnale cryme that clene is.

The strictest Protestant will readily forgive its Mariolatry for the sake of the deep spiritual feeling that pervades and sustains it. There is no evidence that Henryson had taken priest's orders. He is nowhere styled *clericus* or *presbyter;* but his heart is tuned to heavenly music, and he lives "as ever in his great Taskmaster's eye."

Henryson's piety, however, has nothing austere or ascetic about it. It is sweet and natural, and is compatible with sympathies and interests from which a monk would shrink as from sin. An instance in point is the ballad of ***Robene and Makyne,*** one of the loveliest pastorals in all literature. Every stanza has its own particular charm. The green hill with its belt of wood, and flock of sheep, the summer night warm and dry, the yearning passion of the maid, the cruel repulse by the cold-hearted youth, his quick remorse, and unavailing efforts to win the love he had slighted and scorned:

Robene, thow hes hard soung and say,
In gestis and storeis auld,
'The man that will nocht quhen he may,
Sall haif nocht quhen he wald.'
I pray to Jesu, every day,
Mot eik thair cairis cauld,
That first preissis with thee to play,
Be firth, forrest, or fauld:

—all stands out, even in the antique dialect, as clear and vivid as if Burns or Tennyson had penned the verses. How pathetic the sad assurance of these lines—

Robene, that warld is all away,
And quyt brocht till ane end,
And nevir agane thairto perfay
Sall it be as thow wend.

The note here struck is of the truest. The poet leaves Makyne going home "blyth anneuche" "attour" the forest grey, while Robene sits down in dolour and care at the foot of a steep bank to mourn his inexpiable folly. Scotsmen may reasonably be proud that in the department of pastoral poetry their mother tongue is at least the rival of Greece, and the superior of Rome; for there is nothing in the Thyrsis or Amaryllis of Theocritus that can excel, nothing in Virgil that can equal, in point of sweetness and fidelity to nature, Ramsay's *Gentle Shepherd* or Henryson's ***Robene and Makyne.***

The fables ascribed to Æsop have found their way into every European tongue, but they have never been illustrated with such wealth of descriptive imagery and fulness of incident, humorous and sentimental, as in the forgotten version of this gifted Scot. Lord Hailes has censured the prolixity of these renderings and pronounced them tedious; but though they lack the terseness of the classic originals, few will agree with his lordship's criticism. They have the genuine character of such works. The animals are clothed with all the attributes of humanity, and are presented in the guise of the poet's own time. Thus we have, as it were, unintentional delineations of contemporary manners and institutions that are as fresh are they are valuable. Take for example one or two circumstances from

"The Taill of the Uplandis Mous and the Burges Mous." While the former lived solitarily like an outlaw, the latter is "gild-brother" and "ane free burges." When she goes to visit her upland sister, she passes out of town barefooted, with pikestaff in her hand like a poor pilgrim. At their meeting they embrace and kiss each other, now laughing and now crying for joy. The rustic dinner is brought from the "butterie," and excites the scorn of the city-bred "madame." By and by we have an elaborate civic feast "with all the coursis that cuikis culd defyne." In fact take away the element of fable and in every case these poems resolve themselves into pictures of real life by an artist who has a fine eye for "the outward shows of sky and earth," for social usages, and traits of character; and whose shrewdness of observation is sweetened by a kindly humour that makes us love the writer.

In no essential respect does the literary skill of the workmanship seem to us inferior to Chaucer's; but Henryson most nearly approaches the master in his ***Testament of Cresseid.*** It is a continuation of Chaucer's *Troilus and Creseide,* and is inspired by a keener moral sense. The English poet leaves the infidelity of the Trojan maid unpunished. While the noble Troilus perishes on the field of battle, his false bride remains in the possession of the treacherous Diomede. Henryson thought her story should have a different ending, and hence his novel episode, a masterpiece of melodious versification and pathetic sentiment. The introduction is charming. It is a frosty night in early spring. A keen north wind is whistling through the air. Henryson draws near the fire, for he is now old and his blood is thin, and after making himself comfortable with a "drink," he sits down with the poem of "worthie Chaucer glorious," "to cut the winter nicht and mak it schort"; but by and by he takes up another "quhair" (his own, of course), in which he finds "the fatall destenie of fair Cresseid that endit wretchitlie." Deserted by her paramour, she sinks into a slough of vulgar vice, "sa giglotlike, takand thy foull plesance"; but at last, apparently from want rather than remorse, steals home to the house of her father, Calchas, who is "keeper" of the temple of Venus and Cupid. He receives her kindly, but she does not venture to face the people going to the "kirk." She conceals herself in a "secreit orature," where she gives full utterance to her anguish, upbraiding Cupid and his mother as the cause of her misfortune. She then falls into an ecstasy, during which the seven planets or deities descend from their spheres and sit in judgment on her sin. Their portraits are sketched with the free and picturesque touch of one who is a master in the art of vitalizing abstractions. We do not indeed recognise the forms of Grecian mythology and art, though here and there a classic feature has been preserved. They are original creations of a northern and medieval fancy, and may rank with the best allegorical figures in *The Fairy Queene* or *The Mirrour of Magistrates.* . . . Their sentence is, Cresseid shall be punished with leprosy. When she awakes she finds to her horror that the dream has come true. Calchas takes her to the "spittail hous"; and here, as she lies alone at night in a dark corner, she pours forth a lament on her fearful fate, contrasting her present misery with the splendour and happiness of the days when she was the star of beauty and pleasure. The pathos throughout is so sweet and tender, the imagery so rich and various, the word-painting so felicitous, in spite of an excessive alliteration, that we venture to pronounce this part of the poem the highest achievement of Henryson's genius, and unsurpassed by anything in the whole range of Chaucer's works. The interview between Cresseid and Troilus is a most affecting incident, and is admirably managed. The hapless lady, with her companion lepers, is one day sitting by the wayside, begging for alms, when Troilus rides past in triumph to his native city. Something in the miserable face and form of Cresseid reminds him of his lost darling, and an agony of vague remembrance shakes his frame. He drops a purse of gold and a heap of jewels at her skirt, and then rides on without a word. When she learns the name of her generous benefactor (for she had not dared to lift her eyes), there bursts from her lips a storm of self-upbraiding and a passionate eulogium on her former lover, after which she makes her "Testament," and dies. When Troilus hears of her dread fate and death his pity subdues all sense of wrong. Over her remains he reared a temple of grey marble, with this simple inscription in golden letters:—

> Lo, fair ladyis, Cresseid, of Troyis town,
> Sumtyme countet the flour of womanheid,
> Under this stane, late lipper, lyis deid.

No one can read this beautiful poem without a deep admiration, both of the imaginative genius and the moral discernment of the author. We have said that Henryson had no place in contemporary history. Outwardly, that is true; yet we may learn from his writings something that the political annals of his time do not teach. Such men as he are never isolated phenomena. They mark the existence of invisible currents of thought and feeling. They have an audience fit, though few, even in a barbarous age, when might is the only right, and they exercise an influence that is none the less powerful because it is unseeen. Though the fifteenth century produced only one Henryson, we have seen that it was prolific in poets of lesser fame; and we may rest certain that, scattered among the universitics, and abbeys, and schools, and cathedral chapters of Scotland, were some who shared his literary sympathies, though they were not endowed with his diviner mind, and whose own powers were enriched and strengthened by the splendid efforts of his muse. (pp. 161-68)

John M. Ross, "King James, Henryson, and Dunbar," in his Scottish History and Literature to the Period of the Reformation, *edited by James Brown, James Maclehose & Sons, 1884, pp. 132-218.*

G. Gregory Smith (essay date 1900)

[*In the following excerpt, Smith examines Henryson's use of allegory in several works.*]

Robert Henryson . . . is not a voluminous writer, but his literary quality is high and well-sustained throughout; and in this respect he stands in marked contrast with the Southern allegorists. His subjects are theirs in kind: chivalric allegory, as in ***The Bludy Serk;*** *fabliau,* as in ***Orpheus and Eurydice,*** and in the ***Testament of Cresseid,*** an interesting 'continuation' of Chaucer's piece; minor didactic pieces on tattlers, age, the lack of wise men and true, the horrors of pestilence, and notably on death (in ***The Ressoning betwixt Deth and Man,*** and ***The Thrie deid Powis***). To these must be added ***Robene and Makyne,*** a pastoral, and ***The Fables of Esope,*** which are more completely illustrative of the coming literary taste. There is certainly a foretaste of the Renaissance in his choice of such a theme as Orpheus, in his transcription from Aesop, and in his fondness for pagan illustration; but the real divergence from the old ways is seen in his emphatic tendency to moralise his fancy and in the way he does it. He seldom neglects to point the moral of his poem in a stanza or two at the close: allegory of the type of the ***Bludy Serk*** is no longer complete without its explanatory tag; even the conclusion of ***Cresseid,*** though less formal, "monishes"; and the tale of ***Orpheus and Eurydice*** is interpreted in a long 'Moralitas' of over two hundred lines. His didactic mood is shown too in his frequent use, in his minor pieces, of the trick of the 'burden.' All this points to a declension in the spiritual force of allegory. It remains as a poetical form, but it is becoming no longer self-sustaining as a *motif*—as the mystical expression of the love-fervours of the Middle Ages. This change in its character does not necessarily imply a dulling of the poetic spirit, for it is most observable in the times of revival—in Scotland at the close of the century, and in a more advanced phase in the yet greater outburst in Elizabethan England. A comparison of Henryson with, say, Lydgate will show certain differences in the process of deterioration. If Henryson is even less in touch with the old allegory, he has at least a greater appreciation of its literary qualities; and so he escapes from the numbing dulness which settled down on English verse when the old inspiration failed. He is more moral than the 'moral' Gower, and never hesitates to expound his dreams in a way which even Lydgate, had he dreamt as successfully, would not have done; and yet he is less open to the charge of being a tiresome pedagogue masquerading as poet. Not only is the lesson kept apart from the allegory, but the allegory itself, which might have become a mere *pastiche,* is treated anew. This aptitude for the pictorial, which characterises the early Renaissance, begins to appear in Henryson. In a skilful way he makes use of the outworn machinery of the allegory; he treats it as a matter of technique and discovers in it those possibilities of vivid effect which find their fullest expression in the processional panels of the Elizabethans. In other words, he and his contemporaries transform what was originally a mystical cult into a literary engine, and save it from the wreck of mere platitude and "profitable sayings" into which it tended to fall, and did fall, in the hands of Chaucer's English successors. It is this quality which gives his sketches a first-hand interest, whether it be in a description of a pastoral scene, of a grim giant, of a feeble old man, of a mouse, or of Saturn himself. It is notable that Henryson, in his first prologue to the ***Fables,*** emphasises the importance of the pictorial presentment of the moral purpose—

Thocht fenyeit Fabillis of auld Poetrie,
Be nocht all groundit upon treuth, yit than
Thair polite termis of sweit Rhetorie
Ar richt plesand unto the eir of man;
And als the caus that thay first began
Wes to repreif the haill misleving
Of man, be figure of ane uther thing.

I suspect it is this quality, so remarkable henceforth in Scots literature, which has tempted a later criticism to discover throughout things Scottish a strong liking for colour and for natural description. I confess I find it difficult to prove any such monopoly. Some of this artistic energy may have been constitutional, but it was largely the direct result of literary effort which became a tradition within the narrow limits of the national poetry. And it was this very interest in technique, this fondness for 'touching up,' which produced the eccentricities of the 'Flytings' and the parodies on older literary fashions, and probably, too, those experiments in verbal indecency in which the Makaris are unrivalled.

Henryson shows his literary intention most clearly (and he is also at his best) in the ***Fables,*** the ***Testament of Cresseid,*** and ***Robene and Makyne.*** The first two are deliberate. In the ***Fables*** he gives us, as hinted in the quotation above, a series of studies which are of the nature of experiments. So too, and in a more marked way, in his ***Cresseid,*** which he offers as a sequel to Chaucer's *Troilus.* In a certain sense it is a marring of the tragedy of Troilus's sorrow to add the story of the after-sufferings which came upon the inconstant Cresseid, but it is an interesting and successful plea for poetical justice. And it is certainly free, as far as the story of the "lipper" lady's misfortune is concerned, from the offence of having a too obvious purpose. It may be doubted whether the older allegorists would have so deliberately set themselves to humiliate a gentle, though fickle, dame: Chaucer's conclusion is certainly more canonical than critical. ***Robene and Makyne*** is not allegorical in treatment, but it may, not inappropriately, be mentioned here. It is the best known of Henryson's works—because it is our first pastoral of the spontaneous and non-classical type, because it is short and tempting to the anthologist, and because it is a good poem. It is in marked contrast with the stilted *Eclogues* of Barclay, as a dainty sketch of the perennially interesting humours of simple wooing. It is worth noting too that it is almost a 'sport' in Scottish literature, for we find nothing resembling it till we reach the *Gentle Shepherd,* which, however, shows in the main the characteristics of the classical stock. (pp. 44-8)

G. Gregory Smith, "The Scottish Poets," in his The Transition Period, *William Blackwood and Sons, 1900, pp. 35-84.*

Frederic W. Moorman (essay date 1905)

[In the following excerpt, Moorman discusses Henryson's portrayal of nature in his works.]

Robert Henryson whose poetic career probably extended over the greater portion of the latter half of the fifteenth century, is one of the most original and certainly one of the most attractive of our line of poets. Though we think of him chiefly as a fabulist, he was also the author of courtly romances, while, by virtue of his ***Robin and Makyne,*** he may be fitly regarded as the first of our pastoral poets. As an interpreter of Nature Henryson also holds a post of distinction. In this, as in much else, he is the true disciple of Chaucer, but, like the other Scottish poets of the fifteenth and sixteenth centuries, his allegiance to the English master is always tempered with distinct originality, and with the resolve to rely wherever possible upon actual observation. The accent of locality is unmistakable in Henryson, and his landscape painting is never so fine as when it unfolds the scenery of his own northern home.

Most of the ***Fables,*** though they reveal a very shrewd insight into animal life, together with the capacity of looking upon that life on its most attractive and most humorous side, lie somewhat apart from the present field of study. The several fables which introduce the fox—**"Sir Chanteclеer and the Fox", "The Fox, the Wolf and the Moon's Shadow", "The Fox, the Wolf and the Cadger"**—claim comparison with the famous Low German beast-epic, and Henryson can scarcely be said to suffer by the comparison. The first-named fable also recalls Chaucer's *Nun's Priest's Tale,* just as another of the fables—**"The Parliament of Beasts"**—is directly reminiscent of his *Parliament of Fowls.* But it is the fable entitled **"The Preaching of the Swallow"** which chiefly calls for notice in this place. In this poem Henryson anticipates Gawin Douglas in giving to his readers a graphic picture of the different seasons of the year. As we have already seen, Henry the Minstrel does the same thing in his *Wallace,* but there is no evidence to show which of the two poets was the first to write.

Henryson starts his poem with a picture of summer arrayed "in jolye mantill of grene", and in the next stanza passes on to autumn. But it is in depicting winter and spring that he puts forth his chief strength. Nothing is more noticeable in the interpretation of Nature by Scottish poets than the intense realism and zest introduced into descriptions of a wintry landscape. It may easily be argued that these winter scenes are inspired rather by shrinking dread than by appreciation, yet it can scarcely be questioned that the realism of these pictures implies a certain interest and even delight in what is at first sight only repellent. Such at least is the impression which Henryson gives us in his winter landscape:—

> Syne Wynter wan, quhen austern Eolus,
> God of the wynd, with blastes boreall,
> The grene garment of somer glorious
> Hes all to rent and revin in pecis small;
> Than flouris fair, faidit with frost, mon fall,
> And birdis blyith changit thair noitis sweit
> In still murning, neir slane with snaw and sleit.
>
> Thir dailis deip with dubbis drownit is,
> Baith hill and holt heillit with frostis hair;
> And bewis bene are laiffit bair of bliss
> By wickit windis of the Wynter wair.
> All wyld beistis than from the bentis bair
> Drawis for dreid unto their dennis deip,
> Coucheand for cauld in coiffis thame to keip.

Henryson's language is a little quaint—though less so than that of the later poet Douglas—but no quaintness of language can hide the force of the picture. As winter passes into spring, the last of the four landscapes appears, and the poet breaks out into gladness when he sees once more the blossoming of the flowers, and hears the newly awakened voices of the birds:

> Syne cummis Ver, quhen Winter is away,
> The secretar of Somer, with his seeill,
> Quhen columbine up keikis throw the clay,
> Quhilk fleit wes befoir with frostis feeill.
> The maveis and the merle beginnis to mell;
> The lark on loft, with uther birdis small,
> Then drawis furth fra derne, over doun and dail.

In his courtly poem, ***The Testament of Cressid,*** Henryson follows the excellent custom of prefixing to the story an Introduction setting forth the occasion on which the poem was written, and bringing in, incidentally, a good deal of landscape painting. What is most pleasing in this Introduction is the recognition on the poet's part that the tragic theme of his story requires a sombre winter landscape to correspond to it. As he himself expresses it,—

> Ane dooly sesoun to ane cairfull dyte
> Suld correspond, and be equivalent;

and he forthwith proceeds to tell of "shouris of haill", frosts, and bitter blasts that "fra pole Artyk come quhisling loud and shill". This association of a "dooly sesoun" with a "cairful dyte" is not quite such a simple matter as may at first sight appear. It implies, in fact, the recognition of certain moods in Nature, if not also of a certain sense of sympathy between Nature and man.

In the *Prologue* to the ***Fables*** there is no demand for a sombre wintry landscape, and Henryson accordingly gives us one of the most brilliant of his colour-passages, fitly called forth by a description of flaming June:

> Sweit was the smell of flouris quhite and reid,
> The noyis of birdis richt delitious,
> The bewis braid bloomit abone my heid,
> The ground growand with gersis gratious:
> Of all plesance that place wes plenteous,
> With sweit odouris and birdis harmonie,
> The morning myld, my mirth was maire forthy.
>
> The roisis reid, arrayit on rone and ryce,
> The prymerois and the purpour viola;
> To heir it wes ane poynt of Paradice,
> Sic mirth the mavis and the merle couth ma.
> The blossumis blyith brak up on bank and bra,
> The smell of herbis and of foullis cry,
> Contending quha suld haif the victorie.

This is a joyous picture, and the feelings which the June season calls forth from the Scottish poet are wholly spontaneous. There is no suspicion of book-learning in the above description: the birds and the flowers are those of a Scottish woodland, and no false note brings discord into this well-ordered landscape.

Although ***Robin and Makyne*** is the best known of Henryson's poems, it does not call for special attention here. As a faithful and yet romantic picture of shepherd life its charm is perennial; for the scene which it presents is no make-believe, like so many of the pastoral poems of a later and more sophisticated age, but bears throughout the stamp of truth. At the same time, little attempt is made in the course of the pastoral to introduce landscape, even in the form of a scenic background, such as is found in the Robin Hood Ballads, and in many Middle English lyrics. The dialogue form of the poem no doubt accounts for this, for on other occasions, as has already been seen, Henryson paints a landscape with considerable fulness. Yet in reading the poem, we feel that there is everywhere an open-air freshness, and that we are carried away to the greenwood just as surely as in the ballad-poems which open with natural description. It is worthy of notice, too, that in the only stanza in which there occurs anything approaching landscape painting it is the greenwood to which reference is made:

Makyne, the nicht is soft and dry,
The wether warm and fair;
And the grene wod richt neir hard by,
To walk attowre all where.

(pp. 138-41)

Frederic W. Moorman, "The Scottish Poets of the Fifteenth and Sixteenth Centuries," in his The Interpretation of Nature in English Poetry from Beowulf to Shakespeare, *Karl L. Trübner, 1905, pp. 135-57.*

Sir Herbert Grierson (lecture date 1933)

[*Grierson was a Scottish educator and scholar who was a leading authority on John Milton, John Donne, and Sir Walter Scott. In the following excerpt from a 1933 address to the Scottish P.E.N. Club, Grierson appraises the originality of Henryson's* Testament of Cresseid *and other works.*]

Robert Henryson [was] . . . a simple schoolmaster in Dunfermline, a school where, as a later master in the same school declares, "his predecessors have continued maisters and teachers of the youth in letters and doctrine to their great commodity past memory of man". (p. 107)

[It] was doubtless in reading with his pupils the Fables of Æsop, as they were called, in Latin, that the happy idea occurred, or was suggested to him, of translating them into his native vernacular, and of adding to each, as became an instructor of youth, an edifying moral. In the introduction to the **"Tale of the Lion and the Mous,"** he tells us that one beautiful June morning he was visited by no less a person than Æsop himself:

His gowne wes off ane claith als quhyte as milk;
His Chemeis wes off Chambelate Purpour Broun;
His hude off Scarlet, bordourit weill with silk,
On hekillit wyis, untill his girdill doun;
His Bonat round, and off the auld fassoun;
His beird wes quhyte; his Ene wes grit and gray,
With lokker hair, quhilk over his schulderis lay.

But if the schoolmaster in Henryson prompted him to translate the Fables and to add an appropriate moral, it in no way interfered with his dramatic and humorous rendering of them. There is nothing of the rather dreary didactic flatness of a Gower or a Lydgate. Chaucer was his master, "worthy Chaucer glorious", but the Scottish poets generally, and Henryson in particular, were no slavish imitators. In their technique, indeed, their love of alliteration and elaborate rhyming, both Dunbar and Henryson are more akin to the Northern and Western poets of the fourteenth century than to Gower and Chaucer, to the poet or poets who composed the *Pearl* and *Gawayne and the Grene Knight.* If Henryson assimilated what was best in Chaucer's dramatic and humorous method, he gave it a turn of his own. The Scottish poets' handling of their themes, whether narrative or allegorical or lyrical, has a certain Scottish downrightness, which gives the poems of Dunbar and Henryson a flavour of the Scottish character. Their work does not show the courtly over-sophistication of sentiment which one sometimes finds in Chaucer, as in his French models, and their lyrics are more strongly wrought than the filigree work of Chaucer's love lyrics.

Henryson, specially, is not a courtly poet. He has not to waste his time in flattering kings and lords, nor to consider too carefully the refined sentiments of courtly queens and ladies. If the *Moralitas* which he attaches to each Fable is sometimes tedious and far-fetched, nevertheless the moral spirit in which he writes lends solidity to his treatment, without weakening either its dramatic truth or his delightful Scottish humour. A moral Fable could not be better told than his **"Taill of the Uponlandis Mous and the Burges Mous"**, or the two characters be better distinguished and sustained. (pp. 109-11)

It is in the Fables, I think, that one finds Henryson's gifts—easy narrative, playful humour, poetry and gravity—in happiest balance. But his most original poem is the ***Testament of Cresseid.*** There is a little over-elaboration in the aureate style, especially in the description of the gods. But it is to my mind perhaps the most original poem that Scotland has produced. It was no light thing to come after Boccaccio and Chaucer, and to succeed in making a real addition to a great dramatic story, something that without needless challenging of comparison does, in its impressive way, complete that tragic tale.

Chaucer had, in his courtly and detached manner, avoided any moral judgment upon Cresseid. He tells the story and leaves it to speak for itself:

Ne me ne list this sely womman chyde,
Forther than the story wol devyse.
Hire name alas is punysshed so wide
That for hire gilt it oughte ynough suffise.
And if I myghte excuse hire any wise,
For she so sorry was for hire untrouthe,
I wis I wolde excuse hire yit for routhe.

The only moral which Chaucer will enforce at the end of the whole tale is the religious one—that all earthly things are vanity. He speaks as a Christian, but so might a Buddhist. Boccaccio warns young men to beware of women such as Cresseid. Chaucer will not do that. I fancy he thinks at heart that to have loved and been loved by Cresseid was worth while, even if in the end she did desert you:

O blisful night of hem so long ysought,
How blithe unto hem bothe two thou were!
Why ne hadde I swich oon with my soule ybought,
Ye, or the leste ioie that were there.

But all earthly joys are fleeting, bring repentance, the legitimate as well as the illegitimate. The only true joys are in heaven. So Chaucer changes the message of Boccaccio into a pious exhortation:

O yonge fresshe folkes, he or she,
In which that love upgroweth with your age,
Repeyreth hom fro worldly vanitye,
And of your herte up casteth the visage
To thilke god that after his ymage
Yow made, and thynketh al nys but a faire,
This world that passeth soone as floures faire.

And loveth hym which that right for love
Upon a cros, our soules for to beye,
First starf, and roos, and sit in hevene above;
For he nil falsen no wight I dar seye
That wol his herte al hooly on hym leye.

But Henryson is not content with what, after all, is an evasion—he, a Scot and a Schoolemaister, with a Scot's and a schoolmaster's belief in retribution. The result might have been disastrous—a dry or a piously unreal didactic poem. But it is not, and that for two reasons. In the first place, Henryson retains Chaucer's sympathy for Cresseid:

Yit nevertheless quhat ever man deme or say
In scornefull language of thy brukkilnes,
I sal excuse, als far furth as I may,
Thy womanheid, thy wisdom and fairnes;
The quhilk Fortoun hes put to sic distres
As hir pleisit, and nathing throw the gilt
Of the, throw wickit language to be spilt.

In the second place, his morality is sound and sincere, not the preacher's conventional acceptance of standards which he has not made his own. For the retribution which overtakes Cresseid in the poem is the retribution of her own heart. It is from within herself that the stroke which slays her comes. It is not the leprosy we think of as her penalty, but the last encounter with Troilus and its reaction on her own soul. You remember how they met when she the leper begged and he gave alms, neither knowing who the other was, though something in her face makes Troilus' old wound bleed afresh:

Than upon him scho kest up baith hir Ene,
And with ane blenk it come into his thocht
That he sumtime hir face befoir had sene.
Bot scho was in sic plye he knew hir nocht,
Yit than hir luik into his mynd it brocht
The sweit visage and amorous blenking
Of fair Cresseid sumtyme his awin darling.

Ane spark of lufe than till his hart culd spring
And kendlit all his bodie in ane fyre.
With hait Fewir ane sweit and trimbling
Him tuik, quhill he was reddie to expyre.
To beir his Scheild, his Breist began to tyre,
Within ane quhyle he changit mony hew,
And nevertheless not ane ane uther knew.

For Knichtlie pietie and memoriall
Of fair Cresseid, ane Gyrdill can he tak,
Ane Purs of gold, and mony gay Jowall,
And in the Skirt of Cresseid doun can swak;
Than raid away, and not ane word he spak,
Pensive in hart, qhuill he come to the Toun,
And for greit care oft syis almaist fell doun.

Cresseid, too, has not recognized him, but learns from her companions who it is that has given her alms:

"Yes" (quod a Lipper man), "I knaw him weill,
Schir Troylus it is, gentill and fre."

That is the last straw:

Quhen Cresseid understude that it was he,
Stiffer than steill, thair stert ane bitter stound
Throwout hir hart, and fell doun to the ground.

Quhen scho ouircome, with siching sair and sad,
With mony cairfull cry and cald ochane:
"Now is my breist with stormie stoundis stad,
Wrappit in wo, ane wretch full will of wane".
Than swounit scho oft or scho culd refrane,
And ever in hir swouning cryit scho thus:
"O fals Cresseid and trew knicht Troylus.

"Thy lufe, thy lawtie, and thy gentilnes,
I countit small in my prosperitie,
Sa elevait I was in wantones,
And clam upon the fickill quheill sa hie:
All Faith and Lufe I promissit to the,
Was in the self fickill and frivolous:
O fals Cresseid, and trew Knicht Troylus. . . . "

That, it seems to me, is a perfect end to the story, a real *catharsis* leaving us at peace with Cresseid as Chaucer's poem hardly does. Socrates contends in the *Gorgias,* first, that it is better to suffer than to do what is unjust. Troilus, at the end of Chaucer's poem, is happier than Criseyde. Secondly, that if you have done wrong the best thing which can happen to you is to suffer, not to escape, punishment:

> Now the proper office of punishment is twofold: he who is rightly punished ought either to become better and to profit by it, or he ought to be made an example to his fellows, that they may see what he suffers, and fear and become better; those who are punished by gods and men, and improved, are those whose sins are curable; still the way of improving them is by pain and suffering; for there is no other way in which they can be delivered from their evil.

In Chaucer's poem, despite his sympathy, Criseyde is left an example to others. In Henryson's we see her healed and repentant by the way of suffering, and we are left in mind at peace with her as with Troilus. It is no small honour to a Scottish poet to have given this moving and dignified end to one of the great medieval stories.

I shall say nothing of Henryson's other poems. The best are the lyrics, especially ***Robene and Makyne*** and the two allegoric and devotional lyrics, ***The Garmont of Gud Ladeis*** and ***The Bludy Serk.*** One of the finest of Dunbar's lyrics is to my mind that on the Resurrection:

Done is a battle on the dragon blak,
Our campioun Christ counfoundet hes his force;
The yets of Hell ar broken with a crak,
The signe triumphall rasit is of the croce.

I will not say that Henryson's have all the lyrical fervour of that. As a lyrical poet of the Swinburnian kind, a master of every variety of rhyming technique, Dunbar is the greater, but in dramatic power, in gravity of temper, Henryson is the first of early Scottish poets; and his humour, if not so boisterous as Dunbar's, is finer, slyer, more Chaucerian and more Scottish. (pp. 111-16)

Sir Herbert Grierson, "Robert Henryson," in his Essays and Addresses, *Chatto & Windus, 1940, pp. 105-17.*

E. M. W. Tillyard (essay date 1948)

[*Tillyard was an English scholar of Renaissance literature whose studies of John Milton, William Shakespeare, and the epic form are widely respected. In the following excerpt, Tillyard examines both the poetic structure and the medieval context of Henryson's* Testament of Cresseid.]

Although Henryson learnt much of his craft from Chaucer and although his poem continues and assumes in the reader a knowledge of Chaucer's *Troilus and Criseyde,* he does not really compete with his master, nor does his poem suffer when compared with its source. In temper the ***Testament of Cresseid*** is tragic and as such it is nearer akin to some of the ballads and to the later books of Malory's *Morte Darthur* than is the essential comedy of Chaucer. And through being truly tragic it takes itself right out of its medieval setting and allies itself to the tragic writings of all ages. True, when Henryson calls the poem "this tragedie" he meant no more by "tragedie" than the simple medieval notion of a human being, of whatever character and by whatever sequence of events, falling from prosperity into adversity; but in actual fact his poem fulfils more exacting tragic standards. Cresseid's character is not subtle or complicated but it is sufficiently mixed to approximate her to the requirements of Aristotle. She is far from being a saint but she is no villain. Indeed, in herself she is more good than bad, but her errors of weakness and vanity co-operated with the turn of events in causing her ruin. We pity her misfortune and we are afraid because her own misfortune is the type of what may befall the run of humanity.

The tragic emotion is swift and concentrated and can only be conveyed by corresponding poetical means. Henryson is free from the besetting medieval vice of prolixity and joins the successfully tragic writers of all ages by the economy and the emphasis with which he tells his tale. When he is ornate (and he can be so after the fashion of his age) it is in the pauses of the action.

There still exists so strong a prejudice against the notion that a medieval poet (apart from Chaucer) could be an accomplished artist, and the critics have said so little about the art of the ***Testament of Cresseid,*** that I will speak at some length on the economy and emphasis mentioned above and on other matters of style: first in point of language, secondly in point of construction.

The Scottish form of northern English, Henryson's native speech, was naturally powerful and emphatic, but rough; and yet, when skilfully used, it could achieve a surprising degree of sweetness. Henryson achieves emphasis and holds our attention by his great skill in achieving linguistic and rhythmic contrasts. A common habit of rhetoric in the Middle Ages was that of saying the same thing twice in a pattern of balance. It is best known through its survival in the English Prayer Book, it persisted into (for instance) the polite chronicle writing of Hall in the reign of Henry VIII and the prose of Lyly, and it was laughed at in some of the comic writing of Shakespeare. Henryson accepts the convention but puts it to skilful use. He employs it only when he is at leisure and in order to make more emphatic his great power of short intense and moving statements. The poem begins:

> Ane doolie sessoun to ane cairfull dyte
> Suld correspond, and be equivalent.

The second line is rhetorically redundant. But Henryson here is at leisure; he can afford to be conventionally (and for that age decently) expansive. Similarly in stanza 31, describing the horses of Phoebus, he writes

> The third Peros, richt hait and richt fervent,

and again he is at leisure, for it would not do to scant his solemn description of the planetary gods assembled to judge Cresseid. But whenever the action is intense, or even when he merely means business, his language is swift packed and simple. The last line of almost every stanza is of this kind, and these lines give the predominant impression. For emphatic simplicity take the last line of stanza 18,

> Allace that ever I maid yow sacrifice.

This *last* line is the *beginning* of Cresseid's blasphemous speech and is in diction and in rhythm the abrupt blurting out of a sheer blasphemy, one of the crises of the poem. Dramatically it simply could not be bettered. Or take the final line of the penultimate stanza, the final words of the inscription in golden letters on the tomb of Cresseid, who

> Under this stane, lait lipper, lyis deid.

The line is forceful and plain, to brutality; and that this plainness should have been put in golden letters is anything but accidental. Sometimes Henryson puts redundance and packed sense in close proximity. Take the beginning of stanza 14:

> This fair Lady in this wyse destitute
> Of all comfort and consolatioun,
> Richt privelie, but fellowscip, on foot,
> Disagysit, passit far out of the toun—

the first two lines are conventionally rhetorical and redundant: the next seven words recall one of Milton's most concentrated lines:

> Eyeless in Gaza at the Mill with slaves.

It is not only by language and rhetoric that Henryson secures variety and contrast; he also manipulates rhythms with masterly skill. There is no better example in English of sound echoing sense than the description of Venus's double-dealing in stanzas 33 and 34. The very first line is illustration enough:

> Under smyling scho was dissimulait.

The rhythm of the first two words is bolstered up, suggesting the carefully maintained façade: in the last three words the rhythm collapses and disperses, suggesting both the secretiveness of a whisper and the shifts and eddies behind the façade. Or take the fifth line of stanza 49 describing how men avoid the leper,

Quhair thow cummis ilk man sall fle the place.

The first three words suggest the ponderous and painful motion of Cresseid in her sickness; the rest suggest the speed and hurry of the escaping men. Examples could be multiplied indefinitely, since each fresh reading reveals new subtleties.

Sometimes the rhetorical and rhythmic contrasts are on a larger scale. Conspicuous for ornateness and width of vocabulary, for wealth of alliteration, for strong reverberations of sound are the stanzas describing the planets and their judgment. They are followed by the contrasted simplicity and realism of the child coming to call Cresseid to supper. But when a little lower down Cresseid utters her complaint we compare its ornateness with that of the planet-description, but we contrast the wonderfully dulcet tone, its slow and rich and sinuous stanza form, with the grating violence and abrupt cadences of the description of Saturn, her chief enemy, who had robbed her of the gay life she so exquisitely recalls.

The above larger comparisons and contrasts are matters of structure as well as of style. They lead on to other structural details.

The use of irony seems peculiarly appropriate in tragedy: probably because of its astringent effect and of the concentration given by astringency. Irony rests on a contrast between knowledge and ignorance and is usually consummated by the ignorant person's enlightenment. Oedipus cursing the man responsible for the city's plague does not know that he is the man, but the audience does. Later he learns, and his new enlightenment recalls his old ignorance: different parts of the play are drawn together. Added to such specific cases of knowledge and ignorance there can be the general impression that fate knows so much more about the whole business than the people who actually transact it. Both kinds of irony occur in the ***Testament of Cresseid*** and they help to bind the parts of the poem together. The most effective example depends on our recollection of Chaucer's poem. There, one of the most brilliant scenes is of Troilus riding down the street and Cresseid watching him: then, she was in her glory and he her *conscious* slave. When, in Henryson's poem, Troilus rides past a second time, she is a leper and he does not even recognise her. Behind the two episodes is the impression of fate's superior knowledge: when Cresseid was proud and watched Troilus securely, fate was already preparing a contrasting episode. In stanza 72 there is irony that Cresseid, in her extreme sickness and unrecognised by Troilus, should yet arouse to such excess the love symptoms in him. Fate as it were staged this extreme instance of his fidelity to prove to Cresseid how precious a thing she had rejected. A beautiful minor example of irony is in the message the child brings to summon Cresseid to supper, after her doom (stanza 52, 7):

The Goddis wait all your intent full weill.

Calchas meant that Cresseid must have said all the needful prayers by this time. He does not realise that his words can mean with terrible appropriateness that the gods heeded—and punished—the impious tenour of her prayers only too thoroughly. When

He luikit on hir uglie lipper face,

we may take it he was enlightened.

How greatly Henryson minded about knitting his poem tightly can be seen in a single instance of a repeated theme: that of the relations of Esperus, or the evening star Venus, and Saturn. At the beginning the author goes to the window to do homage to the star but he is driven away by the frost, which is the quality of Saturn. In stanza 7 Esperus gives Troilus hope when he has fallen into despair. In stanza 20 Cresseid complains that the seed of love sown in her face has been frozen, and later it is Saturn, the frosty god, who is foremost in punishing her. In stanza 46 Cresseid is described, like the amorous Cleopatra in Shakespeare, as being all air and fire. But now the saturnine chill induces leprosy, which is white like snow though spotted with black. Finally in stanza 58 in the evening after she has entered the lazar-house, the sky is clouded. In other words Esperus cannot be seen, and we are taken back by contrast to the opening of the poem.

The ***Testament of Cresseid*** is, among other things, a tragedy in the medieval sense, the fall from prosperity to misfortune; and Henryson, though dealing principally with the latter, cannot omit the former. His means are simple and brilliantly effective. Into Cresseid's complaint he inserts two stanzas (60 and 61) in which she recalls her old life at court.

Quhair is thy chalmer wantounlie besene
With burely bed and bankowris browderit bene,
Spycis and wyne to thy collatioun,
The cowpis all of gold and silver schene,
The sweit meitis servit in plaittis clene
With saipheron sals of ane gud sessoun,
Thy gay garmentis with mony gudely goun,
Thy plesand lawn pinnit with goldin prene?
All is areir, thy greit royall renoun.

Quhair is thy garding with thir greissis gay
And fresche flowris, quhilk the quene Floray
Had paintit plesandly in everie pane,
Quhair thou was wont full merilye in May
To walk and tak the dew be it was day
And heir the merle and mavis mony ane,
With ladyis fair in carrolling to gane,
And se the royal rinks in thair array
In garmentis gay garnischit on everie grane?

Here the brilliant colours suggest contemporary illumination; and the powerful beat of the verse, the rich alliteration, and the reiterated pressure of the rhyme render with superb success spring and youth at their height when sap and blood flow with the most insistence and jubilation. The stanzas do their work of recollection with great economy and simultaneously set up an emphatic contrast to the loathsomeness of the lazar-house.

Finally, the whole poem is disposed on a firm simple and satisfying plan. There are three clearly articulated crises, each conveyed with strict economy but each relieved by passages of lyrical ornateness. The first is Cresseid's blaspheming the gods (stanzas 18 ff.). This is followed by the elaborate description of the planets. The second is her entry into the lazar-house, the climax of her punishment, and it is followed by her elaborate lyrical complaint. The third is Troilus's passing and alms-giving, by which Cresseid realises the truth and what she has lost. And this is followed by the poem's true resolution: her self-accusation with its lyrical refrain,

> O fals Cresseid and trew knicht Troylus,

and her testament. Her death is no crisis but the fitting conclusion.

The qualities I have mentioned so far are not specifically medieval; they apply to all poetry. And they unite to make the ***Testament of Cresseid*** a very fine poem. Further, they should prompt the reader to be curious about other qualities of the poem, which *are* medieval. These are important, first for being essential to the full understanding of the poem and secondly for their historical and moral interest. (pp. 5-12)

By far the most important of the medieval presuppositions governing the poem is the theological; and all the more because it is not stated at all but quietly taken for granted. Further, it has been passed over, or, if recognised, misunderstood. People often contrast the kindliness and humanity of Chaucer in *Troilus and Criseyde* with Henryson's harshness and legality in the ***Testament of Cresseid.*** Henryson, they say, was the true Scots puritan, who anticipated the harshness of John Knox and his fellow-Calvinists towards the sin of sensuality. He was not content to leave things in the air in the tolerant way Chaucer did; he must have rigid justice, an eye for an eye. They are wrong and misunderstand Chaucer's motive in allowing Criseyde to fade out of the poem. Chaucer is first concerned with the feelings of Troilus, and his Criseyde must subserve them. Any elaborate punishment awarded her would upset his scheme. Further, when it suits him, Chaucer can be quite as moral as Henryson; and pre-eminently when he pictures the soul of Troilus looking down from the heavens onto the business of mortals and seeing how trivial it is compared with the eternal verities. On the other hand Henryson is as kind to his Cresseid as he was free to be within the scheme of orthodox theology.

It remains to point out how full and how precise and how centrally medieval is the morality of the ***Testament of Cresseid.***

Like Malory and other medieval writers Henryson acknowledges two moral codes: the code of Love and the code of the Church. These codes both conflicted and co-operated. Being founded on an exaltation of sex and on adulterous love, the code of Love conflicted with the Church. But provided the conflict was admitted, provided the practice was allowed to be sinful, the Church was not intolerant. . . . [In] the code of Love, once the initial irregularity was granted, the moral rules of service and fidelity were very exacting. And this exactingness was there from the very beginning, being found in the pagan book to which the code of courtly love owed so much, the *Ars Amatoria* of Ovid. This poem, however un-Victorian in temper, has its own morality. At the very beginning Ovid makes it plain that the life of illicit love is hard, that it has its own discipline, and that a vast amount of trouble has to be taken for comparatively insignificant results. The medieval courtly code saw to it that these things were indeed so. It might take several years' probation for the lover to get a kiss, while achievement was comparatively rare. The great principle of the code was the lover's absolute fidelity, which implied a high standard of self-discipline. Indeed, the devotion of the lover to his lady resembled the devotion of the faithful to Mother Church. Hence the code of Love could in its way co-operate with the code of the Church, even preparing its devotees for a transfer of allegiance. This is the doctrine found in Malory's *Morte Darthur;* and it is put with special force in the last chapter of book eighteen, the lyrical passage on May leading to the Queen's Maying in the next book. May is the lover's month,

> for like as herbs and trees bring forth fruit and flourish in May, in like wise every lusty heart that is in any manner a lover springeth and flourisheth in lusty deeds. For it giveth unto all lovers courage, that lusty month of May, in something to constrain him to some manner of thing more in that month than in any other month.

And after enlarging on this theme Malory ends:

> Therefore all ye that be lovers call unto your remembrance the month of May, like as did Queen Guenever, for whom I make here a little mention, that while she lived she was a true lover, and therefore she had a good end.

The second *therefore* in this passage is very important. Guenever's love was adulterous, in accord with the courtly and in conflict with the Church code. But within the courtly code she was a true lover, fulfilling the main condition of absolute fidelity. *Therefore* she was allowed to end her life in the sanctity of a house of nuns.

The two codes operate in the ***Testament of Cresseid*** precisely as they do in *Morte Darthur,* but the Church code is less evident on account of the pagan setting. This setting may prove confusing to a modern reader because the pagan gods here have mixed functions; so I had better explain it before dealing with the poem's general morality. The chief god is Cupid, and his first and obvious function is that of the traditional ruler of the order of lovers. In the most authoritative work of literature concerned with courtly love, the *Roman de la Rose,* Cupid, the god of love, rules in the allegorical garden. . . . But Henryson's Cupid is more than the ruler of the garden of the rose, he is a superior pagan god who convenes a court of other pagan gods, who are also the planets. He is in fact the Eros of Hesiod Plato and Aristotle, oldest of the gods, the creator of order out of chaos, and hence in authority over the others. These other gods are a blend . . . of pagan mythological deities with planetary rulers. Normally, in medieval writing, the pagan gods kept their mythological attributes, merely giving their names to the planets. Henryson approximates them to the beliefs and fashions of his age by making them mainly astrological. He invests them as deities with the powers usually given to the planets as such. In other words his pagan gods are both ornamental in the conventional medieval way and operative in the way the medieval people really believed the planets to work. Now Cupid as creator and the planets with their influence are separate from their other selves as just described and are parts of the general scheme of God's universe. In stanza 42 Cupid says to them

> And sen ye ar all sevin deificait,
> Participant of devyne sapience,

and to Henryson's audience divine sapience or wisdom could only bear a solemn theological meaning. Cupid then and the pagan gods in their planetary function belong to the theological code and when Cresseid offends against them she offends against God's holy laws.

We can now deal with the poem's morality and the nature of Cresseid's offence. First, by her infidelity to Troilus she offended against the code of love and against Cupid in his function of dictator of all lovers. And having thus offended, where Guenever was blameless, her chances of virtue under the other code were much less. That is the position when the poem begins. Further, the temple which Calchas served was a place of general worship, where the "pepill far and neir" used to come: in fact the poetical equivalent of a Christian church. And when Cresseid utters her blasphemies there, she does so in an appropriate way, committing two of the deadly sins. First, pride, in that she blames God for her misfortune instead of herself, and second, anger, for "angerly scho cryit out". And the rest of the poem describes the consequences of these sins. The consequences are not the mere facts that Cresseid was punished and died a leper but that through the working of God's will she was punished, brought to penitence, and ended by taking the blame on herself: in fact the story of her salvation according to the Christian scheme. The process is beautifully contrived. Early in the poem (stanza 17) for all her subsequent arrogance in blaming the gods she was inwardly ashamed and could not face the people in the temple. After this blasphemy she suffers condign punishment. Her sin was pride, and the infliction of leprosy ruined the lovely complexion and the courtly carolling which had been the source of her vanity. However, by itself the leprosy is not enough to make her repent. In stanza 51, although she regrets her blasphemy as an act of rashness that has brought trouble on herself, she does not repent of it but calls the gods "craibit" or unfairly harsh. And when she enters the lazar-house, her state of mind is self-pity: she contrasts her present misery with her past glamour. Then comes the episode of Troilus riding by and of his great generosity; and with the uprush of feeling caused by her recognising his worth and what she had voluntarily rejected, her barrier of pride is quite broken down and she exclaims,

> O fals Cresseid and trew knicht Troylus.

And, most important of all (stanza 80), she blames herself and no one else,

> Nane but myself, as now, I will accuse.

This is the resolution of the poem: the true repentance of Cresseid and the salvation of her soul. In her testament she makes what amends she can. Weaned from the lusts of the flesh she bequeaths her body to be devoured by worms and toads. In sincere pity and unselfishness she bequeaths the gold Troilus gave her to the lepers. She returns Troilus his ring. She dedicates her spirit to Diana, the goddess of chastity: in other words she aspires, as far as she can, to the monastic life. But the thought that Diomede, who forsook her, still has the brooch and belt which Troilus, who was true, gave her and that she cannot restore them is too cruel and she dies.

Guenever in *Morte Darthur* died a holy nun. Her soul went perhaps to Paradise, perhaps to one of the higher regions of Purgatory. Cresseid's aspiration to be a nun was cut off by death. But she had repented and she could not have been damned. Her soul must have gone to Purgatory, yet with much penance to perform. If Henryson had been austere and a Calvinist he would have counted Cresseid's sin as too rank for forgiveness and committed her soul to Hell. Henryson was not hostile to Cresseid, as he tells us in stanza 13, but he does his best for her according to the laws of his religion.

> Yit nevertheles quhat ever men deme or say
> In scornefull language of thy brukkilnes,
> I sall excuse als far furth as I may
> Thy womanheid, thy wisdom and fairnes,
> The quhilk Fortoun hes put to sic distres
> As hir pleisit, and nathing throw the gilt
> Of the, throw wickit langage to be split.

In other words Cresseid's fickleness has been treated too harshly. In extenuation one must remember that she had her good qualities and that fortune was cruel in separating her from Troilus and bringing Diomede in her way. And Henryson goes on to tell how, after all, she was saved.

In this section I set out to speak of religious and ethical matters common to the whole age and exemplified in the ***Testament of Cresseid,*** matters in themselves unconnected with literature. But they turned out to have a literary bearing. Through them a second plot, that of Cresseid's inward purification, was revealed. The first plot was of her outward punishment and death. As we now read the poem we should bear both plots simultaneously in mind, to the great enrichment of the total significance.

I have spoken above of the use Henryson made of Esperus or the planet Venus in constructing his poem and of the poetic majesty of his planet-description. Now good construction and majestic verse are things easily perceived by a modern, and they can be found in the literature of all periods. Yet the influence of the stars meant so much more to Henryson and his contemporaries than to us that we cannot gauge the full effect he produced from it unless we extend our knowledge. We recognise and admire how the story is braced by the repeated references to Esperus, we are pleased and thrilled by the crowded detail and the high colours by means of which Henryson renders his pageant of the seven planets. All this Henryson's contemporaries would have felt much as we do, but their feelings would have been enlarged first by an authentic belief in the power of the stars and by an interest in the ways that power worked, and secondly by the accident that in the epoch of Chaucer and his successors this interest in the stars, always present in the Middle Ages, was especially fashionable.

It is a modern commonplace that astrology and not astronomy was current in the Middle Ages and that men calculated nativities and chose lucky conjunctions of the stars for important actions. So far the commonplace is correct; it is the accompanying assumption that such acts were merely superstitious that is false. There was much superstition and there were many illicit magical practices current, but astrology did not belong here. On the contrary the stars were the instruments of God, and to study them was to study the workings of his will. Henryson's declaration that his planetary deities partook of divine wisdom I found useful above as evidence to put before a modern reader that the planets were more than blind powers; to a contemporary it would merely be a reassuring iteration of the obvious and the accepted. Nothing he said about the stars could have given the least offence to the Benedictine Abbey to which his school was attached.

Far from keeping God and the orthodox scheme of salvation in one department and the irrational workings of the stars in another, the Middle Ages looked on the stars as an organic part of God's creation and as the perpetual instruments and diffusers of his will. And like that will they were unsearchable. The following passage from one of the medieval encyclopedists has the true medieval tone:

> Above Saturn, which is the last plainest and highest from us of all the seven planets, is the heaven that men see so full of stars as it were sown, when it is clear time and weather. This heaven that is so starred is the firmament which moveth and goeth round. Of which moving is so great joy, so great melody and so sweet, that there is no man that, if he might hear it, the never after should have talent ne will to do thing that were contrary unto our Lord in anything that might be; so much should he desire to come thither where he might alway hear so sweet melody and be alway with them. Whereof some were sometime that said that little young children heard this melody when they laughed in their sleep; for it is said that then they hear the angels of Our Lord in heaven sing, whereof they have such joy in their sleep. But hereof knoweth no man the truth save God that knoweth all, which setted the stars on the heaven and made them to have such power. For there is nothing within the earth ne within the sea, how diverse it be, but it is on the heaven figured and compassed by the stars; of which none knoweth the number save God only, which at his pleasure numbreth them and knoweth the name of every each of them, as he that all knoweth and all created by good reason. [Caxton's *Mirrour of the World,* ed. O. H. Prior, 1913]

It was however the planets which had the greatest immediate power over human affairs and about whose behaviour men could learn most:

> These seven planets been such that they have power on things that grow on the earth and abound their virtues more than all the other that been on the firmament and more apparently work, like as the ancient sage philosophers have ensearched by their wits.

We are apt to underestimate the reasonableness with which the theory of planetary influences presented itself to the minds of Chaucer's or Henryson's contemporaries. For instance, the different seasons of the year obviously depended on the varying relations of one of the planets, the sun, to the earth. But though these relations varied they did so constantly. Hence though the climate of January differed from that of May, you would expect all Januaries to be alike. Obviously they were not, and as obviously because the other planets exerted their diversifying influence. What could be more reasonable?

When Henryson used the planets as the instruments of Cresseid's punishment he not only implied that her punishment was by God's will but he used the agents which in contemporary idea were most concerned with human affairs. He was being as natural as a modern novelist would be in explaining the adult acts of his characters through some event of their early years. Further, the conviction that the stars really did work like that would add terror to what without it is already terrific enough. What must have been especially terrifying in Henryson was the concurrence of all the planets. In the normal operation the influence of one planet balanced or impeded that of another. By a singular concurrence they all combine to punish Cresseid.

Henryson's astrological knowledge was correct as far as it went. He gives the planets their proper order; he knows their different attributes; and when it is Saturn and no other planet that strikes Cresseid with leprosy he shows that he understands their different functions. Saturn, with his frosty nature, pale leaden hue, and livid lips was the planet to which the pale disease of leprosy with its black spots was assigned: an assignment valid into the seventeenth century when Lilly, the astrologer, says that Saturn in Leo causes leprosy.

Such accuracy was important because of the fashionable interest in the details of astrology prevalent in Chaucer's day and inherited by his poetical followers. W. C. Curry in his *Chaucer and the Medieval Sciences* has an interesting chapter on the *Knight's Tale,* in which he expounds the full astrological complexity of that story. . . . Curry quite rightly sees that for all its complexity and its topical attraction the machinery of the stars is subsidiary in Chaucer to his interest in his story and in the passions of his characters, but

> in order that this action and these emotions may be rationalised for his readers of the Middle Ages, he has made of scientific astrology a handmaiden to his literary art.

The same is true of Henryson. The ***Testament of Cresseid*** is first of all a human tragedy but the mechanism of the planets was the natural one for Henryson to use. Through this once living and topical, but now outmoded, complex of belief he can present the eternal human drama more freshly than through other means which though in themselves more reasonable would lack the essential stamp of contemporary vogue.

The simple contrast between blossoming and decay, fire and ashes, the bright hair and the skeleton's bone, exists in every age; and I did not mean the earlier mentioned contrast between Cresseid's life at court and her life in the lazar-house to go beyond the perennial commonplace. But in the Middle Ages the contrast took a peculiar form and became rather a conflict. Whereas the Greeks had merely noted and lamented the contrast, with their minds quite easy that blossoming was better than decay, the Middle Ages distrusted the blossoming and the brilliance and thought that decay might really be better as bringing men to perceive a higher blossoming than this world provided. When life was very insecure, such a habit of mind could easily prevail. But with the growth of security, as strong kingdoms arose and orderly towns encircled themselves with walls, and with the revival of art and learning in the twelfth century, men could not help thinking that the present life was very good indeed. The Church, convinced that compared with another life the present life was evil, opposed that thought. It was the special characteristic of the Middle Ages that the two ways of thinking co-existed in a well-developed form; and not merely in opposed groups of people but within the single mind. . . . In some men of the Middle Ages love of life and contempt of the world suffered a different adjustment: not a balance but a state of tension in which both opinions existed in an extreme form and neither predominated. The classic exposition of this tension is Petrarch's prose dialogue, the *Secretum,* between the writer and St Augustine. Both opinions are put forward, but the conflict is indecisive; and we are left with them both in their full potency. Chaucer resembles Petrarch in more than one place. *Troilus and Criseyde* shows as strong a relish for living as any poem, but it is entirely sincere in the final scene of the soul of Troilus looking down on the earth and despising the petty affairs that go on in it. The retraction at the end of the *Canterbury Tales* co-exists with rather than cancels the *Merchant's Tale* or the *Wife of Bath's Prologue.*

Now Henryson (to judge by his work as a whole and especially the ***Fables***) seems naturally to have been a healthy and kindly person. Unlike Dunbar, whose nature was more violent, he could accept the medieval paradox and endure the tension without much trouble. Yet that paradox is there, in the ***Testament of Cresseid,*** in brilliant outline. It comes out in the opening description, so close to life and indicating so sensitive a love for it, of the author mending the fire, taking a drink, and settling to read; in the brilliant colour of Jupiter as described among the planets,

> As goldin wyre sa glitter and was his hair,
> His garmound and his gyis full gay of grene
> With golden listis gilt on everie gair,

contrasted with the unflinching application of an otherworldly morality and with a touch like Cresseid's bequeathing

> my corps and carioun
> With wormis and with taidis to be rent.

This dwelling on the corpse and corruption is only a touch in Henryson's poem yet it allies him to a large medieval tradition and one which continued beyond the Middle Ages proper into Elizabethan drama and Donne. Behind Henryson's touch is the most famous and the most influential of all the works that dwelt on decay with the objects of alienating men from the glamour of this life and of stirring their appetites for a better one, the *De Contemptu Mundi* of Pope Innocent III. . . . Henryson has none of Innocent's savage hatred of the flesh: nevertheless he does arouse the whole medieval context through his reference to worms and toads and corpses.

But Henryson expresses the medieval paradox most aptly and most beautifully in Cresseid's lament, which is a repertory of medieval commonplaces. The delight in life is obvious, in the gaiety and sensuous beauty of the court. There is no more dazzling description in literature than that in the stanzas already quoted of Cresseid walking in her garden in May, to take the dew and hear the birds sing, then going with the other ladies singing, and seeing "the royal rinks in thair array". But even these two stanzas (60 and 61), quite apart from the later stanzas in the lament describing the leper's life, imply the transience and vanity of all this brilliance. They both begin with the words "Quhair is . . . ", and these at once set the stanzas in a large and familiar medieval context. Again and again, and in whatever language—*ubi sunt* or *où sont?*—the medieval writers asked that question; and the answer, whether stated or implied, always was that these things are vanity and that they have passed away. . . . In beginning his stanzas with *Where is?* Henryson would summon up instantly the context of decay and mortality into which Cresseid's once brilliant life is to be set.

Another large context would be suggested when in stanza 64 Cresseid tells people to use her as a *mirror*: and a very moral context too. Medieval mirrors were always didactic, sometimes of what you should imitate, usually of what you should avoid. And like the paradox of love of life and contempt of the world they lasted into Elizabethan days. Hamlet was the glass of fashion, which means that other people ought to imitate him.

These references to medieval commonplaces are a source of strength. They attach the ***Testament of Cresseid*** instantly to a great tradition; they assure us that Henryson spoke the language of all western Europe. Through the repose bred of that assurance Henryson can give us what is unique, what he alone of men is able to give. (pp. 12-27)

E. M. W. Tillyard, "Henryson: 'The Testament of Cresseid', 1470?" in his Five Poems, 1470-1870: An Elementary Essay on the Background of English Literature, *Chatto & Windus, 1948, pp. 5-29.*

Kurt Wittig (essay date 1958)

[*In the following excerpt, Wittig provides an informative study of the* Testament of Cresseid *and the* Morall Fabillis, *particularly praising Henryson's descriptive imagery and poetic style.*]

Any study of Henryson is hampered by the paucity of our knowledge of the poet's life: he is connected with Dunfermline, seems to have been a schoolmaster, flourished *c.* 1480-90, and was dead by 1508, when Dunbar mentions him in his "Lament for the Makars." The numerous prints of his works, however, testify to Henryson's popularity. He was writing from the centre of the thought of his age, but his work is also a keystone in the Scottish tradition, an aspect all too neglected hitherto.

It has hitherto been customary to call Henryson, together with James I, Dunbar and Gavin Douglas, a "Scottish Chaucerian." True, they introduced into Scots literature Chaucer's example and his handling of themes derived from European literature, and recognised him as their master. But they are far from imitating Chaucer in the same way as Lydgate and Occleve; they have so much besides Chaucerian matter that I prefer to call them by their Scots name of "makars." James I alone—if he was the author of the *Kingis Quair*—is a real imitator of Chaucer, but even he shows more originality in doing so than Chaucer's English disciples. (pp. 33-4)

Robert Henryson's debt to Chaucer is great, and he is the first to acknowledge it ([***Testament of Cresseid***], ll. 41 ff.). But he does not imitate. He assimilates Chaucer's conception of poetry and creates from this artistic centre. In a more limited field he achieves (as Tillyard observes [in his *Five Poets 1470-1870,* 1948]) the same artistic level as his master, and there are even passages where Henryson surpasses Chaucer, as in the introduction to the ***Testament*** or the meeting of the lovers. He fertilises Chaucer's heritage with his own native tradition and achieves a new subtlety which is totally his own.

This is obvious from his verse. Henryson writes practically all his poems in the Chaucerian stanza and he is sensitive to its melody and harmony. But he superimposes native alliteration, a common feature of Scots poetry before and after the Renaissance. This gives his rhythm a stronger stress arising from his Scots speech. Henryson uses alliteration, not formally, but as a poetic device to vary the intensity of his expression. In his description of the planets, harsh, icy Saturn is portrayed ([***Testament of Cresseid***], ll. 151 ff.) in rough verse with heavy alliteration of *tch, f(r)*, and such plosives as *p, t, k:* fourfold alliteration is the rule, run-on alliteration or two alliterative patterns in one line frequent. Moreover, massed consonants, heavy stresses, and many shortly ejaculated vowels help (ll. 155 ff.) to suggest a picture of wild, harsh force:

> His face fronsit, his lyre was lyke the leid,
> His teith chatterit, and cheverit with the chin. . . .
>
> Atour his belt his lyart lokkis lay
> Felterit unfair, ouirfret with froistis hoir, . . .
> Under his girdill ane flasche of felloun flanis,
> Fedderit with ice, and heidit with hailstanis.

Jupiter, "richt fair and amiabill," is portrayed (ll. 169 ff.) in gentler rhythms with many tripping dactyls; the vowels are longer, the consonants no longer massed; alliteration is used more economically and does not fall so heavily (ll. 176 f.) on consecutive words:

> His voice was cleir, as cristall wer his ene,
> As goldin wyre sa glitterand was his hair.

With Mars (ll. 183 ff.) a more metallic note is struck, with many monosyllables and richer alliteration, often on fricatives such as *f* and *h;* but there are neither the harshness of accent and alliteration nor (ll. 185 ff.) the knotted consonants of Saturn's picture:

> To chide and fecht, als feirs as ony fyre;
> In hard harnes, hewmond and habirgeoun,
> And on his hanche ane roustie fell fachioun . . .

In such passages as these, the melody, sound harmony and poetic inspiration of Chaucer, and the greater substance, harsher force, and more rugged rhythm of the native metre are welded into a new artistic expressiveness and suggestiveness, which enables Henryson to achieve a subtler modulation even than Chaucer. Henryson's feeling for contrasting rhythms shows in such a line as that ([***Testament of Cresseid***], l. 225) on Venus,

> Under smyling scho was dissimulait,

where the façade of the first half is torn to shreds by the whispering of the second, with its painting of disgust by sibilants and short *i* s. The Complaints of Cresseid (ll. 407 ff.) and also of Orpheus ([***Orpheus and Eurydice***], ll. 134 ff.) are considered metrical masterpieces; but Henryson also knows the effects to be produced by the common metre of the ballads (***Robene and Makyne, The Bludy Serk***). In contrast, however, to Dunbar's enormously richer variety of metres, Henryson's verse always serves the poetic expression and never inclines to virtuosity.

Though no less flexible than Chaucer's, Henryson's verse has a greater austerity. This is simply a characteristic of the Scots language as he wrote it. It is also a national characteristic, and the poet's outlook has the same austere quality as his verses. In his *Troilus and Criseyde,* Chaucer is an observer of the human comedy: whereas Henryson's ***Testament of Cresseid*** has the tragic intensity of a ballad. Even the slightest of Henryson's deviations from Chaucer go to heighten the effect of the "swordstroke tragedy." In the ***Testament,*** Calchas is a priest of Venus (not Apollo) and very fond of his daughter Cresseid. This makes Cresseid's fate all the more pathetic when she is punished for her blaspheming of Venus and Cupid. In his ***Fabillis,*** Henryson is even more independent, digesting his sources rather than following them, and combining elements from different fables to create a new meaning. For ***Robene and Makyne*** no real source or model is known, and Makyne seems to have been his own creation. His creative genius assimilates popular or traditional material so well that his tales read as though they had never been told before. . . . His handling of the plot of **"The Wolf and the Lamb"** is a good example of the manner in which he takes only a general idea, and of the originality he shows in developing it in his own way: though the wolf has his victim in his power he tries to prove legally that the lamb has fouled his water. His legalistic subtleties tear the disguise of allegory, and out comes a sharp satire on the abuse of law against the innocent. The morality—in this case almost half of the whole *Fable*—is even less medieval. Across three centuries we seem to hear the voice of Burns in the fervent indictment of the wolves in human shape, the perverters of right and the oppressors of the common people. The animal has been lost sight of; we get a detailed picture of social conditions, and the poet's whole sympathy is with the sturdy peasants suffering under bondage.

The preiching of the Swallow

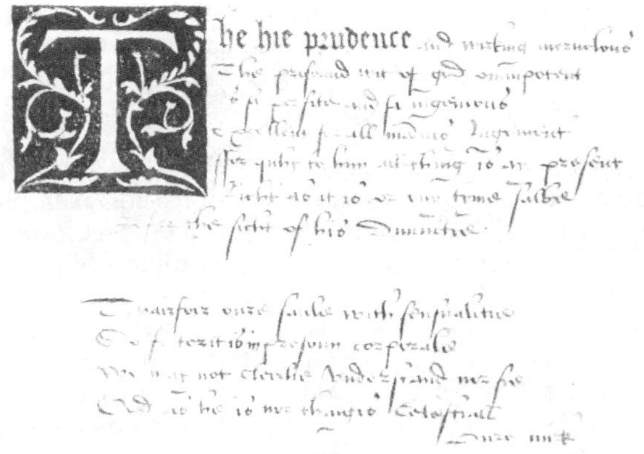

Manuscript version of "The Preiching of the Swallow." Taken from Harleian MS. No. 3865.

Henryson rarely is imitative or conventional. The description of summer and autumn in **"The Preiching of the Swallow"** (**[*Fabillis*]**, ll. 1678 ff.) follows a traditional pattern, with Bacchus, classical gods, and Mediterranean landscape; but those of winter (ll. 1692 ff.) and spring (ll. 1706 ff.) are based on genuine observation of the Lowland scene. The bleak picture of winter, with the wild animals (ll. 1703 ff.) creeping together for warmth in sheltered places, is wonderfully suggestive: so, too, the glimpses of the country folk (ll. 1721. ff.) mending their dykes in spring. With the poet we seem to smell (ll. 1718 f.) the promise of pregnant spring in the soil:

> To se the soill that wes richt sessonabill,
> Sappie, and to resave all seidis abill.

At first sight, the opening of **"The Taill of the Lyonn and the Mous"** looks like the conventional dream allegory, but this introduction of the dream of Æsop, who also pronounces the moral, is due to political caution in a fable that makes dangerous allusion to the weak King James III, and to treason. . . . And even in this dream there is much more individual realism, specific local colour and sharp observation than in Chaucer—or any English poet before the pre-romantics:

> His bonat round, and off the auld fassoun.
>
> 'Displeis you not, my gude maister, thocht I
> Demand your birth, your facultye, and name,
> Quhy ye come heir, or quhair ye dwell at hame?

The beginning of ***The Testament of Cresseid*** is the best evidence of Henryson's sovereign mastery in handling Chaucer's conventions. We have a seasonal opening, but without a trace of conventionality. The action is real, not a dream; it is very specific and highly personal. Instead of the traditional May, we have winter—which has always had a fascination for the Scots poets—with closely observed Scottish characteristics. The cold of winter, and the cold of old age in the poet create the bleak tragic atmosphere necessary for his tale. This use of setting and atmosphere (**[*Testament of Cresseid*]**, ll. 1 ff.) to heighten intensity has no precise equivalent in Chaucer's poetry:

> Ane doolie sessoun to ane cairfull dyte
> Suld correspond, and be equivalent.
> Richt sa it wes quhen I began to wryte
> This tragedie, the wedder richt fervent,
> Quhen Aries, in middis of the Lent,
> Schouris of haill can fra the north discend,
> That scantlie fra the cauld I micht defend.

Looking through the window of his "oratur," the poet sees Venus rising in opposition to the setting sun, and notices that a north wind has dispersed the clouds: but then (ll. 19 ff.):

> The froist freisit, the blastis bitterly
> Fra Pole Artick come quhisling loud and schill
> And causit me remufe aganis my will.
>
> For I traistit that Venus, Luifis Quene,
> To quhome sum tyme I hecht obedience,
> My faidit hart of lufe scho wald mak grene,
> And therupon with humbill reverence,
> I thocht to pray hir hie Magnificence;
> Bot for greit cald as than I lattit was,
> And in my chalmer to the fyre can pas.

In old age, love no longer fires the blood, and "the fyre outward is the best remeid": therefore, he goes on (ll. 36 ff.),

> I mend the fyre and beikit me about,
> Than tuik ane drink my spreitis to comfort,
> And armit me weill fra the cauld thairout.

To shorten the winter night, he reads Chaucer's *Troylus and Criseyde,* but then takes up another book, which tells (ll. 62 ff.)

> the fatall destenie
> Of fair Cresseid, that endit wretchitlie.

"Quha wait [knows]," he reflects (l. 64), "gif all that Chauceir wrait was trew?" And in narrating the "wofull end of this lustie Creisseid," he shows the same consummate mastery. Deserted by Diomeid, Cresseid, "sum men sayis" (l. 77), walked the "Court commoun," but finally returned repentant to her father. In her despair, she curses Venus and Cupid (ll. 126 ff.): but for her blasphemy the Gods, sitting in judgment, strike her (ll. 302 ff.) with leprosy. At the leper-house Troilus (ll. 495 ff.) rides past. Cresseid and he do not recognise each other, but her look suddenly calls up the picture of his Cresseid, and he leaves a rich gift. She inquires (ll. 533 ff.) who it is that has done the lepers "so greit humanitie"—but when she is told it was "Schir Troylus,"

> Stiffer than steill, thair stert ane bitter stound
> Throwout hir hart, and fell doun to the ground.

She acknowledges her own unfaithfulness, makes her testament and dies. Troilus erects a marble tomb where golden letters proclaim (ll. 607 ff.):

> Lo, fair ladyis, Crisseid, of Troyis toun,
> Symtyme countit the flour of womanheid,
> Under this stane lait lipper lyis deid.

The pace is quick and relentless, the whole poem completed in eighty-six stanzas. It is knit still more closely and dramatically by certain recurring themes, such as that of Esperus and Saturn: this note of fate and of cold makes the tragedy inescapable.

If the ***Testament*** is Henryson's tragic masterpiece, the thirteen ***Morall Fabillis of Esope the Phrygian*** are its serene counterpart. Fables were very popular in the Middle Ages; they express the medieval conception of the unity of the world and of all life. . . . Projecting human situations on to a lower and simpler level they facilitate a moral—and allow us to laugh at human weaknesses. Usually, the animal disguise is rather threadbare, a mere allegory. But Henryson's peculiarity is the close observation of *both* the human and the animal detail. He watches his animals intensely. . . . The difference can perhaps best be summed up as follows: in most fables the animals are simply human beings in disguise, but Henryson's animals are closely observed, and they are real animals. True, he endows them with human emotions and human motives, but this is largely in order to make it possible to answer the question how the *animal* would feel in such a situation—if it had human faculties. The animals in Henryson's ***Fabillis*** are thus both creatures and symbols. He has intense sympathy with them, and almost succeeds in entering into their minds—much like Liam O'Flaherty in his animal tales, or Robert Burns in mock-heroic form.

The poet sinks his whole personality in his tale, and **"The Taill of the Uponlandis Mous and the Burges Mous"** is a masterpiece; **"The Preiching of the Swallow"** and **"The Taill of the Wolf, the Foxe and the Cadgear** [hawker]**"** also deserve mention. His fables usually have a twofold moral: one—highly humanitarian and sociological—implicit in the tale; the other, the conventional *moralitas,* at the end. The latter sometimes comes as a surprise: in **"The Taill of the Cok and the Jasp** [precious stone]**"** we sympathise with the cock to whom the jewel, swept carelessly on to the midden by wanton damsels, is of no interest—corn or draff would be more useful. Yet in the *moralitas* the cock is represented as a fool scorning science, the jewel as the love of learning, now lost because men are satisfied with riches and have no patience to seek it. It seems almost as if the poet has allowed his own colourful fable to run away with him, and is now returning to his duty; for it is only the morality that justifies the "fenyeit taill" ([***Fabillis***], ll. 1 ff., 1384 ff.). The moralities of **"The Wolf and the Lamb"** . . . or of **"The Scheip and the Doig** [dog]**"** are a certain exception in their close integration with the tale.

It may come as a surprise that a poet who did not essay a single Scottish subject should hold a key-position in Scotland's literary tradition. But the fact that Henryson gave all his tales a specifically Scottish setting shows how successfully he has digested and assimilated his foreign material. In addition to the native Scottish pictures already mentioned, we have, in ***Orpheus and Eurydice*** (ll. 289 f.),

> Syne owr a mure, with thornis thick and scherp,
> Wepand alone, a wilsum way he went . . .

And on finding a dead fox, the cadger ([***Fabillis***], ll. 2061 f.) dances with joy,

> And all the trace he trippit on his tais;
> As he had hard ane pyper play, he gais;

he will make mittens from its pelt, and not send it to Flanders (l. 2074) to which Scottish fur and wool was shipped. But the fox has only tricked the cadger, who now leaps over a dyke to cut (ll. 2103 f.) a stick of "holyne [holly] grene"—a fine Scottish picture.

Henryson's details are so accurate that they give us a picture of contemporary social conditions: for example, his descriptions ([***Fabillis***], ll. 1825 ff.) of the flax industry—whose centre in Scotland was Dunfermline—of ploughing ([***Fabillis***], ll. 2231 ff.), and of the leper-house outside the gates of the town ([***Testament of Cresseid***], ll, 381 ff.). Henryson's imagery is so concrete that his description of Cresseid's symptoms enabled Sir J. Y. Simpson (the inventor of chloroform) to diagnose Greek elephantiasis, the most incurable variety of leprosis. Whatever he is dealing with—social conditions, astrological medicine, ecclesiastical affairs, contemporary legal abuses—Henryson is truly representative of his time. That is why Stearns could reconstruct a picture of Henryson's age from his poems, and Tillyard took the ***Testament*** as representative of the moral background of the fifteenth century. Henryson has the same keen interest in matters of fact as Barbour, but in rendering account of them he is at once more selective and more concrete. Above all, he is never pedestrian, and is always a consummate artist. His account of the system of the planets ([***Testament of Cresseid***], ll. 141 ff.) and their astronomical, mythological, medical, moral characteristics according to the thinking of his time could have been a dull encyclopædic tract, like Lydgate's in the *Assembly of the Gods.* In fact, it is one of the finest jewels in the treasure-house of Henryson's poetry. With the sure instinct of an artist Henryson selects those traits which best serve his purpose. Individually they lend themselves to the creation of a concrete picture, collectively they symbolise fate, thus heightening the dramatic tension: for the stars reveal the will of God; and in the light of astrology, Cresseid's sin in blaspheming Venus, her trial under Saturn, and her leprosy, form an absolutely natural sequence, and not a single thread could be cut without impairing the intricate weaving of the tragic texture of the poem as a whole.

The condensation of Henryson's stories is largely achieved by his intense power of visualisation. He is never vague or general; he makes us *see* a specific picture, complete in itself. Henryson does not simply report that the husbandman and the wolf take an oath, he makes us see how ([***Fabillis***], ll. 2313 f.)

> The wolff braid furth his fute, the man his hand,
> And on the toddis taill sworne thay ar to stand;

he does not merely state that the flax has grown, but visualises (ll. 1777 ff.) a specific scene:

> And seidis that wer sawin off beforne
> Wer growin hie, that hairis mycht thame hyde,
> And als the quailye craikand in the corne.

Often, too, he tells us (ll. 1743, 1792) where to look:

> 'Se ye yone churll' (quod scho) 'beyond yone pleuch . . .'

> 'Lift up your sicht, and tak gude advertence . . .'

Nothing in this fable of **"The Preiching of the Swallow"** is statement devoid of setting: we watch the crofter work his flax, see a sharply visualised winter scene when he sets his nets, hear the death-song of the birds, and witness the exact movements of the fowler who slays some with a stick, wrings the necks of others, and puts them in his bag.

The reader recreates Henryson's world with his eye, ear, nose. Henryson is keenly alive to the sense of colour. But he does not create static pictures; his quickly moving poetry teems with impressions of motion: the crouching of the fox, the cat playing with the mouse. The latter passage, and **"The Taill of the Paddok and the Mous,"** are, as it were, cinematic masterpieces. Above all, Henryson is fascinated by the manifold, ever-changing effects of light: light shining, shimmering, flashing; again and again these create, in Henryson's eye, a vivid, specific, momentaneous impression. If an imagined scene is not in itself sufficiently concrete, Henryson makes it more completely specific by means of a picturesque comparison. The coining of striking phrases and metaphors in which an image of immediate interest is presented with another suggested by it is one of the chief elements of style in all Scottish literature; and Henryson is a master of the art. Usually, an abstract idea is projected (*F.,* ll. 344 f., 2311 f.) into the vivid world of the senses:

> 'Thy mangerie is mingit all with cair,
> Thy guse is gude, thy gansell sour as gall.'

> 'Ye sall be sworne to stand at my decreit,
> Quhether heirefter ye think it soure or sweit.'

The objects on which Henryson's senses concentrate are those of his immediate surroundings. There is no horizon, no distance, no far-off noise, no general survey of a landscape; the sky ([***Testament of Cresseid***], ll. 1-28, 401; [***Fabillis***], ll. 1657-63) is only mentioned in connexion with the weather, or as a source of astrological data. Henryson presents *genre* pictures of country life with the pictorial sense of the Dutch painters. But in watching the objects around him he is so intent and goes so close to them that the perspective is lost and, as it were, he enters into them himself. The fox and the wolf, in the fable of the cadger, are not really *described;* by numerous intimate observations the poet takes us so close that we enter into, and *feel,* their being, and they assume a life of their own. The picture resulting from such intensity of detail is not an objective one: the poet's own personality permeates the tale, we see with his eyes, hear with his ears, feel his emotions. If Henryson ejaculates (as he often does) an angry comment or a grimly humorous remark, these are almost our own reactions, as when ([***Fabillis***], ll. 694 ff.) he does not want to intrude on the confession of the fox; or when (l. 295) looking through the corner of his eye, he says sardonically,

> Thay taryit not to wesche, as I suppose.

These quick flashes of the poet's personality establish relations of intimacy: the action suddenly concerns us, and the initially objective picture is shot through with subjective feeling. The action becomes life.

Henryson apprehends the world by his senses, not by his reason. In the prologue of **"The Preiching of the Swallow"** the poet tells us (ll. 1642 ff.) to "lat all ressoun be" if we want "to comprehend Him that contenis all":

> Yit nevertheles we may have knawlegeing
> Off God almychtie, be his creatouris,
> That he is gude, ffair, wyis and bening;
> Exempill tak be thir jolie flouris,
> Rycht sweit of smell, and plesant off colouris.
> Sum grene, sum blew, sum purpour, quhyte, and reid,
> Thus distribute be gift off his Godheid.

This explains his innocent delight in the world of the senses. It also shows the strength and the limitation of his vision. Where, in ***Orpheus and Eurydice,*** Henryson gives a survey, a report, he is trite and pale; but where he can intently visualise, *vivify,* a scene, down to the details of his own environment, there he is grand: as in Euridice's flight (ll. 103 ff.), the memories of the Complaint (ll. 134 ff.), the music of the spheres (ll. 219 ff.), the scenes of the search (ll. 247-309). Henryson's strength lies in the reality of his setting, which betrays quite as pronounced a realism of outlook as Barbour's. The presentation of love in ***The Testament of Cresseid*** is realistic, not courtly; the ***Fabillis*** are rich in realism—look at Sprutok's conception of love as compared with Pertok's courtly ideal in **"Schir Chantecleir and the Foxe"** (ll. 509 ff.). ***Robene and Makyne*** is built up on such a conception, and ***Orpheus and Eurydice*** is one of the very few poems of the Middle Ages that tells a classical tale for its own sake, with no allegorical trappings.

The sharp clarity of Henryson's pictures lies partly in the fact that he practises the utmost economy of expression. There is no padding, not a stanza too much, and should the poet digress, he quickly returns to his theme. This concision gives his poems an enormous impact on our mind. Henryson satisfies Edgar Allan Poe's requirement that from the first sentence the writer of a short story must work towards a total effect. Henryson's economy of expression is most remarkable where he deals with deep emotions or with the sublime. Little of the intense feeling or the horror crosses his lips, but there is often immense suggestion in his understatement . . .

> The man leuch na thing, quhen he saw that sicht.

> Quhen Diomeid had all his appetyte,

And mair, fulfillit of this fair ladie,
Upon ane uther he set his haill delyte
And send to hir ane lybell of repudie,
And hir excludit fra his companie.
Than desolait scho walkit up and doun,
And sum men sayis into the court commoun.

. . . I have pietie thou suld fall sic mischance.

Cresseid prays in the temple "with baill aneuch [sorrow enough] in breist" (l. 110); after the hideous deformation of her beauty by the sentence of the gods she looks (ll. 349-50) into a mirror,

And quhen scho saw hir face sa deformait
Gif scho in hart was wa aneuch God wait.

Mute pain reaches its greatest depth when (ll. 372 ff.) Calchas sees his daughter:

He luikit on hir uglye lipper face,
The quhilk befor was quhyte as lillie flour,
Wringand his handis oftymes he said allace
That he had levit to se that wofull hour,
For he knew weill that thair was na succour
To hir seikness, and that dowblit his pane.
Thus was thair cair aneuch betwix thame twane.

This is a specifically Scottish mode of expression. The greatest emotion falls in the pause between two stanzas, and Henryson is a master of the art of making a pause speak. . . . The finest example . . . is during the luxurious banquet of **"The Uponlandis Mous and the Burges Mous"**; they have reached the blissful state of singing "haill yule, haill!" when (ll. 293-4)

The spenser come with keyis in his hand,
Oppinnit the dure, and thame at denner fand.

We feel the petrifying shock in the pause before the next stanza; the subsequent frantic haste is expressed (l. 295) in a sardonic negative understatement:

Thay taryit not to wesche, as I suppose.

This technique of using a pause to intensify dramatic tension closely resembles the ballads, as does the quick shifting of the scene (which one might call "montage").

This tightlipped reticence is partly achieved by Henryson's use of contrast. When pathos seems to rise to the highest pitch, the poet looks abruptly away and sees the common reality of every day. Thus Cresseid has just learnt her fate, and is still dazed with the horror of it, when a child comes from the hall to tell her that supper is ready and that her father (ll. 362 ff.)

'. . . hes mervell sa lang on grouf ye ly,
And sayis your prayers bene to lang sum deill:
The goddis wait all your intent full weill.'

The contrast of tone is heightened by a similar contrast of rhythm: the grating accents of Saturn's sentence, the soft cadences of Cresseid's first soliloquy, and the simplicity of the child bringing the father's message. From the high elegiac note and soft rhythms of her great complaint Cresseid is grimly brought back to earth by a fellow-leper, who says (ll. 475 ff.):

. . . 'Quhy spurnis thow aganis the wall,
To sla thy self, and mend nathing at all?'

'Sen thy weiping dowbillis bot thy wo,
I counsall the mak vertew of ane neid.
To leir to clap thy clapper to and fro,
And leir efter the law of lipper leid.'

From the opening contrast between bleak cold and ardent love to the epitaph "lait lipper lyis deid" written in letters of gold, sustained thematic contrast is the source from which the immense tension of the ***Testament*** arises. It is (as Tillyard points out) a contrast between knowledge and ignorance that underlies the tragic irony of the sublime scene that occurs when the lovers meet for the last time. What a world of difference there is between this chance encounter (ll. 498-525) and their former meetings as lovers! When Troilus, in splendid array, passes the deformed Cresseid at the leper-house:

Than upon him scho kest up baith hir ene,
And with ane blenk it come into his thocht,
That he sumtime hir face befoir had sene.
Bot scho was in sic plye he knew hir nocht,
Yit than hir luik into his mynd it brocht
The sweit visage and amorous blenking
Of fair Cresseid sumtyme his awin darling.

. . . The idole of ane thing, in cace may be
Sa deip imprentit in the fantasy
That it deludis the wittis outwardly,
And sa appeiris in forme and lyke estait,
Within the mynd as it was figurait.

Ane spark of lufe than till his hart culd spring . . .
Within ane quhyle he changit mony hew,
And nevertheless not ane ane uther knew.

Has this passage, with its intense psychology and intimate penetration into the mind, any parallel in medieval literature?

In the ***Fabillis,*** the contrast is not tragic but humorous, as in the opening (ll. 2777 ff.) of **"The Paddok** [frog] **and the Mous"**:

Upon ane tyme (as Esope culd report)
Ane lytill mous come till ane rever syde;
Scho micht not waid, hir schankis were sa schort,
Scho culd not swym, scho had na hors to ryde:
Of verray force behovit hir to bydé,
And to and ffra besyde that revir deip
Scho ran, cryand with mony pietuous peip.

This is wonderfully observed animal life—but like a flash comes the phrase "scho had na hors to ryde." From this intrusion of the human world and the resulting contrast of tall and small arises the tender and pervasive humour, the compassion which subtly points to the human in the animal, or the beast in man. Thus the "uponlandis mous" has (l. 360) her "but and ben," and her town-dwelling sister was (ll. 171 ff.) "gild brother" and "fre burges,"

And fredome had to ga quhair ever scho list,
Amang the cheis in ark, and meill in kist.

In her pantry, the burgess mouse has (l. 265) "flesche and fische aneuch, baith [both] fresche and salt," and when (l.

180) her poor sister comes "bairfute, allone, with pykestaf in hir hand," they feast (ll. 267 ff.) like lords,

> Except ane thing, thay drank the watter cleir.

Much of this is grotesque exaggeration, and the juxtaposition of understatement and overstatement is a characteristic phenomenon in Scottish literature: genuine emotions of the soul are rather suggested than expressed, but the airs that men give themselves are heightened to grotesquerie. This is all the more rollicking here because it is a tiny mouse that lives in a world of pretence. Who does not recognise the hysterics of that other mouse (ll. 2798 ff.) dancing round the paddock [frog], or (ll. 218 ff.) our burgess mouse, indignant at the simple fare her sister offers:

> 'My fair sister' (quod scho), 'have me excusit.
> This rude dyat and I can not accord.
> To tender meit my stomok is ay usit,
> For quhylis I fair alsweill as ony lord.
> Thir wydderit peis, and nuttis, or thay be bord,
> Wil brek my teith, and mak my wame fful sklender,
> Quhilk wes before usit to meitis tender.'

Equally authentic is her taunt (l. 249):

> 'My dische likingis is worth your haill expence.'

The grotesqueness often lies in a comparison, as when the fox (ll. 1051 ff.) answers the inquiries as to the success of a mission by pointing at the bloody head of his companion, the wolf:

> Than Lowrence said: 'My lord, speir not at me!
> Speir at your Doctour off Divinitie,
> With his reid cap can tell yow weill aneuch.

How closely understatement and grotesque exaggeration may combine is shown when despite cheerful invitations by her sister the burgess mouse remains adamant (ll. 239 f.) in her indignation:

> For all hir mery exhortatioun,
> This burges mous had littill will to sing [!].

. . . . .

Henryson's philosophy is rooted in deep religious and moral feeling, and is conspicuously humanitarian, democratic, and independent. Henryson does not speak much about his religion, but it is implicit everywhere. ***The Testament of Cresseid*** does not, as some critics think, reflect the sternness (as compared with Chaucer's humanity) of a puritanical Scottish schoolmaster: rather it holds out a promise of Christian redemption for Cresseid. At the end of Chaucer's *Troilus and Criseyde,* she is a hated outcast and a bad example held up for the cruel scorn of posterity. Henryson says (ll. 87 f.):

> I sall excuse, as far furth as I may,
> Thy womanheid . . .

She has violated the laws of love, and revolts against the planets as set on their courses by God. Even her punishment at first only leads to self-pity: she laments (ll. 351 ff.) *that* she spoke, not *what* she spoke. Only when, as a result of her new meeting with Troilus, she recognises his faithfulness and her own treason, does she *repent* (ll. 542 ff.) and accuse herself: she is saved by her love. Now her *soul* is redeemed—Cresseid leaves it to chaste Diane—even though her body is the prey of toads and worms.

Henryson's creed is summed up (ll. 1647 ff.) in **"The Preiching of the Swallow"**:

> Nane suld presume, be ressoun naturall,
> To seirche the secreitis off the Trinitie,
> Bot trow fermelie, and lat all ressoun be.

He has the firm faith of his time in the divine order of God's creation, where man, animal, and planet all have their appointed place in one and the same universe, and all bear witness that God is "gude, ffair, wyis, and bening." Hence arises Henryson's own innocent delight in nature, of which we have already seen so many examples; hence, too, the righteous indignation with which he observes the failure of the mighty of this world to play the parts that God has allotted to them. For if God is good, he is also just, and those who exploit the poor should dread ([***Fabillis***], l. 2760) "the rychteous Goddis blame":

> O thow grit lord, that riches hes and rent,
> Be nocht ane wolf, thus to devoir the pure;
> Think that na thing cruell nor violent
> May in this warld perpetuallie indure.

Henryson's sharp social and religious satire contains much that is commonplace: the burgess mouse does not say grace; Orpheus finds popes, cardinals, bishops, abbots, in hell; the abuses of the civil as well as the ecclesiastical courts are castigated; in **"The Fox and the Wolf"** there is a hint of abuse of the confession. But there are, however, some remarkable passages. In **"The Wolf and the Lamb,"** the lamb (ll. 2663 ff.) protests against being judged for its father's guilt, while the wolf (ll. 2671 ff.) demands punishment down to the twentieth degree. Like Barbour before him, Henryson does not mention the intercession of the Church or her guardian angels and saints. He, and his creatures, address God directly. The lamb quotes Scripture. In **"The Taill of the Scheip and the Doig,"** the sheep (ll. 1295 f.) reproaches its maker:

> And said, 'Lord God, quhy sleipis thow sa lang?
> Walk, and discerne my cause, groundit on richt,'

and the poet himself exclaims (ll. 1307 f.):

> Seis thow not (Lord) this warld owerturnit is,
> As quha wald change gude gold in leid or tyn?

In addressing God, Henryson uses a tone of intimacy that clearly foreshadows the Presbyterians and their daily reckoning with God. He does not share the Presbyterian tendency to mistrust happiness as such, but he does show a shrewdness that is characteristic of the peasant in all ages, and is very suspicious of all happiness not built up by one's own work—as when (l. 278) the country mouse sees her sister's full larder:

> 'Ye, dame' (quod scho), 'how lang will this lest?'

The swallow warns the birds that they will live to rue their easygoing carelessness; they will pay with their own lives what they ate from the fowler (ll. 1839 ff.). This, however, has already taken us to the secular side of Henryson's philosophy.

Henryson is a countryman; and his philosophy is as firmly rooted in rustic folk wisdom as in religious faith. This gives him poise and the sturdy independence of the peasant who does his work but is too stiff to bow. In the fable—essentially democratic in its appeal—this independence finds an appropriate means of expression. Henryson puts all his love into two of the longest, **"The Taill of the Uponlandis Mous and the Burges Mous"** and **"The Preiching of the Swallow"**; both express the same attitude, the instinctive prudence of the peasant who wants to have both feet on the ground and is suspicious of gambling. Turning her back on "ffeistis delicate" given (ll. 232-3) with "ane glowmand [gloomy] brow," the country mouse returns (ll. 358 ff.)

. . . to hir den,
Als warme as woll, suppose it wes not gret;

though modest, her own way of life is not lacking in happiness and dignity. This is not a cheap common-place, but an almost defiantly, yet unsentimentally, democratic attitude, such as we see also in **"The Cok and the Jasp"** or **"The Wolf and the Lamb."** It is almost the same as that seen in "A Man's a Man for a' that." Never before in medieval literature had the dignity and the rights of the peasant and the common people been proclaimed in such tones. Henryson sees the crofter realistically, in his life and in his work; the simplicity of his outlook and his few fundamental moral principles; his uprightness, his obstinacy, his shrewdness, his homeliness, his suspicion of newfangled things, his gift of making the best of what he finds. This enables him to draw quick character studies of his countrymen, such as the calculating cadger ([***Fabillis***], ll. 2070 ff., 2091 ff.), the fowler (ll. 1839 ff.), the leper lady ([***Testament of Cresseid***], ll. 474 ff.) with no nonsense about her.

With his roots in the people, Henryson shares the old wisdom of the folk, their poetry, proverbs, and lore. His language is popular, his humour that of the people, his quick dialogues colloquial. But at the same time his art is of Chaucer's brilliancy, and his freshness makes even a proverb sound as if we had never heard it, as when (***Robene and Makyne,*** ll. 91 f.) Makyne tartly refuses Robene, who had previously scorned her advances:

The man that will nocht quhen he may
Sall haif nocht quhen he wald.

The closeness of Henryson to folk poetry is most evident in his many points of contact with the ballads; the stark tragedy, the use of contrast, the montage, the grim humour, the drama. For Henryson is rarely the scenic artist (as in the pageant of the planets in the ***Testament***), but presents, without transitions, speech and answer, picture beside picture, resolution and deed, as in **"The Lyonn and the Mous," "The Wolf and the Lamb,"** the ***Ressoning*** poems, or ***Robene and Makyne,*** that remarkable precursor of pastoral drama. Henryson writes art poetry, not folk poetry, but his work contains elements of folk poetry and is based partly on folk tradition. In his assimilation of European subject matter, of Chaucer's conception of poetic art, and of Scottish characteristics, Robert Henryson is one of the greatest poets of the whole of Scottish literature, perhaps the greatest of all, and certainly the one with the most marked personality. (pp. 34-52)

Kurt Wittig, "Full Tide: The Makars," in his The Scottish Tradition in Literature, *Oliver and Boyd Ltd., 1958, pp. 33-90.*

A. M. Kinghorn (essay date 1965)

[*In the excerpt below, Kinghorn surveys Henryson's minor poems, particularly focusing on* Robene and Makyne *and* Sum Practysis of Medecyne.]

Modern critics of Henryson have, in the main, restricted their attention to ***The Testament of Cresseid,*** with some incursions into ***The Morall Fabillis.*** Henryson in fact, wrote at least fourteen other poems, of varying quality and interest, but stamped with their creator's individuality and each worthy of more detailed attention than it has been given. As in the cases of ***The Testament*** and ***The Fabillis,*** the most prominent feature of these minor works is the poet's learning and the rhetorical technique by means of which he incorporates it, quite unobtrusively, into his verse. Henryson's bookishness, far more extensive than Dunbar's, is evident in every poem, and the generally slow tempo induces an impression of weightiness which is absent from Dunbar. Henryson displays the learning of a conservative scholar of his time and country; not a mercurial soul like Dunbar, he is less given to emotional fluctuations of mood and much more of a deliberate preacher. His vocabulary is generally less mannered than Dunbar's and closer to what we believe popular speech to have been like; Henryson's atmosphere is pastoral and of the countryside rather than courtly and of the town and he contemplates the vicissitudes of the world from the point of view of his "rurall mous" whose "sempill lyfe withoutin dreid" is the ideal to be sought and cherished.

Robene and Makyne is perhaps the best illustration of the way in which Henryson marshals his talents as a lyrical poet to make a didactic pastoral. The subject is love between rustics, its form is that of the *débat,* and it is written, though only superficially, in the style of the OF *pastourelles.* The conversational dialogue between the Scots lover and his lass conveys a simple moral of the "gather ye rosebuds" kind, and each stanza is subtly different from its predecessor in mood or in the picture it builds. Robene is keeping his sheep when Makyne reveals her long-standing love for him and tells him that unless he returns it she will certainly die. Robene protests his ignorance of love, whereupon Makyne immediately reveals an unexpected sophistication and shows her familiarity with the language and practices of textbook *amour courtois:*

'be heynd, courtass, and fair of feir,
Wyse, hardy and fre;
So that no denger do the deir,
quhat dule in dern thow dre;
preiss the with pane at all poweir,
be patient and previe.'

Robene is half-hearted and wants to postpone the proferred sexual association until a vague tomorrow; in spite of her entreaties, he leaves her desolate. Later, he has second thoughts, but by this time so has she, and quotes the old saw:

> The man that will nocht quhen he may
> sall haif nocht quhen he wald

Unwilling in his turn to accept rejection, Robene counters this with an enticing picture of dalliance:

> 'Makyne, the nicht is soft and dry,
> The wedder is warme & fair,
> And the grene woid rycht neir us by
> To walk attour all quhair;
> Thair ma na Janglour us espy,
> That is to lufe contrair;
> Thairin, makyne, bath ye & I
> Unsene we ma repair.'

Nevertheless, she remains indifferent and the tables are turned. It is Robene who is finally left to mourn and Makyne to laugh, and we leave him as we found him, looking after his sheep, stricken with remorse because of his casual conduct.

The piece has strong dramatic qualities, for the stanzas are little scenes in themselves and the Scots dialogue is itself colourful and dramatic, but there is no explicit intention on Henryson's part to venture outside the pastoral-lyrical tradition, of which ***Robene and Makyne*** is an elaborate example looking forward to *The Shepheardes Calender.* Althought the inevitable moral purpose is plain and the conventionally named *personae* may mask a significant contemporary allegory, as they do in the ***Fabillis,*** this is Henryson's lightest poem, essentially a song, voicing alternating moods of hope and despair, and conveyed in terms of old-established traditions of ballad, proverb and native irony.

The Bludy Serk has much in common with ***Robene and Makyne,*** though it is more obviously derived from models. It is a narrative with *moralitas* appended, written in the style of the verse romances and telling of a king's beautiful daughter, imprisoned by a foul giant, released by a champion knight who defeated the giant but was so severely wounded in the process that he died. However, before expiring, he bestows on the lady his bloodstained shift, enjoining her to hang it up and think on it and on him whenever suitors beset her. The lady's love for her knight is so great that she vows to remain celibate. The key to the allegory reveals the king as the Trinity, the lady as the soul of Man, the giant as Lucifer, the knight as Christ the martyr, the dungeon as Hell, and the possible suitors as Sin. The blood-stained shift is a symbol of the blood of Christ the Redeemer. The poem is conceived in the ballad-style, and is an instance of an early attempt to create the artificial ballad in direct imitation of known genuine examples which circulated in fifteenth-century Scotland. Many devices of the oral-narrator are built into it—repetition for metrical convenience, conventional descriptive phrases and word-patterns, and a crude sketching of character, but the whole impression is one of a poetical exercise written to illustrate a religious truth.

It is tempting to claim ***Orpheus and Eurydice*** as early work, though there is no real evidence for this. The longest of the minor poems, it is based on Nicholas Trivet's interpretation of the Orpheus legend as told by Boethius and has little in common with the Middle English *Sir Orfeo,* to which it is in any event so inferior as to make comparison pointless. There is little human interest, for Orpheus is a symbol, allegorically justified in the tedious *moralitas,* as the union of Phoebus (wisdom) and Calliope (eloquence), and described as the intellectual part of man's soul. Eurydice represents desire led by temptation and the narrative is an allegory of the early Christian *Psychomachia*—the battle within the soul between the rational and sensual sides of man's nature; Orpheus's inability to resist looking back at Eurydice stands for the triumph of worldly lust and vain prosperity over reason. This is the standard Augustinian interpretation of the legend, popular with theologians from the sixth century onwards, and Henryson adds nothing to it. Just as familiar are the scholarly devices by which he gives the poem weight,—the musical references (taken from Boethius' *De Musica*), the procession of the Muses, the elongated classical allusions, the *mappa mundi,*—all of which are ponderously literary and have parallels in earlier works by both English and Scots writers.

For the critic, the interest of the poem lies in its scenic descriptions. The way in which Scots poetry takes external nature from the life and does not simply sketch in an imagined background of natural lushness is a feature noted by critics from Ramsay onwards. The Scots excel at painting winter and bad weather scenes and Henryson's glance at Orpheus's path towards Hell is an act of memory—the dreary moor, with its thick thorn bushes, and the slippery track through the field have an authenticity about them not matched in English, wherein most late mediaeval climatic descriptions are inclined to be stagy conventional backdrops for the narrative matter which is usually the Southron poet's main concern. Hell is a "dully place," a "grundles deip dungeoun" with all its attendant material horrors, fire and stink and poison and torment, where dwell the undead "ay deand, and nevirmoir sall de." There we encounter the familiar collection of mediaeval sinners, starting with classical and Hebrew tyrants and evildoers and including contemporary prelates convicted of abuses—popes, cardinals, bishops, abbots and other men of religion who had misused their offices, all tormented in the flames. References of this kind are the stock-in-trade of the late mediaeval satirist but the clear domestication of the topography of hell and the importation of mythological personages, such as Cerberus, the Eumenides, Ixion, Tantalus and Titius, together with the unmistakeably Lowland accents of Pluto, Prosperpyne and Orpheus himself place this work squarely in the Scots tradition.

The narrative is sketchy and follows the Ovidian and Vergilian versions; Orpheus only rarely comes alive, as for example in the three opening stanzas of the "Complaint," wherein he cries inconsolably for his vanished wife:

> quhair art thow gone, my luve ewridicess?

and takes his leave of his old haunts. The work shows Henryson to be already an accomplished poet and there is nothing in it suggestive of the 'prentice technician', but its heavy dependence on stock material and a comparison with ***The Testament of Cresseid*** reveals a certain rawness which one associates with immaturity of conception.

The Thre Deid Pollis treats of a familiar mediaeval subject, death—in this instance through its repulsive physical aspects which all men must one day adopt. The poem is strong in pictorial qualities and the reader is asked to imagine the skulls in a row, either real ones or perhaps effigies on a tomb, contemplated by the gloomy poet. They stand out starkly, with cavernous eye sockets and hairless domes and behind them, in a mocking double vision, the "lusty gallandis gay" who will be as they are now, "holkit and how, and wallowit as the weid," and the "ladeis quhyt," their physical charms enhanced by precious stones and jewellery, who shall one day lie "with peilit pollis, and holkit thus your heid."

Having issued this awful reminder, the poet hammers home his moral, warning us against pride, asking us to be humble and seek mercy because earthly vanities and pomp, human achievement and learning are in the end best symbolised by an empty death's head. He makes a special appeal to the aged, who are shortly to die, exhorting them to fall on their knees and ask forgiveness, and concludes with a general injunction to all mankind to pray to the Redeemer for salvation. The piece is a sermon in miniature, which depends for its effect on the pervasive presence of the three grinning skulls and the awful terror of change which affected the mediaeval mind. Henryson keeps the skulls before us in each stanza, thus ensuring the success of an otherwise unremarkable poem through their morbid appeal.

The Ressoning betwix Deth and Man is a dialogue on the same subject, but lacking the force given by the image of the skulls—it reads like a scene from a morality play. Man is full of bounce until he finds out what he is addressing, when he straightway drops his arrogance and obeys death's command to repent and his injunction "edderis, askis and wormis meit for to be." Death is here his own moraliser and man shrinks from his grasp, crying for Christ's mercy on the judgment-day. ***The Ressoning betwix Aige and Yowth*** follows the dialogue pattern but is much more striking. It depends on contrasted portraits of youth and of age and the poet shows how their views of the world differ. Whereas the young man regards it as a place in which to disport himself and to be merry, the old man gazes outward with gloom and despondency and admonishes his companion, telling him that the flower of his youth will soon fade away. The contrast is emphasised in the two refrains which alternate with the speakers:

> O yowth, be glaid in to thy flowris grene.

and

> O yowth, thy flowris fedis fellone sone.

both of which are accepted by the poet, in the final stanza, as true.

The Prais of Aige is a variation on the same theme; this is the point-of-view of an old man, who takes what amounts to a Greek line of argument, rejecting youth's hot-blooded pursuit of vanity and stating a preference for the clear vision of mature years. Although decrepit, the old man is joyful and clear of voice, and inspires the poet who encounters him with his burden of contentment:

> The more of age, the nerar hevynnis blisse.

There is a note of mild protest in this poem which seems to be born of patient endurance of the covetousness of others, and it conveys a personal message usually absent from poems on the theme of earthly vanity.

The same may be said of ***The Abbay Walk,*** the title of which . . . has nothing to do with rambling in the cloisters but is merely a slender prop on which to hang a gloomy moralising poem on the standard pulpit text instructing one to accept one's lot, be it happy or miserable, because all is vanity. Henryson talks like a calm monk, who knows that the world and its values are set at naught and offers consolation from the point-of-view of a man whose faith has matured amidst raw experience. It is this tone in Henryson's religious poems which marks them off from Dunbar's; Henryson is far surer of his place in the scheme of things and he talks without animus as a man enabled by his faith to reject the ultimately worthless and hold fast to what he thinks really valuable; he seems to have little enthusiasm for the shiny attractions of urban life or for the court preferment which cost Dunbar so many sleepless nights. ***The Want of Wyse Men*** and ***Aganis Haisty Credence of Titlaris*** are both closer to Dunbar, or even Lyndsay, in spirit, although the tone is, as we have come to expect from Henryson, more detached and impersonal. The poems throw light on the crude "political" atmosphere of the two "estates," wherein fools were plentiful and loose-tongued, and irresponsible tale-bearers were hearkened to in high places. Henryson is giving a balanced opinion on the causes of administrative corruption, speaking as a poor outsider whose sufferings from the unwisdom of governors are indirect; in the second poem, he warns a governor against listening to unsolicited or lying reports without weighing the evidence; the last stanza paints a grotesque portrait of the "bakbyttar," reminiscent of Langland:

> Within ane hude he hes ane dowbill face,
> Ane bludy tung, undir a fair pretence.

Ane Prayer for the Pest has much in common with the preceding two, for Henryson, in sending up his supplication to God "to preserve us fra this perrelus pestilens," is speaking as spokesman for the ordinary man, later distinguished by Lyndsay under the name of John the Common Weal, whose burdens were unfair, whose treatment by the powerful was unjust and who lacked any protection but the power of prayer. The sentiment in this poem is that of the ***Morall Fabillis,*** particularly of **"The Sheip and the Doig,"** in which, regarding himself as one of them, he pleads specifically for the poor. If Henryson is in any sense a court poet, he is a court poet from a very different stable from the "auld gray horse Dunbar," who is no champion of the oppressed and invariably thinks mainly of himself and his own insecurity at the hands of the king and nobles. Henryson's impersonality is not a sign of remoteness but of selflessness.

The Annunciation and ***The Garmont of Gud Ladeis*** are both excercises on familiar topics—the former stereotyped in theme but elegant in presentation, in fact, the last stanza attains a spontaneity rare among such utterances, drawing attention away from the meticulous care bestowed by the poet on the form of his creation, a hymn of praise for the Virgin:

> O lady lele and lusumest,
> Thy face moist fair & schene Is!
> O blosum blithe and bowsumest,
> Fra carnale cryme that clene Is!
> This prayer fra my splene Is,
> That all my werkis wikkitest
> Thow put away, and mak me chaist
> Fra termigant that teyn Is,
> And fra his cluke that kene Is;
> And syne till hevin my saule thou haist
> Quhar thi makar of michtis mast
> Is kyng, and thow thair quene Is.

The Garmont of Gud Ladeis is a succinct version in short stanzas of a usually long-winded form, namely, the robing of his "gud lady" in various items of clothing each having its moral significance, and although Henryson had precedents, both in French and in English, for this kind of formal personification, he manages to impart a freshness and apparent spontaneity which, as in ***The Annunciation*** masks the triteness of the matter; this he does so well as to give the poem the same hymn-like character, even though in this instance the subject is a moral lesson, designed to be acceptable, perhaps, to the young children taught by Henryson in the Benedictine Abbey school at Dunfermline.

Sum Practysis of Medecyne stands out from all the others because it is a parody of the prescriptions of contemporary apothecaries, aimed at the reader who knows of their ever-complicated character (a legacy of the Arabian compilers and of the medical schools of Salerno and Montpellier who followed the example of these treatises). Henryson achieves his satirical object by listing, in popular alliterative measure, items in a compound which are far-fetched, non-existent, or irrelevant as a cure for the ailment they claim to master. One is momentarily reminded of Villon's *ballade* suggesting a recipe for stewing envious tongues, but unlike Villon, Henryson is not twisted by contempt; instead he is impelled by a good-natured leg-pulling spirit to burlesque the practises of a profession for which he has a strong regard. Henryson is expert at describing the external symptoms of a disease and his account of Cresseid's leprosy was cited by Simpson as evidence of the incidence of Greek elephantiasis in Northern Europe by the sixteenth century. . . . Whatever the sources of the poet's information may have been, ***Sum Practysis of Medecyne*** supplies additional evidence of his keen interest in healing. (pp. 30-8)

All these poems are obviously the work of a skilled *makar,* who tells us little about himself though he obviously moved in the world as an active teacher and helper of men, and whose mainly serious character and steadiness of purpose is mirrored in his handling of stock late mediaeval subjects, rustic love, religious faith, prayer, moral dialogue, incidents of classical legend, complaint against current abuses and of course death, both as a symbol and a stark reality. He is not much given to broad humour, and his sympathetic fastidiousness does not permit him to indulge in Dunbar's satirical scurrility—Henryson's single attempt at burlesque is mild and kindly meant and he lacks the temperament for poetic "flyting." There is no single line in any of his poems which carries a dart with it, and no individual is ever wounded through his righteous indignation. Compared with Dunbar, whose moods vary from scorn to anguish, sometimes within the same poem, Henryson is consistent and predictable throughout the entire canon of his works. The pace of his poetry is leisured but rarely laboured, in spite of the strong moralising character of most of it, and his use of Scots for dialogue, for "aureate" literary passages, and for original descriptive purposes, particularly of harsh weather, is unobtrusively polished, so much so that one scarcely notes how markedly alliterative it is, as for example, in:

> Treuth is all tynt, gyle has the gouvernance,
> Wretchitnes has wroht all welthis wele to wo;
> Fredome is tynt, and flemyt the lordis fro,
> And covatise is all the cause of this.

Henryson does not exercise Dunbar's despotic power over the alliterative long line, and he never risks experimenting with a daring vocabulary in order to justify an otherwise slender offering, so that his verse is less colourful, less dashing and generally more sober than Dunbar's. Not being an innovator in poetic forms and styles, he has not served as a model for later poets, as Dunbar did, and his firm intellectual rooting in the traditional learning of the Middle Ages, together with a saintly conservatism of temperament, has made of him an occasionally admired, but largely neglected *makar.* As a preparation for reading ***The Testament*** and ***The Fabillis,*** these minor poems are invaluable, and now that exactly one hundred years have passed since the first collected edition of his works was published, one feels that it should by this time be possible to discuss Henryson's poems, or at least his lesser pieces, without compulsive references to "Chaucer" and the Chaucerian yardstick. (pp. 39-40)

A. M. Kinghorn, "The Minor Poems of Robert Henryson," in Studies in Scottish Literature, *Vol. III, No. 1, July, 1965, pp. 30-40.*

Edwin Muir (essay date 1965)

[*Muir was a distinguished Scottish novelist, poet, critic, and translator, who was more concerned with the general philosophical issues raised by literary works—such as the nature of time or society—than with the particulars of the work itself, such as style or characterization. In the excerpt below, Muir praises Henryson's "high concise style" and his imaginative creation of the narratives of the* Morall Fabillis *and the* Testament of Cresseid.]

Henryson's poetry has two main virtues; one the property of his age, the other more specifically his own. The first is as important as the second. He lived near the end of a great age of settlement, religious, intellectual and social; an agreement had been reached regarding the nature and meaning of human life, and the imagination could attain harmony and tranquillity. It was one of those ages when everything, in spite of the practical disorder of life, seems to have its place; the ranks and occupations of men; the hierarchy of animals; good and evil; the earth, heaven and hell; and the life of man and of the beasts turns naturally into a story because it is part of a greater story about which there is general consent. Henryson, like Chaucer, exists in that long calm of storytelling which ended with the Renaissance, when the agreement about the great story was broken. There is still an echo of the tranquillity in Spenser. But in *The Faerie Queene* he deals with the delightful creatures of his fancy, and Chaucer and Henryson deal with men and women, wolves and sheep, cats and mice.

The virtue of the story while it lasted was that it made everything natural, even tragedy; so that while pity had a place, there was no place for those outcries against life which fill the tragic drama of the next age. The framework and the nature of the story excluded them. And the pity itself is different from that of the Elizabethans, as deep, but tranquillised by the knowledge that tragedy has its place in the story. The poet accepts life, as the Elizabethans tried to do, but is also resigned to it; the acceptance implying the resignation, and the resignation the acceptance. This attitude makes the age between Chaucer and Henryson the great age of the story. The Elizabethan drama arose when the long peace of storytelling was broken.

The sense that all life, whether of the animals or of men, is a story and part of a greater story, is then one of the surviving virtues of Henryson's poetry, strong enough still, in spite of all that has happened since, to produce a composing effect on us and remind us of a standard of proportion which has been lost. It is the virtue of an age, not ours, and it required to embody it a particular form of art, not ours, and in the practice of that art Henryson was almost perfect.

> Upon ane tyme (as Esope culd Report)
> Ane lytill Mous came till ane Revir syde;
> Scho micht not waid, hir schankis were sa schort,
> Scho culd not swym, scho had na hors to ryde:
> Of verray force behovit hir to byde,
> And to and fra besyde that Revir deip
> Scho ran, cryand with mony pietuous peip.

We recognise the narrative art of an age, which passed with that age. In Henryson what delights us is the perfection with which it is controlled, its speed, which is neither hurried nor lumbering, and the momentary touches of humour and fancy which, while never retarding the story, give it interest and vivacity:

> Scho culd not swym, scho had na hors to ryde.

Henryson's personal contribution to that consummate art was a fanciful eye for detail and a profound sense of situation, most usually comic, but in one or two cases tragic. ***The Moral Fabillis of Esope the Phrygian*** is his great humorous, and ***The Testament of Cresseid*** his great tragic work. During the last century ***The Fables*** have been overshadowed by ***The Testament,*** and their beauties neglected. But to appreciate the sweetness and harmony, the endlessly lively and inventive quality of Henryson's poetry, it is necessary to know them both; otherwise he runs the danger of being considered a poet of moderate capacity who, by a piece of good luck, wrote one great poem.

Most of the fables, though not all, are humorous. Henryson's humour is not quite like anything else in Scottish literature, more subtle and pervasive than the humour of Dunbar or Burns or Scott, more urbane, more indirect, less specialised, and saturated with irony. It is an assumption more than anything else; it remains implicit in the selection of detail and the choice of expression, and rarely comes to the point of statement. The fables transport us into a mood in which we see everything as Henryson sees it, with the same tender ironical humour, but without being able to explain very clearly how the mood has been induced. His sense of the ridiculous is so delicate and exact that the faintest emphasis is sufficient to indicate it, and more than the faintest would distort it. His more obvious strokes of humour, therefore, do not represent him best; as, for instance, when the fox kills a young lamb at Lent, dips it in the stream, and fishes it out, crying:

> 'Ga doun schir Kid, cum up schir salmond agane.'

The quality which transmutes these fables and our mood as we read them is less obvious and more delicate, and consists in a fine decorative sense of the absurd. We find it in the account of the Burgess Mouse on her way to visit her sister in the country:

> Bairfute, allone, with pykestaf in hir hand,
> As pure pylgrime scho passit out of town,
> To seik hir sister baith oure daill and down.

We find it in the lament of Pertok the hen for Chanteclere carried off by the fox:

> 'Allce,' quod Pertok, makand sair murning,
> With teiris grit attour hir cheikis fell;
> 'Yone wes our drowrie, and our dayis darling,
> Our nichtingall, and als our Orloge bell,
> Our walkryfe watche, us for to warn and tell
> Quhen that Aurora with hir curcheis gray
> Put up hir heid betwix the nicht and day.
>
> 'Quha sall our lemman be? quha sall us leid?
> Quhen we ar sad, quha sall unto us sing?
> With his sweit Bill he wald brek us the breid.
> In all this warld wes thair ane kynder thing?
> In paramouris he wald do us plesing,
> At his power, as nature did him geif.
> Now eftir him, allace, how sall we leif?'

In this passage Henryson's sense of the ridiculous is touched with pity, as it often is, and the pity with fantasy. The pity is real, but as we feel it we smile at it, yet without thinking the less of it. The touches in these verses are exquisite:

> Our nichtingall, and als our Orloge bell, . . .
> With his sweit Bill he wald brek us the breid. . . .
> In all this warld wes thair ane kynder thing? . . .

These felicitous inventions run through ***The Fables*** and give the dry stories their delightful life. They stray even into the Moralitas with which each fable ends. These little sermons have been blamed for their dullness, but one suspects that in many of them Henryson retains his irony. It is difficult to believe that a man with such a fine sense of the ridiculous could have written without knowing what he was doing,

> The hennis are warkis that ffra ferme faith
> proceidis,

at the end of a fable where hens and various beasts play their part. And the more serious of the Moralitas have a sincerity that is far from dullness.

The allegory is a form which the modern taste finds stilted and unreal, because the great story as Chaucer and Henryson knew it is dead. But while that story lasted the allegory was a perfectly natural convention—the most convenient device for telling it. ***The Fables*** belong to that modest kind of allegory which finds in the lives of the animals a pattern of human life. It has obvious merits; it simplifies life; it so reduces the dimensions of the human situation that we can easily grasp them; it divests the characters of all adventitious pomp and glory, as well as of all that passes in our time under the name of ideology; it lays bare with a force beyond the reach of literary naturalism the solid egoistic motives of action. This is doubtless what once made it such a popular and democratic form of art.

But in Henryson it assumes virtues of a rarer kind. Human snobbishness becomes touching and forgivable to him when he finds it in the Burgess Mouse. The crimes of the Fox and the Wolf become imaginatively comprehensible, and to that extent excusable, since all the animals act in accordance with their nature. The result is that the animal allegory, when it is not employed satirically, runs the danger of making us indiscriminately indulgent to all the faults and crimes of mankind; and the more lively the imagination of the poet, the more completely he enters into the nature of his allegorical characters, the Lion, the Wolf, the Fox, the Cat, the greater this danger becomes. So the fable has to be followed by the Moralitas, that human proportion may be preserved.

There are one or two fables in which Henryson achieves a profound effect of tragedy and pity, and moves us quite differently. An instance is **"The Preiching of the Swallow."** It is distinguished from the other fables by the solemnity of the opening:

> The hie prudence, and warking mervelous,
> The profound wit of God omnipotent,
> Is sa perfyte, and sa Ingenious,
> Excellend ffar all mannis Jugement;
> For quhy to him all thing is ay present,
> Rycht as it is, or ony tyme sall be,
> Befoir the sicht off his Divinitie.

The argument proceeds in this vein to the conclusion

> That God in all his werkis wittie is.

The seasons are advanced in illustration of this, and Henryson describes how he walked out on a spring day to watch the labourers in the fields; and thereupon he suddenly comes upon the tragic theme of the poem. A flock of birds alights on a hedge near by; they are having a loud dispute with a Swallow, who has been warning them of their danger.

> 'Schir Swallow' (quod the Lark agane) and
> leuch,
> 'Quhat haif ye sene that causis yow to dreid?'
> 'Se ye yone Churll' (quod scho) 'beyond yone
> pleuch,
> Fast sawand hemp, and gude linget seid?
> Yone lint will grow in lytill tyme in deid,
> And thairoff will yone Churll his Nettis mak,
> Under the quhilk he thinkis us to tak.
>
> 'Thairfoir I rede we pas quhen he is gone,
> At evin, and with our naillis scharp and small
> Out off the eirth scraip we yone seid anone,
> And eit it up; ffor, giff it growis, we sall
> Haif caus to weip heirefter ane and all.'

In June Henryson walks out again

> Unto the hedge under the Hawthorne grene

and the birds come and resume their dispute. The Swallow cries:

> 'O, blind birdis! and full of negligence,
> Unmyndful of your awin prosperitie,
> Lift up your sicht, and tak gude advertence;
> Luke to the Lint that growis on yone le;
> Yone is the thing I bad forsuith that we,
> Quhill it wes seid, suld rute furth off the eird;
> Now is it Lint, now is it hie on breird.
>
> 'Go yit, quhill it is tender and small,
> And pull it up, let it na mair Incres;
> My flesche growis, my bodie quaikis all,
> Thinkand on it I may not sleep in peis. . . .
>
> 'The awner off yone lint ane fouler is,
> Richt cautelous and full off subteltie;
> His pray full sendill tymis will he mis,
> Bot giff we birdis all the warrer be;
> Full mony off our kin he hes gart de,
> And thocht it bot ane sport to spill thair blude;
> God keip me ffra him, and the halie Rude.'

The lint ripens and is gathered and spun into thread, and the net is woven for the fowler's use. Winter comes; the fowler clears a place in the snow and strews chaff on it to attract the birds, and while they scrape and scratch he throws the net over them.

> Allace! it was grit hart sair for to se
> That bludie Bowcheour beit thay birdis doun,
> And ffor till heir, quhen thay wist weill to de,
> Thair cairfull sang and lamentatioun;
> Sum with ane staf he straik to eirth on swoun:
> Off sum the heid he straik, off sum he brak the
> crag,
> Sum half on lyve he stoppit in his bag.

The poem produces a strong feeling of approaching danger and of a blindness that no warning can pierce. It is filled with pity and a sort of second-sight which makes one think of Cassandra:

> 'This grit perrell I tauld thame mair than thryis;
> Now ar thay deid, and wo is me thairfoir!'

There is an echo of the last line in ***The Testament of Cresseid.***

The continuous interest and liveliness of the detail makes ***The Fables*** one of the most delightful books in Scottish literature. Detail is a matter of invention, an imaginative conclusion from the facts given; it creates the body of the story, which otherwise would be a mere bare framework. Situation is an imaginative conclusion on a greater scale, and gathers up a larger number and variety of elements. Henryson's genius is shown in his invention in both kinds, and ***The Testament of Cresseid*** is his great achievement in situation. It seems to have been his own invention purely; Mr. Harvey Wood in his consummate edition of Henryson implies it, and Sir Herbert Grierson is of the same opinion. 'It was no light thing', he says [in *Essays and Addresses,* 1940], 'to come after Boccaccio and to succeed in making a real addition to a great dramatic story, something that without needless challenging of comparison does, in its impressive way, complete that tragic tale.'

In his essay Sir Herbert speculates on the reason why Henryson should have been moved to add to a tale already accepted, and in the course of doing so he says the best things that have yet been said about the poem.

> Chaucer had, in his courtly and detached manner, avoided any moral judgment upon Cresseid. . . . The only moral which he will enforce at the end of the whole tale is the religious one—that all earthly things are vanity. . . . But Henryson is not content with what, after all, is an evasion—he, a Scot and a Schoolemaister, with a Scot's and a schoolmaster's belief in retribution. The result might have been disastrous—a dry or a piously unreal didactic poem. But it is not, and that for two reasons. In the first place, Henryson retains Chaucer's sympathy with Cresseid. . . . In the second place, his morality is sound and sincere, not the preacher's conventional acceptance of standards which he has not made his own. For the retribution which overtakes Cresseid in the poem is the retribution of her own heart. . . . It is not the leprosy we think of as her penalty but the last encounter with Troilus and its reaction on her own soul.

And Sir Herbert goes on to say that when the poem ends it has produced 'a real *catharsis* leaving us at peace with Cresseid as Chaucer's poem scarcely does'.

There is only one thing in this criticism with which one is tempted to disagree. I mean the assumption that Scots and schoolmasters have a belief in retribution stronger than that of Italians and Englishmen and playwrights, that Henryson was the retributive kind of Scotsman and schoolmaster, and that the spirit of the poem is in any sense a spirit of retribution. It is filled with pity. Indeed what Sir Herbert brings out so convincingly is that the poem is a more humanly satisfying end to the story than either of the earlier versions had provided, and exhibits a profound humanity which will not rest content with anything less, as the crown of the story, than a genuine reconciliation of the heart. In seeking this reconciliation through retribution Henryson was no more peculiarly Scottish than in refraining from doing so Chaucer was peculiarly English, or Boccaccio peculiarly Italian. This is not a matter of nationality. It would be superfluous to labour the point if there were not a sort of conspiracy to make Henryson a bleak and harsh writer, if Miss Agnes Mure Mackenzie had not called ***The Testament*** stern, and other critics had not cited it as a proof that the Scots have always been dour and harsh in their human judgments. As well call Dante harsh for his treatment of Francesca, or Shakespeare dour for having Desdemona and Cordelia murdered.

The keynote of the poem is sympathy, as Sir Herbert Grierson points out, not judgment, though its theme is judgment. But the judgment is transformed when it is accepted by Cresseid in a moment of realisation; and that, indeed, is what brings about the reconciliation of which Sir Herbert speaks. Henryson's humanity is clear from the beginning of the poem; perhaps indeed humanity is a better word to describe his temper than sympathy: a humanity so simple that it needs only the most ordinary words to give it utterance, the more ordinary the better. He sees misfortune, not guilt, in Cresseid's conduct after she was turned away by Diomede:

> Than desolait scho walkit up and doun,
> And sum men sayis into the Court commoun.

He pities her 'mischance' when she was forced to

> go amang the Greikis air and lait
> Sa gigotlike, takand thy foull plesance!
> I have pietie thou suld fall sic mischance.

He interposes his charity between her and her accusers:

> Yet nevertheless quhat ever men deme or say
> In scornefull language of thy brukkilness,
> I sall excuse, as far furth as I may,
> Thy womanheid, thy wisdome and fairness;
> The quhilk Fortun has put to sic distres
> As hir plesit, and nothing throw the gilt
> Of the, throw wickit language to be spilt.

He attributes Cresseid's misfortunes and faults to chance, and absolves her of all guilt; and this is the assumption running through the poem. He does not bring her to judgment, as some critics have implied; he shows the judgment of fate and of her own heart overtaking her. His humanity in dealing with her is perfectly simple, but its simplicity contains this surprise.

It is this simple and yet surprising humanity that brings about the finest effects of style in the poem; I mean those lines which seem at once the result of exquisite poetic judgment and of a humanity so obvious that it has become sure of itself and seizes at once the ultimate situation, formulating it in the fewest possible words, words which seem just adequate and no more, and in that appear to achieve a more secure finality: all that might have been said being made superfluous by the few simple words that are said. When Cresseid is stricken with leprosy and goes to her father for comfort, Henryson leaves one line to tell of their grief:

> Thus was thair cair aneuch betwix thame twane.

In Cresseid's Complaint one line suffices to draw the contrast between her present and her former condition:

> Quhair is thy Chalmer wantounlie besene?

The incident of Troilus' meeting with her at a corner as he returns to Troy from fighting the Greeks is itself a compressed summary of the tragic situation, and is contained in three lines:

> Than upon him scho kest up baith hir Ene,
> And with ane blenk it come into his thocht,
> That he sumtime hir face befoir had sene.

When she is told by her companions who it was that stopped beside her and threw a purse of gold in her lap, she compresses her fault into the cry:

> 'O fals Cresseid and trew Knicht Troilus!'

Troilus, after hearing of her misfortunes and her death, seems again to be saying all that can be said when he exclaims:

> 'I can no moir.
> Scho was untrew, and wo is me thairfoir.'

The epitaph which he inscribes on her tomb is in the same high concise style:

> Lo, fair Ladyis, Crisseid, of Troyis toun,
> Sumtyme countit the flour of Womanheid,
> Under this stane lait Lipper lyis deid.

No other Scottish poet has risen to this high and measured style, and Henryson himself does not attain it often, though he does as often as the subject requires it. Yet it is a style which one would have expected to suit the Scottish genius, with its seriousness and its love of compressed utterance. And that it does suit that genius is proved by Scottish folk-poetry, and particularly by the Ballads, with their complete seriousness and their extreme compression. But this gift, which belongs to the Scottish people, ceased after Henryson to belong to Scottish poets. Seriousness, though not compression, went for a long time into theology, a theology which was never more than mediocre. To the poet was left only a sort of secondary, official seriousness, that of

> Man was made to mourn

and

> But pleasures are like poppies spread.

The Scottish poets followed the tradition of Dunbar, who expressed the exuberance, wildness and eccentricity of the Middle Ages, not that of Henryson, who inherited the medieval completeness and harmony, and the power to see life whole, without taking refuge in the facetious and the grotesque. Yet Henryson embodies more strikingly than any poet who has lived since the fundamental seriousness, humanity and strength of the Scottish imagination. (pp. 10-21)

Edwin Muir, "Robert Henryson," in his Essays on Literature and Society, *revised edition, Cambridge, Mass.: Harvard University Press, 1965, pp. 10-21.*

Denton Fox (essay date 1966)

[*In the following excerpt, Fox examines Henryson's major works, contending that his natural writing style contradicts what many critics have described as moral seriousness in his poetry.*]

We know little more about Robert Henryson's life than that he was a schoolmaster at Dunfermline and that his name appears towards the end of the list of dead poets in Dunbar's *Lament for the Makers,* which must have been written between 1505 and 1510. The safest guess would seem to be that he died about 1500, and that his poetry was written in the last third of the fifteenth century.

The usual clichés about Henryson are that he is a keen observer of nature and that his genial humanitarianism causes him to be the closest to Chaucer of all the Scottish Chaucerians. There is doubtless some truth in these generalisations, but hardly more than if one were to characterise Chaucer by saying that he was a keen observer of costumes, and had the endearing habit of seeing the best in people. Henryson has been underrated, I think, because his readers have not always extended the parallel with Chaucer far enough to notice that he shares Chaucer's art of concealing his art. Henryson's unobtrusive complexity is particularly evident in his longest work, ***The Morall Fabillis of Esope.*** This collection consists of thirteen fables, some of them derived from the medieval Reynardian stories, but most of them Aesopic, ostensibly translations of the versions in Latin verse by Walter of England. Henryson purports to be telling tales simply and plainly, partly for the 'doctrine wyse', and partly for 'ane merie sport': 'In hamelie language and in termes rude / Me neidis wryte, for quhy of Eloquence / Nor Rethorike, I never Understude.' But in reality his fables are artful, sophisticated and rhetorical; comparable, indeed, to La Fontaine's. From one aspect, they are elegant variations on a standard theme: Walter's fables were a standard school text, and would be well known to most of Henryson's audience. Walter's versions are short and crude; Henryson's, though they average only a little over two hundred lines, are often ten times as long. But on the other hand Henryson's fables are not arcane or precious: as he says of Aesop, he did not want 'the disdane off hie, nor low estate'.

Although it is perhaps not the best of Henryson's fables, the **"Taill of Schir Chantecleir and the Foxe"** is an interesting one to examine, since it has the same plot as *The Nun's Priest's Tale.* The two poems are obviously not very similar: it takes Chaucer about six hundred and forty lines to get from the introduction of the poor widow to the fox's first speech to the cock, but Henryson covers the same ground in twenty-three lines. In these lines Henryson demonstrates his remarkable power of narrating events in a style which is smooth, easy and rapid, but far from flat. The fox is brought to the farmyard, for instance, in these four lines:

> This wylie Tod, quhen that the Lark couth sing,
> Full sair hungrie unto the Toun him drest,
> Quhair Chantecleir in to the gray dawing,
> Werie for nicht, wes flowen ffra his nest.
> 425-8

The two antagonists are balanced against each other, the fox moving into the field of action in the first two lines, and the cock in the last two. But the fox has purposefully set his course ('him drest') *to* the farmyard; the cock has merely flown *from* his place of refuge. The adjectives describing them are linked by alliteration: the fox is 'wylie' and the cock is 'Werie for nicht', ostensibly because, as we have been told, his songs divide the night, but more essentially because, as we later learn, the sexual appetites of his hens make great demands on him. The two details about the dawn serve to make it more vivid, but they are also balanced off with the two animals. For the fox, who is aggressive and cheerful, the lark sings; for the cock, who is going to suffer, the dawn is grey.

Another sort of easy subtlety is shown in the fox's speech to the cock, where, as frequently with Henryson, the superficial meaning of the lines is directly opposed to their true meaning:

> 'Your father full oft fillit hes my wame,
> And send me meit ffra midding to the muris.
> And at his end I did my besie curis,
> To hald his heid, and gif him drinkis warme,
> Syne at the last the Sweit swelt in my arme.'
>
> 441-5

Chantecleir's father had, in truth, often filled the fox's stomach, but by begetting chicks, not by sending presents; the fox doubtless did exert himself in holding the cock's head when he died, but he fails to add that this was also the cause of his death, and that the cock's warm drink was his own blood. The last line is the best: the fox means the cock to take the line's languishing rhythm and the rich chime of 'Sweit swelt' as expressing the fox's grief, but of course they really express the fox pausing delightedly at the recollection of his meal, while 'Sweit' here is not a metaphorical term of affection. This passage is perhaps less delicate than the corresponding point in Chaucer's poem, where the fox remarks that Chantecleir's father and mother 'Han in myn hous ybeen to my greet ese', but it is hardly inferior.

The fox's speech, with its tone of impudent double-tongued sleekness, shows Henryson's remarkable ability to reveal character through dialogue, as does the flattered cock's brief and inane answer: ' "Knew ye my ffather?" quod the Cok, and leuch' (*leuch* here, as often in Henryson, means 'giggled', rather than 'laughed'). A more extended and more important instance of Henryson using different styles to show different speakers and different attitudes towards the world comes a little later in the poem, where seven stanzas are devoted to the hens' reactions after the cock has been kidnapped. First Pertok provides a traditional and ornate lament, worthy of Chaucer's 'Gaufred, deere maister soverayn':

> 'Yone wes our drowrie, and our dayis darling,
> Our nichtingall, and als our Orloge bell,
> Our walkryfe watche, us for to warne and tell
> Quhen that Aurora with hir curcheis gray,
> Put up hir heid betwix the nicht and day.'
>
> 497-501

Then Sprutok, a descendant of the Wife of Bath, speaks in a cheerfully abrupt and downright rhythm, using clichés and proverbs:

> 'We sall ffair weill, I find Sanct Johne to borrow;
> The prouerb sayis, "als gude lufe cummis as gais."
> I will put on my haly dais clais,
> And mak me fresch agane this Jolie may,
> Syne chant this sang, "wes never wedow sa gay!" '
>
> 511-15

After this encouragement, Pertok drops her hypocritical grief and sneers lecherously at Chantecleir: 'off sic as him ane scoir / Wald not suffice to slaik our appetyte.' She promises, in a line which is a nice instance of Henryson's stylistic manoeuvres, that she will quickly be able 'To get ane berne suld better claw oure breik'. *Berne,* 'man, warrior', is an exclusively poetic word, and is usually found in alliterative phrases—though not in combination with *breik,* 'breech'. *Claw* is sometimes used in Middle Scots with the meaning 'scratch gently, caress', but of course has a specially graphic meaning when applied to a cock. The line sums up the various rhetorics of love that we have seen: Pertok's noble and courtly lament, Sprutok's carefree wantonness, and Pertok's change to bestial lust. But instead of letting matters rest here, Henryson brings on a third hen who, 'lyke ane Curate', fulminates against Chantecleir with self-righteous indignation:

> 'rychteous God, haldand the balandis evin,
> Smytis rycht sair, thoct he be patient,
> For Adulterie, that will thame not repent.
>
> . . . it is the verray hand off God
> That causit him be werryit with the Tod.'
>
> 534-6, 542-3

Then, as in *The Nun's Priest's Tale,* all pretensions are destroyed by the reality of the barnyard tumult, which Henryson expresses by giving the widow's commands to her dogs:

> 'How! berk, Berrie, Bawsie Broun,
> Rype schaw, Rin weil, Curtes, Nuttieclyde . . . '
>
> 546-7

One can see how Henryson, like Chaucer, makes the fable into a deflation of human self-importance. The different attitudes towards death expressed by the hens are made ridiculous in numerous ways: by juxtaposition of conflicting rhetorics, by having the most grief-stricken hen turn out to be actually the most lecherous, by having all the attitudes irrelevant, since the cock returns safely, and of course simply by giving poultry human voices. And one can see how Henryson, like Chaucer, relies heavily on changes of style, balancing the voice of one animal against the voice of another, or setting up a heroic style only to puncture it abruptly. But one can also see that there are some fundamental differences between Chaucer's fable and Henryson's which point to a dissimilarity between the two poets.

One difference so obvious that it is easy to overlook is simply that Henryson's poem is written in rhyme royal, not in couplets. Henryson never uses couplets, except in the 'Moralitas' of ***Orpheus and Eurydice,*** where he is explaining an allegory, and his stanzas are stiffer and flow together less easily than Chaucer's usually do. One way to put this difference between the two poets would be to say that time, in Chaucer's poems, tends to move on unobtrusively but continually, where in Henryson there is characteristically a stanza for one instant of time, and then a break before the next stanza. Though of course it is even more dangerous to generalise about Chaucer than about Henryson, and obviously time does not move very fluidly in *The Knight's Tale* or in some of the more stylised stanzaic tales. With these same reservations, another way to put the difference between the two poets is to say that Henryson's verse often seems more impersonal. Beneath Chaucer's poetry one often senses a moving train of thought and constantly changing reactions to what is observed or said; but Henryson seems to change his style only dispassionately, adopting it to the shifts in his subject matter according to the demands of decorum. Chaucer's 'personality' is of course the result of self-conscious art, not involuntary self-revelation, while all of Henryson's poetry manifests his gentle and benevolent mind, but this does not alter the difference of style.

Henryson's style is apt to cause two difficulties for the modern reader. One is that it is easy to look for what is only incidental, the minor touches of realism and humour, and to neglect the large static set pieces which are at the foundation of the structure of his poems. In ***Orpheus and Eurydice*** and ***The Testament of Cresseid*** there are formal laments in special stanzaic forms (the hens' laments are parodies of this genre); much of ***Orpheus*** is devoted to a description of hell; about a third of ***The Testament*** is spent describing the gods and their conference; and the ***Fables*** consist largely of such set speeches as the ones we have seen, together with catalogues and formal descriptions of various kinds. It is impossible to generalise about these passages, except to say that they are all as vital to the meaning of their poems as, for instance, the laments are to the fable of the cock and the fox.

The other, and related, difficulty of Henryson's style is that the reader is apt to take his impersonality for cold and meaningless conventionality. This is particularly true of ***The Testament of Cresseid,*** where the style, so different from Chaucer's, has caused some readers to think that the work is 'by the very strenuousness of its morality in some degree both poetically and morally repulsive' [T. F. Henderson, in his *Scottish Vernacular Literature,* 1910]. But this is to misunderstand the whole meaning of this brilliant and complex poem, and to ignore that it is in many ways a companion to Book V of Chaucer's *Troilus.* Cresseid, like Troilus, comes to self-knowledge and knowledge of the world through suffering, and it is appropriate that Cresseid's suffering should be more physical than Troilus's. The main emotion of both poems is pathos, but Henryson produces this emotion not so much by suggesting his own feelings as by impersonal description and by opposing Cresseid to such bleak figures as Saturn, who says to her, with perfect and chilling finality, that he will change

> 'Thyne Insolence, thy play and wantones
> To greit diseis; thy Pomp and thy riches
> In mortall neid; and greit penuritie
> Thou suffer sall, and as ane beggar die'
>
> 319-22

Another difference between *The Nun's Priest's Tale* and Henryson's fable, equally obvious and I think equally important, is that Henryson concludes his poem with a four-

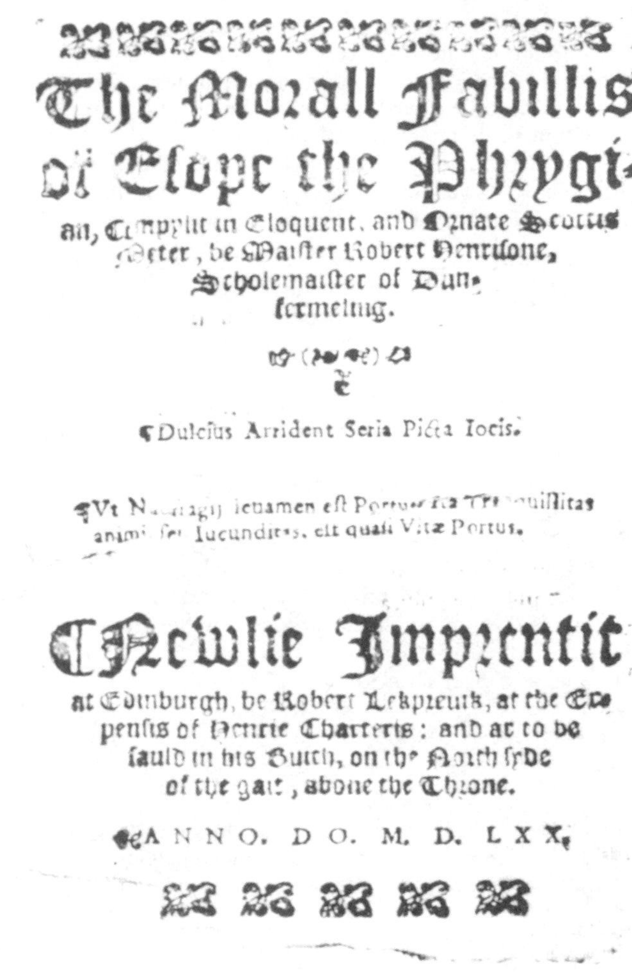
The Morall Fabillis of Esope the Phrygian, Compylit in Eloquent, and Ornate Scottis Meter, be Maister Robert Henrisone, Scholemaister of Dunfermeling.

Dulcius Arrident Seria Picta Iocis.

Newlie Imprentit at Edinburgh, be Robert Lekpreuik, at the Expensis of Henrie Charteris: and ar to be sauld in his Buith, on the North syde of the gait, abone the Throne.

ANNO. DO. M. D. LXX.

Title-page of the Charteris Edition of The Moral Fabillis of Esope the Phrygian, *1570.*

stanza 'Moralitas'. Henryson's characteristic genre, indeed, is the narrative poem to which is appended a passage, sometimes long and never less than twenty lines, which comments in some way on the meaning of the narrative. About three-quarters of the bulk of his poetry, including the ***Fables*** and ***Orpheus and Eurydice,*** falls into this category. And much of his other work comes close to it: many of his short poems are explicitly allegorical, and even the light-hearted pastoral, ***Robene and Makyne,*** points a moral. ***The Testament of Cresseid*** might seem to be the great exception, but in fact it is more similar to the ***Fables*** and ***Orpheus*** than one might think. Although it has no separate 'Moralitas' explaining the action, the events of the poem are given so heavy a symbolic meaning that they become almost allegorical. In her faithlessness, Cresseid sinned against the natural order, *fine amour,* and God, and all these sins are represented in the poem by the compound symbol of her vocal blasphemy against Venus and Cupid. In the same way, the leprosy which results from her blasphemy is meaningful on three levels. The disease destroys her flesh, so punishing her for her misuse of it, but also teaching her of its essential and permanent corruptness. Because of her sin against love she is changed from a sought-after beauty to a loathsome beggar—but this change teaches her to praise Troilus and despise herself. The leprosy is also a divine punishment, for it, above all other diseases, was thought to be a blow from heaven, but because of its medieval association with Job, Christ and the two Lazaruses was also considered a disease of peculiar sanctity, an earthly purgatory which, as the poem hints, renders any future purgatory unnecessary.

No one now, surely, would follow Matthew Arnold in accusing Chaucer of a lack of high seriousness, but it is still true that Henryson is a more immediately and more constantly serious poet. His preoccupation with the need to justify the pleasures of poetry by revealing its 'gude moralitie' comes up explicitly time after time, and all the fables are built on Henryson's desire to show the sad irony that if animals behave like men only in poetry, men too often behave like animals in ordinary life. But Henryson does more than extract morals. As the frequent occurrence in his work of the term 'figure' would indicate, he uses the technique of figural interpretation, which is based on the idea that all objects and events are created by God to be meaningful, and which goes back to the theory that the events of the Old Testament were at once historical happenings and prefigurations of Christianity. So the fox, in our fable, is an actual fox, but also 'may weill be figurate / To flatteraris', while the cock, as a figure for pride, is connected with

> the Feyndis Infernall,
> Quhilk houndit doun wes fra that hevinlie hall
> To Hellis hole, and to that hiddeous hous,
> Because in pryde thay wer presumpteous.
> 596-9

And Henryson never abandons poetry for the sake of morality. He has been blamed for piously tacking inconsequential morals on to his poems, but in fact each 'Moralitas', whether satirical, moral, or allegorical, is an organic and necessary part of its poem. Henryson's moral seriousness, like the rhetorical and conventional aspects of his style, has been disliked and ignored by critics, where it should have been recognised as one of the reasons for the excellence of his poetry. (pp. 171-79)

Denton Fox, "The Scottish Chaucerians," in Chaucer and Chaucerians: Critical Studies in Middle English Literature, *edited by D. S. Brewer, Nelson, 1966, pp. 164-200.*

John MacQueen (essay date 1967)

[*In the following excerpt, MacQueen maintains that* Orpheus and Eurydice *is a morality tale in which Henryson represents Orpheus as the intellectual and Eurydice as the appetitive power of the soul.*]

[Henryson] . . . indicates very precisely his concept of the substance of poetry, a concept which may be seen most readily in the comparatively brief ***Orpheus and Eurydice,*** which reaches its greatest complexity in the ***Testament of Cresseid,*** and which governs the seemingly disparate material of the ***Morall Fabillis of Esope the Phrygian.*** It is nevertheless surprising that even the ***Orpheus and Eurydice*** has received so little in the way of perceptive formal criticism. One writer, for instance, remarks: '***Orpheus and Eurydice*** is one of the very few poems of the Middle Ages that tells a classical tale for its own sake, with no allegorical trappings, [Kurt Wittig, in his *The Scottish Tradition in Literature,* 1958]. As the main narrative of the poem is followed by an allegorical *Moralitas* which in the Bannatyne MS. extends to 218 lines, the assumption, one presumes, is that narrative and *Moralitas* should be considered each in isolation, or at least that the *Moralitas* bears no vital relationship to the narrative. Such an assumption begs several questions, on the answers to which will depend the method of interpreting all Henryson's narrative poetry. Three points must be made. In the first place it has been suggested that the *Moralitas* as it appears in Bannatyne is not wholly Henryson's. The suggestion is unsupported by evidence, but even if it were established, the fact would still remain that Henryson subjoined some kind of allegorical *Moralitas,* and therefore had some kind of allegorical intention. Henryson's sources for the poem seem to indicate the same conclusion. He names Boethius' *De Consolatione Philosophiae* with the standard commentary of Nicholas Trevet (?1258-1328), the English Dominican theologian, biblicist, Hebraist, historian, and classicist, best known for his Anglo-Norman *Chronicle,* used by Chaucer and Gower. . . . Trevet's commentary is entirely allegorical. Moreover, it is almost certain that Henryson used the *De Genealogia Deorum* of Boccaccio as the source at least of his description of the nine Muses. Boccaccio, it is true, himself uses Fulgentius as a source for the allegorical interpretation of the names of the Muses. But Henryson's poem contains matter unrelated to Fulgentius for which some suggestion may be found in Boccaccio. Boccaccio quotes from the commentary of Macrobius on the *Somnium Scipionis* of Cicero the suggestion that the Muses are to be interpreted as the music of the spheres, 'eas equiparans octo sperarum celi cantibus, nonam volens omnium celorum modulationum esse concentum'. In this he is not followed directly by Henryson, who nevertheless introduces the harmony of the spheres unexpectedly in his account of the wanderings of Orpheus in search of Eurydice (vv. 184-239). Nothing similar appears in Fulgentius, and as we have other evidence to suggest that Henryson knew the *Genealogia,* it seems simplest to assume that here too he used Boccaccio—more particularly when he describes the passage as the 'genealogy' of Orpheus. In the *Genealogia,* Boccaccio, it is well known, attempted to defend classical mythology by a moral interpretation in allegorical terms—a third point which suggests allegorical intention on the part of Henryson.

These sources put the poem in a context very different from that which might have been expected, had the immediate source been directly Augustan—Virgil, for instance, or Ovid. In Boethius the story of Orpheus occurs in the poem (Metrum 12) which ends Book III of *De Consolatione,* and which marks an especial difficulty in the development of the argument. Philosophy has led Boethius to a paradoxical double conclusion, that happiness is the highest good, to be equated with God, and that as God is omnipotent, and yet cannot do evil, evil does not exist. She replies to the incredulity of Boethius with the story of Orpheus, put by her into its appropriate context thus: 'Blisful is that man that may seen the clere welle of good! Blisful is he that mai unbynden hym fro the boondes of the hevy erthe!' Her purpose is at least twofold. On the one hand it is to warn Boethius that if at this stage he abandons his faith in the logical structure of the argument, his fate will be similar to that of Orpheus. More important is the second. Orpheus is one who saw 'the clere welle of good' and unbound himself from the bonds of the heavy earth, as is symbolized by his rescue of Eurydice. But as the concluding lines of the poem indicate, Eurydice has an ambiguous, and even sinister, significance. She is the thought which Orpheus sought to lead to the light above; she is also the desire which turned him back to darkness from the bounds of light. Under both aspects she is explicable in terms of the argument which has preceded. Every man naturally desires the highest good which by the exercise of reason he can attain. At the same time, as a temporal fallen creature, man is subject to illusion. As one who desired the highest good, Orpheus rescued Eurydice. As one subject to illusion, he made the mistake by which he lost her again. The figures of the poem, that is to say, are certainly intended by Boethius to be allegorical.

In his commentary, Trevet analyses the allegory, and because, like St. Thomas Aquinas, he was himself a Dominican friar, he interprets in Thomistic and Aristotelian terms. Orpheus is the *pars intellectiva,* the intellectual power of the soul. Eurydice is the *pars affectiva,* the appetitive power of the soul. Trevet stresses, as Boethius does not, the shepherd Aristaeus, whose pursuit of Eurydice led to her death when she trod on a serpent. The connexion between Aristaeus and Greek αριστοσ, 'best', has probably caused the interpretation of Aristaeus as Virtue, which seeks to be united with the appetitive power of the soul, but from which the appetitive shrinks. In Thomistic terms, that is to say, Aristaeus is moral virtue, as opposed to intellectual or theological virtue—'Not every virtue is a moral virtue, but only those that are in the appetitive power.' The serpent is sensuality, by whose sting Eurydice is given over to the powers of hell, and from which it is within the capability of the intellectual power to rescue her. The monsters of hell symbolize the various dangers which beset the intellectual power in its quest. Cerberus is the world, and his three heads are the three ages—childhood, youth, and old age—during which the worldly man is subject to the death of the spirit. The three Furies are the potentiality of sin in thought, word, and deed. Ixion, apparently, is semi-rational human nature, which mistakenly trusts to Fortune, symbolized by the wheel, to win for itself mastery over Nature (Juno). Tantalus is avarice, the root of all evil. Tityos is illegitimate desire to know the future. Orpheus overcomes all these obstructions, only to succumb finally when he is on the very brink of complete success.

Henryson's *moralitas* is enough to show that he accepted this interpretation, but even in his narrative there is evidence to show that he intended Orpheus to represent intellectual, and Eurydice appetitive power. Orpheus, for instance, regards himself as a servant of Venus. Yet in no sense does he win Eurydice; he does not even ask her to marry him. That is the role of the appetitive. Eurydice takes the initiative; it is only after she has offered him her hand that Orpheus becomes a king:

His noble fame so far it sprang and grew,
Till at the last the michty quene of Trace,
Excelland fair, haboundand in richess,
A message send unto that prince so ying,
Requyrand him to wed hir and be king.

Euridices this lady had to name;
And quhene scho saw this prince so glorius,
Hir erand to propone scho thocht no schame,
With wordis sueit, and blenkis amorouss,
Said, 'Welcum, Lord and lufe, schir Orpheuss,
In this provynce ye salbe king and lord!'
(73-83)

The same point is stressed earlier:

And mother to the king schir Orpheouss,
Quhilk throw his wyfe wes efter king of Traiss.
(45-46)

As intellect, Orpheus is divine by descent, but he is sovereign only in so far as Eurydice willingly accepts him. The intellectual power assumes the mastery only at the invitation, and by the consent, of the appetitive. Nor is the mastery more than local and temporary. When Eurydice says to Orpheus

In this provynce ye salbe king and lord,

the metrical accent falls on 'this'. Orpheus, in other words, is restricted to the realm over which Eurydice has previously ruled, that of appetite and its satisfaction. The worldliness of their married joy is stressed:

Betuix Orpheuss and fair Erudices,
Fra thai wer weddit, on fra day to day
The low of lufe cowth kyndill and incress,
With mirth, and blythness, solace, and with play
Off warldly Joy; allace, quhat sall I say?
Lyk till a flour that plesandly will spring,
Quhilk fadis sone, and endis with murnyng.
(85-91)

The death of Eurydice marks the end of Orpheus's kingship:

My rob ryell, and all my riche array,
Changit salbe in rude russet and gray,
My dyademe in till a hate of hair.
(157-9)

The marriage of Orpheus and Eurydice is worldly, but not vicious: morally, it is precariously neutral. For Orpheus it remains so. When Eurydice is taken from him, he does not know whether to look for her in heaven or in hell. With Eurydice it is different, and the difference first becomes apparent with the change of style in stanza 14. Most of the poem is written in the courtly rhyme-royal of Chaucer and James, I, but in the first thirteen stanzas the style is that of moral and panegyric rhetoric rather than of courtly love narrative. In stanza 14 the courtly love style briefly appears:

I say this be Erudices the quene,
Quhilk walkit furth in to a May mornyng,
Bot with a madyn, untill a medow grene,
To tak the air, and se the flouris spring.
(92-95)

Trevet had interpreted the meadow in which Eurydic was

killed as *amena presentis vite.* Henryson found a stylistic equivalent of this in the manner of description usual in the poetry of courtly love. Here, as perhaps always in his writings, the use of this style indicates a failure, a worldliness, of moral judgement on the part of the persons described.

When Eurydice walked in the meadow she was barefooted, and her white shanks were showing. One may perhaps recollect that in Lindsay's *Squyer Meldrum* the Lady of Gleneagles obtained the love of the Squire when she came into his bedroom one May morning,

> Hir schankis quhyte withouttin hois.
>
> (949)

She told her maidens afterwards that she had been walking in her 'Gardine grene':

> (Quod thai) quhair wes your hois and schone:
> Quhy yeid ye with your bellie bair?
> (Quod scho) the morning wes sa fair:
> For be him that deir Iesus sauld
> I felt na wayis ony maner of cauld.
>
> (1016-20)

Henryson only briefly adopts the courtly style, but he puts it in a context strikingly contrasted with that usual in the poetry of courtly love. In the *Knight's Tale* or the *Kingis Quair,* for instance, the May morning serves as background to the courtly lover's first glimpse of his lady and consequent hopeless devotion to her. This for Henryson is the assumed norm of courtly and worldly behaviour. Aristaeus, who sees Eurydice on a May morning, behaves in a way directly opposite. He is a ravisher, whose allegorical function as Virtue is combined with his literal role in a stylistic yoking of apparent incompatibles very characteristic of medieval allegory, and with an effect not dissimilar to that of later metaphysical imagery. The startling combination may well have been regarded by Henryson and his contemporaries as a satisfactory amalgam of wit and imaginative truth.

Henryson took pains to define only to the extent necessary for his allegorical purpose the literal occupation of Aristaeus. Aristaeus is not shepherd, cowherd, or goatherd; he is simply a 'hird' who keeps 'beistis':

> A busteouss hird callit Arresteuss,
> Kepand his beistis, Lay undir a buss.
>
> (97-98)

Allegorically, beasts are the carnal passions, the usually uncontrolled appetitive power of the soul, common to beast and man. Henryson exploits the figure in the ***Fabillis:***

> Na mervell is, ane man be lyke ane Beist,
> Quhilk lufis ay carnall and foull delyte.
>
> (50-51)

As opposed to this, moral virtue is an operative habit (*Summa Theologica,* I-II. LV. 2) which operates on the appetitive power of the soul, and which therefore is appropriately represented by the herd of beasts, Aristaeus. Eurydice has not come under his control, and is therefore his appropriate prey. When she attempts to escape she at once abandons her position of moral neutrality, the serpent stings her, and she passes from the government of Orpheus to that of the king and queen of hell. With the disappearance of the appetitive, Aristaeus also disappears from the story—and so it may be added, does all possibility of a rescue of Eurydice from hell. Intellect alone is insufficient. As moral virtue, Aristaeus cannot come into direct contact with Orpheus, whose moral neutrality is retained when Proserpina is described to him, not as queen of hell, but as queen of fairy.

Hell is the realm of unsatisfied and uncontrolled appetite. Henryson places there two groups of figures, one traditional since the time of Homer, the other a more medieval list of secular and spiritual rulers. The first is wholly pagan, the second, anachronistically with the characteristic timelessness of poetry and drama in the Middle Ages, part pagan, part Christian. The groups differ, however, not so much in this as in allegorical function; they correspond to different aspects of hell as the place of insatiable, or the place of uncontrolled appetite. The purely pagan group represents failure in satisfaction; the defining factor in the other is not so much the inclusion of Christian figures as the fact that all the figures are rulers, whose government has in some way been unjust or unsuccessful. Jezebel appears, but the masculinity which predominates in Henryson's hell indicates a relevance primarily to Orpheus, the masculine intellect which has failed to bring appetitive power under limitation or control. The distinction of pagan and Christian is also irrelevant in so far as the entire concept is obviously Christian—as Christian as Dante's:

> O dully place, and grundles deip dungeoun,
> Furness of fyre, and stink intollerable,
> Pit of dispair, without remissioun,
> Thy meit wennome, Thy drink is pusonable,
> Thy grit panis and to compte unnumerable;
> Quhat creature cumis to dwell in the
> Is ay deand, and nevirmoir sall de.
>
> (310-16)

The stages of Orpheus's journey to hell's house may be compared with those in the *Lyke-Wake Dirge:*

> When thou from hence away art past,
> *Every nighte and alle,*
> To Whinny-muir thou com'st at last;
> *And Christe receive thy saule.*
>
> If ever thou gavest hosen and shoon,
> Sit thee down, and put them on.
>
> If hosen and shoon thou ne'er gav'st nane,
> The whinnes sall prick thee to the bare bane.
>
> From Whinny-muir when thou may'st pass,
> To Brig o' Dread thou com'st at last.

Tityos lies in the middle of Whinny-muir; the Furies torture Ixion on Brig o' Dread. The pagan insatiable appetites appear in the context of Christian morality, or at least Christian folklore.

Ixion, Tantalus, and Tityos are presented with effective symbolic starkness. Each suffers some aspect of the torture of insatiable appetite; Ixion bound to the wheel of the world; Tantalus thirsting for the water and hungry for the food he cannot reach; Tityos with the vulture tearing his organs of desire—stomach, midriff, heart, liver, and tripes. Each is an aspect of the fallen Eurydice, the pangs of which are only to be quieted by the divine authority of intellect—Orpheus, with the new music which he learned in his journey through the spheres. When Orpheus plays music of this kind, appetite is satisfied. Ixion escapes (significantly, Boethius and most other versions have merely that the wheel stood still): Tantalus drinks: the vulture ceases to gnaw. The success of the narrative as symbol depends on its very abruptness:

> And on his breist thair sat a grisly grip,
> Quhilk with his bill his belly throw can boir,
> Both maw, myddret, hart, lever, and trip
> He ruggit out—his panis was the moir.
> Quhen Orpheus thus saw him suffir soir,
> He tuke his herp and maid sueit melody—
> The grip is fled, and Titius left his cry.
> (296-302)

Those who are mentioned in the second list are all rulers—in the first part kings and queens

> Quhilk in thair lyfe full maisterfull had bene,
> And conquerouris of gold, richess, and land.
> (319-20)

The catalogue occupies four stanzas (44-47), and the names are so arranged that with each succeeding stanza moral implications become more and more strongly stressed. Hector, Priam, and Alexander seem to be included (stanza 44) for little reason other than that they were pagan. Antiochus introduces a definite breach of the natural order with his crime of incest. In stanza 45 pagan and Biblical rulers are balanced in alternation; Julius Cæsar, Herod, Nero, Pilate, and Croesus, and the Biblical connotations are the Nativity and Crucifixion. Stanza 46 includes only Old Testament rulers, Pharaoh, Saul, Ahab, and Jezebel, while stanza 47 lists the spiritual rulers of the Christian church who commit offences in the exercise of their power. As has already been noted, Henryson included Jezebel with Eurydice, but it is clear that the stanzas are primarily a catalogue of men who, like Orpheus, have in some way failed in their duty as moral and spiritual leaders.

The poem as we have so far considered it, and as perhaps it most needs to be emphasized, is interior allegorical drama, played with no necessary relevance to the external macrocosm. It would nevertheless be wrong to suppose that Henryson intended his poem to be only a study in analytic moral psychology. Two links, genealogy and music, which as he treats them become almost identical, connect interior drama with exterior universe. The descent of Orpheus from Jupiter represents the descent of human intellect from the divine. Almost equally important is the line—Memory, Apollo, and the Muses—by which Orpheus is able to claim that descent. In particular, his mother is Calliope, 'of all musik maistress', 'finder of all armony'. Among the other Muses, Erato 'drawis lyk to lyk in every thing'; Urania 'is callit armony celestiall'; Clio is 'meditatioun / Of everything that hes creatioun'. Erato and Urania, that is to say, might be thought of as governing powers in the actual physical universe, while Clio links intellect with creation. With the exception of Polyhymnia, the other Muses function as aspects of the abstract intellect. Polyhymnia is poetry, regarded perhaps as the equivalent in musical speech of external harmony. Her function is described, at least, in terms less abstract than those used of the others.

Traditionally, as I have already pointed out, the nine Muses were associated with the nine celestial spheres—an idea which takes its literary origin from the vision of Er with which Plato concludes his *Republic*. There, it will be remembered, the material universe is the Spindle which turns on the knees of Necessity. Upon each circle stood a Siren who uttered a single note: the combination of notes made up the music of the spheres.

Orpheus is man, musician, and intellectual power, whose function in the microcosm corresponds to that of the Muses in the macrocosm. The relevance of the Muses to the physical universe in which Orpheus exists is brought out by the account of Orpheus's journey through the spheres, during which he does not find Eurydice, but does at least learn some music, the 'armony celestiall' which has already been described as Urania.

> Yit be the way sum melody he lerd.
>
> In his passage amang the planeitis all,
> He hard a hevinly melody and sound,
> Passing all intrumentis musicall,
> Causit be rollyn of the speiris round;
> Quhilk armony of all this mappamound,
> Quhilk moving seiss unyt perpetuall,
> Quhilk of this warld Plato the saule can call.
> (218-25)

Orpheus is the intellectual soul of the microcosm; the harmony of the spheres is the Platonic soul of the macrocosm.

The failure of Orpheus is that in his little world he cannot, and does not attempt to, establish a harmony like that of the spheres. Music is part of his inheritance. When he was born his mother sat him on her knee,

> And gart him souk of hir twa paupis quhyte
> The sueit lecour of all musik perfyte.
> (69-70)

The measure of his failure is that between his birth and the death of Eurydice Orpheus is nowhere referred to as a musician. When Eurydice chose him for his fame, stature, and fairness of face, Orpheus remained acquiescent. This is degeneracy.

> It is contrair the Lawis of nature
> A gentill man to be degenerat,
> Nocht following of his progenitour
> The worthe rewll, and the lordly estait.
> (8-11)

The degeneracy takes effect in a corresponding degeneracy of his music. After the death of Eurydice, Orpheus leaves the *amena presentis vite* for the forest:

> Him to reioss yit playit he a spring,
> Quhill that the fowlis of the wid can sing,
> And treis dansit with thair levis grene,
> Him to devod from his grit womenting;
> Bot all in vane, that wailyeit no thing,
> His hairt wes so upoun his lusty quene.
> (144-9)

The dancing of the trees is a traditional feature of the legend, exploited by Henryson with particular effectiveness. The trees are the material world, *silva,* brute matter, over which a degenerate music still has some degree of control. Orpheus himself is more than material, and music of the kind he is now capable of producing has no power to make good a loss, which also is more than material, or even to comfort him. The song is musical in the discipline of its stanzaic structure, but the refrain is a question ('Quhair art thow gone, my luve Ewridicess?'), with no answer stated or implied. Within the stanza the normal structure is again question, or imperative appeal—to his harp, to Phoebus, to Jupiter. Where he makes a statement, it is one merely of loss or of change, and when he does attempt resolution, it is at once qualified by the negation of its contrary—a rhetorical device which strengthens rather than weakens the overall negative impression:

Forsuth seik hir I sall,
And nowthir stint nor stand for stok nor stone.
(178-9)

The operative words are those linked by alliteration on *st*—stint, stand, stok, stone.

The appeal to Phoebus and Jupiter indicates the path, not so much to Eurydice as to regeneration, a path which lies through the spheres. Intellectual discipline is the characteristic of the new music which he learns there, a characteristic expressed stylistically, first in the catalogue form of the description, and secondly in the use of the Latin and Greek terms of musical theory.

Thair leirit he tonis proportionat,
As duplare, triplare, and emetricus,
Enolius, and eik the quadruplait,
Epoddeus rycht hard and curius;
Off all thir sex, sueit and delicius,
Rycht consonant fyfe hevinly symphonyss
Componyt ar, as clerkis can devyse.

Ffirst diatesserone, full sueit, I wiss,
And dyapasone, semple and dowplait,
And dyapenty, componyt with the dyss;
Thir makis fyve of thre multiplicat:
This mirry musik and mellefluat,
Compleit and full of nummeris od and evin,
Is causit be the moving of the hevin.
(219-32)
(pp. 26-42)

As narrator, Henryson disclaims any share in the music which he describes:

Off sic musik to wryt I do bot doit,
Thairfoir of this mater a stray I lay,
For in my lyfe I cowth nevir sing a noit.
(240-2)

The remark is to be taken rhetorically rather than personally; the effect is to emphasize the importance of the passage, the only one upon which such comment is made, and it is worth noting that Henryson repeats the effect when he uses Greek terms to describe the harping of Orpheus before Pluto and Proserpina:

Than Orpheus befoir Pluto sat doun,
And in his handis quhit his herp can ta,
And playit mony sueit proportioun,
With baiss tonis in Ipotdorica,
With gemilling in Yporlerica.
(366-70)

His music has become 'proportioun'.

The link between Orpheus and Eurydice is love; the allegorical significance of Eurydice is appetite. The more intellectual quality, which also is in greater harmony with the order of the universe, is love. It is this intellectual love which Orpheus learns in his journey through the spheres, and which enables him to rescue Eurydice from hell. Orpheus, however, is not merely intellect, he is fallen intellect, which cannot find its appetite in the heavens at any level. He is therefore always liable to confuse love with appetite, as he did on the brink of hell, and his last words are the cry of the blinded intellect seeking a definition of its problems.

Quhat art thow, luve, how sall I the defyne?
Bittir and sueit, crewall and merciable,
Plesand to sum, to uthir plent and pyne,
Till sum constant, to uthir wariable;
Hard is thy law, thy bandis unbrekable;
Quho sservis the, thocht thay be nevir so trew,
Perchance sum tyme thay sall haif causs to rew.
(401-7)
(pp. 43-4)

John MacQueen, in his Robert Henryson: A Study of the Major Narrative Poems, *Oxford at the Clarendon Press, 1967, 229 p.*

J. A. W. Bennett (essay date 1974)

[In the excerpt below, Bennett presents a detailed comparative analysis between Henryson's Testament of Cresseid *and Chaucer's* Troilus and Criseyde, *reproaching Henryson for the "attitudes, beliefs and idioms" which he interpolated into his literary source. For a rebuttal to this essay, see the excerpt by Peter Godman dated 1984.]*

I come to criticise Henryson, not to praise him—or rather, I come to criticise the eulogists of his best-known poem who have obscured his faults by encomiums on its 'delicate moral balance', its 'reflexion of medieval assurance'. In admiration of the author of ***The Fables*** I yield to none. But re-reading Tillyard's exposition of the ***Testament*** [in his *Five Poets 1470-1870,* 1948], I am disturbed by doubts. I shall not dwell on his curious claim that 'through the repose bred of (medieval) assurance Henryson can give us what is unique, what he alone of men is able to give'; or on his conception of 'courtly love', based as that conception is on a passage in Malory that is as confused as Tillyard himself; or on his notion that Henryson presents 'the eternal human drama' through the mechanism of the planets in order to give his work 'the essential stamp of contemporary vogue'. It is enough for the moment to note that Tillyard's essay rests on a version of the Bradleian heresy: we are asked to read the poem in the light of Chaucer's *Troilus;* thus the irony of the 'non-recognition' scene depends, Tillyard claims, on our recollection of the scene in which Chaucer's Troilus rides down the street watched by Criseyde. That Chaucer's lines suggested the episode in the later poem is indeed likely. But it is illegitimate to resort to the *Troilus* to prove irony in ***The Testament***: Chaucer's poem was not so well known in medieval Scotland that Henryson could assume such intimate knowledge in his readers; and to insist on this nexus—as later critics have done—is to diminish rather than to enhance his achievement. We may properly use Chaucer to elucidate Henryson's attitudes, beliefs and idioms. We may profitably compare the two poems. But to treat scenes in Henryson as ironic variations on scenes in Chaucer is to praise the right things for the wrong reason.

Of Henryson's capacity to create arresting scenes there is no question; and even when he takes hints from the *Troilus* he does not depend on it. The opening picture of the poet in his study on a cold clear night . . . ; the assembly and judgement of the planetary deities; the delivery of Cresseid to the spital; Troilus's almsgiving; Cresseid's swoon—all these are vivid and arresting in themselves. It is when we come to locate the several scenes that difficulties arise—and differences from Chaucer's treatment appear. In *Troilus* we always know precisely where we are: it has even been possible to make plans of Chaucer's Troy and of the chief houses in it: for he envisaged it as a medieval city. But the topography of Henryson's poem is vague, not to say perplexing. He will first picture Calchas as living in a fine mansion 'a mile or twa out of toun' (93-6). Here he is perhaps developing the suggestion in Chaucer that Calchas' tent was set outside the Grecian camp on the Troy side: it is the first place that Diomede comes to as he leads Criseyde away from Troy (*Tr.* V. 148-9). Not only does Henryson make the camp a town, he gives it a court with courtesans (76-7)—though the words 'sum men sayis' (that she 'went commoun') (77) do not make it clear (*pace* Fox [*The Testament of Cresseid,* 1968]) that he is 'damning Cresseid': when Chaucer uses that cautious turn of phrase with regard to Cresseid he is careful to add 'I not', ('I don't know') (V. 1058). A few lines later we find that Calchas's 'chalmer' (dwelling) was next to the temple of Venus and Cupid; so this likewise is two miles from town. The suggestion of a temple comes from Chaucer, who mentions the 'observances' in the Temple of Palladion early in the *Troilus:* I. 150ff. . . . Chaucer does not there speak of sacrifices—though later his Cassandra avers that the Greeks refused to sacrifice to Diana (*Tr.* V. 1464); but in the Knight's Tale Palamon offers sacrifices in Venus' temple; and that is certainly located some little distance from the town of Athens—perhaps near the spot where Theseus had come upon Palamon and Arcite, which was in fact 'a mile or tweye' from town (*CT.* A. 1504). The altars in the Knight's Tale are set in oratories (*CT.* A. 1905ff); and it is in an 'orature' that Cresseid kneels (120). The word elsewhere . . . has Christian associations; and Henryson may be envisaging the sacrifice to Venus as a kind of pagan mass. . . . An oratory is an unlikely place to find a mirror in, yet Cresseid finds one (348). Venus, to be sure, is sometimes—though never in Chaucer—depicted with a mirror. We are left uncertain whether Henryson intends an association with that selfregarding goddess; but the incident comes to mind when the leprous Cresseid enjoins other beauties to 'in your mynd ane mirrour mak of me' (457).

The mirror shows her, and us, that the gods' decree has been implemented even while she is dreaming of its promulgation. For the elaborate description of the deities and their court one might make a better case than Tillyard, who sees it as 'decently expansive'; but pedantry intrudes in the two stanzas devoted to the horses of the sun (204-217). Here, as often, Henryson's best effects are in resonant couplets, like those portraying 'Cupid the King ringand ane silver bell / Quhilk men micht heir fra hevin unto hell' (144-5). I can find only one representation of Cupid with a bell, and that is on a little-known mosaic; so it may well be that Henryson was 'ironically' recalling Criseyde's 'throughout the worlde my belle shal be runge' (*Tr.* V. 1062). Yet the truly ironic counterpart to Cupid's bell is to be found in the sad and sullen tones of the cup and clapper that she is to be doomed to carry when the Gods, whom Cupid is summoning, give their verdict. They sound five times in the poem (343, 387, 442, 479, 579), on each occasion in a new context or in the mouth of a new speaker. In more than one sense they make for a unity of tone that is not otherwise easy to demonstrate.

The slow procession of the gods—like the long period of time that elapses before Cresseid awakes—perhaps figures the gradualness of her degradation. Suddenly the poet jerks us back into the everyday world, with a servant knocking at the door of the oratory to say that supper's ready. The door 'closte fast' (as it is in the Miller's Tale, when the carpenter's 'knave' is sent to knock up Absolom); and Calchas' servant, like the carpenter's, has to shout to transmit his impatient master's message:

> He has mervell sa lang on grouf ye ly.
>
> (362)

Yet if the door is shut he cannot know that she is prostrate on the ground, and in fact she is not: she has 'rissin up' (348). As often, Henryson's verisimilitude is imperfect. His true strength, his true irony shows in the concluding couplets of the stanza (assuming that the last line is part of the message):

> And sayis your prayers bene to lang sumdeill;
> The goddis wait all your intent full weill.
>
> (363-4)

They tell us as much of Calchas as of his daughter. Whether or not they are intended to bring comfort (as Mr. MacQueen thinks [*Robert Henryson: A Study of the Major Narrative Poems,* 1967]), they are certainly loaded with dramatic irony. But the last assertion has a Christian flavour that does not altogether sort with the planetary vindictiveness: only the god of Scripture (Heb. 4: 12) knows the intents of the heart.

As a leper Cresseid asks to go 'to yone hospitall at the tounis end' (382). That, to be sure, is where medieval hospitals often stood—just outside the town wall. But in the event Calchas opens a 'secreit yet' (388: 'In his mansioun'?; if it is a mile or two from town there seems little need of secrecy) and takes her to the spital in 'ane village half ane myle thairby' (390: from the said 'mansioun'?). There, Henryson is careful to remark, 'sum knew hir weill': that is, some recognised her at once—whilst the others presumed that because she showed such distress she must be 'of nobill kin': an irony compounded by the next poker-faced line: 'With better will thairfoir thay tuik hir in' (399). To read that line in Tillyard's way, as 'reflecting the old stability of social order' is to miss the sardonic note, which chimes with the leper's later insistance on fair shares (527). But there is no mistaking the emphasis on secrecy—a condition that Henryson has associated with the fallen Cresseid from the beginning, when she:

> Rich privelie but fellowschip, on fute
> Disagysit passit far out of the toun.
>
> (94-5)

Even so Chaucer's Troilus proposes in his anguish 'himselven lik a pilgrim to disgyse' and to visit Calchas (*Tr.* V. 1577). For Tillyard, Henryson's lines recall 'eyeless in Gaza, at the mill, with slaves': a more pertinent comparison would be with Henryson's own figure of the burgess Mouse:

> Bairfute, allone, with pykestaf in hir hand,
> As pure pilgryme scho passit owt off toun.
>
> (***Fables*** 181-2)

He had perhaps learnt the art of re-using such details from the poet who can put the line 'allone, with-outen any companye' to such different effects in the Knight's Tale and the Miller's (*CT.* A. 2779, 3204).

Henryson's Calchas is a Scottish priest—and the characterisation is none the worse for that: as a priest he would know the signs of the leprous condition (367-7) and as a priest he would receive 'almous' of which he could send part to his daughter (392). There is no reason—in terms of Henryson's tale—why she should starve or become a beggar. But the poet is so preoccupied at every stage with Cresseid's plight that he disregards his own pointers; and no attempt to distinguish between poet and stupid narrator can dispose of the difficulty that though Cresseid had asked Calchas to send her 'sum meit for cheritie' (383) and he daily did so (392), hunger soon reduces her to beggary (482-3).

As Chaucer's poem is the tragedy of Troilus, so Henryson's is the tragedy of Cresseid (which is not to say that Tillyard's claim for it as Aristotelian tragedy can stand: Tillyard has confused her with Chaucer's Criseyde). He underlines the likeness by adapting ll. 11-13 of Chaucer's poem in his very opening lines; and when he speaks of Cresseid's 'fatall destenie' (64), he is applying to her the phrase that Chaucer used of Troilus (*Tr.* V. 1)—but weakening its force, since Chaucer has in mind specifically the fatal 'sustren three', the angry Parcas (*Tr.* V. 3); Henryson will use the term 'angry' of Mars (189), of Venus (328), and of Saturn (323). As Chaucer tells 'the double sorwe of Troilus'—his parting from Criseyde and her forsaking of him—so Henryson reports the double sorrow of Cresseid in losing both Troilus and Diomeid. The two stanzas in the ***Testament*** summarising Troilus's grief (43-56) are flat and repetitious. It is only when he turns to Cresseid that Henryson is *engagé.* He piles on the agony. Diomeid 'fulfills all his appetite, and mair' (72); he not only takes another woman, but divorces Cresseid as if she had committed adultery against him. It is half-suggested that she is *forced* to become a strumpet (76-7).

And all of this, says the poet, is due to 'mischance' (84). He even twists the sense of 'fortunait' to make it mean 'destined by Fortune'. Whether or not Henryson is following 'an uther quair', the emphasis here is Henryson's. Here (as at two later crucial points: 323-9 and 505-11) the poet intrudes on the tale:

> Yit nevertheless, quhatever men deme or say
> In scornefull langage of thy brukkilnes,
> I sall excuse, als far furth as I may,
> Thy womanheid, thy wisedome and fairnes—
> The quhilk Fortoun hes put to sic distres
> As hir pleisit, and nathing throw the gilt
> Of the, throw wickit langage to be spilt.
>
> (85-91)

The best one can make of this is: 'Men may say you were morally frail. But I would exempt you from blame, thinking it hard on your womanhood, wisdom and beauty that Fortune should allow wicked tale-tellers to make your name a by-word'. But if the stanza is muddled to the point of imbecility (as Mr. Fox agrees) it is not because the poet is presenting an imbecile narrator, but because he had misread his Chaucer, and misapplied the line in which Chaucer's narrator comments on the same situation (*Troilus* V. 1048-98). When Chaucer's Criseyde, foreseeing that her name will be rolled on many a tongue, cries 'Allas, that swich a cas me sholde falle' (1064), she acknowledges blame: she has 'falsed' Troilus (1058); and when she says 'gilteless, I woot wel, I yow leve' (1084), she is absolving Troilus from guilt, not, as Henryson may have thought, denying her own. If Henryson could misread that line, he may also have misread Chaucer's adjacent comment:

> Ne me ne list this sely womman chyde
> Ferther than the story wol devyse
> Hir name, allas! is publisshed so wyde,
> That for hir gilt it oughte y-now suffyse.
> And if I might excuse hir any wyse,
> For she so sory was for hir untrouthe,
> Y-wis, I wolde excuse hir yet for routhe.
>
> (*Tr.* V. 1094-9)

Here the context forces us to read *sely* as 'hapless', not as 'innocent'. Because Criseyde repented, the narrator feels compassion for her. But this is not to *excuse* her. Mr. Fox sees Henryson 'using the same method as Chaucer for simultaneously revealing the sin and making the sinner sympathetic: a stupid and passionately involved narrator . . . '. But there is nothing stupid in Chaucer's stanza, and it distances rather than involves the narrator. Nor does Chaucer's narrator ever 'blame Cresseid's troubles on a personified Fortune', as Henryson's does when he pities her because she had the hard luck to become a harlot (a state she nonetheless enjoyed: 'sa giglotlike, takand thy foull pleasance' (83-4). As for the wisdom that Henryson attributes to Cresseid, the only ground for it in Chaucer is in Troilus's pitifully naive approval of her supposed decision to return 'pryvely' and 'softely by nighte':

> I comende hir wysdom, by myn hood,
> She wol not maken peple nycely
> Gaure on hir, whan she comth
>
> (*Tr.* V. 1151-3)

That these lines were in Henryson's mind is suggested by

his description of her later secret exit from the Greek camp (94-5, cited above).

If we now turn back to the tale as Henryson tells it we find Cresseid on her knees, perhaps in her father's private chapel: she is evidently afraid of being publicly 'cut' by Diomede, here curiously described as the 'King' (119). Tillyard sees her posture as the first sign of a change of heart. But she is only bewailing, angrily, her destiny (121, 124). The machinery of the story requires that she must do this aloud—so that the deities concerned may hear her accusations, and be affronted. A pagan oratory is the obvious place in which to present them; but she would have no ground for being there were she not thought to be at her devotions.

At this stage Henryson does attend carefully to the development of plot, and his use of motifs from Chaucer is subtle and discriminating. In *Troilus* V. 206ff., it is Troilus who privately curses the gods (amongst them Venus and Cupid) and 'in his throwes frenetyk and madde' curses also 'his burthe, him-self, his fate . . . '—though he later recovers sufficiently to pray for mercy to Cupid (V. 593). Chaucer treats the same theme, more playfully, in *Lenvoy à Scogan,* where 'blaspheme of the goddes' (cf. ***Testament,*** 274, 354) 'through pryde, or through thy grete rakelnesse' is related specifically to Venus and Cupid. The first three stanzas of this balade had been printed by Caxton.

Cresseid's first charge is that the gods:

> gave me anis ane devine responsaill
> that I suld be the flour of luif in Troy
> (127-8)

The lines suggests an oracular answer to prayers; and for that Henryson would find a pertinent precedent in the Knight's Tale, where Palamon prays to Venus in her oratory, and:

> atte laste the statue of Venus shook
> And made a signe, wher-by that he took
> That his preyre accepted was that day.
> (*CT.* A. 2265-7)

Strictly interpreted, the oracular response of l. 128 makes Cresseid's complaint (132) that she is rejected by Diomeid (an enemy to Troy) unwarrantable, as is her further charge that the gods had led her to believe that the love would be always green. Though the gods' indictment may seem vicious, her apostasy is illgrounded.

For the 'uglye visioun' that follows Henryson may also have found a suggestion in Chaucer. Troilus, when in desperate case, has a portentous dream, vouchsafed by the gods:

> The blisful goddess, through hir grete might,
> Han in my dreem y-shewed it ful right.
> (*Tr.* V. 1250-1)

Telling it to Pandarus, he laments his lot in just such rhetorical phrases as Cresseid now uses (1245-74), and it is a similarly self-reflecting dream that she now dreams. In blaming Cupid she has pictured herself as cut down by wintry frost (139). Straightaway she sees 'by appearance' (a phrase that in Chaucer carries the suggestion of the uncanny or the magical: cf. *CT.* F. 218, 1157, 1265) a Cupid who summons as first of the gods Saturn, planet of winter, 'ovirfret with froistis hoir' (165). He gives to Cupid 'litill reverence'—winter is no time for love. Chaucer had noted that it was against Saturn's nature to 'styntén strif and drede' (*CT.* A. 2450), but had also pictured him as compliant to his 'deere doghter Venus' (ib. 2452). His early arrival on the scene is ominous.

If Henryson's deployment of the planetary powers was partly suggested by the presentation of Saturn, Venus, Mars and Jupiter in the Knight's Tale, where we are shown the deities not only in their temples but in 'angry parle' his Venus bears little resemblance to Chaucer's, but much to the very Cresseid who has just blasphemed her: 'dissimulait, Provocative with blenkis amorous, And suddanely changit and alterait, Angrie . . . now grene as leif, now widderit and ago' (225-39). She and Cupid are the only gods directly involved in the case. Cupid argues more like a counsel for the prosecution than a deity; and when he urges that Cresseid, by maligning him and calling his mother blind, blasphemed all the gods, we share the poet's feeling that the final judgement is not divinely fair. His address beginning, 'O cruell Saturne, fraward and angrie' (323) may have been prompted by Chaucer's invocation, 'O influences of these hevenes hye', on the occasion of the conjunction of Cynthia, Saturn and Jupiter (*Tr.* iii, 617-25), and the accomplishment of the gods' will at that earlier stage in Cresseid's story. But Henryson does not present these planetary forces as 'under God' (*Tr.* ib. 619); and there is no ambiguity in his comment on Saturn's judgement:

> Hard is thy dome and to malitious!
> On fair Cresseid quhy hes thow na mercie?
> (324-5)

The disclosure of her plight to her father is finely presented. Henryson's homeliness and economy never show to better effect than in the only phrases he allows Calchas in the whole work—'Douchter, quhat cheir?' (367) and 'How sa?' (369). Yet the emphasis on the help he gives her makes it harder to accept the implication of later stanzas that he soon ceases to support her. Indeed, Henryson seems as unconcerned about the time as he is about the place of the events. Cresseid's long complaint is made, immediately on arrival at the spital 'in a dark corner of the hous allone' (404). A Bentleian commentator—I am thinking of Bentley's matter-of-fact comments on certain passages in *Paradise Lost*—might well complain that in these circumstances the 'ladyis fair of Troy and Greece' whom she begs to take warning by her misery have little chance of doing so. The passage, which corresponds formally to Troilus's complaint at V. 540-553, suffers by comparison with it, and its rhetoric is clogged by alliteration. If this is 'still murning'—whatever that phrase may mean (398)—it is loud and long enough to keep her fellow-lepers awake all night (470-4). Then suddenly, and disconcertingly, she is reduced to follow 'the law of lipper leid' and live by cup and clapper (479-80). A line later cold and hunger have degraded her still further, and she is forced to be 'ane rank beggair'; which evidently means that she is not strong enough to go from place to place, but must sit at one spot (496-7). Yet she is with the lepers when

Troilus passes. They are presumably all waiting for alms outside the gates of Troy.

Weak and almost blind as she is, it is not surprising that she should fail to distinguish him in the company of 'worthy lords' returning victoriously to Troy—though another leper has no difficulty (535); they are on horseback, in armour and the vizored helmets worn for combat. The scene represents an ironic reversal (not noted by Tillyard) of the claim Chaucer's Troilus makes in his last words to Criseyde:

> So lost have I myn hele, and eek myn hewe,
> Criseyde shal nought conne knowe me!
> (*Tr.* V. 1403-4)

It is not this, however, that makes it poignant, but the presentation of a Troilus who *agnoscit veteris vestigia flammae;* and it is perhaps Virgil's phrase that gives us Henryson's 'Ane spark of lufe than till his hart culd spring . . . ' (512). Certainly the only scene that approaches Henryson's climax is the discovery of Tristram as Malory describes it. Isold and Branguyne find him lying in the garden after he has gone mad and run naked in the forest, and 'waxed leane and poore of fleyshe':

> So whan the quene loked uppon Sir Trystramys She was not remembird of hym, but ever she seyde unto Dame Brangnoyue: 'Me semys I shulde have sene thys man here before in many places'. But as sone as Sir Trystramys sye her he knew her well inowe, and than he turned away hys vysage and wept.
> (Malory, *Works,* ll, 501)

When at this point the schoolmaster of Dunfermline inserts his Aristotelian explanation:

> Na wonder was, suppois in mynd that he
> Tuik hir figure sa sone, and lo, now quhy—
> (505-6)

it is as if the pedantic and irrepressible Eagle of the *House of Fame* had suddenly intruded as commentator on the tragedy of the last book of *Troilus.*

But again a terse vernacular word recalls us to the realities of the scene, as with a *swak* (cf. ***Fables,*** 2076, 2146) Troilus's girdle, purse and jewels fall into Cresseid's lap. In much the same way the sharp Gaelic 'ochane' (541) redeems the densely alliterative opening of her last lament. But the drift of that lament is obscure, and it remains an unsuccessful attempt to incorporate a favourite *moralitas* device within the framework of a story that speaks for itself. True, it represents a belated approach to self-knowledge, but at the cost of magnifying her depravity—as if she had *always* 'inclinyt to lustis lecherous'—and of making Troilus almost a Galahad, who 'kept gude continence, Honest and chaist in conversasioun, of all wemen protectour and defence' (554-7). Once again Henryson is extrapolating from various passages in *Troilus* (in particular III, 1772-1806); but how Troilus 'helpit thair opinioun' remains obscure. Formally, the parallel in *Troilus* is with Chaucer's apology:

> Ne I sey not this al-only for these men,
> But most for women that bitraysed be
> Through false folk . . .
> (*Tr.* V. 1779-81)

Cresseid's suggestion that all women are like herself, her 'Take them as you find them', strikes a sour cynical note that jars with her last words: 'Nane but myself as now I will accuse'. It may be argued that this last lament shows Cresseid still like the women she condemns, 'sad as widdercock in wind' (567), and that the oscillation reflects her inner distress. Again the high-flown rhetoric, now jostling with uncertain syntax, leaves us uncertain. The Chaucerian parallel here is with the *litera Criseydi* (*Tr.* V. 1590-1631). But there all the rhetoric accords with the epistolary convention, and neither Troilus nor the modern reader has any difficulty in detecting in it 'Kalendes of chaunge'.

Was it Cresseid's letter that led Henryson to show her making a will (on the spur of the moment, in a place unspecified)? It follows the pattern of medieval wills, though the medieval Christian commended his body to the church, not to 'wormis and taidis' and his 'spirit' to God, not to a goddess. That this brief testament should have given the work its title is inexplicable, and unfortunate. Henryson himself rightly called it a *ballet* (610), for it is a *balade* written in the rhyme royal stanzas that was the customary vehicle for Complaints and so suitable for a poem in which complaint bulks large. Like Criseyde's complaints, the will stanzas mix ambiguous detail and strong dramatic effects. Thus 'myne ornament' (579) suggests that she has taken for herself the girdle and jewels that Troilus has bestowed in answer to the other lepers' prayer for alms (494). The bequest of her soul to Diana is presumably in token of penitence for unchastity, but this goddess is not elsewhere the deity of 'waist woddis' but of 'wodes grene' (KT, 1439). Has Henryson's fondness for the set alliterative phrase (cf. ***Fables*** 1427, 1441) again proved too strong? Or are we to think of waste uninhabited woods as betokening solitary penitence? Since the probable occasion of the introduction of Diana at this point is the prayer of Chaucer's to the chaste goddess who loved 'for to walken in the wodes wilde' (KT, 1481) and hunt therein, it is hardly likely that Henryson had in mind 'the tradition that equated Diana with the Trinity or with the Divine essence'—and still less likely that he conceived of the pagan Cresseid suddenly, in a moment of truth, associating herself with that essence. That she bequeaths 'all my gold' (that is, the purse just dropped in her lap by Troilus), her 'ornament' (his girdle and jewels), and her cup and clapper to her fellow-lepers is hardly the striking proof of her sincerity and unselfishness that Tillyard takes it to be: they would share them in any event; it should count more in her favour that she still has a 'royall ring' sent by Troilus (581-2). But the disposal of the ornaments stirs a recollection that turns her thoughts from the will:

> O Diomed, thou hes baith broche and belt
> Quhilk Troylus gave me in takning
> Of his trew lufe—
> (589)

Once more Henryson is following the Chaucerian story (*Tr.* V. 1040), but not to the end: in *Troilus* Deiphebe snatches the brooch from Diomede in combat, so that Troilus sees it again, and sees it as a symbol of Cresseid's changed love (*Tr.* V. 1670-94). The belt, not mentioned by Chaucer, seems introduced to correspond to the girdle that Troilus has just let fall (520). In any event it is the memory of her bestowal of Troilus' love token on Diomeid that brings the bitterest, the fatal pang. Dying on the words, 'his trew lufe', she brings, by a kind of sympathy, a lesser death to Troilus: 'he swelt for wo and fell doun in ane swoun' when he sees the ring and hears her story (594-99). The epitaph he sets on her marble tomb—it must be at the gates of Troy—is addressed, like her earlier complaint, to the fair ladies of that city, and conveys, though far more concisely and effectively, the stern warning:

> Lo, fair ladyis! Cresseid of Troyis toun,
> Sumtyme countit the flour of womanheid
> Under this stane, lait lipper, lyis deid!

That this is the very last thing Cresseid would have wished is the final irony. She had prayed that oblivion might cover her:

> Under the eirth God gif I gravin wer,
> Quhair nane of Grece nor yit of Troy micht heird!
>
> (414-5)

and that was surely her 'intent' in leaving her gold to her fellow-lepers 'to burie me in grave' (581).

After the weighty conclusion of the epitaph not a word is needed. But Henryson cannot forego his *moralitas,* heavy as it is with laboured polysyllables and padded lines. Even at this point he can take his eye off the object and glance at other purposes, professing that this balade on female fickleness is made not only for the instruction of women but in their honour ('worschip' 611); they are not to mingle their love with false deception (613)—though Cresseid's 'deception' has hardly been the central theme of the story. The terse contrasting last line—'Sen scho is deid, I speik of hir no moir'—adds a final touch of teasing ambiguity. (pp. 5-16)

J. A. W. Bennett, "Henryson's 'Testament': A Flawed Masterpiece," in Scottish Literary Journal, *Vol. 1, No. 1, July, 1974, pp. 5-16.*

Matthew P. McDiarmid (essay date 1981)

[*In the following excerpt, McDiarmid offers general commentary on many of Henryson's shorter poems.*]

Robert Henryson has often been spoken of as an 'impersonal' poet—for example by his modern countryman Edwin Muir who chose to find something of his own remote poetic personality in him ["Robert Henryson," in *Essays on Literature and Society,* 1967]—a voice in which the stability, faith and calm of the great medieval order, as ideally imaged in the doctrinal system for which Dante, it is said, spoke so serenely and Chaucer so happily, can still be heard. To the present writer no one of these poets speaks in quite that way. Certainly Henryson does not.

How much he reveals of himself and his deeply perturbed responses to experience we [see in his] longer poems . . . , and in the dozen or so short ones that he has left similar self-revelation adds to the understanding that should prepare us for a judgment on his work.

Stylistically their method is incantation, often supported by the sharp stress of alliteration, and it is only when they are so recited, aloud, as all poetry should be read, but especially that of his day, that they make their proper impression. It is a various sensibility that comes across, in one or two cases plainly indifferent to a commonplace and dutifully expressed matter, as in ***The Want of Wyse Men, The Ressoning betwix Deth and Man, Agains Haisty Credence of Titlaris*** [idle slanderers], and to a lesser extent ***The Abbey Walk*** ('Is nocht but casualitie and chance'), but in the others, considered together, exhibiting an alternating power, gentleness and deliberate homeliness, that commands respect and liking for both man and artist. Here there is room only for a few appreciative notes.

Doubtless the most famous of them is the wistfully humourous ***Robene and Makyne.*** It has in mind the French Robin and Marie scene and was written to a song-tune of the 'It was a shepherd and his lass' type. The old-world alliterative diction of the opening (soon abandoned) helps to set the mood of 'pastourelle'. The sexually urgent Makyne expounds the 'ABC', as she calls it, of courtly love in a few imploring words: be bold, don't accept 'danger' [standoffishness], and having got your will be 'patient and previe'. Robene, who understands at least what action is expected of him, but is not in the appropriate mood, protests that his sheep will miss his care, and in any case what is this love she makes so much of—it is understood throughout that he has always understood what plain 'sex' is. He goes off and begins to feel that he does understand what love might mean. The situation of Burns's Duncan Gray and his Meg is reversed. It is the woman now who grows 'hale' as he grows 'sick'. But the scene is best played in Henryson's words—

> "Robene, thow hes hard soung and say
> In gestis and storeis auld,
> The man that will nocht quhen he may
> Sall haif nocht quhen he wald.
> I pray to Jesu, every day
> Mot eik thair cairis cauld, [coldly answered]
> That first preisis with the to play [make love]
> Be firth, forrest or fauld" [sheep-cote]
>
> "Makyne, the nicht is soft and dry,
> The wedder is warme and fair,
> And the grene woid rycht neir us by
> To walk attour allquhair;
> Thair may na janglour [gossip] us espy
> That is to lufe contrair;
> Thairin Makyne, bath ye and I
> Unsene we ma repair"
>
> "Robene, that warld is all away
> And quyt brocht till ane end,
> And nevir agane thairto perfay
> Sall it be as thow wend"

Robene has not lost Erudices, and his story does not end with quite the same meaning as that of Orpheus when he leaves his love in hell and 'A wofull wedowe hamwart is he went', but the stories have in common the 'no moir' theme that has been noticed in other contexts too. Missed chances of many kinds is certainly a preoccupation of the poet, and the recurrence of the theme of sex does explain something of his sympathy for both Orpheus and Cresseid.

It recurs in his poems of age and death and in places suggests language for his religious poems. It is directly and frankly applied to his own case, as I believe, in what may be the latest of his poems, and from the stated age of the elder speaker, sixty seven, probably written about 1503, ***The Ressoning betwix Aige and Yowth.*** This has a sung refrain, "O yowth be glaid into thy flowris [growth] grene", set against another sung refrain "O yowth, thy flowris fadis fellone [fearfully] sone!"; the joy of sex will go and "thy manheid sall wendin [pass] as the mone". The duet ends with the older singer watching the younger go off angrily, but of the former it is said that he 'luche [laughed] not but tuk his leif'. We are left with a listening poet who merely repeats both refrains and says how well the singers sang, 'triumphit in thair tone', leaving the reader to his own considerations. Withdrawal without judgment from a scene that, after all, needs only factual statement, something in which Henryson excels, gives it all the more meaning.

A similarly concerned poem that pretends to be a farewell to youth without regrets is the song with this delightful opening,

> Intyl ane garth, under a reid roseir [rose-tree],
> Ane ald man and decrepit hard I sing,
> Gay was the noit, swet wes the voce and cleyr.
> It wes gret joy to heir of sic ane thing;

but the song that follows is completely without gaiety, and is worth mentioning here only for lines that show the comment on youth and passion towards the beginning of the ***Testament*** were indeed the poet's, and not from some fictional and reprehensible narrator:

> Can nane withstand the ragyne of his blud,
> Na yit be stabil on-til he agit be;
> Than in the thing that mast rajoisit he
> Nathing ramanys for to be callit his.

The Thre Deid-Pollis may also address itself to 'lusty gallands' and 'ladeis quhyte, in claithis corruscant' in precisely the fashion that John Knox used to the women in Queen Mary's ante-chamber, but is in the usual *memento mori* style, and is interesting only at points. The line, 'Your fingearis small, quhyte as the quhailis bane', is sensuously striking. The guessing game played by the three skulls with the fascinated observer is a macabre piece of wit:

> This questioun quha can obsolve lat se,
> Quhat phisnamour or perfyt palmester,
> Quha was farest or fowlest of us thre?
> Or quhilk of us of kin was gentillar?

It is possible that Henryson remembered (as did Hamlet) the same question being asked of Alexander by Diogenes. But more macabre is Henryson's sense of a fitness in the question of the three skulls being answered by prayer to the Trinity, 'Thre knit in ane be perfyt unitie'.

The short poems that are purely religious in respect of a certain state of mind being induced, 'quyet in contemplacioun', not the unease of regret or disgust for human weakness, of course not protest, are few, and come as near to pure poetry as his intense and troubled response to experience ever allowed. They are ***The Garmont of Gud Ladeis, The Annunciation*** and ***The Bludy Serk,*** and again I must repeat that for due appreciation they must be read as incantation, and with full awareness of the sophisticated simplicity that they cultivate.

The ***Garmont*** is a gracefully continued conceit relating each item of dress to an inner perfection of the woman that the lover desires to wed. What is extraordinary is that in spite of the itemized spirituality it remains a love poem. It has a muted passion and tenderness. There is a real woman being talked about, and these are the perfections that love would give her. It is only slowly that one realises that they are the listed virtues that a priest might recommend to a woman entering upon the holy state of matrimony, but it is still not a priest's poem but a lover's poem. From the first stanza of promise,

> Wald my gud lady [future wife] lufe me best
> And wirk efter my will,
> I suld ane garmond gudliest
> Gar mak hir body till.

there is an increment of feeling, longing, to the final stanza,

> Wald scho put on this garmond gay,
> I durst sweir by my seill
> That scho woir nevir grene nor gray
> That set hir half so weill.

Again, if more expectedly, one notes how Henryson succeeds in fusing the rhetoric of courtly love with that of Mariolatry in ***The Annunciation***: love can perform such miracles.

> Forcy as deith is likand [pleasing] lufe
> Throuch quhome al bittir swet is;
> Nothing is hard, as Writ can pruf,
> Till him in lufe that letis [dwells].

Or again, 'The miraclis are mekle and meit [natural]/Fra luffis ryver rynnis'. There are hymns to the Virgin in Holland, Dunbar, Kennedy, and other Scots poets; this is much the best because it does not seem to try to outdo others in emotive rhetoric, and keeps to its simple but profound theme of love, whether divine or human, being naturally miraculous and creative.

In ***The Bludy Serk*** the poet turns Christ's dying for man's soul into a tale of old romance, almost a fairy-tale, and with corresponding manner: a prince saves a fair lady from a 'foule gyane', and makes a seemingly unreasonable request on his deathbed that if another wooer come she should think on his bloody mail-shirt and reject him. The manner of simple and sad romance is maintained in the *Moralitas* so that it too seems to belong to the original tale. One notes how it is a specially archaic word at the commencement of the last three lines that sharpens attention, conveys a change in the teller's mood, a new urgency; the minstrel has done with his tale and explanation, now he seizes his audience:

> Hend [courteous] men, will ye nocht herk?
> For his lufe that bocht us deir

Think on the bludy serk!

If it may seem to some readers that the extreme Henryson who conceived the impassioned protests of the suffering Orpheus and rejected Cresseid, and whose bitter theme so often in the ***Fabillis*** was injustice endured by the weak and the poor, is little heard in these generally acquiescent, though sometimes troubled, poems, they should remember that it is his own plight, not that of others, that he is trying to accept, and the divine love and pity that on a few occasions is his theme agrees well enough with what he expected of attitudes to situations in the major poems. At all events, the voice of protest is very clear in ***Ane Prayer for the Pest.***

It begins in the same way as did the **"Preiching,"** stressing God's perfect knowledge of all times, so, of course, he knows of our sins that deserve the punishment of this 'perrelus pestilens', and, of course, if he chooses, his mercy can save us. Christ died to save us from sin, but however great that may be 'Oure deid [death] ma nathing our synnis recompens'. And this appalling death can only endanger souls—

Allais
That we sowld thus be haistely put down,
And dye as beistis without confessioun,
That nane dar mak with uther residence!

God's law must be kept, violation punished, but it is easier to understand punishment of those in high places, responsible for seeing that it is kept, than such indiscriminate punishment. God is an unsuspect judge who will surely free us of this dread. If he must punish, why not by some other way, above all, 'Puneis with pety and nocht with violens!' The theme is justice, and the sights that daily met the poet's eyes on the streets of Dunfermline, during the greatest plague of the century, did not accord with any notion of divine justice that satisfied him. He prayed but he protested, as had Orpheus and Cresseid, not to mention the Lamb of the fables.

With this poem we look directly at the spiritual sources of his poetry, pity, desire for justice, at the basic theme, a world that does not make sense, that is comic or tragic, depending on which bit of its non-sense you choose to see. Sense is in another world. If you see the world in this way, and have the realistic temperament of Chaucer, you write about what is comic, or when you feel a serious comment must be made you write about what is pathetic, an experience such as that of Troilus. The Chaucerian philosophy would seem to give so much life, until you realise that it is only a half-life, and so would exclude the intensest and richest experiences of life, and so most of its greatest art. Doubtless that is why the Wife of Bath is by much the Englishman's greatest creation. She lives not only on the middle ground of experience but at its extremes, as do the greatest creations in literature. It is to the extremes that Henryson's genius naturally turns, where life takes on most meaning; and that is why his Cresseid and his intensely human beast-world, and his own poetic personality, ultimately have more significance for us, than does the work that he thought of when he spoke affectionately of 'worthie Chaucer glorious'.

Henryson like Dante not only has been in hell but has enjoyed a great deal of this upper world's beauty. A recurrent and always heartfelt word is 'joy'—'It was grit joy to him that luifit corne' (as it would shine in the fields of harvest-time), 'The hartlie joy, God geve ye had sene,' etc. Such enjoyment gives a keener voice to his griefs: 'It wes richt hert-sair for to see/That bludie boucheour beit thay birdis doun!', or the description of Troilus's love that seems to imply a thousand sad fables, 'Cresseid of Troyis toun'. He has many styles but the one that has greatness is the simple and the factual: 'For he knew weill that there was na succour/To hir seiknes, and that dowblit his pane./ Thus was thair cair eneuch betwix thame twane.'

Reality is his theme, even in his most fantastic comedy, so that the comic artist always writes from a tragi-comic vision. As regards the presentation of his humanised animals and his people in situations that touch a question of justice, he has been accused of 'piling on the agony', but the language with which he gets his poignant effects—like his comic effects—is of the sparest, and the true occasion of the charge is the fact that his created world is felt to be so much more real than that of his predecessors.

The future of Henryson's reputation not only as a poet but a great poet is assured now that he begins to be better known, and we no longer talk about the stern schoolmaster of Dunfermline. The once neglected, now much loved, poet will have no difficulty in holding his place; in his own words—

The miraclis are mekle [many] and meit [true]
Fra luffis ryver rynnis:
The low [flame] of luf haldand the hete
Unbrynt full blithlie burns.

(pp. 117-25)

Matthew P. McDiarmid, in his Robert Henryson, *Scottish Academic Press Ltd., 1981, 125 p.*

Peter Godman (essay date 1984)

[*In the excerpt below, Godman defends Henryson's* Testament of Cresseid *from J. A. W. Bennett's critical attack, arguing that many of the poet's alleged flaws can also be found in Chaucer's* Troilus and Criseyde.]

Henryson is well served by recent scholarship. His poetry is now available in an edition of rare reliability and finesse by Denton Fox [in his *The Poems of Robert Henryson,* 1981], while his life and works have received from Douglas Gray a sane and subtle interpretation which illuminates Henryson's artistry and sheds light on the character of Middle Scots literature [*Robert Henryson,* 1979]. Doubts persist, none the less, about the nature of Henryson's achievement and, in particular, about the stature of his ***Testament of Cresseid.*** They are voiced most eloquently in the late J. A. W. Bennett's essay, 'Henryson's Testament: a flawed masterpiece' [*Scottish Literary Journal* i, no. I (1974)]. These pages set out to reconsider Bennett's argument, and to emulate its brevity.

'I come to criticise Henryson, not to praise him' is how Bennett's study begins, and the subsequent qualification that his real quarrel is with 'the eulogists . . . who have obscured [Henryson's] faults' does little to temper this opening. Although part of his argument serves as a brisk corrective to the anaemic essay of E. M. W. Tillyard ['The Testament of Cresseid' in *Five Poets 1470-1870,* 1948], most of it is concerned with what Bennett sees as the flaws in Henryson's ***Testament.*** These he distinguishes, with characteristic elegance and economy, as: vagueness, at times amounting to confusion, of detail; imperfections or outright failures of verisimilitude; excessive preoccupation with the fate of Cresseid, frequently leading to muddle and lapsing once into 'imbecility'; stylistic clumsiness ('rhetoric clogged by alliteration', 'uncertain syntax', 'laboured polysyllables and padded lines'); pedantry; and two failed attempts to foist ponderous *moralitates* upon a narrative which speaks for itself. It is true that Bennett finds merit in Henryson's poem, but if these are the flaws he reports in the work he has surveyed, then his description of the ***Testament*** as a masterpiece suggests the sort of structure commended in another context as 'a handyman's paradise'.

Let us follow the course of Bennett's argument. The poem begins well, he acknowledges, with vivid and arresting scenes, but Henryson's topography, unlike Chaucer's, is perplexing. Henryson pictures Calchas as living in a fine mansion a mile or two out of town (93-6), next to the temple of Venus and Cupid (106-9). The location of Calchas' dwelling, notes Bennett, may derive from Chaucer's suggestion that Calchas' tent was set outside the Grecian camp on the Troy side, while the idea of a temple originates from *Troilus,* i. 150 ff. Chaucer does not speak of sacrifices taking place in this building; instead sacrifices to Venus occur in a temple described in the *Knight's Tale*. . . . These points establish that there is some formal correspondence between the setting of *Troilus* and that of the ***Testament,*** and they support Bennett's denial . . . that the relation between the two poets is one of close dependence, but they do not show that Henryson's topography is perplexing when compared with Chaucer's. All they prove is that Henryson and Chaucer, at certain points, differ.

'Not only does Henryson make the [Greek] camp into a town, he gives it a court with courtesans'. . . . At the point in the poem being discussed by Bennett (76-7) Henryson describes Cresseid, after her rejection by Diomeid, walking up and down,

> And sum men sayis, into the court, commoun.
> (77)

There is no suggestion here that Cresseid is one of a number of courtesans; indeed, as Fox points out the word is not recorded in this sense before the mid-sixteenth century. Henryson visualizes, with great compression and vigour, the once cherished mistress of a royal prince rejected by another lover and reduced to promiscuity in a setting calculated to recall her former position of honour. Cresseid's degradation is made complete in lines naturally linked to l. 77:

> To change in filth all thy feminitie,
> And be with fleschelie lust sa maculait,
> And go amang the Greikis air and lait,
> Sa giglotlike takand thy foull plesance!
> (80-3)

Cresseid is a wanton at every level: both 'into the court' and 'amang the Greikis'. The allusion here is not topographical but metaphorical; it refers less to the position of the Greek army than to the indiscriminate range of Cresseid's promiscuity. It is no fairer to tax Henryson with vagueness in this regard than it is to criticize him for calling the Greek camp a 'toun' when he never called it a camp in the first place. Henryson simply invites us to imagine a different setting from Chaucer's.

When the people come to worship in the temple of Venus and Cupid, Cresseid withdraws into 'ane secreit orature' (120). There is no need to postulate her performing there 'a kind of pagan mass' . . . , for the term means a room for private worship or a study, and its Christian connotations are hardly germane to the fact that Cresseid retires into a secluded part of Calchas' mansion for fear and shame that other people might learn of her rejection by Diomeid (116-19). She wants to be alone, but her wish is to be hideously thwarted by what follows. When Cresseid wakes from her vision, she looks at herself in a mirror (348) and finds that she has been stricken by leprosy. Whether it is odd that she has a mirror to hand I cannot tell, but I suspect that Henryson's purpose in placing this detail where he does is not to invite speculation on the furnishings of Calchas' mansion but to provoke a sense of tragic paradox at Cresseid's recognition of her disfigurement. No parallel with depictions of Venus bearing a mirror was required to make Henryson's point that Cresseid becomes aware of the marks of her public disgrace in the privacy of her father's home. She who withdrew to the 'orature' afraid of how others might see her is driven from it by an affliction visible to all the world but first seen by herself, in the mirror.

As Cresseid laments her lot she is interrupted by a child knocking at the door to tell her that supper is ready (358 ff.). Douglas Gray has discussed the pathos and irony of this marvellous scene. For Bennett, it lacks verisimilitude. When the child relays Calchas' message:

> He has merwell sa lang on grouf ye ly'
> (362)

Bennett objects that 'if the door is shut he cannot know that she is prostrate on the ground, and in fact she is not: she has "rissin up" (348)'. But the child does not know that Cresseid is prostrate—he is merely reporting Calchas' surmise—and how can Henryson be accused of a failure of verisimilitude if the surmise is wrong anyway? In fact, Calchas' message is not true or false in a simple way. A pointed irony lies in its near-accuracy. Cresseid *had been* prostrate, but in her dream not in her prayers—Calchas has imagined the scene almost aright. What he has not foreseen is its terrifying character and consequences. The extraordinary circumstances of Cresseid's misfortune are thrown into relief by their chance correspondence to the ordinary events of everyday life, and the verisimilitude is perfect.

Cresseid leaves her father's home for the leper hospital 'at the tounis end' (382). She becomes a beggar (482-3), although she had asked Calchas to send her 'sum meit for cheritie' (383) and he did so daily (392). This is unsatisfactory, as Bennett sees it, because Calchas is presented as a Scottish priest with a regular income. He could send alms to Cresseid: why then should she become a beggar? Henryson, says Bennett, is 'so preoccupied at every stage with Cresseid's plight that he disregards his own pointers'.

When Cresseid enters the leper hospital she was 'ane sorrowfull gest' (402). She took her food and drink alone in a dark corner (404-5), and spent her days in tears and lamentation (406 ff.). It is important to see that this changes. A female leper takes pity on Cresseid. In poignant words, which unmistakably echo Criseyde's own advice to Troilus before leaving Troy:

> I counsall the mak vertew of ane neid
> (478)

she advises Cresseid to join the other lepers; to 'leif efter the law of lipper leid' (480). Cresseid becomes a beggar like the rest (481-3). Her assimilation to their common lot brings with it a further hardship: the qualified solace of companionship deepens her outward degradation. And so, when Troylus comes upon her, Cresseid is no longer even an erstwhile beauty, victim of a hideous affliction. She has fully become a leper. This is relevant to our understanding of why Troylus does not recognize her in the profoundly moving scene in which he gives her alms. To speculate about what had happened to Calchas' food parcels is to disregard Henryson's 'pointers'.

Bennett's view that Henryson is preoccupied with Cresseid leads him to some of his sternest criticisms of the ***Testament***:

> The two stanzas in the ***Testament*** summarising Troilus' grief (43-56) are flat and repetitious. It is only when he turns to Cresseid that Henryson is *engagé.* He piles on the agony.

Henryson's partiality leads him into incoherence, alleges Bennett; the poet is so anxious to attribute Cresseid's actions to 'mischance' (84) that he 'even twists the sense of "fortunait" to make it mean "destined by fortune" '. This can be seen at its worst, says Bennett, in the authorial intrusion at ll. 85-91:

> Yit nevertheless, quhatever men deme or say
> In scornfull langage of thy brukkilnes,
> I sall excuse, als far furth as I may,
> Thy womanheid, thy wisedome and fairnes—
> The quhilk Fortoun hes put in sic distres
> As hir pleisit, and nathing throw the gilt
> Of the, throw wickit langage to be spilt.
> (85-91)

> The best one can make of this is: 'Men may say you were morally frail. But I would exempt you from blame, thinking it hard on your womanhood, wisdom and beauty that Fortune should allow wicked tale-tellers to make your name a by-word.' But if the stanza is muddled to the point of imbecility (as Mr. Fox agrees) it is not because the poet is presenting an imbecile narrator, but because he had misread his Chaucer, and misapplied the line in which Chaucer's narrator comments on the same situation (*Troilus,* V, 1048-98). When Chaucer's Criseyde, foreseeing that her name will be rolled on many a tongue, cries 'Allas, that swich a cas me sholde falle' (1064), she acknowledges blame: she has 'falsed' Troilus (1058); and when she says 'gilteless, I woot wel, I yow leve' (1084), she is absolving Troilus from guilt, not, as Henryson may have thought, denying her own.

If Henryson is guilty here of 'imbecility', Chaucer is no less culpable. The description of Cresseid as 'fortunait' (***Testament,*** l. 79) derives directly from *Troilus.* Denton Fox plausibly detects in this word an ironical reference to Pandarus' enquiry at *Troilus* ii. 280, but the case does not rely on that line alone; it is anticipated by the association of Criseyde's character with the fickleness of fortune at *Troilus,* iv. 8-11 and supported by their virtual identification at *Troilus,* v. 1085. Cresseid, in both Chaucer and Henryson, is not just the victim of Fortune; she is like her.

Bennett sees the cause of what he takes to be the muddle in ll. 85-91 as Henryson's failure to understand Chaucer, and he disagrees with Denton Fox for having said that Henryson is 'using the same method as Chaucer for simultaneously revealing the sin and making the sinner sympathetic . . . '. Criseyde repented, but 'this is not to *excuse* her . . . nor does Chaucer's narrator even blame Cresseid's troubles on a personified fortune, as Henryson's does because she had the hard luck to become a harlot . . . '.

These objections, in one respect, are just. It is not enough to say that Chaucer reveals Criseyde's sin while making her seem sympathetic. In relating Criseyde's deeds by means of a partial narrator Chaucer makes us wary of taking a simple view of them or her. Criseyde was wrong, but lovable; her narrator presents a fond view of her, but his very fondness arouses the suspicions it is superficially intended to allay. *Troilus and Criseyde* is not primarily concerned with the recognition of sin and the effect of compassion; nor is the most taxing question it poses whether we 'excuse' Criseyde but rather whether we understand her. Refashioning the traditional view of Criseyde's infidelity, Chaucer, through the coloured perceptions of his biased narrator, invites us to question how far and how morally we perceive her at all. It is this that Henryson adapts from him. Inherited disapprobation and intense tenderness mingle in ll. 85-91, not because Henryson has misread Chaucer but because he has grasped the function of Chaucer's narrator and applied it to his own. The ***Testament*** opens on a Chaucerian note of febrile sympathy for Cresseid which deliberately leaves us unsure of how to judge her; and in exploiting the ambiguity of Chaucer's picture, in relating her new errors with the old partiality, Henryson recalls a view of Cresseid which he is about to transcend.

On leaving the Greek army and making her way to her father's home Cresseid is 'destitute' (92) but not resourceless. She returns to a comforting welcome from Calchas, and her speech when she retires to the 'orature' (126-40), filled with reproach against the gods of love, does not suggest a superior insight won in her adversities. She is the same self-preoccupied Cresseid; her sufferings are injuries endured at the hands of Venus and Cupid. Bennett has grounds for being scornful of the attribution of wisdom to her at l. 88; the most Cresseid can manage is a low practicality in contriving her secret exit (94-5). And yet of the three attributes listed in l. 88—

> Thy womanheid, *thy wisdome* and fairnes [my italics]

it is only the second and, at this stage of the poem, the least probable which comes to matter at the end.

Two parallel laments by Cresseid dominate the later part of the ***Testament.*** Between them comes the scene in which Troylus, failing to recognize Cresseid, gives her alms. In the first of these laments (407 ff.), self-pity, regret for lost elegance and erstwhile honour, and despair prevail; what is wholly lacking is remorse. Cresseid inveighs against her fortune:

> Fell is thy fortoun, wickit is thy weird
> (412, cf. 454)

She contrasts her past happiness with her present misery, enjoining the 'ladyis fair of Troy and Grece' (452) to learn from what has happened to her; but, at the very moment when she sets herself up as a general example, she is anxious to emphasize her uniqueness:

> My miserie, *quhilk nane may comprehend* . . .
> My greit mischief, *quhilk na man can amend*
> (453, 455, my italics)

In exhorting others to 'exempill mak of me in your memour' (465), Cresseid still asserts a kind of primacy, a primacy of suffering. *She* has been through irreparable hardship; *she* is the victim of a wrong passing others' understanding. At the beginning of the lament Cresseid's subject is her own plight; her conclusion almost asks whether others can profit from so special an example. When Cresseid urges her imagined audience: 'in your mynd *ane mirrour* mak of me' (457), the image is deliberately and delicately chosen. The Cresseid whose first action on waking in the 'orature' was to reach for a mirror becomes a mirror to others in her affliction. Vanity is present in both scenes: the rejected beauty complaining about her fate and railing against the gods has become the ruined beauty inveighing against Fortune. Despite an attempt to lend her sufferings exemplary force, the real subject of Cresseid's speech after her leprosy, as before it, remains herself. Henryson selects his mirrors thoughtfully.

Cresseid's second lament occurs after she has joined the lepers begging in the streets and Troylus has given her his purse. For Bennett 'the drift of that lament is obscure, and it remains an unsuccessful attempt to incorporate a favourite *moralitas* device within the framework of a story that speaks for itself'. . . . Cresseid accuses herself, but exaggerates both her depravity and Troylus' worth; her suggestion that other women are like her is sour, cynical, and discordant with her claim that she alone is to blame; and 'the high-flown rhetoric, now jostling with uncertain syntax, leaves us uncertain'. . . . Let us examine these criticisms.

Cresseid's words at ll. 542 ff. centre upon the repeated contrast:

> . . . fals Cresseid and trew knicht Troylus!
> (546, 553, 560)

As Bennett says, they magnify her depravity and overstate Troylus' virtue. But they are not intended to represent a balanced view of what has happened. So far has Cresseid departed from what she once was that Troylus no longer sees who she is, and his failure to recognize her as she has become brings home to Cresseid her own failure to recognize him as he was. The rhetoric of Cresseid's second lament is the violent rhetoric of self-recrimination.

Cresseid forgets her rejection by Diomeid, her resentment against the gods and Fortune, her own terrible sufferings. Most significantly, she even forgets her flattering image of herself. When Cresseid ventures to counsel others, she now does so not because her case is special and they may profit by it, as she had done in her earlier lament, but because she has become acutely aware of the faults in herself about which she gives general warning:

> Becaus I knaw the greit vnstabilnes,
> Brukkill as glas, into my self, I say—
> Traisting in vther als greit vnfaithfulnes,
> Als vnconstant, and als vntrew of fay—
> Thocht sum be trew, I wait richt few ar thay;
> Quha findis treuth, lat him his lady ruse;
> Nane but my self as now I will accuse.
> (568-74)

Cresseid understands the deepest source of her suffering to be neither her leprosy nor the enmity of Fortune but her own infidelity to and loss of Troylus. Accusing herself, she thinks not of her own lot but of their love. This is not 'a belated approach to self-knowledge', but 'wisdome' gained at a high price. Cresseid, on recognizing her true tragedy, first understands Troylus and herself.

Cresseid goes on to make her will. 'That this brief testament should have given the work its title is inexplicable, and unfortunate'. . . . But the testament is an integral part of Cresseid's reconsideration of her fate:

> Heir I beteiche my corps and carioun
> With wormis and with taidis to be rent;
> (577-8)

Cresseid's physical beauty, source of pride before and of bitter regret after her leprosy, is forgotten. Reduced in her own eyes to 'corps and carioun', it is consigned with weary disgust to the grave.

> My cop and clapper, and myne ornament,
> And all my gold the lipper folk sall haue,
> Quhen I am deid, to burie me in graue.
> (579-81)

Gold, symbol of the elegance and luxury Cresseid so much regretted on seeing her leprosy and realizing its consequences, together with the emblems of her affliction, she relinquishes to 'the lipper folk' who have become her own. To observe that 'they would share in them in any event' . . . is hardly to appreciate the point of Cresseid's bequest; it is not a gratuitous gesture of public munificence but an act symbolic of Cresseid's abandonment of her past and her present states.

> This royall ring, set with this rubie reid,
> Quhilk Troylus in drowrie to me send,

To him agane I leif it quhen I am deid,
To mak my cairfull deid wnto him kend.
(582-5)

'It should count more in her favour that she still has a "royall ring" sent by Troilus' (ibid.). Is Cresseid to be awarded points for having kept Troilus' ruby? Or is it rather that she thinks of him at the last and sends him the only token which remains to her of their love and her remorse?

Thus I conclude schortlie and mak ane end:
My spreit I leif to Diane, quhair scho dwellis,
To walk with hir in waist woddis and wellis.
(586-8)

Whether the leaving of her soul to Diana in this manner is a 'token of penitence for unchastity' . . . , Cresseid wishfully selects the goddess of whom she knows least. The devotee of Venus and Cupid longs at the last for the other world of experience which Diana represents.

O Diomeid, thou hes baith broche and belt
Quhilk Troylus gaue me in takning
Of his trew lufe', and with that word scho swelt.
(589-91)

The painful memory of Troylus' love-tokens in Diomeid's possession causes fresh pain, and with it she dies. At Cresseid's death there is regret, anguish, and self-knowledge, but no peace.

The epitaph which Troylus places on her grave:

Lo, fair ladyis, Cresseid of Troy [the] toun,
Sumtyme countit the flour of womanheid,
Vnder this stane, lait lipper, lyis deid.
(607-9)

is, according to Bennett, 'the final irony', for 'she had prayed that oblivion might cover her' . . . . Worse still, 'Henryson cannot forgo his *moralitas,* heavy with laboured polysyllables and padded lines' . . . :

Now, worthie wemen, in this ballet schort,
Maid for your worschip and instructioun,
Of cheritie, I monische and exhort,
Ming not your lufe with fals deceptioun:
Beir in your mynd this sor[e] conclusioun
Of fair Cresseid, as I haue said befoir.
Sen scho is deid I speik of hir no moir.
FINIS
(610-16)

But the epitaph and the *moralitas* should be considered in relation to one another; it is of some consequence for our understanding of the end of the ***Testament of Cresseid*** that the epitaph is attributed to Troylus and that the *moralitas* is assigned to the narrator.

Cresseid's wish that, after becoming a leper, she might be consigned to oblivion (414-15) had expressed shame and a despairing belief that there was nothing left for her in a life without her good looks and good fortune. Later in the poem Cresseid develops far beyond this, and it is all she comes to understand about herself that Troylus' epitaph omits. Troylus' epitaph tersely recounts the outward facts of her case. It speaks of Cresseid's high reputation and miserable end but says nothing of her infidelity. That is left to the all too explicit narrator and his laboured *moralitas* whose final line pointedly echoes Troylus' words: 'I can no moir' (601). As E. D. Aswell says: 'Cresseid has been dead throughout the poem, and this fact alone is obviously no sufficient reason for ceasing to speak of her now' ['The Role of Fortune in the *Testament of Cresseid',* Philological Quarterly, xlvi (1967)]. The *moralitas,* with its brash simplifications and bald censure of 'fals deceptioun' (613) spells out all that Troylus would not say; to the last, he remains faithful to Cresseid. By placing these final lines in the mouth of his ponderous narrator, seated in front of the fire with glass in hand (36-42), Henryson gracefully implies that the finer part of fidelity is tact.

'We may properly use Chaucer to elucidate Henryson's attitudes, beliefs and idioms. We may profitably compare the two poems. But to treat scenes in Henryson as ironic variations on scenes in Chaucer is to praise the right things for the wrong reasons.' Bennett's formulation could hardly be bettered, and yet it is perhaps not wholly unfair to his essay to suggest that it comes close to reproaching Henryson not only for misunderstanding Chaucer but also for not being him. Considered in context within the poem, every one of the features Bennett distinguishes as a flaw in the ***Testament of Cresseid*** can be seen to have its proper function. It is a quality of good criticism to provoke reconsideration, and this Bennett's essay will have achieved if we can now speak, without inhibition, of Henryson's masterpiece. (pp. 291-300)

Peter Godman, "Henryson's Masterpiece," in The Review of English Studies, *Vol. XXXV, No. 139, August, 1984, pp. 291-300.*

C. David Benson (essay date 1984)

[In the following excerpt, Benson provides a detailed study of The Morall Fabillis, *assessing the influence of Henryson's moral seriousness in several fables.]*

Both the time and place of Robert Henryson's birth were unfortunate for his modern critical reputation. As a Scotsman, he is still sometimes seen as a provincial author whose subjects are *wee beasties* and local social conditions, instead of being recognized as probably the last great medieval poet of Europe. As a fifteenth-century author, he is automatically labeled a "Chaucerian," with the result that he is usually compared exclusively with this single predecessor and only rarely with the other Ricardian poets: John Gower, the *Gawain*-poet, and William Langland. Henryson does owe much to Chaucer, but his verse is not saturated with the older poet's tag phrases as is the work of many English Chaucerians like John Lydgate; the influence is instead deeper and more subtle. Henryson's handling of dialogue, characterization, and word choice, in addition to the complex narrators of the ***Testament of Cresseid*** and some of the ***Fables,*** are certainly indebted to Chaucer, as are his playful stance toward his material and his sense of what need *not* be said. But despite these similarities, Henryson also reveals an equally deep poetic kinship with the other great fourteenth-century English poets.

To call Henryson the last of the Ricardian poets is, of

course, only a metaphor and not a historical fact, but it is astonishing how much his work resembles those characteristics of the Ricardians defined by John Burrow [in his *Ricardian Poetry,* 1971]. Space does not permit a detailed analysis of each, but some of the qualities central to both Henryson and the Ricardians are a "pervasively ironic mode of address," an "authentic story-telling style," use of old stories (all three of Henryson's major works are traditional stories), "a strongly literary sense of form and structure in their handling of text-divisions," effective use of detail, an "elusive way of working within the exemplary mode" (which will be the principal subject herein), an "unheroic image of man," "a sense of humour" (as opposed to wit), and the use of " 'proverbial' similes." Henryson is also like the Ricardians in more specific ways. When he declares that Aesopian ***Fables*** were intended to appeal to both high and low estate, he recalls Gower's claim in *Confessio Amantis* to "go the middel weie," writing "somewhat of lust, somewhat of lore." Similarly, he is like the *Gawain*-poet in his combination of alliteration and rhyme and in his precise, concrete descriptions, especially of nature.

The Ricardian poet that Henryson resembles most closely, however, is William Langland. Their most obvious similarities are the ability to mix strong allegory with detailed, energetic narrative and a real feeling for ordinary life expressed in their compassion for the poor and their indignation at social corruption. The more profound similarities between the two poets, principally their ability to explore serious moral questions in poetry of the highest quality, will be noted throughout these pages.

That Henryson, like Langland, is explicitly and essentially a didactic and moral poet, and not a court, love, or occasional poet, has long been recognized; but the skill and originality of his achievement have not always been sufficiently appreciated. The most obvious manifestation of his desire to instruct and improve is also his longest work: the ***Morall Fabillis of Esope the Phrygian,*** as the early printed editions call it. Henryson's ***Fables,*** which are generally considered the greatest medieval example of this continually popular genre, comprise a prologue and thirteen narratives (the fables proper), each of which is followed by a clearly labeled *moralitas.*

Because the appropriateness of the individual *moralitas* to the events of its narrative is not always clear, the division of each fable has caused problems for commentators. As Richard J. Schrader states [in "Some Backgrounds of Henryson," *Studies in Scottish Literature* 15 (1980)], "No critical problem in Henryson is more important than the relationship of his tales to their *moralitates.*" Three solutions to this problem have been proposed, each of which has the unfortunate effect of simplifying the moral thought of the ***Fables.*** The older view, which is not entirely extinguished today, regards the *moralitates* as conventional, tedious, and irrelevant to Henryson's poetic genius, whose virtues are humor, narrative skill, and human sympathy. This very limited conception of Henryson, which is something like seeing Langland as primarily a poet of medieval English rural life, results in an almost total disregard for the second part of each fable. More recently, other critics

Manuscript version of "The Taill of the Cok and the Jasp." Taken from the Harleian MS. No. 3865.

have gone almost to the opposite extreme in insisting upon the absolute thematic unity between *moralitas* and narrative, despite superficial dissonance. These critics sometimes become overly ingenious in their attempts to harmonize both parts of each fable and run the risk of presenting Henryson as no more than a mechanical versifier, however skillful, of medieval orthodoxies. Nevertheless, they are right to stress both the poet's moral seriousness and the need to include the *moralitates* in any full interpretation of the ***Fables.*** A third group of resolutely modern critics, reacting against the view of Henryson as either kindly or traditional, claims that the gap between story and morality indicates a deep pessimism in Henryson that questions the very order of the universe. This argument, while of real interest, is almost impossible historically and is finally as reductive as the other two. In seeing only a modern despair in the ***Fables,*** these critics rob Henryson of his own serious, complex, and thoroughly medieval moral vision.

All three groups of critics recognize at least some discord, however superficial, between Henryson's narratives and *moralitates,* but none has adequately explained the purpose of these differences. James Kinsley, for example, declares that the "moral applications" are "often too ingenious for modern taste" ["The Medieval Makars" in *Scottish Poetry: A Critical Survey,* 1955]. The ingenuity is there, but it is a reason for congratulation, not complaint. I suggest that what readers like Kinsley take to be a blemish in Henryson's art is the key to the correct understanding of the ***Fables.*** The frequent gaps between story and moral are deliberate and serve to make the reader aware of other tensions and conflicts in the work. Although Henryson is a Christian philosophical poet, he does not offer simple, reductive lessons, as has sometimes been assumed. The *moralitates* alert us to the moral seriousness of the ***Fables,*** but they do not themselves entirely contain it, for Henryson is no dispensor of easy platitudes. Like the Ricardian poets he offers no pat answers, and so his lessons are more difficult and more exhilarating than they seem at first. By exploiting the dissonance between story and moral to lead the reader into the deeper complexities of his work, he teaches us not what to think, but how to think. The result is a justification of the art of the fable and a demonstration that it can be a more entertaining, more demanding, and ultimately more successful teacher than conventional, straightforward moral instruction.

In his prologue to the ***Fables,*** Henryson makes clear that his moral art is not simple. Two images insist that while his *sentences* are delightful, they are only to be discovered with difficulty.

> In lyke manner as throw a bustious eird,
> Swa it be laubourit with grit diligence,
> Springis the flouris and the corne abreird,
> Hailsum and gude to mannis sustenence;
> Sa springis thair ane morall sweit sentence
> Oute of the subtell dyte of poetry,
> To gude purpose, quha culd it weill apply.
>
> The nuttis schell, thocht it be hard and teuch,
> Haldis the kirnell, sueit and delectabill;
> Sa lyis thair ane doctrine wyse aneuch
> And full of frute, vnder ane fenyeit fabill.
> (lines 8-18)

The image of cultivation, developed from a simpler simile in Gualterus Anglicus, emphasizes the great effort needed to bring forth the desired moral product. This effort is one that, as Denton Fox suggests [in his *The Poems of Robert Henryson,* 1981], is probably demanded of the reader: it is he who must struggle with poetry whose complexity is insisted upon ("subtell dyte") in order to make it yield the flower and corn of "ane morall sweit sentence." And that is not the end of his contribution; Henryson declares that the *sentence* will have a good effect only as long as the reader fully participates in the application: "quha culd it weill apply." The second, even more traditional image, that of the nut, emphasizes the pleasant reward for such moral effort. Again Henryson insists on the difficulty of his hard, tough poetry (line 15), but, in contrast to those who find him pessimistic, the poet also promises that the result of his moral poetry will be "delectabill," just as in the previous image it was associated with life and rebirth. Henryson's is not a harsh, dry teaching but one that is "hailsum and gude to mannis sustenence."

After instructing us in the difficulty of reading the ***Fables,*** Henryson significantly begins the collection with his most flagrant and most frequently commented on example of disunity between narrative and morality, **"The Cock and the Jasp."** It becomes the model by which we are taught to read all the fables that follow. In the story, the cock finds a jasper swept into the dirt by careless girls but rejects it as too precious for him and useless in his pursuit of food. His conclusion would seem reasonable enough, but the *moralitas* condemns him for choosing material pleasure over wisdom. Those who say that such a conclusion goes against the tone of the narrative are certainly correct in one sense, but they ignore Henryson's purpose in creating such a conflict.

The tension between the two parts of this fable is itself the most important lesson and shows us by example the difficulty of accomplishing genuine moral instruction. In the *moralitas* to **"The Cock and the Jasp,"** Henryson builds on the apology for fables found in his sources and confronts the wider questions of discovering, recognizing, and using wisdom. "Perfite prudence and cunning" (line 128), symbolized by the jasper, is easy to overlook, as the "damisellis wantoun and insolent" (line 71) do when they sweep it out of the house, but it is also possible to ignore even when seen directly, as by the cock or by an inattentive audience. The first fable demonstrates that real moral teaching is not as simple as it sometimes seems. It is one thing for a preacher or poet to provide a moral lesson, another to have it understood and accepted. Yet unless that is done, all instruction, however true and useful, is merely dust to lazy housekeepers, jasps to cocks, or pearls to swine (line 147). The gap between tale and lesson in the first fable initiates the reader into the difficulty of achieving true wisdom, which is always "tynt and hid" (line 155). To be truly possessed, wisdom must not be merely passively accepted but actively and continually striven for (line 153), as rarely happens: "We seik it nocht, nor preis it for to find" (line 156). The active verbs suggest the same effort and personal involvement demanded in the prologue: a labor of discrimination and judgment that Henryson's indirect method of teaching both advocates and trains.

Another and even more revealing way in which Henryson indicates that the reader needs to go beyond automatic acceptance of the *moralitas* to discover the full wisdom of the ***Fables*** is his practice of including moral instruction within the narratives themselves. This additional level of *sententia* once again stresses the complexity of moral choice and warns us against conclusions that are too facile. Some of these passages, like the warning in **"The Two Mice"** that "efter ioy oftymes cummis cair,/ And troubill efter grit prosperitie" (lines 290-91), serve primarily to emphasize or deepen the concluding *moralitas.* Others, however, are in conflict with the end, such as the quite impassioned stanza in **"The Trial of the Fox"** on the foolishness of risking one's soul for wealth that will be enjoyed by an ungrateful heir (lines 831-37), a lesson that is more worldly than the one in the *moralitas* on the temptations that beset men of religion. Although many such moral passages within the narrative are brief, **"The Preaching of the Swallow"** begins with an elaborate discussion of God's wisdom and the order of the seasons (lines 1622-1712) that is more powerful in itself, and seems to have a more profound relation to the fable, than the concluding *moralitas.*

The most important example of a fable with moral comment within the narrative is **"The Cock and the Fox."** This wonderful tale, which plays with, responds to, and is almost the equal of Chaucer's *Nun's Priest's Tale* (while remaining quite independent), illustrates much about the complexity and wit of Henryson's moral teaching. His most important addition, the speeches of Chantecleir's three wives after they believe he has been killed by the fox (which are for Henryson what the long speeches on dreams are for Chaucer), is not reflected in the *moralitas* at all. These speeches have almost no narrative function (the death they are discussing has not really happened, and all takes place during the stasis of the widow's "swoun"), but they are one of Henryson's most brilliant demonstrations of the difficulties of moral judgment.

The first speech is by Pertok, whose words are undercut before they even begin with an inappropriately human detail that is perhaps better than any in the *Nun's Priest's Tale:* we are told that as she makes her mourning "teiris grit attour hir cheikis fell" (line 496). Her words, highly rhetorical and including "a parody of the formal lament for the dead" [see the note to lines 495-508 in Denton Fox's *The Poems of Robert Henryson,* 1981], regret the loss of one who was for his wives a reliable time piece, an entertainer, a breaker of bread, and as good a lover as nature allowed (lines 495-508). All this is conventional enough, but now Chantecleir's second wife, Sprutok, has her say, in words that are more colloquial in style and very different in content. She dismisses Pertok's sentiments and asserts that she intends to be a gay widow since their husband was not only harsh but a poor lover: "Let quik to quik, and deid ga to the deid" (line 522). That Pertok and Sprutok respond so differently to the same situation already suggests the difficulty any commentator has in interpreting events.

The problem is then further complicated when Pertok responds with a second speech that totally contradicts her first. She now declares that a score of such as Chantecleir could not entirely satisfy his wives (this is especially funny when we remember how cocksure is Chaucer's bird), and she vows to find them a lover within a week who "suld better claw oure breik" (line 529). Now that Henryson has made us begin to doubt the whole procedure of drawing reliable conclusions from events, the third henwife, Coppok (or Toppok), utters "lyke ane curate" (line 530) a sermon which in its simple-minded self-righteousness and haste to draw moral lessons is almost a parody of a conventional *moralitas.* She asserts that Chantecleir was punished by God because he would not repent of his lecherous adultery. In this last speech especially, Henryson the moralist, like Chaucer in his parallel beast fable, suggests the dangers of automatically accepting easy moral certainties. Coppok is a chicken who condemns a sin (adultery) in which she also participates and who sees "the verray hand off God" (line 542) in a death which has not, in fact, even happened. Henryson even goes so far as to make Coppok's moral conclusions ("Prydefull he was, and ioyit off his sin" [line 537]) somewhat resemble his own *moralitas* ("Fy, puft vp pryde, thow is full poysonabill" [line 593]). Likewise, the conclusion to this same *moralitas* ("Thir twa sinnis, flatterie and vaneglore,/ Ar vennomous" [line 612-13]) must raise a smile in the reader who remembers that what is venomous in the *Nun's Priest's Tale* is far less serious, if more unpleasant—laxatives.

Henryson's playing with moral instruction here does not mean that he is cynical or a bitter pessimist, only that he wishes to illustrate the difficulty of attaining true wisdom. Lessons are easy enough to come by (even hens provide them!), but the problem as shown in these four speeches is deciding which lessons apply to which situations ("quha cleirlie vnderstude" [line 610]). The reader must finally teach himself.

The moral complexity of these tales is equalled by the artistic complexity of the *moralitates,* which are variously long, short, satirical, angry, or pleading. Much less detailed critical comment has been expended on this part of each fable than on the narratives (and almost none on their artistry), yet they are not merely mechanical, reductive lessons. They often contain as much wit and art as the fables proper and are as "sueit" and "delectabill" as the prologue promises. For example, in the *moralitas* to the first fable, Henryson compares the cock to one who feeds precious stones to swine (lines 141-47). This is clever use of the human/animal confusion, which is one of the hallmarks of the genre (a rooster feeding pigs?), with a profoundly serious biblical echo (Matthew 7:6). The *moralitas* to the second fable contains an illustration of Henryson's talent for establishing an intimate narrative relationship with the reader: "Thy awin fyre, freind, thocht it be bot ane gleid, / It warmis weill, and is worth gold to the" (lines 389-90). More dramatic, but equally effective appeals to the reader can be found in the description of death and damnation at lines 1930-36 and in the touching prayer to Mary that concludes the abstract allegory of **"The Trial of the Fox"** (lines 1139-45). Henryson frequently demonstrates that he has lavished as much poetic skill on his moralities as on his stories. The *moralitas* to **"The Preaching of the Swallow,"** for example, cleverly develops the image of a seed from the story (lines 1902-08). Likewise, the *moralitas* to **"The Fox, the Wolf, and the Husbandman"** contains two fine allegorical passages: the woods, which play almost no part in the narrative, are carefully presented as a symbol of the dangers of riches (lines 2441-47), and the wolf 's desire for the cheese is described as covetousness, which tempts man into a well of vices leading straight to hell (lines 2448-54). The latter passage is not only a witty expansion of the incident in the fable but is even more dramatically narrated: "Dryuand ilk man to leip in the buttrie/ That dounwart drawis vnto the pane of hell" (lines 2452-53).

Some of the often neglected *moralitates* contain even better and more powerful poetry than their narratives. For example, the moralities to **"The Sheep and the Dog"** and **"The Wolf and the Lamb,"** both of which are quite lengthy and whose numerical sequence (fables VI and XII) may be significant, are passionate denunciations of injustice that reveal an unsentimental but deeply sympathetic compassion for the poor that is reminiscent of Langland. The *moralitas* to the first of this pair contains such sophisticated literary devices as the active involvement of the narrator (lines 1276-85) and speeches and actions that are presented dramatically and without allegorization (for example, lines 1286-92). The sheep's lament to God, which begins, "O lord, quhy sleipis thow sa lang?" (line 1295), is justly famous and makes the reader feel close to the sufferer for the first time in the entire fable. The second *moralitas* (fable XII) contains several direct addresses to the various oppressors of the poor and much precise, emotionally charged poetry whose specific details do not obscure the general application (see for example, lines 2749-55).

Henryson presents his moral teaching with such indirection, complexity, and art because, like the other great Ricardian poets, he knows that it is one thing to state a truth, another to have it accepted, understood, and acted upon. Standard moral lessons, while not wrong, may be too facile or limited to offer real guidance. Such mechanical lessons are like the often contradictory proverbs that Henryson scatters so freely throughout the ***Fables***: they are of limited use because they demand that the reader exercise his own judgment in choosing and applying the correct lesson to a specific situation. To be truly understood a moral question must be explored and experienced, and poetry offers a way of doing that by engaging fully our minds and emotions. The country mouse in **"The Two Mice"** is aware from the first of the tale's *moralitas*—"Ane modicum is mair for till allow,/ Swa that gude will be keruer at the dais,/Than thrawin vult and mony spycit mais" (lines 236-38)—yet at this point she is unable to convince her city sister or even herself to follow this truth. Although her terrifying experiences as a bourgeois beast only bring the mouse to her original conclusion (lines 343-52, which is further developed in the *moralitas*), having actually gone through these events so skillfully told by Henryson, she now understands the same lesson in a more profound way—and so do we as readers. Henryson, like the other Ricardians, knows that real moral knowledge comes only after effort, struggle, and questioning, and this knowledge is finally his justification for the ***Fables.*** They are not merely a pleasant diversion, but, as his images of cultivation and the tough nut in the prologue indicate, something both more organic and more difficult. The poet uses the pleasures of poetry to lead the reader into the complex moral questioning and affirmation that is possible only in the greatest art. As Henryson declares in the prologue, the "subtell dyte" of his poetry leads the reader to a "morall sweit sentence."

How hard it is to make moral teaching truly effective is demonstrated in the fable that is generally recognized as one of Henryson's best and that is often discussed as the key to his collection: **"The Preaching of the Swallow."** The fable opens with a discussion of the "hie prudence" and "profound wit" (lines 1622-23) of God in contrast to the ignorance of man, which suggests the folly of any attempts to rely on our own knowledge. This realization is closely related to what seems to me the most important theme in the tale, although it has largely gone unnoticed: the demonstration of the ineffectuality of standard orthodox moral preaching, even when its message is absolutely correct and of vital importance to its audience. The swallow, who thrice warns the other birds of mortal danger from the fowler, is identified in the *moralitas* as a "halie preichour" (line 1924), and yet Henryson has constructed his tale so that we are forced to question, if not the truth of the swallow's words, at least the manner of their presentation. Unquestionably the birds are foolish to disregard his dire warnings, as events make clear, but some of the responsibility for the deadly outcome rests with the swallow's method of teaching. The swallow's first warning that a farmer is sowing flax seeds which will ultimately become the material for nets (lines 1736-61) may appear unduly alarmist even to the reader because the danger is so remote and the warning is actually sounded (lines 1736-40) before the problem itself (the flax sowing) is even identified (lines 1743-47). The lark's objection that the swallow is only imagining the worst has some truth, even though the proverbs he uses to prove this indicate his own blindness (lines 1762-67). The swallow's second warning is a further example of ineffective preaching (lines 1789-1800). Once more we may assume that his words are literally delivered from on high (see line 1735). Because they are so pompous and insulting ("O blind birds, and full of negligence" [line 1790]), they again fail to reach their audience, even though a truth that is not heard is useless. The birds' concern for their stomachs (lines 1804-06) is certainly unwise, but the preacher himself is not without blame.

The swallow's third warning, which begs the birds not to go into the trap, is the crucial one (lines 1853-59). If they heed him now, they will be safe, but he is no more successful than before. In their hunger, the birds prefer the literal chaff of the fowler to the symbolic fruit of the swallow's preaching. In fact, they totally ignore him (line 1869) and do not even answer as they go to their pitiful deaths, which the narrator describes with great emotion (lines 1874-80). The swallow is left in sorrowful and solitary self-righteousness, uttering a sigh that is like Troilus's at the end of the ***Testament of Cresseid***: "Now ar thay deid, and wo is me thairfoir!" (line 1886). The swallow may blame the birds for ignoring his advice (lines 1882-84), but Henryson has shown that moral teaching, however sound, must reach and involve the audience to be of any use. He elsewhere suggests that his ***Fables,*** which do just that, may, unlike conventional preaching, save us from Satan the Fowler, whose attack is so vividly described in the *moralitas* (lines 1930-36).

Henryson has already alerted us to his justification for fables at the beginning of his previous tale, **"The Lion and the Mouse."** There the poet dreams he meets Aesop, whom he asks for "ane prettie fabill/Concludand with ane gude moralitie" (lines 1386-87). The *auctorite* at first refuses to tell such a tale because of the sinfulness of men who lack devotion to God, "The eir is deif, the hart is hard as stane" (line 1393). He then asks in despair, "For quhat is it worth to tell ane fenyeit taill,/Quhen haly preiching may na thing auaill?" (lines 1389-90). The answer that Henryson suggests with characteristic indirection is that feigned fables are useful precisely because the deaf ears and hard hearts of men often make direct preaching ineffective. The **"Preaching of the Swallow"** demonstrates that such explicit admonition, even when warning of genuine disaster, is often ignored. The solution, however, is not the despair to which Aesop momentarily gives in. Even though preaching, however holy, "may na thing auaill," a fable may avail, as Henryson the dreamer politely and delicately suggests, "Quha wait nor I may leir and beir away/Sum thing thairby heirefter may auaill?" (lines 1402-03). Although Henryson is a poet of moral truth, he also knows, as the fable of the **"Cock and the Fox"** demonstrates, that lies inspired by a "gude spirit" (line 558), just like feigned fables, may be the most efficacious words of all. If Henryson admires as well as disapproves of the clever fox, as Douglas Gray claims [in his *Robert Henryson,* 1979], perhaps it is because deceptive language and tricks played on an audience are not all that far from his own method. Henryson is a poet who teaches us to value what is direct and true through poetry that is frequently neither.

Once we recognize the intricacy of Henryson's moral thought and understand that it goes beyond the apparent lessons of the *moralitates,* it is possible to identify some of the deeper themes of the ***Fables,*** which are presented with his usual indirection. Like Langland, Henryson finds this a harsh world and continually emphasizes the limitations of man's power and his absolute need for God's mercy. The surprising good news of the work, however, is that the almost overwhelming pain of earthly existence is more than compensated for by the love of God.

No one who reads the ***Fables*** carefully can doubt that its world is terribly hard, with little peace, comfort, or companionship—the very opposite of many modern animal stories like *The Wind in the Willows:* "The transience of life and the sudden, unexpected coming of death is strongly felt" [Gray]. Hunger is frequent in the ***Fables,*** as are sudden disasters and traps; mere survival is difficult, and images of the ups and downs of Fortune are common (for example, lines 303-33, 2418-19, 2891-92, 2939-40). If the creation is cruel in the ***Fables,*** its creatures are crueler still. The animals, who are the principal cause of their own misery and destruction because of "lust and appetyte" (line 53), present a frightening picture of sin and its consequence. With one notable exception, desire, will, and selfishness rule characters who are devoid of love or kindness and are frequently described as outlaws, thieves, and lovers of darkness (for example, lines 168, 203, 253-54, 618-20, 959, 2294). Most of the animals seem locked into mechanical enmities and often act out the most primitive and brutal impulses, such as the bizarre, heartless treatment given his father's corpse by the aptly named "Father-war" in **"The Trial of the Fox"** (lines 796-830).

The ***Fables*** are a powerful demonstration of the vanity of human pretensions, revealing again and again in the animal figures the limitations of human power and self-sufficiency. Perhaps the most terrifying example of this is the wether in **"The Wolf and the Wether,"** who protects his flock disguised as a dog and even manages to make a hungry wolf run for his life. His success in only illusory, however, and once his false skin is stripped away his only defense against the indignant wolf is the lame one that he was not in earnest but only playing (lines 2558-59, 2578). For Henryson all practical effort by humans, every attempt to be self-reliant, is finally a joke and nothing but play. Nevertheless, the reward we can expect is deadly earnest indeed, as the fate of the wether proves: "Than be the crag-bane smertlie he [the wolf] him tuke,/Or euer he ceissit, and it in schunder schuke" (lines 2586-87). Men as purely natural beings, as animals, are isolated, unloved, and doomed—neither innocence, as several sheep discover, nor even cleverness, as father and son foxes learn in fables IV and V, can guarantee safety.

Like Langland throughout *Piers Plowman,* Henryson in his narratives and *moralitates* presents rational and practical solutions to the human condition only to show their inadequacy in such a world as this. The apparently sensible *moralitas* of **"The Two Mice,"** for instance, that small possessions bring "sickernes" and "blyithnes" (lines 373-96), is too smug and worldly a final answer. As the narrative and the first stanza of the *moralitas* itself indicate, the deeper answer is the impossibility of real comfort or safety anywhere on this earth (lines 365-72). Although the country mouse may be wise to reject the city mouse's life, we should not overlook the real misery of her own situation (lines 169-70). The same fable continually exposes pretensions that are more human than mouselike. The urban sister is described as a solid bourgeois citizen with rights and privileges (lines 171-75), but, of course, she is really no more than a thief. Similarly, we almost believe in her great feast so lavishly described until the entrances of first the spenser and then the cat reveal how little and vulnerable the mice are. Later fables show even more clearly the inadequacy of the Horatian modesty of life advocated in **"The Two Mice."** The sheep in **"The Sheep and the Dog"** apparently lives humbly, but the law is so perverted—revealing the failure of another human institution—that the poor beast, far from being left with his small possessions, is forced to lose the very wool off his back. Denton Fox notes that the second half of the ***Fables*** is bleaker than the first: "all virtuous persuasions are ineffective, and all evil ones obeyed." The worldly advice of **"The Two Mice,"** which is shown to be ineffective in **"The Sheep and the Dog,"** is fatal in the next to last fable, **"The Wolf and the Lamb."** Neither the lamb's meekness and innocence, nor his appeals to logic and the law (for example, lines 2640-43), are of the slightest good against a foe determined to do evil. In this absolutely clear case of right versus wrong (lines 2624-25), wrong is triumphant to the apparent confusion of the narrator:

> Off his murther quhat sall we say, allace?
> Wes not this reuth, wes not this grit pietie,
> To gar this selie lamb but gilt thus de?
> (lines 2704-06)

Henryson's relentless presentation of the harshness of the world does not mean, as some have recently argued, that the poet is fundamentally a pessimist who sees all as meaningless. Throughout the ***Fables*** there are many indications that beyond the confusion of this world there is order in the universe. An elaborate example is the description of God's power and wisdom and the beneficent harmony of his creation in the opening lines of the **"Preaching of the Swallow"** (lines 1622-1712); a similar effect is created by the account of the heavens and the meaning they reveal in **"The Fox and the Wolf"** (lines 635-48). Furthermore, there is also some indication that those who live below, however steeped in sin, may occasionally possess the capacity to respond to the divine goodness. The one exception to the selfishness in the ***Fables*** is the mutual assistance between the lion and the mouse (and the cooperation of the mice among themselves) in fable VII, which occurs at the very center of the work, suggesting a potential for love in God's creation. Henryson is not given to modern despair; rather, he is what might be called a Northern Christian realist. Like many Anglo-Saxon poets, he recognizes that this life is indeed a brief and often painful passage. We are sinners in a fallen world and on our own are all doomed—but there is hope elsewhere.

Although Henryson's sympathy for human suffering and his anger at social abuses are genuine, he, like Langland, finds the only solution to the human condition to lie beyond this world in the love of God. Henryson is not a simple moralistic poet giving rules for practical conduct, but one whose message is about God's astonishing mercy. His final optimism is real enough, and contains the sweetness promised in the prologue, but it is rarely presented directly. Instead, it is most powerfully seen in negative examples: the misery and self-destruction of beasts (and men acting like beasts) who cut themselves off from God's grace. Henryson forces us to look heavenward because of the absolute absence of justice or security on this earth. In addition, occasionally there are clear expressions of the ultimately hopeful lesson of the ***Fables,*** such as the moving prayer to Mary at the end of fable V (lines 1139-45), which has the same message as ***The Prayer for the Pest***: although we are sinners deserving punishment, we beg for mercy. As in the ***Testament of Cresseid,*** Henryson in the ***Fables*** is neither a Scots puritan nor a modern pessimist. He sees the pain of this world but also the possibility of redemption. The need for mercy and pity is emphasized throughout the central fable, **"The Lion and the Mouse"** (for example, lines 1461, 1537, 1595, 1597). It is even possible that the mysterious lord at whose request the poet says he undertakes the ***Fables*** (line 34) is the Christian Lord, whose redemptive power is cited at the very end of the poem (lines 2973-75).

The first tale, **"The Cock and the Jasp,"** not only demonstrates Henryson's method of moral instruction, as we have already seen, but also his ultimate message. The cock is a lively bird, "cant and crous" (line 65), but his views are too practical and worldly; he is a *coq moyen sensuel* who intends to live on bread alone. He rejects the precious jewel because it is too good for him: "Thow are ane iouell for ane lord or king./It wer pietie thow suld in this mydding/Be buryit thus amang this muke and mold" (lines 81-83). In these words and others like them (see, for example, lines 106ff.), it is difficult not to see a parallel to the mystery of the Incarnation. Like the jasper of wisdom in the dungheap, God, confounding all logic and sense, lowered himself to share our humble state, and thus we are miraculously called to an inheritance equal to that of kings.

Two fables already mentioned that seem extremely pessimistic on the surface actually begin to educate the reader about the poet's message of hope. Fable VI, **"The Sheep and the Dog,"** is in the form of a negative exemplum. The sheep looks for justice (see line 1295 and the lines following), but in vain. Paradoxically, the injustice of the world demonstrates more forcefully than direct statement the need for God's salvation. Nothing else will avail. The last stanza of the *moralitas,* without providing a definite answer to the sheep's problem, suggests where that answer will have to come from: "sen that we ar apprest/In to this eirth, grant vs in heuin gude rest" (lines 1319-20).

Fable XII, **"The Wolf and the Lamb,"** is more pessimistic still, for the tale shows that truth, reason, law, and innocence are no defense against pure evil. The lamb is almost comic as he tries to save himself with formal logic (see especially the *ergo* of line 2650), but his call for strict justice ("Off his awin deidis ilk man sall beir the pais,/As pyne for sin, reward for werkis rycht" [lines 1667-68]) is mistaken and too severe for humankind. The lamb's citation of this Old Testament text simply prompts another harsh precept from the Old Law by the wolf (lines 2672-75). As Saint Paul knew, because all men are carnal they are condemned under the law (Romans 7:14). The only answer is, not strict justice, which must whip us all, but a complete and unmerited mercy. The pitiless world of the ***Fables*** demands the Atonement. Without denying the horror of its story or the seriousness of its call for social reform, I would argue that **"The Wolf and the Lamb"** also shows that the answer to the human condition is not what the lamb says, but what he represents. The lamb is a traditional symbol of Christ and the description of his death seems an undeniable reference to the Eucharist: "Syne drank his blude and off his flesche can eit" (line 2702). This identification is underlined by the oath with which the fox refuses the "reuth" that is the lamb's and our only salvation: "Be Goddis woundis" (line 2697). The hope Henryson expresses here is the familiar Christian paradox that God's mercy and grace, symbolized by the death of the lamb, can offer us the body and blood of salvation even when we act as wickedly as the wolf. Henryson's final lesson, then, is not an applicable moral but a mystery; God's complete goodness and his love of undeserving man confound logic and reason to redeem the terrible world of the ***Fables*** and its bestial creatures. In his excellent book on Henryson, Douglas Gray identifies the final attitude of the ***Fables*** as "wise, realistic, tolerant and religious at once." Without denying this description absolutely, I would suggest it continues the tradition of defining our author in terms more applicable to Chaucer. Henryson is a different kind of poet, less detached and more passionate; like Langland, he is more tortured by the evil of the world and thirstier for God's grace. (pp. 215-29)

C. David Benson, "O Moral Henryson," in Fifteenth-Century Studies: Recent Essays, *edited by Robert F. Yeager, Archon Books, 1984, pp. 215-35.*

David J. Parkinson (essay date 1991)

[In the following excerpt, Parkinson examines Cresseid's trials in the Testament, *asserting that "[the] Middle Scots poets wrote so keenly about disfigurement and exile because these experiences revealed an arbitrary foundation to wordly life."]*

Henryson's ***Testament of Cresseid*** may be "a medieval tragedy in the Senecan mode," as well as "unmistakably Chaucerian"; in its attention to debasement and expulsion, though, it is a quintessentially Scottish poem [Douglas Gray, *Robert Henryson,* 1979; A. C. Spearing, *Medieval to Renaissance in English Poetry,* 1985]. Here as often elsewhere in Middle Scots poetry, sudden, even violent change dominates: youth into age, honor into shame, spring into winter, the paradisal into the hellish. Rhetorical set pieces herald transitions in which style plummets from the most ornate to the plainest. Without warning or explanation, the protagonist is ejected into painful and disgraceful exile. Things go awry: justice is capricious, eloquence suspect, folly endemic. Given such pessimism, it is the more remarkable that Henryson's protagonist Cresseid should at last aspire towards a haunting vision, however qualified, of hope.

Modern commentators have praised both the vigor and the discipline of Middle Scots verse. There may seem to be a tension between the Scottish poet's ambition to prove mastery of the proper forms and techniques—to claim a central place in the community of polite letters—and the confidence to employ this mastery in a range of topics and genres beyond that of, say, English courtly verse of the period. Scottish poets frequently test the limits of style and genre. On occasion they seem to break rudely free from the restrictions accepted by that larger community of courtly making. It is appropriate, then, that the narrative and imagery of exile (with their noble antecedents in Old and Middle English poetry) play a crucial part in Middle Scots poetry. In its fascination with boundaries the younger tradition takes strength and claims independence.

Henryson had an abiding interest in the solitary complainer within the desolate wintry scene: his Orpheus, his tardy lover Robin, as well as the Swallow and the fleeced Sheep of his ***Fables,*** all come to play this role. Nowhere, however, is Henryson so deeply concerned with the course and consequence of punitive suffering as in the ***Testament.*** This is a poem which is almost too articulate about degrees of exclusion.

Even before narration starts, progress has been thwarted, the aged narrator's springtime world having reverted into winter. There is precedent for taking this as a portent: downturns in the weather often signal the onset of a monitory, even macabre vision. . . . Striving to be comfortable despite the cold outside, Henryson's narrator comes upon a "winter's tale" which he proceeds to relate. Despite the horrors outside the window and within the book, he does not seem much disposed toward uncomfortable thoughts about his own mortality: he is a self-indulgent old fellow who is, after all, merely reading and telling this tale to pass time. There is no indication that his wintry experiences will spur him to change his own life.

In the tale itself, the outer world does not revert suddenly from spring to winter. For much of the time, setting is focused upon interiors (the court, the secret oratory, the leper's hospice), within each of which the excluded protagonist Cresseid hides (and is either exclaimed over by the narrator or complains at length herself), and from each of which she must perforce depart. The upset of season in the narrator's preamble corresponds to the moral and then the physical overthrow of the protagonist. In this tale, the forest does not go hoary, the protagonist does.

Being spurned is the first thing to happen to Cresseid in the poem. Having finished with her, Diomede dismisses her; and "than desolait scho walkit vp and doun" (76). At once, the narrator breaks in:

> how was thow fortunait
> To change in filth all thy feminitie,
> And be with fleschelie lust sa maculait.
>
> (79-81)

He will not indulge in "scornefull" or "wickit" language, he insists (86, 91)—having already glanced at her "sa giglotlike takand thy foull plesance!" (83). The level of diction shifting perceptibly, the narrator locates the initial turn from pleasant place to repulsive wilderness inside Cresseid. Alluding to the pollution her behavior brings and to the shunning it earns her from courtly society, the narrator fixes upon Cresseid as a trespasser and rule breaker. The further she goes, the more obvious the danger she poses and the greater the need for further expulsion.

On the other hand, the more obviously polluted Cresseid gets, the more completely she may be purged—a process described by the anthropologist Mary Douglas:

> The attitude to rejected bits and pieces goes through two stages. First they are recognisably out of place, a threat to good order, and so are regarded as objectionable and vigorously brushed away. . . . This is the stage at which they are dangerous; their half-identity still clings to them and the clarity of the scene in which they obtrude is impaired by their presence. But a long process of pulverizing, dissolving and rotting awaits any physical things that have been recognized as dirt. [*Purity and Danger: An Analysis of Concepts of Pollution and Taboo,* 1966]

"Pulverizing, dissolving and rotting" is a fair description of what Henryson has in store for Cresseid. On her path down and outwards, she leaves a trail of the pleasures and advantages her community had allowed her; much later, at the lepers' hospice, her complaint includes a list of these lost things (416-51): *ubi sunt* chamber, bed, cushions, spice and wine, gold and silver cups, saffron sauce, garments, gowns, linen, garden (with all the amenities of springtime; 425-33), fame and honor, singing voice, gracefulness, beauty? For now, though, faded merely from the attentions of the Greek court, Cresseid cannot foresee how far the loss will extend.

Decidedly "destitute" of "comfort and consolatioun", "fellowschip or refute," Cresseid quits the Greeks in disguise and secrecy (92-94). She seeks shelter from disgrace beyond the city walls, at the residence of her father Calchas (here a priest of Venus). Her father's house does not turn out to be a refuge, however; it is instead a way station, the scene of her repudiation of and condemnation by her divine patrons.

"Excludit" by Diomede (75, 133), Cresseid compares her hateful unattached state to the reversion of spring into winter. She casts this reproach particularly at Cupid—her male patron as well as the god "of all thing generabill" (148)—and only secondarily at Venus (to whom Cresseid ascribes Cupid's blindness):

> O fals Cupide, is nane to wyte bot thow
> And thy mother, of lufe the blind goddes!
> Ye causit me alwayis vnderstand and trow
> The seid of lufe was sawin in my face,
> And ay grew grene throw your supplie and grace.
> Bot now, allace, that seid with froist is slane,
> And I fra luifferis left, and all forlane.
>
> (134-40)

The metaphor of seasonal reversion refers to what has already befallen Cresseid; she finds in it no warning of harsher lessons to come. When the planetary deities in their "court and conuocatioun" (346) pass judgement on Cresseid's repudiation of Cupid and Venus, however, they take this metaphor as literally predictive. Giving substance to her bitter rhetoric (and to her stained reputation), they punish her with leprosy, a disease they oppose to youth, beauty, and honor (313-40). If Cresseid must lay blame upon her patrons, let her discover what coldness, dryness, and blackness can mean.

The pattern of events here resembles that of the Scottish poet Richard Holland's *Buke of the Howlat* (c. 1450), in which a parliament of birds despoils the overweening owl of their earlier gift of fine feathers and cast him into his ordained solitude in the wilderness. Likewise, the punishment of an intrusive complainer by the deities of love occupies the center of Part One of Gavin Douglas's *Palice of Honour* (1501). Both Holland's Howlat and Douglas's dreamer suffer disfigurement (limited in the case of the latter to a comic staining, despite threats of a direr metamorphosis) because of their rebellious behavior. So does the allegorical personage Reason in William Dunbar's *The Goldyn Targe:* Venus's servant Presence ("physical closeness")

> kest a pulder in his ene,
> And than as drunkyn man he all forvayit.
> Quhen he was blynd, the fule wyth hym they playit
> And banyst hym amang the bewis grene.
>
> (203-06)

Henryson's arrangement of events at the center of the ***Testament*** would thus seem to contribute to a recurrent topic in Middle Scots poetry, one concerned less with motivation or morality than with the sudden marking out of a troublesome interloper at court.

Like the dreamer of Dunbar's *Goldyn Targe,* Cresseid had assumed that the enclosed garden of polite behavior was paradise; as in *The Goldyn Targe* and *The Palice of Honour,* that garden has revealed itself to be a barren wilderness. Although the imagery of paradise and hell is less explicitly worked out here than in the later poems, Cresseid may still be seen to proceed towards understanding of the hellish consequences of romantic love as she moves further from the heart of her community. Defaced by leprosy now, she again assumes disguise for another departure, this time from her father's house: in "secreit wyse", shrouded in "ane mantill and ane bawer hat," she leaves by "ane secreit yet," and goes "wnto ane village half ane myle thairby" (381, 386, 388, 390). As Cresseid discovers new levels to her isolation, she submits to her necessary removal further and further from the center.

What starts out sweetly ends roughly, Cresseid's progress from court to mansion to village "spittaill hous" (391) towards the grave is marked by various losses: love, reputation and courtly company; health, beauty, youth, and the security of kinship; soon, individuality itself. In a florid complaint (as mentioned above), Cresseid itemizes the various properties she has left and is leaving behind; the shallowness of her concern falls into view when, Cresseid herself in full cry of lament,

> Ane lipper lady rais and till hir wend,
> And said, "Quhy spurnis thow aganis the wall
> To sla thy self and mend nathing at all?"
>
> (474-76)

Once again, the presence of the macabre may be felt: like a preaching corpse, the leprous Cresseid alludes to the imminent falls of those fine ladies still exalted in beauty and love (452-69); her appearance and sentiments recall those of the corpse-queen in the northern alliterative romance *The Awntyrs off Arthure;* and yet, despite all this, circumstances do not permit Cresseid her wished-for impressive effect. As the protagonist is called to face stark necessity, so is the reader. Courtliness gives way to bluntness, as it does again when ("for knichtlie pietie" [519]) a homeward-bound Troilus takes jewels and gold "and in the skirt of Cresseid doun can swak; / Than raid away and not ane word he spak" (522-23). Polite consolations and sentiments are now irrelevant. What matters is that Cresseid pass with growing understanding towards her death.

Soon, in her brief testament, Cresseid will name her last few divestitures: her body ("with wormis and with taidis to be rent" [578]); her remaining possessions—an odd conjunction of leper's things ("cop and clapper" [579]) and relics of court (ornaments, gold, a love token [579-83]); and finally her soul, which she commends "to Diane, quhair scho dwellis, / To walk with hir in waist woddis and wellis" (587-88). The outward and downward journey would seem to be proceeding to its expected goal. Cresseid has consigned her body to a hellish but conventional manner of consumption, and exiled her soul to a wilderness.

Seeing that wilderness as the preserve of Diana (not Mars or Saturn), however, Cresseid envisions a chaste refuge for her soul. Diana's forest may not be quite as civilized as the pleasant if shady grove of Elysian myrtle into which Virgil's Dido flits to rejoin her Sychaeus; it will nevertheless be a place of clean exertion and unchanging greeness. At the point Henryson took up her story, Cresseid was walking up and down, desolate. Now she imagines walking (and staying) with a steadfast female protector. Accompaniment, security: with her physical self about to achieve its "true indiscriminable character," Cresseid seeks an end to the polluting forces of memory, emotion, change, and desire. To be amongst those woods and cleansing wells and not to be alone may in Cresseid's dying, reaching vision seem rather like being in heaven.

"Quha wait gif all that Chauceir wrait was trew?" (64), the narrator had asked upon taking up this story. When the poem draws to its conclusion, truth remains in doubt: "we have almost a picture of the poet as liar" [Denton Fox, "The Coherence of Henryson's Work" in *Fifteenth-Century Studies,* edited by Robert F. Yeager, 1984]. Still, one discovery has been wrung out of experience—by the protagonist if not the narrator. Cresseid has found the source to the "greit vnstabilnes" of her life within herself; "Nane but my self as now I will accuse" (568, 574). This is no "gentle, kind" perception, but one that is disillusioned, even austere. Without this accusing self-awareness, such moralizing as the narrator's warning to ladies to "Ming not your lufe with fals deceptioun" (613) is ignorant and worse than useless. Seeking truth, the poet must proceed tersely, ironically; one can only hope for surer understanding beyond this world.

The Middle Scots poets wrote so keenly about disfigurement and exile because these experiences revealed an arbitrary foundation to worldly life. Loss, winter, and old age are to be considered more lasting and substantial than happiness, youth, and spring. Gorgeous style and the pleasant topics to which it is applied (in secular poetry, at least) exist on the surface of this poetry, as pleasure exists on the surface of life; and even the courtliest of these poems contains some reference to the rudeness and roughness about to jut out from beneath the shiny surface. For Henryson and his immediate successors, this awareness presents a dilemma: given its basic inconsistency, how can even the most disciplined and polished of their secular poems speak with moral authority? By placing this dilemma at the center of a courtly lady's frivolous existence, Henryson attempts to confront it. His narrator tears layer after layer of belonging from Cresseid's life; this savage process manifests a deep pessimism, and has troubled many readers. Still, Henryson has thus gone further than any other Middle Scots poet to liberate his protagonist and his poem from inconsistency. Cresseid's dying aspiration challenged the Middle Scots tradition to take the outcast seriously; it continues to challenge. (pp. 355-61)

David J. Parkinson, "Henryson's Scottish Tragedy," in The Chaucer Review, *Vol. 25, No. 4, 1991, pp. 355-62.*

FURTHER READING

Bennett, H. S. "Fifteenth-Century Verse." In his *Chaucer and the Fifteenth Century,* pp. 124-76. 1947. Reprint. London: Oxford University Press, 1961.

Offers a brief survey of Henryson's principal works.

Burrow, J. A. "Henryson: *The Preaching of the Swallow.*" *Essays in Criticism* XXV, No. 1 (January 1975): 25-37.

Analyzes the structure of "The Preaching of the Swallow", maintaining that the fable "deserves to be counted as one of the minor masterpieces of medieval English poetry."

Canby, Henry Seidel. "The Heirs of Chaucer." In his *The Short Story in English,* pp. 78-102. New York: Henry Holt and Co., 1909.

Praises Henryson's ability as a storyteller in his major works, particularly focusing on the *Morall Fabillis.*

Chalmers, George. Preface to *Robene and Makyne, and The Testament of Cresseid,* by Robert Henryson, edited by George Chalmers, pp. v-xiv. 1824. Reprint. New York: AMS Press, Johnson Reprint Corporation, 1971.

Attempts to trace Henryson's life and the major printings of his works.

Duncan, Douglas. "Henryson's *Testament of Cresseid.*" *Essays in Criticism* XI, No. 2 (April 1961): 128-35.

Posits that *The Testament of Cresseid* "is in many ways an anxious and uncomfortable poem, and that, . . . it questions the divine order quite peremptorily." For a rebuttal to this essay, see the reference to Sydney Harth below.

Elliott, Charles. Introduction to *Robert Henryson: Poems,* by Robert Henryson, edited by Charles Elliott, pp. vii-xv. London: Oxford University Press, 1963.

Detailed study of Chaucer's influence on Henryson.

Eyre-Todd, George. "Robert Henryson." In his *Mediæval Scottish Poetry,* pp. 77-138. London and Edinburgh: Sands & Co., 1892.

Provides an introductory overview of Henryson and his works and reprints his major poems.

Fox, Denton. "Henryson's *Fables.*" *English Literary History* 29, No. 4 (December 1962): 337-56.

Examines the *Morall Fabillis* in a strictly literary fashion in an attempt to reveal a "concealed and highly disciplined complexity" in the verse.

———. Introduction to *Testament of Cresseid,* by Robert Henryson, edited by Denton Fox, pp. 1-58. London: Thomas Nelson and Sons, 1968.

General overview of *The Testament of Cresseid,* including an extensive discussion of early printings of the poem.

Gopen, George D. "The Essential Seriousness of Robert Henryson's *Moral Fables:* A Study in Structure." *Studies in Philology* LXXXII, No. 1 (Winter 1985): 42-59.

Focuses on the seriousness of the *Morall Fabillis* by examining Henryson's use of structural devices.

Gray, Douglas. *Robert Henryson.* Leiden, The Netherlands: E. J. Brill, 1979, 283 p.

Contains seven essays on Henryson's works and their historical context.

Harth, Sydney. "Henryson Reinterpreted." *Essays in Criticism* XI, No. 4 (October 1961): 471-80.

Disagrees with Douglas Duncan's reading of *The Testament of Cresseid* as an " 'anxious and uncomfortable' " poem that " 'questions the divine order' " (see citation listed above). Harth instead contends that Henryson's treatment of Christianity and death in the work is highly ironic.

Henderson, T. F. "The Early Chaucerians, etc." In his *Scottish Vernacular Literature: A Succinct History,* pp. 94-141. 1898. Third rev. ed. Edinburgh: John Grant, 1910.

Assesses the range of Henryson's poetic style in his works.

Jamieson, I. W. A. "The Minor Poems of Robert Henryson." *Studies in Scottish Literature* IX, Nos. 2 and 3 (October-January 1971): 125-47.

Protests A. M. Kinghorn's personalization of Henryson's works (see excerpt dated 1965), asserting that the character of the poems reflects their genre, not the poet's personality.

Ker, W. P. "The Scottish Chaucerians: King James, Henryson, Dunbar." In *Form and Style in Poetry: Lectures and Notes,* edited by R. W. Chambers, pp. 80-94. London: Macmillan, 1928.

Comments on Henryson's use of the Scottish vernacular in his works.

Kinsley, James. "The Mediaeval Makars." In *Scottish Poetry: A Critical Survey,* edited by James Kinsley, pp. 1-32. London: Cassell, 1955.

An appreciative survey of Henryson's major works.

Kratzmann, Gregory. "Henryson and English Poetry." In his *Anglo-Scottish Literary Relations 1430-1550,* pp. 63-103. Cambridge: Cambridge University Press, 1980.

Compares Henryson's *Testament of Cresseid* and the *Morall Fabillis* to various forms of English poetry, particularly focusing on Chaucer's *Troilus and Criseyde* and *The Canterbury Tales.*

McDiarmid, Hugh. Introduction to *Henryson,* edited by Hugh McDiarmid, pp. 7-15. Middlesex, England: Penguin Books, 1973.

Surveys the contemporary critical reception of Henryson.

MacDonald, Donald. "Narrative Art in Henryson's *Fables.*" *Studies in Scottish Literature* III, No. 2 (October 1965): 101-13.

Identifies the narrative structure of the *Morall Fabillis* as the "result of processes of reduction, on the one hand, and of amplification, on the other, consistently [demonstrating] Henryson's unerring recognition of the crucial comic point of the tale, a point that receives additional skillful development and emphasis by his insertion into the tale of new and original elements."

———. "Chaucer's Influence on Henryson's *Fables:* The Use of Proverbs and Sententiae." *Medium Aevum* XXXIX, No. 1 (1970): 21-7.

Observes that both Chaucer's works and Henryson's *Morall Fabillis* exhibit an extensive use of proverbs and *sententiae* by animal characters.

MacQueen, John. "Poetry—James I to Henryson." In *The History of Scottish Literature,* Vol. 1, edited by R. D. S. Jack, pp. 55-72. Aberdeen, Scotland: Aberdeen University Press, 1988.

Judges Henryson a successful poet of comedy and tragedy and documents numerological forms present in his works.

Mann, Jill. "The Planetary Gods in Chaucer and Henryson." In *Chaucer Traditions: Studies in Honour of Derek Brewer,* edited by Ruth Morse and Barry Windeatt, pp. 91-106. Cambridge: Cambridge University Press, 1990.

Detailed study of Chaucer's and Henryson's treatment of the planetary gods in their works.

Marken, Ronald. "Chaucer and Henryson: A Comparison." *Discourse: A Review of the Liberal Arts* VII, No. 4 (Autumn 1964): 381-87.

Analyzes the similarities and differences of craftsmanship in Chaucer's *Troilus and Criseyde* and Henryson's *Testament of Cresseid.*

Mills, Carol. "Romance Convention and Robert Henryson's *Orpheus and Eurydice.*" In *Bards and Makars: Scottish Language and Literature: Medieval and Renaissance,* edited by Adam J. Aiken, Matthew P. McDiarmid, and Derick S. Thomson, pp. 52-60. Glasgow, Scotland: University of Glasgow Press, 1977.

Traces the romantic influences of Henryson's *Orpheus and Eurydice.*

Miskimin, Alice S. "The Renaissance Versions: Henryson's *Testament of Cresseid.*" In her *The Renaissance Chaucer,* pp. 205-14. New Haven, Conn.: Yale University Press, 1975.

Locates Henryson's *Testament of Cresseid* in the "evolution of the Troilus legend" and assesses it as "a distinct departure" from that tradition.

Noll, Dolores L. "*The Testament of Cresseid:* Are Christian Interpretations Valid?" *Studies in Scottish Literature* IX, No. 1 (July 1971): 16-25.

Argues that *The Testament of Cresseid* is "built upon courtly love premises" rather than the Christian tradition.

Reed, Thomas L., Jr. "Introduction: Definitions, Questions, and Methods." In his *Middle English Debate Poetry and the Aesthetics of Irresolution,* pp. 1-40. Columbia: University of Missouri Press, 1990.

Identifies *The Ressoning betuix Deth and Man* and *The Ressoning betuix Aige and Yowth* as two examples of Middle English debate poems.

Ridley, Florence H. "The Treatment of Animals in the Poetry of Henryson and Dunbar." *The Chaucer Review* 24, No. 4 (1990): 356-66.

Comments on the manner in which Henryson portrays animals in the *Morall Fabillis.*

Rowlands, Mary. "The Fables of Robert Henryson." *The Dalhousie Review* XXXIX, No. 4 (Winter 1960): 491-502.

Regards Henryson's *Morall Fabillis* as literary commentary on Scottish society during the late fifteenth century.

Saintsbury, George. "The Four Great Scottish Poets." In his *A Short History of English Literature,* pp. 180-92. London: Macmillan and Co., 1898.

Discusses Henryson's masterful poetic style in *The Testament of Cresseid,* the *Morall Fabillis,* and other works.

Siegmund-Schultze, Dorothea. "Henryson's Departure from the Medieval Norm." In *Life and Literature of the Working Class: Essays in Honour of William Gallacher,* edited by Erika Lingner, pp. 81-91. Berlin: Humboldt University, 1966.

Suggests that Henryson "renounced his allegiance to medieval tradition in favour of an orientation towards more modern trends."

Smith, G. Gregory. "The Scottish Chaucerians." In *The Cambridge History of English Literature,* edited by A. W. Ward and A. R. Waller, pp. 272-303. New York: G. P. Putnam's Sons, 1908.

Survey of Henryson's works, particularly emphasizing the *Morall Fabillis* and the minor poems.

Spearing, A. C. "*The Testament of Cresseid* and the 'High Concise Style'. " *Speculum: A Journal of Mediaeval Studies* XXXVII, No. 2 (April 1962): 208-25.
Probes Henryson's succinct writing style in *The Testament of Cresseid.*

Speirs, John. "Robert Henryson." In his *The Scots Literary Tradition: An Essay in Criticism,* pp. 11-34. London: Chatto & Windus, 1940.
Identifies the sources of Henryson's works as popular, rather than classical, in origin.

Stearns, Marshall W. "Henryson and the Leper Cresseid." *Modern Language Notes* LIX, No. 4 (April 1944): 265-9.
Examines Henryson's "background for and presentation of the leprosy of Cresseid" in *The Testament of Cresseid.*

———. *Robert Henryson.* New York: Columbia University Press, 1949, 155 p.
Collection of seven essays intended to "clear the way for a better understanding and appreciation of [Henryson] and his poetry."

Tillotson, Geoffrey. "The 'Fables' of Robert Henryson." In his *Essays in Criticism and Research,* pp. 1-4. 1942. Reprint. Hamden, Conn.: Archon Books, 1967.
Brief discussion of Henryson's *Morall Fabillis,* focusing on the poet's talent as a storyteller.

Toliver, Harold E. "Robert Henryson: From *Moralitas* to Irony." *English Studies* XLVI, No. 4 (August 1965): 300-09.
Discusses the ironic elements of Henryson's *moralitas* in the *Morall Fabillis* and *The Testament of Cresseid.*

Tytler, Patrick Fraser. "Robert Henryson." In his *Lives of Scottish Worthies,* Vol. III, pp. 76-88. London: John Murray, 1833.
Summary of Henryson's life and works.

Wood, H. Harvey. "Robert Henryson." In his *Two Scots Chaucerians,* pp. 9-23. London: Longmans, Green, and Co., 1967.
Biographical and critical discussion of Henryson.

James I

1394-1437

Scottish monarch and poet.

INTRODUCTION

James is widely recognized as the author of the *Kingis Quair,* an allegorical poem that recounts his experience as a prisoner in England. Critics have praised the *Kingis Quair* for its innovative treatment of the courtly love tradition and for James's skillful universalizing of his personal experience. In addition to making a significant contribution to the development of medieval love poetry, James is credited with introducing the Chaucerian tradition in Scotland.

The second son of King Robert III and Annabella Drummond, James was born in 1394 in Dunfermline. In 1402 he was sent away to be educated by Bishop Henry Wardlaw, the founder of St. Andrews University. James's older brother, heir to the throne, was murdered at the instigation of the boys' uncle, the Duke of Albany; fearing for his younger son's safety, Robert sent James to France in 1406 to complete his education. On its way to France, his ship was intercepted by an English vessel, and James was captured and held for eighteen years in the Tower of London, Nottingham Castle, and Windsor Castle. He was strictly guarded throughout this period and kept under custody for a ransom of 60,000 marks. During his imprisonment, James received an education superior to that available in France at the time. His taste for poetry and music was encouraged, and his related study of Chaucer has been noted as the greatest influence on his writing. Following the death of Robert in 1406, power was given to the Duke of Albany who, in the interest of protecting his own position, did nothing to negotiate James's return to Scotland. James was thus held captive until 1422, when Albany died. While in England, James married Joan (or Jean) Beaufort, daughter of the Earl of Somerset and great-granddaughter of Edward III. Although some historians have speculated that there was no real love between the two and that James's release was contingent upon the marriage, others note that he was one of the few Scottish kings who had no mistresses and interpret Joan's later revenge on James's assassins as a sign of her deep attachment and affection.

Having assumed the throne of Scotland, James was highly regarded for his musical and literary accomplishments, if not for his wisdom and prudence as a ruler. In addition to playing the flute, the harp, and the church-organ, he wrote songs and composed music. As a monarch, he professed his interest in protecting the people, but some historians consider the aggrandizement of the Crown his primary concern. He alienated the majority of his nobles through his violent and illegal confiscations of land, and

his rash impositions of laws made him unpopular with his subjects. James introduced statute law and, with the support of the Church and the middle class, waged an undeclared war on the feudal lords of the Highlands. Throughout his reign, Scotland had troubled relations with England, partly because his ransom was never paid; tensions reached their apex in 1435, when an invading English force was beaten and driven back. However, the greatest danger to James was posed by the Highland chiefs, who assassinated him at Perth in 1437.

John Mair, an early authority on James and the author of *Historia Maioris Britanniae* (1521), praised James as a musician and poet and attributed to him "an ingenious little book about the queen." He referred here to the oldest known copy of the *Kingis Quair,* a manuscript which also contains Chaucer's *Troilus and Criseyde, Parlement of Foules, Legend of Good Women,* and other English and Scottish poems. The manuscript was completed during James IV's reign (1488-1513) and contains the following lines introducing the poem: "Heireftir followis the quair Maid be/ King James of scotland the first/ Callit the kingis quair and/ Maid quhen his Maiestie wes In/ England." Using Mair as their authority, later critics continued to accept James as the author of the *Kingis Quair,* though scholars note that the introductory attribution is not definitive proof of his authorship, because other poems in the manuscript were incorrectly ascribed to Chaucer.

James's authorship of the poem was first questioned in 1896 in *The Authorship of "The Kingis Quair": A New Criticism* by J. T. T. Brown, who believed that the poem was about, but not by, James. He based his claim primarily on a linguistic analysis of the *Kingis Quair* in conjunction with a late fifteenth-century poem, *Court of Love,* concluding that parallels between the two poems indicate the latter's influence on the former; thus, if the *Kingis Quair* dates from the late fifteenth century, James could not have been its author. In addition, Brown found similarities between the *Kingis Quair* and Andrew of Wyntoun's *Origynal Cronykil of Scotland* (1420-24) and posited that if James's poem were an autobiography, he would surely not have relied on other biographical sources. Brown's most forceful argument was that the poem's language—a combination of Midland English and Lowland Scottish—disproves royal authorship, because James would most likely have forgotten his native language during his eighteen-year imprisonment. Brown concluded that the poem dates from the second half of the fifteenth century and suggested that "the claim for the king rests solely on romantic as distinguished from historical criticism." Since the publication of Brown's claim, other critics have defended James's authorship. Robert Sangster Rait rejected the validity of Brown's biographical evidence, claiming that the poem must be read as a literary, rather than a historical, document. John Churton Collins challenged Brown's linguistic evidence on the grounds that the combination of English and Scottish dialect in the *Kingis Quair* could be attributed to the poem's transcribers rather than its author. More recently, Matthew P. McDiarmid claimed that James wrote the *Kingis Quair* in the 1430s, arguing that he would have regained familiarity with the Scottish language after ten years as king. McDiarmid also noted that James's contact with other Scottish captives during his imprisonment would have counteracted the English influence on his language. Although Brown's analysis raised questions about the *Kingis Quair* that can never be satisfactorily answered, scholars accept James's authorship in the absence of evidence to disprove it.

The *Kingis Quair* was first published in 1783 by William Fraser Tytler, who based his edition on a transcription of the James IV manuscript. In his introduction to the poem, Tytler described it as the story of James's youth "set forth by way of allegorical vision." Critics describe the *Kingis Quair* as a spiritual autobiography in which James recounts his personal experience using conventions from the dream-poem genre. In brief, the poem is about a prisoner who falls in love and seeks solace for his situation in the pages of Boethius's *De consolatione philosophiae* (524?). The *Kingis Quair* is characterized by a combination of Christian tenets and Boethian philosophy as a source of strength and faith, an emphasis on the moral and religious aspects of love, and the speaker's acceptance of Fortune as an agent of God. It is written in rhyme royal, and, though James was not the first to use the pattern, scholars speculate that it may have been named in recognition of the royal poet. Literary analyses of the *Kingis Quair* have noted the influence of Chaucer's *Romaunt of the Rose* and "Knight's Tale," as well as John Lydgate's *Temple of Glas,* but most scholars consider the poem original and innovative rather than imitative. Critics have praised James's ability to imbue real events with allegorical significance and his success in involving the reader in the speaker's plight through a technique of direct address. Although the focus of scholarly studies has varied, interpretation of the *Kingis Quair* has continually been oriented by the unavoidable autobiographical content. While some early critics claimed that the poem surpassed any other of the period, praising its romance and elegance, others assessed it as highly conventional and even derivative. Nineteenth-century readers were influenced by the prevailing bias against allegory, and some, like David Irving, expressed hostility to the poem's combination of Christian and pagan mythology. In general, nineteenth-century critics interpreted the *Kingis Quair* as autobiography, equating the anonymous narrator with James and discussing the poem as the real story of his courtship and the expression of his true feelings.

In the early twentieth century, C. S. Lewis described the *Kingis Quair* as "the first modern book of love," praise which is based on the poem's break with the courtly love tradition and what he interprets as its celebration of marriage over adultery. Other early twentieth-century scholars focused on the poem's stylistic qualities, crediting James with introducing the Chaucerian tradition in Scotland and breaking with medieval Scottish poetic conventions. In an interpretation that marked a shift in criticism, John Preston rejected the validity of biographical interpretations and emphasized the speaker's use of Boethian philosophy in his exploration of courtly love. Under Preston's influence, concern has moved from romance to philosophical content in the poem; recent critics have studied James's use of Boethian philosophy, stressing the narrator's progression from despair to faith and his relief from imprisonment through meditation on Fortune. Noting James's skill in combining the philosophical with the personal, critics have praised the *Kingis Quair* as a response to Boethius that applies the philosopher's principles to the experience of love. Scholars point out that this innovative combination marks a new epoch in Scottish poetry, and, in the words of Lois A. Ebin, "renders the experience of Boethius significant to the journey of all men."

PRINCIPAL WORK

**The Kingis Quair* (poetry) 1783; published in *The Poetical Remains of James I, King of Scotland*

*This work was written in the fifteenth century.

Washington Irving (essay date 1819)

[*Irving was an American short story writer, biographer, essayist, historian, and journalist. He is considered the first American man of letters and the creator of the American short story. He is best known for* The Sketch-Book of Geoffrey Crayon, Gent. *(1819-20), which introduced the modern short story form in the United States and was the first work by an American author to gain international recognition. Purportedly the work of Geoffrey Crayon, a genteel American travelling in England, the* Sketch-Book *is a collection of humorous, elegant travel essays in the tradition of Richard Addison and Oliver Goldsmith, Irving's literary models. In the following excerpt from the* Sketch-Book, *Irving discusses the literary qualities of the* Kingis Quair *and praises its "genuine sentiment" and "delightful artlessness."*]

On a soft sunny morning in the genial month of May, I made an excursion to Windsor Castle. It is a place full of storied and poetical associations. (p. 116)

In [a] mood of mere poetical susceptibility, I visited the ancient Keep of the Castle, where James the First of Scotland, the pride and theme of Scottish poets and historians, was for many years of his youth detained a prisoner of state. (p. 117)

[We] may consider the ***King's Quair,*** composed by James during his captivity at Windsor, as another of those beautiful breakings-forth of the soul from the restraint and gloom of the prison-house.

The subject of the poem is his love for the lady Jane Beaufort, daughter of the Earl of Somerset, and a princess of the blood royal of England, of whom he became enamored in the course of his captivity. What gives it a peculiar value, is that it may be considered a transcript of the royal bard's true feelings, and the story of his real loves and fortunes. It is not often that sovereigns write poetry, or that poets deal in fact. It is gratifying to the pride of a common man, to find a monarch thus suing, as it were, for admission into his closet, and seeking to win his favor by administering to his pleasures. It is a proof of the honest equality of intellectual competition, which strips off all the trappings of factitious dignity, brings the candidate down to a level with his fellow-men, and obliges him to depend on his own native powers for distinction. It is curious, too, to get at the history of a monarch's heart, and to find the simple affections of human nature throbbing under the ermine. But James had learnt to be a poet before he was a king: he was schooled in adversity, and reared in the company of his own thoughts. Monarchs have seldom time to parley with their hearts, or to meditate their minds into poetry; and had James been brought up amidst the adulation and gayety of a court, we should never, in all probability, have had such a poem as the ***Quair.***

I have been particularly interested by those parts of the poem which breathe his immediate thoughts concerning his situation, or which are connected with the apartment in the tower. They have thus a personal and local charm, and are given with such circumstantial truth as to make the reader present with the captive in his prison, and the companion of his meditations.

Such is the account which he gives of his weariness of spirit, and of the incident which first suggested the idea of writing the poem. It was the still midwatch of a clear moonlight night; the stars, he says, were twinkling as fire in the high vault of heaven: and "Cynthia rinsing her golden locks in Aquarius." He lay in bed wakeful and restless, and took a book to beguile the tedious hours. The book he chose was Boethius's *Consolations of Philosophy,* a work popular among the writers of that day, and which had been translated by his great prototype, Chaucer. From the high eulogium in which he indulges, it is evident this was one of his favorite volumes while in prison; and indeed it is an admirable text-book for meditation under adversity. It is the legacy of a noble and enduring spirit, purified by sorrow and suffering, bequeathing to its successors in calamity the maxims of sweet morality, and the trains of eloquent but simple reasoning, by which it was enabled to bear up against the various ills of life. It is a talisman, which the unfortunate may treasure up in his bosom, or, like the good King James, lay upon his nightly pillow.

After closing the volume, he turns its contents over in his mind, and gradually falls into a fit of musing on the fickleness of fortune, the vicissitudes of his own life, and the evils that had overtaken him even in his tender youth. Suddenly he hears the bell ringing to matins; but its sound, chiming in with his melancholy fancies, seems to him like a voice exhorting him to write his story. In the spirit of poetic errantry he determines to comply with this intimation: he therefore takes pen in hand, makes with it a sign of the cross to implore a benediction, and sallies forth into the fairy land of poetry. There is something extremely fanciful in all this, and it is interesting as furnishing a striking and beautiful instance of the simple manner in which whole trains of poetical thought are sometimes awakened, and literary enterprises suggested to the mind.

In the course of his poem he more than once bewails the peculiar hardness of his fate; thus doomed to lonely and inactive life, and shut up from the freedom and pleasure of the world, in which the meanest animal indulges unrestrained. There is a sweetness, however, in his very complaints; they are the lamentations of an amiable and social spirit at being denied the indulgence of its kind and generous propensities; there is nothing in them harsh nor exaggerated; they flow with a natural and touching pathos, and are perhaps rendered more touching by their simple brevity. They contrast finely with those elaborate and iterated repinings, which we sometimes meet with in poetry;—the effusions of morbid minds sickening under miseries of their own creating, and venting their bitterness upon an unoffending world. James speaks of his privations with acute sensibility, but having mentioned them passes on, as if his manly mind disdained to brood over unavoidable calamities. When such a spirit breaks forth into complaint, however brief, we are aware how great must be the suffering that extorts the murmur. We sympathize with James, a romantic, active, and accomplished prince, cut off in the lustihood of youth from all the enterprise, the noble uses, and vigorous delights of life, as we do with Milton, alive to all the beauties of nature and glories of art, when he breathes forth brief, but deep-toned lamentations over his perpetual blindness.

Had not James evinced a deficiency of poetic artifice, we

might almost have suspected that these lowerings of gloomy reflection were meant as preparative to the brightest scene of his story; and to contrast with that refulgence of light and loveliness, that exhilarating accompaniment of bird and song, and foliage and flower, and all the revel of the year, with which he ushers in the lady of his heart. It is this scene, in particular, which throws all the magic of romance about the old Castle Keep. He had risen, he says, at daybreak, according to custom, to escape from the dreary meditations of a sleepless pillow. "Bewailing in his chamber thus alone," despairing of all joy and remedy, "fortired of thought and wobegone," he had wandered to the window, to indulge the captive's miserable solace of gazing wistfully upon the world from which he is excluded. The window looked forth upon a small garden which lay at the foot of the tower. It was a quiet, sheltered spot, adorned with arbors and green alleys, and protected from the passing gaze by trees and hawthorn hedges.

> Now was there made, fast by the tower's wall,
> A garden faire, and in the corners set
> An arbour green with wandis long and small
> Railed about, and so with leaves beset
> Was all the place and hawthorn hedges knet,
> That lyf was none, walkyng there forbye
> That might within scarce any wight espye.
>
> So thick the branches and the leves grene,
> Beshaded all the alleys that there were,
> And midst of every arbour might be sene
> The sharpe, grene, swete juniper,
> Growing so fair, with branches here and there,
> That as it seemed to a lyf without,
> The boughs did spread the arbour all about.
>
> And on the small grene twistis set
> The lytel swete nightingales, and sung
> So loud and clear, the hymnis consecrate
> Of lovis use, now soft, now loud among,
> That all the garden and the wallis rung
> Right of their song—

It was the month of May, when everything was in bloom; and he interprets the song of the nightingale into the language of his enamored feeling:—

> Worship, all ye that lovers be, this May,
> For of your bliss the kalends are begun,
> And sing with us, away, winter, away,
> Come, summer, come, the sweet season and sun.

As he gazes on the scene, and listens to the notes of the birds, he gradually relapses into one of those tender and undefinable reveries which fill the youthful bosom in this delicious season. He wonders what this love may be, of which he has so often read, and which thus seems breathed forth in the quickening breath of May, and melting all nature into ecstasy and song. If it really be so great a felicity, and if it be a boon thus generally dispensed to the most insignificant beings, why is he alone cut off from its enjoyments?

> Oft would I think, O Lord, what may this be,
> That love is of such noble myght and kynde?
> Loving his folke, and such prosperitee
> Is it of him, as we in books do find:
> May he oure hertes setten and unbynd:
> Hath he upon our hertes such maistrye?
> Or is all this but feynit fantasye?
>
> For giff he be of so grete excellence,
> That he of every wight hath care and charge,
> What have I gilt to him, or done offense,
> That I am thral'd, and birdis go at large?

In the midst of his musing, as he casts his eye downward, he beholds "the fairest and the freshest young floure" that ever he had seen. It is the lovely Lady Jane, walking in the garden to enjoy the beauty of that "fresh May morrowe." Breaking thus suddenly upon his sight, in the moment of loneliness and excited susceptibility, she at once captivates the fancy of the romantic prince, and becomes the object of his wandering wishes, the sovereign of his ideal world.

There is, in this charming scene, an evident resemblance to the early part of Chaucer's Knight's Tale; where Palamon and Arcite fall in love with Emilia, whom they see walking in the garden of their prison. Perhaps the similarity of the actual fact to the incident which he had read in Chaucer may have induced James to dwell on it in his poem. His description of the Lady Jane is given in the picturesque and minute manner of his master; and being doubtless taken from the life, is a perfect portrait of a beauty of that day. He dwells, with the fondness of a lover, on every article of her apparel, from the net of pearl, splendent with emeralds and sapphires, that confined her golden hair, even to the "goodly chaine of small orfeverye" about her neck, whereby there hung a ruby in shape of a heart, that seemed, he says, like a spark of fire burning upon her white bosom. Her dress of white tissue was looped up to enable her to walk with more freedom. She was accompanied by two female attendants, and about her sported a little hound decorated with bells; probably the small Italian hound of exquisite symmetry, which was a parlor favorite and pet among the fashionable dames of ancient times. James closes his description by a burst of general eulogium:

> In her was youth, beauty, with humble port,
> Bounty, richesse, and womanly feature;
> God better knows then my pen can report,
> Wisdom, largesse, estate, and cunning sure,
> In every point so guided her measure,
> In word, in deed, in shape, in countenance,
> That nature might no more her child advance.

The departure of the Lady Jane from the garden puts an end to this transient riot of the heart. With her departs the amorous illusion that had shed a temporary charm over the scene of his captivity, and he relapses into loneliness, now rendered tenfold more intolerable by this passing beam of unattainable beauty. Through the long and weary day he repines at his unhappy lot, and when evening approaches, and Phœbus, as he beautifully expresses it, had "bade farewell to every leaf and flower," he still lingers at the window, and, laying his head upon the cold stone, gives vent to a mingled flow of love and sorrow, until, gradually lulled by the mute melancholy of the twilight hour, he lapses, "half sleeping, half swoon," into a vision, which occupies the remainder of the poem, and in which is allegorically shadowed out the history of his passion.

When he wakes from his trance, he rises from his stony

pillow, and, pacing his apartment, full of dreary reflections, questions his spirit, whither it has been wandering; whether, indeed, all that has passed before his dreaming fancy has been conjured up by preceding circumstances; or whether it is a vision, intended to comfort and assure him in his despondency. If the latter, he prays that some token may be sent to confirm the promise of happier days, given him in his slumbers. Suddenly, a turtle-dove, of the purest whiteness, comes flying in at the window, and alights upon his hand, bearing in her bill a branch of red gillyflower, on the leaves of which is written, in letters of gold, the following sentence:—

> Awake! awake! I bring, lover, I bring
> The newis glad that blissful is, and sure
> Of thy comfort; now laugh, and play, and sing,
> For in the heaven decretit is thy cure.

He receives the branch with mingled hope and dread; reads it with rapture: and this, he says, was the first token of his succeeding happiness. Whether this is a mere poetic fiction, or whether the Lady Jane did actually send him a token of her favor in this romantic way, remains to be determined according to the faith or fancy of the reader. He concludes his poem by intimating that the promise conveyed in the vision and by the flower is fulfilled, by his being restored to liberty, and made happy in the possession of the sovereign of his heart.

Such is the poetical account given by James of his love adventures in Windsor Castle. How much of it is absolute fact, and how much the embellishment of fancy, it is fruitless to conjecture: let us not, however, reject every romantic incident as incompatible with real life; but let us sometimes take a poet at his word. I have noticed merely those parts of the poem immediately connected with the tower, and have passed over a large part, written in the allegorical vein, so much cultivated at that day. The language, of course, is quaint and antiquated, so that the beauty of many of its golden phrases will scarcely be perceived at the present day; but it is impossible not to be charmed with the genuine sentiment, the delightful artlessness and urbanity, which prevail throughout it. The descriptions of nature, too, with which it is embellished, are given with a truth, a discrimination, and a freshness, worthy of the most cultivated periods of the art.

As an amatory poem, it is edifying, in these days of coarser thinking, to notice the nature, refinement, and exquisite delicacy which pervade it; banishing every gross thought or immodest expression, and presenting female loveliness, clothed in all its chivalrous attributes of almost supernatural purity and grace. (pp. 120-29)

James belongs to one of the most brilliant eras of our literary history, and establishes the claims of his country to a participation in its primitive honors. Whilst a small cluster of English writers are constantly cited as the fathers of our verse, the name of their great Scottish compeer is apt to be passed over in silence; but he is evidently worthy of being enrolled in that little constellation of remote but never-failing luminaries, who shine in the highest firmament of literature, and who, like morning stars, sang together at the bright dawning of British poesy. (p. 130)

Washington Irving, "A Royal Poet," in his The Sketch-Book of Geoffrey Crayon, Gent., *revised edition, 1849. Reprint by J. B. Lippincott & Co., 1873, pp. 116-34.*

Walter W. Skeat (essay date 1884)

[*Skeat was an English philologist and critic whose chief interests were dialect and etymology, and who edited authoritative texts of* Piers Plowman *and the works of Chaucer. In the following excerpt from his introduction to his edition of* The Kingis Quair, *he uses textual evidence from the poem to suggest that it was written over a period of several months.*]

[I believe] that the poem of the ***Kingis Quair,*** that is, of the ***King's Book,*** was composed in 1423. I do not find that it has been observed that we can date it much more exactly than this. A careful study of the poem has led me to believe that it was probably not composed quite all at once; indeed, a poem of 1379 lines must have occupied several days at least, and even at the rate of fifty lines a-day, would have taken up nearly a month. We find, accordingly, that the earlier part of the poem dwells upon the king's state of despondency in the days preceding the month of May, in which he first saw the lady Joan, whilst the closing stanzas refer to a later period. Perhaps we may date its commencement as early as April or March, and its completion, probably, not earlier than June. We also gain some insight into the manner of its composition. It would seem probable that the poem was originally begun as an amusement only, with the avowed hope of beguiling his captivity; he lay awake in bed, thinking *of this and that* (not, at this date, of his lady), and, finding sleep impossible, began to read the treatise of Boethius *De Consolatione Philosophiæ;* he became interested in it (st. 5), and, after shutting it up, continued to think of the variations of Fortune (st. 8). St. 11 follows naturally upon st. 9, and I am inclined to think that st. 10, in which he speaks of Fortune being "afterwards his *friend,*" was interpolated somewhat later. He had, at this time, no very clear idea as to what he was going to write about; he had, indeed, wasted much ink and paper to little effect (st. 13); but, being now ambitious to write "some new thing," and knowing that the best thing to do is to make a good beginning, he made a cross, and so began his book (st. 13). He still bewails his fate, and compares himself to a rudderless ship, since he has no object in life; nothing whereby to guide his voyage (st. 15); so that the poem probably made at first but little progress. St. 19, in which he mentions his torment and his *joy,* may have been slightly altered afterwards; for he seems to have begun his poem by determining to tell the story of his life and lamenting his fate, which continues till st. 28. But in st. 29 there is a great change; he had been bewailing his long days and nights for some time, and I suppose that st. 1 to 28 represent some of his reflections during this period. All at once a new note is struck, one of hope; he now no longer drifts about, but sets to his self-imposed task in good earnest, having found something definite to say; and it is not without some significance that the favourite extract from the poem begins with the thirtieth stanza.

I do not find that any one has noticed a curious expression in st. 191. The lines to which I allude are the third and fourth of that stanza:—

> Thankit mot be the sanctis marciall,
> That me first causit hath this accident.

For *marciall,* the editions by Tytler and others have *merciall,* and there is no note upon the line; nor does the word appear in Thomson's glossary, so that this interesting point has been missed. The "Martial saints" are the saints of the month of Mars, *i.e.* of March; and the poet blesses all the saints of this happy month, because it "first caused him this accident," *i.e.* was the *original cause* of his good fortune. I take this to refer, not to his first sight of his lady (which certainly took place in *May,* as we learn expressly from st. 34, 49, and 65), but to the month in which he first quitted his native land; and I think it highly probable that the recurrence of the 12th of March—the anniversary of the day when he first left home, and all his troubles began (see st. 20)—caused him to turn his thoughts upon the events of his past life. Moreover, it was this retrospect which at last guided him to his new happiness; for it was when he was tired of thinking that he went to the window to seek for rest, or a fresh inspiration (st. 30), and so beheld the garden and the lady. It is further clear that the composition of the poem must have lasted into June, since, after seeing the lady Joan in May, he speaks of his hopes increasing "day by day" (st. 181), of his "long pain and true service in love" (st. 188), which led to his love being reciprocated,—of his "long and true continuance in love and true service" (st. 192), and of his further success in love "day by day" (st. 193). Indeed, if we are to take the words in the *literal* sense, we should have to allow even a still later date for the latter portion of the poem; but perhaps a month or six weeks may fairly be considered a long term of service to a lover who is anxious for the success of his suit. I think it will also appear, upon examination, that the poem may have been intended, at one time, to end with st. 173, which is a sort of Envoy following upon st. 172, where he represents himself as awaking from his dream. I conclude that the poem, or at any rate the first draft of it, was begun at a time, when the poet had little to speak of beyond his past misadventures,—though it is very possible that it was afterwards partially rewritten, owing to the fresh impulse which was given to his fancy on a certain May morning, and that it can hardly have been completed till June.

I believe that this hypothesis is also required by the fragmentary nature of the poem; for, notwithstanding that some art has been shown in giving a certain connectedness to the whole by (as I suppose) the subsequent introduction of occasional connecting phrases, some want of order still remains. The account of Fortune, in st. 158 to 172 with the addition of st. 173, is in a tone in harmony with st. 1 to 28, and might very well have been introduced at an earlier place; whilst st. 152 to 157 have absolutely nothing to do with the subject, and have very much the appearance of having formerly belonged to one of the poet's earlier compositions, over which he spent, as he tells us, so much paper and ink to so little effect. (pp. xi-xiv)

Rev. Walter W. Skeat, in an introduction to The Kingis Quair *by King James I. of Scotland, edited by Rev. Walter W. Skeat, William Blackwood and Sons, 1884, pp. vii-lv.*

John M. Ross (essay date 1884)

[In the following excerpt, Ross praises the Kingis Quair, *claiming that it "marks a new epoch in the history of Scottish poetry."]*

The ***Kingis Quhair*** is generally supposed to have been written during James's captivity, and there can be little doubt that the poem was conceived and mainly composed before he left England; but it may have been retouched about the time of his return to his native country, for in the sixth stanza of canto II. he speaks of his imprisonment as past, while in the epilogue he pours out his profuse thanks for the happiness which his marriage has brought him. The epilogue may well have been added on the occasion of his marriage. It is a kind of epithalamium, and the verse has the rosy bloom of bridal hours. The framework of the poem is an example of that fantastic allegory which enchanted the fancy of the Middle Ages, and which was essentially an incongruous mixture of romantic sentiment and classical fable. This form of allegory was a peculiar product of chivalry—of that vague yet ambitious spirit which sought to surround the poverty and rudeness of medieval life with the glory and grandeur of antiquity. It preceded the revival of learning, which indeed put an end to its daring anachronisms, its grotesque perversions of ancient myths and characters, and its uncritical jumble of crude knowledge. But genius forces its way through every obstacle; and though we can no longer find much pleasure in the phantom world of impossible personages, and in the adventures and pilgrimages of the poet from sphere to sphere, we still delight to trace the presence of imaginative energy in those wonderful descriptions of nature, which seem to us more true and picturesque than anything in our later literature. Chaucer was the first Englishman to give the romantic allegory a home in this country; Gower laboriously seconded the brilliant efforts of his friend and contemporary; and King James became an enthusiastic disciple of both. He calls them his "Maisteris dere," and declares them to be "superlative as poetis laureate." But he is by no means a feeble imitator. He goes his own way, invents his own story, and paints his own pictures with a distinct and original touch. Chaucer and Gower familiarized him with a new form of poetry, which he admired. But he did not copy their productions; he created for himself. In fact, James is a much greater poet than Gower. He did not write so much, but he wrote a great deal better. Nothing in the *Confessio Amantis* is comparable in point of vigour or beauty to the best parts of the ***Kingis Quhair.*** None the less is it creditable to the king's modesty that he spoke with such honest reverence of the twain, whose renown began to fill all England at the time.

A brief outline of the ***Kingis Quhair*** may not be superfluous. The poet, awaking at midnight out of his sleep, takes up the *De Consolatione Philosophiæ* of Boethius, a favourite work of the Middle Ages, of which and of its author we have some account. At last his "eyne 'gan to smert for studying," and he lay down again, revolving in his mind the uncertainty of Fortune, and finding a sad illustration in his own history. Wearied out with his "thoughtis rolling to and fro," he gladly hears "the bell to matins ryng." The "fantasye" took hold of him that the bell was a living voice, and that it commanded him to relate what had befallen him. As he had often before "ink and paper spent" to little purpose, he now resolved to write something new. His strange and woeful lot presses upon his recollection, but he fears that he has not ripeness of wit to describe it properly. The images he uses are taken from the sea. His "feble bote" is steered with doubting heart amid the waves and rocks. All through the dark winter night he waits a favouring wind to fill his sails, and invokes with equal piety the help of Calliope and the Virgin Mary. Resolved, however, to proceed, he asks the Muses to let their "brycht lanternis" shine upon him, and guide "my pen to write my turment and my joye." So ends the first canto.

The second is the gem of the poem. Many of its stanzas are hardly inferior to Chaucer's best work of the same kind, and we read them with heightened feelings of surprise and wonder, that a youth of James's rank could under any circumstances have drunk so deeply of the Pierian spring. In the springtime of the year, when the tender flowers are opening under the sunlight, the young prince amid many friendly farewells sets sail for France. His violent capture and his "strayte ward" in an English prison are then touched upon. He paints his long imprisonment as a season of dolour and pain, that he may more poetically contrast it with the sweet relief of love that is coming. Bird, and beast, and fish all live in freedom; why should he suffer such cruel enthralment? Long days and nights he thus bewails his fortune, "despeired of all joye and remedye." But one bright May morning, when he is gazing in listless mood from the window of his prison-chamber on the fair garden below, girdled with hedges of hawthorn and juniper, he listens to the song of the "lytil suete nyghtingale" as it sat on the "small grene twistis" of the "herbere," and finds himself able by some subtle sympathy to interpret it. It is an amorous chant, calling upon lovers to rejoice in their new-born bliss. The royal captive is bewildered by this rapture. "Quhat lufe is this that makis birdis dote?" While he muses over what he has read in books regarding the power of love, he is insensibly drawn to express a wish that he too might be allowed to enter the service of a god who can "maken thrallis free." At that moment his eye falls upon the fairest flower of womankind he had ever seen. His whole blood starts to his heart, and in an instant he understands the magic mystery of love.

His description of the lady's charms is in the highest style of courtly and chivalrous panegyric. Her sweet face, in which there was no menace, her golden hair, her rich attire, loose and open, yet sparkling with pearls and precious stones, her brilliant head-dress with its spangled love-knots, her white enamelled neck, adorned with a chain of delicate gold work, from which, shaped like a heart, there hung a flawless ruby, that glowed like fire upon her ivory throat, are all descanted upon in a strain of innocent admiration and delight. But above and beyond all this splendour of ornament, there was

> Beautee eneuch to mak a world to dote.

But the graces of her mind surpass even those of her person. Here James perhaps anticipates a later knowledge, but the point is a trivial one; it is poetically finer that all her perfections should be set forth in one dazzling picture, than that they should be noted in the mere order of their discovery. The result is an almost ideal image of maidenly sweetness, prudence, dignity, and grace. Yet the fidelity of the king to his accomplished consort through all his troubled life might lead us to believe that he had not greatly exaggerated the virtues of her character.

Now that he knows the secret of bliss, James pours forth his prayers to Venus, and in his immeasurable joy calls upon the "lytil nyghtingale" again to repeat its gladsome song. In bright and vivid verse, in airy and quaint fancies, he eagerly expostulates with the winged minstrel for delaying its amorous notes. At last the gush of melody bursts forth, to which the impassioned prince sets happy words. All the other choristers of the garden become jubilant, in praise of the tender season of the year and the pastimes of loving hearts. At last the lady retires from the garden, and gloom and despair immediately take possession of the prisoner. He lingers at the window till "Esperus his lampis gan to light," and, according to the fantastic imagery of the times (which was itself a Virgilian reminiscence), weeps and wails piteously. At last, "ourset" with sorrow, he falls into a half sleep, half swoon, during the lapse of which wonderful things happen to him in a vision.

The third, fourth, and fifth cantos are devoted to his adventures in allegorical realms, and may be more briefly sketched. Raised mysteriously into the air, he finds himself "clippit in a cloude of crystall clere and faire," and so passes from sphere to sphere until he reaches "the glad empire off blissful Venus," whose court is described at once with minuteness of detail and vivacity of fancy. All kinds of martyrs and confessors of love are presented to us; the true and the false, the happy and the unhappy; those that would fain have loved, but who were forced into a cloistered life; princes famous for their gallantry, and the poets who recorded their deeds. In a soft retreat he finds the "goddesse of delyte" herself, reclining on her couch, attended by her usher "Fair Calling," and her thrifty chamberer "Secretee." He salutes her in his finest and most copious rhetoric, "sterre of benevolence! Pitouse princesse, and planet merciable!" "suete well off remedye,"

> And in the huge weltering wavis fell
> Off lufis rage, blissful havin, and sure,

and implores her help in his suit. If it were possible for us to take a lively interest in this antiquated form of poetry, we could not fail to be moved by the passionate enthusiasm that here animates James's verse. As it is, we are forced to feel that a true and genuine love fires his bosom, though the literary fashion of his age required a dreary pedantry of expression that chills all modern sympathy.

Venus explains to him at considerable length that the help of more than one goddess is needed in his difficult case, and sends him to the sphere of Minerva under the guidance of "Gude Hope," by whose advice he may "atteyne unto that glad and goldyn floure." He soon reaches "Minerve's Palace, faire and bryt," is admitted by the master porter, "Pacience," and, after admiring "the strenth, the beautee, and the ordour digne" that mark her court, is presented to the wise goddess by his guide. Once more he tells the story of his love. Minerva listens patiently, and when he has finished explains to him that if his passion be founded on virtue and not on "nyce lust," she will lend him her aid. She dilates with great earnestness on the merit of fidelity in love, denounces profligate wooers who employ their wits "the sely innocent woman to begyle," and laments that so few men are true and honourable in their courtship. James declares that the "gude fame" of his lady is dearer to him than all the gold in the world. When Minerva is finally satisfied that his affection is "set in Cristin wise," she promises her most cordial help. It does not seem to amount to much after all, as it chiefly consists of a metaphysical discourse on free will and necessity, winding up with a recommendation to her visitor to seek the help of her whom clerks call Fortune.

His journey in quest of this famous deity is described with Chaucerian richness of imagery and melody of verse. Again and again the pupil in his graphic and graceful pictures imitates and equals his mighty master. The "lusty plane" through which a pleasant river ran, murmuring musically on its lucid course, the flowers fragrant and bright, the glancing motions of the little fishes, the long rows of trees loaded with delicious fruits, the brilliant array of beasts of divers kinds that he passed on his way, are all touched off with the most artistic beauty. At last he spies "Fortune, the goddesse, hufing on the ground." Her great wheel is right before her, and multitudes are clambering upon it. Underneath lay an ugly pit, "depe as ony helle." Whoever fell into it as he climbed, "com no more up agane tidingis to telle"; and very few could keep their footing or their seat on the revolving spokes. The vicissitudes of human life are finely symbolized. When the poet has told her why he has come, she encourages him to step on to the wheel, rallying him kindly on his faint-heartedness. At this critical moment he awakes from his swoon, and the vision comes to an end.

The sixth and last canto is very brief, but it is exquisitely tender and sweet. Opening with an apostrophe to man's "besy goste," that is ever restless till it finds rest in that Heaven from which it came, it goes on to tell how miserable the royal lover felt when he discovered that his happiness was only a dream; but suddenly a white turtle-dove—the bird of Venus—alights on his hand, and looks at him so softly that the "kalendis of confort," or dawn of hope, begins to rise in his heart. In her bill she holds a stalk of "red jerofferis," on whose leaves are written in golden letters the blissful news that his cure is decreed in Heaven, and that Fortune has smiled upon his suit. Then follows the epilogue, of which we have already spoken—a thanksgiving ode, ringing with notes of manly joy, and inspired with a chivalrous devotion that might almost be considered a romantic exaggeration, but for the witness furnished by the king's domestic life.

The ***Kingis Quhair*** marks a new epoch in the history of Scottish poetry. The plain, unadorned, semi-prosaic style of the metrical chronicles gave place to a delicacy and refinement of imaginative feeling, a richness and elegance of diction, and an artistic melody of verse hitherto unknown. The revolution in the national literature was as great as the revolution in the national policy, but it was more benign in its operation and more lasting in its effects. Henceforth Scotland has a share in the culture of western Christendom. All that Chaucer learned from the trouveurs of France and the poets of Italy, who heralded the Renaissance of letters, passed into the spirit of the Scottish prince, and was transmitted by him as an impulse and inspiration to the most gifted of his successors. (pp. 148-56)

John M. Ross, "King James, Henryson, and Dunbar," in his Scottish History and Literature to the Period of the Reformation, *edited by James Brown, James Maclehose & Sons, 1884, pp. 132-218.*

Edmund Gosse (essay date 1898)

[*A distinguished English literary historian, critic, and biographer, Gosse wrote extensively on seventeenth- and eighteenth-century English literature. His commentary in* Seventeenth-Century Studies *(1883),* A History of Eighteenth-Century Literature *(1889),* Questions at Issue *(1893), and other works is generally regarded as sound and suggestive, and he is also credited with introducing the works of the Norwegian dramatist Henrik Ibsen and other Scandinavian writers to English readers. In the following excerpt, Gosse praises James's continuation of the Chaucerian tradition.*]

Of all poems of the fifteenth century . . . that which is most faithful to the tradition of Chaucer, and continues it in the most intelligent way, is the ***King's Quair*** (or Book). The history of this work is as romantic as possible, and yet probably authentic. James I. of Scotland, in 1405, not being yet eleven years old, was treacherously captured by the English, in time of truce, off Flamborough Head, and had been confined, first in the Tower, then in Windsor Castle, for eighteen years, when, seeing Johanne de Beaufort walking in the garden below his prison window, he fell violently in love with her. The match pleased the English Court; they were married early in 1424, and proceeded as King and Queen to Scotland. The poem we are now discussing was written in the spring and early summer of 1423, and it describes, in exquisitely artless art, the progress of the wooing. This poet was murdered, in conditions of heartless cruelty, in 1437. We possess no other indubitable work of his except a Scotch *ballade.*

The King's Quair, in more primitive periods of our literary history, was accepted as a contribution to Scotch poetry. But Dr. Skeat was the first to point out that although the foundation of it is in the Northern dialect, it is carefully composed, as if in a foreign language, in the elaborate Midland or Southern dialect as used, and perhaps not a little as invented, by Chaucer. James I., indeed, is completely under the sway of his great predecessor; no poet of the century repeats so many phrases copied from, or introduces so many allusions to, the writings of Chaucer as he does. He was immersed, it is evident, in the study and almost the idolatry of his master; the first violent emotion of his sequestered life came upon him in that condition, and he burst into song with the language of Chaucer upon his lips. In spite of this state of pupilage, and in spite of his employment of the old French machinery of a dream, allegorical personages and supernatural conventions, the poem of James I. is a delicious one. His use of metre was highly intelligent; he neither deviated back towards the older national prosody, like Lydgate, nor stumbled aimlessly on, like Occleve; he perceived what it was that Chaucer had been doing, and he pursued it with great firmness, so that, in the fifty or sixty years which divided the latest of the *Canterbury Tales* from *The Flower and the Leaf,* the ***King's Quair*** is really the only English poem in which a modern ear can take genuine pleasure.

In its analysis of moods of personal feeling, the ***King's Quair*** marks a distinct advance in fluent and lucid expression. The poem is full, too, of romantic beauty; the description of the garden, of the mysterious and lovely being beheld wandering in its odorous mazes, of the nightingale, "the little sweetë nightingale" on "the smalë greenë twistis," is more accomplished, of its kind, than what any previous poet, save always Chaucer, had achieved. The pathos of the situation, our sympathy with the gallant and spirited royal poet, the historic exactitude of the events so beautifully recorded, the curious chance by which its manuscript was preserved unknown until the end of last century—all combine to give the ***King's Quair*** a unique position in English literature. Alas! as Rossetti sings:

> Alas! for the woful thing
> That a poet true and a friend of man
> In desperate days of bale and ban
> Should needs be born a king.

(pp. 38-40)

Edmund Gosse, "The Close of the Middle Ages (1400-1560)," in his A Short History of Modern English Literature, *William Heinemann, 1898, pp. 33-72.*

G. Gregory Smith (essay date 1908)

[*In the following excerpt, Smith discusses the* Kingis Quair *as an innovative dream-poem which combines a direct personal quality with allegory.*]

It is a critical tradition to speak of the fifteenth century in Scotland as the time of greatest literary account, or, in familiar phrase, "the golden age of Scottish poetry." It has become a commonplace to say of the poets of that time that they, best of all Chaucer's followers, fulfilled with understanding and felicity the lessons of the master-craftsman; and it has long been customary to enforce this by contrasting the skill of Lydgate, Occleve and their contemporaries in the south, with that of James I, Henryson, Dunbar and Gavin Douglas. The contrast does not help us to more than a superficial estimate; it may lead us to exaggerate the individual merits of the writers and to neglect the consideration of such important matters as the homogeneity of their work, and their attitude to the older popular habit of Scottish verse.

We must keep in mind that the work of the greater Scottish poets of the fifteenth century represents a break with the literary practice of the fourteenth. The alliterative tradition dragged on, perhaps later than it did in the south, and the chronicle-poem of the type of Barbour's *Bruce* or the *Legends of the Saints* survived in Henry the Minstrel's patriotic tale of Wallace and in Wyntoun's history. With James I the outlook changes, and in the poems of Henryson, Dunbar, Douglas and some of the minor "makars" the manner of the earlier northern poetry survives only in stray places. It is not that we find a revulsion from medieval sentiment. The main thesis of this chapter will be that these poets are much less modern than medieval. But there is, in the main, a change in literary method—an interest, we might say, in other aspects of the old allegorical tradition. In other words, the poetry of this century is a recovery, consciously made, of much of the outworn artifice of the Middle Ages, which had not yet reached, or hardly reached, the northern portion of the island. The movement is artificial and experimental, in no respects more remarkably so than in the deliberate moulding of the language to its special purpose. Though the consciousness of the effort, chiefly in its linguistic and rhetorical bearings, may appear, at first glance, to reveal the spirit of the renascence, it is nevertheless clear that the materials of this experiment and much of the inspiration of the change come from the Middle Ages. The origin is by no means obscured, though we recognise in this belated allegorical verse the growth of a didactic, descriptive and, occasionally, personal, habit which is readily associated with the renascence. We are easily misled in this matter—too easily, if we have made up our minds to discover signs of the new spirit at this time, when it had been acknowledged, more or less fully, in all the other vernacular literatures of Europe. Gavin Douglas, for example, has forced some false conclusions on recent criticism, by his seeming modern spirit, expressed most strikingly in the prologue to the fifth book of his translation of the *Aeneid:*

> Bot my propyne coym fra the pres fuit hait,
> Unforlatit, not jawyn fra tun to tun,
> In fresche sapour new fro the berrie run.

The renascence could not have had a better motto. Yet there should be little difficulty in showing that Douglas, our first translator of Vergil, was, perhaps, of all these fifteenth century Scots, the gentlest of rebels against the old-world fancies of the Courts of Love and the ritual of the Rose.

The herald of the change in Scottish literary habit is the love-allegory of ***The Kingis Quair,*** or ***King's Book.*** The atmosphere of this poem is that of *The Romance of the Rose:* in general treatment, as well as in details, it at once appears to be modelled upon that work, or upon one of the many poems directly derived therefrom. Closer examination shows an intimacy with Chaucer's translation of the *Romance.* Consideration of the language and of the evidence as to authorship . . . brings conviction that the poem was the direct outcome of study, by some northerner, of Chaucer's *Romaunt* and other works. It was fortunate for Scots literature that it was introduced to this new genre in a poem of such literary competence. Not only is the poem by its craftsmanship superior to any by Chaucer's English disciples, but it is in some respects, in happy phrasing and in the retuning of old lines, hardly inferior to its models. Indeed, it may be claimed for the Scots author, as for his successor, in the *Testament of Cresseid,* that he has, at times, improved upon his master.

The Kingis Quair (which runs to 1379 lines, divided into 197 "Troilus" stanzas, riming *ababbcc*) may be described as a dream-allegory dealing with two main topics—the "unsekernesse" of Fortune and the poet's happiness in love. The contradiction of these moods has led some to consider the poem as a composite work, written at different times: the earlier portion representing the period of the author's dejection, real or imaginary, the latter that of the subsequent joy which the sight of the fair lady in the garden by his prison had brought into his life. . . . [Walter W. Skeat, in his edition of ***The Kingis Quair,***] has expressed the opinion that the poem was begun at a time when the poet "had little to speak of beyond his past misadventures"; and, while allowing that it may have been "afterwards partially rewritten," he finds evidence of its fragmentary origin in the presence of sections which "have absolutely nothing to do with the subject." For these reasons, he disallows Tytler's division (1783) of the poem into six cantos, which had held in all editions for a full century (down to 1884), because it assumes a unity which does not exist. This objection to the parcelling out of the text may be readily accepted—not because it gives, as has been assumed, a false articulation to a disconnected work, but because it interferes unnecessarily with that very continuity which is not the least merit of the poem. The author, early in the work (st. 19), calls upon the muses to guide him "to write his *torment and his joy.*" This is strong evidence by the book in its own behalf, and it is not easily discredited by the suggestion that the line "may have been altered afterwards." If there be any inconsistency observable in the poem, it is of the kind inevitable in compositions where the personal element is strong. In the earlier allegory, and in much of the later (if we think of the Spenserian type) the individuality of the writer is merged in the narrative: in ***The Kingis Quair,*** on the other hand, a striking example of the later dream-poem which has a direct lyrical or personal quality, greater inconsequence of fact and mood is to be expected. Whether that inconsequence be admitted or not by the modern reader, we have no warrant for the conclusion that the work is a mosaic. (pp. 272-75)

A careful examination of this well-constructed poem will show that, to the interest of the personal elements, well blended with the conventional matter of the dream-poem, is added that of its close acquaintance with the text of Chaucer. It is not merely that we find that the author knew the English poet's works and made free use of them, but that his concern with them was, in the best sense, literary. He has not only adopted phrases and settings, but he has selected and returned lines, and given them, though reminiscent of their origin, a merit of their own. Sometimes the comparison is in favour of the later poem, in no case more clearly than in the fortieth stanza, quoted above, which echoes the description, in *The Knight's Tale,* of Palamon's beholding of Emilie. The lines

> And there-with-al he bleynte, and cryde "a!"
> As though he stongen were unto the herte,

are inferior to the Scot's concluding couplet. The literary relationship, of which many proofs will appear to the careful reader, is shown in a remarkable way in the reference at the close to the poems of Gower and Chaucer. This means more than the customary homage of the fifteenth century to Chaucer and Gower, though the indebtedness to the latter is not textually evident. The author of ***The Kingis Quair*** and his Scottish successors have been called the "true disciples" of Chaucer, but often, it must be suspected, without clear recognition of this deep literary appreciation on which their historical position is chiefly based. (pp. 276-77)

G. Gregory Smith, "The Scottish Chaucerians," in The Cambridge History of English Literature: The End of the Middle Ages, Vol. II, *edited by A. W. Ward and A. R. Waller, G. P. Putnam's Sons, 1908, pp. 272-303.*

Owen Barfield (essay date 1921)

[*Barfield is considered by many scholars one of the most underrated men of letters in twentieth-century English literature. An Anthroposophical and Christian philosopher and a close friend of C. S. Lewis, who called him the "wisest and best of my unofficial teachers," Barfield is the author of respected works in many literary genres. His* Poetic Diction *(1929) is considered one of the seminal texts on literary language, while his* Saving the Appearances *(1957) is deemed perhaps the preeminent seminal text on the evolution of consciousness. In the following excerpt, he examines James's improvements of Chaucer and claims that the poetry of the Scottish Chaucerians is superior to that of the English.*]

I often wonder why Boswell never confronted Dr. Johnson with the contrast between the English and Scottish Chaucerians; probably it was because he had never heard of them. No doubt, if he had done so, Johnson would have invented some way of accounting for it, yet it is strange that the poetry of Lydgate and Hoccleve should be so unmemorable beside that of James I., Dunbar and Henryson. I say "unmemorable," because this article is founded on memory rather than criticism. I read them all some time ago, and I find now that some voices still echo and some pictures still remain; others do not.

Chaucer's two English followers are little more than names to me. Lydgate's voice I do not hear at all, save inarticulately, and Hoccleve's only lamenting the loss of Chaucer's "rethorik" and taking last leave of his master with:

> O Maister, Maister, God thy soule reste!

a line which seems to ring across five hundred years with a peculiar sharpness of utterance, because the stanzas it concludes are (for me) such lonely survivors of their author's pen.

It is very different with the Scotch poets, who can never—like the two Englishmen—have known him personally, who lived so many miles away, and who were so much nearer to him in spirit. James I., Dunbar, and Henryson (I omit Gavin Douglas) may be a little known to the average reader through anthologies such as the *Oxford Book of English Verse,* but they are worthy of a very much closer acquaintance, and just as their lines scan better than Lydgate's or Hoccleve's, so are their personalities much more clearly defined in the memory. James I. of Scotland lived a romantic life, and the appeal of ***The King's Quair*** is inevitably heightened by the circumstances under which he wrote it and (with all due respect to His Majesty) by the seeming incongruity of his two claims to fame. The story it tells is true; it was begun in prison, where the English had confined him, and in the poem he describes how, as he tossed one night on the prison bed, the idea came to him to write—how the next morning, looking from the window of his cell, he saw a lady walking in the garden below:

> For quhich sodayne abate, anon asterte
> The blude of all my body to my herte.

How much less melodramatic than Chaucer's description of Palamon:

> And ther-with-al he bleynte and cryde "a"!
> As though he stongen were unto the herte.

and how much better!

The lady was Joan Beaufort, whom he afterwards married, and he seems to have spent the rest of his confinement in writing his long, half-personal, half-allegorical poem, ***The King's Quair.*** He evidently did not finish it till after his release and marriage, and once near the end he says:

> And thus, this floure, I can saye yow no more,
> So hertly hath unto my help attendit
> That fro the deth her man sche has defendit.

History, too, says that on one occasion before his final assassination, Joan saved his life; but the poem is full of such personal touches.

The whole poem is modelled on Chaucer. It has innumerable reminiscences of *Troilus and Criseyde,* which James obviously knew well, since he uses the same metre and is not above transcribing passages, which he sometimes improves. Thus for Chaucer's

> O wery gost, that errest to and fro,
> Why n'iltow flen out of the wofulleste
> Body that evere mighte on grounde go?
> O soule, lurking in this wo, unneste!

he transcribes

> O besy goste, ay flickering to and fro,
> That never art in quiet nor in rest,
> Till thou cum to that place that thou cam fro,
> Quhich is thy first and verray proper nest.

James must also have known the *Romaunt of the Rose* pretty well, and the whole poem is saturated with that "Rose" tradition, which took such hold of the mediæval imagination. It is summed up in the first line of the Bird's Song in ***The King's Quair:***

> Worschippe ye that loveris bene this May,

and there are a thousand echoes of Chaucer in that one line.

All ages have their literary conventions, and the "Rose" tradition, with its exaggerated humility and reverence for women, treated mechanically, is as dull and lifeless as any other, but when genuine passion enters into and works in

An excerpt from the *Kingis Quair*

> Can I not ellis fynd bot giff that he
> Be lord, and as a god may lyve and regne,
> To bynd and louse, and makin thrallis free,
> Than wold I pray his blissful grace benigne
> To hable me unto his service digue,
> And evermore for to be one of tho
> Him trewly for to serve in wele and wo.
>
> And therewith kest I down myn eye ageyne
> Quhare as I saw walkyng under the toure,
> Full secretly, new-cumyn hir to pleyne,
> The fairest or the freschest zoung floure
> That ever I sawe, methocht, before that houre
> For quhich sodayne abate, anon asterte
> The blude of all my body to my hert.
>
> And though I stood abaisit tho a lyte,
> No wonder was: for quhy? my wittis all
> Were so ouercome with plesance and delyte,
> Only through latting of myn eyen fall,
> That sudaynly my hert become hir thrall
> For ever of free wyll; for of menace
> There was no takyn in her suete face.
>
> And in my hede I drew ryght hastily,
> And eft sones I lent it forth ageyne,
> And saw hir walk that verray womanly
> With no wight mo but only women tueyne:
> Than gan I studye in myself and seyne,
> Ah suete! are ze a wardly creature,
> Or hevingly thing in likenesse of Nature?—
>
> Quhen I a lytill thrawe had maid my mone,
> Bewailing myn infortune and my chance,
> Unknawin how or quhat was best to done,
> So ferre I fallyng into lufis dance,
> That sodeynly my wit, my countenance,
> My hert, my will, my nature, and my mind,
> Was changit clene ryght in ane other kind.
>
> Of hir array the form gif I sal write,
> Toward her goldin haire and rich atyre
> In fretwise couchit with perlis quhite,
> And grete balas lemyng as the fyre,
> With mony ane emerant and saphire,
> And on hir hede a chaplet fresch of hewe,
> Of plumys partit rede, and quhite, and blewe;
>
> Full of quaking spangis bryght as gold,
> Forgit of schap like to the amorettis,
> So new, so fresch, so pleasant to behold,
> The plumys eke like to the floure jonettis,
> And other of schap, like to the floure jonettis.
> And, above all this, there-was, wele I wote,
> Beautee eneuch to mak a world to dote.

James I of Scotland, in his The Kingis Quair, *edited by John Norton-Smith, Clarendon Press, 1971.*

it, when the poet, if only for a moment, has lived as well as written in the tradition, it gives forth a lovely sweet tone not heard anywhere else and probably never to be heard again. (pp. 273-74)

Owen Barfield, "The Scottish Chaucerians," in New Statesman, *Vol. XVII, No. 426, June 11, 1921, pp. 273-74.*

C. S. Lewis (essay date 1936)

[Lewis is considered one of the foremost Christian and mythopoeic authors of the twentieth century. Indebted principally to George MacDonald, G. K. Chesterton, Charles Williams, and the writers of ancient Norse myths, he is regarded as a formidable logician and Christian polemicist, a perceptive literary critic, and—perhaps most highly—as a writer of fantasy literature. Also a noted academic and scholar, Lewis held posts at Oxford and Cambridge, where he was an acknowledged authority on medieval and Renaissance literature. A traditionalist in his approach to life and art, he opposed the modern critical movement toward biographical and psychological interpretation, preferring to practice and propound a theory of criticism that stresses the author's intent rather than the reader's presuppositions and prejudices. In the following excerpt from the 1936 edition of The Allegory of Love: A Study in Medieval Tradition, *Lewis discusses the* Kingis Quair *as a poem about real rather than allegorical love and concludes that "it is the first modern book of love" because it advocates the ideal of Christian marriage over the glorification of adultery which was traditional in medieval romances.]*

The importance of [***The Kingis Quair***] does not lie in the fact that it introduced the Chaucerian manner into Scotland. Its importance lies in the fact that it is a new kind of poem—a longish narrative poem about love which is not allegorical, which is not even, like *Troilus* [*and Criseyde*], a romance of lovers who lived long ago, but the literal story of a passion felt by the author for a real woman. It is true that the poem contains a dream, and even an allegorical dream; but the difference between a dream framed in a literal story and an allegorical story framed in a dream is of considerable importance. What makes the novelty even more surprising is the fact that the author seems to be well aware of what he is doing. Careless reading has obscured the fact that the poem opens with what is really a literary preface. The author, after reading Boethius too late at night, falls into a meditation upon Fortune, and reflects

> In tender youth how sche was first my fo,
> And eft my frende . . .

and well he might, if, as the story tells us, he was once a solitary prisoner, and is now a free man and an accepted lover. It is at this point that a brilliantly original idea occurred to him, a novelty that struck with such unpredicted resonance on his mind that the easiest imaginative projection sufficed to identify it with the matin bell striking that same moment in the objective world. As he says

> me thocht the bell
> Said to me, *Tell on man quhat thee befell.*

In our own language, the author, who had long desired to write but spent much ink and paper 'to lyte effect', had suddenly perceived that his own story, even as it stood in real life, might pass without disguise into poetry. He had heard the same voice that called Sidney 'Fool!', bidding him 'Look in thy heart and write'; and making a cross in his old manuscript to distinguish the new dispensation from all his previous attempts, he sat down to write what most emphatically deserves to be called 'sum newe thing'. The authorship of the poem has been disputed, but the dispute need not concern us. Whether the story is taken from the poet's life or from the life of another, the originality of thus telling it at all remains. It is true that the inspiration fails before the end, but the poem is full of beauty and the passage in which the lady is seen from the window is at least as good as its analogue in the *Knights Tale.* The differences between the two are significant. When Palamon sees Emelye his hue becomes 'pale and deedly on to see', and he complains that he has a hurt 'that wol his bane be'. The Scottish poet, in the same predicament, is equally 'abaisit', but he explains that it is because his

> wittis all
> Were so overcome with plesance and delyte.

Again, though both lovers become equally the captives of their ladies, it is only the Scot who says

> sudaynly my hert became hir thrall
> For ever, of free wyll.

In this beautiful oxymoron we see how nature has taught the poet to feel and to express both sides of the complex experience where Chaucer wrote in a tradition that invited him to see only one of them. And so also, even where the two poets approximate most, Palamon cries merely 'as though he *stongen* were unto the herte', and the image is one of pain; the later prisoner says

> anon astert
> The blude of all my body to my hert

recording with singular fidelity that first sense of shock which is common to all vivid emotions as they arise and which transcends the common antithesis of pain and pleasure. In a word, Chaucer for the moment is not looking beyond the lachrymose and dejecting aspects of love which the tradition has made so familiar; the Scottish poet, here far more realistic, telling 'what him befell', recalls us to the essential geniality, the rejuvenating and health-giving virtues of awakened passion, and having thus first presented them directly, goes on to give them that symbolic expression which they demand, in his lyrical address to the nightingale,

> lo here thy golden houre
> That worth were hale all thy lives laboure.

Chaucer himself, and all medieval love poets, had excelled in painting the peace and *solempne* festivity of fruition: but it needed this later and minor poet to remind us that Aphrodite even in her first appearance, when all the future is dark and the present unsatisfied, is still the golden, the laughter-loving goddess. Such is the reward of his literalism, his Scotch fidelity to the hard fact. And this fidelity has another, perhaps a stranger, result. As love-longing becomes more cheerful it also becomes more moral. His Aphrodite loves laughter, but she is a temperate, nay a christened, Aphrodite. There is no question in his poem of adultery, and no trace of the traditional bias against marriage. On the contrary, Venus refers the poet to Minerva, and Minerva will not help him without the assurance that his love is grounded in God's law and set 'in cristin wise'.

About the absolute merits of this little poem we are at liberty to disagree; but we must not misunderstand its historical importance. In it the poetry of marriage at last emerges from the traditional poetry of adultery; and the literal narrative of a contemporary wooing emerges from romance and allegory. It is the first modern book of love. (pp. 235-37)

C. S. Lewis, "Allegory as the Dominant Form," in his The Allegory of Love: A Study in Medieval Tradition, *1936. Reprint by Oxford University Press, London, 1959, pp. 232-96.*

W. Mackay Mackenzie (essay date 1939)

[*In the following excerpt, Mackenzie discusses the* Kingis Quair *in relation to fifteenth-century poetry.*]

The personal nature of the [***Kingis Quair***] undoubtedly tends to the identification of the author with the King, but this judgment is strongly reinforced by the perception that the poem is at its best just where his reputed part is most in evidence—in his imprisonment, his view of the lady, his devotion and final triumph. All this comes with a directness and fervour of emotion that, by association, convey a more lively air even to the staid and conventional matter of the dream.

This characteristic has rightly been stressed and cannot be gainsaid. Of itself, however, it need not be biographical. It may but show how much of an artist the poet was, aiming at and securing just such an effect, fired, too, by the knowledge that this prisoner's case was a real one, not of the sort that other poets had feigned. The reader might claim the qualities mentioned for such a moving line as

> Beautee eneuch to mak a world to dote,

did we not know that already in John Lydgate's *Temple of Glas* had come,

> A world of beaute compassed in her face,

and that, later, in *The Assembly of Ladies* occurs

> It was a world to loke on her visage,

showing this phrasing of eulogy to be current poetic coin.

Where we do get an individual note is in the reaction to love at first sight. Hitherto that had been conventionally of a somewhat painful character. In the *Knight's Tale* (Chaucer) 'Palamon' in such a case becomes 'pale and deedly on to see', while, in his turn, Arcite 'is hurt as moche as he, or moore'. But in the ***Quair*** the hero is 'abaisit' only for a little and only because his wits

> Were so ouercom with plesance and delyte
> . . . . .
> That sudaynly my hert became hir thrall
> For ever of free will.

This is something new in such a context, a contribution of a personal kind—qualities not to be normally expected in mediaeval literature, apart from such a genius as Chaucer. Imitation rather than novelty was the general practice. There was a body of doctrine as to themes and treatment, and the spirit of it is implicit in the identification of poetry and rhetoric, as in st. 197. Much of the ***Quair*** thus follows the established mode. The wakeful night, the prelude to the actual start of the poem, the prisoner viewing the lady, the dream leading to the description of the mythological courts, the close in a summing up of the lessons of the work—all this was in the manner of many other poems before and after. Not artistic self-subsistence nor psychological truth was the mediaeval aim, but a fresh handling of given subjects mainly in the way of literary ornament, with the adducing of similar cases to that in hand, wise or proverbial sayings, and a didactic leaven. Yet it is the mediaeval writers who gave being to that imaginative, mystic treatment of love of which the ***Quair*** is a notable example.

In all this it would be impossible to over-rate the influence of Chaucer, for his successors the master poet, though not perhaps in his most original vein. His very phraseology seemed that of the Muse and of itself inspired imitation. It is a main ingredient of the ***Quair,*** in which the Scottish author [as Walter W. Skeat explains in his introduction to the ***Kingis Quair,***] 'often adopts many of the inflections of the Midland dialect of Chaucer', the result being a 'purely artificial dialect, such as probably was never spoken', or, as the same writer describes it elsewhere, 'a mixed jargon of Northern and Chaucerian English'.

How this peculiarity is to be accounted for has been discussed on the line of how much of the Scottish tongue James may be presumed to have kept from his boyhood, and how much English he must have acquired during his imprisonment, overlooking the qualification that the English he would hear and might speak would not be the Chaucerian language of the ***Quair,*** still less what is mock-Chaucerian. This mechanical formula is both inadequate and unnecessary.

For one thing it cannot account for like characteristics of language in the case of other Scottish poems of that century, such as *The Quare of Jealousy* and *Lancelot of the Laik,* both written in the same sort of artificial dialect, unless, as it has been speculated, all three were written by the same poet.

This possibility has been disputed, but that does not affect the matter of the peculiar nature of the language in all three, whatever minor differences there may be.

To these parallel Scottish cases may be added others from England displaying, in their degree, somewhat similar modes, such as once led to their being attributed, quite wrongly, to Chaucer himself—*The Flower and the Leaf* and *The Assembly of Ladies,* with their [in the words of Skeat] 'archaic embellishment', and *The Court of Love,* where the 'archaisms are affectations and not natural', and with respect to which Skeat admits for the author 'the certainty that he consulted the ***Kingis Quair***'. All three poems are in the metre of the ***Quair***—the rhyme-royal stanza of seven lines—and are anonymous.

These considerations put the case in a different light. None of these poets wrote in a living speech but more or less in what he took to be the language of the master, Chaucer, who had fixed a norm of poetic expression, which itself to some extent was archaic and literary. The language of the ***Quair*** is thus not due to the accidents of the life of King James; it is but one example of a practice illustrated, more or less, in the works of a group of poets in the later fifteenth century, all profoundly influenced by and imitative of Chaucer. The writer was not intruding a word or inflection as it occurred to him; he was consciously composing in a merely pen language with snatches of phrase or even lines taken over directly from his great model. The real issue thus comes to be, where in this group the ***Kingis Quair*** is to be placed and what are its relationships to the others?

The common bond in Chaucer is patent: the English poems in question were once attributed to him as a matter of course. Another link is in Lydgate's *Temple of Glas.* 'As far as I am aware,' wrote Professor Schick, 'the two poems that bear the greatest family-likeness to the *Temple of Glas* are the *Court of Love* and the ***Kingis Quair.***'

The debt to Lydgate is accepted. Most strange, therefore, is it that the author of the ***Quair*** does not name him in his concluding stanza, where instead he finds a place for Gower, with whose work no specific connections have been established. On the other hand, the *Temple* was one of Lydgate's most popular productions and survives in many MSS. But in time his poems tended to be confused with those of Chaucer, which must be the explanation of the omission of his name in the ***Quair.*** Such confusion, however, seems unlikely in Lydgate's life-time, and he outlived King James by a dozen years; least likely for the poet of the ***Quair*** if he had lived for eighteen years in England, had come 'under the influence of its reviving literature', and wrote in 1423.

The case of *The Court of Love* is more complex. Its bearing upon the ***Quair*** was noted in the first printed edition of that poem, when *The Court of Love* was still thought to be by Chaucer. A century or so later Mr Wood could speak of it as one of the pieces connected with ***The Kingis Quair,*** having been among those 'used to obtain the necessary poetical apparatus, the material used for filling in'. Came Dr Brown with his argument that the ***Quair*** was actually dependent upon *The Court of Love* for much of its material and was therefore of later date. To this Skeat opposed his plea that the date of the ***Quair*** was 1423, which we have seen to be irreconcilable with the poem itself, while as to *The Court of Love* he has 'no doubt at all that the true date of the latter is about 1533'. [W. A. Neilson] thought his arguments for that date not 'very cogent', and preferred 'about the end of the first quarter of the sixteenth century', a difference which, for the present purpose, is no great matter: either way *The Court of Love* would definitely be the much later poem. Yet Schick held that as to author and 'exact date . . . we are so sorely puzzled', and for Saintsbury the dates suggested 'some half century or even three quarters of a century later' than 'about the middle of the fifteenth century' are 'admittedly guess-work'.

The problem of some relationship between the poems remains. The passages relied upon by Dr. Brown may be hardily dismissed as mediaeval poetical commonplaces or as mutually derived from Chaucer and Lydgate. But even this critic has to confess that 'it is not easy to deny absolutely a connection between the poems'. Skeat, as quoted above, is more precise.

Avoiding ambiguous resemblances we may offer just a few in which some definite link seems to be implied.

In *The Court of Love* is a long, detailed list of the statutes of that institution, elaborating for the most part traditional material. But of two of these statutes it has to be confessed that there exist no other parallels than certain passages in the ***Quair.*** Their record is confined to the two poems in question.

In the ***Quair*** some rather surprising language is put into the mouth of Venus. She addresses her visitor as 'Yong man'. Now King James in 1424 was twenty-nine years of age, which, if 'young' to-day—and that is questionable—was certainly not so in the fifteenth century. She then goes on to mark the disparity between the lovers:

> And yit, considering the nakitness
>   Both of thy wit, thy persone, and thy myght
> It is no mach of thyne unworthyness
>   To hir hye birth, estate, and beautee bryght.

The closing line is surely an incredible statement coming from one presumed to be a King of Scots speaking of the daughter of an Earl, even though an Earl of royal blood. Her birth could not be 'high' in the sense that his was relatively low, while her 'estate' or social standing was admittedly inferior to that of a King: no one in the fifteenth century would have any doubt as to that, and least of all a King of Scots. True, no rank is mentioned on either side, but the poet calculates upon readers, and these, it is clear, were ready to identify the parties. What then is the point of this stringent humility? The hyperbole of a lover is no answer, if the lover was conscious of its absurdity and knew that others would be aware of it. The irony of the respective positions of the parties is contained in the fact that the lady's grandfather was the eldest of the family of John of Gaunt by Katherine Swinford, and that, though the family had been legitimated, it had been barred from the royal succession.

Now in *The Court of Love* we have the lines in analogous circumstances:

> Thy birth and hers [they] be nothing egall
>
> . . . .
>
> And eik remember thy habilite
>   May not compare with hir, etc.
>
> (ll. 1041, 1044-5)

Here the utterance is quite congruous, marking the disparity between the lady and one who was only 'Of Cambridge clerk' (l.913). It is not mere commonplace, but could be the result of the other poet's presumed 'consultation' of the ***Quair,*** if that was the way of it.

One more case, special in character, must suffice here. Stanza 117 opens with the line,

> And quhen I wepe, and stynten othir quhile,

Obviously bad grammar, since it combines a singular subject with a verb 'stynten' in the plural form. In his first edition Skeat found this misadventure 'quite explicable; it is a translation into Chaucerian language of the Northern word *styntis*', which would be correct in Scots for a verb separated from its subject. By 1911, however, he had substituted a more ingenious accommodation, now printing 'stynt anothir quhile', an emendation, he explains, due to Dr Brown, but which was also independently suggested by [Walter] Wischmann. Now, observe the implications of this course. It is to be assumed that the scribe coming on the word 'stynt', which he had already transcribed correctly in stanzas 53 and 104, thought it proper to detach the first syllable from the word following, change the spelling, and add it to the verb, thus producing a perfectly abnormal construction. Such malpractice is hard to accept. The malevolence of scribes went scarcely to such a length. Nor is the claim [by Wischmann] that 'another quhile' is the adverbial phrase required here, or Skeat's explanation that it means 'at another time, or afterwards', to be accepted. The tears of Venus are the rain, and the idea therefore is not that of a single happening but of a recurrence of the phenomena of weeping and ceasing from time to time, that is 'other quhile' not 'anothir quhile', which would limit us to one set of alternatives.

The strange thing is that no remark has been made upon the circumstance that this false concord of singular subject and plural verb is a peculiar feature of *The Court of Love,* where, for example, we get,

> That goddes chaste I kepen in no wyse
> To serve (ll. 684-5),

and

> For if by me this matter springen out (l. 725).

As Skeat says, 'This cannot be the fault of the scribe.' On what ground, then, is a precisely similar deviation from rectitude in ***The Kingis Quair*** made a scribal offence?

Resemblances rather more than verbal with other poems of the kind might also call for remark. Thus the 'herbere grene' in st. 31 is in its main characteristic of privacy similar to that of *The Flower and The Leaf,* as may be seen in the quotation given in the note to the passage. The particular feature also distinguishes the garden in *Lancelot.* The dress of the lady, too, has details found in *The Assembly of Ladies,* where, however, it gets a fuller description. The date of the English poems is as speculative as that of *The Court of Love,* if not even more so.

Significant for the ***Quair*** are its departures from the traditional treatment of the theme of courtly love. This is no old-world story, like *Troilus and Criseyde,* but one of contemporary life, in which the personages could actually be identified. Nor is it of the so favoured allegorical class, in which not living men and women but the personifications of their desires, impulses, fears, manners, etc., are the actors on the stage of a dream. The dream in the ***Quair*** is incidental to the narrative, not its framework, and the lovers are flesh and blood. Further—and a most important development—the end and sphere of its love is marriage. There is pity for those barred, against their will, from this happy state by a premature vow of celibacy, or yoked in a disastrous union, or robbed of their mates by early death. But in the older manner, under the feudal custom of marriage for territorial or political advantage only, love was accepted as even normally outside the matrimonial tie. All this is changed, and Lydgate had got as far as recognizing the unhappy cases mentioned above. But in the ***Quair*** the reconciliation of love and marriage is achieved. [In the words of C. S. Lewis in *The Allegory of Love,*] 'In it the poetry of marriage at last emerges from the traditional poetry of adultery; and the literal narrative of a contemporary wooing emerges from romance and allegory. It is the first modern book of love.' (pp. 26-38)

W. Mackay Mackenzie, "The King's Quair," in The Kingis Quair *by James I, edited by W. Mackay Mackenzie, Faber & Faber Limited, 1939, pp. 11-42.*

H. S. Bennett (essay date 1947)

[In the following excerpt, Bennett discusses James's experimentation with the Chaucerian style and the question of authorship of the Kingis Quair.]

The chronicle poets . . . belonged essentially to a fast dying state of society. While it was laudable to commemorate in song the exploits of past heroes, much that was of interest lay outside this field, and here the powerful influence of Chaucer and his disciples was of great moment. Both in matter and form English poets were laid under contribution, and outstanding among poems written in the 'Chaucerian' tradition is the ***Kingis Quair.*** That its author owes much to a study of Chaucer cannot be doubted. In places Chaucer's situations are closely copied, in others it is Chaucer's phrasing that is followed. The Chaucerian seven-line stanza (which takes its name 'rhyme royal' from this poem) is adopted, and the poem concludes with a recommendation of the work to 'my maisteris dere, Gowere and Chaucere'. Gower's influence is less marked, but that of Lydgate's *Temple of Glass* is clear enough at times. More important still, the whole work is an allegorical love poem, complete with dream, with interviews with Venus, Minerva, and Fortune, and tricked out with much well-known detail made familiar by the *Romance of the Rose.* In spite of all this it is an original work. In taking over all these stock elements the author has refused to be overcome by them. He uses them for his own purpose and often as freshly as if they had never been used before. The all-important moment of the first sight of the beloved has never been more admirably stated than in the poet's words:

> And therwith kest I doun myn eye ageyne,
> Quhare as I sawe, walking under the toure,
> Full secretly new cummyn hir to pleyne,
> The fairest or the freschest yong floure
> That ever I sawe, me thoght, before that houre,
> For quhich sodayn abate, anon astert

The blude of all my body to my hert.

It is also an original work in its attitude to its subject-matter. Here the lover's suit to the lady finds its consummation in marriage, not in 'courtly love'. The lover is closely questioned by Minerva, who agrees to help him only when he has convinced her that 'in vertew [his] lufe is set with treuth', and that it is 'ground and set in Cristin wis'. Although the poet makes use of a well-worn literary form, he gives it a life of its own because he uses it to tell (or seem to tell) his own story. From the moment he sets out to obey the injunction 'Tell on, man, quhat the befel', the poem has a personal note, and the verses often have an intensity of feeling rarely met with in medieval poetry. The poet is an artist in words. He piles up his adjectives and nouns but makes them effective:

With new fresche suete and tender grene,
Oure lyf, oure lust, oure governoure, oure quene.

He uses the artifices of the rhetoricians with skill, as in the lines above, and as in:

My wele in wo, my frendis all in fone,
  My lyf in deth, my lyght into derkness,
  My hope in feer, in dout my sekirness,
Sen sche is gone: and God mote hir convoye,
  That me may gyde to turment and to joye!

At times he falls back on a cliché: 'the colde stone', 'the rokkes blak', but he is capable of 'a turtur quhite as calk', or of speaking of the fish 'with bakkis blewe as lede', and comparing their bright scales to the glitter of a suit of armour ('That in the sonne on thair scalis bryght As gesserant ay glitterit in my sight'). The management of the stanza and the lyrical quality of many passages denote the work of one who has studied his masters with attention and has gone on to strike out his own music.

Who wrote the ***Kingis Quair***? The scribe who finished copying the unique manuscript now in the Bodleian (MS. Arch. Selden B. 24) wrote at the end of the poem 'Quod Jacobus Primus, Scotorum Rex Illustrissimus', while on a blank space opposite the third stanza of the poem a different hand from any in the manuscript has written: 'Heirefter followis the quair Maid be King James of Scotland ye first callit ye Kingis quair and maid qn his Ma. was In Ingland.' The writer of this second note gives us the title of the poem, which is not stated elsewhere, and also says that it was composed by James while in England. James I of Scotland was a prisoner in England for many years, and the story of the poem parallels in many ways his wooing of Joan Beaufort and marriage. Although attempts have been made to find an author for the poem other than James, these have not been generally accepted. The case for King James has recently been strengthened by Sir William Craigie, who has argued convincingly that the Scottish linguistic features were probably added by scribes, such as the writer of Selden B. 24, and that the poem was originally written in post-Chaucerian Southern English by an author in close touch with the language which he wrote and able to use it correctly. It is highly unlikely that this would have been possible to anyone whose connexions and training were purely Scottish. On the other hand, as Sir William says, 'accepting King James as the author, everything becomes normal and natural; eighteen years' residence in English surroundings, added to an acquaintance with the works of Gower and Chaucer, and no doubt of contemporary English poets, would be amply sufficient to qualify him as a competent maker of poetry after these models'. (pp. 170-73)

H. S. Bennett, "Fifteenth-Century Verse," in his Chaucer and the Fifteenth-Century, *Oxford at the Clarendon Press, 1947, pp. 124-76.*

John Preston (essay date 1956)

[*In the following essay, Preston rejects biographical interpretations of the* Kingis Quair *and suggests that its focus is its allegory about Fortune.*]

Most of the comment on ***The Kingis Quair*** has centred on the question of its authorship. The implication has been that the use of autobiographical material puts the poem on a different footing from other medieval love poems. Even C. S. Lewis, whose account [in *The Allegory of Love,* 1936,] can only lead to fuller understanding and appreciation, takes this view: 'the literal narrative of a contemporary wooing emerges from romance and allegory. It is the first modern book of love.' How fundamentally misleading this approach is becomes clear from the more extended statement by W. Mackay Mackenzie [in his edition of ***The Kingis Quair***]:

> Significant for the ***Quair*** are its departures from the traditional treatment of the theme of courtly love. This is no old-world story, like *Troilus and Criseyde,* but one of contemporary life, in which the personages could actually be identified. Nor is it of the so favoured allegorical class, in which not men and women, but the personifications of their desires, impulses, fears, manners, etc., are the actors on the stage of a dream. The dream in the ***Quair*** is incidental to the narrative not its framework, and the lovers are flesh and blood.

This is certainly wide of the mark. The significance of the poem is that it does not depart at all in essentials from the courtly love tradition. It is certainly no 'old-world story' (nor, of course, is *Troilus*); on the other hand the characters are no more contemporary and identifiable than, say, Blanche or the man in black.

The Kingis Quair must be read with the allegorical tradition in mind. Interest then shifts from the romantic narrative to the way in which this answers the needs of the poem's developing thought. Personal experience dominates general problems; a philosophy of life is achieved by meeting and resolving personal predicaments. Many levels and kinds of experience from the reading of Boethius to the playing out of a romantic adventure are combined in the poem. That James achieved this is due not so much to any unusual poetic gift as to the fact that he wrote in so strong and rich a tradition.

This is not to say that he left that tradition unmodified. When Chaucer uses the dream allegory, for instance, he seems to be unaware of what is happening. He seems to leave the reader to work out for himself the pattern that makes a whole of the separate parts of his poem, the reading, the allegorical visions, and so forth. He poses as a person through whom the truth is for a moment revealed and then, except for a cryptic record which even he does not properly understand, lost again. At the end of the *Parlement of Foules* he returns to perplexity and the barren search for understanding:

> I wok, and othere bokes tok me to
> To reede upon, and yit I rede alway.
>
> (ll. 695-6)

The uselessness of this earnest endeavour stresses that the poet is to cultivate an alert passivity so that he may be ready when the moment comes to record faithfully what he is shown. His guide in the *Parlement of Foules* says to him,

> And if thow haddest connynge for t'endite,
> I shal the shewe mater of to wryte.
>
> (ll. 167-8)

We shall see how at the end of ***The Kingis Quair*** James uses the traditional return to an unsatisfactory normal vision in a new and dramatically effective way. For the moment it is necessary to see that James also brings a new attitude to the co-ordinating pattern of the poem. Instead of insisting on his unconsciousness of imaginative structure he is very much alive to the interrelation of the different parts of the poem. He consciously manipulates the Chaucerian technique, using it as a method to express something already fully apprehended rather than an attitude of mind necessary to the peculiar sort of investigation he is making. This does not mean that James could have presented his full and complex meaning better or even as well in any other way. Yet the greater sophistication in his work is apparent at once: the reading of the book focuses his attention, not on the thoughts by which he is at present disturbed, but on the memory of those that are now past and overcome. The poem is in fact wholly retrospective; it is to tell 'what befell' the poet; it is to be concerned with the development from childhood to maturity of an individual. In the early stages of the poem James weaves together two strands of meaning (the comment on Boethius and on his own state of mind as a boy) and adds yet another (the difficulty of writing about it all) to produce a closeness of texture typical of the whole. This increased density in the imaginative scheme does not obscure three main divisions roughly corresponding to the normal divisions of the dream allegory. The first is concerned with the reading of the book; the second deals with the poet's own experience, which in this case takes the form of a narrative about his early life; the third part, still in the form of a reminiscence, is an account of the dream in which the problems posed by his early experience were resolved.

The reading in Boethius is used partly to introduce James's narrative and partly to establish the themes to be dealt with in the poem. Mackenzie explains this opening sequence as an account of a fate opposite to James's own:

> This leads him to meditate upon the uncertainty of fortune and his own experience, the reverse of that which his noble author had suffered at her hands . . . after a calamitous beginning he is now a happy man, in contrast with Boece, whose fate had gone the opposite way.

A more careful reading of the text is clearly necessary. What chiefly concerns the poet is not Boethius's misfortune but the way in which he overcame it: 'how he, in his poetly report, / In philosophy can him to confort' (st. 4). This history is introduced as an exact parallel to James's own experience: 'nature', he says, 'gave me suffisance in youth' (st. 16) but Fortune became his foe before he was out of this 'tender youth'—his first knowledge of love, that is, brought only 'axis and turment' (st. 67)—and he gained final relief by coming to understand (as Boethius did) the part played by Fortune in the scheme of things. The only difference is that Boethius spoke generally of all experience, whilst James limits his account to the particular experience of love. But James implies all through the poem that this is central to life and that with the full understanding of it goes the understanding of the rest of life; and this view leads to the beautiful restatement of the values of courtly love in Venus's speech, where they are closely related to the divine and natural laws.

For the moment, however, Boethius's history is necessary to help James to arrive at a full consciousness of the issues involved in his experience. Until his reading brought them to the surface there was nothing in what had happened to him that he needed or was able to communicate. It is the Boethian pattern that suggests the pattern his own life has taken: 'I shal the shewe mater of to wryte.'

Further, it is important to note that Boethius's recovery was attained precisely through an acceptance of his misfortune: 'in tham' (his misfortune, poverty, and distress) he 'set his verray sekerness' (his true security). This was only possible because his character was based on a virtuous youth; from it he derived the strength to abandon the 'unsekir warldis appetitis' which alone could make exile distressful:

> And so aworth he takith his penance,
> And of his vertew maid it suffisance.
>
> (st. 6)

James's reflections on the security born of insecurity, the happiness discovered through distress, are clearly meant to be supported by the centrally important discussion of Fortune in the *De Consolatione.* In referring us to the source of his ideas he is also able to imply a fuller and more formal statement of them than he is able to afford at this stage in the poem:

> For I deme that contrarious Fortune profiteth more to men than Fortune debonayre. For alwey, whan Fortune semeth debonayre, thanne sche lieth, falsly byhetynge the hope of welefulnesse; but forsothe contraryous Fortune is alwey sothfast, whan sche scheweth hirself unstable thurw hir chaungynge.
>
> Whoso it be that is cleer of vertu, sad and wel ordynat of lyvynge, that hath put under fote the proude weerdes and loketh, upright, upon either fortune, he may holden his chere undesconfited.

James has invited the reader's attention to this conception, but he now shelves it for the moment and turns to a more commonplace view of uncertainty and insecurity; 'that eche estate, / As fortune lykith, thame will translate' (st.

8). But the general comment is an introduction to James's own history. The threat is greater to the young man; the happiness of youth is not certainly assured; it is an illusory well-being founded on inexperience and immaturity and unable to survive the giddy reverses of chance:

> Thus stant thy confort in unsekerness,
> And wantis it that suld the reule and gye:
> Ryght as the schip that sailith stereles
> Upon the rok(kis) most to harmes hye,
> For lak of it that suld bene hir supplye.
> (st. 15)

'I mene this by myself as in partye', James continues; and it is obvious that the images he chooses relate to his own narrative. What is perhaps more important is that it also recalls Boethius's language:

> Allas how the thought of man, dreynt in overthrowynge depnesse, dulleth and forleteth his propre clernesse, myntynge to gon into foreyne dirknesses as ofte as his anoyos bysynes waxeth withoute mesure, that is dryven to and fro with werldly wyndes.

What is more, the image turns out to be relevant not only to his experience as a youth but also to his sense of unfitness for the imaginative labour.

This is a synthesis which should reveal at once the inadequacy of any approach attaching importance only to the literal historical fact. An account of the narrative which forms the second part of the poem will show to what extent it has the force of symbol and contributes to the whole imaginative scheme.

In the attempt to trace the gradual achievement of some final stability in which human experience will no longer seem disturbing or perplexing, the personal narrative is used to give immediacy and realism. And yet the narrative at once reveals itself as an allegorical as well as a literal statement; the metaphorical pattern already established is now fused with the story in a highly assured interpenetration of dramatic realism and symbolism:

> With mony 'fare wele' and 'Sanct Iohne to borowe'
> Off falowe and frende; and thus with one assent
> We pullit up saile, and furth oure wayis went.
>
> Upon the wawis weltering to and fro,
> So infortunate was us that fremyt day, . . .
> [that] Off inymyis takin and led away
> We weren all, and broght in thair contree;
> Fortune it schupe non othir wayis to be.
> (sts. 23-24)

The subsequent account of his imprisonment brings us to the central image of impotence proceeding from inexperience. Till now the youth has been 'like to the bird that fed is on the nest / And can noght flee' (st. 14); now he finds himself aware of a fuller life and yet still unable to participate in it:

> The bird, the beste, the fisch eke in the see,
> They lyve in fredome everich in his kynd;
> And I a man, and lakkith libertee.
> (st. 27)

This refers to something more than the physical imprisonment; from his window the poet can look into the garden where the nightingale sings of love and the birds rejoice that they have won their mates. But, 'as it semyt to a lyf without, / The bewis spred the herber all about' (st. 32); the boughs still hide the garden from view; knowledge of love is still denied and there is still incredulity:

> Quhat lyf is this, that makis birdis dote? . . .
> It is nothing, trowe I, bot feynit chere,
> And that men list to counterfeten chere.
> (st. 36)

This, with its echoes of Troilus's taunts at love and the easily vulnerable immaturity that produced them, makes it clear that whatever the possibility of James's narrative being literally true it is here offered primarily as a typical courtly love situation. Without sacrificing anything of its dramatic realism James has made the episode a perfect image of still adolescent and unfocused feelings about love.

But the image of imprisonment soon settles into the more conventional thraldom of the courtly love poem; when he first sees the lady his heart at once confesses complete subjection to her. Professor Lewis rightly notices 'the beautiful oxymoron'—'my hert become hir thrall / For ever of free wyll' (st. 41)—in which the poet is able 'to feel and to express both sides of the complex experience'; indeed throughout the account there is a keen awareness of the complexity of the situation. The experience comes at first as a release; the voluntary submission to the lady substitutes for the imprisonment which had isolated him one by which he can express all the new wonder and devotion he feels. This thraldom is not a restraint: 'ar ye god Cupidis owin princesse, / And cummyn ar to lous me out of band?' (st. 43). Yet this new experience brings in a new form the same feelings as before; he is still without sure knowledge, though not now without an object on which his desires may centre:

> Quhat sall I think, allace! quhat reverence
> Sall I minster to your excellence?
> (st. 43)

And lastly the new feelings of delight only heighten the consciousness of restraint; he falls back into 'bewailling myn infortune and my chance' (st. 45).

The passage which follows describing the lady calls for no such delicate balance of responses. It presents an image of sharp and brilliant detail, a beautiful expression of newly-awakened perceptions, but it is considerably less interesting and structurally less closely relevant than the preceding passage. The adoration and homage which do not find clear expression here are better conveyed by the restlessness, the delicately comic agitation of the poet's call to the nightingale:

> Opyn thy throte; hastow no lest to sing?
> Allace! sen thou of resoun had felyng,
> Now, suete bird, say ones to me 'pepe';
> I dee for wo; me think thou gynnis slepe.
> (st. 57)

The language here, unpretentious living speech, is in direct contrast to the elaborate stiffness of the description.

In the superb sixtieth stanza the real strength and flexibility of this language become apparent; at the end of this stanza the humour with its critical balance gives way to a tenderness and eagerness in 'Bot blawe wynd, blawe, and do the levis schake' which recall the naked feeling of 'Western wind, when will thou blow?' The increase in emotional pressure at this point, associated with the return to a more popular, less sophisticated tradition, occurs at the crisis of the poem; the progress from immaturity and ignorance to understanding has reached the point of the first perception of love and its power; and this brings only a clearer perception of powerlessness and a more disturbing doubt:

> So sore thus sighit I with myself allone,
> That turnyt is my strenth in febilness,
> My wele in wo, my frendis all in fone,
> My lyf in deth, my lyght into dirkness,
> My hope in feer, in dout my sekirness,
> Sen sche is gone: and Gode mote hir convoye,
> That me may gyde to turment and to joye!
> (st. 71)

The only way out of the tangle of paradoxes is by the dreams that cut right through it and lead to the final clarification and understanding.

The dream is described, appropriately, as a release: 'and sone, me thoght, furth at the dure in hye / I went my weye, nas nothing me ageyne' (st. 75). In the 'cloude of cristall clere and fair' all things are seen for what they are and in an orderly relationship. Surveying the whole range of love experience the poet is able to test his limited personal knowledge of love against a new and complete knowledge; and this is the right moment for a redefinition of courtly love which Venus herself supplies in reply to the poet's cry for mercy.

Venus seems to offer only another paradox:

> Sen of my grace I have inspirit the
> To knawe my lawe, contynew furth, for oft,
> There as I mynt full sore, I smyte bot soft.
> (st. 105)

But there is a reminder here of what Boethius learnt about Fortune: 'whan Fortune semeth debonayre, thanne sche lieth, falsly byhetynge the hope of welefulnesse.' What Philosophy says of Fortune in the *De Consolatione* could also apply to Love:

> Thou has bytaken thiself to the governaunce of Fortune and forthi it byhoveth the to ben obeisaunt to the maneris of thi lady.

Love and Fortune are seen to be closely linked; their behaviour is puzzling and contrarious in similar ways, the influence of both of them is finally unavoidable and the way to understand them both is simply to experience them fully. That this law of Love or Fortune is taken to be universal is made clear by the myth in which Venus's concern for the lives of men is associated with the natural and divine laws; she describes how, as a token of her weeping, 'cummyth all this reyne, / That ye se on the ground so fast ybete' (st. 116). And the flowers that are watered by her tears 'preyen men, in thair flouris wis, / Be trewe of lufe and worschip my servis' (st. 117). Obedience to the laws of nature means a recognition of the divine law, and the culmination of the whole argument is to be seen in the beautiful stanza 123:

> This is to say, contynew in my servis,
> Worschip my law, and my name magnifye,
> That am your hevin and your paradis.

The definition of courtly love as truly both amorous and divine is a necessary stage in the poetic account of an increasing fullness of understanding and emotional stability.

The final stage is the encounter with Fortune herself when these laws are brought to the test of actual experience. The poet has emphasized throughout that the living and testing of the forces present in life, and not merely their rational acceptance, are of the greatest importance. What matters is the direction given to living and not the formulation of a philosophy. For this reason the direct recommendation to trust in God, to 'Tak him before in all thy governance, / That in his hand the stere has of you all' (st. 130), in spite of its close links with the imagery of the opening of the poem, carries little weight as opposed to the imaginative fusion of values in stanza 123 and the allegory of the encounter with Fortune. After the vision in which the poet seems to be drawn at last into a complete community with the law of kind, the poem proceeds to the brusque comedy of Fortune's wheel:

> 'Now hald thy grippis,' quod sche, 'for thy tyme,
> Ane hour and more it rynnis ouer prime;
> To count the hole, the half is nere away;
> Spend wele, therefore, the remanant of the day.
> . . . Fare wele,' quod sche, and by the ere me toke
> So ernestly, that therwithall I woke.
> (sts. 171-2)

There is nothing conventional about this; the language has the vitality that really fuses comedy and seriousness; the end of a spiritual pilgrimage can be described in near-farcical terms.

James uses the conventional reawakening sequence of the dream poem as a dramatic device, delaying the moment of final understanding:

> Though that my spirit vexit was tofore,
> In suevyng, alssone as ever I woke,
> By twenti fold it was in trouble more
> Bethinking me with sighing hert and sore,
> That nan othir thingis bot dremes had,
> Nor sekernes, my spirit with to glad.
> (st. 174)

But it is the disillusion not the dream which is illusory; a few stanzas later comes the sudden and unexpectedly easy release as the turtle-dove alights on his hand, 'off quham the chere in hir birdis aport / Gave me in hert kalendis of confort' (st. 177).

'Thankit be fortunys exiltree / And quhile, that thus so wele has quhirlit me' (st. 189). If the poet has found personal stability it has been through acquiescence in the changing pattern of life; 'verray welefulnesse' (in Boethius's phrase) consists in knowing life for what it is and accepting it:

> Enforcestow the to aresten or withholden the swyftnesse and the sweigh of hir [Fortune's] turnynge wheel? O thow fool of alle mortel foolis! Yif Fortune bygan to duelle stable, she cessede thanne to ben Fortune.

This conclusion has only been made possible by the imaginative discipline of the dream allegory with its possibilities of organizing and even synthesizing diverse experiences. The narrative, which may or may not be an historical fact, furnishes the basic symbols for a new exploration of the courtly love code and its relations to religion and life. The distinction of the poem lies in the developing meaning of the whole work, not in the romantic story at its core. (pp. 339-47)

John Preston, "Fortunys Exiltree: A Study of 'The Kingis Quair'," in The Review of English Studies, *Vol. VII, No. 28, October, 1956, pp. 339-47.*

Murray F. Markland (essay date 1957)

[*In the following excerpt, Markland analyzes the structure of the* Kingis Quair, *proposing that all elements of the poem combine to illustrate the poet's conception of Fortune.*]

Because it is a strikingly original fifteenth-century poem, ***The Kingis Quair*** is worth repeated evaluation. The author, in a way not common to the usual allegorist, has grounded in a real experience the conventional themes and devices of the dream vision, of the court of love, and of the romance. But the glory of that uncommon realness has for some modern readers obscured the poet's purpose, has caused them to misinterpret the poem, and through that misinterpretation, to come to an incorrect and partially unfavorable judgment of it. When Professor W. W. Skeat [in his introduction to the poem] criticized it for being of a "fragmentary nature" and for "some want of order" he established a mode of evaluating the poem which few have differed from. Only G. Gregory Smith [in "The Scottish Chaucerians," in *Cambridge History of English Literature,* 1907,] and W. M. Mackenzie [in his introduction to the poem] have ventured to add to the accepted remarks on its beauty and originality the opinion that it is well constructed. But in the same breath Mr. Smith must brush aside "whatever inconsistencies are in the poem" as attributable to its personal nature. Mr. Mackenzie, also, is weak in his defense of it. He suggests, contradicting Skeat, that the poem was written in retrospect, that it has not been patched up and added to, but was written as a whole. Although the few stanzas he cites tend to confirm his opinion, so slight an analysis as he makes cannot establish the existence of order everywhere Skeat and others have seen disorder. These, the only efforts to demonstrate the unity of the poem, have been limited to contending that it was written with a foreseen end. None of this criticism helps us to observe the poem's truly unified structure, because underlying it is a mistaken interpretation which seems to have dominated all published criticisms of the poem.

Critics of the poem, reading it as if its purpose were autobiographical, have been forced to judge it ill constructed, because they find that too many passages either do not contribute to that purpose or can be accounted for only as digressions from it. Skeat lists fifteen stanzas (158-173) which "might very well have been introduced at an earlier place," and six (152-157) which "have virtually nothing to do with the subject." These are stanzas which recount the poet's meeting with the goddess Fortune. W. A. Neilson dismisses as a digression six carefully worked out stanzas (145-150) in which Minerva explains to the poet the nature of Fortune and the extent to which he is subject to it. Obviously Skeat and Neilson consider the love story to be the central if not the sole subject of the poem. Mackenzie, however, points out that the poet's reflection on the difference between his fortune and that of Boethius is the stimulus to composition. Smith says that the poem has two main topics, "the 'unsekernes' of Fortune and the poet's happiness in love." One writer, W. J. Courthope, asserts [in *A History of English Poetry,* I, 1895,] that the main theme of the poem is the mutability of Fortune, an insight which he relegates to a footnote. It is upon their suggestive remarks, then, and upon the difficulty other critics have in accounting for the passages devoted to Fortune, that I want to base my interpretation of ***The Kingis Quair*** and my description of its structure. By reinterpreting the poem I hope to redefine the poet's purpose and to demonstrate that the poem is well constructed because each element of it contributes to the accomplishment of that purpose.

I would first take issue with the assumption that the purpose of the poet was biographical. To write with such a purpose he would have had to be much less medieval than he shows himself to be throughout the poem, as uncommon a poet as Chaucer. Although ***The Kingis Quair*** is of the fifteenth century, it is a medieval poem, exemplary and didactic in intent so that it is perfectly in accord with the frequently cited precept, "For Seint Poul seith that al that writen is, to oure doctryne it is y-write." That, remarkably, it tells a real story is for the writer, and should be for the modern critic, secondary, for the function of the story is to illustrate the doctrine. To assume that the writer has a more modernly pleasing purpose than this and then to object because he fails to write in accord with it is to treat him and the poem unfairly. It is a mistake to judge the poem as if its central purpose were to tell the story of James I, because the purpose of the poem is in its doctrine.

The proportions of the poem also indicate that the poet's purpose was other than biographical. Although the story which is usually taken as the central matter is presented in fifty-two stanzas, somewhat less than one third of the poem, twice as many, 100 stanzas, half of the entire poem, are given over to a dream-vision and allegory, featuring Venus, Minerva, and Fortune. It would seem that the poet's interest in the life of James is subordinated to the dream-vision, in which the dreamer receives instruction.

The narrative structure of the poem is further confirmation. The expository framework can be disregarded. Briefly, the story is this: a man is captured and imprisoned. While imprisoned he falls in love. Later, without further action on his part, he is released from prison and wins his love. The statement of his release and his success in love occurs in the closing part of the framework, and it is merely a statement. Clearly, then, the climax of the narrative, the focus of attention, is at the point at which he first knows that he will be released and that he will win his love. That point is at the last of the dream-vision, after the audiences with Venus and Minerva and in the final moments of the encounter with Fortune. If the poet's theme were the romantic story of James and Joan there would have been no need for him to shift from realistic narrative to the more familiar mode of allegory. The narrative could have been extended, the climax appropriately included in it, and moral observations about the nature of Fortune could have concluded it. That the poet chose to do differently can be explained only on the assumption that he had another purpose to which his chosen method was more appropriate.

Once we set aside the notion that the adventures of King James are the central subject, it is not difficult to perceive what the poem is about. The subject is Fortune. The purpose of the poet is to tell a story illustrating Fortune as he comprehends it. The story that he chooses has two linked subjects: the poet's imprisonment and release and the poet's love and its realization, doubly unified in that while the release from prison and the realization of love are dependent upon each other, both are at the disposal of Fortune. He reverses the conventional illustration of Fortune (the story of the fall of a person from a high place, as in Chaucer's *Monk's Tale* and in Lydgate's *Fall of Princes*) to tell the story of a man's rise on the wheel of Fortune through virtuous love and wisdom. He attributes to man, perhaps not free will, but at least a measure of responsibility: a man subject to fortune may affect his fortune by his sinful or virtuous acts. Having thus moralized and christianized the concept of Fortune, he materializes justice so that he receives in this life, in this world, in human love and in physical freedom the reward of his virtue. ***The Kingis Quair*** tells the story of a man who, accepting the discipline of virtuous love and wisdom, attains to good fortune.

Although the use of a true, perhaps personal, story as distinguished from the commonplace "histories" and the poet-dreamer-in-the-mead device is original and remarkable, there is nothing either original or remarkable in the ideas which the poem treats. The poet is accepting a concept of fortune which is conventional and which arises from the same tradition as do the literary conventions he uses.

The controlling purpose of the poem, the intent which gives it form, is the presentation of a philosophical problem which had worried the minds of men throughout the Middle Ages, and which, by the time ***The Kingis Quair*** was written, had been solved in various ways, reducing the philosophical problem to a dramatic problem, a device to motivate action. While Boethius, whom the poet was reading before he began to write, probably felt the need to reconcile Fortune and Providence, and while Boethius' fourteenth-century translator was probably interested in the resolution, Chaucer when he wrote *Troilus and Criseyde* was no longer trying to effect a resolution. What Troilus learns from his experiences is a medieval commonplace. That he learns it without being lectured to is remarkable. That the reader sees it as an idea in action, participating in the structure and controlling the effect of the poem, is even more remarkable. When the paradox appears in later works the resolution of it obviously is without difficulty for the writer. The poet, and this is true of the poet of ***The Kingis Quair,*** is no longer philosophizing, no longer posing a true philosophical problem, because the problem, the statement of it, and the solution of it are ready at hand for him. They are conventional literary devices.

The problem, as the poet of ***The Kingis Quair*** inherits it and poses it, is this: to determine the extent to which a man is subject to Fortune; then to discover the means by which he can free himself from it, and to reconcile the conflicting notions of the pagan concept of Fortune and the Christian concept of divine providence.

The solution that the poet offers, the doctrine of the poem, is that only God has the complete foreknowledge which frees one from the operation of Fortune; however, a man living virtuously, loving virtuously, and having wisdom of a particular kind can influence Fortune or is less subject to it. It is, therefore, a moral problem because a man is thus partially responsible for the outcome of his personal fortune. Furthermore, the poet asserts that Fortune is the working out on earth of God's will in heaven. Wisdom consists in a comprehension of God's plan, an understanding which encourages a patient acceptance of God's will and a conviction that good and ill fortune, being part of the plan, lead to eventual good. (pp. 273-77)

Stanzas 1-13 form a prologue which we should not brush aside as Neilson does, for in the tradition in which the poet writes the prologue is relevant to the matter it introduces. The poet is in bed reading a book by Boethius, who writes of how he fell from prosperity and how he turned to philosophy for comfort. The poet is particularly impressed with Boethius' finding in himself the strength to bear misfortune, and by the realization that the source of this strength was youthful virtue which enabled Boethius in his old age to find comfort in a bad fortune which had released him from "unsekir warldis appetites." (6) The poet says that he will not summarize Boethius but will get on with his matter, which is "how eche estate, / As fortune liketh, thame will translate." (8) Everyone tries to climb on the wheel of Fortune but often loses footing at its least movement. Neither age nor estate aids one, and youth is particularly susceptible to the vagaries of Fortune. This meditation leads him to think of himself: "In tender youth how sche was first my fo / And eft my frende. . . ." (10) He hears the matin bell, which seems to direct him, "Tell on, man, quhat the befell." (11) Although the speaking bell may be a delusion, he accepts its direction, makes a mark, and begins his book.

At this point it would be difficult to anticipate a poem about anything but Fortune. The poet's meditation has been entirely on Fortune. He asserts that Fortune is his subject. The book he reads is *The Consolation of Philosophy,* in which originates much of the concept of Fortune sketched out above. What catches his attention in his reading is Boethius' misfortune and the ameliorative blessing of virtue. He observes that Boethius' fortune was first good then bad, whereas his own was first bad then good. And it is in the midst of thought about the fortunes of his life that he begins to write. The reader is thus prepared for an exemplum of Fortune.

In stanzas 14-16, the first stanzas of the poem proper, the poet restates his subject and theme: himself and his subjection to Fortune because of his lack of reason. He warns young people that they are liable to both good and bad fortune because they lack wisdom, because they are "of wit wyke and unstable." When he was young he was without "the rypenesse of resoun," and so he was like a "stereles ship" when he tried to find his way in the world.

His meditation has narrowed from the general problem of Fortune to its manifestations in his own life. He has also established the basic causes of man's subjection to Fortune, the lack of wisdom and reason. That wisdom, which he is later to receive from Minerva, is the practical knowledge of the divine plan, and that reason seems to be the power to perceive the plan and to govern one's will in accord with it. All of this, he says, is what the poem is to be about.

The narrative begins with stanza 20, after the poet once more anticipates the happy conclusion of his story by saying in stanza 19 that he is to write of "my turment and my joye," and in the following fifty stanzas are presented the biographical facts of the poem, all of which are consistent with the life of James I. The poet first tells of his capture at sea and imprisonment either by God's will or by chance (an anticipation of his resolution of the two). While he was a prisoner he thought much about Fortune and its place in his life. Part of his immediate problem was to distinguish between or to reconcile God's will and Fortune. But a lovely garden, a bird-song, and a beautiful lady bring him to contemplate love, and in his thinking he soon involves love with Fortune and his fate. He has noticed that love is a force which can "both bind and lous and maken thrallis free," (39) and he now considers the lady herself as a means to freedom, "an commyn are to lous me out of band," (43) and "That me may gyde to turment and to joye!" (71) Stanzas 35-39 are an elaboration of the oxymoron expressed again in stanza 41 that in thralldom to love there is freedom, and the poet carefully maintains the ambivalence of the terms of the oxymoron so that they always apply to both his imprisonment and his love. Love then will be an agent of his freedom. It cannot, however, be the only agent, because the chance which has made him a prisoner (24, 26, 27, 29) and which he bewails (45) is the very chance which brought him to love, and that same chance will keep him from attaining his love unless Fortune smiles on him. The good and bad aspects of his Fortune are inseparable. He is still, even in love, subject to Fortune (thus the supremacy of Fortune over love is asserted).

The next section is a dream vision (72-172) which enables the poet to compress and abstract eighteen years of prison tedium and complex negotiation for marriage and liberty. In these one hundred stanzas are most of those, all dealing with Fortune, that Skeat and Neilson have trouble accommodating to their interpretation of the poem; yet it seems to me that Fortune is the central subject here as it has been all along. What we have is an *ars fortunae:* the poet, wanting to win his love (with which freedom from prison is concomitant), in a dream undergoes a discipline of love and wisdom which permits him to mold his future (or which makes him less subject to the whims of Fortune). The dream-vision is a search for freedom through love, wisdom, and Fortune.

The poet is lifted through the heavens to the sphere of Venus, where he enters a roomful of lovers whose "chancis" are mentioned in books. There are those who grew old in the faithful service of love. There are those faithful to love who "happened" to die in middle age, "and othir eke by other divers chance." (87) There are others who are complaining about "fortune and his grete variance." He also sees the blind Cupid and Venus. In petitioning her for help, he addresses her as "O anker and keye of our gude aventure." (100) Venus encourages him to take his "aventure" patiently, humbly, and to be guided by Gude Hope. (106) She informs him that she is supreme in love affairs, but only in conjunction with other powers can she determine the future. In his case some other influences keep him from liberty, and so to free him "It standis noght yit in myn advertence, / Till certeyne coursis endit be and ronne," and when he has in effect won his lady's grace.

Venus concludes the interview by sending him in company of Gude Hope on to Minerva, who has a further influence upon him. In response to his plea Minerva, "the pacient goddesse," promises that if his love is virtuous she will give him her "lore and disciplyne" and he will succeed; if his love is set on "nyce lust" it will be in vain. He is to be virtuous, true, meek, steadfast, diligent in word and deed and to put his trust in God. She warns him to bide his time (patience is a virtue of both Christianity and courtly love), for the hasty man is not wise, "And oft gud fortune flourith with gude wit." (133) Therefore, he is to combine wisdom with his will, and abhor all falseness and deceit. With these conditions fulfilled she will "pray full fair, / That fortune be no more contrair." (144) The discourse on the nature of Fortune with which Minerva continues at this point (145-149), despite Neilson's dismissal of it as a digression, is an integral part of the poem. Having already urged him to virtuous conduct, she continues the poet's instruction by giving him some understanding of the power to which everyone, but he in particular because of his weakness, is subject. Whether Fortune is necessity, or whether man has free will and imposes order on chance by calling it Fortune, she does not determine, but she does assert that where there is the least intelligence and foreknowledge Fortune is strongest and

> To God, that is the first caus onely
> Off every thing, there may no fortune fall:
> And Quhy? for he foreknawing is of all. (148)

It is a power which the poet cannot match but which he may meliorate. With a greater understanding, a greater wisdom, the petitioner is then ready to appeal directly to Fortune. That there is virtue in the discipline is attested by his immediate success with Fortune when he has audience with her.

Having descended from Minerva's palace to the earth, he makes his way along a pleasant river of clear, musical water in which fishes play. Beside the river are green-leaved trees, bearing fine-looking fruit, and fresh flowers. A pleasant scene, still a part of the poet's dream, it is, nevertheless, much like his waking world. But the harmony of the landscape is disturbed when he sees in it many beasts "diverse and strange" (158): the lion, the panther, the squirrel, the ape, the lynx, the unicorn, the porcupine, the tiger, the hare, and others. These stanzas disturb Skeat. Stanzas 152-157, he says, "have virtually nothing to do with the subject." He means, of course, with the love story. But if the subject is Fortune, then these stanzas provide an appropriate setting for that goddess and her wheel. The landscape in which the poet finds her is, at first sight, orderly and consistent, but the natural order of things is not carried on into the animal kingdom. There is a disparity of several kinds among them, and between them and their environment. Surrounded by disparity stands Fortune, the fickle, inconstant goddess. In the poet's dream world as well as in his waking world, Fortune is the center of disorder within an ordered realm where "mich unlikely thing / Full oft about sche sodeynly doth bring." (150) It is not the conventional dwelling-place of Fortune. Although it is undoubtedly derivative of Chaucer's *Parlement of Foules* and of the characteristics of the earthly paradise, it seems to be an original contribution of the poet to the conception of Fortune. What better place to find her embodiment? Just as the description of the garden (31-32), to which Skeat makes no objection (it is conventional), prepares the reader for the appearance of the lady, so this description prepares him for the appearance of Fortune. The given setting is appropriate to each.

Skeat, indeed, objects to the whole encounter with Fortune. Of the scene in which the poet describes the appearance of Fortune and her wheel, and reports her assurance that life will be better for him, Skeat says, "The account of Fortune in st. 158-172 with the addition of st. 173 is in a tone in harmony with st. 1-28 and might well have been introduced at an earlier place." He is right that the tone of the two groups is in harmony, but it does not follow that the second has been given its place without reason. This is the climax of the poem. The prisoner poet, seeking release, has completed the discipline of virtuous love and wisdom and is at the end of his dream-pilgrimage. He has appealed to Venus and Minerva; now he stands before the capricious Goddess whose good will is necessary to his comfort. This is the foreseen end for which the poet's frequent anticipations of joy have prepared the reader. The entire poem has been focused upon an eventual change for the better in his fortune (see stanzas 10, 19, 25, 188, 192, 193). Each of the goddesses has admitted that she has only partial power: Fortune is superior to Venus and Minerva, and Fortune now smiles upon him, a response for which the reader was prepared by stanza 10, "how sche was first my fo / And eft my frende . . ." The poet has chosen to present the approach to this change allegorically through the dream rather than continuing the direct narrative of his imprisonment and the protracted treating for his liberty.

What follows his awakening (173-196) can be called an inartistic continuation only if one insist that the poem end at its point of highest interest. It serves in part as a confirmation to both the poet and the reader of the dream's promise of good fortune. Because of its various functions, however, this closing section is not so well unified as the rest of the poem, but except for several conventional closing gestures, which must be allowed the poet, it is necessary to the poem's completeness. He informs the reader that the promise of the dream was fulfilled, that his fortune did indeed change, that he was rewarded for having undergone the discipline of love and wisdom. Because Fortune favored him he was enabled to attain his liberty and his love. In this manner he completes the narrative motifs. Stanza 196 returns to the idea of stanzas (22, 25, 28, 44, 130) in which the poet has suggested that Fortune is not the supreme authority despite her great power. This subordination of Fortune is reaffirmed here at the end of the poem in stanzas 179 and 196. The fatal influence which has acted upon him, but no longer does, came from God. Having already completed the narrative that illustrated the working of Fortune in his life, he concludes the poem with that generalization, to the effect that Fortune is the working out of God's will. This is his solution to the philosophical problem which he set himself early in the poem: how to reconcile with God's will those things which seem to happen by chance or fortune. What he arrives at is a conventional medieval concept of Christian Fortune.

The value of this reading of the poem is that it does not invalidate the praise of its originality which all critics have given it. The poet has composed a poem which is well constructed by his own standards as well as original by ours. Love and imprisonment have generally been accepted as the central matter of the poem and the concern with Fortune mistaken for digression, interpolation, irrelevance. The effect of that reading has been a general acquiescence in Skeat's unfavorable criticism of the poem's structure. But Fortune, not the love between James I and Joan Beaufort, is the constant focus of the poet's attention. The poem begins in generalizations about Fortune which are first illustrated by the events of James' life and then are restated allegorically, and it concludes with a similar but modified and more positive assertion about the nature of Fortune. Fortune is the only subject of many stanzas, and in others Fortune is constantly mentioned or acting. Furthermore, those passages which would seem inartistic misfits in a poem of love contribute surely to the effect of a poem the subject of which is Fortune. The quality of this poem is that within an elaborate and jaded convention it succeeds in being original. (pp. 280-86)

Murray F. Markland, "The Structure of 'The Kingis Quair'," in Research Studies of the State College of Washington, *Vol. XXV, No. 4, December, 1957, pp. 273-86.*

Mary Rohrberger (essay date 1960)

[*In the following essay, Rohrberger praises the unity of structure and content that yields a totality of meaning in the* Kingis Quair *through the blending of personal experience and philosophy.*]

Such scholarly attention as has been directed to ***The Kingis Quair*** has been more to peripheral problems than

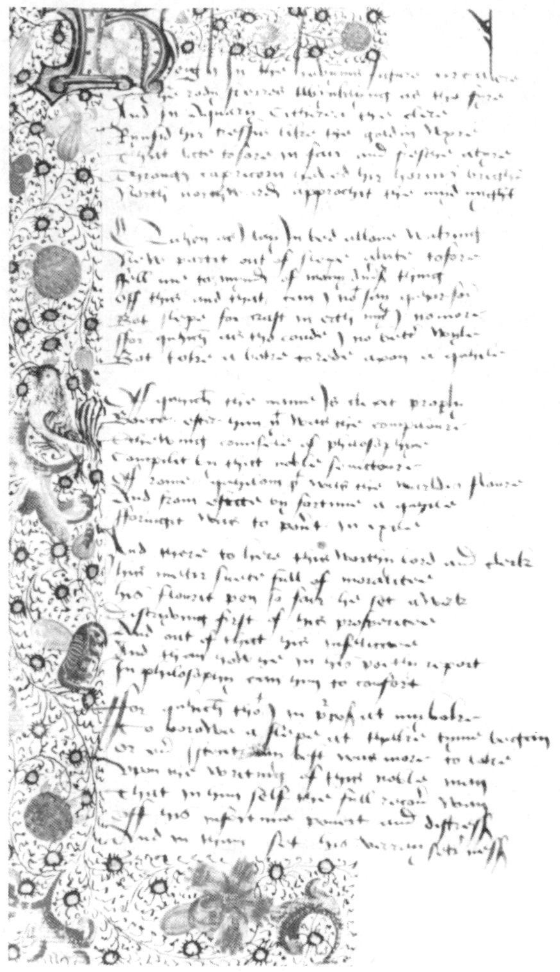

A page from the manuscript of the Kingis Quair.

to attempts to analyze the literary value of the work itself. Consequently assessment of the esthetic value of this poem has been somewhat neglected. Efforts at verifying authorship have led to readings of the poem in terms of the author's life. Scholars have found in the poem allusions that appear to have reference to actual events in the life of the author, James I of Scotland. Captured at an early age, James was a prisoner in England for eighteen years. Upon his release he married Jane Beaufort. References to these events in the poem seem to attest the autobiographical character of ***The Kingis Quair.*** Albert C. Baugh's reading of the poem [in *A Literary History of England,* 1948] is typical of the readings of other scholars who see the work as the story of the author's life. The poem, Baugh states, is about James I of Scotland, who tells of his "capture and imprisonment, his falling in love at first sight when, like Palamon in the *Knight's Tale,* he caught a glimpse of a surpassingly beautiful lady in the garden below his prison window, and the dream in which he is carried aloft, like Chaucer in the *Hous of Fame,* to the palace of Venus and later is advised by Minerva."

Such scholarly activity is invaluable to the literary historian but does little to assert literary worth. Those attempts at evaluation which have been made have been influenced, for the most part, by the poem's allegorical framework and its classification as Chaucerian in tone and style. Scholars have pointed out that the poem has in it many of the characteristics of the allegorical dream vision. These have been listed in an attempt to place the poem within a tradition. [In *The Other World,* 1950,] Howard R. Patch has discussed ***The Kingis Quair*** in terms of the "Other World" tradition and also in terms of literature involving the Goddess Fortuna [in *The Goddess Fortuna in Medieval Literature,* 1927]. C. S. Lewis, on the other hand, has placed the poem somewhat out of the tradition and has argued that its merit lies in the fact that it is new, that it is a "longish narrative poem about love which is not allegorical . . . but the literal story of a passion felt by the author for a real woman." [In *The Allegory of Love,* 1936] Lewis does admit that the poem contains a dream, "even an allegorical dream," but he insists that "the difference between a dream framed in a literal story and an allegorical story framed in a dream" is great. Although Lewis asserts the historical importance of the poem, nevertheless, he refuses to discuss its esthetic value—"about the absolute merits of this little poem we are at liberty to disagree."

James's debt to Chaucer has often been studied and scholars have paid much attention to locating its nature. Discussions of ***The Kingis Quair*** in histories of English literature are located in sections designating the poet as being in the Chaucerian tradition or among the Scottish Chaucerians. Students of Scottish literature, however, are careful to make clear that James far from imitates Chaucer. [In *The Scottish Tradition in Literature,* 1958] Kurt Wittig insists that James shows more originality than Chaucer's English disciples. "Instead of a dream allegory the poet presents us with a real event . . . with a wealth of perception and an eye alert to the fleeting impressions of fire, reflexions, colour, running water, jumping fish." James Kinsley [in "The Mediaeval Makars," in *Scottish Poetry: A Critical Survey,* edited by James Kinsley, 1955] says the same. The poet "draws heavily on stock descriptions, imagery and language of English courtly verse. But the ***Quair*** is not a pastiche. The poet has learnt from Chaucer not only to borrow freely but to handle what he borrows with delicacy and inventiveness."

Despite characteristics, however, which type a poem as part of a particular tradition, or just outside of it but still recognized in relation to it, a particular poem has particular meaning, and different poets make different use of the tradition as they manipulate devices to their own purposes. Certainly James wrote within a tradition; it would have been difficult for him to escape it. Literary conventions of the period are everywhere manifest, and allegory was, as Lewis has shown, the dominant form. ***The Kingis Quair*** contains all of the characteristics of the typical dream vision allegory. [In his edition of ***The Kingis Quair,*** 1939] W. Mackay Mackenzie sums up the relation of this poem to others in the tradition. "The wakeful night, the prelude to the actual start of the poem, the prisoner viewing the lady, the dream leading to the description of the mythological courts, the close in a summing up of the lessons of the work—all this was in the manner of many other poems before and after." But the value of a literary work depends not on the fact that an author uses a certain tradition but on his success in using it to his own ends. As far as esthetic merit is concerned, it does not matter whether the structure is based upon conventional and often used devices or upon techniques startingly new. What does matter is whether meaning emerges from structure and consequently yields unity of effect.

Recently, John Preston in a study of the ***Quair*** took this position, asserting that the allegorical structure of the poem suggests that there is further than autobiographical meaning to be derived from the poem. In his article ["Fortunys Exiltree: A Study of *The Kingis Quair,*" *RES* VII (1956)] Preston points out that the personal experience within the poem illuminates its general problems, but that ***The Kingis Quair*** consists of more than personal experiences. There are many levels and kinds of experience in it. In this paper I shall suggest an interpretation based on the poem's structure, and, in an attempt at evaluation, I shall conclude that a totality of meaning emerges from structure and consequently a unity of effect is achieved.

The Kingis Quair is a poem recording the author's attempt to reconcile his own problems and tribulations with a philosophy of life. His personal experiences are used as a basis for his generalization; thus the poem exhibits both particularity and universality. The poet moves from the specifics of his experience to a dream vision allegory which objectifies in symbolic form the universals of the allegory. The allegory, then, provides meaning for the entire structure and draws together what comes before the vision and what comes after it. The architectonics of the poem are striking. The poet provides an outer framework in which he sets the scene. Mention of "Citherea the clere" is appropriate to the theme of love which is to follow. The second stanza of the poem begins a series which provides motivation and direction for the entire work. Here the action concerns the poet's reading of Boethius. Speculation on the lot of Boethius and on Boethius' consolation in philosophy leads the poet to consider his own unhappiness and pain. The garden scene, which causes the poet to forget his own pain, provides imagery which is clustered symbolically around birds and branches. When the poet takes love as his guide the stage is set for the dream vision. After the vision the poet introduces again the themes of pain, love associated with birds and branches, and philosophy as a guide to action before he closes the poem by returning to an outer frame. The poem is unified, however, not only by this structural balance and logical movement toward a discursive end, but also by a movement in the emotions of the poet. Through the course of the poem he moves from conditions of despair to optimism, from doubt to faith, from questioning to acceptance. At the end of the poem he is secure within himself, able to face life's problems.

The poet states his purpose and introduces his problems in the opening stanzas. Reference to the planet Venus suggests one of the themes to follow. But love is not to be the final answer to the poet's problems, though it is through love that he makes a start. Consequently the poet moves quickly to another theme. It is approaching midnight and he is sleepless; thoughts cram his mind. In an effort to induce sleep he picks up a book. These opening lines motivate the action to come. The book that the poet chooses is important; it is by Boethius, "shewing counsele of philosophye." (Stanza 3) When Boethius wrote the book he was a prisoner, having fallen through Fortune's dictates from high to low estate. His book was an effort to find in philosophy, consolation for his fall. The poet notes that Boethius, working through his problems as he wrote them down, came to find comfort. While reading, the poet becomes interested in what the book says. He had picked it merely to induce sleep; now he finds it worthy of study because it is the account of how a man came to an understanding of his own problems and in himself won full recovery of his misfortune. Boethius, being virtuous in his youth, called upon this virtue to aid him when Fortune turned her back; virtue came at his call and helped him. The poet studies long and hard until his eyes smart. Then he closes the book and ponders on what he has read. These thoughts are "mater new" to him: "how that eche estate, / As fortune lykith, thame will translate." (Stanza 8)

At this point the poet introduces the idea of Fortune's wheel—no man or child is immune to it. Such generalization brings him to thoughts of his own condition. He muses on Fortune's treatment of him. In his mind he reviews the events of his own life. While thus engaged, he hears the matins ring. Strangely, he doubts their reality, thinking them a fantasy that calls him to write of his own adventures. This doubting is characteristic of the poet's nature. He questions his imagination, questions his hearing. He insists that either the matins rang or his thoughts caused the illusion. "It is a bell, or that impressioun / Off my thoght causith this illusioun." (Stanza 12)

There is no doubt that in the progression of his thought here the poet wishes to imply that he desires to repeat the experience of Boethius who found consolation in his writings. The poet determines to write "sum new thing" since his imaginings have thus compelled him. (Stanza 13) The next stanzas concerning the poet's experiences parallel the stanzas about Boethius. The poet describes his own youthful state. He was dependent, "Like to the bird that fed is on the nest," in wit "wayke and unstable," liable to Fortune and Misfortune because he could not care for himself. (Stanza 14) The idea takes on more emphasis when the poet changes his metaphor but carries on the same thought. Now he equates his youth with a rudderless ship, lacking a guide to steer it. As a youth the poet lacked enough reason to govern his will, so that he was rudderless when he embarked on his own voyage of life. The poet skillfully extends his metaphor: as a ship without a guide is liable to crash into the rocks, so his own feeble boat (lacking reason to govern will) was endangered. Since he could not govern it, it had to be directed by the wind. Within this extended metaphor the poet identifies the rocks that are likely to endanger his boat with his own doubtfulness that palls his wits. He lacks direction. Now the voyage of his life is equated with the task of writing his own book. He directs his wit to control the voyage he now begins. His object is to "seke connyng," but with his characteristic doubting, he notes that he may "bot lytill fynd." (Stanza 18) He invokes the Goddesses to help guide him with their "bryght lanternis" in the same way as previously he had invoked the winds to steer his vessel. (Stanza 19)

He begins his voyage in good weather; it is spring, a time of virtue and good. In the seasonal cycle spring follows the frost and flood of winter and promises softness and sweetness, gladness and comfort. These stanzas are a prophecy of his success in his metaphoric journey. From his own winter he will come to the comfort of spring. Such a prophecy is not out of place here. Within the extended metaphor of the boat, two voyages have been described. The first occurred when as a youth he started out completely dependent; his cry for aid then was to the winds to steer him. The winds were the sole guides of his destiny. The second voyage described was that of the projected writing of his book. Here, although doubt palls him, he directs his own wits to steer him; and the aid that he seeks is a lantern to help guide his way. As Boethius found comfort within himself, the poet here begins to seek it out.

The metaphor of the boat is apt, not only because the poet's actual experience does entail a boat and a voyage, but also because the metaphor of the journey foreshadows another journey, the symbolic flight-of-the-mind which the poet will describe in stanzas to come. Now, however, the poet proceeds to describe the actual voyage he took when very young he was taken from his country and put to sea. The voyage started in good weather but did not end well. The ship floundered upon the waves. Another force than its own guided its destiny. Fortune directed its capture. The poet was conveyed to prison and left "without confort, in sorowe abandoun" for eighteen years. (Stanza 25) This situation directly parallels that of Boethius. Both men, through reverses of fortune, found themselves in prison. But Boethius had something to help him—virtue, instilled in him in his youth. Our poet without a basis for comfort suffers for many years. He spends his time bewailing his fate; questioning his own unhappy condition; other things are free; he is imprisoned. He seeks reasons for Fortune's actions, but can find none. The poet needs a base from which he can begin to rise again, as Boethius rose from the base of his virtuous youth. The poet now seeks such a base, and as he seeks, he finds.

It has long been his custom to look through his window at living things below, comparing their freedom with his imprisonment:

> The bird, the beste, the fisch eke in the see,
> They lyve in fredome everich in his kynd;
> And I a man, and lakkith libertee.
>
> (Stanza 27)

These lines provide striking parallelism with lines occurring later in the poem when in the dream sequence the poet wandering in the forest again sees fish and beasts frolicking in freedom. A question arises as to what constitutes freedom for man, but this question is to be answered later. Now when the poet looks down he sees the beauty of the garden; his eyes find a nightingale that sits on the "small grene twistis," and he hears its song of love. (Stanza 33) Association of the bird and twigs with the song of love is important in the structure of the poem. Later a turtle dove carrying a branch of gillyflowers will again provide the poet with comfort, as the bird's song now leads him a step ahead on his metaphoric search for consolation.

The bird calls to the summer to hasten its coming: "Cum, somer, cum, the suete sesoun and sonne." (Stanza 34) The poet hears the bird thank love for this sweet time; but characteristically, the poet questions the song. What has love to do with it? He expresses doubt: "It is nothing, trowe I, bot feynit chere / And that men list to counterfeten chere." (Stanza 36) The author skillfully marks progression from doubt to a kind of faith. The poet begins with rather positive questions and answers: What has love to do with it? It is nothing. In the next question there is a subtle shift in tone: Can love be so important? The poet admits possibility: can all this be "bot feynt fantasye"? (Stanza 37) Now he admits the possibility and questions on the basis of it: if love is in charge of all of this, how has he given love offense? If all this is not true, why is it said as if it were true? The poet moves forward now in his progression of thought to state that if Love is a deity, he would pray to be put into Love's service. It is at this point in his thoughts that he sees the maiden in the garden below and is enthralled by her.

If the poet has moved forward in one series of thoughts, new thoughts begin again with questions. The poet, upon seeing the maiden, again doubts the reality of what he sees. "A! suete, ar ye a wardly creature / Or hevinly thing in likeness of nature?" (Stanza 42) Thus he questions the maiden's identity, but this time he comes to a decision quickly. Whatever she is, he can do nothing to change it. At this decision love moves in. He falls into "lufis dance." (Stanza 45) Suddenly, his wit, his countenance, his heart, his will, his mind, his nature are changed. He describes the beauty of the girl by telling of her youth, bounty, wisdom, and cunning. He knows her now for a real creature and gets intense pleasure from the simple act of beholding her.

Now assured of the deity of Love, the poet prays to Venus and yields her homage. The verses to Venus are structurally balanced with the nightingale's song of love which had previously started the poet's questionings. In a series of stanzas he now calls upon the nightingale to sing again so that the maiden may be pleased. Hearing the bird's response, the poet is filled with joy. His yielding to love, however, is not his final comfort. When the maiden leaves his day is turned into night. Again he is in despair, weeping and wailing. Kneeling in the window, he moans, complains, and sorrows. Something more is necessary to comfort him. But the poet has made a start. He is now in a position exactly parallel with that of Boethius when he was imprisoned. The poet has a base from which he can move forward to find his final consolation. Armed with the virtue of love, he will find as he seeks.

Earlier the poet had invoked bright lanterns to help guide him. Now a beam comes through the window, and he hears a voice say that it brings to him joy and health. He follows the light as it moves through the window. In his flight he journeys up from sphere to sphere until he reaches the empire of Venus. [According to Rob Roy Purdy in *The Platonic Tradition in Middle English Literature,* 1949, this] concept of flight, commonly known as a flight-of-the-mind, is a device often used in medieval literature, and always the purpose of the journey appears to be to gain knowledge. The purpose is no different here—the poet seeks knowledge and gains it.

Since Love is the virtue that he now possesses, it is appropriate that he should begin his search after knowledge with a visit to the Goddess of Love. Coming into Venus' chamber, the poet notices around him millions of lovers who ended their lives in love's service. The poet discerns among the lovers four groups and when he notes them, a voice explains to him the meaning of what he sees. The first group of old lovers are accompanied by Good-will. They had served love from the time they could understand it until their deaths. The second group, made up of young lovers, are accompanied by Courage. They had surrendered to love and died in middle age. The third group, veiled with dark hoods, had loved in secret, half-cowardly, but they had repented and are in company with the figure of Repentance. The fourth group, consisting of a world of folk with discontented looks, are those who had spent their lives complaining about Fortune's treatment of them. The poet appears to learn the meaning of true love, because when he approaches Venus his answers satisfy her. He admits his past ignorance, but pleads his changed condition. Venus, who says she has first inspired him to know the meaning of love, responds to his plea. Her advice is that he should live humbly and serve her, letting Good-hope be his guide. She says that she will help him, but she governs only Love's law. The effects of her beams are bound by others' laws. She alone cannot serve him; he requires other help than hers.

True love, then, is not the final consolation. There is something more. Venus sends the poet to Minerva and lends him Good-hope to guide in his search. When the poet finds Minerva, she, too, agrees to help him, but he must also help himself. Minerva lectures him concerning the nature of his love. She is not as easily satisfied as is Venus. If his love is but lust, his "travail is in veyne." (Stanza 129) The poet should take virtue as his guide and it will steer him. He should be strong, true, and steadfast, not only in words, but also in deeds. He should bide his time and not be hasty, for:

> . . . oft gud fortune flourith with gude wit:
> Quharefore, gif thou will be wel fortunyt,
> Late wisdom ay to thy will be junyt.
>
> (Stanza 133)

The poet protests his constancy and proclaims that his desire is grounded in Christian virtue. Satisfied of his virtue, Minerva agrees to help him: she will pray that Fortune will no longer be contrary with him.

Minerva, then, is not his final consolation, but her advice, like Venus', is helpful. Minerva lectured him concerning Fortune and her place in men's lives. It is said, Minerva tells the poet, that Fortune has direct control over man's weal or woe. Some clerks say that man's life is predestined; but others say:

> . . . that the man
> Has in himself the chos and libertee
> To caus his awin fortune, . . . and no necessitee
> Was in hevin at his nativitee.
>
> (Stanza 147)

Minerva continues explaining wisdom's lesson to the poet. When man has knowledge, Fortune is weak. No fortune may fall on God; God, himself, foreknows all. Fortune is strongest where there is less foreknowing or intelligence in man. The weaker and feebler man is, the more he is in danger of Fortune. This is an important lesson, and if the poet has learned it, he may seek his own Fortune.

The next stanzas involve a test of the poet's knowledge. Following the beam, he lands again on earth in a pleasant and harmonious place. Fish leap and play about; trees are laden with fruit; animals of every nature and condition frolic. Earlier, it will be remembered, the poet had envied the freedom of the birds, the fish, and the animals. Now, however, he is not tempted to join them in their carefree existence; he holds to his purpose, thinking only of from where he has come and where he is going. Having displayed this tenacity of purpose, the poet is led suddenly into the presence of Fortune.

The poet sees first Fortune's wheel. What he observes constitutes another lesson for him. Although there are people who are moved up and down solely through the action of the wheel, there are others: some, who in climbing failed in their footing, and thus fell to the ground; some, who continue to climb despite their falls; and some who, sore from falling, lack courage to continue.

When Fortune calls to the poet, he answers her and asks for help for in his game of life he is about to be checkmated: "Help now my game, that is in poynt to mate." (Stanza 168) Fortune laughs at his metaphoric exclamation of despair. She knows his condition well:

> "Off mate?" quod sche, "o! verray sely wrech,
> I se wele by thy dedely colour pale,
> Thou art to feble of thy-self to streche
> Upon my quhele, to clymbe or to hale
> Withouten help."
>
> (Stanza 169)

But, although he has made a bad beginning, he, himself, has sought her, and she assures him that his turn will come. She helps him on the wheel and cautions him to hold on tight. While saying farewell, she grabs him by the ear, and the poet suddenly awakes.

In his vision the poet has been led progressively from Love, to Wisdom, to Fortune, and the place of each has been explained to him. But all of this has happened in a dream. There must be reconciliation in his conscious waking state. Thus, awake, he worries over the meaning of his dream. Again he is troubled and full of pain:

> Touert myself all this mene I to loke,
> Though that my spirit vexit was tofore
> In suevying, alssone as ever I woke,
> By twenti fold it was in trouble more.
>
> (Stanza 174)

After asking further guidance, he walks to the window, from which the guiding beam had come to him before. Now, a turtle dove lights on his hand, bringing him comfort. The bird symbolically carries a branch of gillyflowers on which a message is written. This message contains a prophecy of the poet's consolation. He reads the message over and over and finally pins it at his bed's head. Gradually his pains go away; day by day his learning quickens; he comes again to his "larges" and "to bliss with hir that is my sovirane." (Stanza 181)

The poet has accomplished his purpose. Through his writing, through his conscious seeking, he has come to an answer: "every wicht his awin suete or sore / Has maist in mynde: I can you no more." (Stanza 182) Concluding his own consolation of philosophy, the poet states, "Now sufficiante is my felicitee." (Stanza 183) The remaining stanzas draw the poem to a close. The poet offers prayers for his brothers to grant them perseverance in their love. He prays for all the people who live in sloth and ignorance with no courage to pull themselves up or to mend their lives and souls. He blesses those things that have directed him to wisdom, and he sends his poem out, hoping it will be accepted and understood.

As Boethius has written his consolation of philosophy, so James I has written his—how he found comfort in knowledge through his faith in virtue. The comparison, of course, is metaphoric and not literal. James's poem is recollected from an experience, while Boethius actually wrote in prison. But James, like Boethius, found solace in philosophy. For James love alone is not enough; nor is wisdom, since Fortune stands over all. But with the help of love and wisdom man can to some extent direct his fate, and with sufficient courage and tenacity, he can again climb the wheel of fortune even if it has already cast him down.

In ***The Kingis Quair*** the poet merges his personal experiences with an allegorical dream vision. The poem leads naturally stanza by stanza to the account of the dream. Skillfully prepared, the early stanzas of the poem set up a situation to be paralleled later. As Boethius wrote, so writes James. But Boethius, imprisoned, carried virtue with him; James was entirely dependent. He spends his time in prison, mourning his fate. It is only when he determines to take some positive action, to seek himself, for his own consolation, that love enters his life and provides a basis for the dream vision. The traditional flight-of-the-mind device is used as a means of objectifying and making real, universal qualities. Thus the poet weaves the universals with the particulars of his experience. The poem is a gradual revelation of truth. The poet seeks it out at the same time that he imparts it to the reader. The reader shares the experience of the poet, who has carefully structured his experiences and has reinforced them with an allegorical dream vision. The experiences and the vision merge within the structure of the poem and yield totality of meaning. (pp. 292-302)

Mary Rohrberger, " 'The Kingis Quair': An Evaluation," in Texas Studies in Literature and Language, *Vol. II, No. 3, Autumn, 1960, pp. 292-302.*

Thomas Humphry Ward on the *Kingis Quair*:

No subject could be better fitted than the love-story of the captive king for a poem in the accepted *trouvère* style. The paganism of romance was fond of representing man as passive material in the hands of two supernatural powers, Fortune and Love; and poetry for two centuries was for ever returning to the theme. James the First was neither original enough to depart from the poetical conventions of his time, nor artist enough to work out his subject without confusion and repetition; and yet the personal interest of his story and its adaptability to the chosen form of treatment would be enough to save ***The King's Quair*** from oblivion, even without the unquestionable beauty of much of the verse. The dress is the common tinsel of the time, but the body beneath is real and human.

Thomas Humphry Ward, in The English Poets, Volume I: Chaucer to Donne, *Macmillan, 1880.*

Matthew P. McDiarmid (essay date 1973)

[*In the following excerpt, McDiarmid interprets the* Kingis Quair *as a spiritual autobiography, emphasizing that the poet's personal experience is the source of the poem's power.*]

The ***Kingis Quair*** is a poetical autobiography, a selective one of course, since the author reviews his life only in order to illustrate the single significant pattern that he has discovered in it. For such a purpose he needed to notice only a few relevant events and the ones that he chose were certainly critical in his career as historians know it. The meaning that he gave to these events in his poem is, however, not easily detachable and indeed the farther interpretation moves from them, in its endeavour to make an independently meaningful statement, the more it loses its way.

Too often critics have considered the poem simply as an attractive collocation of topics, symbolized or conventionalized themes or doctrines, to be identified, abstracted, represented with much the same significance as they have in works of a generally similar content. What is individual tends not to appear as such; the application, which is at least half the poem's meaning, is given less than proper attention and the result is a too simple re-statement of what the poet has to say, clarity being achieved by underplaying certain themes or even omitting them from notice altogether. Examples of this defective treatment are the studies of the ***Quair*** published by John Preston ['Fortunys Exiltree: A Study of *The Kingis Quair*', in *The Review of English Studies* VII (1956)] and John MacQueen ['Tradition and the Interpretation of *The Kingis Quair*', *The Review of English Studies* XII (1961)]. Thus Mr Preston develops the topic of 'fortunys exiltree' with an exclusiveness equal to that of the author of the *Epistola Consolatoria,* addressed to James by the University of Paris in 1414. And Professor MacQueen, relying on convention as a key to interpretation rigorously seeks out and therefore finds only what is conventional. Naturally he concludes that the 'attitude' of the poem is basically that of *The Romance of the Rose,* and that its subject can be generally described as 'the faire cheyne of love' in nature, more particularly, since he has also in mind the precedent of De Guileville's *Pelerinage,* as the action of divine grace in the king's life—not only the grace that is already inherent in nature's order but also that which manifests itself in direct intervention, for example, the saving sight of the beloved and the arrival of the dove with good tidings. Each of these themes (except the notion of special acts of grace) is undoubtedly in the poem but they are presented out of context and therefore disproportionately and misleadingly.

What is notably missing from these and other such accounts is the author and subject of the ***Quair,*** James Stewart. Recent critics have indeed been reluctant to consider the ***Quair*** as a personal document at all. They do not actually say that the history it contains is irrelevant but they write as if it were, and they are quite clear that it is not what the poem is about. Preston objects to C. S. Lewis's praise [in *The Allegory of Love,* 1936,] of its originality as a real-life application of 'the allegory of love' ('the literal narrative of a contemporary wooing emerges from romance and allegory'), and MacQueen asks us to observe that the poet 'does not mention the word marriage'. The latter thus chooses to omit from his discussion a subject that the historians, not to mention the goddess Minerva, think important in the king's life; and Preston prefers to illustrate the Boethian topic of fortune in the ***Quair*** without once referring to the question of free will which gives it significance—a mistake which Minerva naturally does not make—though it was a theme that had more than a philosophical interest for the Scottish king, as for his Roman teacher.

The contrary thesis will be maintained by the present writer in his approach to an interpretation: that the historical narrative, which includes the romantic one, does not merely answer, as Preston believes, 'the needs of the poem's developing thought', but directs it, and explains it to the reader. Not unless we bear firmly in mind that this is a spiritual autobiography, whatever conventions it may employ to tell its story, will we appreciate how impressive a statement it makes. (pp. 48-50)

[The] thought of James . . . reviews a circular course of experience and learning, from a beginning in thoughtless innocence through self-willed and rebellious unreason to a new beginning in Christian reason. Youth 'that seildin ought prouidith' could not consider the whole and wanted the patience to wait and see the wheel come full circle. The circle of experience that he considers particularly is, of course, that of his life from his capture to his liberation, but this has reference also to the larger circle of life turning away from and eventually back to, its natural point of rest, in God—a conception that James might have found in many places, but most conveniently in commentaries on Boethius, the moralizations in copies of Sacrobosco's *Sphere,* and especially in De Guileville's *Pelerinage de la Vie Humaine.*

The controlling concept of the life-circle is not only in the opening and recurring allusion (sts. I, 173, 195) to the return of the heavenly bodies from the unnatural westward course into which they are forced by Primum Mobile (the eastward movement being often compared to the soul's escape from the sensual will to reason and God), but also in the pervading theme of Fortune's wheel and its contrary motions and, most important of all, in the pattern of Boethius's experience, which is like that of the king's (4):

> Descryving first of his prosperitee
> And out of that his infelicitee,
> And than how he in his poleyt report
> In philosophy can him to confort!

Here the likeness in felicity consequent on infelicity is obvious, as also in the spiritual aspect of that felicity, which is an appreciation of providence or divine reason in the changing ways of fortune.

This 'figure circulere' in the poem's narrative has importance for its interpretation. It means that it is the whole of the poet's experience and not this or that particular part or aspect of it, however specially significant, that finally concerns him. Consequently it would be wrong for the critic to direct attention to the theme of love and marriage, which provides the main part of the poem's matter, except as it relates to the king's total comment on his experience. Similarly it would be a mistake to represent the introduction to love and confirmation of its happy future as direct interventions of divine grace, as Professor MacQueen does, when the king's concern is with grace as manifested in the whole course of his life. That this is what the reader is expected to perceive is externally suggested by the responses of both Walter Bower and Hector Boece to the king's English captivity; they see it, in Boece's words, 'non fortuna sed deo ducente'. Since the poet's purpose is to reveal, and not argue, the discovered pattern, the interpreter will simply follow him as he finds it.

It is, of course, as in Boethius and all Boethian poems or testaments, for example, *The Testament of Cresseid,* the complaint of Fortune's injustice that states the issue for comment. Like Boethius or Cresseid the king will cease to question, learn to accept. The main difference in his case, as we have seen, is that he discovers grace not through reasoning or painful correction, but by a change in Fortune's treatment of him that reveals how unhappiness can introduce happiness, even the greatest that can befall a man. He has seen the two faces of Fortune and found them fair.

It is here that his education through love begins. He has experienced something affected by, but more powerful than, Fortune, and in learning the serious duties of love learns also the reality of free will, from which choice of belief and conduct proceeds. The above-mentioned difference in procedure from the *Consolation* can thus be restated: that the enlightenment of reason comes to the king through a personal love which he learns to think of in Christian terms. What James finally preaches is, effectually, salvation through marriage, finding the love of God in the love of a woman, freedom from self in 'the yok that esy is and sure'. It need hardly be said that this is not a 'courtly' love, the love of a Troilus for his Criseyde; it has a doctrinal character that is more easily related to the known importance for the author of the event that inspired it than to any literary convention.

The element of doctrine is as apparent in the poet's Venus as in her sister Minerva, from whom she differs in no way in her thinking about the 'right true end' of love. If it is, admittedly, the quality and observance of love that concerns her most, she gives to her words on these subjects a moral and religious urgency that distinguishes her equally from the goddess Nature of *The Parlement of Foules,* the king and queen of love in the Prologue to *The Legend of Good Women* and the Venus of *The Temple of Glas.* The attitudes of the authors of *The Romance of the Rose,* widely differing as they are, agree in being much less evangelistic. The sacramental view of life and love that inspired these works (it is as basic to the rationalism of Jean de Meun as to the idealism of Guillaume de Lorris), and was the characteristically Christian interpretation of the Boethian 'faire cheyne of love', appears here in its dogmatic form. They exalt faithful love but, unlike King James, set it in the freedom of an ideal world where the bond of marriage need not be specified.

A remarkable instance of this treatment is provided by the monk of Bury's *Temple.* A careful reading is required to discover that its matter is the problem of a married woman and her lover. The heaven that the goddess of the temple offers to these worshippers is naturally indeterminate; it may be eventual marriage made possible by the death of the husband, or simply the consolation of reciprocated love. The problem need not be solved because it is not posed in real terms. In the ***Quair,*** of course, there is no such attempt to disguise, veil or ambiguously distance the subject-matter, and this is not only because the poem is an autobiography, and a marriage is part of its known personal story, but also because its author is frankly and sincerely interested in the meaning of marriage as a sacrament. His Venus accordingly avows that her 'lore' is incomplete without that of Minerva (III), and her promise of a perpetual heaven for the souls of the two lovers echoes the marriage service, and is clearly made to the faithful husband and wife that they will become (123).

It would be wrong to make more of Minerva's sermon than that of Venus, but without doubt it is she who most helps us to understand whatever doctrine or philosophy there is in the poem. Having at once identified herself with Christian teaching on the matter of love, that desire is not to be denied but is to be satisfied only in marriage, since all that men do must be done in the sight of God—'Tak him before in all thy gouernance / That in his hand the stere has of you all' (130)—she proceeds to deal with the basic issue of free will and responsibility. God had foreseen all that would be done to the captive and all that he would do. All has happened by permission of His will and in that sense alone is He responsible for the whole; for His permission included the free choice of good and evil by James, as by others, so that his was the merit of acting according to divine reason, seeking to do 'trew seruis' in his loving, and thus deserving the full happiness denied to those that, in Venus's phrase, 'breken louse and walken at thaire large'. The point is not simply that had he chosen otherwise there would have been no marriage and no liberation, but that there would have been no 'long and trew contynuance' of married love. Yet, the goddess of reason admits, though such a choice was, especially in the captive's case, a pre-condition of his happiness, its full realization in this world was still dependent on the changes of Fortune.

This last very important qualification of reason's power in man has to be understood in the light of what Minerva says about foreknowledge. Since God possesses this faculty to an infinite extent, he is untouched by fortune. To the very limited degree that man has this knowledge he is also beyond her power and may influence her—*sapiens dominabitur astris.* Here Simon reads his Boethius less correctly than James, for the French critic attributes only a counsel of resignation to the philosopher and falsely contrasts this with the king's doctrine of action. This knowledge itself depends on understanding the causes of happiness and unhappiness and these, as we have seen, James has learned, in so far as he now recognizes how the love of God for man works in the natural creation—an understanding that the birds outside the prisoner's window possessed 'in thaire wise'—particularly in the law of love and the necessity for the two faces of Fortune. This, however, is a knowledge of principles and if he has learned how the ones that specially concern love's observance should be applied, there is still the question of what can be done to win good fortune for it.

It is here that a personage in the poem who has been ignored by the critics, Gude Hope, plays his logical rôle. This guide, recommended by Venus (113) to help the lover on his way to Minerva, the support of his happiness in the earthly paradise, and still his companion when at last he encounters Fortune (158), is not only the confidence that comes from a new appreciation of life's happier possibilities, but also the confidence that is based on knowledge of particular favouring circumstances. Just as in theology Good Hope, as the opposite of 'Wanhope' or Despair, ensures God's mercy to the believing suppliant, in the practice of human love the same virtue ensures, to the extent that any virtue in the earthly scene can do so, practical success. This help, according to the contemporary author of the Scots treatise, *Ratis Raving,* discussing the conditions of a successful courtship and marriage, is the same as reasonable expectation. Of 'dame resone' he says that 'gud hop is ay of hire assent' (1045). Gude Hope is thus the good reason a man has to expect success in his wooing and happiness in his marriage. When this guide is absent the object of love is beyond one's reach because of various impediments of character, kinship, rank, and by extension the kind of difficulty that historically beset James.

With this meaning in mind it can be understood that the king set his love where it was acceptable, where marriage was possible, and ensuing happiness might be expected. It is not therefore altogether miraculous that he eventually received the news 'that blisfull bene and sure'. In respect of this personal relationship of fortunate love, as also in respect of the larger relationship of acceptance of God's will in the pattern of life, the theme of the poem may be described as the triumph of reason over foolish will.

With a final paean of thanksgiving, attributing the fortunate circle of his experience to 'the magnificence / Of him that hiest in the hevin sitt', the testament of James Stewart closes. It is patently the record of a man who has known love in marriage, 'that now from day to day / Flourith ay newe', yet more patently the reflective statement of a mature mind whose chief concern is to give this central experience its place in a religious interpretation of 'all myn auenture'. It is neither the narration of a lover's wooing that Lewis assumes it to be—the absence of any of the conventional details or prescribed stages of such a courtship should have checked that reading—nor the impersonal if inspired treatise that Prescott and MacQueen present.

The inadequacy of the former view inevitably provoked the extreme reaction that the latter represents, and the second account was encouraged by mistaken doubts about the poem's claims to be autobiography. That kings do not love their queens seems to have been a wilful article of faith with the sceptics, though singularly unsupported in this case, and the historian's testimony will probably have little weight with them: 'Whether ***The Kingis Quair*** gives an historical version of the wooing or not, the marriage seems to have been of the happiest. The conjugal fidelity of the king is exceptional in early Stewart history'. He is said to have trusted his queen as a partner in the business of government to a quite remarkable extent. For the sincere interest in religion and philosophy, that would have made it natural for James to give to his experience the significance that it has in the ***Quair,*** we have the ample witness of his contemporary and biographer, Abbot Bower.

The king's application of the Boethian theme to his own eventually happier lot has been said to want the profounder significance that a tragic narrative can possess. It is true that Boethius's assertion of an ultimate goodness in the universe to be accepted by any reasonable mind can only be fully tested and illustrated by a more painful account of experience, such as Robert Henryson gives of his unfortunate Cresseid. Her self-criticism, 'Nane but my self as now I will accuse', is made the more impressive by its circumstances. None the less, James's 'divine comedy' is a legitimate and effective treatment.

More, perhaps, might have been made of the eighteen years of exile and frustration in order to give greater weight to the consequent happiness, yet the result might have been only to divide the poem and weaken the celebratory effect, and the change would still not have met Simon's point. The true answer must be that to the Boethian faith the acceptance of fortune for what she is, always the agent of God whichever face she shows, is all that counts. That James learned such acceptance only when the happier face was turned should not deprive his statement of its authority. The vital point is his success in seeing the new friend in the old foe, the two as complementary aspects of the single worthwhile experience of living. Most readers should recognize that the king understands and feels what he says, and that it is personal experience and conviction that allows him to give so significant a pattern to his life's story. (pp. 55-60)

Matthew P. McDiarmid, in an introduction to The Kingis Quair of James Stewart, *edited by Matthew P. McDiarmid, Rowman and Littlefield, 1973, pp. 1-77.*

Lois A. Ebin (essay date 1974)

[*In the following excerpt, Ebin argues that the* Kingis Quair *is not an imitation of, but rather a response to, Boethius and Chaucer, suggesting that the differences between the* Kingis Quair *and its sources are more important than the similarities.*]

Since John Preston's article, " 'Fortunys Exiltree': A Study of the *Kingis Quair,*" [in *Review of English Studies* 7 (1956)] virtually every critic of the ***Quair*** has viewed the poem as an allegory about Fortune rather than simply as an account of James I's own experience. Recently in his informative essay, "Chaucerian Synthesis: The Art of *The Kingis Quair*" [in *Studies in Scottish Literature* 8 (1971)], Walter Scheps has added to our understanding of the poem by developing the suggestions of John MacQueen and other earlier critics that the ***Quair*** is a synthesis of various traditions—Boethian, courtly, allegorical, and Chaucerian. However informative these interpretations may be, none satisfactorily accounts for the ***Quair***'s peculiar features, for example, the relationship of Venus, Minerva, and Fortune, the abruptness of the stanzas which follow the dream, and the conspicuous emphasis on the process of writing in the poem. What critics have not recognized is that the ***Quair*** is a direct response to, rather than an imitation of, Boethius' *Consolation of Philosophy* and Chaucer's *Troilus* and *Knight's Tale.* Like Henryson's *Testament of Cresseid,* a later continuation of *Troilus,* the ***Quair*** takes up questions about the workings of Fortune raised by Boethius and Chaucer but answers them in terms quite different from those of its predecessors. (p. 321)

[The] synthesis of Boethian and courtly materials in the ***Quair*** differs significantly from Chaucer's works particularly with regard to the role of love. In both the *Knight's Tale* and the *Troilus* love increases the characters' susceptibility to Fortune. Palamon's and Arcite's love of Emelye is a source of disorder which both breaks their friendship and heightens the two characters' sense of frustration in a world which appears inexplicable to them. Troilus, though a faithful lover, is unable to escape the turn of Fortune's wheel. His love for Criseyde in fact ensnares him all the more in the world "that passeth soone as floures faire." In the ***Quair,*** however, the narrator's love for his lady leads him to wisdom and ultimately to an understanding of the workings of Fortune. Significantly, as a result of his love he becomes less rather than more subject to Fortune.

James' response to Chaucer and his own view of the relationship between love and Fortune is seen immediately in his use of the passages he borrows. Perhaps the best example of his changes is his manipulation of the incidents adapted from Part I of the *Knight's Tale.* Although James relies heavily on Chaucer in this portion of the ***Quair,*** he makes several important changes in the sequence of Chaucer's episode. In the *Knight's Tale,* Chaucer opens with a description of Emelye in the garden, then turns to Palamon who looks out of the window and spies the lady. Palamon cries out, Arcite sees Emelye, he too is smitten by love and the cousins argue over who has the right to love her. The episode ends with Palamon's and Arcite's long complaints about Fortune.

Significantly, in the ***Quair*** James moves the description of the lady from the beginning to the climax of the episode where he uses the narrator's sight of the lady as an affirmation of Love's power to "bynd and louse and maken thrallis free . . . ." (st. 39). Opening instead with the complaint to Fortune with which Chaucer ends, James restructures the entire episode to reverse the relationship between love and Fortune represented in Part I of the *Knight's Tale.* In the ***Quair,*** Fortune appears unjust to the narrator only before he subjects himself to love. In contrast to Chaucer's characters who complain more bitterly about Fortune after they see the lady, the ***Quair*** narrator bemoans his fate only before he falls in love. Immediately after his opening complaint, he looks out of the window into the garden below where he hears a nightingale welcome the season of love. The nightingale's song makes the narrator wonder about love's powers and he challenges the god to free him from his prison:

Can I noght elles fynd, bot gif that he
Be lord, and as a god may lyue and regne,
To bynd and louse and maken thrallis free,
Than wold I pray his blisfull grace benigne
To hable me vnto his seruice digne.
And euermore for to be one of tho
Him trewly for to serue in wele and wo.
(st. 39)

As if in response to his challenge, the narrator sees the lady. Her appearance confirms love's ability to free men, and unlike the corresponding scene in the *Knight's Tale,* is the first step in the narrator's long journey toward an understanding of the workings of Fortune. Completely transformed by his experience, the narrator no longer feels imprisoned, but is now the "free thrall" of his lady:

. . . forquhy my wittis all
Were so ouercom with plesance and delyte,
Onely throu latting of myn eyen fall,
That sudaynly my hert became hir thrall
For euer, of free wyll—for of manace
There was no takyn in hir suete face.
(st. 41)

The intensity of the narrator's experience is dramatically underscored by his five-stanza description of the lady, much expanded from the corresponding section of the *Knight's Tale.* In contrast to Emelye who is briefly compared to May flowers, the lady appears amid the splendor of gold and jewels. Though human, she is the image of nature's perfection:

In hir was youth, beautee with humble aport,
Bountee, richesse, and wommanly facture,
(God better wote than my pen can report)
Wisedome, largesse, estate, and connyng sure.
In euery poynt so guydit hir mesure,
In word, in dede, in schap, in contenance,
That Nature myght no more hir childe auance.
(st. 50)

The impact of the narrator's experience and his change in outlook are further emphasized by the difference between his two reactions to the nightingale, scenes which James adds to Chaucer's narrative. In the first scene, the nightingale's song prompts him to question, "Quhat lyf is this . . . / Quhat may this be, how cummyth it of ought? / Quhat nedith it to be so dere ybought?" (st. 36). In contrast to his earlier questioning, in stanza 54 he bids the nightingale sing "for Venus sake" "Sing on agane and mak my lady chere" and continues his plea in an emotional outburst of six stanzas. The episode thus ends with the narrator's transformation and positive change in mood rather than with the despair of the corresponding section of the *Knight's Tale.* In the remainder of the ***Quair,*** it will be love which the narrator now so poignantly feels which will lead him to wisdom and an understanding of Fortune.

Even more significant than James' changes in the relation between love and Fortune represented in Chaucer's works is his response to the view of Fortune developed in the material he borrows from Boethius. Just as James invites obvious parallels between the ***Quair*** and the *Knight's Tale* and *Troilus,* at the outset of the poem he introduces several links between his experiences and Boethius'. The book the narrator reads as he lies restlessly in bed is Boethius' *Consolation.* Rather than putting the narrator to sleep, the book keeps him up all night thinking about his own experience in youth when, like Boethius, he suffered an extreme change in Fortune. Like Boethius, he was captured and imprisoned by enemies. He too bitterly lamented his fate but finally won "the full recour" of his "infortune, pouert and distresse" by learning the true nature of Fortune and the limits of her control over men. As he recounts his own experiences, moreover, James borrows expressions and images from Boethius' "fair[e] / Latyne tonge" (st. 7).

But the parallels between the ***Quair*** and the *Consolation,* like James' borrowings from the *Knight's Tale* and *Troilus,* bring into sharper focus the essential differences in emphasis in these works. Rather than returning to Boethian orthodoxy as some critics have suggested, in the ***Quair*** James responds critically to the view of Fortune developed in the *Consolation,* making several significant changes in Boethius' scheme. In the first place, James indicates that it is primarily his youth rather than a preoccupation with the false goods of the world which makes him vulnerable to Fortune. In contrast to Boethius, who was an old man in the height of his career when he suffered his misfortune, James is only a boy of ten years (st. 22), and, the narrator emphasizes, it is during this unstable period of man's life that he is most subject to Fortune (st. 9).

Significantly, when James takes pen in hand to begin his "quair," he underscores this difference between his situation and Boethius'. The first stanza of this book, stanza 14, is loaded with images which suggest the precarious state of youth—"[sely] youth of nature indegest," "Vnrypit fruyte with windis variable," a "bird that fed is on the nest / And can noght flee—of wit wayke and vnstable, / To fortune both and to infortune hable: . . . ." Like a rudderless ship that sails upon the rocks, he lacks the ability to rule and guide himself:

Ryght as the schip that sailith stereles
Vpon the rok[kis,] most to harmes hye
For lak of it that suld bene hir supplye;
So standis thou here in this warldis rage
And wantis that suld gyde all thy viage.
(st. 15)

Expanding this metaphor, James makes it clear that in contrast to the *Consolation,* the ***Quair*** will be a voyage of the youth to find a proper rule and guide for his will:

I mene this by myself, as in partye.
Though nature gave me suffisance in youth,
The rypenesse of resoun lak[it] I

To gouerne with my will, so lyte I couth,
Quhen stereles to trauaile I begouth,
Amang the wawis of this warld to driue:
And how the case anon I will discriue.
(st. 16)

Unlike Boethius who has Philosophy as a mentor from the outset of the *Consolation,* James must actively seek a guide, and it is his search rather than the discussion of the workings of Fortune which occupies the major portion of the vision.

James' emphasis is clear if one compares his use of the ship metaphor with his sources. Boethius, Chaucer, and Lydgate, the authors from whom James borrows most frequently, each use the ship in several ways. On four occasions in the *Consolation,* for example, Boethius introduces the ship to refer to man amid the stormy sea of life. Further developing this metaphor, both Chaucer and Lydgate link the barge amid the tempest with the lover beset by adversity. After he falls in love at the outset of *Troilus and Criseyde,* for example, Chaucer's Troilus laments, "Al sterelees withinne a boot am I / Amydde the see, bitwixen wyndes two, / That in contrarie stonden evere mo." Likewise, the narrator of the *Temple of Glas* refers to his plight as that of a barge amid a tempest:

A nwe tempest for-casteþ now my baarge,
Now vp nov dovne with wind it is so blowe,
So am I p[o]ssid and almost overþrowe,
Fordriue in dirkness with many a sondri wawe.
Alas, when shal þis tempest ouerdrawe
To clere þe skies of myn aduersite . . .
(606-13)

Finally, at the outset of Book II of the *Troilus,* Chaucer again changes the metaphor by linking the ship with the tempestuous matter of his book:

Owt of thise blake wawes for to saylle
O wynd, o wynd, the weder gynneth clere;
For in this see the boat hath swych travaylle,
Of my connyng, that unneth I it steere
This see clepe I the tempestous matere
Of disespeir that Troilus was inne;
Bot now of hope the kalendes bygynne.
(II. 1-10)

James, in contrast to Boethius, Chaucer, and Lydgate, explicitly links the ship with youth. The ship is in danger not because it is in the storm of life or love as in the *Consolation,* the *Troilus,* or the *Temple of Glas,* but because it lacks a guide. It is subject to the waves of the world principally because the narrator does not have ripeness of reason to govern his will. Finally, greatly expanding the suggestions of *Troilus,* II, 1-10, James applies the ship metaphor not only to his actual journey and the journey of the "stereles" youth, but to the writing of the book as well. The ship becomes the matter of his book, the wind his inspiration, and the rocks the "prolixitee of doubilnesse" that cloys his wits:

O empti saile, quhare is the wynd suld blowe
Me to the port, quhare gynneth all my game?
Help, Calyope, and wynd, in Marye name!

The rokkis clepe I the prolixitee
Of doubilnesse that doith my wittis pall:
The lak of wynd is the deficultee
In enditing of this lytill trety small:
The bote I clepe the mater hole of all:
My wit, vnto the saile that now I wynd
To seke conning, though I bot lytill fynd.
(117-26)

The introduction of these three journeys at the outset of the ***Quair*** indicates a focus which will be quite different from Boethius'. The whole issue of Fortune, James suggests, will be seen within the larger context of the youth's journey of life.

A second major change James makes in Boethius' scheme involves the role he assigns to Venus. In the ***Quair*** she is the intermediary between the narrator and Minerva, a position which has no counterpart in Boethius' *Consolation.* Her introduction in the ***Quair*** further underscores James' shift in emphasis from Boethius' experience to the broader vision of man's relation to Fortune in his journey from youth to maturity. In the ***Quair,*** love rather than philosophy is man's first guide. Before the narrator can benefit from wisdom or philosophy, in contrast to Boethius, he must first be prepared by Venus. Prior to his dream, as we have seen, it was love which gave the narrator stability and transformed him from prisoner to free thrall, from one buffeted by Fortune to one capable of determining his own actions. Significantly, when the narrator first addresses Venus during his vision, he makes her role in his journey explicit by echoing his earlier descriptions of himself as a rudderless ship in need of a guide. Venus will be his "havin," his "anker," and his "keye."

As ye that bene the socour and suete well
Of remedye, of carefull hertes cure,
And in the huge weltering wawis fell
Of lufis rage, blisfull havin and sure,
O anker and keye of oure gude auenture, . . .
(st. 100)

In her role as guide, Venus provides two important lessons for the narrator. In the first place, she places his experiences in the larger context of the orderly workings of the universe. Though Love's powers are great, she does not govern alone but is part of an order which the narrator will learn about in greater detail from Minerva:

. . . though it to me pertene
In lufis lawe the septre to gouerne
(That the effectis of my bemes schene
Has thair aspectis by ordynance eterne
With ortheris [to] bynd, and m[e]ynes to discerne),
Quhilum in thingis bothe to cum and gone
That langis noght to me to writh allone.
(st. 107)

Secondly, Venus teaches the narrator the significance of his transformation from prisoner to free thrall and prepares him to govern himself before he turns to the larger questions of fortune and free will. Unlike the majority of men who break her rule and lack governance, the narrator must learn to ground his heart in virtue and discipline his will according to Love's laws:

This is to say, contynew in my seruise,
Worschip my law and my name magnifye

That am your hevin and your paradise,
And I your confort here sall multiplye,
And for your meryt here, pepetualye
Ressaue I sall your saulis of my grace, . . .
(st. 123)

Thus before he is ready to consider the questions Minerva raises, the narrator must achieve the steadfastness and discipline Venus teaches.

In his description of Venus as the intermediary between the narrator and Minerva, James is careful to distinguish her from the Venus of his sources. In contrast to Chaucer in the *Parliament* and *Knight's Tale,* for example, James systematically ignores all of the somber aspects of her passion. Unlike her counterparts in these poems who are found in the questionable company of "Plesaunce," "Aray," "Lust," "Craft," "Delyt," "Messagerye," "Meede," and "Jelosye," Venus in the ***Quair*** is served only by "Gude-Hope," "Fair-Calling," and "Secretee." In both the *Parliament* and the *Knight's Tale,* Chaucer further indicates the pain love can cause through his representation of Venus' temple. Inside the temple in the *Parliament,* the narrator hears:

. . . of skyes hoote as fyr
. . . a swogh that gan aboute renne,
Whiche sikes were engendered with desyr,
That maden every auter for to brenne
Of newe flaume . . .

Likewise, in the *Knight's Tale,* the narrator sees on the walls of Venus' temple pictures of the broken sleep, the cold sighs, the tears, and the lamentation of love.

While James echoes these descriptions in the ***Quair,*** he carefully qualifies his reference to the sighs painted on the temple walls with a parenthetical statement which indicates that the sighs are those of pleasure, not pain:

And in a retrete lytill of compas,
Depeynit all with sighis wonder sad,
(Noght suich sighis as hertis doith manace
Bot suich as dooth lufaris to be glad)
Fond I Venus . . .
(666-70)

Finally, James explicitly changes Chaucer's description of Venus' dress to create a more temperate image of the goddess. In the *Parliament,* the narrator finds Venus in a secret corner lying on a bed alluringly arrayed. Likewise, in the *Knight's Tale,* the statue of Venus is naked, floating in the sea covered only from the waist down by waves. Imitating Chaucer, James' narrator finds Venus "in a retrete lytill of compass" (666) lying in bed. But her body is now covered: "A mantill cast over hir schuldris quhite,— / Thus clothit was the goddesse of delyte." (671-2). Similarly, though his Venus has more in common with Lydgate's in the *Temple of Glas* than Chaucer's, James even changes the long catalogue of lovers he borrows from this poem to one which shows Love in a more flattering light.

Even more significant than James' introduction of Venus in the ***Quair*** is his treatment of the character of Minerva, who many have noted plays a part similar to Philosophy's in the *Consolation.* Like Philosophy, Minerva teaches the narrator the importance of virtue (st. 129), warns him about the doubleness and inconstancy of the world (st. 134-37), and considers questions about the nature of fortune and the relation of free will and necessity (st. 146-47). But Minerva differs from Philosophy in several important ways which have not been recognized. In the first place, she is much less concerned than Philosophy with establishing Fortune's role in an orderly and stable universe. The difference between her focus and Philosophy's is seen vividly by comparing the discussions of free will and necessity with which the two end their dialogues. In the *Consolation,* Philosophy devotes the entire Fifth Book to proving the possibility of man's free will in a world governed by divine providence. She first establishes that rational natures must have free will. Boethius raises the objection that divine foreknowledge and human free will are incompatible. Philosophy counters his objection by showing the difference between divine and human knowledge. Unlike human reason, divine intelligence is not hampered by time; rather it sees all things as eternally present. Thus God does not have foreknowledge, that is, knowledge of future events, but knowledge of an unchanging present. What he sees as happening does happen, but Philosophy demonstrates, the necessity is found only in God's knowledge of the event, not in the nature of the event itself. Thus man does have free choice and must use his will virtuously.

Between Philosophy's discussion and Minerva's, as James was aware, Chaucer's Troilus completely reverses the conclusions of the *Consolation* by repeating only Boethius' arguments in Book 5 without Philosophy's response. Like Boethius, Troilus reasons that if God sees everything in advance and cannot be deceived, whatever His providence foresees will happen. If things could happen in any other way, then God's foreknowledge would not be certain. On the other hand, some argue that Providence foresees what is to come because it will happen and that necessity is thus in the things and not in Providence. Troilus attempts to test this assumption with Boethius' example of a man sitting on a chair, but without Philosophy's aid, he is unable to distinguish between simple and conditional necessity and concludes "That thilke thynges that in erthe falle, / That by necessity they comen alle" (IV, 1049-50).

Drawing from the speeches of Philosophy and Troilus, Minerva briefly sums up both positions (st. 146-47). But in contrast to her predecessors, she does not support either view. Rather she offers a new conclusion: the more foreknowledge or intelligence a person has, the weaker Fortune will be:

And therefore thus I say to this sentence;
Fortune is most and strangest euermore
Quhare leste foreknawing or intelligence
Is in the man; . . .
(1037-40)

Turning to the narrator, she applies her remarks directly:

. . . sone, of wit or lore
Sen thou art wayke and feble, lo, therefore,
The more thou art in dangere and commune
With hir that clerkis clepen so Fortune.
(1040-43)

Minerva's conclusion, as critics have not recognized, underscores the purpose of her entire dialogue with the narrator, not to establish man's free will or the necessity of God's providence but to provide the narrator with "wit or lore" so that he will be less subject to Fortune.

When this emphasis is recognized, James' substitution of Minerva for Philosophy takes on new significance. In contrast to Philosophy who represents only one aspect of man's knowledge, Minerva's scope is much broader. Her domain includes not only the systematized knowledge man acquires but all of his wisdom, all of the wit or reason which he has in "the celles of his brayn." In the later Middle Ages, moreover, Minerva acquired an explicitly Christian emphasis, a change which further distinguishes her from Boethius' Philosophy. Her wisdom, unlike Philosophy's, descends directly from God and leads man ultimately to amend his corrupt nature and live in eternal "joye without strife." As Lydgate explains:

Thys myghty lady and goddesse,
Fro men avoydeth ydelnesse,
And maketh hem ful prudently
For to lyve vertuously,
Her lyfe by wisdom to amende,
And in her wyt to comprehende
Secretys which that be dyvyne.
And she kan folkes eke enclyne,
Both in werre and eke debat,
To ben ewrous and fortunat;
And man, by kynde corumpable,
She kan make pardurable,
Yf she be vertu him gouerne,
Lyk goddys for to be eterne,
To lyven in that perfyt lyfe . . .

(1075-89)

By introducing Minerva instead of Philosophy, James thus draws attention to an essential difference between the *Consolation* and the ***Quair.*** In contrast to Boethius, he suggests that man gains strength against Fortune not by looking outside himself to discover Fortune's nature, powers, and position in the universe, but by developing his own "wit" and reason. Although Minerva's wisdom includes Philosophy's, it goes beyond it. She teaches man virtue, which arms and ennobles him and prepares him to confront Fortune.

When this difference between the two works is recognized, Minerva's role in the ***Quair***—to develop the narrator's wit and reason—is seen clearly as part of a larger scheme of governance in the poem. At the outset, as we have seen, the narrator indicates that the ***Quair*** is a journey of his rudderless ship to find a rule and guide (st. 15). Initially a prisoner of Fortune, in the first stage of his journey he discovers his free will and willingly becomes love's thrall. From Venus, his first anchor or haven, he learns to discipline his will according to her laws and to be constant and steadfast amid the world's rage. By linking the narrator's self-governance with God's governance, Minerva further develops his understanding of this term. Echoing and expanding Venus' instruction, she first bids him ground his heart in virtue if he is to receive her "lore and discipline" (st. 128). She then suggests a new guide for his "stereles" ship:

Tak him before in all thy gouernance,
That in his hand the stere has of you all,
And pray vnto his hye purueyance
Thy lufe to gye . . .

(st. 130)

God's governance is the cornerstone upon which the narrator's must rest. If the narrator is to be "wele fortuynt," he must "Lat wisedom ay [vn] to thy will be iunyt" (st. 133). In other words, he must not merely rely on Love's laws, but on his own wisdom and rule grounded on God's as well. As Minerva's four-stanza digression on the doubleness of the world suggests, few heed this advice. Most are "brukill sort" who feign truth under the shadow of hypocrisy (st. 134). While all are subject to Fortune, through wise governance, one can minimize her effects. Minerva thus warns the narrator of his danger unless he joins wisdom to his will and then sends him on to Fortune. She has, in effect, told the narrator all he needs to know; now he must apply his knowledge.

The confrontation with Fortune which follows is the climax of the vision and not a mere coda as some have assumed. In contrast to Boethius, the ***Quair*** narrator is not finished with his instruction after encountering Minerva. "Wit or resoun" is not sufficient; he must also learn by experience. Thus he descends to the ground to find Fortune. In spite of Minerva's preparation, what he sees as he discovers the goddess hovering over a huge wheel, astonishes and terrifies him:

And vnderneth the quhele sawe I there
An vgly pit, depe as ony helle,
That to behald thereon I quoke for fere.
Bot o thing herd I, that quho therein fell
Com no more vp agane, tidings to telle.
Of quhich, astonait of that ferefull syght,
I ne wist quhat to done, so was I fricht.

(st. 162)

Fortune bluntly mocks the narrator's weakness and warns him though his beginning was "retrograde," he must now be "froward." Half of his time or life is almost gone; he must spend well "the remanant of the day" (st. 171). As she stretches the narrator on her wheel, she bids him learn from the example of its turning, thus demonstrating by experience what Minerva had taught him—the danger of his weakness. Fortune pulls the narrator brusquely by the ear and he awakens just in time before she can spin him about.

Finally, in the frame of the vision which follows, the narrator places his experience in a still larger context. As he indicated at the outset, the ***Quair*** is not only the journey of his "stereless" ship to find a rule and guide but also the journey of his literary endeavor. The relation of these two themes, emphasized again at the end of the poem, provides an important perspective which is not considered in the *Consolation.*

The significance of the narrator's activities as author is first suggested in the rather curious summary of the *Consolation* with which the poem opens. As few critics have noted, James devotes almost as much attention to Boethius as a writer as he does to Boethius as a philosopher. After briefly explaining who Boethius was, he pauses for an enthusiastic account of his poetic skills:

And thereto, here, this worthy lord and clerk
His metir suete, full of moralitee,
His flourit pen so fair he set awerk,
Discryving first of his prosperitee,
And out of that his infelicitee;
And than how he, in his poetly report,
In philosophy can him to confort.

(st. 4)

Two stanzas later, he concludes his summary of the *Consolation* with elaborate praise of Boethius' style:

With mony a noble resoun (as him likit)
Enditing in his fair[e] Latyne tong,
So full of fruyte and rethorikly pykit,
Quhich to declare my scole is ouer yong.

(st. 7)

At the outset of the ***Quair,*** moreover, the narrator introduces himself as a highly self-conscious writer. Like his predecessor in Chaucer's *Troilus,* he repeatedly interrupts the progress of his story to draw conspicuous attention to his craft. In the first twenty stanzas, for example, he provides three rhetorical openings to the poem, an elaborate astrological preface in stanza 1, a formal address in stanza 14, and a new seasonal preface in stanza 20. Between stanzas 13 and 20, moreover, the narrator pauses for a seven-stanza digression about his writing in which he refers briefly to his unsuccessful career as an author, ceremoniously takes his pen in hand "sum new[e] thing to write," and makes a cross to begin his book. With elaborate metaphors, he describes the difficulties of writing and prays to Calyope, Cleo, "Polymye," Thesiphone, and the gods and sisters nine for inspiration. Again after the vision, the narrator interrupts his story to defend his activities as author:

Bot for als moche as sum micht think or seyne:
Quhat nedis me apoun so litill evyn
To writt all this? I ansuere thus ageyne:
Quho that from hell war croppin onys in hevin
Wald efter o thank for ioy mak six or sevin?

(st. 182)

Finally, he closes the ***Quair*** with an envoy to his book, nervously placing it in the tradition of his masters Gower and Chaucer.

James' artistic nervousness, however, as critics have not recognized, is more than just a conventional opening and closing device. In his digression on writing at the outset, the narrator establishes a direct connection between the writing of the book and the central issue of governance in the poem. Significantly, he uses the same metaphors to introduce both themes. The writing of the ***Quair,*** like the search for governance is a "journey" of his "stereles" ship to find "reul and gye." Echoing stanzas 15 and 16 where he applies these metaphors to his philosophic journey, in stanzas 18 and 19, James uses the same terms to refer to the difficulty of his artistic endeavors:

The rokkis clepe I the prolixitee
Of doubilnesse that doith my wittis pall:
The lak of wynd is the deficultee
In enditing of this lytill trety small:
The bote I clepe the mater hole of all:
My wit, vnto the saile that now I wynd
To seke conning, though I bot lytill fynd.

(st. 18)

Thus he bids the gods and muses his "wilsum wittis gye," again echoing stanzas 15 and 16.

After the vision, James makes the link between the two journeys more explicit by further distinguishing his narrator's experience from Boethius'. Unlike Boethius, as James emphasizes, the ***Quair*** narrator does not understand the significance of his dialogue immediately. When he awakens from his vision, he finds himself "twenty-fold" "in trouble more" and demands some token of its validity (st. 176). A turtledove appears bearing gillyflowers and a message of comfort, and, shortly afterwards, the narrator's fortune changes. But it is only in retrospect as he writes that the meaning of his vision becomes clear to him.

By his treatment of the narrative after the vision, James points up the relation of the events of his youth, the book he reads, his dream, and the writing of the ***Quair*** itself. Significantly, when he ends the actual story in stanza 181, he suddenly shifts from the past of his adventures to the present moment of his writing. Though he insists that he has no time to tell all the details of his experience, he continues for sixteen more stanzas before ending the poem. This device has puzzled several of the ***Quair's*** critics [such as M. F. Markland in "The Structure of *The Kingis Quair,*" *Research Studies* 25 (1957)] who find the end of the poem abrupt and "less satisfactory" than the rest. But the last sixteen stanzas in which the narrator returns to the immediate present and his activities as author point up the significance of the events we have witnessed. In the first place, after the vision he makes his role as literary artist extremely conspicuous by providing an elaborate concluding prayer, a rhetorical series of blessings, and a formal envoy for his book. In addition, he radically changes his narrative technique in this portion of the poem by turning away from the specific events of his story to his more distant response. As the narrator looks back on his adventures from his present perspective of author, he indicates that the details of his adventures are less important than their underlying meaning. Thus, rather than relate all that passed between him and his lady as he had done at the outset of the poem, he hastily sums up his change of fortune after the dream in one stanza and concentrates on the broader significance of his love. In his moving prayer, the narrator places his youthful experience explicitly in the larger context of the god's workings:

Eke quho may in this lyfe haue more plesance
Than cum to largesse from thraldom and peyne?—
And by the mene of Luffis ordinance
That has so mony in his goldin cheyne,
Quhich, th[u]s to wyn his hertis souereyne
Quho suld me wite to write tharof, lat se!
Now sufficiante is my felicitee.

(st. 183)

Likewise, the narrator uses the long series of blessings which follow and the literary envoy to draw attention to the meaning of the events he has related. In stanzas 188 to 196, he carefully retraces his steps back to the beginning of the poem, referring in turn to the "goddis all" who helped him, to Fortune, to the nightingale who sang to his lady, to the garden where he first saw his love, to the lady herself, to his youth, to the writing of the book, and finally to the heavens, echoing the first line of the poem, "Hich in the hevynnis figure circulere." But as he threads his way back through the poem linking his own experience, his dream, the book he read, and his writing, he provides an important change in emphasis. In contrast to the opening stanzas of the poem, the narrator's focus is now clearly on God's heaven and His governance. As he bids farewell to his quair as author, he indicates that he understands the significance of his vision:

> And thus endith the f[a]tall influence
> Causit from hevyn quhare powar is commytt
> Of gouirnance, by the magnificence
> Of him that hiest in the hevin sitt.
> To quham we th[a]nk that all oure [lif] hath writt,
> Quho couth it red agone syne mony a yere
> 'Hich in the hevynnis figure circulere'.
>
> (st. 196)

Ending with the appropriate metaphor of God the "writer" of our lives, the narrator provides the conclusion to both of his journeys.

Thus, in the final analysis, the differences between the ***Quair*** and its sources are perhaps more important for an understanding of the poem than are the similarities. Although James borrows freely from Boethius and Chaucer, he defines a view of man's relation to Fortune which differs significantly from theirs. Together, his specific changes in his sources provide a scheme which is a response to rather than an imitation of Boethius' and Chaucer's work. Like Chaucer, James attempts to test the conclusions of the *Consolation* in an area of human experience largely ignored by Boethius. But unlike Chaucer's characters, James' narrator learns to overcome Fortune while he remains in this world. Significantly, he learns not from Philosophy but through his journey from youth to maturity, the journey of every man's life, an experience at once more immediate and credible than Boethius'. Finally, in contrast to Boethius, James demonstrates that man's full recognition of Fortune's role comes from all of the kinds of experience accessible to him—in life, in books, in dreams, and in writing. As the French suggested to the imprisoned King James ten years before he wrote the ***Quair*** in a letter which echoes the *Consolation,* adverse fortune is man's best teacher:

> . . . illustrissime princops ac metuendissime domine, videmus universa sub sole fortune sevientis incursibus fore omniquaque subjecta, preter ea que subnixa sunt in stabili virtutis fundamento . . . Nos vero itaque licet superbientis prodigii sevitiam execramus . . . Si enim utraque fortune conditio, et prospere et adverse, debito ponderentur examine ac equa lance pensemus, ceperimus indubie adversam in omnibus potiorem et omnis vite ac discipline magistram, que veros detigit amicos et mendaces et false felicitatis amatores, quo nichil inter mortales carius existimari potest . . .

The ***Quair,*** however, defines the process which gives validity to these truths and renders the experience of Boethius significant to the journey of all men. (pp. 324-41)

Lois A. Ebin, "Boethius, Chaucer, and 'The Kingis Quair'," in Philological Quarterly, *Vol. 53, No. 3, Summer, 1974, pp. 321-41.*

John MacQueen (essay date 1988)

[*MacQueen is an English educator and critic who specializes in medieval literature. In the following excerpt, he examines the influence of several medieval cultural beliefs and practices evident in the* Kingis Quair. *MacQueen also notes James's experimentation with the five-stress line and rime royal.*]

By English and continental standards, Scots poetry until the end of the first quarter of the fifteenth century had been old-fashioned. The metrical range was limited, as a comparison of Barbour (*c.* 1320-1395) with Chaucer (*c.* 1343–1400) will show. Chaucer's earliest extended works, *The Book of the Duchess, The House of Fame,* and *The Romance of the Rose* (this last, of course, a translation) had been written in an English adaptation of the couplet used by such earlier French authors as Chrétien de Troyes (ob. *c.* 1175) and Guillaume de Lorris (first half of the thirteenth century), that is to say, in a basic octosyllabic, often with feminine rhyme, and with a norm of four stresses. None of Chaucer's later poetry uses this metre; he turned almost exclusively to variations of the five-stress line, commonly in the form of the heroic couplet or stanzaic *rime royal.* His style changed with this change of metre; the date of *The Parliament of Fowls,* written in *rime royal,* is not much later than that of the other poems mentioned, but the structural clarity has much increased, and there is a greater richness of invention to accompany the new metrical form. Italian poetry, in particular that of Dante and Boccaccio, had become an important influence. Chaucer's older contemporary, Barbour, shows originality in the choice of a modern subject for his heroic romance, but metrically and stylistically the ***Bruce*** belongs to the older fashion, as does Wyntoun's later (before 1420) *Cornykkyllys* (the *Original Chronicle*). The first Scots poet to experiment with the newer style is James I (1394-1437).

There is an instinctive reluctance on the part of modern critics to allow that a king might play a significant role in the development of a literature. Such anachronistic feelings are not to be trusted; in Professor Alan Harding's phrase [from "Regiam Majestatem amongst Medieval Law-Books," *Juridical Review* 29 (1984)], they lack 'a true historical sense of the role of kings in the formation of European societies'. Temperamentally, as shown by his political as well as his literary career, James was an innovator, and his kingly status allowed him to exercise a powerful effect on all the workings of the society which depended on him. His poetry, like that of Chaucer, sometimes gives a deliberate impression of *naiveté,* not usually to be taken at face value. Despite its relative brevity, the ***Kingis Quair*** is a complex, powerful, and above all, influential work of art.

The suggestion is sometimes made that during the fifteenth and sixteenth centuries it remained virtually unknown, and cannot therefore have been an influence on Scots literature in general. This seems improbable, even if one ignores the apparent verbal reminiscences which occur in later poets, the direct, if not always perceptive, references made by Walter Bower, John Major, John Bale, George Buchanan and Thomas Dempster, and the fact that the manuscript, written *c.*1488 for Henry Sinclair, 3rd Earl of Orkney, is a wide-ranging collection, which included among much else a text of Chaucer's *Troilus and Criseyde.* This might lead one to the conclusion that the ***Kingis Quair,*** no less than Chaucer's poem, formed a part of the public literary domain. The MS did not remain in the exclusive possession of a single family; in the mid sixteenth century, for instance, it was for a time in the hands of a MacDonald chieftain, Donald Gorm of Sleat in Skye. Two poems, *Lancelot of the Laik* and *The Quare of Jelusy,* neither by James, appear to imitate the distinctive linguistic usage of the ***Quair.*** All fifteenth century poetry, finally, was a public rather than a private art, and it is not likely that a king of James's accomplishments would have confined a major work to a circle which he deliberately had restricted to a few intimates.

The poem is an idealised autobiography, based on James's kidnapping at sea in 1406 and his subsequent eighteen years of captivity in England, which came to an end soon after his marriage to Lady Joan Beaufort in February 1424. The *motif* of captivity is prominent in the two chief literary models which he used, *De Consolatione Philosophiae* of Boethius, and Chaucer's *Knight's Tale.* The first gave him the philosophic emphasis which characterises his poem, the second helped to combine it with a love interest which itself has strong philosophic overtones. James is unusual, although not unique, in the emphasis placed, by way of the speech of Minerva in the dream-vision, on the fulfilment of courtly love in marriage. He is almost hubristic in the confidence with which he offers his own experience as a counterpart and confirmation to that of Boethius, whose virtuous and well-trained youth enabled him to overcome, at least in his mind, the disasters of later life; correspondingly James's own early ignorance and misfortunes were transformed, he claims, by the philosophic miracle of love to set him finally in a position superior to all mischance. Reading this, one becomes uncomfortably conscious of the final scene at Perth, the brutal murder of the king only a few years after the completion of the poem, a murder, the very abruptness of which in a sense sets at nothing all the poetry and philosophy.

'Heirefter followis the quair Maid be King Iames of Scotland the first callit the Kingis Quair and Maid quhen his *Maiestie* wes in Ingland.' The sixteenth century rubric which in the MS precedes the poem recognises that the poem is an offshoot of James's captivity, but is wrong to assert that it was composed during that period. As Professor Norton-Smith notes [in his introduction to ***The Kingis Quair,*** Oxford, 1981], 'The evidence of the poem (11.1264 1351) shows clearly that the poem was written after a marriage had taken place, and after a release from prison had been obtained.' The poem indeed suggests that several years had passed and had given the king the opportunity to develop the philosophic detachment exhibited. Metrically it belongs to the later, more ornate, tradition:

> Unto the impnis of my maisteris dere, [poems]
> Gowere and Chaucere, that on the steppis satt
> Of rethorike quhill thai were lyvand here,
> Superlative as poetis laureate,
> In moralitee and eloquence ornate,
> I recommend my buk in lynis seven,
> And eke thair saulis unto the blisse of hevin.
> (1373-79)

Notably and curiously, James gives Gower precedence over Chaucer, while his own older English contemporary, John Lydgate (1370-1450), as a model at least as important as Gower, remains unmentioned, probably because he was alive when the ***Quair*** was composed. The reason for the position given to Gower may be that the central situation of *Confessio Amantis,* the appeal made by the Lover to Venus and Cupid, which is answered by the appearance of the priest Genius, runs parallel to the prayers made by the captive in the ***Kingis Quair,*** and the divine response which they obtain:

> Than wold I pray his [Cupid's] blisfull grace benigne
> To hable me unto his service digne. [make worthy]
> And evermore for to be one of tho [those]
> Him trewly for to serve in wele and wo.
> (270-73)

> O Venus clere, of goddis stellifyit,
> To quhom I yelde homage and sacrifise,
> Fro this day furth your grace be magnifyit,
> That me ressavit have in swich [a] wise,
> To lyve under your law and do servise.
> Now help me furth, and for your merci lede
> My hert to rest, that deis nere for drede.
> (358-64)

The dream-vision which forms a response to these prayers and which constitutes the greater part of the poem, is the dreamer's visit to the Zodiacal house of Venus and Cupid, and his subsequent journeys to the court of Minerva in the Empyrean, and the garden abode of Fortune on Earth. In a sense, the conversations which he has with these goddesses correspond to the Lover's confession in Gower. It is also, I suppose, possible that James intended the word 'moralitee' to apply particularly to Gower, 'eloquence' primarily to Chaucer, although he is unlikely to have intended an absolute distinction between the two.

C S Lewis noted [in *The Allegory of Love,* 1936,] that in the ***Kingis Quair*** 'the poetry of marriage at last emerges from the traditional poetry of adultery', a point well-made if one ignores the *Franklin's Tale* as a special case, and confines oneself otherwise to literature in English. Gower's French poems, however, in particular the *Traitié . . . pour essampler les amantz marietz* and the opening group of *Cinkante Balades,* devote themselves to the same theme, and it is possible that this also may have led James to give Gower so prominent a position.

His long captivity in England and France had certainly made him acquainted with the vernacular literatures of the southern courts, and with a rhetoric more complex than anything yet produced in Scots. It is certainly poetry of this general kind, emerging from a courtly life resembling that of England and France, which he recommends, through the *persona* of Venus, to the Scots nation:

> Say on than, quhare is becummyn, for shame,
> The songis new, the fresch carolis and dance,

The lusty lyf, the mony change of game,
The fresche array, the lusty contenance,
The besy awayte, the hertly observance, [attendance]
That quhilum was amongis thame so ryf? [once]
Bid thame repent in tyme and mend thaire lyf.
(841-47)

C S Lewis noted that the Boethian prologue to the ***Kingis Quair*** is in effect a literary manifesto, which lays strong emphasis on personal experience as the basis for courtly philosophical poetry. Although at first it may appear an excrescence, the stanza just quoted adds a new dimension to this idea. What has the complaint of Venus, or indeed the court of Venus, to do with the poet's personal development, or with the development in terms of the poem of a philosophic theme? The answer lies in the highest reaches of the poetry of *amour courtois* exemplified, say, by the *Vita Nuova* of Dante, or the *Troilus and Criseyde* of Chaucer. Love, the operation of Venus, was central to the operation of the Mediæval universe. But as the universe was a complex work of art, so the celebrations of the central power of the universe must themselves be complex works of art, and the product of a complex and ornate society. The philosophic subject which emerges from the personal experience of the ***Kingis Quair,*** is the part played by Fortune in

luffis ordinance,
That has so mony in his goldin cheyne.
(1277-78)

The sacrament of matrimony made the service of Venus transcend courtly play, a serious make-believe, philosophically worked out in terms of literature and music; it became something vitally related to the experience of Everyman. The complaint of Venus is that the Scots court has omitted this kind of observance; the remedy which she urges, and which is linked to the sacrament by the homily of Minerva, is that the court should adopt a philosophy, a way of life, and a literature embracing the kinds exemplified in the ***Kingis Quair.*** This is not merely to say extended dream-vision. The poem incidentally contains specimens of other kinds, most notably the songs which punctuate the first autobiographical episode—stanzas 34, 52, 63 and 64-65. In my book, *Ballattis of Lufe* I have tried to show how the Scots courtly lyric developed, in part at least, according to James's example, an example which is strong in the later fifteenth century poets Clerk and Mersar, and which had not entirely lost its power when Alexander Scott (*c.*1515-*c.*1583) was writing for Mary of Guise and her daughter Mary I, nor when Alexander Montgomerie (*c.*1545–1597) was James VI's master poet.

The ***Kingis Quair*** is the earliest Scots poem which we can describe with reasonable certainty as intended for the court, and intended to set an example, which others could follow, of the art appropriate to such poetry. It has long been recognised that this last appears, partly in the elaborate stanza used, partly in the level of diction, imagery and thematic development. Less well recognised, indeed until recently not recognised at all, is the importance of the formal structure, in which a total of 197 stanzas is made up of a Boethian prologue in 13 stanzas, the 60 stanzas of the first autobiographical section, 99 stanzas of the dream-vision, 24 stanzas of the second autobiographical section, and the single dedicatory stanza directed to Gower and Chaucer. The first line of the first stanza, 'Heigh in the hevennis figure circulere', is repeated as the last line of the penultimate 196th stanza, and gives a circular effect to the movement of the entire poem.

The effect is complicated by the fact that 196 which completes the circle, is also a perfect square ($14 \times 14 = 196$), and that 197 is a prime number. James draws a distinction between 'hevin', the Empyrean beyond the Primum Mobile, and 'the hevynnis', the 9 celestial spheres contained by the Empyrean, as may be shown in stanza 196, where he distinguishes between 'him that hiest in the hevin sitt' (God), and 'the hevynnis figure circulere', the 9 celestial spheres of the created universe. In the general context of Mediæval numerology, it may not seem extravagant to suggest that the circular structure of the first 196 stanzas is intended to correspond to that of the spherical created universe, while the extra stanza, which transforms circle and perfect square to a prime number, corresponds to the relationship between the unique Creator and his multiplex but orderly creation, an interpretation which agrees with James's idiosyncratic use of Boethius to illustrate relations between divine Providence, which directly governs the movements of the stars and planets, and Fortune, the apparently arbitrary mistress of affairs in the world below.

The number 99, one of those which tend to appear whenever a literary work deals with the Otherworld or Eternity, makes its appearance as the total number of stanzas (74-172; lines 512-1204) in the dream-vision in which three goddesses, Venus, Minerva and Fortune, advise the imprisoned poet on the progress and significance of his apparently hopeless love for the young woman whom he has seen from his tower window as she walks in the garden below. The vision is decidedly extraterrestrial; he is snatched up through the spheres to one of the Zodiacal houses of Venus; later he goes beyond the Primum Mobile to the palace of Minerva (Heavenly Wisdom—the Fronesis or Prudentia of Alan of Lille's *Anticlaudianus*) in the Empyrean, from which he is returned to the domain of Fortune, Earth—Earth however in an archetypal and symbolic form, which is itself Otherworldly.

Within the dream vision, 50 stanzas are devoted to Venus and her court. Fifty (5×10) is 5, the number of the senses, in a glorified form appropriate to the planetary goddess of love. Twenty-one (thrice the number of the body, seven) stanzas are devoted to Fortune and her realm, and (most significantly) 28, the second perfect number, to Minerva. The 99 stanzas which represent eternal experience, combine with other groups representing temporal existence; the 13 stanzas of the prologue representing the 13 spheres of the created universe (Primum Mobile, Fixed Stars, 7 Planets, 4 Elements), by the movements and relations of which time is measured; the first and second autobiographical groups of stanzas the 60 minutes of the hour and the 24 hours of the day. Other numerological felicities might be mentioned: here it is probably enough to say that such distinctive features of the text are always clearly and accurately pointed.

Although he never forgets eternal values, James's concern is more with the temporal creation, subjected to the whims of Fortune, but ultimately governed by a Boethian and benevolent Providence. His Otherworldly vision enables him to reconcile benevolence with apparent cruel whimsicality, and his ultimate meaning is conveyed by the structure, which subordinates the vision to the circle squared in 196 stanzas, and transformed in 197. (pp. 55-60)

John MacQueen, "Poetry—James I to Henryson," in The History of Scottish Literature: Origins to 1660 (Mediaeval and Renaissance), Vol. I, *edited by R. D. S. Jack, Aberdeen University Press, 1988, pp. 55-72.*

FURTHER READING

Brown, J. T. T. *The Authorship of "The Kingis Quair": A New Criticism.* Glasgow: James MacLehose & Sons, 1896, 99 p.

Uses linguistic and historical evidence to disprove James's authorship of *The Kingis Quair.*

Carretta, Vincent. *"The Kingis Quair* and *The Consolation of Philosophy." Studies in Scottish Literature* XVI (1981): 14-28.

Analyzes James's use of Boethius's work as a "moral touchstone" against which the narrator's ignorance is measured.

Craigie, W. A. "The Language of *The Kingis Quair." Essays and Studies by Members of the English Association* XXV (1939): 22-38.

Surveys the critical reaction to J. T. T. Brown's claim that James did not write *The Kingis Quair* and examines the poem's unique combination of Scottish and English spelling as proof of James's authorship.

"The Poet-King of Scotland." *Fraser's Magazine* n. s. X, No. LVII (September 1874): 378-87.

A biographical interpretation of *The Kingis Quair.*

Irving, David. "James the First." In his *The History of Scotish Poetry,* edited by John Aitken Carlyle, pp. 123-60. Edinburgh: Edmonston and Douglas, 1861.

Discusses the biographical background of *The Kingis Quair* and the debate surrounding the authorship of "Christis Kirk of the Grene" and "Peblis to the Play."

Lewis, C. S. "The *Kingis Quair." The Times Literary Supplement,* No. 1410 (April 18, 1919): 315.

Examines the opening stanzas of the *Kingis Quair* and their function as a preface to the poem.

MacQueen, John. "Tradition and the Interpretation of the *Kingis Quair." The Review of English Studies* XII, No. 46 (May 1961): 117-31.

Compares the *Kingis Quair* to works by Geoffrey Chaucer and John Lydgate, noting James's innovative identification of Fortune with nature.

Noll, Dolores L. " 'The Romantic Conception of Marriage': Some Remarks on C. S. Lewis's Discussion of *The Kingis Quair." Studies in Medieval Culture* III (1970): 159-68.

Agrees with Lewis that the *Kingis Quair* offers insight into the assimilation of courtly love into Christian culture, but claims that "the association of adultery with courtly love was a relatively minor problem. More basic was the struggle between a this-worldly and an otherworldly orientation."

Norton-Smith, John. Introduction to *The Kingis Quair,* by James I of Scotland, pp. xi-xvii. Oxford: Clarendon Press, 1971.

Examines James's emphasis on the imaginative rather than the philosophical and concludes that John Lydgate was a greater influence than Geoffrey Chaucer.

Quinn, William. "Memory and the Matrix of Unity in *The Kingis Quair." The Chaucer Review* 15, No. 4 (Spring 1981): 332-55.

Discusses James's ability to recreate his experience as the source of the poem's unity.

Saintsbury, George. "The Four Great Scottish Poets." In his *A Short History of English Literature,* pp. 180-92. New York: Macmillan, 1898.

A brief discussion of the *Kingis Quair* and James's relation to other Scottish poets.

Scheps, Walter. "Chaucerian Synthesis: The Art of *The Kingis Quair." Studies in Scottish Literature* VIII, No. 3 (January 1971): 143-65.

Examines James's use of Chaucer's technique of combining Boethian philosophy with the courtly poetic tradition.

Spearing, A. C. *"The Kingis Quair."* In his *Medieval Dream Poetry,* pp. 181-86. Cambridge: Cambridge University Press, 1976.

Examines *The Kingis Quair* in the context of medieval dream poems, stressing James's innovative contributions to the genre.

Speirs, John. *"The Kingis Quhair."* In his *The Scots Literary Tradition: An Essay in Criticism,* pp. 5-11. London: Chatto & Windus, 1940.

Examines the allegorical elements of *The Kingis Quair.*

Veitch, John. "National Poets of the Stuart Period: James I. (1394-1437)." In his *The Feeling for Nature in Scottish Poetry,* Vol. I, pp. 186-207. Edinburgh: William Blackwood and Sons, 1887.

Interprets James's poetry as an anticipation of Scottish love-songs in which passion is associated with natural scenery.

Von Hendy, Andrew. "The Free Thrall: A Study of *The Kingis Quair." Studies in Scottish Literature* 11, No. 3 (January 1965): 141-51.

Praises *The Kingis Quair* and rejects autobiographical interpretations.

Sir David Lyndsay

1490-1555

(Also Lindsay) Scottish poet and dramatist.

INTRODUCTION

Lyndsay is widely recognized as the satiric voice of the Reformation in Scotland, and he represents both the last of the medieval Scots poets and the first modern Scottish poet. Presenting humorous commentary on the state of affairs in Scotland and on the corruption of the Church, Lyndsay's works were immensely popular with readers until the nineteenth century, and several verses were proverbialized in the Scottish vernacular. Lyndsay's greatest literary achievement, *Ane Satyre of the Thrie Estaitis* (1540), is a rare example of the transition from the medieval to the modern tradition in drama, for while the work is the only existing Scottish morality play, it also addresses many issues of the Reformation with a complexity never before seen in medieval drama. Although critics agree that Lyndsay was unparalleled as a master of satire, many have argued that much of his verse is uneven and carelessly constructed. Nevertheless, commentators affirm Lyndsay's importance as an influential figure in the history of Scottish literature.

Lyndsay was born into a Scottish noble family, and raised at his father's estate at either the Mount at Cupar-Fife or Garmylton in East Lothian. Lyndsay probably attended grammar school at either Cupar, or Haddington, which was close to Garmylton. His name appears on a register for St. Salvator's College at the University of St. Andrews, and it is believed that Lyndsay attended the university from 1505 to 1508. Lyndsay was a member of James IV's court when Prince James was born in 1512; he was named gentleman-usher, or guardian, to the child, a position he retained even after James IV was killed at Flodden a year later and the prince was crowned James V. In 1522 Lyndsay married Janet Douglas, a seamstress also in the employ of the king. The Earl of Angus named himself James V's regent two years later, dismissing Lyndsay from the court, along with James's other tutors. Lyndsay had inherited both Garmylton and the Mount by this time, and he retired to one of these estates for the duration of the Angus regency. Upon assuming full control of the monarchy in 1528, James appointed Lyndsay chief herald and later knighted him Lyon King of Arms. As the Scottish monarch's chief herald, Lyndsay traveled to the court of Emperor Charles V in the Netherlands in 1531 to renew a treaty between the two countries. He also visited France in 1537 to help arrange a marriage for James V. Lyndsay continued to perform his duties as an ambassador after the king died in 1542, traveling to the courts of Henry VIII of England and Christian III of Denmark, among other places. He died in 1555, shortly after presiding over a chapter of heralds in Edinburgh.

Lyndsay's dismissal from court in the 1520s may have been the catalyst that sparked his literary career. Freed from his duties, Lyndsay meditated on the state of affairs in Scotland, and by 1528, he recorded his musings in a poem entitled *The Dreme. The Dreme* is prefaced by a dedicatory "Epistil to the Kingis Grace," considered by some critics the most appealing passage of the work, which appeals to James V to remember Lyndsay's history of service and affection. The poet then constructs a dream allegory in which Dame Remembrance guides him through hell, purgatory, and heaven before showing him how Scotland has degenerated through ecclesiastical corruption. Similar in many respects to Dante Alighieri's *Divine Comedy,* Lyndsay's vision of hell, which he populates with an abundance of clergymen, satirizes corruption and wrongdoing in the Church. In the concluding "Exhourtatioun to the Kingis Grace," Lyndsay implores the king to have compassion on the poor and to take active measures toward religious reform.

Many commentators surmise that it was only because of Lyndsay's close association with the king that he was allowed to write controversial satires without severe repercussions. Lyndsay took advantage of his preferential status to compose two more works, *The Testament and Complaynt of Our Soverane Lordis Papyngo* (1530) and *The Complaynt and Publict Confessioun of the Kingis Auld Hound, Callit Bagsche* (1536), which explore the precariousness of position and prosperity at court. Lyndsay revives his criticism of ecclesiastical corruption as well as the problem of degeneracy and favoritism at court through the voice of a talking parrot in the *Testament and Complaynt,* a topic elaborated upon by the dog Bagsche in *The Complaynt and Publict Confessioun of the Kingis Auld Hound.*

According to many scholars, *Ane Satyre of the Thrie Estaitis* was first performed in 1540, and its appeal with both aristocrats and common folk established Lyndsay as a leading humorist of Scotland. Lyndsay focused on the theme of reform that often recurs in his works, examining the improbity of the Church and State and periodically alluding to actual events and people. The play consists of two parts interspersed with comic interludes that depict the various abuses of the clergy. The first section of the drama is generally allegorical in tone. Personifying virtues and vices as courtiers, Lyndsay satirizes the profligacy of the king and court, concluding the sequence with the characters' redemption. The second part dramatizes the purgation of corruption in Scotland as a court scene in which the commoners, represented by John the Commonweal, air their grievances against the three estates: Spiritualitie (the clergy), Temporality (the aristocracy), and Merchant (the middle class). During the course of the second section, John the Commonweal's most bitter invectives are directed at the estate of Spiritualitie. The *Satyre* ends with a sermon by Folly, who criticizes all men, even the king, as fools. Lyndsay revised sections of the drama at different stages of his life, and the completed work—at more than 4600 lines—is very long.

Critics generally cite Lyndsay's *Historie and Testament of Squyer Meldrum* (1550?) as another popular work. The poem is a biography of a heroic young squire with whom Lyndsay had been acquainted, and it illustrates the travels, battles, and forbidden love of William Meldrum. Written in the chivalric tradition, vivid battle imagery and the language of courtly love combine to construct a romantic narrative of an historical person. Considered more lighthearted than Lyndsay's other major works, many commentators maintain that *Squyer Meldrum* was probably written to be read aloud. C. S. Lewis glorified the work as a "wholly delightful poem [which] stands, as it were, at the triple frontier where the novel, the romance, and the biography all march together," and concluded that "[we] have greater stories in verse; perhaps none, even in Chaucer, more completely successful." *Ane Dialog betuix Experience and Ane Courteour* (1553), commonly referred to as *The Monarchie,* is the last and longest of Lyndsay's works at over 6000 lines. *The Monarchie* is essentially a poem of religious instruction, surveying the history of the world to its present "Miserabyll Estait." In the course of the work, Lyndsay argues that the Bible should be read to the masses in their native language and that prayers should be conducted in the vernacular as well.

Other than a period of several decades in the late nineteenth and early twentieth centuries, critics have generally tended to overlook Lyndsay's contributions to English literature. The poet's role as a leading satirist remains unimpeachable, but scholars have agreed that his verse is inferior in imagination, descriptive imagery, and grammatical structure in comparison to that of such contemporaries as Gavin Douglas and William Dunbar. Another factor that has contributed to Lyndsay's obscurity is that he wrote in a Scottish vernacular that has become archaic. Indicative of the dualistic critical reaction to Lyndsay's works are John M. Ross's comments on *The Dreme:* that "if the poem were to be judged only by its literary qualities, we should have little to say in its praise, but when we consider the time and the circumstances in which it was composed, we forget its poetic defects and are struck with admiration at its tone. . . . It is the very heroism of patriotic morality." Unlike many of Lyndsay's other works, however, critics have praised the *Satyre* for its masterful technical and stylistic qualities. According to Agnes Mure Mackenzie, "the play as a whole, with all its faults of conventional idea, a humour that sinks too often to mechanized dirt, party one-sidedness, and all the lave, has not only an explosive vitality, but a sure feeling for the actual stage, a technical command of all its devices, that make grievous the general loss of our old drama." Little attention has been given to Lyndsay's works since the early twentieth century. Some interest was revived in the period around 1948 when Tyrone Guthrie successfully produced the *Satyre* at the Edinburgh Festival, but in recent years, scholars have virtually ignored Lyndsay's literary achievements.

While commentators have questioned the literary value of many of Lyndsay's poetic works, his immensely popular satirical invectives against the Church at the height of the Reformation have confirmed his place as an important and transitional figure in Scottish literature. Such an accomplishment led Sir Walter Scott to proclaim: "Still is thy name in high account, / And still thy verse has charms, / Sir David Lindesay of the Mount, / Lord Lion King-at-Arms!"

PRINCIPAL WORKS

The Dreme (poem) 1528
The Complaynt to the King (poem) 1529
The Testament and Complaynt of Our Soverane Lordis Papyngo (poem) 1530
An Answer Quhilk Schir David Lyndsay Maid to the Kingis Flyting (poem) 1536
The Complaynt and Publict Confessioun of the Kingis Auld Hound, Callit Bagsche, Directit to Bawtie, the Kingis Best Belovit Dog, and His Companzeonis (poem) 1536
The Deploratioun of the Deith of Quene Magdalene (poem) 1537
The Justing betuix James Watsoun and Jhone Barbour Servitouris to King James the Fyft (poem) 1538
* *Ane Pleasant Satyre of the Thrie Estaitis in Commendatioun of Vertew and Vituperatioun of Vyce* (drama) 1540
Kitteis Confessioun (poem) 1541?
The Tragedie of the Maist Reverend Father David, Be the Mercy of God, Cardinall, Archbishop of Sanctandrois, and the Haill Realme of Scotland, Primate, Legate, and Chancellor &c. (poem) 1546
The Historie and Testament of Squyer Meldrum (poem) 1550?
† *Ane Dialog betuix Experience and ane Courteour, of the Miserabyll Estait of the World* (poem) 1553
Warkis of the Famous and Worthie Knicht Schir David Lyndsay of the Mont (poetry) 1568
The Poetical Works of Sir David Lyndsay of the Mount, Lyon King of Arms (poetry) 1871
The Works of Sir David Lyndsay of the Mount. 4 vols. (poetry) 1931-36

*While some scholars contend that the *Satyre* was performed as early as 1535, others argue that 1540 is the probable date of the work's composition.

†This work is commonly known as *The Monarchie.*

Sir David Lyndsay (poem date 1530)

[*In the following excerpt from the "Prolog" to his* Complaynt of the Papyngo (1530), *Lyndsay briefly discusses his literary style.*]

[Thocht] I had ingyne, as I have none,
I watt nocht quhat to wryt, be sweit Sanct Jhone;
For quhy? in all the garth of eloquence,
Is no thyng left, bot barrane stok and stone:
The poleit termes are pullit everilk one,
Be thir fornamit Poeitis of prudence;
And sen I fynd none uther new sentence,
I sall declare, or I depart yow fro,
The Complaynt of ane woundit Papingo.

Quharefor, because myne mater bene so rude
Of sentence, and of rethorike denude,
To rurall folke, myne dyting bene directit,
Far flemit frome the sycht of men of gude;
For cunnyng men, I knaw, wyll soune conclude,
It dowe no thyng, bot for to be dejectit:
And, quhen I heir myne mater bene detractit,
Than sall I sweir, I maid it bot in mowis,
To landwart lassis, quhilks kepith kye and yowis.

(pp. 65-6)

Sir David Lyndsay, in his The Poetical Works of Sir David Lyndsay of the Mount, Lyon King of Arms, Vol. I, *revised edition, William Paterson, 1871, pp. 63-106.*

Sir Walter Scott (poem date 1808)

[*Scott was an early nineteenth-century Scottish novelist, poet, historian, biographer, and critic, best known for his popular historical novels. In the excerpt below from his poem* Marmion (1808), *Scott hails Lyndsay as a great satirist who helped further the cause of the Reformation.*]

He was a man of middle age,
In aspect manly, grave, and sage,
As on king's errand come;
But in the glances of his eye
A penetrating, keen, and sly
Expression found its home;
The flash of that satiric rage
Which, bursting on the early stage,
Branded the vices of the age,
And broke the keys of Rome.
On milk-white palfrey forth he paced;
His cap of maintenance was graced
With the proud heron-plume.
From his steed's shoulder, loin, and breast,
Silk housings swept the ground,
With Scotland's arms, device, and crest,
Embroidered round and round.
The double tressure might you see,
First by Achaius borne,
The thistle and the fleur-de-lis,
And gallant unicorn.
So bright the king's armorial coat
That scarce the dazzled eye could note,
In living colors blazoned brave,
The Lion, which his title gave;
A train, which well beseemed his state,
But all unarmed, around him wait.
Still is thy name in high account,
And still thy verse has charms,
Sir David Lindesay of the Mount,
Lord Lion King-at-arms!

(pp. 116-17)

Sir Walter Scott, "The Camp," in his Marmion, *edited by William J. Rolfe, Houghton, Mifflin and Company, 1893, pp. 112-36.*

James Hannay (essay date 1867)

[*Hannay was a Scottish journalist and novelist who contributed critical essays to a number of literary periodicals. His most important work of criticism was* Lectures on Satire and Satirists *(1854). In the following excerpt, Hannay briefly examines Lyndsay's role as a satirist for the Reformation.*]

Sir David Lindsay, of the Mount, . . .is perhaps the most readable of the old Scots poets still. He is fresh and naïf, with a keen pictorial wit, a genuine good nature, and a wholesome contempt for all baseness, cruelty, and pretence. . . . Our business, however, is not . . . with his poetry proper, which has a great deal of pleasant sweetness about it; but with the satires by which he aided the growing spirit of revolt against the old Church. A satirist was wanted in this cause, in Scotland, if anywhere; for in no country had the Romish clergy a larger share of the national wealth, and in none were they more bigoted in belief, or dissolute in morals. (p. 622)

The satire of Sir David Lindsay . . . is of the playful kind. It is not the satire of indignation, but of merriment. It is as free as the satire of [Ulrich von Hutten's] *Epistolæ* in some respects, but is less personal and less gross. There is a real vein of natural fun in his little poem, ***Kittie's Confession,*** where the gravity of the confessor is a touch in the spirit of the *Tartuffe.* Kittie narrates that the good man did not direct her to lead a pure life, or to trust in the merits of Christ, but solely to follow certain observances:—

Bot gave me penance ilk ane day,
Ane Ave Maria for to say,
And Frydayis fyve na fishee to eit,—
Bot butter and eggis are better meit;
And with ane plak to by ane messe
Fra drunken Sschir Jhone Latynless. . . .

Quhen scho was felland as scho wist,
The curate Kittie wald have kist;
But yit ane countenance he bure
Degeist, derote, daign and demure,
Said he, have you any wrongous gear,
Said she, I stole a peck of beir,
Said he, that should restored be,
Therefore deliver it to me! . . .

And mekil Latyne he did mumtaill,
I heard nothing but *hummill bummill.*

The chief satirical work of Sir David Lindsay was a drama called, ***Ane Pleasant Satire of the Three Estaitis,*** which was performed before the Court in 1535, and in 1539. This drama took nine hours in the acting. . . . Some of the characters are real, and some allegorical, and both are made instruments for exposing ecclesiastical abuses, particularly the dilatory proceedings of the Consistory Court. A poor fellow "Pauper" who had lent his mare to an acquaintance who drowned her, seeks redress from this Court; "bot," complains he—

Bot, or they came half way to *concludendum,*

The feind ane plak was left for to defend
him. . . .

Of *pronunciandum* they made me wondrous
fain,
Bot I got never my gude gray mare again!

One of the chief complaints against the Scots prelates was that they never preached, and "the dumb dog the bishop" became a favourite term of abuse among the Protestant clergy. Sir David notices this neglect after his own fashion in a dialogue in his play between the allegorical personages, Gude Connsall and Spiritualitie:—

GUDE-COUNSALL.

And bishop's office is to be ane preacher.
And of the law of God ane public teacher.

SPIRITUALITIE.

Friend, quhare find ye that we suld prechouris
be?

GUDE-COUNSALL.

Luke what St. Paul writes unto Timothie,—
Tak thare the buke, let see gif ye can spell.

SPIRITUALITIE.

I never red that, therefore reid it yourself.

A pardoner, with relics to sell, is also a figure of some prominence in the ***Satire of the Three Estaitis.*** He comes on the stage complaining that the sale of his goods is much interfered with by the circulation of the English New Testament; but proceeds to solicit purchases for some sufficiently remarkable wares:—

My patent pardouns ye may see,
Cam fra the Can of Tartarie,
Weill seald with oster-schellis.
Thocht ye haif na contritioun,
Ye sall haif full remissioun,
With help of bukes and bellis. . . .

Heir is ane cord, baith gret and lang,
Quhilk hangit Johne the Armistrang,
Of gude hemp soft and sound:
Gude haly pepill, I stand for'd
Quhaver beis hangit with this cord
Neidis never to be dround.
The culum of Sanct Bryd's kow,
The gruntill of Sanct Antonis sow,
Quhilk bure his haly bell:
Quha ever he be heiris this bell clink,
Giff me ane ducat for till drink,
He sall never gang to hell,
Without he be of Beliall borne:—
Maisters, trow ye that this be scorne?
Cum win this pardoun, cum.

In spite of all obsoleteness of language and subject, the true spirit of comedy makes its presence felt here. Sir David Lindsay is a rude Scottish Aristophanes; but the genius for dramatic creation which budded in him never came to flower in the cold air of Northern Protestantism. Scotland has never had a dramatic literature, for we suppose nobody now believes in the frigid and unnatural trash of Home's *Douglas.* This is partly due to the fanaticism of the country; and partly to its poverty; but another element must be taken into account in these matters,—the almost constant want of literary attainments and literary sympathy among the modern Scottish clergy. Much as literature did for the Reformation in Scotland as elsewhere, the clergy have done astonishingly little to repay the debt. Yet among Scotch men of letters the memory of Sir David Lindsay of the Mount holds its own:

Still is thy name in high account,
And still thy verse has charms,
Sir David Lindsay of the Mount
Lord Lyon King at Arms!

(pp. 622-24)

James Hannay, "The Satirists of the Reformation," in The Cornhill Magazine, *Vol. XVI, November, 1867, pp. 609-28.*

Alexander Falconer (essay date 1872)

[*In the following excerpt, Falconer offers a mixed appraisal of Lyndsay's works. According to the critic, "[we] cannot claim for him the name of a great poet; as a satirist, he far surpasses any one of the early Scots poets."*]

Thirty years before [the] memorable overthrow [of Catholicism] as the National Church in 1560, and hardly before the word 'heresy' had been heard, Lyndsay had written his ***Dreme,*** and his ***Complaynt to the King.*** In the first poem, a sort of abridged *Divina Commedia,* he supposes himself carried through space, and in the course of his journey visits 'the lowest hell.' The gathering there is motley; but it is significant that churchmen are the most numerous, and that every class of them is well represented!

Thare saw we divers Papis, and Empriouris, . . .
The men of Kirk, lay boundin into byngis;
Thare saw we mony cairfull Cardinall,
And Archebischopis, in thair pontificall;
Proude and perverst Prelatis, out of nummer.
Priouris, Abbottis, and fals flatterand Frieris:
To specify thame all, it wer ane cummer,
Regular Channonis, churle Monkis and
Charteriris,
Curious Clerkis, and Preistis Seculeris:
Thare was sum parte of ilk Religioun,
In Haly Kirk quilk did abusioun. . . .

Rewland that rowt, I sawe, in capis of bras,
Symone Magus, and byschope Cayphas;
Byschope Annas, and the treatour Judas,
Machomete, tha' propheit poysonabyll,
Chore, Dathan, and Abirone thare was;
Heretykis we sawe innumerabyll.
It was ane sycht rycht wonderous lamentabyll.
Quhow that they lay into thay flammis fleityng
With eairfull cryes, girnying and greityng.

To people 'the lowest hell' with the chief rulers of the Holy Church, and to place over them men like Simon Magus and Judas Iscariot, was a daring thing to do, a stroke of satire unequalled in audacity by any previous Scots writer. (p. 96)

[In ***The Dreme***] we have the too often repeated catalogue of misdeeds and crimes which everyone acquainted with

Reformation history so well knows, 'covatyce, luste, and ambitioun,' and their numerous progeny. . . . The same points are handled by him again and again: in all his best known poems they are more or less touched upon; but if with more fulness of treatment in some, with no greater plainness of speech in any. Time and travel did not modify a whit his opinions and his convictions touching the state of the Church: he had seen so much of ecclesiastical life, public and private, before he put pen on paper, that his first judgment was as sound as his last one, his first charge, in this poem in 1528, as distinct and incisive as his last one in the last representation of ***The Satire of the Three Estates,*** twenty-six years later. . . .

In ***The Complaynt to the King,*** written in the year following, occur many interesting passages, descriptive of Lyndsay's early connection with the King, and of the King with the Anguses. These are, occasionally, even homely in their literalness, and might seem as if only meant for the eye of the writer's old pupil and playmate. No state or family papers however, which I have seen, give a distincter idea of the miserable training of the young King; the high-handed tyranny of the Anguses; and the general lawlessness of the nation. Taken along with the two closing poems, ***The Dreme,*** and **'Ane Exhortation to the King's Grace,'** we have materials enough from which to draw a most sorry picture of Scotland under the minority of James V., and also a pretty sure prophecy of the character and reign of the future king. (p. 97)

In the year following he wrote a third poem, ***The Testament and Complaynt of the Papingo,*** more finished and artistic in form than either of the two preceding ones, and more directly personal in its statements. Putting his parable into the mouth of a papingo, or popinjay, or parrot, after the manner of the poets of those days, he complains of the 'covatyce, luste, and ambitioun' of the Church, in words as to the meaning of which there cannot be a doubt. Conjured to declare the truth which she has heard by land or by sea concerning 'us kirkmen,' the poor creature, with some hesitation, complies. She begins with the opinion of 'the commonn people.' They have heard of 'the good old times' when churchmen were indeed the ministers of God and the salt of the earth; when

> Doctrine and deid war both equivolent.

They see nothing of that state of things around them now. The daily life of the clergy testifies unmistakeably that 'doctrine and deid' are no longer 'equivolent.' This degeneracy has naturally followed, she is bold to say, from the wicked alliance of the World and the Church, first made by Constantine; 'one of the weak theories of Wickliffe,' as old Warton thought. Evil upon evil has steadily followed the unhallowed union, until now, in 1530,

> No marvell is, thocht we religious men
> Degenerit be, and in our lyfe confusit;
> Bot sing, and drynk, none uther craft we ken,
> Our Spirituall Fatheris hes as so abusit.
>
> *Gret plesour wer to heir ane Byschope preche,*
> *One Deane, or Doctour in Divinitie,*
> *One Abbot quhilk could weill his Convent teche,*
> *One Persoun flowing in phylosophie:*
> I tyne my tyme, to wys quhilk wyll nocht be;
> *War nocht the preaching of the Begging Frieris,*
> *Tynt war the faith among the Seculeris.*
>
> As for thair precching, quod the Papingo,
> I thame excuse, for quhy, thay bene so thrall
> To Propertie, and hir ding Dochteris two,
> Dame Ryches, and fair lady Sensuall,
> That may nocht use no pastime spirituall;
> And in thair habits, they tak sic delyte,
> Thay have renuncit russat and raploch quhyte.
> Takand to thame skarlote and crammosie,
> With minniver, martrik, grice and rych armyne;
> Thair lawe hartis exaltit ar so hie,
> To see thair Papale pomp, it is ane pyne.
> More ryche arraye is now, with frenzeis fine
> Upon the bardying of ane Bychopis mule
> Nor ever had Paule or Peter agane Yule . . .
>
> Less skaith it ware, with lycence of the Pape.
> That ilke Prelate one wyfe had of his awen
> Nor see thair bastardis ouirhort the countrie
> blawin;
> For now, be thay be weill cumin frome the sculis
> Thay fall to work as they ware commoun bullis.

Now these passages, of which there are many more, were surely very bold words for a Catholic to write of his Church, and were villainous if not true; but if Lyndsay was only versifying openly known facts, as Burns did in *Holy Willie's Prayer* and *The Holy Fair,* then, of course, there was no gainsaying his words. The sort of creature here drawn must have been very numerous at that time in all Christian countries, if we take the abundance of his portraits as a proof. In what literature will you not find them? Lyndsay, like his fellow satirists, generally drew the likeness, and left it to tell its own tale. There was no lofty noble scorn, so ill at all times to brook; no assumption of deeply offended moralities; least of all, no 'new opinions.' ***The Complaynt of the Papingo,*** therefore, was not chargeable with heresy. It was worse to bear with than heresy, but could not be so easily dealt with, nor so thoroughly stamped out.

Was Lyndsay's description of his Church true, however? Are these lines warranted by facts which are undeniable, and on which two opinions are impossible? Was he not merely rhyming words, spiteful words, in hope of pleasing his patron, King James V.? In answer to this, as an historical student, I can honestly say . . . that every word of Lyndsay is true; and that in Church muniments, in State papers, in family records and registers, the various items of the dark catalogue 'covatyee, luste, and ambitioun,' are much too abundantly verified. (pp. 97-9)

For the most decided proof of his influence as a popular poet, and for the fullest illustration of his power as a delineator of contemporary manners, we must look to the most remarkable of his writings, ***Ane pleasant Satyre of the Thrie Estaitis.*** This satire, unlike his other writings, is dramatic in form. Lyndsay, as Lyon King, was required to provide for the royal solace and entertainment as occasion called for it; and the plays and spectacles, the Miracle Plays and Moralities, then everywhere common in Christendom, were matters he had professionally much to do with. Lyndsay of Pitscottie tells us of his skill in devising one of these at St. Andrews, in 1538, in honour of the arrival of Mary of Guise, which had this special feature, that it ended with 'certain orations and exhortations to the Queen, instructing her to serve her God according to God's will and commandments.' The success of this experiment probably decided Lyndsay in the adoption of the simple dramatic dialogue, as the most effective mode of expressing his matured views on men and manners. It was at once safer and bolder: safer, because words spoken by a character in a play are allowed an immunity denied to those spoken in the name of the writer; and bolder, because under this privilege he could hit the heaviest blows, while it told sooner upon the public. In two years, therefore, after the spectacle given at St. Andrews, his famous Satire, the earliest known attempt in Scotland at a Drama, was played, for the first time, before the Court at Linlithgow, during the Feast of Epiphany. It must have been a surprise to most of the audience. In its form it is, as was to be expected, not much unlike the Moralities of the time, the Vices and Virtues, as usual, being represented; but in its spirit and subject it is altogether unlike them. First of all, it could never have been meant for mere amusement. It is throughout pervaded by an earnest practical spirit, which expresses itself on the chief evils in the land in a fearlessly free way, and demands or counsels reform. All that he had written before on the condition of the Church and the Clergy, is told over again, with some additions; the miseries and oppression of the commons coming in for their full share of his notice. In short, it is the sum of all his other satires, blow following blow in language which could have been permitted only on one supposition—its undeniable and half-acknowledged truth. Our astonishment is that, even in spite of this, it was permitted at all. Such plainness of speech to King and Bishop was a new thing in Scotland. . . . (p. 100)

Scott has marked Lyndsay's place and power as a poet with much exactness in his well-known lines in 'Marmion':

> In the glances of his eye,
> A penetrating, keen, and sly
> Expression found its home;
> The flash of *that satiric rage*
> Which, bursting on the early stage,
> *Branded the vices of the age*
> *And broke the keys of Rome.*

It may have occurred more than once to the reader how Lyndsay was allowed to lash the Church with so free a hand, when he himself says it was no jesting matter to complain of priests. And it is a sort of standing wonder. He twice excuses himself, for the freedom of speech, in the ***Satire:***

> Prudent people, I pray you all
> Take no mair grief, in special,
> For we shall speak in general
> For pastime and for play.

But the 'pastime' of free speech like Lyndsay's—for his it was—however disguised, was not then allowed by either Church or State. His words are not sly allusions, nor parodies; they are charges definite and direct, which amount to actual accusation. Mr. Burton finds the explanation in the fact, that Lyndsay 'was but repeating what the authorities of the realm asserted, and the Church itself mournfully confessed. Anything might be said to this purport if he who said it were so skilful as to avoid points of heresy,' &c. I wish I could believe it; and that history did not prove that where the Church could show her hand and crush the free-spoken man, she did not usually do so; and that in Scotland, in that very age, she did not burn friar Kyller, and tried to do her very worst to George Buchanan, for their satires. Moreover, what was confessed by the Church was confessed in the conclave: it was not openly mourned over before the laity. What mattered that confession when public opinion attacked and ridiculed those same things? Was it likely that men, so proud of the privileges of their order, would humbly cry *Peccavimus!* There is nothing we all bridle up at quicker, and forgive slower, than an exposure of our known vices and faults: we cannot deny them, and instinctively strike at the exposer; and we may be quite sure, therefore, that the Latimers and the Lyndsays of those days, unless under royal protection or in high position, and whether there was definable heresy in the satire or not, were certainly silenced. Has not our very pleasant censor, *Mr. Punch,* had experiences, especially across the Channel, which show how far this is true, even in our own day? Some other reason, therefore, than Mr. Burton's must be found for Lyndsay's immunity from everyone of the forms of persecution. (pp. 103-04)

One thing is clear, that Lyndsay was no trimmer. He openly acknowledged himself as the author of his Satires; and if anecdote is to be trusted, he was as sharp at times with his tongue as with his pen. He was not a religious reformer, however; although . . . had he survived for a few years longer, we need scarcely doubt he would have joined himself to the Lords of the Congregation. As to that, we may but guess: as he was, we cannot but admire his boldness, and count him the bravest, clearest-seeing man of his time.

Of his general literary character, it is not proposed to say anything. That, no doubt, has been pretty well gauged from the previous pages. We cannot claim for him the name of a great poet; as a satirist, he far surpasses any one of the early Scots poets. (p. 104)

Alexander Falconer, "Laing's Sir David Lyndsay," in Fraser's Magazine, *Vol. V, January, 1872, pp. 92-104.*

John M. Ross (essay date 1884)

[*In the following excerpt, Ross presents an overview of Lyndsay's principal works, particularly focusing on* The Dreme, Ane Satyre of the Thrie Estaitis, *and* The Monarchie.]

Critics are accustomed to pronounce . . . Lyndsay's [first poem, ***The Dreme,***] the most poetical of his productions, and the *Prolog* is in truth not destitute of descriptive beauty, but we look in vain for anything that will bear comparison with the glowing splendours of Dunbar or the diffuse loveliness of Douglas. It is not Lyndsay's imagery or music that rivets us: it is the strength of his moral convictions, the vigour of his political sketches, the audacity of his satire, the broad light that he throws on the age in which he lived, and the assurance we thus derive that, beneath the turbid surface of feudal life, there were still some men in Scotland who loved justice and mercy and peace; whom the outrages of the great fired with indignation, and the miseries of the poor melted with compassion.

There is nothing original in the structure of the poem. The writer follows the fashion of his craft in the Middle Ages when all aspired to imitate Dante. On a bright winter morning, "lansing ouirthorte the landis, toward the see," because the inland scenery was "unblomit," he hears the plaint of the forlorn songstress of the grove and air, and is filled with a spirit of pensiveness—

> The see was furth, the sand wes smooth and
> dryе;
> Then up and doun, I musit myne allone,
> Tyll that I spyit ane lyttill cave of stone,
> Heych in ane craig: upwart I did approche,
> But tarying, and clam up in the roche.

While he sat here, looking out upon the deep, the "wolteryng of the wallis" suggested to him the instability of the false world . . . , and the current of his thoughts began to set in this direction. At last he is lulled asleep "throw the seyis movyng marvellous," and the "bousteous blastis of Eolus," whereupon he has "ane marvellous visioun." A lady of "portratour perfyte" visits him in his dream, and conducts him through Hell, Purgatory, and Heaven. The sting of the poem lies in what he sees in the first of these regions. "Papis," "cairfull Cardinalls," "Achebischopis in thair pontificall," "proude and perverst Prelatis," "Priouris, Abbottis, and fals flatterand Freris," "churle Monkis," swarm in the "painefull poysonit pytt," and although we are also shown a liberal assortment of the laity "rycht furiouslie fryand"—

> Dukis, Merquessis, Erlis, Barronis,
> Knychtis, . . .
>
> Emprices, Quenis, and ladyis of honouris, . . .
>
> Mansworne merchandis, for their wrangous
> winning, . . .
>
> Fals men of law in cautelis rycht cunning
> Theiffis, revaris, and publict oppressaris;
> Sum part thare was of unleill lauboraris;
> Craftismen, thare saw we, out of nummer;

yet it is with an undisguisedly grim delight that he sees

> The men of Kirk, lay boundin in to byngis.

Perhaps the martyrdom of Patrick Hamilton, which occurred while Lyndsay was writing his ***Dreme,*** and which had rekindled after the lapse of a century the flames of persecution in Scotland, intensified that abhorrence of ecclesiastical cruelty, he is never weary of expressing. In the "satiric rage" of our poet, however, we utterly miss the imaginative richness of Dunbar. Throughout the whole piece there is scarcely what may be called a stroke of genius—a *curiosa felicitas,* or memorable phrase. Classes are outlined with a certain broad force, but we lack the vivid incisive individualism of artistic genius. When persons are mentioned they are names and nothing more—

> Byschope Annas, and the treatour Judas,
> Machomete, that propheit poysonabyll,
> Chore, Dathan, and Abirone thare was.

In this prosaic fashion Lyndsay peoples hell, and if the poem were to be judged only by its literary qualities, we should have little to say in its praise; but when we consider the time and the circumstances in which it was composed, we forget its poetic defects and are struck with admiration at its tone—the earnest, bitter homeliness of accusation against wrong-doers in Church and State, the robust energy of hate, and the intrepidity of speech which Knox himself could not have surpassed. The pictures of the natural capabilities of Scotland, and of the monstrous disorders of the Commonwealth, are the most graphic things in the ***Dreme.*** But nothing appears to us so characteristic of the courage and sincerity of the author as his "Exhortation to the Kyngis Grace" with which he concludes. It is not poetry—but it is something better than poetry. It is the very heroism of patriotic morality. He speaks to his monarch as fearlessly as the old Hebrew prophets spoke to the kings of Judah and Israel; as Knox spoke to Mary, or Melville to her son. The way in which he entreats James to have compassion on the poor is very noble. Nor was his cry uttered in vain. We are fairly entitled to ascribe to Lyndsay, who had much to do with the moulding of his sovereign's character, if not with the direction of his formal studies, the development of those generous and humane instincts which won for him the title of the "King of the Commons." Lyndsay specially denounces the lawlessness of the Borders—

> In to the South, allace! I was neir slain;
> Ouer all the land I culd fynd no releif:
> Almoist betuix the Mers and Lowmabane
> I culde nocht knau ane leill man be ane theif.
> To schaw thair reif, thift, murthour, and mis-
> chief,
> And vicious workis, it wald infect the air;
> And als langsum to me, for tyll declair.

Now, the very next year James undertook his celebrated expedition to the south, in the course of which Scott of Tushielaw, Cockburn of Henderland, Johnnie Armstrong, and many other "minions of the moon," found to their surprise that Justice had still sufficient rope to hang them.

Quite a different note is struck in Lyndsay's next piece, ***The Complaynt to the Kyng,*** which was composed in the following year, 1530. It is a rhyming petition in that easy octo-syllabic measure which is so finely adapted to familiar and satirical narrative. It is chiefly interesting as a record of the author's personal fortunes, of the habits and characters of the Scottish courtiers. The ***Dreme*** is sad and dark with reminiscences of the Douglas tyranny, while the ***Complaynt*** is bright with auguries of future prosperity which unhappily proved false. The vigour and justice of the king's administration are warmly praised, and contrasted with the corrupt condition of things which preceded, when none could hope for preferment who was not "a Douglas or a Douglas's man." (pp. 383-87)

The first result of the ***Complaynt*** was the appointment of Lyndsay to the office of Lyon King of Arms, and his elevation to the dignity of knighthood. The honour had the effect he predicted. It "rubbed the ruste off his ingyne"; and before the year was out another work was written which must have made the ears of churchmen tingle and the faces of courtiers redden with shame. This was ***The Testament and Complaynt of the Kingis Papyngo.*** Beginning with a generous panegyric on his great predecessors in poetry, Chaucer and Gower, "quhose sweit sentence throuch Albione bene sung," and his illustrious contemporaries Dunbar and Douglas, the latter of whom he pronounces "the rose of Inglis rethorick," he next modestly laments his own lack of matter and "ingyne," and apologizes for the insignificance of the subject he has chosen.

> To rurall folke, myne dyting bene directit,
> Far blemit frome the sycht of men of gude;
> For cunnying men, I knaw, wyll soune conclude,
> It dowe no thyng, but for to be dejectit;
> And, quhen I heir myne mater bene detractit,
> Than sall I sweir, I maid it bot in mowis,
> To landwart lassis, quhilks kepith kye and yowis.

The argument of the poem is briefly this: The king has a Papyngo "rycht plesand and perfyte," that could

> Syng lyke the merle, and crawe lyke to the cocke,
> Pew lyke the gled, and chant lyke the laverock,
> Barke lyke ane dog, and kekell like ane ka,
> Blait lyke ane hog, and buller lyke ane bull,
> Gaill lyke ane goik, and greit quhen sho wes wa;
> Clym on ane corde, syne lauch, and play the fule:
> Scho mycht have bene ane Menstrall agane Yule.

This wonderfully clever bird is one morning dashed from a tree-top in the royal gardens by a sudden blast of wind and hurt beyond remeid.

> Upon ane stob scho lychtit on hir breist,
> The blude ruschit out, and scho cryit for a priest.

Her last hours are spent in exhorting the king and courtiers, and in a long sarcastic controversy with her "Holye executouris," the pye, a "channoune regulare," the raven "a blak monk," and the gled "ane holy freir." Sheltering himself under this thin disguise of fable, Lyndsay hurled the javelins of his satire against the clergy with greater force and daring than ever. To the king his language is ever affectionate and free. He counsels him to be honest, diligent, temperate, and virtuous; to gather wise men about him, whether high born or not:

> Cheis thy Counsale of the most sapient,
> Without regarde to blude, ryches, or rent.

to study the art of government for the sake of the "simple multitude," to treat every "true Barroun" as a brother, and above all to seek for help in his heavy work from "that Roye quhilk rent wes on the Rude." (pp. 389-90)

The Second "Epystil of the Papyngo," addressed to the courtiers, is a grave and solemn admonition, reminding them by examples, chosen chiefly from the history of Scotland, how precarious is their tenure of prosperity. The arguments have no great originality. That indeed is not a conspicuous quality of our poet. His sincerity makes his thought simple; his earnestness makes his language plain; yet there is at all times in his serious flights a sermonic vigour that must have struck home to the popular heart. The conclusion of this part is one of the few fine pieces of descriptive poetry in Lyndsay.

> Adew, Edinburgh! thou heych tryumphant toun,
> Within quhose boundis rycht blythful have I bene,
> Of trew merchandis the rute of this regioun,
> Moste reddy to resave Court, King, and Quene!
> Thy polecye and justice may be sene:
> War devotioun, wysedome, and honestie,
> And credence, tynt, thay mycht be found in thee.
>
> Adew, fair Snawdoun! with thy touris hie,
> Thy chapell royall, park, and tabyll rounde!
> May, June, and July, walde I dwell in thee,
> War I one man, to heir the birdis sounde,
> Quhilk doith agane thy royall roche redounde.
> Adew, Lythquo! quhose Palyce of plesance
> Mycht be one patrone in Portingall or France!
>
> Fair weill, Falkland! the fortrace of Fyfe,
> Thy polyte park, under the Lowmound Law!
> Sum tyme in thee I led ane lusty lyfe,
> The fallow deir, to see them raik on raw.
> Court men to come to thee, they stand gret awe,
> Sayand, thy burgh bene, of all burrowis, baill,
> Because, in thee, thay nevir gat gude aill.

But it is when he comes to describe the sentiments and conduct of the "Holye Executouris" that Lyndsay's genius begins to scorch. The fearless way in which he mocks the pretensions to sanctity of the religious orders, proves that he did not purchase the favour of the king by the sale of his conscience. Whatever James might do, our poet was staunch to his convictions, and would on no account yield up the right he enjoyed as an honest man to censure the morals of the Church. In the very dawn of his new prosperity, and thoroughly aware of the perils of speech, he burst into a strain of satire, so broad and plain and rasping that he could never hope for absolution at the hands of a priest. His tone is that of a man who has wholly lost faith in the worth of the clergy. He leaves them not a solitary virtue. They are in his eyes conscious hypocrites, who use the privileges of their order to gratify the most earthly cravings. They would fain make the poor Papyngo believe that they are "holye creaturis," and can bring him "quyke to hevin." They are of course distressed to witness his dying agonies—

> The Ravin come rolpand, quhen he hard the rair;
> So did the gled, with mony pieteous pew.

But the practical conclusion is a greedy advice to the Papyngo to make over to them his "gudis naturall." The rejoinder is a good specimen of Lyndsay's humour—

> The Papyngo said, 'Father, be the Rude,
> Howbeit your rayment be religious lyke,
> Your conscience, I suspect, be nocht gude;
> I did persave, when prevelye ye did pyke
> Ane chekin from ane hen, under ane dyke.'
> 'I grant,' said he, 'that here was my gude friend,
> And I that chekin tuke, bot for my teind.'

The unabashed wretches continue their professional babble about the necessity of confession, and promise that—

> bury we sall your bonis,
> Syne trentalls twenty trattyll all at onis,

besides "cryand for you the cairfull corrynogh,"

> And we sall sing about your sepulture
> Sanct Mongois matynis, and the mekle creid;
> And syne devotely saye, I you assure,
> The auld Placebo bakwart, and the beid;
> And we sall weir for yow the murnying weid;
> And, thocht your spreit with Pluto war profest,
> Devotelie sall your Diregie be addrest.

The impression left on us by this poem is that the Scottish priesthood as a whole had, in Lyndsay's time, become utterly corrupt; not only dead to the spiritual truth of Christianity, but unconscious that such a thing had ever existed. They had apparently ceased to think and feel about the services of religion, and therefore had lost the very capacity of believing in them; so that the whole affair seemed to them a farce which it was their business to keep going. Lyndsay resolved to stop the success of the farce, which was in his eyes a blasphemous burlesque of a solemn tragedy; and we ought to be grateful to the satirist who caused it to be hissed off the stage of Scottish history, and who prepared the way for the revival of the genuine drama of life under the auspices of John Knox.

Passing over some minor pieces belonging to this period, such as ***The Answer to the Kyingis Flyting, The Complaynt of Bagsche, The Justing betuix James Watsoun and Jhone Barbour, Ane Supplicatioun in Contemptioun of Syde Taillis,*** and ***Kitteis Confessioun,*** most of which are mere *jeux d'esprit,* we come upon Lyndsay's masterpiece, ***Ane Pleasant Satyre of the Thrie Estaitis in Commendatioun of Vertew and Vituperatioun of Vyce.*** We do not precisely know when this extraordinary work was composed, nor is it quite certain where it was first performed. Chalmers asserts, without evidence, that the first representation took place at Cupar in 1535. Mr. Laing, on the other hand, with more probability, considering the magnitude of the play and the heavy official duties of the writer, conjectures that the first exhibition was the one at Linlithgow on the feast of Epiphany, 6th January, 1539-40, in presence of the king, queen, the ladies of the court, the bishops, and a great concourse of people of all ranks, "from nine in the morning till six at night." It is not a morality-play, pure and simple; that is to say, the actors are not exclusively personified abstractions. It is rather what is known in the history of our literature as an interlude—something intermediate both in character and time between the morality-play and the regular drama, and representing the transition from the one to the other. It combines in some measure the features of both. Real men and women move about amid allegorical figures. It is at once an echo of the Middle Ages and a prelusion to the "spacious times of great Elizabeth." Lyndsay, however, seems to have properly restricted the term "Interlude" to certain comic and coarse diversions, which were shifted about, altered, multiplied, or diminished, according to the exigencies of time or the inclinations of the audience, and which in no way affected the general movement of the play. An outline of the play, which is rather a succession of independent scenes than a dramatic evolution of incident, may interest some. The prologue is spoken by "Diligence," who winds up with one of those sly humorous sarcasms for which Lyndsay is notable—

> Thairfoir till all our rymis be rung,
> And our mistoinit sangis be sung,
> Let everie man keip weill ane toung,
> And everie woman tway.

"Rex Humanitas" then comes forward, and prays to God for grace to rule himself and his people wisely, but his virtuous desires are rapidly blown to the winds by the allurements of "Wantonness," "Pleasure," and "Solace." These panders introduce the king to "Dame Sensualitie," the star of beauty, and "the fresche fonteine of knichtis amorous"; who describes her own charms with the freedom befitting her character, and assures the monarch that she is nowhere more highly thought of than at the "Court of Rome." When the fatal step is taken and "Rex Humanitas" begins his career of profligacy, "Gude-Counsall" steps on the stage and purposes remonstrance, but he is baffled for the moment by the three villains of the play, "Flatterie," "Falset," and "Dissait," who disguising themselves as "Devotion," "Sapience," and "Discretion," win the ear of the king, and get "Gude-Counsall" expelled from court, and put in prison. While the monarch is in the midst of his wanton revels "Veritie" steps in, and delivers a noble oration on the duties of temporal and spiritual rulers. This excites alarm in the breasts of the three "Vices," who hurry to accuse the new-comer before the spiritualitie of heresy—"in hir hand beirand the New Testament"—and get her put in the stocks. "Chastitie" next makes her appearance, but neither bishop, abbot, prioress, nor parson will acknowledge her, and she is fain to seek refuge among the common people, represented by a "Sowtar" and a "Taylour," whose hospitable intentions, however, are frustrated by the evil passions of their wives, and she finally experiences the same fate as "Veritie." The triumph of wickedness in court and realm now seems secure, when suddenly "Divyne Correction" enters, and a panic seizes the guilty crew, who scurry off in gross disorder, quarrelling as they flee. There is an austere dignity and republican sternness in the speech of "Correction."

> Be me, traitours and tyrants ar put doun,
> Quha thinks na schame of thair iniquitie. . . .
>
> Quhat is ane king? nocht but ane officiar
> To caus his leigis live in equitie;
> And, under God, to be ane punischer
> Of tresspassouris against His Majestie.

As he presents anew to the Monarch, "Gude-Counsall," "Veritie," and "Chastitie," he boldly tells him:

> Now, Schir, tak tent, quhat I will say
> Observe thir same, baith nicht and day,
> And let thame never part yow fray,
> Or else, withoutin dout,
> Turn ye to Sensualitie,
> To vicious lyfe and rebaldrie,
> Out of youre realme richt schamefullie
> Ye sall be ruttit out.

A proclamation is then issued, summoning a parliament

of the Three Estates for the redress of grievances. With this the first part of the satire ends.

The Second Part is more human and is intensely interesting. In it Lyndsay has put forth all his force as a practical reformer. Every mischief, every abuse, every enormity in the national life is pictured, discussed, and condemned. But even this is not enough. He demands reform, and describes the means by which it may be attained. The corruption of the king and the villany of his counsellors form the burden of the first part of the satire; the wrongs, miseries, and wants of the commonwealth, the burden of the second. First enters "Pauper" (The Poor Man), who unfolds to "Diligence" the cause of his wretchedness, and sets forth in touching terms the heartlessness of the clergy in robbing him of his goods in a crisis of domestic agony. Then we have by way of contrast, as if to heighten the pathos of his cry for justice, the brazen-faced proclamation of the "Pardoner" in which Lyndsay's satire of Rome attains its climax of humorous mockery. . . . The altercation between the "Pardoner" and "Pauper," in which the former fleeches the latter out of his last "groat," and Pauper in return tumbles the holy relics into the water, is broadly farcical, and was doubtless received with roars of laughter.

By and by, the three Estates, Clergy, Nobles, and Burgesses, come in to assist the king in doing justice; the first of the three, however, urging delay, as if strongly convinced that their interests were most likely to suffer. "Johne, the Commonweill," hereupon shows face, and immediately begins a fierce assault upon the "kirkmen," the "barons," and the "courtiers," whose representatives, the three Vices, are led to the stocks. "Sensualitie" is next banished, to the great sorrow of the "Spiritualitie," who bid her a tender farewell—

Adew, my awin sweit hart!
Now, duill fell me, that wee twa man depart;

and declare they cannot live without her—for Lyndsay is implacable in his hate, and will not entertain the idea of their reformation. He allows the Temporal Estates—"to wit, the lordis and merchandis"—to be pricked in their consciences as they listen to the passionate accusations of "Johne, the Commonweill," and to promise that they will—

The Commonweill tak he the hand,
And mak with him perpetuall band.

But the clergy are obstinate to the last. They threaten, swear, foam, and rage; with a truly ecclesiastical obstinacy they will acknowledge no fault, abandon no privilege, promise no reform—

Na, na, never till the day of judgement,
We will want nathing that wee have in use,
Kirtil nor kow, teind lambe, teind gryse, nor
 guse.

Then follows an angry and furious discussion on their rights and duties, from which it would appear that in Scotland, as elsewhere, the majority, however worldly-wise or learned in the chicanery of ecclesiastical law, were grossly ignorant of Scripture, and incapable of preaching the Gospel to their flocks—"Dum doggis," as Knox, in imitation of Isaiah, calls them in his wrath.

The flagitious abuses of the consistorial or Church Courts are the subject of endless invective, grave and gay, lively and severe, though these must have been considerably abated by the institution some years before of the Court of Session. Still, the Church had long after this an extensive civil jurisdiction, and it appears to have acted in Lyndsay's time with that singular disregard of justice and humanity which has characterized its judicial procedure in all ages and in all countries of Christendom. There is a merry humour in this bit of hard hitting, which neither the homely jingle of the verse nor the rudeness of the dialect can quite destroy—

Marie! I lent my gossop my mear, to fetch hame
 coills,
And he hir drounit into the Querrell hollis;
And I ran to the Consistorie, for to pleinze,
And thair I happinit amang ane greidie meinze.
Thay gave me first ane thing, thay call *Citendum;*
Within aucht dayis, I gat bot *Lybellandum,*
Within ane moneth, I gat *ad Opponendum,*
In half ane yeir, I gat *Inter loquendum,*
And syne I gat, how call ye it? *ad Replicandum:*
Bot I could never ane word yit understand him.
And than thay gart me cast out many plackis,
And gart me pay for four-and-twentie actis:
Bot or they came half gate to *Concludendum,*
The feind a placke was left far to defend him:
Thus, thay postponit me twa yeir with their
 traine,
Syne, *Hodie ad octo,* bad me cum againe:
And than, thir ruiks, thay roupit wonder fast,
For sentence silver thay cryit at the last.
Of *Pronunciandum,* they maid me wonder faine;
But I got nevir my gude gray meir againe.

The complaint of "Chastitie" against the prelates strikes at one of their vices which had made them specially odious to the Scottish gentry. Nowhere out of Italy were the decencies of life so openly outraged, or the violations of religious vows so gross and shameful as in Scotland. The traditions of the Borgias, with whom the century had opened, were there preserved with shocking fidelity. Not a family was safe—not a matron or a maid. And so shameless had these transgressors become, that they openly paraded the evidence of their guilt. Their progeny were so liberally dowered from the revenues of the Church, that Lyndsay makes the "Temporalitie" declare it cannot get its own daughters married.

For quhy? the markit raisit bene sa hie,
That prelats dochtours of this natioun
Ar maryit with sic superfluetie:
Thay will nocht spair to gif twa thowsand
 pound,
With their dochtours to ane nobill man;
In riches sa thay do superabound.

The king next receives "three famous clarks of greit intelligence"—

For to the common peopill thay can preich,
And in the scuilis, in Latine toung, can teich,

by whose help a further and more searching exposure of the "Spiritualitie" is made. They are forced to describe in detail their manner of life, and thus to pronounce their own condemnation. "Correctioun," who is all through a sort of Master of Ceremony, now asks one of the "famous clarks" to preach a sermon that would really tend to the edification of the laity. The result is a genuine New Testament discourse, "such as Paul, were he on earth, would hear, approve, and own," but the bewilderment and anger of the clergy is something wonderful. They indulge in some captious criticism, but are on the whole stupified and beaten. As a specimen of the picturesque homeliness of Lyndsay's argument, we might quote the clark's reply to the question if the Saviour was really not as rich as a bishop—if he was really a poor man—

Yea brother, be Alhallows:
Christ Jesus had na propertie bot the gallows:
And left not, quhen he yielded up the spreit,
To buy himself ane simpill winding scheit.

Finally the "vices" are stripped of their disguise, and the prelates of their dignities; "Johne the Commonweill," who has been long ill-used, is gorgeously apparelled and takes his seat in Parliament; a proclamation of all the new reforms, with a full account of each, is made by sound of trumpet; even "Pauper" is satisfied, and only begs that "Flatterie," "Dissait," "Falset," "Theft," shall be rigorously punished.

It is impossible to form a just idea of the extraordinary merits of the piece from this meagre outline of its contents. Lyndsay's ***Satyre*** is instinct with life. There is not a dead twig on the whole tree. Under the inspiration of his vital genius, every line quivers like a leaf. His allegorical abstractions are human and speak like men. It is history, not mere poetry, that confronts us in every page. All the phases of Scottish feeling and thought in that perplexed, restless, half-slumbering age which preceded the coming of Knox, are mirrored there with fidelity and homely art. There is not a nation in Christendom which is better off than Scotland in this respect—not one that is in a position to form a clearer notion of the stupidities, superstitions, and impurities from which the Reformation delivered us. Lyndsay's testimony is far above suspicion. If we have set forth his character rightly, he was a man whose opinion was worth more than that of any of his contemporaries—not only because of his moral earnestness, but because of his keen penetration, and deep sagacity. He had nothing to win; he had everything to risk by speaking the truth. He was not a crack-brained enthusiast who courted persecution. On the contrary, he was a careful country squire who wished to add to his estates, and who lost no chance of honestly getting on in the world. And yet, knowing that some had gone to the stake for a tithe of his plain-speaking—that the clergy, weak in Scripture, but strong in craft, clever, unscrupulous, implacable, would be furious at his conduct, he wrote what he thought, and took his chance of their malice. Nothing is concealed, nothing extenuated: he believes them incorrigible and he paints them so. That his language is occasionally obscene is not to be denied, nor is it always possible to advance the apology that he was filthy in order to be natural. There is a way of caricaturing vice which is as bad as vice itself, and Lyndsay sometimes practises it. Let him bear his measure of blame! It was a coarse age; Scotch humour was peculiarly coarse; and if the ladies of the Court did not blush at what they heard, we can only wonder and be silent.

But coarseness like that at which we have glanced occurs only once or twice in the ***Satyre.*** A far more essential feature of the work, throwing a strong light on the individual character of the author, is its earnest humanity. Everywhere indeed Lyndsay shows a tender and generous love of poor men, but here he pleads their cause with persistency and warmth. He had witnessed the reckless cruelties of feudal strife, and the bitter wretchedness of down-trodden labour powerless to redress its wrongs: his heart bled at what he saw, and his spirit sprang up to challenge oppression and to champion the weak. He is neither for king, nor baron, nor priest, but for the Commonwealth, and foreshadows in his feelings that genuine Republicanism which Knox and Buchanan were not afraid to advocate, or Cromwell to enact—in spite of "the right divine of kings to govern wrong"! The peasantry of Scotland long remembered it. It was one of the causes of Lyndsay's immense popularity in the sixteenth and seventeenth centuries, and it is a reason why later ages, in which the sentiment of humanity has acquired greater force, should reverently brush the dust from his memory. (pp. 391-405)

Lyndsay [next] amused himself by composing a poem on the exploits of Squire Meldrum [***The Historie of Squyer Meldrum***], a Fifeshire gentleman of his acquaintance, and whose adventures in Ireland, France, and finally at home, both in war and love, were of a very romantic character. It is singularly unlike all his other writings, and is not to be considered a serious performance, but rather as a *jeu d'esprit,* in which Lyndsay seeks relaxation after the grave and earnest labours of his Muse. The ardour of the Reformer and the gravity of the moralist are forgotten for once. No priest is cursed nor vice denounced; we hear nothing of the miseries of the commonwealth, or the errors of kings. The venerable satirist throws aside his scourge and briskly steps forward as a minstrel of chivalry. There is a fine vivacity in the narrative; the pleasant octo-syllabic lines murmur on with easy music. The play of fancy throughout has a mild radiance, as of autumnal afternoons. In all Froissart there is nothing more delightful in picturesque details than the description of the jousts between Meldrum and the English knight, Talbart, on the plains of Picardy.

The last and longest of Lyndsay's works is ***The Monarchie: ane Dialog betuix Experience and ane Courteour on the Miserabyll Estait of the World.*** It was finished in 1553, but its composition may have extended over many years. It embraces a moral survey of all history, from the creation of Adam to the final Judgment, and closes with a description of the pleasures of glorified saints. As a work of genius or art it is not to be compared with the ***Satyre of the Thrie Estaitis,*** although particular passages possess great merit; for example, the account "Of Imageis usit amang Christin Men" and the "Exclamatioun aganis Idolatrye." In the pictures of priestly pride and greed, and especially of the Court of Rome, the homely but active fancy of the author arranges and combines with wonderful

Sir David Lyndsay reading the prologue to his A Dialog betuix Experience and ane Courteour *(c.1553). An illustration from an edition of 1566.*

effect the materials furnished by a wide, keen, and long-continued observation of society, both secular and ecclesiastical. It is a characteristic of Lyndsay, as of Swift, Defoe, and some other writers, that he does not produce a striking result by brilliant flashes of fancy, but by a series of minute, cunning touches. His strength lies for the most part in details; his imagination can work only in prosaic channels; his satiric humour is raciest in petty familiarities. It is only where hatred of priestly hypocrisy impassions his speech that he rises into eloquence; and even then the elevation of his style comes from the Mount of Sinai and not from the heights of Parnassus.

The ***Monarchie*** is pervaded by a spirit of gloom and sadness, but not of despair. It is the terrible certainty of the Divine Judgments that darkens his vision; not the melancholy conviction that these are the dreams of deluded saints. . . . If there be less sarcasm and more gravity than in his earlier poems, the circumstances of the times, the nature of his subject, and the solemnity of his position at the entrance of the Valley of the Shadow of Death, befit the tone. It is the voice of one who is parting with the world before the struggle is over and the battle won; who cannot see the issues of the future, but who knows that the triumph of the Antichrist will be followed by the terrors of the Lord, and that nations can only hope to flourish by the preaching of the World. (pp. 409-12)

To [Lyndsay] more than to any contemporary we owe that stir of religious thought, that leaven of religious excitement which the eloquence and energy of Knox diffused and impelled to a triumphant issue. He taught his countrymen to regard the Church with courage and honesty and candour, not, as they were wont, with blind servility and ignorant devotion. Institutions and persons were venerable in his eyes only in proportion to their utility and worth. No power on earth could induce this clear-sighted, true-hearted man to worship the false or believe the incredible. Others might wink at the iniquities of kings and barons and priests, but here was a moralist the strength of whose convictions raised him beyond the vacillations of timidity and doubt: who knew that God took cognizance of all forms of wickedness, who felt that the vials of His wrath were reserved for spiritual wickedness in high places. And as he thought of the vain pretences under which popes veiled their ambition, the insolence with which the clergy maintained their immunity from censure, the prostitution of auricular confession, the drivel of saintly invocations, the rascality of indulgences, the ignorance and debauchery of the strolling friars, a fire of sacred scorn was kindled in his heart. To the solidity of his convictions was added the vehemence of hate, to the vigour of his argument, the blister of sarcasm and the mockeries of ridicule, till men learned to wonder at their folly, and, like Clovis the Frank, were at length prepared to burn what they had reverenced and to reverence what they had burned.

Scotland, it has been said, long remembered him. During the sixteenth, seventeenth, and eighteenth centuries upwards of twenty editions of his works were published. His verses were on almost every tongue. Until Burns appeared he was in fact *the* poet of the Scottish people, and was appealed to as an infallible authority on the Scottish language; "Ye'll no fin' that in Davie Lyndsay" was a fatal objection to any new-coined phrase which a speaker ventured to employ. Nothing can surpass his mastery of the vernacular when the subject is homely and the treatment satiric. Rich in picturesque idioms, happy in colloquial ease, his descriptions remind us in their pith and humour and fancy of the Epistles of the Ayrshire Bard. If they lack the higher qualities of pathos, imagination, and tenderness, it should not be forgotten that he deliberately circumscribed the sphere of his poetic activity to serve the cause of God. Every Scot who has since lived has derived an unspeakable advantage from Lyndsay's noble sacrifice of literary ambition to religious duty. (pp. 412-14)

John M. Ross, "Sir David Lyndsay," in his Scottish History and Literature to the Period of the Reformation, *edited by James Brown, James Maclehose & Sons, 1884, pp. 375-414.*

Hugh Walker (essay date 1893)

[*In the excerpt below, Walker traces Lyndsay's emphasis on reform from its inception in* The Dreme *to his final work* The Monarchie.]

[Lindsay's] earliest known poem is ***The Dreme***. . . . In it Lindsay struck at once the notes which characterised his work throughout; and though his satire deepened in his later pieces, he never afterwards reached a higher poetic level. ***The Dreme*** was evidently composed with the double object of bringing before James the evils under which his country was suffering and reminding him that the writer, unlike his fellow-labourer Gawin Dunbar, was still unrewarded for his services; for the pension which he drew was too small to be regarded as a full recompense. But the latter object is with honourable dignity kept in the background. In the prefatory *Epistil,* after reminding the king of his youth spent in the royal service, for which, he says, "hope hes me hecht ane gudlie recompense," he passes on with the usual apology for the absence of "ornate termis" to the *Prolog* to the poem proper. This prologue is one of the few passages in Lindsay that can be fairly reckoned poetical. He narrates how after a sleepless night he walked out on a January morning to the shore. The winter landscape is painted with much feeling—the branches bared by the blast, the snow and sleet "perturbing" all the air, the flowers "under dame Naturis mantyll lurking law," and the birds mourning the absence of summer. The poet reaches the sea, and after pacing for a while up and down on the sand, he takes refuge in a little cave in a cliff, where, musing on the resemblance between the unstable world and the restless waves, he is thrown into the conventional sleep and sees the conventional vision. The machinery of the poem is thus anything but original. The vision is a device worn threadbare in our older poets, and in Lindsay there is the additional improbability of incongruent circumstances. But to atone for this he carries us away from the hackneyed May morning to a fresh scene, and suits his landscape to the complexion of his thoughts if not to the plan of his poem.

While the poet sleeps, a lady who calls herself Dame Remembrance appears before him, and sinks down with him through the earth, "into the lawest Hell." Here Lindsay's preferences begin to peep out. The place of torment is peopled by all sorts and conditions of men, but especially by Churchmen of every description, who are there because of covetousness, lust, and ambition, and because they did not instruct the ignorant by preaching. But above all, here as elsewhere, Lindsay dwells upon temporal wealth as the great source of corruption in the Church. The Emperor Constantine is the fountain and spring of all the evil. As yet however, notwithstanding his clear vision of abuses, Lindsay has no fault to find with the doctrines of the Church. He proclaims his belief "that the trew Kirk can no way erre at all." He has a special class of sufferers for neglect of the confessional. He seats the "Quene of Quenis" next the throne of God. He even accepts, though unwillingly, the doctrine of purgatory, because it rests on the authority of "gret clerkis"; but the stanza in which he expresses this belief concludes significantly—"Quhowbeit my hope standis most in Cristis blude." (pp. 7-9)

Passing from this pit of despair the poet and his guide ascend through purgatory, the limbo of unbaptised babes, and that of pre-Christian mankind. These they leave behind with a speed which marks Lindsay's dislike of the doctrines, and rise through the nine spheres of the old astronomers to heaven itself. But this starry flight is somewhat purposeless. Without learning, or at least without revealing, anything very striking, they descend again to a point from which the whole earth is visible at once. After a rapid description of the world in accordance with mediaeval cosmography the poet fixes his gaze upon Scotland; and here we come upon the kernel and discover the purpose of the poem. It is a political essay meant for the instruction and guidance of James. The poet from his height views the realm of Scotland with her "fructuall" mountains, lusty vales, rich rivers, her abundant game and store of metals, her people fair, able, strong to endure great deeds—everything that ought to create wealth, and yet all producing only poverty. Dame Remembrance assures him that the cause of all the unhappiness is "wanting of justice, polycie, and peace," and that they who are to blame for this want are the nobles. This conclusion is driven home by the appearance of John the Commounweill, a character very familiar to the readers of Lindsay. . . . He is leaving the country, "for Policye is fled again in France," and Justice is almost blind. In the Border there is nothing but theft and murder; in the Highlands and Islands, thriftlessness, poverty, and disorder; while greed and self-seeking have made the Lowlands as bad. There is no redress to be had, therefore he departs to return no more till he sees the country guided "be wysedom of ane gude auld prudent Kyng." Here the vision comes to an end. A ship running into the bay fires her cannon and lets down sails and anchor with crash and clatter, and the poet awakes.

Such is Lindsay on his first appearance in the field of letters, and such he remains to the end. There is more poetic promise than is quite redeemed in later years; but the vigorous sense and the manly courage which dares to utter the truth about the most powerful, qualities which make Lindsay respectable even at his lowest, grow with time. He at once points to the nobles and priests as the source of all the evils under which Scotland was suffering, and he never after hesitates or falters. There is always a purpose in Lindsay's verse, and that purpose is reform. The emphasis falls somewhat differently in later days, when the misdeeds of the nobles have lost [their] prominence . . . , when it has become more evident that the priesthood is the real "plague spot and embossed carbuncle" of the State, and when the hope of reform from within the Church has faded away. But however the parts they play may vary in relative importance, the characters upon Lindsay's stage are always the same. No man ever held to his purpose more faithfully than he.

When next Lindsay wrote, self had a larger place in his thoughts. Already in ***The Dreme*** his youth is "neir ouer blawin"; and when that poem passed, like his previous services, unrewarded, he seems to have felt the necessity of speaking out. He does so in ***The Complaynt to the Kingis Grace*** with bold honesty. It is a vigorous piece of octosyllabic verse, recounting again the personal services mentioned already in ***The Dreme,*** touching upon the same evils in the State, and more especially those connected with religion, but entering into most detail with regard to the Douglas usurpation. The poet was not sparing in his condemnation of it. Without stopping to weigh the risk of offending James, who was still only a boy, Lindsay, in some of the most rapid and forcible lines he ever wrote, denounced the wickedness of taking a mere child from the schools to put in his hands the government of the country, and the selfishness of the nobles in afterwards playing upon his passions and tempting him to vice. His indignation was fired at once by love of his country, and by personal affection for the prince who had grown up under his hands. He evidently regarded James as a boy of promise, and his anger was all the hotter when he saw that promise blasted for the selfish ends of the nobles. This sincerity of passion lifts ***The Complaynt*** above the level of begging poems. Most writers who have attempted such subjects have soiled their fingers with them; but Lindsay rises in personal character, if not in reputation as a poet. It was impossible for him to be self-centred, and there is in every line evidence of the truth of his own assertion that he was still without preferment only because he would not beg.

The Complaynt speedily bore fruit. In the same year in which it was given to the public (apparently 1529), Lindsay was knighted and made Lyon King of Arms. (pp. 9-13)

The first of his writings after his appointment as Lyon King was the curious piece entitled ***The Testament and Complaynt of the Papyngo*** (parrot). It is furnished as usual with an apologetic prologue, in which the poet complains that all poetic matter has been exhausted by his predecessors—"the poleit termes are pullit everilk one." This discloses the secret of the great vice of poetic style in that age. The poet must find or invent "terms rethorycall," "aureait," "poleit," and in straining after them he floods the language with ill-considered and incongruous foreign importations. Lindsay was by no means the only or the chief offender in this way: the mediocrity of his poetic power and the backbone of substance in all his works combined to save him from the flaw which sometimes fatally mars the verse of greater writers; but his adoption of this style whenever his theme admitted, shows that he was as deeply imbued as any with the false taste which it indicates. But the chief interest of the prologue lies in the sketch it furnishes of the state of poetry in Scotland at the time and shortly before. It gives a long list of the names of poets, living and dead, mentioning among the latter most of those whose names appear in Dunbar's *Lament for the Makaris.* The majority of them are mere shades; their works are either entirely lost or exist only in unimportant fragments; but the roll at least affords evidence that there was at that time a great deal of poetic activity about the Scottish court, and a considerable body, if not a high quality of work. Further, a careful examination, with reference to existing fragments, of the terms in which Lindsay refers to his fellow bards, rouses respect for his critical faculty. His allusions are not all as laudatory as they seem: it is possible to detect innuendo and sly hints at weaknesses under the guise of praise. (pp. 13-14)

In ***The Complaynt of the Papyngo*** Lindsay puts into the mouth of the king's parrot those criticisms of Church and State which he had already expressed less fully in his own name. The satire derives some piquancy from the plan of the poem, a plan which Lindsay simply adopts from his predecessors. It is a plan condemned by critics; but criticism has not killed *The Hind and the Panther;* and incongruities which can be overlooked in Dryden are still more pardonable in a writer of the sixteenth century.

Lindsay's parrot, though "rycht fat and nocht weill usit to flee," attempts to climb a tall tree, but falls and is impaled upon a stake. In that condition she addresses two epistles, one to the king, the other to her brethren at court. The former contains much good advice strongly though respectfully put. Plain speaking to the Crown was not as rare in Scotland as it was in England, where from an early period the powers of the sovereign were greater. Still, neither in Scotland nor anywhere else have there been many who, filling a position like Lindsay's, have spoken as openly as he did. Those who have least disguised their opinions have generally been either men somewhat removed from court, or men supported there by a power which had to be respected. Lindsay, on the other hand, had no power except such as the king chose to give him; and all his hopes were centred in royalty. In such circumstances his fearless honesty in addressing a young, self-willed, half-spoilt king was alike honourable to him and to James. Personal affection on both sides probably goes far to explain it. Nor does the long delay in promotion prove any want of regard on the part of the king; for promotion came almost as soon as James was his own master.

The second epistle, still more than the first, is eloquent of the danger which threatens the poet who is too much engrossed with a purpose other than artistic. This epistle points the moral, so often handled in the Middle Ages, of the Falls of Princes; and to do so reviews in most prosaic style the history of Scotland. One of the besetting sins of Lindsay was that he had little artistic sense, and hardly any notion of the necessity of selection. *Quicquid agunt homines* has been at all times the subject of satirists; but few have attempted as persistently as he to mix the whole of their material in the farrago of a single piece. Both epistles however must be regarded as merely preliminary. The poet has relieved his soul for the time of one of its constant burdens, the sense of evils actual or threatening in the State; and he now turns to that which is at present and for ever nearest his heart, the condition of the Church. In his own ***Complaynt*** he had congratulated the king that there was nothing

> Withoute gude ordour in this land,
> Except the Spiritualitie.

With reason, therefore, he might now have passed over temporal affairs; and not without cause is he dull in the treatment of them.

When, in the last and longest section of ***The Complaynt of the Papyngo,*** Lindsay turns to the consideration of matters spiritual, the interest deepens and the style entirely changes. We rise above the atmosphere of respectable commonplace to a region in which abundance of matter and warm present interest give a glow and fire to each phrase. In the earlier parts of this ***Complaynt*** the poet simply utters his own sentiments through an uncouth medium. Now the resources of the plan are developed with considerable ingenuity. Seeing the Papyngo in pain the Pye, the Raven, and the Gled (Kite) come near to shrive her. The Pye proclaims himself

> One Channoun regulare,
> And of my brether Pryour principall:
> My quhyte rocket, my clene lyfe doith declare;
> The blak bene of the deith memoriall:
> Quharefore, I thynk your gudis naturall
> Sulde be submyttit hole into my cure;
> Ye knaw I am ane holye creature.

But the Papyngo is not easy in mind—

> Father, be the rude,
> Howbeit your rayment be religious lyke,
> Your conscience, I suspect, be nocht gude;
> I did persave, quhen prevelye ye did pyke
> Ane chekin from ane hen, under ane dyke.
> I grant, said he, that hen wes my gude freind,
> And I that chekin tuke, bot for my teind.

The Papyngo remaining unconvinced expounds to the Pye and his brethren the Raven (a black monk), and the Gled (a holy friar), the cause of her suspicions and the origin of corruption in the Church. Again the satirist reverts to Constantine. Corruption begins when the Church espouses Property and so begets Riches and Sensuality. These banish Chastity and Devotion. The former is traced in her exile through Italy, France, and England, everywhere rejected and cast out. Her fate is no better in Scotland. She is ousted by one religious order after another until she finds refuge upon the Borough Muir. It is pleasant to notice that the satirist of abuses has still a word of praise for pure life and unfeigned devotion—

> Quhare bene scho now, than said the gredy Gled?
> Nocht amang yow, said scho, I yow assure:
> I traist scho bene upon the Borrow-mure,
> Besouth Edinburgh, and that rycht mony menis,
> Profest amang the Systeris of the Schenis.

At last the Papyngo lies at the brink of death. She shrives herself to the Gled, and bequeaths her various possessions to those who seem to need them most; but she is no sooner dead than her executors, disregarding her bequests, fall to quarrelling over her remains, until in the end the Gled flies away with what is left—

> The lave, with all thair mycht,
> To chace the Gled, flew all out of my sycht.

So far as the chronology of Lindsay's poems can be fixed, there is a gap of several years between ***The Complaynt of the Papyngo*** and the piece which follows next. As there is no known reason why he should have ceased to write, the existence of the gap may fairly be advanced as a ground for suspecting that he was already engaged upon ***The Satyre of the Thrie Estaitis;*** but setting aside for the present the disputed question of the date of this work, it appears that for the next eight or nine years Lindsay is represented only by a few fugitive pieces. In one of these, ***Kittei's Confessioun,*** his favourite note of satire against the Church is repeated, with special reference to auricular confession. In another, the ***Supplicatioun in Contemptioun of Syde Taillis,*** the invective is directed against female luxury in dress, a subject as old as the lament for the decline of manly strength. There are besides one or two pieces connected with public events. From his reputation as a poet, his familiarity with all that related to the king, and the general nature of his duties as a herald, Lindsay might naturally be expected to perform some of those functions which fall to a Poet Laureate. One specimen of such handiwork exists in the ***Deploratioun of the Deith of Quene Magdalene. The Justing betuix James Watsoun and Jhone Barbour,*** widely different as it is, may perhaps be regarded as another. It celebrates a mock tournament which formed part of the rejoicings over the arrival of the successor to Queen Magdalen. (pp. 15-19)

[In 1539], Lindsay is believed to have produced the most curious and on the whole the greatest of his works, the morality entitled ***The Satyre of the Thrie Estaitis.*** Little need be said by way of introduction to it. The historian of Elizabethan literature must inquire into the origin of the English drama; and facts in themselves trivial acquire importance from their relation to the works of Marlowe and Shakespeare and Jonson; but in Scotland the drama never had a history. Lindsay's ***Satyre*** contains the promise of better things to come, but the promise was never redeemed; and in consequence such minute facts as are known with regard to early dramatic exhibitions remain minute and unimportant. Before Lindsay the Scottish drama was very rudimentary, and it remained undeveloped after his day. By a singular irony of fate this was caused by the triumph of the very movement in support of which chiefly ***The Satyre of the Thrie Estaitis*** was written. The Reformation stamped out the spark of dramatic activity in Scotland, as it would have done in England had the Puritan party risen to power half a century earlier than it did. (pp. 21-2)

The Satyre of the Thrie Estaitis is a morality, with the usual mixture of concrete human beings and allegorical impersonations of virtues and vices. It is, like all such compositions, long, rambling, and loosely constructed; but by general consent Lindsay's play, for its vigour and point and sound sense, takes the place of honour in its class. It is less abstract and has more human interest than moralities generally possess: there is interest in the constant reference to the pressing topics of the time; and there is a wealth of unpolished humour which only wants compression to be effective. The characters who appear upon the stage are of very various merit. Some of them are lifeless enough, particularly such personages as Correctioun and the virtues generally; but, on the other hand, there is a certain class of the allegorical figures which in a humbler degree have the same merit as Bunyan's, and for similar reasons. Falset, Dissait, and Flattrie are clothed with flesh and blood because Lindsay was profoundly conscious of the evils against which he directed his satire: they are actual existences to him just as sin and Christian grace are to Bunyan. He is successful in the critical and satirical part: he fails in the suggestions for reconstruction, because he did not realise the way to cure the body politic as vividly as he realised the diseases under which it was suffering.

The body of the ***Satyre*** is divided into two parts; but, so far as its structure can be made out from the authorities upon which the text rests, there are besides two interludes connected with it, one introductory, the other intended to fill the gap between the two parts and to amuse the common throng in the interval while the principal auditors were absent from their places. The play is coarse, the interludes are coarser; but that of *The Puir Man and the Pardoner* is good enough to demand notice. As elsewhere in his works, now with humour sly or broad, now with downright denunciation, Lindsay delights to scorch and flay, to crush and pulverise "religious men" of all classes connected with the Church of Rome; so he utilises the pause between the two parts of ***The Satyre*** to emphasise with scathing sarcasm his conviction that all evil is centred in the Church. The Pardoner, Sir Robert Rome-Raker, enters crying his wares and consigning to the powers of evil "this unsell wickit New Testament" and its translators, Luther and his crew, St. Paul and his books. He has a whole pack of treasures:—

My patent Pardouns, ye ma se,
Cum frae the Cane of Tartarie,
Weill seald with oster schellis.
Thocht ye have na contritioun,
Ye sall have full remissioun,
With help of buiks and bellis.
Heir is ane relict, lang and braid,
Of Fine Maccoull the richt chaft blaid
With teith, and al togidder:
Of Colling's cow, heir is ane horne,
For eating of Makconnal's corne,
Was slane into Balquhidder.
Heir is ane coird, baith great and lang,
Quhilk hangit Johne the Armistrang:
Of gude hemp soft, and sound:
Gude, halie peopill, I stand for'd
Quha ever beis hangit with this cord,
Neids never to be dround.
The culum of Sanct Brydis kow,
The gruntill of Sanct Antonis sow,
Quhilk buir his haly bell;
Quha ever he be heiris this bell clinck,
Gif me ane ducat for till drink,
He sall never gang to hell,
Without he be of Baliell borne:
Maisters, trow ye, that this be scorne!
Cum win this Pardoun, cum.

In the first part of ***The Satyre*** proper the note is struck in the character of Rex Humanitas—a king of noble aspirations falling at the threshold of his career under the sway of evil counsellors and plastic as wax in their hands. Dissait and his fellows, with the ready aid of the Estate Spiritual, put Chastitie and Veritie in the stocks and Vice reigns triumphant. Then enters the *deus ex machina,* Divyne Correctioun. The Virtues are set free, the Vices put to flight; Sensualitie finds refuge and welcome with her friends the spiritual lords; the King is roused from his dreams of luxury and license; and the way is thus prepared for part second. It is remarkable that even at this early date Lindsay seems to have felt it necessary to guard against the excess of reforming zeal. He is the enemy of vice, not of innocent pleasure; and he puts into the mouth of Solace a request readily granted by Divyne Correctioun, to

Give us leave to sing,
To dance, to play at chesse, and tabills,
To reid stories, and mirrie fabils,
For pleasure of our King.

This first part is preliminary. It shows reform begun in high places; but the Three Estates are still to be reduced to order. In the second part, summoned by Diligence, they come upon the stage backwards, led by their Vices; the Spiritual Estate by Covitice and Sensualitie, the temporal lords by Publick Oppressioun, the Commons by Falset and Dissait. When they are challenged for their singular demeanour, Spiritualitie justifies it on the plea that they have gone so for many a year and are very well satisfied to go so still; and when the Vices are led away to the stocks, those of Spiritualitie take a touchingly tender farewell of their superior, assuring him that though they must depart their spirit will remain with him. This over, the reform of abuses proceeds. The temporal lords and the commons, accepting the changes demanded, are soon disposed of. Very different is the attitude of Spiritualitie. "Auld use and wont" covers every corruption—

Wee will want nathing that wee have in use,
Kirtit nor kow, teind lambe, teind gryse, nor guse.

It is needless to go over the ground again. The subjects of complaint are the old familiar themes—the lust, the greed, the ignorance of the religious orders. If the satirist's charges of ignorance seem overdrawn they should be read along with the sober assertion of Knox, that some of the friars thought the New Testament a book written by Martin Luther. The Reformer was unquestionably a deeply prejudiced man, but he was truthful; and he is supported on this point by Buchanan. Johne the Commoun-weill suggests with reason that if King David, the "sair sanct," were living he would repent of his liberality to the Church. The play ends with the passing of a number of wholesome acts and the punishment of the wicked, wherein the representatives of the Spiritual Estate suffer so severely that their vices will acknowledge them no more. (pp. 24-8)

To the declining years of Lindsay's life belong two of his longest works, ***The Historie and Testament of Squyer Meldrum,*** and ***Ane Dialog betuix Experience and ane Courteour,*** commonly known as ***The Monarchie. Squyer Meldrum*** is a tale of chivalrous adventure relating the exploits of a personal friend of the poet. Contrary to his custom Lindsay seems to have written this tale mainly for its own sake. He does indeed proclaim an ethical purpose in the opening lines: as other poets have held up the lives of ancient heroes to be mirrors of virtue and courage, so will he recount the deeds of his contemporary. But there is no burning question in his mind, no immediate reform to be aimed at. We miss therefore that which forms the abiding interest of Lindsay's work, its intimate relation to the history and existing circumstances of his country. The absence of this kind of interest would make most of the author's work unreadable; and though the ***Historie*** is otherwise of much more than average merit, it is on this account less attractive than many a ruder page in his other poems. The story of Squire Meldrum is written, as beseems the subject, in the favourite measure of the old romances. It is of all measures perhaps the easiest to write, up to a certain degree of excellence; and as Lindsay's very moderate powers of rhythm are not strained the octosyllabic lines flow on in a clear and forcible stream. The story is well told: there is less irrelevancy, less redundancy, less false taste than we usually find. But on the other hand no high level is anywhere reached. It is like Scott's poetry, with all the variety of versification, with the colouring, the grace of sentiment, and even with part of the vigour (though Lindsay is vigorous) left out. If, therefore, we accept the view that ***The Historie of Squyer Meldrum*** is his greatest work, the niche of the Lyon King in literature must be small. But this criticism is possible only if we view Lindsay simply and solely as a versifier. In point of fact he was a reformer as much as Knox was, and a versifier chiefly that he might be a reformer. To ignore this is to leave the man himself out, to criticise him without that sympathy which alone makes criticism of any value.

Very different is the last, the longest, the most profoundly earnest of all his works, ***The Monarchie.*** Its date is fixed at the year 1553 by a computation of time within the poem itself. Everywhere there are marks that it is the work of an old man whose task is now to learn to die. It is also the work of a weary man whose dearest hopes have been disappointed. More than once Lindsay breaks out in prayer, dignified from its heartfelt earnestness, for purity, for true religion, for all that may lift his country from its miserable condition. For the gloom which hangs over ***The Monarchie*** is not a personal and selfish one. The author's desire for himself is summed up in the wish to be at rest. But rest was impossible for Lindsay while the country he had served from boyhood was still torn and rent from within and from without, while the evils against which he had consistently striven were still rampant; and so he lifts his dying voice for the last time in a long protest against abuses, civil and spiritual, against the tyranny of nobles, the pride of prelates, the oppression of power in all its forms. But he is too worn in spirit to wield effectually his favourite weapon, satire. In a dialogue between Experience and a Courtier, in the plainest and directest terms, without trick or artifice, he expounds the causes of the evils of the commonweal. He lays his finger on the disordered pulse of the country, and names the disease.

If Lindsay had been an artist, if he had understood the supreme importance of selection and condensation, ***The Monarchie*** would have been a great work, not because of poetic talent, but from sheer weight of earnestness. Unfortunately no man ever less comprehended the importance of selection; and in consequence the poem is in great part worthless. No better plan occurs to him than to throw his ideas into the form of a universal history, in which he traces the fortunes of humanity from Adam to the day of doom, and even a little after it. No one cares to hear in his verse the story of the fall, of the flood, of the building of Babel, of the four great monarchies. It is when from time to time he refers to his own country, or when his earnestness for truth almost rises to a cry, that he shows his genuine strength. He is fully himself only where he warns the tyrant lords and barons that small mercy awaits them at the Judgment, or where he examines the double monarchy, temporal and spiritual, of the Papacy. For more and more as time went on the dispute about religion drew everything else into its vortex, so that men who, like Lindsay, were interested in public affairs, and yet not so immersed in their current as to be drowned in details, fixed their eyes upon this dispute as that the solution of which carried all the rest along with it. (pp. 31-4)

No elaborate summing-up of Lindsay's work and position is necessary: he has spoken for himself. He was not a great poet; although in a few passages, such as the prologue to ***The Dreme*** and the prologue to ***The Monarchie,*** he shows the marks of a poetic mind, imagination was not his strongest faculty. His own words, "I did never sleip on Pernasso," had perhaps a deeper truth than he realised. His work is inartistic, harsh in versification, formless in style, marred by a coarseness which it would be difficult to parallel, impossible to outdo. All attempts to palliate his defects are vain. The appeal to the coarseness of the age is but a partial excuse, and any other is out of the question. The Kirk was not without excuse in putting sternly down exhibitions which admitted of ribaldry and licentiousness such as we find in ***The Satyre of the Thrie Estaitis.*** And yet, the more Lindsay is read, the firmer will be the conviction that all this is external to his work. Despite his faults he still retains a true claim to greatness, namely, that of being the literary leader in the Reformation of the life and faith of his time.

For this task he was much better equipped than he was to enter into competition for the poetic laurel with his predecessor Dunbar or even with Gavin Douglas. He had the keen humour which has characterised his countrymen from Dunbar to Carlyle. He was a close observer with ample opportunities of knowing all classes; and he had the shrewd sense necessary to sift his experience. He was not deeply learned; but he had a sufficient fund of information to supply him with copious historical and traditionary illustrations whenever he wanted them. The result is such as we might expect. Lindsay's satire is by no means highly polished; but it is a sound serviceable weapon, and it cuts. But to the making of *successful* satire—meaning by this, satire which influences action—there go certain moral qualities as well as intellectual powers; and Lindsay possessed these too. He was a man of singular tenacity of character: what his mind once grasped it held. He was single-minded: only once or twice does he speak for personal advancement, and then he does it with vigour and decision but with dignity. Above all, he had the courage to brave the vengeance of powerful enemies and to hold firm although he saw others suffer for offences less than his. It was by virtue of these qualities that Lindsay became not only the first satirist (in the vernacular) of his time, but a power in the State as well. (pp. 38-9)

Hugh Walker, "The Scottish Reformation—Lindsay and the Wedderburns," in his Three Centuries of Scottish Literature: The Reformation to the Union, Vol. I, *Macmillan and Co., 1893, pp. 1-48.*

George Saintsbury (essay date 1898)

[*Saintsbury was a late-nineteenth and early-twentieth-century English literary historian and critic. Hugely prolific, he composed histories of English and European literature, as well as numerous critical works on individual authors, styles, and periods. In the following excerpt, Saintsbury favorably comments on Lyndsay's works despite what he considers their coarseness and lack of poetic style.*]

[Lyndsay] is an interesting, and though not a fully yet a fairly known personality, while they flit as shadows; he has left an abundant supply of work, frequently interesting in itself, and generally characteristic of his time; and in one particular he has the rare good luck to have left the only example, not merely in Scottish but in English literature, of an early *sotie* or political farce-satire in dramatic form. If he had given us nothing but the ***Satire of the Three Estates,*** Lyndsay would be a remarkable figure in English literature; as it is, he has left much else. (p. 176)

Lyndsay's works consist of the above-mentioned ***Satire of the Three Estates,*** of a ***Dialogue between Experience and a Courtier,*** and of the ***History of Squire Meldrum,*** all long poems, with a considerable number of shorter ones. Of the long poems, ***The Dialogue*** (or ***The Monarchie***) consists of more than 6000 lines, chiefly octosyllabic couplets, and gives the history of the world, with comments in the dismallest manner of the fifteenth century. The ***History of Squire Meldrum,*** in the same metre, is an exceedingly pleasant romantic biography of a real person, a sort of cross between Quentin Durward and the Admirable Crichton, whose prowess against Englishmen and others in the field, and his courtesy to ladies in the bower, are very lovingly depicted. The most noteworthy of the three, however (though, like them and Lyndsay's other poems, it is disfigured by the extraordinary coarseness of language which marks most of this early Scottish poetry, and which, except for a very brief time at the Restoration, and then chiefly in anonymous writings, has never been matched in England), is the ***Satire.*** This, as its length, not far short of 5000 lines, makes inevitable, is not a single piece, but, on the model of the French compositions which no doubt suggested it, a set or pentalogy of five different pieces: the first part of the play proper, the First and Second Interludes, the second part of the play, and the Third Interlude, while there is a preliminary interlude of between two and three hundred lines more which has been thought spurious, but with no apparent reason, and which is certainly not less vigorous than the rest, though it is if possible even coarser.

The main play is a "morality" of the familiar kind (see next Book), but with the allegory deflected from its usual ethical tenor to a political bent, Rex Humanitas being tempted by Wantonness, Placebo, and the Vices in the habit of Friars, and saved by Correction, Gude Counsel, and the Virtues. It is in the second part that the Three Estates make a direct appearance; while the Interludes, not losing sight of the moral, enforce it with more farcical and general satire. It has been customary to regard Lyndsay as a partisan of the Reformation, and so, in the merely literal and grammatical sense, he certainly was. But it does not appear very certain that he was a partisan from any doctrinal side.

This sharp satire on abuses in Church and State, perhaps mixed, as satire so often is, with some selfish consideration, appears also in all, or almost all, Lyndsay's minor poems, which, if not over numerous, are very interesting. They scarcely reach a dozen in number, and, as has been said, grace of poetic style and thought is by no means their prominent characteristic. But they all have a certain accomplishment of phrase and form which is extremely noteworthy in contrast with the staggering state of English in both ways at the time, and more noteworthy still when we remember that the Scottish Muse was about to fall almost barren for centuries, while the English was in some fifty years' time to become the fruitful mother of the best poetry in the world. And they are all interesting, more or less, in matter. The ***Dream*** (which is in plain language a begging letter to the King) is in rhyme-royal, and the body of it is simply part of that vast and dreary common form of fifteenth-century allegory through which, as throughout this Book, we have to make our way. But the begging letter by itself has some very interesting biographical touches, reminding James how his master-usher had carried him in his arms and tucked him up in bed; how he had told him not merely "of Hercules the actis honorabill," and much other improving matter, but the Prophecies of Rymour, Beid, and Marlyng, and tales of the Red Etin and the Gyre Carling, for which posterity would very cheerfully give twenty ***Dialogues between Experience and a Courtier.*** The ***Dream*** itself ranges from the centre of the Earth (*i.e.* Hell) and the description of Paradise, to the relations between France and Scotland and the state of Argyle and the Out Isles, which would appear not to have been Paradise at all. The piece, with all its parts included, considerably exceeds 1000 lines, and ends with a direct Exhortation to the King's Grace (in nine-line stanzas, with a different one as *coda*) which is manly and sensible. In fact, both Dunbar and Lyndsay deserve the highest credit for the absence of "assentation" in their addresses to their patrons, James the Fourth and Fifth, though neither father nor son seems to have profited very much thereby.

This manly tone is renewed in the ***Complaint of Sir David Lyndsay***—some 500 lines in octosyllabic couplets—which is again biographical and again suppliant, but does not hesitate to mingle probably unpalatable advice with supplication. Nor is the ***Testament and Complaint of the Papyngo*** (the King's Parrot), which is about the length of the ***Dream,*** and chiefly, but not wholly, in rhyme-royal, very different, being directed largely against various abuses in Church and State, especially the former. The ***Answer to the King's Flyting*** (the ***Flyting*** itself is lost) partakes of the studied coarseness of this singular form of poetical amusement. But Lyndsay's practical honesty makes him still more attentive to warning the "Red Tod of St. Andrews" against vice and disorder than to exercises in curious ribaldry. Another court poem, probably not without special meaning, is the ***Petition*** of the King's old hound "Bagsche" to his successors in favour, Bawtie and others, for "ane portion in Dunfermling," concluding with good advice. The poet's most important attempt in pathetic poetry, the ***Deploration of Queen Magdalene,*** the fair and ill-fated French princess who was James's first wife, and to whom the climate of Scotland was almost at once fatal, is meritorious but hardly successful, Lyndsay being unable to extract from the rhyme-royal that plangent note which it so readily yields to true poets. He is happier, though still not consummately happy, in the comic handling of the ***Justing between Watson and Barbour*** and the ***Supplication in Contempt of Side Tails*** (trains), as well as in the rather famous anticlerical ***Kitty's Confession,*** to which the ***Description of Peddar Coffis*** is a kind of pendant. Lastly has to be mentioned the ***Tragedy of the Cardinal,*** a ferocious attack on the dead Beaton in the style of the *Fall of Princes.* (pp. 177-79)

George Saintsbury, "The Scottish Poets—Historical, Political, and Minor," in his A Short History of English Literature, *The Macmillan Company, 1898, pp. 171-79.*

G. Gregory Smith (essay date 1900)

[*In the following excerpt, Smith examines Lyndsay's transitional position between the literary traditions of the fifteenth and sixteenth centuries and acknowledges the poet's debt to the Chaucerian tradition.*]

The last of [the] Scots school of Allegory is Sir David Lyndsay (1490-1555), who, though, in strict chronology, of the sixteenth century, is yet for critical as well as editorial reasons to be associated with the foregoing writers. Had we accepted the thesis of the classical quality of Gavin Douglas's work, we should have found an excellent companion subject in Lyndsay as the exponent of the theological side of the Renaissance. For the doctrine of 'directness' which Douglas states so pithily . . . , but which he hardly applies in the practice of his own art, was but the literary expression of a general principle which urged others to scrutinise tradition on the side of religious custom and belief and to send the "unlernit" to the sources of sacred knowledge. Of this latter purpose the verse of Lyndsay shows ampler proof. His lateness brought him nearer the time of revolt; and he would from his corner of Northern Europe naturally and more readily incline to the theological phase of the Revival. He feels that the vulgar must get their lesson direct, not from the "cunnyng clerkis" who understand Latin no more "than they do the ravyng of the rukis." As the Latin and Greek writers must not be read in the Arabian paraphrasts but in the best manuscripts which the Poggios may find, so Holy Writ must be freed from the mystification of an unknown tongue and brought to the understanding of all. The analogy is not complete, for the logic of the matter is that the Reformers should have gone straight to the Greek and Hebrew; but what Lyndsay and others meant was that the people should have the opportunity of a more direct and intelligent appreciation of the facts, and that the vernacular alone made this possible.

> Sanct Jerome in his propir toung Romane
> The Law of God he trewlie did translait,
> Out of Hebrew and Greik, in Latyne plane,
> Quhilk hes lene hid from us lang tyme, God wait,
> On to this tyme: but, efter myne consait,
> Had Sanct Jerome bene borne in tyll Argyle,
> Into Yrische toung his bukis had done compyle.

Lyndsay's enthusiasm on this point, united with a general directness of purpose, proclaims him at once as of the New Age, and in purpose the co-worker with Hutten and Luther.

But there is much of the old way in him, more especially in his invention and technique. He uses the "Testament," in the poem so-called and in the ***Papyngo*** piece; the 'Complaint' is the form of three different sets of verses; in the ***Jousting*** and the ***Answer to the King*** he shows the continuing fondness for the "Flyting"; in the ***Dreme,*** the ***Deploratioun,*** and even in the ***Satire of the Thrie Estaitis,*** we find echoes of the Courts of Love; he recalls the *Miseriae Curialium* in his complaint of the old dog Bagsche; he often rides the hobbies of the Schools and revels in those lengthy miscellaneous lists of names, so dear to the mediæval mind. Much of this was general poetic tradition, but most of it is directly modelled on Chaucer, to whom Lyndsay, like all the other Makaris, acknowledges discipleship. Spiritually he has little in common with the older poet; but in the matter of form, and even in word and phrase, he testifies to Chaucer's enduring influence, even into the sixteenth century. Thus his description of Squyer William Meldrum is a careful copy, to the minutest detail, of Chaucer's sketch of the "yong Squyer" in the Prologue to the *Canterbury Tales;* and his praise of the eyes of the lamented Queen Magdalene is in the very words which Chaucer humorously applies to the twinkle of the "wanton and merye" Friar. We should probably not have had the amusing passages between the Papyngo and her executors had we not had the *Parlement of Foules.* His favourite stanza is the seven-lined. Like others of the Chaucerian School he has not a little occasional verse on follies, chiefly feminine, such as ***On Syde Taillis,*** and here and there references to the failings of the fair sex, but in his tone he is rather more acrimonious than the earlier poets. So far, and chiefly in an external and formal way, he stands with the old; yet in essentials he shows important differences. The emphasis of his criticism of women may be the working of the Jean de Meun spirit, or it may be the Lyon King's ungallant way of deploring his royal master's weaknesses; but there is more striking evidence throughout his work how far he had wandered from the old allegorical ideals. He does not use the form, as the early fifteenth-century verse-makers did, merely as a cloak for a general sermon on the Vanities, or, as Dunbar did, because it helped him to pictorial effects. He is on all occasions a preacher for the times; he dreams by courtesy to literary custom, and only as a mere prelude to his serious interest in contemporary politics or historical analogies. In his most conventional passages we suspect that Pride stands for a certain prelate, that his Papyngo is a Scots bird and will have something to say on current events, and that the "ageit man" Experience talks of the worship of Venus and Juno that he may lead up to the idolatry of Edinburgh and the abomination of Loretto. Scotland supplies the stations of his Itinerary. More often he makes no secret of his intention, and rapidly passes through a few colourless stanzas to the business on hand. There his purpose is not exactly satirical, but it suggests the mood of the satirist, and it indicates the presence of the New Spirit. In his purely satirical verse, too, we see a similar development; ***Kitteis Confessioun*** is a more uncompromising burlesque of Church ordinance, and the ***Justing*** mocks the mimic chivalry of the time with a seriousness which we do not find in Dunbar's *Turnament.* His tendency, too, towards the dramatic is further proof that the final stages of crystallisation had begun in the allegory.

Not only does Lyndsay's work show little or nothing of the quality of early allegory, but it illustrates the general paralysis of poetic power which had set in. He is too loud-voiced for reformation to have an ear for the undertones. With blatant honesty he tells us that he "did nevir sleip on Pernasso" nor drink of Helicon, "that mellifluous, famous, fresche fontane"; and his abjuration of the delights of the classical muse meant to him also the abjuration of poesy itself. His age had turned from the ascent of an impossible Parnassus to "the straucht way" to "Mont Calvarie"; and Pegasus had become a sorry hack, drawing the rumbling cart on which politicians and theologians sent their wares to market. If Lyndsay is to call on any Pagan deity for inspiration, it will be on "raveand Rhamnusia, goddes of dispyte." In the prelude to the ***Dreme,*** where his fancy has fullest play, he repeats the old Scottish imagery of a cold stormy night, but instead of taking comfort from fire-light and cordials, or of musing over a book, he wanders forth to the wild seashore, and "for passing of the tyme" climbs into a cave, high in a crag, where, clad in cloak and hood and with mittens on his hands, he gazes on the driving sleet till he falls a-dreaming of the sorrows of Scotland. Denied as he thus is of some of the essential qualities of poet (not that the Muses always require a clear hearth and cordials), he is yet by no means dull and uninteresting; for, though he is a confirmed dyspeptic as far as the matter of his verse is concerned, he makes amends by the energy and vivacity of its form. He is at a disadvantage in the ill-knit and tedious ***Dialogue betwix Experience and a Courtier,*** but elsewhere he shows a remarkable metrical facility. In the stanzas of the ***Testament of the Papyngo*** or of the ***Complaynt of Bagsche*** he runs on without effort; in the poem on Queen Magdalene (in which he most nearly approaches the pageant pictures of Dunbar) his verse rolls in majestic case; and in the ***Historie of Squyer Meldrum*** he outstrips all contemporary romance by the spirit and rush of his lines. In the last poem he forgets the worries of Church and State and throws himself heartily into the frolics of the lusty Squire. He is not lacking in humour, but his occasion is rare. Like Henryson, he amuses a modern reader by the quaintness of epithet and phrase, for which not he but trickish Time must have the credit or the blame. But a discontented sadness is his prevailing mood, and he fittingly marks the boundary between the artistic quickness of the fifteenth century and the severity of the sixteenth—neither quite with the one in its fancy, nor with the other in its quarrel. (pp. 63-8)

G. Gregory Smith, "The Scottish Poets," in his The Transition Period, *William Blackwood and Sons, 1900, pp. 35-84.*

W. Murison (essay date 1938)

[*In the following excerpt, Murison briefly appraises the strengths and weaknesses of Lyndsay's works.*]

Poets sometimes disclaim the title of poet; as Burns in his first *Epistle to John Lapraik:*

I am nae poet, in a sense;
But just a rhymer like by chance.

Such disclaimer, critics have declared, merely exhibits a pleasing modesty on the poet's part. In "The Prolog" to ***The Monarche*** Lyndsay explains why he does not invoke the Muses as do the "pleasand Poetis". He is not one of them,

For I did never sleip on Pernasso,
As did the Poetis of lang tyme ago,
And, speciallie, the ornate Ennius;
Nor drank I never, with Hysiodus,
Of Grece the perfyte poet soverane,
Of Hylicon, the sors of eloquence,
Of that melifluous, famous, fresche fontaine.

In other places Lyndsay calls his writing "rurall ryme", "raggit rurall vers", "barbour rusticall indyte"; and speaks of it as deficient in rhetoric and in ornate terms. Again, he bids his book with its rude unrhetorical style flee to rural folk and not keep company with poets. Yet, while yielding to this conventional modesty, he tacitly claims a place among the Scottish poets, living and dead.

Lyndsay's verse, mostly satiric, didactic and chronicle, amounts to about 18,000 lines, wellnigh all of it written in the midst of his busy public life. He had not time, he may not have had inclination, to revise and polish his verses. Consequently, fault might be found with his limited variety of rhymes, and with his readiness to manipulate forms to suit his rhyme. We must, however, be cautious in judging his rhymes, and his language as a whole, for we cannot be sure that we have the forms he wrote. ***The Monarche*** may have been printed under his supervision. The works printed in his lifetime out of Scotland were not revised by him, and these show variants from the editions printed in Scotland; while Charteris' edition of ***Ane Satyre*** (1602) has many differences in forms from the Bannatyne MSS. text (1568).

Lyndsay has also been charged with weakness, or forgetfulness, because of his fondness for repeating lines and phrases (in battle scenes he has "ruschit rycht rudelie" four times); while other passages are transferred, almost word for word, from one poem to another. In three poems Lyndsay describes the grief of David I of Scotland had he known how religious life would degenerate in the abbeys which he founded. That Constantine ruined the Church by enriching it is stated in ***The Dreme*** and ***The Papyngo,*** two of the earliest works; is repeated in ***Ane Satyre;*** and appears yet again in his latest work, ***The Monarche.*** Such repetition, whatever its stylistic defect, has the advantage of making certain what Lyndsay's opinions were, especially when he utters, as his own, in ***The Complaynt*** or ***The Monarche,*** the views given to characters in ***Ane Satyre.*** His contemporaries would not notice the repetition. Those present at a performance of ***Ane Satyre*** had not necessarily read ***The Dreme:*** readers of ***The Monarche*** were not necessarily auditors of ***Ane Satyre.***

Lyndsay has still marks of mediaevalism: love of astronomical lore, and the conventions of dreams, restless tossing in bed, wandering forth on May mornings, allegories and allegorical personages. He sometimes loads his poetry with pedantic erudition, as catalogues of names. (pp. 75-7)

Though not a poet of the highest type, Lyndsay was a ready versifier with a command of clear and fitting language. He was a quick observer, a man of shrewd sense, a great humorist, a clever painter of life. ***The Monarche*** contains long stretches of dreary chronicling of world-history, but also weighty reflections, well expressed, on life and on affairs in Church and State. ***Squire Meldrum*** has much sprightly narrative and graphic description. Notable for imaginative power is ***The Dreme,*** perhaps because written when exile from Court afforded Lyndsay leisure. As a rule, his subjects do not lend themselves to the pathetic; but ***The Deploratioun,*** though it could not be an expression of personal grief, does show pathos.

But Lyndsay's strength lies in his dramatic skill. Remember the dates of his dramatic work, roughly 1540 to 1554; and what stage plays there were in England during that period. A. W. Ward says that ***Ane Satyre*** "in vigour and variety far outstrips any contemporary or analogous English effort"; and, "Altogether, this dramatic satire is . . . by far the most elaborate as well as in its way the most powerful of all our mediaeval moralities" [*A History of English Dramatic Literature,* vol. I].

Yet one of Lyndsay's fellow-countrymen calls ***Ane Satyre*** "a series of interludes loosely combined into a play" [William Dunbar, in *The Poems of William Dunbar,* Vol. I]. A careful study of ***Ane Satyre*** leaves a totally different impression. The plot is quite good and is well carried out; the varied characters are interesting, even those with abstract names are full of life; there is plenty of lively incidents; the dialogue is grave and gay, its reforming seriousness tempered and enlivened with waggish wit and piercing satire. If some portions of the dialogue are dull to us, we must not forget that the serious matters touched the audiences of Lyndsay's time very intimately. They had suffered from exactions of tithes and other dues; when ecclesiastical immorality was denounced, or ignorance, or neglect of duties, or flaunting of wealth, they could silently think of a culprit, or shout his name aloud. They knew to what friar or pardoner any piece of satire applied, they appreciated topical allusions to marauding Borderers, to Edinburgh merchants and "the brousters of Cowper toun". To understand the full effect and popular appeal of ***Ane Satyre*** we must put ourselves into the position of the men and women of the time. (pp. 77-9)

W. Murison, in his Sir David Lyndsay: Poet, and Satirist of the Old Church in Scotland, *Cambridge at the University Press, 1938, 227 p.*

Lyndsay breaking the Keys of Rome.

Maurice Lindsay (essay date 1948)

[*In the following excerpt, Lindsay compares Lyndsay's poetry to that of Burns and Dunbar. According to the critic, while Lyndsay's poetic ability did not match that of his two contemporaries, his talent as a satirist was vastly superior.*]

[Lyndsay was] a poet whose influence during the two hundred years after his death was probably greater than the influence of Burns. Lyndsay was a vital force in helping on the Reformation. Although he officially remained a Catholic to the end of his days, his poems are full of satirical and angry attacks on the corrupt practices of the clergy of his time.

Probably his popularity—his poems were on the tongues of the ordinary Scottish folk as late as 1820, and, until the advent of Burns, the volumes of his works were as common a piece of furniture in Scottish homes as the Bible—was due to extra-literary reasons. He was, after all, on what proved to be "the winning side," and his continual tilts at "auctorite" must have been relished as long as presbyterianism remained the dominating force in Scottish life. One gets some idea of how much his contemporaries enjoyed these tilts from an appreciative stanza of "Ane Adhortatioun of all Estatis to the Reiding of thir Present Warkis," written by Henry Charteris as a preface to his edition of Lyndsay's poems.

Thocht Gawine Dowglas Bischop of Dunkell
In ornate meter surmount did everilk man:
Thocht Kennedie and Dunbar bure the bell
For the large race of Rethorik they ran.
Yit never Poeit of Scottische clan,
Sa cleirlie schaw that Monstour with his markis.
The Romane God, in quhome all gyle began,
As dois gude David Lyndesay in his Warkis.

With the growth of nineteenth century religious toleration in Scotland, and the gradual decline of the religious influence, that aspect of Lyndsay's work inevitably ceased to have purpose.

Lyndsay's vulgarity and coarseness were regarded as partly (and reprehensibly!) responsible for his popularity by such refined worthies as the nineteenth century Doctors Irving and Small. Lyndsay is, without a doubt, frequently coarse. But he was living in a coarse age, and in such passages as the Interlude between the Pardoner, the Sowtar and his wife in ***Ane Satyre of the Thrie Estaitis,*** he has preserved for us a cross-section of the life of his times—much as Burns does in several of the Kilmarnock poems. . . . The Scot, when not suffering from an attack of Anglified prudishness, is always quick to appreciate the humour in healthy vulgarity. On this count, therefore, Lyndsay achieved undoubted popularity as a mirror of the familiar domestic manners of his day.

A third extra-literary reason may lie in the number of quasi-proverbial moral sayings which Lyndsay, always out to "improve," slipped so neatly and so frequently into his lines. And just as the vast mass of Burnsian devotees worship "the Master" for his platitudes rather than for his poetry, Lyndsay's tags must have won him numerous adherents and stuck easily in many rustic memories.

It has lately been the fashion to cry down Lyndsay's merits in favour of those of Dunbar. Dunbar is, of course, the greater poet by far. But destructive criticism can pull down too many attractive outhouses in its desire to show off the main building to the best advantage. Dunbar, with all his breadth and dignity, was a clumsy battering-ram at satire where Lyndsay was a rapier. And Lyndsay never missed the mark! The anger which he nursed against the corrupt Catholic clergy and against the evil counsellors who led the youthful King James the Fifth into dubious ways, grew in intensity from the relative mildness of ***The Dreme*** (1528) through ***Ane Satyre of the Thrie Estaitis*** (*circa* 1535) to the sarcastic fury of the third book of ***Ane Dialogue betuix Experience and ane Courteour*** (1552-3).

A careless metrist, a writer who would sell his soul for a rhyme, and at times so much a preacher with a purpose that he ceased to be a poet, Lyndsay nevertheless deserves to be read to-day because of his literary merits. He is unequalled as a satirist. His work, except for occasional dreary passages in ***Ane Dialogue betuix Experience and ane Courteour*** is full of vigorous wit, and, if he rarely reaches to the heights of ecstasy and displays little car for the sounds of poetry, he abounds in refreshing good sense. As a mirror of his times he is, of course, quite invaluable. (pp. 6-9)

Maurice Lindsay, in an introduction to Poems. *By Sir David Lyndsay, edited by Maurice Lindsay, Oliver and Boyd Ltd., 1948, pp. 6-10.*

Agnes Mure Mackenzie (essay date 1954)

[*In the excerpt below, Mackenzie examines Lyndsay's* Ane Satyre of the Thrie Estaitis, *assessing its theatrical and literary merits.*]

It has been customary for Lindsay's editors to speak dutifully of his 'religious feeling' [in his ***Ane Satyre of the Thrie Estaits***]: I cannot see in him as much as in Bernard Shaw, who did at all events hold in some regard the mechanized Holy Ghost he calls the Life Force. But his interest in church affairs as political factors—and through most of his manhood they had been major ones—was intense; and he combined with it something else, which has always made for popularity, never more than on the brink of a revolution—a zest in scandal, which he himself no doubt identified with an elevated desire for moral reform.

Many very dead pamphleteers have had as much. What keeps Lindsay's best work alive is his craftsmanship. . . . The ***Estaits*** is a play by a man who knew his stage. . . . [The] sense not only of the image itself, but of the dynamic clash of images which is essential stagecraft, appears in him as far back as the ship's guns crashing into the ***Dreme.***

He did not invent his methods: he did not need to. We do not know if he wrote plays earlier, but certainly, by his later middle age, he swept into his orchestration of technique every element in the preceding sketch of drama, using it swiftly and surely. Take one small instance. When Sensualitie enters with her maids, Fund Jonet—Janet the Foundling—makes a fourth, for that entry only and the song which follows. Sensualitie and the maids are boys dressed as women. Jonet, a singer of reputation enough to perform at least twice at court, is dressed as a boy: and the classic inversion of the Feast of Unreason is clinched when a 'lady', calling her by her well-known professional name, demands a song, and the 'boy', affirming that she will 'bear a bass', leads off at once, no doubt in a high soprano. In print, it is nothing: on the stage it would be considerably funny, and keep the sardonic undertow on the move at a point which threatens a static courtliness.

It is waste of time to fit the play into a 'kind'. You can call it with Saintsbury morality-farce-sotie, or with Mr. Hamer panoramic drama. Both are good enough names if one knows what the words mean: but creative authors do not write a 'kind'. One has something to say—in Lindsay's case that the Old Church was dead and damned and Society rotten but recoverable—and one says it by means of the subject, and the method, that one finds convenient or can achieve. And since most subjects, and methods, are ancient enough, one can seldom use new ones but combines the old, as a musician combines familiar sounds to make new music. Later on, most likely, if one has been successful, or often if not, some earnest soul seeking for a Ph.D. disentangles them, and explains where he thought you stole them.

I shall not try to do as much for Lindsay. I do not think that at any point in the play he said, 'We will do a bit of clerk-play here, some *sotie* there, and a little courtly masque in the other place . . . ' much less 'We'll have some Adam de La Halle here—now that bit of Gringoire, and since nothing Scots can really be admitted to admiration unless it can be said to derive from England, we must get in a little Heywood somewhere'. He probably did have said to him, more or less, 'Here, damn it, we must have a part for X', and 'Look here, that bit drags. Can't you liven it up a little?' And he cursed and looked at his image, and chipped and tinkered: but he clearly had his technique in his bones by then, and the drive of the theme sent him on, one facet after another catching his eye, rising from his subconsciousness bodied already in the image that would serve to put it across to the type of audience he had in mind.

He knew that audience, all the layers of it. He was a Fife laird, of respectable pedigree, who had been at court from his youth, and now was chief herald, Lyon King of Arms, and many times ambassador for his sovereign. But it has always been part of the texture of Scotland that though her class consciousness is, in all classes, keen, a class unselfconsciousness, as in Spain, goes with it, and makes even today for a frank fraternity of intercourse between social unequals. It accounts too for a phenomenon in Scots letters that strangers are apt to consider rather odd. The high tragic ballads, essentially aristocratic, were sung, and often made, in the cottar-house, while a song in Scots as broad as its country humours may be the work of a Duke or a Lord of Session or a world-famous Professor of Economics.

It is true that for all his respectable pedigree, Lindsay lacks the full range. In spite of his quite distinguished place at court, he had, socially, a touch of the 'failed B.A.' It is probably why he nags so at his master, who recalling the young man who sang and told bedtime stories to the sorely harried bairn who was King of Scots, endured the nagging with a surprising patience, though probably with a by no means surprising relief when his Lord Lyon had been packed off for a while as His Excellency the Ambassador. Lindsay had never the deep instinctive gentrice of his social inferiors Henryson or Barbour, or of his exact social equal, Gilbert Hay. But he did understand the crowd. . . . (pp. 15-18)

The thing, we all know, is satire: and satire, the art-form, goes back to the first group of Stone Age lads who caught the Old Man of the Tribe in an off-moment, and later produced some disconcerting mimesis. The word satire, *satura,* is younger, but venerable: and its oldest sense in Latin is fruit salad, or the kind of stew in which anything may occur. To a Roman mind the word, used for an art-form in which everything went, had an echo also of *satyrus,* a satyr: and the satyrs were impolite semi-divinities, whose romps had once relieved the Athenian groundlings who sat under Sophoclean austerities.

With this tradition half-consciously behind it, the play . . . is in places an untidy piece of work. The untidiness comes in part because the thing grew. It began as a court-play, played at Linlithgow to end the Christmas revels of 1540, most probably in the noble Lyon Chamber, whose great triple hearth now confronts the naked sky. We have the English ambassador's description:

> An interlude . . . the hoole matier whereof concluded vpon the Declaratioun of the noughtinesse in Religion / the presumpcion of busshops / . . . and mysusing [misconduct] of preists.

And His Excellency goes on to describe how after the play James called together the Bishop of Glasgow, who was his Chancellor, and other court prelates, and gave them vigorous orders to reform. These were not unneeded, for since the foul tenth century at Rome, when Marozia and her mother governed the Popes, the Church had never been so vilely degraded, largely because it had fallen to a 'spoils system' where its higher places crawled with parasites. Lindsay exaggerates the completeness of squalor: he had seen Bishop Elphinstone of Aberdeen, a scholar and something very like a saint, and a faithful Father in God to his diocese . . . and since Elphinstone had been Chancellor in his day, he had been about the court in Lindsay's young manhood. Nor was Elphinstone the only priest of his kind at either end of David Lindsay's lifetime. We are apt to forget the strong movement for reform alive in the Old Church as well as outside and against it; and Lindsay, with less excuse than we, ignores it. Gross evil there was, though, real and in plenty, not bettered by the common moral landslide of 'post-war' times: and James may well have commissioned the first ***Estaits*** to hold the mirror to those guilty of it before he used his authority against them.

James died. The war came that has been described. England gave up and made peace in 1550, and Scotland tightened her belt with a rationing scheme and began to rebuild the towns 'brint be the auld enemie'. Under the foreign war and the reconstruction, the religious struggle that had now gone on for a quarter-century odd was growing and spreading, its centre in Lindsay's Fife and the shore of the

Firths. Lindsay had taken his place among the attackers, and in 1552 rewrote his play, and had it played on the Castle Hill at Cupar. He enlarged it greatly, and enjoyed himself: its shrewd local and topical hits—many at people who were probably present, and whose customers certainly were—must have rocked the crowd.

Clearly, the thing was a colossal success: as a popular show, in fact, it had everything. Two years later, the brave and able Queen Dowager dispossessed the feeble and treacherous Duke of Châtellerault, her daughter's heir, and assumed the Regency. She may have thought that a little gaiety would be good for the morale of the capital, for she and her court saw a number of plays that summer, not in her palace, but publicly at the Tron. Marie recalled this play, such a long and weary fourteen years before. She had watched it beside her husband at Linlithgow, and may have desired to put it to the same use: it is possible too that a very lonely widow, whose children were growing up in another country, or dead, may have desired to see again Rex Humanitas, who is a candid but kindly sketch of James V. . . . Accordingly, the recent success from Fife was commanded for performance in Edinburgh.

Quite how Lindsay altered it we cannot be sure. Even a fastidious lady of the Renaissance . . . could take a joke of considerable breadth, while the more cerulean parts would be played in her absence. But there may have been some cuts in the interludes, the more as what was topical in Cupar would have no point for the Edinburgh public. And we can also be reasonably sure that some of the weariful repetitive padding that drags the second act out of point and shape was added to live up to the occasion . . . though Charteris's affirmation, fourteen years later, that the thing took nine hours must be exaggeration. (pp. 18-20)

The play was put on in style. Six wrights took a couple of days to lay the boards, instal the royal box and the 'playaris hous' (both probably merely shifted from the Tron), make the 'jebbatis and skaffauld' and the property throne. And there were other properties as well, from the angels' wigs to a live crow for Falset's soul when he is hanged, with tapestry and flowers to dress the stage and the Queen Regent's box, and make-up and costumes (to stand broad daylight) for a cast of some sixty, not counting the musicians.

The show at the Greenside may not have begun, as the one at Cupar did, with a kind of 'trailer', known as the banns. One imagines that this would be played overnight, or earlier still, as advance publicity. It announces that 'gif weddir serve', a King and Estates will arrive in Cupar on the 7th June, at seven a.m. The actual 'crying' comes only to three stanzas: but then a cottar pipes up from the audience that he will be there if he can dodge his wife, and there follows a sequence going back at least to Athens, and forward (with cuts) to the pantomime next Christmas, of the henpecked husband, the braggart old soldier, May cuckolding December, all touched off in a lightning sequence of vignettes, written capably for a capable group of actors, and promising all the familiar delights.

The play opens soberly, in the courtly key. . . . Diligence appears as Presenter (*cf.* Rumour in *Henry V*) no doubt to music, with a grave invocation of the Trinity, and announces the King's arrival to redd all troubles. A change of metre calls up the Estates, with a hint of future action, deftly done, and a call for silence, ceremonially grave till its last word:

> Let euerie man keip weill ane toung,
> And euerie woman tway.

(The trick of anti-climax to formal announcement is exploited elsewhere, especially in this role, which was probably played by a 'dead-pan' actor with a formidable voice.) King Humanitas enters, with members of his Estates: his prayer to be a good King is familiar matter, but very much to the point, and as anti-climax his courtiers Wantonnes and Placebo build up an entry for Solace (we might say Pleasure) who builds in turn for that beryl of beauty, Lady Sensualitie. She now makes a glittering entrance with her maids Danger and Hamelines (we would say Holding-off and Coming-on), and by a curious and effective trick applies to herself the orthodox formulae of the courtly lover, to which the courtiers' by-play with the King gives a counterpoint of the ugly reality that could lie beneath them: the thing is in fact a kind of miniature version of Dunbar's great picture of three expensive lovelies, outside and in. The whole has a balletic quality: it is diagram, but dynamic diagram, with a dream's reality in the fantastic.

The court retire, and there enters the sober figure of Gude Counsall, returning from banishment. He, however, is soon thrust aside by Flatterie, whose part is the leading comedian's henceforward. Flatterie then calls his friends Falset and Dissait; and they disguise themselves with a mock christening, as Devotioun, Sapience and Discretioun. The King, made vulnerable by Sensualitie, returns and becomes their victim: he still means well, and takes them at face value. They chase off Gude Counsall, whereupon Veritie enters, with a large Bible and long golden hair, and preaches a sound and not too wordy sermon on careless rulers—'the pepill follows ay thair principate'. Denounced as a heretic, she is clapped into the stocks, and Chastitie, wandering homeless, fares no better, for though, having been repulsed by each Estate, she is kindly received by a couple of workmen who offer her a drink, their wives see the kindness in the worst possible light, and she flees to the King, to join Veritie on Sensualitie's orders.

The arrival of King Correctioun is announced, and the knaves plot flight, each one to an Estate. Correctioun enters in state, a great winged angel, come to judge the King, who . . . is

> nocht bot ane officiar,
> To caus his Leigis liue in equitie.

Correctioun cleanses the court, Sensualitie fleeing to the Spiritual Estate, and releases Veritie and Chastitie, who with Gude Counsall take the place of the courtiers: and the first act concludes with Rex Humanitas embracing Correctioun, who bids him call an immediate Parliament. The players make formal departure in procession, leaving Diligence to summon the Thrie Estaits. . . .

This first act is a complete play in itself, well made, and for all its infusion of deliberate bathos, with more nobility than Lindsay shows in any other extant work of his save the comparatively early ***Dreme.*** An interlude follows, . . . and, like all that follows, it oscillates between Lindsay's best and worst.

Pauper, complaining, is shoved off stage, and told not to spoil the play. His retort,

> . . . thair is richt lytill play at my hungrie hart,

thrusts like a knife into the comic squabble, and he describes his fleecing by laird and parson. . . . Following him comes the comic pardoner, peddling indulgences, with a profitable side-line in false relics. He was already a traditional figure: Langland and Chaucer in England, for example, had drawn his brothers before 1400. Lindsay now gives him a stretch of brilliant patter that can stand by the famous and anonymous *Droich.* A soutar and his wife apply for divorce, and get it with business gross even for the classic satyr-drama. Pardoner and his boy are suitably and topically lodged, and the interlude ends with a noisy free-for-all.

Diligence now clears the stage for the Second Act. The court having had its paiks, Church and State are now summoned for theirs, although it is soon sufficiently evident that the second will get off with a tactful lightness. King and court re-enter, shepherded by Correctioun and the Virtues: and the Three Estates come before them in procession . . . but walking backward, each led by a Vice. Even to a modern audience, this is effective: a mid-sixteenth-century one had not only been trained to read ceremonial as we do printed words, but saw in the inversion of ceremonial at best a licence for what it formed and restrained, at worst its dedication to the Devil. The 'backwart-ganging' is in fact rather rubbed in, but the speech may have to cover and be lost in a long movement.

They greet the King with formal compliment: and again his answer sets forth in a phrase the traditional Scottish view of the King as Chief:

> Ye ar my members suppois I be your head.

All the rest of the act is shaped upon the pattern of the regular business of a Parliament. The King announces that with Correctioun's help he will reform each Estate. There is comic panic. Then Diligence, who is acting as the macer, calls the 'compleinours', and against the splendour there scrambles on to the stage the lame ragged figure of Johne Commonweill. It is one of the great moments of the play. Lindsay's patriotism could be, and often was, completely gleyed by his party fervencies, but here is that passion for an unhappy country that had sounded generously in the ***Dreme.*** A swift short stichomythic dialogue of the King and the ragged cripple, face to face, leads to John's serio-comic accusation of the Estates and the Vices who captain them. Correctioun orders these last into the stocks, with some dullish scolding. The police chase out Covetise and Sensualitie, who take tearful leave of the Spiritual Estate, each side looking forward to a blythe reunion. The Lords and the Burghs then call for Gude Counsall, who bids John fence the court. By a dream-like shift—audacious, but it comes off—his place as pursuer is now assumed by Pauper, John becoming the pursuer's advocate, who opens his case by pointing out sensibly and forcibly (and topically, in those years of recent and precarious peace) that his client plays a large part in the country's defence: then he attacks the idle of all classes, beginning with 'strang beggers', fiddlers, quacks, and, alas, bards, and passing in the same breath to religious orders (most of whom did at that time deserve no better) goes on to the injustice of secular law, under which small thieves hang while great ones thrive.

Correctioun admonishes the Estates from the Bench. The lay ones promise to mend, embracing John, but the Spiritual make an indignant fuss. John is nervous about pressing his case against them, but now the Lords and the Burghs back him up, and there is a considerable debate. Lindsay's wordiness begins to drown him here. . . . [But] Merchand (the Commissioner for a burgh) drives home the point in three lines:

> Quhat bene the caus of all the heresies
> Bot the abusioun of the prelacies?
> Thay will correct and will nocht be correctit.

Pauper's case being settled, Veritie and Chastitie appear as the pursuers in a new one, the defenders again being the Spiritualitie. Lindsay does not merely repeat his effects, however: their affair (with cuts) stages a good deal better than it reads, for the trick undisguisings, flat on paper, are genuinely funny on the stage.

Gravity breaks in again, most effectively, when the case being disposed of, 'thay cleith Iohne the Common-weil gorgeouslie and set him doun amang them in the Parliament'. Fifteen Acts of Parliament are then proclaimed, just, save for the rhyme, as the Edinburgh people were accustomed to hear them read at the Mercat Cross: the 159 lines of them promise a serious lay-sermon on disorder, but are swamped with a dully shrill anti-clericalism whose point is blunted by its spitefulness. The Vices are now uproariously dealt with, Flatterie, who has talked himself out of a jam, assisting the highly realistic hanging of his late associates, Dissait and Falset, who take touching farewells (full of local Fife allusions in our text)—the former of his kindly patrons the Merchants, the latter of the Crafts, his old good friends, growing suddenly serious and genuinely impressive as the metre swings out and he calls to

> catyfe covetous Kings
> Reauers but richt of vthers Realmis and Rings,

and all 'publick oppressours', fat idle prelates, corrupt judges and lawyers, and then—still in the serious tone and metre—hen-pecking wives. He hangs then, with a crow flapping loose to simulate his black soul. Flatterie remains to congratulate himself . . . and, in logic, the play should end there with his escape and Diligence's dismissal of the crowd to tavern and dance-floor.

Lindsay, unhappily, like too many men of his day all over Europe, found it extremely difficult to leave off. Perhaps, too, he had some speeches he wanted to use, and the popular comedian who played Folie wanted more fat; and there would be the excuse that the crowd must be held while the Queen and her suite mounted and got away down the steep drop to Leith Walk, which riders would have to take with very great care. So he brings on Folie (who had triumphed in the cuckoldry-play of the banns) for a stretch of mechanically grimy back-chat with Diligence and the King, leading on to a *sermon joyeux* of traditional pattern, its text the motto of the Enfans sans souci, *Stultorum numerus infinitus*—americané, there's one born every minute. It is conventional patter, fast and machine-made, and the court who left early cannot be said to have missed much.

Yet the play as a whole, with all its faults of conventional idea, a humour that sinks too often to mechanized dirt, party one-sidedness, and all the lave, has not only an explosive vitality, but a sure feeling for the actual stage, a technical command of all its devices, that make grievous the general loss of our old drama. . . . Faults and all, it is good art, and with flashes too of a nobility Lindsay only once shows elsewhere in his work. And perhaps the good mid-Victorian minister who called Lindsay 'the morning star of the Scots Reformation' had only read portions waled with judicious care by one of his flock with a naughty sense of humour. (pp. 20-6)

Agnes Mure Mackenzie, "The Background and the Play," in Ane Satyre of the Thrie Estaits *by Sir David Lindsay, edited by James Kinsley, Cassell and Company Limited, 1954, pp. 7-26.*

C. S. Lewis (essay date 1954)

[*Lewis is considered one of the foremost Christian and mythopoeic authors of the twentieth century. Indebted principally to George MacDonald, G. K. Chesterton, Charles Williams, and the writers of ancient Norse myths, he is regarded as a formidable logician and Christian polemicist, a perceptive literary critic, and—perhaps most highly—as a writer of fantasy literature. Also a noted academic and scholar, Lewis held posts at Oxford and Cambridge, where he was an acknowledged authority on medieval and Renaissance literature. A traditionalist in his approach to life and art, he opposed the modern critical movement toward biographical and psychological interpretation, preferring to practice and propound a theory of criticism that stresses the author's intent rather than the reader's presuppositions and prejudices. In the following excerpt, Lewis examines Lyndsay's principal works, providing especially favorable commentary on* Squyer Meldrum.]

[Lyndsay's] works are a beautiful example of the 'single talent well employed'. The ***Satyre of the Thrie Estaitis*** . . . holds an important place among our scanty materials for a history of the allegorical drama in Scotland . . . ; here it will be enough to say that this long morality stands apart from the rest of Lyndsay's output by the looseness of the metre and the general popularity of the style, and that it is rich in pathos and low humour. In his remaining works he everywhere keeps well within the lines marked out for him by his great predecessors; there is no novelty in them, and he usually lacks the originality of Henryson and the brilliance of Dunbar and Douglas. But what there is of him is good all through.

His earliest poem, the ***Dreme*** (not before 1528), has grown as logically as the circles made by a pebble thrown in a pond. The centre is a vision of John Commonwealth 'all raggit, revin, and rent, With visage leyne as he had fastit Lent' hastening for the border to leave a Scotland which has no place for him. In order that the poverty of Scotland may be shown as the fault not of nature but of corruption, this is set in a picture of the country as a whole, and the country then set in a complete picture of the earth, earth among the planets, and all in the heavens. Hell is also described, and the total vision, which has thus become a humble relative of the *Somnium Scipionis* and the *Divine Comedy,* is enclosed in a dream and prefaced with a pleasingly realistic account of a winter morning's walk on the sea-shore. It is readable work in a good, though familiar, tradition. The modern reader, no doubt, has to acquire the taste for such things, but the acquisition is easy and worth making. There is a more obvious appeal in the dedicatory epistle where the poet reminds the king how he carried him in his arms as a child, played games with him on the nursery floor, and told him stories about Thomas the Rymer, the *reid etin,* and the *gyir carlyng.* The stanzas on purgatory contain the first indication of Lyndsay's Protestant sympathies.

The ***Complaynt to the King,*** written in octosyllabics that have the spring of Burns or Scott, is a begging poem which shares many of the merits of Dunbar's efforts in the same kind. Like Dunbar, and perhaps in imitation of him, Lyndsay gets great fun out of 'Flyting' the king's evil counsellors; and he knew these lines were good, for he used them over again in the ***Thrie Estaitis.*** But the poem as a whole is gentler than Dunbar would have made it. The repetition of Lyndsay's services to the infant king, which might so easily have reminded us of Mime's *Starenlied* in the opera, is full of humour and affection. The conclusion is graceful in the highest degree. After jokingly asking for a loan, to be repaid

> Quhen kirkmen yairnis no dignitie
> Nor wyffis no soveranitie,

the poet rises into a more serious vein and hopes, in lines which recall the close of *Il Penseroso,* that, if the king after all prove unkind, God will grant him in his *Latter aige* such contentment on his small ancestral estate as Diogenes enjoyed in his tub.

In 1530 came the ***Testament and Complaynt of the Papyngo,*** an account in rhyme royal of the death and last words of the king's parrot. Its *complaynt* is a sermon to its fellow-courtiers and to the king on mutability, with special reference to Scotch history of which the bird displays an extensive knowledge; its *testament* is made in the unwelcome presence of certain birds of prey who turn out to be monks and friars of the feathered world. The dying parrot inveighs against their hypocrisy and avarice, with the usual references to Constantine's unfortunate liberality, while they vigorously defend themselves by throwing the blame on the secular clergy. So far, the satire has been ordinary enough; but we find real satiric invention, and even a strange beauty, when the popinjay, having provided for the poor by leaving her gay coat to the owl, her eyes to the bat, and her voice to the cuckoo, and for herself by committing her spirit to the *Quene of Farie,* is torn in pieces by her carrion executors the moment the breath is out of her body—*hir angell fedderis fleying in the air.* The poem is of historical interest for the list of Scotch poets in the prologue.

The years between 1533 and 1542 saw the production of several occasional poems—a ***Flyting,*** a ***Complaynt*** for Bagsche the king's dog (in which the supposed caninity of the speaker is never lost sight of amid the author's moral and political opinions), an attack on the female fashion of *syde taillis,* and a burlesque ***Justing*** on the lines of Dunbar's 'Tailyeour and Sowtar'. The ***Deploratioun of the Deith of Quene Magdalene*** (1537), which begins dully enough, deserves to be remembered for an excellent concluding stanza and for a stirring picture of the pageantry which would have celebrated the queen's coronation. ***Kitteis Confessioun*** (1542) is an attack on the confessional in which the serious part—that is, the bulk of the poem—tends to be read with some disappointment because the opening has led us to expect a comic treatment. The first forty lines are not unworthy of Prior.

The killing of Cardinal Beaton in 1546 was the occasion of Lyndsay's dullest poem, a ***Tragedie of the Cardinall*** in the tradition of Boccaccio's *De Casibus;* but who could delay on this when we are already in sight of his masterpiece? ***Squire Meldrum*** (after 1550) ought to be in everyone's hands; a lightly modernized and heavily glossed text at a reasonable price is greatly to be desired. This wholly delightful poem stands, as it were, at the triple frontier where the novel, the romance, and the biography all march together. The ideals of love and war are those of romance, but the hero is an historical person whom the author has known, a skilled physician and good footballer as well as a warrior and a lover, whose exploits are kept within the bounds of possibility—though, to be sure, when the enemy are English we may be told that 'The Sutheron wes ay fyve for ane'. The circumstances of Meldrum's battle with the English champion in France might have come straight out of Malory, but there is no leaping up from fallen horses and 'foining like boars' for hours on foot—only the long series of courses with the lance which may actually have occurred and which are described as lovingly as a modern writer of school-stories describes a cricket match. The sea-fight and the mêlée in the streets of a French town, more easily enjoyed by such laymen as ourselves, are among the very best things of their kind. They are in the hammer-like octosyllabics of the *Bruce* and almost any couplet taken from them at random would make the rhetorical battle poetry of Spenser and Drayton look like a tailor's sword beside the sword of a trooper. The strange idea that the poem is a burlesque, unless it is based on the first fifty lines or so, may come from the love scenes where much chivalry, good sense, and wholesome sensuality are mixed with much humour. But the humour is not burlesque; in English medieval romance homely realism thus often blends with courtly love, and *Risus, Focus,* and *Petulantia* are, at all times, the natural attendants of Venus. The hero's ***Testament*** in rhyme royal, which follows the story in octosyllabics, would show, in real life, a levity not very suitable to a death-bed; as a purely poetical fanfare to round off a knightly tale, it is excellent. After committing his soul to God, Meldrum asks for a procession a thousand *hagbutteris in gude ordour* instead of monks and friars; no black for mourning but red for Mars, green for Venus, and blue for Mercury; and instead of requiems *Alleluya with melodie and game* and *cannounis crak,* 'I will that day be heard no hevines'. His farewell to the *sterne of Stratherne, my ladie Soveraine,* whom he had loved *par amors* (with every intention, poor man, of marrying her in the end, but both found it *greit vexatioun to tarrie upon dispensatioun*) almost concludes his speech, but he has time to say quickly at the last 'Sir Curat, gif me incontinent my crysme'. In short, while we are given to understand that he made a good end, we see him with our own eyes die game. It is a fitting conclusion to this unambitious but noble poem. We have greater stories in verse; perhaps none, even in Chaucer, more completely successful.

The ***Dialog betwix Experience and ane Courteour*** (1553?), more familiarly known as the ***Monarche,*** is the last of his poems, and the most medieval in form and spirit, though it refers to Erasmus and to Diodorus Siculus whom Lyndsay had read in one of the early editions of Poggio's Latin version. It opens with a May morning's dream in rhyme royal where Lyndsay attempts, not very successfully, to rival the brilliant colouring of Dunbar and Douglas; it goes on to an octosyllabic history of the five great empires (the papacy being the fifth) preceded by an account of the creation and followed by an account of the Day of Judgement, and relieved from time to time by complaints and apostrophes in decasyllabic stanzas. The presence of these suggests that poets could no longer count on that unjaded appetite in their readers for which the *Cursor Mundi* was written, but the work is substantially true to that old tradition. Nothing is made of the dialogue form; and if the papacy is treated from the point of view of a Reformer, this does not modify the medieval character of the poem. It is a metrical homily on world history, based largely on Orosius, Josephus, and Diodorus. In poems of this type we do not look for 'jewels five words long' nor for any great originality of conception. Their attraction lies in the perennial interest of the matter and in those local variations which it elicits from authors happily ignorant of archaeology and therefore compelled to see the past as if it were part of their own present. They are very seldom dull. From Lyndsay's I gather much that has made it, for me, worth reading. I learn (in answer to a question often raised) that our first parents loved *par amors* in Eden, delighting in each *utheris bodeis soft and quhyte,* and no wonder, says the poet, *consyderyng thare gret bewte;* that in the antediluvian world

> The watter was so strang and yne
> Thay wald nocht laubour to mak wyne;

that the Mediterranean and all other inland seas are relics of the flood; and that when the building of the tower of Babel was abandoned the *schaddow of that hidduous strenth* was already six miles long. It will be seen that Lyndsay usually has his eye on the object. The style of the ***Monarche*** does not rise to very great heights except in some of the lyrical interludes; but he must be a dull reader who finds it dull.

Warton—still our most reliable critic on much later medieval poetry—praises some of Lyndsay's lines as 'nervous, terse, and polished' and claims that they need only a modernized spelling to recommend them to the taste of his own age. This affinity between Lyndsay and the eighteenth century is naturally best seen in the ease and mastery of his lighter octosyllabic pieces; but even where his artistic formulas are most widely removed from those of the Augustans, he might be called a *medieval* Augustan. Decorum, discipline, a perfect understanding of his aim and of the means to that aim—these are his characteristics. (pp. 100-05)

C. S. Lewis, "Late Medieval: The Close of the Middle Ages in Scotland," in his English Literature in the Sixteenth Century, Excluding Drama, *Oxford at the Clarendon Press, 1954, pp. 66-119.*

Agnes Mure Mackenzie (essay date 1955)

[*In the following excerpt, Mackenzie comments on the sermonic elements of many of Lyndsay's works.*]

As with many writers who succeed by their faults as much as by their virtues, Lindsay's early work is a good deal the more attractive. There is something very likeable in ***The Dreme,*** in which he reminds the lad new come to power [James V] of the days when its writer would comfort and amuse a harried bairn whose crown had crashed on to his head at eighteen months old, tucking him up in bed, singing to him—

The first sillabis that thow didst mute
Was 'Pa, Da Lyn.' Upon the lute
Then played I twenty springis—

and telling him stories of Greek and Roman and biblical heroes, of Merlin and Thomas the Rhymer and the Reid Etin. Now he offers a new tale, opening with the long fashionable dream, this time on the wintry shore on a New Year's Day. . . . Dame Remembrance takes him to Hell, where the 'men of kirk lay bounden into bingis' and the other two Estates are no better off, nor are their wives. They pass on swift Dantean journey through Purgatory, Limbo, the Elements, the Spheres and the Heavenly Court, returning to Earth for a geographical survey, all most ornamentally erudite. Then comes the cake within this elaborate icing. Lindsay asks to see Scotland, and does, with its rich possibilities of wealth in the widest sense, and its grim actualities. Remembrance tells him

it lakkis na uthir thing
Bot labour and the pepillis governing,

which lack comes from the 'want of justice, polycie, and peace' in 'sleuthful hirdis': the heads of the State care only for their own profit—which happened, at the time, to be perfectly true. Against them as witness comes the lean ragged man Jhone Comoun Weill, whose bitter complaint, spoken here with harsh and moving sincerity, laments 'the realm that hes owr young ane King'. Then a ship comes to anchor off the shore, and the guns of her salute to the New Year, and reign, rouse the dreamer, who, waking, advises his young master in a very sound exposition of a king's duties, candid, sensible and with real affection in it for king and kingdom.

It was the first, and the best, of many sermons. Between the ***Dreme*** and the Glorious Revolution of 1688, to preach at the sovereign . . . was a sport as popular, in some quarters, as golf: and Lindsay might well have captained the national team. He even preaches in the begging letters that most poets then and long after bestowed on their patrons: when, next year or so, he is asking for a rise, he not only recalls his nursery services and gives a candid picture of the Douglas régime, including Angus's deliberate debauching of his young King and stepson, to keep him quiet: he tells the King that since he is trying to achieve good order, he should cause it too in the 'spiritualitie' . . . and now will he lend his old playmate £1000 till the Bass and the May forgather on Mount Sinai? Failing that, will God at least make his Sovereign oblige with the wherewithal 'of quiet lyf and sober rent'? A similar piece, of the middle thirties, is set in the mouth of the ***Kingis auld hound callit Bagsche,*** whose nose has been put out by that new pup Bawtie. It is one of the pleasantest of begging letters, for it lacks the self-righteous shrillness that grew on Lindsay, and its dry humour can still turn on himself, blending the canine and human agreeably.

But Bagsche owns that he has 'maid bludie sarkis' in his time. Lindsay, in fact, as he rose into his forties, was setting up as *le Caton de nos jours,* and that is always a dangerous trade for Cato—most of all, perhaps, when his skin is fairly safe. ***The Testament and Complaynt of our Soverane Lordis Papyngo*** is a polemic piece in the cause of that Reformation for which many both within and without the Old Church were striving. The decoration, at once traditional and topical, is possibly a little overweight. Its bright background is the royal aviary: James had a liking for fantastic birds, keeping not only herons, cranes and peacocks but so many coloured parrots and parroquets that they needed the services of a whole-time warden. The thing opens with a procession of vernacular poets, dead and living, with in its forefront a very handsome tribute to 'Gawane Dowglas, Bischope of Dunkell', and as ghostly a rear-rank of dead fashionables as those in Dunbar's 'Lament: Quhen he wes sek'. He will not compete with such distinguished writers, so falls back on the sad tale of the King's pet parrot, who on her death-perch after an accident has to scold not only the King but also his father, who is saddled surprisingly with the guilt for Flodden—not for fighting the battle with obsolescent armament, but actually for fighting it at all. The Papyngo bids farewell, with an immortal line, to Edinburgh, 'thow heich triumphant toun', to the other palaces, Stirling, Linlithgow and Falkland with its lovely park but shocking ale in the pubs, and then gets to business by calling three canon lawyers to make her will. They prove to be the Pye, the Gled [kite], and the Raven, and there follows the conventional onslaught on clerical greed, with a careful exception in favour of the new Priory of the Sciennes.

Lindsay's attitude still, however, is less that of the political polemist than of the professionally outspoken person with the tail of an eye upon the muckle pierglass. In the middle thirties the King and his Lord Lyon . . . held a formal *flyting.* Lindsay's half survives, and though the shrillness is growing, there is still affection under the invective. Of course, like all prophets since (and before) Isaiah, he had to have a shot at women's fashions. ***Ane Supplicatioun in Contemplatioun of Syde Taillis*** [voluminous trains], written between 1537 and 1542, is famous, foul, and (as increases on him) far too long for its point. Quite as heartfelt and possibly rather earlier—the Queen married and died in 1537—is ***The Deploratioun of the Dethe of Quene Magdalene,*** a duty-piece by the recognized laureate. There is a certain dramatic colour in the panorama of painted scaffolds ready to hold the players, of wine wherewith the fountains should have flowed, of the craftsmen's green coats, the burgesses' crimson and scarlet, the purple, black and brown silk of the Town Council, that the Queen should have passed below her canopy of cloth of gold, 'all turnit into sable', the music to dirges. But 'Da Lin' shows less grief for his master's charming bride of not quite seventeen than does the Lord Lyon for his wasted labour in stage-managing pomps that are not going to come off.

The King died in the end of 1542. Lindsay saw him turn, with that 'litill smyle of lauchtir', to the wall. Thereafter the growing shrillness gains upon him, and the humour is apt to be stock sculduddery and stock invective. ***Kitteis Confessioun,*** of the 1540s, is a tolerably nasty piece of work. The attack on abuses of the confessional was not unjustified, but the self-righteous dirt is far from endearing. An uglier specimen, to those at least who happen to know the facts, is ***The Tragedie of the Umquhyle maist Reuerend Father David . . . Cardinall and Archibyschope of Sanctandrois,*** which gloats, at more length than Knox though with better manners, on the murder of that prelate. To the Extreme Left in religion at that time, England was much what Russia is nowadays to their political equivalent. The reader who knows what Henry VIII said of Scotland (a subject on which he was in fact not sane) and what his troops, by their own showing, did there, finds his jaw dropping at the damnation of Beaton for opposing the quisling Earls of Arran and Angus and as the warmonger who caused the sack and burning of Edinburgh . . . for which Beaton was responsible in the same sense as Sir Winston Churchill for the bombing of London. But the public to whom the ***Tragedie*** was addressed had not read Henry's official communiqués, far less his careful orders to his troops, and as propaganda the thing is quite brilliantly done, 'carrying' the better for the sound and genuine sense of its conclusion, where the bishops are adjured to keep their oaths and the 'princes' to take as much trouble in choosing them as they would do in choosing a cook or a tailor.

Of the other three late works which have survived, ***The Historie of ane nobil and wailyeand squyer William Meldrum vmquhyle Laird of Cleische and Bynnis*** (written about 1550) is pleasanter reading. Even there, to be sure, the taste is somewhat doubtful: it is *biographie romancée,* with fairly frank detail, of a man newly dead and a lady who was possibly still alive: but at any rate it is both kindly and lively. His hero is an agreeable young soldier, of a type that for centuries was a standard export—a tall man of his hands, a favourite with the ladies, and the lover of a wealthy young widow, Lady Haldane of Gleneagles, who is reft from him by her recalcitrant kinsmen. The octosyllabic couplet has straightforward vigour, and the thing is a really spirited novel in verse.

Its readability does not carry over (at any rate for the twentieth-century reader) to the more ambitious work of about the same time, ***Ane Dialogue betuix Experience and ane Courteour off the Miserabyll Estait of the Warld,*** commonly known as the ***Monarche,*** which Lindsay probably thought his supreme achievement. It is dedicated to the Regent Arran, his half-brother Archbishop Hamilton (the heads of the civil and spiritual powers) and the Estates, and professes to show that the ghastly total war which their friend Henry VIII had loosed upon the country is no more than the just reward for Scotland's sins, which will be much worse if she imports arms from France. There are over six thousand mortal lines of it, mainly octosyllabic couplet with 'exclamatiounis' and other trimmings in assorted stanza. Their main substance, with much parade of information, is a pious summary of world history, from Eden through the Four Monarchies of Babylon and Persia, Greece and Rome, to the fall of the Papal Fifth, and the Last Judgment . . . with a wipe at the old grievance of ladies' trains. Its informativeness, its often really eloquent abuse, made it long popular, even as a school-book. . . . (pp. 40-3)

Dead popular learning is very dead indeed, and to tackle the ***Monarche*** now needs firm resolution and strong black coffee. This is not true of a very different work whose purpose was not dissimilar in the main, though here Lindsay keeps clear of foreign politics. Though the plan of this book excludes discussion of drama, one cannot in fairness to Lindsay leave out all mention of the great morality-play ***Ane Satyre of The Thrie Estaits*** (probably first performed in 1540), which is by far his most important work: it seems to have been to the Scottish Reformation what *Le Mariage de Figaro* was to the French Revolution, but its quality does not depend on its political effect on its own time. . . . [Even in its untidiness], the thing has an actuality and verve beyond any drama in England and most in France until Lindsay had been dead for a generation. (pp. 43-4)

Agnes Mure Mackenzie, "The Renaissance Poets: (1) Scots and English," in Scottish Poetry: A Critical Survey, *edited by James Kinsley, Cassell and Company Ltd., 1955, pp. 33-67.*

Kurt Wittig (essay date 1958)

[In the following excerpt, Wittig discusses the significance of Scottish colloquialism and democratic themes in Lyndsay's works.]

Till the days of Walter Scott, Sir David Lyndsay of the Mount (1486/90-1555) was the most widely read and frequently printed of the Makars; among the Scots peasantry his name was almost proverbial. The reasons for this popularity are highly revealing. (p. 91)

[None] has so eloquently championed the common people as this influential courtier. When he says that his verse and language are rough and rustic, and that they lack the aureate elegance of Dunbar or Douglas, he is not showing conventional modesty. His works were meant for "rurall folk" (***Papyngo,*** 66). When he uses a courtly style, it often is almost in order to parody it, as in the "First Epystyll" of the ***Papyngo;*** in ***Ane Satyre of the Thrie Estaitis,*** Sensualitie speaks in aureate Chaucerian stanzas as long as she keeps up her pretence (ll. 499 ff.), but in Braid Scots tail-rhyme as soon as she drops her mask. Lyndsay's natural medium is colloquial Scots, with occasional drastic violence. Listen to John the Common Weill, who is half-incredulous, half-stammering with happiness, when he hears (***Thrie Estaitis,*** ll. 2417-8) the good tidings of reform, and, pushing his way through the crowd to get closer, exclaims:

> Out of my gait, for Gods saik let me ga:
> Tell me againe, gude maister, quhat ye say.

It is when, as in this passage, Lyndsay's ear is tuned in to the language of common folk that he finds his true inspiration and achieves his most genuinely dramatic effects. He reflects the sound common sense of the folk, including their proverbs, their shrewdness, their desire for firm ground under their feet, and their realistic suspicion of gambling. "Wo to the realme that hes ouir young ane king" (***Dreme,*** l. 1011)—that is the keynote of Lyndsay's political complaint, and in ***The Complaint and public Confessioun of the Kingis auld Hound, callit Bagsche,*** instead of the Wheel of Fortune, he gives us (l. 151) a picturesque Scots proverb: "Hiest in Court, nixt the weddie [gallows]." Lyndsay's humour consequently inclines to coarseness and obscenity, but it also has (***Thrie Estaitis,*** l. 1527) the grim dramatic quality of folk speech:

> Na cuir thow nocht, man, for my thrift.
> Trows thou that I be daft?

Lyndsay's metres are commonly of the more popular variety. He does use the Chaucerian stanza and a few other courtly forms, and the framework of his poems is usually modelled on courtly originals. There are occasional instances of decorative alliteration, and one (***Papyngo,*** ll. 647 ff., 1172 ff.) of ornate internal rhyme. In the ***Thrie Estaitis,*** however, Lyndsay shows that he is more at home with bob-and-wheel stanzas and tail-rhymes, which go to meet popular taste. Among the latter, there are many with curtailed second parts (for example, *a a b a b*), and one of these is the earliest occurrence of the Burns-stanza in Scotland ($a\ a\ a_4\ b_2\ a_4\ b_2$).

Not that Lyndsay had neglected the study of Chaucer and his contemporaries. His earliest extant poem, the ***Dreme*** (1528), begins with the conventional sleepless night and the dream vision; but, apart from this, its realistic and intimate specification of local and personal details is quite un-Chaucerian. Moreover, it is a January night . . . with snow and hail, and the contrast of the bleakness of nature with the poet's colourful memories of summer creates the desired atmosphere of "mutability" for his dream. In passages like this, where he conjures up a concretely visualised scene, Lyndsay has the sensuous suggestiveness and intensity that we found characteristic of Douglas, Dunbar and Henryson; but, unlike them, he has too much to say, and all too easily becomes prolix. Perhaps being a teacher to the prince had made him dogmatic and encyclopædic.

The dream proper, a vision of Hell, Paradise, the elements, and earth, seems to follow the European pattern. But the longest single part of the poem (ll. 799-1015) is a view of Scotland and her fate, seen with common sense and realism. This harnessing of allegory to a popular patriotic purpose is quite out of accord with the older convention, and it was one of the ways in which "Davie Lyndsay" endeared himself to the common folk of Scotland. The poet asks his guide, Remembrance, why Scotland is so poor. He sees fish, mountains with "bestiall," valleys of corn, rivers, lochs, hunting, "halkyng," deer, springs, rich finds of metals, even gold, silver and precious stones. The luxury of wine and spices she may lack, but food, drink, clothing are abundant, nor are there (ll. 834-5)

> More fairer peple, nor of gretar ingyne,
> Nor of more strenth gret dedis tyll indure.

The answer is that Scotland suffers (ll. 847 ff.) from lack of "governyng," of due enforcement of her laws, of far-seeing policies, and consequently of peace. If the shepherd sleeps, the flock will fall prey to the wolves. In his dream the poet sees a gaunt, rugged "berne [man]" coming across the fields, a "pyikstaff" in his hand as if he had gone from his home. It is "Jhone the Comoun Weill," whom we meet again in the ***Thrie Estaitis:*** the fact that Lyndsay twice personifies the Common Weill as a peasant or bonnet laird is highly significant. John is "disgysit," "disherissit," neglected. Polecye has fled to France, his sister Justice is all but blind (ll. 947 f.). In the lawless Border John had almost been slain, the "sweir swyngeoris [lazy rogues]" of the Highlands drove him away, in the outer Islands and in Argyll he found "unthrift, sweirnes [sloth], falset, pouertie, stryfe" (l. 965). From the Lowlands he was expelled by profit; the clergy practice simony; "Covatice" is everywhere. John the Common Weill will not, he says, be able to return home (ll. 1004-5)

> . . . tyll that I see the countre gydit
> Be wysedome of ane gude auld prudent kyng.

This is a new use of allegory; the allegorical figures enable Lyndsay to express abstract political ideas in concrete pictures with sharp contemporary and local characteristics. Lyndsay is the most eloquent and convinced exponent of the "democratic attitude" that is such a marked feature in Scottish literature. Henryson had expressed the dignity of the peasant; to Lyndsay, a cobbler or tailor has greater ethical worth than bishop or prelate, because they thoroughly *know* their trade (***Thrie Estaitis,*** ll. 3127 ff., 3344 ff.). Lyndsay's manly independence has its noblest ring in ***Bagsche*** (1533-36) and in the ***Complaynt*** (*c.* 1529). He has never been able to beg favours, he says, and even now (***Complaynt,*** l. 31) "I wyll nocht flyte." In the ***Papyngo*** (1530), the dying parrot appeals (l. 303) to his monarch, James V, to choose his council regardless of "blude, ryches or rent," and urges him to read history, the chronicles, and statecraft for half an hour a day. "Lerne to be ane kyng," he cries (l. 287); and in the ***Thrie Estaitis*** Lyndsay explains (l. 1605) what he means:

> Quhat is ane king? nocht bot ane officiar,

To caus his leiges live in equitie.

This is the true state doctrine of the Reformation, but it is also the state doctrine of the Declaration of Arbroath and of Barbour's *Bruce:* it is the task of a king to defend the God-given "fredome" and "richt" of the people. The supreme effort must be for peace, which best serves the common weal. Most of the reforms in the ***Thrie Estaitis*** are designed to promote the common weal, by strengthening the rule of law on which the security of the common man depends. (pp. 91-4)

Democracy and social justice are Lyndsay's main themes. They induced him to champion the cause of the Reformation; and his criticism of the Old Church was the greatest single cause of the immense popular vogue that he enjoyed. Biting satire against abuses among the clergy occurs in ***The Dreme*** and ***Papyngo,*** and is the essence of the ***Satyre of the Thrie Estaitis.*** The latter was performed before the royal family on 6 January 1540, fully twenty years before the Scottish Reformation, in a version of which no text survives. In 1552 followed an open-air performance in Lyndsay's native Cupar (Fife), from which Bannatyne gives us extracts, and in 1554 yet another version was performed before the burgesses of Edinburgh and probably also the Queen Regent. For the public performances at Cupar and Edinburgh the text was much enlarged. It is full of allusions to local and contemporary events, and conveys a sharp picture of the social conditions of the time: abuses in the Church; the pest (ll. 2594 ff.) of beggars, pardoners, bards, pipers and other retainers; the tricks (l. 4056) of the merchants who "mix Ry-meill amang the saip [soap]" and cheat the simple peasant women; the Border cattle-thieves who flourish under the protection of the great lords. Perhaps because they had fewer opportunities for whole-sale corruption, the burgesses are let off more leniently than the two other Estates. Even so, all three come in for caustic satire.

The play opens with Rex Humanitas pampered and led by the nose by Flatterie, Falset, Sensualitie, Dissait (in disguise), while Veritie and Chastitie are shut in the stocks and lawlessness is rampant. In an interlude, the extortion of "corpse-present [death duty]" by the priest makes the peasant a Puir Man whom the Pardoner robs of his last groat. But Divyne Correction is on the way (l. 1594),

To teill the ground that hes bene lang vnsawin;

and the Parliament of the Thrie Estaitis is summoned for reform measures. They come in walking backward, but John the Common Weill shows up their true leaders: Covetice and Sensualitie among the clergy; Publick Oppressioun among the secular Lords; Falset and Dissait among the burgesses. When these all have been put behind lock and key, the reform measures advocated by John the Common-Weill are carried—against the violent opposition of the clergy, where their own vested interests are threatened. The ignorant prelates are replaced by learned preachers; Flatterie, under his mask as a Freir, expelled; and the other vices hanged. And Pauper fervently implores the King not to let these good laws be a dead letter only. But what here looks like the dreichest of dreich fare is in fact an ample and spicy banquet.

Lyndsay does not break with the Old Church, but he wants to see it reformed. To him, the roots of the evil are ecclesiastical property, which leads to covetice and worldliness ("First Act," §§ 7, 10-13, 15), and compulsory celibacy, which produces immorality (§§ 6, 14). Learning and preaching should be the inalienable mark of the clergy (§§ 8-9, 12)—then the whole people will stand up to defend its Kirk (§ 1).

Most of Lyndsay's reforms are social. He does not touch dogma—let the Doctores explain the Trinity (***Dreme,*** l. 546). Still, he calls for the translation of the Bible as a source of truth. Characteristically, the Vices in the ***Thrie Estaitis*** quote the saints more frequently than the Virtues do. In the ***Papyngo,*** Lyndsay exposes the abuse of the confessional; in ***Kitteis Confessioun*** (1540s) . . . he advocates voluntary confession, not to a priest, but to God Himself. In the ***Thrie Estaitis*** John the Common Weill says his creed to his Lord directly, and adds the article concerning the Church (ll. 3024 ff.) only after renewed command:

I trow *Sanctam Ecclesiam,*
Bot nocht in thir Bischops nor thir Freirs,
Quhilk will, for purging of thir neirs,
Sard up the ta raw, and doun the uther.
The mekill Devill resave the fidder.

To which Divyne Correction himself replies (ll. 3029 f.):

Say quhat ye will, Sirs, be Sanct Tan,
Me think Johne ane gude Christian man.

Elsewhere (ll. 1160-1) Veritie speaks to God in a tone we know from Henryson:

Get up, thow sleipis all too lang, O Lord,
And mak sum reasonabill reformatioun.

(pp. 96-8)

To Lyndsay his own poetry was less important than the message which it conveyed. Therefore he repeats himself in characters, ideas, episodes, phrases, rhymes, and his 18,000 lines are wholly unrevised. Lyndsay is not a formal artist; to him, poetry serves a purpose—as it was to do under the Presbyterians. At first sight, the ***Thrie Estaitis*** may be of the same type as the slightly older English *King Johan* by John Bale, who also employs the morality play as a weapon for the Reformation. In *King Johan,* abstract moral and political conceptions are transformed into symbolic figures, which then disguise themselves as historical personalities: thus, Privat Welth becomes Nobility, which then disguises itself as Cardinal Pandulphus; Sedition becmes a Monk, who subsequently assumes the guise of Stephen Langton. This brings the drama within striking distance of the chronicle play. There is admittedly a certain resemblance to it in the first part of the ***Thrie Estaitis,*** when Flatterie and his consorts disguise themselves as a Freir, and so on; but Lyndsay does not specifically identify these symbolic figures with particular historical personalities or events. On the other hand, his satire is saturated with local, social, political details that add up to a precise picture of the conditions of the age. Bale's figures are chessmen in an allegorico-historico-political game; Lyndsay's are men of real life, of his own environment, in an allegorical cloak.

But Lyndsay does not think allegorically. Allegory is not, in his hands, a conventional way of expressing, in poetry, an intricate and subtle system of thought, or of representing abstract vices and virtues with their innumerable attributes: it is a means of presenting a real social and political problem in terms of a concrete picture that we can actually visualise, and it enables Lyndsay himself, in presenting it, to keep his feet on the ground. The abstract thought that the common weal is suffering poverty is translated (ll. 2438, 2456) into a picturesque, proverbial image that leaves a lasting impression in the mind—it "gars John the Common Weill want his warm clais [clothes]." Similarly, Flatterie (ll. 602 ff.) is "new landit out of France"; Dissait (l. 656) is "counsallor to the Merchand-men"; only John the Common Weill (ll. 2543 f.) shall stand at the bar of the tribunal, and so forth. This sharper realism favours a stronger dramatic quality: Falset (ll. 793, 849 ff.) follows the example of the other vices, disguises himself as a monk, and calls himself Sapience—but then forgets his new name. In the heat of the argument, Spiritualitie is provoked into saying (l. 2910) that he himself has never read the New Testament; and on being told that this is the Apostle Paul's own commandment, hotly retorts (ll. 2915):

> Sum sayis be him that wore the croune of thorne,
> It had been gude that Paull had neir bene borne.

The ***Satyre of the Thrie Estaitis*** is a rather isolated example of early Scottish drama. Among Lyndsay's tasks at Court was the arrangement of plays: he directed the pageant to welcome James V's second Queen, Marie de Lorraine, and ***The Iusting betuix Watson and Barbour*** was part of these festivities. Lyndsay shows considerable dramatic talent—more, certainly, than his English contemporaries. Though it could stand thorough pruning, the ***Thrie Estaitis*** has, despite its length, a remarkable unity. Lyndsay at least sees things dramatically, in terms of action and tension, and he enters the minds of his figures so as to make them speak in character: Flatterie's report of the voyage from France (ll. 602 ff.) is a fine example. This makes the characters sufficiently individual—look at Spiritualitie thundering his "How dare you!" The chief source of Lyndsay's dramatic power is the tension of argument, that good Scots art. It is this that gives the second part its strength, and the dispute between the Thrie Estaitis themselves is one of the highlights of the play: how well observed is the intervention (ll. 2928 ff.) of the Third Estait. Compared with this, the more allegorical first part looks old-fashioned. The learned disputations, on the other hand, may be an essential part of Lyndsay's message, but are apt to become dogmatic and boring. But when he is visualising a realistic and definite scene, and comes closest to the sharp, precise Scots speech, Lyndsay is brilliant.

Lyndsay's racy dramatic idiom fits naturally into the conception of the Scots literary tradition that we have already formed. His subject-matter only occasionally affords scope for understatement (***Papyngo,*** l. 171):

> God wat gyff than my hart wes wo begone.

But we find examples of the tension that arises from contrast (***Complaynt,*** "Prolong" [*sic*] to the ***Dreme***); of extravaganza (***The Iusting betuix Watsoun and Barbour***); and of the spirit of flyting, if not of its artistic formalism. When, in ***The Answer quhilk Schir Dauid Lindesay maid to the Kingis Flyting*** (*c.* 1535), he puts on his Sabbath braws and uses the Chaucerian stanza, he is speaking with his tongue in his cheek. In other places (***Dreme,*** ll. 211, 224, 266) he wields the whip of alliteration with the best of them. And in the ***Thrie Estaitis*** (ll. 2444 ff.), listen to the rumbling anger of Johne the Common Weill:

> Thair canker cullours I ken them be the heads . . .
>
> Loe quhair the loun lyis lurkand at his back . . .
>
> Thou feinyeit Flattrie, the feind fart in thy face!

Lyndsay's animal poems are, too, an essential link in the Scottish tradition. Though it clearly foreshadows the later Scottish species of animal testaments and mock elegies, his ***Papyngo*** echoes the true medieval style; but ***Bagsche*** is distinctively Scottish. It is the first dog-poem in Scots or English; it considers the sturdily independent dog as a kind of equal, a comrade; and it has much in common with Henryson's *Fabillis,* or Dunbar's most manly "Petition of the Gray Horse, Auld Dunbar," the Gaelic poets, or Burns. Here I do not postulate a literary influence, but rather a popular traditional attitude towards animals. (pp. 98-101)

Kurt Wittig, "Ebbing: David Lyndsay," in his The Scottish Tradition in Literature, *Oliver and Boyd Ltd., 1958, pp. 91-102.*

James Kinsley (essay date 1959)

[In the excerpt below, Kinsley focuses on Squyer Meldrum, *praising it as "the most delightful of Lindsay's poems, and the last and most novel of the medieval Scottish essays in verse romance."]*

The Historie of Squyer Meldrum is a Scottish romance with a pendant poetical ***Testament,*** written in the mid sixteenth century by Sir David Lindsay of the Mount to celebrate the heroic life of a Fifeshire laird. A vigorous tale of love and war, it is the most delightful of Lindsay's poems, and the last and most novel of the medieval Scottish essays in verse romance. (p. 1)

William Meldrum, the hero of the ***Historie,*** came of an ancient Fifeshire family. He was heritor of lands in the barony of Cleish near Lochleven, granted to an earlier William Meldrum in the reign of Robert III, and of another estate called the Binns. Meldrum witnessed a document for the transfer of land in June 1506, and was therefore then of legal age. On Lindsay's evidence, he served with the Scottish army in France in 1513; and after his return to Scotland he settled *paramours* with the widowed Lady of Gleneagles. As a result of this liaison he was viciously assaulted in 1517, and parted from his mistress. In 1522 he became Sheriff-depute of Fife under his patron Patrick, fourth Lord Lindsay of the Byres and a kinsman of the Lord Lyon, and seems to have lived at Struther, the Fifeshire home of the Lindsays, until his death. The last record we have of him is his signature to a charter dated

Struther, 25 July 1550, and it may be assumed that he died soon after. The Lady of Gleneagles survived him, and died in 1553.

The ***Historie*** has a simple narrative sequence: a prologue in which Lindsay sets out his intention and his theme (ll. 1-64); a character-sketch of Meldrum and an account of the chivalrous part he played in the Scottish raid on Carrickfergus in 1513 (ll. 65-212); a brief description of his success in love and war when the Scottish force reached France (ll. 213-44); the campaign against the English in Picardy and Meldrum's combat with the English champion Talbart at Montreuil (ll. 245-600); further feats of arms, and Meldrum's conduct of a street fight with the English at Amiens (ll. 601-90); his return to Scotland, with an account of a victory at sea over an English pirate (ll. 691-848); his love affair at Gleneagles (ll. 849-1052); service to the lady in reclaiming her Highland castle from the lawless Macfarlane (ll. 1053-1152); a description of lovers' bliss (ll. 1153-82); a tragic reverse of fortune in the ambush near Edinburgh (ll. 1183-518); and the *vita quieta* at Struther (ll. 1519-94).

Lindsay knew Meldrum in the Struther period of his life, if not earlier. Of his character he writes at first hand; and for his career he drew on the Squyer's confidences. The ***Historie*** is a serious biography celebrating the virtues and deeds of a great man intimately known and lately dead, and there is no reason to doubt its essential truth. For all his witchery as a teller of tales in the royal nursery, Lindsay was . . . a reliable man. George Buchanan ends his account of the fatal apparition which appeared to James IV at Linlithgow:

> Amongst [those present] there was David Lindsay of the Mount, a man of approved honesty and of a learned education, who in the whole course of his life abhorred lying; and if I had not received this story from him as a certain truth, I had omitted it as a romance of the vulgar.

The historical documents illustrating Meldrum's life are few: family charters and other legal papers, and the account of the ambush of 1517 in Pitscottie's *Cronicles of Scotland.* As far as they go, the records bear out Lindsay's version of the affair at Gleneagles and its sequel, and of Meldrum's last years. The earlier events in Ireland and France, in which the Squyer (apparently on his own testimony) was involved, are quite historical; the combat with Talbart at Montreuil has at least a historical context, and is described with the precision to be expected from a poet who was also chief herald and a student of chivalry; and the street-fight at Amiens, the sea-fight, and the skirmish with Macfarlane, though unsubstantiated, have an air of probability. Moreover, Lindsay does not show a highly developed sense of literary form anywhere in his poetry, and there is no sign in the ***Historie*** of a distortion of the *ordo naturalis* to make an artificial pattern. His story, within the natural framework of good and ill fortune and a quiet end, is episodic; its shape seems to be merely and strictly that of Meldrum's life. The affair of love and valour at Carrickfergus is not completed in the happy sequel which a writer of fictitious romance would have concocted for his audience: the exigences of the service force Meldrum to leave his 'dayis darling', and 'aventure' combines with 'youth and insolence' to prevent his return. Nor does the climacteric episode of the ambush look as though it has been adjusted to a literary design: Meldrum's lady vanishes as abruptly as she seems to have done in fact, and history forbids the expected revenge and triumph.

Yet the ***Historie*** belongs to the category of chivalric romance. It stands 'at the triple frontier where the novel, the romance, and the biography all march together' [C. S. Lewis, in his *English Literature in the Sixteenth Century,* 1954]. Lindsay uses many of the narrative and descriptive methods of romance, and much of its stock vocabulary, to set forth his hero's life. For this novel artifice he had no important precedent in French or English romance, which deals mainly with legendary or remotely historical matter. He had, however, a notable example of *biographie romancée* in his native literature, in John Barbour's *Actes and Life of the most Victorious Conquerour, Robert Bruce King of Scotland* (1376), and another, inferior but no less popular, in Blind Harry's *Actes and Deidis of . . . Schir William Wallace, Knicht of Ellerslie* (MS 1488). (pp. 5-8)

The purpose of Lindsay's ***Historie*** is . . . to give Meldrum his place 'amangis the laif' of

> our Nobill Progenitouris
> Quhilk suld to vs be richt mirrouris,
> Thair verteous deidis to ensew
> And vicious leuing to eschew.

The stories with which he entertained the boy king long ago were of 'dedis marciall' and 'leill Luffaris'—all matter of romance; and the literary form in which these tales had come down was the natural and appropriate one for the history of the Squyer, a modern hero worthier in love than Lancelot and more valorous in battle than Tydeus, Roland, Oliver, Gawain or 'onie Knicht of the round Tabill'. Like Barbour, Lindsay is writing 'not . . . a conventional romance with historic persons and incidents for his material [but] history which has all the qualities of romance in real life'.

We must not think of the chivalric romances as concerned with 'far-off things and battles long ago', and therefore as imaginatively distant from the everyday life of the men who wrote and read or listened to them. For their own time they were realistic narrative, whether their matter was wholly fictitious or not, 'modern novels—studies of contemporary life, characters and emotions, mixed up with adventures more or less surprising' [W. P. Ker, in his *English Literature: Medieval,* 1922]. There is nothing melodramatic about Meldrum. He is essentially a soldier of fortune, a familiar type of wandering Scot in sixteenth- and seventeenth-century Europe, like Quentin Durward 'seeking my fortune in France, or elsewhere, after the custom of my countrymen'. His profession is that of another laird's son, James Henderson, writing from the Low Countries in 1608: 'I am a young man, and gif I haif litill, I haif als litill to fear. I have my swerd undishonorit, and that is aneuch to me; yit gif evir God send me a fortune, I hoip to use it weill' [see Agnes M. Mackenzie, in her *Scottish Pageant 1513-1625,* 1948]. The lady of Gleneagles too is a realistic figure, living out her quietly cultivated life in household management, ready to 'luik hir maidinnis all amang' and keep them up to the mark, skilled in the provision of 'daintie dischis', and beguiling 'the nicht if it be lang' with music and 'talk and merie mowis [*lively chatter*]' in her chamber. There is no extravagance either in her appearance and dress or in her entertainment; she wears the kirtle and the loose cloak fashionable among the wellborn Scotswomen of her day; and the meals and recreations of her household are described without the exaggeration to which many romancers are given.

The events of Meldrum's foreign service are circumstantially described; the details of battle on land and sea, and the process of the combat with Talbart, are familiar to readers of Pitscottie and other chroniclers. Nor is there anything fanciful in the physical background to Meldrum's Scottish adventures. The 'Castell' at Gleneagles is the familiar castellated house of the Scottish lairds—a tower with its outbuildings and a small garden in which 'to tak the hailsum Air' within the peel, and inside a great hall with private apartments reached by a spiral stair rising through a projecting turret. The 'Castell . . . fair and strang' in the Lennox, on the other hand, is the simpler defensive stone tower still to be seen on the Border and the Highland Line—a gaunt roofed and embattelled 'Fortres' to withstand lawless forays and the attacks of aggressive neighbours.

The morality and *moeurs* of the story are those of Lindsay's Scotland: a country accustomed to sudden alarms and excursions, its peace disturbed by the violence of a wild and self-seeking aristocracy . . . , its rulers ready for quick repressive action, and its lesser gentry equipped with their tenants to defend hearth and home.

Although the authors of romance told their tales in contemporary terms, they did not aim at 'realism' quite in our modern sense. Like the writers of heroic poetry and drama in the seventeenth century, they wished to give 'a just and lively Image of human nature, in its Actions, Passions, and traverses of Fortune . . . for the delight and benefit of Mankind'; but they realised their design by heightening character and conduct 'above the Life' in accordance with the traditional ideals of *amour courtois* and chivalry [*Essays of John Dryden,* Vol. I, ed. W. P. Ker, 1926]. In Lindsay's eyes, the gallant Squyer at Struther deserved a memorial with all the trappings of romance, and there was no need in doing this to distort the essential truth of either character or action. The only valid distinction we may make in reading the ***Historie*** is not the modern one between fact and fiction, but the medieval one between 'suthfast' matter and poetic 'carping'. The delightfulness of even a 'suthfast' story, says Barbour, depends on its being told 'on gud maner'; and Lindsay makes a romance of Meldrum's life by conforming to literary tradition in characterisation and style. The Squyer is a paragon of resourceful 'hie courage' in war, equally accomplished in the lists, in a street brawl, a sea-fight, a siege, and an ambush. His virtues of hand and heart bring him nearer the national heroes Bruce and Wallace than the 'gentil knyghtes' of high romance, but they exalt him 'above the Life'. He faces odds with marvellous assurance—two 'cruell men and kene' at Carrickfergus, a gigantic English champion at Montreuil, superior English forces at Amiens and at sea, and Stirling of Keir's assassins in the appalling ratio of three score to eight. He is moreover a model of courtesy and compassion, and shows generosity to the vanquished. Though eminently a man of war—his heart goes to Venus, but his epitaph is 'the maist inuincibill weiriour heir lyis'—he is expert in the art of love, and wins a woman's devotion in Ireland, England, France, and at home.

In his treatment of the Squyer's love Lindsay moves away from the courtly tradition. He shows the ambivalence of several medieval Scots poets in his attitude to love—of Dunbar, for example, who understands the conventions perfectly but puts them to brilliantly comic or satirical use, and of the authors of the *pastourelle* dialogues which open in courtly style and end in grossness. Lindsay is familiar with the ideals and the vocabulary of *amour courtois,* but he cannot—or will not—use them with consistent seriousness. In ***Ane Satyre of the Thrie Estaits*** Danger, traditionally the embodiment of a woman's defensive reticence in love, cynically admits that

> . . . I was nocht sweir
> To Venus observance,
> Howbeit I mak Dangeir:
> Yit be continuance
> Men may haue thair pleasance:
> Thairfoir let na man fray:
> We will tak it perchance,
> Howbeit that wee say nay;

and Lindsay's picture of chambering and wantonness at court is frankly animal. There is neither delicacy nor subtlety in Meldrum's lady of Gleneagles. She shows a passing anxiety about reputation and the prohibitions of canon law; but she is an artlessly passionate and responsive woman, nearer to Boccaccio's Criseida than to Chaucer's wonderfully complex Criseyde. Lindsay learnt little of feminine psychology from his reading 'Off Troilus the sorrow and the Ioye'. The Squyer himself is presented as a courtly lover, striving to 'stonden in his lady grace', vowing eternal devotion, stricken by Cupid's darts into sleeplessness and despair; but his approach to the lady has more soldierly abruptness and despatch than a sophisticated lover should display, and Lindsay's own sly humour intensifies the contrast between courtly sentiment and brisk 'chalmer glew'. Some have objected to the comic glint in this love scene. But Pandarus jests in Criseyde's bedroom; '*Risus, Focus,* and *Petulentia* are, at all times, the natural attendants of Venus'; and Scott rightly saw Lindsay as a man

> In aspect manly, grave, and sage,
> As on King's errand come;
> But in the glances of his eye
> A penetrating, keen, and sly
> Expression found its home.

Nor does the sense of fun in the ***Historie*** justify the suspicion that Lindsay's intention is burlesque; his laughter is fitful, a 'sudden glory' breaking from the sustained energy of the tale. (pp. 9-14)

To the Fifeshire lairds and Edinburgh courtiers who listened to Lindsay's tale in the 1550s, the exploits of Squyer Meldrum in France did more than recall an old and ineffectual campaign. 'Hary the aucht' and his chivalry were still the objects of a lively hatred. Meldrum had demonstrated Scottish superiority, man for man, to the English knights who had persistently and lately ravaged the country; a mere squire had overcome the English champion at Montreuil—David against Goliath—and taken an English man-of-war, displaying in the hour of victory a generosity to his foe which had seldom been reciprocated in the recent campaigns. And d'Arcy's reminder of how a Frenchman and a Scot 'dang seir Sutheroun to the ground' was a tribute to the still triumphant Auld Alliance.

The vocabulary of the ***Historie,*** like the characters, is traditional. *Men of weir* are *bauld and stout, bauld and wicht, stalwart and stout, worthie and wicht, wyse and wicht, brym as beiris,* and (if they are not on the right side) *cruell and kene;* knights are *nobill* and barons *bauld;* ladies are *bricht, lustie,* and *quhyte as milk.* The poem is packed with stock phrases: *hie on hicht, hand for hand, on the bent, vpon the grene; nouther Barn nor Byre, dule and cair, on horse nor fute, hose and schone, Ioy and blis, musick and menstrallie, Trump and Clarioun, Speir and Scheild, sword nor knyfe.* Such phrases become established, of course, mainly as labour-saving devices in poetry composed for recitation; but, as the vigorously unconventional narrative passages in ***Ane Satyre*** show, Lindsay's tags are not a symptom of linguistic inadequacy. They are, rather, part of a conscious stylisation, helping as much as the use of traditional sentiments and situations to place the Squyer in the context of romance. Moreover, Lindsay depends on speed for much of his effect, and the recurrence of familiar and expected phrases, particularly in short couplet verse, aids the onward flow of the story.

An important and distinctive feature of his style in this poem is alliteration. What had once been fundamental to the structure of English verse had become merely a type of stylistic ornament popular with the authors of rhyming romances. Many of Lindsay's alliterative phrases are, on the evidence of earlier romances, part of the stock vocabulary referred to above, and perform the same functions, e.g., *birneist brand, douchtie deidis, with duntis sa derflie on him dang* and similar phrases, *fair of face, faucht in feild, lap delyuerlie* and *lichtlie lap, pertlie to preif thair pith thay preist, rent and riches, stand in stour* and *stand in monie stalwart strife, strang and stout, his sword he swappit sa, Taburne and Trumpet, wyse and wicht* and similar phrases. But Lindsay's verse is more strongly (and more subtly) 'with lel letteres loken' than these isolated phrases suggest. Alliterative patterns of varying complexity run through the whole fabric of the ***Historie,*** and are particularly noticeable in descriptions of conflict. This exhilarating device for communicating the violence and clash of battle had been borrowed from the alliterative romances by Chaucer for his accounts of the tournament in the Knight's Tale and the sea-fight in the Legend of Cleopatra, but it was familiar to Lindsay from many passages in the *Brus* and *Wallace*. . . . Like Barbour and Blind Harry, Lindsay uses alliterative patterns to bind lines together: sometimes carrying a single alliterative unit on into the next line:

> And *b*ait me till he gart me *b*leid
> And drew me *b*ackwart fra my steid
>
> That straik was with sic *m*icht and fors
> That on the ground lay *m*an and hors,

where the recurring consonants supplement other kinds of repetition; sometimes doubling the alliteration within the couplet:

> Wes neuer *m*an *b*uir *b*etter hand:
> Thair *m*icht na *B*uckler *b*yde his *b*rand
>
> And *s*a did *s*laik that *m*ortall feid
> *S*a that na *m*an wes put to deid
>
> Defendand me wi*th*in ane *s*tound
> *Th*ow dang *s*eir *S*utheroun to the ground;

and sometimes weaving more complex patterns:

> *S*ayand, for *h*ym that *h*eryit *H*ell,
> *H*elp me, *s*weit *S*ir, I am ane *M*ayd.
> Than *s*oftlie to the *m*en he said,
> I pray zow giue againe hir *s*ark.

Despite the accumulation of conventional phrases, and the contrivance of alliterative patterns, Lindsay's language is simple and colloquial. He gives his whole tale actuality as the ballad poets do, by using the vocabulary and reproducing the tones of everyday speech. His master here was doubtless Barbour, though the main strength of the Scottish tradition in poetry from the early Stewart poets to Burns lies in the artistic manipulation of the spoken language. Lindsay's concern is to tell a good story to an audience; character is tersely expressed in speech and action, without sententious commentary, and no room is given to the set descriptions in which so many romancers delight. He avoids matters which 'it wer to lang for to declair', in the urgent spirit of Barbour:

> For suld I tell all thar effer,
> Thair countynans and thar maner,
> Thouch I couth, I suld cummerryt be.

His characters, like their creator, talk naturally and economically in the language of Fife. Even when the champion Talbart 'blawis greit boist' on the battlefield, he expresses himself with the masculine simplicity of a soldier. Meldrum is no more effusive when he tosses on his bed at Gleneagles or when he makes his 'sailye' on Marjorie Lawson—a pleasing contrast with the interminably rhetorical Troilus; and the minstrel had fine material for humorous dramatic recitation in the give-and-take of Marjorie and her persistent maids. The ***Historie*** was written to be read aloud. Lindsay is always aware of his audience, and he entertains them with the humour, zest, and easy familiarity of the practised story-teller.

The pendant verse ***Testament,*** in a higher, aureate style, is obviously fictitious—'a purely poetical fanfare to round off a knightly tale' [according to Lewis]—but not, as some have supposed, satiric in intention. Lindsay, it is true, parodies the pious legal testament, and mixes the sacred and the profane. But the blend is common, if not indeed inevitable, in the context of courtly love; and it does not detract from the effect of the poem as a summary and a memorial. In origin the literary testament is a parody of a religious form, and there were French precedents for replacing Christian symbols by those of *amour courtois.* The genre became common in late fifteenth-century France, reaching the level of high art in Villon; and it seems to have been popular thereafter in Scotland, if not in England. Lindsay doubtless knew Henryson's serious *Testament of Cresseid,* written in the rhyme-royal stanza he uses for Meldrum, and Dunbar's satire on Andro Kennedy.

He had already tried the form himself in rhyme-royal, in ***The Testament and Complaynt of our Souerane Lordis Papyngo*** (1530), a mixture of comedy, satire, and instruction. The king's parrot, wounded by a fall from a tree, leaves her master 'counsale' on right government, and grave advice to her 'brether of court'. She discourses solemnly with her executors, and finally directs them in the disposal of her body and effects. Her mantle goes to the owl, 'indigent and pure', her bright eyes to the bat, her beak to the pelican, her music and 'voce Angelycall' to the gowk, her 'Eloquence and toung Rhetoricall' to the goose, her bones in 'one cais of Ebure fyne' to the phoenix, and her heart to the king.

There are the same elements of parody and wit in Meldrum's ***Testament,*** and he borrows some of the Papyngo's notions. But the primary purpose of the poem, like that of the ***Historie,*** is memorial and panegyrical; and the man of love and valour dies in a mood of tender recollection, martial pride and 'hie courage', with time for the sacrament and a devout commitment of his soul to God. (pp. 14-19)

James Kinsley, in an introduction to Squyer Meldrum *by Sir David Lindsay, edited by James Kinsley, Thomas Nelson and Sons Ltd., 1959, pp. 1-19.*

FURTHER READING

Brown, Ivor. "*Ane Satyre of the Thrie Estaitis* at the Edinburgh Festival." In *Ane Satyre of the Thrie Estaitis,* by Sir David Lyndsay, edited by James Kinsley, pp. 27-33. London: Cassell and Co., 1954.

Discusses the modern appeal of *Ane Satyre of the Thrie Estaitis* based on a 1948 production of the drama at the Edinburgh Festival.

"Studies in Scottish Literature: Sir David Lyndsay." *The Dublin University Magazine* LXXXVIII (July 1876): 76-88.

Surveys Lyndsay's major works, particularly commenting on the uneven quality of his poems.

Hannay, James. "Erasmus, Sir David Lyndsay, and George Buchanan." In his *Satire and Satirists: Six Lectures,* pp. 55-106. London: David Bogue, 1854.

Biographical and critical survey of Lyndsay's career, including an examination of his satiric influence in Scotland.

Henderson, T. F. "Gavin Douglas and Sir David Lyndsay." In his *Scottish Vernacular Literature: A Succinct History,* pp. 188-231. 1898. Third revised edition. Edinburgh: John Grant, 1910.

Presents an overview of Lyndsay's life and works, with an emphasis on *Ane Satyre of the Thrie Estaitis.*

Irving, David. "Sir David Lyndsay." In his *The History of Scotish Poetry,* pp. 329-81. 1861. Reprint. New York: Johnson Reprint Corporation, 1972.

Observes that Lyndsay's works "exhibit considerable inequalities; but where they are not distinguished by any superior force of imagination, they are often entertaining by their strokes of humour, or instructive by their views of life and manners."

James VI of Scotland, I of England. "The Phoenix." In his *Essayes of a Prentise, in the Divine Art of Poesie: A Counterblaste to Tobacco,* edited by Edward Arber, pp. 40-50. London: n. p., 1869.

Cites Lyndsay as an influence on his own writing style.

Laing, David. "Memoir of Sir David Lyndsay." In *The Poetical Works of Sir David Lyndsay of the Mount, Lyon King at Arms,* by Sir David Lyndsay, edited by David Laing, pp. vii-lii. Edinburgh: William Paterson, 1871.

Biographical introduction to a collection of Lyndsay's works.

Mackenzie, George. "The Life of Sir David Lindsay of the Mount, Lyon King at Arms." In his *Lives and Characters of the Eminent Writers of the Scots Nation,* vol. III, pp. 35-40, 1722. Reprint. New York: Garland Publishing, Inc., 1971.

Brief summary of Lyndsay's life and literary career, with excerpts of his poems.

Mill, Anna J. "The Influence of the Continental Drama on Lyndsay's *Satyre of the Thrie Estaitis.*" *The Modern Language Review* XXV, No. 4 (October 1930): 425-42.

Examines the relationship of Lyndsay's *Satyre of the Thrie Estaitis* to the tradition of French morality drama.

———. "Representations of Lyndsay's *Satyre of the Thrie Estaitis.*" *PMLA* XLVII, No. 3 (September 1932): 636-51.

Traces possible performances of *Ane Satyre of the Thrie Estaitis* during Lyndsay's lifetime.

Minto, William. "Chaucer's Contemporaries and Successors: Scottish Successors." In his *Characteristics of English Poets from Chaucer to Shirley,* pp. 93-115. Boston: Ginn and Co., 1904.

Focuses on the various sources that influenced Lyndsay's writing style and discusses the satirical elements of his major works.

Morley, Henry. "Chapter V." In his *An Attempt towards a History of English Literature,* vol. VIII, pp. 102-42. London: Cassell and Co., 1892.

Brief biographical and critical essay, placing Lyndsay's works in relation to John Knox's career.

Sampson, George. "Renascence and Reformation: Sir David Lyndsay." In his *The Concise Cambridge History of English Literature,* pp. 112-14. 1941. Third edition. London: Cambridge University Press, 1970.

Generally appreciative introduction to Lyndsay's life and works.

Veitch, John. "National Poets of the Stuart Period: Sir David Lyndsay (1490-1557)." In his *The Feeling for Nature in Scottish Poetry,* pp. 283-306. Edinburgh: William Blackwood and Sons, 1887.

Discusses Lyndsay's treatment of nature in his works.

Scottish Chaucerians

INTRODUCTION

The period between the late fifteenth century and the mid sixteenth century is known as the golden age of Scottish poetry, an era in which, according to George Eyre-Todd, "the mediæval spirit reached its highest expression." The major poets of the age—James I, Robert Henryson, William Dunbar, and Gavin Douglas—are commonly known as the Scottish Chaucerians because they embraced the higher standards for craftsmanship embodied by Geoffrey Chaucer's works. Their poetry reflects a transitional phase in Scottish literary history; for while it is in many ways thoroughly medieval, some of its elements herald a new literary tradition.

Scholars have noted the difficulty of discussing the Scottish Chaucerians as a cohesive school since they were a diverse and dissimilar group of poets whose works encompass a broad range of styles and formats. Each of them relied on Chaucer to some degree, either for textual elements or for inspiration. Their individuality was such that the manifestations of Chaucer's influence varied widely among them, though they all shared with Chaucer the goal of establishing English as a literary language. A number of commentators assert that similarities between Chaucer's works and those of his Scottish successors stem from reliance on common source materials, particularly French courtly literature as embodied in *Le Roman de la Rose.*

The earliest of the Scottish Chaucerians, James I, returned to Scotland after years of captivity in England, bringing with him an appreciation for the new literary trends of the South. His only known work, *The Kingis Quair,* is a dream allegory which, while written in the French courtly tradition, recalls Chaucer's works in both style and spirit. James Kinsley notes that "the poet has learnt from Chaucer not only to borrow freely but to handle what he borrows with delicacy and inventiveness." *The Kingis Quair* is written in rhyme royal, as are many of Chaucer's works; and critics point out similarities in plot between James's poem and Chaucer's "The Knight's Tale," but they also emphasize that James's innovative approach to courtly love literature sets his work apart. According to G. Gregory Smith, *The Kingis Quair* "represents the first phase of Scottish Chaucerianism, in which the imitation, though individualised by the genius of its author, is deliberate and direct." Chaucer remained the inspiration behind the poetry of James's literary successors, but each continued to develop his own unique style of expression. Writing several years after James, Henryson is remembered primarily for his *Morall Fabillis,* a collection of thirteen fables chiefly based on those of Aesop, and *The Testament of Cresseid,* a continuation of Chaucer's *Troilus and Criseyde.* Although generations of critics have debated the extent of Henryson's debt to Chaucer, they generally concur that his works share with Chaucer's a delicate subtlety and stylistic agility. In discussions of Henryson's works, commentators praise the poet's ability to inform an existing story with renewed élan, as well as his detailed treatment of nature which makes use of traditional elements but also reflects close and careful personal observation.

Commentators generally assert that Dunbar, considered the finest of the Scottish Chaucerian poets, has the least in common with Chaucer. Critics laud Dunbar's versatility, noting that he displays a distinct and consistent approach to poetry regardless of genre: whether a religious hymn, or a catalog of abuse, Dunbar viewed each type of poetry as a craft to be mastered. His best known works include the ceremonial poem "The Goldyn Targe," the satire "The Tretis of the Tua Mariit Wemen and the Wedo," and the elegy "Lament for the Makaris." While scholars acknowledge that certain technical facets of Dunbar's works reflect Chaucer's influence, they concede that the two poets are very different. Denton Fox has suggested that "it is a desperate endeavour to trace Dunbar's relationship to Chaucer, or for that matter to any of his predecessors, since he appears on the one hand to have written in every possible poetic tradition, and on the other hand to have borrowed only very slightly from any specific poet." Like Dunbar, James, and Henryson, Douglas is considered a transitional poet: his dream allegory, *The Palice of Honour,* is thoroughly Chaucerian in both plot and diction, yet his translation of Virgil's *Aeneid* anticipates the Renaissance interest in revival of the classics. Douglas's version of this epic poem is historically notable as the first translation of a verse classic into an English dialect, but commentators assert that the translation itself, as well as Douglas's original compositions that precede each book of the *Aeneid,* deserve mention as significant poetic accomplishments in their own right. The prologues especially exhibit Douglas's versatility; their broad range of topics comprises explanations of translation techniques, literary criticism, philosophical musings, and descriptive nature scenes.

A number of critics have argued that the term Scottish Chaucerians is misleading and inaccurate because it seems to imply that Chaucer is their only influence and that their poetry is purely imitative. Several scholars refer to these poets not as Scottish Chaucerians but as *makars,* a term used by Dunbar to refer to his fellow literary craftsmen. Florence Ridley has averred that discussing them as Chaucerians "puts them in the wrong time and the wrong place, assigns them characteristics they do not have, and denies them talents they do." Most critics agree, however, that though the final results differed broadly with each poet, the Scottish Chaucerians approached their works in a similar manner. As Fox has written, "their poetry is a poetry of craftsmanship, and they are united by their devotion to their craft. . . . These poets, in their different ways, all seem to have channelled their passion towards the idea that a poem ought to be as finely wrought as possible."

George Eyre-Todd

[*In the following essay, Eyre-Todd outlines the political and historical circumstances which led up to the "golden age" of Scottish poetry.*]

The history of Scottish poetry divides itself naturally into certain strongly marked periods corresponding to periods in the political history of the country. The most interesting of these poetic periods in many respects is that in which the mediæval spirit reached its highest expression. Almost the sole subject of the country's early muse had been the deeds of arms and heroes. After the great struggle with England there had ensued the century of the chronicler-poets, and in their hands Scottish verse had drawn its inspiration entirely from the national patriotism. James I., however, among other advantages, brought home with him from his captivity a new poetic influence—the influence of Petrarch and Chaucer. From that time, beginning with James' own kingly composition, a fresh life seemed to be abroad in Scottish poetry. It was as if a soft summer wind had come blowing out of the south. In the heart of the north there began to throb new pulses of thought and desire. Imagination stirred again and woke. Beside the old stem of heroic narrative sprang new poetic forms—pastoral, allegory, satire, ballad. And presently, passionate, rich and exuberant, this later poesy of the Middle Ages burst into prodigal flower.

In the fifteenth century there was passing over Europe one of those great waves of vitality which from time to time have made and marked the eras of history. A later wave of the same sort, yet unnamed, made its political mark in the French Revolution, and finding early expression in Scotland in the poetry of Burns, gave birth to the romantic genius of Byron, Scott, Balzac and Goethe, and the world of modern thought. The moving event in the fifteenth century, perhaps, was the capture of Constantinople by the Turks in 1453. For hundreds of years the ancient capital of the Eastern Empire had been the chief repository of the traditions of Greek literature and civilization; and the scattering of Byzantine scholarship over Europe upon the fall of the city largely helped to bring about that revival of thought and art which in the south took the form of the Renaissance and in the north of the Reformation.

The Scottish poets of the last decades of the fifteenth and the first of the sixteenth century cannot, it is true, be reckoned singers of the new era. There is about the work of Henryson, Dunbar and Douglas a mournful note that betokens it of an age about to pass away. They are not the prophets of a morning-time, and the soul that shines in their verse has the splendid weariness of full experience, not the hot enthusiasm of an epoch's youth. It would seem, however, as if a breath of the coming life had touched the air, and to the ripeness of the older time had added a flush of colour and strength. There is reason to believe that all the great Scottish poets of the period had visited the Continent, and there, it is probable, they had felt something of the quickening of the new era that was about to dawn. At any rate it is certain that the poetry of mediæval Scotland found its fullest and richest expression at the last, when feudalism in church and state had reached its climax, and when, before the kindling of the Reformation, the old order was about to disappear.

The political circumstances of the period in Scotland throw their own light upon the subject.

In the history of every nation which has perfected a national life there can be distinguished a golden era. Athens had her time of Pericles, Rome her Augustan age, Later Italy her Renaissance, England her reign of Elizabeth. A regular likeness may be noticed in the circumstances of all these periods. When a Philosophy of History, Aristotle's ambitious dream, at last is written, the phenomena of national growth and decay may be discovered to be as regular, even to minute details, as the growth, flourish and decay of the forest oaks. It is enough here to remark that, after an infancy of obscure development and a youth of storm and struggle, there appears always to come a national manhood of exuberant spirit and strength. A new sense of power seems to awaken. While conquest flushes the country's arms, and wealth floats in upon a flowing tide, the national genius of poetry and art breaks into splendid fire.

Scotland reached this era of her history towards the end of the fifteenth century. Out of its Celtic, Saxon, Cymric and Norman elements the nation had been born into a new existence amid the early Wars of Independence. Afterwards, for one hundred and fifty years, the Stewarts had been making their way from the position of little more than party leaders among a turbulent nobility to the actual sovereignty of the state. But towards the close of the fifteenth century the royal house had at last secured for itself unquestioned power. A firm, strong government was established under the sceptre of James IV. To its more ancient acquisitions of the Western Isles and the Isle of Man the crown had lately added the isles Orkney and Shetland. By the rapid increase of the country's maritime enterprise possibilities of wealth had recently developed to an extent before unknown. And in the eyes of Europe just then, chiefly because of the foothold she afforded for checkmating the movements of Henry VII., Scotland had assumed a position of large consideration.

These were the greater political influences at work to bring about the ripeness of the time. Some minor circumstances were perhaps not less important.

James IV. had inherited the hoarded wealth of his unfortunate father, as Augustus Cæsar inherited the wealth of the dead Julius; and, like Augustus, the Scottish king sought by all available means to encourage the arts of civilization in his realm. James himself was no mean scholar, speaking Latin, French, German, Flemish, Italian, Spanish, and Gaelic, besides his native Scottish, and his tastes and his policy alike were towards refinement. Never before had there been so brilliant a court in Scotland, and never was there to be so brilliant a court again. For the fourth time a Scottish king had married an English princess, and for the fourth time a consequent wave of civilization seemed to pass across the country. Gay tournaments, huntings, feastings, were the pursuits of the nobility; and amid the quickening of social life the arts that elevate and the arts that charm rose into high esteem. At the same time—as great an influence, perhaps, of another sort—the discovery of printing was introduced into Scotland during the reign of James IV.

It was in circumstances like these—the national pulse beating with its fullest life, and the fortunes of the country a rising flood—that the national poetry might be expected to put forth its brightest blossoms. This in fact was what came to pass. Fifty years earlier than the great revival of letters in the southern half of the island the golden age of her poetry arrived in Scotland. (pp. 1-6)

George Eyre-Todd, "Mediaeval Scottish Poetry," in his Mediaeval Scottish Poetry, *Sands & Company, 1892, pp. 1-6.*

G. Gregory Smith

[In the essay below, Smith surveys the lives and works of the Scottish Chaucerians, asserting that, although their works represent a break with the literary tradition of the fourteenth century, they are essentially more mediaeval than modern.]

It is a critical tradition to speak of the fifteenth century in Scotland as the time of greatest literary account, or, in familiar phrase, "the golden age of Scottish poetry." It has become a commonplace to say of the poets of that time that they, best of all Chaucer's followers, fulfilled with understanding and felicity the lessons of the master-craftsman; and it has long been customary to enforce this by contrasting the skill of Lydgate, Occleve and their contemporaries in the south, with that of James I, Henryson, Dunbar and Gavin Douglas. The contrast does not help us to more than a superficial estimate; it may lead us to exaggerate the individual merits of the writers and to neglect the consideration of such important matters as the homogeneity of their work, and their attitude to the older popular habit of Scottish verse.

We must keep in mind that the work of the greater Scottish poets of the fifteenth century represents a break with the literary practice of the fourteenth. The alliterative tradition dragged on, perhaps later than it did in the south, and the chronicle-poem of the type of Barbour's *Bruce* or the *Legends of the Saints* survived in Henry the Minstrel's patriotic tale of Wallace and in Wyntoun's history. With James I the outlook changes, and in the poems of Henryson, Dunbar, Douglas and some of the minor "makars" the manner of the earlier northern poetry survives only in stray places. It is not that we find a revulsion from medieval sentiment. The main thesis of this [essay] will be that these poets are much less modern than medieval. But there is, in the main, a change in literary method—an interest, we might say, in other aspects of the old allegorical tradition. In other words, the poetry of this century is a recovery, consciously made, of much of the outworn artifice of the Middle Ages, which had not yet reached, or hardly reached, the northern portion of the island. The movement is artificial and experimental, in no respects more remarkably so than in the deliberate moulding of the language to its special purpose. Though the consciousness of the effort, chiefly in its linguistic and rhetorical bearings, may appear, at first glance, to reveal the spirit of the renascence, it is nevertheless clear that the materials of this experiment and much of the inspiration of the change come from the Middle Ages. The origin is by no means obscured, though we recognise in this belated allegorical verse the growth of a didactic, descriptive and, occasionally, personal, habit which is readily associated with the renascence. We are easily misled in this matter—too easily, if we have made up our minds to discover signs of the new spirit at this time, when it had been acknowledged, more or less fully, in all the other vernacular literatures of Europe. Gavin Douglas, for example, has forced some false conclusions on recent criticism, by his seeming modern spirit, expressed most strikingly in the prologue to the fifth book of his translation of the *Aeneid:*

> Bot my propyne coym fra the pres fuit hait,
> Unforlatit, not jawyn fra tun to tun,
> In fresche sapour new fro the berrie run.

The renascence could not have had a better motto. Yet there should be little difficulty in showing that Douglas, our first translator of Vergil, was, perhaps, of all these fifteenth century Scots, the gentlest of rebels against the old-world fancies of the Courts of Love and the ritual of the Rose.

The herald of the change in Scottish literary habit is the love-allegory of *The Kingis Quair,* or King's Book. The atmosphere of this poem is that of *The Romance of the Rose:* in general treatment, as well as in details, it at once appears to be modelled upon that work, or upon one of the many poems directly derived therefrom. Closer examination shows an intimacy with Chaucer's translation of the *Romance.* Consideration of the language and of the evidence as to authorship . . . brings conviction that the poem was the direct outcome of study, by some northerner, of Chaucer's *Romaunt* and other works. It was fortunate for Scots literature that it was introduced to this new genre in a poem of such literary competence. Not only is the poem by its craftsmanship superior to any by Chaucer's English disciples, but it is in some respects, in happy phrasing and in the retuning of old lines, hardly inferior to its models. Indeed, it may be claimed for the Scots author, as for his successor, in the *Testament of Cresseid,* that he has, at times, improved upon his master.

The Kingis Quair (which runs to 1379 lines, divided into 197 "Troilus" stanzas, riming *ababbcc*) may be described as a dream-allegory dealing with two main topics—the "unsekernesse" of Fortune and the poet's happiness in love. The contradiction of these moods has led some to consider the poem as a composite work, written at different times: the earlier portion representing the period of the author's dejection, real or imaginary, the latter that of the subsequent joy which the sight of the fair lady in the garden by his prison had brought into his life. One writer has expressed the opinion that the poem was begun at a time when the poet "had little to speak of beyond his past misadventures"; and, while allowing that it may have been "afterwards partially rewritten," he finds evidence of its fragmentary origin in the presence of sections which "have absolutely nothing to do with the subject." For these reasons, he disallows Tytler's division (1783) of the poem into six cantos, which had held in all editions for a full century (down to 1884), because it assumes a unity which does not exist. This objection to the parcelling out of the text may be readily accepted—not because it gives, as has been assumed, a false articulation to a disconnected work, but because it interferes unnecessarily with that very continuity which is not the least merit of the poem. The author, early in the work (st. 19), calls upon the muses to guide him "to write his *torment and his joy.*" This is strong evidence by the book in its own behalf, and it is not easily discredited by the suggestion that the line "may have been altered afterwards." If there be any inconsistency observable in the poem, it is of the kind inevitable in compositions where the personal element is strong. In the earlier allegory, and in much of the later (if we think of the Spenserian type) the individuality of the writer is merged in the narrative: in *The Kingis Quair,* on the other hand, a striking example of the later dream-poem which has a direct lyrical or personal quality, greater inconsequence of fact and mood is to be expected. Whether that inconsequence be admitted or not by the modern reader, we have no warrant for the conclusion that the work is a mosaic.

The poet, lying in bed "alone waking," turns to the pages of *Boethius,* but soon tires of reading. He thinks of Fortune and recalls

In tender youth how sche was first my fo
And eft my frende.

He is roused by the matins-bell, which seems to say "tell on, man, quhat the befell." Straightway he resolves "sum newë thing to write," though he has in his time spent ink and paper to small purpose. He begins his tale of early misfortune with an elaborate metaphor of a ship at the mercy of the elements; then narrates how the actual ship in which he was sailing from his own country was captured by the enemy, and how he was sent into confinement. From his window, he looks upon a fair garden and hears the love-song of the birds. This song, which is given as a *cantus,* prepares the reader for the critical passage of the poem in which the poet sees the lady who from that moment brings sunshine into his life:

And there-with kest I doun myn eye ageyne,
 Quhare as I sawe, walking under the toure,
Full secretly new cummyn hir to pleyne,
 The fairest or the freschest yong[ë] floure
 That euer I sawe, me thoght, before that houre,
For quhich sodayn abate, anon astert
The blude of all my body to my hert. XL.

When the lady, unconscious of her lover's prayer, departs, she leaves him the "wofullest wicht," plunged again in the misery from which her coming had raised him. At night, tired out, he dreams that he is carried high into the heavens to the house of Venus. The goddess receives him graciously, but sends him with Good Hope to Minerva for further advice. This, the learned goddess gives, with quotations from *Ecclesiastes* and observations on predestination; and she sends him, as he is "wayke and feble," to consult Fortune. He returns to earth, and, passing by a plain, stocked, in the conventional way, with all kinds of animals, he meets again his guide Good Hope, who takes him to Fortune's citadel. He finds the dame, and sees the great wheel. This is described to him, and he is ordered to take his place upon it.

"Fare wele," quod sche, and by the ere me toke
So ernestly, that therewithall I woke.

Distracted by the thought that all may be but a vain dream, he returns to the window from which he had seen the lady. To him comes a turtle-dove with a sprig of gilly-flower, bearing the tidings, inscribed in gold on the edges, that, in heaven, the cure of all his sorrow is decreed. The poem concludes with the lover's hymn of thanks to each and every thing which has contributed to his joy, even to the castle-wall and the "sanctis marciall" who had guided him into the hands of the enemy; and, lastly, he commends his book to the poems ("impnis") of his masters Gower and Chaucer, and their souls to heaven.

A careful examination of this well-constructed poem will show that, to the interest of the personal elements, well blended with the conventional matter of the dream-poem, is added that of its close acquaintance with the text of Chaucer. It is not merely that we find that the author knew the English poet's works and made free use of them, but that his concern with them was, in the best sense, literary. He has not only adopted phrases and settings, but he has selected and returned lines, and given them, though reminiscent of their origin, a merit of their own. Sometimes the comparison is in favour of the later poem, in no case more clearly than in the fortieth stanza, quoted above, which echoes the description, in *The Knight's Tale,* of Palamon's beholding of Emilie. The lines

And ther-with-al he bleynte, and cryde "a!"
As though he stongen were unto the herte,

are inferior to the Scot's concluding couplet. The literary relationship, of which many proofs will appear to the careful reader, is shown in a remarkable way in the reference at the close to the poems of Gower and Chaucer. This means more than the customary homage of the fifteenth century to Chaucer and Gower, though the indebtedness to the latter is not textually evident. The author of *The Kingis Quair* and his Scottish successors have been called the "true disciples" of Chaucer, but often, it must be suspected, without clear recognition of this deep literary appreciation on which their historical position is chiefly based.

The only MS. text of *The Kingis Quair* is preserved in the Bodleian Library, in the composite MS. marked "Arch. Selden. B. 24," which has been supposed to belong to the last quarter of the fifteenth century. It is there described in a prefatory sentence (fol. 191) as "Maid be King Iames of scotland the first callit the kingis quair and Maid quhen his Maiestie Wes In England." This is confirmed in the

Latin *explicit* on fol. 211. The ascription to James I, king of Scots, remains uncontroverted. A recent attempt to place the text later than *The Court of Love,* has led to a careful sifting of all the evidence, actual and circumstantial, with the result that the traditional view has been established more firmly, and something beyond a suspicion raised that, if there be any borrowing, *The Court of Love* is the debtor. The story of the poem is James's capture in March 1405, his imprisonment by the English and his wooing of Joan Beaufort. There is no reason to doubt that the story was written by James himself, and the date of composition may be fixed about the year 1423. During his exile the king had found ample opportunity to study the work of the great English poet whose name was unknown in the north, and whose influence there might have been delayed indefinitely. This literary intimacy enhances the autobiographic interest of *The Kingis Quair.*

The influence of Chaucer is hardly recognisable in any of the other works which have been ascribed to James, unless we accept a recent suggestion that fragment B (ll. 1706-5810) of the *Romaunt* was written by him. The short piece of three stanzas, beginning "Sen trew Vertew encressis dignytee" is unimportant; and the "popular" poems *Peblis to the Play* and *Christis Kirk on the Grene,* if really his, belong to a genre in which we shall look in vain for traces of southern literary influence. The contrast of these pieces with *The Kingis Quair* is, indeed, so marked as to have led many to assume that James cannot be the author of both. This is, of course, no argument; nor does the suggestion that their tone sorts better with the genius of his royal successor, "the Gudeman of Ballengeich," count for much. On the other hand, the identification of *Peblis to the Play* with the poem *At Beltayne,* which Major ascribes to James, and the acceptance of the statement in the Bannatyne MS. that he is the author of *Christis Kirk,* must be counterbalanced by the evidence of language and prosody, which appear to point to a later origin than the first decades of the fifteenth century.

The Kingis Quair represents the first phase of Scottish Chaucerianism, in which the imitation, though individualised by the genius of its author, is deliberate and direct. Even the personal and lyrical portions do not destroy the impression that the poem is a true birth of the old allegory. In other words, allegory is of the essence of the conception: it is not introduced for the sake of its interpretation, or as a decorative aid. In the second stage, as disclosed in the poems of Henryson, Dunbar and Douglas, we recognise an important change. Some of the pieces appear to have the old outlook and the old artistic purpose; yet, even in these, the tone is academic. They are breaking away from the stricter and more self-contained interest of the literature of the *Rose;* they adapt both sentiment and style to more individual, or national, purpose, and make them subservient to an ethical thesis. Yet Chaucer remains the inspiring force, not merely in turns of phrase and in fashion of verse, but in unexpected places of the poetic fabric. Even as late as the mid-sixteenth century, in such a sketch as Lyndsay's *Squyer Meldrum,* we are, at times, reminded of the vitality of Chaucerian tradition.

Of Robert Henryson, in some respects the most original of the Scottish Chaucerians, we know very little. He is described, on the title-page of the earliest extant edition of his *Fables* (1570), as "scholemaister of Dunfermeling." His birth has been dated about 1425. A "Master Robert Henryson" was incorporated in 1462 in the university of Glasgow, which had been founded in 1451. The entry states that the candidate was already a licentiate in arts and bachelor in degrees. It is probable, therefore, that his earlier university education was received abroad, perhaps at Paris or Louvain. His mastership at the Benedictine abbey grammar-school in Dunfermline and his notarial office (if he be the Robert Henryson who witnesses certain deeds in 1478) would lead us to infer that he was in lower orders. His death, which may have taken place about 1500, is alluded to in Dunbar's *Lament for the Makaris.* There are no dates to guide us in tracing the sequence of his poems, and the internal evidence is inconclusive. Yet we cannot be far out in naming 1450 as the earlier limit of the period during which they were composed.

Henryson's longest and, in some ways, his best work is his *Morall Fabillis of Esope.* The material of the book is drawn from the popular jumble of tales which the Middle Ages had fathered upon the Greek fabulist; much of it can be traced directly to the edition of Anonymus, to Lydgate's version and to English Reynardian literature as it appeared in Caxton's dressing. In one sense, therefore, the book is the least original of Henryson's works; but, in another, and the truer, it may take precedence of even *The Testament of Cresseid* and *Robene and Makyne* for the freshness of its treatment, notably in its adaptation of hackneyed *fabliaux* to contemporary requirements. Nor does it detract from the originality of presentation, the good spirits, and the felicity of expression, to say that here, even more than in his closer imitations of Chaucer, he has learnt the lesson of Chaucer's outlook on life. Above all, he shows that fineness of literary taste which marks off the southern poet from his contemporaries, and exercised but little influence in the north even before that later period when the rougher popular habit became extravagant.

The *Fables,* as we know them in the texts of the Charteris print of 1571 and the Harleian MS. of the same year, are thirteen in number, with a general prologue prefixed to the tale of the Cock and the Jewel, and another introducing that of the Lion and the Mouse. They are written in the familiar seven-lined stanza, riming *ababbcc.* From the general prologue, in which he tells us that the book is "ane maner of translatioun" from Latin, done by request of a nobleman, he justifies the function of the fable

> to repreue the haill misleuing
> Of man, be figure of ane uther thing.

And again he says,

> The nuttis schell, thocht it be hard and teuch,
> Haldis the kirnell, and is delectabill.
> Sa lyis thair ane doctrine wyse aneuch,
> And full frute, vnder ane feinyeit fabill.
> And clerkis sayis, it is richt profitabill
> Amangis eirnist to ming ane mery sport,
> To licht the spreit, and gar the tyme be schort.

As the didactic element is necessarily strong in the fable, little may be said of its presence in Henryson's work, except, perhaps, that his invariable habit of reserving all reflections for a separate *moralitas* may be taken as evidence of the importance attached to the lesson. Earlier English fabulists, such as Lydgate, mixed the story and the homily, to the hurt of the former. Henryson's separation of the two gives the narrative greater directness and a higher artistic value. Indeed, the merit of his *Fables* is that they can be enjoyed independently and found self-satisfying, because of the contemporary freshness, the unfailing humour, and the style which he weaves into familiar tales. The old story of the sheep in the dog's skin has never been told in such good spirits; nor is there so much "character" in any earlier or later version of the Town and Country Mouse as there is in *The Uponlandis Mous and the Burges Mous.*

In his treatment of nature he retains much of the traditional manner, as in the "processional" picture of the seasons in the tale of the Swallow and the other Birds, but, in the minor touches in the description of his "characters," he shows an accuracy which can come only from direct and careful observation. His mice, his frog with

> hir fronsit face,
> Hir runkillit cheikis, and hir lippis syde,
> Hir hingand browis, and hir voce sa hace,
> Hir logerand leggis, and hir harsky hyde,

his chanticleer, his little birds nestling in the barn against the storm, even his fox, are true to the life. It is, perhaps, this realism which helps his allegory and makes it so much more tolerable to the modern reader. There is, too, in his sketches more than mere felicity: he discloses, again and again, that intimacy and sympathy with nature's creatures which we find fully expressed in Burns, and, like his great successor, gently draws his readers to share the sentiment.

Orpheus and Eurydice, based on *Boethius,* may be linked with the *Fables* in type, and in respect of its literary qualities. The *moralitas* at the close, which is irksome because of its undue length, shows that the conception is similar: the title *moralitas fabulae sequitur* indicates that the poet was unwilling to let the story speak for itself. This, however, it does, for it is well told, and it contains some lyrical pieces of considerable merit, notably the lament of Orpheus in ten-lined stanzas with the musical burden "Quhar art thow gane, my luf Erudices?" or "My lady Quene and luf, Erudices." Even in the processional and catalogue passages, in which many poets have lost themselves or gone aground, he steers a free course. When he approaches the verge of pedantic dulness in his account of the musical technicalities which Orpheus learnt as he journeyed amid the rolling spheres, he recovers himself, as Chaucer would have done,

> Off sik musik to wryte I do bot dote,
> Tharfor at this mater a stra I lay,
> For in my lyf I coud nevir syng a note.

In *The Testament of Cresseid,* he essays the bold part of a continuator. Having turned, for fireside companionship on a cold night, to the "quair"

> Writtin be worthie Chaucer glorious
> Of fair Cresseid and lustie Troylus,

he meditates on Cresseid's fate, and takes up another "quair" to "break his sleep,"

> God wait, gif all that Chauceir wrait was trew.
> Nor I wait nocht gif this narratioun
> Be authoreist, or fenyeit of the new,
> Be sum Poeit, throw his inventioun
> Maid to report the Lamentatioun
> And wofull end of this lustie Cresseid;
> And quhat distres scho thoillit, and quhat deid!

After this introduction, he proceeds, obviously on a hint from Chaucer's text, to give the sequel to the Diomede episode. Chaucer had prayed each "lady bright of hewe,"

> That al be that Criseyde was untrewe,
> That for that gilt she be not wrooth with me.
> Ye may hir gilt in othere bokes see;
> And gladlier I wol wryten, if yow leste,
> Penelopëes trouthe and good Alceste.
> *Troilus,* v, ll. 1774-8;

and he had chivalrously passed on to the closing scene in the tragedy of Troilus. Henryson supplements this with the tragedy of Cresseid. Cast off by Diomede, the distressed woman retires to an oratory and prays to Venus and Cupid, till she falls into an ecstasy. She dreams of her judgment by Saturn, that she shall be stricken with disease, and shall drag out her days in misery. She awakes, to find that she is a leper. A child comes to tell her that her father bids her to supper. She cannot go; and her father appears by her side, and learns how Cupid has taken his vengeance upon her. Sad at heart, he grants her wish to pass straightway with "cop and clapper" to the spital. There, in a dark corner, she "chides her dreary destiny." On a day there passes Troilus and his company in triumph; and the lepers beg for alms.

> Than upon him scho kest up baith her ene,
> And with ane blenk it come in to his thocht
> That he sum tyme hir face befoir had sene,
> Bot scho was in sic plye he knew hir nocht;
> Yit than hir luik into his mynd it brocht
> The sweit visage and amorous blenking
> Of fair Cresseid, sumtyme his awin darling.

He trembles, and changes colour, but no one sees his suffering. To Cresseid he throws rich alms, and passes on. The lepers marvel at his affection for "yone lazarous"; and Cresseid discovers that her friend is Troilus. Not the least effective part of the poem is that which contrasts the sensitiveness of the lovers; or the concluding passage in which the penitent Cresseid makes her testament, and a leper takes her ring from her corpse and carries it to Troilus.

> He swelt for wo, and fell doun in ane swoun;
> For greit sorrow his hairt to birst was boun:
> Siching full sadlie, said, "I can no moir,
> Scho was untrew, and wo is me thairfoir!"

The felicity of the simple style of the next stanza is unmistakable—

> Sum said he maid ane tomb of merbell gray,
> And wrait hir name and superscriptioun,
> And laid it on hir grave, quhair that scho lay,
> In goldin letteris, conteining this ressoun:
> "Lo, fair ladyis, Cresseid of Troyis toun,
> Sumtyme countit the flour of womanheid,

Under this stane, late lipper, lyis deid."

The thirteen shorter poems which have been ascribed to Henryson are varied in kind and verse-form. The majority are of a reflective cast, dealing with such topics as Want of Wise Men, Age, Youth, Death, Hasty Credence and the like—topics which are the delight of the fifteenth century minor muse. There are allegorical poems, such as *The Bludy Serk,* with the inevitable *moralitas,* a religious piece on the annunciation, and *A Prayer for the Pest.* Two of the poems, the pastoral dialogue of *Robene and Makyne* and the burlesque *Sum Practysis of Medecyne,* deserve special mention for historical reasons; the former, too, for its individual excellence. The *estrif* between Robene (Robin) and Makyne (Malkin) develops a sentiment, thus expressed in the girl's own words—

The man that will nocht quhen he may
Sall haif nocht quhen he wald—

which is probably an echo of the *pastourelles.* In literary craftsmanship, the poem excels its later and more elaborate analogue *The Nut Brown Maid.* The older and simpler language, and the ballad *timbre* (which runs throughout many of Henryson's minor poems) place *Robene and Makyne* almost entirely outside Chaucerian influence. This is even more obvious in *Sum Practysis of Medecyne;* and, for this reason, some have doubted Henryson's authorship. The divergence is, however, of no evidence against the ascription. Taken with the pieces the same type which are known to be by his contemporaries, it gives us an earlier link in the chain of popular alliterative (or neo-alliterative) verse which resisted the Chaucerian infusion and was destined to exert a strong influence upon later Scottish poetry. These burlesque pieces in Henryson, Dunbar and Douglas and, later, in Lyndsay (in each case a single and disconnected effort) appear to have been of the nature of experiments or exercises in whimsicality, perhaps as a relief from the seriousness or more orderly humour of the muse. The roughness in tone resembles that of the "flytings," in which it is intentional, and, in many cases, without parallel in English literature. The persistence of this form throughout the century, and in places least expected, may supply an argument for James I's authorship of *Peblis to the Play* and *Christis Kirk on the Grene.* At least, the dissimilarity between these and the *Kingis Quair* would not, did other reasons not interfere, disprove that they came from the same pen.

William Dunbar has held the place of honour among the Scottish "makars." It may be that his reputation has been exaggerated at the expense of his contemporaries, who (for reasons now less valid) have not received like critical attention. Scott's statement that he is "unrivalled by any which Scotland ever produced" strikes the highest note of praise, and is, perhaps, responsible for much of the unvaried appreciation which has followed. Russell Lowell's criticism has arrested attention because it is exceptional, and because it is a singular example of extravagant depreciation. It has, however, the indirect value that it prompts us to test our judgments again, and weigh the value of such popular epithets as "the Scottish Chaucer" and "the Scottish Skelton." There is generally a modicum of truth in easy titles of this kind, though the essence of the epithet is too often forgotten or misunderstood.

Of the personal history of William Dunbar, we have only a few facts; and of the dates of his writings or of their sequence we know too little to convince us that any account of his literary life is more than ingenious speculation. As Dunbar appears to have graduated bachelor of arts at St. Andrews in 1477, his birth may be dated about 1460. Internal evidence, for the most part indirect, points to his having survived the national disaster at Flodden, perhaps till 1520. Like Kennedy, his poetic rival in the *Flyting,* Gavin Douglas and Lyndsay, and, indeed, like all the greater poets from James I, with the exception of the schoolmaster of Dunfermline, he was connected with the court and, like most of them, was of noble kin. These facts must be kept in mind in a general estimate of the courtly school of Scottish verse, in explaining its artificialities and in understanding the separation in sentiment and technique from the more popular literature which it superseded for a time. This consideration supplies, among other things, part of the answer to the problem why the national or patriotic note, which is strongly characteristic of later writers, is wanting at a period when it might be expected to be prominent. In preceding work, with the exception, perhaps, of *Wallace,* the appeal to history is in very general terms; during "the golden age," when political forces were active and Border memories might have stirred the imagination, the poets are wholly absorbed in the literary traditions of romance, or in the fun and the disappointments of life at court; only in the mid-sixteenth century, and, first, most unmistakably in the French-made *Complaynt of Scotlande,* do we find that perfervid Scotticism which glows in later literature.

Dunbar's kinship with the house of Dunbar did not bring him wealth or place. After his college course he became a novice, subject to the strict rule of the Observantines of the Franciscan order. He appears, however, to have fretted under the restraint of his ascetic calling. In a poem entitled *How Dumbar wes desyrd to be ane freir* he makes frank confession of his difficulties, and *more suo* describes the exhortation to him to "refuse the world" as the work of the devil.

This freir that did Sanct Francis thair appeir,
Ane feind he wes in liknes of ane freir;
He vaneist away with stynk and fyrie smowk;
With him me thocht all the houshend he towk,
And I awoik as wy that wes in weir.

He found some relief in the roving life of a friar, and he appears to have spent a few years in Picardy and other parts of France, where he certainly was in 1491 with Bothwell's mission to the French court for a bride for the young James IV. There among the many Scots then haunting Paris, he may have met Gavin Douglas, Elphinstone, bishop of Aberdeen, Hector Boece and John Major; but the Sorbonne, where they were to be found, had, probably, few attractions for him. It is tempting to speculate that the wild life of the faubourgs and the talent of Bohemians like François Villon (whose poems had just been printed posthumously, in 1489) had the strongest claim upon the restless friar. It has been assumed, not without some plausibility, that there are traces in the Scot's poems of direct French influence, in other and deeper ways than in the choice of subjects which Villon had made his own. By 1500, he was back in Scotland, no longer an Observantine, but a priest at court, pensioned by the king, and moving about as a minor official in royal business. The title "rhymer of Scotland," in the English privy council accounts during the sojourn in London of the Scottish embassy for the hand of Margaret Tudor, has been taken by some to mean that, beyond his being the poetical member of the company who praised London in verse, he was recognised to some extent as laureate. Of his literary life, which appears to have begun with his association with the court in 1500, we know nothing beyond what the poems tell us indirectly; but of the sentiment of his age, as seen by a courtier, we have the fullest particulars.

Dunbar's poems fall into two main divisions—the allegorical and occasional. Both show the strength of Chaucerian tradition, the former in a more immediate way, the latter (with full allowance for northern and personal characteristics) in the continuance of the satirical, moral and religious themes of the shorter poems of Chaucer's English followers. There is, however, a difference of atmosphere. Dunbar's work is conditioned by the circumstance that it was written by a courtier for the court. Poetry had fallen, as has been hinted, into close association with a small royal and aristocratic coterie. But life at court, though it showed a political and intellectual vigour which contrasts favourably with that of earlier reigns, and had grown more picturesque in serving the exuberant taste of the "redoubted roye," was circumscribed in its literary interests, and, with all its alertness, added little or nothing to the sum of poetic endeavour. The age may have been "golden"; it was not "spacious." Literary consciousness, when it existed, turned to the romantic past or to the old ritual of allegory, or to the re-editing, for contemporary purposes, of plaints of empty purses, of the fickleness of woman, of the vanity of the world and of the lack of piety; or it was absorbed in the merely technical task of illuminating or aureating the "rude" vernacular. If, however, the area was not enlarged, it was worked more fully. From this experience, at the hands of writers of great talent, much was gained for Scottish verse which has the appearance of newness to the literary historian. What is, therefore, outstanding in Dunbar, is not, as in Henryson, the creation of new genres or fresh motives. Compared with Henryson, Dunbar shows no advance in broad purpose and sheer originality. He is, apart from all question of vocabulary, more artificial in the stricter historical sense; and he might have deserved no better from posterity than Lydgate and Occleve have deserved had he not supplied the rhythms and added life and humour to the old matter.

Dunbar's debt to Chaucer is less intimate and spiritual than Henryson's or King James's. He could not have given us the after tale of Cresseid, or caught so clearly the sentiment of the master in a new *Quair.* Chaucer is, to him, the "rose of rethoris all" (as every poet of the century admitted), but he follows him at a distance and, perhaps, with divided affection for the newer French writers. Still, the Chaucerian influence is there, though the evidence of direct drawing from the well of English is less clear.

The Goldyn Targe has the simple *motif* of the poet's appearance (in a dream, on a conventional May morning) before the court of Venus, where he endeavours to resist the arrows of Dame Beauty and her friends with the aid of Reason's "scheld of gold so schene." He is wounded near to death and taken prisoner. Then he knows that the lady is "lustiar of chere": when she departs, he is delivered over to Heaviness. As she sails off, the noise of the ship's guns wakes him to the enjoyment, once more, of the May morning and the singing birds. The allegory is of the simplest; the contemporary didacticism has hardly invaded it, and the abstractions which the poet introduces are in closer kinship with the persons of courtly allegory than with the personages in the moralities of the period. A similar theme appears in his well-known short poem, *Sen that I am a presoneir* (sometimes known as *Beauty and the Prisoner*); but there didactic and personal elements have been added. It is probable that criticism has been over busy in seeing references to the king, to his liaison with Margaret Drummond and to her suspicious death. In *The Thrissil and the Rois,* the intrusion of the *moralitas* is at once obvious. The setting is heraldic: the theme is the marriage of James IV and Margaret Tudor. The familiar machinery of the dream-poem is here; but the general effect is that of an elaborate prothalamium. It is an easy stage from this poetic type to the pageant and masque; but in the single example of Dunbar's "dramatic" endeavour—in the fragment of *The Interlude of the Droichis Part of the Play*—the allegory is used merely to enhance the whimsicality of the design.

In Chaucer's simpler narrative manner, we have the tale of *The Freiris of Berwik,* dealing with the old theme of an untrue wife caught in her own wiles. The ascription of this piece to Dunbar has been doubted, but there is nothing in it unworthy of his metrical art or his satiric talent. The *Tretis of the Tua Mariit Wemen and the Wedo,* which is certainly his, echoes the gossip of the Wife of Bath, but it speaks with a freedom from which Chaucer would have shrunk. Its antique line and alliteration connect it formally with the popular poetry which Chaucer parodied and undid; yet the association is remote. For it is essentially a literary exercise, perhaps a burlesque *pastiche* to satisfy the romantic fashion of the court. The art of this remarkable poem is always conscious. In the fierce thrusts of sarcasm, in the warping of words, uncouth and strong, we seem to see the personal satisfaction of the craftsman in his triumph of phrase and line.

I haue ane wallidrag, ane worme, ane auld wobat carle,
A waistit walroun, na worth bot wourdis to clatter;
Ane bumbart, ane dron bee, ane bag full of flewme,
Ane skabbit skarth, ane scorpioun—

So hurtle the words in this dialogue on matrimonial risks. In some respects, it is difficult to differentiate this *tour de force* from a "flyting"; but the husbands are not present, and may not (if they could) meet the torrents of abuse.

In considering the satirical and occasional poems of Dunbar, which constitute at once the greater and more important portion of his work, it is well, in the first place, to see how far the Chaucerian influence holds. Here, at least, it is difficult to allow the aptness of the title "the Scottish Chaucer," unless it mean nothing more than that Dunbar, by analogical compliment, has the first place in Early and Middle Scots, as Chaucer has in Middle English. It cannot mean that he shows Chaucer's spirit and outlook, as Henryson has shown; nor that Dunbar is, in these satirical and occasional pieces, on which his wider reputation rests, a whole-hearted pupil in the craft of verse. The title would have appeared more fitting in his own day, when his appeal to contemporaries (apart from any acknowledged debt to his forerunner) was of the same technical kind which Chaucer had made to his; but a comparison, nowadays, has to take account of other matters. Both poets are richly endowed with humour: it is the outstanding quality of each; but in no respect do their differences appear more clearly. Here, Dunbar is unlike Henryson in lacking the gentler and more intimate fun of their master. He is a satirist in the stronger sense; more boisterous in his fun, and showing, in his wildest frolics, an imaginative range which has no counterpart in the southern poet. His satirical powers are best seen in his *Tidings from the Session,* an attack on the law courts, and in his *Satire on Edinburgh,* in which he denounces the filthy condition of the capital; in his verses on his old friends the Franciscans, and on the flying friar of Tungland who came to grief because he had used hens' feathers; in his fiercer invectives of the *General Satire* and *The Epitaph on Donald Owre;* and in the vision of *The Dance of the Sevin Deidlie Synnis.* The last is one of the best examples of Dunbar's realism and literary cunning in suiting the word and line to the sense, as in the description of Sloth—

> Syne Sueirnes, at the secound bidding,
> Come lyk a sow out of a midding,
> Full slepy wes his grunyie:
> Mony sweir bumbard belly-huddroun,
> Mony slute daw and slepy duddroun,
> Him serwit ay with sounyie.

In all, but especially in the *Dance,* there is not a little of the fantastic ingenuity which appears in his more purely comic sketches. And these again, though mainly "fooleries," are not without satirical intention, as in his *Joustis of the Tailseour and the Sowtar* and his *Black Lady,* where the fun is a covert attack on the courtly craze for tourneys. Of all the pieces in this category, his *Ballad of Kynd Kittok* best illustrates that elfin quality which relieves his "busteous" strain of ridicule. The waggish description of the thirsty alewife, her journey on a snail, her arrival in heaven and her sojourn there till, desiring a "fresh drink," she wanders forth and is not allowed to return, her going back to her alehouse and the poet's concluding request—

> Frendis, I pray you hertfully,
> Gif ye be thirsty or dry,
> Drink with my Guddame, as ye ga by,
> Anys for my saik—

strike a note, of which the echoes are to be often heard in later northern verse. There is more than an accidental likeness between this roguish request to the reader and the close of Burns's *Address to the Deil* and *The Dying Words of Poor Mailie.* The reach of Dunbar's fancy is at its greatest in *The Interlude.* There, in his description of Fyn, he writes—

> He gat my grauntschir Gog Magog;
> Ay quhen he dansit, the warld wald schog;
> Five thousand ellis yeid in his frog
> Of Hieland pladdis, and mair.
> yit he was bot of tendir youth;
> Bot eftir he grewe mekle at fouth,
>
> Ellevyne myle wyde met was his mouth,
> His teith was ten ell sqwair.
> He wald apon his tais stand,
> And tak the sternis doune with his hand
> And set them in a gold garland
> Above his wyfis hair.

This is a triumph of the grotesque on the grand scale which the creator of Gargantua would have admired, and could not have excelled. Something of the same quality is seen in his wild picture of the birth of Antichrist in mid-air, in his *Vision,* which opens with the customary dream-setting and gives no hint of this turn in the poet's fancy.

Of lyrical, as of strictly dramatic, excellence, there is little in Dunbar. His love poems are few and, taken as a whole, undistinguished. His religious and moral verses, the one of the hymn type, the other on the hackneyed themes of Good Counsel, *Vanitas vanitatum* and (when he is cheery in mood) Blitheness, deserve commendation for little beyond their metrical facility. They are too short to be tedious to the modern reader. He uses the old device of the "testament" to good purpose in the comic poem on the physician Andrew Kennedy; and, here again, his imagination transforms the old convention. In all Goliardic literature there is nothing to excel this stanza:

> A barell bung ay at my bosum,
> Of varldis gud I bad na mair;
> *Et corpus meum ebriosum*
> I leif onto the toune of Air;
> In a draf mydding for euer and ay
> *Ut ibi sepeliri queam,*
> Quhar drink and draff may ilka day
> Be cassyne *super faciem meam.*

In *The Dance,* already referred to, Dunbar works up the familiar material of the *Danse Macabre.* In his *Flyting of Dunbar and Kennedie* (his poetic rival Walter Kennedy) we have a Scottish example of the widely-spread European genre in its extremest form. It remains a masterpiece of scurrility. The purpose of the combatants in this literary exercise was to outdo each other in abuse, and yet not to quarrel. It is hard for the most catholic modern to believe that they kept the peace, though Dunbar speaks kindly of his "friend" in his *Lament.* The indirect value of *The Flyting* is great—linguistically, in its vocabulary of invective; biographically, for it tells us more of the poet than we derive from any other source; historically, in respect of its place in the development of this favourite genre in Scots, and its testimony to the antipathies of Celtic and Lowland civilisations in the early sixteenth century. A like indirect interest attaches to *The Lament for the Makaris,* which Dunbar wrote "quhen he was seik." It is a poem on the passing of human endeavour, a *motif* which had served the purpose of scores of fifteenth century laments. If it was written under the influence of Villon's master ballades, praise must be allowed to Dunbar that he endenised the Frenchman's art with some success. The solemn effect of the burden, *Timor mortis conturbat me,* occasional happy turns, as

> He takis the campioun in the stour,
> The capitane closit in the tour,
> The lady in bour full of bewte;
> *Timor Mortis conturbat me*

and a sense of literary restraint give the piece distinction above the average poem of this type. Much of its reputation nowadays is as a historical document, which tells us nearly all that we know of some of Dunbar's contemporaries. He names his greater predecessors, and, properly, puts Chaucer first on the roll.

Dunbar, we have said, has been called the "Scottish Skelton." There is some justice in the likening, but the reasons are not consistent with those which give him the title of the "Scottish Chaucer." His allegiance to Chaucer is shown in literary reminiscence, whether of *motif,* or phrase, or stanza—a bookish reminiscence, which often helps us to distinguish the fundamental differences in outlook. There is a spiritual antithesis; but there are textual bonds. With Skelton, on the other hand, who must have been the borrower, had any contact been possible, he stands in close analogy, in two important respects. In the first place, both poets, in their unexpected turns of satire and in their jugglery of words, anticipate the Rabelaisian humour in its intellectual audacity and inexhaustible resource. Whether in wider excursions of fancy, or in verbal orgies, such as in the *Complaint to the King*—

> Bot fowll, jow-jowrdane-hedit jevellis,
> Cowkin-kenseis, and culroun kewellis;
> Stuffettis, strekouris, and stafische strummellis;
> Wyld haschbaldis, haggarbaldis, and hummellis;
> Druncartis, dysouris, dyvouris, drewellis,
> Misgydit memberis of the dewellis; *etc.*

We are constantly reminded of the rector of Diss, and often of the historian of Gargantua and his son Pantagruel. In the second place, their metrical purposes have much in common. The prosodic variety of both is always our first impression—of Dunbar, without parallel in range and competence in any English writer before his time. The interest of the matter in him, as in Skelton, is that the variety is not the effect of mere literary restlessness, but the outcome of experiment to extend the capabilities of English verse in counterpart to what was being done by "aureation" and other processes for poetic diction and style. If Dunbar's prosodic cunning were less remarkable, and if Skelton's so-called "doggerel" were even less palatable than it is to those who take a narrow view of this problem of English, the endeavour of both poets, and of the Scot in particular, would lose none of its historical value. Dunbar borrows from all quarters, chiefly from Chaucer, but also from older popular forms, and from French models found in that other Bohemian genius, François Villon. Yet he is not a mere copyist: his changes in the grouping of the lines in the stanza, his varying the length of the verses and his grafting of one form upon another, are evidence of the literary artist at work. It is useless to attempt to illustrate this by selection from the hundred and one poems, which are ascribed to him, for a selection cannot disclose his kaleidoscopic ingenuity. The remarkable range and resource of his technique and the vitality of his imagination must redeem his work in the eyes of the most alien modern of the charges which have been brought against the art of Lydgate and Occleve. His was not the heavy-headed fancy of a moribund medievalism. The explanation of the difference may be, after all, largely personal. Only so far is he of the renascence. The chief interest to us lies in the old things which he has chosen and recast, as genius may do at any time, whether the age be "dark" or "new."

If no serious effort has been made to claim Dunbar as a child of the renascence, except in respect of his restlessness, in which he shows something of the human and individual qualities associated with that movement, his contemporary Gavin Douglas has been frequently described as the embodiment the fullest and also the first among Scottish poets, of the principles of neoclassicism. A critic of high consideration has recently said that "no poet, not even Dante himself, ever drank more deeply of the spirit of Virgil than Gavin Douglas." Others who consent to this have laid stress on the fact that Douglas was the first translator of a great verse classic into the vernacular. If this conclusion were as just as it is, at first sight, plausible, Douglas could have no place, or only a very minor place in this chapter, which assumes a fundamental homogeneity in medieval method, in most respects incongruent with the literary intention of the new learning.

Like Dunbar, Douglas was of good family, and a cleric; but he had influence and fortune which brought him a large measure of worldly success. He had become a dignitary of the church when the erst-friar was riming about the court and writing complaints of his empty purse. Unlike Dunbar, he had no call to authorship. His literary career, if we may so speak of the years when all his work was written, is but a part of a busy life, the early experience of a man destined to lose his leisure in the strife of politics. He was the third son of Archibald, fifth earl of Angus, the "great earl," better known as "Bell-the-Cat." He was born *c.* 1475, and completed his early training in 1494, when he graduated at St. Andrews. In 1501, after spending some time in cures in Aberdeenshire and the Lothians, he became provost of the collegiate church of St. Giles in Edinburgh, his tenure of which partly synchronised with his father's civil provostship of the capital. Between this date and 1513 (that defining year in all Scottish biography of this period) he did all his literary work, *The Palice of Honour, King Hart, Conscience* and the translation of the *Aeneid,* begun early in 1512 and printed in 1513. Other writings have been ascribed to him—a translation of Ovid (though, in one place, he speaks of this work as a task for another), plays on sacred subjects and sundry *Aureae orationes;* but none are extant, and we have his testimony (in the "Conclusion" of the *Aeneid*), which may be accepted as valid, that he made Vergil his last literary task.

> Thus vp my pen and instrumentis full yoyr
> On Virgillis post I fix for evirmore,
> Nevir, from thens, syk materis to discryve:
> My muse sal now be cleyn contemplatyve,
> And solitar, as doith the byrd in cage;
> Sen fer byworn is all my childis age,

And of my dayis neir passyt the half dait
That natur suld me grantyn, weil I wait.

His later history is exclusively political, a record of promotions and oustings. He was bishop of Dunkeld from 1516 to 1520, when he was deprived of his see because he had gone to the English court for aid in the Douglas-Albany quarrels. Two years later, he died of plague in London, in the house of his friend lord Dacre. Just before his death, he had sent to another friend, Polydore Vergil, material for the latter's *History,* by way of correction of Major's account, which Vergil had proposed to use.

The Palice of Honour, Douglas's earliest work, is an example, in every essential sense, of the later type of dream-poem, already illustrated in the *Goldyn Targe.* It is, however, a more ambitious work (extending to 2166 lines); and it shows more clearly the decadence of the old method, partly by its over-elaboration, partly by the inferior art of the verse, partly by the incongruous welding of the pictorial and moral purposes. The poem is dedicated to James IV, who was probably expected to read between the lines and profit from the long lesson on the triumph of virtue. The poem opens in a "gardyne of plesance," and in May-time, as of yore. The poet falls asleep, and dreams of a desert place "amyd a forest by a hyddeous flude, with a grysly fische." Queen Sapience appears with her learned company. This is described by the caitiffs Sinon and Achitophel, who wander in its wake. Solomon, Aristotle, Diogenes, Melchisedech and all the others are there and are duly catalogued. The company passes on to the palace. Then follow Venus and her court with Cupid, "the god maist dissauabill." The musical powers of this company give the poet an opportunity for learned discourse. We recall several earlier passages of the kind, and especially Henryson's account in the *Orpheus.* Douglas's remark,

Na mair I vnderstude thir numbers fine,
Be God, than dois a gukgo or a swine,

almost turns the likeness into a plagiarism from his predecessor. The procession of lovers moves the poet to sing a "ballet of inconstant love," which stops the court and brings about his arrest. His pleas that "ladyis may be judges in na place" and that he is a "spiritual man" avail nothing; he is found guilty. Reflecting sorrowfully on what his punishment may be, he sees another procession approach, that of the muses with their court of poets. Calliope pleads for him, and he is released on condition that he will sing in honour of Venus. Thereafter, the poet proceeds to the palace, in companionship with a nymph, bestowed by Calliope. They pass through all countries and by all historic places, and stop for festivity at the well of the muses. Here Ovid, Vergil and others, including Poggio and Valla, recite by command before the company. The palace lies beyond on a rock of "slid hard marbell stone," most difficult of ascent. On the way up, the poet comes upon the purgatory of idle folk. The nymph clutches him by the hair and carries him across this pit to the top, "as Abacuk was brocht in Babylone." Then he looks down on the wretched world and sees the carvel of the State of Grace struggling in the waters. After a homily from the nymph on the need of grace, he turns to the palace, which is described with full architectural detail. In it, he sees Venus on her throne; and he looks in her mirror and beholds a large number of noble men and women (fitly described in a late rubric as a "lang cathalogue"). Venus observes her former prisoner, and, bidding him welcome, gives him a book to translate.

Tuichand this buik perauenture ye sall heir
Sum tyme eftir, quhen I haue mair laseir.

So it would appear that Douglas had his *Aeneid* then in mind. Sinon and Achitophel endeavour to gain an entrance. Catiline, pressing in at a window, is struck down by a book thrown by Tully. Other vicious people fail in their attempts. Then follows a description of the court of the prince of Honour and of secretary Conscience, comptroller Discretion, ushers Humanity and True Relation and many other retainers. The glories of the hall overcome the poet, who falls down into a "deidlie swoun." The nymph ministers to him, and gives him a thirteen-stanza sermon on virtue. Later, she suggests that they should take the air in the palace garden. When following her over the tree-bridge which leads to this spot, the poet falls "out ouir the heid into the stank adoun," and (as the rime anticipates) "is neir to droun." Then he discovers that all has been a dream. A ballad in commendation of honour and virtue concludes the poem.

The inspiration of the poem is unmistakable; and it would be easy to prove that not only does it carry on the Chaucerian allegory, but that it is directly indebted to

Geffray Chauceir, as A *per se* sans peir
In his vulgare,

who appears with Gower, Lydgate, Kennedy, Dunbar and others in the court of poets. There is nothing new in the machinery to those who know the *Rose* sequence, *The House of Fame* and *The Court of Love.* The whole interest of the poem is retrospective. Even minor touches which appear to give some allowance of individuality can be traced to predecessors. There is absolutely nothing in *motif* or in style to cause us to suspect the humanist. Douglas's interest in Vergil—if Venus's gift be rightly interpreted—is an undiscriminating interest which groups the Mantuan, Boccaccio and Gower together, and awards like praise to each. He introduces Ovid and Vergil at the feast by the well of the muses, much as they had been introduced by the English poets, though, perhaps, with some extension of their "moral" usefulness, as was inevitable in the later type of allegory. The *Palice of Honour* is a medieval document, differing from the older as a *pastiche* must, not because the new spirit disturbs its tenor.

Of *King Hart,* the same may be said, though it must be allowed to be a better poem, better girded as an allegory, and surer in its harmony of words. Its superiority comes from a fuller appreciation of Chaucerian values: it cannot be explained, though some have so considered it, as an effect of Vergilian study. There is not the faintest trace of renascence habit in the story of king Heart in his "comlie castle strang" and of his five servitors (the senses), queen Pleasance, Foresight and other abstractions. The setting and sentiment recall the court of the prince of Honour in the *Palice of Honour;* and that, again, repeats the picture of the court of the palace in all the early continental versions of the *cours d'amour.*

Conscience is a four-stanza conceit telling how the moral sense has grown dull in men. "Conscience" they had; then they slipped away the "con," and had "science" and "na mair." Then, casting off "sci," they were left with "ens,"

Quhilk in our language signifies that schrew
Riches and geir, that gart all grace go hens.

Douglas's translation of the twelve books of the *Aeneid* and of the thirteenth by Mapheus Vegius is his most interesting work, apart from the question how far his tone is Vergilian in the stricter humanistic sense. In respect of the thirteen prologues and supplementary verses of a more personal character, it may be said to be more original than the so-called "original" allegories. Not all of these are introductory to the "books" to which they are attached; and those which are most pertinent are concerned with the allegory of Vergil's poem. Some may be called academic exercises, which may have been written at odd times, and, perhaps, for other purposes. A picture of a Scottish winter, which has been often quoted, introduces book VI; another, of May, book XII; and another, of June, book XIII. The subjects may have been suggested by the time of the year when the poet reached these stages in translation; if they were deliberately introduced for pictorial relief, they are the nearest approach to renascence habit in the whole work and in all Douglas's writings. A *tour de force* in the popular alliterative stanza, not without suspicion of burlesque intention, is offered as the appropriate preface to the eighth book!

Sum latit lattoun, but lay, lepis in laud lyte;
Sum penis furth a pan boddum to prent fals plakkis;
Sum goukis quhill the glas pyg grow full of gold yit,
Throw cury of the quentassens, thocht clay mugis crakis;
Sum warnour for this warldis wrak wendis by his wyt;
Sum trachour crynis the cunye, and kepis corn stakis;
Sum prig penny, sum pyk thank wyth privy promyt;
Sum garris wyth a ged staf to jag throw blak jakkis.
Quhat fynyeit fayr, quhat flattry, and quhat fals talis!
Quhat misery is now in land!
How mony crakyt cunnand!
For nowthir aiths, nor band,
Nor selis avalis.

This audacious break in the web of the *Aeneid* may have served some purpose of rest or refreshment, such as was given by the incongruous farce within the tedious moralities of the age; but it is not the devising of a humanist. The dialogue between the translator and Mapheus Vegius, in the thirteenth prologue, follows the medieval fashion, which was familiar before Henryson conversed with Aesop about his *Fables.* The first, or general, prologue is the most important, and is frequently referred to for evidence of Douglas's new outlook. The opening homage to Vergil is instructive.

Laude, honor, prasingis, thankis infynite
To the, and thi dulce ornate fresch endite,
Mast reuerend Virgill, of Latyne poetis prince,
Gemme of ingine and fluide of eloquence,
Thow peirles perle, patroun of poetrie,
Rois, register, palme, laurer, and glory,
Chosin cherbukle, cheif flour and cedir tree,
Lanterne, leidsterne, mirrour, and A *per se,*
Master of masteris, sweit sours and springand well.

It is not difficult to underline the epithets which have done good service in the Chaucerian ritual. Indeed, were we to read "Chaucer" for "Virgill" and "English" for "Latyne" in the third line, we should have a straightforward "Chaucerian" passage, true in word and sentiment. But Chaucer is really not far away. Douglas names him ere long, and loads him with the old honours, though he places him second to Vergil. The reason for this is interesting. Chaucer, in telling the story of Dido in *The Legend of Good Women,* had said,

I coud folwe, word for word, Virgyle,
But it wolde lasten al to long a whyle.

This, Douglas politely disputes, especially as Chaucer had said, rather "boldly," that he followed Vergil in stating that "Eneas to Dido was forsworne." Douglas is careful to disprove this, because it distorts Vergil's purpose to teach all kind of virtue by the consistent goodness of his hero, and to point out (as Henryson seems to have thought in his *Cresseid*) that Chaucer "was ever, God wait, wemenis frend." We are a long way from Vergil here; as we are when the poet complains that Caxton's translation does not do justice to what is hidden "under the cluddes of dirk poetry." Douglas makes a more plausible claim to be a modern in a further objection that Caxton's translation (taken from a French version) is bad, that it is out in its words and its geography, and marred by omissions; in quoting Horace on the true method of rendering a foreign author; and in urging the advantages to vernacular style from the reading of the Latin poet. Yet, after all, his aim was to make Vergil's book a literary bible, as Boccaccio's and Chaucer's were. He desires to be thanked by schoolmasters and by "onletterit" folk, to whom he has given a new lesson; he joins St. Gregory's opinion with Horace's; he sees a Christian purpose in his work, and he prays for guidance to Mary and her Son, "that heavenlie Orpheus." His Vergil is, for the most part, the Vergil of the dark ages, part prophet, part wizard, master of "illusionis by devillich werkis and coniurationis." These, he confesses, are now more rare for "the faith is now mair ferme"; but the circumstances should have been allowed for by the dullard Caxton. When he returns in the prologue to the sixth book to chide those who consider that book but full of "gaistis and elriche fantaseis" and "browneis and bogillis," he says of Vergil—

As tuiching hym, writis Ascencius:
Feill of his wordis bene lyk the appostillis sawis;
He is ane hie theolog sentencius,
And maist profound philosophour he hym schawis.
Thocht sum his writis frawart our faith part drawis,
Na wondir; he was na cristin man, per de;
He was a gentile, and leifit on payane lawis,
And yit he puttis ane God, Fadir maist hie.

So it would appear, only too clearly, from these interesting prologues, that Douglas's literary attitude was not modern, and that he is not even so much a Janus-poet as his position and opportunities would warrant. When we separate him from his literary neighbours, it must be as a dilettante.

Probably, the main interest of the translation, and of most of Douglas's work, is philological. No Scot has built up such a diction, drawn from all sources, full of forgotten tags of alliterative romance, Chaucerian English, dialectal borrowings from Scandinavian, French, Latin. No one is harder to interpret. Literary merit is not wanting; yet, in those passages, and especially in his *Aeneid,* which strike the reader most, by the vigorous, often onomatopoeic force of the vocabulary, the pleasure is not what he who knows his Vergil expects, and must demand. The excellence of such a description as that of Acheron—

> With holl bisme, and hiduus swelth wnrude,
> Drumlie of mud, and scaldand as it wer wod,
> Popland and bullerand furth on athir hand
> Onto Cochitus all his slik and sand,

is not the excellence of the original. We are sometimes reminded of Stanyhurst's later effort, in which, however much we may admire the verbal briskness in the marshalling of his thunder and storm passages, we feel that all "wanteth the trew *decorum*" of Vergilian sentiment. The archaic artifices, the metrical looseness and the pedestrian tread, where Vergil is alert, destroy the illusion. Still, if we may not give Douglas more than his due, we must not give him less. His *Aeneid* is a remarkable effort, and is gratefully remembered as the first translation of a great classical poet into English, northern or southern.

Douglas's work, considered as a whole, expresses, in the amplest way, the content of the allegorical literature. He has lost the secret of the older devices, and does not understand the new which were about to usurp their place. He has not the artistic sense of Henryson, or the resource of Dunbar. His pictorial quality, on which so much stress has been laid by some who would have him to be a modern, is not the pagan delight, nor is its use as an interpretation of his mood after the fashion of the renascence. Some passages which have been cited to prove the contrary are but copies from Henryson and earlier work. In him, as in Hawes (to quote a favourite metaphor of both) "the bell is rung to evensong." If Lyndsay and others in the next period still show Chaucerian influence, with them it is a reminiscence, amid the turmoil of the new day.

The minor contemporaries of Henryson, Dunbar and Douglas add nothing to our sketch of Middle Scots poetry. What information we have of these forgotten writers is derived from Dunbar's *Lament for the Makaris,* Douglas's *Palice of Honour* and Lyndsay's *Testament of the Papyngo.* Historians have probably exaggerated the extent and importance of this subordinate literature. It is true we know little of the authors or of their works, but what we do know shows that to speak of "nests of singing birds," or to treat Dunbar as a kind of Shakespearean eminence overtopping a great range of song, is amiable hyperbole. What is extant of this "Chaucerian" material lies in the lower levels of Lydgate's and Occleve's work. The subjects are of the familiar fifteenth century types, and, when not concerned with the rougher popular matter, repeat the old plaints on the ways of courts and women and on the vanity of life. Walter Kennedy, Dunbar's rival in *The Flyting,* and the most eminent of these minors, has left five poems, *The Passioun of Christ, Ane Ballat in praise of Our Lady, Pious Counsale, The Prais of Aige* and *Ane agit Manis invective against Mouth-thankless.* His reputation must rest on the *Flyting* rather than on the other pieces, which are conventional and dull; and there only because of the antiquarian interest of his "billingsgate" and his Celtic sympathies. With Kennedy may be named Quintyne Schaw, who wrote an *Advyce to a Courtier.*

In a general retrospect of this Chaucerian school it is not difficult to note that the discipleship, though sincere, was by no means blind. If the Scottish poets imitated well, and often caught the sentiment with remarkable felicity, it was because they were not painful devotees. In what they did they showed an appreciation beyond the faculty of Chaucer's southern admirers; and, though the artistic sense implied in this appreciation was dulled by the century's craving for a "moral" to every fancy, their individuality saved them from the fate which befel their neighbours. Good as the *Testament of Cresseid* is, its chief interest to the historical student is that it was written, that Henryson dared to find a sequel to the master's well-rounded story. Douglas's protest in the general prologue to his *Aeneid,* though it fail to prove to us that Vergil was much more to him than Chaucer was, shows an audacity which only an intelligent intimacy with the English poet could allow. The vitality of such appreciation, far from undoing the Chaucerian tradition, gave it a fresh lease of life before it yielded, inevitably, to the newer fashion. (pp. 272-303)

G. Gregory Smith, "The Scottish Chaucerians," in The Cambridge History of English Literature: The End of the Middle Ages, Vol. II, *edited by A. W. Ward and A. R. Waller, G. P. Putnam's Sons, 1908, pp. 272-303.*

Louis Golding

[*In the following essay, Golding defends the Scottish Chaucerians from criticism traditionally leveled against them, asserting that their works have been both diminished and misunderstood by comparison to Chaucer.*]

Unhappy are the poets of dialect. They might be conceived as seated unsteadily upon a three-legged stool, whereof the legs are their master language, the dialect of it they have adopted or that has adopted them, and their one sure support of poetry. How much happier had the fate of the Scottish Chaucerians been had they taken the precaution to be born in China or Peru. Alas for that lovely company, King James and Henryson, Dunbar and Douglas! The obscurest poet of the obscurest Mongolian race is sure of his Judith Gautier or Arthur Waley or Powys Mathers, to detach him from his darkness sooner or later, and to set him burning among some constellation of 'Coloured Stars.' If Dunbar had been a Chinese waiter in a London restaurant, if James had but been a railway-porter in Bath, what praise would have been too lavish for so distinguished a music as they devised? I have always felt that they are set dubiously upon a border-line of appreciation, these Scottish post-Chaucerians. They are not read with enthusiasm in Scotland. Is it because the forms they wrote in were imported from a foreign land then so hostile? They are hardly read in England at all, saving in the Universities. Is it because their dialect is too difficult? But it is a tenth as difficult, perhaps, as the Romance poetries that Englishmen read so assiduously. Shall Mr. Scott Moncrieff need to transfer his attentions from the *Chanson de Roland* to *The Thrissil and the Rois*? An examination of the forgotten virtues of these poets may not be without interest in an age sickening of those new virtues, so loudly thrust upon it, which are neither virtuous nor novel.

On the difference between English and Scottish Chaucerians:

Perhaps the most obvious general difference between the Chaucerians of England and Scotland is in their rhythmic traditions. The iambic tetrameter of Dunbar is as characteristic of the Scots as the Lydgate line is of the English. The very assured tradition of metrical regularity in which Dunbar writes is at once more impressive and less potentially expressive than the balanced pentameters south of the border. One of the achievements of Chaucer's verse is to create an enormous range of the tones of speech within verse. Dunbar, at his best anyway, is not divorced from the life of the spoken language, but his speech-accents are those of the formal occasion in the great hall or even the open-air pulpit. This certainly implies a healthier tradition than was to be found in contemporary England, where the Chaucerians seem very in-bred and restricted to what can be said confidentially in a small room: at the same time it prevents an achievement of the magnitude of Chaucer's, or Dante's or even Langland's.

Ian Robinson, in his Chaucer and the English Tradition, *Cambridge at the University Press, 1972.*

In the weak eyeballs of academicians the virtues of the Scottish Chaucerians are blurred in the glory thrown about them by the sun of Chaucer. But it is possible to overestimate even Shakespeare as we can impute thirty thousand feet to Everest. So Chaucer is rather lost wholly than loved wholly by the declaration that he was greater in each respect than each member of this community of poets who derive their immortality, alas! more from his name than from their own high merits. Chaucer's greatness lies not in his detail but in his mass, in so much being less than Shakespeare, whose greatness is surpassed in neither mass nor detail. It is the multiplicity of the man, Chaucer, the abundance of his large lungs breathing, this laughing colossus standing wind-towsled over his age, that so cheats the airs from our puny pinnaces. Obviously enough none of the Scottish company is a colossus. They are great in their detail rather than their mass. And it is in the beauty of their texture, their delight in the threads they weave into comely silken patterns like Henryson's 'Robene and Makyne,' stout tapestries like the *Prologues* of Douglas, that they anticipate the marvellous housewifery of Spenser, and, at their highest, in the sweetness and strength of *The Golden Targe,* that they anticipate John Keats, the last of their line.

Their mediaevalism is imputed to them now as a virtue, now a fault. It is no more a virtue than a man's skin. Or the term is applied to them as a statement of their limitations. This seems a graver consideration. They are not, we learn, original "makers." Without Chaucer they fall to the ground; once more these poets seize the antiquated orange of allegory, attempting once more to squeeze thence new drops of invention. James has his allegory, *The Kingis Quair,* Henryson his Chaucerian Testament; Dunbar and Douglas, poets who should have known better, still embrace their fruits of allegory. These critics state an obvious enough truth. These poets certainly made use of long-familiar forms. Yet apart from the fact that at least three of them were highly original elsewhere in their writings (and who knows but that Time has ruthlessly swallowed other work of James than his *Quair* and 'Good Counsel,' and work no less original than a prologue of Douglas?), yet the criticism is parallel to a condemnation of the Elizabethans for not forging entirely new plots. Whether the form of the Scottish Chaucerians was native or derivative, or their language a blend of northern and southern modes, their achievement was poetry, of which there is so little in the world, of which there cannot be too much. One feels that if Gower had lived to-day, he would not have attempted Parnassus's slope. He would have found the cinema a more effective instrument of moral suasion and have written scenarios for films of religious propaganda. Lydgate would have been a Civil Servant writing letters to the reviews mildly repudiating Mr. Bayfield on Shakespearian versification. The Scottish Chaucerians, who were poets of the fifteenth century, would have been poets to-day.

It is the fashion to sneer at the Chaucerians, when any attention is paid them at all, for their "aurification" of the English tongue—their deliberate introduction of Latinisms. No critic who finds this a fault can have a keen insight into the making of poetry. These poets were conscious of an abounding sensuous delight in the world. It was perhaps a courtly, almost a sophisticated delight; yet it was sincere and urgent; they sought for a vocabulary to express their emotion in the language as left by Chaucer; but the language of Chaucer was not meticulous enough, not adequately jewelled. Hence we find in them that deliciously inquisitive search for musical Latin trisyllables, for fine melodies—a process which, though essentially smaller in nature, anticipates the majestic Latinizings of Milton and the later trilingual symphonies of Francis Thompson.

Of these poets the simplest and most naïve was James; simplest that is, in spirit. For the stanzas of the *Kingis Quair* are constructed with so clear a music and the architecture of the poem is so gracefully poised that James displays himself a craftsman of high rank. The poem manifests a charming and precocious sympathy for living things outside his royal self:

> The bird, the beste, the fisch eke in the see,
> They lyve in fredome, everich in his kind:
> And I a man, and lakkith libertee!

So is his 'lytill swete nightingale' heard by him to chant its feat love-ditty; so can no strain be sadder than his attempt at self-delusion:

> It is nothing, trowe I, but feynit chere,
> And that men list to counterfeten chere.

Or when fortune finally favours his suit, he utters thanksgiving in a passage among the most exquisite of early love-poetry—thanks to the nightingale, it may be, and to the gillyflower, and thanks to the fair castell wall.

Henryson is as delicate as James, but he has more variety and skill. 'Robene and Makyne' holds an important place as the first of English pastorals, but it is intrinsically a worthy sire to 'The Shepheard's Calendar' and 'Comus.' It is full of modulations effected with fine artistry. Nothing could be chaster than its concluding silhouette:

> And so left him boyth wo and wreuch
> In dolour and in cair,
> Kepand his bird under a huche
> Amang the holtis hair.

We have to travel far before we discover the precedent established by Henryson adopted; such a continuation of another man's work as *The Testament of Cresseid* is the continuation of Chaucer's *Troilus.* We must go further than Chapman, who did no more than conclude the fragment left by his brother poet. One cannot help wondering whether Sir Harry Johnstone remembered the dim poet who first came that way, when he set to work upon the novels of Dickens and the drama of Shaw. At all events Henryson was not to have the last word for all his:

> Of fair Cresseid, as I have said befoir
> Sen scho is deid I speik of hir no moir.

A greater than he, but in sour mood, was to tell her fortunes again.

It would be idle to refuse to Dunbar's forehead the laurel of Scottish Chaucerian poetry. He has neither James's simplicity nor Henryson's grace, but he has a range and power and originality which elect him high among the second ranks of poets, beside a Marvell, a Clare, a John Davidson. Never was poetry more "thick inlaid with patines of bright gold" than his *Golden Targe.* It is like the canvasses of the Italian goldsmith-painters, like the gem-encrusted bosom of a Sforza lady:

> The cristall air, the sapher firmament,
> The ruby skies of the Orient,
> Kest beriall bemes on emerant bewis grene;
> The rosy garth, depaynt and redolent
> With purpur, azure, gold and goulis gent. . . .

That this same poet should have written also his *Tua Mariit Wemen and the Wedo,* with its more than Rabelaisian candour, its immense zest, its clever parody of and improvement upon the antique alliterative measure, is a problem in literary psychology. Nor does the tale end here. There follows the grotesque and powerful 'Dance of the Sevin Deidly Synnis,' with its massive thrust in the jaw for Highlanders in general and the miserable Macfadyans in particular. Or, at the opposite pole in the bewildering spirit of this man, his dolorous litany of dead poets, *"Timor mortis conturbat me." Timor mortis* no longer disturbeth him. Not many are they who love this poet, but these love him well.

Douglas in some senses marks the decadence of this burst of poetry briefly examined here. He is more of a litterateur, an Alexandrian, than the rest. We feel that the tremendous versatility of Dunbar, his feverish experimentation with many techniques is implicit in the man, native to him. In Douglas we feel a sense of deliberation, form a greater stimulus than matter. Take, for instance, the amazing virtuosity of the "Ballade in Commendation of Honour"; how the rhymes dance and sparkle like ascending and descending watery arrows in a sunlit fountain!

> Haill, rois maist chois til clois thy fois greit
> micht!
> Haill, stone quhilk schone upon the throne of
> licht!
> Vertew, quhais trew sweit dew ouirthrew al
> vice . . .

Not that even here poetry is lacking. But the tone here is of cunning silver rather than of plain fine gold.

So too we find a new formalism invading, not unpleasantly, the prologues to his translation of the *Æneid.* The prologues describing the winter landscapes and the May morning are adjectival poetry *in excelsis.* Never was there such a plethora of adjectives. Whilst, in sooth, adjectives are not lacking from *The Golden Targe,* they are subordinate to the scheme. In Douglas the scheme is subordinate to the adjectives. *Passing away,* saith simplicity, *passing away.* And yet never was the adaptation of sound to meaning carried to a more masterly degree. The poem on winter, in its each syllable, is a translation of winter's essential music, hard, dry, jagged, craggy. The sea spumes bitterly, howls along livid coasts. Marrow freezes. A man reading in summer crouches for warmth over his empty fire-grate.

. . . Until the reader recalls the May morning of this same poet, this May morning of English poetry:

> The twinkling stremowris of the orient
> Sched purpour sprangis with gold and asure
> ment. . . .
> And al smal foulis singis on the spray
> Welcome the lord of licht and lampe of day!

The freshness of Chaucer, the lyric of Henryson, the skill of Dunbar, are fused in this *aubade.* Spring poets since that day seem curiously belated. When Shakespeare came, he sang the summer of his race. There are moments when it seems that to Shelley, wild, dying bird, was left only the threnody of autumn:

> Sad storm whose tears are vain,
> Bare woods whose branches stain,
> Deep caves and dreary main,
> Wail for the world's wrong!

(pp. 782-83)

Louis Golding, "The Scottish Chaucerians," in The Saturday Review, *London, Vol. 134, No. 3500, November 25, 1922, pp. 782-83.*

Agnes Mure Mackenzie

[*In the excerpt below, Mackenzie evaluates the poetry of James I, Robert Henryson, William Dunbar, and Gavin Douglas. She asserts that, while the literature of their period has "little of the spiritual depth that marks the highest type of poetry," it does display "enormous vigour" and a "brilliant technical accomplishment."*]

[It] is certainly true that fifteenth and sixteenth century Scots literature shows, as the former century advances, the breakdown of the mediaeval moral code and the onset of that moral callousness or imperceptiveness that goes alongside the intellectual quickening of the Renaissance, the age's contentment, save at illuminated moments, with the lust of the flesh, the lust of the eye and brain, and the pride of life. Thus, Henryson apart, the literature of that age, accomplished and vigorous as it is, has little of the spiritual depth that marks the highest type of poetry. What it has is enormous vigour, very brilliant technical accomplishment—brilliant is in fact the word—and at its best, strong emotion to lift it from mere distinguished construction to real creation.

The four major names of the tradition are James I, Robert Henryson, William Dunbar, and Gavin Douglas. King James is the oldest, and, as poet, the least. It is he who is the Chaucerian among them. Henryson goes back, though very much in his own fashion, to an older tradition than Chaucer, Dunbar to that of the *Rose,* and Douglas, in his own manner, to the *Rose* and the classics. James precedes the others by a good deal, having been born in the fourteenth century, in 1394, and murdered in 1436, nearly a quarter of a century before Dunbar was born.

None of the four was a "whole-time" man of letters, and James was least so: indeed, in his short twelve years of active reign he proved himself one of the most vigorous and capable sovereigns of a country that required an efficient government. If he had lived for another twenty years, he would certainly have saved us from many of the troubles of the mid-century, and consolidated his work both at home and abroad. But he was a Stewart, and it was not to be.

An efficient King of Scots had much to do besides writing poetry. James' work, even with what is lost, does not seem to have been copious, though he was always, like his daughters and so many of his descendants, a lover of the arts. According to Hector Boece, "he was well lernit to fecht with the sword, to just, to tournay, to worsle, to sing and dance, was an expert mediciner, richt crafty in playing baith of lute and harp and sindry other instrumentis of music. He was expert in gramer, oratory, and poetry, and made sae flowand and sententious versis: he was ane natural and borne poete." He seems to have been a musician of great merit. Nearly two hundred years later an Italian, Tassoni, speaks of him as one of the pioneers of "modern" music, saying that "he invented a new kind, plaintive and melancholy, in which he was imitated by Carlo Gesualdo, Prince of Verona, who in our age has improved music with many new and admirable inventions." It is possible that the new songs were based on Highland airs: James was a noted performer upon the clarsach. He did write many songs, whether set to his own music or to Highland, but these are lost, and his only surviving writings are a rather fine ballade on *Trust in God,* much in the key of Chaucer's gnomic work, and a very modish allegoric vision-piece, *The Kingis Quhair,* written about the time of his return, in 1424, from his long imprisonment. In spite of its traditional celebrity, it came near enough joining his songs, for it exists only in one MS. of nearly the end of the century, long hidden in an English library.

The Quhair (=quire, book) has always had a sort of popular fame by reason of its romantic history, of the young captive king looking from his window on the garden beneath, and straightway "striken to the herte" by fair Joan Beaufort. It has been said by scholars that the story cannot be true, because the same thing happened to Arcyte: it is extraordinarily difficult to convince a certain type of mind that a thing which occurs in fiction can do so in fact. This may not have, but it is not an unlikely thing to happen to an ardent, imaginative, and imprisoned young man in his twenties, with the Stewart susceptibility to a fair face. In any case, if it is not a literal account of his first sight of a lady he undoubtedly did love, to the point of being one of the few Stewart kings who did not complicate Scots politics by the production of several illegitimate offspring, the prison window and the free lovely garden make a true image of their circumstances. We know that the poem was written for Queen Joan: and the parts that speak of her are very much the best of it, bringing sincerity into its graceful convention. Literary imitation is not inconsistent with that: it is a mere naivety to deny it.

The poem uses the same convention as *The Pearl, The Hous of Fame, The Goldyn Targe,* and *The Divine Comedy,* to take a varied batch of its applications: the dream-allegory made popular nearly two centuries before by Guillaume de Lorris. The elaborate ornament, like the pageantry of symbolical figures in the tapestry, fresco, sculpture, and illumination of the time, is a regular feature of the type, and not by any means confined to Chaucer, as discussions of the *Quhair* sometimes imply. None the less, Chaucer is clearly James's master in verse, and he uses the gracious seven-lined stanza Chaucer had devised for *The Parlement of Foules* and used so exquisitely in *Troylus* that it was popular till the seventeenth century. James writes it gracefully, but he never quite succeeds in getting Chaucer's lovely plangent note. Blind Harry (though not in that metre) beats him there. The language also shows, very strongly, Chaucerian influence. It is much less decorated than that of *The Pearl* or of Dunbar, but is a definitely "poetic diction," though possibly less artificial than it looks, for the strong southern element is only what might be expected of a man who had lived in England from twelve to thirty, at a time when the fifteenth-century change in English speech, that approximated its accidence to the Scottish, had scarcely begun.

The poem begins with the prisoner unable to sleep. He sits down to read Boethius, and recalls his capture, with a real emotion: although the imprisonment was a gilded one, the shock of its treachery, to a sensitive boy, the eighteen years of forced inaction to a youth of James' fiery disposition, must have been bitter, beside the glittering success of Henry V, his senior only by half a dozen years. Then, as he looks from the window, he sees a lady, and the graceful conventional verse fires with real passion:

> Onely throu latting of myn eyen fall. . . .
> My hert, my will, my nature, and my mynd
> War changit clene ryght in ane ithir kynd.

It is the old, recurrent astonishment, "l'image toujours neuve."

The vision that follows, after the lady has gone and he has fallen asleep with his head on the stone, is conventional enough, after the modish forms, though graceful in its tapestry-patterning. One has to remember, reading these many visions, the pictorial imagery of the age. One can never understand any one art, in a given period, without knowing something of what the rest were like: the best commentary on Milton is Wren's St Paul's. The sleeper finds himself at Venus' court: the goddess cheers him and sends him to Minerva, who discourses on wise and unwise love, on honesty in love, on Fortune and free-will. He passes on by a river to a meadow, then to a garden, the rich formal garden that was one of the major mediaeval delights, where Fortune is in the midst above her wheel. She pities him, and bids him mount the wheel and take his chance. . . . But he wakes, seeing nothing of the Charterhouse of Perth on a winter night, and a white dove flies to him with a wall-flower bearing a message of comfort in golden letters. Then he explains that Fortune has been kind, and he is writing as a thank-offering, and ends by praying to Venus for all lovers and for those too dull of soul to love, and commending his book humbly to those of Chaucer and Gower, in rather the spirit of Charles IX's lines to Ronsard. The classical imagery all through has the mediaeval *presentness,* that sees nothing incongruous in invoking Calliope in the name of Our Lady. That was absurd to the post-Renaissance mind. But looking back from the twentieth century one wonders at times if we have not, perhaps, lost something in losing that irrecoverable power of unity of vision—not "changeden substance into accidente"?

James of the Fiery Face,

> —le roy scotiste,
> Qui demy face euct, dit-on,
> Vermeil comme une amathiste—

and who was killed at thirty, was less an amateur of the arts than his father, his son, his brilliant grandson, or even his sisters. His reign, with its jangle of Queen Joan's fierce vengeance, of Crichton and Livingstone, of the Douglas wars, did not make for peaceful letters, though it saw the foundation, four years before Arkinholm, of Glasgow University. His sister, the young Dauphine Margaret, one of the most tragic figures in her tragic family, was, like her father, a poet, but the little of her rather copious work that has survived is all in French, as is the very touching little lament for "la sienne suer o cuer courtois" ascribed to her sister Isobel Duchess of Brittany. Another sister, Eleanor, translated *Ponthus et Sidoine* into German for the benefit of her husband, Sigismund Duke of Austria. Nothing in vernacular letters survives from James' reign except *Wallace* and some scraps of popular song, including the ominous tag

> Edinborough Castle, tour and toun,
> Guid grant thow sink for sin,
> And that even for the blake dinner
> Erl Douglas gat therinne.

Very early in the minority of James' successor, in 1462, we first hear of Robert Henryson, matriculating at Glasgow, but already a graduate in arts and law. We know little of him but that he was schoolmaster in Dunfermline, possibly in its great Benedictine Abbey, and apparently also practised as a notary. His life was a long one, and since his extant poems are clearly those of a man no longer young, they probably belong to the later years of James III and the reign of James IV. We know that he was dead by 1506.

Of the major poets of his century, Henryson is, superficially, most like Chaucer in temper and outlook and in the peculiar quality of his humour. The likeness, however—the more as it extends to choice of subject—throws strongly into relief his very marked individuality both as man and as poet, which shows most clearly in, precisely, the poem whose subject is avowedly suggested by Chaucer. Chaucer's *Troylus and Criseyde* had been a version of a favourite mediaeval addition to the tale of Troy—how the young prince Troilus loved a fair Greek hostage, how they were happy, and then she was exchanged and returned, and betrayed him with Diomed, so that he died despairing. Shakespeare was to take it up again, with its passion and pity turned to a sardonic anger of disillusionment. Henryson set himself to continue Chaucer's poem, in a spirit that is neither Chaucer's nor Shakespeare's: it is nearer, in fact, the temper of Shakespeare's own tragedies. Instead of the novelist's analysis of emotion in Chaucer's *Troylus,* which is in fact the first great English novel, there is a fierce condensation, a darker and sterner pity, not pathos but the swordstroke tragedy of the ballads. The poem takes its note at once. It is winter: he sees the planet Venus rise on a cold clear night of wind, the east wind of Fife, then mends the fire and "beikis him about,"

> And toke ane drink, my spreitis to conforte,

and then reads *Troylus and Criseyde* and after it, another, imaginary, tale of the end of the story, whose substance he recounts. Cresseid is jilted in turn by her new lover, and goes back to her father: their brief interview has a fine sense of the dramatic. Calchas is Venus' priest, but Cresseid is too shamed to show herself in the temple. She prays instead in a secret oratory, reproaching Venus who has led her to trust in the beauty that has betrayed her. There is the inevitable vision then, without which no large-scale poem was complete—a gorgeous procession of the Old Gods that recalls the pageants of the *Faerie Queene.* Cupid charges her with blasphemy of his mother, and the eldest and the youngest planet, the cold star Saturn and the Moon, are bidden to judge her. Saturn strikes her with his frosty wand, and she is filled with the leprosy that was so insistent a mediaeval horror. She wakes from her dream, goes to the glass to reassure herself, and learns the truth of it, and her ruined beauty. There follows a scene of wild misery with her father, who takes her privily to "the hospitall at the tounis end," where her fellow-lepers comfort her with hard-won philosophy. She who has been fair and desired and lived daintily, must e'en make the best of it, and live "eftir the law of lipparleid." Then comes the climax. As she begs with them at the gate, Troilus rides past them from victorious battle. She is too blind by now to recognise him, and her face so marred he cannot know her either. Yet something about her recalls to him Cresseid: he changes colour, and moved by the memory, throws her his purse and rides away in silence. From her fellows' chatter over the good fortune she learns who he is and swoons, rousing before she dies to send him, by a fellow-leper, the ruby ring that had been his first gift to her. He hears the story, crying "Scho was untrew, and wo is me thairfoir," and has her buried richly under marble, with the curt sufficient epitaph,

> Lo, ladyis fair, Cresseid of Troyis toun,
> Sumtyme countit the flour of womanheid,
> Undir this stane, late lippar, lyis deid.

The whole thing has a stark sense of the east wind—one of those bleak Fife days with white water on the Firth. But its stern justice has a profound and aching pity, and something also of the sense of redemption that comes at the close of a tragedy of Shakespeare's.

It is not, by any means, Henryson's only note. He can write things of the shrewdest and liveliest humour, with a homely realism instead of the stately pageant of the gods: but even under their most whimsical there is always a certain sense of the ironies—below the mirth a sense of the tragic littleness of humanity, and below that again, what is not common anywhere in that century, a grave underlying assurance of stable law. One has it beneath the whimsy of the *Fables,* delightful *remaniements* of "Esope myne autour," in the vein of the *Nonnes Preestes Tale.* It is interesting to see how Henryson's own temperament informs their lively and homely realism of humour as much as the tragic fantasy of *The Testament of Cresseid.* They have the same humanity, but it is comic, not tragic, as in the genteel *refanement* of the "burgess mouss:" yet there is a tenderness in the amusement, for the innocent terrors of the "rural mous." They show also another quality of Henryson, the sharp perception of surroundings, not merely as decoration, as in romanticism, not merely as something to put down, as with most realists, who remind one so often of a small boy with a camera who must keep letting it off at no matter what, but as an essential element of the complex experience he is portraying. This is notably so in his handling of natural phenomena. The English climate is no better than the Scots,—that of London, in fact, is more treacherous than that of any Scottish district known to me: but for centuries English literature ignores wet weather, storm, the wilder aspects of the country, rather as in another century it ignored the wilder aspects of sex so much that when they became mentionable again it could scarcely bring itself to talk of anything else. It liked nature, but tidy and obliging nature: it had forgotten, or felt only as horror, the fierce sense of the storm, of moor country, that shows again and again in pre-Conquest poetry, West Saxon and Northumbrian alike, as in *The Seafarer*:

> Nap nihtscua, norpan sniwde,
> hrim hrusan band: hægl feoll on eorpan,
> corna caldast.

—and the next lines are not revulsion, but the stir that moves a man to seek *elpeodigra eard,* the country of strange folk, over the steep seas. This receptiveness to nature in all its aspects, not merely in the kindly, is a constant note in Scots poetry for centuries before James Thomson carried south of the Border a fashion that was to produce Wordsworth, and which, reduced to a popular sentimentality, looks like burying all the wild nature we have left under a layer of sardine-tins and paper bags.

Less important than either *Cresseid* or the *Fables* is *A Traitie of Orpheus Kyng and how he came to yeid to Hewyn and to Hel to seik his Quene.* It is graceful enough, and more classical in feeling than the *Kyng Orfeo* of the fourteenth century, but is marred by too much learning—in this case, theory of music. The intrusion no doubt pleased the scientific fashion of the age, like Chaucer's flourishes of astrology or the 1920 novelists' of the subconscious. Nothing goes out of date so quickly as science, or makes a work of art so soon look obsolete.

Henryson's shorter poems are generally meditative and didactic rather than lyrical, their verse in the tone of recitative rather than song. The exception is his best, which has lyrical movement with the dramatic feeling of the *Testament,* though it is love's comedy now instead of tragedy, a dry ironic comedy that does not empty passion but encloses it. *Robene and Makyne* is a pastoral duologue of a type popular in mediaeval France. Its verse has a delightful impish dance, unusual in Henryson, and largely due to the fact that he has "swung" it by using a blend of metrical and alliterative form, in the manner of *The Pearl* and of much of Dunbar. The theme is conventional, but there is more than convention in the wicked humour of Robin's semi-surrender and the denouement. The indifferent Robin is wooed by his passionate fair, and submits at last: since the lady wants it so much, he will oblige—if his sheep don't happen to stray at the crucial moment. There is a certain devilment in Makyne's remark, when the tables are turned and he has become the wooer, "As thow hes done, sa sall I say."

The man who wrote *The Testament of Cresseid* was a greater *man* than William Dunbar, with a type of imagination that in "literary" poetry—there is plenty in the ballads—Scotland was scarcely to see again until the closing chapters of *Waverley.* But of all the Scots writers of his age, Dunbar is, taking him all round, the most considerable. Mrs Annand Taylor, in a charming if slightly exasperating book, has scolded him severely for not being either Malory or Rossetti. The charge, if irrelevant, is true. He was certainly neither, but he was much himself, and no less what was the essence of his own time. He had in fact the makings of a great poet: that he is one in the lesser kinds of poetry is as true of him as of Alexander Pope, and in both because they abound so exceedingly in the sense of their age and of their society. He has a fine firm intellectual quality; an intense degree of the "more than ordinary organic (=sensory) sensibility" that Wordsworth considered the essential of the creative temperament; and a spectacular technical accomplishment. But he comes in an age that all over Europe is almost devoid of spiritual intensity, and his experience rarely brought him the intensity of emotion that, poetically speaking, might have made up for it. He was a priest and a courtier together, one of

> Those gay abati with the well-turned leg
> And rose i' the hat-brim, not so much St Paul
> As saints of Caesar's household—

—the type of the eighteenth century *abbé de salon.* Now, priests have written great poems, and so have courtiers, but the combination is a hampering one for the highest kind of poetry. The man who is both can never be wholly either, can never, at heart, desire wholly what is of either, with a sense that the desire, however far from his power, is within his right. Dunbar thus remains below the pinnacles: he writes superb court-poetry, but though he can dance divinely he seldom soars. And partly because of that very limitation it is he of all Northern European poets who most fully expresses the spirit of his own age, its intricate, rather brutal gorgeousness, its hard intellectual quality, its intense vitality of the will and the senses and its numbness of the finer spiritual perceptions. Emotionally, he is nearer Dryden (who, by the way, was partly of Scots descent) than anyone else who writes the common language, and he would have been completely at home in the Paris of the Fronde. (His views on the *Carte du Tendre* might have been unacceptable in the Hôtel de Rambouillet . . . yet I don't know. He liked both allegory and a pretty woman.) Indeed, though I have compared him to Pope and Dryden, he is nearer the French seventeenth century than anything in English except, significantly, Ben Jonson. The likeness, however, is in spirit, not in literary technique. The great French writing of the *Grand Siècle* has a quality of marble, of wrought bronze. Dunbar's is like gorgeous many-coloured enamel, hard, glittering, and full of reflected lights. His greatest work would have staggered Jean Racine: and yet, perhaps, it has a good deal in common with the rooms that lead onwards from the Salon d'Hercule, the rooms through which a court passed to see *Georges Dandin.*

We have a considerable body of Dunbar's work, although its survival, as usual, was rather a near thing. Chepman and Myllar printed *The Goldyn Targe, The Twa Maryit Wemen, Quhen he wes Seik,* and four other pieces, in 1508. The rest of him is in the Bannatyne, Maitland, Asloan and Reidpath MSS., and there was no collected edition till 1834. His life is more distinct than those of his predecessors. He was probably born in the last years of James II, and the main associations of his maturity are with the brilliant court of James IV. His restless vigour gave him a wandering youth. He turned to the Franciscan order, and as a novice tramped all over England, preaching in Canterbury Cathedral, but he never took the vows, becoming instead, unfortunately for himself and for the Church, a secular priest—secular, in fact, in more senses than the technical. Like Chaucer before him he went into what we should call the Civil Service. We know that he went with the Scots Ambassador to France in 1491, and after James had declined the Spanish match, to England with the envoy who arranged the King's marriage to Margaret Tudor. Diplomatic business also took him to Germany, Italy, Spain, and Norway, on the coast of which country he claims to have been wrecked. Although he never held any important post, he was a personal favourite with both King and Queen—little as their tastes, for the most part, agreed—and although James steadily refused him the benefice for which he clamoured, he was pensioned in 1500. In his later years he was a sort of official court-poet, turning out a good deal of brilliant "occasional" verse for official functions, the official compliments of a royal or ambassadorial visit. A good deal of his unofficial work is also more or less occasional, and between that and his laureate pieces he gives a shrewd, witty, vigorously coloured picture of the Scots court life of the time, on its less serious side. There was a serious side. James was the true Renaissance prince, avid of beauty as his father had been, an impassioned scholar (Ayala says he spoke six languages besides the two that were native to his country), and as interested in science as his descendants Prince Rupert and Charles II—a religious man, too, in strange passionate alternations between the love-affairs that (save perhaps for Margaret Drummond's) suggest vivid energy and a heart too twisted in youth to find any peace: he never, to his last day, forgot that at fifteen he had helped, however unwittingly, to kill his father. Something fated about the man, more than in most of his line, suggests the White King, who was also Scot crossed with Dane. It is in Holbein's strangely haunting portrait. But James had far the finer brain of the two, and that intense power of vitality that was coming to be applauded under the misconception of it called *virtù.* The Renaissance and Middle Ages fuse in him, in one of those personalities who suggest that a reason why Scotland has little great poetry or drama is that she has never needed to create it as enlargement of experience. Her passions found outlet in immediate action, and the impulses that elsewhere made epic and tragedy, in her made the naked fact of her history.

But in spite of its brilliance, and of the King's personality, the splendour of that court was of its age, and soulless. It was gorgeous, but corrupt. Margaret of Denmark was dead, and the women who led it were the King's fleeting mistresses, or Margaret of England, who had the Tudor vulgarity without the Tudor brains: Holbein reveals her with disastrous completeness. (Cross *that* with Douglas arrogance, not too intelligent, in Angus, and the shrillness of Lennox, and you may well breed Darnley.) Dunbar had plenty of material for the satire that is the note of his greatest work, and plenty of cause for the weariness under his laughter. And the reckless magnificence of his style was in the picture. Scots architecture, between the climate and the hard native stone, was severer than French or English, but its builders took out the difference in gorgeousness of person. Grafton Herald remarks with patriotic annoyance that at the handing over of Queen Margaret the Scots outshone his countrymen in "apparell and riche jewels and massy Chaynes"—and Henry's court did not go Quakerish.

All these things show in the greatest, and grimmest, satire in our literature, *The Twa Maryit Wemen and the Wedo.* The subject is one that has occupied writers from the Prophet Isaiah to Mr Noel Coward. To use a phrase that is now become old-fashioned, it deals with the expensive Bright Young Person, and one could wish that our own contemporaries, who are so fond of writing of similar types, could do so with Dunbar's force and concision. It is one of the most flaying things in literature, and of uncommon technical interest, not merely because it is the last important piece in unrhymed alliterative verse, but because of the way in which its many-coloured brilliance of decoration is made an integral part of the satire itself, made to be "burning instead of beauty," though it is beauty and recognised for that.

It begins with the splendour of midsummer night in a palace garden, all green and coloured flowers and glittering lights, and three lovely delicate ladies as gay as the flowers, and as exquisite:

> I saw thre gay ladeis sit in ane grene arbeir,
> All graithit in to garlandis of fresche gudelie flouris.
> So glitterand as the gold wer thair glorius gilt tressis,
> Quhill all the gressis did gleme of thair glaid hewis.
> Kemmit wes thair cleir hair, and curiouslie sched,
> Attour thair schuldres doun schyne, schyning full brycht,
> With curches, cassin thame aboue, of kirsp cleir and thin.
> Thair mantillis grein war as the gress that grew in May sesoun,
> Fetrit with thair quhyt fingaris about thair fair sydes.
> Of ferlifull fyne favour war their faceis meik,
> All full of flurist fairheid, as flouris in June,
> Quhyt, seimlie, and soft, as the sweit lilies,
> New vpspred vpon spray, or new spynist rose,
> Arrayit ryally about with mony rich vardour,
> That nature, full nobillie, annamallit fine with flouris
> Of alkin hewis under hewin, that ony heynd knew,
> Fragrant, all full of fresch odours, fynest of smell.
> Ane marbre tabile coverit was befoir thai thre ladeis
> With ryall coupis upon rawis, full of ryche wynys.

They solace themselves with the wines until their tongues are loosened, and they chatter of the subject in which they take most interest. There are no men about: it is strictly *inter augures.* They are of the type for whom harlotry is a hobby rather than a profession, but skilled amateurs who make a good thing out of it. And they discuss their methods as they might their service at tennis, completely satisfied with their own outlook as a natural and adequate view of life.

Then, when they have said enough to strip themselves naked, without a word of comment we are made to visualise them again, their delicate loveliness in the rich setting.

> The morow myld wes and meik, the mavis did sing,
> And all remuffit the myst, and the meid smellit.
> Siluer schouris doun schake, as the schene cristall,
> And berdis schoutit in schaw, with thair shrill notis.
> The golden glitterand gleme so gladit thair hertis
> Thai made a glorius gle amang the grene bewis.
> The soft souch of the swyr, and soune of the stremis,
> The sweit savour of the sward and singing of foulis,
> Myght confort any creature of the kyn of Adam,
> And kindill agane his curage, thocht it was cald slokynt.
> Then rais thir ryall wivis, in thair riche wedis,
> And rakit hame to thair rest, through the rise blosmyt.

There is not a word of condemnation. We simply see both the inside and the out, *together.* And that is devastating. The thing is ghastly, but superb in its kind. It makes most modern work on the subject extraordinarily thin, diffuse, and flat.

It is the greatest of his satires. There is a pair to it, a companion-piece "forty years on," in *Rycht early on Ash Wednesday,* where two old cummers whose sensual delights are reduced to food and drink hold forth on the unwholesomeness of fasting. It has the same grim detachment, but naturally cannot achieve the superb horror of the contrasts in the other, using instead a hard-bitten black and white, like certain woodcuts. Satire dominates the greater part of his work. Although Dunbar was a man of family, there is a certain bourgeois strain in him: it is one of his seventeenth-century qualities, and perhaps one of the reasons why he got on better with Margaret Tudor than with her husband, who tolerated and probably liked him, but steadily refused the advancement for which he clamoured. And the favourite bourgeois emotion is disapproval, which is not at all the same thing as contempt. Contempt is sure of itself, and its note, in art, is "Non ragionam di lor, ma guarda, e passa." You find that, magnificently, in *The Twa Maryit Wemen,* where he does look and pass, without a word, but the look sees everything, and assesses it. There are times, however, when he does *ragionare,* in a grumble not without envy of what he dislikes. To be fair, one must distinguish this from the mere joyful virtuosity of invective for its own sake, in which he is a master. But the element shows its head in him now and then, as it was to do increasingly in Scots society in the next generation, until some century later it swamped Scots art and drowned it: one has glimpses at times of its authentic differentia, the hatred with an envy of the thing hated, a self-conscious self-assertion in the hater, that leads—though not as yet, and not in Dunbar—to the rancorous loathing of all things that are gracious and assured, from fine manners to the carved work of the sanctuary.

As yet it is only here and there, however, that one catches this unpleasing quality, unless there is perhaps a little of it in the very predominance of satire in Dunbar's work. His subjects are the customary ones, the Church, the law, the court, and of course women. After the dispassionate venom and the sheer decorative quality of the *Twa Maryit Wemen,* the best, artistically, are the very dissimilar *Feinzit Freir of Tungland,* where satire, or rather lampoon, caracoles in exultant vehemence of the grotesque, and *The Dans of the Sevin Deidly Sinnis,* which has the Cellini exuberance of decoration that marks his pageant-poetry, to which this, in fact, is a sort of anti-masque.

The *Freir* is a topical caricature, of one of the King's scientific protégés, an Italian physician who made unsuccessful experiments in both alchemy and aviation, damaging himself badly in an attempt to "glide" from the Rock of Stirling. Dunbar, who had not the type of mind that is sympathetic to attempt at the unachieved—as I say, he has a touch of the smug Lallan bailie—gives a lively if libellous account of his medical and clerical past, and a really joyful gallopade of his adventures among the fowls of the air, who are astonished at this strange creature in feathered wings:

Sum held he had bene Daedalus,
Sum the Minotaur mervalus,
Sum the Martis smith Wlcanus,
And sum Saturnus kuke.
And evir the cushattis at him tuggit,
The rukes him rent, the ravynis him ruggit,
The hudit crawis his hair furth druggit,
The hevyn he micht nat bruik.

The myttane, and Sanct Martynis fowle
Wend he had been the horned owle:
They set apone him with a yowle,
And gaif him dynt for dynt.
The golk, the gormaw, and the gled
Beft him with buffettis quhill he bled,
The sparhawk to the spring him sped
Als fers as fyre of flynt.

Thik was the clud of kayis and crawis,
Of marleyonis, mittanis, and of mawis,
That bikkrit at his berd with blawis,
In battaill him abowt.
They nibblit him with noyis and cry,
The rerd of them raiss to the sky,
And evir he cryit on Fortune, Fy.
His lyfe wes into dout.

It has the headlong grotesquerie that is a recurrent note in Scots literature, from *Colkelbie's Sow* to Outram's *Annuity,* and since, to *Juan in America*: one finds it again, and with more sympathy, in *Kynd Kittok,* which is not so much satire as grotesquerie for its own sake, like *Tam o' Shanter.* The lady is an alewife who dies of drouth, and sets out for Heaven: she meets a newt riding on a snail, who gives her a lift, and dodging St Peter, contrives to get through the gate. The Deity is so amused at the way she jouked the saint that He lets her be, and she lives soberly for seven years as Our Lady's henwife. Then, looking out, she is homesick for her own ale—"the aill of Hevin wes sour." She slips out for a drink, and this time St Peter is more on the alert, so she is keeping a pub to this day between earth and Heaven, and Dunbar begs his friends to stop there as they go by, and have a drink for the good of the house.

The Sevin Deidly Sinnis is, as I have said, an anti-masque to such things as *The Thrissil and the Rois* and *The Goldyn Targe.* Its allegorical pageant-procession goes back to Lorris, or rather to Jehan de Meung, and the Seven Sins themselves were a favourite mediaeval subject in all the arts. There is no greater test of an artist's originality than the way in which he deals with such stock material. Dunbar's handling of this has splendid vigour, with the same glittering solidity, in a strong and rather angular design, that one finds in contemporary Flemish painting. But this is not painting: it is a dance, and it moves, with a sort of violent ballet-wheel, the rapid couplets, mostly on double rhymes, caught back hard against the four-times-repeated rhyme of the short lines, that gives its verse the strange harmonised movement of concurrent rhythms of which few men are masters but Dunbar a great one:

Nixt him in dans cum Covatyce,
Rut of all evill and grund of vyce,
That nevir cowd be content.
Caityvis, wreches, and okkeraris,
Hud-pykis, hurdaris, and gadderaris,
All with that warlo went.
Out of thair throtis they schot on oder
Het moltin gold, me thocht a fudder,
As fireflawcht maist fervent.
Ay as they tomit them of schot,
Feyndis filld them new up to the throt,
With gold of alkyn prent.

His other pageant-work is very unlike this, being courtly decorative stuff, the equivalent in verse of the masque and ballet that all through the fifteenth and sixteenth and (out of Scotland) the seventeenth centuries, till the Roi Soleil grew too old to dance, were a regular part of any festival, whether civic, courtly, or academic. *The Thrissil and the Rois* was written for the King's wedding. It is completely traditional stuff in the same convention as Chaucer's wedding-masque, *The Parlement of Foules,* and beautifully done, with a lovely opening of landscape, "anamellit richly with new azure lycht," just touched with dry realism in a hint at the contrast between the May of poetry and the May of East Coast fact. After the crowning by Nature of the Lion and the Eagle as Kings of Beasts and of Fowls, the "awful Thrissil," "kepit with a busche of speiris" is given "a radius crown of rubeis" and wedded to "the fresche Rois, of cullour reid and quhyt," and the close is an enchanting chorus of bird-song whose rhyme-royal takes on a strange chiming harmony, not Chaucer's plangent note, but individual and beautiful, the suggestion of the choiring of many voices that is one of Dunbar's greatest gifts. One has something of it again in the little song sung after dinner on the wedding-day, with the refrain, "Welcome of Scotland to be Queen." There is nothing in it, but the enchanting pattern of sound, unresolved until its close, has grace enough to make it a fitter offering for Margaret's granddaughter.

Dunbar's greatest thing in this masque-type, however, is the magnificent *Goldyn Targe,* the finest thing of its kind in the language, above even Chaucer's work in this type of poem. It is not an "occasional" piece, but a love-allegory, and in fact an odd production for a priest, though to be sure he does seem to have resembled the Abbé d'Herblay, better known as Aramis, and his relations with pretty ladies like Mrs Musgrave may not all have been on the spiritual plane. But it may have been written for the King or some other patron. There is a sort of rueful sincerity under the convention, but it need not mean that Dunbar was, on that occasion, speaking for himself—at any rate in more than the expression of his habitual delight in certain forms of beauty. There is no doubt about that. From its lovely opening in a May dawn it is full of the jewelled glittering colour, the *net* enamelled luminescence, that he loved.

Full angelike thir birdis sang thair houris
Within thair courtyns grene into thair bouris,
  Apparalit quhyte and reid wyth blumis suete.
Anamellit was the felde with all colouris,
The perly droppis shuke in siluer schouris,
  Quhill all in balm did branch and levis flete.
  Depairt fra Phebus, did Aurora grete:
Her cristall teris I saw hing on the flouris,
  Quhilk he for lufe all drank vp with his hete.

Above all there is his joy in clear water and the clear lights of Northern sun under a washed sky.

Doun throw the ryss ane ryuir ran with stremys
Sa lustily agayn thae likand lemys,
  That all the lake as lamp did leme of licht,
Quhilk schadovit all about with twynkling glemis
That bewis bathit wer in secund bemis,
  Throw the reflex of Phebus visage brycht.
  On every syde the hegis raise on hicht,
The bank wes grene, the bruke was full of bremys,
  The stanneris clere as stern in frosty nycht.

His eye for it shows in the play of *reflected* light in

The roch agayn the ryuir resplendent
  As low enlumynit all the levis schene.

The patterning of the sense of colours is notable: they are not merely chance bright splashes, but parts of a visualised design, built up before the mind's eye like architecture. These glinting reflections of water succeed a perfect rainbow of jewel-names and heraldic tinctures, and then, out of the richness,

I saw approach agayn the orient sky
  Ane saill als quhyte as blossum vpon spray

is climax and resolution of the symphony of colour as much as close to the action of this iridescent prelude. The ship bears "all the chois of Venus cheualry," and Jean Fouquet made no more decorative design in those lovely miniatures of the castled Loire country. The transparent quality Dunbar gives all his lights may seem faintly unnatural to an English reader, if he has any: but Dunbar was a man of East Scotland, where light does give that sense of being seen through crystal. Chaucer's "Al the Orient laugheth of the lighte" is deservedly famous. But it can be paralleled, and surpassed, a hundred times in Dunbar, from what is obviously his own direct observation, not a remembrance of

Lo bel pianeta . . .
Faceva rider tutto l'oriente.

In praising *The Goldyn Targe* above Chaucer, I do not mean to call Dunbar the greater poet. He was not. He has a much lesser range, nothing of Chaucer's great narrative gift, his pity, and consequently his humanity. But in this pure decorative verse, the equivalent, in letters, of the Cellini tradition of goldsmith's work, Dunbar's only equal, at his best, is Spenser, whose set-pieces rival him in the softer, more flowing and ample Italian manner, as against Dunbar's French and Flemish *netteté.* It is not the greatest kind of poetry: but Dunbar is on the pinnacle of the kind.

It is in some of the shorter pieces that his note is deepest. They are not all deep: some of them are occasional compliment, like the description of the elaborate pageants that graced a royal visit to Aberdeen, or the stately praise of London: one observes, by the way, that he has *seen* the city—seen it, no doubt, in highly complimentary terms and without any reference to the local stenches, but seen it undoubtedly. There are the sufficiently numerous begging-pieces: Dunbar was as impecunious as most poets. Not all are either begging or compliment. Things like the famous *Flyting of Dunbar and Kennedy* are the precise reverse of any aureation of praise. These cursing-matches in verse were a literary game that goes back to the *tenso* of the Troubadours, and Dunbar's immense vocabulary and swinging verve of metre made him a formidable antagonist. His metrical skill seldom left him. Some of the finest examples of it are in the graceless and probably tactless *Dregie,* a parody, sufficiently profane, of a requiem, addressed to the King, who had gone into retreat at Stirling. Listen to the peal of the bells in the *responsiones.* (The *-ion* termination is in two syllables.)

Tak consolatioun in zour pane.
In tribulatioun tak consolatioun,
Out of vexatioun come hame agane.
Tak consolatioun in zour pane.

The serious lyrics are sometimes very lovely. Some of these are occasional pieces also, like the lament for Bernard Stuart d'Aubigny, Commander of the Garde écossaise, Marshal of France, and one of the great captains of his day, who came to his own country as French Ambassador, and died there of fever in 1508. (It was he once, captured in Spain, who made terms for his command, that they should go free with the honours of war, but "fier comme un Ecossais," refused them for himself, and "sharply rebuked two young lords his kinsmen, for that more faintly than was fit for men, namely for their being Scotsmen and of the blood royal, they did bewail the unfortunate success of the war.") "Laureate" work as it is, it has genuine feeling. Indeed, it is usually in the darker moods that his lyrics are best, though there are exceptions like the lovely Hymn to Our Lady that begins *Rorate coeli desuper,* happily using the introit for the Annunciation to open a Nativity Carol like a tall painted window in winter sunlight—a Strachan window with silver lights in it.

Rorate celi desuper!
  Hevinis distill zour balmy schouris,
For now is rissin the bricht day ster
  Fro the rois Mary, flour of flouris.
  The cleir Sone, quhome no clud devouris
Surmounting Phebus in the est,
  Is cumin of his hevinly touris,
Et nobis Puer natus est.

The companion *Ballat of Our Lady* is perhaps less lovely, though it is a marvellous tour de force as metre. It has not the organ-roll of

Dame du ciel, régente terrienne,
Emperière des infernaux palus:

it is in fact the equivalent of the crazy richness of decoration in Roslin Chapel, but like Roslin it is not "pretty:" there is an arrogant vigour under the wild intricacy.

Haile, qwene serene, haile, maist amene,
  Haile, hevinlie hie empryss.
Haile, schene, vnseyne with carnale eyne,
  Haile, rois of paradys.
Haile, clene, bedene, ay till conteyne,
  Haile, fair fresche flour-de-lyce.
Haile, grene daseyne, haile, fro the splene,
  Of Jhesu genetrice.
    Ave Maria, gratia plena,
  Thow bair the Prince of pryss,
Our teyne to meyne, and ga betweyne,
  Ane hevinlie oratrice.

These are not his only "divine" poems, though they are the best known, and *Rorate coeli* is perhaps the most beautiful. In his older years, perhaps when the shock of Flodden had sobered him and turned his mind towards the *Summa rerum,* he made a *Ballat of the Passioun of Christ,* a fine thing, nowise conventional, that marches through stark steady detail of vision, like a Flemish painting, with a deep sense in it of pity and of contrition, rising to a grave hope in the Resurrection, to be ratified in the Communion of Easter.

With greiting glaid be than come Grace,
  With wourdis sweit saying to me,
Ordane for Him ane resting place,
  That is so werie wrocht for the.
  The Lord within this dayis thrie
    Sall law undir thy lyntell bou,
  And in thy hous sall herbrit be
    The blissit Salvator Jesu.

Among the more serious of the "lay" lyrics, there is a bitter grace in the song to a lady who has no rue in the garden of her beauties, but as far as love-poetry goes, Dunbar's best outside the *Targe* is the *débat* of *The Merle and the Nichtingale,* who hold the poetic equivalent of the formal academic disputes the flytings parodied, this time between sacred and profane love. The matter is conventional, though it does not sound insincere. The form has nothing second-hand about its use of the familiar octave, and the conclusion, where the two sing together, has something of the harmonic quality of the bird-song in *The Thrissil and the Rois.* One hears it again in the piece that has some of his sincerest feeling in it, the Ash Wednesday bird-song with the famous

Come nevir yet May sa fresche and grene
But Januar come als wode and kene.
Wes nevir sic drowth but anes cam rain.
All erdly joy returnis in pane.

He revolts at times, worldling though he is, against "the wavering of this wrechit warld of sorrow." Sometimes there is a reconciliation, as in the famous *Meditatioun in Wyntir.* But it is never a very deep or lasting reconciliation. He was a man of his age, intensely conscious of the black gulf of nothing that stretched around its violent opulence and with little hold on the ultimate Sense of the Cross to bridge its dark night. He knows, as the rest know—the remembrance of it is passionate and recurrent—that "thy pomp shall go down to the grave, and the noise of thy viols, the worm be spread under thee, and the worm cover thee." They could not but see the skull behind the beauty, yet could not sit easily enough to mortality to accept it, as the true Middle Age had done, and reach out beyond. There is a grim and profound sense of evanescence in the sombre procession of the dead that is perhaps his most famous piece of work, where all his jewellery of rhythm and colour subdue themselves to a stark grey onward movement, like the vaulting of a crypt. It is not the defiant fantasy of the *danse macabre,* but a march of hooded shadows that have been men.

The dirge of dead poets that is its epilogue was grim enough for Dunbar, "quhen he wes seik." Our history has made it grimmer still, for out of twenty-five poets that he mentions, how many mean anything to a modern Scot? Of five, indeed—and he speaks of them with praise—not a single letter of their work is left, and more than half the rest are only shadows.

In that world of ghosts, the two others that are clearest in that generation are Walter Kennedy of the *Flyting* with Dunbar, and Gavin Douglas, Bishop of Dunkeld. And one of these is as much a *memento mori* as the lost men, Heriot and Traill and Ross and Stobo. Kennedy was a man of family, and a scholar, Master of Arts of Glasgow, where he served as examiner in 1481. He was a figure at the brilliant court of a king still Invictissimus: Douglas—no mean judge—puts him above Dunbar, as "the greit Kennedie." But scarcely a linc is left of him but his share in the *Flyting*—and what would Dunbar's be as sample of Dunbar? We know that he could write with vigour, and his *Prais of Age,* a sober acquiescent elegiac, shows that flyting was not his only mood. But whether he may have written a *Goldyn Targe . . . Autant en emporte ly vens.* He may have lived to see Chepman and Myllar print, but even much later it was the common habit of court-poets, in all countries, to circulate their works in MS. and print only when their friends took to mangling what they copied. "Literary" literature, at any time, appeals to only a small proportion of a nation. In a country whose total population was just about that of the modern City of London in working hours—that is, a million—that proportion, even if relatively high, is numerically small. And the court of the Stewarts was very much, by the time the monasteries were degenerate, the cultural centre of Scotland. Even the Highland gentry came about it: one of my forebears, whose habitat was a far cry beyond Lochow, was on James's Privy Council. The war on the arts that was so soon to follow had a very vulnerable enemy.

Gavin Douglas is much less shadowy. In fact, we know more of him, as a man, than we do of Dunbar, and we have at least the greater part of his work, which places him among the traditional major Four of the middle Stewarts. He was an important person, a Red Douglas—a son of Archibald Bell-the-Cat, no less, so that it is scarcely surprising that Erasmus comments on his regal dignity of bearing. He was born under James III, about 1475, graduated at St Andrews, became a priest, held charges in the North-east and in the Lothians, became Provost of St Giles and a freeman of Edinburgh, and seems to have had a peaceful and honourably successful career in the Church and in letters, until middle age, when Flodden threw him into the storms of James V's minority. As a Lord of the Council of Regency he helped the Queen Dowager's marriage with Angus his nephew. It made him Bishop of Dunkeld, with a promise, never kept, of the Primacy: but Albany's return from France couped the Douglas creel, and sent Douglas, with Angus and the Queen, into exile. He died of plague in 1522, at the court of his niece-in-law's brother, and was buried in the Royal Chapel of the Savoy, as became a grand-uncle of the Margaret Douglas who was more than once proclaimed heir to the English throne, to which her grandson in fact was to succeed. His epitaph is *Patria sua exul.*

The only work we know definitely for his consists of two poems in the pageant-allegory tradition, *King Hart* and *The Palice of Honour,* and his remarkable translation of Vergil, the first in verse in either form of English. He translated also the *Remedium Amoris,* but this is lost: he is also said, on rather doubtful authority, to have written certain *Comoediae Sacrae,* but if he ever did, they have disappeared.

The Palice is a dream of the difficult path to true glory, and the less elaborate *King Hart* sees the Heart of Man as a king in his castle, with a suggestion of the tumultuous Stewart minorities in the courtiers, Strength, Wantonness, Disport, and so forth, who attempt to control him. They are court-pieces in the aureate tradition, but although their morality sounds sincere enough, they have not the glittering beauty of Dunbar. None the less, there are strokes of fine imaginative quality in things like the picture of King Hart's castle, the contrast of the feasting within and the salt sour water circling it about. There is considerable dramatic sense, too, in the handling of the narrative, and its figures are given a certain concreteness of personality. In his method of handling allegory he recalls Spenser so strongly that it seems probable the latter was his pupil: the *Palice* was printed in London in 1553, and Douglas's reputation in England was considerable, so that the younger poet must have known him . . . must have liked him, too, for there is real poetry in Douglas, of a kind and quality by no means common in the English poets in the century-and-three-quarters between Spenser and his greatest master, Chaucer. Sackville, in fact, is the only Englishman of the period one can put beside him, and Sackville is admittedly one of Spenser's models. But the general artistic method of the *Faerie Queene* is closer to *King Hart* than to *The Mirror for Magistrates.*

The deeper poetic qualities of Douglas's work show to more advantage, in his *Eneidos.* His version of the famous passage in Book VI will serve as example:

> Thay walkit furth so derk oneath thay wist
> Quhidder thay went amyddis dim schadowis thare,
> Quhare evir is nicht, and nevir licht dois repair,
> Throwout the waste dungeoun of Pluto king,
> Thay roid boundis and the gousty ring,
> Siklyke as quha wald throw thik woodis wend,
> In obscure licht quhare none may nat be kend,
> As Jupiter the king etherial
> With erdis skug hidis the hevynnys al,
> And the mirk nicht with her vysage grey
> From every thing has reft the hew away.

The translation itself is notable enough: perhaps it northernises Vergil to some extent, gives him a certain colour of something like *Beowulf.* (But Vergil, after all, was not a Latin.) He does not achieve the Vergilian music, however. His couplets are competent, but they have no more chant than Pope's—much less indeed, than his own rhyme-royal in *King Hart*: his visual imagination is stronger than his auditory. It appears, very notably, in the famous interludes between the books, which are the best of his original work, and show him not only a poet but a pioneer, in more than the great group of Renaissance translators. He is the first poet in our language to take landscape in itself and for itself as a subject—not merely a setting for a subject—of poetic emotion. The quality and the reality of the emotion—his own, with no tradition to guide or arouse it—show in the famous summer night-piece of the Thirteenth Prologue:

> Yondir doun dwinis the evin sky away,
> And vpspringis the brycht dawing of the day,
> Intill ane other place nocht far in sondir,
> Quhilk to behald was pleasans and half wondir.

The late W. P. Ker, that teacher *valde deflendus,* says of it: "He sees a new thing in the history of the world . . . and in naming it he gives the interpretation, also, the spirit of poetry: pleasance and half wonder." The Seventh Prologue, of Winter, is perhaps more famous, and as description more original.

> Bewtie wes lost, and barrand schew the landis.
> With frostis haire ourfret the feildis standis.
> Soure bitter bubbis, and the schowris snell
> Semyt on the sward ane similitude of hell,
> Reducyng to our mynd, in every steid,
> Goustly schadowis of eild and grisly deid.
> Thik drumly scuggis derknit so the hevyne,
> Dim skyis oft furth-warpit ferful levyne,
> Flaggis of fyir, and mony felloun flaw,
> Scharp soppis of sleit, and of the snipand snaw.
> The dowy diches war all donk and wait,
> The law vaillé flodderit al with spait. . . .
> Broun muris kithit thair wysnit mossy hewe. . . .
> The wynd maid wayfe the reid weyd on the dyke. . . .
> The grund stude barrand, widderit, dosk, and grey.
> Wide-quhair with fors so Eolus schouttis schyll
> In this congealit sessoune scharp and chyll,
> The callour air, penetrative and pure,
> Dasyng the bluide in every creature,
> Made seik warm stovis, and beyn fyris hot,
> In double garment clad and wylycoat,
> With mychty drink, and meytis confortive,
> Agayn the storme wyntre for to strive.

This is not new to us. But it *was* quite new. Douglas is the first poet in any form of the language deliberately to paint wild weather—indeed to paint landscape on any considerable scale—for its own sake, to find the aesthetic pleasure in it as such, not merely as the appropriate setting for some thrill of adventure among wildness. He is thus a figure of cardinal importance in the development of all nature-poetry, not only in English. (And after the Gulf, it was a Scotsman, James Thomson, the forerunner of the eighteenth-century Risorgimento, who recovered that note and brought it into England, making it one of the main elements in the great Romantic movement that was to colour the literature of Europe.) Once, too, as I, or rather Ker, have just said, he states in a line the very core of that movement. And he brought Vergil into our language, not as a remote enchanter or a distant quarry for tales, but as a piece of literature. It is not an inconsiderable achievement for a bishop-diplomat of an age in the main fundamentally unpoetic. None the less, although he is the dawn of that Renaissance we were never to possess, he is, as artist, less considerable than Dunbar. His verse is rougher, less finished, less professional, and his mass of observation, as close and true as it is, does sometimes overload and blur his design.

There is, by the way, an interesting point about his language. Perhaps because he was an exile, he calls it "Scottis." He is the first to use the word in that sense. Dunbar and Henryson—Barbour for that matter—do not write the same language as Chaucer, and presumably were aware of the fact, as Mr Hergesheimer is aware that a Scot or an Englishman takes his luggage by railway while he takes his baggage by railroad, and (quite rightly) considers both idioms correct for the country of their respective use. So Dunbar considers Chaucer's speech and his own both forms of "Inglis"—and Lindsay, writing a generation later, but before the anglicising movement begun by Knox, calls Douglas himself "of our *Inglis* rhetorike the rose." In practice, of course, the patriotic poet tries no tariff measures of vocabulary. Like his brethren, he took his wealth where he found it. If no native word was to hand, he imported one—French, Latin, English, or Scandinavian, "as the Romans did Greek." The analogy happens to be Douglas' own, when he had to apologise to his purist conscience. The language in fact was in the later fifteenth century passing into the almost violent stage of growth that English in England was to know a little later, in preparation for the great Elizabethans. But Scotland had Knox and Melville for Marlowe and Spenser, and they tickled her muses othergates than the latter.

Douglas outlived Dunbar, and is not in that ghost-procession of dead makaris, who drift, *da morte disfatti . . . come d'autunno le foglie,* in the rear of Dunbar's lament, pitiful echoes of the court of a king who so loved music and the gracious arts. They were, for the opening sixteenth century, the conspicuous names of the last century and a quarter, the men who, to a chief poet of his day, were the memorable figures of that time in Scottish letters, or at any rate enough to conjure up these, for the list is not necessarily a librarian's catalogue: we know it is incomplete, for one of the most conspicuous of all, the poet great-grandfather of Dunbar's chief patron, is omitted, although earlier names are there.

Three of the twenty-five are distinguished foreigners. "The noble Chaucer, of makaris flour," has the preeminence that was his due, and the English Gower and Lydgate, fashionable and successful men of letters in their day, and the former a writer of considerable talent, go with him. Then come twenty-two of his own fellow countrymen,

> Throwout the waste dungeoun of Pluto king.

Barbour and Blind Harry, Henryson and Wyntoun and (if he is Hucheon) Sir Hew of Eglinton, are less "bereavit" than the rest, though we know for a fact that about half of Barbour's work is lost. But as for the others . . . these ghosts are all but voiceless. Ettrick and Heriot, Lockhart, Ross, and "gude gentill Stobo" have been sunk without trace. They may have been responsible for some of the anonymous verse that survives, and is often of beauty. Some of the rest are scarcely less unsubstantial. James Affleck *may* be the author of one poem in the Selden MS. John Clerk, who like him practised "ballat-making and tragedie," is a shade more fortunate. He *may* have been the gentleman to whom Dunbar describes Andro Kennedy as leaving "Guid's braid malison and mine," and he *may* also be the author of five pieces in the Bannatyne MS.—varied, for the five include religious, amorous, and satiric-humorous. One of them is the pleasant *Wowyng of Jok and Jinny,* a lively rustic affair with a burlesque description of the tocher, in a tradition that comes down through Burns to Violet Jacob and Charles Murray. Clerk of Tranent I have spoken of already as among the last romancers. Holland was a priest, exiled to England with the Douglases. We have a political allegory of his, *The Boke of the Howlat,* but its allusions are so intricately up-to-the-minute it is difficult to follow. Hay, a knight, a graduate in arts and law, and Chamberlain to Charles VII of France, wrote poems, and is one of the claimants for *Alexander,* but his known work survives only in prose, which is described elsewhere. Johnstone has one religious piece in the Bannatyne MS., and he acted plays before James IV: we know no more of him. Mersar is highly praised as a poet of love, and was still famous a generation later, but all that is left of him appears to be one grim recension, in the Maitland MS., of the old "Earth upon earth" poem, on the text

> Eird gois apone eird glitterand in gold,
> yit sall eird go to eird sonar nor he wold,

and three pieces in Bannatyne, one a warning to women against lightness, in a curious hitched metre, one another warning against the wiles of inconstant men, and the third a sermon in verse on the Whole Duty of Lovers: it is pleasantly sententious, but none of the four suggest a technique on the level of Dunbar's. Of the two Rules all that we know is where they lived, that they were good fellows, that one of them is presumably the author of a religious satire in the Bannatyne and Maitland MSS., and that he, or the other one, wrote a rather endearing piece of invective, *The Cursing of Schir John Ruill apone the Stelaris of his Foulis*: the two are not much as the total "remains" of a brace of poets. Brown is so vague that there has been serious argument as to whether he was a man or merely a misprint: Bannatyne reads "tane Broun" where Maitland has "done roun." But one religious poem in the former's collection is attributed to him. Shaw, the last to die, has at least an identity, as the son of James III's Ambassador to Denmark—in fact, a person of some social standing: but all that remains of his writings is one shrewd satire, on the text "Knaw courtis, and wynd, has oftsys vareit." And as for Dunbar himself, it is true that we have what may be most of his work. But if four manuscripts had chanced to be lost before 1834, in three centuries of assorted (and Scottish) history, he would be almost as ghostly as most of his neighbours. And he was the laureate of a brilliant court, at one of the pinnacles of our history, very little more than four centuries ago.

To these ghosts may be added Prior Henry of Kelso, who *floruit* about 1500 and is said to have made a translation of Rutilius' *De Re Rustica,* and a Greek poem on Our Lady for Lorenzo de' Medici; and one or two other names which appear in Bannatyne, and may belong more or less to this time. A patriotic poem, *the Ring* (règne) *of the Roy Robert,* describes the pointed retort of Robert III to a claim for homage made by Henry IV of England, who is forcibly reminded both of past treaties and of that habit of his own country, of being perpetually under foreign rulers, that in fact is one of the curiosities of its history. It is ascribed to one Dean David Steill, but we know no more of him, nor even whether his deanery was ecclesiastical or municipal: one may guess the latter, as two love-poems are ascribed to *Steil* in the Bannatyne MS. As Queen Caroline said, however, "Cela n'empêche pas," at that period: but there may have been another man of the same name, and in any case, no one is born in orders. Lichtoun, a monk, has a couple of poems in Bannatyne, one with the stately opening, "O mortal man, remember nicht and day," not ill followed up, the other a rather tedious nonsense-piece, remarkably like some ultra-modern poetry of the nineteen-twenties. The printer's advertisement of *The Thrie Talis of the Thrie Prestis of Peblis,* three "moral stories" resembling in manner the more decent ones in the *Decameron,* and printed in 1603, though written, apparently, before 1491, mentions a "delectabill discourse," *Biblo,* which is lost. No reference to it has been traced anywhere else.

On the assumptions of an age that believed more fully in the trousered god Progress than in the Trinity, the fact that these men and their works are lost shows that they could not have mattered. But the exquisite work of Alexander Scott survived precariously for centuries in one MS. copy, that might have vanished in any siege or spring-cleaning or fit of religious fervour that happened to come to one of its various owners. And if all but one of my works were to be lost I think I should like to choose which was to survive. One wonders how blindly the poppy has been scattered. (pp. 70-109)

Agnes Mure Mackenzie, "The Last of the Middle Ages," in her An Historical Survey of Scottish Literature to 1714, *Alexander Maclehose & Co., 1933, pp. 61-109.*

A. M. Kinghorn

[Kinghorn is an English critic and educator who has written extensively on medieval Scottish literature. In the following essay, he examines works by the group of poets whom he asserts should be known as the "mediaeval makars," rather than Scottish Chaucerians. He suggests that, though their methods differed, the "makars" shared the objective of establishing Scots as a literary language.]

Scots poetry of the fifteenth and sixteenth centuries presents both linguistic and literary problems. The term "Middle Scots" itself is one used by scholars to describe the language of written communication in the Scottish Lowlands from the reign of James I until James VI's accession to the English throne. Nineteenth-century philologists, such as W. W. Skeat, lent authority to the tradition, still disseminated in the Schools, that claimed Middle Scots as a literary language never actually spoken. Modern studies of the work of the makars indicate that their poetic vocabulary is made up of at least three levels of usage: "aureate" language; the language of the educated classes; and the language of the peasants. Dunbar's "The Merle and the Nychtingaill" provides only one instance of the combination of all three in the same poem. He and his contemporaries wrote for an educated audience in and around the Court and aimed at creating a literary language capable of supporting the weight of meaning which a social poetry demanded. Their medium, reinforced by direct borrowings from modern French and colloquial Latin—both of which were part of the vocabulary of every literate Scotsman—was certainly not remote from popular speech. In effect, their object was the same as Chaucer's: to rival French as a language of literature, just as Chaucer tried to do in English.

This similarity of aim has given rise to another historical *mésalliance:* the unqualified application of the term "Scottish Chaucerians" to the representatives of the literary period 1470-1550 in Scotland. Although the poets themselves gave formal recognition to Chaucer, calling him their "maistere dere" and the "rose of rethoris all," in much the same manner as Spenser later acknowledged Chaucer as his master, it was really inspiration, not instruction, which the Scots poets (and for that matter Spenser also) received from Chaucer. Chaucer himself assimilated from France the dream-allegory of *Le Roman de la Rose,* the *fabliau* or short humorous satirical tale of which the beast-fable is one form, and from Italy the social narrative poem of Boccaccio with its Southern warmth and delight in the more voluptuous side of human nature. Yet we do not call Chaucer an "imitator" of the French or Italian traditions which he modified and which contributed to the making of the English literary tradition. Thus when we look for "Chaucerian" characteristics in the poetry of James I, Henryson, Dunbar, and Gawain Douglas, we are really seeking the nature of many dissimilar elements under one artificial heading, since, apart from the obvious linguistic and conventional similarities, found mainly in James I's *Kingis Quair,* "Chaucerianism" is a spiritual quality which transcends artifice and defies definition in simple terms.

A similar objection can be made to the word "Scottish." When we refer to "Scottish" literature we mean the literature produced by lowland Scotland as distinct from Gaelic literature. The Scots language is a development from the Northern dialect of Middle English which did not occur until after 1400, so that there is no difference between the dialect of John Barbour, who was strongly anti-English, and that of Lawrence Minot, who was strongly anti-Scots. In fact, the lowland Scots themselves referred to their tongue as "Inglis," and though Henryson exhibits a transitional difference between English and Scots it was not until 1512 that Gawain Douglas actually took pains to call his language "Scottis" as distinct from "Inglis." What is meant by the word "Scottish," therefore, has to do less with language than with national character and topography. An anti-sentimental hardheadedness and a sense of the grimmer realities of life emerge as positive qualities in the poetry of the "makars." Moreover, the background setting of their works is not one of lush Italian or French landscape or of any imported Mediterranean scene. When Henryson writes about Orpheus' descent to the underworld, the topography of Hell is distinctly that of Scotland:

> Syne our a mure, with thornis thik and scherp,
> Wepand allone, a wilsum way he went,
> And had nocht bene throw suffrage of his harp,
> With fell pikis he had bene schorne and schent;

while Dunbar frequently mentions Scottish place names and landmarks. Though David Daiches' statement [in *Robert Burns,* 1952] that "the poetry of the mediaeval Scottish poets is the only mediaeval poetry in Europe which consistently keeps its eye on the poet's native landscape" ignores, for example, early Welsh poetry such as the Mabinogion, it nevertheless expresses a dominant characteristic of Middle Scots poetry. With the above in mind, one hopes that the term "Scottish Chaucerians" will disappear and "mediaeval makars" take its place.

The Kingis Quair is the most challenging example of the poems attributed to the makars. It is a work of no single language, it poses many problems, and it may not even be a Scottish poem, although the unique manuscript is the work of Scottish scribes of about 1500. It is traditionally attributed to James I (*c.* 1423), who is supposed to have written it during his imprisonment in England; but there are too many echoes in it of late fifteenth-century English poetry to make such evidence as exists of his authorship entirely acceptable. The theme of the work is unusual for its time; it pretends to autobiography and it deals with a husband's love for his own wife, which, in the mediaeval tradition of courtly love, was almost a discreditable emotion. C. S. Lewis said [in *The Allegory of Love,* 1951] that in the *Quair* "the poetry of marriage at last emerges from the traditional poetry of adultery" for the author seems to be describing his own love and, unlike Chaucer, obtrudes himself throughout the poem. His originality lies in the use of allegory and other conventional devices to celebrate a real courtship and not, as was usual, a fanciful, idealized and impersonal one. The color, rhythm, and richness look forward to Spenser's "Epithalamion" and even to Keats and the pre-Raphaelites; and the lyrical impact is much more intense and concentrated than that of Chaucer. The music of nature, the coloration of the fishes, beasts, and trees, and the uninhibited revelations of the writer recall the English secular songs of the fourteenth century.

Nevertheless, the *Quair* bears the closest resemblance of all the works of the "makars" to Chaucer's style of composition; but since all mediaeval poets shared common conventions, wrote and learned from the same works, and were educated to the same habits of mind—of which allegory was the normal expression—this poem cannot be considered simply on one level as an imitation of Chaucer's allegorical method by a writer with a talent for *pastiche.* Its fidelity to truth of experience communicates a vitality which the works of Chaucer's direct imitators do not possess, and it culminates, not in the time-honored erotic hangover of *Le Roman de la Rose,* but in marriage, now viewed in retrospect with continued satisfaction:

> Quhich has my hert for evir sett abufe
> In perfyte joy, that nevir may remufe
> Bot onely deth.

This personal note was continued by Robert Henryson, said to have been a schoolmaster in Dunfermline, who was not mastered by Chaucerian diction and was an original adaptor of various literary traditions. Much of his work is infused with a genial but retiring quality (as presumably befits the scholastic life) and, although in terms of quantity he did not write much, in emotional content he surpassed his contemporary makars and did not shy away from realistic treatment of a tragic theme. His masterpiece is "The Testament of Cresseid," in which his direct debts to Chaucer are limited to the skeleton of the plot itself and to the use of the English poet as a model for rhetorical composition. Whereas Chaucer translated and developed Boccaccio's *Il Filostrato* in order to make his *Troilus and Criseyde,* Henryson took up the old story at the point where Chaucer left off and applied his talents to the creation of an original imaginative work. Cresseid has broken the moral and the theological laws and her sin is punished by the physical affliction of leprosy, but through her eventual repentance and her testament relinquishing earthly things she is permitted to die in the purified state of an aspirant to the conventual life. Whereas Chaucer saw the real values of life as religious and makes his Troilus see human efforts as wasteful. Henryson promotes sympathy for Cresseid's miserable lot on this earth but the stern moralist is always in control and, as a matter of principle, displays little sympathy for the shortcomings of fallen humanity. Chaucer's inconclusiveness may be closer to life, but Henryson's strong and unyielding sense of justice in the Platonic sense of giving each man his due is aesthetically more satisfying.

The Morall Fabillis, written by Henryson in about 1485, are in a lighter vein. They are rehandled versions of *Aesop's Fables* but include others, such as "The Fox, the Wolf and the Cadger," which may possibly have been his own original invention. The heavy, moral Aesop is transformed in his hands and a fresh cast is given to the old stories, which now become the vehicles for political and social commentary. Historical investigations into the subject matter of the fables suggest that they were closely connected with the vicissitudes of the times. "The Taill of the Uponlandis Mous, and the Burges Mous" stands out as illustrative of Henryson's ability to make the mice speak and act like human beings while at the same time preserving their animal traits. "The Taill of the Fox, the Wolf and the Cadger" plays off human and animal qualities against each other, and "The Taill of the Wolf and the Lamb," upholding a thinly disguised political allegory, points out that real justice is to be found only in heaven—on earth might is right, in spite of the civil law. "The Taill of the Scheip and the Doig" draws a realistic picture of the effects of tyranny on the powerless. In such pieces Henryson is anticipating the feeling behind Lyndesay's *Ane Pleasant Satyre of the Thrie Estaitis,* first performed in 1540, which communicates its author's sympathy for the common man. The *Moralitas* following each tale does nothing to detract from the human sympathy in the narrative itself. As R. L. Mackie observes: "the poet's heart goes out to the weak and foolish, the victims of injustice and cruelty, whether they be mice or sheep, or little birds hovering above the fowler's snare, or 'the puir commons, that daily are oppressed be tyrant men.' "

Henryson's language is a good deal less "literary" than that of other makars, in the *Fabillis* at least, and is more clearly rooted in the speech of the peasantry. Unlike the others, he was not strictly of the Court circle and is often thought to have been little affected by Chaucer, though such a view fails to take into account the more subtle direct influences of tone, rhetoric, and verse-formation, as well as the art of reflecting his own personality in his poems without seeming to do so, itself a strong characteristic of Chaucer. The *Fabillis* emphasize character and action rather than setting, for Henryson gives only slender hints of the Northern landscape; but his straightforward narrative and colloquial dialogue are squarely in the native Scots tradition. Though he may lack the versatility and the glitter of his fellow poet William Dunbar, Henryson reveals a more profound poetic character that is less prone to enslavement by the wizardry of words:

> In hamelie language and in termes rude
> Me neidis wryte, for quhy of Eloquence
> Nor Rethorike, I never Understude.

Dunbar affords us the clearest indication of what is really meant by "Chaucerian." Chaucer invented a poetic diction when he translated *Le Roman de la Rose* and Dunbar is fully conscious of that; his "aureate style" and, later, Gawain Douglas' "sugurit sang" is the result of the Scots poets' own experimentation with European rhetorical conventions and Chaucerian modifications of them. In his freedom of expression Dunbar is lively and modern, and his ability to turn his hand to almost any kind of verse on almost any subject makes him the first Scottish poet to impress his readers with a dynamic mental agility. He jumps from one topic to another, writing comic lyrics like "On His Heid-ake," parodies like "The Sowtar and Tailyouris War," serious lyrics on the transience of human life, devotional lyrics, allegories like "The Goldyn Targe" or "The Thrissil and the Rois," formal obsequies such as his address "To Aberdein," poems praising women and other poems chuckling ironically at women, sardonic petitions for overdue preferment, pieces which owe their inspiration to personages at the Stuart Court as, for example, "A Dance in the Quenis Chalmer" or "Of Sir Thomas Norny," macaronic compositions in the European tradition using two or three languages as "The Testament of Mr Andro Kennedy," and so on. There seems to be no limit to his versatility. When C. M. Grieve, writing in 1927, issued his manifesto for the revival of Scots language and literature in the present century, it was to Dunbar, not to Burns, that he looked for example, for in linguistic and thematic variety the former is the richest of Scots poets.

Dunbar's longest and most ambitious effort is "The Tretis of the Tua Mariit Wemen and the Wedo," a burlesque on the confession convention of the innocent fair maids of romance. In form it is not "Chaucerian" and it takes its metrical structure from the Northern English alliterative tradition of verse romances like "Rauf Coilyear," "The Cursing of Sir John Rowell," or "Colkelbie's Sow," all of which are briefly mentioned or referred to by Dunbar or by other "makars" such as Douglas or Lyndesay. Though alliterative verse did not make more than sporadic appearances in England after the Norman Conquest, it flourished once more in the middle of the fourteenth century—mainly in the West Midlands and the North, where there was a greater resistance to French influences than in the South. The alliterative measure was more dignified and magnificent than rhyming stanzas, and suited spacious heroic themes; the same qualities made it a fit medium for satire and burlesque, and in the hands of a skilled makar like Dunbar it was remarkably effective.

"The Tua Mariit Wemen and the Wedo" stresses the gulf separating appearances from reality, and the contrast is made between the outer show and the inner minds of the three women. The problem of evil beneath a fair exterior was one which occupied the Renaissance poets—particularly Shakespeare—but Dunbar was not a philosophical poet, and it is more likely that he was drawing pictures from the life of James IV's Court. Formally, the piece is a mediaeval debate among three ladies celebrating Midsummer's Eve in a garden bower, which is overheard in conventional wise by the poet eavesdropping behind a hedge. The garden is the earthly paradise of the Rose, and the ladies, pure heroines of romance; Dunbar describes them in lavish terms and shows their familiarity with the diction of *amour courtois* and with the art of adultery, along with the virtues of secrecy and "pity" so dear to the heart of mediaeval convention. The reader soon discovers, however, that despite their superficial courtliness, the trio regard marriage as no more than licensed harlotry. Their attitude has to be considered against the background of mediaeval society, in which the giving of dowries played an important role in the arrangement of marriages and in which the wife was often made the sole executrix of her deceased husband's estate. This state of affairs affected not only the nobility and the bourgeosie, but even poor girls, who sought to acquire a suitable dowry through the receiving of alms. The impact of Dunbar's satire is for this reason probably more savage and less comic in its effect in this age than it was in his own time, and although for the modern reader the rose-garden maidens are golddiggers (of a type presumably common in James's materialistic Court), the coarseness of their sentiments and conversation must be considered against its appropriate social background and not judged in accordance with late Renaissance poetic idealization of the married state.

Dunbar's poetic energy is best revealed in "The Flyting of Dunbar and Kennedy," a cursing-match in the course of which Dunbar argues for the "Inglis" against the "Yrysch" or Gaelic as the national tongue, and which depends for its success not upon any intellectual argument, but on the composer's ability to maintain a succession of vituperative words so that the effect becomes comic. Not only Dunbar, but also Lyndesay and Montgomerie wrote flytings; Burns made notes for one, and there are even one or two contemporary examples of the genre. It takes its source from the mediaeval pulpit and rudely burlesques clerical rhetoric. As such, it is a descendant of the Goliardic Latin poems which, under the name *sermones,* and using the same techniques, castigated the corruptions of the age. The influence of the pulpit is evident in the expressions of Henryson, Dunbar, Douglas, Lyndesay, and other makars who were in holy orders or took a keen interest in ecclesiastical affairs during the years of polemic preceding the Reformation. This tendency emerges, not only in its extreme form as flyting, but also in a certain morbidity and obsession with the ugly and repellent. We see it in Henryson's "Thre Deid Pollis" (death's heads):

> Behold oure heidis thre,
> Oure holkit ene, oure peilit pollis bair;
> As ye ar now, Into this warld we wair,
> Als fresche, als fair, als lusty to behald;
> Quhan thow lukis on this suth examplair
> Off thy self, man, thow may be richt unbald.

and in Dunbar's "Of Manis Mortalitie":

> Thocht now thow be maist glaid of cheir,
> Fairest and plesandest of port,
> Yit may thow be, within ane yeir,
> Ane ugsum, uglye tramort,

with its sinister refrain,

> Quod tu in cinerem reverteris.

The theme of life as but a brief pathway to the fearsome and permanent state of death was common during the Middle Ages and Renaissance; the "Ubi sunt?" tradition permeated both ascetic and poetic meditation. Villon's

> Mais où sont les neiges d'antan?

and Dunbar's

> Quhat is this lyfe bot ane straucht way to deid?

reveal one ever-present side of their poetic characters. Dunbar's inclination to make hay while the sun shines is tempered by a sad musing over life's disappointments and the primitive image of "timor mortis."

His serious works, often glossed over by commentators in favor of his comic or mercurial verses, transcend the Stewart Court and his own personal difficulties within its confines. "Of the Nativitie of Christ" combines the aureate and literary styles and is a masterpiece of sheer incision of language, anticipating, at the same time, the Renaissance symmetry of "Epithalamion." "On the Resurrection of Christ," a hymn for the morning of Easter Sunday, is a fierce demonstration of poetic energy:

> Done is a battell on the dragon blak,
> Our campioun Chryst confountet hes his force:
> The yettis of hell ar brokin with a crak,
> The signe triumphall rasit is of the croce.

Here we have Dunbar's etching of an allegory in swift strokes, appealing to the mind's eye as well as to the ear, and looking forward to Bunyan's description of Christian's combat with Apollyon.

"Meditatioun in Wyntir" is an intensely personal lyric by the mediaeval, rather than the Renaissance, Dunbar. It seems to have been directly inspired by the gloom of the Scottish winter which, by taking away the poet's will to write "sangis, ballattis, and . . . playis," has prompted him to capture his downcast mood and to make a poetic confession of his nocturnal fears. The external transience of the court and the uncertainty of his own future there hold but a passing interest for him; far more pressing is the account he will have to give of his life after death:

> And than sayis Age, "My freind, cum neir,
> And be not strange, I the requier;
> Cum brodir, by the hand me tak,
> Remember thow hes compt to mak
> Off all thi tyme thow spendit heir."

Death's appearance in the following stanza is something of an anti-climax, but for Dunbar it is the concrete symbol of all his fears, from which there is no escape. The best that can be made of this situation is to look forward to the vivid enjoyments and ephemeral delights of the warm season. This poem brings us closer to the real Dunbar than do either his formal allegories or his wayward burlesques.

[When] we look for "Chaucerian" characteristics in the poetry of James I, Henryson, Dunbar, and Gawain Douglas, we are really seeking the nature of many dissimilar elements under one artificial heading, since, apart from the obvious linguistic and conventional similarities, found mainly in James I's *Kingis Quair,* "Chaucerianism" is a spiritual quality which transcends artifice and defies definition in simple terms.

—A. M. Kinghorn

Gawain Douglas, Bishop of Dunkeld, wrote two allegorical poems, "The Palice of Honour" and "King Hart," in the conventional manner which are interesting chiefly for their promise of better things to come. They should be considered as trial runs, deliberately contrived experiments with stock material, which reveal the writer's command of language and his store of classical learning. Douglas' reputation rests on his translation of Virgil's *Aeneid* into Scots, completed in 1513, shortly before Flodden and the virtual extinction of the flower of Scotland. Because it was produced in a period of political and linguistic transition it has—until recently, at any rate—been regarded as a literary curiosity and as a part of literary history rather than of literature itself. It has been praised by critics of the "beauties and blemishes" school for its exuberant richness and Spenserian pictorial qualities, and then passed over as a quaint relic of the late Middle Ages in Scotland.

Douglas wrote it under the spell of a righteous patriotism, at a time when military and political threats from England were growing rapidly. His immediate object was to stabilize and enrich his native language which, as we have noted before, he called "Scottis," and to give it eminence as a European literary medium fitted, like Latin, for heroic utterance. To the existing Scots vocabulary he added Latin, French, and Northern English words—in fact, he created a Lallans with much the same character and aims as modern Lallans has, and demonstrated that it had enough scope and power to bridge the gap between Roman and mediaeval Scots civilization. Far from being influenced by English poetry, the Scots *Aeneid* influenced English poets. The Earl of Surrey tried his hand at rendering the second and fourth books of the *Aeneid* into English. Much of the result, which appeared in 1557, was directly plagiarized—even to the extent of whole passages—from the Douglas version. An edition of the latter, printed by Thomas Ruddiman in 1710, served as a Jacobite patriotic symbol in Edinburgh after the 1707 Union, and Allan Ramsay called himself "Gawain Douglas" while he was a member of the "Easy Club" for the revival of Scots language and literature. The strongly nationalist atmosphere which has always surrounded Douglas' great work has largely inhibited and frustrated attempts to examine it on purely literary criteria.

C. S. Lewis is not prevented by national ties from taking an objective view of the work [in *English Literature in the Sixteenth Century,* 1954] and remarks that the Scots *Aeneid* is a mediaeval poem in its own right, written in a courtly medium which loses its "quaint" associations as soon as the modern reader finds himself able to make certain mental adjustments. One adjustment is concerned with the language itself—Scots has since become a *patois,* and critics are prejudiced against it as a literary medium. Words like "gudeman" or "braes" have taken on their rustic associations since the translation was made—in sixteenth-century Scotland Douglas' vocabulary did not bear the stamp of the provincial. The other adjustment which Lewis recommends is that the reader forget his schoolroom training in the classics, with all its insistence upon the solemnity and decorum of the ancient world and its writings. The briskness of Douglas' version will then seem less undignified and unheroic to readers brought up on notions that Virgil represents "the grand style." Lewis suggests that many lines in the free translation "so pierce to the very heart of the *Aeneid* " that the whole effect is one of a freshness lacking in later standard English versions like Dryden's, and that it may well be that the modern world has less affinity with the classical world than humanist tradition would have us believe.

Apart from the actual rendering, there is an extra book—translated not, of course, from Virgil, but from a fifteenth-century continuation by Maffeo Vegio—and "Prologues" to each of the thirteen books. The *Prologues* are original additions, and many of them tell us about the poet himself and reflect his intimate views on life and literature. The language of the *Prologues* is more directly related to the aureate diction of Dunbar's allegorical and devotional poetry than to the language of the actual translation, but the sentiments owe little to the study. In *Prologue* VII, Douglas is expressing what he himself felt about the Scottish winter:

Widequhair with fors so Eolus schouttis schyll
In this congelyt sessioune scharp and chyll,
The callour air penetrative and puire
Dasyng the bluide in every creature,
Made seik warm stovis, and beyne fyris hoyt,
In double garmont cled and wyly-coyt
Wyth mychty drink and meytis confortive,
Agayne the storme wyntre for to strive,

although, as might be expected of a Scot writing in Scotland, his description of summer in *Prologue* XII relies somewhat more on the resources of a scholarly vocabulary:

Mysty vapour upspringand, sweit as sens,
In smoky soppis of donk dewis wak,
Moich hailsum stovis ourheildand the slak;
The aureat fanys of hys troue soverane
With glytrand glans ourspred the occiane,
The large fludis lemand all of lycht
Bot with a blenk of his supernale sycht.

Even so, this is obviously far from being a conventional Mediterranean portrait. The Scottish countryside becomes a living, moving thing, and its seasonal changes are faithfully conveyed with a realistic attention to details and linguistic overtones which draw the reader emotionally into a "native" atmosphere.

The key to the whole work, both as a translation and as a poem in its own right, is the author's statement in the *Prologue* to Book I on the difficulties of translation. Referring to "our tongis penuritie" in comparison with the rich resources of Latin, the "maist perfyte language fyne," he says that he will not translate word for word but will instead take the advice of St. Gregory and of Horace and give a free rendering. As a translator he is a "Renaissance man," regarding the classics as literature rather than as the mystically inspired productions of genius akin to divinity. Emotionally, as a poet, he is mediaeval Christian and wholly in the tradition of linguistic experimentation in Scots. Temperamentally, he is a Scots idealist in the patriotic tradition, intellectually aware of the classical peak of culture and language to which his own civilization might aspire. As a result of the work of Henryson and Dunbar, Douglas found the Scots language in a state of considerable fluidity, and his translation is poetically as well as academically original. The *Prologues,* in fact, show far less poetic originality than the translation does. As C. S. Lewis observes: "He is not always great in the great passages; but he has often rendered the sublimity of Virgil in lines that no translator, and not many original poets, have surpassed." There is an effortlessness about Douglas' handling of his classical themes which Henryson, his closest relation among the makars, cannot approach without lapsing into self-consciousness. Orpheus' descent into the underworld is a studied performance compared with Aeneas' descent as translated from Book VI:

But lo! a litle before the son-rising,

The ground begouth to rummys, croyn, and
ring,
Undir thair feit, and woddy toppis hie
Of thir hillis begyn to mufe thai se;
Amang the shaddowis and the skuggis mark
The hell houndis hard thai yowll and bark,
At the cuming of the goddes Proserpyne.

The force of Douglas' rendering can be felt even more directly by stressing the gulf between his Scots version and Dryden's English version of the same passage:

nor ended till the next returning sun.
Then earth began to bellow, trees to dance,
And howling dogs in glimmering light advance,
Ere Hecate came.

The contrast between these two passages brings up the question of the blatant difference between English and Scots poetry; the trend of the former has been towards "the grand style" centuries before Arnold coined that phrase, and with a few exceptions, such as Donne and Byron, English poets have approached their task in a spirit of solemnity and have achieved expression by means of a sensuous association of words. Scots poets infuse their verse with a literary quality of another kind—the sheer quality of life, of which aesthetic ideals are but manifestations. Douglas, fulfilling the tradition of the makars, made the fullest possible use of the unadorned expressive power of the Scots language as it then was, so that his translation has strength and virility rather than the graceful suggestiveness of the Southern tradition. It is part of Scotland's tragic history that the very year in which the *Aeneid* translation was finished was the last year of her short-lived prosperity. The malleable medium which Douglas essayed to perfect as a vehicle for the long poem began to lose its *raison d'être* with the gradual decline of national independence during the sixteenth century. Though the tradition of the makars continued in the hands of a group of post-Flodden men, Lyndesay, Alexander Scott, Montgomerie, Stewart of Baldynneis, and a score of anonymous poets whose remains appear in the Bannatyne and Maitland manuscripts, by 1600 it had become a slender thing, kept alive in the court or driven underground to await the attentions of Watson and Ramsay in the early years of the eighteenth century.

Of those who followed Douglas, the only major figure is that of Lyndesay, whose name today conjures up the memory of one work, *Ane Pleasant Satyre of the Thrie Estaitis,* which has survived as a testament to its author's vivid personality. Like Dunbar before him, Lyndesay succeeded in imprinting his remarkable vigor on the reader's mind, and he has come down through the years as a representative of characteristic Protestant feeling. His activities as a courtier and diplomat during the years of decision preceding the Reformation are reflected in *The Dreme* (1527) and *The Monarche* (1552). In both of these Lyndesay is distinguished by a statesmanlike preoccupation with his country's progress; his aim was the reform of the Church and State to the detriment of the corrupt clergy and nobility and towards the improvement of the lot of the commons. Lyndesay's theme is social justice and so great was the degree of corruption in the relations between Church and State that he and other moderates were compelled to attack the existing system root and branch. His work soon reveals that its value is to be found in its modern revolutionary content and not in its form, which is superficially allegorical. His verse-satires are reformatory in intention and he has scant respect for poetic worth as such. His poetry suffers from the literary sacrifices which he made to his intense social and evangelical consciousness, but he knew exactly what he was sacrificing—he wished to write moral and critical propaganda, and any literary preoccupation was subordinated to this main aim. The personal experience of Dunbar was replaced in Lyndesay by a positive world of combative ideas. The Rose gave way to the controversialists and the personal complaint became a public one. Lyndesay wrote to be read and understood rather than to be enjoyed and, of all the makars, he was the only one whose works survived in the popular mind as a monument to pre-Reformation Scots literature.

The Dreme is a complete example of a "non-poetically" inspired poem, and it contains none of the customary references to poetical predecessors and favorable Muses. The superficial allegory does little to conceal the apocalyptic visionary character of John the Common Weill, almost a Shavian figure

Quhose rayment wes all raggit, revin, & rent;
With visage leyne, as he had fastit lent,

whom we meet for the second time in *Ane Satyre of the Thrie Estaitis.* Not since Langland's *Piers Plowman* has such a revolutionary figure come to guide a poet's Muse. John personifies Lyndesay's human feeling for the common man who ought, in the ideal Church-State relationship, to be served by both, and not, as was the case in pre-Reformation Scotland, crushed beneath their weight. Lyndesay makes John complain of the injustices done to the common people in the name of the Church and the Civil Law and *The Thrie Estaitis* emerges as a vision of the writer's ideal government. The work is political propaganda cast in dramatic verse-form, and its periodic vulgarity is an invitation to the masses. The dramatic method of communicating his democratic ideas is the root of all his verse from *The Dreme* to *The Monarche.* Lyndesay's natural bent was the drama, and his appeals are direct and factual, as, for example, in the dialogue between the Pauper and the Pardoner which bridges the two parts of *Ane Satyre:*

PAUPER. My haly father, quhat wil that pardon
cost?

PARDONER. Let se quhat mony thow bearest in
thy bag,

or in *The Testament of the Papyngo,* an unsubtle attack on ecclesiastical abuses which is essentially dramatic in spirit:

Than, wyt ye weill, my hart wes wounder sair,
For to behalde that dolent departyng,
Hir Angell fedderis fleyng in the air:
Except the hart, was left of hir no thyng.

The Monarche is his last poem and today it is a literary curiosity. Its form is indicated in the subtitle—it is "a dialogue between experience and the courtier" that prophesies the end of the world with extreme urgency. In it Lyndesay throws over all pretence to making poetry in favor of the colloquial language of straightforward communication, unornamented and bald. At the end of the *Fourth Book,* there follows an exhortation given by Experience to the courtier, in the course of which one solitary poetic passage occurs. It describes an evening scene, and might have been written by Henryson or even Douglas:

> The blysfull byrdis bownis to the treis,
> And ceissis of thare hevinlye armoneis:
> The Cornecraik in the croft, I heir hir cry;
> The bak, the Howlat, febyll of thare eis,
> For thare pastyme, now in the evinnyng fleis.

(pp. 73-88)

A. M. Kinghorn, "The Mediaeval Makars," in Texas Studies in Literature and Language, *Vol. I, Spring, 1959, pp. 73-88.*

Denton Fox

[In the essay below, Fox focuses on the major works of Henryson, Dunbar, and Douglas, discussing in particular the misconceptions that result from their designation as Scottish Chaucerians. He concludes that despite their dissimilarities, the three poets share a passion for poetic craftsmanship that unites their works.]

The term 'Scottish Chaucerians' is a traditional name which is in some respects misleading, but it does have the merit of suggesting a few basic problems. It raises first the question of who these poets are, and whether they are a sufficiently homogeneous group to be given any single label, let alone this one; then the question of in what ways, if at all, they are 'Chaucerians', or for that matter 'Scottish'.

The name has usually been applied to the Scottish poets of the fifteenth and early sixteenth centuries who wrote, at least occasionally, in the formal 'aureate' style and who inserted references to Chaucer into their poems: the author of *The Kingis Quair,* Henryson, Dunbar, Douglas, perhaps Lyndsay. But it is impossible to give the term any definite boundaries, for it could certainly be applied to the mostly anonymous predecessors and imitators of these poets. I would like arbitrarily to limit myself here to Henryson, Dunbar and Douglas, who are in several ways the central figures. They are central chronologically: all their poems were probably written during a period of less than fifty years, the most brilliant period of Scottish poetry; and they are the most representative figures, as well as the most outstanding ones. Each is a poet of a different type, and between them they exemplify most of the important kinds of poetry written in Scotland during this period, but there are also some clear and fundamental resemblances binding them together. It should be remembered, of course, that by limiting ourselves to these three poets we are neglecting a good deal of Chaucer's influence on Scottish verse. On the one hand, there is the early *Kingis Quair,* more Chaucerian if less certainly Scottish than any later poem, but a work which, except for its great merit and the spellings of its surviving manuscript, seems to belong with the English Chaucerians. Then there are the poets who came after Douglas, most notably Sir David Lyndsay. But Lyndsay and the other Scots poets of the middle of the sixteenth century wrote at a time when the Chaucerian tradition had become thoroughly naturalised. The most serious omission, perhaps, is that of the large bulk of poetry, either anonymous or by almost unknown poets, which is roughly contemporaneous with Henryson, Dunbar and Douglas. Authors' names have often counted for more than a poem's intrinsic merit: if a poem has been attributed to a well known poet (and the attributions of Middle Scots poems are frequently far from certain) it has at least been given the dubious immortality of being repeatedly edited, but the anonymous poems tend to slip into oblivion. Yet these anonymous poems are sometimes both Chaucerian and excellent: the fabliau *The Freiris of Berwick,* for instance, has justly been said to be 'above all other attempts to continue the tradition of the comic Canterbury Tales'.

The 'Scottish' part, at least, of the label 'Scottish Chaucerians' ought to be clear enough. But even this is misleading: almost all of the connotations which 'Scottish' has for a modern Englishman or American are utterly irrelevant to the Middle Scots poets. When we think of Scotland we tend to think either of post-medieval inventions—Presbyterianism, Bonnie Prince Charlie, the myth of Scottish frugality—or of the Highlands, with their modern paraphernalia of kilt, bagpipes, and sentimentality. But the poets and their audience felt more affinity with the English on the other side of the border than with the Gaelic-speaking Highlanders whom they despised as wretched savages. *Iersch,* 'Highland', is the first insult that Dunbar throws at Kennedy in their *Flyting.*

Yet 'Scottish', when attached to 'Chaucerian', does have some meaning: it indicates first the language that these poets wrote in, and secondly the literary tradition that was behind them. Even here, however, a modern reader is likely to be misled. It is important to remember the obvious fact that the Middle Scots writers, unlike Burns and the later Scots poets, did not consciously choose to write in a dialect, but wrote in Middle Scots for the same reasons that Middle English writers wrote in their various dialects of Middle English. If Middle Scots should seem at first sight quaint, or provincial, or difficult to a modern reader, this is a quality in the modern reader, not in the language. Middle Scots is of course simply a development of Northern English, and the poets who wrote in it (except for the politically conscious Douglas) spoke of it as 'Inglis', not as 'Scottis'. On the other hand, it is not only a dialect but also a literary language, consciously improved, polished, and stabilised. Yet though sophisticated and artificial, it is at the same time an immensely flexible and variable language into which the grossest rustic terms or the most ornate Latin words can be assimilated.

The Middle Scots poets are also differentiated from their English contemporaries by having a specifically Scottish literary tradition. Perhaps the best way to explain this tradition is by an oversimplification: Chaucer influenced immediately and profoundly the English tradition, so that the bulk of the more pretentious fifteenth-century English verse is Chaucerian; his influence on Scottish verse was slower and less overwhelming, so that the pre-Chaucerian ways of writing are still fashionable in Scotland in the fifteenth century. This is of course an inexact statement: the influence of Gower and especially Lydgate on both English and Scottish verse is not negligible; there is plenty of fifteenth-century English poetry which is not Chaucerian, most obviously among the lyrics; on the other hand, *The Kingis Quair* and, in places, Blind Harry's *Wallace* (c. 1475) are Chaucerian. But it remains true that the pre-Chaucerian tradition was more available to Dunbar, for instance, than it was to his English contemporaries. The most obvious sign of this is that alliterative poetry, which in England was essentially dead by the fifteenth century, was still influential in Scotland at the beginning of the sixteenth century. There is, first, the ordinary unrhymed alliterative line, as in *Piers Plowman,* which occurs in Dunbar's *The Tua Mariit Wemen and the Wedo.* Then there is the rhymed alliterative stanza, ending in a group of short lines, which is used by Henryson, Douglas and numerous anonymous poets, often for humorous purposes. A more indirect symptom is the habit which Henryson, Dunbar and Douglas have of using alliteration very heavily in verse which is structurally non-alliterative. But of course the Scottish literary tradition consisted of much more than an alliterative technique. Since we possess few of the earlier poems, and are usually unable to date those which we do have, it is hard to be very precise about the nature of this tradition. But one can distinguish a few types of poetry that were flourishing in Scotland before Henryson: narrative verse in pronouncedly end-stopped couplets, octosyllabic in Barbour's *Bruce* (c. 1375), decasyllabic in the *Wallace;* comic verse of an exuberant and fantastic nature; and religious lyrics—usually more religious than lyric.

The 'Chaucerian' part of 'Scottish Chaucerian' is so equivocal as to be almost meaningless. It is clear, at least, that the Scots poets, unlike some of the English ones, were not 'Chaucerians' in the sense of being submerged in Chaucer, and trying vainly to imitate him. It is also clear that they were 'Chaucerians' in the same way that we now are all, perforce, Cartesians, Marxists, Freudians. Henryson, Dunbar and Douglas wrote about a century after Chaucer had fundamentally changed the course of English poetry, and they could no more ignore this change than we can ignore the changes for which we hold Descartes, Marx and Freud responsible. In order to determine more precisely how, and in what ways, Chaucer influenced the Scots poets, it is necessary to examine the individual poets, though one can make some preliminary cautions and generalisations. No one would wish to deny the profound influence which Chaucer had on later poetry, but it is perhaps possible to exaggerate his importance, and to make him solely responsible for a movement in which he was only the outstanding figure. Chaucer, surely, was not the only conduit through which French and Italian influence, and the 'new poetry', came into England. Gower, Lydgate, and the English Chaucerians all helped to change the native tradition, while the Scots poets, inhabitants of an independent country traditionally allied with France against England, were perfectly capable of going directly to French poetry.

Each age creates for itself its own image of Chaucer, and fortunately both Dunbar and Douglas have described their, and I think their age's, Chaucer. Dunbar, in *The Golden Targe,* writes:

O reverend Chaucere, rose of rethoris all,
As in oure tong ane flour imperiall,
That raise in Britane evir, quho redis rycht,
Thou beris of makaris the tryumph riall;
Thy fresch anamalit termes celicall
This mater coud illumynit have full brycht:
Was thou noucht of oure Inglisch all the lycht,
Surmounting eviry tong terrestriall,
Alls fer as Mayis morow dois mydnycht?

O morall Gower, and Ludgate laureate,
Your sugurit lippis and tongis aureate,
Bene to oure eris cause of grete delyte;
Your angel mouthis most mellifluate
Oure rude langage has clere illumynate,
And faire ourgilt oure speche, that imperfyte
Stude, or your goldyn pennis schupe to wryte;
This Ile before was bare and desolate
Off rethorike or lusty fresch endyte.

253-70

Douglas has a similar passage in the prologue to the first book of his translation of the *Aeneid,* and though he may have borrowed some of his vocabulary from Dunbar, the passage agrees so well with his other statements on poetry that it can safely be taken as expressing his own opinion:

venerabill Chauser, principal poet but peir,
Hevynly trumpat, orlege and reguler,
In eloquens balmy cundyt and dyall,
Mylky fontane, cleir strand and roys ryall
Of fresch endyte, throu Albion iland braid . . .

339-43

Dunbar has been sneered at for calling Chaucer 'rose of rethoris', as if he thought that Chaucer was a mere rhetorician. Modern critics are beginning to think that Dunbar had a very good point, and that Chaucer's rhetorical skill was not the least of his qualities. But in any case, both Dunbar and Douglas plainly value Chaucer not for his humour, nor for his genial insight into humanity, nor for his interesting stories, but for his use of and improvement of English as a poetic language. The metaphors with which they describe Chaucer are very interesting. Both Dunbar and Douglas associate him with flowers, freshness, royalty and heaven, and agree in calling him the chief of all poets. They both imply that he has given life to poetry throughout Britain: Dunbar says that before Chaucer, Gower and Lydgate 'This Ile . . . was bare and desolate'; Douglas says that Chaucer was the life-giving (*Mylky*) fountain and river of poetry, running through all Britain. And they both provide images for the qualities they value in Chaucer. Dunbar's principal term is light: Gower and Lydgate, lesser luminaries, 'Oure rude langage has clere illumynate', while Chaucer is almost the sun, 'Mayis morow', and 'of oure Inglisch all the lycht'. Douglas speaks of Chaucer as a *reguler* ('regulator', perhaps a nonce-use), and equates him with instruments for telling time, *orlege* and *dyall,* and also with the *Hevynly trumpat,* God's regulator.

It is fair, I think, to extrapolate from these passages the general feelings of the Middle Scots poets about Chaucer.

They considered him to be, in a very essential sense, the father of modern English poetry, the man who purified, regularised, and clarified English, and so made it possible for highly civilised and highly wrought poetry to be written in the vernacular. From the troubadours to the Pléiade, European poets were engaged in a constant struggle to make their native tongues into languages with the beauty, precision and stability of Latin. Henryson, Dunbar and Douglas were fully conscious of the debt they owed to Chaucer, and to a lesser extent to Gower and Lydgate, for their part in this task. One can see, too, why Dunbar and Douglas (in another passage), like so many other poets, group together Chaucer, Gower and Lydgate, a rather oddly balanced triumvirate by modern tastes. One reason is of course simply that the late medieval writers did not know very much, perhaps often did not care very much, about the canons of these three poets, so that they did not make clear or accurate distinctions between them. To take two Scottish examples, in the earliest surviving dated printed book in Scotland (1508), Lydgate's *Complaint of the Black Knight* is ascribed to Chaucer; and in the Bannatyne Manuscript, the most important anthology of Middle Scots verse, there are nine poems attributed to Chaucer, all incorrectly, as well as one genuine Chaucerian poem, which is not attributed to him. But the most important reason for the traditional triumvirate is that the Scots and English poets that came after Lydgate had, like all poets, a utilitarian interest in their predecessors. They did not wish to make comparative evaluations, but to use the new modes of poetry which Gower, Chaucer and Lydgate had introduced, and to steal from them anything that seemed useful: diction, rhetoric, genres. Lydgate, voluminous, dilute, and easy to improve upon, was in many ways more immediately useful to his successors than Chaucer who, like other poets of the very first rank, did not always have a beneficent influence on his followers.

If the passages quoted above tell us something about the Scots poets' opinion of Chaucer, they also tell us something about their own poetry. The praise of bygone poets is of course a highly traditional *topos,* but this does not make it either obligatory or meaningless. The Middle Scots poets are addicted to praising Chaucer, Lydgate and Gower, surely, because they wish to announce that they are following in their footsteps, and that they too are modern, sophisticated and technically skilful poets. In a similar way, Henryson, Dunbar and Douglas all give encomiums of the Greek and Latin poets in order to demonstrate that they are cosmopolitan and learned poets, writing poetry which is comparable to, and in the same tradition with, classical poetry. The English Augustan poets provide an obvious parallel here: just as the Scots praise the earlier English poets, so Dryden, for instance, praises 'Mr. Waller and Sir John Denham . . . those two fathers of our English poetry . . . our numbers were in their nonage till these last appeared', while both the Scots and the Augustans revere the classical poets, as models to be imitated and as standards of excellence. The Scots, like the Augustans, were poets of profound originality but of equally profound and more obvious devotion to traditional styles, subjects and genres. It is interesting to look at the genres in which Henryson, Dunbar and Douglas wrote. The greater part of Henryson's work consists of his *Fables,* which he describes as a 'maner of Translatioun' (the other important fables in English are by John Gay); his other two major works are a reworking of the familiar Orpheus and Eurydice legend, and *The Testament of Cresseid,* which as a continuation of Chaucer's *Troilus* is a sufficiently bookish work. Dunbar is primarily an occasional poet, and he writes in the usual genres: short moral, religious, satirical, petitionary, and humorous poems. One of his favourite forms is the standard dream-vision, which he often subverts for humorous or satirical purposes, as the Augustan poets did with the epic. Douglas's major works are his translation of the *Aeneid* (the other important English translation of it is of course by Dryden) and *The Palace of Honour,* which is in the traditional form of an allegorical dream-vision.

The other side of the coin to the Scots' and Augustans' agreement in preferring traditional genres is their agreement on the fundamental importance of poetic technique and craftsmanship. Like the Augustans, the Scots took very seriously the traditional doctrine that poetry is thought dressed in beautiful language and rhetorically ornamented. As a result, the most outstanding common quality of Henryson, Dunbar, and Douglas seems to me to be their preoccupation with style, the 'artificiality', in the best sense, of their poetry.

We know little more about Robert Henryson's life than that he was a schoolmaster at Dunfermline and that his name appears towards the end of the list of dead poets in Dunbar's *Lament for the Makers,* which must have been written between 1505 and 1510. The safest guess would seem to be that he died about 1500, and that his poetry was written in the last third of the fifteenth century.

The usual clichés about Henryson are that he is a keen observer of nature and that his genial humanitarianism causes him to be the closest to Chaucer of all the Scottish Chaucerians. There is doubtless some truth in these generalisations, but hardly more than if one were to characterise Chaucer by saying that he was a keen observer of costumes, and had the endearing habit of seeing the best in people. Henryson has been underrated, I think, because his readers have not always extended the parallel with Chaucer far enough to notice that he shares Chaucer's art of concealing his art. Henryson's unobtrusive complexity is particularly evident in his longest work, *The Morall Fabillis of Esope.* This collection consists of thirteen fables, some of them derived from the medieval Reynardian stories, but most of them Aesopic, ostensibly translations of the versions in Latin verse by Walter of England. Henryson purports to be telling tales simply and plainly, partly for the 'doctrine wyse', and partly for 'ane merie sport': 'In hamelie language and in terms rude / Me neidis wryte, for quhy of Eloquence / Nor Rethorike, I never Understude.' But in reality his fables are artful, sophisticated and rhetorical; comparable, indeed, to La Fontaine's. From one aspect, they are elegant variations on a standard theme: Walter's fables were a standard school text, and would be well known to most of Henryson's audience. Walter's versions are short and crude; Henryson's, though they average only a little over two hundred lines, are often ten times as long. But on the other hand Henryson's fables are not arcane or precious: as he says of Aesop, he did not want 'the disdane off hie, nor low estate'.

Although it is perhaps not the best of Henryson's fables, the *Taill of Schir Chantecleir and the Foxe* is an interesting one to examine, since it has the same plot as *The Nun's Priest's Tale.* The two poems are obviously not very similar: it takes Chaucer about six hundred and forty lines to get from the introduction of the poor widow to the fox's first speech to the cock, but Henryson covers the same ground in twenty-three lines. In these lines Henryson demonstrates his remarkable power of narrating events in a style which is smooth, easy and rapid, but far from flat. The fox is brought to the farmyard, for instance, in these four lines:

> This wylie Tod, quhen that the Lark couth sing,
> Full sair hungrie unto the Toun him drest,
> Quhair Chantecleir in to the gray dawing,
> Werie for nicht, wes flowen ffra his nest.
>
> 425-8

The two antagonists are balanced against each other, the fox moving into the field of action in the first two lines, and the cock in the last two. But the fox has purposefully set his course ('him drest') *to* the farmyard; the cock has merely flown *from* his place of refuge. The adjectives describing them are linked by alliteration: the fox is 'wylie' and the cock is 'Werie for nicht', ostensibly because, as we have been told, his songs divide the night, but more essentially because, as we later learn, the sexual appetites of his hens make great demands on him. The two details about the dawn serve to make it more vivid, but they are also balanced off with the two animals. For the fox, who is aggressive and cheerful, the lark sings; for the cock, who is going to suffer, the dawn is grey.

Another sort of easy subtlety is shown in the fox's speech to the cock, where, as frequently with Henryson, the superficial meaning of the lines is directly opposed to their true meaning:

> 'Your father full oft fillit hes my wame,
> And send me meit ffra midding to the muris.
> And at his end I did my besie curis,
> To hald his heid, and gif him drinkis warme,
> Syne at the last the Sweit swelt in my arme.'
>
> 441-5

Chantecleir's father had, in truth, often filled the fox's stomach, but by begetting chicks, not by sending presents; the fox doubtless did exert himself in holding the cock's head when he died, but he fails to add that this was also the cause of his death, and that the cock's warm drink was his own blood. The last line is the best: the fox means the cock to take the line's languishing rhythm and the rich chime of 'Sweit swelt' as expressing the fox's grief, but of course they really express the fox pausing delightedly at the recollection of his meal, while 'Sweit' here is not a metaphorical term of affection. This passage is perhaps less delicate than the corresponding point in Chaucer's poem, where the fox remarks that Chantecleir's father and mother 'Han in myn hous ybeen to my greet ese', but it is hardly inferior.

The fox's speech, with its tone of impudent double-tongued sleekness, shows Henryson's remarkable ability to reveal character through dialogue, as does the flattered cock's brief and inane answer: ' "Knew ye my ffather?" quod the Cok, and leuch' (*leuch* here, as often in Henryson, means 'giggled', rather than 'laughed'). A more extended and more important instance of Henryson using different styles to show different speakers and different attitudes towards the world comes a little later in the poem, where seven stanzas are devoted to the hens' reactions after the cock has been kidnapped. First Pertok provides a traditional and ornate lament, worthy of Chaucer's 'Gaufred, deere maister soverayn':

> 'Yone wes our drowrie, and our dayis darling,
> Our nichtingall, and als our Orloge bell,
> Our walkryfe watche, us for to warne and tell
> Quhen that Aurora with hir curcheis gray,
> Put up hir heid betwix the nicht and day.'
>
> 497-501

Then Sprutok, a descendant of the Wife of Bath, speaks in a cheerfully abrupt and downright rhythm, using clichés and proverbs:

> 'We sall ffair weill, I find Sanct Johne to borrow;
> The prouerb sayis, "als gude lufe cummis as gais."
> I will put on my haly dais clais,
> And mak me fresch agane this Jolie may,
> Syne chant this sang, "wes never wedow sa gay!" '
>
> 511-15

After this encouragement, Pertok drops her hypocritical grief and sneers lecherously at Chantecleir: 'off sic as him ane scoir / Wald not suffice to slaik our appetyte.' She promises, in a line which is a nice instance of Henryson's stylistic manoeuvres, that she will quickly be able 'To get ane berne suld better claw oure breik'. *Berne,* 'man, warrior', is an exclusively poetic word, and is usually found in alliterative phrases—though not in combination with *breik,* 'breech'. *Claw* is sometimes used in Middle Scots with the meaning 'scratch gently, caress', but of course has a specially graphic meaning when applied to a cock. The line sums up the various rhetorics of love that we have seen: Pertok's noble and courtly lament, Sprutok's carefree wantonness, and Pertok's change to bestial lust. But instead of letting matters rest here, Henryson brings on a third hen who, 'lyke ane Curate', fulminates against Chantecleir with self-righteous indignation:

> 'rychteous God, haldand the balandis evin,
> Smytis rycht sair, thoct he be patient,
> For Adulterie, that will thame not repent.
>
> . . . it is the verray hand off God
> That causit him be werryit with the Tod.'
>
> 534-6, 542-3

Then, as in *The Nun's Priest's Tale,* all pretensions are destroyed by the reality of the barnyard tumult, which Henryson expresses by giving the widow's commands to her dogs:

> 'How! berk, Berrie, Bawsie Broun,
> Rype schaw, Rin weil, Curtes, Nuttieclyde . . . '
>
> 546-7

One can see how Henryson, like Chaucer, makes the fable into a deflation of human self-importance. The different attitudes towards death expressed by the hens are made ridiculous in numerous ways: by juxtaposition of conflicting rhetorics, by having the most grief-stricken hen turn out to be actually the most lecherous, by having all the attitudes irrelevant, since the cock returns safely, and of course simply by giving poultry human voices. And one can see how Henryson, like Chaucer, relies heavily on changes of style, balancing the voice of one animal against the voice of another, or setting up a heroic style only to puncture it abruptly. But one can also see that there are some fundamental differences between Chaucer's fable and Henryson's which point to a dissimilarity between the two poets.

One difference so obvious that it is easy to overlook is simply that Henryson's poem is written in rhyme royal, not in couplets. Henryson never uses couplets, except in the 'Moralitas' of *Orpheus and Eurydice,* where he is explaining an allegory, and his stanzas are stiffer and flow together less easily than Chaucer's usually do. One way to put this difference between the two poets would be to say that time, in Chaucer's poems, tends to move on unobtrusively but continually, where in Henryson there is characteristically a stanza for one instant of time, and then a break before the next stanza. Though of course it is even more dangerous to generalise about Chaucer than about Henryson, and obviously time does not move very fluidly in *The Knight's Tale* or in some of the more stylised stanzaic tales. With these same reservations, another way to put the difference between the two poets is to say that Henryson's verse often seems more impersonal. Beneath Chaucer's poetry one often senses a moving train of thought and constantly changing reactions to what is observed or said; but Henryson seems to change his style only dispassionately, adopting it to the shifts in his subject matter according to the demands of decorum. Chaucer's 'personality' is of course the result of self-conscious art, not involuntary self-revelation, while all of Henryson's poetry manifests his gentle and benevolent mind, but this does not alter the difference of style.

Henryson's style is apt to cause two difficulties for the modern reader. One is that it is easy to look for what is only incidental, the minor touches of realism and humour, and to neglect the large static set pieces which are at the foundation of the structure of his poems. In *Orpheus and Eurydice* and *The Testament of Cresseid* there are formal laments in special stanzaic forms (the hens' laments are parodies of this genre); much of *Orpheus* is devoted to a description of hell; about a third of *The Testament* is spent describing the gods and their conference; and the *Fables* consist largely of such set speeches as the ones we have seen, together with catalogues and formal descriptions of various kinds. It is impossible to generalise about these passages, except to say that they are all as vital to the meaning of their poems as, for instance, the laments are to the fable of the cock and the fox.

The other, and related, difficulty of Henryson's style is that the reader is apt to take his impersonality for cold and meaningless conventionality. This is particularly true of *The Testament of Cresseid,* where the style, so different from Chaucer's, has caused some readers to think that the work is 'by the very strenuousness of its morality in some degree both poetically and morally repulsive. But this is to misunderstand the whole meaning of this brilliant and complex poem, and to ignore that it is in many ways a companion to Book V of Chaucer's *Troilus.* Cresseid, like Troilus, comes to self-knowledge and knowledge of the world through suffering, and it is appropriate that Cresseid's suffering should be more physical than Troilus's. The main emotion of both poems is pathos, but Henryson produces this emotion not so much by suggesting his own feelings as by impersonal description and by opposing Cresseid to such bleak figures as Saturn, who says to her, with perfect and chilling finality, that he will change

> 'Thyne Insolence, thy play and wantones
> To greit diseis; thy Pomp and thy riches
> In mortall neid; and greit penuritie
> Thou suffer sall, and as ane beggar die.'
>
> 319-22

Another difference between *The Nun's Priest's Tale* and Henryson's fable, equally obvious and I think equally important, is that Henryson concludes his poem with a four-stanza 'Moralitas'. Henryson's characteristic genre, indeed, is the narrative poem to which is appended a passage, sometimes long and never less than twenty lines, which comments in some way on the meaning of the narrative. About three-quarters of the bulk of his poetry, including the *Fables* and *Orpheus and Eurydice,* falls into this category. And much of his other work comes close to it: many of his short poems are explicitly allegorical, and even the light-hearted pastoral, *Robene and Makyne,* points a moral. *The Testament of Cresseid* might seem to be the great exception, but in fact it is more similar to the *Fables* and *Orpheus* than one might think. Although it has no separate 'Moralitas' explaining the action, the events of the poem are given so heavy a symbolic meaning that they become almost allegorical. In her faithlessness, Cresseid sinned against the natural order, *fine amour,* and God, and all these sins are represented in the poem by the compound symbol of her vocal blasphemy against Venus and Cupid. In the same way, the leprosy which results from her blasphemy is meaningful on three levels. The disease destroys her flesh, so punishing her for her misuse of it, but also teaching her of its essential and permanent corruptness. Because of her sin against love she is changed from a sought-after beauty to a loathsome beggar—but this change teaches her to praise Troilus and despise herself. The leprosy is also a divine punishment, for it, above all other diseases, was thought to be a blow from heaven, but because of its medieval association with Job, Christ and the two Lazaruses was also considered a disease of peculiar sanctity, an earthly purgatory which, as the poem hints, renders any future purgatory unnecessary.

No one now, surely, would follow Matthew Arnold in accusing Chaucer of a lack of high seriousness, but it is still true that Henryson is a more immediately and more constantly serious poet. His preoccupation with the need to justify the pleasures of poetry by revealing its 'gude moralitie' comes up explicitly time after time, and all the fables are built on Henryson's desire to show the sad irony that if animals behave like men only in poetry, men too often behave like animals in ordinary life. But Henryson does more than extract morals. As the frequent occurrence in his work of the term 'figure' would indicate, he uses the technique of figural interpretation, which is based on the idea that all objects and events are created by God to be meaningful, and which goes back to the theory that the events of the Old Testament were at once historical happenings and prefigurations of Christianity. So the fox, in our fable, is an actual fox, but also 'may weill be figurate / To flatteraris', while the cock, as a figure for pride, is connected with

> the Feyndis Infernall,
> Quhilk houndit doun wes fra that hevinlie hall
> To Hellis hole, and to that hiddeous hous,
> Because in pryde thay wer presumpteous.
> 596-9

And Henryson never abandons poetry for the sake of morality. He has been blamed for piously tacking inconsequential morals on to his poems, but in fact each 'Moralitas', whether satirical, moral, or allegorical, is an organic and necessary part of its poem. Henryson's moral seriousness, like the rhetorical and conventional aspects of his style, has been disliked and ignored by critics, where it should have been recognised as one of the reasons for the excellence of his poetry.

We know only a little more about Dunbar's life than about Henryson's. There is some evidence to suggest that he was born about 1456 and died about 1515, and it is fairly certain that he graduated as a Master of Arts from St Andrews. His name appears more than thirty times in the records between 1500 and 1513, usually as the recipient of a pension from James IV, and all of his poems which can be dated from internal evidence (about a third of the eighty or so which survive) fall within this period. Attempts have been made to construct his biography from his poetry, but this is a speculative enterprise.

One of the most surprising things about Dunbar is that he wrote so many different sorts of poetry: scatological abuse, the stiffest and most bejewelled panegyric, and everything in between. Scholars have tried to sort out his poetry by periods, with a frivolous youth and a pious old age, but there is no evidence to support this, and a good deal to contradict it. One might as well postulate an afternoon Dunbar, who wrote formal and ceremonial verse, an evening Dunbar, who wrote bawdry in the taverns, and a morning-after Dunbar, who wrote moral lyrics and petitions for money. The truth, of course, is simply that Dunbar wrote happily and skilfully in almost any genre. A great repertory of styles seems to be a characteristic of Middle Scots poets: among Henryson's short poems are an obscene burlesque and a hymn to Mary, not to mention the variety of styles in his longer poems, and Douglas also writes in a number of different ways. Dunbar's contemporary, Walter Kennedy, furnishes a concise example: of his six poems, one is a flyting, two are moral and didactic, one is pornographic, one is a hymn to Mary, and one a long narrative on the Passion. The stylistic virtuosity of the Middle Scots poets is a result of their attitude towards poetry: they regard it less as a means of self-expression than as a craft which has to be learned. And just as a good carpenter can build either a house or a chair, so a competent poet should be able to work in any genre. Dunbar, who seems the most representative of the Middle Scots poets, the one who carries their characteristic qualities to the furthest extreme, is only the most conspicuous of a number of virtuosos.

It is, I think, completely hopeless to speculate on Dunbar's personality by affirming that some of his poems are 'sincere', while others are merely exercises. But this is not to say that he lacks individuality, or that his poetry is not in some ways a fairly homogeneous body of work. Even from a purely technical viewpoint Dunbar's loftiest poems are not unlike his most vulgar ones. The resemblance is, indeed, clearest in the most extreme cases, as one can see by comparing passages from a hymn to Mary, *Ane Ballat of Our Lady,* and from the *Flyting:*

> Empryce of prys, imperatrice,
> Brycht polist precious stane;
> Victrice of vyce, hie genetrice
> Of Jhesu, lord soverayne . . .
> 61-4

> Baird rehator, theif of natour, fals tratour, feyindis gett;
> Filling of tauch, rak sauch, cry crauch, thow art our sett;
> Muttoun dryver, girnall ryver, yadswyvar, fowll fell the . . .
> 244-6

These passages would be less startling to Dunbar's contemporaries than they are to us: the first is in a tradition which derives from Latin hymns with internal rhyme, while the *Flyting* is a member of an equally orthodox genre, one which may also derive from medieval Latin verse, and perhaps is remotely connected with the intricately worked scaldic lampoons. But they are still passages of a sufficiently extreme sort. It is true, of course, that they represent extremes of lofty and of vulgar poetry, but it is equally true, and I think more basic, that they are both at the same end of the spectrum, and represent poetry at its most artificial. The pounding internal rhyme of these passages is certainly intolerable for very long (and Dunbar did not use it long or often), and we need not take them any more seriously than I expect their author did, but they are useful because they demonstrate, in an exaggerated form, the rhetorical and metrical prestidigitation which, used less obtrusively, is important to all of Dunbar's work.

These two passages also raise the problem of Dunbar's vocabulary. *Ane Ballat of Our Lady* is one of the *loci classici* of 'aureation', or what scholars think of as the vicious habit which became common among Chaucer's followers of sprinkling their verse with newfangled and obtrusive Latinate words. But there are several objections to this sweeping condemnation. One is simply that this poem is plainly a *tour de force,* and not a fair representative of Dunbar's usual 'aureate' style. A more basic objection is that 'aureation' has, I think, been misunderstood by modern readers. The term, as used by Lydgate and later poets, does not seem to have any necessary direct reference to

Latinate words, but means merely 'golden'. These poets wished to make their verse golden and sweet (another favourite adjective), in the new Continental and Chaucerian manner, and they also wished to refine, purify, and gild their native tongue. One of the devices they used for this purpose, perhaps one more obvious to a modern reader than their other rhetorical techniques, was the use of strikingly Latinate words. Some critics have objected to this device, perhaps because they followed too literally Wordsworth's dictum that poets ought to use 'the language really spoken by men', and so distrusted any formal poetic diction, whether medieval or Augustan. But surely exotic Latinisms are permissible and even normal in English verse: no one, for instance, would now object to 'this my hand will rather / The multitudinous seas incarnadine, / Making the green one red'.

Like Shakespeare, if perhaps unlike some of the English fifteenth-century poets, Dunbar only uses Latinate words to serve a specific purpose. They occur with some frequency in his loftier poems, particularly where he is aiming at a precise and glittering richness. *The Golden Targe* is the most sustained and most successful example of this richness, but it appears occasionally in other poems, as for example *The Merle and the Nychtingaill:* 'Undir this brench ran doun a revir bricht, / Of balmy liquour, cristallyne of hew, / Agane the hevinly aisur skyis licht . . . ' But in the humorous satire, *Epitaph for Donald Owre,* Dunbar uses Latinisms partly for their powerful weight when they are preceded by short and light native words, and partly for their sibilant alliteration:

Thocht he remissioun
Haif for prodissioun,
Schame and susspissioun
Ay with him dwellis.

3-6

And in the moral poem, *Learning Vain Without Good Life* (sometimes called *Dunbar at Oxinfurde*), he uses Latinate words to give a suggestive description of the various branches of learning:

The curious probatioun logicall,
The eloquence of ornat rethorie,
The naturall science philosophicall,
The dirk apperance of astronomie . . .

9-12

One might guess that Dunbar had a theory of poetic diction the opposite of Wordsworth's, and believed that one way to make poetry effective was to use language which contrasted conspicuously with ordinary unpoetic speech. His Latinisms seem more frequent than, statistically, they are, because he makes them so obtrusive. Again, his techniques can be seen most clearly by looking at extreme examples. This stanza is from *None May Assure in this Warld:*

Vbi ardentes anime,
Semper dicentes sunt Ve! Ve!
Sall cry Allace! that women thame bure,
O quante sunt iste tenebre!
In to this warld may none assure.

71-5

The burning souls are taken out of the ordinary speech and time of this world by being described in Latin, but then the third line, though equally biblical, makes them disturbingly immediate by having them cry the English 'Allace' instead of 'Ve', and by having them refer to their mothers. And both the grave immutability of the Latin and the pathos of the English fall onto the last line, which is effective because of its simplicity and because one is forced by the preceding lines to read it very slowly and heavily.

This playing off of English against Latin is used in many of Dunbar's greatest poems: *On the Resurrection of Christ,* for instance, with its refrain, 'Surrexit Dominus de sepulchro', or *Of the Nativitie of Christ,* with its 'Et nobis Puer natus est'. But it is also used in his macaronic parodies, such as *The Testament of Mr Andro Kennedy,* which seem to me in their own way no less great:

I, Maister Andro Kennedy,
Curro quando sum vocatus,
Gottin with sum incuby,
Or with sum freir infatuatus;
In faith I can nought tell redly,
Unde aut ubi fui natus,
Bot in treuth I trow trewly,
Quod sum dyabolus incarnatus.

1-8

The opening solemnity of 'I, Maister Andro Kennedy' is carried on by the heavy and rhythmical syllables of the second line, but at the same time is rendered ridiculous by the meaning of the Latin. And the idiotic and redundant pomposity of 'Bot in treuth I trow trewly' clashes marvellously with the preposterously different pomposity of 'sum dyabolus incarnatus'.

If we turn back to the passage from the *Flyting* quoted above, we find there a diction equally exotic, though of course very different. Dunbar's terms of abuse were presumably more familiar to his contemporaries than they are to us, though the variations and mistakes in the manuscripts indicate that these terms troubled his scribes, as well as the modern lexicographers. But in any case it is obvious that in poetry these violent and often obscene slang words are as alien and conspicuous as any Latinisms. One might adduce as a parallel Ezra Pound, who jolts his reader as much by his harsh colloquialisms as by his fragments of Chinese. But if Dunbar and Pound are both motivated by a desire to use the full resources of English (as well as of any other language that happens to be handy), there is the difference that Dunbar follows a traditional decorum, and, except when he writes parodies, reserves his different styles and dictions for different genres.

Northrop Frye has aptly said that Dunbar is a 'musical' poet, meaning not that his poems are smooth and mellifluous, but that in their reliance on 'the rhythm, movement, and sound of words' they show similarities to music. Both his ornate and his humorous poems are obviously musical, in their different ways, but the term fits equally well the group of poems, mostly moral and satirical lyrics, together with some petitionary and occasional verse, which are written in what might be called Dunbar's 'middle style'. The poem *Inconstancy of Luve* provides a minor but neat example:

In luve to keip allegance,
It war als nys an ordinance,
As quha wald bid ane deid man dance
In sepulture.

21-4

The effect of the passage comes mainly from the way in which the rising rhythm of the first three lines is balanced against the thud of the unexpectedly short last line.

A stanza from the *Lament for the Makers* gives a more subtle example of Dunbar's musical qualities, and also demonstrates some of his rhetorical techniques:

He takis the campion in the stour,
The capitane closit in the tour,
The lady in bour full of bewte;
Timor mortis conturbat me.

29-32

Death's three victims are bound closely together by parallel construction, rhyme (*stour—tour—bour*), and alliteration (though the masculine and warlike series, *campion—capitane—closit,* is opposed by the feminine and domestic *bour—bewte*). But there is also a logical progression. The champion is strong to fight against death, yet might well expect to meet death in the thick of battle. The captain of a castle should be more secure, 'closit in the tour', but still, castles are closed because they are attacked. The lady, at least, should be safe, for surely a boudoir is one place that death would not be unmannerly enough to enter, and yet she, if the farthest removed from the scenes of violent death, is also the most fragile. This line has two rhyme words, *bour* and *bewte,* so that it simultaneously closes the list of victims and connects them with the fourth line.

This stanza consists of a series of simple statements, and its success comes from the precise and economical way in which the statements are first created, and then played off against each other. All of Dunbar's moral lyrics might be described as being a 'poetry of statement', in the phrase which has been applied to Dryden, another 'musical' poet. These poems contain only traditional and even hackneyed ideas, without a trace of any complicated intellectual development. Instead, Dunbar devotes all of his immense rhetorical and metrical skill to giving these ideas a perfect and immutable form. But Dunbar's use of language in the moral poems does not seem very different from his use of language in the ornate or humorous poems, although to be sure the diction itself varies immensely. Dunbar's high style, for all its richness, is not vague or highly connotative, but works to produce a glittering and precise surface. And his low style, for all of its apparent uncouth vigour, is successful because each word is locked into place by rhetorical and metrical restraints. One might describe Dunbar's poetry by saying the same thing in three different ways: it is a poetry of statement—Dunbar never describes, or evokes, or suggests, but simply states; it is a poetry of surfaces—precise, static, and two-dimensional; and it is a musical poetry—its meaning is not philosophical, or even discursive, but is like the meaning of a piece of music.

It is a desperate endeavour to trace Dunbar's relationship to Chaucer, or for that matter to any of his predecessors, since he appears on the one hand to have written in every possible poetic tradition, and on the other hand to have borrowed only very slightly from any specific poet. But one can make a few generalisations. First, it seems clear that Dunbar and Chaucer are about as unlike as any two poets can be. Chaucer's poems are typically narrative, philosophical, richly suggestive, and lengthy; Dunbar's poems are just the opposite. Secondly, it seems clear that Dunbar is immensely indebted to Chaucer. His debts are of two kinds, neither of which is very susceptible to measurement. On the technical level, Dunbar's sophisticated metrics, rhetorical devices and diction surely descend, in part, from Chaucer. The question here is not so much of Chaucer inventing new techniques as of his naturalising some of the graces of Continental verse and of his emphasising, and so strengthening, certain features of the native tradition. One could be precise, and point to certain words and stanzaic forms which Dunbar borrowed from Chaucer, or very often from Lydgate, but the more important part of the debt is more intangible: Dunbar's prevailingly syllabic metrics, for instance, and his willingness to accept into his poetry rhetorical figures and learned words.

Dunbar's second debt to Chaucer is no more than a matter of genres. The situation here is very similar: Chaucer did not so much invent new genres as naturalise Continental ones, or embellish and refine pre-existent native genres. A large number of Dunbar's poems are written in Chaucerian genres: allegorical poems about spring and love, dream-visions, moral lyrics, and witty begging poems. But Dunbar's poetry stands in a special and almost a parasitic relationship to the traditional genres. Most typically he writes parodies or near-parodies, as, for example, his frequent humorous adaptations of the dream-vision form, or *The Tua Mariit Wemen and the Wedo,* which is among other things a parody of a *chanson d' aventure,* of a *chanson de mal mariée,* and of a *demande d' amour.* Even Dunbar's serious poems tend to be highly 'literary': Dunbar expects his readers to be acquainted with the traditional genres and themes, and to appreciate his novel rehandling of them. *The Golden Targe,* for instance, and the poems similar to it, contain very traditional matter reworked into flamboyant and brilliant exercises where the style and the poetical techniques are all-important, and the meanings traditionally connected with the matter are scarcely bothered with. One feels, finally, that Dunbar's expressions of obligations to Chaucer are almost symbolic: he praises that mythical figure, 'Chaucer-the-father-of-English-poetry', because he is so aware of his reliance on the traditional genres and styles of English verse.

Gavin Douglas, the third of our poets, seems in some ways to be set apart from Henryson and Dunbar, though this may be partly an illusion arising from the fact that we know a good deal about Douglas's life where we know practically nothing about Henryson's or Dunbar's. Douglas was born about 1475, a son of the powerful Archibald 'Bell-the-Cat', fifth Earl of Angus. After graduating from St Andrews, he took orders, perhaps more because he was a younger son than because of any particular vocation. He rose rapidly, becoming Provost of St Giles' in Edinburgh about 1501, and after Flodden (1513), when his nephew married the widowed queen of James IV, the world seemed his oyster. He became Bishop of Dunkeld, briefly (and perhaps only by his own styling) Chancellor of Scotland, and he had expectations of becoming Archbishop of St Andrews and guardian of the young James V. But his hopes all came to nought, and he died in London, unsuccessfully intriguing, in 1522. So apart from his poetry he survives only as a minor footnote to Scottish history—though it is true that his faction came back into power less than two years after his death, and that if he had lived a little longer he might well have obtained more of his eagerly pursued 'pompe of eirdlie dignitie'.

Both of Douglas's major poems, *The Palace of Honour* and his translation of the *Aeneid,* seem to have some affinities with later English poetry. In *The Palace of Honour* we see a world that is immensely rich but confusing and baffling, a world in which the traditional ways of acting and perceiving no longer appear effective. Dunbar's poems, on the other hand, tend to be either amoral or to follow a simple and traditional morality, while Henryson is an extremely subtle but also very traditional moralist. Douglas's *Aeneid* is in many ways a Renaissance translation: he is interested in Virgil's *Aeneid* as a literary whole, and in Aeneas as 'the mast soueran man', a pattern of conduct. He follows the Latin text conscientiously, although he does not aim at a literal translation: 'Sum tyme the text mon haue ane expositioun, / Sum tyme the collour will caus a litill additioun, / And sum tyme of a word I mon make thre . . . ' (Prologue to Book I). Here again, Douglas is very different from Henryson, who allegorises the myth of Orpheus and Eurydice, from Dunbar, with his lighthearted and traditional references to the 'ornate stilis so perfyte' of 'Omer', and, as Douglas self-righteously points out at length, from Chaucer's rather lop-sided treatment of the *Aeneid* in *The House of Fame.*

Douglas's aristocratic, self-seeking and mercurial life is appropriate to his poetry, for with him we seem to have a new image, the poet as gifted amateur, rather than the old image of the poet as a professional and semi-anonymous bard. It is not that his poetry is technically casual or incompetent, but that he gives the impression of writing only at his own pleasure, and only on subjects which interest him. It is curiously fitting, in view of his transitional position in Scottish literature, that his poetry should be exactly contemporary with Dunbar's (*The Palace of Honour* was written about 1501, and his *Aeneid* was finished in 1513), but that most of his public life should take place in the radically changed new world of James V.

The most important thing to say about Douglas's *Aeneid* is what Ezra Pound and C. S. Lewis have already said loudly, just that it is an exceedingly good poem. It seems likely, especially now that a competent edition has appeared, that the poem will in the future be valued for what it is: one of the first and best of the English translations of the Renaissance; a translation of the *Aeneid* which is at least as good as Dryden's; and therefore necessarily an important English work in its own right. C. S. Lewis has helped to clear away two misapprehensions about the poem which a modern reader is likely to fall into. One is that Douglas's language may seem to us quaint and rustic, because 'We forget that in his day it was a courtly and literary language'. The other is that the characters in the translation may seem to us too brisk, colloquial and modern because we have been falsely trained to see them as venerable, antique and stiff. Lewis's point here is surely sound, though perhaps Douglas went a little too much to the opposite extreme from us. One suspects that Aeneas seemed more of a contemporary to Douglas than he did to Virgil.

But there is still a third misapprehension which may block our understanding of the poem. It is easy to think of Douglas as an untaught genius who forcibly, brilliantly and instinctively threw the *Aeneid* into English. But nothing could be farther from the truth, since Douglas's *Aeneid* is an exceptionally self-conscious and rhetorical translation. He warns us of this clearly enough in his prologue to the first book, a critical and polemical general introduction running to more than five hundred lines. The first few lines show both Douglas's opinion of Virgil, as a master of rhetoric, and Douglas's ambition to raise his own language to an equal pitch of eloquence.

> Lawd, honour, praysyngis, thankis infynyte
> To the and thy dulce ornat fresch endyte,
> Maist reuerend Virgill, of Latyn poetis prynce,
> Gem of engyne and flude of eloquens,
> Thow peirles perle, patroun of poetry,
> Roys, regester, palm, lawrer and glory,
> Chosyn charbukkill, cheif flour and cedyr
> tre . . .

Modern readers have been misled, perhaps, by the contrast which Douglas goes on to draw between his 'blunt endyte' and the 'scharp sugurate sang Virgiliane', between his 'ignorant blabryng imperfyte' and Virgil's 'polyst termys redymyte' ('wreathed' or 'adorned'). But this conventional mock-modesty is of course itself a rhetorical flourish. In the rest of the prologue Douglas demonstrates rather ostentatiously the range and skilfulness of his styles, and at the same time takes up some technical matters. He states that he will use some Latin, French and southern English words, which means that he will use an artificial poetic diction; he discusses, with examples, the difficulty of translating some Latin words; and he derides the blunders of earlier translators. Douglas provides a most revealing image when he remarks,

> Quha is attachit ontill a staik, we se,
> May go na ferthir bot wreil about that tre:
> Rycht so am I to Virgillis text ybund . . .
> 297-9

His translation, then, is a green plant winding around a stake, ornamenting and covering it, but attached to it at all points—or almost all, for Douglas says he may 'mak digressioun sum tyme'. The simile also works in a way which Douglas may not have intended, for a plant's stake is designed, of course, to support and guide the plant. Douglas laments that he could have made a poem 'twys als curyus' if he had not been constrained to follow Virgil's text, but if he had attempted to write a poem of this magnitude without a support and guide, the results would surely have been more curious than organised.

Douglas's famous prologues, original poems which are prefixed to each book of the *Aeneid,* offer another guide-post to the nature of the translation. These prologues are in a great variety of metrical forms, and on a great variety of subjects: some provide literary criticism; some are satirical, moral, philosophical, or religious; and some are descriptions of nature at different seasons. Critics have usually concentrated on these last ones, and complimented Douglas on his feeling for nature and his close observation of the Scottish landscape. But this is to put the emphasis on the wrong place, for the prologues are above all a series of set pieces intended to demonstrate Douglas's competence at writing in various styles on various subjects. To be sure, the seasonal prologues are very good, but Douglas wrote them more because the seasons were a standard topic for Scottish poets than because he had any eighteenth-century feeling for nature. The prologues might be compared with the *Shepherd's Calendar:* in both cases there is the same purposive and partly experimental variety of forms, the same self-conscious use, and abuse, of traditional genres, and the same obtrusive concern with poetical techniques.

Douglas's *Aeneid* is so huge and so variegated that it is impossible to treat it in any detail here, but perhaps a single quotation will indicate some of the qualities, as well as some of the problems, of the translation.

> The rage of Silla, that huge swelth in the see,
> ye haue eschapit, and passit eik haue yhe
> The euer rowtand Charibdis rolkis fell;
> The craggis quhar monstruus Ciclopes dwell
> Yhe ar expert. Pluk vp your hartis, I you pray,
> This dolorus dreid expell and do away.
>
> I iv 73-8

> vos et Scyllaeam rabiem penitusque sonantis
> accestis scopulos, vos et Cyclopia saxa
> experti; revocate animos maestumque timorem
> mittite . . .
>
> I 200-3

One notices first Douglas's characteristic habit of expanding and elucidating his original. *Mittite* is doubled into the downright 'expell and do away'; *accestis* into the explicit 'eschapit, and passit eik'. These expansions seem reasonable enough, but a purist would object that Douglas has unwarrantably introduced Charybdis into the passage, and moreover has mistakenly made Scylla, instead of Charybdis, into a whirlpool (*swelth*). This confusion is unimportant, but the passage shows how he generally takes a freer approach to the Latin than a modern translator would. If one reads Douglas's translation while holding an annotated edition of Virgil, one will find that Douglas incorporates directly into his text many of the modern annotations. Usually, though not always, these additions are correct and helpful. But a modern translator would no more dare to do this than he would dare to insert his own original compositions between each book. Douglas often throws new and valuable light on the meaning of a particular passage, just as his translation as a whole brings out powerfully and unexpectedly some overlooked aspects of Virgil, but he is not a reliable guide to Virgil's actual words. To an unusually large degree, the excellence of Douglas's translation is derived more from the translator than from the original.

This passage also shows some of the reasons for Douglas's excellence. One of them, rather ironically, is precisely the quality which makes him difficult for a modern reader: his vocabulary. In some cases he was simply fortunate in his inheritance: *rowtand,* for instance, is an admirable word for *sonantis,* being more exact than *roaring* and less bookish than *resounding,* while *dolorus dreid* is a very happy equivalent for *maestum timorem.* Douglas is particularly skilful in taking advantage of the flexibility of literary Scots: he moves freely from the most colloquial to the most ornate diction and makes a forceful but never pedantic use of Latinisms and neologisms. The first four lines of this passage, for instance, lead up to the emphatic Latinism, *expert* (which ordinarily meant 'experienced' in Middle Scots, but is here used in a Latinate construction), and then this climax is followed by the semi-colloquial *Pluk vp.* Similarly, in the last line the Latinate *expell* is complemented by *do away.*

Douglas's felicitous handling of rhetoric and rhythm is also demonstrated in this passage. There are, for instance, two separate patterns in the first three lines. On the one hand, the first and third lines, describing the dangers, are balanced against the second line, describing the safety. On the other hand, these three lines are divided syntactically into two clauses, each a line and a half long, and arranged in a careful chiasmus: object, subject, auxiliary verb, past participle—past participle, auxiliary verb, subject, object. The next phrase, *The craggis . . . ar expert,* is parallel with the first line and a half, so that the reader expects Douglas to repeat the whole three-line pattern again. But instead there is an abrupt and rhythmically jarring full stop, emphasising the *expert,* and a shift into a broken and colloquial rhythm, imitating the tone of Aeneas's earnest plea. Throughout the passage there runs an alliteration so constant as to be almost structural, but used purposefully to link words together: *Silla—swelth—see, craggis—Ciclopes, dolorus dreid—do away.*

Douglas's *Palace of Honour,* though a less important poem than his *Aeneid,* is especially interesting here because it so clearly stands in the Chaucerian tradition. In genre, it is like *The House of Fame:* a dream-vision about a journey to a lofty and allegorical building. Douglas seems to have borrowed many of the details of his plot from Chaucer, though of course one cannot always be certain that he did not go directly to Chaucer's sources, or on the other hand borrow from *The Temple of Glass* or other fifteenth-century imitations of Chaucer, some of which are perhaps no longer extant. But there are enough verbal reminiscences of Chaucer in *The Palace of Honour,* and enough direct references to Chaucerian characters, to make us safe in assuming that Douglas, most of the time, was borrowing immediately from Chaucer.

By looking at the plot of *The Palace of Honour* one can see not only how much Douglas was indebted to Chaucer, but also how well he understood him—Douglas's poem is a very useful commentary on *The House of Fame. The Palace of Honour* has the same traditional beginning as *The Legend of Good Women:* the narrator goes out on a May morning, sees the spring flowers, hears spring songs, and then has a visionary dream. But Douglas's narrator, like the narrator in *The House of Fame,* dreams that he is in a 'desert terribill'. In both poems, this desert stands for the desolate and barren spiritual condition of the narrator, caught in the wastes of the temporal world, and is equivalent to Dante's *selva oscura* or Eliot's wasteland, though the actual detailed description of Douglas's desert makes it seem oddly like the landscape in Browning's *Childe Roland.* Douglas's narrator sees Minerva, the 'Quene of Sapience', go by with her train, on the way to the 'Palace of Honour', and then Diana, but he himself remains and does not follow either the way of wisdom or the way of asceticism. Then, after a learned digression on sound waves, in imitation of the lecture which Chaucer's eagle gives, Venus appears, with Mars, Cupid and the rest of the court of love. This court is composed mostly of the heroines of *The Legend of Good Women* and of the figures from the temple of Venus in *The House of Fame,* together with a few characters who are even more Chaucerian: Arcite, Palamon and Emily, Troilus and Criseyde, and Griselda. The narrator finally feels constrained to sing a song, set off from the narrative by being in a different stanzaic form, in which he laments his own woes and denounces Venus. As a result, he is seized by the court, tried and condemned. There is an obvious parallel here with *The Legend of Good Women,* where Chaucer's narrator is condemned by the god of love for having made songs against love, and the parallel is carried on by the sequel. In Douglas's poem the 'court rethoricall' of muses and famous poets appears, and Calliope intercedes for mercy, using the same arguments that Chaucer's Alceste uses: the sin is small, the victim is unworthy of a god, and he won't do it again. So Douglas's narrator, like Chaucer's, goes free after having promised to make poetic amends.

Douglas makes it clear that he is using this material because it is meaningful, not simply because it is traditional. He emphasises, for instance, the difference between sexual love, with its power to brutalise or destroy (the dreamer is afraid that Venus will transform him into an animal or kill him) and the intercessory charity of Calliope. The complicated relationships between love and poetry are neatly implied, too: they are at odds, not only because poetry is often anti-feminist, but also because perfection of the work conflicts with perfection of the life; yet they are reconcilable, partly because poetry celebrates and immortalises love, and partly because poetry is a parallel but independent road to the Palace of Honour. So after the narrator is saved by Calliope and her band of muses and poets, who sweep on stage almost like a rescuing army, Calliope entrusts him to the charge of a nymph and they go off together on their way to the palace.

This guiding nymph fulfils the same functions as Chaucer's eagle and, though less loquacious, shows her similarity to him by encouraging the fearful narrator and telling him where to look. Their journey is a terrestrial one, yet no less extraordinary and extensive than Chaucer's aerial one: 'Now into Egypt, now into Italie, / Now in the realme of Trace, and now in Spane.' But at one place there seems to be a humorous glance at Chaucer's air transport, for the nymph seizes the narrator by the hair and carries him over a hell-like ditch and up to the palace at the top of a hill.

The third and last part of *The Palace of Honour,* as of *The House of Fame,* is concerned with the narrator's adventures at his destination. Douglas's building is obviously modelled on Chaucer's: both are very beautiful, are made out of beryl, have intricately carved golden gates, and have immensely rich interiors which are full of precious stones. But they are also very different, as the titles of the poems suggest: 'Palace' is grander than 'House', and 'Honour' less equivocal than 'Fame'. The difference is neatly symbolised by the hills the buildings are on: both hills appear to be made of glass, but where Chaucer's turns out to be of ice, Douglas's is of hard marble, and so equally hard to climb but infinitely more durable. Chaucer emphasises the arbitrariness of earthly fame and, with his revolving wicker house, gives an image of mutability. Douglas's honour is supernatural, just and eternal (it is always the same season at the palace), and so is contrasted with earthly mutability: from the top of the hill one can look down and see the earth, which appears in the guise of a stormy sea filled with drowning mariners.

But there is a curious similarity between the climactic revelations of the two poems. In *The House of Fame,* of course, Chaucer breaks off just as the 'man of great auctorite' is apparently about to make an important statement. Although *The Palace of Honour* is a finished poem, the climax is almost as equivocal and tantalising: the narrator peers through a hole, sees 'ane God omnipotent', swoons, and is laughed at by his nymph for being such a coward. It would seem as though each poet was forced by the very nature of his poem to produce such an ambiguous climax, or perhaps more exactly such a lack of climax. Dante could end his serious and Christian poem with a Paradiso, but Chaucer and Douglas can only make an ironic gesture towards an ultimate revelation in their half-humorous and ostensibly unchristian poems. Dante, the pilgrim, is educated by his travels so that he can understand the truths of the Paradiso, but neither Chaucer's nor Douglas's narrators are very educable, and perhaps neither the eagle nor the nymph are the best possible pedagogues.

It would be possible to show other Chaucerian borrowings in *The Palace of Honour*—it seems likely, for instance, that there is a bond of relationship between the Chaucerian *persona* and Douglas's narrator, who is shown as being dazed, curious, timid, and, as he himself admits, knowing no more than a sheep. But for all of Chaucer's influence, it must be admitted that the poem seems to a modern reader profoundly un-Chaucerian. In *The House of Fame,* for all its preposterous plot, there is a smooth and plausible narrative line, and the narrator always seems to be present in his flesh and blood. But *The Palace of Honour* is a glittering and artificial poem: Douglas seems to make no effort to preserve any reasonable narrative coherence, or to impart any feeling of verisimilitude.

Douglas's metrical forms are partly responsible for the special quality of his poem, and they also give us an indication of his purposes. The first two books are in the nine-line stanza, rhymed *aabaabbab,* which Chaucer used in *Anelida and Arcite,* and which Dunbar was to use in *The Golden Targe,* a poem very similar to some parts, particularly the prologue, of *The Palace of Honour.* The third book is in the different nine-line stanza, rhymed *aabaabbcc,* which Chaucer used in *The Complaint of Mars.* In several places Douglas uses a ten-line stanza to mark off rhetorically ornate songs, and at the end of the poem, perhaps taking a hint from the internal rhyme in *Anelida and Arcite,* he has three stanzas, the first with double internal rhyme, the second with triple and the third with quadruple, while he preserves in all of them the normal end-rhyme of the *Anelida* stanza. Douglas's use of the forms of these two poems reminds us of an aspect of Chaucer which was very important in the fifteenth century but which has often been overlooked: Chaucer as a metrical innovator and as a technical virtuoso. And these intricate stanzaic forms show us that Douglas is not trying to conduct a realistic narrative, but to achieve a highly wrought poetic brilliance. The elaborate burst of rhyme with which Douglas concludes *The Palace of Honour* is only an extreme example of the artificial splendour which he has been striving for throughout the whole work.

It is surely no accident that Douglas's narrator is rescued and given a guide by Calliope, the muse of epic poetry and so, as Douglas says, of the 'kinglie stile'. Douglas's narrator rises above the world by the aid of a muse, not by the aid of a philosophical and humanly loquacious eagle: Douglas himself raises his poem off the ground by sheer rhetoric, not by structural design or by sympathetically human characters. Douglas's preoccupation with rhetoric and style is of course very evident throughout the poem. The prologue is a dazzling set piece in the aureate mode, and Douglas begins the first book with a dramatically rhetorical stanza—in which he pretends to disclaim any rhetorical ability. The poem is filled with rhetorical figures and with explicit comments on the styles of Douglas himself, of his characters and of other poets, while at the end there is a three-stanza epilogue that is largely Douglas's mock-apology for his 'barrant termis' and 'vile indite'.

But there is also a connection between the poem's emphasis on rhetoric and its very structure. Visionary poems about allegorical journeys tend to be richly variegated and comprehensive, as if their authors wished to set up allegorical worlds that were as complex and multitudinous as our ordinary world. Dante and the author of *Piers Plowman* achieve this comprehensiveness by the sheer magnitude and seriousness of their poems; Chaucer, in *The House of Fame,* uses a variety of devices—the re-telling of the *Aeneid,* which brings a metamorphosed classical world into the poem, the exhaustive logical rigour with which the various applicants to Fame are classified, and the stupidity of the narrator, which allows Chaucer to hint at worlds seen but not understood. *The Parliament of Fowls* offers a tidier example, with its three figures of Scipio, Venus and Nature balanced against each other so as to form the corners of an all-embracing triangle. But Douglas has a simpler way to make his poem inclusive. He merely brings every possible sort of subject matter into his poem, fits it all neatly into the tissue of his rhetoric, and passes on. One of the most characteristic parts of the poem is the section where the narrator looks into Venus's magic mirror and sees 'The deidis and fatis of euerie eirdlie wicht': Satan's fall, Noah's flood, over thirty Old Testament figures, about fifty figures from classical history and mythology, medieval falconers and necromancers, and the heroes of contemporary popular poetry.

The basic structural device of *The Palace of Honour,* then, is the list: the different parts of the poem are joined together by simple juxtaposition and these parts are themselves largely made up of catalogues. Chaucer himself is a great master of lists—one thinks of the description of the House of Fame, or of the more brilliant description of the temples in *The Knight's Tale*—but the difference between the two poets is shown by their methods of describing a journey. Chaucer conveys the length and the marvellousness of the flight in *The House of Fame* by letting us see it through the surprised eyes of the narrator; Douglas achieves something of the same effect by simply giving a long, preposterous, but skilful list of the geographical places through which his narrator passes.

One may, if one wishes, repeat the old truism to the effect that medieval critical theories perniciously emphasised rhetoric and ornamentation at the expense of structure and unity. But it is perhaps more helpful to note that Douglas's techniques are justified by their results. The suddenness of his scene shifting, for instance, the quick juxtaposition of apparently disparate passages, works to produce the strange mixture of clarity and lack of causality that is so typical of dreams, and also is used to reinforce Douglas's themes. In particular, the pervasive theme of the contrast between earthly mutability and transcendental perfection is repeatedly brought out by the juxtaposition of contrasting scenes. And even Douglas's catalogues are something more than a medieval vice: it is interesting to observe that Auden, another poet who is fond of allegory and ostentatious rhetoric, uses catalogues frequently. Like Dunbar, who is also addicted to lists, Douglas uses them to group similar or contrasting elements, to balance entities against each other and to freeze them into a comprehensive and rigid rhetorical form. Dunbar's catalogues perhaps reveal a finer ear and a greater meticulousness, but Douglas's are far from slovenly. The following passage, for instance, shows not only Douglas's skilful variation of pace and rhythm, but also his ability to lead a catalogue up to a climax:

> The miserie, the crueltie, the dreid,
> Pane, sorrow, wo, baith wretchitnes and neid,
> The greit inuy, couetous dowbilnes,
> Tuitchand warldlie vnfaithfull brukilnes.
>
> I p. 64

The Palace of Honour is doubtless not one of the world's great poems, but it is, I think, a very deft and interesting piece which has been undervalued because misunderstood: readers have hunted in it for a philosophical richness or a Chaucerian humanity which is not there, and have dismissed as faults and digressions the obtrusive rhetoric and the perpetually shifting subject matter which are actually the poem's essential qualities.

Even if Douglas is not the most typical of Middle Scots poets, he serves well enough as a text on which to conclude. Like the other Scots poets, he can be seen in several contexts. One is the familiar 'History of English Literature'. Here Douglas, Henryson and Dunbar appear as poets inheriting the Chaucerian wealth, partly through fifteenth-century intermediaries, but using it for profoundly un-Chaucerian purposes: there is a vast gulf between *The*

House of Fame and *The Palace of Honour.* These poets seem themselves to leave no direct heirs, except for some relatively minor sixteenth-century Scots, but Douglas, at least, foreshadows the Elizabethan poets. Just as his *Aeneid* is the precursor of the Elizabethan translations (and was plagiarised by Surrey), so the prologues to it seem to point towards the experiments in different metres and dictions of the sixteenth-century English poets, and so his *Palace of Honour* makes a bit more evident the connection between Chaucer and the *Faerie Queene.*

Another context is the general European background, the tradition that Dante suggested in his famous phrase for Arnaut Daniel: 'fu miglior fabbro del parlar materno' (*Purgatorio* XXVI, 117). Douglas, Henryson and Dunbar have an honourable place among the countless medieval and Renaissance poets who tried to refine their various maternal tongues by concentrating arduously on perfection of form and rhetoric, and who successfully attempted to produce a literature that could rival their classical inheritance.

But Dante's phrase, with its use of the word *fabbro,* 'smith, craftsman, maker', for *poet,* leads us back again to Douglas, Henryson, Dunbar and the short-lived apogee of Scottish literature which they represent. The word *poet* itself, of course, like many of its synonyms in different languages, has an etymological meaning of something like *maker,* but it is surely not coincidental that in modern English the term *maker,* in the sense of *poet,* is reserved almost exclusively for the Middle Scots poets. Their poetry is a poetry of craftsmanship, and they are united by their devotion to their craft, even though each poet manifests it differently: Henryson with his pervading decorum and his art that conceals art; Dunbar with his succinct brilliance; Douglas with his gaudy rhetorical flowers. These poets, in their different ways, all seem to have channelled their passion towards the idea that a poem ought to be as finely wrought as possible. This implies their limitations: these poets are not profoundly interested in philosophy, in nature, or in self-revelation. But their poems are well made, which is perhaps all the praise that any poet can demand. (pp. 164-200)

Denton Fox, "The Scottish Chaucerians," in Chaucer and Chaucerians: Critical Studies in Middle English Literature, *edited by D. S. Brewer, Nelson, 1966, pp. 164-200.*

Florence H. Ridley

[*In the essay below, Ridley asserts that the term Scottish Chaucerians is misleading and inappropriate because it implies that the Scottish poets merely copied Chaucer. She focuses on Henryson's* The Testament of Cresseid, *comparing it with Chaucer's* Troilus and Criseyde *to illustrate the differences between Chaucer's work and that of the late fifteenth-century Scottish poet.*]

For over four hundred years the greatest poets of medieval Scotland have stood in the shadow of Chaucer, their work judged in the light of his, they themselves categorized as "Scots Chaucerians," a term which puts them in the wrong time and the wrong place, assigns them characteristics they do not have, and denies them talents they do. This intellectual Chaucerian straitjacket, presupposing the nature of their work and forestalling its objective appraisal, has resulted in persistent neglect of the Scots' poetry. Admittedly the dialect of these writers, Robert Henryson, Gawin Douglas, and William Dunbar, is difficult for us today; but so is the dialect of *Sir Gawain and the Green Knight,* and that poem is neglected by neither students nor critics. In the present space the effect and extent of the Chaucerian blight can perhaps be best suggested by representative quotes from a great body of commentary and a detailed analysis of the actual as opposed to the traditionally accepted relationship between one Scots poem widely touted as "Chaucerian" and the relevant English poem.

Chaucer is a giant among poets, surpassed in English literature only by Shakespeare and perhaps Milton, though the point is arguable. Comparison between him and the Scots would inevitably make them appear in some way inferior—F. P. Magoun once suggested that making such a comparison was to put a New York skyscraper in a California patio. Both accommodations have their uses, and the Scots have excellences of their own; yet even when they do not aim at those of the master, time and again in appraising them critics drag in Chaucer whether his presence is relevant or not. Dunbar is criticized because he lacks Chaucer's chivalry and figures, "admirable in the ways of the parson, Constance, or Griseld." Why not criticize Chaucer for lacking Dunbar's vitriolic bite and figures admirable in the ways of the Lady Solistaris who dance their minuet of vice at court? Henryson "was incapable of rising to the refinements, or conceiving the delicacies" of Chaucer. But Henryson gives no indication of ever attempting such refinements and delicacies. In "The Thrissil and the Rois" and "The Goldyn Targe" "there is nothing . . . to recall the discursive dialogues between 'Geoffrey' and the eagle in upper space." Why on earth should there be? Relevant or not, Chaucer's presence seems inescapable in criticism of Middle Scots poetry and has resulted in misinterpretation of the poets' work and persistent underestimation of their achievement both as individuals and as a school. Chaucer, sole begetter of the movement, is the master influence who brought fresh literary life to Scotland, "quickened the fallow ground" making it "sessonabill, sappie, and to resave all seidis abill," and only thus able to produce the likes of Henryson, Douglas, and Dunbar. The critics' name is legion, but perhaps G. G. Smith speaks best for those who give Chaucer full credit for the flowering of Scotland's poetry. In discussing "the Chaucerian revival," Smith says: " . . . the North deliberately put itself to school and by a rhetorical, and somewhat bookish, discipline, rather than by a natural facility, reproduced, and at times improved upon, the models."

The nature of the conventionally conceived relationship is illuminated by the terms in which it is described. Chaucer is the master and lantern, moulder, model, and king; the Scots are his pupils, disciples, followers, successors, and liegemen. To his genius first, their ability second, is due their high achievement; they are dependent upon him as inspiration, stimulus, source. Their great works are modeled upon, borrowed from, suggested and inspired by those of Chaucer. They are good when they imitate most, bad when they imitate least. Frequently it is suggested that without Chaucer the Scots would never have been poets at all, much less good poets! Even when critics praise them, they often do so in terms of Chaucer, making him the standard of excellence, "Chaucerian" a synonym for "good," and assigning Dunbar and the rest certain ill-defined, but inevitably Chaucer-related, traits. Henryson has humor finer, slyer, more Chaucerian than Dunbar's, and is "the only one of the major Makars who is really Chaucerian in his breadth of mind and largeness." Douglas "attains a robuster versification than you are like to find in Chaucer." Why must the praise always be by comparison, and why must the comparison always be with Chaucer?

Why should commonplaces of content, meter, and language be taken as evidence of dependency? Henryson is "prone, like Chaucer, to draw a comic parallel between the bestial and the human." The assemblage of creatures in "The Thrissil and the Rois" is "in imitation of Chaucer's 'Parliament of Fowls' "; Douglas' pentameter couplets are "Chaucer's rhyming couplets of ten-syllabled lines"; the southern forms of his dialect, the result of Chaucer's influence. But other such parallels were commonly drawn in the great body of beast epic and fable; other assemblages were described, other pentameter couplets composed by poets other than Chaucer; and the southern forms of Douglas' dialect were frequently enough found from Edinburgh to the channel during the late fourteenth, fifteenth, and early sixteenth centuries. (pp. 175-78)

Consistently Henryson, Douglas, and Dunbar are held up to Chaucer and found wanting. Of course not all critics interpret the Scots solely in this manner; recently a number have been at pains to reject both the term "Scots Chaucerian" and the concept. Yet they have remained curiously persistent, and even these critics seem unable to escape entirely the Chaucerian set. Fox says, "The 'Chaucerian' part of 'Scottish Chaucerian' . . . [is] so equivocal as to be almost meaningless" but entitles his essay "The Scottish Chaucerians," calls the *Testament of Cresseid* a continuation and companion piece, an analysis of and parallel to *Troilus* which uses Chaucer's characters and situation "to explore the same problems that Chaucer deals with." MacQueen asserts that Henryson is not the disciple of but rather a fellow innovator with Chaucer, yet describes the *Testament* as the "most Chaucerian" of Henryson's works, "The Cok and the Fox," as an "adaptation" of "The Nun's Priest's Tale," "The Taill of the Lyon and the Mous" as "directly modelled on the 'Prologue' to Chaucer's 'Legend of Good Women,' " and finds Henryson's burgess mouse reminiscent of the Wife of Bath. Even the redoubtable Agnes Mure Mackenzie, after firmly stating "the Scottish Chaucerians are a myth," feels compelled to point out that Henryson is "superficially, most like Chaucer in temper and out-look and in the peculiar quality of his humour," and she approaches the Scots poet by comparing him to Chaucer.

Yet, evidence of the Scots' indebtedness is surprisingly slim. Douglas and Dunbar call Chaucer "master." Henryson refers to him, occasionally uses rime royal as he does, and bases two poems on narratives which derive either from Chaucer or sources common to both. Douglas' "Palice of Honour," like Chaucer's "House of Fame," is a dream vision involving the journey of a comic persona to the palace of a personified abstraction. Dunbar's "Goldyn Targe," like Chaucer's "Legend of Good Women," is a dream vision involving a company of ladies and a dreamer attacked by a god of love; the ladies in his "Twa Marriet Wemen and the Wedo" appear to be descended, as was the Wife of Bath, from La Vieille in *Romance of the Rose,* and his satire on the court fool, Thomas Norny, employs a mock-heroic technique and meter comparable to those in Chaucer's "Rime of Sir Thopas." But the purpose of Henryson's "Cok and the Fox" and the *Testament of Cresseid* is quite different from that of Chaucer's comparable poems; Douglas' "Palice of Honour" is minor work, perhaps one tenth as long as his *Eneados* and one hundredth as significant; and there are indicative resemblances to Chaucer in no more than four, at most five, of over one hundred poems attributed to Dunbar. On the whole, the main reason for calling the Scots "Chaucerian" seems to be that they were the first to write good verse in the British Isles after Chaucer.

Nearly anyone who wrote English poetry for two hundred years after Chaucer would have been hard put not to show his influence somehow. Spenser's Acrasia bears a family likeness to Chaucer's Venus—though it is possible that both enchantresses hark back to Prudentius' glowing Luxuria. Should we then call Spenser "Chaucerian," or both Chaucer and Spenser "Prudentian"? Shakespeare tells of Troilus and Criseyde; and it is doubtful that he would have described Troilus on the Trojan walls gazing toward the Grecian tents had Chaucer not done so before him. Donne's aubade to the sun reflects that of Chaucer, and Dryden, like Henryson, retold the tale of Chauntecleer and Pertelote. But neither Shakespeare nor Donne nor Dryden is called "Chaucerian." Why the Scots? Because, says H. H. Wood, "it is quite impossible to overestimate their debt in inspiration, in form, and in doctrine, to their master and original, Chaucer . . . without [whose] inspiring and fructifying influence . . . the movement would never have been." Without *Troilus* there would have been no *Testament;* without the Wife of Bath, no "Twa Marriet Wemen and the Wedo." Sprutok's song, "Was never wedow sa gay," reminds Wood of Chauntecleer's "My leif is faren on lande"; Makyne reminds him of Criseyde. We may well agree with Golding, "happier had the fate of the Scottish Chaucerians been had they . . . been born in China," set as they are "dubiously upon a border-line of appreciation," their virtues "blurred in the glory thrown about them by the sun of Chaucer," deriving "their immortality, alas! more from his name than from their own high merits" ["The Scottish Chaucerians," *The Saturday Review of Politics, Literature, Science, and Art,* 134 (1922), 782].

Despite its Scottish idiom, Henryson's *Testament of Cresseid* was long attributed to Chaucer, and in 1803 William Godwin established the standard mode of its criticism in writing that the poem had "a degree of merit calculated to make us regret that it is not a performance standing by itself, instead of serving merely as an appendage to the work of another." Subsequently Bennett designated it "a not unworthy pendant," Huxley, "merely a short sequel" to Chaucer's *Troilus and Criseyde,* McDermott, "the most successful of Chaucerian imitations." The *Testament* begins its story where Chaucer left off, is in the same stanzaic form as *Troilus,* and was first printed as Book VI of that poem. Beyond that what is Henryson's actual debt? If the two poems are compared in detail, it becomes apparent that the *Testament* is neither a slender appendage to nor an imitation of *Troilus.* Henryson perceived in Chaucer embryonic concepts which he developed and carried through to their logical end. In a sense, his poem takes its departure from Chaucer's, but achieves great dramatic force by means of contrast with rather than resemblance to it. Chaucer tells of the birth, blossoming, and betrayal of a love which is an earthly shadow of the cosmic force that creates, vitalizes, and binds together the universe. Henryson tells of the corruption and death that follow the betrayal of such love and its debasement into lust.

He must have meant to set his poem against Chaucer's, for he tells initially of reading Chaucer's account of the sorrow of Troilus; then throughout he inserts echoes from *Troilus* which call it persistently to mind and help to make clear that his poem is at once consistent with it and yet quite different. Despite his title, Chaucer is concerned primarily with Troilus, whose growth he traces from ignorance of any sort of love through the puppy love of a young Romeo, to adult passion and a mature but finite questioning of God's ordinance, to final, reconciled comprehension of the nature of all human happiness—including love. But Chaucer presents a static Criseyde who never learns and never changes, who simply disappears from the story with her fate left obscure. Henryson traces the progress of Criseyde become Cresseid, a figure whose corrupt end grows logically and inevitably from seeds in Chaucer's poem. However, by continually pointing up the contrast between that poem and his own, between what love and Criseyde had been and what they become, he enhances the grimness of his heroine's lot, underscores the lesson it illustrates, and explores an irony left undeveloped by Chaucer: we make our own fate, but are blind to that fact until it is too late.

Chaucer commences his tragedy of Troilus with a plea to Tesephone for aid in writing, for the manner of its telling should suit a tale; and Henryson in the first lines of his tragedy of Cresseid strikes the same note, "Ane doolie sessoun to ane cairfull dyte / Suld correspond and be equiualent." Both poets then set their narratives in spring, the appropriate season for each, but with a notable difference. For Chaucer spring is an English April, filled with new green and the sweet scent of flowers, a suitable setting for the birth of Troilus' idealistic love. For Henryson spring is the very opposite, a northern mid-Lent of hail, frost, and bitter wind, at once an effective setting for his story and a means of emphasizing the difference between it and Chaucer's: the warm, fresh, young love of which Chaucer wrote has now passed, to be succeeded by age, cold lust, disease, and death.

Henryson disposes quickly and, in the light of Chaucer's account, logically of the affair between Criseyde and Diomede. Chaucer had presented Diomede's speedy wooing, begun in the short space of a ride from Troy to the Greek camp, as a parody of Troilus' long, formal courtship, and suggested Criseyde's incipient falsity in her early responses to the Greek warrior:

"But as to speke of love, ywis," she seyde.
"I hadde a lord, to whom I wedded was,
The whos myn herte al was, til that he deyde."
(V.974-976)

After her husband, as we know, came Troilus; but Criseyde continues, "And other love, as help me now Pallas, / Ther in myn herte nys, ne never was" (V.977-978). Thus we see that she can lie, and having denied a previous betrayal, she concludes:

I say nat therfore that I wol yow love,
N'y say nat nay; but in conclusioun,
I mene wel, by God that sit above!
(V.1002-04)

It is the utterance of a woman tragically weak; and surely any love between such a one and Chaucer's Diomede would from the start have been doomed to end as Henryson perceived and, in resuming her story, depicts in a few devastating lines:

Quhen Diomeid had all his appetyte,
And mair, fulfillit of this fair ladie,
Vpon ane vther he set his haill delyte,
And send to hir ane lybell of repudie
And hir excludit fra his companie.
(71-75)

The most consistent motivation of Chaucer's Criseyde is a proud concern for honor which she equates with her reputation, as Pandarus says, initially that of a saint. Having accepted Troilus, her greatest fear is that "Men myghten demen that he loveth me" (II.730), although she reasonably concludes:

May ich hym lette of that? Why, nay, parde!
I knowe also, and alday heere and se,
Men loven wommen al biside hire leve;
And whan hem leste namore, la them byleve!
(II.732-735)

Her refusal of his plea that they flee Troy together is based on this concern:

And also thynketh on myn honeste,
That floureth yet, how foule I sholde it shende
And with what filthe it spotted sholde be,
If in this forme I sholde with yow wende.
Ne though I lyved unto the werldes ende,
My name sholde I nevere ayeynward wynne.
(IV.1576-81)

Near the end of the story she does give over care for the Mrs. Grundys of the world and resolves to return to Troilus; but Diomede's persuasion suffices to change her resolve, and Criseyde herself predicts the loss of the name she has so jealously guarded, "O, rolled shal I ben on many a tonge!" (V. 1061). In the *Testament* Henryson shows the heroine's regard for her hallowed reputation debased to fear lest men know, not that a great prince loves her, but that the surfeited Diomede has indeed "when hem liste namore" thrown her out. Chaucer's Criseyde once stood proudly among the other worshippers in the temple of the Palladion. Henryson's Cresseid will not enter a temple to sacrifice as she should, but hides outside, afraid the people may suspect her disgrace. And she will endure the fate Criseyde predicted: her name foully ruined, spotted with filth, will be rolled on every tongue.

Chaucer's Criseyde is almost never alone. She lives surrounded by ladies, is visited by Pandarus, sought out by Troilus and Diomede. But Henryson emphasizes the isolation of Cresseid, who journeys to her father's house without fellowship and alone in a secret oratory angrily cries out against the gods for her lack of lovers:

> Vpon Venus and Cupide angerly
> Scho cryit out, and said on this same wyse,
> "Allace, that euer I maid yow sacrifice!
>
> "ye gaue me anis ane deuine responsaill
> That I suld be the flour of luif in Troy;
> Now am I maid ane vnworthie outwaill,
> And all in cair translatit is my joy.
> Quha sall me gyde? Quha sall me now conuoy,
> Sen I fra Diomeid and nobill Troylus
> Am clene excludit, as abiect odious? . . .
> And fra luifferis left, and all forlane."
> (124-33, 140)

The Scots poet, recognizing that a woman with the character Chaucer assigned Criseyde would inevitably lose her company of ladies and lovers and be isolated, assigns just such a fate to Cresseid.

Following her outburst, Henryson tells how in a vision Cresseid sees a convocation of gods to whom Cupid appeals for justice:

> "Lo," quod Cupide, "quha will blaspheme the name
> Of his awin god, outher in word [or] deid,
> To all goddis he dois baith lak and schame,
> And suld haue bitter panis to his meid.
> I say this by yone wretchit Cresseid,
> The quhilk throw me was sum tyme flour of lufe,
> Me and my mother starklie can reprufe, . . .
> This greit iniure done to our hie estait
> Me think with pane we suld mak recompence; . . .
> Thairfoir ga help to reuenge, I yow pray!"
> (274-280, 290-291, 294)

One of the more troubling aspects of Henryson's poem is the cause assigned here for the punishment of his heroine. Since Criseyde's sin was infidelity, Cupid's charge of blasphemy seems somewhat inconsistent. But again, I believe, Henryson is developing a rudimentary concept of Chaucer's and, by so doing, suggesting that it is not mere angry words against two pagan gods which bring down punishment upon Cresseid's head. The crux of the matter would seem to be against whom or what she blasphemes, and how.

Chaucer identifies love with an omnipotent life force, "Thorugh which that thynges lyven alle and be." Book III of *Troilus* opens with an invocation which moves from praise of Venus to that of the power whose emanations vitalize the universe, to that of God's redemptive love, and closes with further praise of love which, as Troilus says, governs earth and sea, holds peoples joined, knits the law of company, diversifies the seasons, and binds together the discordant elements, bringing forth day and night and keeping the sea in check (III.1-16, 1744-64). Clearly it is no subjective passion to which the young prince responds, but a cosmic creative force of which his own emotion, at once physical yet spiritualizing, is at least a shadow if not a part. Henryson does not identify love in these explicit terms; rather, he assigns something of the same role Chaucer had assigned love to the seven planet gods who judge and punish Cresseid,

> Quhilk hes power of all thing generabill,
> To reull and steir be thair greit influence
> Wedder and wind, and coursis variabill . . .
> . . . seuin deificait,
> Participant of deuyne sapience.
> (147-150, 288-289)

In crying out against the gods of love, Cresseid has, as Cupid says, done shame to all these gods, violence "Asweill for yow as for my self," and thus has blasphemed against the power that generates and rules the world. Her blasphemy, however, consists not just of words, but of a series of actions which began with Criseyde's lies, betrayal of Troilus's ennobling love and response to Diomede's debased wooing, and has now progressed to Cresseid's prostitution and sacrilegious outcry. The wrongness of these actions is underscored by the rightness of those of Troilus.

Troilus speaks and acts perfectly in accordance with the laws of love, is ennobled by and faithful to it. For aid he prays devoutly to the same gods who punish Cresseid; for his happiness, he thanks Venus, Cupid, and "Benigne Love, thow holy bond of thynges," with a reverent acknowledgment of its power, "Whoso wol grace, and list the nought honouren, / Lo, his desir wol fle withouten wynges" (III.1261-63), which ironically suggests the nature of Cresseid's later offense. On the other hand, Criseyde breaks the laws of love and feels but little of its ennoblement. Henryson then makes clear the full significance of these contrasting actions, showing to what end the course upon which Criseyde embarks would lead, if indeed love be as Chaucer describes it. Having dishonored the divine power Troilus honors, she will inevitably suffer.

In her vision Saturn and Cynthia, representatives of the gods, decree that Cresseid is to be afflicted "with seiknes incurabill, / And to all louers be abhominabill" (307-308). What she seems to see here is a metaphorical statement of her crime and its punishment, for just as the gods represent the creating, ruling force of the universe, which Chaucer interpreted as love and against which she has blasphemed in action and word, so the punishment they mete out represents the logical consequences of such blasphemy. With or without the intervention of pagan gods, Cresseid would experience loss of beauty, disease, abandonment, and death because those are the natural results of her behavior, of her violation of the laws which govern "all thing generabill." Her dream represents dawning comprehension of what she has done and the beginning of a new self-awareness.

Relevant or not, Chaucer's presence seems inescapable in criticism of Middle Scots poetry and has resulted in misinterpretation of the poets' work and persistent underestimation of their achievement both as individuals and as a school.

—Florence H. Ridley

Blindness to herself and to the nature of true love is the hallmark of Chaucer's heroine, blindness which for Cresseid is gradually mitigated. Initially Criseyde, a widow, has greater maturity and common sense—shrewdness might be a better term—than Troilus. Yet despite her experience, her comprehension of love never equals that he achieves, but remains instead comparable to that of Pandarus. For the uncle love is but "casuel plesaunce" (IV.419), for the niece it begins in nothing and ends in nothing, "That erst was nothing, into nought it torneth" (II.798). When Antigone praises love, the right life, which leads one to flee all vice and live in virtue, Criseyde can only wonder, "Lord, is ther swych blisse among / Thise loveres" (II.885-886). Moreover, despite her shrewdness, Criseyde's understanding of human nature, including her own, remains limited. She is certain she can trick her father and return to Troy—were she not she would die on the spot. But of course Criseyde cannot trick Calkas, and she neither returns nor dies. She swears to mourn forever should Troilus die:

> And, Troilus, my clothes everychon
> Shul blake ben in tokenyng, herte swete,
> That I am as out of this world agon.
> (IV.778-780)

But she has worn black before for another man, and as Troilus had displaced that dead husband in her heart, Diomede displaces him. When Criseyde promises, "To Diomede algate I wol be trewe" (V. 1071), inevitably we wonder who will be next.

Perceiving in Criseyde's words and actions the implications for subsequent development, Henryson tells us most graphically what, if not precisely who, will be next in her downward progress. While Chaucer's heroine ends as she began, "slydinge of corage" and totally unaware of it, Henryson's learns and changes, her mind's eye ironically becoming ever clearer as her physical eyes become blurred with disease. After sentence is passed upon her, Saturn blasts Cresseid's beauty with a touch of his frosty wand and Cynthia inflicts disease upon her:

> Thy cristall ene mingit with blude I mak,
> Thy voice sa cleir vnplesand hoir and hace,
> Thy lustie lyre ouirspred with spottis blak,
> And lumpis haw appeirand in thy face:
> Quhair thow cummis, ilk man sall fle the place.
> (337-341)

This is the concrete expression of the ultimate degradation which would befall Chaucer's lovely heroine, for the ravaging of beauty symbolizes corruption which began with Criseyde's falsity and grew with Cresseid's lust and irreverence. With the vision and the disease, Cresseid's understanding of the significance of her actions begins, and again it is a development partially anticipated but left unrealized by Chaucer. Pandarus had once urged Criseyde to love, warning that beauty would pass:

> 'And sende yow than a myrour in to prye,
> In which that ye may se youre face a morwe!'
> Nece, I bidde wisshe yow namore sorwe.
> (II.404-406)

Now Cresseid wakes from her dream:

> . . . than rais scho vp and tuik
> Ane poleist glas, and hir schaddow culd luik;
> And quhen scho saw hir face sa deformait,
> Gif scho in hart was wa aneuch, God wait!
> (347-350)

Pandarus' idle prayer has been fulfilled, and indeed he could have wished his niece no more sorrow.

Still pathetically concerned to protect her reputation, Cresseid asks Calkas:

> . . . Father, I wald not be kend;
> Thairfoir in secreit wyse ye let me gang
> To yone hospitall at the tounis end,
> (380-382)

and retires to the spital house. There as she remembers her fairness, lovers, riches, honor, fame, all irrevocably lost, Cresseid feels the force of another of Pandarus' earlier warnings:

> The worste kynde of infortune is this,
> A man to han ben in prosperitee,
> And it remembren, whan it passed is,
> (III.1626-28)

and offers herself as a mirror wherein other women may see the truth of such an admonition:

> . . . in your mynd ane mirrour mak of me:
> As I am now, peraduenture that ye
> For all your micht may cum to that same end.
> (457-459)

Of course to be aware that such loss may come is not necessarily to know how to avoid it; and Cresseid still, accepting no responsibility for her plight, blames the "craibit Goddis" and, like Criseyde, fortune and fate. But Cresseid keeps on learning. As she continues to weep and chide her destiny, she is counseled by a leper lady to make virtue of necessity, "[G]o leir to clap thy clapper to and fro, / And lei[f] efter the law of lipper leid" (479-480); and having broken the law of lovers, Cresseid learns to follow that of lepers.

Her moment of final illumination comes with recognition of Troilus, which brings full awareness of what he represents and is, and of the contrast, so damning to herself, between them. The passage describing these reactions (498-546) has caused some difficulty, but I believe the key to its meaning may be found in Henryson's adroit development of another suggestion in Troilus, where the psychological ground for this recognition is laid. Chaucer describes the manner in which Troilus was affected by his first sight of Criseyde in all her beauty and pride:

> And of hire look in him ther gan to quyken
> So gret desir and such affeccioun,
> That in his hertes botme gan to stiken
> Of hir his fixe and depe impressioun . . .
> [He] Was ful unwar that Love hadde his dwel-
> lynge
> Withinne the subtile stremes of hir yen;
> That sodeynly hym thoughte he felte dyen,
> Right with hire look, the spirit in his herte.
> (I.295-298, 304-307)

Then upon this concept of the onset of love Henryson builds, telling how when Troilus rides past a leper huddled by the roadside, although he does not recognize her, those bleared eyes where love once dwelt bring to mind, "The sweit visage and amorous blenking / Of fair Cresseid, sumtyme his awin darling" (503-504). And as once before his lady's look had seemed to slay his spirit, so now:

> Ane spark of lufe than till his hart culd spring
> And kendlit all his bodie in ane fyre;
> With hait fewir, ane sweit and trimbling
> Him tuik, quhill he was reddie to expyre.
> (512-515)

Henryson explains:

> Na wonder was, suppois in mynd that he
> Tuik hir figure sa sone, and lo, now quhy:
> The idole of ane thing in cace may be
> Sa deip imprentit in the fantasy
> That it deludis the wittis outwardly,
> And sa appeiris in forme and lyke estait
> Within the mynd as it was figurait.
> (505-511)

It is the sense impression of Criseyde fixed in his heart long ago as Chaucer had told which moves Troilus, and he tosses the beggar alms.

Criseyde had once felt the aspect of Troilus sink into her heart, seeing him ride from the battlefield among the cheering Trojans. But Chaucer had not said that the image became fixed in its depths; and now the figure of Troilus, which could be but dimly perceived by leprous eyes, rouses no impression in Cresseid's imagination as she asks, "Quhat Lord is yone . . . / Hes done to vs so greit humanitie?" (533-534). Only with the revelation, "Schir Troylus it is, gentill and fre" (536), does she feel a bitter pang of memory, understanding, and self-knowledge and see at last what Criseyde never saw: the difference between love like that of Diomede and that of Troilus and the significance of her actions. Seeing that she has shaped her own destiny, she no longer blames fortune or the gods but only herself, and for the first time laments the wrong done Troilus rather than her own misery:

> All faith and lufe I promissit to the
> Was in the self fickill and friuolous:
> O fals Cresseid and trew knicht Troilus!
> (551-553)

This marks a considerable advance over Criseyde's blindness, but even Cresseid's understanding never approaches the cosmic wisdom of Troilus who, as Chaucer tells, not only comprehends true love but ultimately sees all earthly felicity, of which love is a part, in proper perspective. Only at the moment of death does Cresseid comprehend anything of the nature of real love; and she ends as Henryson knew, given the character Chaucer originally assigned his heroine, she would, not like Troilus laughing in the heavens but comparatively unenlightened, dead beneath a stone. Thus the *Testament,* primarily through the relationship between the two heroines, develops consistently yet in an unexpected way action and character anticipated in *Troilus,* and by so doing evokes pathos and powerful dramatic irony.

The narrator of Chaucer's *Troilus* displays no attitude of significance for any major theme of that poem; but the attitudes of Henryson's narrator serve to emphasize further the lesson of the *Testament,* particularly by their contrast with those of Cresseid. This narrator first appears trying humbly to invoke Venus, whom he has promised to obey and now trusts will renew his success in love. But he is repelled by frost and bitter wind for the fire of passion is no longer for him—he is old, and "Thocht lufe be hait, yit in ane man of age / It kendillis nocht sa sone as in youtheid" (29-30). Lovelessness on the part of Chaucer's narrators is a standard joke, the result of ineptness; here it is the natural result of age which the narrator, blaming no one, accepts philosophically. Cresseid too had once worshipped Venus, trusting that the goddess would always prosper her suit. Now she too is loveless, but in sharp contrast to the narrator she blames the gods for infelicity she has brought upon herself and is neither obedient, humble, nor reverent. Initially the narrator shares Cresseid's blindness as to the cause of her fate, attributing to cruel fortune the distress which, he says, has come about "nathing throw the gilt / Of the," and anticipating her protest against the crabbed gods by himself upbraiding Saturn, "O cruell Saturne, fraward and angrie, / Hard is thy dome and to malitious!" (323-324). In his concluding admonition to women, however, the narrator again like Cresseid reproves no one and nothing save her own false deception.

Obviously Henryson considered the deception of Troilus important, for his final words relate Cresseid's punishment specifically to that offense. Yet, it had been committed only in Chaucer's poem and is not included among those sins of blasphemy, slander, defamation, injury, and violence done the gods which Cupid cites as reasons for punishing Cresseid. I believe the apparent contradiction is resolved by the fact that Henryson considered this specific sin against love to be only one aspect, though perhaps the most important, of a whole complex of wrongdoings, of blasphemy in word and deed which began in *Troilus* and continued in the *Testament.* This woman's end about which Chaucer remained silent is the just, inevitable result of a progress spanning both poems. "Troilus moot wepe in cares colde," says Chaucer's narrator:

Swich is this world, whoso it kan byholde:
In ech estat is litel hertes reste.
God leve us for to take it for the beste!
(V.1747-50)

When youthful passion ends as it must, Henryson's narrator takes it for the best. He does not rail against fortune, fate, or the gods, but turning to comforts appropriate to old age—a fire, a drink, warm wraps, and a book—wisely adapts himself to natural law. Cresseid in violating all the laws of love violates the natural law of gods and men; by infidelity she brings down lovelessness, by lecherous living disease upon herself; she attacks the gods and dies a disgraced outcast. Perhaps the lesson is best stated in "The Knight's Tale," where Theseus says:

Thanne is it wysdom, as it thynketh me,
To maken vertu of necessitee,
And take it weel that we may nat eschue,
And namely that to us alle is due.
And whoso gruccheth ought, he dooth folye,
And rebel is to hym that al may gye.
(*The Canterbury Tales, I* (A) 3041-46)

The leper lady who counseled Cresseid would have agreed. Such is the testament illustrated by the downward course of a heroine whose character is consistently developed from the beginning of Chaucer's poem to the end of Henryson's, a testament for anyone who "gruccheth," rebels or blasphemes in word or deed against the gods—or, as the masque of seven planets suggests, the laws which rule and steer all things generable in the world.

Now if in light of this comparison of the two poems we again ask what was Henryson's debt to Chaucer, perhaps it will be apparent how misleading "Scots Chaucerian," with its connotations of dependency, really is. For in the *Testament* Henryson did not imitate Chaucer, did not adopt his material or manner or themes. He found in Chaucer's poem a latent idea and the outline of a static character which he proceeded to develop fully in such a way as to illustrate that idea and make it a lesson universally applicable. The greatest teachers point the way for others; and that, I believe, is what Chaucer did for Henryson, though it is a way he himself did not, perhaps even could not, go. To see the *Testament of Cresseid* as weaker because it begins where *Troilus and Criseyde* leaves off and gains irony from its contrast with that poem—much less because it is not a perfect imitation—is to miss the point and artistry of Henryson's achievement and do far less than credit to a poet who was a genius completely in his own right. (pp. 179-96)

Florence H. Ridley, "A Plea for the Middle Scots," in The Learned and the Lewed: Studies in Chaucer and Medieval Literature, *edited by Larry D. Benson, Cambridge, Mass.: Harvard University Press, 1974, pp. 175-96.*

FURTHER READING

Aitken, Adam J.; McDiarmid, Matthew P.; and Thomson, Derick S., eds. *Bards and Makars.* Glasgow: University of Glasgow Press, 1977, 250 p.

Collection of essays focusing on the language and literature of mediaeval and renaissance Scottish writers.

Blake, N. F. "The Fifteenth Century Reconsidered." *Neuphilologische Mitteilungen* LXXI, No. 1 (1970): 146-57.

Judges Scottish literature of the fifteenth century superior to English literature of the same period, crediting the stability of the "literary language" in Scotland. Blake maintains that Chaucer's influence on these writers "was limited to nonlinguistic features like the use of allegory and stanza."

Kinsley, James. "The Mediaeval Makars." In *Scottish Poetry: A Critical Survey,* edited by James Kinsley, pp. 1-32. London: Cassell and Co., 1955.

Surveys mediaeval Scottish poetry, asserting that "its historical interest and its permanent appeal lie not in any bold departures from the general European tradition, but in the adaptation of stock themes and styles in ways which are congenial to the Scottish temper and appropriate to Scottish life."

MacQueen, John. Introduction to *Ballatis of Luve,* pp. xi-lxix. Edinburgh: Edinburgh University Press, 1970.

Detailed introduction and explication of courtly love lyrics from fifteenth- and sixteenth-century Scotland.

———. "The Literature of Fifteenth-Century Scotland." In *Scottish Society in the Fifteenth Century,* edited by Jennifer M. Brown, pp. 184-208. London: Edward Arnold, 1977.

Describes the notable literary figures of the period, discussing the artistic, historical, and linguistic significance of their works.

Millar, J. H. *A Literary History of Scotland,* London: T. Fisher Unwin, 1903, 703 p.

Historical and critical examination of Scottish literature up to 1900, including a substantial section on the Scottish Chaucerians.

Robinson, Ian. "Scotland." In his *Chaucer and the English Tradition,* pp. 234-47. London: Cambridge University Press, 1972.

Discusses the works of Dunbar, Henryson, and Douglas in relation to the Chaucerian tradition.

Smith, Janet M. *The French Background of Middle Scots Literature.* London: Oliver and Boyd, 1934, 186 p.

Surveys Scottish literature in the Middle Ages, noting the extent to which the Scots poets looked to France for method and inspiration. Smith concludes that "there was very little foreign influence on the spirit" of Scottish poetry.

Wittig, Kurt. *The Scottish Tradition in Literature.* Edinburgh and London: Oliver and Boyd, 1958, 352 p.

Studies Scottish literature not as an isolated entity, but "as a product of that particular community in which it originated."

Literature Criticism from 1400 to 1800

Cumulative Indexes

This Index Includes References to Entries in These Gale Series

Contemporary Literary Criticism Presents excerpts of criticism on the works of novelists, poets, dramatists, short story writers, scriptwriters, and other creative writers who are now living or who have died since 1960.

Twentieth-Century Literary Criticism Contains critical excerpts by the most significant commentators on poets, novelists, short story writers, dramatists, and philosophers who died between 1900 and 1960.

Nineteenth-Century Literature Criticism Offers significant passages from criticism on authors who died between 1800 and 1899.

Literature Criticism from 1400 to 1800 Compiles significant passages from the most noteworthy criticism on authors of the fifteenth through eighteenth centuries.

Classical and Medieval Literature Criticism Offers excerpts of criticism on the works of world authors from classical antiquity through the fourteenth century.

Short Story Criticism Compiles excerpts of criticism on short fiction by writers of all eras and nationalities.

Poetry Criticism Presents excerpts of criticism on the works of poets from all eras, movements, and nationalities.

Drama Criticism Contains excerpts of criticism on dramatists of all nationalities and periods of literary history.

Children's Literature Review Includes excerpts from reviews, criticism, and commentary on works of authors and illustrators who create books for children.

Contemporary Authors Series Encompasses five related series. *Contemporary Authors* provides biographical and bibliographical information on more than 97,000 writers of fiction, nonfiction, poetry, journalism, drama, motion pictures, and other fields. Each new volume contains sketches on authors not previously covered in the series. *Contemporary Authors New Revision Series* provides completely updated information on active authors covered in previously published volumes of *CA*. Only entries requiring significant change are revised for *CA New Revision Series. Contemporary Authors Permanent Series* consists of updated listings for deceased and inactive authors removed from the original volumes 9-36 when these volumes were revised. *Contemporary Authors Autobiography Series* presents specially commissioned autobiographies by leading contemporary writers. *Contemporary Authors Bibliographical Series* contains primary and secondary bibliographies as well as analytical bibliographical essays by authorities on major modern authors.

Dictionary of Literary Biography Encompasses three related series. *Dictionary of Literary Biography* furnishes illustrated overviews of authors' lives and works and places them in the larger perspective of literary history. *Dictionary of Literary Biography Documentary Series* illuminates the careers of major figures through a selection of literary documents, including letters, notebook and diary entries, interviews, book reviews, and photographs. *Dictionary of Literary Biography Yearbook* summarizes the past year's literary activity with articles on genres, major prizes, conferences, and other timely subjects and includes updated and new entries on individual authors.

Concise Dictionary of American Literary Biography A six-volume series that collects revised and updated sketches on major American authors that were originally presented in *Dictionary of Literary Biography.*

Something about the Author Series Encompasses three related series. *Something about the Author* contains well-illustrated biographical sketches on juvenile and young adult authors and illustrators from all eras. *Something about the Author Autobiography Series* presents specially commissioned autobiographies by prominent authors and illustrators of books for children and young adults.

Yesterday's Authors of Books for Children Contains heavily illustrated entries on children's writers who died before 1961. Complete in two volumes.

Literary Criticism Series Cumulative Author Index

This index lists all author entries in the Gale Literary Criticism Series and includes cross-references to other Gale sources. References in the index are identified as follows:

AAYA: *Authors & Artists for Young Adults,* Volumes 1-8
BLC: *Black Literature Criticism,* Volumes 1-3
CA: *Contemporary Authors* (original series), Volumes 1-136
CAAS: *Contemporary Authors Autobiography Series,* Volumes 1-15
CABS: *Contemporary Authors Bibliographical Series,* Volumes 1-3
CANR: *Contemporary Authors New Revision Series,* Volumes 1-37
CAP: *Contemporary Authors Permanent Series,* Volumes 1-2
CA-R: *Contemporary Authors* (first revision), Volumes 1-44
CDALB: *Concise Dictionary of American Literary Biography,* Volumes 1-6
CLC: *Contemporary Literary Criticism,* Volumes 1-72
CLR: *Children's Literature Review,* Volumes 1-26
CMLC: *Classical and Medieval Literature Criticism,* Volumes 1-9
DC: *Drama Criticism,* Volumes 1-2
DLB: *Dictionary of Literary Biography,* Volumes 1-114
DLB-DS: *Dictionary of Literary Biography Documentary Series,* Volumes 1-9
DLB-Y: *Dictionary of Literary Biography Yearbook,* Volumes 1980-1990
LC: *Literature Criticism from 1400 to 1800,* Volumes 1-20
NCLC: *Nineteenth-Century Literature Criticism,* Volumes 1-36
PC: *Poetry Criticism,* Volumes 1-5
SAAS: *Something about the Author Autobiography Series,* Volumes 1-14
SATA: *Something about the Author,* Volumes 1-69
SSC: *Short Story Criticism,* Volumes 1-10
TCLC: *Twentieth-Century Literary Criticism,* Volumes 1-46
WLC: *World Literature Criticism, 1500 to the Present,* Volumes 1-6
YABC: *Yesterday's Authors of Books for Children,* Volumes 1-2

A. E. 1867-1935 .... **TCLC 3, 10**
See also Russell, George William
See also DLB 19

Abbey, Edward 1927-1989 ...... **CLC 36, 59**
See also CANR 2; CA 45-48; obituary CA 128

Abbott, Lee K., Jr. 19??- .... **CLC 48**

Abe, Kobo 1924- .... **CLC 8, 22, 53**
See also CANR 24; CA 65-68

Abell, Kjeld 1901-1961 .... **CLC 15**
See also obituary CA 111

Abish, Walter 1931- .... **CLC 22**
See also CA 101

Abrahams, Peter (Henry) 1919- ..... **CLC 4**
See also CA 57-60

Abrams, M(eyer) H(oward) 1912- ... **CLC 24**
See also CANR 13; CA 57-60; DLB 67

Abse, Dannie 1923- .... **CLC 7, 29**
See also CAAS 1; CANR 4; CA 53-56; DLB 27

Achebe, (Albert) Chinua(lumogu) 1930- .... **CLC 1, 3, 5, 7, 11, 26, 51**
See also BLC 1; CLR 20; WLC 1; CANR 6, 26; CA 1-4R; SATA 38, 40

Acker, Kathy 1948- .... **CLC 45**
See also CA 117, 122

Ackroyd, Peter 1949- .... **CLC 34, 52**
See also CA 123, 127

Acorn, Milton 1923- .... **CLC 15**
See also CA 103; DLB 53

Adamov, Arthur 1908-1970 ...... **CLC 4, 25**
See also CAP 2; CA 17-18; obituary CA 25-28R

Adams, Alice (Boyd) 1926- ... **CLC 6, 13, 46**
See also CANR 26; CA 81-84; DLB-Y 86

Adams, Douglas (Noel) 1952- ... **CLC 27, 60**
See also CA 106; DLB-Y 83

Adams, Francis 1862-1893 .... **NCLC 33**

Adams, Henry (Brooks) 1838-1918 .... **TCLC 4**
See also CA 104; DLB 12, 47

Adams, Richard (George) 1920- .... **CLC 4, 5, 18**
See also CLR 20; CANR 3; CA 49-52; SATA 7

Adamson, Joy(-Friederike Victoria) 1910-1980 .... **CLC 17**
See also CANR 22; CA 69-72; obituary CA 93-96; SATA 11; obituary SATA 22

Adcock, (Kareen) Fleur 1934- ...... **CLC 41**
See also CANR 11; CA 25-28R; DLB 40

Addams, Charles (Samuel) 1912-1988 .... **CLC 30**
See also CANR 12; CA 61-64; obituary CA 126

Addison, Joseph 1672-1719 .... **LC 18**
See also DLB 101

Adler, C(arole) S(chwerdtfeger) 1932- .... **CLC 35**
See also CANR 19; CA 89-92; SATA 26

Adler, Renata 1938- .... **CLC 8, 31**
See also CANR 5, 22; CA 49-52

Ady, Endre 1877-1919 .... **TCLC 11**
See also CA 107

Andrewes, Lancelot 1555-1626 .... **LC 5**

Andrews, Cicily Fairfield 1892-1983
See West, Rebecca

Andreyev, Leonid (Nikolaevich)
1871-1919 .... **TCLC 3**
See also CA 104

Andrezel, Pierre 1885-1962
See Dinesen, Isak; Blixen, Karen (Christentze Dinesen)

Andric, Ivo 1892-1975 .... **CLC 8**
See also CA 81-84; obituary CA 57-60

Angelique, Pierre 1897-1962
See Bataille, Georges

Angell, Roger 1920- .... **CLC 26**
See also CANR 13; CA 57-60

Angelou, Maya 1928- .... **CLC 12, 35, 64**
See also BLC 1; CANR 19; CA 65-68; SATA 49; DLB 38

Annensky, Innokenty 1856-1909... **TCLC 14**
See also CA 110

Anouilh, Jean (Marie Lucien Pierre)
1910-1987 ...... **CLC 1, 3, 8, 13, 40, 50**
See also CA 17-20R; obituary CA 123

Anthony, Florence 1947-
See Ai

Anthony (Jacob), Piers 1934- ...... **CLC 35**
See also Jacob, Piers A(nthony) D(illingham)
See also DLB 8

Antoninus, Brother 1912-
See Everson, William (Oliver)

Antonioni, Michelangelo 1912- ..... **CLC 20**
See also CA 73-76

Antschel, Paul 1920-1970....... **CLC 10, 19**
See also Celan, Paul
See also CA 85-88

Anwar, Chairil 1922-1949 .... **TCLC 22**
See also CA 121

Apollinaire, Guillaume
1880-1918 .... **TCLC 3, 8**
See also Kostrowitzki, Wilhelm Apollinaris de

Appelfeld, Aharon 1932- .... **CLC 23, 47**
See also CA 112

Apple, Max (Isaac) 1941-........ **CLC 9, 33**
See also CANR 19; CA 81-84

Appleman, Philip (Dean) 1926- ..... **CLC 51**
See also CANR 6; CA 13-16R

Apuleius, (Lucius) (Madaurensis)
125?-175?.................. **CMLC 1**

Aquin, Hubert 1929-1977.......... **CLC 15**
See also CA 105; DLB 53

Aragon, Louis 1897-1982........ **CLC 3, 22**
See also CA 69-72; obituary CA 108; DLB 72

Arany, Janos 1817-1882......... **NCLC 34**

Arbuthnot, John 1667-1735.......... **LC 1**

Archer, Jeffrey (Howard) 1940- .... **CLC 28**
See also CANR 22; CA 77-80

Archer, Jules 1915- .... **CLC 12**
See also CANR 6; CA 9-12R; SAAS 5; SATA 4

Arden, John 1930- .... **CLC 6, 13, 15**
See also CAAS 4; CA 13-16R; DLB 13

Arenas, Reinaldo 1943- .... **CLC 41**
See also CA 124, 128

Arendt, Hannah 1906-1975 .... **CLC 66**
See also CA 19-20R; obituary CA 61-64

Aretino, Pietro 1492-1556 .... **LC 12**

Arguedas, Jose Maria
1911-1969 .... **CLC 10, 18**
See also CA 89-92

Argueta, Manlio 1936- .... **CLC 31**

Ariosto, Ludovico 1474-1533......... **LC 6**

Aristophanes
c. 450 B. C.-c. 385 B. C. ..... **CMLC 4; DC 2**

Arlt, Roberto 1900-1942 .... **TCLC 29**
See also CA 123

Armah, Ayi Kwei 1939- .... **CLC 5, 33**
See also BLC 1; CANR 21; CA 61-64

Armatrading, Joan 1950- .... **CLC 17**
See also CA 114

Arnim, Achim von (Ludwig Joachim von Arnim) 1781-1831 .... **NCLC 5**
See also DLB 90

Arnold, Matthew
1822-1888 .... **NCLC 6, 29; PC 5**
See also WLC 1; DLB 32, 57; CDALB 1832-1890

Arnold, Thomas 1795-1842 ...... **NCLC 18**
See also DLB 55

Arnow, Harriette (Louisa Simpson)
1908-1986 .... **CLC 2, 7, 18**
See also CANR 14; CA 9-12R; obituary CA 118; SATA 42, 47; DLB 6

Arp, Jean 1887-1966............... **CLC 5**
See also CA 81-84; obituary CA 25-28R

Arquette, Lois S(teinmetz) 1934-
See Duncan (Steinmetz Arquette), Lois
See also SATA 1

Arrabal, Fernando 1932- ... **CLC 2, 9, 18, 58**
See also CANR 15; CA 9-12R

Arrick, Fran 19??- .... **CLC 30**

Artaud, Antonin 1896-1948 ..... **TCLC 3, 36**
See also CA 104

Arthur, Ruth M(abel) 1905-1979.... **CLC 12**
See also CANR 4; CA 9-12R; obituary CA 85-88; SATA 7; obituary SATA 26

Artsybashev, Mikhail Petrarch
1878-1927 .... **TCLC 31**

Arundel, Honor (Morfydd)
1919-1973 .... **CLC 17**
See also CAP 2; CA 21-22; obituary CA 41-44R; SATA 4; obituary SATA 24

Asch, Sholem 1880-1957 .... **TCLC 3**
See also CA 105

Ashbery, John (Lawrence)
1927- ... **CLC 2, 3, 4, 6, 9, 13, 15, 25, 41**
See also CANR 9; CA 5-8R; DLB 5; DLB-Y 81

Ashton-Warner, Sylvia (Constance)
1908-1984 .... **CLC 19**
See also CA 69-72; obituary CA 112

Asimov, Isaac 1920- .... **CLC 1, 3, 9, 19, 26**
See also CLR 12; CANR 2, 19; CA 1-4R; SATA 1, 26; DLB 8

Astley, Thea (Beatrice May)
1925- .... **CLC 41**
See also CANR 11; CA 65-68

Astley, William 1855-1911
See Warung, Price

Aston, James 1906-1964
See White, T(erence) H(anbury)

Asturias, Miguel Angel
1899-1974 .... **CLC 3, 8, 13**
See also CAP 2; CA 25-28; obituary CA 49-52

Atheling, William, Jr. 1921-1975
See Blish, James (Benjamin)

Atherton, Gertrude (Franklin Horn)
1857-1948 .... **TCLC 2**
See also CA 104; DLB 9, 78

Attaway, William 1911?-1986
See also BLC 1; DLB 76

Atwood, Margaret (Eleanor)
1939- .... **CLC 2, 3, 4, 8, 13, 15, 25, 44; SSC 2**
See also WLC 1; CANR 3, 24; CA 49-52; SATA 50; DLB 53

Aubin, Penelope 1685-1731? .... **LC 9**
See also DLB 39

Auchincloss, Louis (Stanton)
1917- .... **CLC 4, 6, 9, 18, 45**
See also CANR 6; CA 1-4R; DLB 2; DLB-Y 80

Auden, W(ystan) H(ugh)
1907-1973 ..... **CLC 1, 2, 3, 4, 6, 9, 11, 14, 43; PC 1**
See also WLC 1; CANR 5; CA 9-12R; obituary CA 45-48; DLB 10, 20

Audiberti, Jacques 1899-1965 ...... **CLC 38**
See also obituary CA 25-28R

Auel, Jean M(arie) 1936- .... **CLC 31**
See also CANR 21; CA 103

Auerbach, Erich 1892-1957 .... **TCLC 43**
See also CA 118

Augier, Emile 1820-1889 .... **NCLC 31**

Augustine, St. 354-430........... **CMLC 6**

Austen, Jane
1775-1817 .... **NCLC 1, 13, 19, 33**
See also WLC 1

Auster, Paul 1947- .... **CLC 47**
See also CANR 23; CA 69-72

Austin, Mary (Hunter)
1868-1934 .... **TCLC 25**
See also CA 109; DLB 9

Averroes 1126-1198 .... **CMLC 7**

Avison, Margaret 1918- .... **CLC 2, 4**
See also CA 17-20R; DLB 53

Ayckbourn, Alan 1939- .... **CLC 5, 8, 18, 33**
See also CA 21-24R; DLB 13

Aydy, Catherine 1937-
See Tennant, Emma

Ayme, Marcel (Andre) 1902-1967... **CLC 11**
See also CA 89-92; DLB 72

Booth, Martin 1944-.............. **CLC 13**
See also CAAS 2; CA 93-96

Booth, Philip 1925-............... **CLC 23**
See also CANR 5; CA 5-8R; DLB-Y 82

Booth, Wayne C(layson) 1921- ..... **CLC 24**
See also CAAS 5; CANR 3; CA 1-4R;
DLB 67

Borchert, Wolfgang 1921-1947 ..... **TCLC 5**
See also CA 104; DLB 69

Borges, Jorge Luis
1899-1986 ... **CLC 1, 2, 3, 4, 6, 8, 9, 10, 13, 19, 44, 48; SSC 4**
See also WLC 1; CANR 19; CA 21-24R;
DLB-Y 86

Borowski, Tadeusz 1922-1951 ...... **TCLC 9**
See also CA 106

Borrow, George (Henry)
1803-1881 .... **NCLC 9**
See also DLB 21, 55

Bosschere, Jean de 1878-1953..... **TCLC 19**
See also CA 115

Boswell, James 1740-1795 .... **LC 4**
See also WLC 1

Boto, Eza 1932-
See Beti, Mongo

Bottoms, David 1949-............. **CLC 53**
See also CANR 22; CA 105; DLB-Y 83

Boucolon, Maryse 1937-
See Conde, Maryse
See also CA 110

Bourget, Paul (Charles Joseph)
1852-1935 .... **TCLC 12**
See also CA 107

Bourjaily, Vance (Nye) 1922- .... **CLC 8, 62**
See also CAAS 1; CANR 2; CA 1-4R;
DLB 2

Bourne, Randolph S(illiman)
1886-1918 .... **TCLC 16**
See also CA 117; DLB 63

Bova, Ben(jamin William) 1932-.... **CLC 45**
See also CLR 3; CANR 11; CA 5-8R;
SATA 6; DLB-Y 81

Bowen, Elizabeth (Dorothea Cole)
1899-1973 ..... **CLC 1, 3, 6, 11, 15, 22; SSC 3**
See also CAP 2; CA 17-18;
obituary CA 41-44R; DLB 15

Bowering, George 1935-........ **CLC 15, 47**
See also CANR 10; CA 21-24R; DLB 53

Bowering, Marilyn R(uthe) 1949-... **CLC 32**
See also CA 101

Bowers, Edgar 1924- .... **CLC 9**
See also CANR 24; CA 5-8R; DLB 5

Bowie, David 1947- .... **CLC 17**
See also Jones, David Robert

Bowles, Jane (Sydney)
1917-1973 .... **CLC 3, 68**
See also CAP 2; CA 19-20;
obituary CA 41-44R

Bowles, Paul (Frederick)
1910- .... **CLC 1, 2, 19, 53; SSC 3**
See also CAAS 1; CANR 1, 19; CA 1-4R;
DLB 5, 6

Box, Edgar 1925-
See Vidal, Gore

Boyd, William 1952-........ **CLC 28, 53, 70**
See also CA 114, 120

Boyle, Kay 1903- .. **CLC 1, 5, 19, 58; SSC 5**
See also CAAS 1; CA 13-16R; DLB 4, 9, 48

Boyle, Patrick 19??-.............. **CLC 19**

Boyle, Thomas Coraghessan
1948- .... **CLC 36, 55**
See also CA 120; DLB-Y 86

Brackenridge, Hugh Henry
1748-1816 .... **NCLC 7**
See also DLB 11, 37

Bradbury, Edward P. 1939-
See Moorcock, Michael

Bradbury, Malcolm (Stanley)
1932- .... **CLC 32, 61**
See also CANR 1; CA 1-4R; DLB 14

Bradbury, Ray(mond Douglas)
1920- .... **CLC 1, 3, 10, 15, 42**
See also WLC 1; CANR 2, 30; CA 1-4R;
SATA 11, 64; DLB 2, 8;
CDALB 1968-1988

Bradford, Gamaliel 1863-1932..... **TCLC 36**
See also DLB 17

Bradley, David (Henry), Jr. 1950- .. **CLC 23**
See also BLC 1; CANR 26; CA 104;
DLB 33

Bradley, John Ed 1959-........... **CLC 55**

Bradley, Katherine Harris 1846-1914
See Field, Michael

Bradley, Marion Zimmer 1930-..... **CLC 30**
See also CANR 7; CA 57-60; DLB 8

Bradstreet, Anne 1612-1672.......... **LC 4**
See also DLB 24; CDALB 1640-1865

Bragg, Melvyn 1939- .... **CLC 10**
See also CANR 10; CA 57-60; DLB 14

Braine, John (Gerard)
1922-1986 .... **CLC 1, 3, 41**
See also CANR 1; CA 1-4R;
obituary CA 120; DLB 15; DLB-Y 86

Braithwaite, William Stanley 1878-1962
See also BLC 1; CA 125; DLB 50, 54

Brammer, Billy Lee 1930?-1978
See Brammer, William

Brammer, William 1930?-1978 ..... **CLC 31**
See also obituary CA 77-80

Brancati, Vitaliano 1907-1954..... **TCLC 12**
See also CA 109

Brancato, Robin F(idler) 1936-..... **CLC 35**
See also CANR 11; CA 69-72; SATA 23

Brand, Millen 1906-1980........... **CLC 7**
See also CA 21-24R; obituary CA 97-100

Branden, Barbara 19??-........... **CLC 44**

Brandes, Georg (Morris Cohen)
1842-1927 .... **TCLC 10**
See also CA 105

Brandys, Kazimierz 1916-......... **CLC 62**

Branley, Franklyn M(ansfield)
1915- .... **CLC 21**
See also CLR 13; CANR 14; CA 33-36R;
SATA 4

Brathwaite, Edward 1930-......... **CLC 11**
See also CANR 11; CA 25-28R; DLB 53

Brautigan, Richard (Gary)
1935-1984 .... **CLC 1, 3, 5, 9, 12, 34, 42**
See also CA 53-56; obituary CA 113;
SATA 56; DLB 2, 5; DLB-Y 80, 84

Braverman, Kate 1950- .... **CLC 67**
See also CA 89-92

Brecht, (Eugen) Bertolt (Friedrich)
1898-1956 .... **TCLC 1, 6, 13, 35**
See also WLC 1; CA 133;
brief entry CA 104; DLB 56

Bremer, Fredrika 1801-1865 ..... **NCLC 11**

Brennan, Christopher John
1870-1932 .... **TCLC 17**
See also CA 117

Brennan, Maeve 1917-............. **CLC 5**
See also CA 81-84

Brentano, Clemens (Maria)
1778-1842 .... **NCLC 1**
See also DLB 90

Brenton, Howard 1942-........... **CLC 31**
See also CA 69-72; DLB 13

Breslin, James 1930-
See Breslin, Jimmy
See also CA 73-76

Breslin, Jimmy 1930-........... **CLC 4, 43**
See also Breslin, James

Bresson, Robert 1907-............ **CLC 16**
See also CA 110

Breton, Andre 1896-1966... **CLC 2, 9, 15, 54**
See also CAP 2; CA 19-20;
obituary CA 25-28R; DLB 65

Breytenbach, Breyten 1939-..... **CLC 23, 37**
See also CA 113, 129

Bridgers, Sue Ellen 1942- .... **CLC 26**
See also CANR 11; CA 65-68; SAAS 1;
SATA 22; DLB 52

Bridges, Robert 1844-1930......... **TCLC 1**
See also CA 104; DLB 19

Bridie, James 1888-1951 .... **TCLC 3**
See also Mavor, Osborne Henry
See also DLB 10

Brin, David 1950-................ **CLC 34**
See also CANR 24; CA 102

Brink, Andre (Philippus)
1935- .... **CLC 18, 36**
See also CA 104

Brinsmead, H(esba) F(ay) 1922-.... **CLC 21**
See also CANR 10; CA 21-24R; SAAS 5;
SATA 18

Brittain, Vera (Mary) 1893?-1970... **CLC 23**
See also CAP 1; CA 15-16;
obituary CA 25-28R

Broch, Hermann 1886-1951....... **TCLC 20**
See also CA 117; DLB 85

Brock, Rose 1923-
See Hansen, Joseph

Brodkey, Harold 1930-............ **CLC 56**
See also CA 111

Brodsky, Iosif Alexandrovich 1940-
See Brodsky, Joseph (Alexandrovich)
See also CA 41-44R

Brodsky, Joseph (Alexandrovich)
1940- .... **CLC 4, 6, 13, 36, 50**
See also Brodsky, Iosif Alexandrovich

Burroughs, William S(eward) 1914- .... **CLC 1, 2, 5, 15, 22, 42**
See also WLC 1; CANR 20; CA 9-12R; DLB 2, 8, 16; DLB-Y 81

Busch, Frederick 1941- ... **CLC 7, 10, 18, 47**
See also CAAS 1; CA 33-36R; DLB 6

Bush, Ronald 19??-............... **CLC 34**

Butler, Octavia E(stelle) 1947- ..... **CLC 38**
See also CANR 12, 24; CA 73-76; DLB 33

Butler, Samuel 1612-1680 .... **LC 16**
See also DLB 101

Butler, Samuel 1835-1902 ...... **TCLC 1, 33**
See also WLC 1; CA 104; DLB 18, 57

Butor, Michel (Marie Francois) 1926- .... **CLC 1, 3, 8, 11, 15**
See also CA 9-12R

Buzo, Alexander 1944-............ **CLC 61**
See also CANR 17; CA 97-100

Buzzati, Dino 1906-1972 .... **CLC 36**
See also obituary CA 33-36R

Byars, Betsy 1928-............... **CLC 35**
See also CLR 1, 16; CANR 18; CA 33-36R; SAAS 1; SATA 4, 46; DLB 52

Byatt, A(ntonia) S(usan Drabble) 1936- .... **CLC 19, 65**
See also CANR 13, 33; CA 13-16R; DLB 14

Byrne, David 1953?-.............. **CLC 26**

Byrne, John Keyes 1926-
See Leonard, Hugh
See also CA 102

Byron, George Gordon (Noel), Lord Byron 1788-1824 .... **NCLC 2, 12**
See also WLC 1

Caballero, Fernan 1796-1877..... **NCLC 10**

Cabell, James Branch 1879-1958 ... **TCLC 6**
See also CA 105; DLB 9, 78

Cable, George Washington 1844-1925 .... **TCLC 4; SSC 4**
See also CA 104; DLB 12, 74

Cabrera Infante, G(uillermo) 1929- .... **CLC 5, 25, 45**
See also CANR 29; CA 85-88

Cade, Toni 1939-
See Bambara, Toni Cade

CAEdmon fl. 658-680............ **CMLC 7**

Cage, John (Milton, Jr.) 1912- ..... **CLC 41**
See also CANR 9; CA 13-16R

Cain, G. 1929-
See Cabrera Infante, G(uillermo)

Cain, James M(allahan) 1892-1977 .... **CLC 3, 11, 28**
See also CANR 8; CA 17-20R; obituary CA 73-76

Caldwell, Erskine (Preston) 1903-1987 .... **CLC 1, 8, 14, 50, 60**
See also CAAS 1; CANR 2; CA 1-4R; obituary CA 121; DLB 9, 86

Caldwell, (Janet Miriam) Taylor (Holland) 1900-1985 .... **CLC 2, 28, 39**
See also CANR 5; CA 5-8R; obituary CA 116

Calhoun, John Caldwell 1782-1850 .... **NCLC 15**
See also DLB 3

Calisher, Hortense 1911- .... **CLC 2, 4, 8, 38**
See also CANR 1, 22; CA 1-4R; DLB 2

Callaghan, Morley (Edward) 1903-1990 .... **CLC 3, 14, 41, 65**
See also CANR 33; CA 9-12R; obituary CA 132; DLB 68

Calvino, Italo 1923-1985 .... **CLC 5, 8, 11, 22, 33, 39; SSC 3**
See also CANR 23; CA 85-88; obituary CA 116

Cameron, Carey 1952- .... **CLC 59**

Cameron, Peter 1959-............. **CLC 44**
See also CA 125

Campana, Dino 1885-1932........ **TCLC 20**
See also CA 117

Campbell, John W(ood), Jr. 1910-1971 .... **CLC 32**
See also CAP 2; CA 21-22; obituary CA 29-32R; DLB 8

Campbell, Joseph 1904-1987 .... **CLC 69**
See also CANR 3, 28; CA 4R; obituary CA 124; AAYA 3

Campbell, (John) Ramsey 1946- .... **CLC 42**
See also CANR 7; CA 57-60

Campbell, (Ignatius) Roy (Dunnachie) 1901-1957 .... **TCLC 5**
See also CA 104; DLB 20

Campbell, Thomas 1777-1844 .... **NCLC 19**

Campbell, (William) Wilfred 1861-1918 .... **TCLC 9**
See also CA 106

Camus, Albert 1913-1960 ... **CLC 1, 2, 4, 9, 11, 14, 32, 63, 69; DC 2; SSC 9**
See also WLC 1; CA 89-92; DLB 72

Canby, Vincent 1924-............. **CLC 13**
See also CA 81-84

Canetti, Elias 1905- .... **CLC 3, 14, 25**
See also CANR 23; CA 21-24R; DLB 85

Canin, Ethan 1960-............... **CLC 55**

Cape, Judith 1916-
See Page, P(atricia) K(athleen)

Capek, Karel 1890-1938 .... **TCLC 6, 37; DC 1**
See also WLC 1; CA 104

Capote, Truman 1924-1984 ..... **CLC 1, 3, 8, 13, 19, 34, 38, 58; SSC 2**
See also WLC 1; CANR 18; CA 5-8R; obituary CA 113; DLB 2; DLB-Y 80, 84; CDALB 1941-1968

Capra, Frank 1897-.............. **CLC 16**
See also CA 61-64

Caputo, Philip 1941-............. **CLC 32**
See also CA 73-76

Card, Orson Scott 1951- .... **CLC 44, 47, 50**
See also CA 102

Cardenal, Ernesto 1925-........... **CLC 31**
See also CANR 2; CA 49-52

Carducci, Giosue 1835-1907....... **TCLC 32**

Carew, Thomas 1595?-1640 .... **LC 13**

Carey, Ernestine Gilbreth 1908- .... **CLC 17**
See also CA 5-8R; SATA 2

Carey, Peter 1943-............ **CLC 40, 55**
See also CA 123, 127

Carleton, William 1794-1869...... **NCLC 3**

Carlisle, Henry (Coffin) 1926-..... **CLC 33**
See also CANR 15; CA 13-16R

Carlson, Ron(ald F.) 1947-......... **CLC 54**
See also CA 105

Carlyle, Thomas 1795-1881 ...... **NCLC 22**
See also DLB 55

Carman, (William) Bliss 1861-1929 .... **TCLC 7**
See also CA 104

Carpenter, Don(ald Richard) 1931- .... **CLC 41**
See also CANR 1; CA 45-48

Carpentier (y Valmont), Alejo 1904-1980 .... **CLC 8, 11, 38**
See also CANR 11; CA 65-68; obituary CA 97-100

Carr, Emily 1871-1945........... **TCLC 32**
See also DLB 68

Carr, John Dickson 1906-1977 ...... **CLC 3**
See also CANR 3; CA 49-52; obituary CA 69-72

Carr, Virginia Spencer 1929-....... **CLC 34**
See also CA 61-64

Carrier, Roch 1937- .... **CLC 13**
See also DLB 53

Carroll, James (P.) 1943-.......... **CLC 38**
See also CA 81-84

Carroll, Jim 1951- .... **CLC 35**
See also CA 45-48

Carroll, Lewis 1832-1898......... **NCLC 2**
See also Dodgson, Charles Lutwidge
See also CLR 2; WLC 1; DLB 18

Carroll, Paul Vincent 1900-1968.... **CLC 10**
See also CA 9-12R; obituary CA 25-28R; DLB 10

Carruth, Hayden 1921- .... **CLC 4, 7, 10, 18**
See also CANR 4; CA 9-12R; SATA 47; DLB 5

Carson, Rachel 1907-1964 .... **CLC 71**
See also CANR 35; CA 77-80; SATA 23

Carter, Angela (Olive) 1940-..... **CLC 5, 41**
See also CANR 12; CA 53-56; DLB 14

Carver, Raymond 1938-1988 ... **CLC 22, 36, 53, 55; SSC 8**
See also CANR 17; CA 33-36R; obituary CA 126; DLB-Y 84, 88

Cary, (Arthur) Joyce (Lunel) 1888-1957 .... **TCLC 1, 29**
See also CA 104; DLB 15

Casanova de Seingalt, Giovanni Jacopo 1725-1798 .... **LC 13**

Casares, Adolfo Bioy 1914-
See Bioy Casares, Adolfo

Casely-Hayford, J(oseph) E(phraim) 1866-1930 .... **TCLC 24**
See also BLC 1; CA 123

Casey, John 1880-1964
See O'Casey, Sean

Dabydeen, David 1956?- .... **CLC 34**
See also CA 106

Dacey, Philip 1939- .... **CLC 51**
See also CANR 14; CA 37-40R

Dagerman, Stig (Halvard)
1923-1954 .... **TCLC 17**
See also CA 117

Dahl, Roald 1916-............ **CLC 1, 6, 18**
See also CLR 1, 7; CANR 6; CA 1-4R; SATA 1, 26

Dahlberg, Edward 1900-1977... **CLC 1, 7, 14**
See also CA 9-12R; obituary CA 69-72; DLB 48

Daly, Elizabeth 1878-1967......... **CLC 52**
See also CAP 2; CA 23-24; obituary CA 25-28R

Daly, Maureen 1921- .... **CLC 17**
See also McGivern, Maureen Daly
See also SAAS 1; SATA 2

Daniken, Erich von 1935-
See Von Daniken, Erich

Dannay, Frederic 1905-1982
See Queen, Ellery
See also CANR 1; CA 1-4R; obituary CA 107

D'Annunzio, Gabriele
1863-1938 .... **TCLC 6, 40**
See also CA 104

Dante (Alighieri)
See Alighieri, Dante

Danvers, Dennis 1947-............ **CLC 70**

Danziger, Paula 1944- .... **CLC 21**
See also CLR 20; CA 112, 115; SATA 30, 36

Dario, Ruben 1867-1916 .... **TCLC 4**
See also Sarmiento, Felix Ruben Garcia
See also CA 104

Darley, George 1795-1846........ **NCLC 2**

Daryush, Elizabeth 1887-1977.... **CLC 6, 19**
See also CANR 3; CA 49-52; DLB 20

Daudet, (Louis Marie) Alphonse
1840-1897 .... **NCLC 1**

Daumal, Rene 1908-1944......... **TCLC 14**
See also CA 114

Davenport, Guy (Mattison, Jr.)
1927- .... **CLC 6, 14, 38**
See also CANR 23; CA 33-36R

Davidson, Donald (Grady)
1893-1968 .... **CLC 2, 13, 19**
See also CANR 4; CA 5-8R; obituary CA 25-28R; DLB 45

Davidson, John 1857-1909........ **TCLC 24**
See also CA 118; DLB 19

Davidson, Sara 1943- .... **CLC 9**
See also CA 81-84

Davie, Donald (Alfred)
1922- .... **CLC 5, 8, 10, 31**
See also CAAS 3; CANR 1; CA 1-4R; DLB 27

Davies, Ray(mond Douglas) 1944- .. **CLC 21**
See also CA 116

Davies, Rhys 1903-1978........... **CLC 23**
See also CANR 4; CA 9-12R; obituary CA 81-84

Davies, (William) Robertson
1913- .... **CLC 2, 7, 13, 25, 42**
See also WLC 2; CANR 17; CA 33-36R; DLB 68

Davies, W(illiam) H(enry)
1871-1940 .... **TCLC 5**
See also CA 104; DLB 19

Davis, Frank Marshall 1905-1987
See also BLC 1; CA 123, 125; DLB 51

Davis, H(arold) L(enoir)
1896-1960 .... **CLC 49**
See also obituary CA 89-92; DLB 9

Davis, Rebecca (Blaine) Harding
1831-1910 .... **TCLC 6**
See also CA 104; DLB 74

Davis, Richard Harding
1864-1916 .... **TCLC 24**
See also CA 114; DLB 12, 23, 78, 79

Davison, Frank Dalby 1893-1970 ... **CLC 15**
See also obituary CA 116

Davison, Peter 1928- .... **CLC 28**
See also CAAS 4; CANR 3; CA 9-12R; DLB 5

Davys, Mary 1674-1732............. **LC 1**
See also DLB 39

Dawson, Fielding 1930- .... **CLC 6**
See also CA 85-88

Day, Clarence (Shepard, Jr.)
1874-1935 .... **TCLC 25**
See also CA 108; DLB 11

Day, Thomas 1748-1789............. **LC 1**
See also YABC 1; DLB 39

Day Lewis, C(ecil)
1904-1972 .... **CLC 1, 6, 10**
See also CAP 1; CA 15-16; obituary CA 33-36R; DLB 15, 20

Dazai Osamu 1909-1948 .... **TCLC 11**
See also Tsushima Shuji

De Crayencour, Marguerite 1903-1987
See Yourcenar, Marguerite

Dee, John 1527-1608 .... **LC 20**

Deer, Sandra 1940-............... **CLC 45**

De Ferrari, Gabriella 19??- .... **CLC 65**

Defoe, Daniel 1660?-1731 .... **LC 1**
See also WLC 2; SATA 22; DLB 39

De Hartog, Jan 1914-............. **CLC 19**
See also CANR 1; CA 1-4R

Deighton, Len 1929-....... **CLC 4, 7, 22, 46**
See also Deighton, Leonard Cyril
See also DLB 87

Deighton, Leonard Cyril 1929-
See Deighton, Len
See also CANR 19; CA 9-12R

De la Mare, Walter (John)
1873-1956 .... **TCLC 4**
See also CLR 23; WLC 2; CA 110; SATA 16; DLB 19

Delaney, Shelagh 1939- .... **CLC 29**
See also CA 17-20R; DLB 13

Delany, Mary (Granville Pendarves)
1700-1788 .... **LC 12**

Delany, Samuel R(ay, Jr.)
1942- .... **CLC 8, 14, 38**
See also BLC 1; CANR 27; CA 81-84; DLB 8, 33

de la Ramee, Marie Louise 1839-1908
See Ouida
See also SATA 20

De la Roche, Mazo 1885-1961 ..... **CLC 14**
See also CA 85-88; DLB 68

Delbanco, Nicholas (Franklin)
1942- .... **CLC 6, 13**
See also CAAS 2; CA 17-20R; DLB 6

del Castillo, Michel 1933- .... **CLC 38**
See also CA 109

Deledda, Grazia 1871-1936 .... **TCLC 23**
See also CA 123

Delibes (Setien), Miguel 1920- ... **CLC 8, 18**
See also CANR 1; CA 45-48

DeLillo, Don
1936- .... **CLC 8, 10, 13, 27, 39, 54**
See also CANR 21; CA 81-84; DLB 6

De Lisser, H(erbert) G(eorge)
1878-1944 .... **TCLC 12**
See also CA 109

Deloria, Vine (Victor), Jr. 1933-.... **CLC 21**
See also CANR 5, 20; CA 53-56; SATA 21

Del Vecchio, John M(ichael)
1947- .... **CLC 29**
See also CA 110

de Man, Paul 1919-1983 .... **CLC 55**
See also obituary CA 111; DLB 67

De Marinis, Rick 1934-........... **CLC 54**
See also CANR 9, 25; CA 57-60

Demby, William 1922-............ **CLC 53**
See also BLC 1; CA 81-84; DLB 33

Denby, Edwin (Orr) 1903-1983..... **CLC 48**
See also obituary CA 110

Dennis, John 1657-1734............ **LC 11**

Dennis, Nigel (Forbes) 1912-........ **CLC 8**
See also CA 25-28R; obituary CA 129; DLB 13, 15

De Palma, Brian 1940-............ **CLC 20**
See also CA 109

De Quincey, Thomas 1785-1859 ... **NCLC 4**

Deren, Eleanora 1908-1961
See Deren, Maya
See also obituary CA 111

Deren, Maya 1908-1961........... **CLC 16**
See also Deren, Eleanora

Derleth, August (William)
1909-1971 .... **CLC 31**
See also CANR 4; CA 1-4R; obituary CA 29-32R; SATA 5; DLB 9

Derrida, Jacques 1930-........... **CLC 24**
See also CA 124, 127

Desai, Anita 1937- .... **CLC 19, 37**
See also CA 81-84

De Saint-Luc, Jean 1909-1981
See Glassco, John

Descartes, Rene 1596-1650 .... **LC 20**

De Sica, Vittorio 1902-1974 .... **CLC 20**
See also obituary CA 117

Author Index

Gold, Herbert 1924- . . . . **CLC 4, 7, 14, 42**
See also CANR 17; CA 9-12R; DLB 2; DLB-Y 81

Goldbarth, Albert 1948- . . . . **CLC 5, 38**
See also CANR 6; CA 53-56

Goldberg, Anatol 1910-1982 . . . . **CLC 34**
See also obituary CA 117

Goldemberg, Isaac 1945- . . . . **CLC 52**
See also CANR 11; CA 69-72

Golding, William (Gerald) 1911- . . . . . **CLC 1, 2, 3, 8, 10, 17, 27, 58**
See also WLC 3; CANR 13; CA 5-8R; DLB 15

Goldman, Emma 1869-1940 . . . . **TCLC 13**
See also CA 110

Goldman, William (W.) 1931- . . . . **CLC 1, 48**
See also CA 9-12R; DLB 44

Goldmann, Lucien 1913-1970 . . . . . . **CLC 24**
See also CAP 2; CA 25-28

Goldoni, Carlo 1707-1793 . . . . **LC 4**

Goldsberry, Steven 1949- . . . . **CLC 34**

Goldsmith, Oliver 1728?-1774 . . . . **LC 2**
See also WLC 3; SATA 26; DLB 39, 89, 104, 109

Gombrowicz, Witold 1904-1969 . . . . **CLC 4, 7, 11, 49**
See also CAP 2; CA 19-20; obituary CA 25-28R

Gomez de la Serna, Ramon 1888-1963 . . . . **CLC 9**
See also obituary CA 116

Goncharov, Ivan Alexandrovich 1812-1891 . . . . **NCLC 1**

Goncourt, Edmond (Louis Antoine Huot) de 1822-1896 . . . . **NCLC 7**

Goncourt, Jules (Alfred Huot) de 1830-1870 . . . . **NCLC 7**

Gontier, Fernande 19??- . . . . **CLC 50**

Goodman, Paul 1911-1972 . . . . **CLC 1, 2, 4, 7**
See also CAP 2; CA 19-20; obituary CA 37-40R

Gordimer, Nadine 1923- . . . . **CLC 3, 5, 7, 10, 18, 33, 51, 70**
See also CANR 3, 28; CA 5-8R

Gordon, Adam Lindsay 1833-1870 . . . . **NCLC 21**

Gordon, Caroline 1895-1981 . . . . **CLC 6, 13, 29**
See also CAP 1; CA 11-12; obituary CA 103; DLB 4, 9; DLB-Y 81

Gordon, Charles William 1860-1937
See Conner, Ralph
See also CA 109

Gordon, Mary (Catherine) 1949- . . . . **CLC 13, 22**
See also CA 102; DLB 6; DLB-Y 81

Gordon, Sol 1923- . . . . **CLC 26**
See also CANR 4; CA 53-56; SATA 11

Gordone, Charles 1925- . . . . **CLC 1, 4**
See also CA 93-96; DLB 7

Gorenko, Anna Andreyevna 1889?-1966
See Akhmatova, Anna

Gorky, Maxim 1868-1936 . . . . **TCLC 8**
See also Peshkov, Alexei Maximovich
See also WLC 3

Goryan, Sirak 1908-1981
See Saroyan, William

Gosse, Edmund (William) 1849-1928 . . . . **TCLC 28**
See also CA 117; DLB 57

Gotlieb, Phyllis (Fay Bloom) 1926- . . . . **CLC 18**
See also CANR 7; CA 13-16R; DLB 88

Gould, Lois 1938?- . . . . **CLC 4, 10**
See also CA 77-80

Gourmont, Remy de 1858-1915 . . . . **TCLC 17**
See also CA 109

Govier, Katherine 1948- . . . . **CLC 51**
See also CANR 18; CA 101

Goyen, (Charles) William 1915-1983 . . . . **CLC 5, 8, 14, 40**
See also CANR 6; CA 5-8R; obituary CA 110; DLB 2; DLB-Y 83

Goytisolo, Juan 1931- . . . . **CLC 5, 10, 23**
See also CA 85-88

Gozzi, (Conte) Carlo 1720-1806 . . **NCLC 23**

Grabbe, Christian Dietrich 1801-1836 . . . . **NCLC 2**

Grace, Patricia 1937- . . . . **CLC 56**

Gracian y Morales, Baltasar 1601-1658 . . . . **LC 15**

Gracq, Julien 1910- . . . . **CLC 11, 48**
See also Poirier, Louis
See also DLB 83

Grade, Chaim 1910-1982 . . . . **CLC 10**
See also CA 93-96; obituary CA 107

Graham, Jorie 1951- . . . . **CLC 48**
See also CA 111

Graham, R(obert) B(ontine) Cunninghame 1852-1936 . . . . **TCLC 19**

Graham, W(illiam) S(ydney) 1918-1986 . . . . **CLC 29**
See also CA 73-76; obituary CA 118; DLB 20

Graham, Winston (Mawdsley) 1910- . . . . **CLC 23**
See also CANR 2, 22; CA 49-52; obituary CA 118

Granville-Barker, Harley 1877-1946 . . . . **TCLC 2**
See also CA 104

Grass, Gunter (Wilhelm) 1927- . . **CLC 1, 2, 4, 6, 11, 15, 22, 32, 49**
See also WLC 3; CANR 20; CA 13-16R; DLB 75

Grau, Shirley Ann 1929- . . . . **CLC 4, 9**
See also CANR 22; CA 89-92; DLB 2

Graver, Elizabeth 1965- . . . . **CLC 70**

Graves, Richard Perceval 1945- . . . . **CLC 44**
See also CANR 9, 26; CA 65-68

Graves, Robert (von Ranke) 1895-1985 . . . **CLC 1, 2, 6, 11, 39, 44, 45**
See also CANR 5; CA 5-8R; obituary CA 117; SATA 45; DLB 20; DLB-Y 85

Gray, Alasdair 1934- . . . . **CLC 41**
See also CA 123

Gray, Amlin 1946- . . . . **CLC 29**

Gray, Francine du Plessix 1930- . . . . **CLC 22**
See also CAAS 2; CANR 11; CA 61-64

Gray, John (Henry) 1866-1934 . . . . **TCLC 19**
See also CA 119

Gray, Simon (James Holliday) 1936- . . . . **CLC 9, 14, 36**
See also CAAS 3; CA 21-24R; DLB 13

Gray, Spalding 1941- . . . . **CLC 49**

Gray, Thomas 1716-1771 . . . . **LC 4; PC 2**
See also WLC 3

Grayson, Richard (A.) 1951- . . . . **CLC 38**
See also CANR 14; CA 85-88

Greeley, Andrew M(oran) 1928- . . . . **CLC 28**
See also CAAS 7; CANR 7; CA 5-8R

Green, Hannah 1932- . . . . **CLC 3, 7, 30**
See also Greenberg, Joanne
See also CA 73-76

Green, Henry 1905-1974 . . . . **CLC 2, 13**
See also Yorke, Henry Vincent
See also DLB 15

Green, Julien (Hartridge) 1900- . . **CLC 3, 11**
See also CA 21-24R; DLB 4, 72

Green, Paul (Eliot) 1894-1981 . . . . . . **CLC 25**
See also CANR 3; CA 5-8R; obituary CA 103; DLB 7, 9; DLB-Y 81

Greenberg, Ivan 1908-1973
See Rahv, Philip
See also CA 85-88

Greenberg, Joanne (Goldenberg) 1932- . . . . **CLC 3, 7, 30**
See also Green, Hannah
See also CANR 14; CA 5-8R; SATA 25

Greenberg, Richard 1959?- . . . . **CLC 57**

Greene, Bette 1934- . . . . **CLC 30**
See also CLR 2; CANR 4; CA 53-56; SATA 8

Greene, Gael 19??- . . . . **CLC 8**
See also CANR 10; CA 13-16R

Greene, Graham (Henry) 1904-1991 . . . **CLC 1, 3, 6, 9, 14, 18, 27, 37, 70, 72**
See also CANR 35; CA 13-16R; obituary CA 133; SATA 20; DLB 13, 15, 77, 100; DLB-Y 85

Gregor, Arthur 1923- . . . . **CLC 9**
See also CANR 11; CA 25-28R; SATA 36

Gregory, J. Dennis 1925-
See Williams, John A.

Gregory, Lady (Isabella Augusta Persse) 1852-1932 . . . . **TCLC 1**
See also CA 104; DLB 10

Grendon, Stephen 1909-1971
See Derleth, August (William)

Grenville, Kate 1950- . . . . **CLC 61**
See also CA 118

Greve, Felix Paul Berthold Friedrich 1879-1948
See Grove, Frederick Philip
See also CA 104

Grey, (Pearl) Zane 1872?-1939 . . . . . **TCLC 6**
See also CA 104; DLB 9

Henley, Beth 1952- .... **CLC 23**
See also Henley, Elizabeth Becker
See also CABS 3; DLB-Y 86

Henley, Elizabeth Becker 1952-
See Henley, Beth
See also CA 107

Henley, William Ernest
1849-1903 .... **TCLC 8**
See also CA 105; DLB 19

Hennissart, Martha
See Lathen, Emma
See also CA 85-88

Henry, O. 1862-1910 ... **TCLC 1, 19; SSC 5**
See also Porter, William Sydney
See also YABC 2; CA 104; DLB 12, 78, 79; CDALB 1865-1917

Henryson, Robert 1430?-1506? ...... **LC 20**

Henry VIII 1491-1547 .... **LC 10**

Henschke, Alfred 1890-1928
See Klabund

Hentoff, Nat(han Irving) 1925- ..... **CLC 26**
See also CLR 1; CAAS 6; CANR 5, 25; CA 1-4R; SATA 27, 42; AAYA 4

Heppenstall, (John) Rayner
1911-1981 .... **CLC 10**
See also CANR 29; CA 1-4R; obituary CA 103

Herbert, Frank (Patrick)
1920-1986 .... **CLC 12, 23, 35, 44**
See also CANR 5; CA 53-56; obituary CA 118; SATA 9, 37, 47; DLB 8

Herbert, George 1593-1633 .... **PC 4**

Herbert, Zbigniew 1924- .... **CLC 9, 43**
See also CA 89-92

Herbst, Josephine 1897-1969 .... **CLC 34**
See also CA 5-8R; obituary CA 25-28R; DLB 9

Herder, Johann Gottfried von
1744-1803 .... **NCLC 8**

Hergesheimer, Joseph
1880-1954 .... **TCLC 11**
See also CA 109; DLB 9

Herlagnez, Pablo de 1844-1896
See Verlaine, Paul (Marie)

Herlihy, James Leo 1927- .... **CLC 6**
See also CANR 2; CA 1-4R

Hermogenes fl.c. 175- .... **CMLC 6**

Hernandez, Jose 1834-1886 ...... **NCLC 17**

Herrick, Robert 1591-1674 .... **LC 13**

Herriot, James 1916- .... **CLC 12**
See also Wight, James Alfred
See also AAYA 1

Herrmann, Dorothy 1941- .... **CLC 44**
See also CA 107

Hersey, John (Richard)
1914- .... **CLC 1, 2, 7, 9, 40**
See also CA 17-20R; SATA 25; DLB 6

Herzen, Aleksandr Ivanovich
1812-1870 .... **NCLC 10**

Herzl, Theodor 1860-1904 .... **TCLC 36**

Herzog, Werner 1942- .... **CLC 16**
See also CA 89-92

Hesiod c. 8th Century B.C.- ...... **CMLC 5**

Hesse, Hermann
1877-1962 ... **CLC 1, 2, 3, 6, 11, 17, 25, 69; SSC 9**
See also CAP 2; CA 17-18; SATA 50; DLB 66

Heyen, William 1940- .... **CLC 13, 18**
See also CAAS 9; CA 33-36R; DLB 5

Heyerdahl, Thor 1914- .... **CLC 26**
See also CANR 5, 22; CA 5-8R; SATA 2, 52

Heym, Georg (Theodor Franz Arthur)
1887-1912 .... **TCLC 9**
See also CA 106

Heym, Stefan 1913- .... **CLC 41**
See also CANR 4; CA 9-12R; DLB 69

Heyse, Paul (Johann Ludwig von)
1830-1914 .... **TCLC 8**
See also CA 104

Hibbert, Eleanor (Burford) 1906- .... **CLC 7**
See also CANR 9, 28; CA 17-20R; SATA 2

Higgins, George V(incent)
1939- .... **CLC 4, 7, 10, 18**
See also CAAS 5; CANR 17; CA 77-80; DLB 2; DLB-Y 81

Higginson, Thomas Wentworth
1823-1911 .... **TCLC 36**
See also DLB 1, 64

Highsmith, (Mary) Patricia
1921- .... **CLC 2, 4, 14, 42**
See also CANR 1, 20; CA 1-4R

Highwater, Jamake 1942- .... **CLC 12**
See also CLR 17; CAAS 7; CANR 10; CA 65-68; SATA 30, 32; DLB 52; DLB-Y 85

Hijuelos, Oscar 1951- .... **CLC 65**
See also CA 123

Hikmet (Ran), Nazim 1902-1963 .... **CLC 40**
See also obituary CA 93-96

Hildesheimer, Wolfgang 1916- ..... **CLC 49**
See also CA 101; DLB 69

Hill, Geoffrey (William)
1932- .... **CLC 5, 8, 18, 45**
See also CANR 21; CA 81-84; DLB 40

Hill, George Roy 1922- .... **CLC 26**
See also CA 110, 122

Hill, Susan B. 1942- .... **CLC 4**
See also CANR 29; CA 33-36R; DLB 14

Hillerman, Tony 1925- .... **CLC 62**
See also CANR 21; CA 29-32R; SATA 6

Hilliard, Noel (Harvey) 1929- ...... **CLC 15**
See also CANR 7; CA 9-12R

Hillis, Richard Lyle 1956-
See Hillis, Rick

Hillis, Rick 1956- .... **CLC 66**
See also Hillis, Richard Lyle

Hilton, James 1900-1954 .... **TCLC 21**
See also CA 108; SATA 34; DLB 34, 77

Himes, Chester (Bomar)
1909-1984 .... **CLC 2, 4, 7, 18, 58**
See also BLC 2; CANR 22; CA 25-28R; obituary CA 114; DLB 2, 76

Hinde, Thomas 1926- .... **CLC 6, 11**
See also Chitty, (Sir) Thomas Willes

Hine, (William) Daryl 1936- .... **CLC 15**
See also CANR 1, 20; CA 1-4R; DLB 60

Hinton, S(usan) E(loise) 1950- ..... **CLC 30**
See also CLR 3, 23; CA 81-84; SATA 19, 58; AAYA 2

Hippius (Merezhkovsky), Zinaida (Nikolayevna) 1869-1945 ...... **TCLC 9**
See also Gippius, Zinaida (Nikolayevna)

Hiraoka, Kimitake 1925-1970
See Mishima, Yukio
See also CA 97-100; obituary CA 29-32R

Hirsch, Edward (Mark) 1950- ... **CLC 31, 50**
See also CANR 20; CA 104

Hitchcock, (Sir) Alfred (Joseph)
1899-1980 .... **CLC 16**
See also obituary CA 97-100; SATA 27; obituary SATA 24

Hoagland, Edward 1932- .... **CLC 28**
See also CANR 2; CA 1-4R; SATA 51; DLB 6

Hoban, Russell C(onwell) 1925- .. **CLC 7, 25**
See also CLR 3; CANR 23; CA 5-8R; SATA 1, 40; DLB 52

Hobson, Laura Z(ametkin)
1900-1986 .... **CLC 7, 25**
See also CA 17-20R; obituary CA 118; SATA 52; DLB 28

Hochhuth, Rolf 1931- .... **CLC 4, 11, 18**
See also CA 5-8R

Hochman, Sandra 1936- .... **CLC 3, 8**
See also CA 5-8R; DLB 5

Hochwalder, Fritz 1911-1986 ...... **CLC 36**
See also CA 29-32R; obituary CA 120

Hocking, Mary (Eunice) 1921- ..... **CLC 13**
See also CANR 18; CA 101

Hodgins, Jack 1938- .... **CLC 23**
See also CA 93-96; DLB 60

Hodgson, William Hope
1877-1918 .... **TCLC 13**
See also CA 111; DLB 70

Hoffman, Alice 1952- .... **CLC 51**
See also CA 77-80

Hoffman, Daniel (Gerard)
1923- .... **CLC 6, 13, 23**
See also CANR 4; CA 1-4R; DLB 5

Hoffman, Stanley 1944- .... **CLC 5**
See also CA 77-80

Hoffman, William M(oses) 1939- ... **CLC 40**
See also CANR 11; CA 57-60

Hoffmann, E(rnst) T(heodor) A(madeus)
1776-1822 .... **NCLC 2**
See also SATA 27; DLB 90

Hoffmann, Gert 1932- .... **CLC 54**

Hofmannsthal, Hugo (Laurenz August Hofmann Edler) von
1874-1929 .... **TCLC 11**
See also CA 106; DLB 81

Hogg, James 1770-1835 .... **NCLC 4**

Holbach, Paul Henri Thiry, Baron d'
1723-1789 .... **LC 14**

Holberg, Ludvig 1684-1754 .... **LC 6**

Holden, Ursula 1921- .... **CLC 18**
See also CAAS 8; CANR 22; CA 101

Johnson, Diane 1934- . . . . **CLC 5, 13, 48**
See also CANR 17; CA 41-44R; DLB-Y 80

Johnson, Eyvind (Olof Verner) 1900-1976 . . . . **CLC 14**
See also CA 73-76; obituary CA 69-72

Johnson, Fenton 1888-1958
See also BLC 2; CA 124; brief entry CA 118; DLB 45, 50

Johnson, James Weldon 1871-1938 . . . . **TCLC 3, 19**
See also Johnson, James William
See also BLC 2; CA 125; brief entry CA 104; SATA 31; DLB 51; CDALB 1917-1929

Johnson, James William 1871-1938
See Johnson, James Weldon
See also SATA 31

Johnson, Joyce 1935- . . . . **CLC 58**
See also CA 125, 129

Johnson, Lionel (Pigot) 1867-1902 . . . . **TCLC 19**
See also CA 117; DLB 19

Johnson, Marguerita 1928-
See Angelou, Maya

Johnson, Pamela Hansford 1912-1981 . . . . **CLC 1, 7, 27**
See also CANR 2, 28; CA 1-4R; obituary CA 104; DLB 15

Johnson, Samuel 1709-1784. . . . . **LC 15**
See also DLB 39, 95

Johnson, Uwe 1934-1984 . . . . **CLC 5, 10, 15, 40**
See also CANR 1; CA 1-4R; obituary CA 112; DLB 75

Johnston, George (Benson) 1913- . . . **CLC 51**
See also CANR 5, 20; CA 1-4R; DLB 88

Johnston, Jennifer 1930- . . . . **CLC 7**
See also CA 85-88; DLB 14

Jolley, Elizabeth 1923- . . . . **CLC 46**
See also CA 127

Jones, D(ouglas) G(ordon) 1929- . . . . **CLC 10**
See also CANR 13; CA 29-32R, 113; DLB 53

Jones, David 1895-1974 . . . . **CLC 2, 4, 7, 13, 42**
See also CANR 28; CA 9-12R; obituary CA 53-56; DLB 20

Jones, David Robert 1947-
See Bowie, David
See also CA 103

Jones, Diana Wynne 1934- . . . . **CLC 26**
See also CLR 23; CANR 4, 26; CA 49-52; SAAS 7; SATA 9

Jones, Gayl 1949- . . . . **CLC 6, 9**
See also BLC 2; CANR 27; CA 77-80; DLB 33

Jones, James 1921-1977. . . . **CLC 1, 3, 10, 39**
See also CANR 6; CA 1-4R; obituary CA 69-72; DLB 2

Jones, (Everett) LeRoi 1934- . . . . **CLC 1, 2, 3, 5, 10, 14, 33**
See also Baraka, Amiri; Baraka, Imamu Amiri
See also CA 21-24R

Jones, Louis B. 19??- . . . . **CLC 65**

Jones, Madison (Percy, Jr.) 1925- . . . **CLC 4**
See also CAAS 11; CANR 7; CA 13-16R

Jones, Mervyn 1922- . . . . **CLC 10, 52**
See also CAAS 5; CANR 1; CA 45-48

Jones, Mick 1956?- . . . . **CLC 30**
See also The Clash

Jones, Nettie 19??- . . . . **CLC 34**

Jones, Preston 1936-1979 . . . . **CLC 10**
See also CA 73-76; obituary CA 89-92; DLB 7

Jones, Robert F(rancis) 1934- . . . . **CLC 7**
See also CANR 2; CA 49-52

Jones, Rod 1953- . . . . **CLC 50**
See also CA 128

Jones, Terry 1942?- . . . . **CLC 21**
See also Monty Python
See also CA 112, 116; SATA 51

Jong, Erica 1942- . . . . **CLC 4, 6, 8, 18**
See also CANR 26; CA 73-76; DLB 2, 5, 28

Jonson, Ben(jamin) 1572(?)-1637. . . . . . **LC 6**
See also DLB 62

Jordan, June 1936- . . . . **CLC 5, 11, 23**
See also CLR 10; CANR 25; CA 33-36R; SATA 4; DLB 38; AAYA 2

Jordan, Pat(rick M.) 1941- . . . . **CLC 37**
See also CANR 25; CA 33-36R

Josipovici, Gabriel (David) 1940- . . . . **CLC 6, 43**
See also CAAS 8; CA 37-40R; DLB 14

Joubert, Joseph 1754-1824 . . . . **NCLC 9**

Jouve, Pierre Jean 1887-1976. . . . . . **CLC 47**
See also obituary CA 65-68

Joyce, James (Augustine Aloysius) 1882-1941 . . . . . . **TCLC 3, 8, 16, 26, 35; SSC 3**
See also CA 104, 126; DLB 10, 19, 36

Jozsef, Attila 1905-1937. . . . . **TCLC 22**
See also CA 116

Juana Ines de la Cruz 1651?-1695 . . . . **LC 5**

Julian of Norwich 1342?-1416? . . . . **LC 6**

Jung Chang 1952- . . . . **CLC 71**

Just, Ward S(wift) 1935- . . . . **CLC 4, 27**
See also CA 25-28R

Justice, Donald (Rodney) 1925- . . **CLC 6, 19**
See also CANR 26; CA 5-8R; DLB-Y 83

Juvenal c. 55-c. 127 . . . . **CMLC 8**

Kacew, Romain 1914-1980
See Gary, Romain
See also CA 108; obituary CA 102

Kacewgary, Romain 1914-1980
See Gary, Romain

Kadare, Ismail 1936- . . . . **CLC 52**

Kadohata, Cynthia 19??- . . . . **CLC 59**

Kafka, Franz 1883-1924 . . . . **TCLC 2, 6, 13, 29; SSC 5**
See also CA 105, 126; DLB 81

Kahn, Roger 1927- . . . . **CLC 30**
See also CA 25-28R; SATA 37

Kaiser, (Friedrich Karl) Georg 1878-1945 . . . . **TCLC 9**
See also CA 106

Kaletski, Alexander 1946- . . . . **CLC 39**
See also CA 118

Kalidasa fl. c. 400- . . . . **CMLC 9**

Kallman, Chester (Simon) 1921-1975 . . . . **CLC 2**
See also CANR 3; CA 45-48; obituary CA 53-56

Kaminsky, Melvin 1926-
See Brooks, Mel
See also CANR 16; CA 65-68

Kaminsky, Stuart 1934- . . . . **CLC 59**
See also CANR 29; CA 73-76

Kane, Paul 1941-
See Simon, Paul

Kanin, Garson 1912- . . . . **CLC 22**
See also CANR 7; CA 5-8R; DLB 7

Kaniuk, Yoram 1930- . . . . **CLC 19**

Kant, Immanuel 1724-1804 . . . . . . **NCLC 27**

Kantor, MacKinlay 1904-1977 . . . . . . **CLC 7**
See also CA 61-64; obituary CA 73-76; DLB 9

Kaplan, David Michael 1946- . . . . . . **CLC 50**

Kaplan, James 19??- . . . . **CLC 59**

Karamzin, Nikolai Mikhailovich 1766-1826 . . . . **NCLC 3**

Karapanou, Margarita 1946- . . . . **CLC 13**
See also CA 101

Karl, Frederick R(obert) 1927- . . . . . **CLC 34**
See also CANR 3; CA 5-8R

Kassef, Romain 1914-1980
See Gary, Romain

Katz, Steve 1935- . . . . **CLC 47**
See also CANR 12; CA 25-28R; DLB-Y 83

Kauffman, Janet 1945- . . . . **CLC 42**
See also CA 117; DLB-Y 86

Kaufman, Bob (Garnell) 1925-1986 . . . . **CLC 49**
See also CANR 22; CA 41-44R; obituary CA 118; DLB 16, 41

Kaufman, George S(imon) 1889-1961 . . . . **CLC 38**
See also CA 108; obituary CA 93-96; DLB 7

Kaufman, Sue 1926-1977 . . . . **CLC 3, 8**
See also Barondess, Sue K(aufman)

Kavan, Anna 1904-1968 . . . . **CLC 5, 13**
See also Edmonds, Helen (Woods)
See also CANR 6; CA 5-8R

Kavanagh, Patrick (Joseph Gregory) 1905-1967 . . . . **CLC 22**
See also CA 123; obituary CA 25-28R; DLB 15, 20

Kawabata, Yasunari 1899-1972 . . . . **CLC 2, 5, 9, 18**
See also CA 93-96; obituary CA 33-36R

Kaye, M(ary) M(argaret) 1909?- . . . . **CLC 28**
See also CANR 24; CA 89-92

Kaye, Mollie 1909?-
See Kaye, M(ary) M(argaret)

Kaye-Smith, Sheila 1887-1956. . . . . **TCLC 20**
See also CA 118; DLB 36

Kaymor, Patrice Maguilene 1906-
See Senghor, Leopold Sedar

Klinger, Friedrich Maximilian von 1752-1831 .... **NCLC 1**

Klopstock, Friedrich Gottlieb 1724-1803 .... **NCLC 11**

Knebel, Fletcher 1911- .... **CLC 14**
See also CAAS 3; CANR 1; CA 1-4R; SATA 36

Knight, Etheridge 1931-1991 .... **CLC 40**
See also BLC 2; CANR 23; CA 21-24R; DLB 41

Knight, Sarah Kemble 1666-1727 ..... **LC 7**
See also DLB 24

Knowles, John 1926- ...... **CLC 1, 4, 10, 26**
See also CA 17-20R; SATA 8; DLB 6; CDALB 1968-1987

Koch, C(hristopher) J(ohn) 1932- ... **CLC 42**
See also CA 127

Koch, Kenneth 1925- .... **CLC 5, 8, 44**
See also CANR 6; CA 1-4R; DLB 5

Kochanowski, Jan 1530-1584 .... **LC 10**

Kock, Charles Paul de 1794-1871 .... **NCLC 16**

Koestler, Arthur 1905-1983 .... **CLC 1, 3, 6, 8, 15, 33**
See also CANR 1; CA 1-4R; obituary CA 109; DLB-Y 83

Kohout, Pavel 1928- .... **CLC 13**
See also CANR 3; CA 45-48

Kolmar, Gertrud 1894-1943 .... **TCLC 40**

Konigsberg, Allen Stewart 1935-
See Allen, Woody

Konrad, Gyorgy 1933- .... **CLC 4, 10**
See also CA 85-88

Konwicki, Tadeusz 1926- ..... **CLC 8, 28, 54**
See also CAAS 9; CA 101

Kopit, Arthur (Lee) 1937- .... **CLC 1, 18, 33**
See also CA 81-84; CABS 3; DLB 7

Kops, Bernard 1926- .... **CLC 4**
See also CA 5-8R; DLB 13

Kornbluth, C(yril) M. 1923-1958 .... **TCLC 8**
See also CA 105; DLB 8

Korolenko, Vladimir (Galaktionovich) 1853-1921 .... **TCLC 22**
See also CA 121

Kosinski, Jerzy (Nikodem) 1933-1991 ... **CLC 1, 2, 3, 6, 10, 15, 53, 70**
See also CANR 9; CA 17-20R; obituary CA 134; DLB 2; DLB-Y 82

Kostelanetz, Richard (Cory) 1940- .. **CLC 28**
See also CAAS 8; CA 13-16R

Kostrowitzki, Wilhelm Apollinaris de 1880-1918
See Apollinaire, Guillaume
See also CA 104

Kotlowitz, Robert 1924- .... **CLC 4**
See also CA 33-36R

Kotzebue, August (Friedrich Ferdinand) von 1761-1819 .... **NCLC 25**

Kotzwinkle, William 1938- ... **CLC 5, 14, 35**
See also CLR 6; CANR 3; CA 45-48; SATA 24

Kozol, Jonathan 1936- .... **CLC 17**
See also CANR 16; CA 61-64

Kozoll, Michael 1940?- .... **CLC 35**

Kramer, Kathryn 19??- .... **CLC 34**

Kramer, Larry 1935- .... **CLC 42**
See also CA 124, 126

Krasicki, Ignacy 1735-1801 .... **NCLC 8**

Krasinski, Zygmunt 1812-1859 .... **NCLC 4**

Kraus, Karl 1874-1936 .... **TCLC 5**
See also CA 104

Kreve, Vincas 1882-1954 .... **TCLC 27**

Kristofferson, Kris 1936- .... **CLC 26**
See also CA 104

Krizanc, John 1956- .... **CLC 57**

Krleza, Miroslav 1893-1981 .... **CLC 8**
See also CA 97-100; obituary CA 105

Kroetsch, Robert (Paul) 1927- .... **CLC 5, 23, 57**
See also CANR 8; CA 17-20R; DLB 53

Kroetz, Franz Xaver 1946- .... **CLC 41**
See also CA 130

Kropotkin, Peter 1842-1921 .... **TCLC 36**
See also CA 119

Krotkov, Yuri 1917- .... **CLC 19**
See also CA 102

Krumgold, Joseph (Quincy) 1908-1980 .... **CLC 12**
See also CANR 7; CA 9-12R; obituary CA 101; SATA 1, 48; obituary SATA 23

Krutch, Joseph Wood 1893-1970 .... **CLC 24**
See also CANR 4; CA 1-4R; obituary CA 25-28R; DLB 63

Krylov, Ivan Andreevich 1768?-1844 .... **NCLC 1**

Kubin, Alfred 1877-1959 .... **TCLC 23**
See also CA 112; DLB 81

Kubrick, Stanley 1928- .... **CLC 16**
See also CA 81-84; DLB 26

Kumin, Maxine (Winokur) 1925- .... **CLC 5, 13, 28**
See also CAAS 8; CANR 1, 21; CA 1-4R; SATA 12; DLB 5

Kundera, Milan 1929- .... **CLC 4, 9, 19, 32, 68**
See also CANR 19; CA 85-88; AAYA 2

Kunitz, Stanley J(asspon) 1905- .... **CLC 6, 11, 14**
See also CANR 26; CA 41-44R; DLB 48

Kunze, Reiner 1933- .... **CLC 10**
See also CA 93-96; DLB 75

Kuprin, Aleksandr (Ivanovich) 1870-1938 .... **TCLC 5**
See also CA 104

Kureishi, Hanif 1954- .... **CLC 64**

Kurosawa, Akira 1910- .... **CLC 16**
See also CA 101

Kuttner, Henry 1915-1958 .... **TCLC 10**
See also CA 107; DLB 8

Kuzma, Greg 1944- .... **CLC 7**
See also CA 33-36R

Kuzmin, Mikhail 1872?-1936 ...... **TCLC 40**

Labrunie, Gerard 1808-1855
See Nerval, Gerard de

La Bruyere, Jean de 1645-1696 ...... **LC 17**

Laclos, Pierre Ambroise Francois Choderlos de 1741-1803 .... **NCLC 4**

La Fayette, Marie (Madelaine Pioche de la Vergne, Comtesse) de 1634-1693 .... **LC 2**

Lafayette, Rene
See Hubbard, L(afayette) Ron(ald)

Laforgue, Jules 1860-1887 .... **NCLC 5**

Lagerkvist, Par (Fabian) 1891-1974 .... **CLC 7, 10, 13, 54**
See also CA 85-88; obituary CA 49-52

Lagerlof, Selma (Ottiliana Lovisa) 1858-1940 .... **TCLC 4, 36**
See also CLR 7; CA 108; SATA 15

La Guma, (Justin) Alex(ander) 1925-1985 .... **CLC 19**
See also CANR 25; CA 49-52; obituary CA 118

Lamartine, Alphonse (Marie Louis Prat) de 1790-1869 .... **NCLC 11**

Lamb, Charles 1775-1834 .... **NCLC 10**
See also SATA 17

Lamming, George (William) 1927- .... **CLC 2, 4, 66**
See also BLC 2; CANR 26; CA 85-88

LaMoore, Louis Dearborn 1908?-
See L'Amour, Louis (Dearborn)

L'Amour, Louis (Dearborn) 1908-1988 .... **CLC 25, 55**
See also CANR 3, 25; CA 1-4R; obituary CA 125; DLB-Y 80

Lampedusa, (Prince) Giuseppe (Maria Fabrizio) Tomasi di 1896-1957 .... **TCLC 13**
See also CA 111

Lampman, Archibald 1861-1899 .. **NCLC 25**
See also DLB 92

Lancaster, Bruce 1896-1963 .... **CLC 36**
See also CAP 1; CA 9-12; SATA 9

Landis, John (David) 1950- .... **CLC 26**
See also CA 112, 122

Landolfi, Tommaso 1908-1979 ... **CLC 11, 49**
See also CA 127; obituary CA 117

Landon, Letitia Elizabeth 1802-1838 .... **NCLC 15**

Landor, Walter Savage 1775-1864 .... **NCLC 14**

Landwirth, Heinz 1927-
See Lind, Jakov
See also CANR 7; CA 11-12R

Lane, Patrick 1939- .... **CLC 25**
See also CA 97-100; DLB 53

Lang, Andrew 1844-1912 .... **TCLC 16**
See also CA 114; SATA 16

Lang, Fritz 1890-1976 .... **CLC 20**
See also CANR 30; CA 77-80; obituary CA 69-72

Langer, Elinor 1939- .... **CLC 34**
See also CA 121

Langland, William 1330?-1400? ...... **LC 19**

Lanier, Sidney 1842-1881 .... **NCLC 6**
See also SATA 18; DLB 64

Lanyer, Aemilia 1569-1645 . . . . **LC 10**

Lao Tzu c. 6th-3rd century B.C. . . . **CMLC 7**

Lapine, James 1949- . . . . **CLC 39**
See also CA 123, 130

Larbaud, Valery 1881-1957 . . . . **TCLC 9**
See also CA 106

Lardner, Ring(gold Wilmer)
1885-1933 . . . . **TCLC 2, 14**
See also CA 104; DLB 11, 25, 86; CDALB 1917-1929

Larkin, Philip (Arthur)
1922-1985 . . . **CLC 3, 5, 8, 9, 13, 18, 33, 39, 64**
See also CANR 24; CA 5-8R; obituary CA 117; DLB 27

Larra (y Sanchez de Castro), Mariano Jose de
1809-1837 . . . . **NCLC 17**

Larsen, Eric 1941- . . . . **CLC 55**

Larsen, Nella 1891-1964 . . . . **CLC 37**
See also BLC 2; CA 125; DLB 51

Larson, Charles R(aymond) 1938- . . . **CLC 31**
See also CANR 4; CA 53-56

Latham, Jean Lee 1902- . . . . **CLC 12**
See also CANR 7; CA 5-8R; SATA 2

Lathen, Emma . . . . **CLC 2**
See also Hennissart, Martha; Latsis, Mary J(ane)

Latsis, Mary J(ane) . . . . **CLC 2**
See also Lathen, Emma
See also CA 85-88

Lattimore, Richmond (Alexander)
1906-1984 . . . . **CLC 3**
See also CANR 1; CA 1-4R; obituary CA 112

Laughlin, James 1914- . . . . **CLC 49**
See also CANR 9; CA 21-24R; DLB 48

Laurence, (Jean) Margaret (Wemyss)
1926-1987 . . **CLC 3, 6, 13, 50, 62; SSC 7**
See also CA 5-8R; obituary CA 121; SATA 50; DLB 53

Laurent, Antoine 1952- . . . . **CLC 50**

Lautreamont, Comte de
1846-1870 . . . . **NCLC 12**

Lavin, Mary 1912- . . . . . . **CLC 4, 18; SSC 4**
See also CA 9-12R; DLB 15

Lawler, Raymond (Evenor) 1922- . . . **CLC 58**
See also CA 103

Lawrence, D(avid) H(erbert)
1885-1930 . . . . **TCLC 2, 9, 16, 33; SSC 4**
See also CA 104, 121; DLB 10, 19, 36

Lawrence, T(homas) E(dward)
1888-1935 . . . . **TCLC 18**
See also CA 115

Lawson, Henry (Archibald Hertzberg)
1867-1922 . . . . **TCLC 27**
See also CA 120

Laxness, Halldor (Kiljan) 1902- . . . . **CLC 25**
See also Gudjonsson, Halldor Kiljan

Laye, Camara 1928-1980 . . . . **CLC 4, 38**
See also BLC 2.; CANR 25; CA 85-88; obituary CA 97-100

Layton, Irving (Peter) 1912- . . . . . **CLC 2, 15**
See also CANR 2; CA 1-4R; DLB 88

Lazarus, Emma 1849-1887. . . . . **NCLC 8**

Leacock, Stephen (Butler)
1869-1944 . . . . **TCLC 2**
See also CA 104; DLB 92

Lear, Edward 1812-1888 . . . . **NCLC 3**
See also CLR 1; SATA 18; DLB 32

Lear, Norman (Milton) 1922- . . . . . . **CLC 12**
See also CA 73-76

Leavis, F(rank) R(aymond)
1895-1978 . . . . **CLC 24**
See also CA 21-24R; obituary CA 77-80

Leavitt, David 1961?- . . . . **CLC 34**
See also CA 116, 122

Lebowitz, Fran(ces Ann)
1951?- . . . . **CLC 11, 36**
See also CANR 14; CA 81-84

Le Carre, John 1931- . . . **CLC 3, 5, 9, 15, 28**
See also Cornwell, David (John Moore)
See also DLB 87

Le Clezio, J(ean) M(arie) G(ustave)
1940- . . . . **CLC 31**
See also CA 116, 128; DLB 83

Leconte de Lisle, Charles-Marie-Rene
1818-1894 . . . . **NCLC 29**

Leduc, Violette 1907-1972 . . . . **CLC 22**
See also CAP 1; CA 13-14; obituary CA 33-36R

Ledwidge, Francis 1887-1917. . . . . . **TCLC 23**
See also CA 123; DLB 20

Lee, Andrea 1953- . . . . **CLC 36**
See also BLC 2; CA 125

Lee, Andrew 1917-
See Auchincloss, Louis (Stanton)

Lee, Don L. 1942- . . . . **CLC 2**
See also Madhubuti, Haki R.
See also CA 73-76

Lee, George Washington
1894-1976 . . . . **CLC 52**
See also BLC 2; CA 125; DLB 51

Lee, (Nelle) Harper 1926- . . . . . . **CLC 12, 60**
See also CA 13-16R; SATA 11; DLB 6; CDALB 1941-1968

Lee, Lawrence 1903- . . . . **CLC 34**
See also CA 25-28R

Lee, Manfred B(ennington)
1905-1971 . . . . **CLC 11**
See also Queen, Ellery
See also CANR 2; CA 1-4R; obituary CA 29-32R

Lee, Stan 1922- . . . . **CLC 17**
See also CA 108, 111

Lee, Tanith 1947- . . . . **CLC 46**
See also CA 37-40R; SATA 8

Lee, Vernon 1856-1935 . . . . **TCLC 5**
See also Paget, Violet
See also DLB 57

Lee-Hamilton, Eugene (Jacob)
1845-1907 . . . . **TCLC 22**
See also CA 117

Leet, Judith 1935- . . . . **CLC 11**

Le Fanu, Joseph Sheridan
1814-1873 . . . . **NCLC 9**
See also DLB 21, 70

Leffland, Ella 1931- . . . . **CLC 19**
See also CA 29-32R; DLB-Y 84

Leger, (Marie-Rene) Alexis Saint-Leger
1887-1975 . . . . **CLC 11**
See also Perse, St.-John
See also CA 13-16R; obituary CA 61-64

Le Guin, Ursula K(roeber)
1929- . . . . **CLC 8, 13, 22, 45, 71**
See also CLR 3; CANR 9, 32; CA 21-24R; SATA 4, 52; DLB 8, 52; CDALB 1968-1987

Lehmann, Rosamond (Nina) 1901- . . . **CLC 5**
See also CANR 8; CA 77-80; DLB 15

Leiber, Fritz (Reuter, Jr.) 1910- . . . . **CLC 25**
See also CANR 2; CA 45-48; SATA 45; DLB 8

Leimbach, Marti 1963- . . . . **CLC 65**

Leino, Eino 1878-1926 . . . . **TCLC 24**

Leiris, Michel 1901- . . . . **CLC 61**
See also CA 119, 128

Leithauser, Brad 1953- . . . . **CLC 27**
See also CANR 27; CA 107

Lelchuk, Alan 1938- . . . . **CLC 5**
See also CANR 1; CA 45-48

Lem, Stanislaw 1921- . . . . **CLC 8, 15, 40**
See also CAAS 1; CA 105

Lemann, Nancy 1956- . . . . **CLC 39**
See also CA 118

Lemonnier, (Antoine Louis) Camille
1844-1913 . . . . **TCLC 22**
See also CA 121

Lenau, Nikolaus 1802-1850 . . . . . . **NCLC 16**

L'Engle, Madeleine 1918- . . . . **CLC 12**
See also CLR 1, 14; CANR 3, 21; CA 1-4R; SATA 1, 27; DLB 52; AAYA 1

Lengyel, Jozsef 1896-1975. . . . . **CLC 7**
See also CA 85-88; obituary CA 57-60

Lennon, John (Ono)
1940-1980 . . . . **CLC 12, 35**
See also CA 102

Lennon, John Winston 1940-1980
See Lennon, John (Ono)

Lennox, Charlotte Ramsay
1729?-1804. . . . . **NCLC 23**
See also DLB 39

Lentricchia, Frank (Jr.) 1940- . . . . . . **CLC 34**
See also CANR 19; CA 25-28R

Lenz, Siegfried 1926- . . . . **CLC 27**
See also CA 89-92; DLB 75

Leonard, Elmore 1925- . . . . . . **CLC 28, 34, 71**
See also CANR 12, 28; CA 81-84

Leonard, Hugh 1926- . . . . **CLC 19**
See also Byrne, John Keyes
See also DLB 13

Leopardi, (Conte) Giacomo (Talegardo Francesco di Sales Saverio Pietro)
1798-1837 . . . . **NCLC 22**

Lerman, Eleanor 1952- . . . . **CLC 9**
See also CA 85-88

Lerman, Rhoda 1936- . . . . **CLC 56**
See also CA 49-52

Lermontov, Mikhail Yuryevich
1814-1841 . . . . **NCLC 5**

Leroux, Gaston 1868-1927. . . . . **TCLC 25**
See also CA 108

Lesage, Alain-Rene 1668-1747........ **LC 2**

Leskov, Nikolai (Semyonovich) 1831-1895 .... **NCLC 25**

Lessing, Doris (May) 1919- .... **CLC 1, 2, 3, 6, 10, 15, 22, 40; SSC 6**
See also CA 9-12R; DLB 15; DLB-Y 85

Lessing, Gotthold Ephraim 1729-1781 .... **LC 8**

Lester, Richard 1932-............. **CLC 20**

Lever, Charles (James) 1806-1872 .... **NCLC 23**
See also DLB 21

Leverson, Ada 1865-1936......... **TCLC 18**
See also CA 117

Levertov, Denise 1923- ...... **CLC 1, 2, 3, 5, 8, 15, 28, 66**
See also CANR 3, 29; CA 1-4R; DLB 5

Levi, Peter (Chad Tiger) 1931- ..... **CLC 41**
See also CA 5-8R; DLB 40

Levi, Primo 1919-1987......... **CLC 37, 50**
See also CANR 12; CA 13-16R; obituary CA 122

Levin, Ira 1929- .... **CLC 3, 6**
See also CANR 17; CA 21-24R

Levin, Meyer 1905-1981 .... **CLC 7**
See also CANR 15; CA 9-12R; obituary CA 104; SATA 21; obituary SATA 27; DLB 9, 28; DLB-Y 81

Levine, Norman 1924- .... **CLC 54**
See also CANR 14; CA 73-76; DLB 88

Levine, Philip 1928- .. **CLC 2, 4, 5, 9, 14, 33**
See also CANR 9; CA 9-12R; DLB 5

Levinson, Deirdre 1931-........... **CLC 49**
See also CA 73-76

Levi-Strauss, Claude 1908- .... **CLC 38**
See also CANR 6; CA 1-4R

Levitin, Sonia 1934-.............. **CLC 17**
See also CANR 14; CA 29-32R; SAAS 2; SATA 4

Lewes, George Henry 1817-1878 .... **NCLC 25**
See also DLB 55

Lewis, Alun 1915-1944............ **TCLC 3**
See also CA 104; DLB 20

Lewis, C(ecil) Day 1904-1972
See Day Lewis, C(ecil)

Lewis, C(live) S(taples) 1898-1963 .... **CLC 1, 3, 6, 14, 27**
See also CLR 3; CA 81-84; SATA 13; DLB 15

Lewis (Winters), Janet 1899-....... **CLC 41**
See also Winters, Janet Lewis
See also CANR 29; CAP 1; CA 9-10R; DLB-Y 87

Lewis, Matthew Gregory 1775-1818 .... **NCLC 11**
See also DLB 39

Lewis, (Harry) Sinclair 1885-1951 .... **TCLC 4, 13, 23, 39**
See also CA 104; DLB 9; DLB-DS 1; CDALB 1917-1929

Lewis, (Percy) Wyndham 1882?-1957................. **TCLC 2, 9**
See also CA 104; DLB 15

Lewisohn, Ludwig 1883-1955...... **TCLC 19**
See also CA 73-76, 107; obituary CA 29-32R; DLB 4, 9, 28

L'Heureux, John (Clarke) 1934-.... **CLC 52**
See also CANR 23; CA 15-16R

Lieber, Stanley Martin 1922-
See Lee, Stan

Lieberman, Laurence (James) 1935- .... **CLC 4, 36**
See also CANR 8; CA 17-20R

Li Fei-kan 1904-................. **CLC 18**
See also Pa Chin
See also CA 105

Lifton, Robert Jay 1926- .... **CLC 67**
See also CANR 27; CA 17-18R

Lightfoot, Gordon (Meredith) 1938- .... **CLC 26**
See also CA 109

Ligotti, Thomas 1953- .... **CLC 44**
See also CA 123

Liliencron, Detlev von 1844-1909 .... **TCLC 18**
See also CA 117

Lima, Jose Lezama 1910-1976
See Lezama Lima, Jose

Lima Barreto, (Alfonso Henriques de) 1881-1922 .... **TCLC 23**
See also CA 117

Limonov, Eduard 1943- .... **CLC 67**

Lincoln, Abraham 1809-1865..... **NCLC 18**

Lind, Jakov 1927-......... **CLC 1, 2, 4, 27**
See also Landwirth, Heinz
See also CAAS 4; CA 9-12R

Lindsay, David 1876-1945........ **TCLC 15**
See also CA 113

Lindsay, (Nicholas) Vachel 1879-1931 .... **TCLC 17**
See also CA 114; SATA 40; DLB 54; CDALB 1865-1917

Linney, Romulus 1930- .... **CLC 51**
See also CA 1-4R

Li Po 701-763.................. **CMLC 2**

Lipsius, Justus 1547-1606 .... **LC 16**

Lipsyte, Robert (Michael) 1938- .... **CLC 21**
See also CLR 23; CANR 8; CA 17-20R; SATA 5

Lish, Gordon (Jay) 1934-.......... **CLC 45**
See also CA 113, 117

Lispector, Clarice 1925-1977....... **CLC 43**
See also obituary CA 116

Littell, Robert 1935?-............. **CLC 42**
See also CA 109, 112

Little, Malcolm 1925-1965
See also BLC 2; CA 125; obituary CA 111

Liu E 1857-1909................ **TCLC 15**
See also CA 115

Lively, Penelope 1933-......... **CLC 32, 50**
See also CLR 7; CANR 29; CA 41-44R; SATA 7; DLB 14

Livesay, Dorothy 1909- .... **CLC 4, 15**
See also CAAS 8; CA 25-28R; DLB 68

Lizardi, Jose Joaquin Fernandez de 1776-1827 .... **NCLC 30**

Llewellyn, Richard 1906-1983....... **CLC 7**
See also Llewellyn Lloyd, Richard (Dafydd Vyvyan)
See also DLB 15

Llewellyn Lloyd, Richard (Dafydd Vyvyan) 1906-1983
See Llewellyn, Richard
See also CANR 7; CA 53-56; obituary CA 111; SATA 11, 37

Llosa, Mario Vargas 1936-
See Vargas Llosa, Mario

Lloyd, Richard Llewellyn 1906-
See Llewellyn, Richard

Locke, Alain 1886-1954.......... **TCLC 43**
See also CA 124, 106; DLB 51

Locke, John 1632-1704 .... **LC 7**
See also DLB 31

Lockhart, John Gibson 1794-1854 .... **NCLC 6**

Lodge, David (John) 1935-......... **CLC 36**
See also CANR 19; CA 17-20R; DLB 14

Loewinsohn, Ron(ald William) 1937- .... **CLC 52**
See also CA 25-28R

Logan, John 1923- .... **CLC 5**
See also CA 77-80; obituary CA 124; DLB 5

Lo Kuan-chung 1330?-1400? .... **LC 12**

Lombino, S. A. 1926-
See Hunter, Evan

London, Jack 1876-1916 ...... **TCLC 9, 15, 39; SSC 4**
See also London, John Griffith
See also SATA 18; DLB 8, 12, 78; CDALB 1865-1917

London, John Griffith 1876-1916
See London, Jack
See also CA 110, 119

Long, Emmett 1925-
See Leonard, Elmore

Longbaugh, Harry 1931-
See Goldman, William (W.)

Longfellow, Henry Wadsworth 1807-1882 .... **NCLC 2**
See also SATA 19; DLB 1, 59; CDALB 1640-1865

Longley, Michael 1939-........... **CLC 29**
See also CA 102; DLB 40

Longus fl. c. 2nd century- .... **CMLC 7**

Lopate, Phillip 1943- .... **CLC 29**
See also CA 97-100; DLB-Y 80

Lopez Portillo (y Pacheco), Jose 1920- .... **CLC 46**
See also CA 129

Lopez y Fuentes, Gregorio 1897-1966 .... **CLC 32**

Lord, Bette Bao 1938-............ **CLC 23**
See also CA 107; SATA 58

Lorde, Audre (Geraldine) 1934-..... **CLC 18**
See also BLC 2; CANR 16, 26; CA 25-28R; DLB 41

Matthiessen, Peter 1927- . . . . **CLC 5, 7, 11, 32, 64**
See also CANR 21; CA 9-12R; SATA 27; DLB 6

Maturin, Charles Robert 1780?-1824. . . . . **NCLC 6**

Matute, Ana Maria 1925- . . . . **CLC 11**
See also CA 89-92

Maugham, W(illiam) Somerset 1874-1965 . . . . **CLC 1, 11, 15, 67; SSC 8**
See also CA 5-8R; obituary CA 25-28R; SATA 54; DLB 10, 36, 77, 100

Maupassant, (Henri Rene Albert) Guy de 1850-1893 . . . . **NCLC 1; SSC 1**

Mauriac, Claude 1914-. . . . . **CLC 9**
See also CA 89-92; DLB 83

Mauriac, Francois (Charles) 1885-1970 . . . . **CLC 4, 9, 56**
See also CAP 2; CA 25-28; DLB 65

Mavor, Osborne Henry 1888-1951
See Bridie, James
See also CA 104

Maxwell, William (Keepers, Jr.) 1908- . . . . **CLC 19**
See also CA 93-96; DLB-Y 80

May, Elaine 1932- . . . . **CLC 16**
See also CA 124; DLB 44

Mayakovsky, Vladimir (Vladimirovich) 1893-1930 . . . . **TCLC 4, 18**
See also CA 104

Mayhew, Henry 1812-1887 . . . . . . **NCLC 31**
See also DLB 18, 55

Maynard, Joyce 1953- . . . . **CLC 23**
See also CA 111, 129

Mayne, William (James Carter) 1928- . . . . **CLC 12**
See also CA 9-12R; SATA 6

Mayo, Jim 1908?-
See L'Amour, Louis (Dearborn)

Maysles, Albert 1926- and **Maysles, David** 1926- . . . . **CLC 16**
See also CA 29-32R

Maysles, Albert 1926- . . . . **CLC 16**
See also Maysles, Albert and Maysles, David
See also CA 29-32R

Maysles, David 1932-. . . . . **CLC 16**
See also Maysles, Albert and Maysles, David

Mazer, Norma Fox 1931- . . . . **CLC 26**
See also CLR 23; CANR 12; CA 69-72; SAAS 1; SATA 24

Mazzini, Guiseppe 1805-1872 . . . . **NCLC 34**

McAuley, James (Phillip) 1917-1976 . . . . **CLC 45**
See also CA 97-100

McBain, Ed 1926-
See Hunter, Evan

McBrien, William 1930- . . . . **CLC 44**
See also CA 107

McCaffrey, Anne 1926- . . . . **CLC 17**
See also CANR 15; CA 25-28R; SATA 8; DLB 8

McCarthy, Cormac 1933-. . . . . **CLC 4, 57**
See also CANR 10; CA 13-16R; DLB 6

McCarthy, Mary (Therese) 1912-1989-. . . **CLC 1, 3, 5, 14, 24, 39, 59**
See also CANR 16; CA 5-8R; obituary CA 129; DLB 2; DLB-Y 81

McCartney, (James) Paul 1942- . . . . **CLC 12, 35**

McCauley, Stephen 19??-. . . . . **CLC 50**

McClure, Michael 1932- . . . . **CLC 6, 10**
See also CANR 17; CA 21-24R; DLB 16

McCorkle, Jill (Collins) 1958-. . . . . . **CLC 51**
See also CA 121; DLB-Y 87

McCourt, James 1941-. . . . . **CLC 5**
See also CA 57-60

McCoy, Horace 1897-1955 . . . . **TCLC 28**
See also CA 108; DLB 9

McCrae, John 1872-1918. . . . . **TCLC 12**
See also CA 109; DLB 92

McCullers, (Lula) Carson (Smith) 1917-1967 . . **CLC 1, 4, 10, 12, 48; SSC 9**
See also CANR 18; CA 5-8R; obituary CA 25-28R; CABS 1; SATA 27; DLB 2, 7; CDALB 1941-1968

McCullough, Colleen 1938?- . . . . **CLC 27**
See also CANR 17; CA 81-84

McElroy, Joseph (Prince) 1930- . . . . **CLC 5, 47**
See also CA 17-20R

McEwan, Ian (Russell) 1948- . . . **CLC 13, 66**
See also CANR 14; CA 61-64; DLB 14

McFadden, David 1940-. . . . . **CLC 48**
See also CA 104; DLB 60

McFarland, Dennis 1956- . . . . **CLC 65**

McGahern, John 1934-. . . . . **CLC 5, 9, 48**
See also CANR 29; CA 17-20R; DLB 14

McGinley, Patrick 1937-. . . . . **CLC 41**
See also CA 120, 127

McGinley, Phyllis 1905-1978 . . . . . . **CLC 14**
See also CANR 19; CA 9-12R; obituary CA 77-80; SATA 2, 44; obituary SATA 24; DLB 11, 48

McGinniss, Joe 1942-. . . . . **CLC 32**
See also CANR 26; CA 25-28R

McGivern, Maureen Daly 1921-
See Daly, Maureen
See also CA 9-12R

McGrath, Patrick 1950-. . . . . **CLC 55**

McGrath, Thomas 1916- . . . . **CLC 28, 59**
See also CANR 6; CA 9-12R, 130; SATA 41

McGuane, Thomas (Francis III) 1939- . . . . **CLC 3, 7, 18, 45**
See also CANR 5, 24; CA 49-52; DLB 2; DLB-Y 80

McGuckian, Medbh 1950- . . . . **CLC 48**
See also DLB 40

McHale, Tom 1941-1982 . . . . **CLC 3, 5**
See also CA 77-80; obituary CA 106

McIlvanney, William 1936- . . . . **CLC 42**
See also CA 25-28R; DLB 14

McIlwraith, Maureen Mollie Hunter 1922-
See Hunter, Mollie
See also CA 29-32R; SATA 2

McInerney, Jay 1955- . . . . **CLC 34**
See also CA 116, 123

McIntyre, Vonda N(eel) 1948- . . . . . **CLC 18**
See also CANR 17; CA 81-84

McKay, Claude 1889-1948 . . . . **TCLC 7, 41; PC 2**
See also BLC 3; CA 104, 124; DLB 4, 45, 51

McKay, Claude 1889-1948
See McKay, Festus Claudius

McKay, Festus Claudius 1889-1948
See also BLC 2; CA 124; brief entry CA 104

McKuen, Rod 1933- . . . . **CLC 1, 3**
See also CA 41-44R

McLuhan, (Herbert) Marshall 1911-1980 . . . . **CLC 37**
See also CANR 12; CA 9-12R; obituary CA 102; DLB 88

McManus, Declan Patrick 1955-
See Costello, Elvis

McMillan, Terry 1951- . . . . **CLC 50, 61**

McMurtry, Larry (Jeff) 1936- . . . . **CLC 2, 3, 7, 11, 27, 44**
See also CANR 19; CA 5-8R; DLB 2; DLB-Y 80, 87; CDALB 1968-1987

McNally, Terrence 1939-. . . . . . **CLC 4, 7, 41**
See also CANR 2; CA 45-48; DLB 7

McNamer, Deirdre 1950-. . . . . **CLC 70**

McNeile, Herman Cyril 1888-1937
See Sapper
See also DLB 77

McPhee, John 1931-. . . . . **CLC 36**
See also CANR 20; CA 65-68

McPherson, James Alan 1943- . . . . . **CLC 19**
See also CANR 24; CA 25-28R; DLB 38

McPherson, William 1939- . . . . **CLC 34**
See also CA 57-60

McSweeney, Kerry 19??- . . . . **CLC 34**

Mead, Margaret 1901-1978 . . . . **CLC 37**
See also CANR 4; CA 1-4R; obituary CA 81-84; SATA 20

Meaker, M. J. 1927-
See Kerr, M. E.; Meaker, Marijane

Meaker, Marijane 1927-
See Kerr, M. E.
See also CA 107; SATA 20

Medoff, Mark (Howard) 1940- . . . **CLC 6, 23**
See also CANR 5; CA 53-56; DLB 7

Megged, Aharon 1920-. . . . . **CLC 9**
See also CANR 1; CA 49-52

Mehta, Ved (Parkash) 1934- . . . . **CLC 37**
See also CANR 2, 23; CA 1-4R

Mellor, John 1953?-
See The Clash

Meltzer, Milton 1915- . . . . **CLC 26**
See also CLR 13; CA 13-16R; SAAS 1; SATA 1, 50; DLB 61

Melville, Herman 1819-1891 . . . . . . **NCLC 3, 12, 29; SSC 1**
See also SATA 59; DLB 3, 74; CDALB 1640-1865

Membreno, Alejandro 1972- . . . . **CLC 59**

Menander
c. 342 B.C.-c. 292 B.C. . . . . **CMLC 9**

Mencken, H(enry) L(ouis)
1880-1956 . . . . **TCLC 13**
See also CA 105, 125; DLB 11, 29, 63; CDALB 1917-1929

Mercer, David 1928-1980. . . . . **CLC 5**
See also CANR 23; CA 9-12R; obituary CA 102; DLB 13

Meredith, George 1828-1909 . . . . . . **TCLC 17**
See also CA 117; DLB 18, 35, 57

Meredith, George 1858-1924 . . . . . . **TCLC 43**

Meredith, William (Morris)
1919- . . . . **CLC 4, 13, 22, 55**
See also CANR 6; CA 9-12R; DLB 5

Merezhkovsky, Dmitri
1865-1941 . . . . **TCLC 29**

Merimee, Prosper
1803-1870 . . . . **NCLC 6; SSC 7**

Merkin, Daphne 1954- . . . . **CLC 44**
See also CANR 123

Merrill, James (Ingram)
1926- . . . . **CLC 2, 3, 6, 8, 13, 18, 34**
See also CANR 10; CA 13-16R; DLB 5; DLB-Y 85

Merton, Thomas (James)
1915-1968 . . . . **CLC 1, 3, 11, 34**
See also CANR 22; CA 5-8R; obituary CA 25-28R; DLB 48; DLB-Y 81

Merwin, W(illiam) S(tanley)
1927- . . . . . . **CLC 1, 2, 3, 5, 8, 13, 18, 45**
See also CANR 15; CA 13-16R; DLB 5

Metcalf, John 1938- . . . . **CLC 37**
See also CA 113; DLB 60

Mew, Charlotte (Mary)
1870-1928 . . . . **TCLC 8**
See also CA 105; DLB 19

Mewshaw, Michael 1943- . . . . **CLC 9**
See also CANR 7; CA 53-56; DLB-Y 80

Meyer-Meyrink, Gustav 1868-1932
See Meyrink, Gustav
See also CA 117

Meyers, Jeffrey 1939- . . . . **CLC 39**
See also CA 73-76

Meynell, Alice (Christiana Gertrude Thompson) 1847-1922 . . . . **TCLC 6**
See also CA 104; DLB 19

Meyrink, Gustav 1868-1932. . . . . . . **TCLC 21**
See also Meyer-Meyrink, Gustav

Michaels, Leonard 1933- . . . . **CLC 6, 25**
See also CANR 21; CA 61-64

Michaux, Henri 1899-1984 . . . . . . **CLC 8, 19**
See also CA 85-88; obituary CA 114

Michelangelo 1475-1564. . . . . **LC 12**

Michelet, Jules 1798-1874 . . . . **NCLC 31**

Michener, James A(lbert)
1907- . . . . **CLC 1, 5, 11, 29, 60**
See also CANR 21; CA 5-8R; DLB 6

Mickiewicz, Adam 1798-1855 . . . . . **NCLC 3**

Middleton, Christopher 1926- . . . . . . **CLC 13**
See also CANR 29; CA 13-16R; DLB 40

Middleton, Stanley 1919- . . . . **CLC 7, 38**
See also CANR 21; CA 25-28R; DLB 14

Migueis, Jose Rodrigues 1901- . . . . . **CLC 10**

Mikszath, Kalman 1847-1910 . . . . . **TCLC 31**

Miles, Josephine (Louise)
1911-1985 . . . . **CLC 1, 2, 14, 34, 39**
See also CANR 2; CA 1-4R; obituary CA 116; DLB 48

Mill, John Stuart 1806-1873 . . . . . **NCLC 11**
See also DLB 55

Millar, Kenneth 1915-1983 . . . . **CLC 14**
See also Macdonald, Ross
See also CANR 16; CA 9-12R; obituary CA 110; DLB 2; DLB-Y 83; DLB-DS 6

Millay, Edna St. Vincent
1892-1950 . . . . **TCLC 4**
See also CA 103; DLB 45; CDALB 1917-1929

Miller, Arthur
1915- . . . . . . **CLC 1, 2, 6, 10, 15, 26, 47; DC 1**
See also CANR 2, 30; CA 1-4R; CABS 3; DLB 7; CDALB 1941-1968

Miller, Henry (Valentine)
1891-1980 . . . . **CLC 1, 2, 4, 9, 14, 43**
See also CA 9-12R; obituary CA 97-100; DLB 4, 9; DLB-Y 80; CDALB 1929-1941

Miller, Jason 1939?- . . . . **CLC 2**
See also CA 73-76; DLB 7

Miller, Sue 19??- . . . . **CLC 44**

Miller, Walter M(ichael), Jr.
1923- . . . . **CLC 4, 30**
See also CA 85-88; DLB 8

Millett, Kate 1934- . . . . **CLC 67**
See also CANR 32; CA 73-76

Millhauser, Steven 1943- . . . . **CLC 21, 54**
See also CA 108, 110, 111; DLB 2

Millin, Sarah Gertrude 1889-1968 . . **CLC 49**
See also CA 102; obituary CA 93-96

Milne, A(lan) A(lexander)
1882-1956 . . . . **TCLC 6**
See also CLR 1, 26; YABC 1; CA 104, 133; DLB 10, 77, 100

Milner, Ron(ald) 1938- . . . . **CLC 56**
See also BLC 3; CANR 24; CA 73-76; DLB 38

Milosz Czeslaw
1911- . . . . **CLC 5, 11, 22, 31, 56**
See also CANR 23; CA 81-84

Milton, John 1608-1674. . . . . **LC 9**

Miner, Valerie (Jane) 1947- . . . . **CLC 40**
See also CA 97-100

Minot, Susan 1956- . . . . **CLC 44**

Minus, Ed 1938- . . . . **CLC 39**

Miro (Ferrer), Gabriel (Francisco Victor)
1879-1930 . . . . **TCLC 5**
See also CA 104

Mishima, Yukio
1925-1970 . . . . **CLC 2, 4, 6, 9, 27; DC 1; SSC 4**
See also Hiraoka, Kimitake

Mistral, Gabriela 1889-1957 . . . . **TCLC 2**
See also CA 104

Mistry, Rohinton 1952- . . . . **CLC 71**

Mitchell, James Leslie 1901-1935
See Gibbon, Lewis Grassic
See also CA 104; DLB 15

Mitchell, Joni 1943- . . . . **CLC 12**
See also CA 112

Mitchell (Marsh), Margaret (Munnerlyn)
1900-1949 . . . . **TCLC 11**
See also CA 109, 125; DLB 9

Mitchell, S. Weir 1829-1914 . . . . . . **TCLC 36**

Mitchell, W(illiam) O(rmond)
1914- . . . . **CLC 25**
See also CANR 15; CA 77-80; DLB 88

Mitford, Mary Russell 1787-1855. . **NCLC 4**

Mitford, Nancy 1904-1973. . . . . **CLC 44**
See also CA 9-12R

Miyamoto Yuriko 1899-1951 . . . . . . **TCLC 37**

Mo, Timothy 1950- . . . . **CLC 46**
See also CA 117

Modarressi, Taghi 1931- . . . . **CLC 44**
See also CA 121

Modiano, Patrick (Jean) 1945- . . . . . **CLC 18**
See also CANR 17; CA 85-88; DLB 83

Mofolo, Thomas (Mokopu)
1876-1948 . . . . **TCLC 22**
See also BLC 3; brief entry CA 121

Mohr, Nicholasa 1935- . . . . **CLC 12**
See also CLR 22; CANR 1; CA 49-52; SAAS 8; SATA 8

Mojtabai, A(nn) G(race)
1938- . . . . **CLC 5, 9, 15, 29**
See also CA 85-88

Moliere 1622-1673 . . . . **LC 10**

Molnar, Ferenc 1878-1952. . . . . **TCLC 20**
See also CA 109

Momaday, N(avarre) Scott
1934- . . . . **CLC 2, 19**
See also CANR 14; CA 25-28R; SATA 30, 48

Monroe, Harriet 1860-1936. . . . . . . **TCLC 12**
See also CA 109; DLB 54, 91

Montagu, Elizabeth 1720-1800 . . . . **NCLC 7**

Montagu, Lady Mary (Pierrepont) Wortley
1689-1762 . . . . **LC 9**

Montague, John (Patrick)
1929- . . . . **CLC 13, 46**
See also CANR 9; CA 9-12R; DLB 40

Montaigne, Michel (Eyquem) de
1533-1592 . . . . **LC 8**

Montale, Eugenio 1896-1981 . . . **CLC 7, 9, 18**
See also CANR 30; CA 17-20R; obituary CA 104

Montesquieu, Charles-Louis de Secondat
1689-1755 . . . . **LC 7**

Montgomery, Marion (H., Jr.)
1925- . . . . **CLC 7**
See also CANR 3; CA 1-4R; DLB 6

Montgomery, Robert Bruce 1921-1978
See Crispin, Edmund
See also CA 104

Montherlant, Henri (Milon) de
1896-1972 . . . . **CLC 8, 19**
See also CA 85-88; obituary CA 37-40R; DLB 72

Ochs, Phil 1940-1976 .... **CLC 17**
See also obituary CA 65-68

O'Connor, Edwin (Greene) 1918-1968 .... **CLC 14**
See also CA 93-96; obituary CA 25-28R

O'Connor, (Mary) Flannery 1925-1964 ... **CLC 1, 2, 3, 6, 10, 13, 15, 21, 66; SSC 1**
See also CANR 3; CA 1-4R; DLB 2; DLB-Y 80; CDALB 1941-1968

O'Connor, Frank 1903-1966 .... **CLC 14, 23; SSC 5**
See also O'Donovan, Michael (John)
See also CA 93-96

O'Dell, Scott 1903- .... **CLC 30**
See also CLR 1, 16; CANR 12; CA 61-64; SATA 12; DLB 52

Odets, Clifford 1906-1963 .... **CLC 2, 28**
See also CA 85-88; DLB 7, 26

O'Donovan, Michael (John) 1903-1966 .... **CLC 14**
See also O'Connor, Frank
See also CA 93-96

Oe, Kenzaburo 1935- .... **CLC 10, 36**
See also CA 97-100

O'Faolain, Julia 1932- .... **CLC 6, 19, 47**
See also CAAS 2; CANR 12; CA 81-84; DLB 14

O'Faolain, Sean 1900-1991 .... **CLC 1, 7, 14, 32, 70**
See also CANR 12; CA 61-64; obituary CA 134; DLB 15

O'Flaherty, Liam 1896-1984 .... **CLC 5, 34; SSC 6**
See also CA 101; obituary CA 113; DLB 36; DLB-Y 84

O'Grady, Standish (James) 1846-1928 .... **TCLC 5**
See also CA 104

O'Grady, Timothy 1951- .... **CLC 59**

O'Hara, Frank 1926-1966 .... **CLC 2, 5, 13**
See also CA 9-12R; obituary CA 25-28R; DLB 5, 16; CDALB 1929-1941

O'Hara, John (Henry) 1905-1970 .... **CLC 1, 2, 3, 6, 11, 42**
See also CA 5-8R; obituary CA 25-28R; DLB 9; DLB-DS 2; CDALB 1929-1941

O'Hara Family
See Banim, John and Banim, Michael

O'Hehir, Diana 1922- .... **CLC 41**
See also CA 93-96

Okigbo, Christopher (Ifenayichukwu) 1932-1967 .... **CLC 25**
See also BLC 3; CA 77-80

Olds, Sharon 1942- .... **CLC 32, 39**
See also CANR 18; CA 101

Olesha, Yuri (Karlovich) 1899-1960 .... **CLC 8**
See also CA 85-88

Oliphant, Margaret (Oliphant Wilson) 1828-1897 .... **NCLC 11**
See also DLB 18

Oliver, Mary 1935- .... **CLC 19, 34**
See also CANR 9; CA 21-24R; DLB 5

Olivier, (Baron) Laurence (Kerr) 1907- .... **CLC 20**
See also CA 111, 129

Olsen, Tillie 1913- .... **CLC 4, 13**
See also CANR 1; CA 1-4R; DLB 28; DLB-Y 80

Olson, Charles (John) 1910-1970 .... **CLC 1, 2, 5, 6, 9, 11, 29**
See also CAP 1; CA 15-16; obituary CA 25-28R; CABS 2; DLB 5, 16

Olson, Theodore 1937-
See Olson, Toby

Olson, Toby 1937- .... **CLC 28**
See also CANR 9; CA 65-68

Ondaatje, (Philip) Michael 1943- .... **CLC 14, 29, 51**
See also CA 77-80; DLB 60

Oneal, Elizabeth 1934- .... **CLC 30**
See also Oneal, Zibby
See also CLR 13; CA 106; SATA 30

Oneal, Zibby 1934- .... **CLC 30**
See also Oneal, Elizabeth

O'Neill, Eugene (Gladstone) 1888-1953 .... **TCLC 1, 6, 27**
See also CA 110; DLB 7; CDALB 1929-1941

Onetti, Juan Carlos 1909- .... **CLC 7, 10**
See also CA 85-88

O'Nolan, Brian 1911-1966
See O'Brien, Flann

O Nuallain, Brian 1911-1966
See O'Brien, Flann
See also CAP 2; CA 21-22; obituary CA 25-28R

Oppen, George 1908-1984 .... **CLC 7, 13, 34**
See also CANR 8; CA 13-16R; obituary CA 113; DLB 5

Oppenheim, E. Phillips 1866-1946 .... **TCLC 45**
See also brief entry CA 111; DLB 70

Orlovitz, Gil 1918-1973 .... **CLC 22**
See also CA 77-80; obituary CA 45-48; DLB 2, 5

Ortega y Gasset, Jose 1883-1955 ... **TCLC 9**
See also CA 106, 130

Ortiz, Simon J. 1941- .... **CLC 45**

Orton, Joe 1933?-1967 .... **CLC 4, 13, 43**
See also Orton, John Kingsley
See also DLB 13

Orton, John Kingsley 1933?-1967
See Orton, Joe
See also CA 85-88

Orwell, George 1903-1950 .... **TCLC 2, 6, 15, 31**
See also Blair, Eric Arthur
See also DLB 15

Osborne, John (James) 1929- .... **CLC 1, 2, 5, 11, 45**
See also CANR 21; CA 13-16R; DLB 13

Osborne, Lawrence 1958- .... **CLC 50**

Osceola 1885-1962
See Dinesen, Isak; Blixen, Karen (Christentze Dinesen)

Oshima, Nagisa 1932- .... **CLC 20**
See also CA 116

Oskison, John M. 1874-1947 .... **TCLC 35**

Ossoli, Sarah Margaret (Fuller marchesa d') 1810-1850
See Fuller, (Sarah) Margaret
See also SATA 25

Ostrovsky, Alexander 1823-1886 .... **NCLC 30**

Otero, Blas de 1916- .... **CLC 11**
See also CA 89-92

Otto, Whitney 1955- .... **CLC 70**

Ouida 1839-1908 .... **TCLC 43**
See also de la Ramee, Marie Louise
See also DLB 18

Ousmane, Sembene 1923-
See also BLC 3; CA 125; brief entry CA 117

Ousmane, Sembene 1923- .... **CLC 66**
See also Sembene, Ousmane
See also CA 125; brief entry CA 117

Ovid 43 B.C.-c. 18 A.D. .... **CMLC 7; PC 2**

Owen, Wilfred (Edward Salter) 1893-1918 .... **TCLC 5, 27**
See also CA 104; DLB 20

Owens, Rochelle 1936- .... **CLC 8**
See also CAAS 2; CA 17-20R

Owl, Sebastian 1939-
See Thompson, Hunter S(tockton)

Oz, Amos 1939- ... **CLC 5, 8, 11, 27, 33, 54**
See also CANR 27; CA 53-56

Ozick, Cynthia 1928- .... **CLC 3, 7, 28, 62**
See also CANR 23; CA 17-20R; DLB 28; DLB-Y 82

Ozu, Yasujiro 1903-1963 .... **CLC 16**
See also CA 112

P. V. M. 1912-1990
See White, Patrick (Victor Martindale)

Pa Chin 1904- .... **CLC 18**
See also Li Fei-kan

Pack, Robert 1929- .... **CLC 13**
See also CANR 3; CA 1-4R; DLB 5

Padgett, Lewis 1915-1958
See Kuttner, Henry

Padilla, Heberto 1932- .... **CLC 38**
See also CA 123

Page, Jimmy 1944- .... **CLC 12**

Page, Louise 1955- .... **CLC 40**

Page, P(atricia) K(athleen) 1916- .... **CLC 7, 18**
See also CANR 4, 22; CA 53-56; DLB 68

Paget, Violet 1856-1935
See Lee, Vernon
See also CA 104

Paglia, Camille 1947- .... **CLC 68**

Palamas, Kostes 1859-1943 .... **TCLC 5**
See also CA 105

Palazzeschi, Aldo 1885-1974 .... **CLC 11**
See also CA 89-92; obituary CA 53-56

Paley, Grace 1922- .... **CLC 4, 6, 37; SSC 8**
See also CANR 13; CA 25-28R; DLB 28

Palin, Michael 1943- .... **CLC 21**
See also Monty Python
See also CA 107

Palliser, Charles 1948?- .... **CLC 65**

Author Index

Puig, Manuel 1932-1990 . . . . **CLC 3, 5, 10, 28, 65**
See also CANR 2, 32; CA 45-48

Purdy, A(lfred) W(ellington) 1918- . . . . **CLC 3, 6, 14, 50**
See also CA 81-84

Purdy, James (Amos) 1923- . . . . **CLC 2, 4, 10, 28, 52**
See also CAAS 1; CANR 19; CA 33-36R; DLB 2

Pushkin, Alexander (Sergeyevich) 1799-1837 . . . . **NCLC 3, 27**

P'u Sung-ling 1640-1715 . . . . **LC 3**

Puzo, Mario 1920- . . . . **CLC 1, 2, 6, 36**
See also CANR 4; CA 65-68; DLB 6

Pym, Barbara (Mary Crampton) 1913-1980 . . . . **CLC 13, 19, 37**
See also CANR 13; CAP 1; CA 13-14; obituary CA 97-100; DLB 14; DLB-Y 87

Pynchon, Thomas (Ruggles, Jr.) 1937- . . **CLC 2, 3, 6, 9, 11, 18, 33, 62, 72**
See also CANR 22; CA 17-20R; DLB 2

Quarrington, Paul 1954?- . . . . **CLC 65**
See also CA 129

Quasimodo, Salvatore 1901-1968 . . . **CLC 10**
See also CAP 1; CA 15-16; obituary CA 25-28R

Queen, Ellery 1905-1982 . . . . **CLC 3, 11**
See also Dannay, Frederic; Lee, Manfred B(ennington)

Queneau, Raymond 1903-1976 . . . . **CLC 2, 5, 10, 42**
See also CA 77-80; obituary CA 69-72; DLB 72

Quin, Ann (Marie) 1936-1973 . . . . **CLC 6**
See also CA 9-12R; obituary CA 45-48; DLB 14

Quinn, Simon 1942-
See Smith, Martin Cruz
See also CANR 6, 23; CA 85-88

Quiroga, Horacio (Sylvestre) 1878-1937 . . . . **TCLC 20**
See also CA 117

Quoirez, Francoise 1935-
See Sagan, Francoise
See also CANR 6; CA 49-52

Raabe, Wilhelm 1831-1910 . . . . **TCLC 45**

Rabe, David (William) 1940- . . . **CLC 4, 8, 33**
See also CA 85-88; CABS 3; DLB 7

Rabelais, Francois 1494?-1553 . . . . **LC 5**

Rabinovitch, Sholem 1859-1916
See Aleichem, Sholom
See also CA 104

Rachen, Kurt von 1911-1986
See Hubbard, L(afayette) Ron(ald)

Radcliffe, Ann (Ward) 1764-1823 . . **NCLC 6**
See also DLB 39

Radiguet, Raymond 1903-1923 . . . . **TCLC 29**
See also DLB 65

Radnoti, Miklos 1909-1944 . . . . **TCLC 16**
See also CA 118

Rado, James 1939- . . . . **CLC 17**
See also CA 105

Radomski, James 1932-
See Rado, James

Radvanyi, Netty Reiling 1900-1983
See Seghers, Anna
See also CA 85-88; obituary CA 110

Rae, Ben 1935-
See Griffiths, Trevor

Raeburn, John 1941- . . . . **CLC 34**
See also CA 57-60

Ragni, Gerome 1942- . . . . **CLC 17**
See also CA 105

Rahv, Philip 1908-1973 . . . . **CLC 24**
See also Greenberg, Ivan

Raine, Craig 1944- . . . . **CLC 32**
See also CANR 29; CA 108; DLB 40

Raine, Kathleen (Jessie) 1908- . . . **CLC 7, 45**
See also CA 85-88; DLB 20

Rainis, Janis 1865-1929 . . . . **TCLC 29**

Rakosi, Carl 1903- . . . . **CLC 47**
See also Rawley, Callman
See also CAAS 5

Ramos, Graciliano 1892-1953 . . . . . **TCLC 32**

Rampersad, Arnold 19??- . . . . **CLC 44**

Ramuz, Charles-Ferdinand 1878-1947 . . . . **TCLC 33**

Rand, Ayn 1905-1982 . . . . **CLC 3, 30, 44**
See also CANR 27; CA 13-16R; obituary CA 105

Randall, Dudley (Felker) 1914- . . . . . . **CLC 1**
See also BLC 3; CANR 23; CA 25-28R; DLB 41

Ransom, John Crowe 1888-1974 . . . . **CLC 2, 4, 5, 11, 24**
See also CANR 6; CA 5-8R; obituary CA 49-52; DLB 45, 63

Rao, Raja 1909- . . . . **CLC 25, 56**
See also CA 73-76

Raphael, Frederic (Michael) 1931- . . . . **CLC 2, 14**
See also CANR 1; CA 1-4R; DLB 14

Rathbone, Julian 1935- . . . . **CLC 41**
See also CA 101

Rattigan, Terence (Mervyn) 1911-1977 . . . . **CLC 7**
See also CA 85-88; obituary CA 73-76; DLB 13

Ratushinskaya, Irina 1954- . . . . **CLC 54**
See also CA 129

Raven, Simon (Arthur Noel) 1927- . . . . **CLC 14**
See also CA 81-84

Rawley, Callman 1903-
See Rakosi, Carl
See also CANR 12; CA 21-24R

Rawlings, Marjorie Kinnan 1896-1953 . . . . **TCLC 4**
See also YABC 1; CA 104; DLB 9, 22

Ray, Satyajit 1921- . . . . **CLC 16**
See also CA 114

Read, Herbert (Edward) 1893-1968 . . **CLC 4**
See also CA 85-88; obituary CA 25-28R; DLB 20

Read, Piers Paul 1941- . . . . . . **CLC 4, 10, 25**
See also CA 21-24R; SATA 21; DLB 14

Reade, Charles 1814-1884 . . . . **NCLC 2**
See also DLB 21

Reade, Hamish 1936-
See Gray, Simon (James Holliday)

Reading, Peter 1946- . . . . **CLC 47**
See also CA 103; DLB 40

Reaney, James 1926- . . . . **CLC 13**
See also CA 41-44R; SATA 43; DLB 68

Rebreanu, Liviu 1885-1944 . . . . **TCLC 28**

Rechy, John (Francisco) 1934- . . . . **CLC 1, 7, 14, 18**
See also CAAS 4; CANR 6; CA 5-8R; DLB-Y 82

Redcam, Tom 1870-1933 . . . . **TCLC 25**

Reddin, Keith 1956?- . . . . **CLC 67**

Redgrove, Peter (William) 1932- . . . . **CLC 6, 41**
See also CANR 3; CA 1-4R; DLB 40

Redmon (Nightingale), Anne 1943- . . . . **CLC 22**
See also Nightingale, Anne Redmon
See also DLB-Y 86

Reed, Ishmael 1938- . . . . **CLC 2, 3, 5, 6, 13, 32, 60**
See also BLC 3; CANR 25; CA 21-24R; DLB 2, 5, 33; DLB-DS 8

Reed, John (Silas) 1887-1920 . . . . . . **TCLC 9**
See also CA 106

Reed, Lou 1944- . . . . **CLC 21**

Reeve, Clara 1729-1807 . . . . **NCLC 19**
See also DLB 39

Reid, Christopher 1949- . . . . **CLC 33**
See also DLB 40

Reid Banks, Lynne 1929-
See Banks, Lynne Reid
See also CANR 6, 22; CA 1-4R; SATA 22

Reiner, Max 1900-
See Caldwell, (Janet Miriam) Taylor (Holland)

Reizenstein, Elmer Leopold 1892-1967
See Rice, Elmer

Remark, Erich Paul 1898-1970
See Remarque, Erich Maria

Remarque, Erich Maria 1898-1970 . . . . **CLC 21**
See also CA 77-80; obituary CA 29-32R; DLB 56

Remizov, Alexey (Mikhailovich) 1877-1957 . . . . **TCLC 27**
See also CA 125

Renan, Joseph Ernest 1823-1892 . . . . **NCLC 26**

Renard, Jules 1864-1910 . . . . **TCLC 17**
See also CA 117

Renault, Mary 1905-1983 . . . . **CLC 3, 11, 17**
See also Challans, Mary
See also DLB-Y 83

Rendell, Ruth 1930- . . . . **CLC 28, 48**
See also Vine, Barbara
See also CA 109; DLB 87

Renoir, Jean 1894-1979 . . . . **CLC 20**
See also CA 129; obituary CA 85-88

Resnais, Alain 1922- . . . . **CLC 16**

Author Index

Vaculik, Ludvik 1926- . . . . **CLC 7**
See also CA 53-56

Valenzuela, Luisa 1938- . . . . **CLC 31**
See also CA 101

Valera (y Acala-Galiano), Juan
1824-1905 . . . . **TCLC 10**
See also CA 106

Valery, Paul (Ambroise Toussaint Jules)
1871-1945 . . . . **TCLC 4, 15**
See also CA 104, 122

Valle-Inclan (y Montenegro), Ramon (Maria) del 1866-1936 . . . . **TCLC 5**
See also CA 106

Vallejo, Cesar (Abraham)
1892-1938 . . . . **TCLC 3**
See also CA 105

Van Ash, Cay 1918- . . . . **CLC 34**

Vance, Jack 1916?- . . . . **CLC 35**
See also DLB 8

Vance, John Holbrook 1916?-
See Vance, Jack
See also CANR 17; CA 29-32R

Van Den Bogarde, Derek (Jules Gaspard Ulric) Niven 1921-
See Bogarde, Dirk
See also CA 77-80

Vandenburgh, Jane 19??- . . . . **CLC 59**

Vanderhaeghe, Guy 1951- . . . . **CLC 41**
See also CA 113

Van der Post, Laurens (Jan) 1906- . . . **CLC 5**
See also CA 5-8R

Van de Wetering, Janwillem
1931- . . . . **CLC 47**
See also CANR 4; CA 49-52

Van Dine, S. S. 1888-1939 . . . . **TCLC 23**

Van Doren, Carl (Clinton)
1885-1950 . . . . **TCLC 18**
See also CA 111

Van Doren, Mark 1894-1972 . . . . . **CLC 6, 10**
See also CANR 3; CA 1-4R;
obituary CA 37-40R; DLB 45

Van Druten, John (William)
1901-1957 . . . . **TCLC 2**
See also CA 104; DLB 10

Van Duyn, Mona 1921- . . . . **CLC 3, 7, 63**
See also CANR 7; CA 9-12R; DLB 5

Van Itallie, Jean-Claude 1936- . . . . . . **CLC 3**
See also CAAS 2; CANR 1; CA 45-48;
DLB 7

Van Ostaijen, Paul 1896-1928 . . . . . **TCLC 33**

Van Peebles, Melvin 1932- . . . . . . **CLC 2, 20**
See also CA 85-88

Vansittart, Peter 1920- . . . . **CLC 42**
See also CANR 3; CA 1-4R

Van Vechten, Carl 1880-1964 . . . . . . **CLC 33**
See also obituary CA 89-92; DLB 4, 9, 51

Van Vogt, A(lfred) E(lton) 1912- . . . . . **CLC 1**
See also CANR 28; CA 21-24R; SATA 14;
DLB 8

Varda, Agnes 1928- . . . . **CLC 16**
See also CA 116, 122

Vargas Llosa, (Jorge) Mario (Pedro)
1936- . . . . **CLC 3, 6, 9, 10, 15, 31, 42**
See also CANR 18; CA 73-76

Vassa, Gustavus 1745?-1797
See Equiano, Olaudah

Vassilikos, Vassilis 1933- . . . . **CLC 4, 8**
See also CA 81-84

Vaughn, Stephanie 19??- . . . . **CLC 62**

Vazov, Ivan 1850-1921 . . . . **TCLC 25**
See also CA 121

Veblen, Thorstein Bunde
1857-1929 . . . . **TCLC 31**
See also CA 115

Verga, Giovanni 1840-1922 . . . . **TCLC 3**
See also CA 104, 123

Vergil 70 B.C.-19 B.C. . . . . **CMLC 9**

Verhaeren, Emile (Adolphe Gustave)
1855-1916 . . . . **TCLC 12**
See also CA 109

Verlaine, Paul (Marie)
1844-1896 . . . . **NCLC 2; PC 2**

Verne, Jules (Gabriel) 1828-1905 . . . **TCLC 6**
See also CA 110; SATA 21

Very, Jones 1813-1880 . . . . **NCLC 9**
See also DLB 1

Vesaas, Tarjei 1897-1970 . . . . **CLC 48**
See also obituary CA 29-32R

Vian, Boris 1920-1959 . . . . **TCLC 9**
See also CA 106; DLB 72

Viaud, (Louis Marie) Julien 1850-1923
See Loti, Pierre
See also CA 107

Vicker, Angus 1916-
See Felsen, Henry Gregor

Vidal, Eugene Luther, Jr. 1925-
See Vidal, Gore

Vidal, Gore
1925- . . . . . **CLC 2, 4, 6, 8, 10, 22, 33, 72**
See also CANR 13; CA 5-8R; DLB 6

Viereck, Peter (Robert Edwin)
1916- . . . . **CLC 4**
See also CANR 1; CA 1-4R; DLB 5

Vigny, Alfred (Victor) de
1797-1863 . . . . **NCLC 7**

Vilakazi, Benedict Wallet
1905-1947 . . . . **TCLC 37**

Villiers de l'Isle Adam, Jean Marie Mathias Philippe Auguste, Comte de
1838-1889 . . . . **NCLC 3**

Vinci, Leonardo da 1452-1519 . . . . **LC 12**

Vine, Barbara 1930- . . . . **CLC 50**
See also Rendell, Ruth

Vinge, Joan (Carol) D(ennison)
1948- . . . . **CLC 30**
See also CA 93-96; SATA 36

Visconti, Luchino 1906-1976 . . . . **CLC 16**
See also CA 81-84; obituary CA 65-68

Vittorini, Elio 1908-1966 . . . . . . **CLC 6, 9, 14**
See also obituary CA 25-28R

Vizinczey, Stephen 1933- . . . . **CLC 40**

Vliet, R(ussell) G(ordon)
1929-1984 . . . . **CLC 22**
See also CANR 18; CA 37-40R;
obituary CA 112

Voight, Ellen Bryant 1943- . . . . **CLC 54**
See also CANR 11; CA 69-72

Voigt, Cynthia 1942- . . . . **CLC 30**
See also CANR 18; CA 106; SATA 33, 48;
AAYA 3

Voinovich, Vladimir (Nikolaevich)
1932- . . . . **CLC 10, 49**
See also CA 81-84

Voltaire 1694-1778 . . . . **LC 14**

Von Daeniken, Erich 1935-
See Von Daniken, Erich
See also CANR 17; CA 37-40R

Von Daniken, Erich 1935- . . . . **CLC 30**
See also Von Daeniken, Erich

Vonnegut, Kurt, Jr.
1922- . . . . . . **CLC 1, 2, 3, 4, 5, 8, 12, 22, 40, 60; SSC 8**
See also CANR 1, 25; CA 1-4R; DLB 2, 8;
DLB-Y 80; DLB-DS 3;
CDALB 1968-1988; AAYA 6

Vorster, Gordon 1924- . . . . **CLC 34**

Voznesensky, Andrei 1933- . . . **CLC 1, 15, 57**
See also CA 89-92

Waddington, Miriam 1917- . . . . **CLC 28**
See also CANR 12, 30; CA 21-24R;
DLB 68

Wagman, Fredrica 1937- . . . . **CLC 7**
See also CA 97-100

Wagner, Richard 1813-1883 . . . . **NCLC 9**

Wagner-Martin, Linda 1936- . . . . **CLC 50**

Wagoner, David (Russell)
1926- . . . . **CLC 3, 5, 15**
See also CAAS 3; CANR 2; CA 1-4R;
SATA 14; DLB 5

Wah, Fred(erick James) 1939- . . . . . . **CLC 44**
See also CA 107; DLB 60

Wahloo, Per 1926-1975 . . . . **CLC 7**
See also CA 61-64

Wahloo, Peter 1926-1975
See Wahloo, Per

Wain, John (Barrington)
1925- . . . . **CLC 2, 11, 15, 46**
See also CAAS 4; CANR 23; CA 5-8R;
DLB 15, 27

Wajda, Andrzej 1926- . . . . **CLC 16**
See also CA 102

Wakefield, Dan 1932- . . . . **CLC 7**
See also CAAS 7; CA 21-24R

Wakoski, Diane
1937- . . . . **CLC 2, 4, 7, 9, 11, 40**
See also CAAS 1; CANR 9; CA 13-16R;
DLB 5

Walcott, Derek (Alton)
1930- . . . . **CLC 2, 4, 9, 14, 25, 42, 67**
See also BLC 3; CANR 26; CA 89-92;
DLB-Y 81

Waldman, Anne 1945- . . . . **CLC 7**
See also CA 37-40R; DLB 16

Waldo, Edward Hamilton 1918-
See Sturgeon, Theodore (Hamilton)

Walker, Alice
1944- . . . . . . **CLC 5, 6, 9, 19, 27, 46, 58; SSC 5**
See also BLC 3; CANR 9, 27; CA 37-40R;
SATA 31; DLB 6, 33;
CDALB 1968-1988; AAYA 3

Walker, David Harry 1911- . . . . **CLC 14**
See also CANR 1; CA 1-4R; SATA 8

Walker, Edward Joseph 1934-
See Walker, Ted
See also CANR 12; CA 21-24R

Walker, George F. 1947- . . . . **CLC 44, 61**
See also CANR 21; CA 103; DLB 60

Walker, Joseph A. 1935- . . . . **CLC 19**
See also CANR 26; CA 89-92; DLB 38

Walker, Margaret (Abigail)
1915- . . . . **CLC 1, 6**
See also BLC 3; CANR 26; CA 73-76; DLB 76

Walker, Ted 1934- . . . . **CLC 13**
See also Walker, Edward Joseph
See also DLB 40

Wallace, David Foster 1962- . . . . **CLC 50**

Wallace, Irving 1916- . . . . **CLC 7, 13**
See also CAAS 1; CANR 1; CA 1-4R

Wallant, Edward Lewis
1926-1962 . . . . **CLC 5, 10**
See also CANR 22; CA 1-4R; DLB 2, 28

Walpole, Horace 1717-1797 . . . . **LC 2**
See also DLB 39

Walpole, (Sir) Hugh (Seymour)
1884-1941 . . . . **TCLC 5**
See also CA 104; DLB 34

Walser, Martin 1927- . . . . **CLC 27**
See also CANR 8; CA 57-60; DLB 75

Walser, Robert 1878-1956 . . . . **TCLC 18**
See also CA 118; DLB 66

Walsh, Gillian Paton 1939-
See Walsh, Jill Paton
See also CA 37-40R; SATA 4

Walsh, Jill Paton 1939- . . . . **CLC 35**
See also CLR 2; SAAS 3

Wambaugh, Joseph (Aloysius, Jr.)
1937- . . . . **CLC 3, 18**
See also CA 33-36R; DLB 6; DLB-Y 83

Ward, Arthur Henry Sarsfield 1883-1959
See Rohmer, Sax
See also CA 108

Ward, Douglas Turner 1930- . . . . **CLC 19**
See also CA 81-84; DLB 7, 38

Warhol, Andy 1928-1987 . . . . **CLC 20**
See also CA 89-92; obituary CA 121

Warner, Francis (Robert le Plastrier)
1937- . . . . **CLC 14**
See also CANR 11; CA 53-56

Warner, Marina 1946- . . . . **CLC 59**
See also CANR 21; CA 65-68

Warner, Rex (Ernest) 1905-1986 . . . . **CLC 45**
See also CA 89-92; obituary CA 119; DLB 15

Warner, Susan 1819-1885 . . . . **NCLC 31**
See also DLB 3, 42

Warner, Sylvia Townsend
1893-1978 . . . . **CLC 7, 19**
See also CANR 16; CA 61-64; obituary CA 77-80; DLB 34

Warren, Mercy Otis 1728-1814 . . . **NCLC 13**
See also DLB 31

Warren, Robert Penn
1905-1989 . . . **CLC 1, 4, 6, 8, 10, 13, 18, 39, 53, 59; SSC 4**
See also CANR 10; CA 13-16R. 129. 130; SATA 46; DLB 2, 48; DLB-Y 80; CDALB 1968-1987

Warshofsky, Isaac 1904-1991
See Singer, Isaac Bashevis

Warton, Thomas 1728-1790 . . . . **LC 15**

Warung, Price 1855-1911 . . . . **TCLC 45**

Washington, Booker T(aliaferro)
1856-1915 . . . . **TCLC 10**
See also BLC 3; CA 114, 125; SATA 28

Wassermann, Jakob 1873-1934 . . . . . **TCLC 6**
See also CA 104; DLB 66

Wasserstein, Wendy 1950- . . . . . . **CLC 32, 59**
See also CA 121; CABS 3

Waterhouse, Keith (Spencer)
1929- . . . . **CLC 47**
See also CA 5-8R; DLB 13, 15

Waters, Roger 1944-
See Pink Floyd

Wa Thiong'o, Ngugi
1938- . . . . **CLC 3, 7, 13, 36**
See also Ngugi, James (Thiong'o); Ngugi wa Thiong'o

Watkins, Paul 1964- . . . . **CLC 55**

Watkins, Vernon (Phillips)
1906-1967 . . . . **CLC 43**
See also CAP 1; CA 9-10; obituary CA 25-28R; DLB 20

Waugh, Auberon (Alexander) 1939- . . **CLC 7**
See also CANR 6, 22; CA 45-48; DLB 14

Waugh, Evelyn (Arthur St. John)
1903-1966 . . . **CLC 1, 3, 8, 13, 19, 27, 44**
See also CANR 22; CA 85-88; obituary CA 25-28R; DLB 15

Waugh, Harriet 1944- . . . . **CLC 6**
See also CANR 22; CA 85-88

Webb, Beatrice (Potter)
1858-1943 . . . . **TCLC 22**
See also CA 117

Webb, Charles (Richard) 1939- . . . . . . **CLC 7**
See also CA 25-28R

Webb, James H(enry), Jr. 1946- . . . . **CLC 22**
See also CA 81-84

Webb, Mary (Gladys Meredith)
1881-1927 . . . . **TCLC 24**
See also CA 123; DLB 34

Webb, Phyllis 1927- . . . . **CLC 18**
See also CANR 23; CA 104; DLB 53

Webb, Sidney (James)
1859-1947 . . . . **TCLC 22**
See also CA 117

Webber, Andrew Lloyd 1948- . . . . . . **CLC 21**

Weber, Lenora Mattingly
1895-1971 . . . . **CLC 12**
See also CAP 1; CA 19-20; obituary CA 29-32R; SATA 2; obituary SATA 26

Webster, John 1580?-1634? . . . . **DC 2**
See also DLB 58

Webster, Noah 1758-1843 . . . . **NCLC 30**
See also DLB 1, 37, 42, 43, 73

Wedekind, (Benjamin) Frank(lin)
1864-1918 . . . . **TCLC 7**
See also CA 104

Weidman, Jerome 1913- . . . . **CLC 7**
See also CANR 1; CA 1-4R; DLB 28

Weil, Simone 1909-1943 . . . . **TCLC 23**
See also CA 117

Weinstein, Nathan Wallenstein 1903-1940
See West, Nathanael

Weir, Peter 1944- . . . . **CLC 20**
See also CA 113, 123

Weiss, Peter (Ulrich)
1916-1982 . . . . **CLC 3, 15, 51**
See also CANR 3; CA 45-48; obituary CA 106; DLB 69

Weiss, Theodore (Russell)
1916- . . . . **CLC 3, 8, 14**
See also CAAS 2; CA 9-12R; DLB 5

Welch, (Maurice) Denton
1915-1948 . . . . **TCLC 22**
See also CA 121

Welch, James 1940- . . . . **CLC 6, 14, 52**
See also CA 85-88

Weldon, Fay
1933- . . . . **CLC 6, 9, 11, 19, 36, 59**
See also CANR 16; CA 21-24R; DLB 14

Wellek, Rene 1903- . . . . **CLC 28**
See also CAAS 7; CANR 8; CA 5-8R; DLB 63

Weller, Michael 1942- . . . . **CLC 10, 53**
See also CA 85-88

Weller, Paul 1958- . . . . **CLC 26**

Wellershoff, Dieter 1925- . . . . **CLC 46**
See also CANR 16; CA 89-92

Welles, (George) Orson
1915-1985 . . . . **CLC 20**
See also CA 93-96; obituary CA 117

Wellman, Mac 1945- . . . . **CLC 65**

Wellman, Manly Wade 1903-1986 . . **CLC 49**
See also CANR 6, 16; CA 1-4R; obituary CA 118; SATA 6, 47

Wells, Carolyn 1862-1942 . . . . **TCLC 35**
See also CA 113; DLB 11

Wells, H(erbert) G(eorge)
1866-1946 . . . . . . **TCLC 6, 12, 19; SSC 6**
See also CA 110, 121; SATA 20; DLB 34, 70

Wells, Rosemary 1943- . . . . **CLC 12**
See also CLR 16; CA 85-88; SAAS 1; SATA 18

Welty, Eudora (Alice)
1909- . . . . **CLC 1, 2, 5, 14, 22, 33; SSC 1**
See also CA 9-12R; CABS 1; DLB 2; DLB-Y 87; CDALB 1941-1968

Wen I-to 1899-1946 . . . . **TCLC 28**

Werfel, Franz (V.) 1890-1945 . . . . . . **TCLC 8**
See also CA 104; DLB 81

Wergeland, Henrik Arnold
1808-1845 . . . . **NCLC 5**

Wersba, Barbara 1932- . . . . **CLC 30**
See also CLR 3; CANR 16; CA 29-32R; SAAS 2; SATA 1, 58; DLB 52

Wertmuller, Lina 1928- . . . . **CLC 16**
See also CA 97-100

Wescott, Glenway 1901-1987....... **CLC 13**
See also CANR 23; CA 13-16R; obituary CA 121; DLB 4, 9

Wesker, Arnold 1932- .... **CLC 3, 5, 42**
See also CAAS 7; CANR 1; CA 1-4R; DLB 13

Wesley, Richard (Errol) 1945-....... **CLC 7**
See also CA 57-60; DLB 38

Wessel, Johan Herman 1742-1785 .... **LC 7**

West, Anthony (Panther) 1914-1987 .... **CLC 50**
See also CANR 3, 19; CA 45-48; DLB 15

West, Jessamyn 1907-1984 ...... **CLC 7, 17**
See also CA 9-12R; obituary CA 112; obituary SATA 37; DLB 6; DLB-Y 84

West, Morris L(anglo) 1916-..... **CLC 6, 33**
See also CA 5-8R; obituary CA 124

West, Nathanael 1903-1940 .... **TCLC 1, 14, 44**
See also CA 104, 125; DLB 4, 9, 28; CDALB 1929-1941

West, Paul 1930- .... **CLC 7, 14**
See also CAAS 7; CANR 22; CA 13-16R; DLB 14

West, Rebecca 1892-1983 .. **CLC 7, 9, 31, 50**
See also CANR 19; CA 5-8R; obituary CA 109; DLB 36; DLB-Y 83

Westall, Robert (Atkinson) 1929-... **CLC 17**
See also CLR 13; CANR 18; CA 69-72; SAAS 2; SATA 23

Westlake, Donald E(dwin) 1933- .... **CLC 7, 33**
See also CANR 16; CA 17-20R

Westmacott, Mary 1890-1976
See Christie, (Dame) Agatha (Mary Clarissa)

Whalen, Philip 1923- .... **CLC 6, 29**
See also CANR 5; CA 9-12R; DLB 16

Wharton, Edith (Newbold Jones) 1862-1937 .... **TCLC 3, 9, 27; SSC 6**
See also CA 104; DLB 4, 9, 12, 78; CDALB 1865-1917

Wharton, William 1925-........ **CLC 18, 37**
See also CA 93-96; DLB-Y 80

Wheatley (Peters), Phillis 1753?-1784................ **LC 3; PC 3**
See also BLC 3; DLB 31, 50; CDALB 1640-1865

Wheelock, John Hall 1886-1978 .... **CLC 14**
See also CANR 14; CA 13-16R; obituary CA 77-80; DLB 45

Whelan, John 1900-
See O'Faolain, Sean

Whitaker, Rodney 1925-
See Trevanian

White, E(lwyn) B(rooks) 1899-1985 .... **CLC 10, 34, 39**
See also CLR 1; CANR 16; CA 13-16R; obituary CA 116; SATA 2, 29, 44; obituary SATA 44; DLB 11, 22

White, Edmund III 1940-......... **CLC 27**
See also CANR 3, 19; CA 45-48

White, Patrick (Victor Martindale) 1912-1990 .. **CLC 3, 4, 5, 7, 9, 18, 65, 69**
See also CA 81-84; obituary CA 132

White, T(erence) H(anbury) 1906-1964 .... **CLC 30**
See also CA 73-76; SATA 12

White, Terence de Vere 1912-...... **CLC 49**
See also CANR 3; CA 49-52

White, Walter (Francis) 1893-1955 .... **TCLC 15**
See also BLC 3; CA 115, 124; DLB 51

White, William Hale 1831-1913
See Rutherford, Mark
See also CA 121

Whitehead, E(dward) A(nthony) 1933- .... **CLC 5**
See also CA 65-68

Whitemore, Hugh 1936-........... **CLC 37**

Whitman, Sarah Helen 1803-1878 .... **NCLC 19**
See also DLB 1

Whitman, Walt 1819-1892 .... **NCLC 4, 31; PC 3**
See also SATA 20; DLB 3, 64; CDALB 1640-1865

Whitney, Phyllis A(yame) 1903-.... **CLC 42**
See also CANR 3, 25; CA 1-4R; SATA 1, 30

Whittemore, (Edward) Reed (Jr.) 1919- .... **CLC 4**
See also CAAS 8; CANR 4; CA 9-12R; DLB 5

Whittier, John Greenleaf 1807-1892 .... **NCLC 8**
See also DLB 1; CDALB 1640-1865

Wicker, Thomas Grey 1926-
See Wicker, Tom
See also CANR 21; CA 65-68

Wicker, Tom 1926-................ **CLC 7**
See also Wicker, Thomas Grey

Wideman, John Edgar 1941- .... **CLC 5, 34, 36, 67**
See also BLC 3; CANR 14; CA 85-88; DLB 33

Wiebe, Rudy (H.) 1934-...... **CLC 6, 11, 14**
See also CA 37-40R; DLB 60

Wieland, Christoph Martin 1733-1813 .... **NCLC 17**

Wieners, John 1934-............... **CLC 7**
See also CA 13-16R; DLB 16

Wiesel, Elie(zer) 1928-..... **CLC 3, 5, 11, 37**
See also CAAS 4; CANR 8; CA 5-8R; SATA 56; DLB 83; DLB-Y 87

Wiggins, Marianne 1948-.......... **CLC 57**

Wight, James Alfred 1916-
See Herriot, James
See also CA 77-80; SATA 44

Wilbur, Richard (Purdy) 1921- .... **CLC 3, 6, 9, 14, 53**
See also CANR 2; CA 1-4R; CABS 2; SATA 9; DLB 5

Wild, Peter 1940-................ **CLC 14**
See also CA 37-40R; DLB 5

Wilde, Oscar (Fingal O'Flahertie Wills) 1854-1900 .... **TCLC 1, 8, 23, 41**
See also CA 119; brief entry CA 104; SATA 24; DLB 10, 19, 34, 57

Wilder, Billy 1906-............... **CLC 20**
See also Wilder, Samuel
See also DLB 26

Wilder, Samuel 1906-
See Wilder, Billy
See also CA 89-92

Wilder, Thornton (Niven) 1897-1975 ..... **CLC 1, 5, 6, 10, 15, 35; DC 1**
See also CA 13-16R; obituary CA 61-64; DLB 4, 7, 9

Wiley, Richard 1944-............. **CLC 44**
See also CA 121, 129

Wilhelm, Kate 1928-............... **CLC 7**
See also CAAS 5; CANR 17; CA 37-40R; DLB 8

Willard, Nancy 1936-........... **CLC 7, 37**
See also CLR 5; CANR 10; CA 89-92; SATA 30, 37; DLB 5, 52

Williams, C(harles) K(enneth) 1936- .... **CLC 33, 56**
See also CA 37-40R; DLB 5

Williams, Charles (Walter Stansby) 1886-1945 .... **TCLC 1, 11**
See also CA 104

Williams, Ella Gwendolen Rees 1890-1979
See Rhys, Jean

Williams, (George) Emlyn 1905-1987 .... **CLC 15**
See also CA 104, 123; DLB 10, 77

Williams, Hugo 1942-............. **CLC 42**
See also CA 17-20R; DLB 40

Williams, John A(lfred) 1925-.... **CLC 5, 13**
See also BLC 3; CAAS 3; CANR 6, 26; CA 53-56; DLB 2, 33

Williams, Jonathan (Chamberlain) 1929- .... **CLC 13**
See also CANR 8; CA 9-12R; DLB 5

Williams, Joy 1944- .... **CLC 31**
See also CANR 22; CA 41-44R

Williams, Norman 1952- .... **CLC 39**
See also CA 118

Williams, Paulette 1948-
See Shange, Ntozake

Williams, Sherley Anne 1944-
See also BLC 3; CANR 25; CA 73-76; DLB 41

Williams, Shirley 1944-
See Williams, Sherley Anne

Williams, Tennessee 1911-1983 .... **CLC 1, 2, 5, 7, 8, 11, 15, 19, 30, 39, 45, 71**
See also CANR 31; CA 5-8R; obituary CA 108; CABS 3; DLB 7; DLB-Y 83; DLB-DS 4; CDALB 1941-1968

Williams, Thomas (Alonzo) 1926-... **CLC 14**
See also CANR 2; CA 1-4R

Williams, Thomas Lanier 1911-1983
See Williams, Tennessee

Williams, William Carlos 1883-1963 ... **CLC 1, 2, 5, 9, 13, 22, 42, 67**
See also CA 89-92; DLB 4, 16, 54, 86; CDALB 1917-1929

Williamson, David 1932- .... **CLC 56**

Williamson, Jack 1908- .... **CLC 29**
See also Williamson, John Stewart
See also DLB 8

Williamson, John Stewart 1908-
See Williamson, Jack
See also CANR 123; CA 17-20R

Willingham, Calder (Baynard, Jr.) 1922- .... **CLC 5, 51**
See also CANR 3; CA 5-8R; DLB 2, 44

Wilson, A(ndrew) N(orman) 1950- .. **CLC 33**
See also CA 112, 122; DLB 14

Wilson, Andrew 1948-
See Wilson, Snoo

Wilson, Angus (Frank Johnstone) 1913- .... **CLC 2, 3, 5, 25, 34**
See also CANR 21; CA 5-8R; DLB 15

Wilson, August 1945- .... **CLC 39, 50, 63; DC 2**
See also BLC 3; CA 115, 122

Wilson, Brian 1942- .... **CLC 12**

Wilson, Colin 1931- .... **CLC 3, 14**
See also CAAS 5; CANR 1, 122; CA 1-4R; DLB 14

Wilson, Edmund 1895-1972 .... **CLC 1, 2, 3, 8, 24**
See also CANR 1; CA 1-4R; obituary CA 37-40R; DLB 63

Wilson, Ethel Davis (Bryant) 1888-1980 .... **CLC 13**
See also CA 102; DLB 68

Wilson, Harriet 1827?-?
See also BLC 3; DLB 50

Wilson, John 1785-1854 .... **NCLC 5**

Wilson, John (Anthony) Burgess 1917-
See Burgess, Anthony
See also CANR 2; CA 1-4R

Wilson, Lanford 1937- .... **CLC 7, 14, 36**
See also CA 17-20R; DLB 7

Wilson, Robert (M.) 1944- .... **CLC 7, 9**
See also CANR 2; CA 49-52

Wilson, Sloan 1920- .... **CLC 32**
See also CANR 1; CA 1-4R

Wilson, Snoo 1948- .... **CLC 33**
See also CA 69-72

Wilson, William S(mith) 1932- .... **CLC 49**
See also CA 81-84

Winchilsea, Anne (Kingsmill) Finch, Countess of 1661-1720 .... **LC 3**

Wingrove, David 1954- .... **CLC 68**
See also CA 133

Winters, Janet Lewis 1899-
See Lewis (Winters), Janet
See also CAP 1; CA 9-10

Winters, (Arthur) Yvor 1900-1968 .... **CLC 4, 8, 32**
See also CAP 1; CA 11-12; obituary CA 25-28R; DLB 48

Winterson, Jeannette 1959- .... **CLC 64**

Wiseman, Frederick 1930- .... **CLC 20**

Wister, Owen 1860-1938 .... **TCLC 21**
See also CA 108; DLB 9, 78

Witkiewicz, Stanislaw Ignacy 1885-1939 .... **TCLC 8**
See also CA 105; DLB 83

Wittig, Monique 1935?- .... **CLC 22**
See also CA 116; DLB 83

Wittlin, Joseph 1896-1976 .... **CLC 25**
See also Wittlin, Jozef

Wittlin, Jozef 1896-1976
See Wittlin, Joseph
See also CANR 3; CA 49-52; obituary CA 65-68

Wodehouse, (Sir) P(elham) G(renville) 1881-1975 ... **CLC 1, 2, 5, 10, 22; SSC 2**
See also CANR 3; CA 45-48; obituary CA 57-60; SATA 22; DLB 34

Woiwode, Larry (Alfred) 1941- ... **CLC 6, 10**
See also CANR 16; CA 73-76; DLB 6

Wojciechowska, Maia (Teresa) 1927- .... **CLC 26**
See also CLR 1; CANR 4; CA 9-12R; SAAS 1; SATA 1, 28

Wolf, Christa 1929- .... **CLC 14, 29, 58**
See also CA 85-88; DLB 75

Wolfe, Gene (Rodman) 1931- .... **CLC 25**
See also CAAS 9; CANR 6; CA 57-60; DLB 8

Wolfe, George C. 1954- .... **CLC 49**

Wolfe, Thomas (Clayton) 1900-1938 .... **TCLC 4, 13, 29**
See also CA 104; DLB 9; DLB-Y 85; DLB-DS 2

Wolfe, Thomas Kennerly, Jr. 1931-
See Wolfe, Tom
See also CANR 9; CA 13-16R

Wolfe, Tom 1931- ... **CLC 1, 2, 9, 15, 35, 51**
See also Wolfe, Thomas Kennerly, Jr.

Wolff, Geoffrey (Ansell) 1937- .... **CLC 41**
See also CA 29-32R

Wolff, Tobias (Jonathan Ansell) 1945- .... **CLC 39, 64**
See also CA 114, 117

Wolfram von Eschenbach c. 1170-c. 1220 .... **CMLC 5**

Wolitzer, Hilma 1930- .... **CLC 17**
See also CANR 18; CA 65-68; SATA 31

Wollstonecraft Godwin, Mary 1759-1797 .... **LC 5**
See also DLB 39

Wonder, Stevie 1950- .... **CLC 12**
See also Morris, Steveland Judkins

Wong, Jade Snow 1922- .... **CLC 17**
See also CA 109

Woodcott, Keith 1934-
See Brunner, John (Kilian Houston)

Woolf, (Adeline) Virginia 1882-1941 .... **TCLC 1, 5, 20, 43; SSC 7**
See also CA 130; brief entry CA 104; DLB 36, 100

Woollcott, Alexander (Humphreys) 1887-1943 .... **TCLC 5**
See also CA 105; DLB 29

Wordsworth, Dorothy 1771-1855 .... **NCLC 25**

Wordsworth, William 1770-1850 .... **NCLC 12; PC 4**
See also DLB 93, 107

Wouk, Herman 1915- .... **CLC 1, 9, 38**
See also CANR 6; CA 5-8R; DLB-Y 82

Wright, Charles 1935- .... **CLC 6, 13, 28**
See also BLC 3; CAAS 7; CANR 26; CA 29-32R; DLB-Y 82

Wright, Charles (Stevenson) 1932- .. **CLC 49**
See also CA 9-12R; DLB 33

Wright, James (Arlington) 1927-1980 .... **CLC 3, 5, 10, 28**
See also CANR 4; CA 49-52; obituary CA 97-100; DLB 5

Wright, Judith 1915- .... **CLC 11, 53**
See also CA 13-16R; SATA 14

Wright, L(aurali) R. 1939- .... **CLC 44**

Wright, Richard (Nathaniel) 1908-1960 ... **CLC 1, 3, 4, 9, 14, 21, 48; SSC 2**
See also BLC 3; CA 108; DLB 76; DLB-DS 2; CDALB 1929-1941; AAYA 5

Wright, Richard B(ruce) 1937- ...... **CLC 6**
See also CA 85-88; DLB 53

Wright, Rick 1945-
See Pink Floyd

Wright, Stephen 1946- .... **CLC 33**

Wright, Willard Huntington 1888-1939
See Van Dine, S. S.
See also CA 115

Wright, William 1930- .... **CLC 44**
See also CANR 7, 23; CA 53-56

Wu Ch'eng-en 1500?-1582? .... **LC 7**

Wu Ching-tzu 1701-1754 .... **LC 2**

Wurlitzer, Rudolph 1938?- ..... **CLC 2, 4, 15**
See also CA 85-88

Wycherley, William 1640?-1716 ...... **LC 8**
See also DLB 80

Wylie (Benet), Elinor (Morton Hoyt) 1885-1928 .... **TCLC 8**
See also CA 105; DLB 9, 45

Wylie, Philip (Gordon) 1902-1971 ... **CLC 43**
See also CAP 2; CA 21-22; obituary CA 33-36R; DLB 9

Wyndham, John 1903-1969 .... **CLC 19**
See also Harris, John (Wyndham Parkes Lucas) Beynon

Wyss, Johann David 1743-1818 .. **NCLC 10**
See also SATA 27, 29

X, Malcolm 1925-1965
See Little, Malcolm

Yanovsky, Vassily S(emenovich) 1906-1989 .... **CLC 2, 18**
See also CA 97-100; obituary CA 129

Yates, Richard 1926- .... **CLC 7, 8, 23**
See also CANR 10; CA 5-8R; DLB 2; DLB-Y 81

Yeats, William Butler 1865-1939 .... **TCLC 1, 11, 18, 31**
See also CANR 10; CA 104; DLB 10, 19

Yehoshua, A(braham) B. 1936- .... **CLC 13, 31**
See also CA 33-36R

Literary Criticism Series Cumulative Topic Index

This index lists all topic entries in the Gale Literary Criticism Series *Contemporary Literary Criticism, Literature Criticism from 1400 to 1800, Nineteenth-Century Literature Criticism,* and *Twentieth-Century Literary Criticism.*

LC Cumulative Nationality Index

LC Cumulative Title Index

Title Index

Title Index

Title Index

Title Index

Title Index

Title Index

Title Index

Title Index

Title Index

Title Index

Title Index

Title Index

Title Index

Title Index

Title Index

Title Index

Title Index

Title Index

ISBN 0-8103-7962-7
90000
9 780810 379626